D1240889

COMPOSITES DESIGN

COMPOSITES DESIGN
FOURTH EDITION

STEPHEN W. TSAI

Director, Mechanics and Surface Interactions Branch
Nonmetallic Materials Division
United States Air Force Materials Laboratory
Dayton, Ohio

THINK COMPOSITES: DAYTON, PARIS, AND TOKYO

513-429-4594

COMPOSITES DESIGN
FOURTH EDITION

Cover: The home card for HyperComposites, a database for composite materials using Apple Computer Company's HyperCard. HyperComposites, in Section 29, is a completely new section, and can be the beginning of a novel way of communication, teaching and learning.

PUBLISHERS

THINK COMPOSITES
P. O. Box 581
Dayton, Ohio 45419
Telephone: (513) 429–4594

THINK COMPOSITES FRANCE
155 Boulevard Brune
75014 Paris
Telephone (1) 45.39.56.67

THINK COMPOSITES JAPAN
3–14–17 Wada
Suginami–ku, Tokyo 166
Telephone (1) 422.47.5911

Paper Back: ISBN 0–9618090–2–7

Printed in USA

LIST OF CONTRIBUTORS

RODOLFO M. AOKI, Deutsche Forschungs und Versuchsanstalt für Luft–
und Raumfahrt (DFVLR), Stuttgart, West Germany

RAN Y. KIM, University of Dayton Research Institute, Dayton, Ohio,
USA

THIERRY N. MASSARD, Commissariat à l'Energie Atomique (CAE),
Paris, France

FRANK L. MATTHEWS, Centre for Composite Materials, Imperial
College of Science and Technology, London, UK

JOCELYN M. PATTERSON, U. S. Air Force Materials Laboratory,
Dayton, Ohio, USA

K. P. RAO, U. S. Air Force Materials Laboratory, Dayton, Ohio, USA, (on
leave from Indian Institute of Science, Bangalore, India)

AJIT K. ROY, University of Dayton Research Institute, Dayton, Ohio,
USA

FORREST A. SANDOW, U. S. Air Force Flight Dynamics Laboratory,
Dayton, Ohio, USA

PETER O. SJÖBLOM, University of Dayton Research Institute, Dayton,
Ohio, USA

GEORGE S. SPRINGER, Department of Aeronautics and Astronautics,
Stanford University, Stanford, California, USA

IPPEI SUSUKI, National Aerospace Laboratory, Tokyo, Japan

SENG C. TAN, AdTech Systems Research Inc., Fairborn, Ohio, USA

STEPHEN W. TSAI, U. S. Air Force Materials Laboratory, Dayton,
Ohio, USA

PREFACE TO THE FOURTH EDITION

The fourth edition is a natural extension of our last edition. Aside from correcting errors and improving our presentation, this edition features our initial attempt at using Apple Computer's HyperCard software. HyperCard is a graphics database that offers new horizons in communication and information retrieval, and numerous features which we do not yet know how to define. The hard copies of Composites Design in HyperCard, which we call HyperComposites, are in Section 29. While the topics covered there should be of interest to designers and engineers, the dynamic features of HyperComposites even in its very elementary forms offer many exciting opportunities to make the composite materials design process easy and rewarding.

Section 29 is merely a "static display," which does not do justice to HyperCard's total capability. Like in the Paris Air Show, a "fly-by" is needed to get the full impact. We expect HyperCard to advance composites design in a manner equal to what Macintosh's desk top publishing has done for this book since 1984. We are much indebted to Bill Atkinson and Apple Computer Company for developing HyperCard.

Failure criteria have been the focus of improvement in this edition. Sections 11 on ply strength and Section 12 on laminate strength have been rewritten. References are made to relevant topics presented in Section 29 on HyperComposites, and all three sections should be studied as a unit. Discussions on the interaction term in the quadratic failure criterion, the matrix degradation factor, and the associated test methods have all been further elaborated upon in Section 29.

Our composites design software packages continue to be accepted by thousands of users. Less than adequate documentation has been one deficiency which we have tried to correct in this edition. In fact, manuals for GenLam, LamRank, and Mic-Mac in much expanded forms can be found in Sections 25, 26, and 27, respectively. Since we often preach that calculation is a must for designing with composite materials, the required software must be user friendly. We believe that the manuals in this edition are making the ability to calculate available to more users than ever before. In Section 29, HyperComposites, we also show the sensitivity of Mic-Mac in Subsection 29.18, and that of the constituent materials modifications in Subsection 29.19. Hopefully, the examples given in these subsections further illustrate the need for calculation.

As much as HyperCard has made Section 29 possible, the use of macros with spreadsheets has made answering "what's best?" as easy as answering "what if?" The particular macro, Chart-quick, is a version of Chart-all, which was given to us by Dan Molligan, Composites Division, Du Pont Company in

Wilmington. We are grateful for his contribution.

We also wish to acknowledge the support of our work by the US Air Force Materials Laboratory, the US Air Force Sacremento Air Logistics Center, the US Army Ballistic Research Laboratory, and the US National Research Council Postdoctoral program. Like last year, special thanks are due to Dr. Ajit Roy, Dr. Ran Kim and Lt Jocelyn Patterson.

We also wish to thank the University of California at Berkeley for continuing to sponsor the annual Composite Materials Workshop, now in its twelveth year; and to the Society of Advanced Materials and Process Engineering for sponsoring the pre-symposium tutorial, now in its third year. We are also indebted to Prof. George Springer of the Department of Aeronautics and Astronautics at Stanford University for using our book to teach his class of one hundred post graduate students. An audience of that size must be a record in composite materials education. The opportunity to reach hundreds of participants and students is what has provided us with the challenge and impetus to publish another edition of this book.

Stephen W. Tsai

May 1988

PREFACE TO THE THIRD EDITION

After having published the 1985 and 1986 editions of Composites Design, we have decided to publish this as the third edition instead of the 1987 edition. We were able to reach more students and practicing engineers in 1986 than in 1985. Nearly 30 universities in the US now use our book and software. Our 1986 Composite Materials Workshop at the University of California in Berkeley had the best attendance in ten years. Our pre–conference tutorial at the annual meeting of the Society for the Advancement of Materials and Processing Engineering (SAMPE) was attended by nearly 300 people. We received equally enthusiastic participation of our tutorials at the European SAMPE, and the ASM International and the Engineering Society of Detroit conferences.

The most noticeable improvement of the present edition is the text printed by the Apple Laserwriter. The integrated graphics of Microsoft's Excel worksheet provided us with a new dimension in presentation. Other hardware and software improvements made writing and editing much faster and more flexible.

In technical content, Section 22 on pressure vessels, and Section 23 on buckling are completely new, and deal with design oriented topics. Section 10 on micromechanics has been simplified. Section 12 on the limit and ultimate strengths is essentially new, and provides a rational foundation for design. The laminate ranking now includes choices of variable sublaminate thickness and ply angles. The new Section 14 covers all aspects of ranking including a new round off routine.

New graphics have been added to Section 15 on residual stresses. Life prediction and data analysis have been added to Section 19 on fatigue. The strength of holes with bonded inclusion forms the basis of a repair technology has been added to Section 20 on notched strength.

Sections 25 to 27 have been added to provide the much needed documentation of the software packages such as GENLAM, LAMRANK, Mic–Mac's, and easy–to–learn tutorials. Sections on glossary, symbols and index have been expanded and updated. In the 1985 edition, we have 220 pages; in 1986, 380 pages; and in 1987, about 530 pages. With 15 percent higher word density of Laserwriter over that of Imagewriter, the actual increase of content of this edition over the last is about 150 percent.

International outlines of composites design in the form of "viewrolls" are presented in Section 28. The multilingual presentations include English, French, German and Japanese versions. The viewrolls are run by Microsoft's Excel, and contain smart viewgraphs to facilitate training and self–teaching. When these software packages were presented by the phenomenal Graphics Projector 700 by Hughes Aircaft Company, we achieved an incredible speed and efficiency in training engineers to design with composite materials. The generous support by the Hughes Aircraft Company during 1986 is hereby acknowledged.

We also wish to acknowledge the support of our work from the US Air Force Materials Laboratory, the US Air Force Sacremento Air Logistic Center, the US Army Ballistic Research Laboratory, and the US National Research Council Postdoctoral program. The dedication and drive of our team to finish this ediction on time is much appreciated. Special thanks are due to Dr. Roy, Dr. Kim and Lt Patterson.

To the hundreds of students and engineers whom we have met face to face during many of our presentations, and to others who have used our book and software, we wish to thank them for their enthusiastic response and constructive feedback. We feel very happy and positive about composite materials. There remain issues which we must overcome. But they are solvable. We see exciting opportunities for composite materials in the years ahead.

Stephen W. Tsai

February 1987

PREFACE TO THE 1986 EDITION

Composites Design–1985 was first distributed at our annual Composite Materials Workshop at the University of California, Berkeley, in February, 1985. In less than one year, thousands of this soft–cover book have reached students and practicing engineers. Society for the Advancement of Material and Process Engineering played a major role in promoting this book. Numerous other organizations such as the Japan Society of Composite Materials, the American Institute of Metallurgical Engineers, the European Association of Composite Materials, the Detroit Society of Engineers, the European Space Agency, the Commissariat à l'Energie Atomique of France, and others also helped us in making this book available to the users.

From numerous direct contacts with the designers in industry, we have received many important feedbacks which will influence the future directions of our book. The 1986 edition has incorporated some of the suggestions. As rational design of composites continued to grow, we were happy to receive contributions from a few active researchers who were able to reduce the high technology of composites to an easy–to–use format. Important topics like moisture effects, joints, fatigue, notched strength, test methods, interlaminar stresses, and many refinements have been included in the 1986 edition.

We are happily surprised by the popularity of the Think Composites Softwares Users Club. Hundreds of engineers have access to our programs. While any one can write and debug programs, it is no longer cost effective to duplicate what is readily available. Even students can better use their time learning the essence of composites design than calculating the strength of a laminate with residual stresses.

We are also pleased to have the opportunity to interact with Stanford, Renselear Polytechnic Institute, Drexel University, and others where composite materials are taught. Thus far our book has greater success with industry than with government and academia. We also have greater success with individuals than with the library. We hope that our 1986 edition will have a broader appeal.

When we showed our book to the Apple Computer Company, we were surprised to find that our book represented one of the major milestones in computer publishing. We expect to grow with the advances of hardwares and softwares in personal computers. Only a small part of the 1986 edition is done by the laser printer. We hope that the next edition will be totally laser printed.

Stephen W. Tsai

February 1986

TABLE OF CONTENTS

TABLE OF CONTENTS

TABLE OF CONTENTS

TABLE OF CONTENTS

TABLE OF CONTENTS

TABLE OF CONTENTS

TABLE OF CONTENTS

TABLE OF CONTENTS

TABLE OF CONTENTS

Section 1

INTRODUCTION

1.1 BACKGROUND

The rapidly expanding applications of composites in the recent past have provided much optimism for the future of our technology. Although man–made composites have existed for thousands of years, the high technology of composites has evolved in the aerospace industry only in the last twenty years. Filament–wound pressure vessels using glass fibers were the first strength critical application for modern composites. Then came boron filaments in the 1960's which started many US Air Force programs to promote aircraft structures made of composites. The F–111 horizontal stabilizer was the first flight–worthy composite component.

Production of composite stabilizer for the F–14 in the early 1970's was another major milestone. That was followed by the composite stabilator for the F–15, and composite rudder and stabilizer for the F–16. In the early 1980's, Boeing 767 used nearly two tons of composite materials in its floor beams and all of its control surfaces. The USSR giant transport, Antonov 124, has a total of 5500 kg of composite materials, of which 2500 kg are graphite composites. The all–composite fin box of the Airbus Industrie A310–300 is an impressive structure in its simplicity. Nearly all emerging aircraft have extensive use of composites; examples include the Dassault–Breguet's Rafale, Saab–Scania JAS–39 Gripen, the European Fighter Aircraft (EFA) of Britain, West Germany, Italy and Spain, and a new generation of commercial aircraft Airbus 320, McDonnell–Douglas MD–11, and Boeing 7J7. The Beech Aircraft's Starship 1 is an all–composite airplane, and is currently undergoing flight test.

In 1986, another all–composite airplane that set a world record in nonstop flight around the world was the Voyager designed and built by Burt Rutan and his coworkers. The plane was ultra light as expected. But it also showed amazing toughness and resilience against many stormy encounters. Graphite composites are used in the dual rudders of the revolutionary 12–meter yacht, the USA, of the St. Francis Yacht Club's entry to the 1987 America's Cup challenge. For the 1988 Cup challenge, more entensive use of composites has been planned. These applications have converted composite materials from a high technology domain into household words. High visibility is an important ingredient for the growth and acceptance of composite materials as viable engineering materials.

Materials and processing advances have been instrumental to the growth of our technology. Graphite and aramid fibers became commercially available in the early 1970's. Epoxies are available for various use conditions. More recently, higher temperature matrix materials and thermoplastics have emerged for more demanding applications of the future.

In the mean time, the high technology of composites has spurred applications outside the aerospace industry. The sporting goods is a major outlet of our material. Hundreds of tons of graphite composites were used for tennis and squash rackets, and golf shafts each year since 1983. These rackets and composites are synonymous. Other applications include bicycles, oars for rowing, and just about any equipment where weight, stiffness, and strength are important.

At a recent conference held by the Engineering Society of Detroit an automotive executive saw the impact of composite materials on his industry to be as great as if not greater than that of electronics. Such high expectation of composites is good for our technology. We should dedicate ourselves to promote composites for as many product lines as possible.

It is our belief that the acceptance of composites can be greatly enhanced if the cost is lowered; the design, simplified. We would like to address primarily the design issue which is intimately related to the cost.

1.2 DESIGNING WITH COMPOSITES

Designing with any material is often more art than science; that with composites is no exception and one has much to learn. Universities prefer teaching analysis to design. Books on analysis outnumber those on design by a wide margin. Research topics are rarely design–oriented. But products are made with or without rational design. Netting analysis is still considered useful for design. Same holds true for the carpet plot. Furthermore, design limit is often based on some strain level; one level for laminates without holes, and a reduced level for those with holes or for damage tolerance. Workers in numerous emerging composite materials, such as metal–matrix composites, ceramic composites, molecular composites, and carbon–carbon composites, have been preoccupied with their particular problems, and resorted to oversimplified theories of shear lag, pull out, and their version of the netting analysis. These are typical practices in the US industry. They are not rationally developed. In fact most of them are misleading if not wrong. They are still in use because the practices are simple. Fortunately the polymer–matrix composites are so strong that they have been reliable and competitive in spite of the less–than–perfect design practice. For the emerging composite materials, workers not familiar with existing micro and macromechanics are well advised to seek sound theory and valid experimental techniques. Self–made, simplistic theories such as the netting analysis, and test methods such as the pull out or push in tests should not be pursued.

Our desire is to use as much science as possible for designing with composites. For this reason, netting analysis, carpet plots, and strain limits are not used. We rely on laminated plate theory. In fact we can treat netting analysis as a special case of laminated plate theory by degrading the matrix. For both the limit and ultimate strengths we will use the interacting quadratic criterion. We do not recommend the use of the noninteracting, non–scalar maximum stress or maximum strain criterion. The choice of criterion is of course based on test data. Reliable data from which the best criterion can be selected are unfortunately difficult to obtain.

To us rationality is as important as practicality. We must have both if we are to succeed. We cannot afford to penalize composites by using the wrong design. By the same token we should not deny ourselves of the extraordinary properties of composite materials by using outmoded tools. As we see it, the basic issue in designing with composites is to learn to use the directionally dependent properties. The scalar approach for the design of isotropic materials is acceptable because stiffness and strength can each be represented by one parameter; i.e., the Young's modulus and the uniaxial strength, respectively. Poisson's ratio can be assumed to remain constant at 0.3. Strength under combined stresses based on the von Mises or Tresca criterion does not deviate significantly from the uniaxial tensile or pure shear strength.

But for composites, the number of constants increase to four for the stiffness and at least five for the strength of an on–axis unidirectional ply. In a multidirectional laminate, the stiffness constants can be as many as 21, and the strength is five times the number of ply groups. We must use matrix in place of scalar operations. This is the challenge that all of us must face when we work with anisotropic materials. Netting analysis, carpet plots, and the limit or maximum strain criterion ignore the effects of combined stresses. Matrix algebra is not used. Such approaches are at least 25 years out of date.

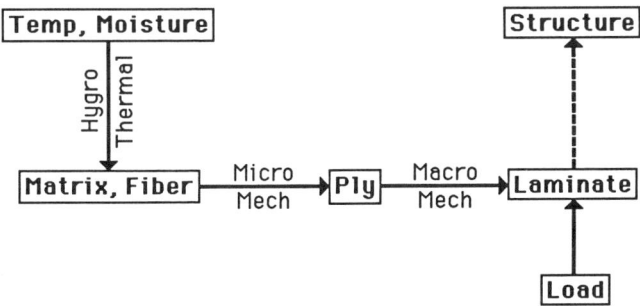

FIGURE 1.1 AN INTEGRATED FRAMEWORK FOR COMPOSITES DESIGN.

How can we make our design conceptually simple and analytically proper? This can be achieved by setting up a rational framework. An example is shown in Figure 1.1. Designing with composites required several additional factors which do not exist in the conventional material. Specifically, we need three bridges to link materials and environmental characteristics to the final stiffness and strength of a laminated composite. The bridges are: hygrothermal analysis and data, micromechanics, and macromechanics. The framework in Figure 1.1 is to minimize the number of variables and their functional dependency. We believe that a full–featured design process must consider all the variables. We will outline these variables in the next subsection.

1.3 OUR APPROACH

First, we want to expand Figure 1.1 to show key variables and their functional relations. Our approach is to use the simplest framework that still contains all the variables and then connect them with the simplest relations. Then it becomes feasible to optimize composite laminates with all the features. The expanded Figure 1.1 is shown in Figure 1.2. The symbols used in this chart are defined in Section 2 and listed in Appendix A at the end of this book.

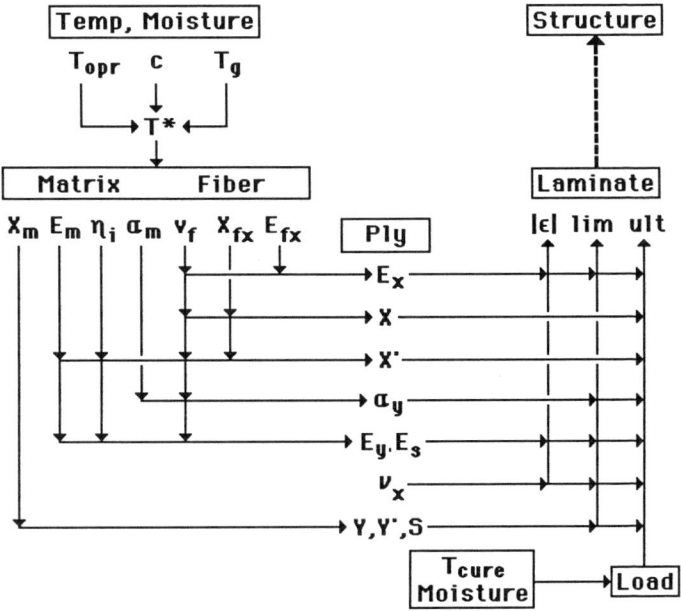

FIGURE 1.2 PRINCIPAL VARIABLES AND RELATIONS OF COMPOSITES.

Our intent is to establish the functional relations of these variables and show how full–featured design of composite materials can be achieved.

The most efficient configuration is the unidirectional composite. We will develop the method of the use of on– and off–axis unidirectional composites to carry combined loads. If the loads are such that unidirectional composites are inadequate and inefficient, we will go to bidirectional laminates. The process continues as we increase the ply angles to 3, 4 and higher.

Obviously, the number of angles must be balanced between considerations of manufacturing and cost, and the requirement for stiffness and strength. We take the highly directional composites as the upper bound; the quasi–isotropic laminate, the lower bound.

The simplification of our design approach can be divided into several levels:

* For materials optimization, simplified micromechanics formulas are essential so that the contribution of fiber and matrix and the effects of hygrothermal variables can be related to the stiffness and strength of a chosen laminate.
* For stiffness optimization, a simplified laminated plate theory, based on thin wall construction and repeating sublaminates, is useful in providing a rapid selection of symmetric and unsymmetric design.
* For strength optimization, the principal stress approach is recommended for single load cases; and the laminate ranking approach, for both single and multiple load cases. Design should be verified at the limit and ultimate strengths of laminates derived from the FPF (first–ply–failure), the LPF (last–ply–failure), and the desired safety margin.

Although these are by no means all inclusive, they represent a good beginning of making designing with composites on a consistent and rational basis. More importantly, the salient features of composite materials can now be fully exploited. The methodology described in this book represents the minimum required. Obviously more will be forthcoming. But sufficient information has become available that designing with composite materials can be as confidently as that with conventional materials.

Matrix inversions are involved in the determination of laminate stiffness. It is impossible to anticipate the effects of simple operations such as the adding and subtracting plies, and the rigid body rotation of a laminate. These effects can be systematically established and should not be surprises. Instead of guessing or using intuition we recommend calculation.

In order to enhance confidence in our design calculations, we make constant comparison of our optimum composite with the quasi–isotropic laminate of the same composite as a lower bound. This comparison is also important because the same calculation is needed to compare our laminate with isotropic materials like aluminum. We also make sure that calculations can be easily and accurately performed. We see in the 1980's the personal computer or work station as the most effective tool to aid design. We have mentioned repeatedly that formulas must be simplified, and the number of design variables reduced. The use of micromechanics, for example, reduces the number of material and geometric variables. With simplification, many more design iterations can be effectively exercised than what is possible with outmoded tools.

1.4 COMPUTERS

Personal computers and work stations play a special role in our approach. Due to the increased number of material constants over the isotropic case, computers are ideally suited to provide designers with timely information. The spreadsheet, database and integrated graphics capabilities of computers can be utilized to make designing with composites easy, fast and rewarding.

We encourage full utilization of whatever computer that is available. It was not very long ago, in fact in 1976, we were using Texas Instruments SR–52 for our laminate calculations. We were attracted to the programmable calculators by their ease and consistency of operation because we could barely invert by hand a 3x3 matrix without errors. The chronology of our calculator/computer experience can be briefly summarized as follows.

TABLE 1.1 EVOLUTION OF COMPUTING TOOLS FOR COMPOSITES DESIGN

Year	Instrument	Memory/steps	Recorder	Computer Cost
1976	TI SR–52	20/120	Mag cards	$300
1978	TI–59	60/480	Mag cards	$300
1980	Sharp 1500	2k RAM/Basic	Cassette	$700
1982	Sinclair	4k RAM/Basic	Cassette	$200
1983	Apple II	64k RAM/Basic	Floppy disk	$3000
1984	IBM PC	128k RAM	Floppy disk	$4000
1984	Macintosh	128k RAM	Micro disk	$3000
1985	IBM, Mac, etc	>10 megabyte	Hard disk	$4000

In the late 1980's, we expect major innovations in hardware and software to be commercially available. There are so many advances in computational capability that updating Table 1.1 can no longer be by one or two lines.

Our low cost, unprotected software packages have become as popular as our book. We believe that students and professionals in the field of composite materials can accelerate their learning by working with the available, preprogrammed software, which contain tutorials, smart viewgraphs, and other learning aids. Samples of our software packages are shown later in this book. It is more cost effective to learn to design composite materials than to spend hours debugging programs.

As an example of the growth in computer technology, we use Apple Computer's HyperCard software to cover a wide variety of subjects related to composites design. This graphical database, which we call HyperComposites, a term coined from Apple's designation, offers new dimensions in teaching, learning, and communication. Among the many outstanding features of HyperCard are the ease of use to integrate and diseminate information with the aid of smart graphics, sound, speech, music, and animation. The examples that we have used are on the most elementary level.

Section 2

NOTATION AND SYMBOLS

2.1 OUR SYSTEM

We follow the notation and symbols used in the textbook: *Introduction to Composite Materials,* by S. W. Tsai and H. T. Hahn, Technomic, Lancaster, Pennsylvania 17604 (1985). We are bound by the following rules required by the contracted notation:

- Single subscript for second–rank tensors; double subscripts for fourth–rank tensors. Shear component for stress and strain has only single subscript.
- Engineering shear strain is used. Same applies to the twisting curvature– displacement relation, i.e.,

$$k_s = -2\partial^2 w/\partial x \partial y \qquad (2.1)$$

Note that the factor of 2 is added to the tensorial relation. Like the engineering shear strain, the twisting curvature here is an engineering rather than tensorial curvature. Our sign convention calls for a negative sign in this relation.
- Letter subscripts x, y, z, t, u and s designate the on–axis coordinates; numeric subscripts 1, 2, 3, 4, 5 and 6 designate the off–axis coordinates.

In addition, we use the following conventions:

- Engineering constants are defined from the components of the normalized compliance. Definitions are also given for the unsymmetric laminates. The coupling coefficients are normalized by columns, not by rows; Poisson's ratios are defined differently from other authors.
- Other symbols include:
  Asterisk [*] means a normalized variable.
  Prime ['] means compressive or negative.
  Superscript o [°] means in–plane.
  Superscript f [f] means flexural.
- We use normalized variables (those with *) for properties in addition to the absolute. Normalized properties are required to compare one property with another. Stiffness components for example are expressed in Pa.
- We use dimensionless variables whenever possible. Then we do not have to be concerned with SI versus English units. We prefer to represent thickness by the number of plies instead of m or mm, failure envelopes in strain space instead of stress space, and loss of stiffness or strength due to changes are expressed in ratios of material properties, nondimensional temperature, etc.

2.2 CONTRACTED NOTATION

Contracted notation is a simplification of the usual tensorial notation. Instead of having the same number of indices to match the rank of the tensor, like having 2 indices for the second–rank tensor, and 4 for the 4th–rank, the contracted notation reduces the number of indices by one half. Single index is used for the second–rank tensors; double indices, for the fourth–rank. Contracted notation cannot be applied to the first–rank and other odd–rank tensors.

When we use contracted notation, we should use engineering shear strain, in place of the tensorial shear strain. Thus the factor of two must be properly and consistently applied. Twisting curvature in Equation 2.1 is of the engineering rather than the tensorial type. The components of the compliance must also be corrected in addition to the contraction of the indices. The numeric correction factors of 1, 2 and 4 must be applied in accordance with the relations in Figure 2.1 (see page 2.5). Incorrectly or inconsistently applied correction factors can lead to unnecessarily complicated unsymmetric matrices, and uncertainties and confusion.

2.3 CONTRACTED STRESS

This contraction is straightforward. No numeric correction is necessary. There are two systems of notations for the stress components; viz., the letter and numeric subscripts; see Table 2.1.

The contraction of the normal stress components is natural and well accepted, but that of the shear is not universally accepted. Our contraction of the numeric subscripts is more popular because it follows the same order of 1–2–3 if the plane of the shear stress is designated by its normal; e.g., the 2–3 plane by 1. The contraction of the letter subscripts is arbitrary but consistent with the purpose of contraction. Mixing of single and double subscripts is not recommended.

TABLE 2.1 CONTRACTION OF SUBSCRIPTS FOR STRESS COMPONENTS

Regular letter subscripts	σ_{xx}	σ_{yy}	σ_{zz}	σ_{yz}	σ_{zx}	σ_{xy}
Regular numeric subscripts	σ_{11}	σ_{22}	σ_{33}	σ_{23}	σ_{31}	σ_{12}
Contracted numeric subscripts	σ_1	σ_2	σ_3	σ_4	σ_5	σ_6
Contracted letter subscripts	σ_x	σ_y	σ_z	σ_q	σ_r	σ_s

2.4 CONTRACTED STRAIN

This contraction needs a numeric correction factor of 2 for the shear components because engineering shear is used. The usual definition of the tensorial strain–displacement relation is:

$$\varepsilon_{ij} = (u_{i,j}+u_{j,i})/2 \tag{2.2}$$

The definition of engineering shear strain is analogous to Equation 2.1:

$$\varepsilon_6 = 2\varepsilon_{12} = \partial u/\partial y+\partial v/\partial x$$

$$\varepsilon_5 = 2\varepsilon_{31} \tag{2.3}$$

$$\varepsilon_4 = 2\varepsilon_{23}$$

The strain contraction is summarized in Table 2.2.

2.5 CONTRACTED STIFFNESS

The stiffness matrix for the generalized Hooke's law in its uncontracted form is:

$$\{\sigma\} = [C]\{\varepsilon\}, \quad \text{or} \quad \sigma_{pq} = C_{pqrs}\varepsilon_{rs}, \quad p,q,r,s = 1,2,3 \tag{2.4}$$

This can be represented by a matrix multiplication table, in Table 2.3.

TABLE 2.2 CONTRACTION OF SUBSCRIPTS FOR STRAIN COMPONENTS

Regular letter subscripts	ε_{xx}	ε_{yy}	ε_{zz}	ε_{yz}	ε_{zx}	ε_{xy}
Regular numeric subscripts	ε_{11}	ε_{22}	ε_{33}	ε_{23}	ε_{31}	ε_{12}
Contracted numeric subscripts	ε_1	ε_2	ε_3	$\varepsilon_4/2$	$\varepsilon_5/2$	$\varepsilon_6/2$
Contracted letter subscripts	ε_x	ε_y	ε_z	$\varepsilon_q/2$	$\varepsilon_r/2$	$\varepsilon_s/2$

TABLE 2.3 GENERALIZED HOOKE'S LAW IN UNCONDENSED FORM

	ε_{11}	ε_{22}	ε_{33}	ε_{23}	ε_{32}	ε_{31}	ε_{13}	ε_{12}	ε_{21}
σ_{11}	C_{1111}	C_{1122}	C_{1133}	C_{1123}	C_{1132}	C_{1131}	C_{1113}	C_{1112}	C_{1121}
σ_{22}	C_{2211}	C_{2222}	C_{2233}	C_{2223}	C_{2232}	C_{2231}	C_{2213}	C_{2212}	C_{2221}
—									
—									
σ_{21}	C_{2111}	C_{2122}	C_{2133}	C_{2123}	C_{2132}	C_{2131}	C_{2113}	C_{2112}	C_{2121}

Since both stress and strain are symmetric; i.e.,

$$\sigma_{pq} = \sigma_{qp} \, , \quad \varepsilon_{pq} = \varepsilon_{qp} \tag{2.5}$$

a typical row in Table 2.3 can be read as:

$$\sigma_{11} = C_{1111}\varepsilon_{11}+C_{1122}\varepsilon_{22}+C_{1133}\varepsilon_{33}+(C_{1123}+C_{1132})\varepsilon_{23}$$

$$+(C_{1131}+C_{1113})\varepsilon_{31}+(C_{1112}+C_{1121})\varepsilon_{12} \tag{2.6}$$

If we now introduce the engineering shear strain and the contracted notation for all the indices, we have:

$$\sigma_1 = C_{11}\varepsilon_1+C_{12}\varepsilon_2+C_{13}\varepsilon_3+C_{14}\varepsilon_4+C_{15}\varepsilon_5+C_{16}\varepsilon_6 \tag{2.7}$$

In summary, the generalized Hooke's law in contracted notation is:

$$\{\sigma\} = [C]\{\varepsilon\}, \quad \text{or} \quad \sigma_i = C_{ij}\varepsilon_j, \quad i,j = 1,2,3,4,5,6 \tag{2.8}$$

Thus the indices for the stiffness components follow precisely those for the contraction of stress. No correction factor for the contraction is needed. This easy conversion from four to two indices is made possible by having:

• Symmetry of stress and strain,
• Symmetry of the stiffness matrix, and
• Use of engineering shear strain.

2.6 CONTRACTED COMPLIANCE

The generalized Hooke's law in terms of compliance is:

$$\{\varepsilon\} = [S]\{\sigma\}, \quad \text{or} \quad \varepsilon_{pq} = S_{pqrs}\sigma_{rs}, \quad p,q,r,s = 1,2,3 \tag{2.9}$$

The first and the eighth rows for this uncondensed, uncontracted form of the generalized Hooke's law are:

$$\varepsilon_{11} = S_{1111}\sigma_{11}+S_{1122}\sigma_{22}+S_{1133}\sigma_{33}+S_{1123}\sigma_{23}+S_{1132}\sigma_{32}$$

$$+S_{1131}\sigma_{31}+S_{1113}\sigma_{13}+S_{1112}\sigma_{12}+S_{1121}\sigma_{21} \tag{2.10}$$

$$\varepsilon_{12} = S_{1211}\sigma_{11}+S_{1222}\sigma_{22}+S_{1233}\sigma_{33}+S_{1223}\sigma_{23}+S_{1232}\sigma_{32}$$

$$+S_{1231}\sigma_{31}+S_{1213}\sigma_{13}+S_{1212}\sigma_{12}+S_{1221}\sigma_{21} \tag{2.11}$$

If we now apply the contracted notation of stress and strain (with engineering shear), and assume symmetry for the compliance matrix, we will have:

$$\{\varepsilon\} = [S]\{\sigma\}, \quad \text{or} \quad \varepsilon_i = S_{ij}\sigma_j, \quad i,j = 1,2,3,4,5,6 \tag{2.12}$$

But the contraction of the compliance matrix requires additional numeric corrections. The contracted forms for Equations 2.10 and 2.11 are:

$$\bar{\varepsilon}_1 = S_{11}\sigma_1 + S_{12}\sigma_2 + S_{13}\sigma_3 + S_{14}\sigma_4 + S_{15}\sigma_5 + S_{16}\sigma_6 \qquad (2.13)$$

$$\bar{\varepsilon}_6 = S_{61}\sigma_1 + S_{62}\sigma_2 + S_{63}\sigma_3 + S_{64}\sigma_4 + S_{65}\sigma_5 + S_{66}\sigma_6 \qquad (2.14)$$

If we compare term by term between Equations 2.13 and 2.10, and 2.14 and 2.11, we will arrive at the following numeric correction factors of 1, 2 and 4:

$$S_{11} = S_{1111}, \ldots S_{12} = S_{1122}, \ldots$$

$$S_{14} = 2S_{1123}, \; S_{15} = 2S_{1131}, \ldots S_{61} = 2S_{1211}, \ldots \qquad (2.15)$$

$$S_{44} = 4S_{2323}, \; S_{45} = 4S_{2331}, \ldots$$

Thus the contracted compliance matrix can be viewed as having four equal 3x3 sub–matrices. The correction factor is unity for the upper–left sub–matrix; 2, for the lower–left, and the upper–right; and 4, for the lower–right; see Figure 2.1 for the correction factors for compliance matrix. These factors are necessary and are the results of the symmetry of stress and strain, the symmetry of the compliance matrix, and the use of engineering shear.

i \ j	1	2	3	4	5	6
1 2 3	$S_{ij} = S_{pqrs}$			$S_{ij} = 2S_{pqrs}$		
4 5 6	$S_{ij} = 2S_{pqrs}$			$S_{ij} = 4S_{pqrs}$		

FIGURE 2.1 CORRECTION FACTORS BETWEEN THE CONTRACTED AND UNCONTRACTED COMPLIANCE MATRICES.

If engineering shear is not used, a factor of 2 must be applied to the last three columns of the stiffness matrix and the last three rows of the compliance matrix. These matrices are no longer symmetric. In contrast to the compliance matrix the stiffness matrix requires no correction factors between the contracted and uncontracted notations. This is shown in Figure 2.2 to illustrate the difference from Figure 2.1.

j \ i	1	2	3	4	5	6
1						
2		$C_{ij} = C_{pqrs}$			$C_{ij} = C_{pqrs}$	
3						
4						
5		$C_{ij} = C_{pqrs}$			$C_{ij} = C_{pqrs}$	
6						

FIGURE 2.2 THERE IS NO CORRECTION FACTOR BETWEEN THE CONTRACTED AND UNCONTRACTED STIFFNESS MATRICES.

2.7 CONCLUSIONS

The use of contracted notation reduces the number of indices resulting in simpler mathematical expressions. But it must be applied consistently. We do not recommend mixing single and double indices such as the use of single indices for the normal components and double indices for the shear. Furthermore, engineering shear strain is recommended for the contracted notation (Table 2.2). While the contracted stiffness matrix is derived from the uncontracted without correction factors (Table 2.3), the contracted compliance matrix requires correction factors of 1, 2 and 4 (Equation 2.15).

2.8 LIST OF PRINCIPAL SYMBOLS – SEE APPENDIX A

Section 3

GENERALIZED HOOKE'S LAW

3.1 MATRIX MULTIPLICATION TABLES

The generalized Hooke's law is the linear stress–strain relation for an anisotropic material. It is derived from the elastic energy as a basic postulate in the theory of elasticity. It is convenient to use the contracted notation described in the last section and to represent matrix multiplication such as:

$$\{\sigma\} = [C]\{\varepsilon\}, \quad \text{or} \quad \sigma_i = C_{ij}\varepsilon_j, \quad i,j = 1,2,3,4,5,6 \tag{3.1}$$

by the following matrix multiplication table:

TABLE 3.1 GENERALIZED HOOKE'S LAW IN TERMS OF STIFFNESS

	ε_1	ε_2	ε_3	ε_4	ε_5	ε_6
σ_1	C_{11}	C_{12}	C_{13}	C_{14}	C_{15}	C_{16}
σ_2	C_{21}	C_{22}	C_{23}	C_{24}	C_{25}	C_{26}
σ_3	C_{31}	C_{32}	C_{33}	C_{34}	C_{35}	C_{36}
σ_4	C_{41}	C_{42}	C_{43}	C_{44}	C_{45}	C_{46}
σ_5	C_{51}	C_{52}	C_{53}	C_{54}	C_{55}	C_{56}
σ_6	C_{61}	C_{62}	C_{63}	C_{64}	C_{65}	C_{66}

This is the most general law for an anisotropic linearly elastic material. There are 36 components or constants required to completely describe this material. It has no material symmetry. It is also called a triclinic material. This stiffness matrix however is symmetric from energy consideration; i.e.,

$$C_{ij} = C_{ji} \tag{3.2}$$

By symmetry or the reciprocal relation only 21 of the 36 constants are independent.

3.2 MONOCLINIC SYMMETRY

If any material symmetry exists, the number of constants will reduce. For example, if the 1–2 or z=0 plane is a plane of symmetry, all constants associated with the positive 3– or z–axis must be the same as those with the negative 3– or z–axis. Shear strain components ε_4 and ε_5, or ε_{yz} and ε_{xz} in the uncontracted notation, respectively, are coupled only with shear stress components σ_4 and σ_5. The Hooke's law in Table 3.1 can be simplified for a monoclinic material; i.e., a material having symmety with respect to the z = 0 plane, as follows:

TABLE 3.2 STIFFNESS MATRIX OF A MONOCLINIC (z = 0) MATERIAL

	ε_1	ε_2	ε_3	ε_4	ε_5	ε_6
σ_1	C_{11}	C_{12}	C_{13}	0	0	C_{16}
σ_2	C_{21}	C_{22}	C_{23}	0	0	C_{26}
σ_3	C_{31}	C_{32}	C_{33}	0	0	C_{36}
σ_4	0	0	0	C_{44}	C_{45}	0
σ_5	0	0	0	C_{54}	C_{55}	0
σ_6	C_{61}	C_{62}	C_{63}	0	0	C_{66}

When expressed in this coordinate system there are 20 nonzero constants, of which 13 are independent. If the coordinate system changes, for example, to an arbitrary plane, the number of nonzero constants will increase up to 36. But the independent constants remain 13, which is the case of a monoclinic material for all coordinate systems.

3.3 ORTHOTROPIC SYMMETRY

As the level of material symmetry increases, the number of independent constants continues to reduce. If we have symmetry in three orthogonal planes we have an orthotropic material. The number of independent constants is now 9. If the planes of symmetry coincide with the reference coordinate system, the nonzero components are 12; this is shown in Table 3.3. If the symmetry planes are not coincident with the reference coordinates, the nonzero components can be those shown in Table 3.1. If one of the symmetry planes coincide with the 3– or z–coordinate axis, the nonzero components will be those shown in Table 3.2. The number of independent constants remains 9 for orthotropic materials irrespective of the orientation of the symmetry planes.

3.4 TRANSVERSELY ISOTROPIC SYMMETRY

The next level of material symmetry is the transversely isotropic material, which has 5 independent constants. If the isotropic plane coincides with one of the planes of the coordinate system, the nonzero components are 12; this is shown in Table 3.4. If the symmetry planes are not coincident with the reference coordinates, the nonzero components will be those shown in Table 3.1. If one of the symmetry planes coincide with the 3– or z–coordinate axis, the nonzero components will be those shown in Table 3.2. The number of independent constants remain 5 for the transversely isotropic material irrespective of the orientation of the symmetry planes.

TABLE 3.3   STIFFNESS MATRIX OF AN ORTHOTROPIC MATERIAL

	ε_1	ε_2	ε_3	ε_4	ε_5	ε_6
σ_1	C_{11}	C_{12}	C_{13}	0	0	0
σ_2	C_{21}	C_{22}	C_{23}	0	0	0
σ_3	C_{31}	C_{32}	C_{33}	0	0	0
σ_4	0	0	0	C_{44}	0	0
σ_5	0	0	0	0	C_{55}	0
σ_6	0	0	0	0	0	C_{66}

This is an important anisotropic material symmetry. It is frequently used to describe the elastic constants of anisotropic fibers, and unidirectional composites. The isotropic plane for both cases is normal to the axis of the fibers.

TABLE 3.4   STIFFNESS MATRIX OF A TRANSVERSELY ISOTROPIC (x = constant) MATERIAL

	ε_1	ε_2	ε_3	ε_4	ε_5	ε_6
σ_1	C_{11}	C_{12}	C_{12}	0	0	0
σ_2	C_{21}	C_{22}	C_{23}	0	0	0
σ_3	C_{21}	C_{32}	C_{22}	0	0	0
σ_4	0	0	0	$(C_{22}-C_{23})/2$	0	0
σ_5	0	0	0	0	C_{66}	0
σ_6	0	0	0	0	0	C_{66}

Because of transverse isotropy, the following four relations were used in reducing the number of independent constants from 9 for the orthotropic material to 5 for the transversely isotropic material:

$$C_{22} = C_{33}, \quad C_{13} = C_{12},$$
$$C_{55} = C_{66}, \quad C_{44} = (C_{22}-C_{23})/2$$

(3.3)

Since the 2–3 or yz–plane is isotropic, indices 2 equal to 3, and 5 equal to 6 in the contracted notation. The last of Equation 3.3 is derived from the equivalence between pure shear, and the combined tension and compression.

3.5 ISOTROPIC SYMMETRY

If a material is fully isotropic the number of independent constants reduce from 5 to 2 resulting from the following three relations:

$$C_{11} = C_{22} = C_{33}$$

$$C_{12} = C_{23} = C_{31} \tag{3.4}$$

$$C_{44} = C_{55} = C_{66} = (C_{11} - C_{12})/2$$

This is shown in Table 3.5. There are 12 nonzero constants, same as those in Tables 3.3 and 3.4. This is apparently the minimum number of nonzero constants regardless of material symmetry.

TABLE 3.5 STIFFNESS MATRIX OF AN ISOTROPIC MATERIAL

	ε_1	ε_2	ε_3	ε_4	ε_5	ε_6
σ_1	C_{11}	C_{12}	C_{12}	0	0	0
σ_2	C_{21}	C_{11}	C_{12}	0	0	0
σ_3	C_{21}	C_{21}	C_{11}	0	0	0
σ_4	0	0	0	$(C_{11}-C_{12})/2$	0	0
σ_5	0	0	0	0	$(C_{11}-C_{12})/2$	0
σ_6	0	0	0	0	0	$(C_{11}-C_{12})/2$

We have shown that the stiffness components are functions of material symmetries. The compliance components follow the same pattern of the nonzero and the number of independent components. They have the same appearance as the stiffness components in Tables 3.1 through 3.5. We merely replace C_{ij} by S_{ij}.

There is however one exception; i.e., the equivalence of pure shear, and the combined tension and compression applied at a 45-degree orientation would lead to the following relation for the compliance component:

$$S_{44} = 2(S_{22} - S_{23})$$

$$S_{55} = 2(S_{33} - S_{31}) \tag{3.5}$$

$$S_{66} = 2(S_{11} - S_{12})$$

In terms of engineering constants, we can express the equivalence as:

$$G = E/2(1+v) \tag{3.6}$$

where G, E, v are the shear modulus, Young's modulus, and Poisson's ratio, respectively.

In Table 3.6 we show the compliance matrix of an isotropic material. Note that the column and row headings are interchanged with those in Table 3.5. Equation 3.5 can be simplified for the isotropic material:

$$S_{44} = S_{55} = S_{66} = 2(S_{11}-S_{12}) \qquad\qquad (3.7)$$

TABLE 3.6 COMPLIANCE MATRIX OF AN ISOTROPIC MATERIAL

	σ_1	σ_2	σ_3	σ_4	σ_5	σ_6
ε_1	S_{11}	S_{12}	S_{12}	0	0	0
ε_2	S_{21}	S_{11}	S_{12}	0	0	0
ε_3	S_{21}	S_{21}	S_{11}	0	0	0
ε_4	0	0	0	$2(S_{11}-S_{12})$	0	0
ε_5	0	0	0	0	$2(S_{11}-S_{12})$	0
ε_6	0	0	0	0	0	$2(S_{11}-S_{12})$

3.6 SUMMARY OF MATERIAL SYMMETRIES

We now present a summary of the Hooke's law in Table 3.7. The on–axis refers to the symmetry axes; the off–axis, the rotation about one of the reference axes; and the general, rotation about any axis.

TABLE 3.7 SUMMARY OF 3–DIMENSIONAL MATERIAL SYMMETRIES

Type of Material Symmetry	Number of Independent Constants	Number of Nonzero: On–axis	Number of Nonzero: Off–axis	Number of Nonzero: General
Triclinic	21	36	36	36
Monoclinic	13	20	36	36
Orthotropic	9	12	20	36
Transversely Isotropic	5	12	20	36
Isotropic	2	12	12	12

The behavior of an anisotropic material depends not as much on the number of independent constants as on the nonzero components. For example, the on–axis orthotropic and the on–axis transversely isotropic materials behave the same qualitatively as an isotropic material. They all have 12 nonzero components, and are geometrically arranged like those in Table 3.3, 3.4, or 3.5. For these materials, the shear and normal components of stress and strain are not coupled. When an orthotropic or transversely isotropic material rotates away from its symmetry axes about the 3– or z–axis, this off–axis orientation results in 20 nonzero components. Now shear coupling is present and this material will behave like a monoclinic material in its on–axis orientation. If the orthotropic or transversely isotropic material rotates about an axis other than the three reference axes, the nonzero components are now 36 and will behave like a triclinic material shown in Table 3.1.

In Figure 3.1 we show graphically the nature of the three most common material symmetries.

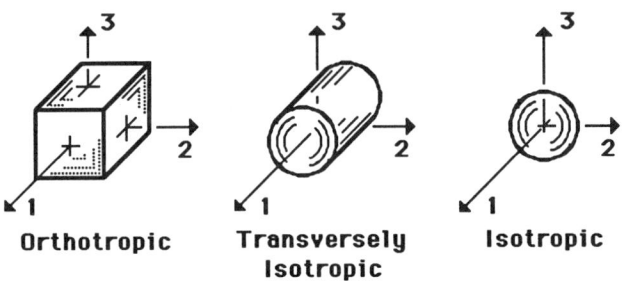

Orthotropic   **Transversely**   **Isotropic**
                       Isotropic

FIGURE 3.1 GRAPHICAL REPRESENTATIONS OF THREE MATERIAL SYMMETRIES.

3.7 ENGINEERING CONSTANTS

The definitions of the Young's moduli of an anisotropic material are straightforward, as follows:

$$E_1 = 1/S_{11}, \quad E_2 = 1/S_{22}, \quad E_3 = 1/S_{33} \tag{3.8}$$

But the definition of shear moduli is arbitrary. We show two definitions; using one or two subscripts:

$$E_4 = G_{23} = 1/S_{44}, \quad E_5 = G_{31} = 1/S_{55},$$
$$E_6 = G_{12} = 1/S_{66} \tag{3.9}$$

We prefer the single subscript definition because it is consistent with the intent of the contracted notation.

The definitions of the Poisson and shear couplings are even less standardized and are in fact conflicting. We will show two definitions for a monoclinic material, in the following Tables 3.8 and 3.9. An off–axis orthotropic, and an off–axis transversely isotropic materials have the same nonzero components as the monoclinic material.

In Table 3.8 each column is normalized by the same engineering constant. We prefer this definition because the interpretation of simple tests such as a uniaxial test can be readily done. But many authors use the row normalization for the definition of engineering constants. This is shown in

Table 3.9. Here we are bound by the accepted convention of the subscripts that the first subscript i refers to the row; the second subscript, the column.

TABLE 3.8   COLUMN–NORMALIZED ENGINEERING CONSTANTS OF A MONOCLINIC MATERIAL

	σ_1	σ_2	σ_3	σ_4	σ_5	σ_6
ε_1	$1/E_1$	$-v_{12}/E_2$	$-v_{13}/E_3$	0	0	v_{16}/E_6
ε_2	$-v_{21}/E_1$	$1/E_2$	$-v_{23}/E_3$	0	0	v_{26}/E_6
ε_3	$-v_{31}/E_1$	$-v_{32}/E_2$	$1/E_3$	0	0	v_{36}/E_6
ε_4	0	0	0	$1/E_4$	v_{45}/E_5	0
ε_5	0	0	0	v_{54}/E_4	$1/E_5$	0
ε_6	v_{61}/E_1	v_{62}/E_2	v_{63}/E_3	0	0	$1/E_6$

Thus the definition of the coupling coefficients v_{ij} depends how the normalizing factor is applied. In Table 3.8 each column is normalized by the same Young's modulus or shear modulus. For the case of E_1 larger than in E_2:

v_{21} = major or longitudinal Poisson's ratio

     = the larger Poisson's ratio

$$= -S_{21}/S_{11} \tag{3.10}$$

v_{12} = minor or transverse Poisson's ratio

     = the smaller Poisson's ratio

     $= v_{21}E_2/E_1$

$$= -S_{12}/S_{22} \tag{3.11}$$

TABLE 3.9   ROW–NORMALIZED ENGINEERING CONSTANTS OF A MONOCLINIC MATERIAL

	σ_1	σ_2	σ_3	σ_4	σ_5	σ_6
ε_1	$1/E_1$	$-v_{12}/E_1$	$-v_{13}/E_1$	0	0	v_{16}/E_1
ε_2	$-v_{21}/E_2$	$1/E_2$	$-v_{23}/E_2$	0	0	v_{26}/E_2
–						
–						
–						
ε_6	v_{61}/E_6	v_{62}/E_6	v_{63}/E_6	0	0	$1/E_6$

In Table 3.9 each row is normalized by the same Young's modulus or shear modulus, we have the definitions for the coupling coefficients defined just the opposite of those in Equation 3.10; where again we assume E_1 larger than E_2.

$$v_{12} = \text{major Poisson's ratio}$$

$$= \text{the larger of the Poisson's ratio}$$

$$= -S_{21}/S_{22} \tag{3.12}$$

$$v_{21} = \text{minor Poisson's ratio}$$

$$= v_{12}E_2/E_1$$

$$= -S_{12}/S_{11} \tag{3.13}$$

As indicated earlier, we do not recommend the coupling coefficients by row normalization shown in Table 3.9. Unfortunately many authors choose this normalization by rows even though it is less rational and consistent than that by columns.

3.8 STIFFNESS IN TERMS OF ENGINEERING CONSTANTS

The expressions of C_{ij} in terms of the engineering constants in the last section are lengthy because of the matrix inversion of the compliances. Such expressions for materials with orthotropic, transversely isotropic and isotropic symmetries can be found in the US Air Force Materials Laboratory report (AFML–TR–66–149, Part II): *Mechanics of Composite Materials*, by Stephen W. Tsai. For example, an orthotropic material in Table 3.3 can be expressed:

$$C_{11} = (1-v_{23}v_{32})VE_1$$

$$C_{22} = (1-v_{31}v_{13})VE_2$$

$$C_{33} = (1-v_{21}v_{12})VE_3$$

$$C_{12} = (v_{12}+v_{13}v_{32})VE_1 = (v_{21}+v_{23}v_{31})VE_2 \tag{3.14}$$

$$C_{13} = (v_{13}+v_{12}v_{23})VE_1 = (v_{31}+v_{32}v_{21})VE_3$$

$$C_{23} = (v_{23}+v_{21}v_{13})VE_2 = (v_{32}+v_{31}v_{12})VE_3$$

$$C_{44} = G_{23}, \ C_{55} = G_{31}, \ C_{66} = G_{12} = E_6$$

where $V = 1/(1-v_{12}v_{21}-v_{32}v_{23}-v_{13}v_{31}-2v_{21}v_{13}v_{32})$

All the engineering constants are defined in Table 3.8. A transversely isotropic material in Table 3.4 can be expressed:

$$C_{11} = (1-v_{23}{}^2)VE_1, \ C_{22} = C_{33} = (1-v_{21}v_{12})VE_2$$

$$C_{12} = C_{13} = v_{21}(1+v_{23})VE_2 = v_{12}(1+v_{23})VE_1 \tag{3.15}$$

$$C_{23} = (v_{23}+v_{21}v_{12})VE_2$$

$$C_{44} = (1-v_{23}-2v_{21}v_{12})VE_2/2, \; C_{55} = C_{66} = G_{12} = E_6$$

where $V = 1/[(1+v_{23})(1-v_{23}-2v_{21}v_{12})]$

For an isotropic material Equations 3.15 above can be further simplified:

$$C_{11} = C_{22} = C_{33} = (1-v)VE$$

$$C_{12} = C_{13} = C_{23} = vVE \qquad\qquad (3.16)$$

$$C_{44} = C_{55} = C_{66} = G = E/[2(1+v)]$$

where $V = 1/[(1+v)(1-2v)]$

These relations are relatively simple because shear coupling is absent in the matrix in Table 3.4. Similar closed–form expressions for a monoclinic material shown in Table 3.2 would be nearly impossible because shear coupling terms like C_{16}, et al are present. The inversion of this matrix is quite lengthy. Numerical values for a CFRP composite (T300/5208) will be shown at the end of the next section.

3.9 CONCLUSIONS

Generalized Hooke's law in three dimensions can be simplified by the presence of material symmetry and the chosen orientation of the reference coordinates. Material behavior however is dictated more by the number of nonzero components than by the number of independent constants. We strongly recommend that the intent of contracted notation be followed faithfully. Inconsistent use of this notation can lead to unnecessary confusion and complication. We must also be sure when we define the coupling coefficients. There are two commonly used definitions, shown in Equations 3.10 through 3.13. We use Equations 3.10 and 3.11.

Section 4

PLANE STRESS AND PLANE STRAIN

Stress analysis is done in two dimensions for most materials including composites. Plane stress and plane strain are the most common two dimensional cases. The generalized Hooke's law can be greatly simplified for these two dimensional cases.

4.1 PLANE STRESS

The assumed zero and nonzero stress and strain components for various anisotropic materials are listed in Table 4.1. The term on– or off– refer to the coordinate axes placed on or off the material symmetry axes, respectively. The off axis is a rotation about the 3– or z–axis, the normal to the 1–2 or x–y plane, respectively.

TABLE 4.1 STRESS AND STRAIN COMPONENTS UNDER PLANE STRESS IN THE 1–2 PLANE.

Type of Material Symmetry	No symmetry, Triclinic, Off–monoclinic	On–monoclinic, Off–ortho, Off–trans–iso	On–ortho, On–trans–iso, Isotropic
Nonzero Constants	36	20*	12
$\sigma_1, \sigma_2, \sigma_6$	$\neq 0$	$\neq 0$	$\neq 0$
$\sigma_3, \sigma_4, \sigma_5$	$= 0$	$= 0$	$= 0$
$\varepsilon_1, \varepsilon_2, \varepsilon_3, \varepsilon_6$	$\neq 0$	$\neq 0$	$\neq 0$
$\varepsilon_4, \varepsilon_5$	$\neq 0$	$= 0$	$= 0$

* for off–orthotropic and off–transversely isotropic symmetries if the plane containing plane stress is not perpendicular to the axis of rotation then all six strain components exist.

It is assumed that the 1–2 plane is the plane of interest, and the nonzero stress and strain components in this plane can be related by a specialized Hooke's law, as follows:

$$\{\varepsilon\} = [S]\{\sigma\}, \text{ or } \varepsilon_i = S_{ij}\sigma_j, \quad i,j = 1,2,6 \tag{4.1}$$

where the compliance for plane stress has the same components as that for the

3–dimensional Hooke's law because stress components are specified. Because of Poisson or shear coupling the normal strain in the thickness or the 3 direction is not zero. From the specialized Hooke's law we can show:

$$\varepsilon_3 = S_{31}\sigma_1 + S_{32}\sigma_2 + S_{36}\sigma_6 \tag{4.2}$$

If the material is isotropic, the two Poisson couplings are equal and the shear coupling vanishes:

$$\varepsilon_3 = -\nu(\sigma_1 + \sigma_2)/E \tag{4.3}$$

The stiffness matrix for plane stress for triclinic material symmetry which is the most general material symmetry is beyond the scope of this section. For other material symmetries, we use the 3–dimensional stress–strain relations for materials with 20 or less nonzero components, shown for example in Table 3.2. For plane stress in 1–2 plane, the stresses in terms of the stiffness matrix are as follows:

$$\sigma_1 = C_{11}\varepsilon_1 + C_{12}\varepsilon_2 + C_{13}\varepsilon_3 + C_{16}\varepsilon_6$$

$$\sigma_2 = C_{21}\varepsilon_1 + C_{22}\varepsilon_2 + C_{23}\varepsilon_3 + C_{26}\varepsilon_6$$

$$\sigma_6 = C_{61}\varepsilon_1 + C_{62}\varepsilon_2 + C_{63}\varepsilon_3 + C_{66}\varepsilon_6 \tag{4.4}$$

$$\sigma_3 = C_{31}\varepsilon_1 + C_{32}\varepsilon_2 + C_{33}\varepsilon_3 + C_{36}\varepsilon_6 = 0$$

$$\sigma_4 = \sigma_5 = 0$$

We can eliminate the normal strain in the 3–direction as a dependent variable by solving the fourth line in Equation 4.4:

$$\varepsilon_3 = -(C_{31}\varepsilon_1 + C_{32}\varepsilon_2 + C_{36}\varepsilon_6)/C_{33} \tag{4.5}$$

By substituting Equation 4.5 into 4.4, we now have the stress–strain relation for plane stress in the 1–2 plane in terms of reduced stiffness:

$$\{\sigma\} = [Q]\{\varepsilon\}, \text{ or } \quad \sigma_i = Q_{ij}\varepsilon_j, \quad i,j = 1,2,6 \tag{4.6}$$

where $\quad Q_{ij} = C_{ij} - C_{i3}C_{j3}/C_{33}$ $\qquad\qquad$ (4.7)

$\qquad\qquad$ = reduced stiffness for plane stress

If the plane stress is in the 2–3, or the 1–3 plane, we have respectively:

$$Q_{ij} = C_{ij} - C_{i1}C_{j1}/C_{11}, \quad i,j = 2,3,4$$
$$Q_{ij} = C_{ij} - C_{i2}C_{j2}/C_{22}, \quad i,j = 1,3,5 \tag{4.8}$$

The three cases of plane stress that lie in the planes of symmetry are shown in Figure 4.1. Plane stress can exist on the symmetry planes only. If a material has no symmetry, the last two shear stresses in Equation 4.4 will not vanish. Then we cannot have plane stress.

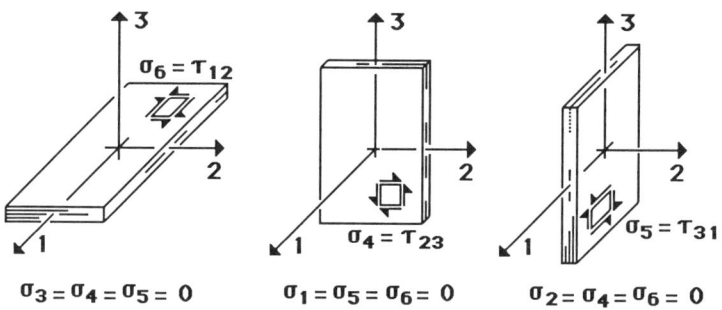

$\sigma_6 = \tau_{12}$

$\sigma_4 = \tau_{23}$

$\sigma_5 = \tau_{31}$

$\sigma_3 = \sigma_4 = \sigma_5 = 0$ $\sigma_1 = \sigma_5 = \sigma_6 = 0$ $\sigma_2 = \sigma_4 = \sigma_6 = 0$

FIGURE 4.1   GRAPHICAL REPRESENTATION OF PLANE STRESS WITH THEIR PLANES COINCIDENT WITH THE SYMMETRY PLANES. THE ZERO NORMAL AND THE SHEAR COMPONENTS IN THE CONTRACTED NOTATION ARE SHOWN.

4.2 MATERIAL SYMMETRIES FOR PLANE STRESS

The number of independent and nonzero constants for each symmetry is listed in Table 4.2. The behavior of materials is controlled more by the number of nonzero constants than by the number of independent constants. For example, the nonzero constants will appear as coefficients of the equation of equilibrium of a plate. The governing equations of a laminated plate with holes or cracks contain all six components of the compliance matrix; see Section 21 Notch Strength. These coefficients will dictate the behavior of the plate under a given set of boundary conditions. It does not matter if these nonzero coefficients are related or not. Thus for plane stress, the principal difference between the 6–constant material and the 4–constant one is the existence or absence of shear coupling.

TABLE 4.2 ELASTIC MODULI UNDER PLANE STRESS

Material Anisotropic(6) Symmetry (independent constants)	On–orthotropic(4) Off–orthotropic(4) Off–square symm(3)	On–square symm(3) Isotropic(2)
Nonzero Components	6	4
$Q_{11}, Q_{22}, Q_{12}, Q_{66}$ $S_{11}, S_{22}, S_{12}, S_{66}$	$\neq 0$	$\neq 0$
Q_{16}, Q_{26} S_{16}, S_{26}	$\neq 0$	$= 0$

The square symmetric material has equal stiffness on its symmetry axes, but unlike the isotropic material the in–plane shear is independent. So there are 3 independent constants. A fabric with balanced weave is a square symmetric material.

4.3 PLANE STRESS ENGINEERING CONSTANTS

Engineering constants are defined from the components of compliance:

$$E_1 = 1/S_{11}, \quad E_2 = 1/S_{22}, \quad E_6 = G_{12} = 1/S_{66} \qquad (4.9)$$

The coupling coefficients above are defined using normalization by columns as in Table 3.8, not by rows as in Table 3.9.

$$v_{21} = -S_{21}/S_{11}, \quad v_{12} = -S_{12}/S_{22} = v_{21}E_2/E_1$$

$$v_{61} = S_{61}/S_{11}, \quad v_{16} = S_{16}/S_{66} = v_{61}E_6/E_1 \qquad (4.10)$$

$$v_{62} = S_{62}/S_{22}, \quad v_{26} = S_{26}/S_{66} = v_{62}E_6/E_2$$

Finally explicit relations between engineering constants and the stiffness components exist through the inversion of the compliance matrix. But these relations are simple only for the on–axis orthotropic material. Simple relations for anisotropic and off–axis orthotropic materials do not exist; i.e.,

$$Q_{11} \neq E_1/(1-v_{21}v_{12}), \quad Q_{22} \neq E_2/(1-v_{21}v_{12})$$

$$Q_{12} \neq v_{21}Q_{11} \neq v_{12}Q_{22}, \quad Q_{66} \neq E_6 \neq G_{12} \qquad (4.11)$$

In order to avoid confusion we designate the on–axis orthotropic constants by letter subscripts to distinguish them from numeric subscripts of the anisotropic and off–axis orthotropic constants:

$$Q_{xx} = E_x/(1-v_xv_y), \quad Q_{yy} = E_y/(1-v_xv_y)$$

$$Q_{xy} = v_xQ_{yy} = v_yQ_{xx}, \quad Q_{ss} = E_s \qquad (4.12)$$

For the on–axis square symmetric material:

$$Q_{xx} = Q_{yy} = E_x/(1-v_x^2),$$

$$Q_{xy} = v_xQ_{xx}, \qquad (4.13)$$

$$Q_{ss} = E_s \neq E_x/2(1+v_x)$$

where the shear modulus is not dependent on the Young's modulus and Poisson's ratio, making this a 3–constant material. These constants are all defined relative to the symmetry axes. There are two sets of such axes, one 45 degrees from the other.

For the isotropic material:

$$Q_{xx} = Q_{yy} = E/(1-v^2)$$

$$Q_{xy} = vE/(1-v^2) \qquad (4.14)$$

$$Q_{ss} = G = E/2(1+v)$$

The last equation is derived from Equation 3.3:

$$G = (Q_{xx} - Q_{xy})/2 \tag{4.15}$$

The basic differences between the square symmetric versus isotropic materials are: the 3 versus 2 independent constants, and that the engineering constants must be measured from the symmetry axes versus those from any axes, respectively. The subscripts in the engineering constants in Equation 4.13 are there to signify nonisotropic constants.

4.4 PLANE STRAIN

This is the other 2–dimensional state very analogous to the state of plane stress.

TABLE 4.3 STRESS AND STRAIN COMPONENTS UNDER PLANE STRAIN IN THE 1–2 PLANE.

Type of Material Symmetry	No symmetry, Triclinic, Off–monoclinic	On–monoclinic, Off–ortho, Off–trans–iso	On–ortho, On–trans–iso, Isotropic
Nonzero Constants	36	20*	12
$\varepsilon_1, \varepsilon_2, \varepsilon_6$	$\neq 0$	$\neq 0$	$\neq 0$
$\varepsilon_3, \varepsilon_4, \varepsilon_5$	$= 0$	$= 0$	$= 0$
$\sigma_1, \sigma_2, \sigma_3, \sigma_6$	$\neq 0$	$\neq 0$	$\neq 0$
σ_4, σ_5	$\neq 0$	$= 0$	$= 0$

* for off–orthotropic and off–transversely isotropic symmetries if the plane containing plane strain is not perpendicular to the axis of rotation then all six stress components exist.

Since strain components are specified in plane strain, the stiffness components for 2–dimensional plane strain are the same as those for the 3–dimensional Hooke's law. Therefore, the stress and strain components in the 1–2 plane, for example, are related as follows:

$$\{\sigma\} = [C]\{\varepsilon\}, \text{ or } \quad \sigma_i = C_{ij}\varepsilon_j, \quad i,j = 1,2,6 \tag{4.16}$$

For materials other than the triclinic, 20–constants type, we can show that the stress component normal to the 1–2 plane can be determined:

$$\sigma_3 = C_{31}\varepsilon_1 + C_{32}\varepsilon_2 + C_{36}\varepsilon_6 \tag{4.17}$$

The compliance components, however, must be modified for the plane strain state. This modification can be derived by substituting Equation 4.17 into the generalized Hooke's law to eliminate σ_3 as an independent variable. This derivation is analogous to the reduced stiffness matrix for the plane stress case. Now we have the reduced compliance case for the plane strain. Assuming that the 1–2 plane is the plane strain, we have

$$\{\varepsilon\} = [R]\{\sigma\}, \text{ or } \varepsilon_i = R_{ij}\sigma_j, \quad i,j = 1,2,6 \tag{4.18}$$

where $R_{ij} = S_{ij} - S_{i3}S_{j3}/S_{33}$ \hfill (4.19)

= reduced compliance for plane strain.

Like the case of plane stress, the reduced compliance matrix for plane strain for triclinic material symmetry is also beyond the scope of this section and thus is not obtained. Similar to Equation 4.8 and Figure 4.1, we can have the reduced compliance for plane strain in the other two symmetry axes. This is shown in Figure 4.2.

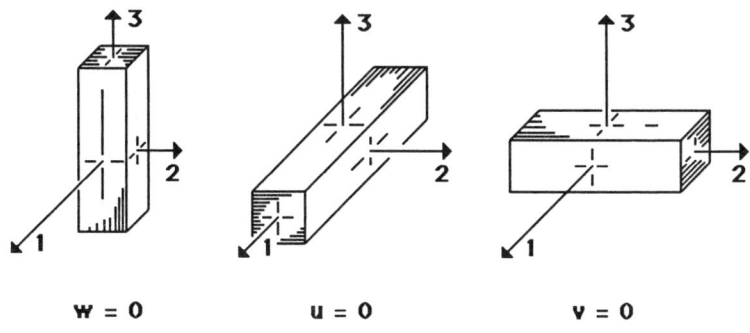

w = 0   **u = 0**   **v = 0**

FIGURE 4.2   GRAPHICAL REPRESENTATION OF PLANE STRAIN IN THE PLANES OF ORTHOGONAL SYMMETRY. ASSUMED ZERO DISPLACEMENT IS SHOWN FOR EACH CASE.

4.5 PLANE STRAIN ENGINEERING CONSTANTS

We can derive the engineering constants associated with plane strain same as those with plane stress; e.g.,

$$E_1 = 1/R_{11}, \ldots v_{21} = -R_{21}/R_{11}, \ldots \tag{4.20}$$

The coupling coefficients are based on normalization by columns as in Table 3.8 and Equation 4.10. Again we wish to emphasize that there are at least two systems of normalization, one by columns and one by rows. We recommend the former.

The relations between engineering constants and the stiffness components are not as straightforward because matrix inversion is involved.

The independent and nonzero constants of anisotropic materials under plane strain, analogous to those in Table 4.2 for plane stress, are shown in Table 4.4.

TABLE 4.4 ELASTIC MODULI UNDER PLANE STRAIN

Material Symmetry (independent constants)	Anisotropic(6) Off–orthotropic(4) Off–square symm(3)	On–orthotropic(4) On–square symm(3) Isotropic(2)
Nonzero Components	6	4
$C_{11}, C_{22}, C_{12}, C_{66}$ $R_{11}, R_{22}, R_{12}, R_{66}$	$\neq 0$	$\neq 0$
C_{16}, C_{26} R_{16}, R_{26}	$\neq 0$	$= 0$

4.6 SAMPLE PROBLEMS IN PLANE STRESS

We can compute all the elastic constants from a given set of engineering constants. We take the following values for unidirectional CFRP laminate, T300/5208 (values for this and other composite materials can be found in Table 6.5):

$$E_x = 181 \text{ GPa}, \; E_y = 10.3 \text{ GPa}, \; v_x = 0.28, \; E_s = 7.17 \text{ GPa}$$

Then, from Equation 4.12

$$v_y = v_x E_y/E_x = 0.28(10.3/181) = 0.0159$$

$$Q_{xx} = E_x/(1 - v_x v_y) = 181/(1 - 0.28 \times .0159) = 181.81 \text{ GPa}$$

$$Q_{yy} = E_y/(1 - v_x v_y) = 10.3/(1 - 0.28 \times .0159) = 10.346 \text{ GPa}$$

$$Q_{xy} = v_x Q_{yy} = v_y Q_{xx} = 0.28 \times 10.346 = 2.897 \text{ GPa} \tag{4.21}$$

$$Q_{ss} = E_s = 7.17 \text{ GPa}$$

From Equation 4.9

$$S_{xx} = 1/E_x = 1/181 = 5.52 \; 1/\text{TPa}$$

$$S_{yy} = 1/E_y = 1/10.3 = 97.09 \; 1/\text{TPa}$$

$$S_{xy} = -v_x/E_x = -v_y/E_y = -1.55 \; 1/\text{TPa} \tag{4.22}$$

$$S_{ss} = 1/E_s = 1/7.17 = 139.47 \; 1/\text{TPa}$$

The product of the stiffness matrix and compliance matrix should be a unity matrix because one matrix is the inverse of the other; i.e.,

$$[Q] = [S]^{-1} \tag{4.23}$$

4.7 SAMPLE PROBLEMS IN PLANE STRAIN

Find the reduced compliance matrix and stiffness matrix of an on–axis transversely isotropic material. We assume that the 2–3 plane is isotropic. If we further assume that the 1–2 plane is under plane strain, shown as the case on the left in Figure 4.2, we need the following two additional components of the compliance matrix in order to complete Equation 4.19:

$$S_{zz} = S_{yy} = 97.09 \text{ 1/TPa, from } E_z = E_y$$

$$v_{yz} = 0.5, \text{ from which } S_{yz} = -v_{yz}/E_y = -48.54 \text{ 1/TPa}$$

$$(4.24)$$

The transverse–transverse Poisson's ratio, v_{yz}, for this material was found slightly higher than 0.5 by M. Knight, *Journal of Composite Materials*, Volume 16 (March 1982), p. 153. This Poisson's ratio was shown to be bounded between 0 and 1. The frequently assumed value of 0.3 is lower than what we have found.

From Equation 4.19, and letting 1 = x, 2 = y, 3 = z, we can compute the reduced compliance matrix for a plane strain in the 1–2 plane:

$$R_{xx} = S_{xx} - S_{xz}^2/S_{zz} = 5.52 - 1.55^2/97.09 = 5.51 \text{ 1/TPa}$$

$$R_{yy} = S_{yy} - S_{yz}^2/S_{zz} = 97.09 - 48.54^2/97.09$$

$$= 72.82 \text{ 1/TPa} \qquad (4.25)$$

$$R_{xy} = S_{xy} - S_{xz}S_{yz}/S_{zz} = -1.55 - 1.55 \times 48.54/97.09$$

$$= -2.325 \text{ 1/TPa}$$

$$R_{ss} = S_{ss} = 139.47 \text{ 1/TPa, where } S_{zs} = S_{36} = 0$$

Reverting to numeric subscripts to conform to Table 3.4, the following 3–dimensional stiffness matrix components can be computed from Equation 3.15

$$V = 1/(1+v_{23})(1-v_{23}-2v_{21}v_{12})$$

$$= 1/(1+0.5)(1-0.5-2 \times 0.28 \times 0.0159) = 1.36$$

$$C_{11} = (1-v_{23}^2)VE_1 = (1-0.5^2) \times 1.36 \times 181 = 184.6 \text{ GPa}$$

$$C_{22} = C_{33} = (1-v_{21}v_{12})VE_2 = (1-0.28 \times 0.0159) \times 1.36 \times 10.3$$

$$= 13.94 \text{ GPa}$$

$$C_{12} = C_{13} = v_{21}(1+v_{23})VE_2 = v_{12}(1+v_{23})VE_1$$

$$= 0.28 \times (1+0.5) \times 1.36 \times 10.3 = 5.88 \text{ GPa}$$

$$(4.26)$$

$$C_{23} = (v_{23}+v_{21}v_{12})VE_2 = (0.5+0.28 \times 0.0159) \times 1.36 \times 10.3$$

$$= 7.06 \text{ GPa}$$

$C_{44} = (1-v_{23}-2v_{21}v_{12})VE_2/2$

$\quad\quad = (1-0.5-2\text{x}0.28\text{x}0.0159)\text{x}1.36\text{x}10.3/2 = 3.44 \text{ GPa}$

$C_{55} = C_{66} = G_{12} = E_6 = 7.17 \text{ GPa}$

For the plane strain case, the compliance and stiffness matrices are the inverse of each other. Their product must produce a unity matrix; i.e.,

$$[C] = [R]^{-1} \tag{4.27}$$

where the stiffness matrix is 3x3, with indices 1, 2 and 6.

4.8 CONCLUSIONS

The stiffness and compliance matrices in the generalized Hooke's law for 3–dimensional stress and strain cannot be transferred directly to plane stress and plane strain. Modifications to the 3–dimensional state are necessary. The reduced stiffness for the plane stress case, and the reduced compliance for the plane strain case are examples of the modifications, and are summarized in Table 4.5.

TABLE 4.5 SUMMARY OF 3– AND 2–DIMENSIONAL ELASTIC MODULI

Dimensions	3–Dimension	2–D Plane Stress	2–D Plane Strain
Stiffness	C_{ij}	Q_{ij}	C_{ij}
Compliance	S_{ij}	S_{ij}	R_{ij}

Section 5

STRESS AND STRAIN TRANSFORMATIONS

5.1 TRANSFORMATION EQUATIONS

Stress and strain at a point are functions of the reference coordinate axis. This coordinate axis dependence is of fundamental importance not only because the true nature of stress and strain is explained, but also the relations between laminate stress and strain and ply stress and strain can be explicitly stated. One outstanding feature of composite materials is the highly directional or anisotropic property. It is often advantageous to rotate unidirectional or laminated composites to some off–axis orientation. The transformation equations are necessary to calculate the stress and strain in this off–axis and the principal axis orientations. The latter can be used as one design method of selecting the optimum laminate orientation.

Applied loads to a structure are usually given in the laminate axes while failure criteria, for example, are usually applied to the stress or strain relative to the ply axes. The transformation equations allow us to go from one coordinate system to another.

The components of stress and strain change in accordance with specific transformation equations. The equations for stress are different from those for strain because we have elected to use the contracted notation which requires the use of engineering shear strain. The transformation equations in both the matrix and index notations are, as follows:

$$
\begin{aligned}
\{\sigma'\} &= [J]\{\sigma\} & \sigma_i' &= J_{ij}\sigma_j, \ i,j = 1,2,6 \\
\{\sigma\} &= [J]^{-1}\{\sigma'\} & \sigma_i &= J_{ij}^{-1}\sigma_j' \\
\{\varepsilon\} &= [J^T]\{\varepsilon'\} & \varepsilon_i &= J_{ji}\varepsilon_j' \\
\{\varepsilon'\} &= [J^T]^{-1}\{\varepsilon\} & \varepsilon_i' &= J_{ji}^{-1}\varepsilon_j
\end{aligned}
\tag{5.1}
$$

$$
\text{where} \quad [J] =
\begin{vmatrix}
m^2 & n^2 & 2mn \\
n^2 & m^2 & -2mn \\
-mn & mn & m^2-n^2
\end{vmatrix}
\tag{5.2}
$$

$$[J]^{-1} = \begin{vmatrix} m^2 & n^2 & -2mn \\ n^2 & m^2 & 2mn \\ mn & -mn & m^2-n^2 \end{vmatrix} \qquad (5.3)$$

$$[J^T] = \begin{vmatrix} m^2 & n^2 & -mn \\ n^2 & m^2 & mn \\ 2mn & -2mn & m^2-n^2 \end{vmatrix} \qquad (5.4)$$

$$[J^T]^{-1} = \begin{vmatrix} m^2 & n^2 & mn \\ n^2 & m^2 & -mn \\ -2mn & 2mn & m^2-n^2 \end{vmatrix} \qquad (5.5)$$

where $m = \cos\theta$, $n = \sin\theta$

Typical values for transformation matrices of frequently used ply angles of 0, 90, 45 and –45 degrees are:

$$[J]^{(0)} = \begin{matrix} 1 & 0 & 0 \\ 0 & 1 & 0 \\ 0 & 0 & 1 \end{matrix} \qquad [J^T]^{-1(0)} = \begin{matrix} 1 & 0 & 0 \\ 0 & 1 & 0 \\ 0 & 0 & 1 \end{matrix} \qquad (5.6)$$

$$[J]^{(90)} = \begin{matrix} 0 & 1 & 0 \\ 1 & 0 & 0 \\ 0 & 0 & -1 \end{matrix} \qquad [J^T]^{-1(90)} = \begin{matrix} 0 & 1 & 0 \\ 1 & 0 & 0 \\ 0 & 0 & -1 \end{matrix} \qquad (5.7)$$

$$[J]^{(45)} = \begin{matrix} 0.5 & 0.5 & 1 \\ 0.5 & 0.5 & -1 \\ -0.5 & 0.5 & 0 \end{matrix} \qquad [J^T]^{-1(45)} = \begin{matrix} 0.5 & 0.5 & 0.5 \\ 0.5 & 0.5 & -0.5 \\ -1 & 1 & 0 \end{matrix} \qquad (5.8)$$

$$[J]^{(-45)} = \begin{matrix} 0.5 & 0.5 & -1 \\ 0.5 & 0.5 & 1 \\ 0.5 & -0.5 & 0 \end{matrix} \qquad [J^T]^{-1(-45)} = \begin{matrix} 0.5 & 0.5 & -0.5 \\ 0.5 & 0.5 & 0.5 \\ 1 & -1 & 0 \end{matrix} \qquad (5.9)$$

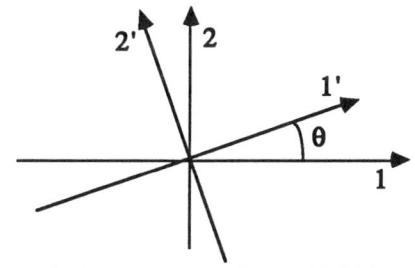

FIGURE 5.1 RELATION BETWEEN THE 1–2 AND 1'–2' COORDINATES.

5.2 MULTIPLE–ANGLE TRANSFORMATION

This is an alternative form using linear combinations of the stress components:

$$p_\sigma = (\sigma_1 + \sigma_2)/2, \quad q_\sigma = (\sigma_1 - \sigma_2)/2, \quad r_\sigma = \sigma_6 \tag{5.10}$$

For the strain components, we have analogous combinations except that tensorial strain must be used. The factor of 1/2 is needed.

$$p_\varepsilon = (\varepsilon_1 + \varepsilon_2)/2, \quad q_\varepsilon = (\varepsilon_1 - \varepsilon_2)/2, \quad r_\varepsilon = \varepsilon_6/2 \tag{5.11}$$

We can rewrite the stress transformation equations in matrix form using the linear combinations in Equation 5.10:

$$\{p',q',r'\}_\sigma = [K]\{p,q,r\}_\sigma$$

$$\{p,q,r\}_\sigma = [K]^{-1}\{p',q',r'\}_\sigma \tag{5.12}$$

Similarly, we can write the strain transformation in matrix form:

$$\{p',q',r'\}_\varepsilon = [K^T]^{-1}\{p,q,r\}_\varepsilon$$

$$\{p,q,r\}_\varepsilon = [K^T]\{p',q',r'\}_\varepsilon \tag{5.13}$$

where
$$[K] = [K^T]^{-1} = \begin{vmatrix} 1 & 0 & 0 \\ 0 & \cos 2\theta & \sin 2\theta \\ 0 & -\sin 2\theta & \cos 2\theta \end{vmatrix} \tag{5.14}$$

$$[K]^{-1} = [K^T] = \begin{vmatrix} 1 & 0 & 0 \\ 0 & \cos 2\theta & -\sin 2\theta \\ 0 & \sin 2\theta & \cos 2\theta \end{vmatrix} \tag{5.15}$$

These transformations are simpler than those with the second power of sines and cosines because the matrices are rigid–body rotations with double angles. In fact, Mohr's circles are constructed by this double angle rotation. Stress and strain now have the same transformation because tensorial shear strain is used in Equation 5.11.

5.3 PRINCIPAL STRESS AND STRAIN

For every state of stress, there is one particular orientation of the coordinate axes when the normal components reach extremum values and the shear vanish. Using Equation 5.12, this orientation θ_0 is found by letting:

$$r' = 0 = -q\sin2\theta_0 + r\cos2\theta_0, \quad \text{or}$$

$$\tan2\theta_0 = r/q = 2\sigma_6/(\sigma_1 - \sigma_2)$$

$$\sigma_1^{prin} = \sigma_I = p+R$$

$$\sigma_2^{prin} = \sigma_{II} = p-R \tag{5.16}$$

$$R^2 = q^2 + r^2$$

$$\sigma_6^{prin} = 0$$

Subscript σ is left out here; all quantities are related to stress.

At 45 degrees from the principal axes, the shear reaches maximum and the normal components are equal.

At $\theta = \theta_0 \pm 45$

$$\sigma_1^{max\ shear} = \sigma_2^{max\ shear} = p$$

$$\sigma_6^{max\ shear} = \pm R \tag{5.17}$$

The Mohr's circle representation of stress components and their variation with orientation is shown in Figure 5.2.

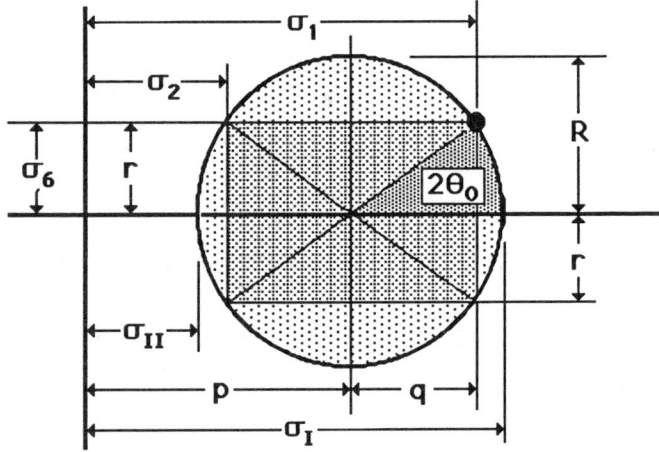

FIGURE 5.2 MOHR'S CIRCLE REPRESENTATION OF STRESS AND ITS PRINCIPAL
COMPONENTS.

Similar relations for the principal strain exist. But unlike stress our strain is not a tensorial entity. We use engineering shear strain as defined in Equation 2.3. The traditional Mohr's circle for stress must be modified to take into account the engineering shear strain.

The relations analogous to Equation 5.16 are:

$$r' = 0 = -q\sin2\theta_0 + r\cos2\theta_0, \text{ or}$$

$$\tan2\theta_0 = r/q = \varepsilon_6/(\varepsilon_1 - \varepsilon_2)$$

$$\varepsilon_1^{prin} = \varepsilon_I = p+R, \qquad \varepsilon_2^{prin} = \varepsilon_{II} = p-R$$

$$R^2 = q^2 + r^2, \qquad \varepsilon_6^{prin} = 0$$

(5.18)

At $\theta = \theta_0 \pm 45$

$$\varepsilon_1^{max\ shear} = \varepsilon_2^{max\ shear} = p$$

$$\varepsilon_6^{max\ shear} = \pm R$$

(5.19)

The vertical axis r in Figure 5.2 is one half the engineering shear strain. This is shown in Figure 5.3.

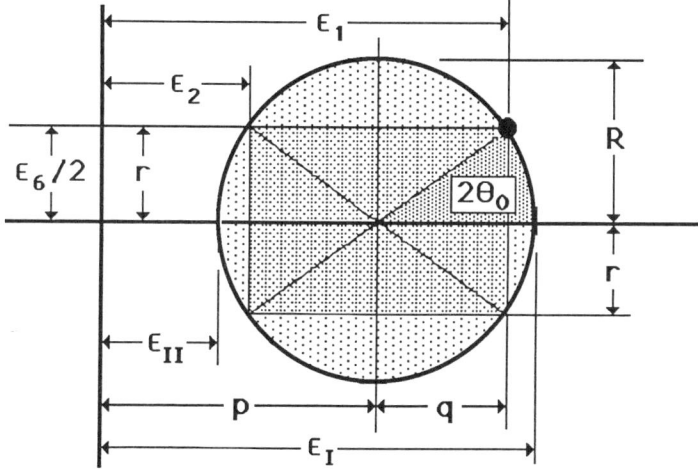

FIGURE 5.3   MOHR'S CIRCLE REPRESENTATION OF STRAIN AND ITS PRINCIPAL COMPONENTS. NOTE THAT ENGINEERING SHEAR STRAIN IS TWICE THE TENSORIAL SHEAR STRAIN.

The Mohr's circle representation is of importance to failure and strength envelopes in strain space. Those envelopes will be discussed in detail in Sections 11 and 12. But we do like to point out that the rotation of a ply angle can be portrayed by identical rotation by doubled angle in the Mohr's space. With such simple relation, it is easy to generate failure and strength envelopes by rigid body rotation if such rotation is done about the p–axis, where p is defined in Equation 5.11. This is shown in Figure 12.16.

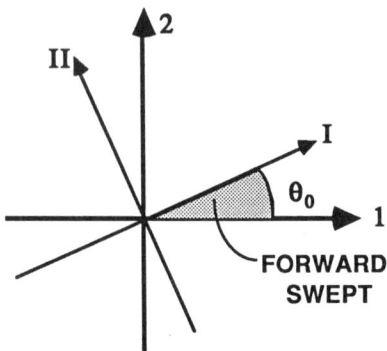

FIGURE 5.4   RELATION BETWEEN THE 1–2 AND I–II AXES. COUNTER CLOCKWISE
PHASE ANGLES FROM THE REFRENCE AXIS TO THE PRINCIPAL AXIS IN
MOHR'S CIRCLES IN FIGURES 5.2 AND 5.3 CORRESPOND TO A
CLOCKWISE ROTATION IN THIS FIGURE OR A FORWARD SWEPT
DIRECTION WHEN WE 'FLY' OR HEAD ALONG THE 2–AXIS.

5.4 STRESS AND STRAIN INVARIANTS

Invariants are combinations of stress or strain components that remain
constant under coordinate transformation. For example, linear invariants are
the first terms in Equations 5.10 and 5.11; i.e., $\mathbf{p}$. Quadratic invariants
include those in Equations 5.16 and 5.18; i.e., $\mathbf{R}$. Geometrically, $\mathbf{p}$ is the
center of the Mohr's circle; $\mathbf{R}$, the radius. Both remain invariant when
transformation angle θ changes.

Invariants are useful for the design of composites. We can easily show that
the following are invariant:

$$|\sigma^{mises}|^2 = |\sigma|^2 = \sigma_1{}^2 - \sigma_1\sigma_2 + \sigma_2{}^2 + 3\sigma_6{}^2 \tag{5.20}$$

$$|\varepsilon^{iso}|^2 = (1+v^2)/E^2 \ \{(\sigma^{mises})^2 + ((1-4v+v^2)(\sigma_1\sigma_2-\sigma_6)^2 \ /(1+v^2)\} \tag{5.21}$$

$$|\varepsilon|^2 = \varepsilon_1{}^2 + \varepsilon_2{}^2 + \varepsilon_6{}^2/2 \tag{5.22}$$

We may call $|\sigma|$ in Equation 5.20 the von Mises invariant, which can be used
as an effective stress or strength of a material under combined stresses. We
may call $|\varepsilon|$ in Equation 5.22 an effective strain invariant, which can be used
as a measure of deformation or susceptibility to buckling of a material under
combined strains. Both invariants are useful indicators to rank composite
laminates.

Using the effective strain in Equation 5.22 as a basis for design is better than
using one of the normal strain components. The former is a scalar, and the
latter is not. The difference is fundamental but ignored by many practicing
engineers. We must design with invariants in order to arrive at an invariant
design. If we do not use invariants, such as the use of the maximum normal
strain of a laminate, our design will depend on the choice of the coordinate
system. For example, the thickness of an aircraft wing cover will be

different if we use the leading edge instead of the trailing edge as our reference. It is that wrong.

Geometrically, the effective strain |ε| derived from the strain invariant is a vector originating from the origin of the strain space. This vector can also be related to strength, and would be a much better choice than using one of the strain components.

5.5 SAMPLE PROBLEMS

Prob 1: Given the following state of stress:

$$\{\sigma\} = \{100, -30, 50\} \tag{5.23}$$

Find the transformed components and the principal and the maximum shear axes.

SOLUTION: Results shown in the following charts are obtained by substituting the values in Equation 5.23 into the first of Equation 5.1.

Figure 5.5 shows the variation of the stress components as a function of coordinate axes, as measured by the angle θ in Figure 5.1. The true essence of transformation is the principal axes, which, in this example, are analogous to the symmetry axes of the material.

From Equation 5.16, the phase angle based on the initial stress in Equation 5.23 is:

$$\theta_0 = [arctan(r/q)]/2 = [arctan(2\times50/130)]/2$$

$$= 18.8 \text{ degree} \tag{5.24}$$

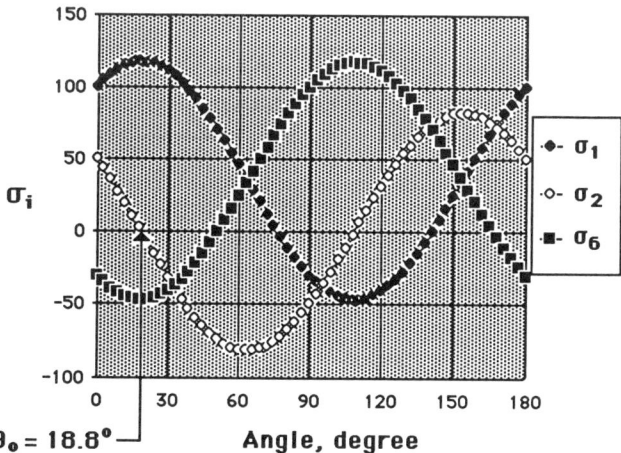

FIGURE 5.5 TRANSFORMED STRESS COMPONENTS OF EQUATION 5.23.

The nature of stress transformation from the principal axes is graphically illustrated in Figure 5.6:

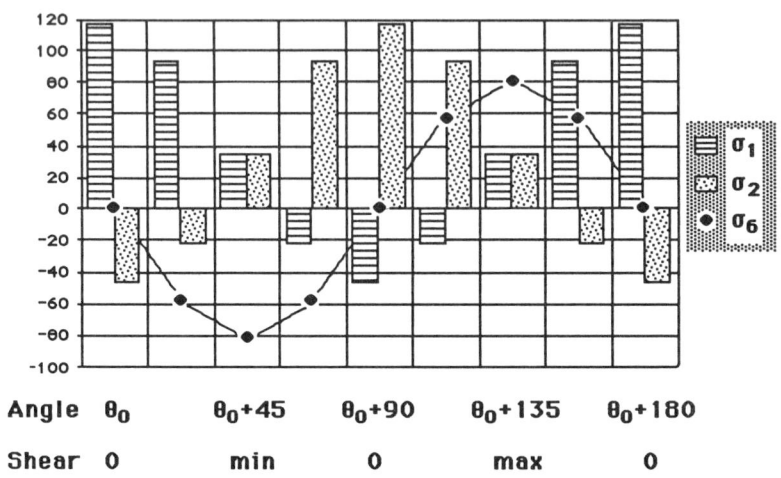

Angle	θ_0	θ_0+45	θ_0+90	θ_0+135	θ_0+180
Shear	0	min	0	max	0

FIGURE 5.6 TRANSFORMED STRESS FROM THE PRINCIPAL AXES.

5.6 CONCLUSIONS

The stress and strain transformations are simple algebraic equations. We want to emphasize the definition of the angle: θ is positive if the new axis is reached by a counterclockwise rotation. This is shown in Figure 5.1. An inverse transformation, as shown in Equation 5.3 for example, merely changes the sign of angle θ, therefore $\sin\theta$.

The concept of principal stress is sometimes used in the failure criteria of isotropic materials. For anisotropic materials, principal stress or strain do not offer anything special in failure criteria. But for highly directional materials, principal stress can be effectively used as an efficient orientation to carry certain combined stresses. The invariants of stress and strain are also important for assessing the performance of composite laminates. We do not recommend the use of stress or strain components by themselves. Use the invariants derived from them.

Finally, the sign of the angle of transformation is critical: we must know if the laminate is to swing forward or backward.

Section 6

PLY STIFFNESS

6.1 TRANSFORMATION OF STIFFNESS

The on–axis plane stress stiffness and compliance of a unidirectional or fabric ply can be computed from the engineering constants as follows:

$$[Q] = \begin{vmatrix} E_x/(1-v_xv_y) & v_xQ_{yy} & 0 \\ v_yQ_{xx} & E_y/(1-v_xv_y) & 0 \\ 0 & 0 & E_s \end{vmatrix} \tag{6.1}$$

where $Q_{12} = Q_{21}, Q_{16} = Q_{61} = 0, Q_{26} = Q_{62} = 0$ (6.2)

$$[S] = \begin{vmatrix} 1/E_x & -v_y/E_y & 0 \\ -v_x/E_x & 1/E_y & 0 \\ 0 & 0 & 1/E_s \end{vmatrix} \tag{6.3}$$

where $S_{12} = S_{21}, S_{16} = S_{61} = 0, S_{26} = S_{62} = 0$ (6.4)

The off–axis stiffness matrix can be derived from the stress–strain relation, Equation 4.6, and stress and strain transformation Equations 5.1:

$$\{\sigma\} = [Q]\{\varepsilon\}, \quad [J]\{\sigma\} = [J][Q]\{\varepsilon\}, \quad \{\sigma'\} = [J][Q][J^T]\{\varepsilon'\}$$

therefore $\{\sigma'\} = [Q']\{\varepsilon'\}$,

where $[Q'] = [J][Q][J^T]$ (6.5)

This stiffness matrix transformation is to go from the 1–axis to the 1'–axis, with the angle of rotation positive in the counterclockwise direction. This is shown as angle ϕ in Figure 6.1. The material symmetry axes coincide with the 1–2 axes.

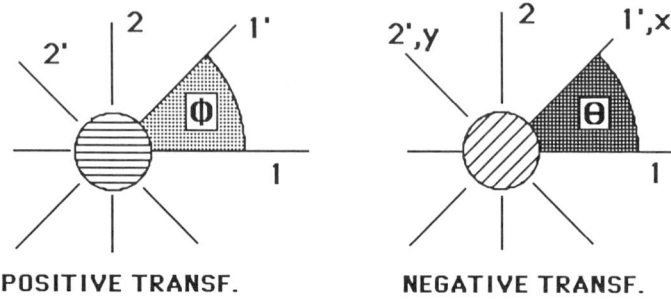

POSITIVE TRANSF.   **NEGATIVE TRANSF.**

FIGURE 6.1 ANGLES FOR POSITIVE AND NEGATIVE TRANSFORMATION MATERIAL
SYMMETRY OR FIBER DIRECTION IS SHOWN IN THE SMALL CIRCLE.

The transformation relation in Equation 6.5 can be shown in the following matrix multiplication table:

TABLE 6.1 POSITIVE TRANSFORMATION OF STIFFNESS MATRIX

On–axis	Q_{xx}	Q_{yy}	Q_{xy}	Q_{ss}
Off–axis				
Q_{11}	m^4	n^4	$2m^2n^2$	$4m^2n^2$
Q_{22}	n^4	m^4	$2m^2n^2$	$4m^2n^2$
Q_{12}	m^2n^2	m^2n^2	m^4+n^4	$-4m^2n^2$
Q_{66}	m^2n^2	m^2n^2	$-2m^2n^2$	$(m^2-n^2)^2$
Q_{16}	$-m^3n$	mn^3	m^3n-mn^3	$2(m^3n-mn^3)$
Q_{26}	$-mn^3$	m^3n	mn^3-m^3n	$2(mn^3-m^3n)$

$m = \cos\phi$, $n = \sin\phi$; see Figure 6.1.
ϕ is positive counterclockwise from the 1– to 1'–axis; see

If a ply material with axes x–y is rotated away from a laminate axes 1–2; the transformation from this off–axis ply to the laminate system is defined as negative in Figure 6.1. The angle is then the ply orientation θ. Any term with odd power of sine changes sign as we go from Table 6.1 to 6.2. This occurs with the 61 and 62 components, the shear coupling components, of the stiffness matrix.

We believe that the negative transformation shown in Table 6.2 is more natural for material properties because it shows the contribution of an off–axis ply to a laminate. Bold face letters are used in Table 6.2 to indicate our preference. Either table can be used but consistency is most important and must be maintained.

TABLE 6.2 NEGATIVE TRANSFORMATION OF STIFFNESS MATRIX

On–axis	Q_{xx}	Q_{yy}	Q_{xy}	Q_{ss}
Off–axis				
Q_{11}	m^4	n^4	$2m^2n^2$	$4m^2n^2$
Q_{22}	n^4	m^4	$2m^2n^2$	$4m^2n^2$
Q_{12}	m^2n^2	m^2n^2	m^4+n^4	$-4m^2n^2$
Q_{66}	m^2n^2	m^2n^2	$-2m^2n^2$	$(m^2-n^2)^2$
Q_{16}	m^3n	$-mn^3$	mn^3-m^3n	$2(mn^3-m^3n)$
Q_{26}	mn^3	$-m^3n$	m^3n-mn^3	$2(m^3n-mn^3)$

$m = \cos\theta$, $n = \sin\theta$; θ is ply orientation, positive in counter–clockwise direction; see Figure 6.1.

The most important relation between the positive and negative transformations or that between Tables 6.1 and 6.2 is:

$$\theta = -\phi \qquad (6.6)$$

6.2 MULTIPLE–ANGLE TRANSFORMATION

We introduce the following linear combinations of the stiffness components so we can express their transformation in multiple angles. The multiple angles functions are derived from the following trigonometric identities :

$$m^4 = (3+4\cos2\theta+\cos4\theta)/8, \qquad m^3n = (2\sin2\theta+\sin4\theta)/8$$

$$m^2n^2 = (1-\cos4\theta)/8, \qquad mn^3 = (2\sin2\theta-\sin4\theta)/8 \qquad (6.7)$$

$$n^4 = (3-4\cos2\theta+\cos4\theta)/8$$

TABLE 6.3 LINEAR COMBINATIONS OF ON–AXIS STIFFNESS MODULI

On–axis	Q_{xx}	Q_{yy}	Q_{xy}	Q_{ss}
Linear comb				
$U_1 = U_4+2U_5$ *	3/8	3/8	1/4	1/2
U_2	1/2	–1/2	0	0
U_3	1/8	1/8	–1/4	–1/2
$U_4 = U_1-2U_5$ *	1/8	1/8	3/4	–1/2
$U_5 = (U_1-U_4)/2$ *	1/8	1/8	–1/4	1/2

* These combinations are invariant.

The transformation in Table 6.2 can now be rewritten:

TABLE 6.4 TRANSFORMATION OF STIFFNESS IN MULTIPLE ANGLES

Trig func Off–axis	Invariant	$\cos 2\theta$	$\cos 4\theta$	$\sin 2\theta$	$\sin 4\theta$
Q_{11}	U_1	U_2	U_3	0	0
Q_{22}	U_1	$-U_2$	U_3	0	0
$Q_{12} = Q_{21}$	U_4	0	$-U_3$	0	0
Q_{66}	U_5	0	$-U_3$	0	0
$Q_{16} = Q_{61}$	0	0	0	$U_2/2$	U_3
$Q_{26} = Q_{62}$	0	0	0	$U_2/2$	$-U_3$

6.3 QUASI–ISOTROPIC CONSTANTS

Associated with every anisotropic material are quasi–isotropic constants derived from the invariants of coordinate transformation. The quasi–isotropic constants represent the lower bound performance of each composite. They are used as a guide in design to insure that, whatever ply angle orientations we may select for a given load, the laminate performance is at least equal if not better than the quasi–isotropic laminate. These quantities are invariant which are better design parameters than any component of a stiffness matrix.

$$[Q]^{\text{iso}} = \begin{vmatrix} U_1 & U_4 & 0 \\ U_4 & U_1 & 0 \\ 0 & 0 & U_5 \end{vmatrix} \qquad (6.8)$$

$$[S]^{\text{iso}} = \begin{vmatrix} U_1/D & -U_4/D & 0 \\ -U_4/D & U_1/D & 0 \\ 0 & 0 & 1/U_5 \end{vmatrix} \qquad (6.9)$$

$$D = U_1{}^2 - U_4{}^2$$

$$E^{\text{iso}} = D/U_1 = (U_1{}^2 - U_4{}^2)/U_1 = U_1[1 - (v^{\text{iso}})^2]$$

$$v^{\text{iso}} = U_4/U_1$$

$$G^{\text{iso}} = U_5$$

(6.10)

6.4 MATRIX INVERSION

$$[S] = [Q]^{-1} \qquad (6.11)$$

$$|Q| = (Q_{11}Q_{22} - Q_{12}{}^2)Q_{66} + 2Q_{12}Q_{26}Q_{16} - Q_{11}Q_{26}{}^2 - Q_{22}Q_{16}{}^2$$

$$S_{11} = (Q_{22}Q_{66}-Q_{26}{}^2)/|Q|, \qquad S_{22} = (Q_{11}Q_{66}-Q_{16}{}^2)/|Q|$$

$$S_{12} = (-Q_{12}Q_{66}+Q_{16}Q_{26})/|Q|, \qquad S_{66} = (Q_{11}Q_{22}-Q_{12}{}^2)/|Q|$$

$$S_{16} = (Q_{12}Q_{26}-Q_{22}Q_{16})/|Q|, \qquad S_{26} = (Q_{12}Q_{16}-Q_{11}Q_{26})/|Q|$$

6.5 ENGINEERING AND COUPLING CONSTANTS

$$E_1 = 1/S_{11}, \quad E_2 = 1/S_{22}, \quad E_6 = G_1 = G_{12} = 1/S_{66}$$

$$\nu_{21} = -S_{21}/S_{11}, \qquad \nu_{12} = -S_{12}/S_{22}$$

$$\nu_{61} = S_{61}/S_{11}, \qquad \nu_{16} = S_{16}/S_{66} \tag{6.12}$$

$$\nu_{62} = S_{62}/S_{22}, \qquad \nu_{26} = S_{26}/S_{66}$$

$$\nu_{21}/\nu_{12} = S_{22}/S_{11} = E_1/E_2$$

$$\nu_{61}/\nu_{16} = S_{66}/S_{11} = E_1/E_6 = E_1/G_1 = E_1/G_{12} \tag{6.13}$$

$$\nu_{62}/\nu_{26} = S_{66}/S_{22} = E_2/E_6 = E_2/G_1 = E_2/G_{12}$$

The coupling constants are derived by using the same normalizing factor for each column of the compliance matrix. As explained in Section 2, we prefer this normalization by columns. Note that others use the normalization by rows; then they have for example:

$$\nu_{12} = -S_{12}/S_{22}, \ \nu_{21} = -S_{21}/S_{11},$$

$$\nu_{12}/\nu_{21} = S_{22}/S_{11} = E_1/E_2 \tag{6.14}$$

Although other authors use this system, we do not think it is rational.

6.6 SAMPLE PROBLEMS

Similar to the data used in the sample problems for plane stress in Section 4.6, we will use the same basic data for CFRP T300/5208 shown in Equation 4.21 and repeated here:

$$[Q] = \begin{vmatrix} 181.81 & 2.897 & 0 \\ 2.897 & 10.346 & 0 \\ 0 & 0 & 7.17 \end{vmatrix} \tag{6.15}$$

From Table 6.2 for $\theta = 45°$, $m = n = 0.707$, we show here how to calculate two of the six components of the off–axis plane stress stiffness:

$$Q_{11} = 1/4(181.81+10.34+2\times2.90+4\times7.17) = 56.66 \ \text{GPa}$$

$$Q_{26} = 1/4(181.81-10.43) = 42.87 \ \text{GPa} \tag{6.16}$$

If the angle is –45 degrees, Q_{11} remains the same but Q_{26} becomes negative.

For multiple–angle transformation listed in Table 6.4, we must first calculate the linear combinations of the plane stress stiffness, such as U_1, in accordance with the first formulas (the first line) in Table 6.3:

$$U_1 = 1/8(3Q_{xx}+3Q_{yy}+2Q_{xy}+4Q_{ss})$$

$$= 1/8(3\times181.81+3\times10.34+2\times2.90+4\times7.17)$$

$$= 76.37 \text{ GPa} \tag{6.17}$$

Similarly,

$$U_2 = 1/2(181.81-10.34) = 85.73 \text{ GPa}$$

$$U_3 = 19.71, U_4 = 22.61, U_5 = 26.88 \text{ GPa} \tag{6.18}$$

Instead of the formulas in Table 6.2, we can now use those in Table 6.4 to calculate the off–axis stiffness components. We will use the 45–degree example as before:

$$Q_{11} = U_1+U_2\cos2\theta+U_3\cos4\theta$$

$$= 76.37+85.73\times0+19.71\times(-1) = 56.66 \text{ GPa} = Q_{22}$$

$$Q_{26} = U_2/2\sin2\theta-U_3\sin4\theta \tag{6.19}$$

$$= 85.73/2-19.71\times0 = 42.87 \text{ GPa} = Q_{16}$$

Similarly,

$$Q_{12} = 42.32 \text{ GPa}, Q_{66} = 46.59 \text{ GPa} \tag{6.20}$$

From Equations 6.8 and 6.10, we can calculate the quasi–isotropic constants which establish the minimum stiffness potential of anisotropic and orthotropic materials:

$$[Q]^{iso} = \begin{vmatrix} 76.37 & 22.61 & 0 \\ 22.61 & 76.37 & 0 \\ 0 & 0 & 26.88 \end{vmatrix} \text{ GPa} \tag{6.21}$$

$$\nu^{iso} = U_4/U_1 = 22.61/76.37 = 0.30$$

$$G^{iso} = U_5 = 26.88 \text{ GPa} \tag{6.22}$$

$$E^{iso} = U_1[1-(\nu^{iso})^2] = 76.37(1-0.30^2) = 69.68 \text{ GPa}$$

If we wish to calculate the compliance of the 45–degree CFRP, we can invert the stiffness matrix in accordance with the formulas in Section 6.4:

$$|Q| = (Q_{11}Q_{22}-Q_{12}^2)Q_{66}+2Q_{12}Q_{26}Q_{16}-Q_{11}Q_{26}^2-Q_{22}Q_{16}^2$$

$$= (56.66^2-42.32^2)\times46.59+2\times(42.32-26.66)\times42.87^2$$

$$= 1.3427 \quad 10^{30}(Pa)^3 \text{ or } (GPa)^2(TPa) \tag{6.23}$$

$$S_{11} = (Q_{22}Q_{66}-Q_{26}^2)/|Q| = (56.66\times46.59-42.87^2)/|Q|$$

$$= 59.75 \text{ 1/TPa} = S_{22}$$

$$S_{12} = (-Q_{12}Q_{66}+Q_{16}Q_{26})/|Q| = (-42.32\times46.59+42.87^2)/|Q|$$

$$= -9.99 \text{ 1/TPa}$$

$$S_{66} = (Q_{11}Q_{22}-Q_{12}{}^2)/|Q| = (56.66^2-42.32^2)/|Q| \qquad (6.24)$$

$$= 105.71 \ 1/TPa$$

$$S_{16} = (Q_{12}Q_{26}-Q_{22}Q_{16})/|Q| = (42.32-56.66)\times42.87/|Q|$$

$$= -45.78 \ 1/TPa = S_{26}$$

For the 45–degree off–axis engineering constants, we use Equation 6.12:

$$E_1 = 1/S_{11} = 1/59.75 = 16.74 \ GPa = E_2$$

$$E_6 = 1/S_{66} = 1/105.71 = 9.46 \ GPa$$

$$v_{21} = -S_{21}/S_{11} = 9.99/59.75 = 0.17 = v_{12} \qquad (6.25)$$

$$v_{61} = S_{61}/S_{11} = -45.78/59.75 = -0.77 = v_{62}$$

$$v_{16} = S_{61}/S_{66} = -45.78/105.71 = -0.43 = v_{26}$$

The importance of the sample problems above is the numerous sets of constants that can represent the elasticity of a composite material. The relations among these sets are fixed and must be followed without deviation. There are no short cuts. We have not shown the transformation relations of the compliance components. They are not necessary here because we have shown how to obtain the off–axis compliance components by inverting the off–axis stiffness components. We emphasize the stiffness components because in laminated plate theory, which we will explain in the next few sections, we take the average of the plane stress stiffness components rather than that of the corresponding compliance components.

The sequence of operations goes from the stiffness matrix as defined in Table 6.2 or 6.4, to the compliance matrix by inversion in Section 6.4 or Equation 6.11, and finally to the engineering constants in Section 6.5. The stiffness components are not directly related to engineering constants except in the case of orthotropic or on–axis materials as defined in Equation 6.1.

The on–axis stiffness components Q_{xx} and Q_{yy} are nearly equal to the corresponding engineering constants E_x and E_y for all highly orthotropic materials. Numerically, the values are 181.00 versus 181.81 GPa for the longitudinal components; and 10.30 versus 10.34 GPa for the transverse components. But in off–axis orientation, Q_{11} is 56.66 GPa for 45 degree angle, and E_1 is 16.74 GPa for the same ply angle. There is a difference of 380 percent!

For proper utilization and design of composite materials, the off–axis plies pose the most formidable barrier for the beginner. We must learn to deal with the transformation of properties with precise relations and avoid guesswork.

6.7 ELASTIC CONSTANTS OF TYPICAL COMPOSITE PLIES

In Table 6.5 a variety of composite materials are listed. The first eight ply materials are unidirectional; the last two, fabric. These elastic constants are average values gathered from different sources. Other proerties of the same composite plies and fabrics listed in Table 6.5 can be found in other sections. In Table 6.5a, the units are in SI; in Table 6.5b, in English.

- Strength properties in Table 11.1.
- Volume and mass fractions in Table 10.1.
- Constants for micromechanics parameters in Table 10.5.
- Hygrothermal expansion coefficients in Table 15.1.

TABLE 6.5a ELASTIC PROPERTIES OF VARIOUS COMPOSITE MATERIALS IN SI

Type	CFRP	BFRP	CFRP	GFRP	KFRP	CFRTP	CFRP	CFRP	CCRP	CCRP
Fiber/cloth	T300	B(4)	AS	E-glass	Kev 49	AS 4	IM6	T300	T300	T300
Matrix	N5208	N5505	H3501	epoxy	epoxy	PEEK	epoxy	Fbrt 934	Fbrt 934	Fbrt 934
Ply eng'g constants and data						APC2		4-mil tp	13-mil c	7-mil c
Ex,GPa	181.0	204.0	138.0	38.6	76.0	134.0	203.0	148.0	74.0	66.0
Ey,GPa	10.30	18.50	8.96	8.27	5.50	8.90	11.20	9.65	74.00	66.00
nu/x	0.28	0.23	0.30	0.26	0.34	0.28	0.32	0.30	0.05	0.04
Es,GPa	7.17	5.59	7.10	4.14	2.30	5.10	8.40	4.55	4.55	4.10
v/f	0.70	0.50	0.66	0.45	0.60	0.66	0.66	0.60	0.60	0.60
rho	1.60	2.00	1.60	1.80	1.46	1.60	1.60	1.50	1.50	1.50
ho,mm	0.125	0.125	0.125	0.125	0.125	0.125	0.125	0.100	0.325	0.175
[Q]*0,GPa										
Qxx	181.8	205.0	138.8	39.2	76.6	134.7	204.2	148.9	74.2	66.1
Qyy	10.35	18.59	9.01	8.39	5.55	8.95	11.26	9.71	74.19	66.13
Qxy	2.90	4.28	2.70	2.18	1.89	2.51	3.60	2.91	3.71	2.91
Qss	7.17	5.59	7.10	4.14	2.30	5.10	8.40	4.55	4.55	4.10
[S]*0,1/TPa										
Sxx	5.5	4.9	7.2	25.9	13.2	7.5	4.9	6.8	13.5	15.2
Syy	97.1	54.1	111.6	120.9	181.8	112.4	89.3	103.6	13.5	15.2
Sxy	-1.5	-1.1	-2.2	-6.7	-4.5	-2.1	-1.6	-2.0	-0.7	-0.7
Sss	139.5	178.9	140.8	241.5	434.8	196.1	119.0	219.8	219.8	243.

Type	CFRP	BFRP	CFRP	GFRP	KFRP	CFRTP	CFRP	CFRP	CCRP	CCRP
Fiber/cloth	T300	B(4)	AS	E-glass	Kev 49	AS 4	IM6	T300	T300	T300
Matrix	N5208	N5505	H3501	epoxy	epoxy	PEEK	epoxy	Fbrt 934	Fbrt 934	Fbrt 934
						APC2		4-mil tp	13-mil c	7-mil c
Linear combinations of [Q],GPa										
U1*	76.37	87.70	59.66	20.45	32.44	57.04	85.88	62.47	58.84	52.37
U2	85.73	93.20	64.90	15.39	35.55	62.88	96.44	69.58	0.00	0.00
U3	19.71	24.08	14.25	3.33	8.65	14.78	21.83	16.82	15.34	13.75
U4*	22.61	28.36	16.96	5.51	10.54	17.28	25.43	19.73	19.05	16.66
U5*	26.88	29.67	21.35	7.47	10.95	19.88	30.23	21.37	19.89	17.85
* invariant										
Quasi-isotropic constants										
E,GPa	69.68	78.53	54.84	18.96	29.02	51.81	78.35	56.24	52.67	47.07
nu	0.30	0.32	0.28	0.27	0.32	0.30	0.30	0.32	0.32	0.32
G,GPa	26.88	29.67	21.35	7.47	10.95	19.88	30.23	21.37	19.89	17.8

$E_{ISO} \rightarrow$

TABLE 6.5b   ELASTIC PROPERTIES OF VARIOUS COMPOSITE MATERIALS IN ENGLISH UNITS

Type	CFRP	BFRP	CFRP	GFRP	KFRP	CFRTP	CFRP	CFRP	CCRP	CCRP
Fiber/cloth	T300	B(4)	AS	E-glass	Kev 49	AS 4	IM6	T300	T300	T300
Matrix	N5208	N5505	H3501	epoxy	epoxy	PEEK	epoxy	Fbrt934	Fbrt934	Fbrt934
						APC2		4-mil tp	13-mil c	7-mil c
Ply eng'g constants and data										
E_x, msi	26.25	29.58	20.01	5.60	11.02	19.43	29.44	21.46	10.73	9.57
E_y, msi	1.49	2.68	1.30	1.20	0.80	1.29	1.62	1.40	10.73	9.57
nu/x	0.28	0.23	0.30	0.26	0.34	0.28	0.32	0.30	0.05	0.04
E_s, msi	1.04	0.81	1.03	0.60	0.33	0.74	1.22	0.66	0.66	0.59
v/f	0.70	0.50	0.66	0.45	0.60	0.66	0.66	0.60	0.60	0.60
rho	1.60	2.00	1.60	1.80	1.46	1.60	1.60	1.50	1.50	1.50
ho,mil	4.925	4.925	4.925	4.925	4.925	4.925	4.925	3.94	12.805	6.895
[Q]*0, msi										
Q_{xx}	26.36	29.73	20.13	5.68	11.11	19.53	29.61	21.59	10.76	9.58
Q_{yy}	1.50	2.70	1.31	1.22	0.80	1.30	1.63	1.41	10.76	9.59
Q_{xy}	0.42	0.62	0.39	0.32	0.27	0.36	0.52	0.42	0.54	0.42
Q_{ss}	1.04	0.81	1.03	0.60	0.33	0.74	1.22	0.66	0.66	0.59

Type	CFRP	BFRP	CFRP	GFRP	KFRP	CFRTP	CFRP	CFRP	CCRP	CCRP
Fiber/cloth	T300	B(4)	AS	E-glass	Kev 49	AS 4	IM6	T300	T300	T300
Matrix	N5208	N5505	H3501	epoxy	epoxy	PEEK	epoxy	Fbrt 934	Fbrt 934	Fbrt 934
[S]*0, 1/10^9 psi										
S_{xx}	37.9	33.8	49.7	178.6	91.0	51.7	33.8	46.9	93.1	104.8
S_{yy}	670	373	770	834	1254	775	616	714	93	105
S_{xy}	-10.3	-7.6	-15.2	-46.2	-31.0	-14.5	-11.0	-13.8	-4.8	-4.8
S_{ss}	962	1234	971	1666	2999	1352	821	1516	1516	1682
Linear combinations of [Q], msi										
U1*	11.07	12.72	8.65	2.97	4.70	8.27	12.45	9.06	8.53	7.59
U2	12.43	13.51	9.41	2.23	5.15	9.12	13.98	10.09	0.00	0.00
U3	2.86	3.49	2.07	0.48	1.25	2.14	3.17	2.44	2.22	1.99
U4*	3.28	4.11	2.46	0.80	1.53	2.51	3.69	2.86	2.76	2.42
U5*	3.90	4.30	3.10	1.08	1.59	2.88	4.38	3.10	2.88	2.59
* invariant										
Quasi-isotropic constants										
E, msi	10.10	11.39	7.95	2.75	4.21	7.51	11.36	8.15	7.64	6.83
nu	0.30	0.32	0.28	0.27	0.32	0.30	0.30	0.32	0.32	0.32
G, msi	3.90	4.30	3.10	1.08	1.59	2.88	4.38	3.10	2.88	2.59

6.8 TRANSFORMED STIFFNESS OF TYPICAL COMPOSITES

We list in Table 6.6 the elastic moduli of a ply oriented at 45 degrees. The equality between the 11 and 22, and that of 16 and 26 is noted. Indices 1 and 2 are interchangeable.

TABLE 6.6   TRANSFORMED ELASTIC MODULI OF 45-DEGREE PLY ORIENTATION OF VARIOUS COMPOSITE MATERIALS

Type	CFRP	BFRP	CFRP	GFRP	KFRP	CFRTP	CFRP	CFRP	CCRP	CCRP
Fiber/cloth	T300	B(4)	AS	E-glass	Kev 49	AS 4	IM6	T300	T300	T300
Matrix	N5208	N5505	H3501	epoxy	epoxy	PEEK	epoxy	Fbrt 934	Fbrt 934	Fbrt 934
[Q']^45,GPa						APC2		4-mil tp	13-mil c	7-mil c
11=22	56.66	63.62	45.41	17.12	23.79	42.26	64.06	45.65	43.50	38.62
12	42.32	52.44	31.21	8.84	19.19	32.06	47.26	36.55	34.40	30.42
66	46.59	53.76	35.60	10.80	19.60	34.66	52.05	38.19	35.24	31.61
16=26	42.87	46.60	32.45	7.69	17.77	31.44	48.22	34.79	0.00	0.00
[S']^45,1/TPa										
11=22	59.7	58.9	63.8	93.7	155.2	77.9	52.5	81.5	61.4	68.2
12	-10.0	-30.5	-6.6	-27.0	-62.2	-20.1	-7.0	-28.4	-48.5	-53.7
66	105.7	61.2	123.2	160.3	203.9	124.0	97.4	114.4	28.4	31.6
16=26	-45.8	-24.6	-52.2	-47.5	-84.3	-52.4	-42.2	-48.4	0.0	0.0
Eng'g constants at 45 degree										
E1=E2,GPa	16.74	16.98	15.66	10.67	6.44	12.83	19.04	12.27	16.30	14.6
E6 GPa	9.46	16.34	8.12	6.24	4.90	8.06	10.27	8.74	35.24	31.6
nu/21	0.17	0.52	0.10	0.29	0.40	0.26	0.13	0.35	0.79	0.79
nu/61	-0.77	-0.42	-0.82	-0.51	-0.54	-0.67	-0.80	-0.59	0.00	0.
nu/62	-0.43	-0.40	-0.42	-0.30	-0.41	-0.42	-0.43	-0.42	0.00	0.

In Figures 6.2 and 6.3 we show the transformation of Q_{11} and Q_{66} components of typical composites. In Figure 6.4, we show the shear coupling component, Q_{16}, of the same composites.

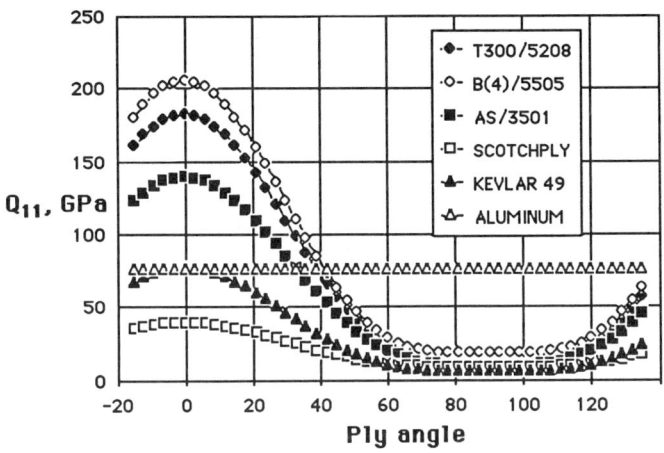

FIGURE 6.2   TRANSFORMATION OF Q_{11} FOR VARIOUS COMPOSITES AND ALUMINUM.

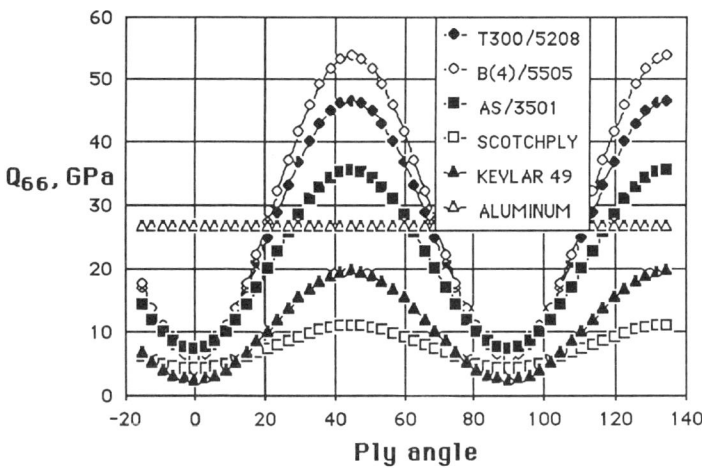

FIGURE 6.3 TRANSFORMATION OF Q_{66} FOR VARIOUS COMPOSITES AND ALUMINUM.

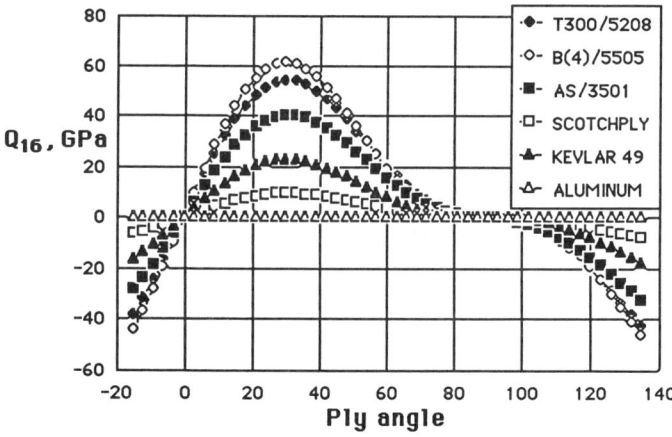

FIGURE 6.4 TRANSFORMATION OF Q_{16} FOR VARIOUS COMPOSITES AND ALUMINUM (WHICH IS ZERO).

6.9 TRANSFORMED STIFFNESS OF CFRP T300/5208

In Table 6.7 we list the key elastic constants of CFRP T300/5208 at 15 degree invervals. The following constants are included:

Plane stress elastic moduli Q_{ij}
Plane stress elastic compliance S_{ij}
Engineering constants E_i
Coupling coefficients v_{ij}
Thermal expansion coefficient α_i

TABLE 6.7 STIFFNESS VALUES AS A FUNCTION OF PLY ANGLE IN SI

θ, degree	Ply orientation							
	0.00	15.00	30.00	45.00	60.00	75.00	90.00	105.00
	Off–axis stiffness, in GPa							
Q_{11}	181.81	160.47	109.38	56.66	23.65	11.98	10.35	11.98
Q_{22}	10.35	11.98	23.65	56.66	109.38	160.47	181.81	160.47
$Q_{12}=Q_{21}$	2.90	12.75	32.46	42.32	32.46	12.75	2.90	12.75
Q_{66}	7.17	17.03	36.74	46.59	36.74	17.03	7.17	17.03
$Q_{16}=Q_{61}$	0.00	38.50	54.19	42.87	20.05	4.36	0.00	–4.36
$Q_{26}=Q_{62}$	0.00	4.36	20.05	42.87	54.19	38.50	0.00	–38.50
	Off–axis compliance, in 1/(TPa)							
S_{11}	5.52	13.77	34.75	59.75	80.53	93.06	97.09	93.06
S_{22}	97.09	93.06	80.53	59.75	34.75	13.77	5.52	13.77
$S_{12}=S_{21}$	–1.55	–3.66	–7.88	–9.99	–7.88	–3.66	–1.55	–3.66
S_{66}	139.47	131.03	114.15	105.71	114.15	131.03	139.47	131.03
$S_{16}=S_{61}$	0.00	–30.20	–46.96	–45.78	–32.34	–15.58	0.00	15.58
$S_{26}=S_{62}$	0.00	–15.58	–32.34	–45.78	–46.96	–30.20	0.00	30.20
	Off–axis engineering constants, in GPa							
E_1	181.00	72.63	28.78	16.74	12.42	10.75	10.30	10.75
E_2	10.30	10.75	12.42	16.74	28.78	72.63	181.00	72.63
E_6	7.17	7.63	8.76	9.46	8.76	7.63	7.17	7.63
	Off–axis Poisson, shear and normal couplings							
v_{21}	0.28	0.27	0.23	0.17	0.10	0.04	0.02	0.04
v_{12}	0.02	0.04	0.10	0.17	0.23	0.27	0.28	0.27
v_{61}	0.00	–2.19	–1.35	–0.77	–0.40	–0.17	0.00	0.17
v_{16}	0.00	–0.23	–0.41	–0.43	–0.28	–0.12	0.00	0.12
v_{62}	0.00	–0.17	–0.40	–0.77	–1.35	–2.19	0.00	2.19
v_{26}	0.00	–0.12	–0.28	–0.43	–0.41	–0.23	0.00	0.23
	Thermal and moisture expansion coefficients, in E–6/deg C and absolute							
α_1	0.02	1.53	5.64	11.26	16.88	20.99	22.50	20.99
α_2	22.50	20.99	16.88	11.26	5.64	1.53	0.02	1.53
α_6	0.00	–11.24	–19.47	–22.48	–19.47	–11.24	0.00	11.24

In Figure 6.5 we show the transformed sitffness constants. On the left hand side of this figure, we compare the plane stress stiffness Q_{11} with the engineering constant E_1. Note that the two have essentially identical values at 0 and 90 degrees, but differ significantly in intermediate angles. Also shown in this figure is the corresponding invariant U_1 (from Table 6.5) which is the average value of the transformed Q_{11}; i.e., the areas under U_1 and Q_{11} are equal. On the left hand side of this figure, the shear modulus Q_{66} are compared with the transformed shear E_6 and invariant U_5. Again the shear moduli at 0 and 90 are the same, but differ significantly in the angles in between. The areas under the Q_{66} and invariant U_5 are equal.

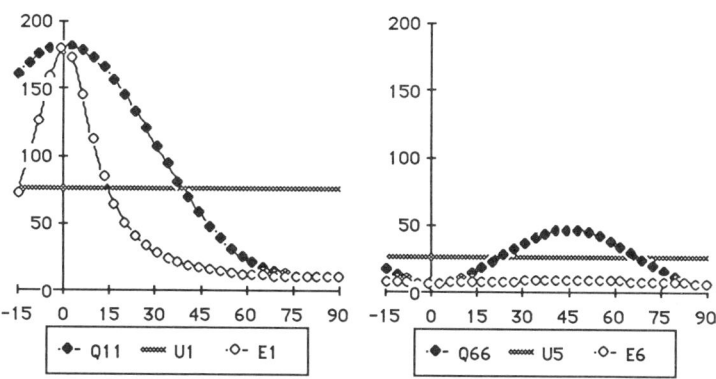

FIGURE 6.5 STIFFNESS CONSTANTS AS FUNCTIONS OF PLY ANGLE.

In Figure 6.6, we show the Poisson and shear coupling coefficients, v_{21} and v_{61}, respectively. For isotropic material the shear coupling coefficient is identically zero.

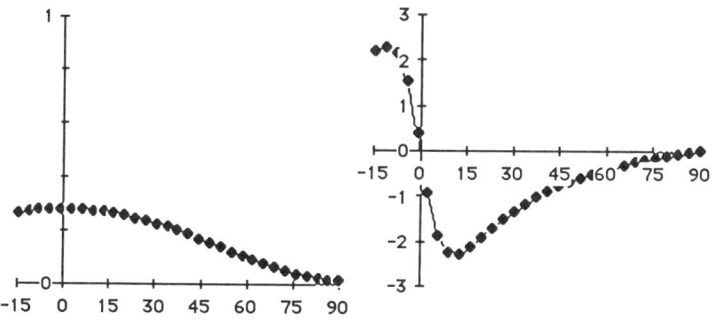

FIGURE 6.6 MAJOR POISSON'S RATIO AND SHEAR COUPLING COEFFICIENT AS FUNCTIONS OF PLY ANGLE.

6.10 CONCLUSIONS

The key elastic properties of composite materials lies in those of the plies in laminates. The invariants are important because they define the limits of the elastic capability of a composite material. The transformed properties are exact and require no approximation. The unidirectional plies are significantly different from isotropic materials. It is not accurate to compare the longitudinal Young's modulus with the Young's modulus of isotropic materials directly. The invariants should be used to represent composite materials. This basis of comparison between materials is fair, and conservative for composite materials.

Section 7

IN–PLANE STIFFNESS OF SYMMETRIC LAMINATES

7.1 LAMINATE CODE

Laminate code is needed for design and manufacturing, but it is difficult to standardize. The code may be based on one of the following conventions:

- The limits of integration of an unsymmetric construction go from the bottom of the laminate to the top.
- The limits of integration of a symmetric construction go from the mid–plane to the top surface. The value of the integral is then doubled.
- The ply laying process in manufacturing goes from the outer surface toward the mid–plane. So the process can start either from the bottom or from the top.
- The use of repeating sublaminates is easier if the lamination begins from the outer surface and goes toward the mid–plane.

For symmetric laminates subjected to in–plane loads only, the stacking sequence of plies is not important. Therefore we can use any convention for the laminate code. When we are building symmetric laminates for flexure, or unsymmetric laminates for any load, explicit code is essential.

We prefer a laminate code that goes from the top surface to the bottom surface. For the present the following codes represent the same laminate, where subscript T stands for total, and S, symmetric:

$$[0_3/90_2/45/-45_3/-45_3/45/90_2/0_3]_T,$$

$$[0_3/90_2/45/-45_6/45/90_2/0_3]_T, \text{ or } [0_3/90_2/45/-45_3]_S \tag{7.1}$$

If a laminate consists of repeating sublaminates, a number representing the multiple units may be placed before the letter T or S. Using the laminate above as a sublaminate, we can represent a laminate consisting of 4 such units where the repeating index is 2 for this example:

$$[0_3/90_2/45/-45_3]_{2S}, \quad \{[0_3/90_2/45/-45_3]_2\}_S, \text{ or}$$

$$[0_3/90_2/45/-45_3/0_3/90_2/45/-45_3/-45_3/45/90_2/0_3/-45_3/45/90_2/0_3]_T \tag{7.2}$$

7.2 LAMINATED PLATE THEORY

In addition to the usual assumptions of a linearly elastic material and linear strain–displacement relations, three principal geometric assumptions are:

1. **Laminate is symmetric.**
2. **Laminate is thin: h << a, b**
   where h = thickness, a = length, and b = width.
3. **Ply strain is constant** and equal to the laminate strain:

$$\{\varepsilon\} = \{\varepsilon^o\}, \text{ or } \varepsilon_i = \varepsilon_i^o, \, i = 1,2,6 \tag{7.3}$$

We can define in–plane stress, stress resultant, and laminate stiffness by integration:

$$\{N\} = \int_{-h/2}^{h/2} \{\sigma\}dz = \int_h [Q]\{\varepsilon\}dz = \left[\int_h [Q]dz\right]\{\varepsilon\} \tag{7.4}$$

$$\{N\} = [A]\{\varepsilon\}, \text{ in N/m} \tag{7.5}$$

$$\{\varepsilon^o\} = [a]\{N\} \tag{7.6}$$

$$[A] = \int_{-h/2}^{h/2} [Q]dz \tag{7.7}$$

$$[a] = [A]^{-1}, \text{ in m/N} \tag{7.8}$$

We define normalized variables in Pa:

$$\{\sigma^o\} = \{N\}^* = \{N\}/h$$

$$[a^*] = h[a] \tag{7.9}$$

$$[A^*] = [A]/h$$

The effective stress–strain relations for in–plane behavior are:

$$\{\sigma^o\} = [A^*]\{\varepsilon^o\}$$

$$\{\varepsilon^o\} = [a^*]\{\sigma^o\} \tag{7.10}$$

The normalized material properties are useful for direct comparison with other materials because the properties are intensive, independent of the thickness of the laminate.

7.3 MATRIX INVERSION

$$[a] = [A]^{-1}, \, [a^*] = [A^*]^{-1}$$

$$|A| = (A_{11}A_{22}-A_{12}^2)A_{66}+2A_{12}A_{26}A_{16}-A_{11}A_{26}^2-A_{22}A_{16}^2$$

$$a_{11} = (A_{22}A_{66}-A_{26}{}^2)/|A|$$

$$a_{22} = (A_{11}A_{66}-A_{16}{}^2)/|A|$$

$$a_{12} = (A_{16}A_{26}-A_{12}A_{66})/|A| \qquad (7.11)$$

$$a_{66} = (A_{11}A_{22}-A_{12}{}^2)/|A|$$

$$a_{16} = (A_{12}A_{26}-A_{22}A_{16})/|A|$$

$$a_{26} = (A_{12}A_{16}-A_{11}A_{26})/|A|$$

7.4 IN–PLANE ENGINEERING CONSTANTS

Engineering constants are defined from the components of normalized compliance:

$$E_1{}^o = 1/a_{11}{}^*, \qquad E_2{}^o = 1/a_{22}{}^*, \qquad E_6{}^o = 1/a_{66}{}^*$$

$$\nu_{21}{}^o = -a_{21}/a_{11}, \qquad \nu_{12}{}^o = -a_{12}/a_{22}$$

$$\nu_{61}{}^o = a_{61}/a_{11}, \qquad \nu_{16}{}^o = a_{16}/a_{66} \qquad (7.12)$$

$$\nu_{62}{}^o = a_{62}/a_{22}, \qquad \nu_{26}{}^o = a_{26}/a_{66}$$

Again, the normalization by columns is used for the coupling constants.

7.5 PLY STRESS AND PLY STRAIN

For a symmetric laminate under in–plane stress or deformation, ply strain and laminate strain are assumed to be equal. Ply stress varies from ply angle to ply angle; see Figure 7.1.

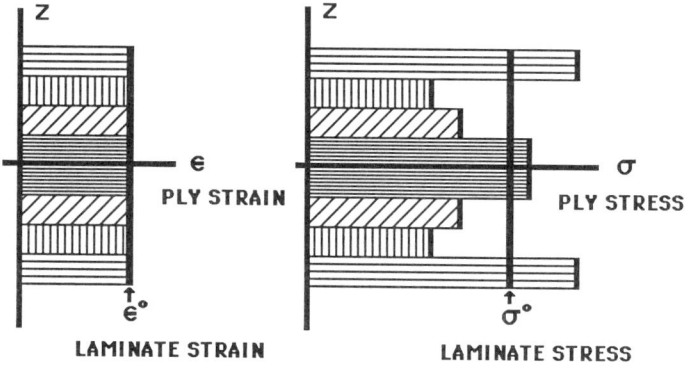

FIGURE 7.1 STRESS AND STRAIN ACROSS LAMINATE THICKNESS.

$\{\epsilon^o\} = \{\epsilon'\}$ = laminate– and off–axis ply strain

$\{\epsilon\}^{(i)}$ = on–axis strain of the i–th ply = $[J^T]^{-1(i)}\{\epsilon'\}$,

$\{\sigma\}^{(i)}$ = on–axis stress of the i–th ply = $[Q]\{\epsilon\}^{(i)}$,

[Q] = on–axis ply stiffness matrix (Equation 6.1),

$\{\sigma'\} = [Q']\{\epsilon^o\}$ = laminate– or off–axis ply stress,

[Q'] = off–axis ply stiffness matrix (Table 6.2).

(7.13)

where, from Equation 5.4:

$$[J^T]^{-1} = \begin{vmatrix} m^2 & n^2 & mn \\ n^2 & m^2 & -mn \\ -2mn & 2mn & m^2-n^2 \end{vmatrix}$$

(7.14)

where **m = cosθ, n = sinθ** and **θ = ply angle**, as shown in Figure 7.2.

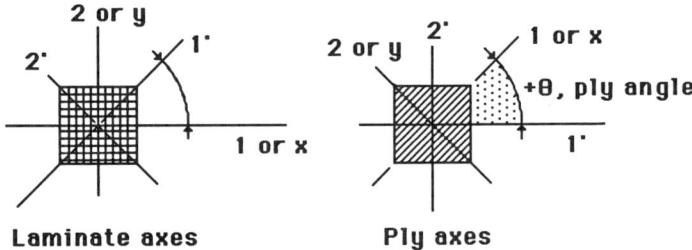

FIGURE 7.2 LAMINATE AND PLY COORDINATE AXES.

The integrated ply stress must be in static equilibrium with the applied loads. This was shown graphically in Figure 7.1.

$$\{\sigma^o\} = 1/h \int_{-h/2}^{h/2} \{\sigma\}dz,$$

(7.15)

$$\{\sigma^f\} = 6/h^2 \int_{-h/2}^{h/2} \{\sigma\}zdz = 0$$

(7.16)

7.6 STIFFNESS MATRIX EVALUATION

The integration of Equation 7.7 can be performed using many different methods. Four methods will be shown and their features described. We define a ply group as plies with same angle grouped or banded together. For a laminate with m ply groups, the integration can be replaced by a summation:

$$[A] = \sum_{i=1}^{m} [Q']^{(i)} \left[z^{(i)} - z^{(i-1)} \right], \tag{7.17}$$

$[Q']^{(i)}$ = off–axis stiffness of the i–th ply group with angle θ measured from the laminate axes (Table 6.2 or 6.4).

This is a direct summation replacing the integration. This is a good method if the flexural stiffness and coupling matrices of the laminate are also being evaluated at the same time. From this summation we can develop three other methods of integration; viz., the multiple angle method, the cash register method, and the rule–of–mixtures method.

The multiple angle method is an extension of the multiple angle transformation of the stiffness matrix shown in Table 6.4. Instead of integrating the variation of the stiffness matrix across the laminate thickness, we integrate the variation of the trigonometric functions as shown as follows and summarized in Table 7.1:

$$V_1 = \int_{-h/2}^{h/2} \cos2\theta dz, \qquad V_2 = \int_{-h/2}^{h/2} \cos4\theta dz$$

$$\tag{7.18}$$

$$V_3 = \int_{-h/2}^{h/2} \sin2\theta dz, \qquad V_4 = \int_{-h/2}^{h/2} \sin4\theta dz$$

$$V_i^* = V_i/h \tag{7.19}$$

TABLE 7.1 IN–PLANE STIFFNESS BY MULTIPLE ANGLE METHOD

$[A^*]$	1	V_1^*	V_2^*	V_3^*	V_4^*
A_{11}^*	U_1	U_2	U_3	0	0
A_{22}^*	U_1	$-U_2$	U_3	0	0
A_{12}^*	U_4	0	$-U_3$	0	0
A_{66}^*	U_5	0	$-U_3$	0	0
A_{16}^*	0	0	0	$U_2/2$	U_3
A_{26}^*	0	0	0	$U_2/2$	$-U_3$

The second method of summation is an extension of Equation 7.17, which we call the cash register method:

$$[A] = \sum_{i=1}^{m} [Q']^{(i)} h^{(i)} \tag{7.20}$$

where $h^{(i)}$ = thickness of the i-th ply group.

We can further simply Equation 7.20:

$$[A] = \sum_{i=1}^{m} [Q']^{(i)} h_o n^{(i)}$$

where h_o = unit ply thickness, $n^{(i)}$ = ply number in the i-th group.

Finally,

$$[A] = \sum_{i=1}^{m} [A^o]^{(i)} n^{(i)}, \tag{7.21}$$

where $[A^o]^{(i)}$ = the i-th unit ply stiffness = $[Q']^{(i)} h_o$

This is the cash register method; i.e., a summation of the products of the ply number and the unit ply stiffness, component by component. This is easier to use than the direct summation. We can add and subtract plies. We can also evaluate hybrids, a laminate with two or more materials. The unit of stiffness is N/m. If we use the laminate code for symmetric laminate, like the last of Equation 7.1, the letter S means doubling the laminate matrix resulting from 7.17.

The last method of summation, the rule-of-mixtures method, is derived as follows:

$$[A^*] = [A]/h$$

$$= \sum_{i=1}^{m} [Q']^{(i)} h^{(i)}/h$$

$$[A^*] = \sum_{i=1}^{m} [Q']^{(i)} v^{(i)} \tag{7.22}$$

where $v^{(i)}$ = fraction of the i-th group.

This is the rule-of-mixtures method. Since the normalized stiffness is intensive, independent of the absolute laminate thickness, it can be used for a direct comparison with other materials, and for stiffness input data to finite element analysis. Unlike the absolute matrix in Equation 7.21, the resulting normalized matrix need not be doubled for symmetric laminates.

7.7 MULTIPLE ANGLE METHOD FOR π/4 LAMINATES

For a family of laminates with only ply angles of 0, 90, 45, and –45 degrees, the evaluation of the stiffness matrix is greatly simplified. Equations 7.17 and 7.18 are:

$$V_1{}^* = v_0 - v_{90}, \quad V_2{}^* = v_0 + v_{90} - v_{45} - v_{-45}$$

$$V_3{}^* = v_{45} - v_{-45}, \quad V_4{}^* = 0 \tag{7.23}$$

Table 7.2 shows the simplified in–plane stiffness. Note that when volume fractions are equal, V's vanish and only invariant terms in Table 7.2 remain. The laminate is QUASI–ISOTROPIC. Its stiffness is the same as the quasi–isotropic stiffness of the unidirectional composite in Equation 6.8. Thus quasi–isotropic constants are material properties of a composite material independent of the layup of the laminate.

TABLE 7.2 IN–PLANE STIFFNESS BY MULTIPLE ANGLE METHOD

[A*]	1	$V_1{}^*$	$V_2{}^*$	$V_3{}^*$
		$v_0 - v_{90}$	$v_0 + v_{90} - v_{45} - v_{-45}$	$v_{45} - v_{-45}$
$A_{11}{}^*$	U_1	U_2	U_3	0
$A_{22}{}^*$	U_1	$-U_2$	U_3	0
$A_{12}{}^*$	U_4	0	$-U_3$	0
$A_{66}{}^*$	U_5	0	$-U_3$	0
$A_{16}{}^* = A_{26}{}^*$	0	0	0	$U_2/2$

EXAMPLE: Find [A*] of [0₃/90] for T300/5208 (see Table 6.5 for data).

SOLUTION: $v_0 = 0.75$, $v_{90} = 0.25$, $v_{45} = v_{-45} = 0$

$$V_1{}^* = 0.5, \quad V_2{}^* = 1, \quad V_3{}^* = 0$$

$$A_{11}{}^* = U_1 + .5U_2 + U_3 = 76.37 + .5 \times 85.73 + 19.71 = 138.95 \text{ GPa}$$

$$A_{22}{}^* = U_1 - .5U_2 + U_3 = 53.22 \text{ GPa}$$

$$A_{12}{}^* = U_4 - U_3 = 22.61 - 19.71 = 2.9 \text{ GPa} \tag{7.24}$$

$$A_{66}{}^* = U_5 - U_3 = 26.88 - 19.71 = 7.17 \text{ GPa}$$

$$A_{16} = A_{26} = 0$$

From Table 7.2, we see that the shear coupling components are equal; i.e.,

$$A_{16} = A_{26}$$

for all values of the volume fractions of the ±45 degree plies. This simple condition however is not carried over to the shear coupling components of the compliance matrix. The reason for this can be seen from the matrix inversion shown in Equation 7.11, repeated here as follows:

$$a_{16} = (A_{12}A_{26} - A_{22}A_{16})/|A| = (A_{12} - A_{22})A_{16}/|A|$$

$$a_{26} = (A_{12}A_{16} - A_{11}A_{26})/|A| = (A_{12} - A_{11})A_{16}/|A|$$

In the last steps in the equations above, we assumed that the shear coupling components are equal. We can thus conclude that unless

$$A_{11} = A_{22}$$

the shear coupling components a_{16} and a_{26} will have different values. This multiple angle method cannot be applied to hybrids.

7.8 EXAMPLE OF CASH REGISTER METHOD

Repeating the formula for this method of summation from Equation 7.21:

$$[A] = \sum_{i=1}^{m} [A^o]^{(i)} n^{(i)} \qquad (7.25)$$

We need only the $[A^o]$ for the unit plies with appropriate angles and ply numbers to obtain the laminate stiffness immediately. The unit ply data for typical composites are shown in Table 7.3 for 0, 90, 45, and –45 degree ply angles.

EXAMPLE: Find [A] for $[0/90/45_2]_S$ for T300/5208 (from Table 7.3).

SOLUTION: $h = 8h_0 = 0.001$ m, $[A^*] = [A]/h = 1000[A]$

$$A_{ij} = 2x(A_{ij}{}^{o(0)} + A_{ij}{}^{o(90)} + 2A_{ij}{}^{o(45)}) \qquad (7.26)$$

$$A_{11} = 2x(22.73 + 1.29 + 2x7.08) = 76.36 \text{ MN/m}$$

or $A_{11}{}^* = 76.36$ GPa

$$A_{22} = 2x(1.29 + 22.73 + 2x7.08) = 76.36 \text{ MN/m}$$

or $A_{22}{}^* = 76.36$ GPa

$$A_{12} = 2x(0.36 + 0.36 + 2x5.29) = 22.6 \text{ MN/m}$$

or $A_{12}{}^* = 22.6$ GPa $\qquad (7.27)$

$$A_{66} = 2x(0.9 + 0.9 + 2x5.82) = 26.88 \text{ MN/m}$$

or $A_{66}{}^* = 26.88$ GPa

$$A_{16} = A_{26} = 2x2x(5.36) = 21.44 \text{ MN/m}$$

or $A_{16}{}^* = A_{26}{}^* = 21.84$ GPa

TABLE 7.3 PLY STIFFNESS/CASH REGISTER METHOD IN SI AND ENGLISH UNITS

Type	CFRP	BFRP	CFRP	GFRP	KFRP	CFRTP	CFRP	CFRP	CCRP	CCRP
Fiber	T300	B(4)	AS	E-glass	Kev 49	AS 4	IM6	T300	T300	T300
Matrix	N5208	N5505	H3501	epoxy	epoxy	PEEK	epoxy	Fbrt934	Fbrt934	Fbrt934
h_o, mm	0.125	0.125	0.125	0.125	0.125	0.125	0.125	0.100	0.325	0.175
[A°]/0 (unit ply stiffness), MN/m								tape	cloth	cloth
11	22.73	25.62	17.35	4.90	9.58	16.84	25.52	14.89	24.11	11.57
22	1.29	2.32	1.13	1.05	0.69	1.12	1.41	0.97	24.11	11.57
21=12	0.36	0.53	0.34	0.27	0.24	0.31	0.45	0.29	1.21	0.51
66	0.90	0.70	0.89	0.52	0.29	0.64	1.05	0.46	1.48	0.72
16=26	0.00	0.00	0.00	0.00	0.00	0.00	0.00	0.00	0.00	0.00
[A°]/90, MN/m										
11	1.29	2.32	1.13	1.05	0.69	1.12	1.41	0.97	24.11	11.57
22	22.73	25.62	17.35	4.90	9.58	16.84	25.52	14.89	24.11	11.57
21=12	0.36	0.53	0.34	0.27	0.24	0.31	0.45	0.29	1.21	0.51
66	0.90	0.70	0.89	0.52	0.29	0.64	1.05	0.46	1.48	0.72
16=26	0.00	0.00	0.00	0.00	0.00	0.00	0.00	0.00	0.00	0.00
[A°]/45, MN/m										
11=22	7.08	7.95	5.68	2.14	2.97	5.28	8.01	4.57	14.14	6.76
21=12	5.29	6.56	3.90	1.11	2.40	4.01	5.91	3.66	11.18	5.32
66	5.82	6.72	4.45	1.35	2.45	4.33	6.51	3.82	11.45	5.53
16=26	5.36	5.82	4.06	0.96	2.22	3.93	6.03	3.48	0.00	0.00
[A°]/-45, MN/m										
11=22	7.08	7.95	5.68	2.14	2.97	5.28	8.01	4.57	14.14	6.76
21=12	5.29	6.56	3.90	1.11	2.40	4.01	5.91	3.66	11.18	5.32
66	5.82	6.72	4.45	1.35	2.45	4.33	6.51	3.82	11.45	5.53
16=26	-5.36	-5.82	-4.06	-0.96	-2.22	-3.93	-6.03	-3.48	0.00	0.00

h_o, mil	5.	5.	5.	5.	5.	5.	5.	4.	13.	7.
[A°]/0 (unit ply stiffness), kip/in								tape	cloth	cloth
11	129.77	146.31	99.08	27.96	54.70	96.14	145.71	85.01	137.67	66.08
22	7.38	13.27	6.43	5.99	3.96	6.39	8.04	5.54	137.67	66.08
21=12	2.07	3.05	1.93	1.56	1.35	1.79	2.57	1.66	6.88	2.91
66	5.12	3.99	5.07	2.95	1.64	3.64	6.00	2.60	8.44	4.10
16=26	0.00	0.00	0.00	0.00	0.00	0.00	0.00	0.00	0.00	0.00
[A°]/90, kip/in										
11	7.38	13.27	6.43	5.99	3.96	6.39	8.04	5.54	137.67	66.08
22	129.77	146.31	99.08	27.96	54.70	96.14	145.71	85.01	137.67	66.08
21=12	2.07	3.05	1.93	1.56	1.35	1.79	2.57	1.66	6.88	2.91
66	5.12	3.99	5.07	2.95	1.64	3.64	6.00	2.60	8.44	4.10
16=26	0.00	0.00	0.00	0.00	0.00	0.00	0.00	0.00	0.00	0.00
[A°]/45, kip/in										
11=22	40.44	45.41	32.41	12.22	16.98	30.17	45.72	26.07	80.72	38.59
21=12	30.20	37.43	22.27	6.31	13.70	22.89	33.73	20.87	63.83	30.40
66	33.25	38.37	25.41	7.71	13.99	24.74	37.15	21.81	65.39	31.59
16=26	30.60	33.26	23.16	5.49	12.69	22.44	34.42	19.87	0.00	0.00
[A°]/-45, kip/in										
11=22	40.44	45.41	32.41	12.22	16.98	30.17	45.72	26.07	80.72	38.59
21=12	30.20	37.43	22.27	6.31	13.70	22.89	33.73	20.87	63.83	30.40
66	33.25	38.37	25.41	7.71	13.99	24.74	37.15	21.81	65.39	31.59
16=26	-30.60	-33.26	-23.16	-5.49	-12.69	-22.44	-34.42	-19.87	0.00	0.00

Note that the factor of 2 is needed for symmetric laminates, and that the two shear coupling components are always equal for $\pi/4$ laminates. The shear coupling components for the compliance matrix, a_{16} and a_{26}, are not equal unless $A_{11} = A_{22}$. (See Equation 7.11 for the inverted matrix.)

EXAMPLE: Find A_{11} of $\{[0/90]^{cfrp}/45_2^{bfrp}\}_S$. (Use T300 and Boron data)

SOLUTION: Follow the same formula in Equation 7.26 except the use of boron composite for the 45–degree plies.

$$A_{11} = 2x(22.73+1.29+2x7.95) = 79.84 \text{ MN/m} \tag{7.28}$$

7.9 EXAMPLE OF RULE–OF–MIXTURES METHOD

The formula for this method is shown in Equation 7.22 and repeated here:

$$[A^*] = \sum_{i=1}^{m} [Q']^{(i)}v^{(i)}, \tag{7.29}$$

The stiffness moduli for the same four ply angles, 0, 90, 45, and –45, are shown in Table 7.4. The rule–of–mixtures method is based on the product of the ply stiffness and the ply fraction.

EXAMPLE: Find $[A^*]$ of $[0_3/90]$ for T300/5208 (see Table 7.4 for data).

SOLUTION: $v_0 = 0.75$, $v_{90} = 0.25$, $v_{45} = v_{-45} = 0$

$$A_{11}^* = 0.75x181.81+0.25x10.35 = 138.95 \text{ GPa}$$

$$A_{22}^* = 0.75x10.35+0.25x181.81 = 53.22 \text{ GPa}$$

$$A_{12}^* = 0.75x2.9+0.25x2.9 = 2.9 \text{ GPa} \tag{7.30}$$

$$A_{66}^* = 0.75x7.17+0.25x7.17 = 7.17 \text{ GPa}$$

$$A_{16} = A_{26} = 0$$

Note that the results are the same as those in Equation 7.24. If the laminate is a hybrid, this method is equally applicable provided that the correct ply material data and ply fractions are used. Care must be exercised if the unit ply thicknesses are different. This occurs when unidirectional and fabric composites are combined.

7.10 SAMPLE PROBLEMS OF IN–PLANE STIFFNESS

Prob 1: Find engineering constants of $[0_3/90]$ for T300/5208.

From Equation 7.24, we know $[A^*]$:

$$[A^*] = \begin{vmatrix} 138.95 & 2.90 & 0 \\ & 53.22 & 0 \\ \text{symm} & & 7.17 \end{vmatrix} \text{ GPa} \tag{7.31}$$

TABLE 7.4 [A*]/RULE OF MIXTURES METHOD IN SI AND ENGLISH UNITS

Type	CFRP	BFRP	CFRP	GFRP	KFRP	CFRTP	CFRP	CFRP	CCRP	CCRP
Fiber	T300	B(4)	AS	E-glass	Kev 49	AS 4	IM6	T300	T300	T300
Matrix	N5208	N5505	H3501	epoxy	epoxy	PEEK	epoxy	Fbrt934	Fbrt934	Fbrt934
						APC2		4-mil	13-mil	7-mil
[Q]^0,GPa								tape	cloth	cloth
Qxx	181.81	204.98	138.81	39.17	76.64	134.70	204.15	148.87	74.19	66.13
Qyy	10.35	18.59	9.01	8.39	5.55	8.95	11.26	9.71	74.19	66.13
Qxy	2.90	4.28	2.70	2.18	1.89	2.51	3.60	2.91	3.71	2.91
Qss	7.17	5.59	7.10	4.14	2.30	5.10	8.40	4.55	4.55	4.10
[Q]^90,GPa										
Q11	10.35	18.59	9.01	8.39	5.55	8.95	11.26	9.71	74.19	66.13
Q22	181.81	204.98	138.81	39.17	76.64	134.70	204.15	148.87	74.19	66.13
Q12	2.90	4.28	2.70	2.18	1.89	2.51	3.60	2.91	3.71	2.91
Q66	7.17	5.59	7.10	4.14	2.30	5.10	8.40	4.55	4.55	4.10
Q16=Q26	0.00	0.00	0.00	0.00	0.00	0.00	0.00	0.00	0.00	0.00
[Q']^45,GPa										
11=22	56.66	63.62	45.41	17.12	23.79	42.26	64.06	45.65	43.50	38.62
12	42.32	52.44	31.21	8.84	19.19	32.06	47.26	36.55	34.40	30.42
66	46.59	53.76	35.60	10.80	19.60	34.66	52.05	38.19	35.24	31.61
16=26	42.87	46.60	32.45	7.69	17.77	31.44	48.22	34.79	0.00	0.00
[Q']^-45,GPa										
11=22	56.66	63.62	45.41	17.12	23.79	42.26	64.06	45.65	43.50	38.62
12	42.32	52.44	31.21	8.84	19.19	32.06	47.26	36.55	34.40	30.42
66	46.59	53.76	35.60	10.80	19.60	34.66	52.05	38.19	35.24	31.61
16=26	-42.87	-46.60	-32.45	-7.69	-17.77	-31.44	-48.22	-34.79	0.00	0.00

[Q]^0, msi								tape	cloth	cloth
Qxx	26.36	29.72	20.13	5.68	11.11	19.53	29.60	21.59	10.76	9.59
Qyy	1.50	2.70	1.31	1.22	0.80	1.30	1.63	1.41	10.76	9.59
Qxy	0.42	0.62	0.39	0.32	0.27	0.36	0.52	0.42	0.54	0.42
Qss	1.04	0.81	1.03	0.60	0.33	0.74	1.22	0.66	0.66	0.59
[Q]^90, msi										
Q11	1.50	2.70	1.31	1.22	0.80	1.30	1.63	1.41	10.76	9.59
Q22	26.36	29.72	20.13	5.68	11.11	19.53	29.60	21.59	10.76	9.59
Q12	0.42	0.62	0.39	0.32	0.27	0.36	0.52	0.42	0.54	0.42
Q66	1.04	0.81	1.03	0.60	0.33	0.74	1.22	0.66	0.66	0.59
Q16=Q26	0.00	0.00	0.00	0.00	0.00	0.00	0.00	0.00	0.00	0.00
[Q']^45, msi										
11=22	8.22	9.23	6.58	2.48	3.45	6.13	9.29	6.62	6.31	5.60
12	6.14	7.60	4.53	1.28	2.78	4.65	6.85	5.30	4.99	4.41
66	6.76	7.79	5.16	1.57	2.84	5.03	7.55	5.54	5.11	4.58
16=26	6.22	6.76	4.71	1.12	2.58	4.56	6.99	5.04	0.00	0.00
[Q']^-45, msi										
11=22	8.22	9.23	6.58	2.48	3.45	6.13	9.29	6.62	6.31	5.60
12	6.14	7.60	4.53	1.28	2.78	4.65	6.85	5.30	4.99	4.41
66	6.76	7.79	5.16	1.57	2.84	5.03	7.55	5.54	5.11	4.58
16=26	-6.22	-6.76	-4.71	-1.12	-2.58	-4.56	-6.99	-5.04	0.00	0.00

Using Equation 7.11, we obtain the compliance matrix:

$$[a*] = \begin{vmatrix} 7.20 & -.39 & 0 \\ & 18.81 & 0 \\ \text{symm} & & 139.5 \end{vmatrix} \ 1/\text{TPa} \qquad (7.32)$$

From Equation 7.12 we find the engineering constants:

$$E_1{}^o = 1/7.20 = 138.88 \ \text{GPa}$$

$$E_2{}^o = 1/18.81 = 53.15 \ \text{GPa} \qquad (7.33)$$

$$v_{21}{}^o = 0.39/7.20 = 0.0544$$

The laminate Poisson's ratio is nearly zero. This is a consequence of the 90–degree ply that limits the Poisson's contraction. Because of the low Poisson's ratio of this orthotropic laminate

$$A_{11}*/E_1{}^o = 138.95/138.88 = 1.001 \qquad (7.34)$$

We can go directly from the engineering constants of plies to those of a laminate with less that 0.1 percent error. This is only true for cross–ply laminates; e.g., apply the rule–of–mixtures equation using the engineering constants:

$$E_1{}^o = 0.75\text{x}181 + 0.25\text{x}10.3 = 138.33 \ \text{GPa} \qquad (7.35)$$

Prob 2: Find engineering constants of [0/90/45$_2$], T300/5208.

From Equation 7.27, we know [A*]:

$$[A*] = \begin{vmatrix} 76.36 & 22.60 & 21.44 \\ & 76.36 & 21.44 \\ \text{symm} & & 26.88 \end{vmatrix} \ \text{GPa} \qquad (7.36)$$

Using Equation 7.11, we obtain the compliance matrix:

$$[a*] = \begin{vmatrix} 17.02 & -1.58 & -12.31 \\ & 17.02 & -12.31 \\ \text{symm} & & 56.83 \end{vmatrix} \ 1/\text{TPa} \qquad (7.37)$$

From Equation 7.12 we find the engineering constants:

$$E_1{}^o = 1/17.02 = 58.76 \ \text{GPa} = E_2{}^o$$

$$E_6{}^o = 1/56.83 = 17.60 \ \text{GPa}$$

$$v_{21}{}^o = 1.58/17.02 = 0.093 \qquad (7.38)$$

$$v_{61}{}^o = -12.31/17.02 = -0.723$$

Although the laminate Poisson's ratio is still small, the $A_{11}*$ is no longer close to $E_1{}^o$ because this laminate is anisotropic.

Note that because $A_{11} = A_{22}$ and $A_{16} = A_{26}$, we have $a_{11} = a_{22}$ and $a_{16} = a_{26}$.

We can show that for [0$_2$/90/45$_2$], we have

$$A_{11}/A_{22} = 1.54, \ A_{16}/A_{26} = 1$$

$$a_{11}/a_{22} = 0.595, \; a_{16}/a_{26} = 0.565 \qquad (7.39)$$

Again, the message is that all components are involved in a matrix inversion and it is impossible to guess the results by intuition.

Prob 3: Find engineering constants of [45/–45] for T300/5208.

SOLUTION: From Equation 7.27, we know [A*]:

$$[A*] = \begin{vmatrix} 56.66 & 42.32 & 0 \\ & 56.66 & 0 \\ symm & & 46.59 \end{vmatrix} \; GPa \qquad (7.40)$$

Using Equation 7.11, we obtain the compliance matrix:

$$[a*] = \begin{vmatrix} 39.92 & -29.82 & 0 \\ & 39.92 & 0 \\ symm & & 21.46 \end{vmatrix} \; 1/TPa \qquad (7.41)$$

From Equation 7.12 we find the engineering constants. This laminate is frequently used for shear test specimens.

$$E_1^{\circ} = 1/39.92 = 25.05 \; GPa = E_2^{\circ}$$

$$E_6^{\circ} = 1/21.46 = 46.59 \; GPa \qquad (7.42)$$

$$v_{21}^{\circ} = 29.82/39.92 = 0.747$$

From the off–axis stiffness of [45] in the Section 6,

$$E_1 = 16.74 \; GPa, \quad E_6 = 9.46 \; GPa, \quad v_{21} = 0.17 \qquad (7.43)$$

Comparing Equations 7.42 and 7.43, we can certainly see the difference between [45] and [±45]. The parallel springs model or the simple rule–of–mixtures equation is certainly not applicable.

For a [0$_2$/±45] laminate using laminated plate theory, we have:

$$E_1^{\circ} = 103.98 \; GPa$$

$$E_2^{\circ} = 29.22 \; GPa \qquad (7.44)$$

$$E_6^{\circ} = 26.88 \; GPa$$

If we apply the rule–of–mixtures equation to a [0$_2$] and [±45] we will have:

$$E_1^{\circ} = [181+25.05]/2 = 103 \; GPa \quad (1 \; percent \; error)$$
$$E_2^{\circ} = [10.3+25.05]/2 = 17.68 \; GPa \quad (60 \; percent \; error) \qquad (7.45)$$

The values for the normal stiffness components in Equation 7.44 are exact while those in Equation 7.45 are not reliable, as shown by the relative errors indicated in the parenthesis.

But the shear modulus using the rule–of–mixtures is exact; e.g.,

$$E_6^{\circ} = [7.17+46.59]/2 = 26.88 \; GPa \quad (no \; error) \qquad (7.46)$$

This simple relation provides the correct answer because the sublaminates of [0] and [±45] are orthotropic. The relation will not be valid for unbalanced laminates.

Prob 4: Can laminates have unusual Poisson's ratios?

Poisson's ratios for anisotropic materials are not limited to the range between 0 and 1/2 imposed on isotropic materials.

We have seen that a [±45] has a Poisson's ratio of 0.747. For this CFRP, that of the [±30] is 1.37. Physically we may relate this large Poisson's ratio to the scissoring effect of the off–axis plies. Through micromechanics, we can show that the Poisson's ratio for [±30] can approach 3.0 if the matrix stiffness of the normal epoxy resin is reduced to zero.

We mentioned in Section 4.7 that in three dimensions the transverse–transverse Poisson's ratio of a transversely isotropic material was bounded between 0 and 1.

We can also show that

for $[15_2/60]$, $v_{21}^\circ = -0.366$ (7.47)

We are not aware of a simple explanation of this negative Poisson's ratio. Again the interaction between plies of a laminate is complex and nearly impossible to visualize in many instances.

7.11 RANKING IN–PLANE STIFFNESSES

It is useful to examine the range of variability of the stiffness of laminates as the ply orientations change. This unique feature of composites can be illustrated by ranking families of the following $\pi/4$ sublaminates:

35, 8–ply, quadri–directional sublaminates:
starting with code [5111], [4211], . . . [1115];

40, 6–ply, tridirectional sublaminates:
starting with code [4110], [3210], . . . [0114];

                                                        (7.48)

18, 4–ply, bidirectional sublaminates:
starting with code [3100], [2200], . . . [0013]; and

4, unidirectional: with code [1000], [0100], [0010], [0001].

where the sublaminate code designates the number of plies in the order of 0, 90, 45 and –45 degrees. Thus

[5111] designates $[0_5/90/45/{-45}]$ (7.49)

There are 97 sublaminates among the four families above. We wish to show the ranking of the elastic moduli of these laminates, as follows:

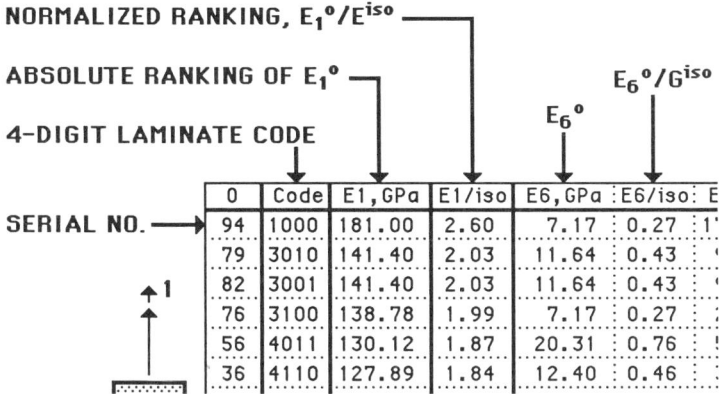

Figure 7.3 shows the top and bottom seven E_1^0 within the family of 97 CFRP laminates. Both the absolute and relative values are shown.

There are no surprises for the laminates with the highest E_1 which also corresponds to those with the lowest E_2. Netting analysis seems to yield the ranking based on the percentage of 0–degree plies. But the rule of mixtures relation is not able to predict quantitatively the resulting stiffness. The prediction of the lowest E_1 or the highest E_2 based on the laminated plate theory cannot be simplified using any form of netting analysis or the rule–of–mixtures relation.

	0	Code	E1,GPa	E1/iso	E6,GPa	E6/iso	E1/E2	E1/E6
MAX→	94	1000	181.00	2.60	7.17	0.27	17.58	25.24
	79	3010	141.40	2.03	11.64	0.43	9.48	12.14
↑1	82	3001	141.40	2.03	11.64	0.43	9.48	12.14
	76	3100	138.78	1.99	7.17	0.27	2.61	19.36
	56	4011	130.12	1.87	20.31	0.76	5.43	6.41
	36	4110	127.89	1.84	12.40	0.46	3.00	10.32
	46	4101	127.89	1.84	12.40	0.46	3.00	10.32
	87	130	16.63	0.24	12.55	0.47	0.28	1.32
	90	103	16.63	0.24	12.55	0.47	0.28	1.32
	86	220	16.11	0.23	12.70	0.47	0.16	1.27
	89	202	16.11	0.23	12.70	0.47	0.16	1.27
	85	310	14.92	0.21	11.64	0.43	0.11	1.28
	88	301	14.92	0.21	11.64	0.43	0.11	1.28
MIN→	95	100	10.29	0.15	7.17	0.27	0.06	1.44

FIGURE 7.3   THE HIGHEST AND THE LOWEST RANKINGS OF E1 OF 97–LAMINATE FAMILY IN TERMS ABSOLUTE AND RELATIVE STIFFNESS OVER THE QUASI–ISOTROPIC LAMINATE.

Highly anisotropic or highly directional laminates control both the highest and lowest stiffnesses. Unidirectional and bidirectional laminates are among those listed in Figure 7.3. Three tridirectional ones are among the top seven, but no quadri–directional ones appear.

In Figure 7.4 we show the ranking of the highest and the lowest seven laminates based on the laminate shear modulus. Again, both absolute and relative values are shown. The highest shear modulus is that from [±45], which is not surprising. Again quadri–directional laminates are not rated among the highest or the lowest.

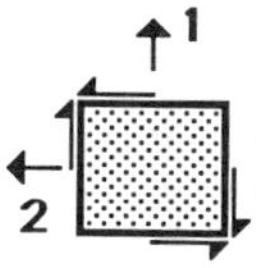

0	Code	E1,GPa	E1/iso	E6,GPa	E6/iso	E1/E2	E1/E6
92	22	25.05	0.36	46.59	1.73	1.00	0.54
63	1032	51.31	0.74	38.90	1.45	1.60	1.32
64	1023	51.31	0.74	38.90	1.45	1.60	1.32
73	132	32.08	0.46	38.90	1.45	0.63	0.82
74	123	32.08	0.46	38.90	1.45	0.63	0.82
91	31	24.29	0.35	37.31	1.39	1.00	0.65
93	13	24.29	0.35	37.31	1.39	1.00	0.65
96	10	16.73	0.24	9.45	0.35	1.00	1.77
97	1	16.73	0.24	9.45	0.35	1.00	1.77
94	1000	181.00	2.60	7.17	0.27	17.58	25.24
76	3100	138.78	1.99	7.17	0.27	2.61	19.36
77	2200	95.99	1.38	7.17	0.27	1.00	13.39
78	1300	53.15	0.76	7.17	0.27	0.38	7.41
95	100	10.29	0.15	7.17	0.27	0.06	1.44

$45_2/-45_2$ MAX →

↑1
← 2

MIN →

FIGURE 7.4　THE HIGHEST AND LOWEST RANKED LAMINATE SHEAR MODULUS IN ABSOLUTE AND RELATIVE VALUES.

In Figure 7.5, the ratios of the two normal stiffness components are ranked. Again, the highest and the lowest seven laminates are shown.

	0	Code	E1,GPa	E1/iso	E6,GPa	E6/iso	E1/E2	E1/E6
MAX→	94	1000	181.00	2.60	7.17	0.27	17.58	25.24
	79	3010	141.40	2.03	11.64	0.43	9.48	12.14
	82	3001	141.40	2.03	11.64	0.43	9.48	12.14
	80	2020	100.29	1.44	12.70	0.47	6.23	7.90
	83	2002	100.29	1.44	12.70	0.47	6.23	7.90
	56	4011	130.12	1.87	20.31	0.76	5.43	6.41
	57	3021	103.76	1.49	25.30	0.94	3.71	4.10
	68	312	27.94	0.40	25.30	0.94	0.27	1.10
	66	411	23.94	0.34	20.31	0.76	0.18	1.18
	86	220	16.11	0.23	12.70	0.47	0.16	1.27
	89	202	16.11	0.23	12.70	0.47	0.16	1.27
	85	310	14.92	0.21	11.64	0.43	0.11	1.28
	88	301	14.92	0.21	11.64	0.43	0.11	1.28
MIN→	95	100	10.29	0.15	7.17	0.27	0.06	1.44

FIGURE 7.5 THE HIGHEST AND LOWEST RANKED RATIOS OF THE NORMAL STIFFNESS COMPONENTS.

Finally, we show in Figure 7.6, the ranked ratios of the normal stiffness over the shear modulus. Again quadri–directional laminates are not ranked because these laminates tend to be less anisotropic.

	0	Code	E1,GPa	E1/iso	E6,GPa	E6/iso	E1/E2	E1/E6
MAX→	94	1000	181.00	2.60	7.17	0.27	17.58	25.24
	76	3100	138.78	1.99	7.17	0.27	2.61	19.36
	77	2200	95.99	1.38	7.17	0.27	1.00	13.39
	79	3010	141.40	2.03	11.64	0.43	9.48	12.14
	82	3001	141.40	2.03	11.64	0.43	9.48	12.14
	36	4110	127.89	1.84	12.40	0.46	3.00	10.32
	46	4101	127.89	1.84	12.40	0.46	3.00	10.32
	72	141	28.54	0.41	29.98	1.12	0.57	0.95
	75	114	28.54	0.41	29.98	1.12	0.57	0.95
	73	132	32.08	0.46	38.90	1.45	0.63	0.82
	74	123	32.08	0.46	38.90	1.45	0.63	0.82
	91	31	24.29	0.35	37.31	1.39	1.00	0.65
	93	13	24.29	0.35	37.31	1.39	1.00	0.65
MIN→	92	22	25.05	0.36	46.59	1.73	1.00	0.54

FIGURE 7.6 RANKED RATIOS OF NORMAL STIFFNESS OVER SHEAR.

7.12 SAMPLE PROBLEMS IN PLY STRESS AND PLY STRAIN

It is useful to examine the ply stress and ply strain defined earlier in this section. Figure 7.1 is repeated here to the uniform ply strain and the piece–wise constant ply stress across the laminate thickness.

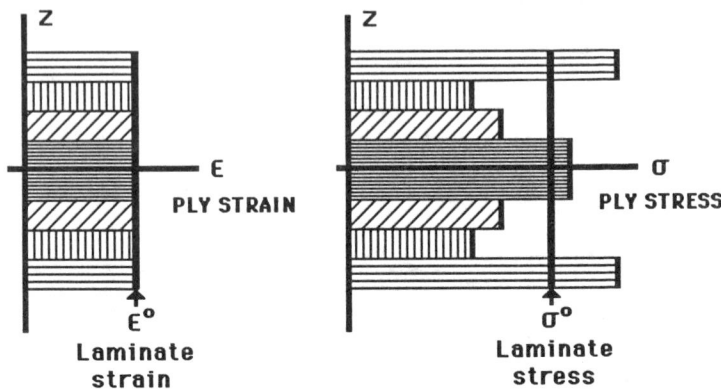

FIGURE 7.6 PLY STRESS AND PLY STRAIN ACROSS LAMINATE THICKNESS.

EXAMPLE: We will use the data developed earlier in Problem 2 of Section 7.10 for [0/90/45$_2$]:

$$[A^*] = \begin{vmatrix} 76.36 & 22.60 & 21.44 \\ & 76.36 & 21.44 \\ \text{symm} & & 26.88 \end{vmatrix} \text{ GPa} \qquad (7.50)$$

$$[a^*] = \begin{vmatrix} 17.02 & -1.58 & -12.31 \\ & 17.02 & -12.31 \\ \text{symm} & & 56.83 \end{vmatrix} \text{ 1/TPa} \qquad (7.51)$$

Let us impose a biaxial load:

$$\{N\} = \{100, \ 50, \ 0\} \text{ kN/m}$$
$$\{N^*\} = \{N/h\} = \{\sigma^o\} = \{100, \ 50, \ 0\} \text{ MPa} \qquad (7.52)$$

where   h = thickness = 8h$_0$ = 8x125x10^{-6} = 1x10^{-3} m = 1 mm

      h$_0$ = unit ply thickness = 125x10^{-6} m

Now we can calculate the laminate strain from Equations 7.13 and 7.10:

$$\{\varepsilon^o\} = \{\varepsilon'\} = \text{laminate– and off–axis ply strain}$$

$$\{\varepsilon^o\} = [a^*]\{\sigma^o\}$$

$$\varepsilon_1{}^o = a_{11}{}^*\sigma_1{}^o + a_{12}{}^*\sigma_2{}^o + a_{16}{}^*\sigma_6{}^o$$

$$= 17.02 \text{x} 100 - 1.58 \text{x} 50 - 12.31 \text{x} 0 = 1.622 \text{x} 10^{-3} \qquad (7.53)$$

$$\varepsilon_2{}^o = 0.692 \text{x} 10^{-3}$$

$$\varepsilon_6{}^o = -1.846 \text{x} 10^{-3}$$

We now compute the on–axis ply strain using Equations 7.13, 5.1 and 5.5:

$\{\varepsilon\}^{(i)}$ = on–axis strain of the i–th ply = $[J^T]^{-1(i)}\{\varepsilon'\}$

$\theta = 0$, $\{\varepsilon\} = \{1.62, 0.69, -1.85\}\times10^{-3}$

$\theta = 90$, $\{\varepsilon\} = \{0.69, 1.62, 1.85\}\times10^{-3}$ (7.54)

$\theta = 45$, $\{\varepsilon\} = \{0.235, 2.08, -0.93\}\times10^{-3}$

We now calculate the on–axis ply stress using Equations 7.13 and 4.6:

$\{\sigma\}^{(i)}$ = on–axis stress of the i–th ply = $[Q]\{\varepsilon\}^{(i)}$

where $[Q]$ = on–axis ply stiffness matrix (Equation 6.1)

$\theta = 0$, $\{\sigma\} = \{296.99, 11.86, -13.23\}$ MPa

$\theta = 90$, $\{\sigma\} = \{130.60, 18.79, 13.23\}$ MPa   (7.55)

$\theta = 45$, $\{\sigma\} = \{48.67, 22.20, -6.67\}$ MPa

We can calculate the ply stress in the laminate axes from Equation 7.13:

$\{\sigma'\} = [Q']\{\varepsilon^o\}$ = laminate– or off–axis ply stress

where $[Q']$ = off–axis ply stiffness matrix (Table 6.2)

or directly from stress transformation using Equations 5.1 and 5.3:

$\theta = 0$, $\{\sigma\} = \{296.99, 11.86, -13.23\}$ MPa

$\theta = 90$, $\{\sigma\} = \{18.79, 130.60, -13.23\}$ MPa   (7.56)

$\theta = 45$, $\{\sigma\} = \{42.11, 28.77, 13.23\}$ MPa

We need to satisfy the equilibrium of ply stresses and the applied laminate stresses following Equation 7.15:

$$\{\sigma^o\} = 1/h \int_{-h/2}^{h/2} \{\sigma\}dz,$$

$\{\sigma_1{}^o\} = [296.99+18.79+2\times42.11]/4 = 100$ MPa

$\{\sigma_2{}^o\} = [11.86+130.60+2\times28.77]/4 = 50$ MPa   (7.57)

$\{\sigma_6{}^o\} = [-13.23-13.23+2\times13.23]/4 = 0$

Note that the the average stresses here agree with the applied stress in Equation 7.52. Equilibrium is thus satisfied. We must further verify that the moments are zero as indicated in Equation 7.16:

$$\{\sigma^f\} = 6/h^2 \int_{-h/2}^{h/2} \{\sigma\}zdz = 0 \qquad (7.58)$$

The integration is not necessary since all ply stresses are piece–wise constant, as shown in Figure 7.7. Then the following integral will be identically zero; i.e.

$$\{\sigma^f\} = \int_{-h/2}^{h/2} z dz = \{[h^2]-[h^2]\}/8 = 0 \qquad (7.59)$$

7.13 PRESSURE VESSELS

It is simple to extend the in–plane stiffness to the membrane stresses of a pressure vessel subjected to axisymmetrical loads such as internal or external pressure, axial force, and torque. The dimensions of the pressure vessel is shown in Figure 7.8.

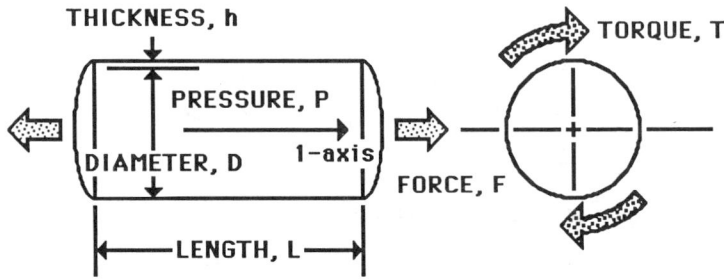

FIGURE 7.8   A CYLINDRICAL PRESSURE VESSEL SUBJECTED TO   PRESSURE
AXIAL FORCE AND TORQUE.

Let the 1–axis be the longitudinal or axial direction; the 2–axis, the circumferential or hoop direction; the z–axis, across the wall thickness. The membrane, or in–plane stresses, are:

$$\sigma_1^o = PD/4h + F/\pi Dh \quad \mathit{long} = \frac{PD}{4h} = \frac{Pr}{2t} = axial$$

$$\sigma_2^o = PD/2h \quad \mathit{hoop} = \frac{PD}{2h} = \frac{P}{h}\frac{D}{2} = \frac{Pr}{h} \qquad (7.60)$$

$$\sigma_6^o = 2T/\pi D^2 h \quad \mathit{radial}$$

The resulting membrane, or in–plane strain, is simply

$$\{\varepsilon^o\} = [a^*]\{\sigma^o\} \qquad (7.61)$$

The displacements, or changes in lengths, are

$$\delta L = L\varepsilon_1^o$$
$$\delta D = D\varepsilon_2^o \qquad (7.62)$$

The angle of twist in radians is

$$\theta = 2(L/D)\varepsilon_6^o \qquad (7.63)$$

In terms of degrees, we must multiply the results in Equation 7.63 by $180/\pi$ or 57.5 degrees/radian.

If the cylinder is orthotropic, there will be no shear coupling. The angle of twist is the result of the applied torque only; i.e.,

$$\theta = 2(L/D)\varepsilon_6^{\,o} = 2(L/D)(\sigma_6^{\,o}/E_6^{\,o}) = TL/GJ \qquad (7.64)$$

where $G = E_6^{\,o}$

J = polar moment of inertia = $\pi(D^4-d^4)/32$

where d = inside diameter

For thin shells

$$J = \pi D^3 h/4 \qquad (7.65)$$

If we wish to find the growth and twist of the vessel due to change in temperature and moisture content, the mechanically applied stresses in Equation 7.60 will be replaced by nonmechanical stresses. The calculation of resulting strains and displacements remain the same. The calculation of the nonmechanical stresses will be covered in Section 15, Residual Stresses and Strains.

7.14 CONCLUSIONS

It is useful to emphasize that the analysis and design of composite laminates is based on laminated plate theory. In this section, the simplest version of this theory is outlined. This represents the minimum level of skill that is required to fully appreciate that composite materials can have not only superior structural performance but also unique features. Shear coupling, for example, has no counter part in isotropic materials.

The sample problems in this section also point out the need of computers to perform many of the routine calculations. Doing them by hand is time consuming and often frustrating. It is difficult to avoid errors. This is the reason for acquiring computer programs.

Section 8

FLEXURAL STIFFNESS OF SYMMETRIC LAMINATE

8.1 LAMINATED PLATE THEORY

Three assumptions analogous to those used in the in–plane behavior of a laminate are:

- **Laminate is symmetric.** The laminate may have a honeycomb core with a total thickness measured in number of plies. One half of the core thickness expressed in number of unit plies will appear in the laminate code; e.g., for a 6–ply thick core:

$$\{[0_3/90_2/45/-45_3]_r/c_3\}_S \tag{8.1}$$

The total laminate is 24–ply thick if the repeat index r is unity. If $r = 2$, the 9–ply sublaminate is repeated once making the facing 18–ply thick. The total laminate now is 42–ply thick.
- **Laminate is thin:** $h \ll a, b$
where h = thickness, a = length, and b = width.
- **Ply strain is linear** in the thickness coordinate z:

$$\{\varepsilon\} = z\{k\}, \text{ or } \varepsilon_i = zk_i \tag{8.2}$$

We can define moment, flexural stress, laminate flexural stiffness, and effective engineering constants by integrating over the thickness h of the laminate:

$$\{M\} = \int_{-h/2}^{h/2} \{\sigma\}zdz = \int_{-h/2}^{h/2} [Q]\{\varepsilon\}zdz = \int_{-h/2}^{h/2} [Q]z^2dz\{k\}$$

$$\{M\} = [D]\{k\}, \text{ in N} \tag{8.3}$$

$$\{k\} = [d]\{M\}, \text{ in 1/m} \tag{8.4}$$

$$[D] = \int_{-h/2}^{h/2} [Q]z^2dz, \text{ in Nm} \tag{8.5}$$

$$[d] = [D]^{-1}, \text{ 1/Nm} \tag{8.6}$$

In terms of normalized variables which are useful in comparing different materials:

$\{\sigma^f\} = 6\{M\}/h^2$ = effective stress at outer surfaces, in Pa $\qquad$ (8.7)

$\{\epsilon^f\} = h\{k\}/2$ = actual strain at outer surfaces $\qquad$ (8.8)

$[D^*] = 12[D]/h^3 = [D]/I^*$ = normalized flexural stiffness, in Pa $\qquad$ (8.9)

$[d^*] = [d]h^3/12 = [d]I^*$ = normalized flexural compliance, in 1/Pa $\qquad$ (8.10)

$I^* = h^3/12$ = normalized moment of inertia $\qquad$ (8.11)

In the case of a beam I^* is equal to I/b, where b = width, or

$$I = bh^3/12, \text{ or } E_1^f I = b/d_{11} = bI^*/d_{11} = I/d_{11}{}^* \qquad (8.12)$$

The effective stress–strain relations in flexure are:

$$\begin{aligned} \{\sigma^f\} &= [D^*]\{\epsilon^f\} \\ \{\epsilon^f\} &= [d^*]\{\sigma^f\} \end{aligned} \qquad (8.13)$$

8.2 FLEXURAL ENGINEERING CONSTANTS

$$\begin{aligned} E_1^f &= 1/d_{11}{}^*, \quad E_2^f = 1/d_{22}{}^*, \quad E_6^f = 1/d_{66}{}^* \\ \nu_{21}^f &= -d_{21}/d_{11}, \quad \nu_{12}^f = -d_{12}/d_{22} \\ \nu_{61}^f &= d_{61}/d_{11}, \quad \nu_{16}^f = d_{16}/d_{66} \\ \nu_{62}^f &= d_{62}/d_{22}, \quad \nu_{26}^f = d_{26}/d_{66} \end{aligned} \qquad (8.14)$$

Again, the normalization by columns is used for the definition of the coupling constants.

8.3 PLY STRESS AND PLY STRAIN

Analogous to Equation 7.13 for the ply stress and ply strain for the in–plane loading, we now have for flexure:

$\{\epsilon'\}^{(z)} = z\{k\}$ = laminate– and off–axis ply strain

$\{\epsilon\}^{(z)} = [J^T]^{-1(z)}\{\epsilon'\}^{(z)} = [J^T]^{-1(z)}z\{k\}$

$\qquad$ = on–axis ply strain at z for a given ply angle

$\{\sigma\}^{(z)} = [Q]^{(z)}\{\epsilon\}^{(z)}$ = on–axis ply stress at z $\qquad$ (8.15)

$[Q]^{(z)}$ = on–axis stiffness matrix at z (Equation 6.1)

$\{\sigma'\}^{(z)} = [Q']^{(z)}\{\epsilon'\}^{(z)}$ = laminate– or off–axis ply stress

$[Q']^{(z)}$ = off–axis stiffness matrix at z (Table 6.2 or 6.3)

where the strain transformation is given by Equation 5.5, repeated here:

$$[J^T]^{-1} = \begin{vmatrix} m^2 & n^2 & mn \\ n^2 & m^2 & -mn \\ -2mn & 2mn & m^2-n^2 \end{vmatrix} \tag{8.16}$$

The static equilibrium of the ply and laminate stresses must satisfy:

$$\{\sigma^o\} = \{N\}/h = 1/h \int_{-h/2}^{h/2} \{\sigma\}dz = 0 \tag{8.17}$$

$$\{\sigma^f\} = 6\{M\}/h^2 = 6/h^2 \int_{-h/2}^{h/2} \{\sigma\}zdz \tag{8.18}$$

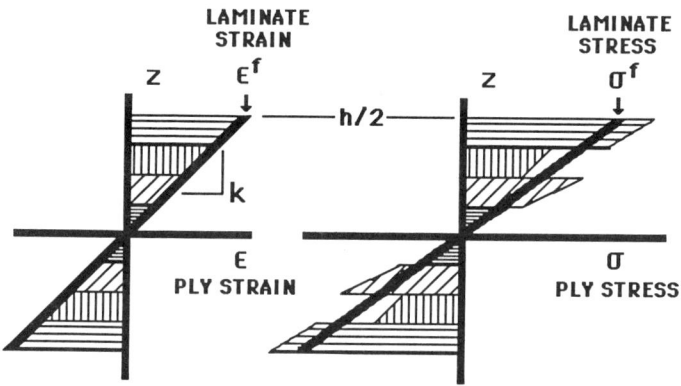

FIGURE 8.1   PLY STRESS AND PLY STRAIN AND THEIR EQUIVALENT LAMINATE STRESS AND LAMINATE STRAIN.

8.4 FLEXURAL STIFFNESS EVALUATION

The integration of Equation 8.5 can be replaced by the summation of a laminate with m ply groups:

$$[D] = 1/3 \sum_{i=1}^{m} [Q']^{(i)}\left[(z^{(i)})^3 - (z^{(i-1)})^3\right] \tag{8.19}$$

where $[Q']^{(i)}$ = off-axis stiffness of the i-th ply group with angle θ measured from the laminate axes (Table 6.2 or 6.3). Index i begins from the bottom surface, $z = -h/2$.

For symmetric laminates:

$$[D] = 2/3 \sum_{j=1}^{m/2} [Q']^{(j)} \left[(z^{(j)})^3 - (z^{(j-1)})^3 \right] \qquad (8.20)$$

The summation may be from either the bottom surface to the mid–plane, or the mid–plane to the top surface of the laminate. We recommend the latter summation for symmetric laminates in which case the ply group must be in reversed order of that in the laminate code. Index j is used here to differentiate from index i used for the entire laminate in Equation 8.19. Unlike the in–plane stiffness, the order of the ply groups is critical for the flexural stiffness. If all plies have the same unit ply thickness and are of the same material, the summation above can be simplified by use of ply number t in place of ply coordinate z:

$$z = th_o$$

where $t = 1,2,3, \ldots n/2$ measured from the midplane,

h_o = unit ply thickness   (8.21)

Equation 8.20 becomes:

$$[D] = 2h_o^3 \sum_{t=1}^{n/2} [Q']^{(t)} \left[t^3 - (t-1)^3 \right]/3 \qquad (8.22)$$

where $t^3 - (t-1)^3 = 3t^2 - 3t + 1$ (8.23)

We can use the normalized stiffness:

$$[D^*] = [D]/I^* = 12[D]/h^3$$

$$= 12[D]/(nh_o)^3 \qquad (8.24)$$

$$[D^*] = 8/n^3 \sum_{t=1}^{n/2} [Q']^{(t)}(3t^2 - 3t + 1) \qquad (8.25)$$

where n is the total number of plies; index t, increases with the number of unit plies from the mid–plane. This index is different from indices i and j, which designate the ply groups in Equations 8.19 and 8.20, respectively.

Similar to the summation of the in–plane stiffness in Table 7.1, that of the flexural stiffness can also be formulated using the multiple angle method.

TABLE 8.1 FLEXURAL STIFFNESS BY MULTIPLE ANGLE METHOD

[D*]	1	$W_1{}^*$	$W_2{}^*$	$W_3{}^*$	$W_4{}^*$
$D_{11}{}^*$	U_1	U_2	U_3	0	0
$D_{22}{}^*$	U_1	$-U_2$	U_3	0	0
$D_{12}{}^*$	U_4	0	$-U_3$	0	0
$D_{66}{}^*$	U_5	0	$-U_3$	0	0
$D_{16}{}^*$	0	0	0	$U_2/2$	U_3
$D_{26}{}^*$	0	0	0	$U_2/2$	$-U_3$

$$\text{where} \quad W_1 = \int_{-h/2}^{h/2} \cos2\theta z^2 dz, \quad W_2 = \int_{-h/2}^{h/2} \cos4\theta z^2 dz$$
$$W_3 = \int_{-h/2}^{h/2} \sin2\theta z^2 dz, \quad W_4 = \int_{-h/2}^{h/2} \sin4\theta z^2 dz$$

(8.26)

$$W_i{}^* = W_i/I^* = 12W_i/h^3 \tag{8.27}$$

For symmetric laminates, the limits of integration can be replaced as follows:

$$W_1 = 2\int_0^{h/2} \cos2\theta z^2 dz, \quad \ldots \quad W_4 = 2\int_0^{h/2} \sin4\theta z^2 dz \tag{8.28}$$

8.5 SANDWICH PLATES

For a symmetric laminate with a symmetric core, the ply stress and strain distributions are very similar to those shown in Figure 8.1, except in the space provided by the core. This is shown in Figure 8.2.

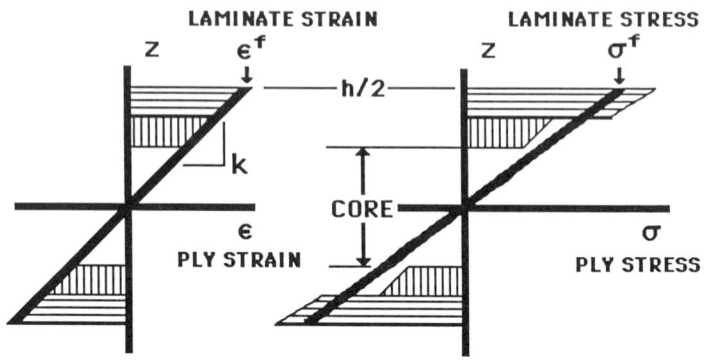

FIGURE 8.2 PLY STRESS AND STRAIN IN A PLATE WITH SANDWICH CORE.

The flexural stiffness is:

$$[D] = 2\int_{z_c}^{h/2} [Q]z^2dz \qquad (8.29)$$

where the top face of the core is z_c.

In case of a symmetric laminate with homogeneous plies, the summation can be done for the top half of the laminate, with index j from top face of the core to the top face of the laminate:

$$[D] = 2/3 \sum_{j=c}^{m/2} [Q']^{(j)}\left[(z^{(j)})^3-(z^{(j-1)})^3\right] \qquad (8.30)$$

In place of ply groups, a new index t for a ply by ply summation can be done:

$$[D] = 2h_o^3/3 \sum_{t=c}^{n/2} [Q']^{(t)}\left[t^3-(t-1)^3\right] \qquad (8.31)$$

If all plies have the same unit ply thickness and are of the same material

$$[D^*] = 8/n^3 \sum_{t=c}^{n/2} [Q']^{(t)}(3t^2-3t+1) \qquad (8.32)$$

where c is the half core depth measured in the number of plies; i.e., equal to the subscript after c (for core) in Equation 8.1.

The difference between a symmetric laminate with or without a core is the lower limit of the integration, 0 or c, respectively. The normalizing constant is the same, as shown in Equation 8.24. The multiple angle method shown in Table 8.1 must be modified to reflect the existence of a symmetric core as follows:

TABLE 8.2 FLEXURAL STIFFNESS WITH A CORE BY MULTIPLE ANGLE METHOD

[D*]	$1-c*^3$	W_1*	W_2*	W_3*	W_4*
$D_{11}*$	U_1	U_2	U_3	0	0
$D_{22}*$	U_1	$-U_2$	U_3	0	0
$D_{12}*$	U_4	0	$-U_3$	0	0
$D_{66}*$	U_5	0	$-U_3$	0	0
$D_{16}*$	0	0	0	$U_2/2$	U_3
$D_{26}*$	0	0	0	$U_2/2$	$-U_3$

where $c* = 2z_c/h$ = core thickness ratio = percent core   (8.33)

$$W_1 = 2\int_{z_c}^{h/2} \cos2\theta z^2 dz, \qquad W_2 = 2\int_{z_c}^{h/2} \cos4\theta z^2 dz$$

(8.34)

$$W_3 = 2\int_{z_c}^{h/2} \sin2\theta z^2 dz, \qquad W_4 = 2\int_{z_c}^{h/2} \sin4\theta z^2 dz$$

$$W_i* = W_i/I* = 12W_i/h^3$$ (8.35)

8.6 BEAMS

The determination of the deflection and strength of statically determinate beams made of composite laminates is a simple extension of laminated plate theory.   The only difference from the homogeneous beam arises from that of the material properties.

For statically determinate beams, we know the bending moment M at each point along the beam. We can calculate the stress in the beam from

$$\sigma = Mc/I$$ (8.36)

Let the axis of the beam run along the 1–axis. The stress in a laminated composite beam from a given bending moment M can be determined from Equations 8.7 derived from laminated plate theory:

$M_1 = M/b$, where b is the width of the beam.   (8.37)

$M_2 = M_6 = 0$

$\sigma_1^f = 6M_1/h^2$ (8.38)

$\sigma_2^f = \sigma_6^f = 0$

From any strength of materials book we can find the maximum moment and maximum deflection for beams with simple loads and simple end conditions. We will show the formulas for the following six beams in Table 8.3:

• Three beams with concentrated load.
• Three beams with uniformly distributed load:

The maximum moment and deflection δ are normalized with respect to the cantilever beam with concentrated and distributed loads. They are designated as M* and δ*, respectively. The concentrated load is P in Newton, and the distributed load is q, in Newton/meter.

LOADED BEAMS	M_{max}	M*	δ_{max}	δ*
	PL	1	$PL^3/3EI$	1
	PL/4	1/4	$PL^3/48EI$	1/16
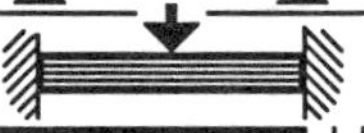	PL/8	1/8	$PL^3/192EI$	1/64
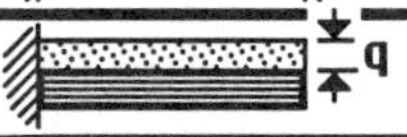	$qL^2/2$	1	$qL^4/8EI$	1
	$qL^2/8$	1/4	$5qL^4/384EI$	5/48
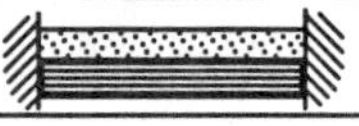	$qL^2/12$	1/6	$qL^4/384EI$	1/48

FIGURE 8.3 MAXIMUM MOMENTS AND DEFLECTIONS OF SIX SIMPLE BEAMS.

Formulas for the moments and deflections are easy, and are the same for homogeneous as well as laminated composite materials. The Young's modulus along the beam axis is the only constant that distinguishes one material from another. For the composite beam the Young's modulus is defined in Equation 8.14; i.e.,

$E = E_1^f$ (8.39)

The difference in the stress distribution across the beam is, however, significantly different. The difference between a homogeneous and a laminated composite material is shown in Figure 8.4. Having plies with different elastic constants, the stress in each ply is piece–wise linear, and varies from ply to ply.

The ply stress and ply strain determination in a laminated composite material is done following the laminated plate theory, as stated in Equation 8.4 and outlined in Section 8.4.

$k_1 = d_{11}M_1$, where d_{11} is a compliance component.

$$= (d_{11}/b)M = (d_{11}*/I)M = M/E_1^f I \qquad (8.40)$$

$$k_2 = d_{21}M_1 = v_{21}^f k_1$$

$$k_6 = d_{61}M_1 = v_{61}^f k_1 \qquad (8.41)$$

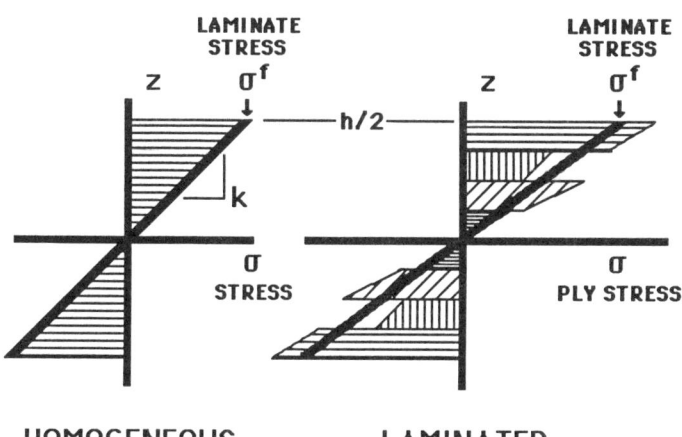

HOMOGENEOUS   LAMINATED

FIGURE 8.4 STRESS DISTRIBUTIONS IN HOMOGENEOUS AND LAMINATED COMPOSITE BEAMS; THE FORMER IS LINEAR, THE LATTER IS PIECE-WISE LINEAR.

We can calculate the ply strain in the beam from Equation 8.15:

$$\{\varepsilon'\}^{(z)} = z\{k\} = \text{beam- and off-axis ply strain} \qquad (8.42)$$

From the calculated strain we can determine the strength/stress ratio or the margin of safety, including the residual stress due to curing and moisture absorption. The strength/stress ratio calculation will be covered in Section 11, and the residual stress in Section 15.

If we want to know the ply stress in the beam, like that in Figure 8.4, the calculation follows the formulas in Equation (8.15):

$$\{\sigma'\}^{(z)} = [Q']^{(z)}\{\varepsilon'\}^{(z)} = \text{laminate- or off-axis ply stress} \qquad (8.43)$$

where $[Q']^{(z)}$ = off-axis stiffness matrix at z (Table 6.2 or 6.3)

It is a recommended practice to verify equilibrium of the in-plane and flexural stresses; the integrals in Equations 7.15 and 7.16 must be equal to the applied load and moment. For the simple beams described above, the in–plane load is zero, and the flexural stress must be balanced by the applied moment per Equation 8.7.

For more complicated beams, the approach remains the same as long as they are statically determinate. When this is not satisfied, more complicated methods are required.

8.7 TUBINGS

There are many useful applications of composite laminates formed in thin wall tubing of symmetric cross sections. The analysis of the bending of tubing is very analogous to the beams of the previous subsection. The Young's modulus of the laminate along the tubing will be that of the E_1^o. We only need to define the section modulus of various cross sections. Then the product $E_1^o I$ is the beam stiffness we need. We will defined a few simple cross sections in Figure 8.5. The wall thickness must be symmetric and thin for this one–dimensional solution; i.e.,

$$h \ll a \qquad (8.44)$$

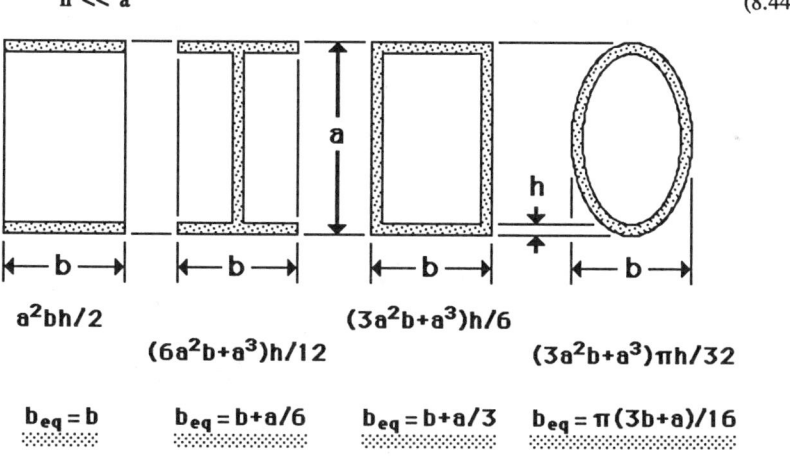

FIGURE 8.5 AREA MOMENT OF INERTIA AND EQUIVALENT WIDTH OF VARIOUS THIN WALL TUBINGS.

Using the moment of inertia in Figure 8.4 in conjunction with Table 8.3 the maximum moment and deflection of the six beams can be readily computed. The Young's modulus of the thin wall along the tube axis is determined by in–plane modulus E_1^o from the laminated plate theory, as defined in Equation 7.12 for symmetric, balanced (orthotropic) tubing wall:

$$E = E_1^o \qquad (8.44)$$

In Figure 8.5 we also show the equivalent width or width correction for each of the three cross sections on the right. The baseline width is the open sandwich construction on the extreme left of this figure. The added material in the remaining three sections can be represented by an increase in the width. The wall thickness h remains the same for all sections.

Analogous to Equation 8.41, we can determine the curvature using the correct Young's modulus and the moment of inertia, such as those in Figure 8.5:

$$k_1 = d_{11}M_1 = M/E_1{}^o I \tag{8.45}$$

The other induced curvatures would be functions of the Poisson and shear coupling of the in–plane modulus:

$$k_2 = -v_{21}{}^o k_1, \qquad k_6 = v_{61}{}^o k_1 \tag{8.46}$$

The different sections in Figure 8.5 will each have a different area moment of inertia as indicated in the figure. We can also treat the increase in the sectional stiffness by claiming a higher equivalent width, or a reduced applied moment; i.e., the moment in Equation 8.45 can be replaced by an equivalent moment:

$$M_{eq} = b_{eq}M_1 \tag{8.47}$$

Regardless of which method we use for determining the curvature, we can calculate the maximum ply strain in the tubing from Equation 8.8:

$$\{\varepsilon^o\} = a\{k\}/2 \tag{8.48}$$

This strain at the outer fiber of the tubing will be used for the calculation of the strength/stress ratio to be described in Section 11. The quadratic failure criterion is preferred because the two conjugate roots correspond to the strength ratios at the top and bottom faces, where $z = \pm a/2$. The roots are obtained from the same calculation. Equation 10.15 shows this relationship. We only have to apply the criterion once and obtain both roots, R^+ and R^-, immediately. If we use maximum stress or maximum strain criterion, we must apply the criterion twice.

Thin wall tubing are susceptible to buckling. The Euler–type column buckling is easy to determine. We only need to use the same sectional stiffness in Equation 8.45. For a column with fixed/free end conditions:

$$P_{critical} = \pi^2 E_1{}^o I/4L^2$$

where $P_{critical}$ = critical axial load.

   $E_1{}^o$ = in–plane stiffness of the symmetric tubing wall.
   I = area moment of inertia, such as those in Figure 8.4.

   L = length of column.

For a hinged/hinged end condition:

$$P_{critical} = \pi^2 E_1{}^o I/L^2 \tag{8.49}$$

Solutions for cases with more complicated end conditions can be found in strength of materials books, for example, in R. J. Roark, *Formulas for Stress and Strain*, McGraw–Hill. But, the local buckling of the wall is not an easy problem.

When the cross section of the tubing is not symmetric with respect to the mid–plane, the solution is simple if the tubing is under bending. We will cover this problem in Section 9. If torque is applied to the tubing, the formulas for the rectangular and elliptic cross–sections can be found, for example, in R. J. Roark. For other sections such as the I–beam and unsymmetric sections, we are not aware of simple formulas. Buckling of tubing under torque is also difficult.

8.8 CONCLUSIONS

There are no shortcuts in the evaluation of the flexural stiffness of symmetric laminates. The position of each ply must be evaluated and summed. Unlike the in–plane stiffness matrix which can be orthotropic for balanced laminates, flexural stiffness cannot be orthotropic if off–axis plies, such as plies with 45 degree angle, exist. The application of the flexural behavior to the analysis and design of beams is simple and direct, provided the structure is statically determinate.

We illustrated examples of practical problems can be solved using this simple theory. The beam bending is limited to symmetric laminates. The anisotropy due to the shear coupling in bending is included in the stress and strain analysis; see Equations 8.41–8.43. The bending of tubing is a simplified one–dimensional solution, and only the in–plane Young's modulus is needed. The tubing wall is limited to symmetric, balanced laminate. If the cross section of the tubing is not symmetric, the thin wall theory will have to be modified.

Section 9

STIFFNESS OF UNSYMMETRIC LAMINATES

The laminate code of this most general laminate is typified by the letter T for total. Ply groups go from the bottom surface to the top in accordance with the limits of definite integrals:

$$[0_3/90_2/45]_T \tag{9.1}$$

This convention however is often modified for specialized laminates, such as the symmetric sandwich and the unsymmetric thin wall construction.

9.1 LAMINATED PLATE THEORY

It remains valid if the plate is thin and the strains are linear:

$$\{\varepsilon\} = \{\varepsilon^o\}+z\{k\}, \quad \text{or} \quad \varepsilon_i = \varepsilon_i{}^o+zk_i, \quad i = 1,2,6 \tag{9.2}$$

We define stress resultants and moments as before and derive the generalized stress–strain relation for our unsymmetric laminates:

$$\{N\} = \int_{-h/2}^{h/2} \{\sigma\}dz = \int_h [Q]\{\varepsilon\}dz = \int_h [Q]dz\{\varepsilon^o\}+\int_h [Q]zdz\{k\}$$

$$= [A]\{\varepsilon^o\}+[B]\{k\}, \text{ in N/m} \tag{9.3}$$

$$\{M\} = \int_{-h/2}^{h/2} \{\sigma\}zdz = \int_h [Q]\{\varepsilon\}zdz = \int_h [Q]zdz\{\varepsilon^o\}+\int_h [Q]z^2dz\{k\}$$

$$= [B]\{\varepsilon^o\}+[D]\{k\}, \text{ in N} \tag{9.4}$$

When discrete, homogeneous plies are used, integration can be replaced by summation:

$$[A] = \sum_{i=1}^{m} [Q'] \left[z^{(i)}-z^{(i-1)} \right], \text{ in N/m} \tag{9.5}$$

$$[B] = 1/2 \sum_{i=1}^{m} [Q'] \left[(z^{(i)})^2 - (z^{(i-1)})^2 \right], \text{ in N} \tag{9.6}$$

$$[D] = 1/3 \sum_{i=1}^{m} [Q'] \left[(z^{(i)})^3 - (z^{(i-1)})^3 \right], \text{ in Nm} \tag{9.7}$$

m = total number of ply groups

$[Q']$ = off–axis ply stiffness

$[B]$ = coupling matrix between in–plane and flexure.

= 0 when laminate is symmetric

9.2 PARTIAL INVERSION

$$\{\epsilon^o\} = [a]\{N\} - [a][B]\{k\}$$
$$\{M\} = [B][a]\{N\} + ([D] - [B][a][B])\{k\}, \text{ in N} \tag{9.8}$$

This partially inverted relation is useful when curvature remains unchanged; i.e.,

$$\{k\} = 0, \qquad \{\epsilon^o\} = [a]\{N\} \tag{9.9}$$

for all laminates, symmetric or not. This simple relation is applicable to cylindrical shells subjected to axisymmetric loading such as internal or external pressure, axial tension or compression, and torque. For the purpose of saving materials and mass, there is no need to use a symmetric wall if the load is axisymmetric.

9.3 COMPLIANCE

The fully inverted stiffness matrix is:

$$\{\epsilon^o\} = [\alpha]\{N\} + [\beta]\{M\}$$
$$\{k\} = [\beta^T]\{N\} + [\delta]\{M\}, \text{ in 1/m} \tag{9.10}$$

where
$$[\alpha] = [a] + [a][B]([D] - [B][a][B])^{-1}[B][a], \text{ in m/N}$$
$$[\beta] = -[a][B]([D] - [B][a][B])^{-1}, \ 1/N$$
$$[\beta^T] = -([D] - [B][a][B])^{-1}[B][a], \ 1/N \tag{9.11}$$
$$[\delta] = ([D] - [B][a][B])^{-1}, \ 1/Nm$$

For symmetric laminates:

$$[B] = 0: \qquad [\alpha] = [a], \qquad [\delta] = [d] \tag{9.12}$$

9.4 NORMALIZED STRESS–STRAIN RELATIONS

Equations 9.3 and 9.4, and 9.10 can be expressed in normalized quantities:

In–plane stress in Pa:

$$\{\sigma^o\} = \{N^*\} = \{N\}/h \tag{9.13}$$

Flexural stress in Pa:

$$\{\sigma^f\} = \{M^*\} = 6\{M\}/h^2 \tag{9.14}$$

Flexural or surface strain:

$$\{\varepsilon^f\} = \{k^*\} = z^{(max)}\{k\} = h\{k\}/2 \tag{9.15}$$

Normalized height:

$$z^* = 2z/h, \quad -1 \leq z^* \leq 1 \tag{9.16}$$

Total strain, equal to the actual strain; See Figure 9.1:

$$\{\varepsilon\} = \{\varepsilon^o\} + z^*\{\varepsilon^f\} \tag{9.17}$$

Total average stress (not equal to the actual stress):

$$\{\sigma^*\} = \{\sigma^o\} + z^*\{\sigma^f\} \tag{9.18}$$

Normalized stiffness, all in units of Pa:

$$[A^*] = [A]/h, \qquad [B^*] = 2[B]/h^2, \qquad [D^*] = 12[D]/h^3 \tag{9.19}$$

Normalized compliance, all in units of 1/Pa:

$$[\alpha^*] = h[\alpha], \qquad [\beta^*] = h^2[\beta]/2, \qquad [\delta^*] = h^3[\delta]/12 \tag{9.20}$$

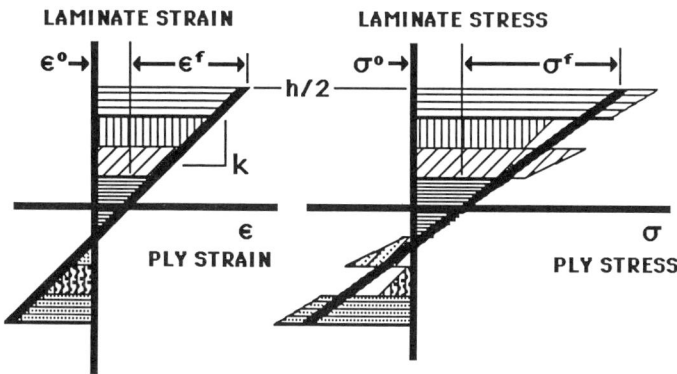

FIGURE 9.1 PLY STRESS AND STRAIN AND LAMINATE STRESS AND STRAIN.

The final normalized stress–strain relations are (factors of 3 and 1/3 in the coupling terms are the results of normalization):

$$\{\sigma^o\} = [A^*]\{\varepsilon^o\}+[B^*]\{\varepsilon^f\}$$
$$\{\sigma^f\} = 3[B^*]\{\varepsilon^o\}+[D^*]\{\varepsilon^f\}$$

(9.21)

$$\{\varepsilon^o\} = [\alpha^*]\{\sigma^o\}+[\beta^*]\{\sigma^f\}/3$$
$$\{\varepsilon^f\} = [\beta^{*T}]\{\sigma^o\}+[\delta^*]\{\sigma^f\}$$

(9.22)

9.5 ENGINEERING CONSTANTS

Engineering constants for unsymmetric laminates are uncommon and difficult to measure because in–plane and flexural deformations are coupled. Instead of three strain measurements we now need six, three on each surface. We then have:

$$\{\varepsilon^o\} = (\{\varepsilon^+\}+\{\varepsilon^-\})/2$$
$$\{\varepsilon^f\} = (\{\varepsilon^+\}-\{\varepsilon^-\})/2$$

(9.23)

where superscript + and − refer to the strain at the top and bottom surfaces, respectively. Engineering constants are those derived from simple tests such as uniaxial loading, pure shear loading, simple bending or pure twisting. For combined stresses, these constants cannot be defined. The constants should not be improperly used; e.g., a direct comparison with equivalent constants of symmetric laminates should not be made.

$$E_1^o = \sigma_1^o/\varepsilon_1^o = 1/\alpha_{11}^*, \text{ when } \sigma_1^o \neq 0$$
$$E_2^o = \sigma_2^o/\varepsilon_2^o = 1/\alpha_{22}^*, \text{ when } \sigma_2^o \neq 0$$
$$E_6^o = \sigma_6^o/\varepsilon_6^o = 1/\alpha_{66}^*, \text{ when } \sigma_6^o \neq 0$$

(9.24)

$$E_1^f = \sigma_1^f/\varepsilon_1^f = 1/\delta_{11}^*, \text{ when } \sigma_1^f \neq 0$$
$$E_2^f = \sigma_2^f/\varepsilon_2^f = 1/\delta_{22}^*, \text{ when } \sigma_2^f \neq 0$$
$$E_6^f = \sigma_6^f/\varepsilon_6^f = 1/\delta_{66}^*, \text{ when } \sigma_6^f \neq 0$$

(9.25)

Coupling coefficients are derived from the off–diagonal components in the compliance matrix. There are so many constants (up 15 off–diagonal components resulting in possibly 30 coupling constants) in the case of the most general unsymmetric laminates, we will only show the Poisson's ratios:

$$\nu_{21}^o = -\varepsilon_2^o/\varepsilon_1^o = -\alpha_{21}/\alpha_{11}, \text{ when } \sigma_1^o \neq 0$$
$$\nu_{12}^o = -\varepsilon_1^o/\varepsilon_2^o = -\alpha_{12}/\alpha_{22}, \text{ when } \sigma_2^o \neq 0$$
$$\nu_{21}^f = -\varepsilon_2^f/\varepsilon_1^f = -\delta_{21}/\delta_{11}, \text{ when } \sigma_1^f \neq 0$$
$$\nu_{12}^f = -\varepsilon_1^f/\varepsilon_2^f = -\delta_{12}/\delta_{22}, \text{ when } \sigma_2^f \neq 0$$

(9.26)

9.6 STIFFNESS EVALUATION

The integrations of the stiffness components defined in Equations 9.3 and 9.4, or the corresponding summations shown in Equations 9.5, 9.6 and 9.7 do not have shortcuts for unsymmetric laminates and must be done for the entire laminate. The limits of integration, comparable to those in Equations 7.18 and 8.26, cannot be reduced to one half of the laminate thickness like the case of symmetric laminates. The location of the sandwich core is in general unsymmetric. As expected, the stiffness evaluation of unsymmetric laminates is time–consuming. The highly coupled in–plane and flexural behavior is also conceptually different. This can be viewed as an opportunity to provide unique structural performances not possible with conventional constructions.

9.7 THE PARALLEL AXIS THEOREM

To find the applied stress resultants, applied moments, and the stiffness matrix of a laminate with respect to a plane other than the midplane:

$$\{N'\} = \{N\}$$

$$\{M'\} = \{M\}-d\{N\}$$

$$[A'] = [A]$$

$$[B'] = [B]-d[A]$$

$$[D'] = [D]-2d[B]+d^2[A]$$

(9.27)

where primed matrices are the new reference plane; d the distance between the new and old reference planes, see Figure 9.2:

$$d = z-z' = \text{transfer distance} \tag{9.28}$$

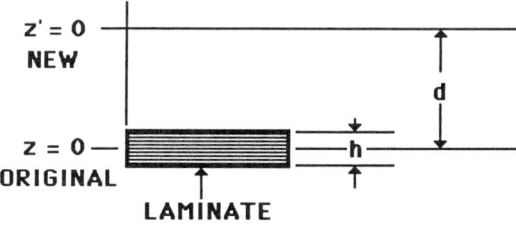

FIGURE 9.2 ORIGINAL AND NEW MIDPLANES FOR THE PARALLEL AXIS THEOREM.

This theorem can also be expressed in terms of normalized quantities:

$$d^* = d/h = \text{normalized transfer distance, h = thickness} \tag{9.29}$$

$$[A^{*\prime}] = [A^*]$$

$$[B^{*\prime}] = [B^*]-2d^*[A^*] \qquad (9.30)$$

$$[D^{*\prime}] = [D^*]-12d^*[B^*]+12d^{*2}[A^*]$$

where $[A^*] = [A]/h$, $[B^*] = 2[B]/h^2$, $[D^*] = 12[D]/h^3$ as in Equation 9.19.

9.8 REPEATED SUBLAMINTES

Sublaminates consist of a small assemblage of plies that can be repeated to form a thick laminate. Typical sublaminates may have up to 8 plies and 4 ply angles, like those in Equation 7.48, and later in Table 14.3. The advantages of sublaminates are:

• Easier selection of optimum ply angles.
• A more damage tolerant laminate resulting from maximum splicing or mixing of plies.
• Simpler layup resulting in lower cost and fewer error in production.

The design process consists of two steps: determine first the optimum ply angles, and secondly, the required number of repeating sublaminates. The laminate code with sublaminates in brackets, index r for repeat, and z_c for half–depth of sandwich core is:

$$\{[\text{sublaminate}]r/z_c\}_s \qquad (9.31)$$

where $[\text{sublaminate}] = [\theta_1/\#_1, \theta_2/\#_2, - - -]$

For unsymmetric constructiozs, different sublaminates and different repeat indices can be used for the top and bottom faces:

$$\{[\text{sublaminate}^+]r^+/c/[\text{sublaminate}^-]r^-\}_T \qquad (9.32)$$

where c is the core.

In the case of symmetric laminates in Equation 9.31, we can use the parallel axis theorem to derive the laminate stiffness matrix. The definition of terms are shown in Figure 9.3.

The following formulas are derived using the following series for the repeating index r:

$$\Sigma r = r(r+1)/2, \qquad \Sigma r^2 = r(r+1)(2r+1)/6 \qquad (9.33)$$

The stiffness matrices for the sublaminate in the location shown in Figure 9.3 (from the bottom surface) are:

$$[A^o], [B^o], [D^o] \qquad (9.34)$$

where Limits of integration are from $-h/2$ to $-(h/2)+u$.

u = thickness of sublaminate

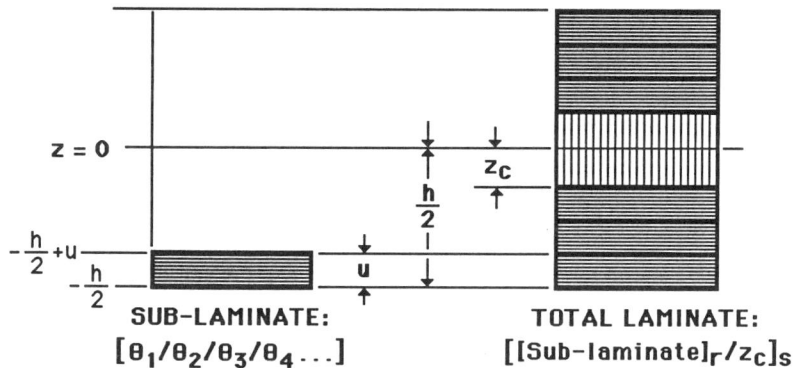

FIGURE 9.3 RELATION BETWEEN SUBLAMINATE AND TOTAL LAMINATE

The stiffness matrices of the total laminate in Figure 9.3 are:

$$[A] = 2r[A^\circ]$$

$$[B] = 0 \tag{9.35}$$

$$[D] = 2r\big[[D^\circ]+(r-1)u[B^\circ]+(r-1)(2r-1)u^2[A^\circ]/6\big]$$

If the total construction is unsymmetric but is built with the same sublaminate, Equation 9.32 can be modified and leads to the following:

$$[A] = (r^++r^-)[A^\circ]$$

$$[B] = (r^+-r^-)\big[-[B^\circ]-(r^++r^--1)u[A^\circ]/2\big]$$

$$[D] = (r^++r^-)[D^\circ]+\big[r^+(r^+-1)+r^-(r^--1)\big]u[B^\circ] \tag{9.36}$$

$$+\big[r^+(r^+-1)(2r^+-1)+r^-(r^--1)(2r^--1)\big]u^2[A^\circ]/6$$

The advantages, cited above, of repeated sub–laminates to form a thick laminate are almost self–evident for in–plane loading. For bending and twisting, the use of sublaminates will also lead to a stronger laminate resulting from a higly dispersed laminate. Having fewer plies in a sublaminate makes optimization of ply angles considerably simpler. In fact, sublaminates do not need to have more than ten plies. This is shown in Sections 14.10 (repeated in 29.18). The effect of stacking sequence of a thick laminate is important only when sublaminates are not used. If sublaminates are used, the stacking sequence effect is reduced when the number of repeated sublmainates are increased. This is also shown in Section 29.18. Thus, the use of sublaminates can be a very powerful option in the design of composite laminates for both in–plane and flexural loadings. The closed form relations above make the use of sublaminates easy and simple.

9.9 THIN WALL CONSTRUCTION

A thin wall construction has negligible wall or face sheet thicknesses relative to the total thickness or depth of a sandwich or stiffened construction. Since we are uncoupling the face sheets, they should be symmetric laminates in order to avoid stretching/flexure coupling. The theory of laminated plate theory for symmetric and unsymmetric constructions can be considerably simplified. This simplification makes design of such construction easy to achieve; a typical construction is shown in Figure 9.4:

$$d^+=h/2, \quad d^-=-h/2 \tag{9.37}$$

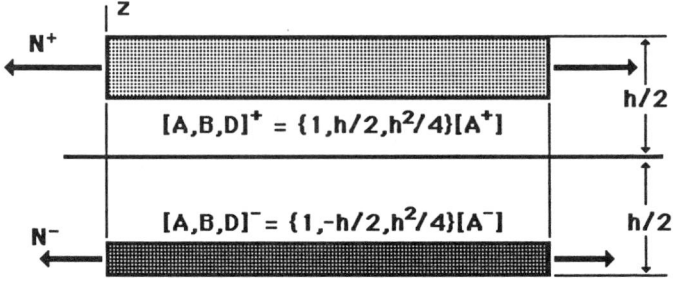

FIGURE 9.4 A THIN WALL, UNSYMMETRIC CONSTRUCTION

Equations 9.27, and 9.30 are simplified because the in–plane stiffness matrix will control the stiffness of the entire construction. The coupling and flexural stiffness matrices make negligible contribution to the total stiffness. But they remain significant in the local buckling of the face sheet. The stiffness of the top and bottom sheets are:

$$[A, B, D]^+ = \{1, d^+, (d^+)^2\}[A^+] = \{1, h/2, h^2/4\}[A^+]$$
$$[A, B, D]^- = \{1, d^-, (d^-)^2\}[A^-] = \{1, -h/2, h^2/4\}[A^-] \tag{9.38}$$

The total stiffness of this construction is simply the sum of the top and bottom faces in Equation 9.38.

$$[A, D] = \{1, h^2/4\}[A^++A^-]$$
$$[B] = h/2[A^+-A^-] \tag{9.39}$$

When the in–plane stiffness of the face sheets are equal, we have a symmetric construction, for which [B] vanishes.

The in–plane and flexural loads imposed on the construction are:

$$\{N\} = \{N^++N^-\}, \qquad \{M\} = \{N^+-N^-\}h/2 \tag{9.40}$$

or $\quad \{N^+\} = \{N/2+M/h\}, \qquad \{N^-\} = \{N/2-M/h\} \tag{9.41}$

The resulting stresses and strains at the top and bottom surfaces are:

$$\{N^+\} = [A^+]\{\varepsilon^+\}, \qquad \{N^-\} = [A^-]\{\varepsilon^-\} \qquad (9.42)$$

$$\{\varepsilon^+\} = [a^+]\{N^+\}, \qquad \{\varepsilon^-\} = [a^-]\{N^-\} \qquad (9.43)$$

We can write the in–plane and curvature of our construction as:

$$\{\varepsilon^o\} = \{\varepsilon^+ + \varepsilon^-\}/2, \qquad \{k\} = \{\varepsilon^+ - \varepsilon^-\}/h$$

or $\{\varepsilon^+\} = \{\varepsilon^o\} + h\{k\}/2, \qquad \{\varepsilon^-\} = \{\varepsilon^o\} - h\{k\}/2$ (9.44)

By combining the relations above, we can show in addition to Equation 9.39 the following stiffness and compliance matrices:

$$[\alpha, \delta] = \{1/4, \ 1/h^2\}[a^+ + a^-]$$

$$[\beta] = [a^+ - a^-]/2h \qquad (9.45)$$

In normalized terms, we have:

$$[A^*, D^*] = \{1, \ 3\}[A^+ + A^-]/h$$

$$[B^*] = [A^+ - A^-]/h \qquad (9.46)$$

$$[\alpha^*, \delta^*] = \{1, \ 1/3\}[a^+ + a^-]h/4$$

$$[\beta^*] = [a^+ - a^-]h/4 \qquad (9.47)$$

These relations for unsymmetric construction are more easily obtained than the complete laminated plate theory which requires a 6x6 inversion; see Equation 9.11.

9.10 THIN WALL CONSTRUCTION WITH SUBLAMINATES

If our thin wall construction consists of the same sublaminate for the top and bottom faces, but with different repeating indices, say, r^+ and r^-, respectively, we have:

$$[A^+] = r^+[A^o], \qquad [A^-] = r^-[A^o]$$

$$[a^+] = 1/r^+[a^o], \qquad [a^-] = 1/r^-[a^o] \qquad (9.48)$$

$$[A^{o*}] = [A^o]/u, \qquad [a^{o*}] = u[a^o] \qquad (9.49)$$

Sublaminates simplify the calculation of the stiffness of thick laminates. The thin wall construction is intended to further simplify design but it is limited to particular configurations. Errors are introduced if the walls are thick.

The stress–strain relations of this special thin wall construction are:

$$[A, D] = (r^+ + r^-)\{1, h^2/4\}[A^\circ]$$

$$[B] = (r^+ - r^-)[A^\circ]h/2 \tag{9.50}$$

$$[\alpha, \delta] = (1/r^+ + 1/r^-)\{1/4, 1/h^2\}[a^\circ]$$

$$[\beta] = (1/r^+ - 1/r^-)[a^\circ]/2h \tag{9.51}$$

In normalized terms, we have:

$$[A^*, D^*] = (r^+ + r^-)\{1, 3\}[A^{\circ *}]u/h$$

$$[B^*] = (r^+ - r^-)[A^{\circ *}]u/h \tag{9.52}$$

$$[\alpha^*, \delta^*] = (1/r^+ + 1/r^-)\{1/4, 1/12\}[a^{\circ *}]$$

$$[\beta^*] = (1/r^+ - 1/r^-)[a^{\circ *}]/2 \tag{9.53}$$

Note that when the construction is symmetric; i.e., $r^+ = r^-$, the coupling matrices vanish. The flexural stiffness is three times the in–plane stiffness for thin wall construction, for both symmetric and unsymmetric constructions.

9.11 ACCURACY OF THE THIN WALL THEORY

The simplified theory of thin wall laminate is useful for design but the limits of its utility must be clearly understood. We will make comparisons between the unabridged and simplified theories to illustrate the errors introduced by our simplification.

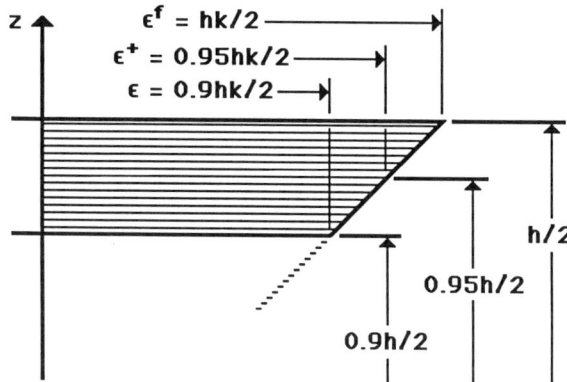

FIGURE 9.5 STRAIN ACROSS THE TOP FACE OF A THIN WALL CONSTRUCTION.

The simplest comparison is the strain variation across a thin face sheet shown in Figure 9.5. Let us assume that the top face shown is 10 percent of the half–thickness h/2 of the total construction. Since linear strain across the entire construction is assumed, it varies from 0.9 to unity. The average strain would be 0.95 of the top surface or flexural strain, or with 5 percent error. We can generalize that the error introduced by the approximation of the strain in a thin wall construction is the same as the ratio of the face sheets to the total thicknesses.

A comparison of the elastic constants of the construction can be made. We will compute the elastic moduli for a thin wall construction:

$$[90/c_8/0] \text{ and } [90/c_{98}/0] \tag{9.54}$$

These laminates have 80 and 98 percent core, respectively. The results using the unabridged theory of Equations 9.5–7 and 9.11, and the normalization by Equation 9.19, and the results of the thin wall theory of Equations 9.46 and 47 are listed in Table 9.1.

TABLE 9.1 COMPARISON OF ELASTIC MODULI BETWEEN THEORIES.

$[90/c_8/0]$, $z_c{}^* = 0.80$ $[90/c_{98}/0]$, $z_c{}^* = 0.98$

	UNA–BRIDGED	THIN WALL	PERCENT ERROR	UNA–BRIDGED	THIN WALL	PERCENT ERROR
$A_{11}{}^*$	19.1	19.1	0.0	1.91	1.91	0.0
$B_{11}{}^*$	15.4	17.1	11.0	1.70	1.71	0.6
$D_{11}{}^*$	47.7	57.3	20.0	5.65	5.73	1.4
$\alpha_{11}{}^*$	252	256.5	0.2	2564	2565	0.1
$\beta_{11}{}^*$	249	229	8.7	220	229	0.4
$\delta_{11}{}^*$	103	85.5	21.0	872	855	2.0

We can say that a thin wall construction with 98 percent core will have about 2 percent error. For "thick wall" construction, say, 80 percent core, the error of simplified theory can bring 20 percent error. The error is about the same as that of the strain shown in Figure 9.5. Thus a simplified theory of unsymmetric construction is a useful design process that can effectively utilize the salient features of composite materials without the burden of a complete laminated plate theory.

9.12 STIFFENED PANELS

The repeating section of a panel stiffened with one rib along the 1–axis is shown in Figure 9.6. The stiffness of this panel can be obtained by applying the parallel axis theorem of Equation 9.27 to the plate and the rib.

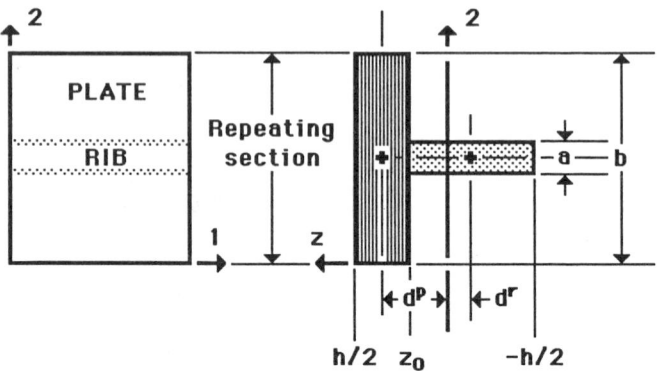

FIGURE 9.6   A REPEATING SECTION OF STIFFENED PANEL BY A RIB IN THE
1-DIRECTION.

The stiffness of the plate about its own midplane at $z = d^p$ is:

$$[A,B,D]^p = \int_{-h'/2}^{h'/2} [Q]^p(1,z,z^2)dz \qquad (9.55)$$

where $h' = 2(h/2-d^p) = h-2d^p$

Similarly the stiffness of the rib (with laminae parallel to 1–2 plane) with respect to its midplane at $z = d^r$ can be obtained. Since the rib is one dimensional, only the 11–components are computed.

$$[A_{11},B_{11},D_{11}]^r = (a/b) \int_{-h''/2}^{h''/2} [Q_{11}]^r(1,z,z^2)dz \qquad (9.56)$$

where $h'' = |2(-h/2-d^r)| = |-h-2d^r|$

a/b = width correction between the rib and the plate.

If the rib laminae are perpendicular to 1–2 plane, then

$$[A_{11}]^r = (h''/b) \int_{(b-a)/2}^{(b+a)/2} [Q_{11}]^r \, dy$$

$$[B_{11}]^r = 0 \qquad (9.57)$$

$$[D_{11}]^r = [A_{11}]^r \, [h'']^2/12$$

Using the parallel axis theorem, we can combine the stiffness of the plate and the rib:

$$A_{11} = A_{11}{}^{p} + A_{11}{}^{r}$$

$$B_{11} = B_{11}{}^{p} + d^{p}A_{11}{}^{p} + B_{11}{}^{r} + d^{r}A_{11}{}^{r} \qquad (9.58)$$

$$D_{11} = D_{11}{}^{p} + 2d^{p}B_{11}{}^{p} + (d^{p})^{2}A_{11}{}^{p} + D_{11}{}^{r} + 2d^{r}B_{11}{}^{r} + (d^{r})^{2}A_{11}{}^{r}$$

If the plate and the rib are symmetrical with respect to their own midplanes, the coupling matrix [B] will be identically zero, and Equation 9.58 becomes

$$A_{11} = A_{11}{}^{p} + A_{11}{}^{r}$$

$$B_{11} = d^{p}A_{11}{}^{p} + d^{r}A_{11}{}^{r} \qquad (9.59)$$

$$D_{11} = D_{11}{}^{p} + (d^{p})^{2}A_{11}{}^{p} + D_{11}{}^{r} + (d^{r})^{2}A_{11}{}^{r}$$

The other components of the stiffness of the stiffened panel are assumed to be unaffected by the rib; i.e., Equation 9.58 can be modified for components other than the 11–components:

$$A_{ij} = A_{ij}{}^{p}$$

$$B_{ij} = B_{ij}{}^{p} + d^{p}A_{ij}{}^{p} \qquad (9.60)$$

$$D_{ij} = D_{ij}{}^{p} + 2d^{p}B_{ij}{}^{p} + (d^{p})^{2}A_{ij}{}^{p}$$

Note that the contribution of the rib is zero for these components, valid when the rib is small relative to the plate; i.e., a/b is small.

If the plate is symmetric about its midplane, Equation 9.60 can be further simplified. If the rib runs in the 2–direction, the subscript 1 will be replaced by subscript 2 in Equations 9.58 and 9.59. All the 11–components will be changed to the 22–components. If we have ribs in both directions, both 11– and 22–components will appear in Equations 9.58 and 9.59.

If the stiffened panel is used as the top cover of the thin wall construction described in Section 9.9, the in–plane stiffnesses of the plate and the rib will be that of the face sheet; i.e., from Equation 9.58

$$A_{11} = A_{11}{}^{p} + A_{11}{}^{r} = A_{11}{}^{+}$$

$$A_{21}{}^{p} = A_{21}{}^{+}, \; A_{22}{}^{p} = A_{22}{}^{+}, \; A_{66}{}^{p} = A_{66}{}^{+} \qquad (9.61)$$

$$A_{16}{}^{p} = A_{16}{}^{+}, \; A_{26}{}^{p} = A_{26}{}^{+}$$

$$0 < A_{12}{}^{+} < A_{21}{}^{+}$$

Similar expressions can be obtained for the bottom face. Then Equations 9.39 and 9.45 can be applied accordingly.

The method for the stiffened panel shown Figure 9.6 can be applied to a more complicated geometry than the plate and the rib. For example, pultruded sections of complex geometry can be similarly analyzed. The width of the repeating section b has not entered the calculation. Only the ratio a/b has been used. The calculation is intended to apply to unit width.

If the actual width is needed, all components of the stiffness matrix [A] must be multiplied by the actual width; e.g., if the width is less than 1 meter, the panel stiffness will be reduced proportionally.

As a sample problem, find the 11–component in the stiffness matrix of a stiffened panel consisting T300/5208, 160 plies of [±45] as the plate, and 40 plies of [0] as the rib. The dimensions are shown in Figure 9.7. The total thickness of the panel, $h = 0.04$m; the width of the rib, $a = 0.005$m; and the width of the repeating section, $b = 0.05$m.

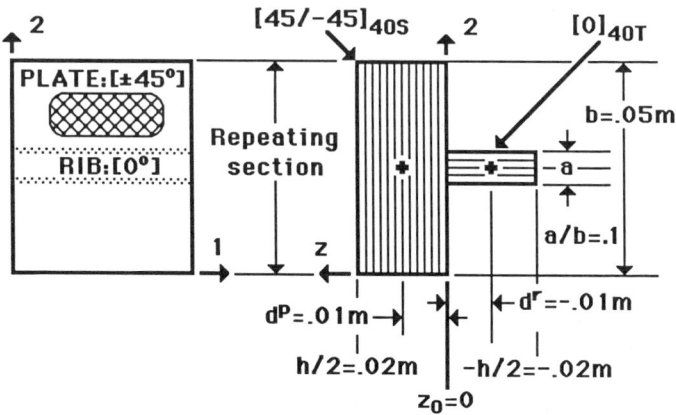

FIGURE 9.7 SAMPLE STIFFENED PANEL.

For the 160–ply [45/–45] plate,

$$h' = 160h_0 = 0.02m, \qquad (h')^3/12 = 0.666 \times 10^{-6} m^3$$

From Prob 3 in Section 7.10, **$A_{11}* = 56.66$ GPa**

$$A_{11}{}^p = A_{11}*h' = 56.66 \times 0.02 = 1133 \text{ MN/m}$$

$$B_{11}{}^p = 0 \qquad\qquad\qquad\qquad (9.62)$$

$$D_{11}{}^p = A_{11}*(h')^3/12 = 37.77 \text{ kNm}$$

For the 40–ply [0] rib, with the same depth of 0.02m as the plate.

$$h'' = 0.02m, \quad (h'')^3/12 = 0.666 \times 10^{-6} m^3$$

For T300/5208, $Q_{xx} = 181.81$ GPa. From Equation 9.56 with $a/b = 0.1$

$$A_{11}{}^r = (a/b)Q_{xx}h'' = 0.1 \times 181.81 \times .02 = 363.6 \text{ MN/m}$$

$$B_{11}{}^r = 0 \qquad\qquad\qquad\qquad (9.63)$$

$$D_{11}{}^r = (a/b)Q_{xx}(h'')^3/12 = 12.11 \text{ kNm}$$

We can find the 11–components of the stiffness matrix by using the values above in Equation 9.59, where

$d^P = -d^r = 0.01$ m

$h = h'+h'' = 0.04$ m, $h^3/12 = 5.33 \times 10^{-6}$ m^3

$A_{11} = A_{11}{}^P + A_{11}{}^r = 1133 + 364 = 1497$ MN/m

$B_{11} = d^P A_{11}{}^P + d^r A_{11}{}^r = 0.01(1133 - 364) = 7.69$ MN   (9.64)

$D_{11} = D_{11}{}^P + (d^P)^2 A_{11}{}^P + D_{11}{}^r + (d^r)^2 A_{11}{}^r$

$= 37.77 \times 10^3 + 0.0001 \times 1133 \times 10^6 + 12.11 \times 10^3 + 0.0001 \times 364 \times 10^6$

$= (151.0 + 48.5) 1 \times 10^3 = 199.5$ kNm

It is more meaningful to convert the absolute stiffness components to normalized ones in accordance with Equation 9.19. Since all normalized stiffness components have the same unit, direct comparison of their influence can be assessed.

$A_{11}{}^* = A_{11}/h = 1497/0.04 = 37.4$ GPa

$B_{11}{}^* = 2B_{11}/h^2 = 2 \times 7.69/0.0016 = 9.6$ GPa   (9.65)

$D_{11}{}^* = 12D_{11}/h^3 = 199.5/5.33 \times 10^{-6} = 37.4$ GPa

Note that the coupling component is small relative to the in–plane and flexural stiffness.

The other components of the stiffness matrix are the same as the comparable components for the plate only. We will not do them here.

9.13 CONCLUSIONS

Unsymmetric laminates represent the ultimate utilization of composite materials. Such laminates provide a unique structural behavior which does not exist with conventional materials. Designers often avoid them because their highly coupled deformation is difficult to analyze. Unsymmetric laminates should not be confused with unbalanced laminates. Some designers also avoid the latter for the same reason.

Our recommendation is that we should select the most efficient laminate construction and should not arbitrarily outlaw unsymmetric laminates. At least we should be aware of the penalty that we must pay when we avoid unbalanced and/or unsymmetric laminates. There is however no reason for using symmetric construction of cylindrical shells if the loading is axisymmetric.

Section 10

MICROMECHANICS

10.1 BACKGROUND

Micromechanics establishes the relation between the properties of the constituents and those of the unit composite ply; see Figure 1.1. Extensive literature is available. The law or rule of mixtures is the simplest relation and often sufficiently accurate for many micromechanics problems. This rule states that the composite property is the sum of the property of each constituent multiplied by its volume fraction.

Micromechanics has been used extensively to guide materials improvement by materials engineers. But the designer of laminates and composite structures use only macromechanics which rely on the measured ply data to establish optimum laminates for a structure. We believe that the designer can be benefited by using micromechanics as design tools as well. We propose the use of an integrated micro- and macromechanics which can include the following features:

- The prediction of the last–ply–failure can be readily achieved by replacing plies with cracks with continuous plies having a lower effective matrix modulus. This will be covered in Section 11.
- The empirical data fit of hygrothermal properties of composite materials can be readily achieved by using power–law approximations applied to micromechanical variables. This will be covered in Section 17.
- Using micromechanics, optimization of materials and geometry on a micromechanical level can be achieved, which leads to a general description of failure modes in the fiber, in the matrix, and at the interface. More will be said later in this Section.

All available micromechanics analyses are approximate. In addition, many properties of the constituents called for in micromechanics formulas cannot be measured. The most common models of micromechanics include:

- Parallel model which gives the upper–bound prediction.
- Series model which gives the lower–bound prediction. The bounds may be far apart to render useful information.
- Modified rule–of–mixtures model which is easy to use and recommended in this book.
- Numerous other strength–of–materials models which may serve special purposes.
- Concentric cylinders model which yield easy results for composite bulk modulus but complicated results for composite shear modulus.
- Square–packing model provides not only effective composite modulus, but also stress distribution. But this analysis is not easy to use for materials sensitivity studies.
- Self–consistent model gives some insight on the interaction between the constituents, and is not difficult to use.

The limitations of micromechanics arise from the idealized fiber cross section and fiber packing symmetry, as well as the assumed continuity at the interface and approximations used in the stress analysis. Micromechanics is further limited by the unmeasurable properties of anisotropic fibers, and the often ignored shrinkage stresses. Detail descriptions of local failure modes are difficult and require further research.

We therefore believe that the realistic use of the micromechanics formulas is for sensitivity study; i.e., the change of a known properties due to some micromechanical change. The relative rather than the absolute change is often adequate for the purpose of design. Figure 10.1 illustrates the back–calculation of constituent properties from a baseline ply data.

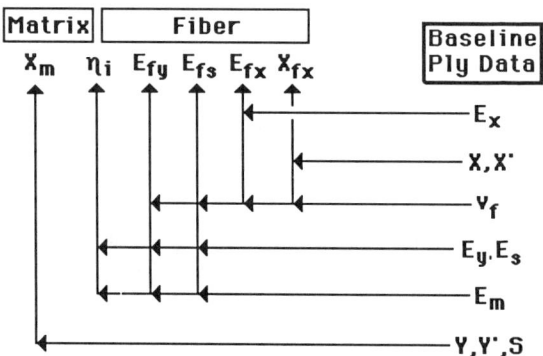

FIGURE 10.1   MICROMECHANICS RELATIONS FOR THE CALCULATION OF THE
CONSTITUENT DATA FROM THE MEASURED BASELINE PLY DATA.

10.2 DENSITY

The composite density as a function of the constituents and their volume fractions can be computed using the rule of mixtures relation:

$$\rho = v_f \rho_f + v_m \rho_m \qquad (10.1)$$

where ρ = density, v = volume fraction,
Subscript f for fiber, m for matrix.

In terms of mass factions which are often measured and reported:

$$\rho = 1/(m_f/\rho_f + m_m/\rho_m + v_v/\rho)$$

$$v_v = \text{void volume fraction} = 1 - \rho(m_f/\rho_f + m_m/\rho_m) \qquad (10.2)$$

where   m = mass fraction of the constituents f and m.

A void content of 0.5 percent is assumed in the Table 10.1. Such low void content has negligible effect on the composite density, and the relation between the volume and mass fractions of each constituent.

TABLE 10.1 VOLUME AND MASS FRACTIONS OF VARIOUS COMPOSITES

Type	CFRP	BFRP	CFRP	GFRP	KFRP	BFRA
Fiber	T300	B(4)	AS	E–glass	Kev 49	Boron
Matrix	N5208	5505	3501	epoxy	epoxy	Al
Fiber density	1.750	2.600	1.750	2.600	1.440	2.600
Matrix dens	1.200	1.200	1.200	1.200	1.200	3.500
ρ_f/ρ_m	1.458	2.167	1.458	2.167	1.200	0.743
void, v_v	0.005	0.005	0.005	0.005	0.005	0.000
Fiber volume	0.700	0.500	0.666	0.450	0.700	0.450
Matrix vol	0.295	0.495	0.329	0.545	0.295	0.550
Comp dens, ρ	1.579	1.894	1.560	1.824	1.362	3.095
Fiber mass	0.776	0.686	0.747	0.641	0.740	0.378
Matrix mass	0.224	0.314	0.253	0.359	0.260	0.622

10.3 LONGITUDINAL YOUNG'S MODULUS AND POISSON'S RATIO

The micromechanics formula for this stiffness of a unidirectional composite follows the rule–of–mixtures relation:

$$E_x = v_f E_f + v_m E_m \qquad (10.3)$$

where E's are the Young's moduli.

Since the fiber stiffness is many times the matrix stiffness, the second term in Equation 10.3 can often be ignored:

$$E_x = v_f E_f \qquad (10.4)$$

The formula for the longitudinal Poisson's ratio also follows the rule–of–mixtures:

$$v_x = v_f v_f + v_m v_m \qquad (10.5)$$

The fiber Poisson's ratio is difficult to determine. We can back calculate from the measured composite Poisson's ratio; i.e.,

$$v_f = (v_x - v_m v_m)/v_f \qquad (10.6)$$

The measured Young's modulus and Poisson's ratio of epoxy are:

$$E_m = 3.45 \text{ GPa}, \ v_m = 0.35 \qquad (10.7)$$

We can now back calculate the fiber Poisson's ratio of the following epoxy–matrix composites:

TABLE 10.2 IMPLIED FIBER POISSON'S RATIOS OF VARIOUS COMPOSITES

Type	CFRP	BFRP	CFRP	GFRP	KFRP
Fiber	T300	B(4)	AS	E–glass	Kev 49
Matrix	N5208	5505	3501	epoxy	epoxy
v_x	0.28	0.23	0.30	0.26	0.34
v_f	0.70	0.50	0.66	0.45	0.60
v_f	0.25	0.11	0.27	0.15	0.33

The implied fiber Poisson's ratios, back–calculated using Equation 10.6 and the measured composite Poisson's ratios listed in Table 6.5, vary from .11 to .33. It is commonly accepted to assume a constant Poisson's ratio for unidirectional composites. It is not a sensitive micromechanical variable.

Woven fabrics have very low Poisson's ratios because the fibers in the transverse direction withhold the Poisson contraction.

10.4 LONGITUDINAL SHEAR MODULUS

The micromechanics formula for this stiffness modulus also follows the rule–of–mixtures relation except the variables are now the compliance, the reciprocal of the stiffness. This a series–connected model, as opposed to the parallel connected model in Equations 10.1 and 10.3. One most often cited formula is:

$$1/E_s = v_f/G_f + v_m/G_m \qquad (10.8)$$

where E_S is the shear modulus of a unidirectional ply, G's are the shear moduli of the fiber and matrix.

Being the lower bound, this equation gives value lower than measured data. One way of correcting this deficiency without giving up the simplicity of the rule–of–mixtures relation is to add an empirical constant to this equation. An example of this constant is the easy–to–use stress partitioning parameter proposed by Hahn, where

η_s = stress partitioning parameter

= (Average matrix stress)/(Average fiber stress)

$$= <\sigma_m>/<\sigma_f> \qquad (10.9)$$

The value of this parameter lies between 0 and 1. We can now modify the rule–of–mixtures relation in Equation 10.8:

$$(1+v^*)/E_s = 1/G_f + v^*/G_m \qquad (10.10)$$

where $v_s^* = \eta_s v_m/v_f$ = reduced matrix/fiber volume ratio $\qquad (10.11)$

We recover Equation 10.8 from 10.10 when η is 1. Typical values of the reduced volume ratio v* are shown and tabulated in following figure and table:

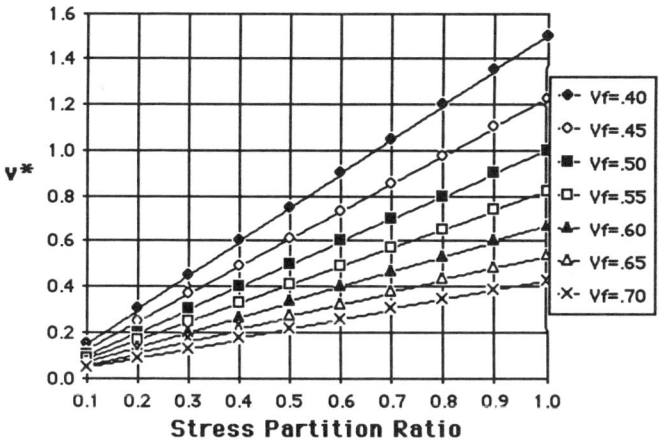

FIGURE 10.3 REDUCED VOLUME RATIO AS A FUNCTION OF STRESS PARTITIONING RATIO OR PARAMETER AND FIBER VOLUMES.

TABLE 10.3 REDUCED VOLUME RATIO AS FUNCTION OF FIBER VOLUME AND STRESS PARTITIONING PARAMETER

v_f	0.40	0.45	0.50	0.55	0.60	0.65	0.70	0.75
η				v^*				
0.1	0.15	0.12	0.10	0.08	0.07	0.05	0.04	0.03
0.2	0.30	0.24	0.20	0.16	0.13	0.11	0.09	0.07
0.3	0.45	0.37	0.30	0.25	0.20	0.16	0.13	0.10
0.316*	0.47	0.38	0.32	0.26	0.21	0.17	0.14	0.10
0.4	0.60	0.49	0.40	0.33	0.27	0.22	0.17	0.13
0.5	0.75	0.61	0.50	0.41	0.33	0.27	0.21	0.17
0.516**	0.77	0.63	0.52	0.42	0.34	0.28	0.22	0.17
0.6	0.90	0.73	0.60	0.49	0.40	0.32	0.26	0.20
0.7	1.05	0.86	0.70	0.57	0.47	0.38	0.30	0.23
0.8	1.20	0.98	0.80	0.65	0.53	0.43	0.34	0.26
0.9	1.35	1.10	0.90	0.74	0.60	0.48	0.39	0.30
1.0	1.50	1.22	1.00	0.82	0.67	0.54	0.43	0.33

* η_s for GFRP from Eq. 10.17; ** η_y for GFRP from Eq. 10.29

In order to establish the stress partitioning parameter of a practical composite, we are fortunate to have a very common composite in glass–epoxy composite which possesses isotropic fibers.

From the longitudinal stiffness of the composite of 38.4 GPa and fiber volume faction of 0.45 in Table 6.5, we use Equation 10.4 to back–calculate the fiber stiffness:

$$E_f = 38.4/0.45 = 85.3 \text{ GPa}$$

$$E_m = 3.4 \text{ GPa} \tag{10.12}$$

From Equation 3.6, and using $v_f = 0.2$, $v_m = .35$

$$G_f = 85.3/2(1+.2) = 35.5 \text{ GP}$$

$$G_m = 3.4/2(1+.35) = 1.26 \text{ GPa} \tag{10.13}$$

We rewrite Equation 10.10 to back–calculate the v^*:

$$v_s{}^* = (1/E_s - 1/G_f)/(1/G_m - 1/E_s) \tag{10.14}$$

Using the values in Equation 10.12 and reported E_s (=4.14 in Table 6.5), we can back–calculate v^*:

$$v_s{}^* = (1/4.14 - 1/35.5)/(1/1.26 - 1/4.14) = 0.386 \tag{10.15}$$

From Equation 10.11,

$$\eta_s = v_s{}^* v_f/v_m \tag{10.16}$$

$$= 0.386(0.45/0.55) = 0.316 \tag{10.17}$$

With the this stress partitioning parameter, the micromechanics formula of Equation 10.10 is reliable for performing sensitivity study of micromechanics variables such as constituent properties and volume fractions. This parameter can be applied to both isotropic and anisotropic fibers provided the shape, size, and volume fraction of the fiber are similar to baseline glass–epoxy composite. This micromechanics formula and other similar ones are not recommended for predicting absolute composite properties; i.e., they should be used for sensitivity studies from a baseline composite material.

10.5 SHEAR MODULUS OF PLIES WITH ANISOTROPIC FIBERS

The elastic moduli of an anisotropic fiber are not easily measured. Assuming the fiber to be transversely isotropic, there are five independent constants. Only its longitudinal Young's modulus is measurable. Its longitudinal shear and transverse moduli are needed for micromechanics predictions but are nearly impossible to measure. The remaining two constants can be two Poisson's ratios, which do not have significant contribution to the composite moduli.

It is therefore practical to predict the shear modulus of a composite with anisotropic fibers by back–calculation. We would first establish the missing fiber moduli through back–calculation by assuming a reasonable value for the stress partitioning parameter such as that in Equation 10.17 derived from GFRP.

The shear and transverse moduli of the fiber can be back-calculated using Equation 10.10, which can be easily rearranged as follows:

$$G_{fx} = \left[(1+v_s^*)/E_s - v_s^*/G_m\right]^{-1} \tag{10.18}$$

The longitudinal shear modulus for T300/5208 composite is 7.17 GPa from Table 6.5; the shear modulus of epoxy matrix is 1.28 GPa, shown in Equation 10.13; a stress partitioning parameter of 0.316 will be assumed. With,

$$v_f = 0.7, \; v_s^* = 0.316(0.3/0.7) = 0.1355 \tag{10.19}$$

$$G_{fx} = 1/[(1+0.1355)/7.17 - 0.1355/1.26] = 19.6 \text{ GPa} \tag{10.20}$$

If we have assumed that the fiber is isotropic, the shear modulus can be calculated using the following moduli:

Longitudinal modulus = 181 GPa

Poisson's ratio = 0.2

From Equation 10.4,

Fiber longitudinal modulus = 181/0.7 = 258 GPa $\tag{10.21}$

From Equation 3.6,

$$G_{f(iso)} = E/2(1+v) = 258/2(1+0.2) = 108 \text{ GPa} \tag{10.22}$$

This shear is more than five times the implied shear in Equation 10.20.

We would recommend the following equation for sensitivity studies of the longitudinal shear modulus of T300/5208:

$$E_s = [1+0.316(v_m/v_f)]/[1/19.6+0.316(v_m/v_f)/G_m] \tag{10.23}$$

In this formula we keep the stress partitioning parameter and the fiber shear modulus constant. We can vary the volume fractions and the matrix shear modulus. Only modest variation on these variables are allowed because the stress partitioning parameter and the back-calculated fiber shear modulus will change if the variables in Equation 10.23 change drastically.

Figure 10.3 can be used to calculate the shear moduli of a unidirectional composite with epoxy matrix. The reduced volume ratio is the parameter in the figure. It can be obtained in Figure 10.2 or Table 10.3.

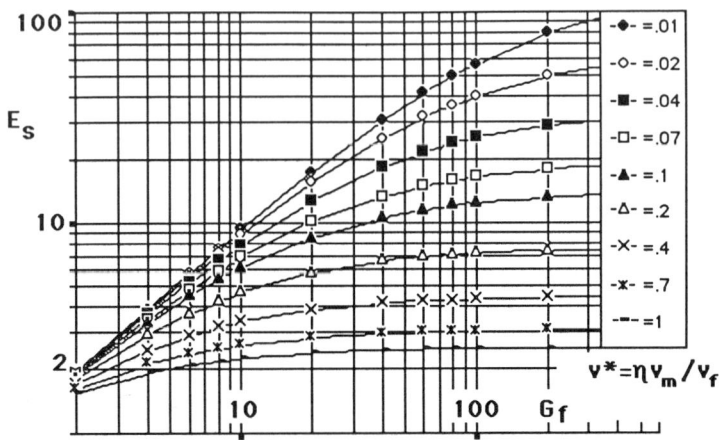

FIGURE 10.3 SHEAR MODULUS OF EPOXY MATRIX UNIDIRECTIONAL COMPOSITES
AS FUNCTIONS OF REDUCED VOLUME V*.

10.6 TRANSVERSE MODULUS

The micromechanics method for the transverse modulus follows precisely
that for the longitudinal shear modulus. In place of Equations 10.10 et al,
we have:

$$(1+v_y*)/E_y = 1/E_{fy} + v_y*/E_m \tag{10.24}$$

where $v_y* = \eta_y v_m/v_f$ = reduced matrix/fiber volume ratio   (10.25)

The numerical example for the shear modulus in Section 10.4 are applicable
to the transverse modulus. For example, comparable to Equations 10.15 and
10.19 we now have, respectively:

$$v_y* = (1/E_y - 1/E_{fy})/(1/E_m - 1/E_y) \tag{10.26}$$

$$E_{fy} = \left[(1+v_y*)/ E_y - v_y*/ E_m\right]^{-1} \tag{10.27}$$

Using same determination of the stress partitioning parameter for the shear
modulus from GFRP, we assume that glass fiber is isotropic and have the
same longitudinal and transverse stiffness as that in Equation 10.12:

$$E_{fx} = E_{fy} = 85.3 \text{ GPa}$$

$$E_y = 8.27 \text{ GPa from Table 6.4, } E_m = 3.4 \text{ GPa} \tag{10.28}$$

Substituting these values in Equation 10.26

$$v_y^* = (1/8.27 - 1/85.3)(1/3.4 - 1/8.27) = 0.630$$

$$\eta_y = v_y^*(v_f/v_m) = 0.516 \tag{10.29}$$

Figure 10.2 and Table 10.3 are applicable for both the transverse and shear moduli. The stress partitioning parameters are different in these two cases.

Figure 10.4 can be used to calculate the transverse moduli of epoxy matrix unidirectional composites.

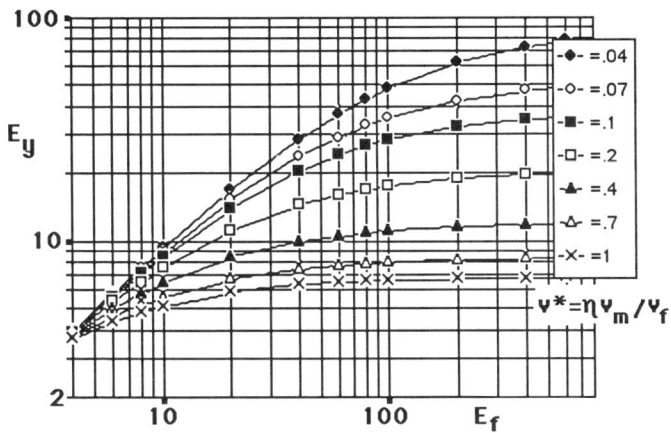

FIGURE 10.4 TRANSVERSE MODULUS OF EPOXY MATRIX UNIDIRECTIONAL COMPOSITES AS A FUNCTION OF REDUCED VOLUME V*.

10.7 EXPANSION COEFFICIENTS

The thermal and moisture expansion coefficients of unidirectional epoxy matrix composites can be expressed in the following simplified micromechanics formulas:

$$\alpha_x = \beta_x = 0 \tag{10.30}$$

where the fiber is assumed to be insensitive to temperature and moisture.

$$\alpha_y = v_m(1+v_m)\alpha_m, \quad \beta_y = v_m(1+v_m)\beta_m \tag{10.31}$$

Both transverse thermal and moisture expansions is proportional to v_m.

10.8 MICROMECHANICS OF STRENGTHS

The predictions of strengths of an orthotropic ply from the constituents are more complicated that those of elastic constants. We will again resort to back–calculation, and devise some easy–to–use formulas for sensitivity studies.

Let us assume that we have measured the five strengths of a unidirectional ply at a reference state, say room temperature with 0.5 percent moisture (c = 0.005). We will designate this reference state by superscript o. The five strengths are:

$$X^o, \; X'^o, \; Y^o, \; Y'^o, \text{ and } S^o \tag{10.32}$$

We can assume that the rule–of–mixtures equation holds for the longitudinal strength as well, we will have

$$X^o = v_f^o X_f^o \tag{10.33}$$

In fact, fiber strength is difficult to measure because: (1) the fiber diameter is small, (2) fiber strength has a scatter, and (3) it also decreases with the length of the test specimen. For a given baseline material, we can back–calculate the fiber strength; i.e.,

$$X_f^o = X^o/v_f^o \tag{10.34}$$

If we have a new fiber material we expect:

$$X = v_f X_f \tag{10.35}$$

Thus the variation of the longitudinal strength from a baseline material is:

$$X/X^o = (v_f/v_f^o)(X_f/X_f^o) \tag{10.36}$$

For longitudinal compressive strength, we expect the same relation holds. The micro–buckling mode can be included by adding to Equation 10.36 the change in the ply shear modulus, the foundation modulus:

$$X'/X'^o = (v_f/v_f^o)(X_f/X_f^o)(E_s/E_s^o)^c \tag{10.37}$$

The exponent c is added to the shear moduli ratio. This exponent is to be empirically determined. We recommend a value 0.2, which means that the relative reduction of the compressive strength is less than that of the shear modulus.

It is equally difficult to establish micromechanics equations for the transverse and shear strengths. They are more dependent on the matrix and interfacial strengths than on the fiber strength. If the baseline and modified matrix strengths, and their ratios are, respectively:

$$X_m^o, \; X_m, \text{ and } \; X_m/X_m^o \tag{10.38}$$

we can assume that

$$Y/Y^o = Y'/Y'^o = S/S^o = X_m/X_m^o \tag{10.39}$$

If we wish to include the effect of the interfacial strength, we can postulate that the strength will affect the transverse tensile and shear strength more than the transverse compressive, longitudinal tensile and compressive strength. We can modify Equation 10.39 to include an index for the interface

$$Y/Y^o = S/S^o = (i)(X_m/X_m^o) \tag{10.40}$$

where $0 < i < 1$. $\tag{10.41}$

The formulas above will be used in the integrated micro–macromechanics analysis including the hygrothermal effects. Numerical examples will be given. If experimentally observed behavior cannot be described by these simple formulas, they can be modified accordingly. One simple modification is the use of exponents for each dimensionless parameter; e.g., Equation 10.39 can be modified:

$$Y/Y^o = (i)^a(X_m/X_m^o)^b$$
$$S/S^o = (i)^c(X_m/X_m^o)^e \tag{10.42}$$

In Equation 10.40, these exponents are unity. When their values are greater than unity, they accentuate the effect of the associated dimensionless parameter; when their values are less than unity, they reduce the effect.

10.9 MICROMECHANICS OF WOVEN COMPOSITES

The predictions of elastic constants and strength of fabrics, filament–wound and braided structures can be made using classical micro and macro mechanics with appropriate empirical correction factors. We propose to replace the woven composite by a multidirectional laminate consisting of the fiber angles. Then the micromechanics formulas for the stiffness and strength are applied to the plies as before.

We first show where this replacement approach gives accurate prediction. From Table 11.1, we can observe the measured stiffness and strength of a unidirectional tape and two woven cloths all made of the same T300/F934 composite. They are listed in Columns 9, 10 and 11 in Table 11.1.

If we treat the fabric as a cross–ply or [0/90] laminate we simply take the average of the longitudinal and transverse modulus we have:

$$(E_x+E_y)/2 = (148+10)/2 = 79 \text{ GPa} \tag{10.43}$$

Compared with the 13–mil and 7–mil fabrics we have the following errors:

$$79/74 = 1.07, \ 79/66 = 1.20 \tag{10.44}$$

or 7 and 20 percent errors, respectively. As expected, the laminated plate theory prediction in Equation 10.43 gives the upper bound value.

As we have seen in the examples given in Section 7, the Poisson's ratio of cross–ply laminates is nearly zero. The measured Poisson's ratios for the two fabrics are indeed close to zero, with actual values of 0.05 and 0.04. We can expect this near–zero Poisson's ratio to hold true for all square fabrics.

The shear modulus is carried over from the unidirectional to the fabrics with the following errors:

$$4.55/4.55 = 1.00, \quad 4.55/4.10 = 1.11 \tag{10.45}$$

Shear strength is also carried over well from the cross–ply laminate to the fabrics with a error about 4 percent.

The tensile and compressive strengths of the fabrics, however, are much lower than what the simple rule–of–mixtures equation would yield. The tensile strength of the fabric is closer to the cross–ply laminate than the compressive strength. This is not unexpected because the fibers are not straight in fabrics.

10.10 MICROMECHANICS OF RANDOM COMPOSITES

The predictions of the elastic constants of random composites can be based on the quasi–isotropic composites. For two–dimensional random composites the quasi–isotropic constants are those listed in Equation 6.10. Those constants are the same of a quasi–isotropic $\pi/4$ laminate. The uniaxial strength of the two–dimensional composite can be based on the first–ply–failure strength because we do not expect any post first–ply–failure capability. An approximate method for the determination of the composite tensile strength is the product of the quasi–isotropic constant and the transverse tensile failure strain. For example, for CFRP T300/5208 from Tables 6.5 and 10.1, respectively:

$$E^{iso} = 69.68 \text{ GPa}, \quad \varepsilon_x{}^* = 3.88 \times 10^{-3}$$
$$\sigma^{iso} = 69.68 \times 3.88 = 270 \text{ MPa} \tag{10.46}$$

For three–dimensional random composites, an approach similar to the two–dimensional composites can be applied. In place of Equation 6.10, the three–dimensionally random composites has been addressed in the literature; see for example R. M. Christensen's Mechanics of Composite Materials, John Wiley, 1979. The effective quasi–isotropic Young's modulus for the 3–D is about one half of that of the 2–D. For T–300/5208, it would be about 35 GPa. The uniaxial strength can also be approximated by the modulus multiplied by the transverse tensile failure strain, analogous to Equation 10.46. For the 3–D, the strength would be about 135 MPa.

10.11 CONCLUSIONS

The micromechanics formulas in this section are simple to use. While they may not be the most sophisticated in form but are expected to provide sufficient insight for determining the trend in sensitivity studies and giving direction to materials improvement. In Figures 1.1 and 1.2, micromechanics also play a critical role in establishing the hygrothermal dependency of the stiffness and strength of composites. With readily workable micromechanics formulas we can successfully integrate micro and macro mechanics to provide a powerful tool for efficient use of composite materials. Examples of the integrate micro–macro analysis, Mic–Mac for short, will be demonstrated later.

Section 11

FAILURE CRITERIA

11.1 INTRODUCTION

Failure criteria are needed for design and for guiding materials improvement. The most frequently used criteria are extensions of similar criteria for isotropic materials, which include the maximum stress, maximum strain, and quadratic criteria. Unlike the analytical formulation of the elastic deformation of previous sections, these criteria are empirical. But the criteria must still be consistent with the principles of mechanics and mathematics.

The failure criterion of an on–axis unit ply is relatively easy to determine, analogous to the stiffness of the unit ply. Once the on–axis failure criterion is known, the off–axis or laminate–axis criterion can be obtained by the coordinate transformation of stress or strain.

The effects of curing stress are additive to the mechanically applied stress following the conventional analysis of thermoelasticity. The temperature and moisture dependent properties can also be readily integrated into the quasi–static stress analysis if these properties are essentially time–independent. If properties are time–dependent and nonlinear, more complex mathematical models than the static analysis will be required. With failure criteria, ply–by–ply strength analysis can be determined, from which the first–ply–failure, last–ply–failure, design limit and ultimate can all be derived. In this section, we will cover various failure criteria of a unidirectional ply, and the first–ply–failure of laminated composites. Plies are intact with the FPF envelope. In the next section we will describe a matrix degradation model for laminate load carrying capability beyond the FPF.

11.2 BASIC STRENGTH DATA

It is assumed that the following strengths of a unidirectional or fabric ply can be determined from relatively simple tests:

> X – Longitudinal tensile strength
> X' – Longitudinal compressive strength
> Y – Transverse tensile strength   (11.1)
> Y' – Transverse compressive strength
> S – Longitudinal shear strength

Using these data we can establish two–dimensional failure criteria and predict the strength of an orthotropic ply subjected to combined stresses or strains.

We can recover the von Mises failure criterion for isotropic materials by setting:

$$X = X' = Y = Y', \qquad S = X/\sqrt{3} = 0.57X \qquad (11.2)$$

where the $\sqrt{3}$ comes from the von Mises invariant in Equation 5.20.

The modes of failure of composite materials are more complicated than the modes under simple tests listed in Equation 11.1. Longitudinal tensile failure of a unidirectional ply can be related to the fiber failure by the rule of mixtures in Equation 10.35. Longitudinal compressive strength, on the other hand, involves more than one mode. Fibers can fail under axial compression, by micro–buckling, or by kinking of a group of fibers. The matrix stiffness and interfacial bond contribute to the foundation that affects the buckling and kinking modes of failure. So, while we may be able to define the fiber failure in terms of the longitudinal tensile failure, we cannot extend this to characterize the longitudinal compressive failure. Similarly transverse tensile strength is a combination of matrix strength under complex stresses, interfacial strength between the fiber and matrix, and the curing stresses on the micromechanical level. The transverse compressive strength involves multiple modes as well. The same applies to the longitudinal shear strength.

Recognizing the complexity involved in the failure modes of unidirectional composites, we should try to avoid oversimplifying the physically observed phenomena. Failure modes operate interactively, concurrently as well as sequentially. Until we have more controlled experiments, it is difficult to describe most of these failure modes. In the mean time we can rely on appropriate failure criteria to guide design and materials improvement.

11.3 STRENGTH/STRESS RATIO

The strength/stress ratio R or strength ratio, for short, is the ratio between the maximum, ultimate or allowable strength, and the applied stress. We postulate that our material is linearly elastic, and then for each state of combined stresses there is a corresponding state of combined strains. We also assume proportional loading; i.e., all components of stress and strain increase by the same proportion.

$$\{\sigma\}_{max} = R\{\sigma\}_{applied}, \quad \text{and} \qquad (11.3)$$

$$\{\varepsilon\}_{max} = R\{\varepsilon\}_{applied} \qquad (11.4)$$

Numerically R can have any positive value but only that with a value greater than or equal to unity has physical meaning. This multipurpose ratio can be used in a variety of ways to aid design. Its utility is further explained in Section 29, HyperComposites. Its advantages over the von Mises stength index is shown in Subsections 29.14; and its use in 29.15. The use of the strength ratio is valid for all common failure criteria.

•When R = 1, failure occurs.

•When R >1, say R = 2, the safety factor is two; i.e., the applied stress can increase by a factor of two before failure occurs.

•When R < 1, say R = 0.5, the applied stress has exceeded the strength by a factor of two. This is not physically possible. The ratio is a useful information for design; e.g., reduce the load by one half, or double the number of plies for a new design.

•Note that when the applied stress or strain component is unity, the resulting strength ratio is the strength. This is an easy method of calculating strength.

Proportional loading means that the loading vectors in stress and strain space are kept in the same direction. Typically such vectors would radiate from the origin of stress or strain space, and extend like rays when the applied stress or strain increases. Examples of these vectors illustrated as hands in a clock can be seen in Subsection 29.10. If initial or residual stresses are present, the applied vectors will radiate from a point different from the origin. Modifications to the strength ratio calculation will have to be made.

We will examine three failure criteria: maximum stress, maximum strain, and quadratic criteria. In the first two criteria, the strength ratio is applied to each stress or strain component in the symmetry or on–axis orientation of the ply. The lowest ratio of the three stress or strain components controls the failure. In the quadratic criterion, each combined state of stress and the corresponding state of strain has a unique strength ratio. It can be applied in any reference axes, on or off the symmetry axes. The quadratic criterion is more flexible than the maximum stress or strain criterion.

11.4 MAXIMUM STRESS CRITERION

This criterion is applied by calculating the strength/stress ratio for each stress component. In the principal stress space where shear is zero, the four measured strengths, X, X', Y, and Y' for T300/5208 are shown as solid squares in the left of Figure 11.1. As shown in the right of Figure 11.1, the maximum stress failure criterion is simply a box drawn through these points.

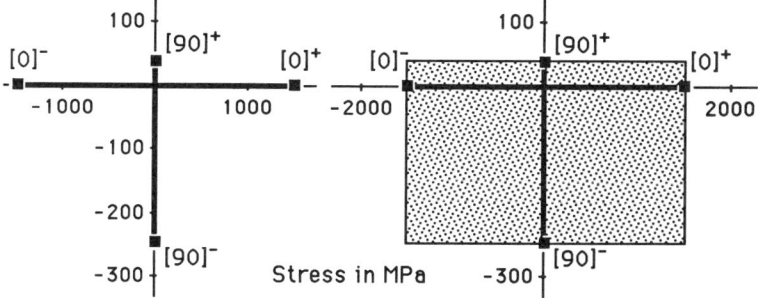

FIGURE 11.1   MAXIMUM STRESS CRITERION OF AN ORTHOTROPIC PLY IN
PRINCIPAL STRESS SPACE. THE UNAXIAL DATA POINT ARE
IDENTIFIED BY [0]+ AS THE LONGITUDINAL TENSILE STRENGTH, ETC.

The lowest strength ratio among the following three equations determines the ratio that controls the failure of the ply:

$$R_x = X/\sigma_x \text{ if } \sigma_x>0, \text{ or } R_x' = X'/|\sigma_x| \text{ if } \sigma_x<0 \quad (11.5)$$

$$R_y = Y/\sigma_y \text{ if } \sigma_y>0, \text{ or } R_y' = Y'/|\sigma_y| \text{ if } \sigma_y<0 \quad (11.6)$$

$$R_s = S/|\sigma_s| \quad (11.7)$$

From orthotropic symmetry consideration, shear strength is not sign dependent. It is often assumed that there are five independent modes of failure, one assigned to each positive and negative stress component, such as longitudinal tensile, longitudinal compressive, etc.

11.5 MAXIMUM STRAIN CRITERION

The maximum strain criterion is very similar to the maximum stress criterion. The maximum strain from each simple test is either measured or computed from the measured strength divided by the tangent modulus:

$$\varepsilon_x^* = X/E_x, \text{ or } \varepsilon_x^{*'} = X'/E_x$$

$$\varepsilon_y^* = Y/E_y, \text{ or } \varepsilon_y^{*'} = Y'/E_y \quad (11.8)$$

$$\varepsilon_s^* = S/E_s$$

Plotting the maximum strain criterion in strain space is simply analogous to drawing a box for the maximum stress criterion. In Figure 11.2 we show the typical boxy envelope on the zero shear strain plane. Each line of the envelope defines the appropriate allowable strain listed in Equation 11.8.

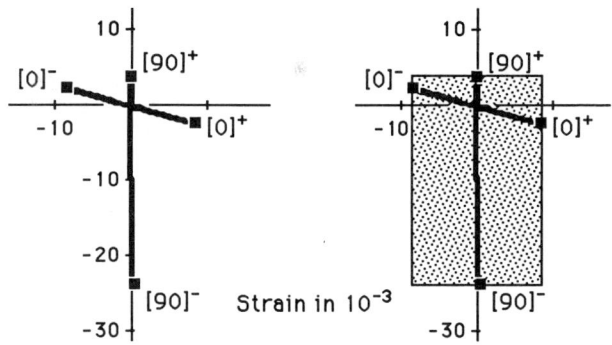

FIGURE 11.2   MAXIMUM STRAIN CRITERION OF AN ORTHOTROPIC PLY IN PRINCIPAL STRAIN SPACE. THE UNAXIAL DATA POINT ARE IDENTIFIED BY [0]+ AS THE LONGITUDINAL TENSILE STRENGTH, ETC.

Strength ratio of this criterion is also decided from the lowest of three ratios of the maximum strain divided by the applied strain.

$$R_x = \varepsilon_x*/\varepsilon_x \text{ if } \varepsilon_x > 0, \text{ or } R_x' = \varepsilon_x*/|\varepsilon_x| \text{ if } \varepsilon_x < 0$$

$$R_y = \varepsilon_y*/\varepsilon_y \text{ if } \varepsilon_y > 0, \text{ or } R_y' = \varepsilon_y*/|\varepsilon_y| \text{ if } \varepsilon_y < 0 \qquad (11.9)$$

$$R_s = \varepsilon_s*/|\varepsilon_s|$$

Like the maximum stress criterion, the sign of the normal strain component determines whether the tensile or compressive ultimate strain should be used. A failure mode is also implicitly assigned to each strain component. Interactions among the possible five modes are assumed to be nonexistent by this and the maximum stress criteria. The boxy appearance of the envelope implies no interaction.

Because Poisson's ratio is not zero, there is always coupling between the normal strain components which leads to disagreement between these two criteria as to both the magnitude of the load and the assigned mode responsible for the failure. Agreements between the two criteria exist only on the shear plane and along the four lines of constant failures due to uniaxial stresses. Since deformation of a body is always coupled, by the nonzero Poisson's ratio, we would like to think that failure is also coupled.

11.6 QUADRATIC CRITERION IN STRESS SPACE

One way to incorporate a coupled or interacting failure criterion is to use the quadratic criterion, which can be rationalized as a generalization of stress or strain invariants. We no longer depend on failure criteria to define the modes of failure, and recognize failure criteria as useful design tools based on fitting available data. We postulate that the criterion in stress space consists of the sum of linear and quadratic invariants as follows:

$$F_{ij}\sigma_i\sigma_j + F_i\sigma_i = 1, \qquad i,j = 1,2,3,4,5,6 \qquad (11.10)$$

For a thin orthotropic ply under plane stress relative to the symmetry axes x–y, the strength parameters F's can be computed from the following:

$$F_{xx} = 1/XX', \qquad F_{yy} = 1/YY', \qquad F_{ss} = 1/S^2$$

$$F_x = 1/X - 1/X', \qquad F_y = 1/Y - 1/Y', \quad F_s = 0 \qquad (11.11)$$

The absolute interaction term, or its normalized term $F_{xy}*$, can be determined only by biaxial tests.

$$F_{xy} = F_{xy}*[F_{xx}F_{yy}]^{1/2} \qquad (11.12)$$

These tests are difficult to perform; some simple versions are recommended in Subsections 29.22, 29.23, and 29.24. In the mean time we can treat the interaction term as an empirical constant. The numerical value of the normalized interaction term can be $-1/2$ for the generalized von Mises criterion, and zero for approximately the Hill/Hoffman criterion. For highly anisotropic composite materials, the failure envelope in stress space is a very elongated ellipsoid. It is difficult to show it graphically because it looks like a hot dog. We therefore prefer to use the strain space representation, which we will discuss later. We will illustrate the sensitivity of this interaction term in the next subsection.

The strongest recommendation of the use of quadratic criterion is that the non–interacting criteria are limiting cases of the quadratic. This can be seen in Subsection 29.9.

Since each combination of stress components in Equation 11.10 reaches its maximum when the left–hand side reaches unity, we can substitute Equation 11.3 into 11.10:

$$[F_{ij}\sigma_i\sigma_j]R^2+[F_i\sigma_i]R-1=0 \tag{11.13}$$

The value of the stress components in Equation 11.13 are that of the applied stress. For a given material, the F's are specified. For a given state of applied stresses, the σ's are known. We only need to solve the quadratic equation in the strength/stress ratio R in Equation 11.13. The correct answer is the positive square root in the quadratic formula; i.e.,

$$aR^2+bR-1 = 0, \quad a = F_{ij}\sigma_i\sigma_j, \quad b = F_i\sigma_i \tag{11.14}$$

$$R = -(b/2a)+[(b/2a)^2+1/a]^{1/2} \tag{11.15}$$

The absolute value of the conjugate root from negative square root yields the strength ratio when the sign of all the applied stress components is reversed. This is useful for the bending of a symmetric plate because the resulting ply stresses change signs between the positive and negative distance from the mid–plane; designated R^+ and R^-, respectively; i.e.,

$$R^+ = -(b/2a)+[(b/2a)^2+1/a]^{1/2}$$
$$R^- = |-(b/2a)-[(b/2a)^2+1/a]^{1/2}| \tag{11.16}$$

11.7 QUADRATIC CRITERION IN STRAIN SPACE

The plane stress criterion in Equation 11.10 can be represented in strain space by a straightforward substitution of the stress–strain relation. The resulting failure criterion is not one based on plane strain because we ignore the nonzero strain along the thickness direction. We are actually representing the plane stress failure criterion in strain space. This is acceptable if we recognize that all failure criteria are purely empirical, and are not analytical or derivable from fundamental principles.

The resulting failure criterion in strain space is:

$$G_{ij}\varepsilon_i\varepsilon_j+G_i\varepsilon_i = 1 \tag{11.17}$$

where $G_{xx} = F_{xx}Q_{xx}^2+2F_{xy}Q_{xx}Q_{xy}+F_{yy}Q_{xy}^2$

$G_{yy} = F_{xx}Q_{xy}^2+2F_{xy}Q_{xy}Q_{yy}+F_{yy}Q_{yy}^2$

$G_{xy} = F_{xx}Q_{xx}Q_{xy}+F_{xy}(Q_{xx}Q_{yy}+Q_{xy}^2)+F_{yy}Q_{xy}Q_{yy} \tag{11.18}$

$$G_{ss} = F_{ss}Q_{ss}{}^2$$

$$G_x = F_xQ_{xx}+F_yQ_{xy}$$

$$G_y = F_xQ_{xy}+F_yQ_{yy}$$

Since we assume that the strength ratio based on combined stresses is equal to that on combined strains, we can determine the strength ratio using the failure criterion in strain space:

$$[G_{ij}\varepsilon_i\varepsilon_j]R^2+[G_i\varepsilon_i]R-1 = 0 \tag{11.19}$$

We can apply the same solution of this quadratic equation as before:

$$aR^2+bR-1 = 0, \quad a = G_{ij}\varepsilon_i\varepsilon_j, \quad b = G_i\varepsilon_i \tag{11.20}$$

$$R = -(b/2a)+[(b/2a)^2+1/a]^{1/2} \tag{11.21}$$

Constants a and b are invariant and have the same values in stress and strain spaces because we use a linear theory. The representation of failure envelopes in strain space is preferred because strain is usually specified in laminated plate theory; i.e., strain is at most a linear function of the thickness. Failure envelopes are fixed in strain space, and are independent of other plies with different angles which may exist in a laminate. They can thus be regarded as material properties. On the other hand, the stress space failure envelopes of the individual plies in a multidirectional laminate are functions for each laminate; see Subsection 29.10 for examples. In Figure 11.3 we show the quadratic failure envelopes in the principal strain space of T300/5208 for two values of the normalized interaction terms; –0.5 and 0.

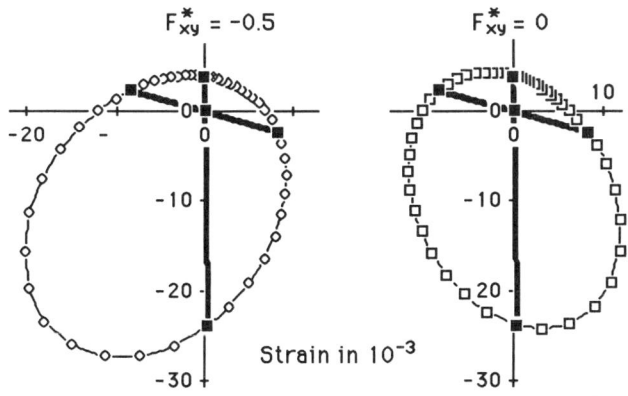

FIGURE 11.3   QUADRATIC FAILURE CRITERION OF AN ORTHOTROPIC PLY IN
PRINCIPAL STRAIN SPACE OF TWO VALUES OF INTERACTION TERMS.

11.8 TYPICAL PLY STRENGTH DATA

We will show in Table 11.1a and b typical strength data for the same composite materials as those in Table 6.5a and b for the elastic constants, in SI and English units, respectively.

TABLE 11.1a   STRENGTH OF VARIOUS COMPOSITE MATERIALS IN SI

Fiber	T300	B(4)	AS	E-glass	Kev 49	AS 4	H-IM6	T300	T300	T300
Matrix	N5208	N5505	3501	epoxy	epoxy	PEEK	epoxy	F934	F934	F934
Engineering constants, GPa or dimensionless								4-mil tp	13-mil c	7-mil c
Ex	181.00	204.00	138.00	38.60	76.00	134.00	203.00	148.00	74.00	66.00
Ey	10.30	18.50	8.96	8.27	5.50	8.90	11.20	9.65	74.00	66.00
nu/x	0.28	0.23	0.30	0.26	0.34	0.28	0.32	0.30	0.05	0.04
Es	7.17	5.59	7.10	4.14	2.30	5.10	8.40	4.55	4.55	4.10
Max stress, MPa										
X	1500	1260	1447	1062	1400	2130	3500	1314	499	375
X'	1500	2500	1447	610	235	1100	1540	1220	352	279
Y	40	61	51.7	31	12	80	56	43	458	368
Y'	246	202	206	118	53	200	150	168	352	278
S	68	67	93	72	34	160	98	48	46	46
Max strain, eps*, E-03										
x	8.29	6.18	10.49	27.51	18.42	15.90	17.24	8.88	6.74	5.68
x'	8.29	12.25	10.49	15.80	3.09	8.21	7.59	8.24	4.76	4.23
y	3.88	3.30	5.77	3.75	2.18	8.99	5.00	4.46	6.19	5.58
y'	23.88	10.92	22.99	14.27	9.64	22.47	13.39	17.41	4.76	4.21
s	9.48	11.99	13.10	17.39	14.78	31.37	11.67	10.55	10.11	11.22

TABLE 11.1b   STRENGTH OF VARIOUS COMPOSITE MATERIALS IN ENGLISH

Fiber	T300	B(4)	AS	E-glass	Kev 49	AS 4	H-IM6	T300	T300	T300
Matrix	N5208	N5505	3501	epoxy	epoxy	PEEK	epoxy	F934	F934	F934
Engineering constants, msi or dimensionless								4-mil tp	13-mil c	7-mil c
Ex	26.25	29.58	20.01	5.60	11.02	19.43	29.44	21.46	10.73	9.57
Ey	1.49	2.68	1.30	1.20	0.80	1.29	1.62	1.40	10.73	9.57
nu/x	0.28	0.23	0.30	0.26	0.34	0.28	0.32	0.30	0.05	0.04
Es	1.04	0.81	1.03	0.60	0.33	0.74	1.22	0.66	0.66	0.59
Max stress, ksi										
X	217.5	182.7	209.82	153.99	203	308.85	507.5	190.53	72.355	54.375
X'	217.5	362.5	209.82	88.45	34.075	159.5	223.3	176.9	51.04	40.455
Y	5.8	8.845	7.4965	4.495	1.74	11.6	8.12	6.235	66.41	53.36
Y'	35.67	29.29	29.87	17.11	7.685	29	21.75	24.36	51.04	40.31
S	9.86	9.715	13.485	10.44	4.93	23.2	14.21	6.96	6.67	6.67
Max strain, eps*, E-03										
x	8.29	6.18	10.49	27.51	18.42	15.90	17.24	8.88	6.74	5.68
x'	8.29	12.25	10.49	15.80	3.09	8.21	7.59	8.24	4.76	4.23
y	3.88	3.30	5.77	3.75	2.18	8.99	5.00	4.46	6.19	5.58
y'	23.88	10.92	22.99	14.27	9.64	22.47	13.39	17.41	4.76	4.21
s	9.48	11.99	13.10	17.39	14.78	31.37	11.67	10.55	10.11	11.22

In Table 11.2, we show the vlaues of the strength parameters in strain space for various composite materials. Since the values are dimensionless, they are the same for the SI and English units. Two values for the interactions terms are shown; viz., the von Mises and Hill/Hoffman.

TABLE 11.2   STRENGTH PARAMETERS IN STRAIN SPACE OF VARIOUS COMPOSITE MATERIALS

Type	CFRP	BFRP	CFRP	GFRP	KFRP	CFRTP	CFRP	CFRP	CCRP	CCRP
Fiber	T300	B(4)	AS	E-glass	Kev 49	AS 4	H-IM6	T300	T300	T300
Matrix	N5208	N5505	3501	epoxy	epoxy	PEEK	epoxy	F934	F934	F934
Strength parameters $Fxy* = -0.5$ (Generalized von MISES)								4-mil tp	13-mil c	7-mil c
Gxx	12004	10374	7376	1914	13454	6394	5822	10971	29783	40019
Gyy	10681	27646	7467	18882	47657	4890	14914	12786	32580	40965
Gxy	-3069	-2989	-1746	1712	2069	-1584	-495	-2570	-13120	-17455
Gss	11118	6961	5828	3306	4576	1016	7347	8985	9784	7944
Gx	61	130	39	25	-150	-40	-34	42	-65	-63
Gy	217	214	131	198	351	66	125	168	-52	-61
Strength parameters $Fxy* = 0$ (Modified HILL)										
Gxx	15544	14823	9889	3669	23445	8136	9259	14999	31418	41879
Gyy	10882	28050	7630	19258	48380	5005	15104	13049	34216	42825
Gxy	3280	6728	2467	5137	16885	1545	4938	4183	3273	3720
Gss	11118	6961	5828	3306	4576	1016	7347	8985	9784	7944
Gx	61	130	39	25	-150	-40	-34	42	-65	-63
Gy	217	214	131	198	351	66	125	168	-52	-61

11.9 FAILURE SURFACE OF OFF–AXIS PLIES

We know how to transform an off–axis stress and strain to an on–axis orientation. Failure criteria are usually applied in this fashion. But we can just as easily transform the failure stress or strain from an on–axis orientation (a point on the failure surface) to an off–axis orientation equal to the particular ply angle. We then have created a point on the failure surface of an off–axis ply. In fact, the off–axis surface can be generated from the on–axis surface through a rigid–body rotation equal to twice the ply angle, as shown in Equations 5.14 and 5.15. This relation is precisely that in the Mohr's circle space. Thus, once a failure envelope in the symmetry or orthotropic axes of a ply is determined, the off–axis plies can be easily generated. We need off–axis failure surfaces because composite laminates always have off–axis plies.

We will illustrate the failure envelope in strain space using an example similar to that shown in Figure 11.2. We can easily generate the [90] from the [0] by a rigid–body rotation about the p–axis. It is a rotation via the shear space; i.e., the third dimension. By comparing the boxy shapes and the labels on each line of the two envelopes in Figures 11.4 the symmetry is self–evident.

The next easiest off–axis ply is the 45–degree ply. The failure envelope of this ply is bounded by allowable values of p and q, defined in Equation 5.11;

$$p = (\varepsilon_1 + \varepsilon_2)/2$$

$$q = (\varepsilon_1 - \varepsilon_2)/2 \qquad\qquad (11.22)$$

$$r = \varepsilon_6/2$$

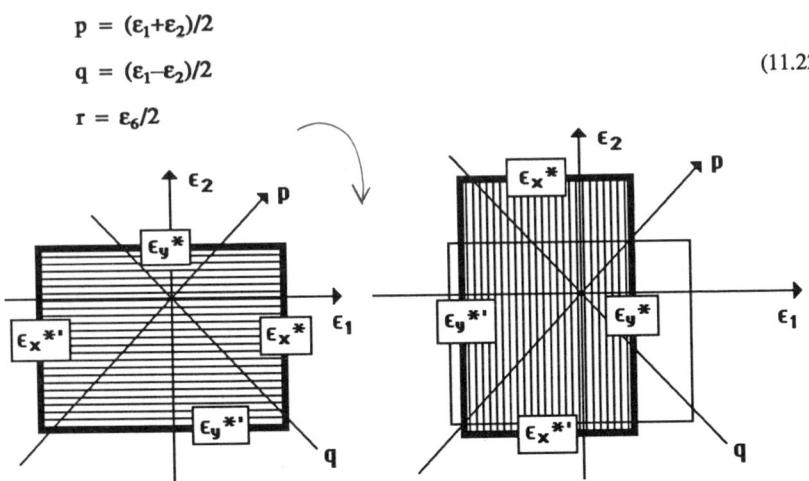

FIGURE 11.4   MAXIMUM STRAIN ENVELOPES FOR [0] AND [90] ON THE PRINCIPAL STRAIN PLANE.

These linear combinations of strain components are shown graphically in a Mohr's circle in Figure 5.2. As representative unidirectional plies shown in Table 11.1, we can see that the transverse tensile strain is lower than the longitudinal tensile strain (compare eps y* versue eps x*, or 3.88 versus 8.29xE–03). The positive p value would most likely be different from the negative p. In Figure 11.5, we show the case of the positive p lower than the negative p. This is the case for T300/5208, shown in Table 11.1. For this material the negative p is controlled by the longitudinal compressive strain, equal to 8.29 xE–03. The allowable q would be symmetric about the p–axis and has a numerical value equal to the allowable r; i.e., one half of the allowable shear strain, equal to (9.48/2)xE–03.

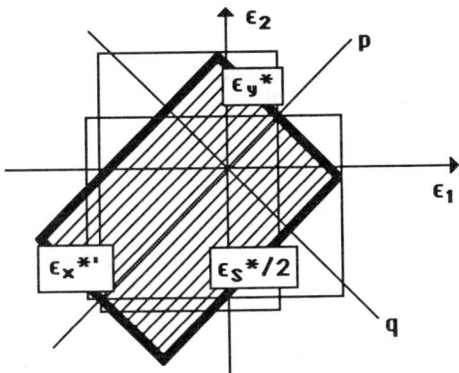

FIGURE 11.5   MAXIMUM STRAIN ENVELOPE FOR [45] ON PRINCIPAL STRAIN PLANE.

11.10 SUCCESSIVE PLY FAILURES

Whatever failure criterion is used, it is applied to each ply within a laminate. The ply with the lowest strength ratio will fail first, thus, the first–ply–failure. This inner envelope is shown in Figure 11.6. It is important to point out that the FPF is the inner envelope of intact plies. Once the applied stress or strain exceeds the FPF envelope plies will be degraded with matrix/interfacial cracks.

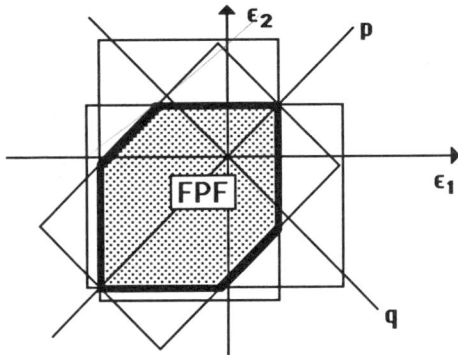

FIGURE 11.6   FIRST–PLY–FAILURE ENVELOPE OF [0/90/+45] USING THE MAXIMUM STRAIN CRITERION.

At the first–ply–failure point the failure mode most probably consists of cracks propagating parallel to the fibers in the case of a unidirectional ply. The cracks can be within the matrix and/or at the fiber–matrix interface. As load increases, more cracks are generated. According to a shear lag analysis these cracks are spaced at certain minimum distance, about seven times the thickness of the ply group; i.e., the distance between adjacent cracks cannot be smaller than seven times the thickness. Within a failed or cracked ply or ply group there is an estimated maximum crack density, from 10 to 15 cracks per centimeter.

Operationally, the quadratic criteria are easier to use because each ply is governed by one strength ratio for each applied load. There will be as many strength ratios as there are plies for in–plane loading. Successive ply failures will proceed from the ply with the lowest strength ratio until the ultimate strength of the laminate is reached, which we call the last–ply–failure. The maximum stress or maximum strain criterion is more difficult to operate because for each ply we must take three out of five strength ratios, the lowest of which is the governing ratio. As the number of plies increase, three times more strength ratios than those for the quadratic must be computed. In addition the quadratic calculation is based on equalities rather than inequalities which are more difficult to compute.

11.11 EXAMPLES OF PLY FAILURE ENVELOPES

We will show typical quadratic failure envelopes in stress and strain spaces. In stress space, the envelope for nearly all composites is highly elongated due to their high longitudinal strengths. It is therefore difficult to plot the failure envelopes of highly anisotropic materials in stress space. Bar charts of the polar radius of the failure envelope would be an easier way of showing the strength variation as function of ply angles. In Figure 11.7, this is done for CFRP T300/5208 in the first and fourth quadrants in the principal stress space. The figure shows how drastic the off–axis uniaxial tensile strength drops in the first quadrant (between 0 and 90 degrees). The drop in strength in the fourth quadrant is not as drastic because the transverse compressive strength of most unidirectional composites is much higher than the transverse tensile. The basic strength data are taken from Table 11.1, where the interaction term is −1/2 (the generalized von Mises criterion) is selected.

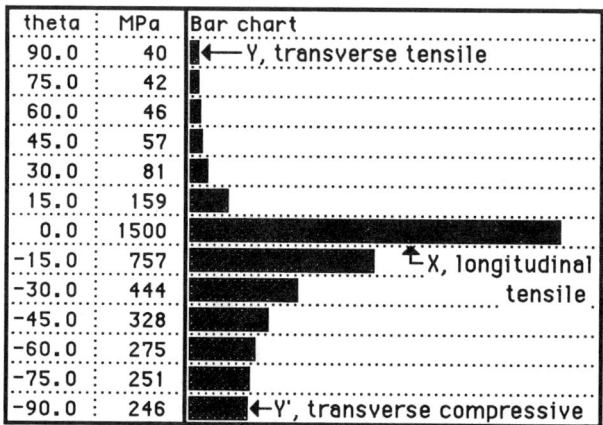

FIGURE 11.7 POLAR RADIUS OF T300/5208 QUADRATIC FAILURE ENVELOPE ALONG
THE LONGITUDINAL TENSILE STRESS.

The failure envelope of the same graphite/epoxy composite is plotted in Figure 11.8 for two shear strain levels, at zero and 0.009; in Figure 11.9 the envelope of E–glass/epoxy is plotted for shear strains at zero and 0.016.

The strain space representation has several advantages:

- It is easier to plot because the envelope is less elongated.
- It is invariant; i.e., remains fixed for all laminates.
- It is dimensionless; the same in SI and English units.
- It is easier to define design limit and ultimate, to be covered in the next section.

The flexibility in the quadratic failure criterion is derived from the interaction term, the values for which lie between −1 and 1. The experimental determination requires a state of combined stresses. Such tests are not easy to perform. The traditional approach is to use a tubular specimen. Unfortunately, the cost of specimen and that of testing can be prohibitively high and impratical for design data generation.

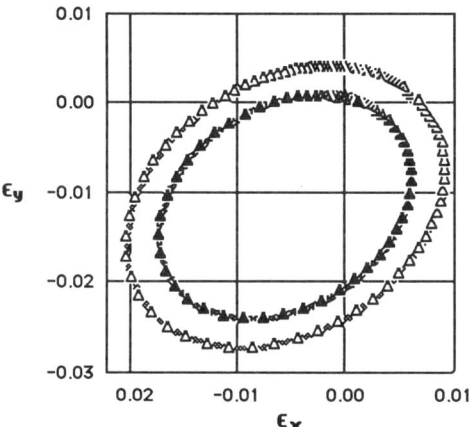

FIGURE 11.8   QUADRATIC FAILURE ENVELOPES OF 0 AND 0.009 SHEAR IN STRAIN SPACE OF T300/5208. THE ZERO SHEAR IS THE LARGER ELLIPSE.

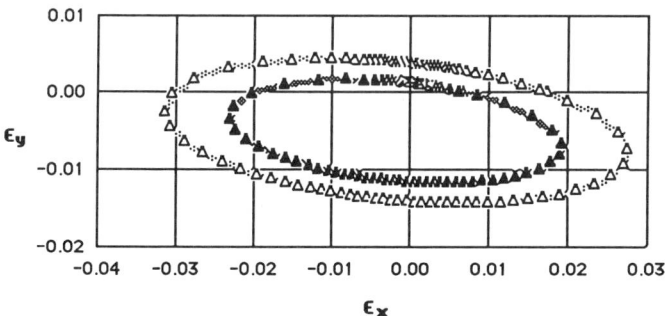

FIGURE 11.9   QUADRATIC FAILURE ENVELOPES OF E–GLASS/EPOXY FOR SHEAR STRAINS OF ZERO AND 0.0016, THE LARGER AND SMALLER ELLIPSES, RESPECTIVELY.

In Subsection 29.22 to 29.24, several alternative approaches that can measure the value for the interaction term are proposed. These tests are relatively easy to perform, and are amenable for testing large samples for design data and for possible quality control tests.

It should be emphasized that failure criteria are empirical schemes to fit available experimental data. Since they are not derived from fundamental principles, it is not a question of having a correct or incorrect criterion. The quadratic criterion is better because it is easier to use, and more flexible.

11.12 EXAMPLES OF MULTIDIRECTIONAL ENVELOPES

We show in Figures 11.10 and 11.11 the failure envelopes of $\pi/4$ laminates of T300/5208 in strain space, with normalized interaction term equal to $-1/2$ and 0, respectively. The data for these envelopes are listed in Table 11.1. The shaded area is the first–ply–failure region. All plies are intact. Laminated plate theory cannot be applied beyond the FPF because cracks begin to form and the internal force distribution is altered. A modified theory dealing with degraded plies will be covered in the next section.

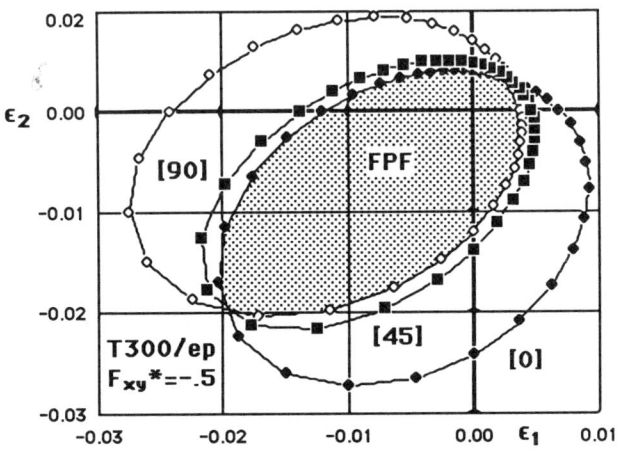

FIGURE 11.10   FIRST–PLY–FAILURE ENVELOPES OF T300/5208 $\pi/4$ LAMINATES, WITH INTERACTION TERM OF $-1/2$.

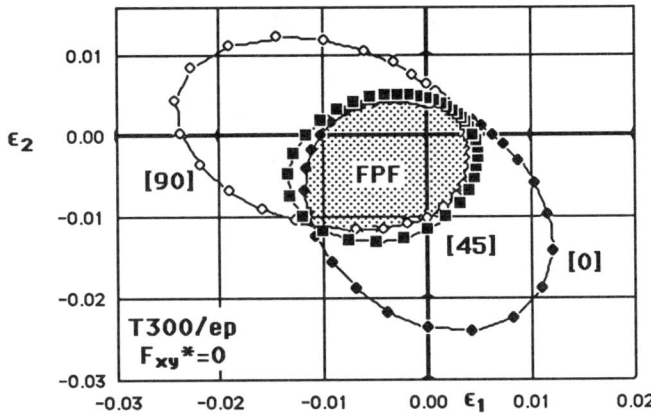

FIGURE 11.11   FIRST–PLY–FAILURE ENVELOPES OF T300/5208 $\pi/4$ LAMINATES, WITH INTERACTION TERM OF 0.

We also show similar envelopes for AS/PEEK in Figures 11.12 and 11.13.

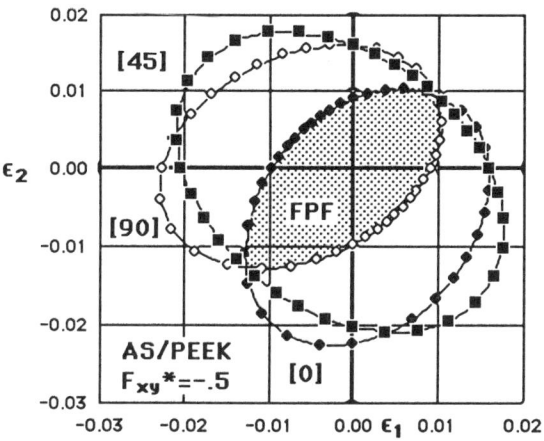

FIGURE 11.12 FIRST–PLY–FAILURE ENVELOPES OF AS/PEEK $\pi/4$ LAMINATES, WITH INTERACTION TERM OF –1/2.

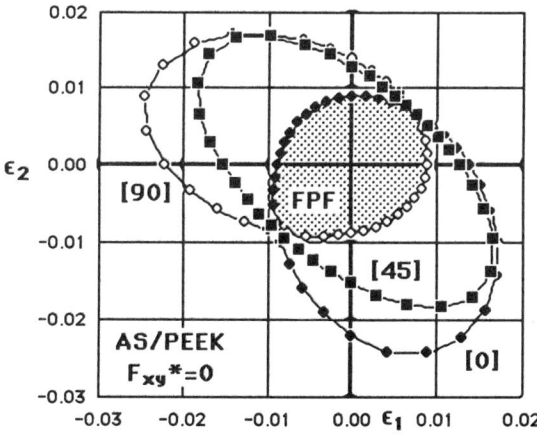

FIGURE 11.13 FIRST–PLY–FAILURE ENVELOPES OF AS/PEEK $\pi/4$ LAMINATES, WITH INTERACTION TERM OF 0.

Similar envelopes for IM6/epoxy are shown in Figures 11.14 and 11.15.

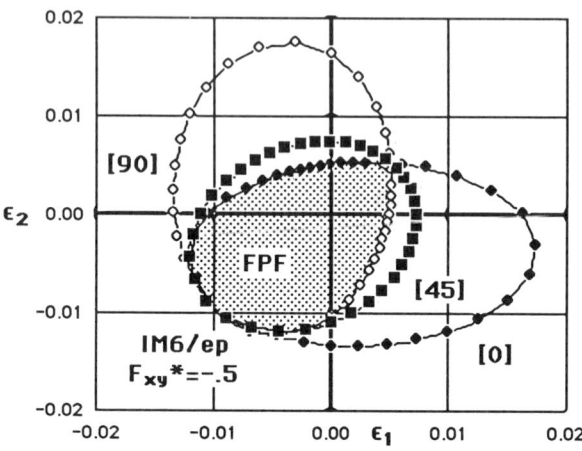

FIGURE 11.14   FIRST–PLY–FAILURE ENVELOPES OF IM6/EPOXY $\pi/4$ LAMINATES, WITH INTERACTION TERM OF –1/2.

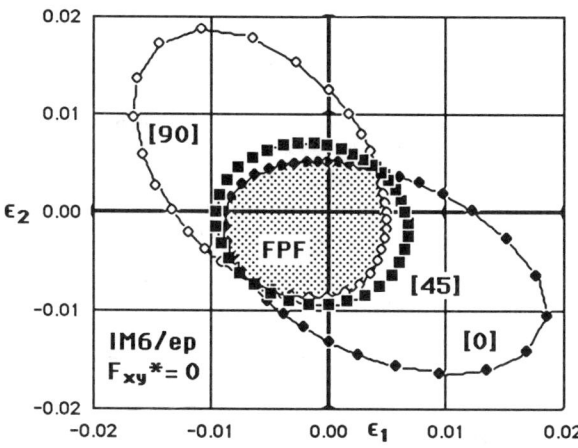

FIGURE 11.15   FIRST–PLY–FAILURE ENVELOPES OF IM6/EPOXY $\pi/4$ LAMINATES, WITH INTERACTION TERM OF 0.

11.13 CONCLUSIONS

We would like to emphasize again the utility and limitations of failure criteria. We need the criteria to guide us in design and materials improvement. We can calculate the safety factor and determine the weakness in our strength characteristics so the direction of improvement in materials can be made.

In Figure 11.16 we show the development of the FPF envelope of a multidirectional laminate from the ply properties. For the quadratic failure criterion a value for the interaction term must be added. From plies of different angles, the FPF envelope of a laminate is easily developed.

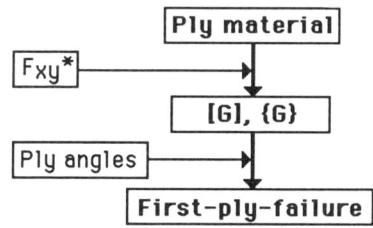

FIGURE 11.16   FLOW DIAGRAM OF FPF ENVELOPE FROM THE QUADRATIC FAILURE CRITERION OF AN ANISOTRTOPIC PLY.

In Subsection 29.9, different values of the interaction term for various composite materials are shown. The effect of the interaction term for a unidirectional E–glass/epoxy is shown in more detail in Subsections 29.26 for [0], and 29.28 for [π/4]; that for T300/5208, in Subsections 29.27 and 29.29, respectively. Proposed tests for the determination of the interaction term are listed in Section 29.17.

In conclusion, failure criteria are empirical and phenomenological. They cannot be readily related to failure modes. The physical phenomena of the failure of composites are much too complicated to be described by any of the simple criteria mentioned in this section. We prefer the quadratic criterion for its easy application, for its continuous extension to a last–ply–failure prediction in Section 12, for its systematic incorporation of residual stresses in Section 15 and hygrothermal stresses in Section 17, for its recovery of the maximum stress and maximum strain criterion in the limit shown in Section 29.9 and 29.10, and above all, for its mathematically simplicity, invariance, and internal consistency.

If maximum stress or maximum strain criterion must be used, we recommend in place of the boxy envelopes, shown in Figures 11.1 and 11.2, the truncated envelopes analogous to the Tresca criterion for isotropic materials. The truncation occurs in the second and fourth quadrants in the zero shear plane.

It will make the failure criterion more conservative than the boxy envelopes, and includes some interaction among failure modes. Examples of the truncated envelopes can be seen in Section 29.8 for T300/5208. The use of the truncated maximum stress and maximum strain criterion will not be as simple as that without the truncation. Instead of a six-sided box (having only five independent strength parameters), we will have two additional slanted sides.

Section 12

DESIGN LIMIT AND ULTIMATE STRENGTHS OF LAMINATES

12.1 INTRODUCTION

The first–ply–failure (FPF) envelopes of the last section are a straightforward application of laminated plate theory and a given failure criterion. If the applied load exceeds the FPF, a laminate may or may not be able to sustain additional load. In this section we will examine the post–FPF load carrying capability of any laminate subjected to a monotonically increasing load. Various approaches to rationalize limit and ultimate strengths for laminated composites will be discussed. A matrix degradation model is proposed to distinguish intact plies from those with cracks. The limit and ultimate strength envelopes can then be derived from this degradation model.

12.2 MODELING OF DEGRADED PLIES

We repeat Figure 11.6 of the last section here in Figure 12.1 to show the FPF envelope of a typical $\pi/4$ laminate in the principal strain plane obtained using the maximum strain failure criterion. In the last section we also showed numerous examples of the FPF envelopes using the quadratic failure criterion. Again we wish to emphasize that failure envelopes based on intact plies are valid only up to the FPF.

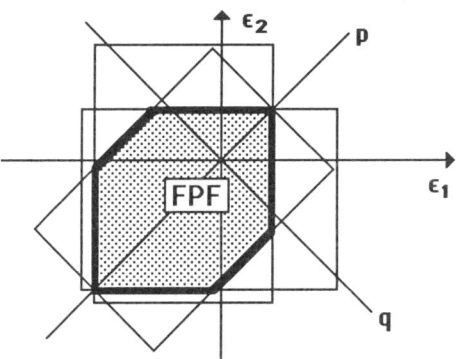

FIGURE 12.1 FIRST–PLY–FAILURE ENVELOPE OF $[0/90/\pm45]_s$ USING THE MAXIMUM STRAIN CRITERION.

In principle, we can load, unload, and reload a laminate and experience no irreversible effects so long as we do not go beyond the FPF region, which describes the maximum capability of the intact plies. When we pass the first–ply–failure envelope, cracks begin to form parallel to the fibers in the unidirectional plies. The cracks run within the matrix, at the fiber–matrix interface, and in some cases across the fibers. As the load increases, more cracks are generated until a saturation level is reached just before the ultimate failure of the laminate.

A ply or ply group with cracks will change the internal stress distribution of the laminate. The cracks result in local stress concentrations which may lead to cracks or fracture in neighboring plies. The effective stiffness of the laminate will also reduce, but not by any noticeable degree because the transverse and shear moduli of a unidirectional ply are small compared with that of the longitudinal modulus. We will show later that the quasi–isotropic Young's modulus of most $\pi/4$ laminates can remain at nearly 90 percent of the initial modulus based on intact plies. As long as the plies are embedded in the laminate they will continue to affect the stiffness of the laminate. A ply with transverse cracks is not the same as having it completely removed from the laminate. This practice is not acceptable. Another approach to model cracked plies is to lower the transverse and shear moduli of the plies to nearly zero. This practice is also not reasonable because cracked plies are not totally disintegrated.

We are not aware of a simple, systematic method for assessing the effect of a failed ply because conventional stress analysis like laminated plate theory by definition is limited to a continuum or plies without cracks. We propose replacing the cracked plies with a continuum of lower stiffness so that the conventional stress analysis can be applied. Our approach is graphically illustrated in Figure 12.2.

Ply is degraded by transverse cracks resulting from matrix and/or interface failure.

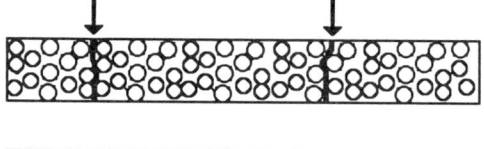

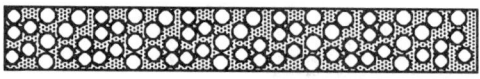

Degraded ply is modeled by a quasi-homogeneous ply with reduced matrix modulus.

FIGURE 12.2   REPLACEMENT OF DEGRADED PLIES BY QUASI-HOMOGENEOUS PLIES WITH LOWER MATRIX STIFFNESS.

The use of lower stiffness values for the plies or for the matrix is not entirely arbitrary. In fact, the observed stiffness of the laminate having partially and totally degraded plies is used to estimate the degree of the ply stiffness reduction. Thus, the replacement of cracked plies by quasi–homogeneous plies is done semi–empirically. The micromechanics analysis in Section 10 can be applied directly to predict the loss in transverse and shear moduli due to the reduction in matrix modulus. The results of the stiffness reductions for CFRP T300/5208 are shown in dimensionless quantities in Figure 12.3. It is observed from the Figure 12.3 that the relative reduction in the transverse and shear moduli is less than that in the matrix modulus. This is reasonable because the fiber stiffness remains constant. For example, if the matrix reduction is to 40 percent, the transverse stiffness would reduce to 55 percent; the shear modulus to 45 percent. This approach is simple and has the added advantage of including the hygrothermal properties within the same integrated micro–macromechanics framework.

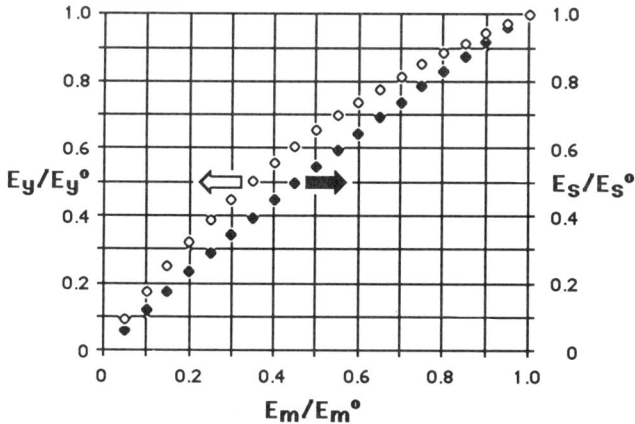

FIGURE 12.3   RELATIVE REDUCTION IN TRANSVERSE AND SHEAR MODULI DUE TO REDUCTION IN MATRIX YOUNG'S MODULUS FOR CFRP T300/5208 BASELINE PLY.

As plies are degraded through a reduced matrix modulus, the longitudinal stiffness is not affected in accordance with Equation 10.3 or 10.4. The major Poisson's ratio is probably uncoupled as cracks are generated. In the absence of a micromechanics model, the Poisson's ratio is assumed to reduce by the same percentage as the matrix modulus is reduced.

It is also assumed that the failure criterion is also affected by the matrix degradation. The interaction term in the quadratic criterion, like Poisson's ratio, will also reduce linearly with the matrix modulus. The longitudinal compressive strength will also reduce as the shear modulus of the degraded ply is reduced. Based on available data, an exponent of 0.2 to the matrix degradation factor is recommended; see Equation 12.19.

12.3 LAST–PLY–FAILURE PREDICTION

As a simple approach to predict ultimate failure of a multi–directional laminate, we propose the following additional steps beyond the replacement of the failed plies as just discussed. If we can load and unload laminates after successive ply failures, we could expect a $[0/90]_s$ laminate to have stress–strain curves shown schematically in Figure 12.4.

While we will defer to the experimental determination of the matrix degradation factor, we can examine the effects of this factor on the laminate stiffness. We will continue to use laminated plate theory assuming that plies are homogeneous but have reduced moduli. The three stress–strain curves in Figure 12.4 are calculated and the failure stress for each ply can also be predicted using appropriate failure criteria. The accumulation of transverse cracks reaches a maximum level as the stress approaches the ultimate strength. We can view this saturation level as the end point of this particular failure mode. By reducing the matrix modulus while keeping the matrix strength constant, we are in effect suppressing further matrix failure in fully cracked plies. In the case of our $[0/90]_s$ laminate, the 90 degree ply is expected to crack first in the intact laminate. This is shown in Figure 12.4. The failure stress of the 0 degree ply for the intact case is higher than that of the 90 degree ply, and is therefore not expected to have cracks before the 90 degree ply.

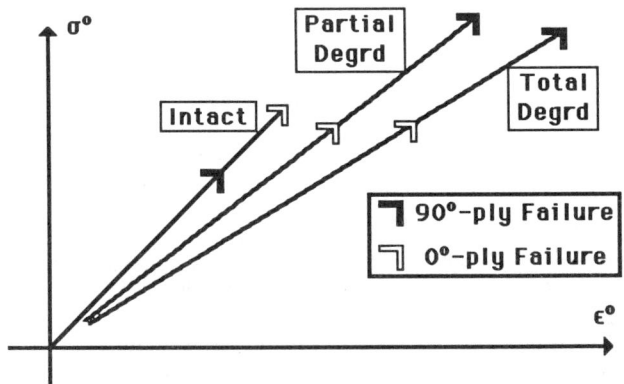

FIGURE 12.4 SCHEMATIC IN–PLANE STRESS–STRAIN CURVES OF A $[0/90]_s$
LAMINATE FOR VARIOUS DEGREES OF DAMAGE. THE PLY FAILURES
FOR EACH DEGREE OF DAMAGE ARE ALSO INDICATED.

If the applied uniaxial load is then decreased to zero and reloaded, we would expect the stress–strain curve to follow the partially degraded curve in Figure 12.4. The laminate stiffness would be reduced. If we use laminated plate theory again and use a reduced matrix stiffness for the 90 degree ply, we will see the shift in the failure levels for the 0 and 90 degree plies. This shift for our $[0/90]_s$ laminate can be rationalized because the stress level to cause further failure in the cracked 90 degree ply would be very high. We have reduced the matrix modulus without reducing matrix strength. In effect, we have suppressed the matrix failure mode. The fiber failure in compression is probably the only mode by which a ply can fail after the saturation of transverse cracks in the 90 degree ply in this laminate. We assume that the ultimate strength of the laminate is reached when all plies are saturated with transverse cracks, and the ply with the lowest failure load will be the ultimate load of the laminate. When the matrix/interface failure mode is suppressed, the only remaining failure mode must be associated with the fibers.

We believe that it is only necessary to calculate the first and last ply failures. Intermediate ply failures can be very involved for laminates with many ply angles. It may be overextending the validity of our simplified approach. We therefore recommend the procedure shown schematically in Figure 12.5 where intermediate or partial ply failures are ignored. If the applied load increases monotonically, the stress–strain curve is expected to go from the origin to the FPF point on the "intact" line, then deviate to the LPF point on the "totally degraded" line. The jump from the intact to the degraded stress–strain curves is not as drastic as the gap shown in Figure 12.5. For practical laminates, the loss of laminate stiffness due to matrix degradation is less than 10 percent. The jump is small, and the FPF and LPF points appear to be on the same stress–strain curve. A more detailed discussion of this transition from the intact to the degraded stress–strain curves is covered in Section 29.10.

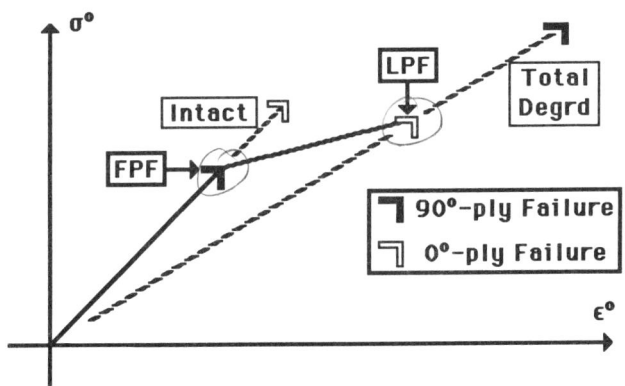

FIGURE 12.5   SIMPLIFIED PREDICTION OF THE LAST–PLY–FAILURE IS BASED ON
THE LAMINATE WITH TOTALLY DEGRADED PLIES.

12.4 FAILURE MODES

The use of our matrix degradation model is a semi–empirical method of extending laminated plate theory to the final failure of the laminate. The degraded plies exist only in laminated forms. The identification of the failure modes is unfortunately more complicated than simple labels of fiber and matrix/interface failures. Failure modes interact and occur simultaneously as well as sequentially. Additional modes such as delamination can arise from nonuniform curing, and local impact transverse to the laminate, and also can occur at free edges and at points of ply drop off.

Our degradation model is useful in predicting the ultimate failure with the aid of empirically determined matrix degradation factor, and that of micromechanics, shown in Figure 12.3.

The frequently used netting analysis for burst pressure and the fiber stress calculation of a pressure vessel subjected to internal pressure is not a theory. It is derived from the consideration of the equilibrium of a balanced angle ply construction. It does not satisfy strain compatibility. It does not depend on the stress–strain relation of the material. The notion that the fibers carry all the load in the uniaxial tension of a unidirectional composite is valid, but the extension of this simple model to off–axis plies without laminated plate theory is incorrect. We recommend a consistent theory that can analyze a pressure vessel as well as any laminated construction. We do not recommend two theories to analyze the same structure. The use of netting analysis for burst pressure determination, and that of laminated plate theory for deformation is internally inconsistent, and does not enhance the rational and confident use of composite materials.

The LPF prediction is usually greater than that of FPF in the tension–tension and tension–shear domains. In compression–compression and tension–compression domains, LPF may be less than FPF. Then FPF would be the ultimate strength. If loading is followed by unloading and reloading the failure modes become complicated. The same is true for fatigue loading and nonproportional loading (reloading follows a path different from the loading and unloading).

Plies in a laminate that fail simultaneously will have LPF equal to FPF. This occurs when a balanced angle ply laminate is subjected to any combination of normal stresses, with no shear. This also occurs when a laminate is subjected to hydrostatic tension or compression. Then the strain values of LPF and FPF are equal for all ply orientations. The focal points in the first and third quadrants along the p–axis in Figure 12.1 are the hydrostatic points. Simultaneous ply failures however does not mean optimum laminate configuration. When multiple loads are considered as a design basis of a composite laminate, simultaneous failure cannot and should not be considered as a criterion for optimization.

We have shown the FPF and LPF of a T300/5208 $[0/90]_s$ laminate subject to a uniaxial tensile load in Figure 12.5. The 90 degree ply fails before the 0 degree ply. But if we apply uniaxial compression, by symmetry of this material, the 0 degree ply must fail before the 90 degree ply. The mode of failure in the 0 degree ply can be the matrix cracking, fiber compressive failure, fiber micro–buckling, kink band formation, or a combination of these modes. The load carrying capability of the 0 degree ply after the initial failure is going to be less. Thus the LPF prediction will be lower than that of the FPF. As stated earlier, the FPF will then be the ultimate strength for a monotonically loaded laminate. This is shown in Subsection 29.11. Also in this subsection, we show the failure envelopes of E–glass/epoxy composite. The shape of the envelope is such that 90 degree ply failure occurs first in both uniaxial tension and compression of a $[0/90]_s$ laminate.

Failure modes in laminates depend not only on the ply layup but also on the particular ply material. If matrix cracking in the 0 degree ply in the $[0/90]_s$ laminate is induced through uniaxial tensile load beyond the FPF, subsequent reloading of a uniaxial compressive load will induce failure in the degraded 0 degree ply, which is lower than the FPF based on the intact model. The mode of failure also depends on the history of loading.

The damage due to tension–tension and tension–compression fatigue, as will be discussed in Section 19, is more severe than that for static loading. The number of transverse cracks and the loss of laminate stiffness for fatigue are higher than those in static tests, because fatigue loading is more damaging than static loading and delamination also occurs along the free edges of the test specimen. The compression–compression fatigue of the same $\pi/4$ laminates show no cracks, and negligible loss in laminate stiffness. We therefore recommend the use of our matrix degradation model as a means of describing the failure modes and predicting the ultimate load of laminated composites. In addition, we can use the same approach of defining the limit and safety factor for the design of laminates.

12.5 LAST–PLY–FAILURE ENVELOPES

The last–ply–failure envelopes are plotted using the following approaches which are analogous to the FPF envelopes:

 • Strain space representation, because it is independent of ply layup, and easy to plot as
   compared with that in stress space.
 • Same representation as used for FPF envelopes, so direct comparison can be made.
 • Simple extension to define limit and ultimate strength envelopes.
 • Simple sensitivity studies of laminate layup, micromechanical variables, normalized
   interaction term F_{xy}^*, and residual stresses from lamination.
 • The quadratic failure criterion, because it is easy to calculate and easy to plot. In
   Section 29.10, the LPF based on both the quadratic and maximum strain are shown.

Unless otherwise noted in the figure caption, the failure envelopes are evaluated based on the following assumptions, explained later in this Section:

 • The material considered is CFRP T300/5208
 • The stress interaction term equals –0.5
 • The matrix degradation equals 0.3 (This value has been found to differ for various ply
   materials; see Subsection 29.12 for more current values. The envelopes in this section,
   however, are based on 0.3.)

In Section 11, we showed the failure envelopes of the intact 0, 90, +45 and –45 degree plies that comprise a $\pi/4$ laminate, an example of which is shown again in Figure 12.6. Note that the +45 and –45 failure envelopes are coincident in this principal strain plane. Recall that the inner envelope represents the first–ply–failure envelope, and the envelopes beyond the FPF are not physically meaningful.

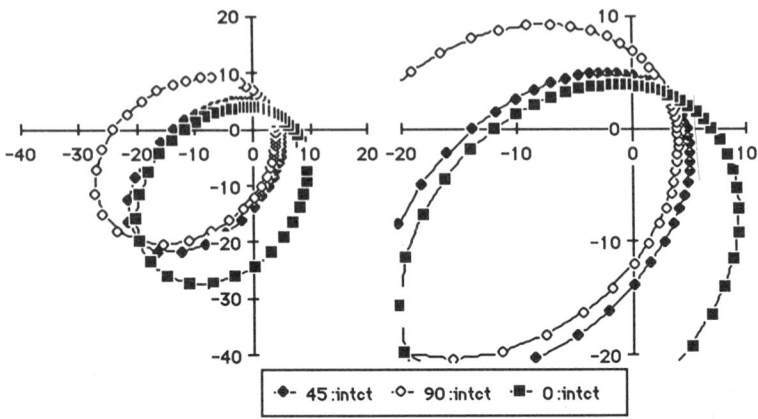

FIGURE 12.6   (a) INTACT FAILURE ENVELOPES FOR 0, 90, AND ±45 DEGREE PLIES
OF A π/4 CFRP T300/5208 LAMINATE AND (b) CLOSEUP OF THE FPF
ENVELOPE DEFINED BY THE INNERMOST REGION.

In Figure 12.7, we show the failure envelopes for degraded 0, 90, and ±45 degree plies which define the LPF envelope for π/4 laminate of CFRP T300/5208. The LPF envelope is a function of the degradation factor. In this figure, it is 0.3. If the factor is unity, we have no degradation, and LPF and FPF will be identical. Since we define LPF as the inner envelope of a laminate having degraded plies, the failure envelopes beyond the LPF are not meaningful except for the easy identification of the ply that controls a particular section of the LPF.

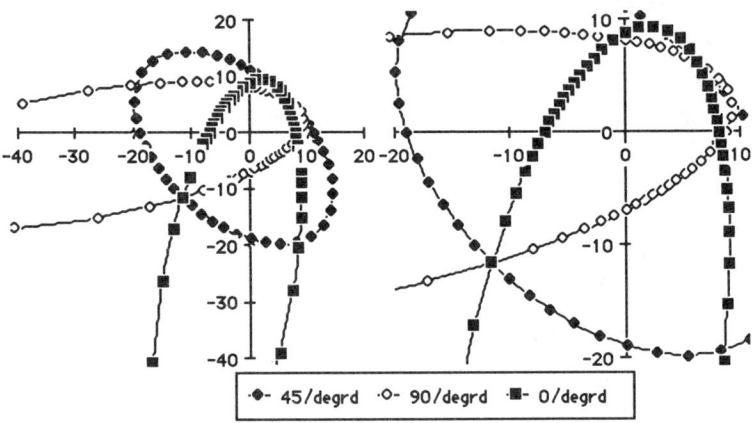

FIGURE 12.7   (a) DEGRADED FAILURE ENVELOPES FOR 0, 90, AND ±45 DEGREE
PLIES OF A π/4 CFRP T300/5208 LAMINATE AND (b) CLOSEUP OF THE
LPF ENVELOPE DEFINED BY THE INNERMOST REGION.

The much reduced compressive strength of the degraded plies, shown in the third quadrant in Figure 12.7, is the result of the loss of shear modulus as the matrix degrades. The micro–buckling of fibers will be more likely to occur as the shear modulus decreases. If there is no reversal in loading, the LPF that is lower than FPF can be overlooked in design. But if load reversal occurs, the lowered compressive strength must be considered.

12.6 ULTIMATE STRENGTH ENVELOPES

As mentioned in the last section, the LPF envelope does not necessarily represent the ultimate load carrying capability of the laminate because a portion of this envelope may be equal to or less than the FPF envelope. In the region of compression–compression, the LPF is often less than the FPF. It is assumed here that only monotonic loading is considered. We do not consider changes or reversals in loading path which may result in complicated and mixed failure modes, such as tensile followed by compressive loads.

We define the ultimate strength as the larger of the FPF and LPF. In Figure 12.8a, we repeat the FPF and LPF strength envelopes from the last two figures. In Figure 12.8b, we show the ultimate strength envelope. This envelope is simply the outer of the two envelopes in Figure 12.8a. The ultimate strength envelope for this material is controlled by the LPF in the positive p domain in the principal strain plane; by the FPF, in the negative p domain. Invariant p, defined in Equation 5.11 and Figure 5.2, is measured along an axis that bisects the first and third quadrants; see Figure 12.1.

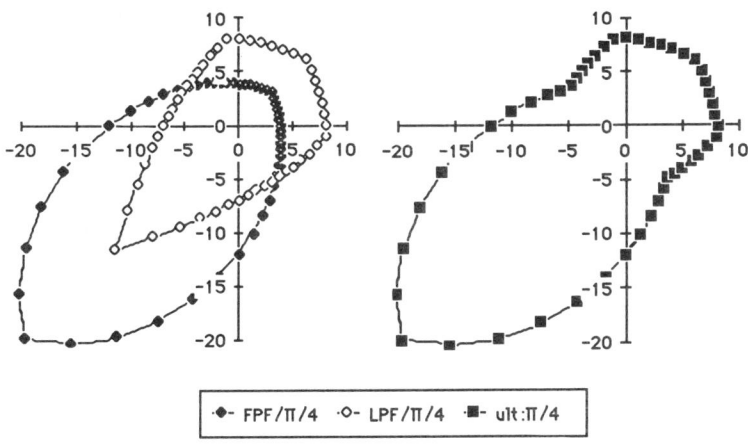

$$\boxed{\text{-•- FPF/}\pi/4 \quad \text{-○- LPF/}\pi/4 \quad \text{-■- ult:}\pi/4}$$

FIGURE 12.8   (a) FPF AND LPF ENVELOPES OF π/4 CFRP T300/5208 LAMINATE AND
(b) THE ULTIMATE STRENGTH ENVELOPE DEFINED BY THE
OUTERMOST BOUNDARY OF THE FPF AND LPF ENVELOPES.

12.7 LIMIT STRENGTH ENVELOPES

Definition of a limit strength using the FPF and ultimate strength envelopes can be based on more than one rule. We are not aware of a universally

load carryg cap = ultimate strength

accepted definition of limit load. We define limit strength as that induced by the maximum load which a structure is expected to encounter during its lifetime. We further define safety factor as the ratio of the load carrying capability of a structure to the limit load. For a design rule commonly encountered in the aerospace industry, the factor is often 1.5. The limit envelopes can be determined by one or both of the following rules:

Rule 1: FPF based design: No matrix degradation at limit.
Rule 2: FPF/LPF based design: limit derived from ultimate, the higher of FPF and LPF.

In Figure 12.9 we show the relationship among the limit, limit* and ultimate strengths of laminates and the traditional FPF criterion. The critical element for the LPF determination is the matrix degradation factor which is a semi–empirical constant. By the same token, the critical element for the FPF is the failure criterion selected. If the quadratic criterion is selected, the critical element would be the interaction term.

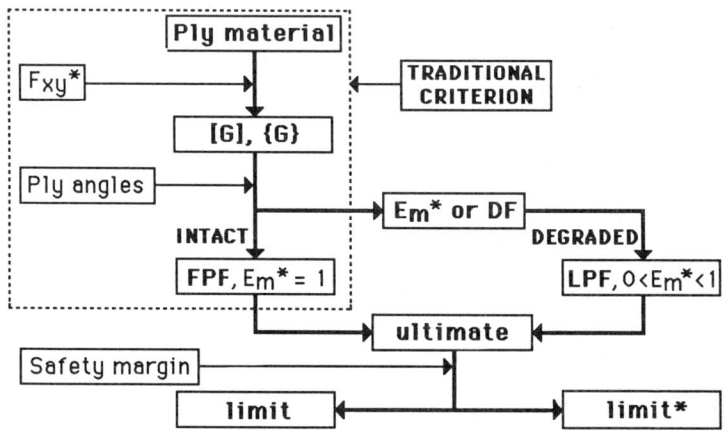

FIGURE 12.9 FLOW DIAGRAM FROM THE TRADITIONAL FAILURE CRITERION TO THE LIMIT AND ULTIMATE STRENGTH OF A MULTIDIRECTIONAL LAMINATE.

The FPF and LPF are laminate strength envelopes, based on intact and degraded matrix, respectively. The two envelopes become coincident when the degradation factor is unity. The matrix degradation factor is labeled E_m^* or E_m/E_m°; the ply degradation factor DF can also be applied directly to the sitffness and strength of the ply with cracks without using micromechanics. This will be covered later in this section.

The ultimate envelope is defined:

$$\text{ultimate} = \text{MAX(FPF, LPF)} \qquad (12.1)$$

Two interpretations on limit strength of a laminate are here defined.

The ultimate based limit envelope, designated limit*, is simply

limit* = ultimate/safety   *(SF)(limit*) = ult*   (12.2)

Finally, the design limit envelope, designated limit, is

limit = MIN(FPF, limit*)   (12.3)

From Equations 12.2 and 12.3, we can state two expressions for safety factor:

safety factor = ultimate/limit*   (12.4)

safety factor ≥ ultimate/limit   (12.5)

Figure 12.10a shows the limit and ultimate strength envelopes of CFRP T300/5208. Figure 12.10b shows, in addition to limit and ultimate, the limit* strength envelope using a factor of safety of 1.5.

For T300/5208 and many comparable composite materials, the difference between limit and limit* envelopes occurs mainly in the first quadrant in the principal strain plane. If limit* is used for design, matrix cracking would occur when loading goes beyond the FPF. In quadrants other than the first, limit and limit* envelopes essnetially coincide. Loading beyond the limit envelope in the third quadrant, for exmaple, will not result in matrix cracking because a safety factor is imposed. Thus the difference between limit and limit* depends on the value of safety factor. The gap between limit and limit* will reduce and eventually disappear when the safety factor is increased.

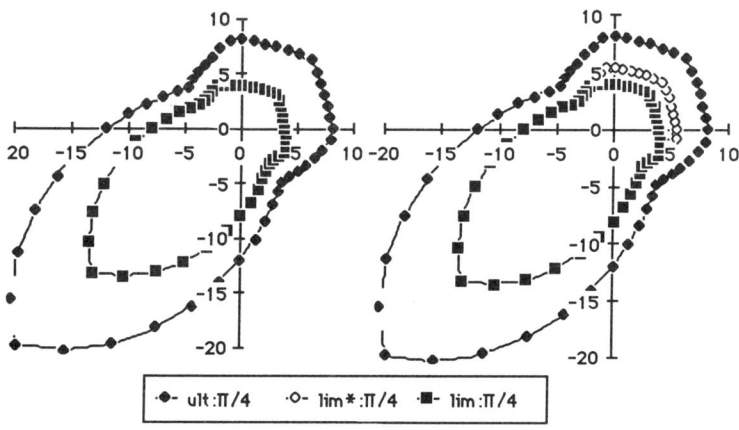

FIGURE 12.10   LIMIT, LIMIT*, AND ULTIMATE STRENGTH ENVELOPES OF π/4 CFRP T300/5208 LAMINATE IN PRINCIPAL STRAIN PLANE.

Other parameters which also affect the shape and size of limit and ultimate strength envelopes are listed as follows:

- Choice of composite material, and laminate layup
- Limit definition options; i.e., limit and limit*
- Choice of the failure criteria, and the interaction term if the quadratic criteria is used
- Matrix degradation factor
- Safety factor
- Choice of the plane of strains to show the failure envelopes (we will limit to the principal strains and the q–r planes)
- Effect of curing stresses due to lamination (to be covered in Section 15)

12.8 STRENGTH ENVELOPES FOR [0/45/–45] LAMINATE

Figure 12.11a shows the FPF and LPF envelopes for a [0/±45] laminate. When the 90 degree ply is deleted from a π/4 laminate, a [0/±45] laminate remains. Accordingly, looking at Figures 12.6 and 12.7 and ignoring the 90 degree failure envelope, the envelopes of the FPF and LPF for the [0/±45] laminate can be visualized. The ease of generating strength envelopes of different laminates is a credit to the strain space representation of the envelopes. If stress space is used, we cannot go from one laminate to another without recalculation. In Subsection 29.10, failure envelopes for several cross–ply laminates are there to illustrate this point. The ultimate envelope for this laminate is the outermost envelope of Figure 12.11a.

Figure 12.11b shows the limit, limit* and ultimate strength envelopes. Again we see a gap between the limit and limit* envelope in the first and fourth quadrants in the principal strain plane. This gap represent a higher actual safety factor than 1.5 if design limit is used in design.

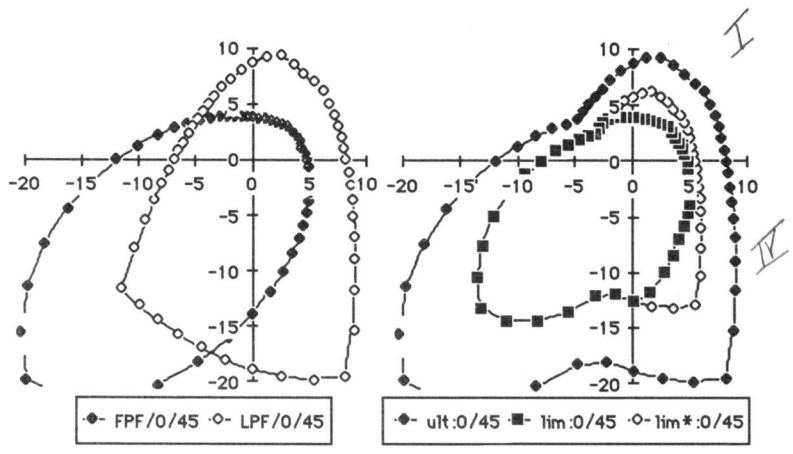

FIGURE 12.11   (a) FPF AND LPF, AND (b) LIMIT, LIMIT* AND ULTIMATE STRENGTH ENVELOPES OF [0/±45]$_s$ CFRP T300/5208 LAMINATE.

12.9 PARAMETER SENSITIVITY STUDY

In this section we will examine the sensitivity of several parameters on the strength envelopes of CFRP T300/5208. The first is the normalized interaction term in the quadratic failure criterion. We superposed the limit and ultimate envelopes to show the differences resulting from the values of the normalized interaction term of –0.5 and 0..

In Figure 12.12a the limit envelope from Figure 12.10 is shown in solid diamonds. The normalized interaction term equals to –0.5. The open diamonds represent the term equal to zero. A major difference between the two values of this term exists only in the third quadrant in the principal strain plane.

In the ultimate strength envelope, shown in Figure 12.12b, the same comment applies. Unless laminates are subjected to compression–compression load, the choice of value for the interaction term does not appear to be critical. Again for more exact determination of this interaction term, several relatively simple tests are suggested in Subsection 29.22 to 29.24.

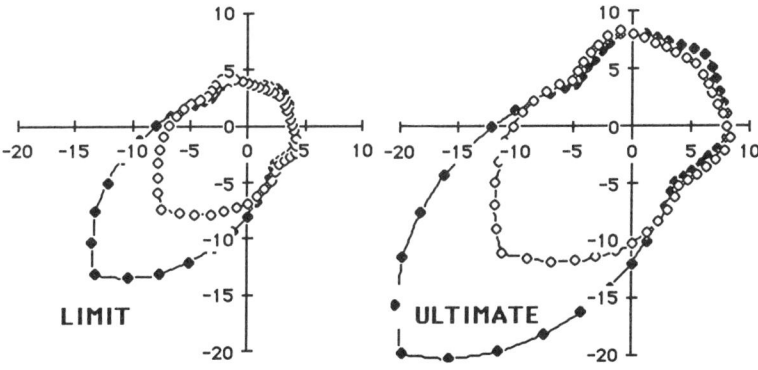

FIGURE 12.12   (a) LIMIT AND (b) ULTIMATE STRENGTH ENVELOPES OF π/4 CFRP
T300/5208 LAMINATE WITH STRESS INTERACTION FACTOR EQUAL
TO –0.5 (SOLID DIAMOND) AND 0 (OPEN DIAMOND).

In Figure 12.13, we show the sensitivity of the matrix degradation factor on LPF in the principal strain plane. When the degradation factor is unity, there is no degradation. We recover the FPF envelope. There is a slight difference between the π/4 laminate in Figure 12.13a, and [0/45/–45] laminate in Figure 12.13b because the segment of the controlling ply switches from the 90 in the former to the 45 degree ply in the latter.

In the other extreme when the degradation factor approaches zero, we recover a maximum strain envelope or that based on netting analysis (noninteracting failure criteria). In order to avoid singularity, we use a degradation factor of 0.01. The controlling plies for the π/4 laminate are the 0 and 90 degree plies. The square shaped strength envelope in Figure 12.13a is bounded by the 0 degree ply along the vertical lines; the 90 degree ply, the horizontal lines. Again the lower compressive strains are caused by the reduced shear modulus of the degraded plies. A comparable illustration of the degraded laminate based on the maximum strain criterion can be found in Section 29.10. A variation of the LPF as a function of degradation factor for T300/5208 is shown in small increments in Section 29.11.

In the [0/45/–45] laminate, shown in Figure 12.13b, the strength envelope looks like a parallelogram. The vertical sides represent the 0 degree ply, as before. Since the 90 degree ply is no longer present, the slanted lines are the 45 degree plies. The slanting of the plus and minus 45 degree plies in the failure envelope can be seen in Figure 12.7a.

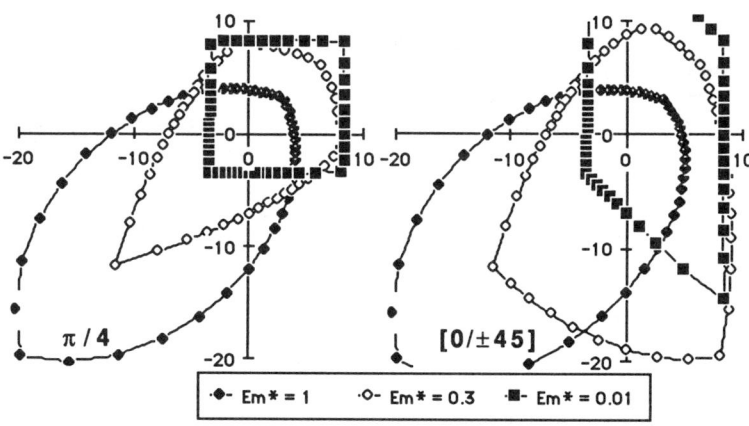

FIGURE 12.13   LPF ENVELOPES FOR $\pi/4$ AND [0/±45]$_s$ CFRP T300/5208 LAMINATE
WITH DEGRADATION FACTOR EQUAL TO 1, 0.3, AND 0.01.

The continuous variation of LPF as a function of the degradation factor is an important feature of our matrix degradation model. This is different from a practice of two separate and distinct models commonly accepted in the design of filament–wound vessels, where FPF is based on intact plies but LPF is derived empirically from measured burst pressure or netting analysis. The latter corresponds to the case of having a degradation factor near zero. In Section 29.10 we show that the range of values for this factor for various composite materials can be between nearly zero and 0.3. With the exception of glass/ and Kevlar/epoxy composites, most composite materials have interaction terms between 0.1 and 0.3.

In Table 12.1, we show the fractional reduction of the quasi–isotropic Young's modulus E_1^o of various $\pi/4$ laminates as the degradation factor approaches zero. They represent the worst–case values for these laminates. The conclusion is that for most multidirectional laminates, the loss of laminate stiffness due to matrix degradation is relatively small; i.e., less than 15 percent. For this reason, the slopes in the stress–strain curves in Figure

12.5 between the intact and totally degraded laminates would be much smaller than those listed in Table 12.1.

TABLE 12.1 REDUCTION OF LAMINATE UNIAXIAL STIFFNESS OF $\pi/4$ LAMINATES AS MATRIX DEGRADATION FACTOR APPROACHES ZERO.

Ply Material	CFRP T300/5208	BFRP B/5505	CFRP AS/3501	GFRP Scotchply	KFRP Kev 49	CFRP T300/934
Modulus Reduction	0.87	0.87	0.84	0.68	0.87	0.88

The modulus reduction however can be greater than those listed in the table if failure modes other than matrix degradation occurs. In some test coupons, edge delamination can cause further modulus and strength reduction. In Section 19 on fatigue, physical evidence of delamination in addition to matrix cracking, and the observed loss of stiffness can be seen.

In Figure 12.14 we compare the limit and ultimate strength envelopes using two matrix degradation factors. The solid diamonds are those with a factor of 0.3; the open diamonds, 0.01. There is practically no difference in the limit envelope in Figure 12.14a. The difference in the ultimate envelope in Figure 12.14b is significant only in the first quadrant in the principal strain plane. This is not unexpected since LPF is controlled by matrix degradation factor; and FPF, by the interaction term.

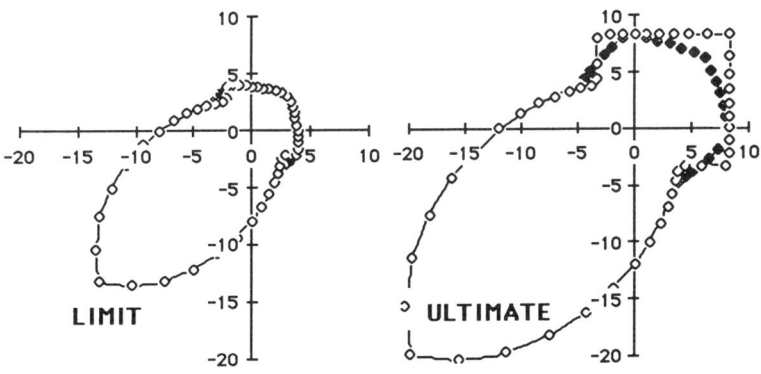

FIGURE 12.14   LIMIT AND ULTIMATE STRENGTH ENVELOPES OF $\pi/4$ CFRP T300/5208 LAMINATE WITH DEGRADATION FACTOR EQUAL TO 0.3 AND 0.01.

The last parameter that affects the limit and limit* strength envelopes is the safety factor. In Figure 12.15a we show the limit envelopes with safety margins of 1.5 and 2. In the first quadrant, the two envelopes are coincident. This is due to having an actual ratio between the ultimate and limit strengths greater than the desired safety factor. This appears as a gap between the limit and limit* envelopes in Figure 12.9b. In the limit* strength envelopes shown in Figure 12.15b, the envelopes are based on the ultimate strength divided by the safety factor. Therefore as the factor increases from 1.5 to 2, for example, the envelope reduced in size proportionally.

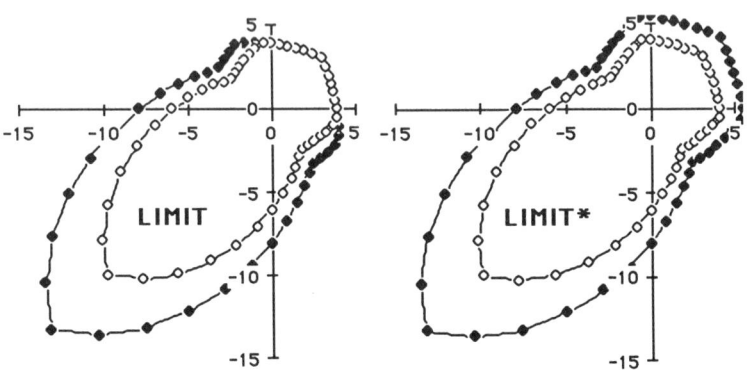

FIGURE 12.15   LIMIT AND LIMIT* ENVELOPES OF $\pi/4$ CFRP T300/5208 LAMINATE
WITH SAFETY FACTOR EQUAL TO 1.5 (SOLID DIAMOND) AND 2 (OPEN
DIAMOND).

12.10 FAILURE ENVELOPES IN THE p=0 PLANE

Up to now all failure and strength envelopes are displayed in the principal strain space. It is important to have a different view of the three dimensional envelopes. The p–axis is significant because p is the first strain invariant. Mohr's circle rotates about this axis, with an angular displacement equal to twice the angle of coordinate rotation; see for example Figure 5.2, where the phase angle in Figure 5.3 is doubled. The ply angle appears as a rigid body rotation in the p=constant plane. For this reason the representation of failure and strength envelopes is simple and easy to visualize. We show in Figure 12.16 the geometric relations between the principal strain plane and the p=0 plane.

The bisectors in the principal strain plane are the p– and q–axis; the shear strain is measured along the r–axis, out of the principal or p–q plane. The relevance of the p–axis to the failure envelope is that the failure envelope of each ply angle rotates about this axis with no change in shape; i.e., a rigid body rotation. This is very convenient because if we know the envelope for a 0 degree ply, a 90 degree ply will be a 180 degree rotation within the plane while the shape remains fixed. The rotation between the 0 and 90 degree plies in the material symmetry plane, defined by the x–y axes, as illustrated in Figure 11.2, is an improper rotation; i.e., out of the symmetry plane. This rotation is different from the rigid–body rotation in the q–r plane.

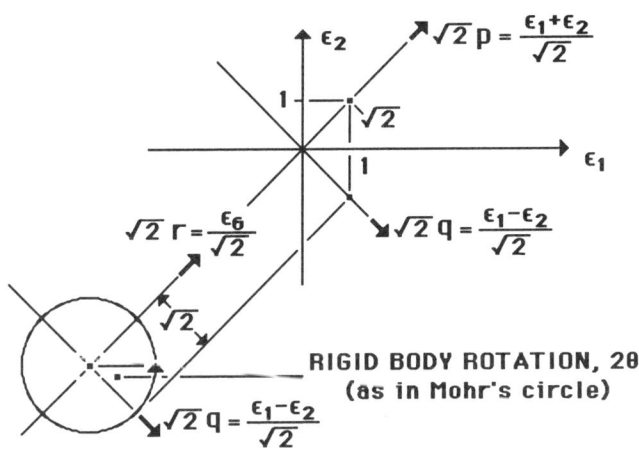

FIGURE 12.16   THE RELATIONSHIP BETWEEN p,q,r–AXES AND STRAIN COMPONENT STRAIN SPACE

In Figure 12.17a and b, we show the FPF and LPF strength envelopes for a $\pi/4$ laminate, respectively. The rigid body rotation of the plies is indicated by a circle drawn around the four ply orientations. The ply that controls the failure in the strength envelope can be seen more clearly in the LPF envelope on the right. Each ply controls a segment.

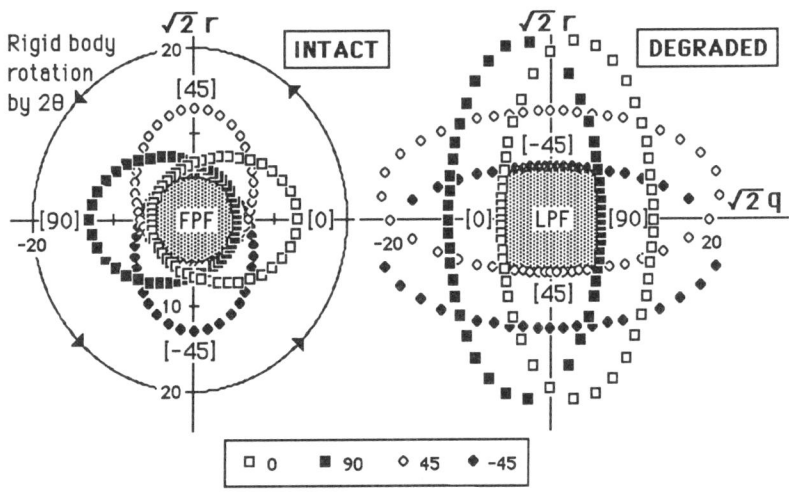

FIGURE 12.17   FPF AND LPF ENVELOPES OF $\pi/4$ CFRP T300/5208 LAMINATE IN p=0 PLANE. THE CIRCLE SHOWS THE DIRECTION OF RIGID BODY ROTATION OF ENVELOPES AS PLY ANGLE INCREASES IN THE POSITIVE DIRECTION.

The 0 degree ply becomes limiting at negative q, which is the horizontal axis in the p=0 plane. Negative q is located in the second quadrant in the principal strain plane; see Figure 12.16. The strain of negative q is the result of a combined longitudinal compressive and transverse tensile strains acting on the 0 degree ply. Conversely, the 90 degree ply becomes limiting at positive q, which is subjected to the same transverse tensile and longitudinal compressive strains on the 90 degree ply. The failure strains for both plies must be equal, as shown in Figure 12.17.

It also should be pointed out that due to the coordinate transformation of 45 degrees, the strain values shown in the p=0 plane must be corrected by a factor of $\sqrt{2}$. For example, the limiting strain for the 0 degree in Figure 12.17a is –5.34. With the correction factor, the strains in the principal plane would be $-5.34/\sqrt{2} = -3.78 = \varepsilon_1 = -\varepsilon_2$.

Similarly we can see that the 45 degree ply imposes the strain limits of the FPF and LPF envelopes at the negative r; that of –45 degree ply, at positive r. The numerical value of r is one half of the shear strain, which for the latter case is equal to 6.70 in Figure 12.17a. The shear strain is twice this value; i.e., 13.4. But this value must be reduced by the same $\sqrt{2}$ applied to the normal strains. Thus the actual shear strain at failure is $13.4/\sqrt{2} = 9.48$, which equals to the failure strain in shear listed in Table 11.1 for this CFRP (Row 26, Column 2). The positive 45 degree ply, by symmetry, can be interpreted similarly.

In Figure 12.18a, the FPF and LPF strength envelopes for a $\pi/4$ laminate are shown. Since the FPF is completely enclosed by the LPF, the ultimate is simply the LPF, which is shown in Figure 12.18b.

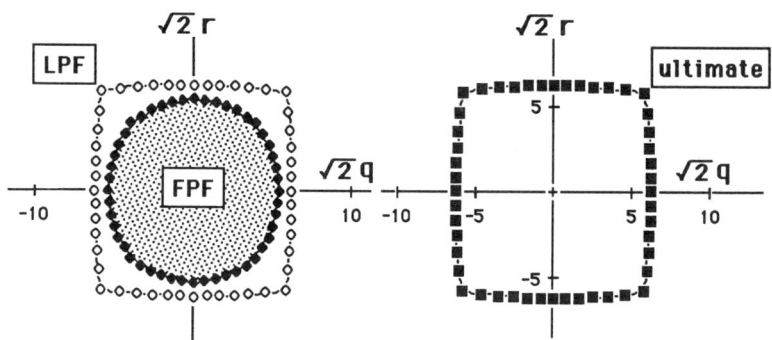

FIGURE 12.18   FPF, LPF AND ULTIMATE STRENGTH ENVELOPES OF $\pi/4$ CFRP
T300/5208 LAMINATE IN p=0 PLANE.

In Figure 12.19a, the FPF and LPF strength envelopes [0/±45]$_s$ are shown. Since the FPF is completely enclosed by the LPF, the ultimate is simply the LPF, which is shown in Figure 12.18b. Using a safety margin of 1.5, there is a gap between the limit and limit* envelopes. As safety margin increases, the gap will be reduced. Then the limit and limit* envelopes will coincide.

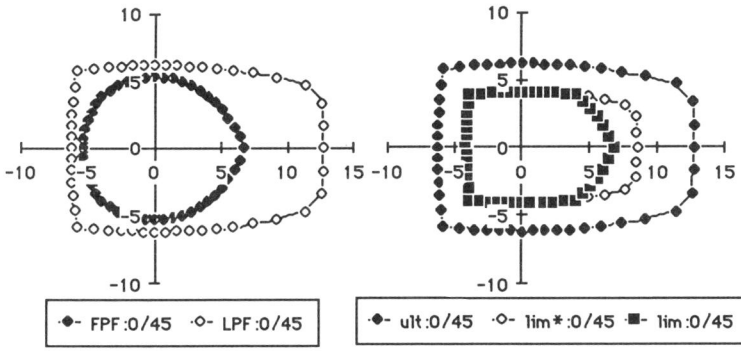

FIGURE 12.19   FPF AND LPF, AND LIMIT, LIMIT* AND ULTIMATE STRENGTH
ENVELOPES OF [0/±45]$_s$ CFRP T300/5208 LAMINATE IN p=0 PLANE.

The relative sizes of limit and limit* envelopes are shown in Figure 12.20 for the same material but with a $\pi/4$ laminate for the illustration.

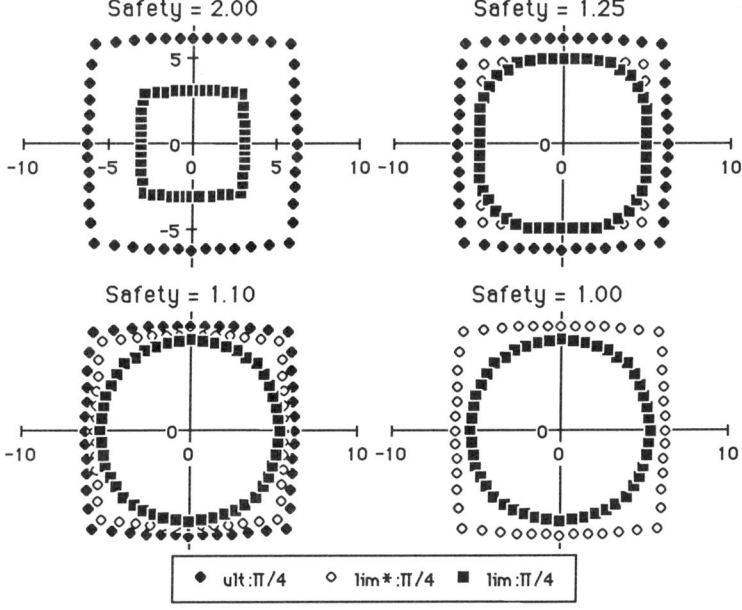

FIGURE 12.20   LIMIT, LIMIT* AND ULTIMATE STRENGTH ENVELOPES OF $\pi/4$ CFRP
T300/5208 LAMINATE IN p=0 PLANE FOR VARIOUS SAFETY FACTORS.

The safety factors of 2, 1.25, 1.1 and 1 are shown. The figure in the upper left corner has the highest safety factor of 2. The limit and limit* envelopes coincide. In the upper right corner, the safety factor is reduced to 1.25. A small gap can be seen between the limit and limit* envelopes. As safety factor continues to reduce to 1.1, all three envelopes are distinct in the lower left corner figure. Finally when safety factor is unity in the lower right corner the FPF and LPF envelopes are recovered.

12.11 STRENGTH ENVELOPES OF E–GLASS/EPOXY COMPOSITES

We wish to present the key strength envelopes for an E–glass/epoxy composite material, in the principal strain plane. In Figure 12.21, the FPF and LPF envelopes are shown for a π/4 laminate and a degradation factor of 0.3. Similar to CFRP T300/5208 in previous examples, the controlling plies are the 0 and 90 degrees for both the FPF and LPF.

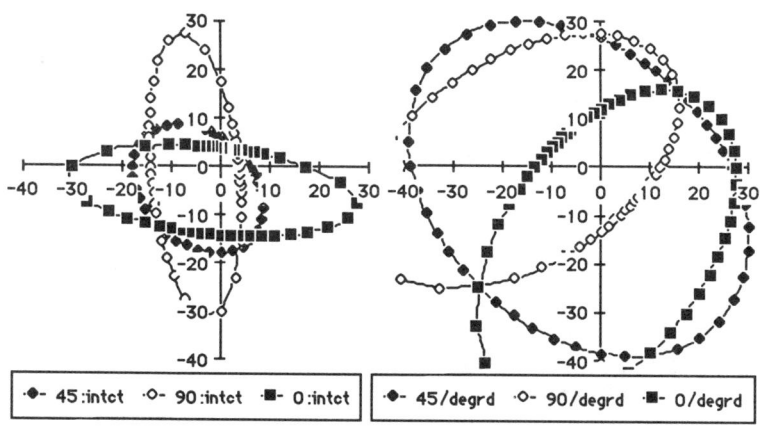

FIGURE 12.21   FPF AND LPF ENVELOPES OF π/4 E–GLASS/EPOXY LAMINATE.

Additional figures on the strength envelopes for E–glass/epoxy, and other composite materials, can be found in Subsections 29.11, 29.12, and 29.17. Degradation factors different from 0.3 have been used for the examples shown in Section 29. However, the method of developing various strength envelopes such FPF, LPF, limit and ultimate remains the same.

In Figure 12.22a, we show the FPF and LPF envelopes, from which the ultimate envelope can be derived. Protrusions by the FPF envelope occur in the second and fourth quadrants. This accounts for the unsmooth limit, limit* and ultimate strength envelopes in Figure 12.22b.

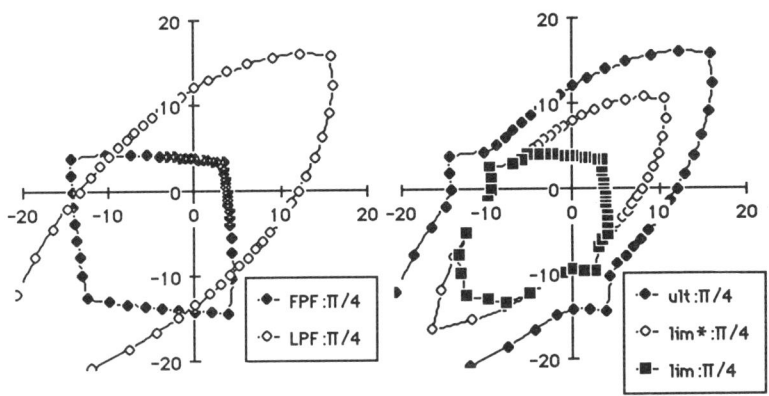

FIGURE 12.22   FPF AND LPF, AND LIMIT, LIMIT* AND ULTIMATE STRENGTH
ENVELOPES OF π/4 E–GLASS/EPOXY LAMINATE.

The gap between limit and limit* appears in both the first and third
quadrants. It is important to capitalize on the strength potential in the first
quadrant. For example, the filament–wound pressure vessel relies on an
inner rubber liner to prevent leakage and more fully utilize the fiber strength
beyond the FPF envelope.

In Figure 12.23, we show the FPF, LPF and the resulting ultimate strength
envelopes for a $[0/\pm45]_s$ laminate. The protrusion by the FPF envelope is
present in the second quadrant only. Again, we can visualize the removal of
the 90 degree ply from Figure 12.21 in order to generate the results in Figure
12.23. By the same token the strength envelopes for $[0/90]_s$ or $[\pm45]_s$
laminate can be similarly generated by observation.

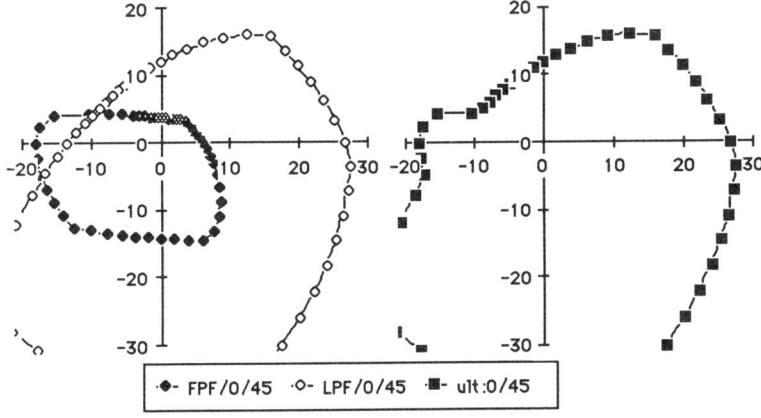

FIGURE 12.23   FPF, LPF AND ULTIMATE STRENGTH ENVELOPES OF $[0/\pm45]_s$
E–GLASS/EPOXY LAMINATE.

In Figure 12.24a, the limit and ultimate strength envelopes in the principal strain space are shown. In Figure 12.24b, the limit, limit* and ultimate envelopes are shown. The large gap between the limit and limit* envelopes presents another opportunity of exploiting the strength of composite materials.

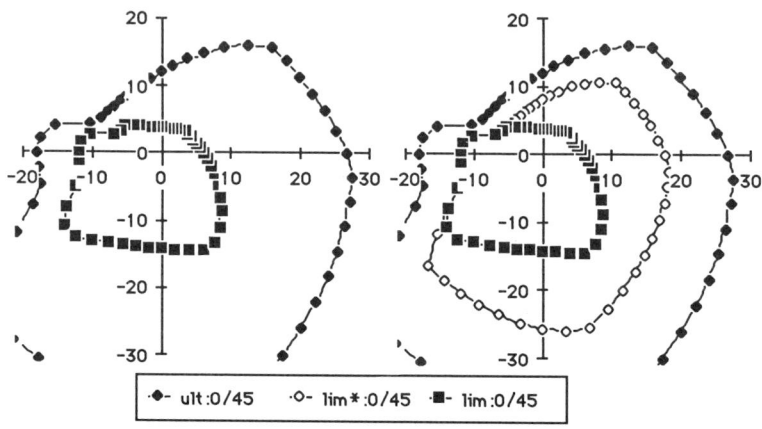

FIGURE 12.24   LIMIT, LIMIT* AND ULTIMATE STRENGTH ENVELOPES OF [0/±45]$_s$
E–GLASS/EPOXY LAMINATE.

12.12 DEGRADATION FACTOR FOR PLY MODULI

The matrix degradation is used as a model for plies with cracks and was discussed in Section 12.2. The relative reduction in the matrix modulus can be related to comparable reductions in the transverse and shear moduli of a damaged ply through micromechanics calculations. The results are shown in Figure 12.3.

For the analysis of laminated composite materials, we recommend two approaches: one is the integrated micro–macromechanics analysis (Mic–Mac); the other, the traditional laminated plate theory (macromechanics) using the ply properties as a starting point. In the Mic–Mac, the matrix degradation factor can be used to predict the LPF, from which the limit and ultimate strengths can be derived.

Most macromechanics analysis programs do not include micromechanics. The principal reason is the uncertainty in the micromechanics formulas, and that in the nonisotropic fiber properties. Without a built–in micromechanics in a macromechanics analysis, the matrix degradation model proposed here must be modified.   A different degradation factor DF is proposed for macromechanics. This factor is applied directly to the stiffness and strength of unidirectional plies. The relations for these three degraded ply stiffness properties are given below:

$$E_y = (DF)E_y{}^\circ \qquad\qquad (12.6)$$

$$E_s = (DF)E_s{}^\circ \qquad\qquad (12.7)$$

$$v_x = (DF)v_x{}^\circ \qquad\qquad (12.8)$$

where superscript zero denotes moduli of intact plies. The longitudinal stifffness is assumed to remain intact. In order to take into account of the effect of the loss of the foundation modulus on the microbuckling mode of failure shown in Equation 10.37, the same degradation factor is applied to the compressive failure strength, X'. Combining Equations 12.7 with 10.37 we have

$$X' = X'^\circ (DF)^{0.2} \qquad\qquad (12.9)$$

where the exponent c takes a value of 0.2 here. The effect of degradation is reduced by this exponent; i.e., the effect is less than linear.

If maximum strain criterion is used in macromechanics analysis, the failure strain in longitudinal compression must also be adjusted to reflect the loss of compressive strength, as follows:

$$\varepsilon_x{}^{*'} = \varepsilon_x{}^{*''}(DF)^{\,0.2} \qquad\qquad (12.10)$$

This is illustrated in Subsection 29.11 for the maximum strain criterion. We further propose the uncoupling of the failure modes in the quadratic criterion by linearly degrading the interaction term as well; i.e.,

$$F_{xy}{}^* = (DF)F_{xy}{}^{*\circ} \qquad\qquad (12.11)$$

For convenience we propose the use of the same numerical value for the DF as the matrix degradation factor $E_m/E_m{}^\circ$; typical values for which can be found in Subsection 29.12.

We want to use the degradation factors calculated from micromechanics. The values for the degraded transverse and shear moduli can be found in Subsection 29.12. For this approach, the degradation factor in Equations 12.6 and 12.7 will be increased. For example, for T300/5208 using a matrix degradation factor of Em* of 0.2, the micromechanics–calculated transvserve stiffness degradation will be 0.31; and that for the shear modulus, 0.27. The degradation fators for Poisson's ratio, compressive strength and the interaction term remain the same as 0.2. The DF values in Equations 12.8 through 12.11 will remain unchanged.

Based on our experience such as the sensitivity study shown in Figure 12.12, the LPF prediction is not sensitive to small changes in these degradation factors. Thus for macromehanics calculation such as GenLam and LamRank, we recommend the use of the matrix degradation factor for the DF. It is a common practice to use a DF value close to zero. We do not believe that such low value is justifiable. The degraded laminate stiffness, like those in

Table 12.1, can also be used to select the best degradation factor.

12.13 CONCLUSIONS

A systematic and internally consistent criterion for defining limit, limit* and ultimate strength envelopes has been demonstrated. The envelopes are easy to generate and provide designers with a pictorial view of the performance of a family of laminates. While strain space representation has many convenient features, any applied load which appears as a vector in this space will rotate as the layup of the laminate changes. In stress space, the applied load vector is unique and not affected by the laminate layup. A comparison of the load vectors in stress– and strain–space in the form of a clock is shown in Subsection 29.10.

In Section 15 on residual stresses we will continue by showing the effects of cure temperature and moisture content on the strength envelopes of composite materials. We believe that visualization of the laminate strength is important to designers.

Our approach used in the definition of strength envelopes can be summarized as follows:

- The quadratic failure criterion using an empirically determined interaction term.

- First–ply–failure envelope as defined from intact plies.

- Last–ply–failure envelope as defined from degraded plies, using an empirically determined matrix degradation factor.

- Ultimate envelope, derived from the greater of the FPF and LPF, which defines the maximum load carrying capability.

- Limit envelopes can be either the limit or limit*, an ultimate–based limit. A factor of safety is imbedded in the limit and limit* strengths. We recommend the former for general applications, and the latter for specialized applications like filament–wound pressure vessels.

- The difference between these two limits is significant in the tension–tension quadrant for GFRP and KFRP, but becomes less significant as the safety factor increases.

The limit envelopes are not smooth because the ply that controls the laminate failure changes as the loading changes. When such a change is abrupt, the laminate may have many local minimums. This situation makes laminate optimization difficult. We will show in the section on laminate design that an optimization routine can be highly influenced by the prescribed starting laminate. The quasi–isotropic laminate is frequently used for this purpose. This starting laminate, however, does not always ensure that a global minimum can be reached.

While failure envelopes of isotropic materials or unidirectional plies are convex, the limit and ultimate envelopes of composite laminates are not. We have just cited that the ply that controls the limit and ultimate envelopes also changes. This can be treated as the pointed vertices in the yield surface of a polycrystalline metal where many slip planes can be operative. The lack of convexity of laminate envelopes makes it difficult to define secondary loads. Our recommendation is that as many multiple loads as practical should be included initially. It is no longer intuitive to select the best laminate. A rational, systematic method like LamRank is recommended.

Finally, we have strongly advocated the quadratic failure criterion as the most flexible and the easiest to use. In addition, it is more general than both the maximum stress and the maximum strain criteria. For intact plies, we can recover the noninteracting criteria by increasing the longitudinal strengths, or decreasing the transverse and shear moduli. These limiting cases are shown in Subsection 29.9. For the degraded plies, we uncouple both the stiffness and failure modes by letting the Poisson's ratio and the interaction term reduce llically with the degradation factor. For the fully degraded plies the failure envelopes for the noninteracting and the quadratic will become the same in the limit. This is shown in Subsection 29.13 and 29.17. For these and other reasons cited earlier in this and the last sections, we believe that the quadratic criterion is better than both the maximum stress and the maximum strain criteria.

Section 13

PRINCIPAL STRESS DESIGN

13.1 SINGLE LOADS

When a structure is to be used under one load condition, then the structure is said to be subjected to a single load. A single load results in a combined stress state, and in the case of plane stress all three components may be present.

Unidirectional composites have exceedingly high stiffness and strength combined with light weight. But their properties are limited to the direction along the parallel fibers. The load must be uniaxial, not biaxial. When the load is applied slightly off the fiber direction, precipitous drop in properties occurs. We call this material and its properties directional.

Depending on the nature of the single load it is possible to take advantage of the superior properties of a highly directional composite. This design process is easily done by using the principal stress direction. When a structure must carry different loads under different conditions the directional material is in general not adequate. This multiple load condition will require different design methods; one such is based on the ranking or sorting large number of laminates which will be covered in the next section.

13.2 ISOTROPIC DESIGN

The design of isotropic materials is most frequently based on the von Mises failure criterion. For plane stress:

$$\sigma_1{}^2 - \sigma_1\sigma_2 + \sigma_2{}^2 + 3\sigma_6{}^2 = X^2 \tag{13.1}$$

where X = uniaxial yield or ultimate strength.

In terms of principal stresses Equation 13.1 becomes:

$$\sigma_I{}^2 - \sigma_I\sigma_{II} + \sigma_{II}{}^2 = X^2 \tag{13.2}$$

In Figure 13.1 the yield or failure criterion normalized by the uniaxial strength X is plotted. The tensile and compressive strengths are equal.

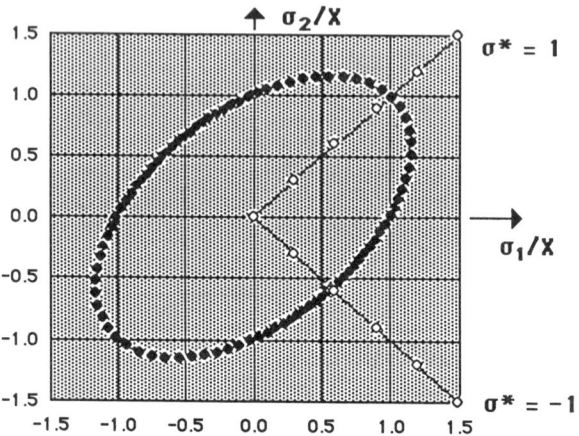

FIGURE 13.1 VON MISES FAILURE CRITERION ON PRINCIPAL PLANE.

Symmetry exists with reference to principal stress ratios ($\sigma^*=\sigma_2/\sigma_1$) of ±1; this is shown as $\sigma^* = \pm1$ in Figure 13.1. The strength capability as measured by σ_I between these stress ratios is shown in Figure 13.2 for aluminum with tensile strength of 200 MPa.

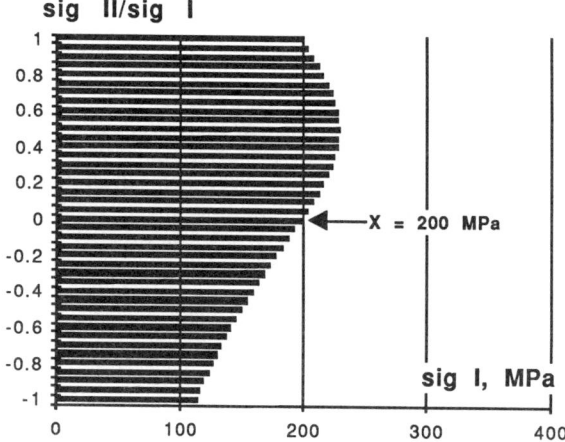

FIGURE 13.2 STRENGTH CAPABILITY UNDER BI–AXIAL STRESSES.

Each strength under biaxial principal stresses in Figure 13.2 corresponds to a point on the failure envelope in Figure 13.1. Like all isotropic materials the strength under biaxial stresses is relatively flat, not highly directional. The maximum and minimum values are at:

when stress ratio, $\sigma^* = 1/2$: $\sigma_I = (2/\sqrt{3})X = 1.154X$

when stress ratio, $\sigma^* = -1$: $\sigma_I = (1/\sqrt{3})X = 0.577X$

(13.3)

The latter corresponds to the shear strength of this material. For our aluminum with strength of 200 MPa:

1:2 biaxial strength = 231 MPa

Shear strength = 115 MPa

(13.4)

13.3 PRINCIPAL STRESS DESIGN

For a single load design of composite materials, we recommend the use of principal stress as the criterion. For each state of stress there is a principal direction when shear stress vanishes. This orientation is easily determined, as shown in Section 5.3 and Figure 5.2. The Mohr's circle, repeated here, provides a quick estimate of the principal stresses and the phase angle θ_0:

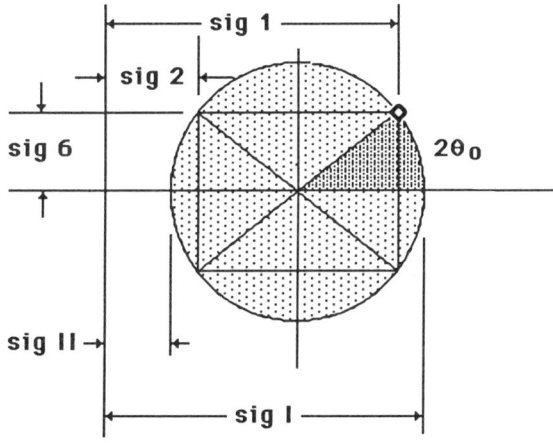

FIGURE 13.3 RELATION BETWEEN APPLIED AND PRINCIPAL STRESSES.

The phase angle can be confusing in two aspects: its sign and the factor of two in the Mohr's circle space. The phase angle in both Figures 13.3 and 13.4 are positive.

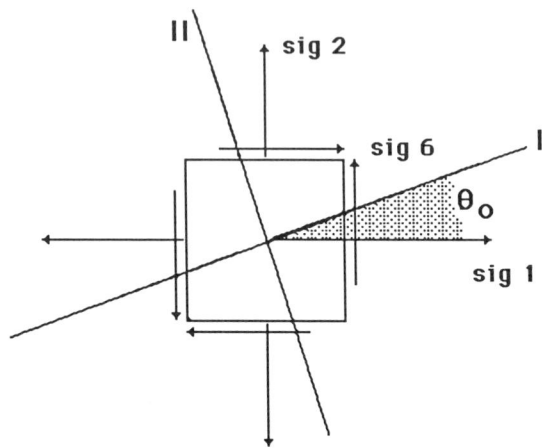

FIGURE 13.4   ORIENTATION OF THE PRINCIPAL AXES FROM THOSE OF THE
APPLIED STRESS.

The principal stress design is to utilize the highly directional properties of
unidirectional and laminated composites. This concept is useful for single
load design.

13.4 DESIGN WITH DIRECTIONAL MATERIALS

We will show the design options of a CFRP (T300/5208) for single loads.
Like the isotropic material, each strength under biaxial principal stresses
corresponds to a point on the failure envelope. We use the quadratic failure
criterion with a normalized interaction term of $-1/2$; i.e., the generalized von
Mises criterion. The strength data for are taken from Table 11.1. The
strengths under combined principal stresses comparable to Figure 13.2 are
shown in Figure 13.5. The material is highly directional and shows the
precipitous change in strength as σ^*'s move away from zero. The drop in
strength in the positive σ^*'s is greater that that in the negative ratios. This is
caused by the transverse tensile strength being smaller than the transverse
compressive strength.

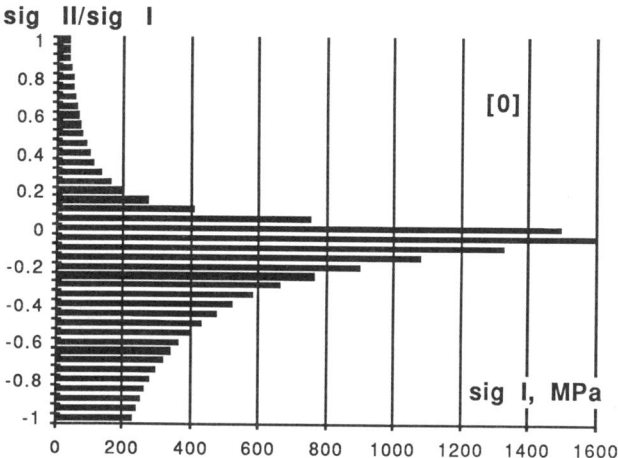

FIGURE 13.5 STRENGTH OF [0] T300/5208 VERSUS σ*.

There is a factor of 4 difference between the horizontal scale of this figure for the 0–degree CFRP and that for the aluminum. The 40 percent lighter in density of the CFRP than aluminum will increase the specific strength of CFRP over aluminum by a factor of 10.

This figure is limited to the following values of stresses:

$$\sigma_I > \sigma_{II}, \text{ and } \sigma_I > 0. \tag{13.5}$$

We did not show the compressive stress in the longitudinal direction because for this composite the transverse compressive strength is much higher than the tensile strength. The advantage of CFRP over aluminum is even greater for the case of $\sigma_I < 0$.

The highly directional nature of this CFRP and composites in general represents an opportunity. Our design concept is simply orient the material in the principal axes of the applied stress. Preferred orientation for isotropic materials does not exist. If we rotate our composite laminates to the principal stress direction, they will be anisotropic in the new laminate axes. We will have shear coupling resulting in beneficial or detrimental strains. As mentioned earlier the highly directional material has one inherent weakness: its precipitous loss in strength when the actual stress deviates from that anticipated in design.

13.5 SAMPLE PROBLEMS

Prob 1: Find strength ratios for aluminum and CFRP T300/5208 for an applied load of $\sigma_i = \{100, 100, 100\}$, MPa.

SOLUTION: Given the following state of stress:

$\sigma_i = \{100, 100, 100\}$ MPa   (13.6)

First we must find the principal stresses and the phase angle using Equations 5.10 and 5.16:

$p = 100, q = 0, r = 100, R = 100$

therefore $\sigma_I = 200, \sigma_{II} = 0, \theta_0 = [\arctan(100/0)]/2 = 45$ degree.

Using the definition of strength ratio in Equation 11.3 and the von Mises failure criterion in Equation 13.2 for aluminum:

$R^{alum} = 1$ (13.7)

The strength ratio for our CFRP is simply the ratio between the longitudinal strength X (=1500 MPa) and the applied stress:

$R^{cfrp} = 1500/200 = 7.5$ (13.8)

Phase angle $\theta_0 = +45$ degree   (13.9)

This is the required rigid body rotation from the laminate axis in order to take advantage of the directional strength of CFRP.

The angle of rotation is positive or forward swing in Figure 5.3.

If the applied stress has negative shear; i.e.,

$\sigma_i = \{100, 100, -100\}$ MPa   (13.10)

Then $p = 100, q = 0, r = -100, \theta_0 = -45$ degree.

Phase angle $\theta_0 = -45$ degree   (13.11)

The angle of rotation is negative or swept backward.

In Figure 13.6 we plotted the state of stress in both aluminum and CFRP to scale. The 7.5:1 ratio in their relative strengths is shown by the different sizes of the two Mohr's circles.

For composite materials the superior longitudinal strength can be utilized by orienting the material axis. The required rigid body rotations of forward or backward swing are shown in the figure for various combined stresses. The longitudinal strengths for the plus and minus 45 degree, shown in Equations 13.9 and 13.11, respectively, are multiplied by the strength ratio of 7.5 in Equation 13.8 to reflect the strength of CFRP composite.

Prob 2: **What are the resulting strains of our rotated composite? Is shear coupling beneficial or not?**

SOLUTION: For the applied stress in Equation 13.6, we can easily compute the resulting strain from the compliance of aluminum, and T300/5208 in Table 6.5:

For aluminum, $E = 69$ GPa, $\nu = .3, G = 69/2.6 = 26.5$ GPa

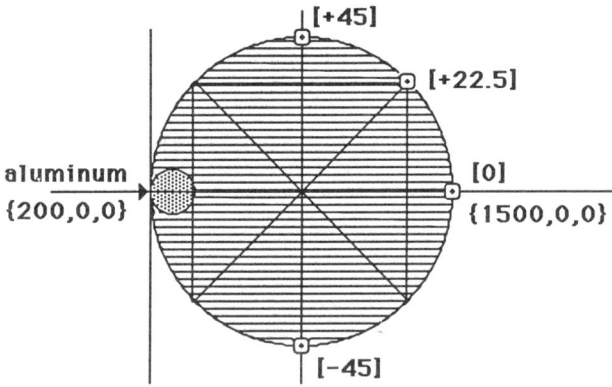

FIGURE 13.6 MOHR'S CIRCLE PLOTS OF UNIAXIAL STRENGTH OF ALUMINUM AND T300/5208, OR $\sigma^* = 0$. COMBINED STRESS CAPABILITY AND THE SWING ANGLES ARE ALSO SHOWN.

$\varepsilon_1 = \varepsilon_2 = (1/69-.3/69)x100 = 0.001014$

$\varepsilon_6 = 100/26.5 = .00377$

(13.12)

For T300/5208 at $\theta = 45$ degree,

$\varepsilon_1 = \varepsilon_2 = (59.57-9.99-45.78)x100 = .00038$

$\varepsilon_6 = (-45.78-45.78+105.71)x100 = .0014$

(13.13)

Although the strain components are much smaller for the CFRP, it is better to compare the effective strain from a strain invariant; see section 5.4. Among numerous invariants we may select for the present purpose:

$|\varepsilon| = [\varepsilon_1^2+\varepsilon_2^2+(\varepsilon_6^2/2)]^{1/2}$

(13.14)

For aluminum: $|\varepsilon| = [2x.00141^2+(.00377)^2/2]^{1/2}$

$= .003045$

(13.15)

For CFRP: $|\varepsilon| = [2x.00038^2+(.0014)^2/2]^{1/2}$

$= .001126$

(13.16)

The ratio of $\varepsilon^{al}/\varepsilon^{cfrp} = 2.70$

(13.17)

CONCLUSION: the resulting strain is smaller and shear coupling beneficial.

If we make a mistake in swinging backward (–45 degree):

For CFRP at –45, $S_{16} = S_{26} = +45.78$:

$\varepsilon_1 = \varepsilon_2 = (59.75-9.99+45.78)x100 = .00815$

$\varepsilon_6 = (2x45.78+105.71)x100 = .0197$

(13.18)

$$|\epsilon| = [2x.00815^2 + (.0197)^2/2]^{1/2} = .01808 \tag{13.19}$$

This is higher than that in Equation 13.15 by a factor of 16.

CONCLUSION: Wrong swing angle is catastrophic!

Prob 3: **Can we use the unidirectional CFRP for a load different from the uniaxial stress shown in Figure 13.6? How would a stress ratio, σ^*, of –0.2 perform relative to aluminum?**

SOLUTION: From Figure 13.5, we can find that:

$$\sigma_2/\sigma_1 = -0.2, \text{ the effective strength } \sigma_1 = 900 \text{ MPa.} \tag{13.20}$$

The combined stress capability is {900,–180,0)

The combined stress capability of aluminum is (170,–34,0)

The relative strength is illustrated in Figure 13.7 which is comparable to the relative Mohr's circles in Figure 13.6.

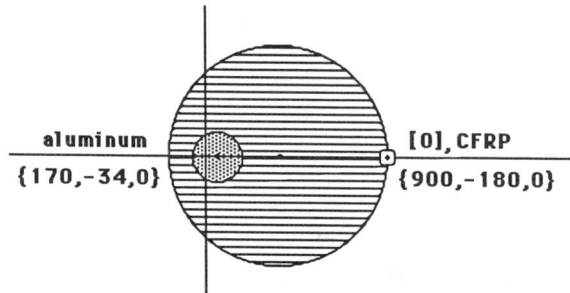

FIGURE 13.7 SAME SCALE AS IN FIG 13.6 EXCEPT $\sigma^* = -.2$.

The advantage of CFRP over aluminum although smaller is still obvious.

CONCLUSION: Unidirectional composites are capable of carrying combined stresses effectively with proper laminate axes rotation; i.e., forward or backward swing.

Prob 4: **What are the strength capability of CFRP laminates?**

SOLUTION: Highly directional properties can also be derived from simple laminates such as   angle–ply and tridirectional laminates. Typical results for CFRP T300/5208 are shown below:

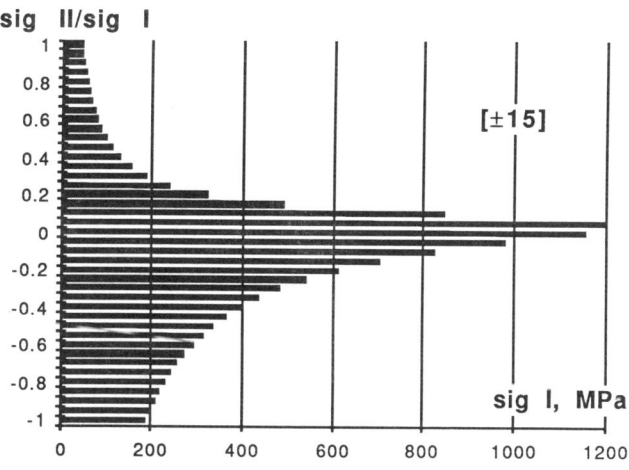

FIGURE 13.8 STRENGTH OF [±15] CFRP FOR VARIOUS σ*.

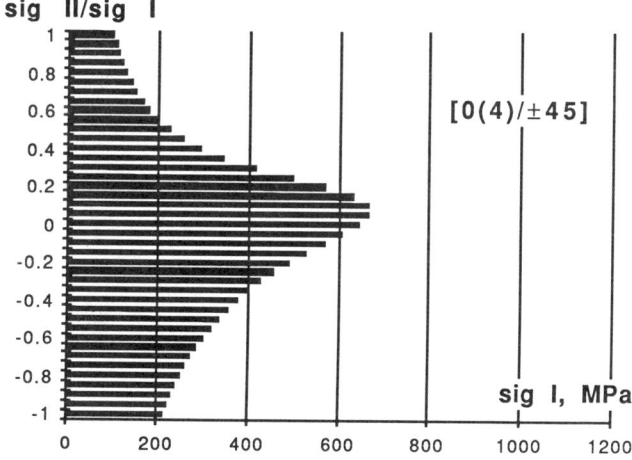

FIGURE 13.9 STRENGTH OF [0₄/±45] FOR VARIOUS σ*.

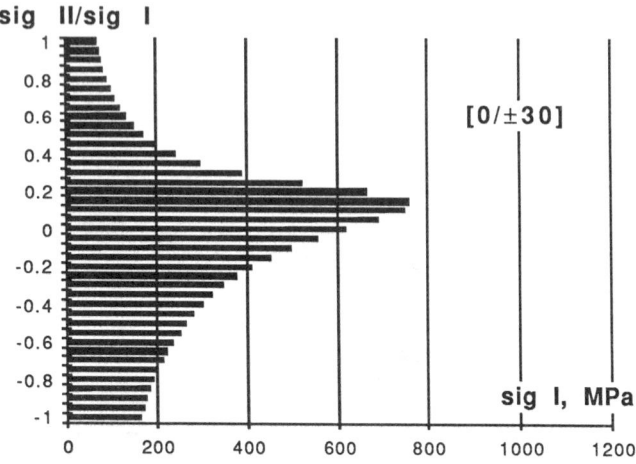

FIGURE 13.10 STRENGTH OF [0/±30] CFRP FOR VARIOUS σ*.

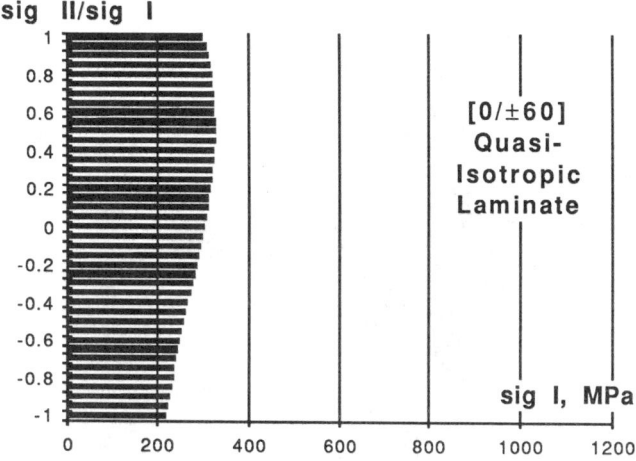

FIGURE 13.11 STRENGTH FOR CFRP QUASI–ISOTROPIC LAMINATES.

All the laminates with the exception of the quasi–isotropic laminate can be used for principal stress design. Only the highly directional ones show unusual benefit. But the less directional laminates are more suitable for multiple or wide–spectrum loads.

13.6 THE MAGIC ROD

Shear coupling is an unusual feature of an anisotropic material. A rod can be made with a properly designed shear coupling so bending and twisting of the rod are coupled to render "magic" motion, which is not possible with the isotropic rod.

Under uniaxial stress, say, σ_1 the resulting strains are:

$$\varepsilon_1 = a_{11}{}^*\sigma_1, \quad \varepsilon_2 = a_{21}{}^*\sigma_1, \quad \varepsilon_6 = a_{61}{}^*\sigma_1 \tag{12.21}$$

We are primarily interested in the shear coupling which is the ratio of normal to shear strains:

$$v_{61} = \varepsilon_6/\varepsilon_1 = a_{61}/a_{11} \tag{12.22}$$

For a rod with a thin wall circular cross–section, the bending curvature and twisting angle are related by this shear coupling and the section moduli.

$$\textbf{Moment of inertia} = I = \pi D^3 h/8 = \pi R^3 h \tag{12.23}$$

where   D = diameter, R = radius, h = wall thickness << D, R.

Under the influence of pure bending moment M,

$$\sigma^{max} = Mc/I = MR/I = 4M/\pi D^2 h \tag{12.24}$$

$$\varepsilon^{max} = a_{11}{}^*\sigma^{max} \tag{12.25}$$

$$\varepsilon^{ave}/\varepsilon^{max} = 1/\pi \int_0^\pi \sin\theta d\theta = 2/\pi \tag{12.26}$$

$$\varepsilon^{ave} = 2\varepsilon^{max}/\pi = 8a_{11}{}^*M/\pi^2 D^2 h \tag{12.27}$$

$$\varepsilon_6 = v_{61}\varepsilon^{ave} \tag{12.28}$$

$$\textbf{Angle of twist in radian} = (L/R)\varepsilon_6$$

$$= [8(L/R)v_{61}a_{11}{}^*/\pi^2 D^2 h]M \tag{12.29}$$

$$\textbf{Angle of twist in degree} = [2(L/R)v_{61}a_{11}{}^*/45\pi D^2 h]M \tag{12.30}$$

where   L = length of rod, v_{61} = shear coupling.

The magic rod can also be used as screw or threaded rod; i.e., with an applied torque to the rod, the rod would change its length. For most common composite materials, an anisotropic rod would behave like a rod with left–handed screw. A clockwise twist would cause a reduction in length.

13.7 CONCLUSIONS

The principal design takes advantage of the highly directional properties of composites. It is a very efficient design but is limited to a single–load design. It is also limited to a structure subjected to homogeneous state of stress; i.e., the stress distribution is reasonably uniform. Once these limitations are satisfied the outstanding features of composite materials can be fully exploited.

Section 14

DESIGN BY RANKING

14.1 LAMINATE RANKING

Another method of design can be based on the ranking of a family or families of laminates. This is an alternative to the conventional optimization, and the principal stress design of the last section. The strength ranking is analogous to that of in–plane stiffness illustrated in Section 7.11. The method appears to be one of the most powerful design tools to emerge, and it is based on:

- Laminated plate theory for a family of symmetric laminates subjected to in–plane load only.
- Quadratic failure criterion using –1/2 for the normalized interaction term.
- Instead of using the matrix degradation factor through micromechanics, the ply are degraded by a ply degradation factor DF, defined in Section 12. Laminate strength ranking is based on either limit and limt* also described in Section 12.
- Room temperature properties only; curing stresses due to lamination is included.
- Single or multiple loads.
- CFRP T300/5208 as the sample material for this section.
- Up to 1000 member sublaminate family, and 2 to 4 ply angles.

As in Section 7, the 4–digit laminate code for the sublaminate is used. The digits in the code represent the number of plies in the sublaminate, and in the order of the ply angles selected. For a generalized $\pi/4$ laminate, code [4211] means $[0_4/90_2/45/-45]_s$; and [1023], $[0/45_2/-45_3]_s$. The code may also be applied to angles other than multiples of $\pi/4$ if the angles are specified. If we use two or three angles instead of four, the last one or two digits would be zero, respectively. For example a $[0/90]_s$ laminate is designated by code [1100]. We purposely keep our sublaminate between 2 and 10 ply so the single digit–code will suffice. It turns out that the use of sublaminate with more than ten plies is not justified from the standpoint of optimization, and cost.

A special $\pi/4$ laminate is the [1111], $[0/90/45/-45]_s$, or the $\pi/4$ quasi–isotropic laminate. Similarly, a special $\pi/3$ laminate is the [1110], $[0/60/-60]_s$, or the $\pi/3$ quasi–isotropic laminate. Both laminates represent the minimum performance of the composite material without taking the advantage of anisotropy. The ranking of the laminates includes not only the absolute strength of each laminate within the family, but also the relative strength over the quasi–isotropic laminate. These strength ratios not only show the benefit of anisotropy, but also provide a comparison among composite and isotropic materials.

14.2 LAMINATE DATABASE

A database is generated with the following parameters:

- Material properties
- Number of plies in the sublaminates
- Number and value of orientations to be used

The number of sublaminates in each family is a function of the number of plies and the number of orientations in each sublaminate. If we have a 2–ply sublaminate having two angles: 0 and 90. There are then three possible combinations: $[0_2]$, $[90_2]$, $[0/90]$. If we have a 3–ply sublaminate with the same two angles, we will have four combinations: $[0_3]$, $[0_2/90]$, $[0/90_2]$, $[90_3]$.

Table 14.1 shows the number of possible sublaminates in a family of given number of orientations (between 2 and 4) and total number of plies (between 2 and 10).

TABLE 14.1   NUMBER OF SUBLAMINATES IN A FAMILY FOR GIVEN NUMBER OF PLY ORIENTATIONS AND PLIES

Number of Plies	Family of 2 orientations	Family of 3 orientations	Family of 4 orientations
2	3	6	10
3	4	10	20
4	5	15	35
5	6	21	56
6	7	28	84
7	8	36	120
8	9	45	165
9	10	55	220
10	11	66	286
Total	65	285	1000

The sublaminates in each family can be either unidirectional, bidirectional, tridirectional or quadri–directional.

For instance, given a unidirectional ply, 6 plies in each sublaminate and the four orientations 0, 90, 45, –45 we generate the following database of 84 laminates shown in Table 14.2

The four digit laminate code is used. The leading zeros are not shown in the table; e.g., laminate number 1 is [0006] which is a [–45] laminate. The next number if the number of ply groups, which is one for this unidirectional laminate. Then the "ortho" means orthotropy. Elsewhere we have "aniso" for anisotropy, and "Q–iso" for quasi–isotropy.

With 8 plies in each sublaminate and the four orientations 0, 90, 45,–45 we generate the following database of 165 sublaminates shown in Table 14.3.

The notations follow those of Table 14.2.

TABLE 14.2 SUMMARY OF 84 SUBLAMINATES WITH 6 PLIES AND 4 ANGLES.

No.	Code	QUADRI	No.	Code	QUADRI	No.	Code	QUADRI	No.	Code	QUADR
1	6	1 Ortho	22	330	3 Ortho	43	1230	4 Ortho	64	2400	4 Ortho
2	15	2 Ortho	23	402	3 Ortho	44	1302	4 Ortho	65	3003	4 Ortho
3	24	2 Ortho	24	411	3 Ortho	45	1311	4 Ortho	66	3012	4 Ortho
4	33	2 Ortho	25	420	2 Ortho	46	1320	3 Ortho	67	3021	3 Ortho
5	42	2 Aniso	26	501	2 Aniso	47	1401	3 Aniso	68	3030	2 Aniso
6	51	2 Aniso	27	510	2 Aniso	48	1410	3 Aniso	69	3102	3 Aniso
7	60	1 Ortho	28	600	1 Ortho	49	1500	2 Ortho	70	3111	4 Ortho
8	105	2 Aniso	29	1005	2 Ortho	50	2004	2 Aniso	71	3120	3 Aniso
9	114	3 Aniso	30	1014	3 Aniso	51	2013	3 Aniso	72	3201	3 Aniso
10	123	3 Aniso	31	1023	3 Aniso	52	2022	3 Ortho	73	3210	3 Aniso
11	132	3 Aniso	32	1032	3 Aniso	53	2031	3 Aniso	74	3300	2 Ortho
12	141	3 Aniso	33	1041	3 Aniso	54	2040	3 Aniso	75	4002	2 Aniso
13	150	2 Aniso	34	1050	2 Aniso	55	2103	3 Aniso	76	4011	3 Ortho
14	204	2 Aniso	35	1104	3 Aniso	56	2112	4 Aniso	77	4020	2 Aniso
15	213	3 Aniso	36	1113	4 Aniso	57	2121	4 Aniso	78	4101	3 Aniso
16	222	3 Ortho	37	1122	4 Ortho	58	2130	3 Aniso	79	4110	3 Aniso
17	231	3 Aniso	38	1131	4 Aniso	59	2202	3 Aniso	80	4200	2 Ortho
18	240	2 Aniso	39	1140	3 Aniso	60	2211	4 Ortho	81	5001	2 Aniso
19	303	2 Aniso	40	1203	3 Aniso	61	2220	3 Aniso	82	5010	2 Aniso
20	312	3 Aniso	41	1212	4 Aniso	62	2301	3 Aniso	83	5100	2 Ortho
21	321	3 Aniso	42	1221	4 Aniso	63	2310	3 Aniso	84	6000	1 Ortho

14.3 PRINCIPAL STRESS VERSUS RANKING METHODS

In Section 13 it was shown that laminates can be designed using the principal stresses for single loads. We can use the laminate ranking to achieve similar results. The two approaches are complementary. Both are based on the same theory. But we may arrive at different answers because the constraints imposed by the selection of laminates. The principal stress approach is dependent on the particular basic laminates selected; i.e., [0], [15/–15], etc., and the rigid body rotation, or the forward or backward swing angle. For a given load we have to explore several laminates to arrive at an optimum construction. In general this approach is effective for the highly directional laminates.

When the anticipated load is not well defined, a less directional composite may be preferred to reduce the sudden drop in strength when the load changes. The laminate ranking method may be most effective for this situation. The method is easily extended to treat multiple load conditions. Another important advantage of the ranking approach is the listing of alternate laminates for the same applied load.

The ranking approach is however limited by the families of laminates selected that to be ranked. The number of plies in a sublaminate and the ply angles allowed determine a laminate family. Presently we have limited the possibilities to 2 to 4 different angles and 2 to 10 plies in the sublaminates. For a given set of 4 angles this gives nearly 1000 possible designs. Having a finite combination of plies in the sublaminate and ply angles turns out not as severe a limitation as anticipated.

TABLE 14.3 SUMMARY OF 165 SUBLAMINATES WITH 8 PLIES AND 4 ANGLES

No.	Code	QUADRI	No.	Code	QUADRI	No.	Code	QUADRI	No.	Code	QUADR.
1	8	1 Ortho	43	701	2 Aniso	85	2033	3 Ortho	127	3320	3 Aniso
2	17	2 Aniso	44	710	2 Aniso	86	2042	3 Aniso	128	3401	3 Aniso
3	26	2 Aniso	45	800	1 Ortho	87	2051	3 Aniso	129	3410	3 Aniso
4	35	2 Aniso	46	1007	2 Aniso	88	2060	2 Aniso	130	3500	2 Orthoo
5	44	2 Ortho	47	1016	3 Aniso	89	2105	3 Aniso	131	4004	2 Aniso
6	53	2 Aniso	48	1025	3 Aniso	90	2114	4 Aniso	132	4013	3 Aniso
7	62	2 Aniso	49	1034	3 Aniso	91	2123	4 Aniso	133	4022	2 Ortho
8	71	2 Aniso	50	1043	3 Aniso	92	2132	4 Aniso	134	4031	3 Aniso
9	80	1 Ortho	51	1052	3 Aniso	93	2141	4 Aniso	135	4040	2 Aniso
10	107	2 Aniso	52	1061	3 Aniso	94	2150	3 Aniso	136	4103	3 Aniso
11	116	3 Aniso	53	1070	2 Aniso	95	2204	3 Aniso	137	4112	4 Aniso
12	125	3 Aniso	54	1106	3 Aniso	96	2213	4 Aniso	138	4121	4 Aniso
13	134	3 Aniso	55	1115	4 Aniso	97	2222	4 Q-iso	139	4130	3 Aniso
14	143	3 Aniso	56	1124	4 Aniso	98	2231	4 Aniso	140	4202	3 Aniso
15	152	3 Aniso	57	1133	4 Ortho	99	2240	3 Aniso	141	4211	4 Aniso
16	161	3 Aniso	58	1142	4 Aniso	100	2303	3 Aniso	142	4220	3 Aniso
17	170	3 Aniso	59	1151	4 Aniso	101	2312	4 Aniso	143	4301	3 Aniso
18	206	3 Aniso	60	1160	3 Aniso	102	2321	4 Aniso	144	4310	4 Aniso
19	215	3 Aniso	61	1205	3 Aniso	103	2330	3 Aniso	145	4400	2 Ortho
20	224	3 Aniso	62	1214	4 Aniso	104	2402	3 Aniso	146	5003	2 Aniso
21	233	3 Ortho	63	1223	4 Aniso	105	2411	4 Ortho	147	5012	3 Aniso
22	242	3 Aniso	64	1232	4 Aniso	106	2420	3 Aniso	148	5021	3 Aniso
23	251	3 Aniso	65	1241	4 Aniso	107	2501	3 Aniso	149	5030	2 Aniso
24	260	2 Aniso	66	1250	3 Aniso	108	2510	3 Aniso	150	5102	3 Aniso
25	305	2 Aniso	67	1304	3 Aniso	109	2600	2 Ortho	151	5111	4 Aniso
26	314	3 Aniso	68	1313	4 Aniso	110	3005	2 Aniso	152	5120	3 Aniso
27	323	3 Aniso	69	1322	4 Ortho	111	3014	3 Aniso	153	5201	3 Aniso
28	332	3 Aniso	70	1331	4 Aniso	112	3023	3 Aniso	154	5210	3 Aniso
29	341	3 Aniso	71	1340	3 Aniso	113	3032	3 Aniso	155	5300	2 Ortho
30	350	2 Aniso	72	1403	4 Aniso	114	3041	3 Aniso	156	6002	2 Aniso
31	404	2 Aniso	73	1412	4 Aniso	115	3050	2 Aniso	157	6011	3 Aniso
32	413	3 Aniso	74	1421	4 Aniso	116	3104	4 Aniso	158	6020	2 Aniso
33	422	3 Aniso	75	1430	3 Aniso	117	3113	4 Aniso	159	6101	3 Aniso
34	431	3 Aniso	76	1502	4 Aniso	118	3122	4 Ortho	160	6110	3 Aniso
35	440	2 Aniso	77	1511	4 Ortho	119	3131	4 Aniso	161	6200	2 Ortho
36	503	3 Aniso	78	1520	3 Aniso	120	3140	3 Aniso	162	7001	2 Aniso
37	512	3 Aniso	79	1601	3 Aniso	121	3203	3 Aniso	163	7010	2 Aniso
38	521	3 Aniso	80	1610	3 Aniso	122	3212	4 Aniso	164	7100	2 Ortho
39	530	2 Aniso	81	1700	2 Ortho	123	3221	4 Aniso	165	8000	1 Ortho
40	602	3 Aniso	82	2006	2 Aniso	124	3230	3 Aniso	166		
41	611	3 Ortho	83	2015	3 Aniso	125	3302	3 Aniso	167		
42	620	2 Aniso	84	2024	3 Aniso	126	3311	4 Ortho	168		

14.4 A ROUND OFF PROCEDURE FOR THE RANKING METHOD

Designing with symmetric sublaminates, we are forced with making discrete increase in the number of sublaminates as dictated by the laminated plate analysis. Such discrete increase may involve as many as twice the number of plies in the sublaminate, i.e., for a 10–ply sublaminate, this increase can be up to 20 plies. It is therefore desirable to reduce such increase when the number of plies in the sublaminate is large or when the number of repeats is low.

We define a sublaminate (**a b c d**) as the number of plies oriented in each of the selected ply angle. To remove this potentially unnecessary jump to the next integer in the repeat index we propose an additional laminate selection process applied to the required fractional sublaminate. For example if the repeat index is 4.3, we will not advance to 5.0 as the final design. Instead, we will attempt to select the best laminate that would satisfy the 0.3 sublaminate. The additional fraction of the sublaminate should be designed using the same criterion and ply angles as the sublaminate, but could also include other constraints such as minimizing free edge delamination.

To achieve optimum sizing of the laminate, we propose the use of a round off laminate, (**A B C D**), for which the number of plies is less than those in the sublaminate and such that the laminate has these following criteria:

- Repeated sublaminate $(a\ b\ c\ d)_{rs}$ does not meet the design criteria;

- With an additional sublaminate, $(a\ b\ c\ d)_{(r+1)s}$ overshoots the design criteria;

- $[(a\ b\ c\ d)_r + (A\ B\ C\ D)]_s$ or $[(a\ b\ c\ d)_{r+1} - (A\ B\ C\ D)]_s$ just meets the design criteria;

- Round off laminate (A B C D) has the minimum number of plies, such that A≤a, B≤b, C≤c, and D≤d.

The algorithm is brute force: investigate all the possible 1–ply laminates for each of the ply angle orientations of the sublaminate, [a b c d], to see if the additional ply of plies meet the requirements. If not, investigate the 2–ply laminates and so on until a laminate which meets the design criteria is found. Of course, the number of possible round off laminates increases very quickly with the number of plies in the original sublaminate.

Fortunately the family size of the round off laminates is relatively small. For a 10 ply sublaminate, the maximum number of round off laminates to be investigated is 250. It is however easier to use round off laminates in positive and negative ways; that is, laminates can be added to the original repeated sublaminates, or subtracted from the latter plus one sublaminate.

14.5 DISPLAY OF RESULTS

We will show in Figure 14.1 explanations of the tabular results of a laminate ranking. In the first column, the ranking of strength is identified in descending order. In the second column, the layup of the chosen family is shown. The family is defined by the number of plies in the sublaminate from 2 to 10, the the number and values of the angle in each ply group. The number of ply group in each laminate is 2, 3 or 4. The first laminate is Figure 14.1 is $[45_4/\text{-}45_4]_S$ laminate.

Column 3 shows the next larger integer of the repeat index. If the theoretical repeat index for the loading is 15.4, it is advanced to the next integer which is 15. As mentioned earlier, this increase may make the laminates overly conservative.

Column 4 is the relative strength between the particular laminate of the family and the quasi–isotropic laminate of the same composite material. The comparison in this figure is the strength ratio based on design limit, not limit*. We can of course elect to rank in terms of limit*. The relative strength shows the advantage of anisotropy. It should never be less than unity.

If the strength ratio at limit for the quasi–isotropic laminate is 1.4, and that for a particular laminate is 2.5, the relative strength of the latter laminate over the former is 2.5/1.4 = 1.78.

Column 5 is the theoretical number of plies required for the loading. It is simply the total thickness of the laminate divided by the strength ratio at limit. If we start with an 8–ply laminate, the strength ratio at limit is 0.52, the total number of plies would be 8/0.52 = 15.4.

Column 6 is the ratio of the ultimate over the FPF strength. This number is greater than or equal to unity. By referring to Figure 12.8a, the region where this ratio is greater than unity is seen in the first quadrant; that equal to unity, in the third quadrant. For multiple loads, there will be one ratio for each load. The value shown in this column is the lowest ratio among all loads for each laminate within the family. If this ratio is less than the safety margin the limit load is lower than the FPF. If this ratio is higher than the safety margin, like laminates 3,4 and 5, the limit load is at FPF, and the actual safety margin is higher than the minimum specified.

Columns 7 and 8 are analogous to Columns 4 and 5 except the strength criterion for ranking has changed from limit to limit*. As we know, at limit* matrix degradation is allowed.

Column 9 and 10 identifies the critical or controlling load among all possible loads. This is useful for designing with multiple loads. If ranking is based on limit, the applicable critical load is listed under column labeled Lmt; that based on limit*, column Lmt*.

LAMINATE RANKING   **CONTROL.**

LAMINATE LAYUP

NEXT LARGER REPEAT INTEGER

R^{lam}/R^{iso} at lim R^{lam}/R^{iso} at lim*

h/R^{lim} h/R^{lim*}

(1) (2) (3) (4) (5) (6) (7) (8) (9)

No	Laminate		Limit			Limit*		Crit. Lo.	
	Layup	Repeat	relative	# plies	Ult/FPF	relative	# plies	Lmt.	Lmt
1	44	14	1.91	212.5	1.41	1.91	212.5	1	1
2	53	16	1.66	244.1	1.12	1.66	244.1	1	1
3	35	16	1.62	250.5	1.79	1.93	210.1	1	1
4	1034	16	1.6	253.9	1.61	1.72	236.2	1	1
5	134	16	1.6	253.9	1.61	1.72	236.2	1	1

No	Laminate with Round off	# plies	R-Limit	R-Limit*	R-Ult
1	[(44) X 13 + (2)]S	212.0	1.00	1.00	1.50
2	[(53) X 15 + (2)]S	244.0	1.02	1.02	1.52
3	[(35) X 15 + (30)]S	246.0	1.02	1.18	1.77
4	[(1034) X 15 + (30)]S	246.0	1.00	1.04	1.57
5	[(134) X 15 + (30)]S	246.0	1.00	1.04	1.57

$[(a\ b\ c\ d)_{repeat} + (A\ B\ C\ D)]_s$ **R-VALUES**

TOTAL PLIES

FIGURE 14.1   EXPLANATION OF RESULTS OF LAMINATE RANKING. ALL
LAMINATES ARE CFRP T300/5208, 8-PLY SUBLAMINATES, P/4 LAYUP,
DEGRADATION FACTOR OF 0.3, AND SAFETY FACTOR OF 1.5.

In the lower half of Figure 14.1 we show in the second column the final
laminate which consists of two part: the repeated sublaminate, and the round
off laminate. The third column shows the total number of plies, which now
are even integers. The final laminates can have can have lower number of
plies than the theoretical laminate in column 5 of the upper half. This is
possible because the round off laminates can be more efficient than the
multiples of the sublaminate.

The last three columns in the lower half of Figure 14.1 shows the
recalculated strength ratios of the final laminate. The example shown in this
figure is ranked by limit, the R-limit values should always be equal or
greater than unity. If ranking is based on limit* the R-limit* values will
always be equal or greater than unity. Then the corresponding R-limit may
be less than unity. This is consistent because under limit* matrix degradation
is allowed. Finally the R-ultimate should be equal or greater than the safety
margin if ranking is based on limit. If ranking is based on limit* R-ultimate
is equal to the product of safety margin and R-limit*.

14.6 SINGLE LOADS

We will show the results of our ranking method for a number of simple and
representative loads. Most results are difficult if not impossible to predict.

..erefore think that calculation is better than intuition or guessing.

...ign for strength can be based on one of two definitions of the limit ...ength. These criteria are the limit and limit* strengths described in ...ction 12. Although the strength ranking can be based on either limit or ...mit*, we prefer the former because its calculation is based on a more ...ccurate theory than that of the limit*. Furthermore, limit is conservative because limit load cannot exceed the FPF envelope. The results are displayed in terms of the number of repeated sublaminates required for one half of a symmetric laminate, and the ratio of plies of the quasi–isotropic laminate over those of each laminate. As before, the residual stresses are based on a temperature difference is –100 °C and moisture content is 0.005.

Although it is not illustrated here, we may design our laminate based on stiffness, or elastic stability. In addition to the ranking of stiffness moduli in Section 7.11, ranking strain invariant of Equations 5.21 and 13.14 may be a good choice for complex strains. It is assumed here that with a smaller induced strain invariant, the resulting laminate has a higher stiffness and more elastic stability.

The ratio over isotropy shows the advantage of laminate anisotropy over the quasi–isotropic laminate of the same composite. This ratio can also be used to show directly the strength advantages over isotropic materials such as aluminum and steel. The weight advantage of composites over metals can be included to show an additional benefit of composites.

The results of a simple uniaxial tensile load {10,0,0} in MN/m are shown in Figure 14.2. The material is CFRP T300/5208, having the usual room temperature properties as those used in preceding sections. In this study, 8–ply sublaminates, with four ply angles of $\pi/4$ increments, are ranked.

No	Laminate		Limit			Limit*		Crit. Load	
	Layup	Repeat	relative	# plies	Ult/FPF	relative	# plies	Lmt.	Lmt*
1	8000	6	3.39	80.0	1.12	2.78	80.0	1	1
2	7001	7	2.62	103.5	1.75	2.51	88.7	1	1
3	7010	7	2.62	103.5	1.75	2.51	88.7	1	1
4	6011	7	2.54	106.9	1.64	2.27	98.0	1	1
5	7100	7	2.47	109.7	1.81	2.44	91.2	1	1

No	Laminate with Round off		# plies	R–Limit	R–Limit*	R–Ult
1	[(8000) X	5 + (1000)]S	82.0	1.02	1.02	1.54
2	[(7001) X	6 + (4000)]S	104.0	1.02	1.19	1.78
3	[(7010) X	6 + (4000)]S	104.0	1.02	1.19	1.78
4	[(6011) X	6 + (5000)]S	106.0	1.02	1.11	1.67
5	[(7100) X	6 + (7000)]S	110.0	1.02	1.23	1.84

FIGURE 14.2 HIGHEST STRENGTH LAMINATES UNDER {10,0,0}, MN/m.

The figure, with its format repeated in this section, contains two parts: the upper part contains the results of the ranking using laminated plate theory, and the limit, limit* and ultimate strengths; and the lower part, the results of the round off.

In Figure 14.3, we show the strength ranking of laminates subjected to uniaxial compression {–10,0,0} in MPa. The best laminate now is [7100] having 87.5 percent 0–degree plies. It shows that a cross–ply laminate with a small amount of 90–degree plies will have a higher compressive strength than a laminate with all 0–degree plies.

No	Laminate		Limit			Limit*		Crit. Load	
	Layup	Repeat	relative	# plies	Ult/FPF	relative	# plies	Lmt.	Lmt*
1	7100	4	3.56	60.4	1	3.56	60.4	1	1
2	8000	4	3.49	61.7	1	3.49	61.7	1	1
3	6200	5	3.11	69.2	1	3.11	69.2	1	1
4	5300	6	2.62	82.0	1	2.62	82.0	1	1
12	5111	7	1.93	111.8	1	1.93	111.8	1	1

No	Laminate with Round off	# plies	R–Limit	R–Limit*	R–Ult
1	[(7100) X 3 + (6000)]S	60.0	1.01	1.01	1.52
2	[(8000) X 3 + (7000)]S	62.0	1.01	1.01	1.51
3	[(6200) X 4 + (2000)]S	68.0	1.00	1.00	1.50
4	[(5300) X 5 + (1000)]S	82.0	1.01	1.01	1.52

FIGURE 14.3 HIGHEST STRENGTH LAMINATES UNDER {–10,0,0}, MN/m.

In Figure 14.4, we show the result of laminate ranking for pure shear.

No	Laminate		Limit			Limit*		Crit. Load	
	Layup	Repeat	relative	# plies	Ult/FPF	relative	# plies	Lmt.	Lmt*
1	35	16	1.95	250.5	1.53	1.99	246.5	1	1
2	44	17	1.91	256.2	1.17	1.91	256.2	1	1
3	53	18	1.8	272.3	1	1.8	272.3	1	1
4	134	18	1.74	280.6	1.36	1.74	280.6	1	1
13	2033	22	1.46	336.2	1.17	1.46	336.2	1	1

No	Laminate with Round off	# plies	R–Limit	R–Limit*	R–Ult
1	[(35) X 15 + (30)]S	246.0	1.00	1.00	1.50
2	[(44) X 16 + (1)]S	258.0	1.01	1.01	1.51
3	[(53) X 17 + (10)]S	274.0	1.01	1.01	1.51
4	[(134) X 17 + (4)]S	280.0	1.00	1.00	1.51

FIGURE 14.4   HIGHEST STRENGTH AND STIFFNESS LAMINATES UNDER
{0,0,10}, MN/m.

Two biaxial loadings cases are shown in Figures 14.5 and 14.6. The load is 1:2 biaxial membrane stress. In a cylindrical vessel, they are produced by internal and external pressures. For internal pressure, laminate [0233] is the best for strength, but due to the lack of 0 degree plies the axial stiffness is low.

No	Laminate		Limit		Ult/FPF	Limit*		Crit. Load	
	Layup	Repeat	relative	# plies		relative	# plies	Lmt.	Lmt*
1	233	12	1.35	179.6	1.67	1.23	161.4	1	1
2	3500	12	1.29	187.0	1.97	1.39	142.1	1	1
3	2411	12	1.29	187.9	1.96	1.38	144.0	1	1
4	1322	12	1.27	190.0	1.92	1.34	148.1	1	1
5	4400	14	1.15	210.9	1.89	1.18	167.7	1	1

No	Laminate with Round off	# plies	R–Limit	R–Limit*	R–Ult
1	[(233) X 11 + (200)]S	180.0	1.01	1.16	1.74
2	[(3500) X 11 + (500)]S	186.0	1.00	1.33	2.00
3	[(2411) X 11 + (411)]S	188.0	1.01	1.33	1.99
4	[(1322) X 11 + (322)]S	190.0	1.01	1.30	1.95
5	[(4400) X 13 + (100)]S	210.0	1.00	1.26	1.89

FIGURE 14.5 HIGHEST STRENGTH AND STIFFNESS LAMINATES UNDER INTERNAL PRESSURE OF A CYLINDRICAL VESSEL {5,10,0}, MN/m.

Biaxial compressive load laminates are different from those for biaxial tension (see Figure 14.6). A greater difference exists in the number of plies required; e.g., 52 plies for compression versus 180 plies for tension.

No	Laminate		Limit		Ult/FPF	Limit*		Crit. Load	
	Layup	Repeat	relative	# plies		relative	# plies	Lmt.	Lmt*
1	3500	4	1.91	51.6	1	1.91	51.6	1	1
2	2411	4	1.87	52.7	1	1.87	52.7	1	1
3	1322	4	1.78	55.6	1	1.78	55.6	1	1
4	2600	4	1.6	61.6	1	1.6	61.6	1	1
5	332	4	1.57	62.9	1	1.57	62.9	1	1

No	Laminate with Round off	# plies	R–Limit	R–Limit*	R–Ult
1	[(3500) X 3 + (200)]S	52.0	1.04	1.04	1.56
2	[(2411) X 3 + (200)]S	52.0	1.03	1.03	1.55
3	[(1322) X 3 + (200)]S	52.0	1.02	1.02	1.53
4	[(2600) X 3 + (2000)]S	52.0	1.01	1.01	1.52
5	[(332) X 3 + (2)]S	52.0	1.01	1.01	1.52

FIGURE 14.6 HIGHEST STRENGTH LAMINATES UNDER BIAXIAL COMPRESSION {–5,–10,0}, MN/m.

A truly combined or complex stresses {–10,2,3} in MN/m have all three components present, and is shown in Figures 14.7. For this particular loading, the advantage of using a composite material over an isotropic material is less than 20 percent. Yet, if the weight advantage of 40 percent over aluminum is considered, the composite material is still attractive.

14.7 MULTIPLE LOADS

Multiple loads can be viewed in several ways. Traditionally such an analysis considers different loads at a point in a structure. Each load corresponds to one of the conditions that the structure is likely to be exposed to during its manufacturing, installation, operation, or maintenance. Alternatively multiple loads can also be viewed as the variation of loads at different locations within a structure. Multiple load design can then provide a rational basis to select ply drop–off (change in number of plies) from point to point within a structure.

No	Laminate		Limit			Limit*		Crit. Load	
	Layup	Repeat	relative	# plies	Ult/FPF	relative	# plies	Lmt.	Lmt*
1	5030	14	1.52	209.7	1.72	1.74	183.4	1	1
2	4040	14	1.48	216.1	1.45	1.48	216.1	1	1
3	6020	15	1.35	236.3	2.02	1.82	175.7	1	1
4	5120	16	1.32	242.5	1.66	1.46	219.1	1	1
15	5111	18	1.14	281.1	1.38	1.14	281.1	1	1

No	Laminate with Round off	# plies	R–Limit	R–Limit*	R–Ult
1	[(5030) X 13 + (10)]S	210.0	1.00	1.14	1.71
2	[(4040) X 13 + (3000)]S	214.0	1.01	1.01	1.52
3	[(6020) X 14 + (3020)]S	234.0	1.00	1.33	2.00
4	[(5120) X 15 + (10)]S	242.0	1.01	1.10	1.65

FIGURE 14.7   HIGHEST STRENGTH LAMINATES UNDER {–10,2,3}, MN/m

We have mentioned repeatedly that the selection of laminates using the carpet plot method is not reliable. We will compare the combined stress example of the last section, {–10,2,3} (Figure 14.7), with the multiple load method. The carpet plot method assumes that a laminate sized from 3 independently operating stress; i.e.,

$$\{-10,0,0\}, \{0,2,0\}, \text{ and } \{0,0,3\} \quad \textbf{MN/m} \tag{14.2}$$

is the same as that sized from a combined stress state. The results of the three independent loads are shown in Figure 14.8. It is impossible to guess the ranking and the controlling load of the laminates.

No	Laminate		Limit			Limit*		Crit. Load	
	Layup	Repeat	relative	# plies	Ult/FPF	relative	# plies	Lmt.	Lmt*
1	3230	12	1.17	184.2	1	1.17	184.2	1	1
2	4130	12	1.15	187.2	1.54˙	1.18	182.3	3	3
3	4112	12	1.15	187.2	1.39	1.15	187.2	3	3
4	3212	12	1.15	187.7	1.34	1.15	187.7	3	3
10	3122	13	1.09	198.2	1	1.09	198.2	1	1

No	Laminate with Round off	# plies	R–Limit	R–Limit*	R–Ult
1	[(3230) X 11 + (2000)]S	180.0	1.01	1.01	1.52
2	[(4130) X 11 + (130)]S	184.0	1.01	1.05	1.57
3	[(4112) X 11 + (12)]S	182.0	1.02	1.02	1.53
4	[(3212) X 11 + (12)]S	182.0	1.02	1.02	1.53
10	[(3122) X 12 + (1100)]S	196.0	1.02	1.02	1.52

FIGURE 14.8   HIGHEST STRENGTH LAMINATES FOR MULTIPLE LOADS OF {10,0,0}, {0,2,0}, AND {0,0,3}, MN/m.

This example of a multiple load condition is intended to follow the rationale of netting analysis and the carpet plot. The implicit assumption in netting analysis and carpet plot is that loads do not interact. We can size laminates by one load or stress component at a time. But if the applied stresses act simultaneously, the laminate must be sized by considering the combined stresses. This is required by the laminated plate theory, and the results are shown in Figure 14.7. Among the top laminates, not a single laminate appear in common in both figures, Figures 14.7 and 14.8. Even for these laminates the number of plies required are entirely different. The approximation made by the carpet plot leads to serious errors, namely an unconservative estimate for the number of plies required.

14.8 DEEP BEAMS

The ranking method for multiple loads can be used to select the desired sublaminate for a deep beam, shown in Figure 14.9. The plane stress solution of this problem can be found in S. G. Lekhnitskii's *Anisotropic Plates*, second edition, pp 60–62 (Gordon and Breach, 1968). The notation and the coordinate axes are redefined here to conform to our system of notation and symbols.

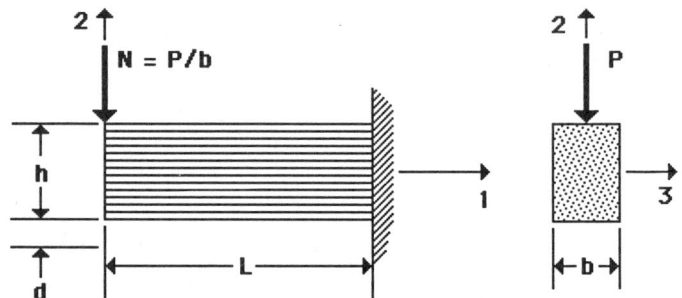

FIGURE 14.9   A CANTILEVER BEAM WITH END FORCE.

$$\sigma_1 = [12x^*y^* + \nu_{61}(12y^{*2} - 1)](N/h)$$

$$\sigma_2 = 0 \tag{14.3}$$

$$\sigma_6 = (3/2)[1 - 4y^{*2}](N/h)$$

where $x^* = x/h$, $x^{*(max)} = L/h$

$y^* = y/h$, $y^{*(max)} = 1/2$, $y^{*(min)} = -1/2$

$\nu_{61} = a_{61}/a_{11}$.

At top face: $\sigma_1^{(max)} = [6L/h + 2\nu_{61}](N/h)$, $\sigma_2 = \sigma_6 = 0$

At mid–plane: $\sigma_6^{(max)} = (3/2)(N/h)$, $\sigma_1 = \sigma_2 = 0$ \tag{14.4}

For our 165 laminates, given in Table 14.1 for the 8–ply, 4–angle sublaminate; the shear coupling coefficients are less than one. For beams with aspect ratios L/h greater than 5, the shear coupling contribution to the normal stress is negligible. The elementary strength of materials solution is adequate.

We can also show that the maximum deflection under the applied load is:

$$d = 4Na_{11}*(L/h)^3 \qquad (14.5)$$

where compliance $a_{11}*$ includes the contribution of every component of the stiffness matrix of the laminate.

By ignoring the shear coupling term in Equation 14.4, we can apply our ranking method for the design of a deep beam by assuming the following stress distribution at the root of the beam; i.e., $x_1 = L$:

at y = h/2, $N_1 = 10$ MN/m, $N_2 = N_6 = 0$

at y = –h/2, $N_1 = –10$MN/m, $N_2 = N_6 = 0$ (14.6)

at y = 0, $N_6 = 3$ MN/m, $N_1 = N_2 = 0$

The load variation across a beam is treated as a multiple load condition. The resulting laminate ranking based on strength is shown in Figure 14.10.

No	Laminate		Limit			Limit*		Crit. Load	
	Layup	Repeat	relative	# plies	Ult/FPF	relative	# plies	Lmt.	Lmt*
1	4112	12	1.45	187.2	1.39	1.19	187.2	2	2
2	5012	13	1.31	206.4	1.62	1.16	191.6	2	3
3	4220	13	1.31	206.5	1.97	1.42	157.0	1	1
4	3122	13	1.31	207.7	1.57	1.12	198.2	1	3
5	4130	13	1.3	208.0	1.71	1.22	182.3	1	2

No	Laminate with Round off	# plies	R–Limit	R–Limit*	R–Ult
1	[(4112) X 11 + (12)]S	182.0	1.02	1.02	1.53
2	[(5012) X 12 + (1010)]S	196.0	1.00	1.02	1.53
3	[(4220) X 12 + (4120)]S	206.0	1.01	1.32	1.99
4	[(3122) X 13 + (0)]S	208.0	1.00	1.05	1.57
5	[(4130) X 12 + (4000)]S	200.0	1.00	1.06	1.59

FIGURE 14.10 HIGHEST STRENGTH LAMINATE FOR A DEEP BEAM.

14.9 BENDING OF THIN WALL CONSTRUCTIONS

As mentioned earlier, multiple load design can also be applied to a variety of design problems, which includes the design of unsymmetric thin wall construction. The theory of this special construction has been covered in Section 9. We will now apply the laminate ranking method to this unsymmetric construction. The relation between the in–plane and flexural loads applied to the entire construction and the in–plane loads applied to the face sheets is shown in Equation 9.41 and repeated here:

$$\{N^+\} = \{N/2+M/h\}$$

$$\{N^-\} = \{N/2-M/h\}$$
(14.7)

If we only have applied moments,

$$\{N^+\} = -\{N^-\} = \{M\}/h \tag{14.8}$$

Because of the simple relation between N^+ and N^-, it is easy to apply the laminate ranking method for single or multiple moments by checking the strength ratios of both the top and bottom faces.

Such simple strength calculation is not applicable if we have simultaneously applied moments and in–plane loads. Then the in–plane loads applied to the top face are unrelated to those applied to the bottom face, not just a sign change as in Equation 14.8. But the laminate ranking method remains valid. The strength ratio or the number of plies required must be calculated separately for the top and the bottom faces.

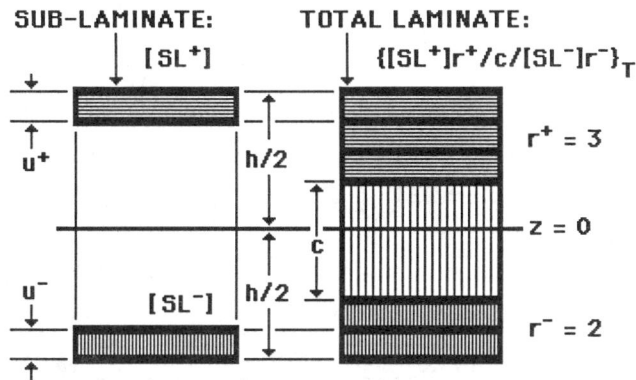

FIGURE 14.11   AN UNSYMMETRIC THIN WALL CONSTRUCTION WITH

In Figure 14.11, we show the unsymmetric thin wall construction. Note that the validity of the thin wall theory requires a thickness of core c nearly equal to the total thickness of the construction h. The superscript + and − refer to the top and the bottom face sheets. The sublaminates (SL^+ and SL^-) and repeating indices (r^+ and r^-) are shown. A sandwich core or a substructure of spars and ribs that is assumed to support the face sheets. If the construction is a "thick wall" variety, simple relations like those in Equations 14.7 and 14.8 are no longer valid.   A full laminated plate theory in place of the simplified one will be needed.

The case of a single applied moment is displayed in Figures 14.12 and 14.13 for the top and bottom faces respectively. We assume that the applied moment is resolved into a positive load of $\{10,0,-2\}$ MN/m at the top face; and an opposite load of $\{-10,0,2\}$ at the bottom face. Each face is ranked individually. The lightest structure would be the lightest top and bottom faces. But other constraints may dictate the use of face laminate other than the lightest. But for the particular case, the weight advantage of the lightest is 2x(61+57) = 236 plies. The number of plies must be doubled because both faces are symmetric laminates.

No	Laminate		Limit			Limit*		Crit. Load	
	Layup	Repeat	relative	# plies	Ult/FPF	relative	# plies	Lmt.	Lmt*
1	5012	12	1.58	179.7	1.69	1.41	159.2	1	1
2	4103	12	1.56	182.2	1.45	1.23	182.2	1	1
3	5102	12	1.55	183.0	1.6	1.31	171.5	1	1
4	4202	12	1.55	183.2	2.05	1.67	134.2	1	1
7	4022	12	1.5	188.7	1.96	1.55	144.5	1	1

No	Laminate with Round off	# plies	R–Limit	R–Limit*	R–Ult
1	[(5012) X 11 + (1010)]S	180.0	1.01	1.17	1.75
2	[(4103) X 11 + (100)]S	178.0	1.01	1.01	1.52
3	[(5102) X 11 + (102)]S	182.0	1.01	1.08	1.62
4	[(4202) X 11 + (1002)]S	182.0	1.01	1.34	2.01
7	[(4022) X 11 + (4001)]S	186.0	1.00	1.32	1.99

FIGURE 14.12   HIGHEST STRENGTH LAMINATES UNDER A SINGLE APPLIED MOMENT AT THE TOP FACE. THE EFFECTIVE LOAD IS {10,0,–2}.

No	Laminate		Limit			Limit*		Crit. Load	
	Layup	Repeat	relative	# plies	Ult/FPF	relative	# plies	Lmt.	Lmt*
1	3302	11	1.41	168.1	1	1.41	168.1	1	1
2	3203	11	1.38	171.9	1	1.38	171.9	1	1
3	5021	12	1.32	179.3	1.15	1.32	179.3	1	1
4	4202	12	1.3	181.6	1.07	1.3	181.6	1	1
10	6011	13	1.22	194.4	1.38	1.22	194.4	1	1

No	Laminate with Round off	# plies	R–Limit	R–Limit*	R–Ult
1	[(3302) X 10 + (102)]S	166.0	1.00	1.00	1.51
2	[(3203) X 10 + (3200)]S	170.0	1.00	1.00	1.50
3	[(5021) X 11 + (2000)]S	180.0	1.01	1.01	1.52
4	[(4202) X 11 + (2000)]S	180.0	1.00	1.00	1.50
10	[(6011) X 12 + (1)]S	194.0	1.03	1.03	1.55

FIGURE 14.13   HIGHEST STRENGTH LAMINATES UNDER A SINGLE APPLIED MOMENT AT THE BOTTOM FACE. THE EFFECTIVE LOAD IS {–10,0,2} IN MN/m.

If the applied moment is fully reversible, the required number of plies for both faces will have to be identical. The moment is resolved into two multiple loads of {10,0,–2} and {–10,0,2} in MN/m. The result of the ranking is shown in Figure 14.14. We see that the positive moment, the first load, is the controlling one for all top laminates. Complete stress reversals demand different laminates to sustain the moment.

No	Laminate		Limit			Limit*		Crit. Load	
	Layup	Repeat	relative	# plies	Ult/FPF	relative	# plies	Lmt.	Lmt*
1	4202	12	1.55	183.2	1.51	1.3	181.6	1	2
2	5102	12	1.51	187.6	1.5	1.26	187.6	2	2
3	5021	12	1.51	188.2	1.57	1.32	179.3	1	2
4	6011	13	1.46	194.4	1.38	1.22	194.4	2	2
5	4112	13	1.44	197.2	1.04	1.2	197.2	2	2

No	Laminate with Round off	# plies	R–Limit	R–Limit*	R–Ult
1	[(4202) X 11 + (2001)]S	182.0	1.00	1.01	1.51
2	[(5102) X 11 + (102)]S	182.0	1.01	1.02	1.52
3	[(5021) X 11 + (4001)]S	186.0	1.00	1.04	1.56
4	[(6011) X 12 + (1)]S	194.0	1.03	1.03	1.55
5	[(4112) X 12 + (2000)]S	196.0	1.01	1.01	1.51

FIGURE 14.14   HIGHEST STRENGTH LAMINATES FOR FULLY REVERSIBLE MOMENT.
THE EFFECTIVE IN–PLANE LOADS ARE MULTIPLE LOADS WITH THE
SAME MAGNITUDES AS THOSE IN FIGURES 14.12 AND 14.13.

In Figures 14.15 and 14.16 we show the case of designing two moments for
our thin wall construction. The multiple moments are not reversible. Thus
the loads imposed on the top face are {–4,2,1} and {7,0,1}. The opposite
loads will be applied to the bottom face; i.e., {4,–2,–1} and {–7,0,–1}.
The laminate ranking is applied individually. It is apparent that guessing will
be useless. The effects of the moments on the top and bottom faces are quite
different. The first moment controls most of the top laminates in the bottom
face; and the second moment, the top face.

No	Laminate		Limit			Limit*		Crit. Load	
	Layup	Repeat	relative	# plies	Ult/FPF	relative	# plies	Lmt.	Lmt*
1	5120	8	1.36	116.5	1.16	1.36	116.5	2	2
2	4211	8	1.34	118.6	1	1.34	118.6	2	2
3	3221	8	1.33	118.9	1	1.33	118.9	2	2
4	4130	8	1.24	127.4	1	1.24	127.4	2	2
5	3311	8	1.24	127.9	1	1.24	127.9	2	2

No	Laminate with Round off	# plies	R–Limit	R–Limit*	R–Ult
1	[(5120) X 7 + (1100)]S	116.0	1.01	1.01	1.51
2	[(4211) X 7 + (2010)]S	118.0	1.01	1.01	1.52
3	[(3221) X 7 + (3000)]S	118.0	1.02	1.02	1.53
4	[(4130) X 8 + (0)]S	128.0	1.01	1.01	1.51
5	[(3311) X 8 + (0)]S	128.0	1.00	1.00	1.50

FIGURE 14.15   HIGHEST STRENGTH LAMINATES FOR THE TOP FACE SUBJECTED TO
MULTIPLE RESOLVED MOMENTS OF {–4,2,1} AND {7,0,1}.

No	Laminate		Limit			Limit*		Crit. Load	
	Layup	Repeat	relative	# plies	Ult/FPF	relative	# plies	Lmt.	Lmt*
1	5120	7	1.81	107.3	1.51	1.49	106.6	2	1
2	4220	8	1.65	117.9	1.57	1.41	112.3	2	1
3	4130	8	1.6	121.2	1.24	1.31	121.2	1	1
4	4121	8	1.57	123.9	1.42	1.28	123.9	1	1
6	5111	9	1.41	137.6	1.81	1.39	114.2	1	1

No	Laminate with Round off		# plies	R–Limit	R–Limit*	R–Ult
1	[(5120) X	6 + (3120)]S	108.0	1.01	1.01	1.51
2	[(4220) X	7 + (2000)]S	116.0	1.00	1.05	1.58
3	[(4130) X	7 + (3100)]S	120.0	1.02	1.02	1.53
4	[(4121) X	7 + (3100)]S	120.0	1.00	1.00	1.50
6	[(5111) X	8 + (110)]S	132.0	1.02	1.18	1.77

FIGURE 14.16   HIGHEST STRENGTH LAMINATES FOR THE BOTTOM FACE
SUBJECTED TO MULTIPLE RESOLVED MOMENTS OF {4,–2,–1} AND
{–7,0,–1}.

The variation in the required ply number in the bottom face is again much less than that in the top face; i.e., 2X(58–51) = 14 versus 2X(85–59) = 52.

If the moments are reversible, totally or partially, the resulting in–plane loads applied to the top and bottom faces are treated as additional loads, in an identical manner as for the case shown in Figure 14.14.

It may be more economical to use the same laminate for the top and bottom faces. For this multiple load case, either the [4110] laminate can serve both faces with 2x(59+53) = 224 plies, or the [5111] laminate with 2x(66+51) = 234 plies.

14.10 SENSITIVITY OF RANKING PARAMETERS

The purpose of this section is to examine the sensitivity of various parameters of the laminate ranking method. Examples using both single and multiple complex loads are given. From these, some conclusions about the design of composite materials can be made.

NUMBER OF PLIES IN THE SUBLAMINATE

A sublaminate can vary from 2 to 10 plies. The symmetric hypothesis of the design process requires that the thickness of the laminate be atleast twice the thickness of its sublaminate. A question arises as to whether a small or a large sublaminate should be used. Figures 14.17 and 14.18 illustrate, for typical loads, the influence of the number of plies in the sublaminate. The loads used are defined as follows:

	N_1	N_2	N_6
Load 1	10	5	–2
Load 2	0	5	–2
Load 3	–3	0	4
Load 4	0	10	–4

Note that in Figure 14.17, single load conditions are considered. The angles are fixed to four orientations $[0/90/45/-45]_s$. The number of plies in the sublaminates vary from 6 to 10. For comparison, the solution provided by **CLASSIC**, an optimization program developed by Gerald V. Flanagan, and modified by Thierry N. Massard, is shown as horizontal lines. The theoretical plies (shown in the fourth column of the top table in Figure 14.1) are shown slightly higher than the CLASSIC lines. The practical plies are those without round off (shown in the third column of the top table in Figure 14.17). For these loads and laminates, the practical laminates require higher plies than the theoretical. But with the round off procedure described in Section 14.4, we have shown that the final laminate can be as low if not lower in ply number than the theoretical laminate. The laminated plate theory calculations are based on room temperature properties and do not include residual stresses.

The plies in the sublaminates did not drastically change the total number of plies in the final laminate. Therefore it is preferred to keep the number of plies in the sublaminate to a minimum. The implication is that the lower the plies in the sublaminate, the simpler the laminate, the lower the cost of fabrication, the fewer ply to consider for the ply drop off, and tougher the laminate.

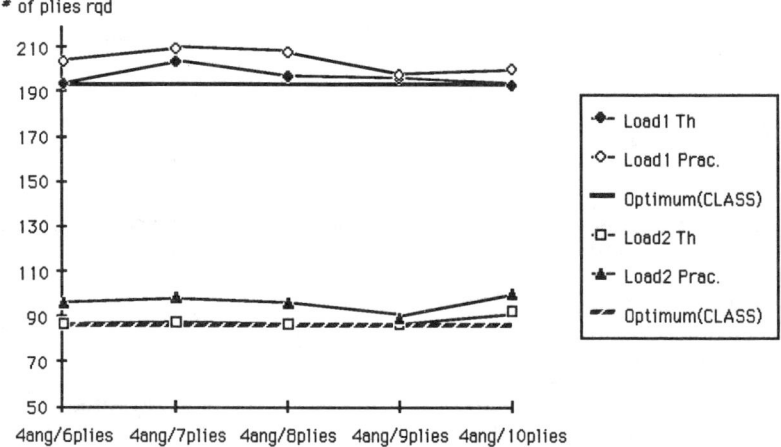

FIGURE 14.17 INFLUENCE OF THE NUMBER OF PLIES IN THE SUBLAMINATE ON THE DESIGN THICKNESS OF THE LAMINATE FOR TWO LOAD CASES: LOAD 1 {10,5,–2}, AND LOAD 2 {0,5,–2}.

In Figure 14.18, the lower curves are the results for a single load of {–3,0,4}, Load 3. Same comments can be made concerning the desirability of a 6–ply sublaminate over a 10–ply sublaminate. In the upper curves in Figure 14.18, a multiple loading condition is considered {10,5,–2} and {0,10,–4}, Load 1 and Load 4. The best is the 9–ply sublaminate. Even here the variations in the total number of plies are about 10 percent. For comparison, the solutions provided by **CLASSIC** are also shown as horizontal lines. Again with round off laminates, we can expect that the final laminate will be as low in the number of plies as the theoretical laminates.

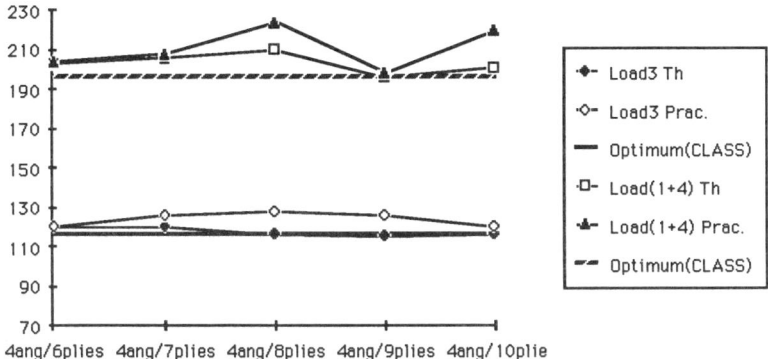

FIGURE 14.18 INFLUENCE OF THE NUMBER OF PLIES IN THE SUBLAMINATE ON THE DESIGN THICKNESS OF THE LAMINATE FOR TWO LOAD CASES (LOAD 3 AND LOAD 1 + LOAD 4).

Figures 14.17 and 14.18 confirm that the solution predicted by **CLASSIC**, an optimization method, is very nearly approximated by the theoretical laminate ranking method.

Most importantly it can be concluded that the number of plies in the sublaminate is not a critical parameter in the design process. Although the ratios between ply angle orientations may be different (not explicitly indicated in Figures 14.17 and 14.18), the total number of plies in the laminate required remains constant. As mentioned above that for practical reasons such as round off, edge effects, or manufacturing considerations, it might be better to work with smaller sublaminates.

NUMBER OF ORIENTATIONS IN THE SUBLAMINATE

The sublaminate families can include ply angles of any orientation. The number of orientations is limited, however, to four different angles. Figure 14.19 shows the influence of the number and selection of angles on the design requirements of two typical loads.

It can be observed that equivalent results are found using sublaminates consisting of three and four ply angles. Laminates comprised of only two angles, however, are severely penalized, presumably because of the inability to support shear loads. Again consistent with the results of Figures 14.17 and 14.18, it also appears that increasing the number of plies in the sublaminate has little effect on the total number of plies required for the laminate and cannot compensate for the lack of orientation.

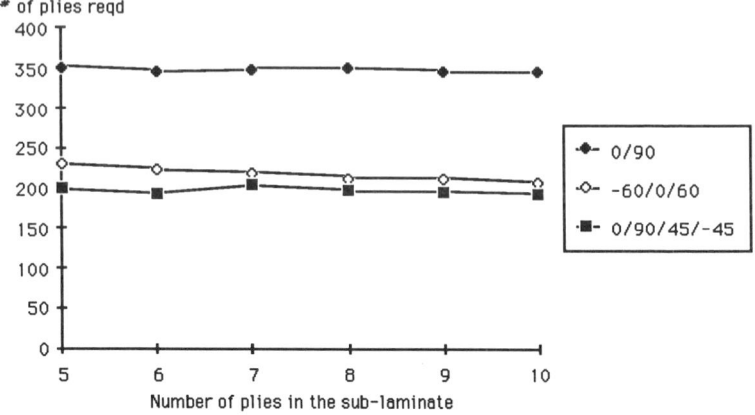

FIGURE 14.19 INFLUENCE OF NUMBER OF PLY GROUPS IN SUBLAMINATE.

ORIENTATION OF THE PLY ANGLES

Rigid body rotation of a given family of sublaminates

Figure 14.20 shows an example on the effect of rigid body rotation of an 8–ply family of sublaminates with $\pi/4$ orientations. The optimum sublaminates in the figure are identified for each angle of rotation. The ply angles refer to the original sublaminate.

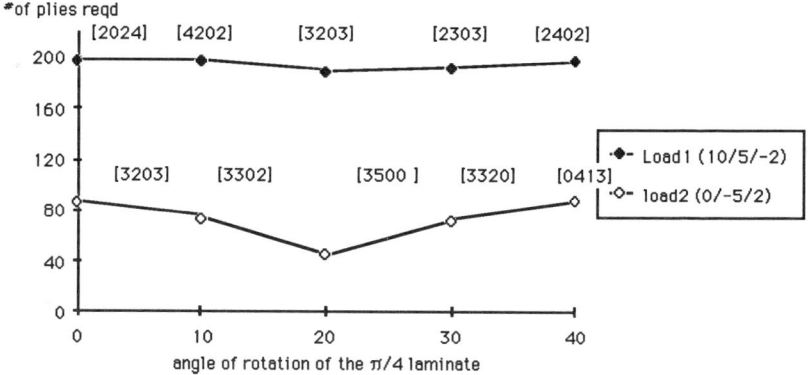

FIGURE 14.20 INFLUENCE OF RIGID BODY ROTATION ON 8–PLY SUBLAMINATES.

From Figure 14.20, it appears that the influence of the rigid body rotation is negligible. It must be emphasized that the laminate design is very different from one point to another, as indicated in this figure by the laminate code of each data point, even though the total ply thickness does not vary. Knowing that a composite material is by definition a higly oriented material, it can be foreseen that the choice of orientation is critical in the design process. Figure 14.20 shows, however, that it is not critical as long as a good optimization process is used to determine the right ratio between the different orientations.

Selection of q in [0/90/q/–q] sublaminates

Figure 14.21 shows the design for two typical load cases using the sublaminate [0/90/q/–q] where q varies between zero and 75 degrees. It can be seen that for Load 1 (the upper curve) the resulting laminate is nearly constant for five different orientations (q≠0). The design is independent of q. Although the total thickness of the laminate is constant, note that the layup may be significantly different according to the value of q (although not explicitly indicated in Figure 14.21). In the lower curve for Load 2, the variations in the ply number are greater than that of Load 1. It is a matter of many factors that dictate the sensitivity of the ranking parameter.

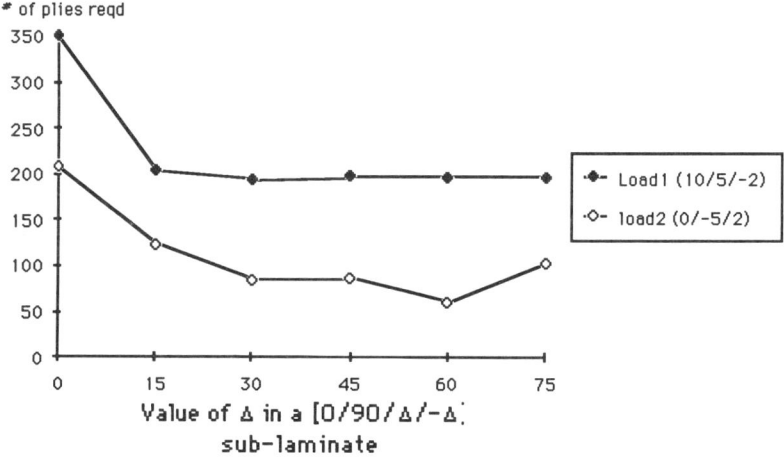

FIGURE 14.21 INFLUENCE OF θ IN [0/90/±45] SUBLAMINATE.

MATERIAL SELECTION

The most delicate choice in design is probably the material selection. A wide range of materials are available on the market. Technical and economic criteria have to be considered. Figure 14.22 shows the design thickness required to sustain a given complex load based on the limit strength, the ultimate strength, and a safety factor of 1.5 for eight different materials.

Figure 14.22 shows that the final design depends on the criteria chosen by the designer. The three criteria often lead to significantly different sublaminates. The difference between the number of plies required by the three criteria reflects how the different ratios of ply angle orientations affect the relationship of First–Ply–Failure and Last–Ply–Failure. For example, except for the fiberglass and the Kevlar system, the layup is very different between the First–Ply–Failure and the design Limit criteria. This can be explained by pointing out that high stiffness systems like graphite or boron are more affected by degradation than low stiffness systems.

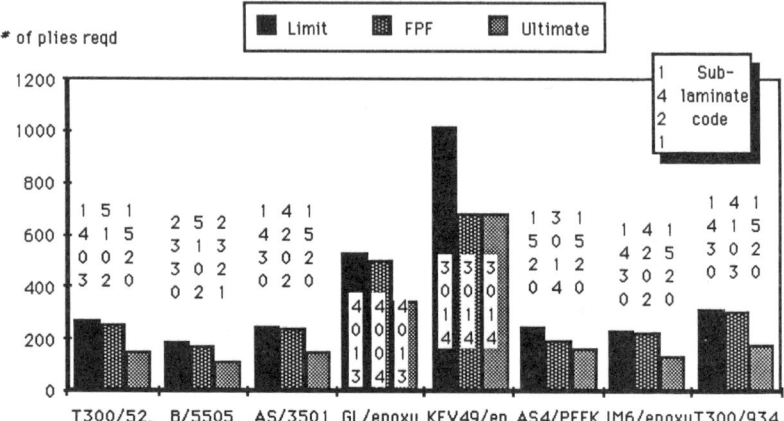

FIGURE 14.22 INFLUENCE OF MATERIAL SELECTION.

The large disparity in thickness among the different materials in Figure 14.22 clearly shows the importance of choosing the right material. Layup can be very different for different materials. Limit design calls for [1 4 0 3] for T300/5208 and [3 0 1 4] for Kevlar 49. Translating a laminate design from one material to another by some simple ratio inferred from comparing a presumably dominant property such as longitudinal strength or stiffness is erroneous. From this example it can be seen that high compressive loads can be better supported by off–axis reinforcement of Kevlar, while graphite is able to support the same type of loads by on–axis reinforcements.

A sophisticated analysis can be built from this method. For instance, economic considerations can be included by giving the cost to weight ratio of each material as a parameter of the design. Table 14.4 shows some typical product and manufacturing cost ratios. In Figure 14.23, the limit design for the same load considered in Figure 14.22 and the cost ratios shown in Table 14.4 are plotted as an efficiency value for each material. Figure 14.23 shows that the most cost effective design would be to use glass/epoxy (ignoring weight). Boron is the most expensive design (ignoring stiffness). It can also be observed that even though Kevlar is cheaper than graphite, Kevlar in this case is not as effective as the graphite designs.

14.11 CONCLUSIONS

We have shown that the ranking method can be viewed as an electronic carpet plot. This approach is reliable, consistent with the laminated plate theory, and, above all, easy to implement. The conventional carpet plot is not correct because strength under combined stresses cannot be analyzed as independent stresses. It cannot be done as a superposition of uniaxial and shear strengths. The unique feature of composites and the difficulties with the design process can often be traced to the externally applied combined stresses. We must learn to accept systematic calculation as the only reliable method. We are not aware of any shortcut.

TABLE 14.4 COST FOR DIFFERENT MATERIALS, RELATIVE TO COST FOR CFRP

Material		Cost*
graphite/epoxy	T300/N5208	1
boron/epoxy	B4/5505	5
graphite/epoxy	AS/3501	1
glass/epoxy	E-glass	0.2
Kevlar49/epoxy	Kev49/epoxy	0.5
graphite/epoxy	APC2	2
graphite/epoxy	IM6/epoxy	1.5
graphite/epoxy	T300/934	1

*   normalized by cost of graphite/epoxy

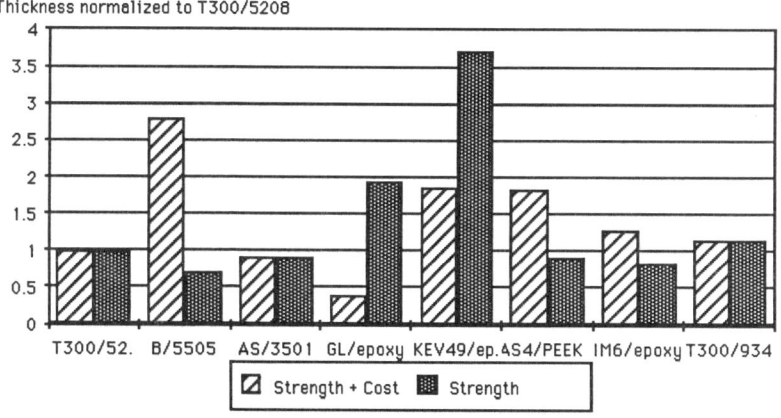

FIGURE 14.23 EFFICIENCY RATING CALCULATED AS THE COST (NORMALIZED TO COST OF CFRP T300/5208 SHOWN IN TABLE 14.12) PER UNIT STRENGTH AND THE STRENGTH RATIO AT FPF (NORMALIZED TO STRENGTH RATIO OF CFRP T300/5208) AS A FUNCTION OF THE MATERIAL SELECTION.

Laminate ranking is an alternative to conventional optimization methods and appears to be an emerging design tool of high potential. The number of sublaminates in each family is a function of the number of plies and the number of ply angle orientations in each sublaminate. A 165 laminate family of 8–ply sublaminates comprised of four angles (at 45 degree increments) is recommended.

Finally, single load design by a laminate ranking method can be combined with that by the principal stress method. The laminate selected from the ranking method can undergo a rigid body rotation or a sweep angle similar to that used in the principal stress method. The two methods are complementary.

We have shown a number of applications of the ranking method for single and multiple loads. It can be applied to the variation of loads at a point within a structure. It can also be applied to the variation of loads from point to point within a structure as a result of a single externally applied load. The deep beam is one example of this application.

We also show the application of multiple loads to the flexure of a thin wall construction. We only indicated the ranking method based on strength, but not on stiffness. First, there is no intrinsic limitation on the applicability of the method to flexure. We did not rank the stiffness because of the space limitation of our figures. Secondly, for the thin wall construction, the stiffness ranking for the in–plane loading is directly applicable. But, for the "thick wall" construction, the stacking sequence of the plies becomes important. Specific positions of the plies within a laminate have a strong influence on the stiffness and strength of the laminate. The present ranking method must be modified take into account the ply positions.

The multiple load approach can be extended to many other applications. Relatively simple extensions include tapered plates and hybrids. We believe that the fabrication of laminates can be simplified if tapered plates are built with repeating sublaminates. Such construction will be more damage tolerant because the maximum ply splicing is achieved. In addition such construction is easier to assemble and less prone to errors than the current practice of not using the repeating sublaminates.

Hybrids are used for two primary reasons; viz., to use a less costly composite, and to compensate for the weakness of a composite. The synergistic effects of hybrids have often been cited but are rarely explained systematically. We believe that opportunities exist for using the multiple load approach to examine the contribution of hybrids.

Many practicing engineers are bound by rules. The use of balanced laminate is one. The 10 percent rule is another. As a simple interpretation of this rule, a 10–ply sublaminate with fully populated laminate codes is recommended; i.e., having at least one ply in every ply orientation. Then there are attempts to further simply the carpet plot or the transformation equations of orthotropic plies. We believe that the rules are arbitrary and serve no purpose. The ranking method is quicker and certainly more reliable than unwarranted shortcuts. The examples of the sensitivities of various laminate parameters can provide designer with much needed information to lead to effective use of composite materials.

Section 15

RESIDUAL STRESSES AND STRAINS

15.1 RESIDUAL STRESSES

Organic and inorganic matrix composites will have very complicated residual stresses after processing or curing. On the micromechanical level, processing or curing stresses are caused by the volumetric contraction of the matrix, the differential thermal contraction between the matrix and the fiber after cooldown, and nonuniform consolidation or solidification. For organic matrix composites, moisture is absorbed which further complicates the residual stresses. The effects of these stresses are difficult to assess and cannot be measured directly. The empirically measured ply strengths are very much affected by the residual stresses. The effects are, in fact, reflected in the measured strengths. Until reliable predictions of strength based on micromechanics become available, we will back–calculate residual stresses from the temperature–dependent strength data.

Another type of residual stresses originates from the macromechanical or laminate level. Because composite plies are anisotropic, the thermal contraction in the longitudinal direction is much less than that in the transverse direction. This differential contraction after cooldown, and expansion after moisture absorption will give rise to macromechanical residual stresses. Using the laminated plate theory, these stresses are relatively easy to calculate.

We are only concerned with the macromechanical residual stresses in this section. We assume that temperatures before and after curing and moisture absorbed after curing remain uniform across the laminate thickness. We can extend the theory to deal with a linearly varying temperature across a symmetric plate as a special case.

15.2 FREE HYGROTHERMAL EXPANSION

The stress–free expansion of a unidirectional ply is shown in Figure 15.1. The on–axis expansions, e_x and e_y, of a ply are:

$$e_x = \alpha_x \Delta T + \beta_x c$$

$$e_y = \alpha_y \Delta T + \beta_y c$$

(15.1)

where α_i = thermal expansion coefficients.

β_i = moisture expansion coefficients.

ΔT = room (or operating) temperature – cure temperature.

c = moisture content.

The Equation 15.1 is referred to the on– or ply–axes, which differ from the laminate axes.

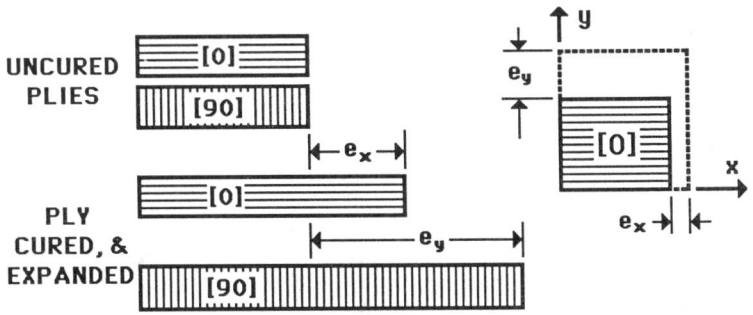

FIGURE 15.1   STRESS–FREE EXPANSIONS OF A UNIDIRECTIONAL PLY. THE
REFERENCE STATE IS UNCURED PLIES AT CURE TEMPERATURE; THE
EXPANDED STATE IS BASED ON DIFFERENCES IN TEMPERATURE AND
MOISTURE CONTENT AFTER CURING.

15.3 PLY STRENGTH AFTER EXPANSION

Strengths of unidirectional composites are commonly measured after cooldown and possible exposure to moisture. While temperature is usually uniform within the composite, the moisture is almost always nonuniform. The slow diffusion of moisture is responsible for this nonuniformity. The measured strength or the corresponding ultimate strain is depicted in Figure 15.2.   The strain from the original stress–free state at the cure temperature must be the sum of the free expansional and the measured mechanically applied strain at room temperature.

15.4 RESIDUAL STRAINS AFTER CURING

The curing of a multidirectional laminate induces macromechanical curing stresses. This is shown in Figure 15.3. Although the laminate in this figure is a simple cross–ply, the principle is applicable to all laminates. The mathematical formulation in this section is approximate because the process of curing of an organic matrix is in general time–dependent and nonlinear. We use only time–independent, linear theory.   One simple way to compensate this deficiency is to use the stress–free temperature in place of the actual cure temperature. We have found that the stress–free temperature can be as much as 30 degree C below the cure temperature. The simplest method of determining the stress–free temperature is to observe the elevated temperature at with a warped unsymmetric laminate becomes flat.

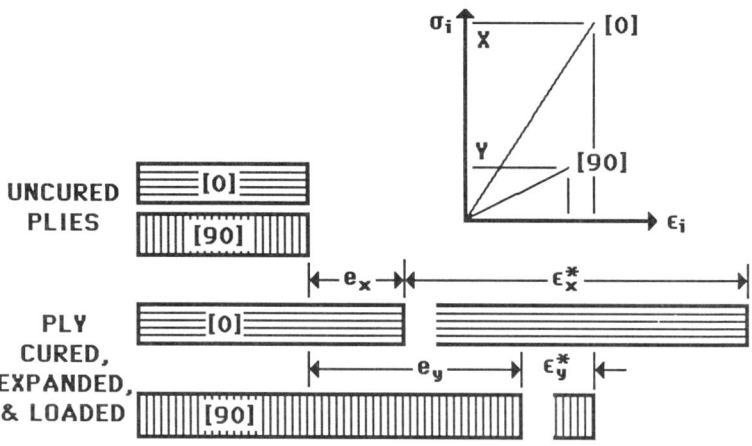

FIGURE 15.2   MEASURED ULTIMATE STRAINS AFTER FREE HYGROTHERMAL
EXPANSION OR CONTRACTION.

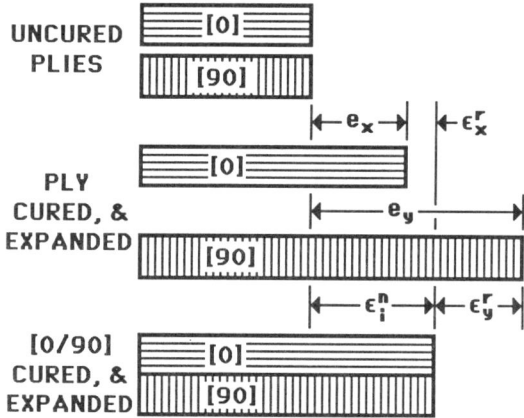

FIGURE 15.3   RELATION BETWEEN NONMECHANICAL, RESIDUAL, AND FREE
EXPANSIONAL STRAINS AS DEFINED IN EQUATION 15.9 WHERE ALL
THE STRAINS ARE IN–PLANE AND RELATIVE TO THE MATERIAL
AXES. THE LAMINATE IS SYMMETRIC.

In order for the strain components to be additive in Figure 15.3, they all
must be in the on– or symmetry axes of the plies. The nonmechanical strain
is the laminate strain measured from the stress–free state. The residual strain
is simply the difference between the nonmechanical strain and the free
expansional strain. We will now derive these strains from the laminated plate
theory.

The nonmechanical stresses are derived from the nonmechanical strains given in Equation 15.1:

$$\sigma_i^n = Q_{ij} e_j \qquad (15.2)$$

For the on– or symmetry–axis of each ply:

$$\sigma_x^n = Q_{xx} e_x + Q_{xy} e_y$$
$$\sigma_y^n = Q_{yx} e_x + Q_{yy} e_y \qquad (15.3)$$

For a on–axis orthotropic material, there is no nonmechanical shear stress.

The transformed nonmechanical stress from the ply– to the laminate–axis:

$$\sigma_1^n = p^n + q^n \cos 2\theta$$
$$\sigma_2^n = p^n - q^n \cos 2\theta \qquad (15.4)$$
$$\sigma_6^n = q^n \sin 2\theta$$

where $\quad p^n = [\sigma_x^n + \sigma_y^n]/2 = [(Q_{xx} + Q_{xy}) e_x + (Q_{xy} + Q_{yy}) e_y]/2$

$$q^n = [\sigma_x^n - \sigma_y^n]/2 = [(Q_{xx} - Q_{xy}) e_x + (Q_{xy} - Q_{yy}) e_y]/2 \qquad (15.5)$$

We can now derive the nonmechanical stress components:

$$\sigma_1^{(o)n} = N_1^n/h = (1/h) \int \sigma_1^n dz = p^n + q^n V_1^*$$

$$\sigma_2^{(o)n} = N_2^n/h = (1/h) \int \sigma_2^n dz = p^n - q^n V_1^* \qquad (15.6)$$

$$\sigma_6^{(o)n} = N_6^n/h = (1/h) \int \sigma_6^n dz = q^n V_3^*$$

where V_1^* and V_2^* are defined in Equations 7.18 and 7.19, and repeated as follows:

$$V_1^* = (1/h) \int_{-h/2}^{h/2} \cos 2\theta dz, \quad V_3^* = (1/h) \int_{-h/2}^{h/2} \sin 2\theta dz \qquad (15.7)$$

We use this multiple–angle formulation because the V_1 and V_3 are needed for the in–plane stiffness of any laminate and may have already been calculated. If we limit this calculation to symmetric laminates, the nonmechanical in–plane strains shown in Figure 15.3 are:

$$\varepsilon_i^{(o)n} = a_{ij} N_j^n \qquad (15.8)$$

Residual in–plane strains are:

$$\varepsilon_i^{(o)r} = \varepsilon_i^{(o)n} - e_i, \qquad i = x, y, s \qquad (15.9)$$

The strains here are in the on– or symmetry–axis, not in the laminate–axis; i.e.,

$$\varepsilon_x^{(o)r} = \varepsilon_x^{(o)n} - e_x$$

$$\varepsilon_y^{(o)r} = \varepsilon_y^{(o)n} - e_y \quad\quad (15.10)$$

$$\varepsilon_s^{(o)r} = \varepsilon_s^{(o)n}$$

The residual strain is a function of ΔT (usually negative) and moisture c. If both are zero, the residual strain is of course zero. If we have a unidirectional composite (no lamination), the residual strain is also zero.

If the operating temperature is equal to the cure temperature, ΔT is zero. There will be no residual strain due to curing. In this case, the residual strain due to moisture will be a linear function of the moisture content c. If moisture content is zero, the residual strain will be a linear function of ΔT. If both ΔT and c are not zero, the residual strain will be a nonlinear function. This nonlinearity is important if we wish to calculate the "self–destruct" temperature or moisture level.

15.5 EXPANSION COEFFICIENTS

The effective in–plane expansion coefficients are formulated by assuming either ΔT or c is zero; i.e., the free expansion is computed by assuming that it is either due to temperature or moisture, but not both:

$$\alpha_i^o = a_{ij} \int_{-h/2}^{h/2} Q_{jk}\alpha_k dz \quad\quad (15.11)$$

$$\beta_i^o = a_{ij} \int_{-h/2}^{h/2} Q_{jk}\beta_k dz \qu\quad (15.12)$$

For a laminate the nonmechanical or expansional in–plane strain is analogous to that for the ply in Equation 15.1:

$$\varepsilon_i^{(o)n} = \alpha_i^o \Delta T + \beta_i^o c \qu\quad (15.13)$$

where $i = 1, 2, 6$. These laminate expansions can be positive, zero, and negative, and can induce shear by having nonzero 6–components. By properly designing the laminate layup, unique expansional behavior is possible.

15.6 PLY FAILURES AND STRENGTH RATIOS

The strain that will determine the failure of a ply in a laminate is the total strain which can be defined as the sum of the mechanical and residual strains. The residual strain is in turn related to the nonmechanical and expansional strains as follows:

$$\varepsilon_i{}^* \geq \varepsilon_i{}^{total} = \varepsilon_i{}^m + \varepsilon_i{}^r = \varepsilon_i{}^m + \varepsilon_i{}^n - e_i \qquad (15.14)$$

A graphical representation of these relations are shown in Figure 15.4. The mechanical strains corresponding to the failure or maximum strains of the 0– and 90–degree plies are shown in this figure. Residual strains must be added or subtracted from the mechanical strains in order to determine the total strain, like Equation 15.14.

The first, last and intermediate ply failures, described in Figure 12.4, are shown again here in Figure 15.5. We wish to emphasize again that the first–ply–failure calculation is reliable and internally consistent with the laminated plate theory, but the ply failures after the FPF, including the last–ply–failure, are semi–empirical and, therefore, approximate.

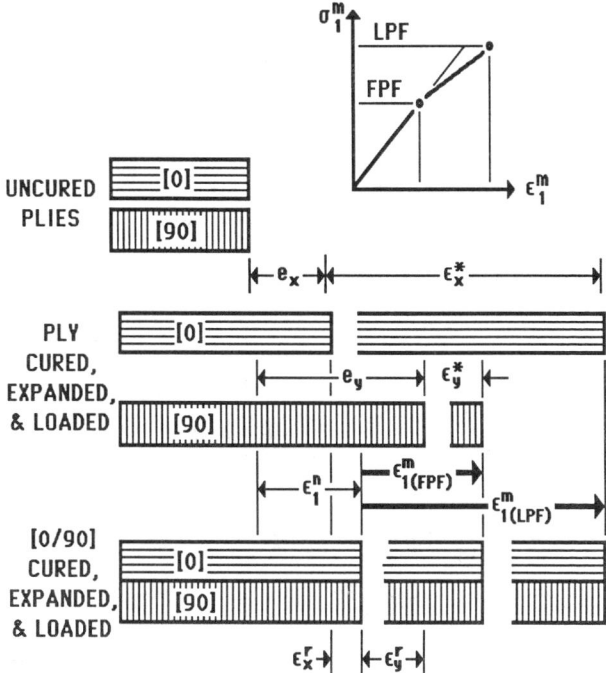

FIGURE 15.4   MECHANICALLY APPLIED STRAINS TO A LAMINATE ARE SHOWN TO HAVE REACHED THE MAXIMUM STRAINS HERE.

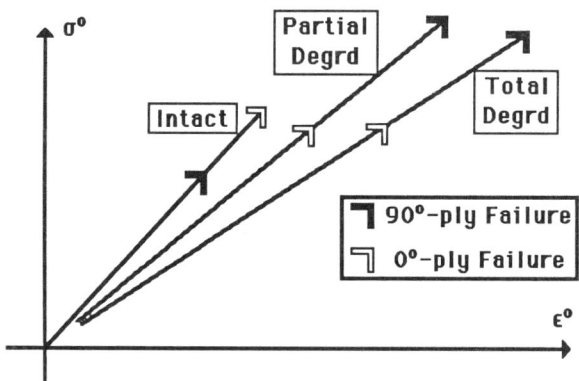

FIGURE 15.5   STRESS–STRAIN CURVES OF A [0/90] LAMINATE WITH VARYING
DEGREE OF DEGRADATION. SAME AS FIGURE 12.4.

Before we apply the failure criteria, we need to define strength ratio again. The failure strain in Equation 15.14 consists of two components: the mechanical and residual strains.   In the last Section (Section 15.5), we discussed the relations between the residual strain, and ΔT and c.   It is not appropriate to define a strength ratio for the total strain because mechanical loads, temperature and moisture do not vary proportionally at the same time. We can have several strength ratios:

R^m, the mechanical strength ratio, from which the maximum mechanical load can be computed. ΔT and c can be arbitrary, but have fixed values.

R^t, the thermal strength ratio, from which the self–destruct temperature can be computed.   Mechanical load and moisture content should be held fixed.

R^c, the moisture strength ratio, from which the self–destruct moisture content can be computed.   The mechanical load and ΔT should be held fixed.

R^r, the residual strength ratio, which we will use here to designate either the thermal or moisture strength ratio.   This takes the place of R^t or R^c, and will be used in subsequent derivation.

For the present, we will use only the mechanical and residual strength ratios and apply the following strain to both the quadratic and maximum strain failure criteria:

$$\varepsilon_i^* = \varepsilon_i^{max} = R^m\varepsilon_i^m + R^r\varepsilon_i^r \qquad (15.15)$$

The most general failure criterion with both mechanical and residual stresses is a generalization of the quadratic failure criterion in strain space shown in Equation 11.17.

$$G_{ij}(R^m\varepsilon_i^m + R^r\varepsilon_i^r)(R^m\varepsilon_j^m + R^r\varepsilon_j^r) + G_i(R^m\varepsilon_i^m + R^r\varepsilon_i^r) - 1 = 0 \qquad (15.16)$$

We can solve this quadratic equation for only one strength/stress ratio at a time; i.e., setting one strength ratio equal to unity and solving for the other. It is convenient to define the following scalar products similar to those in Equation 11.19 for simpler representation of the quadratic solutions, where the superscripts m and r designate mechanical and residual, respectively, and superscript mix, the mixture or cross–multiplication products of m and r:

$$a^m = G_{xx}(\varepsilon_x{}^m)^2 + 2G_{xy}\varepsilon_x{}^m\varepsilon_y{}^m + G_{yy}(\varepsilon_y{}^m)^2 + G_{ss}(\varepsilon_s{}^m)^2$$

$$a^r = G_{xx}(\varepsilon_x{}^r)^2 + 2\ G_{xy}\varepsilon_x{}^r\varepsilon_y{}^r + G_{yy}(\varepsilon_y{}^r)^2 + G_{ss}(\varepsilon_s{}^r)^2$$

$$b^m = G_x\varepsilon_x{}^m + G_y\varepsilon_y{}^m + G_s\varepsilon_s{}^m$$

$$b^{mix} = 2\Big[G_{xx}\varepsilon_x{}^m\varepsilon_x{}^r + G_{xy}\varepsilon_x{}^m\varepsilon_y{}^r + G_{xy}\varepsilon_y{}^m\varepsilon_x{}^r + G_{yy}\varepsilon_y{}^m\varepsilon_y{}^r$$
$$+ G_{ss}\varepsilon_s{}^m\varepsilon_s{}^r\Big]$$

$$b^r = G_x\varepsilon_x{}^r + G_y\varepsilon_y{}^r + G_s\varepsilon_s{}^r$$

(15.17)

15.7 QUADRATIC CRITERION FOR MAXIMUM MECHANICAL STRESS WITH RESIDUAL STRAINS

Equation 15.16 is solved for $\mathbf{R^m}$ while holding $\mathbf{R^r = 1}$. This case corresponds to the strength analysis of the mechanically applied stress at specified levels of temperature and moisture.

$$a(R^m)^2 + bR^m + c = 0 \tag{15.18}$$

$$R^m = [(b/2a)^2 - c/a]^{1/2} - (b/2a) \tag{15.19}$$

where $a = a^m$

$$b = b^{sum} = b^m + b^{mix} = \Big[G_x\varepsilon_x{}^m + G_y\varepsilon_y{}^m\Big] + \Big\{2\Big[G_{xx}\varepsilon_x{}^m\varepsilon_x{}^r$$
$$+ G_{xy}\varepsilon_x{}^m\varepsilon_y{}^r + G_{xy}\varepsilon_y{}^m\varepsilon_x{}^r + G_{yy}\varepsilon_y{}^m\varepsilon_y{}^r + G_{ss}\varepsilon_s{}^m\varepsilon_s{}^r\Big]\Big\} \tag{15.20}$$

$$c = -1 + a^r + b^r = -1 + \Big[G_{xx}(\varepsilon_x{}^r)^2 + 2\ G_{xy}\varepsilon_x{}^r\varepsilon_y{}^r + G_{yy}(\varepsilon_y{}^r)^2$$
$$+ G_{ss}(\varepsilon_s{}^r)^2\Big] + \Big[G_x\varepsilon_x{}^r + G_y\varepsilon_y{}^r + G_s\varepsilon_s{}^r\Big] \tag{15.21}$$

15.8 QUADRATIC CRITERION FOR MAXIMUM RESIDUAL STRESS

Equation 15.16 is solved for R^r while holding $R^m = 1$. This case corresponds to the strength analysis of the residual stress at a specified mechanical stress. The residual stress is due to either temperature or moisture, but not both.

$$a(R^r)^2 + bR^r + c = 0 \tag{15.22}$$

where $a = a^r$

$b = b^r + b^{mix}$

$c = -1 + a^m + b^m$

Note that the scalar products are defined in Equation 15.17 as before. Note also that the superscripts m and r are simply interchanged for the R^m and R^r calculations.

If mechanical stress is zero (no externally applied stress), the maximum temperature or moisture that would lead to a self–destruct level is simply the quadratic root of Equation 15.22 with

$$a = a^r, \quad b = b^r, \quad c = -1 \tag{15.23}$$

15.9 MAXIMUM STRAIN CRITERION FOR MECHANICAL STRESS WITH RESIDUAL STRESSES

Instead of the quadratic criterion which involves many cross product terms, the maximum strain criterion may be simpler to use. In place of Equation 10.8, we have:

$$R_x = (\varepsilon_x{}^* - \varepsilon_x{}^r)/\varepsilon_x{}^m = (\varepsilon_x{}^* - \varepsilon_x{}^n + e_x)/\varepsilon_x{}^m$$

$$\text{if } \varepsilon_x{}^m > 0, \text{ or}$$

$$R_x{}' = (\varepsilon_x{}^{*'} - \varepsilon_x{}^r)/|\varepsilon_x{}^m| = (\varepsilon_x{}^{*'} - \varepsilon_x{}^n + e_x)/|\varepsilon_x{}^m| \tag{15.24}$$

$$\text{if } \varepsilon_x{}^m < 0$$

$$R_y = (\varepsilon_x{}^* - \varepsilon_y{}^r)/\varepsilon_y{}^m = (\varepsilon_y{}^* - \varepsilon_y{}^n + e_y)/\varepsilon_y{}^m$$

$$\text{if } \varepsilon_y{}^m > 0, \text{ or}$$

$$R_y{}' = (\varepsilon_x{}^{*'} - \varepsilon_y{}^r)/|\varepsilon_y{}^m| = (\varepsilon_y{}^{*'} - \varepsilon_y{}^n + e_y)/|\varepsilon_y{}^m| \tag{15.25}$$

$$\text{if } \varepsilon_y{}^m < 0$$

$$R_s = (\varepsilon_s{}^* - \varepsilon_s{}^r)/|\varepsilon_s{}^m| = (\varepsilon_s{}^* - \varepsilon_s{}^n)/|\varepsilon_s{}^m| \tag{15.26}$$

15.10 SIGNIFICANCE OF RESIDUAL STRESSES

In order to assess the effects of residual stresses on the failure of composite materials, we must know the hygrothermal expansion coefficients. Typical values are shown in Table 15.1. The elastic constants of the materials in this table can be found in Table 6.5.

TABLE 15.1 HYGROTHERMAL EXPANSION COEFFICIENTS FOR TYPICAL COMPOSITE MATERIALS

Ply Material	T300/ 5208	B/ 5505	AS/ 3501	Scotch 1002	Kevlar/ epoxy
α_x, μ/K	0.02	6.1	–0.3	8.6	–4.0
α_y, μ/K	22.5	30.3	28.1	22.1	79.0
β_x	0.0	0.0	0.0	0.0	0.0
β_y	0.6	0.6	0.44	0.6	0.6

As a sample calculation of the residual stresses, the following data for CFRP T300/5208 are used:

• Elastic modulus listed in Table 6.5.
• Strength data listed in Table 11.1 for the case of $F_{xy}^* = -0.5$.
• Expansion coefficients:

$$\alpha_x = 0.02 \times 10^{-6}/K, \quad \alpha_y = 22.5 \times 10^{-6}/K$$
$$\beta_x = 0, \quad \beta_y = 0.6$$

(15.27)

In Figure 15.6, we plot the effects of cure temperature and moisture content on the limit and ultimate strength envelopes of the CFRP $\pi/4$ laminate. These envelopes follow the same method used in those shown in Section 12. In this figure, we show the limit envelope on the right hand side; the ultimate, the left hand side.

Three cases are shown. First is the case when residual stress is ignored. This corresponds to zero temperature difference between the cure and operation temperature, and zero moisture.

The second case is dry, defined by a –100 degree C temperature difference, and zero moisture. This dry state is representative of a freshly cure laminate which still does not have time for moisture absorption. It can also represent a long time service in space when all moisture may have escaped.

The third case is wet, defined by a –100 degree C temperature difference, and 0.005 or 0.5 percent moisture content. This moisture is the saturation level of many epoxy matrix materials. This wet state represent a long time exposure of organic matrix composite materials on earth.

The results in Figure 15.6 show that if the curing stress is ignored in the design calculation, it is unsafe for the dry state, but conservative for the wet state. The effect of residual stress on the limit envelope is more severe than that on the ultimate.

The residual stress effect of moisture can reduce or cancel that of the cure temperature. For room temperature operation of CFRP T300/5208, the residual stress is canceled at about 0.3 percent for cure temperatures up to 100°C, and about 0.8 percent for temperatures up to 150°C.

For applications in space, for example, where moisture is zero initially or in the long run of a wet composite, cure temperature should be kept as low as possible.

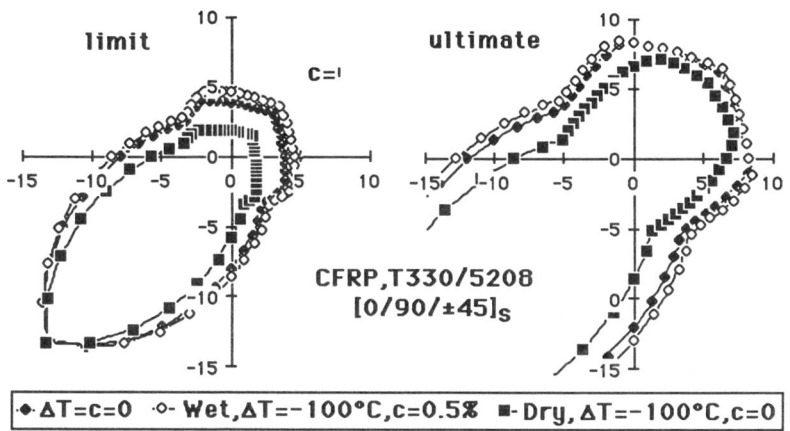

FIGURE 15.6 EFFECT OF CURE TEMPERATURE AND MOISTURE CONTENT ON THE LIMIT AND ULTIMATE STRENGTH ENVELOPES OF [π/4] CFRP.

Although moisture is beneficial as an agent to offset the curing stresses, this is not always true if the moisture distribution is highly nonuniform.

Moisture diffusion is several orders of magnitude slower than that of temperature. Moisture absorption is like filling a huge reservoir with a small pump. The water level stays nearly constant and can change only very slowly with time. Moisture desorption or dehydration is the same time–consuming process except that the process is reversed. For the assessment of the long term effects of moisture and temperature we have assumed that both moisture and temperature distributions are uniform across the laminate. The calculation of the residual stresses is made with this assumption.

For long term applications of organic matrix composite materials, nonuniform moisture distribution occurs in the one or two plies on the surface of the laminate. The moisture content there tries to adjust to the ambient condition. It therefore fluctuates as the environment fluctuates. But in the interior of the laminate, the moisture migration is slow and does not fluctuate. Instead, it moves slowly along the gradient of moisture concentration. The figures above are intended to describe the long time behavior of laminates. The outer surface plies are assumed to be of transient nature only and have no major effect on the bulk properties of the laminate.

For laminates with only a few plies, the assumed constant moisture content may have to be modified.

In Figure 15.7 we show the effects of curing for a [0/45/–45] laminate of the same material and conditions as those in the last figure. The trend remains the same. The effect on the limit envelope for a dry laminate appears to be more severe than that on the π/4 laminate.

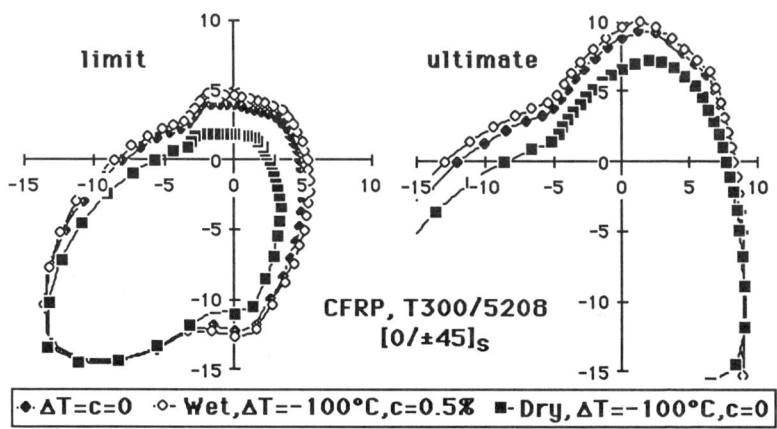

FIGURE 15.7 EFFECT OF CURE TEMPERATURE AND MOISTURE CONTENT ON THE LIMIT AND ULTIMATE STRENGTH ENVELOPES OF [0/45/–45] CFRP.

In Figure 15.8 we show the effects of curing for a π/4 laminate of GFRP Scotchply and conditions similar to those of the last two figures. The expansion-coefficients of this GFRP can be found in Table 15.1 above. The trend again remains the same. The effect on the limit envelope for a dry laminate appears to be more severe than that on the CFRP π/4 laminate.

15.11 PLY STRESS WITH RESIDUAL STRESSES

If residual stresses are to be included in the calculation of the ply stress we must be certain that equilibrium is satisfied. From Equation 15.14,

$$\{\varepsilon\}^{total} = \{\varepsilon^m + \varepsilon^r\} = \{\varepsilon^m + \varepsilon^n - e\} \tag{15.28}$$

The ply stress with the i–th ply angle will be:

$$\{\sigma\}^{(i)} = [Q]^{(i)}\{\varepsilon\}^{total} = [Q]^{(i)}\{\varepsilon^m + \varepsilon^r\} \tag{15.29}$$

The numerical example of ply stress calculation without residual stresses was given in Section 7.12. The same laminate under the same applied stress resultant will be calculated with residual stresses in a sample problem given at the end of this section. Again we must emphasize that the sum of various strains in the last two equations must share the common coordinate axes. If the on–axis free expansions in Equation 15.1 are used, the other strain such as the mechanical and nonmechanical strains must also be the on–axis strains.

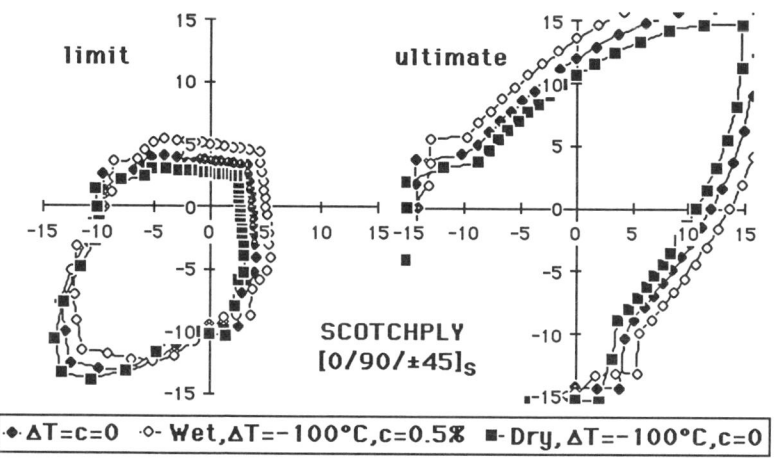

FIGURE 15.8 EFFECT OF CURE TEMPERATURE AND MOISTURE CONTENT ON THE LIMIT AND ULTIMATE STRENGTH ENVELOPES OF [π/4] GFRP.

15.12 SIGNIFICANCE OF TEMPERATURE GRADIENTS

For a nonuniform temperature distribution across the laminate thickness, we can use the same laminated plate theory, and the linear thermoelastic relation of Equation 15.1.   A linear temperature distribution is an accurate approximation for one–dimensional heat conduction across the laminate. Let the temperature distribution shown in Figure 15.9 be:

$$T = \Delta T + (2\delta T/h)z \tag{15.30}$$

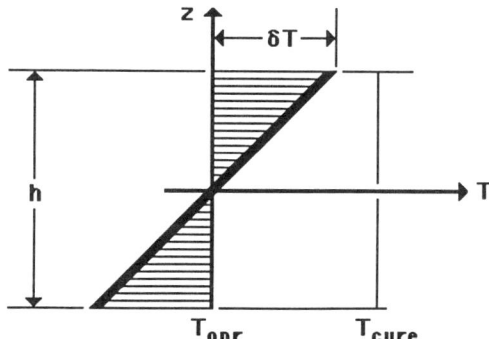

FIGURE 15.9 LINEAR TEMPERATURE GRADIENT ACROSS LAMINATE.

where $\Delta T = T_{opr} - T_{cure}$

δT = (temperature gradient)/2

In place of Equation 15.1, we have

$$\{e\} = \{\alpha\}[\Delta T + (2\delta T/h)z] + \{\beta\}c \tag{15.31}$$

From Equation 7.4 or 15.6

$$\{N\}^n = \int \{\sigma\}^n dz = \int [Q]\{e\} dz$$

$$= \left[\int [Q]\{\alpha\} dz\right] \Delta T + \left[\int [Q]\{\alpha\} z dz\right](2\delta T/h)$$

$$+ \left[\int [Q]\{\beta\} dz\right]c \tag{15.32}$$

For symmetric laminates $\int [Q]\{\alpha\} z dz = 0$ (15.33)

Therefore $\{\varepsilon^o\}^n = [a]\{N\}^n$

$$= \left\{ [a] \int [Q]\{\alpha\} dz \right\} \Delta T + \left\{ [a] \int [Q]\{\beta\} dz \right\} c$$

$$= \{\alpha^o\}\Delta T + \{\beta^o\}c \tag{15.34}$$

$$\{M\}^n = \int \{\sigma\}^n z dz = \int [Q]\{\varepsilon\}^n z dz$$

$$= \left[\int [Q]\{\alpha\} z dz\right] \Delta T + \left[\int [Q]\{\alpha\} z^2 dz\right](2\delta T/h)$$

$$+ \left[\int [Q]\{\beta\} z dz\right]c \tag{15.35}$$

For symmetric laminates $\int [Q]\{a\} z dz = \int [Q]\{\beta\} z dz = 0$ (15.36)

Therefore $\{k\}^n = [d]\{M\}^n$ (15.37)

where $\{M\}^n = \left[\int [Q]\{\alpha\} z^2 dz\right](2\delta T/h)$ (15.38)

This nonmechanical moment is due to the unsymmetric thermal expansion caused by the linear gradient.

Finally $\{\varepsilon\}^n = \{\alpha^o\}\Delta T + \{\beta^o\}c + z\{k\}^n$

$$= \{\alpha^o\}\Delta T + \{\beta^o\}c + z[d]\{M\}^n \tag{15.39}$$

Note that the moment is proportional to the temperature gradient; if the gradient vanishes we recover the case of uniform temperature in Equation 15.13.

15.13 SAMPLE PROBLEMS

Prob 1: Find the free hygrothermal expansions of CFRP T300/5208 at room temperature (22°K) and moisture content of 0.5 percent, assuming cure temperature is 122°K.

SOLUTION: From Equations 15.1 and 15.27 for the expansion coefficients:

$$e_x = \alpha_x \Delta T + \beta_x c = 0.02 \times 10^{-6} \times (-100) = -2 \times 10^{-6}$$

$$e_y = \alpha_y \Delta T + \beta_y c = 22.5 \times 10^{-6} \times (-100) + 0.6 \times 0.005$$

$$= 0.75 \times 10^{-3}$$

(15.40)

Note that tranverse expansional strain can be canceled when:

At $c = 0.005$, $\Delta T = 0.6 \times 0.005 / 22.5 \times 10^{-6} = 133°K$, or

At $\Delta T = -100°K$, $c = 22.5 \times 10^{-6} \times 100 / 0.6 = 0.00375$

Prob 2: Find the nonmechanical stress and strain, and residual strain based on the inputs above for [0/90/45₂].

SOLUTION: The stiffness and compliance of this laminate can be found in Section 7, Problem 2, and will not be repeated here.

From Equation 15.7,

$$V_1^* = (1/h) \int_{-h/2}^{h/2} \cos 2\theta \, dz = [\cos 0 + \cos 180 + 2\cos 90]/4 = 0$$

(15.41)

$$V_3^* = (1/h) \int_{-h/2}^{h/2} \sin 2\theta \, dz = [\sin 0 + \sin 180 + 2\sin 90]/4 = 0.5$$

Substituting the expansional strains in Equations 15.40 into 15.6 and 15.7:

$$\sigma_1^{(o)n} = p^n + q^n V_1^* = -15.1 \text{ MPa}$$

$$\sigma_2^{(o)n} = p^n - q^n V_1^* = -15.1 \text{ MPa}$$

(15.42)

$$\sigma_6^{(o)n} = q^n V_3^* = 4.1 \text{ MPa}$$

The nonmechanical strain can be found using Equation 15.8:

$$\{\varepsilon^o\}^n = [a^*]\{\sigma^o\}^n = \{-0.283, -0.283, 0.604\} \times 10^{-3}$$

(15.43)

The residual strain is found using Equation 15.10, or for th on–axis 0–degree ply, subtracting Equation 15.40 from 15.43

$$\{\varepsilon\}^{(0)r} = \{\varepsilon^{(0)n} - e\} = \{-0.281, 1.97, 0.604\} \times 10^{-3}$$

(15.44)

For the on–axis 90–degree ply we must first transform Equation 15.43 before we subtract the free expansions

$$\{\varepsilon\}^{(90)n} = \{-0.283, -0.283, -0.604\}x10^{-3} \tag{15.45}$$

$$\{\varepsilon\}^{(90)r} = \{\varepsilon^{(90)n}-e\} = \{-0.281, 1.97, -0.604\}x10^{-3} \tag{15.46}$$

For the on–axis 45–degree ply we must transform the nonmechanical strain, then subtract the expansional strain:

$$\{\varepsilon\}^{(45)r} = \{\varepsilon^{(45)n}-e\} = \{0.0209, 1.66, 0\}x10^{-3} \tag{15.47}$$

Prob 3: **Find the effective thermal expansion coefficients of this laminate:** $[0/90/45_2]$.

SOLUTION: The thermal expansion coefficients can be obtained by using Equation 15.11, or by finding the nonmechanical strain due to one degree temperature change. We will show the latter method. From Equation 15.1, one degree change in temperature yields:

$$e_x = \alpha_x x1 = 0.02x10^{-6}, \quad e_y = \alpha_y x1 = 22.5x10^{-6} \tag{15.48}$$

From Equation 15.5,

$$p^n = [(Q_{xx}+Q_{xy})e_x+(Q_{xy}+Q_{yy})e_y]/2 = 0.151 \text{ MPa}$$
$$q^n = [(Q_{xx}-Q_{xy})e_x+(Q_{xy}-Q_{yy})e_y]/2 = -0.082 \text{ MPa} \tag{15.49}$$

From Equation 15.7 and the V_1 and V_2 in Equation 15.41

$$\{\sigma^o\}^n = \{0.151, 0.151, -0.041\} \text{ MPa} \tag{15.50}$$

The nonmechanical strain per one degree is the thermal expansion coefficient. Thus from Equation 15.8

$$\{\alpha^o\} = \{\varepsilon^o\}^n = \{2.83, 2.83, -8.04\}x10^{-6} \tag{15.51}$$

Prob 4: **Find the effective moisture expansion coefficients of the laminate:** $[0/90/45_2]$.

SOLUTION: Moisture expansion coefficients can be obtained by using Equation 15.12, or by finding the nonmechanical strain due to a unit change. We will show the latter method.

From Equation 15.1, 100 percent change moisture yields

$$e_x = \beta_x x1 = 0, \quad e_y = \beta_y x1 = 0.6 \tag{15.52}$$

From Equation 15.5,

$$p^n = [(Q_{xx}+Q_{xy})e_x+(Q_{xy}+Q_{yy})e_y]/2 = 3970 \text{ MPa}$$
$$q^n = [(Q_{xx}-Q_{xy})e_x+(Q_{xy}-Q_{yy})e_y]/2 = -2230 \text{ MPa} \tag{15.53}$$

From Equation 15.6 and the V^* in Equation 15.41

$$\{\sigma^o\}^n = \{3970, 3970, -1120\} \text{ MPa} \tag{15.54}$$

The nonmechanical strain per 100 percent moisture absorption is the moisture expansion coefficient. Thus from Equation 15.8

$$\{\beta^o\} = \{\epsilon^o\}^n = \{7.51, 7.51, -1.61\} \times 10^{-2} \tag{15.55}$$

Comparing the moisture expansion coefficients with those thermal coefficients in Equation 15.50, the former is four orders of magnitude higher than the latter. This is expected because moisture absorption is about 1 percent, and the temperature difference between room and cure is about −100. There is the factor of 10000. Thus moisture expansion of the laminate is about the same magnitude as that of temperature and opposite in sign. One offsets the other under room temperature and long time (so moisture can be absorbed). The tables in Section 15.9 showing the effects of residual stresses led to the same conclusions.

Prob 5: Find the ply stress and strain under applied load of {100, 50, 0} kN/m, same as that in Section 7.12, and see if equilibrium is satisfied.

SOLUTION: The resulting mechanical strain in the laminate axes is the same as before; i.e.,

$$\{\epsilon\}^m = \{1.622, 0.692, -1.846\} \times 10^{-3} \tag{15.56}$$

The on–axis mechanical strains are:

$$\theta = 0, \quad \{\epsilon\}^m = \{1.622, 0.692, -1.846\} \times 10^{-3}$$

$$\theta = 90, \quad \{\epsilon\}^m = \{0.692, 1.622, 1.846\} \times 10^{-3} \tag{15.57}$$

$$\theta = 45, \quad \{\epsilon\}^m = \{0.235, 2.08, -0.930\} \times 10^{-3}$$

From Equations 15.44 15.46, and 15.47 we have the on–axis residual strains. The total strain is the sum of the mechanical and residual per Equation 15.28.

$$\theta = 0, \quad \{\epsilon\}^{total} = \{1.34, 2.66, -1.24\} \times 10^{-3}$$

$$\theta = 90, \quad \{\epsilon\}^{total} = \{0.411, 3.59, 1.24\} \times 10^{-3} \tag{15.58}$$

$$\theta = 45, \quad \{\epsilon\}^{total} = \{0.255, 3.75, -0.930\} \times 10^{-3}$$

Since these strain are on–axis, we can use Equation 15.3 or 15.29 to determine the on–axis stress of each ply.

$$\theta = 0, \quad \{\sigma\}^{total} = \{252, 31.4, -8.9\} \text{ MPa}$$

$$\theta = 90, \quad \{\sigma\}^{total} = \{85.2, 38.3, 8.9\} \text{ MPa} \tag{15.59}$$

$$\theta = 45, \quad \{\sigma\}^{total} = \{57.3, 39.5, -6.67\} \text{ MPa}$$

Note that these stresses are different from those in Equation 7.55 which had no residual stresses.

In order to check equilibrium, the on–axis stresses must be transformed to the laminate–axis using Equation 5.1 and 5.2

$\theta = 0$, $\{\sigma\}^{\text{total}} = \{252, 31.4, -8.9\}$ MPa

$\theta = 90$, $\{\sigma\}^{\text{total}} = \{38.3, 85.2, -8.9\}$ MPa   (15.60)

$\theta = 45$, $\{\sigma\}^{\text{total}} = \{55.1, 41.7, 8.9\}$ MPa

We need to satisfy equilibrium by balancing between the ply stresses and the externally applied stresses, similar to the results of Equation 7.57. The laminate is $[0/90/45_2]$:

$\{\sigma_1{}^o\} = [252+38.3+2\text{x}55.1]/4 = 100$ MPa

$\{\sigma_2{}^o\} = [31.4+85.2+2\text{x}41.7]/4 = 50$ MPa   (15.61)

$\{\sigma_6{}^o\} = [-8.9-8.9+2\text{x}8.9]/4 = 0$

Note that equilibrium is satisfied because the 8–ply laminate has a thickness of 1 mm resulting in the applied stress precisely $\{100, 50, 0\}$ MPa. As a basis of comparison of the ply stresses with and without residual stresses, we can compare the results of Equation 15.58, and those on–axis ply stresses without residual stresses listed in Equation 7.55 and repeated as follows:

$\theta = 0$, $\{\sigma\} = \{296.99, 11.86, -13.23\}$ MPa

$\theta = 90$, $\{\sigma\} = \{130.60, 18.79, 13.23\}$ MPa   (15.62)

$\theta = 45$, $\{\sigma\} = \{48.67, 22.20, -6.67\}$ MPa

Although the hygrothermal expansions in Equation 15.40 are small, the ply stresses due to residual stresses are quite significant. They are certainly not negligible.

15.14 CONCLUSIONS

We have tried to show the effects of residual stresses due to the difference between the operating and cure temperatures, and due to absorption and desorption of moisture. The theory is a direct extension of the laminated plate theory. Residual strains can be integrated into the limit and ultimate strength envelopes. We must know if the curing stresses are in fact offset by absorbed moisture. Residual stresses are not difficult conceptually but require discipline is to balance various strains. The equilibrium check in on of the sample problems is one way to ascertain that all the ply stresses and strains are correctly calculated. The fact that the effects of cure temperature and moisture can offset each other for long time exposure on earth must still be examined for each application. The linear theory used in this section must be tempered with the actual time–dependent, nonlinear phenomenon of curing and moisture absorption. Carefully conceived test and data interpretation are still recommended.

Section 16

ENVIRONMENTAL EFFECTS

George S. Springer
STANFORD UNIVERSITY, STANFORD

16.1 INTRODUCTION

When an organic matrix composite is exposed to humid air or to a liquid, both the moisture content and the temperature of the material may change with time. These changes, in turn, affect the thermal and mechanical properties, resulting in a decrease in performance. Therefore, to utilize the full potential of composite materials their response to environmental exposure must be known. Specifically, answers to the following problem are sought.

A composite material is exposed to an environment in which the temperature and the moisture level vary with time in a prescribed manner. It is required to find the following parameters:

a) Temperature inside the material as a function of position and time,
b) Moisture concentration inside the material as a function of position and time,
c) Total amount (mass) of moisture inside the material as a function of time,
d) Moisture and temperature induced ("hygrothermal") stresses inside the material as a function of time,
e) Dimensional changes of the material as a function of time, and
f) Changes in the "performance" of the material as a function of time.

Here the word "performance" is used in a broad sense to denote any mechanical, chemical, thermal, or electrical property of interest, such as strength, modulus, fatigue life, glass transition temperature, thermal, and electrical conductivities.

Generally, the problem is attacked in three steps, as illustrated in Figure 16.1. First, the temperature distribution and the moisture content inside the material are calculated. Second, from the known temperature and moisture distributions the hygrothermal deformations and stresses are calculated. Third, the changes in performance due to temperature and moisture are determined. In this section, we will concentrate on the determination of the moisture distribution inside the material. The hygrothermal stresses and their effects are covered in Section 15 on Residual Stresses and Strains, and Section 17 on Hygrothermal Effects.

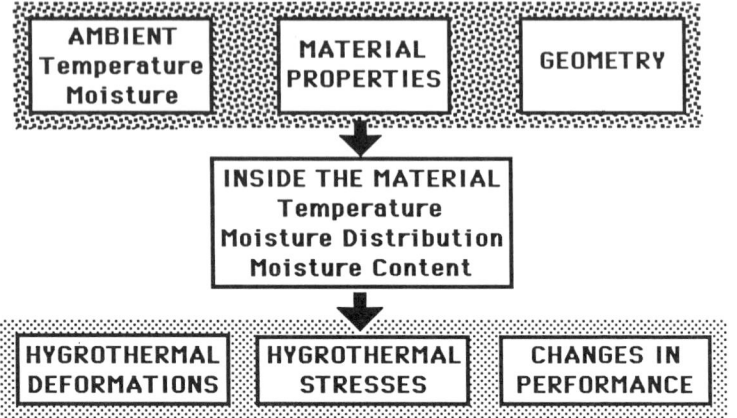

FIGURE 16.1 PROCEDURE FOR ASSESSING ENVIRONMENTAL EFFECTS.

16.2 TEMPERATURE AND MOISTURE DISTRIBUTIONS

The temperature and moisture distributions inside the composite can readily be calculated when moisture penetrates into the material by "Fickian" diffusion. Such diffusion is assumed to take place when the following conditions are met:

- a) Heat transfer through the material is by conduction only and can be described by Fourier's law.
- b) The moisture diffusion can be described by a concentration dependent form of Fick's law.
- c) The temperature inside the material approaches equilibrium much faster than the moisture concentration and hence the energy (Fourier) and mass transfer (Fick) equations are decoupled.
- d) The thermal conductivity and mass diffusivity depend only on temperature and are independent of the moisture concentrations or the stress levels inside the material.

Below, solutions are presented for the temperature and moisture distributions in single and multilayered composites under Fickian diffusion.

Single–Layer Composite——Constant Environmental Conditions

The following problem is considered (Figure 16.2):

- a) The composite is a single–layer plate in which the moisture content and temperature vary only in the direction normal to the face of the plate.
- b) The ambient temperature and ambient moisture content are constant and are the same on both sides of the plate.
- c) The temperature inside the material approaches equilibrium much faster than the moisture concentration and hence the temperature inside the material can be taken to be the same as the ambient temperature.
- d) Initially, the temperature and moisture distributions are uniform inside the material.

e) The thermal conductivity and the mass diffusivity depend only on temperature and are independent of the moisture concentrations and the stress levels inside the material.

f) The plate is made of a single layer only and the material is quasi–homogeneous, so that variations of the material properties with position inside the material may be neglected.

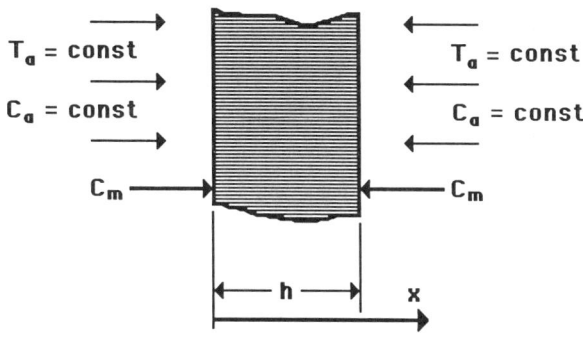

FIGURE 16.2 SINGLE–LAYER—CONSTANT ENVIRONMENTAL CONDITIONS.

For the problem specified above, the temperature distribution is uniform across the plate and, at all times, the temperature equals the ambient temperature:

$$T_{inside} = T_{ambient} = T_a \tag{16.1}$$

The moisture concentration c as a function of position x and time t is [16–1]

$$c^* \equiv \frac{c - c_i}{c_m - c_i} = 1 - \frac{4}{\pi} \sum_{j=0}^{\infty} \frac{1}{2j+1} \sin\frac{(2j+1)\pi x}{h} \exp\left[-\frac{(2j+1)^2 \pi^2 Dt}{h^2}\right] \tag{16.2}$$

where c_i is the uniform, initial moisture concentration inside the material, c_m is the maximum moisture concentration that is reached in the material for a given ambient condition, h is the plate's thickness, and D is the mass diffusivity in the direction normal to the plate.

The total mass of moisture inside the plate is

$$m = A \int_0^h c\,dx \tag{16.3}$$

where A is the exposed surface area.

Equations 16.2 and 16.3 yield the following expression for the total mass

$$G \equiv \frac{m-m_i}{m_m-m_i} = 1 - \frac{8}{\pi^2} \sum_{j=0}^{\infty} \frac{1}{(2j+1)^2} \exp\left[-\frac{(2j+1)^2 \pi^2 Dt}{h^2}\right]$$

(16.4)

where m_i is the initial mass of the material (that is, the mass prior to exposure to the moist environment) and m_m is the mass of moisture in the material when the material is fully saturated, in equilibrium with its environment

$$m_m = (A)(c_m)(h)$$

(16.5)

The parameter G may conveniently be approximated by

$$G = 1 - \exp\left[-7.3(Dt/h^2)^{0.75}\right]$$

(16.6)

This expression is simpler to use than Equation 16.4.

A parameter of practical interest is the percent weight gain, defined as

$$M = (W-W^o)/W^o \times 100 = m/m^o \times 100$$

(16.7)

where W = weight of moist material
               W^o = weight of dry material
               m = mass of absorbed water
               m^o = mass of dry material

Equations 16.4 and 16.7 give

$$M = G(M_m - M_i) + M$$

(16.8)

The subscripts refer to the uniform initial and fully saturated conditions, respectively. Accordingly, we have

$$M_m = m_m/m_{dry} \times 100 = c_m/\rho \times 100$$

$$M_i = m_i/m_{dry} \times 100 = c_i/\rho \times 100$$

(16.9)

where ρ is the density of the dry material.

Note that the moisture concentration and the total moisture content can be calculated by the above expressions even when one side of the plate is insulated so that moisture enters through one face only. In this case the thickness h must be replaced by twice the thickness $2h$ in Equations 16.2, 16.4, and 16.6.

Multilayered Composites——Time Varying Environmental Conditions

The following problem is considered (Figure 16.3)

a) The temperature and moisture content inside the material vary only in the direction normal to the face of the plate.
b) The temperature inside the material equilibrates much faster than the moisture

concentration, and hence at each instant of time the temperature distribution inside the material corresponds to the instantaneous ambient temperature.

c) The material properties depend only on temperature, and are independent of moisture concentration and stress level.

d) The environmental conditions (temperature, moisture level) vary in arbitrary but known manner.

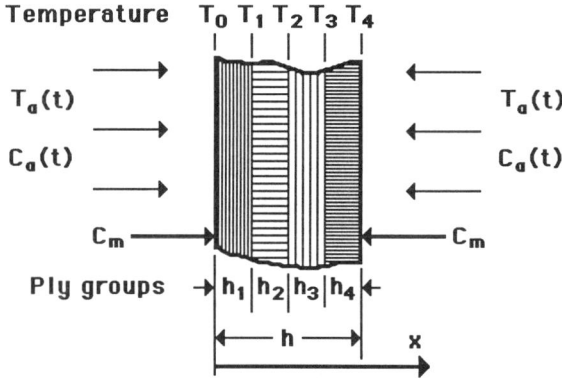

FIGURE 16.3.   MULTILAYERED COMPOSITE—TIME VARYING ENVIRONMENTAL CONDITIONS.

The temperature distribution inside the plate is [16–2]

$$T_0 - T_1 = qR_1, \quad T_2 - T_1 = qR_2$$
$$T_3 - T_2 = qR_3, \quad T_4 - T_3 = qR_4$$

(16.11)

where $R_i = K_i / h_i$

$$q = (T_4 - T_1)/(R_1 + R_2 + R_3 + R_4)$$

T_0 through T_4 are the surface temperatures, K_i is the thermal conductivity of the i–th layer (in the direction normal to the face of the plate).

Although the above expressions are written for a plate consisting of four layers, the results can readily be extended to plates consisting of arbitrary number of layers.

The moisture concentration and the moisture content must be obtained by numerical methods. A computer code (designated as W8GAIN) was developed for performing the calculations. The program listing and a sample input–output can be found in [16–1].

The required input parameters for the program are:

a) The ambient temperature and relative humidity as a function of time on both sides of the plate.

b) The initial moisture concentration and initial temperature distribution inside the plate; these concentrations need not be uniform.

c) The density of each layer.
d) The maximum moisture content of each layer as a function of ambient conditions.
e) The thermal conductivity and mass diffusivity as a function of temperature for each layer.

The outputs of the program are:

a) Moisture concentration as a function of position and time in each layer.
b) Weight (mass) change of each layer as a function of time.
c) Total weight (mass) change as a function of time.

Non–Fickian Diffusion

The aforementioned calculation procedures can be used only if the moisture diffusion is by a Fickian process. The conditions under which Fickian diffusion exists must be determined by tests. Generally, Fickian diffusion takes place at low temperatures and for materials exposed to humid air. Deviations from Fickian diffusion occur at elevated temperatures and for materials immersed in liquids. It is noteworthy that Fickian diffusion is a reasonable approximation for many materials, including graphite–epoxy composites.

16.3 TEST PROCEDURES FOR DETERMINING D AND M_m

The following test procedure may be used to determine the diffusivity D and the maximum moisture content M_m

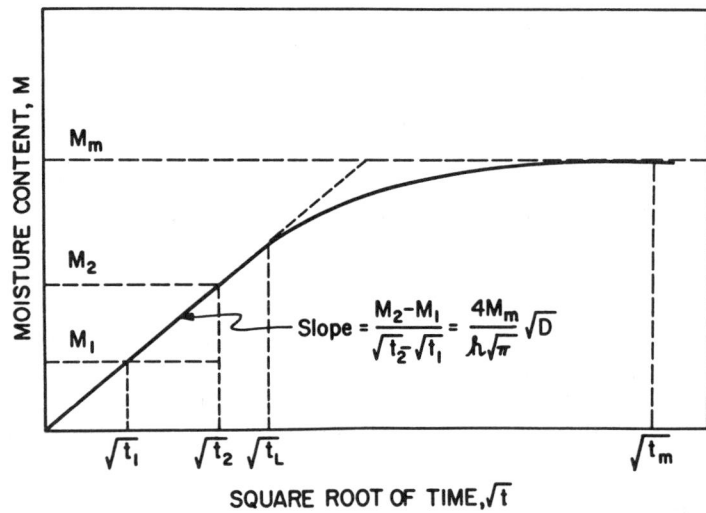

FIGURE 16.4 ILLUSTRATION OF THE CHANGE OF MOISTURE CONTENT WITH THE SQUARE ROOT OF TIME FOR FICKIAN DIFFUSION. FOR $t < t_L$ THE SLOPE IS CONSTANT.

a) A test specimen is fabricated in the form of thin plate.
b) The specimen is completely dried in an oven and the dry weight W_{dry} is measured.
c) The specimen is placed in a constant temperature, constant moisture level environment and the weight is recorded as a function of time.
d) The moisture content M (see Equation 16.7) is plotted versus the square root of time (see Figure 16.4).

In case of Fickian diffusion, after a long period of time the M versus square–root time curve approaches asymptotically the maximum moisture content M_m. The initial slope of the curve is proportional to the diffusivity

$$D = \pi(h/4M_m)^2[(M_2-M_1)/(\sqrt{t_2}-\sqrt{t_1})]^2 \qquad (16.13)$$

Alternately, the value of D can be found using Equation 16.8. An arbitrary value of D is selected and M is calculated by Equations 16.8 and 16.6 for different times. The calculated results are compared with the data. The procedure is repeated with different D values until a "best fit" to the data is obtained. The error introduced in the value of D due to diffusion through the edges can be estimated by the procedure given in [16–1].

16.4 MAXIMUM MOISTURE CONTENT

The value of M_m is nearly constant when the material is submerged in a liquid. For materials exposed to humid air, M_m can be related to the relative humidity f by the expression

$$M_m = a(\phi)^b \qquad (16.14)$$

where a and b are constants, and their values are given in Tables 16.1–16.3.

TABLE 16.1   MAXIMUM MOISTURE CONTENTS OF SELECTED GRAPHITE–EPOXY COMPOSITES IMMERSED IN LIQUID [16–1]

Liquid	Maximum moisture content, M_m (percent)		
	T300/1034	AS/3501–5	T300/5208
Distilled water	1.70	1.90	1.50
Saturated salt water	1.25	1.40	1.12
No. 2 diesel fuel	0.50	0.55	0.45
Jet A fuel 0.45	0.52	0.40	0.40
Aviation oil 0.65	0.65	0.60	0.60

TABLE 16.2 MAXIMUM MOISTURE CONTENT OF SELECTED GRAPHITE–
EPOXY COMPOSITES AND EPOXY RESINS EXPOSED TO HUMID AIR*

Material	a	b
T300/1034	0.017	1
AS/3501–5	0.019	1
T300/5208	0.015	1
934 (resin)	0.060	1.4 ϕ<60 percent, 1.8 ϕ>60 percent
3501–5 (resin)	0.060	1.4 ϕ<60 percent, 1.8 ϕ>60 percent
5208 (resin)	0.060	1.4 ϕ<60 percent, 1.8 ϕ>60 percent

* where $M_m = a\phi^b$ if b = 1
$M_m = a(\phi/100)^b \times 100$ if b ≠ 1

TABLE 16.3 THE APPARENT MAXIMUM MOISTURE CONTENT OF SELECTED
POLYESTER E–GLASS AND VINYLESTER E–GLASS COMPOSITES
(PERCENT) [16–1]

Substance	Temp (°C)	SMC–R25	VE SMC–R50	SMC–R50
Humid air, 50 percent	23	0.17	0.13	0.10
	93	0.10	0.10	0.22
Humid air, 100 percent	23	1.00	0.63	1.35
	93	0.30	0.40	0.56
Distilled water	23	3.60	–	–
	50	3.50	–	–
Salt water 23		0.85	0.50	1.25
	93	2.90	0.75	1.20
No. 2 diesel fuel	23	0.29	0.19	0.45
	93	2.80	0.45	1.00
Lubricating oil	23	0.25	0.20	0.30
	93	0.60	0.10	0.25
Antifreeze 23		0.45	0.30	0.65
	93	4.25	3.50	2.25
Indolene 23		3.50	0.25	0.60
	93	4.50	5.00	4.25

16.5 MASS DIFFUSIVITY

When the diffusion is Fickian and **D** is a function of temperature only, the diffusivity is related to temperature by the Arrhenius relationship

$$D = D_o \exp[-C/T] \tag{16.15}$$

where D_0 and **C** are constants, and **T** is the absolute temperature. Values of the constants are given in Tables 16.4–16.6.

The transverse diffusivity of a unidirectional composite is

$$D_y = D_o \exp[-C/T] \tag{16.15}$$

where D_0 is in $mm^2 s^{-1}$; **C** in K.

TABLE 16.4 TRANSVERSE DIFFUSIVITIES OF SELECTED GRAPHITE EPOXY
COMPOSITES IMMERSED IN LIQUIDS AND HUMID AIR [16–1]

LIQUID/AIR	T300/1034 D_o	C	AS/3501–5 D_o	C	T300/5208 D_o	C
Distilled water	16.3	6211	768	7218	132	6750
Saturated salt water	5.85	6020	5.38	6472	6.23	5912
Humid air	2.28	5554	6.51	5722	0.57	4993

TABLE 16.5 DIFFUSIVITIES OF EPOXY RESINS EXPOSED TO HUMID AIR [16–1]

RESIN	934 D_o	C	3501–5 D_o	C	5208 D_o	C
Humid air	4.85	5113	16.1	5690	4.19	5448

For fiber reinforced composites the diffusion coefficients in the direction parallel and perpendicular to the fibers (D_x and D_y) may be estimated by the expressions [16–1]

$$D_x = (1-v_f)D_m + v_f D_f \tag{16.16}$$

where D_m is the diffusivity of the resin matrix, D_f is the diffusivity of the fiber and v_f is the volume fraction of the fibers. A more lengthy expression is required for the transverse diffusivity. These expressions become invalid if moisture propagates along fiber–resin interfaces or through cracks and voids.

Generally, the diffusivity of the fiber is small compared to the diffusivity of the matrix and we may simplify the expression in [16–1]

$$D_x = (1-v_f)D_m \tag{16.17}$$

$$D_y = [1-\sqrt{(v_f/\pi)}]D_m \tag{16.18}$$

In a direction making α degrees with the orientation of the fibers the off–axis diffusivity is

$$D_1 = D_x \cos^2\alpha + D_y \sin^2\alpha \tag{16.19}$$

Similar expressions for the thermal conductivities of unidirectional composites can be derived. Other approximations can also be found in Reference [16–1].

TABLE 16.6 APPARENT TRANSVERSE DIFFUSIVITIES OF SELECTED POLYESTER
E–GLASS AND VINYLESTER E–GLASS COMPOSITES [16–1]

Substance	Temp (°C)	SMC–R25	VE SMC–R50	SMC–R50
Humid air, 50_s	23	10.0	10.0	30.0
	93	50.0	50.0	30.0
Humid air, 100_s	23	10.0	5.0	9.0
	93	50.0	50.0	50.0
Salt water	23	10.0	5.0	15.0
	93	5.0	30.0	80.0
No. 2 diesel fuel	23	6.0	5.0	5.0
	93	6.0	10.0	5.0
Lubricating oil	23	10.0	10.0	10.0
	93	10.0	10.0	10.0
Antifreeze	23	50.0	30.0	20.0
	93	5.0	0.8	10.0
Indolene	23	1.0	10.0	10.0
	93	10.0	1.0	3.0

Values of D_y are given in 10^7 mm²s⁻¹.

16.6 ACCELERATED MOISTURE CONDITIONING

The mechanical, thermal, and chemical properties of organic matrix
composites change during environmental exposure. To determine the
magnitudes of these changes the usual procedure is to expose the material to a
moist environment until the moisture level inside the material reaches the
required value. The material is then subjected to the appropriate tests to
measure the changes in properties caused by the absorbed moisture.
Unfortunately, moisture conditioning of the material may last months or
years. Under most circumstances such long conditioning times are
unacceptable. In the following a procedure is described which reduces the
time required to moisturize the material during environmental conditioning.

Problem Statement

We consider a plate of thickness **h** made of a fiber reinforced organic matrix
composite. The moisture concentration c and the temperature **T** inside the
plate is taken to vary only in the direction normal to the face of the plate.
Initially (at time t < 0), the temperature T_i and the moisture concentration
c_i are known at every point inside the plate. At time t = 0 the plate is
exposed to humid air. Both the ambient temperature T_a and the ambient
humidity f_a may vary with time. As time progresses the temperature and
moisture distributions inside the plate and the total moisture content of the
plate change. After some time t_f the temperature, moisture concentration,
and the total moisture content reach the values T_d, c_d, and M_d.

The objective is to establish the environmental conditions (temperature,
relative humidity) which yield the same T_d, c_d, and M_d values as the actual

ambient, but yield these in a shorter time, i.e., in a time t_t which is less than t_f ($t_t < t_f$).

Here, a procedure for accelerated environmental conditioning is presented for the case when

    a) The moisture distribution to be reached is uniform across the plate, and
    b) At any instant of time, the temperature inside the plate corresponds to the ambient temperature.

For this problem the temperature distribution is uniform across the plate and, at all times, the temperature equals the ambient temperature

$$T_{inside} = T_{ambient} = T_a \qquad (16.20)$$

The required uniform moisture concentration c_d inside the plate can be established by several different environments. Commonly, the plate is exposed to humid air in which the humidity is constant and corresponds to the required value of c_d ("regular" method, see Figure 16.5). The time to reach c_d by the regular method is t_f.

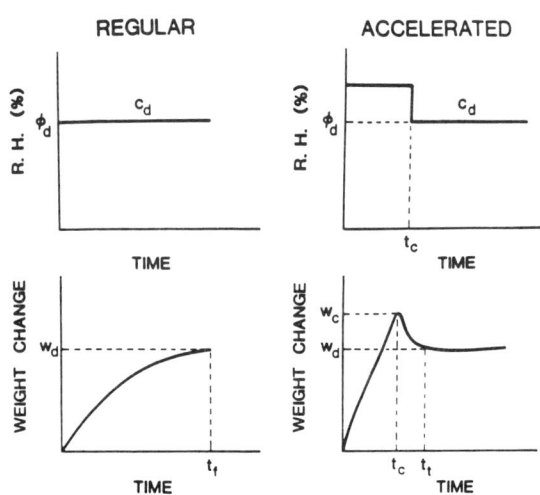

FIGURE 16.5.   ILLUSTRATION OF THE RELATIVE HUMIDITY EMPLOYED IN REGULAR AND ACCELERATED TESTS, AND THE CORRESPONDING WEIGHT CHANGE OF THE MATERIAL.

The procedure for establishing c_d in a time t_t which is less than t_f consists of two major steps:

    a) The plate is exposed to air at 100 percent relative humidity for a period of time t_c (Figure 16.5).
    b) At time t_c the relative humidity of the ambient air is reduced to the value which

corresponds to c_d, and the plate is exposed to this ambient until time t_t. The relationship between c_d and ϕ_d is (see Equations 16.3, 16.7, and 16.14)

$$c_d = \rho M_d/100 = \rho a(\phi_d)^b/100 \tag{16.21}$$

It is necessary to select the "change over" time t_c and the "conditioning time" t_t. These times must be selected to satisfy the following:

a) At the end of the exposure (time $t = t_t$) at every point inside the plate the moisture concentration c agrees (within a prescribed limit) with the desired uniform moisture concentration c_d, and
b) The desired uniform moisture concentration c_d is reached in the shortest possible time t_t.

Selection of the "Change–Over" and "Conditioning" Times

The change–over time and the conditioning time can be determined by the solution of the partial differential equations describing moisture diffusion through the material [16–4]. The results can conveniently be summarized in charts. To accomplish this we introduce a dimensionless moisture concentration and dimensionless time

$$c^* = c/c_{100} \tag{16.22}$$

$$t^* = Dt/h \tag{16.23}$$

where, as before h is the thickness of the plate and c_{100} is the maximum uniform moisture concentration which is reached in the material after exposure to air at 100 percent relative humidity.

The dimensionless "change–over time" t_c^* versus the dimensionless desired moisture concentration c_d^* is given in Figure 16.6.

The dimensionless conditioning time t_t^*, required to ensure that the moisture concentration is everywhere within a prescribed limit of c_d^*, is presented in Figure 16.7. The results in Figure 16.7 are for the three cases when the moisture concentrations everywhere are within 99, 95, or 90 percent of the desired, constant value of c_d^*.

Once the dimensionless times t_c^* and t_t^* are known (Figures 16.6 and 16.7) the actual times t_c and t_t can be calculated by Equation 16.23. These calculations require a knowledge of the diffusivity D. Unfortunately, there is always an uncertainty in the value of D, 100 percent variation in D is quite common [16–1]. Any error in D also manifests itself in the values of t_c and t_t. More accurate values of t_c and t_t can be obtained by placing a test coupon (often referred to as the "witness coupon") into the environmental chamber and by monitoring the weight change of this coupon. The change in humidity from $\phi = 100_s$ to $\phi = \phi_d$ is made when the weight change (percent) of the coupon M reaches the value M_c.

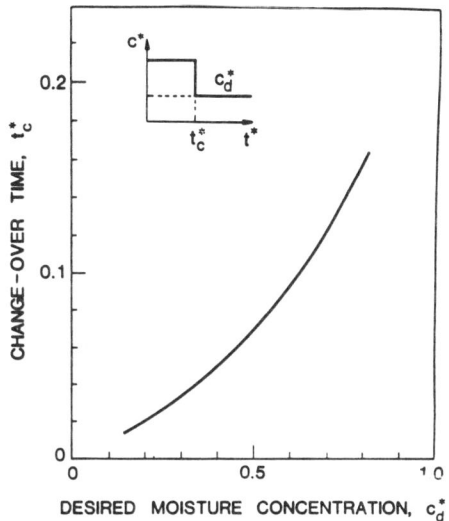

FIGURE 16.6.   THE DIMENSIONLESS CHANGE–OVER TIME T_C VERSUS THE
DIMENSIONLESS DESIRED MOISTURE CONCENTRATION C_D

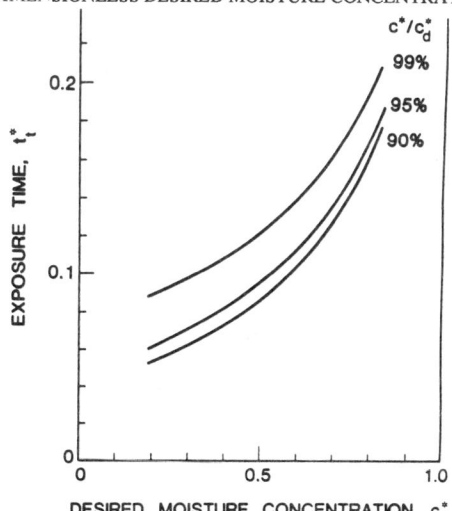

FIGURE 16.7. THE DIMENSIONLESS EXPOSURE TIME T_T VERSUS THE
DIMENSIONLESS DESIRED MOISTURE CONCENTRATION C_D. THE
THREE CURVES CORRESPOND TO THE CONDITIONS WHERE THE
MOISTURE CONCENTRATION AGREES WITHIN 90, 95, AND 99 PERCENT
OF THE DESiRED MOISTURE CONCENTRATION AT EVERY POINT
INSIDE THE COMPOSITE.

$$M_c = (M_{100})(M_c^*) \tag{16.24}$$

where M_{100} is the maximum moisture content corresponding to 100 percent relative humidity (Equation 16.14)

$$M_{100} = a(100)^b \tag{16.25}$$

M_c^* is the moisture content in the material at the change over time $t = t_c^*$. The change over time t_c^* is given by Figure 16.6. At time t_c^* the moisture concentration c_c^* as well as the moisture content M^* can be calculated [16–5]. The calculated values of M_c^* are summarized in Figure 16.8. The value of M_c^* at which the change over from $\phi = 100_s$ to $\phi = \phi_d$ is performed can readily be determined from Figure 16.8 and Equations 16.24 and 16.25. The weight of the witness coupon also indicates the end of the conditioning. The conditioning is complete when the weight of the coupon becomes constant.

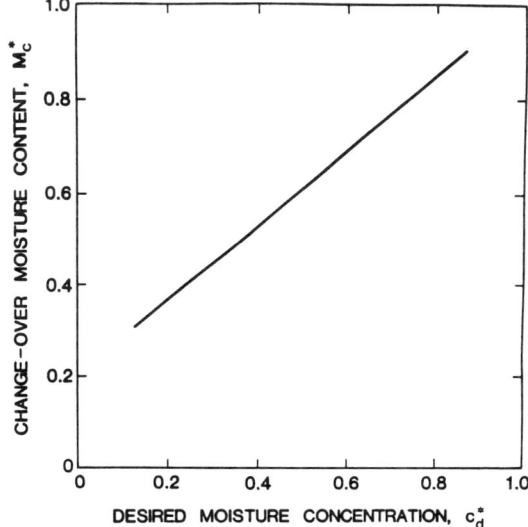

FIGURE 16.8   THE DIMENSIONLESS CHANGE–OVER MOISTURE CONTENT Mc*
VERSUS THE DIMENSIONLESS MOISTURE CONCENTRATION Cd*.

Sample Problem

The following example illustrates the use of the method described above in choosing the conditions for accelerated moisture conditioning.

We consider a 0.25 inch thick plate made of Fiberite T300/1034 graphite epoxy composite. The material properties are specified in Tables 16.2 and 16.5. The plate is exposed to humid air in which both the temperature and relative humidity vary with time. Let us suppose that after a long period of time the weight gain of the plate becomes nearly constant, having the value of $M_d = 0.68$ percent. It is desired to establish the test conditions which result in the same moisture content (0.68 percent) as well as the same moisture distribution as the actual ambient. Solution to the problem proceeds as follows:

1) The dimensionless desired moisture concentration is calculated (see Equations 16.21 and 16.25)

$$M_d = c_d/c_{100} = M_d/M_{100} = 0.68/0.017/100 = 0.4 \qquad (16.26)$$

2) The relative humidity corresponding to M_d is calculated

$$\phi_d = (M)^{1/b}/a = 0.68/0.017 = 40 \text{ percent} \qquad (16.27)$$

3) The dimensionless change–over time is selected. From Figure 16.6 the value of t_c^* corresponding to c_d^* is

$$t_c^* = 0.05 \qquad (16.28)$$

4) The change–over time is calculated. The accelerated test is assumed to take place at 170°F. Then Equation 16.23 and the data in Table 16.5 give

$$t_c = t_c^* h^2/D = 0.05 \times (0.25)^2/1.56 \times 10^{-6}$$

$$= 2000 \text{ hrs} = 84 \text{ days} \qquad (16.29)$$

5) The dimensionless conditioning time is determined. From Figure 16.7 (corresponding to the 99 percent level), we obtain

$$t_t^* = 0.104 \qquad (16.30)$$

6) The actual conditioning time is calculated

$$t_t = t_t^* h^2/D = 0.104 \times (0.25)^2/1.56 \times 10^{-6}$$

$$= 4200 \text{ hrs} = 170 \text{ days} \qquad (16.31)$$

If a "witness coupon" were to be placed in the chamber, steps 3–6 would be as follows

3a)   The dimensionless change over weight M_c^* is determined from Figure 16.8

$$M_c^* = 0.43 \qquad (16.32)$$

4a)   The actual change over weight M_c calculated. Equations 16.24 and 16.25 give

$$M_c = (M_{100})(M_c^*) = 1.7 \times 0.43 = 0.73 \text{ percent} \qquad (16.33)$$

5a)—6a) The final conditioning time is determined from the observed weight change of the witness coupon.

According to this example the plate is to be kept in humid air at 100 percent relative humidity for 84 days. The relative humidity is to be changed then to 40 percent. After 170 days the moisture concentration will be within 99 percent of the desired concentration throughout the plate.

The desired moisture concentration could also be achieved by exposing the plate to humid air at 40 percent relative humidity and 170°F. As can be seen from Figure 16.9, under this condition the desired moisture concentration would be reached in 800 days. This is a long time compared to the 180 days needed to reach c_d by the present method.

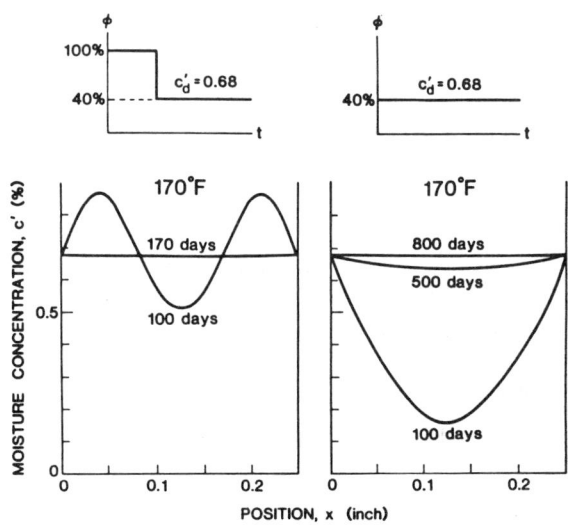

FIGURE 16.9.   THE VARIATION OF MOISTURE WITH TIME IN A 1/4 IN THICK FIBERITE T300/934 GRAPHITE/EPOXY COMPOSITE EXPOSED TO TWO DIFFERENT AMBIENTS. NOTE THAT BOTH AMBIENTS RESULT IN THE UNIFORM MOISTURE CONCENTRATION OF 0.68 PERCENT ($c'=c/\rho \times 100$).

16.7 GLASS TRANSITION TEMPERATURE

Fickian diffusion is more likely to occur in rubbery polymers than in glassy polymers. Transition from glassy to a rubbery state occurs at the glass transition temperature. Hence the glass transition temperature T_g is an important parameter in the moisture transfer process.

The absorbed moisture may change (generally decrease) the glass transition temperature, thereby affecting the diffusion behavior of the material. The Bueche–Kelley theory provides the following estimate of T_g

$$T_g = [\beta_m(1-v_f)T_{gm}+\beta_f v_f T_{gf}]/[\beta_m(1-v_f)+\beta_f v_f)] \tag{16.34}$$

where β_m, β_f, and v_f are the moisture expansion coefficients and the volume fraction of the fiber. Typical values of the glass transition temperature are presented in Figures 16.10 and 16.11.

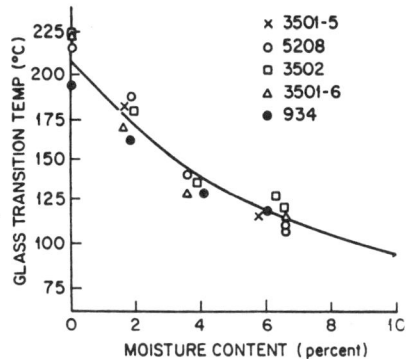

FIGURE 16.10. GLASS TRANSITION TEMPERATURE VERSUS MOISTURE CONTENT
FOR DIFFERENT NEAT RESINS. [16–4]

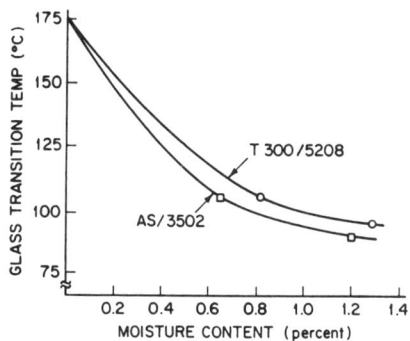

FIGURE 16.11. GLASS TRANSITION TEMPERATURE VERSUS MOISTURE CONTENT
FOR TWO TYPES OF GRAPHITE COMPOSITES. [16–4]

16.8 ENVIRONMENTAL CYCLES

The moisture transport characteristics as well as the properties of composites
may change when the material is exposed to slowly changing environments
for long–time periods, or if it is subjected to suddenly changing
environments for short–time periods. Environmental cycles have generally
been found to increase the rate of moisture uptake and decrease the
mechanical properties. However, the relationships between cycles and
material behavior are not yet understood clearly. In fact, some of the
evidence is contradictory. Significant changes have been observed in some
materials subjected to environmental cycles while only minor changes were
found in some other materials under presumably similar conditions.

REFERENCES

16–1. Springer, G. S., ed. *Environmental Effects on Composite Materials, vol. 1.* Technomic, 1981.

16–2. Kreith, F. *Principles of Heat Transfer.* International Textbook, 1966.

16–3. Springer, G. S., ed. *Environmental Effects on Composite Materials, vol. 2.* Technomic, 1984.

16–4. Springer, G. S. "Moisture Absorption in Fibre–Resin Composites", in *Developments in Reinforced Plastics.* Ed. G. Pritchard. Applied Science, 1982, pp. 43—65.

16–5. Ciriscioli, P. R., W. I. Lee, and G. S. Springer. "Accelerated Environmental Testing of Composites," *Journal of Composite Materials.*

16–6. Doxsee, L. E., W. J. Lee, G. S. Springer, and S. S. Chang. "Temperature and Moisture Induced Deformations in Composite Sandwich Panels". *Journal of Reinforced Plastics and Composites, vol. 5,* January 1985.

Section 17

HYGROTHERMAL EFFECTS

17.1 MICROMECHANICS APPROACH

We showed in Figure 1.2 our overall framework for composites design. In this section Figure 1.2 is split in three parts to illustrate the integrated micro–macromechanics framework and how the temperature– and moisture–dependent material properties are introduced. In Figure 17.1 the improved macromechanics analysis is shown.

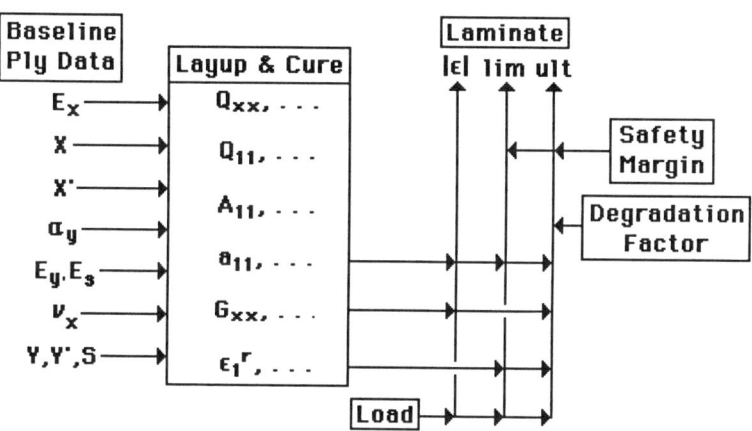

FIGURE 17.1 IMPROVED MACROMECHANICS ANALYSIS.

The laminate stiffness, expansion coefficients, and the strength under a given applied load can be determined from the laminate layup and the particular curing process of a specific composite material. This figure shows the flow of the traditional analysis process from the ply data to the performance characteristics of any multidirectional laminate. The added features of the improved analysis are the limit and ultimate strengths using the safety margin and degradation factor described in Section 12.12. We have covered the relations required to complete this process in earlier sections of this book. From four elastic constants, four hygrothermal expansion coefficients, and five strengths for a unidirectional composite, we can determine the stiffness, the expansion, and the limit and ultimate strengths of a multidirectional laminate under any combined in–plane and flexural loads.

We have also covered the micromechanics relations in Section 10. Our use of micromechanics is different from the traditional flow from the constituent properties to those of the ply. Knowing the limitation of the idealized relations and the unknown fiber properties, we recommend back–calculation of the fiber properties using simple micromechanics relations. Figure 17.2 is a duplicate of Figure 10.1. This flow chart shows the determination of the constituent properties calculated from the measured ply properties.

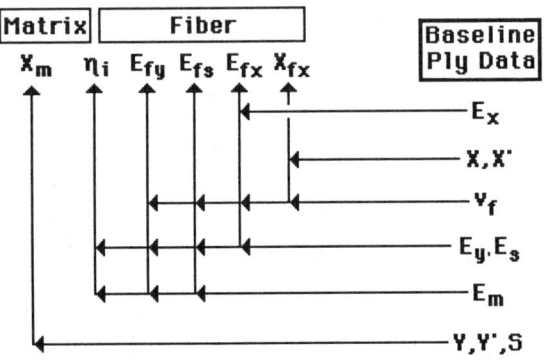

FIGURE 17.2   MICROMECHANICS RELATIONS TO BACK–CALCULATE
CONSTITUENT DATA FROM MEASURED BASELINE PLY DATA.

From the measured temperature–moisture dependent ply properties we will rely on micromechanics to back–calculate the implied changes in the constituent properties. This is done through a nondimensional temperatures, and assumed exponential functions for this temperature. Figure 17.3 shows the hygrothermal exponents to be back–calculated from the baseline ply data.

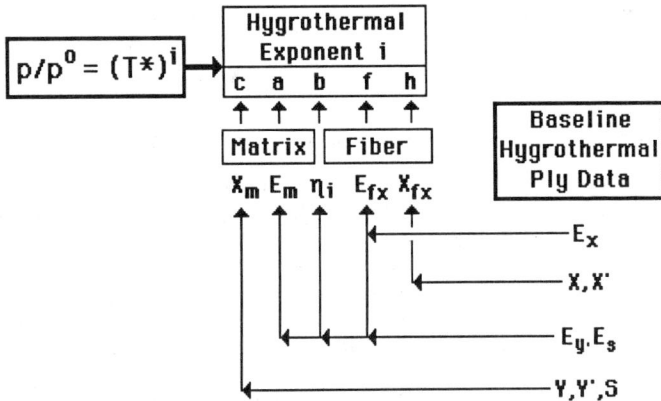

FIGURE 17.3   BACK–CALCULATION OF THE HYGROTHERMAL EXPONENTS USING
MICROMECHANICS RELATIONS AND THE MEASURED BASELINE PLY
DATA AS FUNCTIONS OF TEMPERATURE AND MOISTURE.

We can summarize our integrated micro–macromechanics framework by presenting in Figure 17.4 a duplicate of Figure 1.2. Once the constituent properties and the hygrothermal exponents are determined from a baseline material, we can forward–calculate the micro– and macro–mechanical variables for the same baseline material.

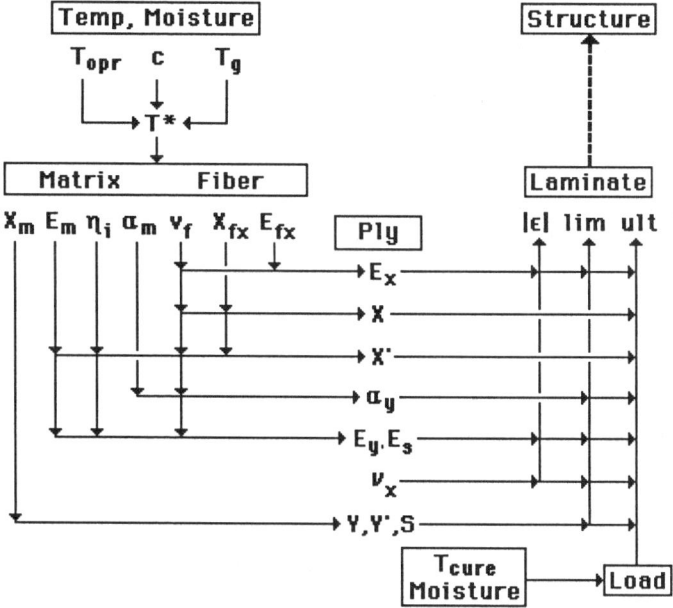

FIGURE 17.4   THE INTEGRATED MICRO–MACRO FRAMEWORK OF COMPOSITES ANALYSIS AND DESIGN.

Since we are not aware of any mechanics theory that governs the hygrothermal effects we will use the following assumptions to simplify the modeling of temperature and moisture effects:

- Hygrothermal effects can be fitted by a power law of a nondimensional temperature T^*.
- Changes in stiffness and strength of constituents can be approximated by exponents of T^*.
- Micromechanics formulas remain valid for the range of hygrothermal changes. Properties of materials remain linear and are not time dependent.
- Laminated plate theory and failure criteria remain valid and only the stiffness and strength properties are changed.

We use micromechanics because we can reduce the number of variables. If we ignore micromechanics and assess the hygrothermal effects on the ply or laminate levels, we will have to run many more tests and will find sensitivity studies of materials design much more difficult.

17.2 NONDIMENSIONAL TEMPERATURE

We define a key parameter:

$$T^* = [T_g - T_{opr}]/[T_g - T_{rm}] \tag{17.1}$$

where T^* = nondimensional temperature.

T_g = glass–transition temperature of the organic matrix.

T_{opr} = operating temperature.

T_{rm} = room or reference temperature.

We further assume that moisture suppresses the glass transition temperature by a simple temperature shift, as shown in Figure 17.5:

$$T_g = T_g^0 - gc \tag{17.2}$$

where T_g^0 = glass–transition temperature at dry state.

g = temperature shift per unit moisture absorbed.

c = moisture absorbed.

In Figure 17.5 we show a linear relation between the nondimensional temperature and the operating temperature. If we wish to have nonlinear relations, a power law would be simple and takes only one exponent. The sensitivity of the value of this exponent is shown in Figure 17.6.

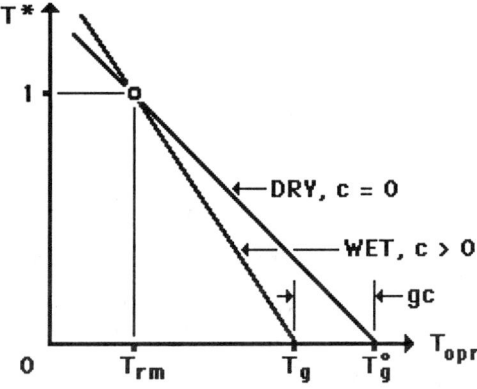

FIGURE 17.5   NONDIMENSIONAL TEMPERATURE AS A LINEAR FUNCTION OF OPERATING TEMPERATURE AND MOISTURE CONTENT.

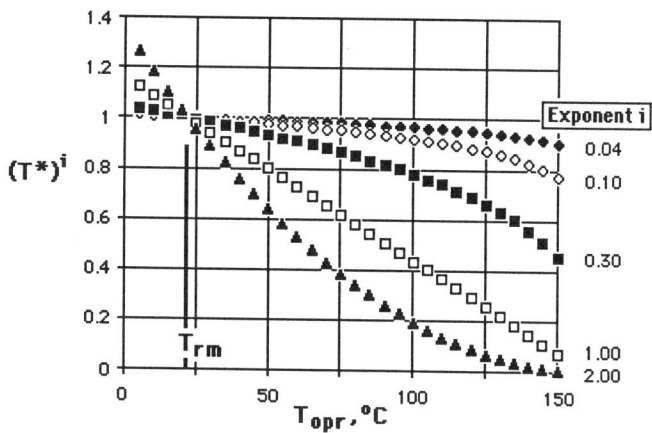

FIGURE 17.6   SENSITIVITY OF THE POWER LAW OF THE NONDIMENSIONAL
                 TEMPERATURE AS A FUNCTION OF THE OPERATING TEMPERATURE.

The effect of moisture content on the nondimensional temperature T^* is shown in Figure 17.7 below.

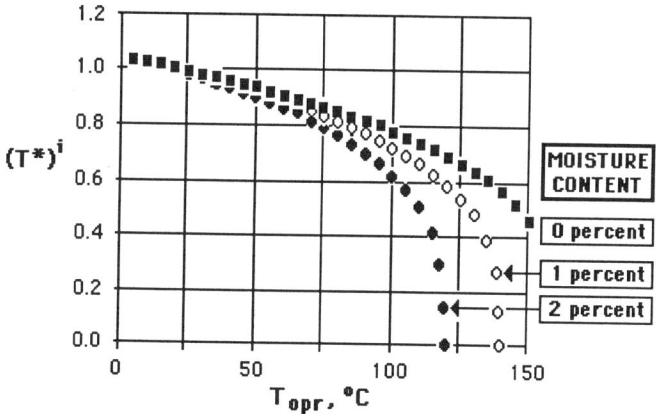

FIGURE 17.7   EFFECTS OF MOISTURE CONTENT ON THE NONDIMENSIONAL
                 TEMPERATURE FUNCTION FOR A CONSTANT EXPONENT OF 0.3.

17.3 MATRIX AND FIBER PROPERTIES

We can use the exponents of T^* to empirically fit the matrix and fiber stiffness and strength data as functions of moisture and temperature:

$$E_m/E_m{}^0 = (T^*)^a \tag{17.3}$$

$$\eta_y/\eta_y{}^0 = \eta_s/\eta_s{}^0 = (T^*)^b \tag{17.4}$$

$$X_m/X_m{}^0 = (T*)^c \tag{17.5}$$

$$E_{fx}/E_{fx}{}^0 = E_{fy}/E_{fy}{}^0 = G_{fx}/G_{fx}{}^0 = (T*)^f \tag{17.6}$$

$$X_f/X_f{}^0 = (T*)^h \tag{17.7}$$

With these back–calculated constituent properties as functions of T*, we can derive the ply stiffness and strength in terms of T* and appropriate exponents following the relationships postulated in Section 10 on micromechanics.

$$E_x/E_x{}^0 = (v_f/v_f{}^0)(T*)^f \tag{17.8}$$

$$E_y/E_y{}^0 = \text{a nonlinear function of } (T*)^a, (T*)^b, \text{ and } v_f. \tag{17.9}$$

$$v_x = \text{constant} \tag{17.10}$$

$$E_s/E_s{}^0 = \text{a nonlinear function of } (T*)^a, (T*)^b, \text{ and } v_f. \tag{17.11}$$

The function for the shear modulus ratio is not necessarily the same as that for the transverse stiffness.

We can derive the longitudinal tensile strengths of a unidirectional composite by combining the micromechanics formula in Equations 10.36 with the hygrothermal effect on the fiber strength in Equation 17.7:

$$X/X^0 = (v_f/v_f{}^0)(T*)^h \tag{17.12}$$

We can also derive the longitudinal compressive strength by combining the micromechanics formula in Equation 10.37 with Equation 17.7:

$$X'/X'^0 = (v_f/v_f{}^0)(T*)^h(E_s/E_s{}^0)^e \tag{17.13}$$

As mentioned in Section 10, the inclusion of the shear modulus ratio is intended to compensate for the micro–buckling of the fiber. The same correction is included the degradation factor DF discussed in Section 12.12 where the exponent c is replaced by e, having a value of 0.2.

Finally, the matrix–controlled strength is derived from the postulate in Equation 10.39 and the power law of Equation 17.5:

$$Y/Y^0 = Y'/Y'^0 = S/S^0 = (T*)^c \tag{17.14}$$

17.4 HYGROTHERMAL EFFECTS ON A UNIDIRECTIONAL COMPOSITE

We assume the following data to demonstrate the hygrothermal effects on the stiffness and strength of a CFRP, T300/5208 composite:

- Dry–state glass–transition temperature, $T_g{}^0 = 160^oC$ (17.15)
- T_{opr} = input data, but should be lower than the
  glass–transition temperature of the matrix. (17.16)

- $T_{rm} = 22^{\circ}C$ (17.17)

- g = temperature shift due to moisture = 2000° C/c

  = 20° C/percent moisture.   (17.18)

- c = moisture content in absolute fraction; i.e. 0.01
  for 1 percent.   (17.19)

- Matrix exponents in Equations 17.3, 17.4, and 17.5:

  a = 0.5, b = 0.2, c = 0.9.   (17.20)

- Fiber exponents in Equations 17.6 and 17.7:

  f = h = 0.04.   (17.21)

The values of these exponents must be determined empirically. It is always a matter of judgement how many exponents are needed to accurately describe of observed phenomenon. We believe that these constants are the minimally required. The effect of residual stresses due to lamination described in Section 15 are highly interlocked with the hygrothermal properties of this section.

In the absence of extensive data, we will only indicate the trends of the hygrothermal effect for typical laminates. The [±45] laminate is a very sensitive specimen to determine matrix related exponents in Equation 17.20. The uniaxial tensile strength of this laminate can be expressed as a function of temperatures and moisture contents. The prediction is based on the integrated micro–macromechanics analysis formatted on a spreadsheet (Mic–Mac in Section 27) using the room temperature data of CFRP T300/5208. The fiber stiffness and strength are back–calculated.

- Young's modulus of the matrix = 3.4 GPa   (17.22)

- Young's modulus of the fiber = 259 GPa*   (17.23)

- Tensile strength of the matrix = 40 MPa   (17.24)

- Tensile strength of the fiber = 2143 MPa*   (17.25)

- Fiber volume fraction = 0.70   (17.26)

- Glass–transition temperature of the matrix = 160°C

      (17.27)
- Baseline material is based on 122°C cure and 0.5 percent
  moisture.   (17.28)

The predicted results are shown in Table 17.1. The limit and ultimate strengths are normalized by a baseline strengths of 91 and 136 MPa, respectively. The latter strengths are calculated using an opterating temperature of 22 °C and moisture content of 0.005.

TABLE 17.1   NORMALIZED UNIAXIAL TENSILE STRENGTH OF [±45] AT VARIOUS OPERATING TEMPERATURES AND MOISTURE CONTENTS.

	c, percent	0.0	0.5	1.0
T_{opr}	dT			
–28	–50	1.0	1.3	1.4
22	0	0.8	1.0	1.2
122	100	0.3	0.4	0.3

The hygrothermal exponents in Equation 17.20 have made major reduction in strength in hot/wet conditions, and increase in low temperatures. The data in this table can be used to determine the value of the exponents. The exponents however cannot be entirely arbitrary. Exponent **a** governs the matrix modulus. It should be lower than exponent **c** for the matrix strength if the linearized failure strain at elevated temperature is lower. Exponent **b** for the stress partitioning parameter should not be much different from exponent **a** because the average stress ratio between the fiber and matrix should not be much different from the stiffness ratio between the fiber and the matrix. In Table 17.2, we show the change in ply data resulting from the hygrothermal conditions using the exponents in Equations 17.20 and 17.21.

TABLE 17.2   HYGROTHERMAL EFFECTS ON CFRP, T300/5208 UNIDIRECTIONAL COMPOSITE.

c, percent	**0.5**	**0.5**	**1.0**
T_{opr}	**–28**	**22**	**122**
E_x, GPa	181	181	180
E_y, GPa	11.0	10.3	7.4
v_x	0.28	0.28	0.28
E_s, GPa	7.7	7.2	5.0
X, MPa	1502	1500	1491
X', MPa	1532	1500	1386
Y, MPa	53	40	10
Y', MPa	325	246	63
S, MPa	90	68	17

17.5 HYGROTHERMAL EFFECTS ON A LAMINATE

The following laminate, cure temperature and loads will be used to assess the hygrothermal effects, and the results are listed in Tables 17.3 and 17.4:

- Laminate: $\pi/4$ quasi–isotropic.
- Cure temperature = 122^0 K
- Applied loads:
  Uniaxial tensile load: {1,0,0}
  Uniaxial compressive load: {–1,0,0}
  Pure shear load: {0,0,1}
  Internal pressure of a cylindrical vessel: {1,2,0}

For the baseline uniaxial tensile strength of a $\pi/4$ laminate at room temperature and moisture content of 0.5, the limit strength is 325 MPa, and the ultimate strength is 498 MPa. These strengths are used to normalize the strength at limit and ultimate under various temperature moisture combinations. Based on our results, there is only a small difference between two normalized values of the limit and ultimate strengths. For simplicity, we will show in Table 17.3 the average of the two normalized values.

TABLE 17.3   NORMALIZED UNIAXIAL TENSILE STRENGTH AT VARIOUS OPERATING
              TEMPERATURES AND MOISTURE CONTENTS.

c, percent		0.0	0.5	1.0
Topr	dT			
–28	–50	0.6	1.0	1.1
22	0	0.6	1.0	1.1
122	100	0.5	0.8	0.8

We see strength reduction at high temperature as well as at dry conditions. The high temperature effect is due to the reduced matrix strength. The reduction in strength at zero moisture (dry condition) is due to increased curing stresses.

For the baseline uniaxial compressive strength of a $\pi/4$ laminate at room temperature and moisture content of 0.005, the limit strength is 419 MPa, and the ultimate strength is 629 MPa. These strengths will be used to normalize the strengths at limit and ultimate under various temperature moisture combinations. For simplicity, we will show in Table 17.4 the average values between the two normalized strengths.

TABLE 17.4   NORMALIZED UNIAXIAL COMPRESSIVE STRENGTH AT VARIOUS
               OPERATING TEMPERATURES AND MOISTURE CONTENTS.

	c, percent	0.0	0.5	1.0
Topr	dT			
−28	−50	0.5	1.0	1.2
22	0	0.5	1.0	1.2
122	100	0.5	0.8	0.6

For the baseline shear strength of a $\pi/4$ laminate at room temperature and moisture content of 0.5, the limit strength is 157 MPa, and the ultimate strength is 235 MPa. These strengths will be used to normalize the strengths at limit and ultimate under various temperature moisture combinations. For simplicity, we will again show in Table 17.5 the average values.

TABLE 17.5   NORMALIZED SHEAR STRENGTH AT VARIOUS OPERATING
               TEMPERATURES AND MOISTURE CONTENTS.

	c, percent	0.0	0.5	1.0
Topr	dT			
−28	−50	0.6	1.0	1.4
22	0	0.6	1.0	1.4
122	100	0.6	1.0	0.8

For the baseline circumferential strength of a pressure vessel subjected to internal pressure, using a $\pi/4$ laminate at room temperature and moisture content of 0.5, the limit strength is 359 MPa, and the ultimate strength is 603 MPa. These strengths will be used to normalize the strengths at limit and ultimate under various temperature moisture combinations.

TABLE 17.6   NORMALIZED CIRCUMFERENTIAL STRENGTHS AT LIMIT/ULTIMATE
               OF A PRESSURE VESSEL AT VARIOUS OPERATING TEMPERATURES
               AND MOISTURE CONTENTS.

	c, percent	0.0	0.5	1.0
Topr	dT			
−28	−50	0.4/0.9	1.0/1.0	1.2/1.0
22	0	0.4/0.9	1.0/1.0	1.2/1.0
122	100	0.4/0.5	0.9/0.8	1.1/1.0

17.5 CONCLUSIONS

Based on the results of Tables 17.3 to 17.6 we can assess the effects of operating temperature and the moisture content on the strength of composite laminates.

• Hygrothermal effects on the limit and ultimate are similar, and follow the trend from the lowest stress level at cold/dry conditions due to residual stress to the highest at cold/wet conditions where absorbed moisture cancels the residual stress resulting from high temperature cure.

• Moisture absorption relieves curing stresses, and increases both the limit and ultimate strengths. The effect on the limit is greater than that on the ultimate.

• Hygrothermal effects on the ply are not translated directly to laminates. Both laminate layup and the nature of the applied load have as much effect as the temperature and moisture conditions. We must rely on laminated plate theory to estimate these effects.

• The proposed method of assessing hygrothermal effects requires many assumptions. First is the nondimensional temperature, with a built–in temperature shift due to moisture absorption. The second is the power law relations shown in Equations 17.3 et al. Material constants are divided in groups in order to reduce the number of exponents. Then the value of the exponents must be determined.

• We would like to emphasize the need for extensive data and improved calculations to assess all these highly interacting parameters. Hygrothermal effects are important because composite materials do expect to operate under different environmental conditions. Furthermore, more severe conditions are anticipated in the future. Thus a rational and consistent methodology is essential.

Section 18

BOLTED JOINTS

Frank L. Matthews
IMPERIAL COLLEGE OF SCIENCE AND TECHNOLOGY, LONDON

18.1. GENERAL BEHAVIOR OF BOLTED JOINTS

The design methods that have been established for structural joints in metals are applicable, in a general fashion, to fiber–reinforced plastics (FRP). However, as is to be expected, the physical nature of FRP does introduce problems that are not encountered with metals, and, although trends can be established [18–1], it is usually not possible to "read across" from one composite system to another. The anisotropic stiffness and strength, the low interlaminar shear, and through–thickness tensile strengths mean that unexpected failure modes may be introduced.

The behavior of the joint could also be influenced by the fiber type and form (random mat, woven fabric, unidirectional, etc.), resin type and fiber volume fraction. In addition the strength of the joint is determined by the joint type (single or double lap, etc.) and geometry, bolt size, washer size, clamping force, hole size and tolerance. Of all these parameters the clamping force, namely the force in the through–thickness direction caused by tightening the bolt, is of critical importance.

Four basic failure modes, as shown in Figure 18.1, can be identified. Ideally, one would like the corresponding failure loads to occur at the same load. If this is not possible, bearing failure is preferred, if only because this mode is not catastrophic. However, this may not produce the lightest joint.

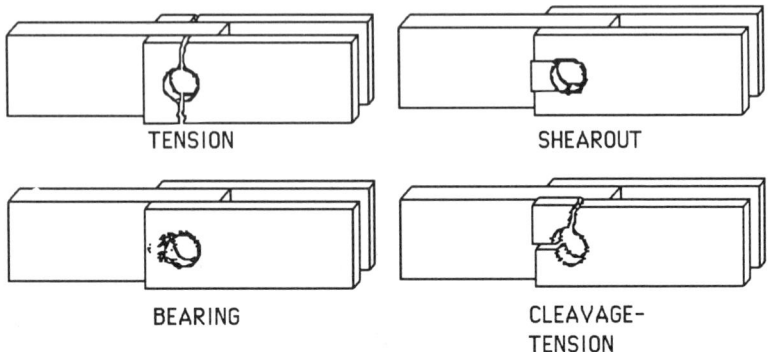

TENSION   SHEAROUT

BEARING   CLEAVAGE-
                                     TENSION

FIGURE 18.1   FAILURE MODES IN A SINGLE BOLT JOINT

For reasons of cost and convenience, basic experimental data is usually obtained from single bolt specimens, loaded in double shear, with the geometry shown in Figure 18.2. Stresses are defined in terms of the failure load (P), normally taken as the maximum tensile load sustained by the joint.

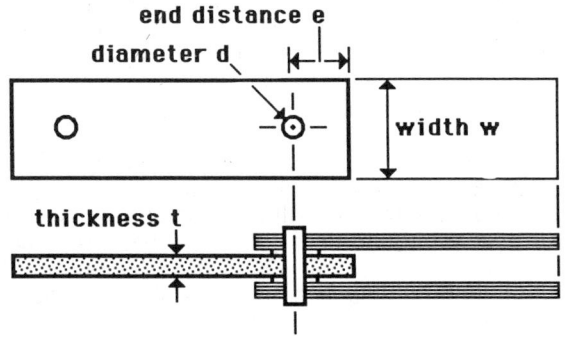

FIGURE18.2 DEFINITION OF GEOMETRY OF SINGLE BOLT JOINT

For a multi–bolt joint the width (w) is replaced by the pitch (p). Even when failure is in a mode other than bearing, the strength is usually expressed in terms of the bearing stress σ_b (=P/dt).

18.2 INFLUENCE OF VARIOUS PARAMETERS

GEOMETRY

The geometric factors that influence joint strength are width (w), end distance (e), laminate thickness (t) and bolt diameter (d). Width and end distance must be above a certain minimum if full bearing strength is to be attained. Below these minima, tensile failure will occur if the width is too small, and shear out or cleavage failure if the end distance is too small.

The effect of altering **d/t** varies with material. As a general rule, the ratio of bolt hole diameter to thickness should be greater than unity to avoid failure of the bolt.

LOAD DIRECTION

The strength of a bolted joint will vary with load direction due to the anisotropic nature of the material. Ideally, the direction of the applied load should coincide with the direction of maximum strength, although in practice such coincidence cannot be guaranteed. The more "isotropic" a lay–up, the less sensitive it is to load direction.

Joints loaded in compression are not sensitive to geometry changes and are generally stronger than joints loaded in tension. The latter approaches the strength of the former at large values of **e** and **w**.

LOADING TYPE AND RATE

Joint strength appears insensitive to changes within the normal range of loading rates corresponding to static testing. Although very little information is available about impact and creep loading, it is likely that in both cases strength will be less than for static loading.

The limited information available on fatigue loading suggests that lifetimes of several million cycles can be expected for loads as high as 70 percent of static ultimate, for joints loaded in double shear. Single shear loading causes a drastic reduction in fatigue strength.

BOLT FIT

For maximum strength the bolt hole should ideally be reamed to size. Likewise, the fit of the bolt in the washer influences strength, and again the ideal situation would be for the washer hole to be reamed to fit the bolt.

A "normal fit" for the hole and washer can reduce the bearing strength by up to 25 percent from the ideal situation. Some of the scatter in test results can be attributed to this effect, the strength being dependent on the relative position of washer and hole.

Clamping Force

For a given configuration and material the most significant factor is the through–thickness clamping force provided by tightening the bolt. The presence of washers prevents the laminate from splitting through the thickness on the loaded side of the hole, as happens with a plain pin offering no such restraint.

It is possible that a grossly over tightened bolt could damage the laminate by forcing the washers into the surface. For normal volume fractions this does not appear to be a serious problem. Indeed, for a reasonable value of d/t it is more likely that the bolt threads will strip before laminate damage occurs.

The bearing strength of a fully tightened bolt can be up to four times that of a pin joint. Even a "finger tight" nut can show a strength twice that of a pin joint. The ratio between fully tight and finger tight strengths depends on the material; typical data is shown in:

- Figure 18.3 for woven roving GRP (glass/polyester)
- Figure 18.4 for GFRP (unidirectional glass/epoxy laminate)
- Figure 18.5 for CFRP (unidirectional carbon/epoxy laminate)
- Figure 18.6 for woven fabric KFRP (Kevlar/epoxy laminate)

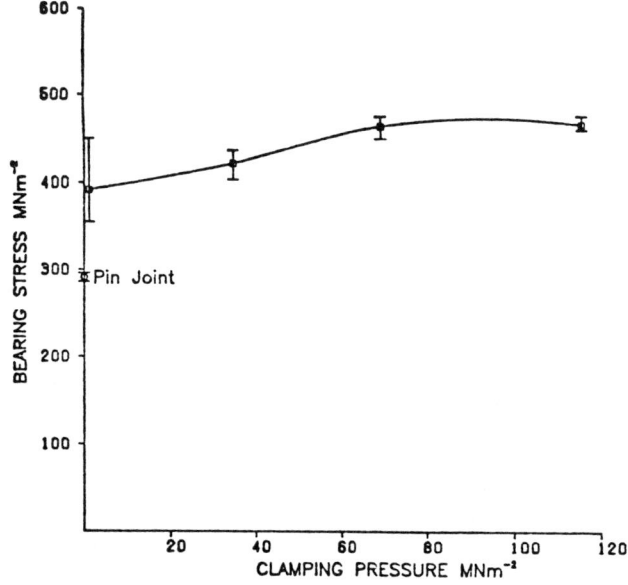

FIGURE 18.3. VARIATION OF BEARING STRESS WITH BOLT CLAMPING PRESSURE FOR WOVEN GRP LAMINATES

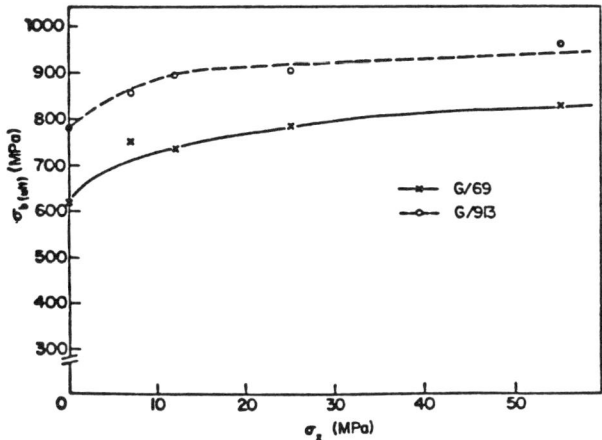

FIGURE 18.4   VARIATION OF BEARING STRENGTH OF [0/±45] GFRP LAMINATES WITH BOLT CLAMPING PRESSURE. d=6.35mm, t=3mm

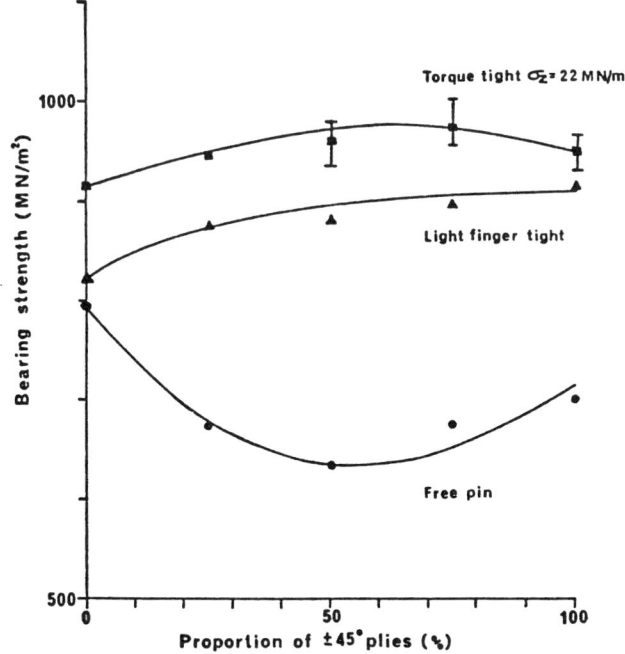

FIGURE 18.5   EFFECT OF LATERAL CONSTRAINT ON THE BEARING STRENGTH OF HTS/914 [0/±45] CFRP LAMINATES

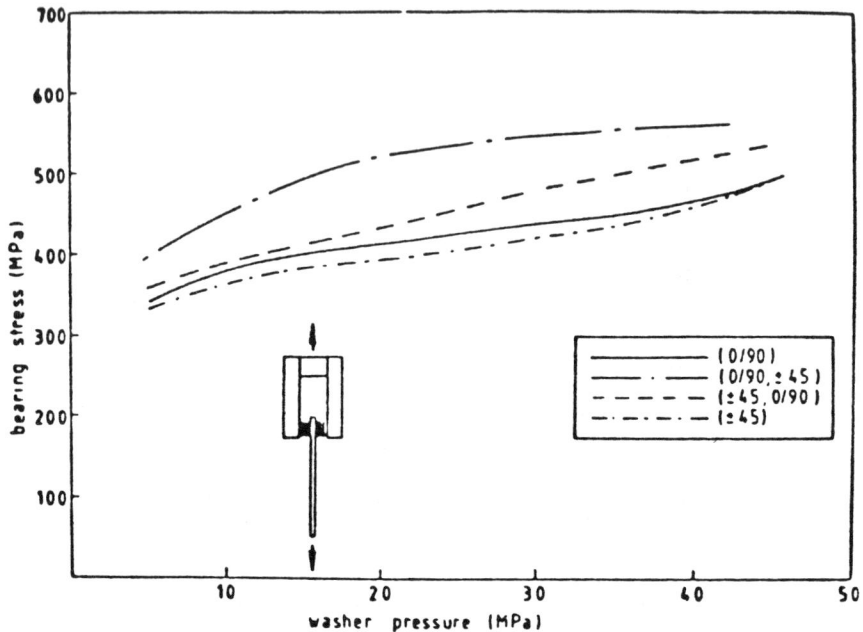

FIGURE 18.6   BEARING STRESS AS A FUNCTION OF LATERAL CONSTRAINT FOR WOVEN KFRP LAMINATES

Fiber and Resin Type

The type of resin, fiber, ply orientation and stacking sequence clearly play an important role in determining strength. The resin becomes relatively more important as the proportion of the ±45 degree fibers increases. Contrary to what might be expected, such a lay–up has a high bearing strength if it is adequately restrained (by washers).

The highest bearing strengths are attained for lay–ups containing around 50 percent of 0 degree plies. Here the presence of ±45 degree plies is also beneficial in improving the compressive strength of the constrained 0 degree plies.

Typical data for GRP, GFRP, CFRP, and KFRP are given in Figures 18.7–18.14 in which the variation of bearing strength with w/d and e/d is shown. More complete information on the behavior of these materials can be found in [18–2 to 5], respectively.

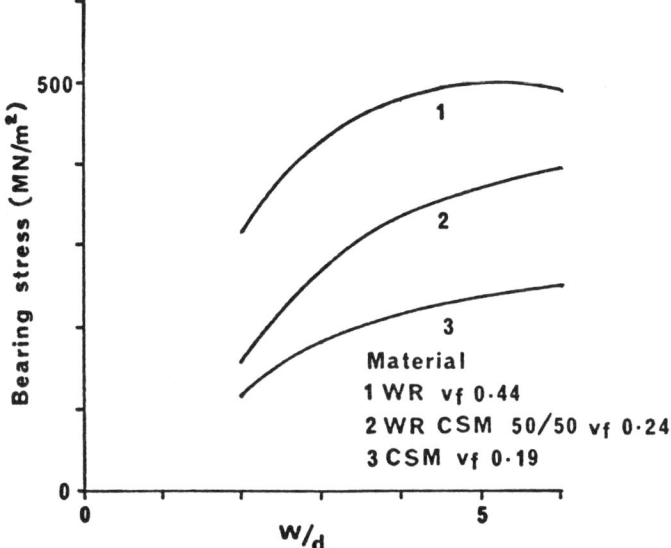

FIGURE 18.7   VARIATION OF BEARING STRESS VERSUS w/d FOR GRP

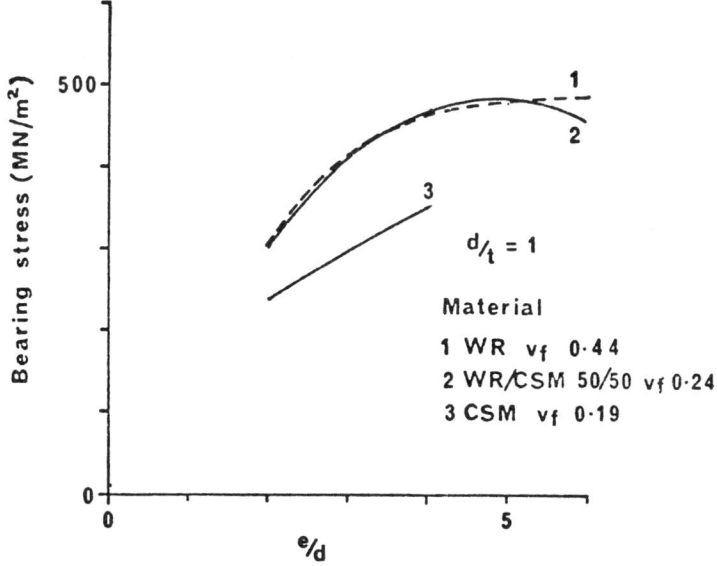

FIGURE 18.8   VARIATION OF BEARING STRESS VERSUS e/d FOR GRP

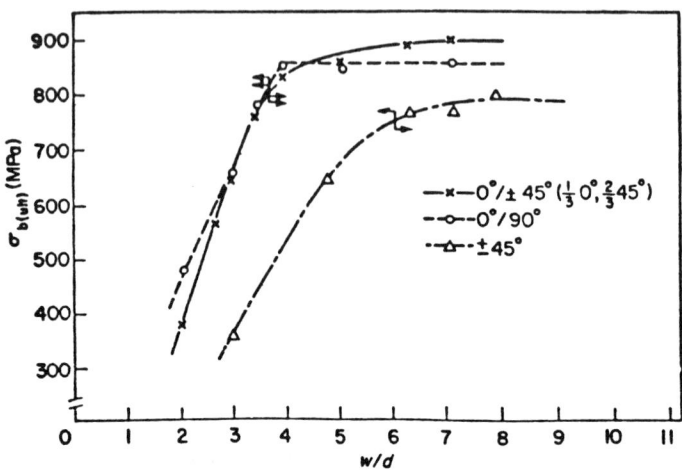

FIGURE 18.9   BEARING STRESS VERSUS w/d RATIO FOR VARIOUS G/913 GFRP
LAMINATES, d=6.35mm, t= 3 mm, s_z= 12 MPa

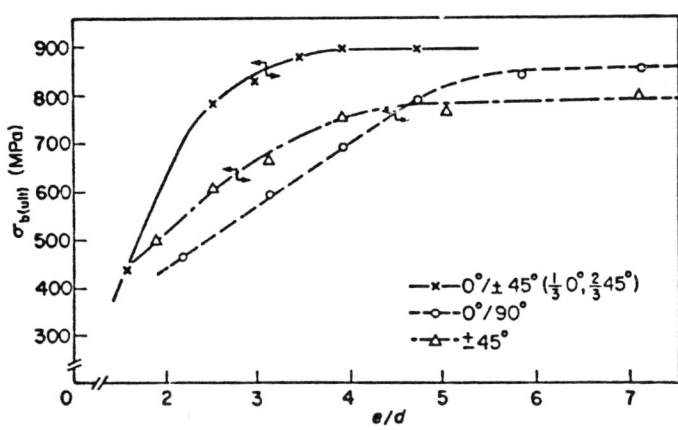

FIGURE 18.10 BEARING STRESS VERSUS e/d RATIO FOR VARIOUS G/913 GFRP
LAMINATES. d=6.35mm, t=3mm, s_z=12 MPa

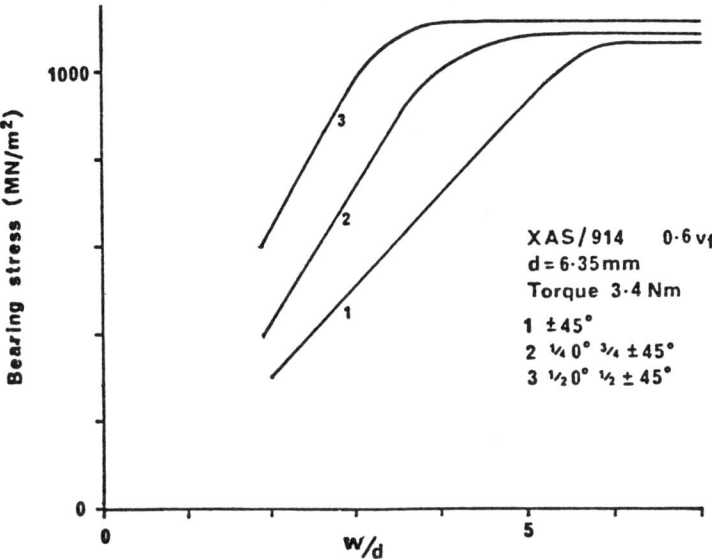

FIGURE 18.11 VARIATION OF BEARING STRESS WITH w/d FOR [0/±45] CFRP

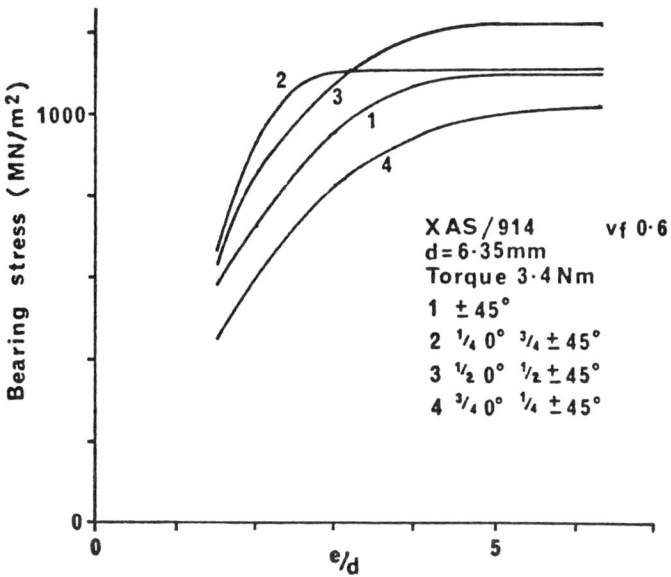

FIGURE 18.12 VARIATION OF BEARING STRESS WITH e/d FOR [0/±45] CFRP

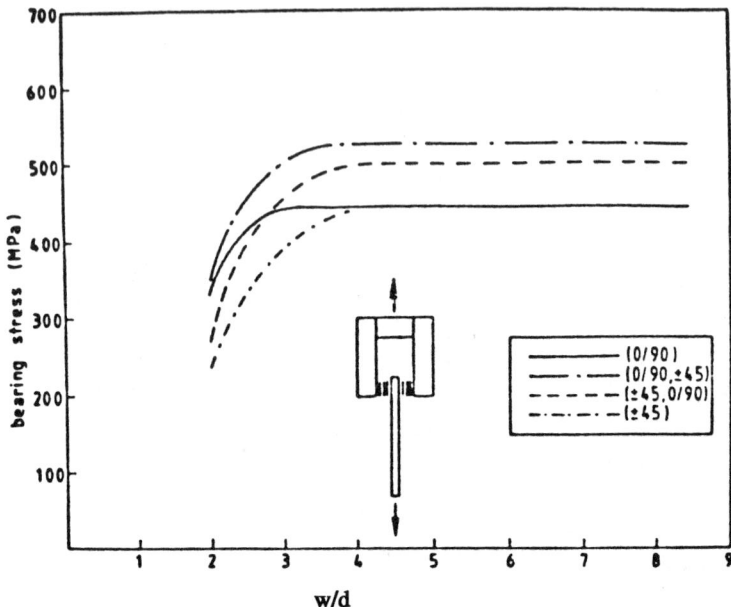

FIGURE 18.13 BEARING STRESS AS A FUNCTION OF w/d FOR WOVEN KFRP

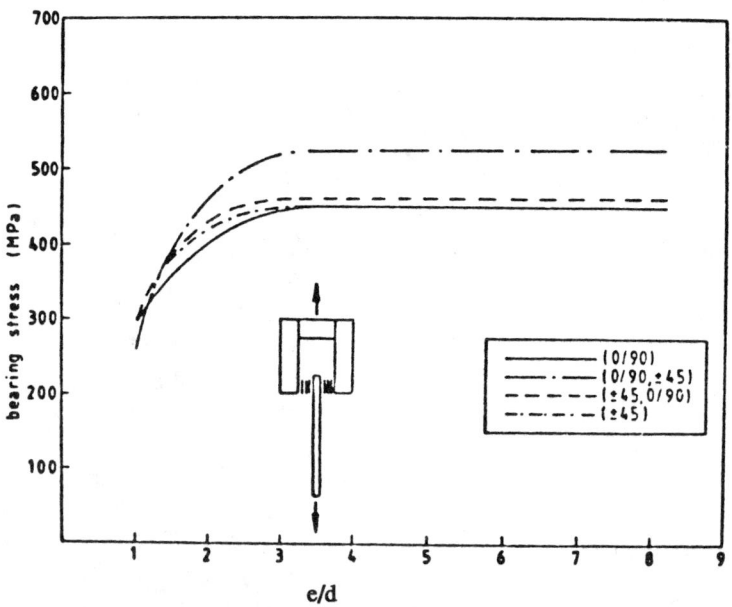

FIGURE 18.14 BEARING STRESS AS A FUNCTION OF e/d FOR WOVEN KFRP

The strength values given in Figures 18.7–18.14 are for fully tightened bolts and are averages of results from 3–5 replicates at each data point. The standard deviation to be expected on such data is probably about 10 percent of the mean.

A more complete test program to obtain B–Basis allowables on GRP [18–2] indicates strengths around 80 percent of the values given. This could probably be taken as typical for the other materials.

Due to relaxation of the matrix, the bolt clamping force will decrease with time. Work with GRP [18–2] indicates that this should not be a serious problem at room temperature.

18.3 MULTI–BOLT JOINTS

Unless the pitch is greater than four bolt diameters, the strength per bolt in a row or line joint (see Figure 18.15) will be less than that of a single bolt joint. Again, data is scarce, but based on work with GRP [18–2] a strength reduction factor, **K**, as shown in Figure 18.16 can be assumed. The strength of the joint, **P**, is then;

$$P = nKP_{min} \qquad (18.1)$$

where **n** represents the number of bolts, and P_{min} is obtained from curves such as those shown in Figures 18.8, 18.10, 18.12, or 18.14 using the appropriate end distance for the joint under consideration.

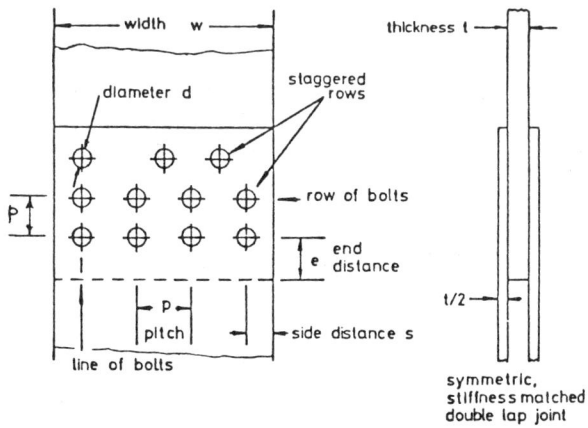

FIGURE 18.15 DEFINITION OF GEOMETRY FOR A MULTI–BOLT JOINT

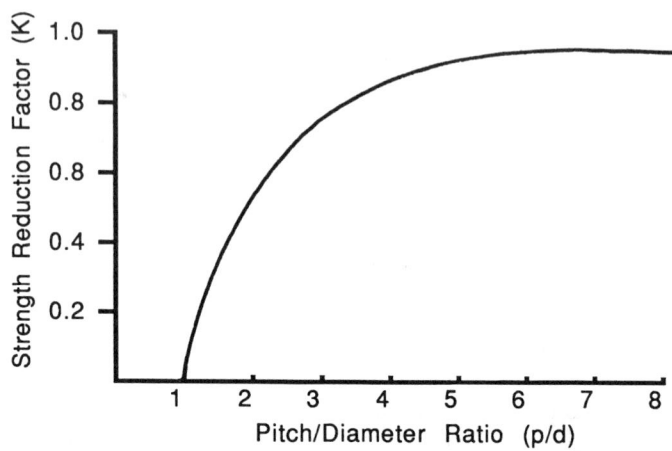

FIGURE 18.16.   VARIATION OF STRENGTH REDUCTION FACTOR, K, FOR
MULTI–BOLT JOINTS VERSUS PITCH/DIAMETER RATIO

Single Lap Joints

Curves of bearing stress versus width or end distance follow the same form as those for double lap, single bolt, configurations (Figures 18.7–18.14). As a general rule, the 'plateau' value will be about 15 percent lower for single lap joints.

18.4   DESIGN METHODS FOR SINGLE BOLT JOINTS IN DOUBLE SHEAR

General Information

The results presented in Section 18.1 indicate that the strengths can be obtained corresponding to a fully tight bolt. The design curves presented in this section use an idealized form of that data. In practice, 'B–Basis' curves would probably be used.

Use of such design curves allows the prediction of the maximum joint strength that can be expected. Suitable reduction factors can then be applied, where appropriate, to allow for fall–off in bolt tension, hole tolerance, multi–bolts, etc.

It is assumed here that the laminate has been designed and thus its thickness and load capacity are known. We wish to determine the size of bolt needed to transmit this load for a given geometry, or vice versa. It is assumed that data is available for a range of d/t. Figures 18.17–18.22 are taken from Reference 18–2 for GRF which showed σ_b increases with d/t. Other materials show the opposite trend. This should not invalidate the general approach.

Determine the Load that can be carried for a given geometry.

(a) The width is fixed but end distance can be varied (or vice versa)

First, select a bolt to give **d/t**=1 and calculate **w/d**. Use the curves of σ_b versus **w/d** to obtain the corresponding bearing stress. Transfer this value to the curve of σ_b versus **e/d**, and obtain, **e/d** for the same **d/t**. Next select a larger bolt, recalculate **d/t** and **w/d**, and repeat the process (**d/t** will be higher and **w/d** lower than before). Then check the usefulness of the second value of σ_b for a **P/t–d–σ_b** chart (Figure 18.17) or, if preferred, by calculation. The initial values of stress (σ_{b1}) and diameter (d_1) will give the corresponding failing load per unit thickness (**P$_1$/t**). The second set, σ_{b2} and d_2, will give an alternative strength (**P$_2$/t**). The process can be repeated with other bolt sizes, the largest value of **P/t** then being selected. The strength (**P**) and geometry (**e**) are now known.

The whole process may also be used if the end distance is fixed but the width is varied.

This procedure can be applied to a multi–bolt joint by making use of the reduction factor quoted above.

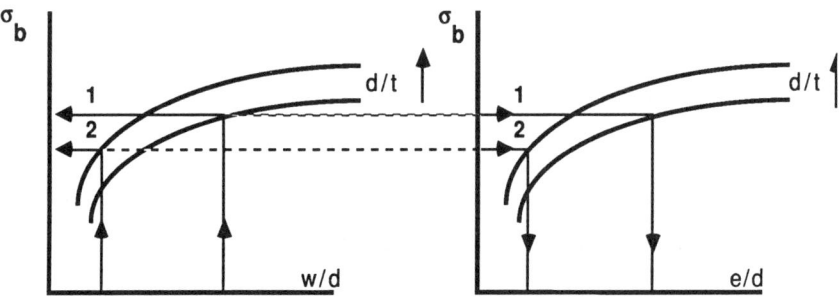

FIGURE 18.17 DETERMINING LOAD WITH FIXED WIDTH BUT VARIED END DISTANCE

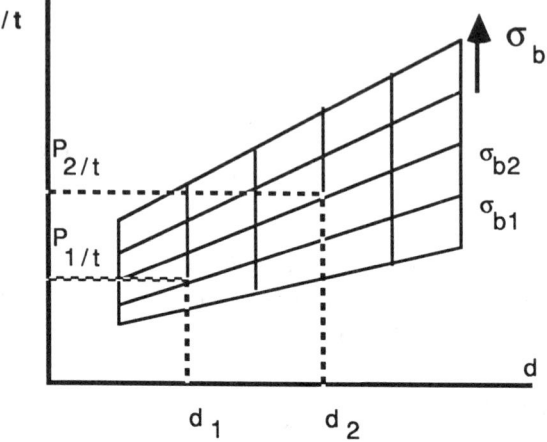

FIGURE 18.18 CHART OF P/t VERSUS D FOR VALUES OF σ_b

(b) <u>The width and end distance are both fixed</u>

First, select a bolt, as in (a) above, to give a **d/t**=1, and calculate **w/d** and **e/d**. Find the corresponding bearing stress from the curves. The failure load will correspond to the smaller of the two values of σ_b and can be found from the **P/t–d–σ_b** chart. For a second iteration, larger bolt is chosen, and the whole procedure repeated, as in (a).

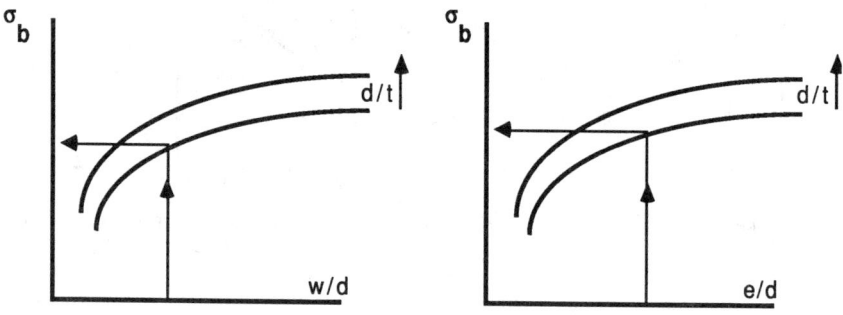

FIGURE 18.19 DETERMINING LOAD WITH WIDTH AND END DISTANCE BOTH FIXED

Determine the Geometry needed to carry a given load

(a) <u>No restrictions on width and end distance</u>

Select, as above, a bolt to give **d/t**=1 and calculate the corresponding bearing stress (**P/dt**). If this stress is above the "plateau" on the curves, choose a larger bolt and repeat the process. The intercept with the appropriate **d/t** curve will give the required geometry.

If it is impossible to get an intercept with any reasonable bolt size, then a multi–bolt joint is required.

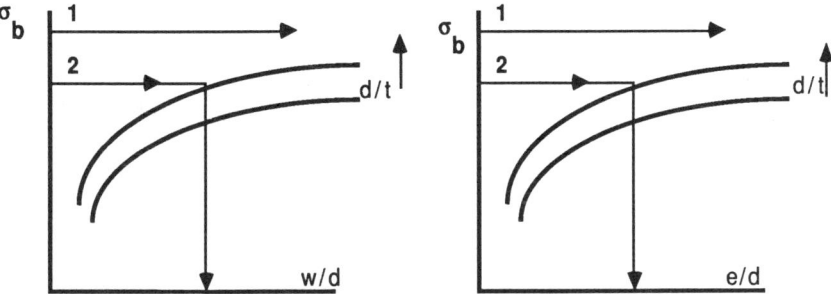

FIGURE 18.20   DETERMINING THE GEOMETRY NEEDED TO CARRY A GIVEN LOAD
WITH NO RESTRICTIONS ON WIDTH OR END DISTANCE

(b) Restriction on end distance or width

Suppose there is an upper limit on **e** (i.e. on **e/d**). The procedure is similar to (a) above in that increasing values of **d** are selected until an intercept on the curve, below the limiting **e/d**, is obtained. The limiting value of **e/d** will decrease as **d** increases. The corresponding value of **w** is found from the other curve. The curves are used in the other order if the restriction is on width.

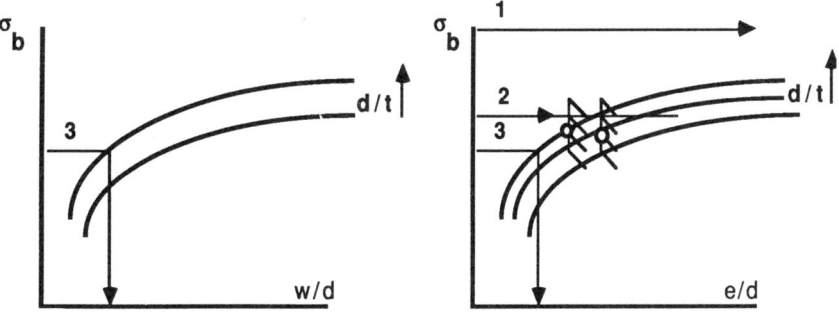

FIGURE 18.21   DETERMINING THE GEOMETRY NEEDED TO CARRY A GIVEN LOAD
WITH RESTRICTIONS ON END DISTANCE OR WIDTH

(c) Restriction on end distance and width

In this case the procedure follows as in (b) above, but continues until an
intercept is obtained below limits. Thus, in the illustration given, "3" would
be acceptable, but "2" would not, because the intercept is above the e/d limit.

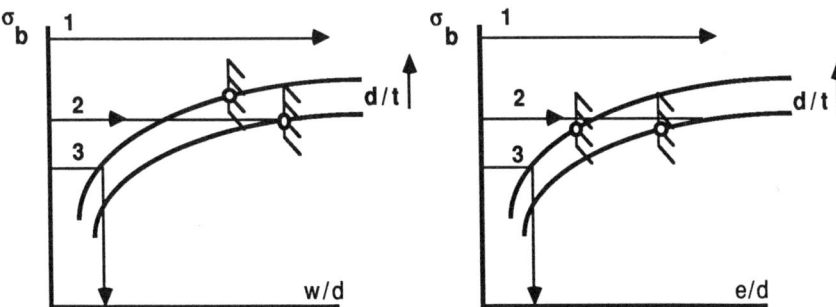

FIGURE 18.22   DETERMINING THE GEOMETRY NEEDED TO CARRY A GIVEN LOAD
WITH RESTRICTIONS ON END DISTANCE AND WIDTH

REFERENCES

18–1.   Godwin, E. W. and Matthews, F. L., 'A Review of the Strength of Joints in
Fibre–Reinforced Plastics. Part 1: Mechanically Fastened Joints', *Composites*, 11, 3,
July 1980, p. 155.

18–2.   Matthews F. L., Godwin, E. W. and Kilty, P. F., 'The Design of Bolted Joints in
GRP.' Technical Note TN 82–105, Dept. of Aeronautics, Imperial College,
London, UK, 1982.

18–3.   Kretsis, G. and Matthews, F. L., 'The Strength of Bolted Joints in Glass
Fibre/Epoxy Laminates'. *Composites*, 16, 2, April 1985, p. 92.

18–4.   Collings, T. A., 'On the Bearing Strength of CFRP Laminates', *Composites*, 13, 3,
July 1982, p. 241.

18–5.   Hodgkinson, J. M., DeBeer, D. L. and Matthews, F. L., 'The Strength of Bolted
Joints in 'Kevlar' RP', Proc Workshop, Composites Design for Space Applications,
Noordwijk, Holland, 16/18 October 1985, The European Space Agency, ESTEC.

Section 19

FATIGUE BEHAVIOR

Ran Y. Kim

UNIVERSITY OF DAYTON RESEARCH INSTITUTE, DAYTON

19.1 FAILURE MECHANISMS

Composite materials exhibit very complex failure mechanisms under static and fatigue loading because of anisotropic characteristics in their strength and stiffness. Fatigue failure is usually accompanied with extensive damages which are multiplied throughout specimen volume instead of a predominant single crack, which is often observed in most isotropic brittle materials. The four basic failure mechanisms are matrix cracking, delamination, fiber breakage, and interfacial debonding. Any combination of these is mainly responsible for fatigue damages which may result in reduced fatigue strength and stiffness. The type and degree of these damages vary widely depending upon material properties, laminations including stacking sequence, type of fatigue loading, etc. It has been observed that the damage development under fatigue and static loading is similar except that fatigue at a given stress level causes additional damages to occur as a function of cycles.

19.2 MATRIX CRACKING

In multidirectional laminates under in–plane loading, the failure usually occurs successively from the weakest ply to the strongest ply. As an example, consider the matrix cracking process of a $[0/90/\pm45]_s$ graphite/epoxy laminate, subjected to uniaxial tension. We would expect successive transverse cracks in the respective off–axis ply as the load applied to the laminate increases. The first cracks occur in the 90 degree plies to be followed by the ±45 degree plies. The stress level at the initiation of the first crack in the respective ply can be predicted using analytical approaches. The correlation between analysis and experiment is reasonably good for the 90 degree plies but found to be rather poor for the ±45 degree plies. The main reason for this large discrepancy for the ±45 degree plies appears to be due to the influence of cracks developed earlier in the 90 degree ply.

Figure 19.1 shows micrographs of transverse cracks observed at free edges. The first crack occurred in the 90 degree plies and propagated to the interfaces. With increasing load, new cracks occur in the ±45 degree plies adjacent to the 90 degree plies. Most of these cracks appear at the tip of the 90 degree cracks and are extended to the interface of the ±45 degree plies.

Subsequently, the number of such cracks increases with the load until laminate failure. However, prior to laminate failure the number of cracks in some cases reaches a limiting case where no further new cracks occur in spite of additional loading. Figure 19.2 presents the number of cracks in the 90 degree and +45 degree plies as function of applied stress. Most specimens did not show any cracks in the –45 degree ply until final failure, although the lamination theory predicts the same stress state in both the +45 degree and –45 degree plies. The main reason for this discrepancy is the redistribution of ply stress due to the cracks developed.

 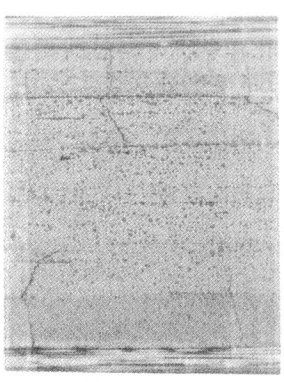

(a) 345 MPa   (b) 552 MPa

FIGURE 19.1   MICROGRAPHS SHOWING CRACK PATTERNS UNDER STATIC LOADING: $[0/90/\pm45]_s$.

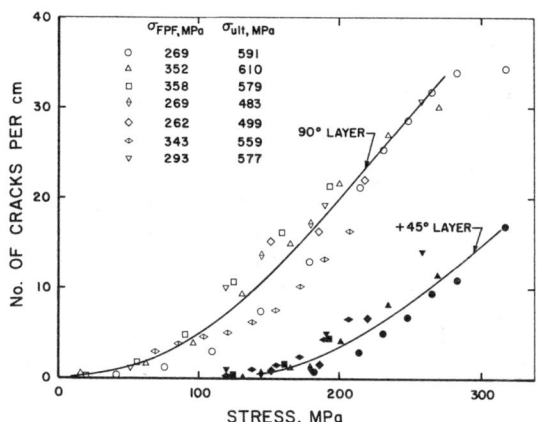

FIGURE 19.2   STRESS VERSUS NUMBER OF CRACKS FOR $[0/90/\pm45]_s$ LAMINATE SUBJECTED TO STATIC LOADING. THE STRESS REPRESENTS DIFFERENTIAL STRESS OBTAINED BY SUBTRACTING STRESS AT FIRST PLY FAILURE (σ_{FPF}) FROM APPLIED STRESS.

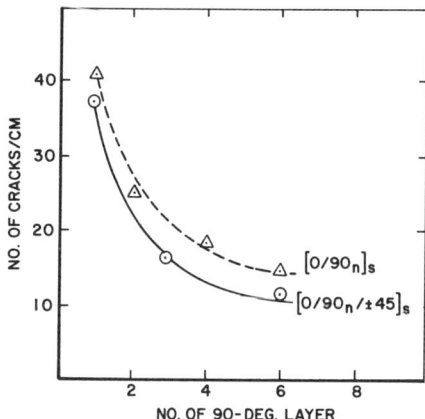

FIGURE 19.3   EFFECTS OF THE 90 DEGREE PLY THICKNESS ON THE CRACK
DENSITY AT LIMITING CASE.

Figure 19.3 also shows the effect of ply thickness on the number of cracks in
the limiting case.   The crack density for a given ply appears to be
independent of laminate type.   The multiple cracking behavior can also be
predictable by analytical models based on shear lag analysis.   However, there
exists a large discrepancy between prediction and experiment, especially in
high stress regions.

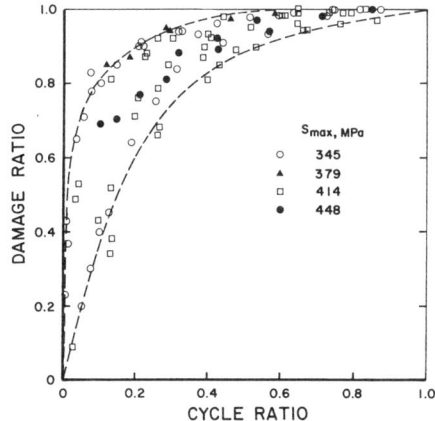

FIGURE 19.4   INCREASE OF CRACK DENSITY FOR $[0/90/\pm45]_s$ LAMINATE SUBJECTED
TO FATIGUE LOADING

In fatigue loading, the number of cracks in each angle ply is higher compared with that in static loading and reaches a limiting case. The multiplication process of transverse cracks in the course of fatigue cycle are shown in Figure 19.4. The damage ratio is defined here as the ratio of the crack density at "n" cycles to the crack density at final failure. Cracks in all off–axis plies were lumped together. Most of crack multiplication (approximately 60 to 90 percent) occurred during the first 20 percent of the fatigue life. A good amount of fatigue life is seen to remain after reaching the crack density.

The stacking sequence in a laminate plays a significant role in the development of cracks as shown in Figure 19.5.

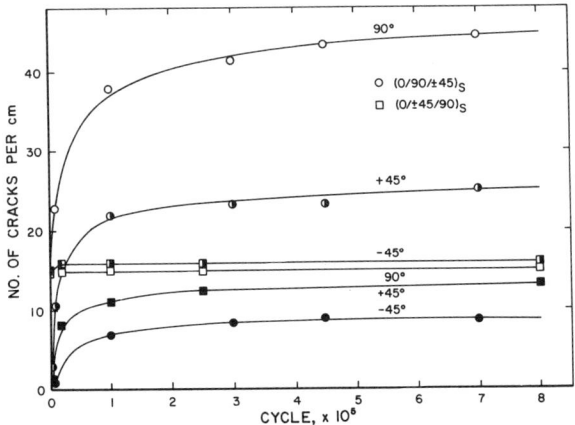

FIGURE 19.5   FATIGUE CYCLES VERSUS NUMBER OF CRACKS FOR [0/90/±45]$_s$ AND [0/±45/90]$_s$ LAMINATES.

There is a considerable difference in the development of the 90 degree cracks between the two stacking sequences of a quasi–isotropic laminate. The [0/90/±45]$_s$ laminate has more cracks in the 90 degree ply than the [0/±45/90]$_s$ laminate. This can be explained by consideration of the ply thickness and stress relaxation from free edge delamination. The thickness of the lumped 90 degree ply in the [0/±45/90]$_s$ is twice that of the dispersed 90 degree ply in the other laminate. The multiplication of 90 degree cracks was nearly arrested after free–edge delamination in the [0/±45/90]$_s$ laminate. The thickness effect is also seen in the +45 degree and –45 degree (twice as thick) plies in the [0/90/±45]$_s$ laminate. Figure 19.6 presents a series of micrographs of transverse cracks observed at the free–edge of the specimen in the course of fatigue loading. Unlike the static loading, transverse cracks in the –45 degree ply and numerous axial cracks, are shown. The axial cracks were initiated at the tip of the transverse crack and extended along the axial direction as increasing fatigue cycles. Interlaminar shear stress and transverse cracks in the +45 degree and –45 degree plies seem to be responsible for the delamination shown at 650,000 cycles in Figure 19.6.

Cracks in the 90 degree plies in the [0/90/±45]$_s$ laminate were also found less than one million cycles at the fatigue stress level of 172 MPa, which is much smaller than the stress level at the first ply failure under static loading (approximately 206 MPa). The first ply failure cycles are related to the transverse S–N relation.

The 0 degree plies are also susceptible to cracking in the fiber direction, due to transverse stress in the 0 degree ply of a multidirectional laminate. Because the transverse stress is usually small, axial cracking in 0 degree plies may not occur under static loading. However, under fatigue this axial cracking in cross laminates has been observed.

19.3 DELAMINATION

Delamination along the straight free–edge of composite laminates under an in–plane uniaxial load has been observed since the early 1970's. Since then a great amount of work has been reported on the free–edge problem in composite laminates, indicating that free–edge delamination is attributed to the existence of interlaminar stresses which are highly localized in the neighborhood of a free–edge under an in–plane loading. The nature of interlaminar stresses with regard to their magnitude and sign can be accurately calculated using analytical models. The magnitude and distribution of interlaminar stress components varies widely, depending on the type of laminate, stacking sequence, properties of the constituent materials and type of loading. For instance, crossply [0/90]$_s$ laminate shows much smaller interlaminar stress components than does the [±30/90]$_s$ laminate. Consequently, extensive delamination is observed in the [±30/90]$_s$ laminate under applied uniaxial tension. Whereas, very little or no delamination has been observed in crossply laminates except for thick laminates where the 90 degree plies stacked together rather than separated by 0 degree plies. The laminate stacking sequence determines whether interlaminar normal stresses will result in tension or compression at the free–edges and influences the magnitude of interlaminar stress components. As an example, consider a quasi–isotropic laminate with two stacking sequences, [0/90/±45]$_s$ and [0/±45/90]$_s$. The latter stacking sequence produces tensile normal stress along the free edges of a coupon, whereas the former produces compressive normal stresses at the same free–edges. Thus, the [0/±45/90]$_s$ laminate shows extensive delamination under tension before final failure, but does not show any delamination under compression because of compressive interlaminar normal stress produced. For the same reason, delamination occurs in the [0/90/±45]$_s$ laminate under uniaxial compression but not under uniaxial tension. By employing an appropriate failure theory in conjunction with stress analysis, the location and stress level at the onset of delamination can be predicted.

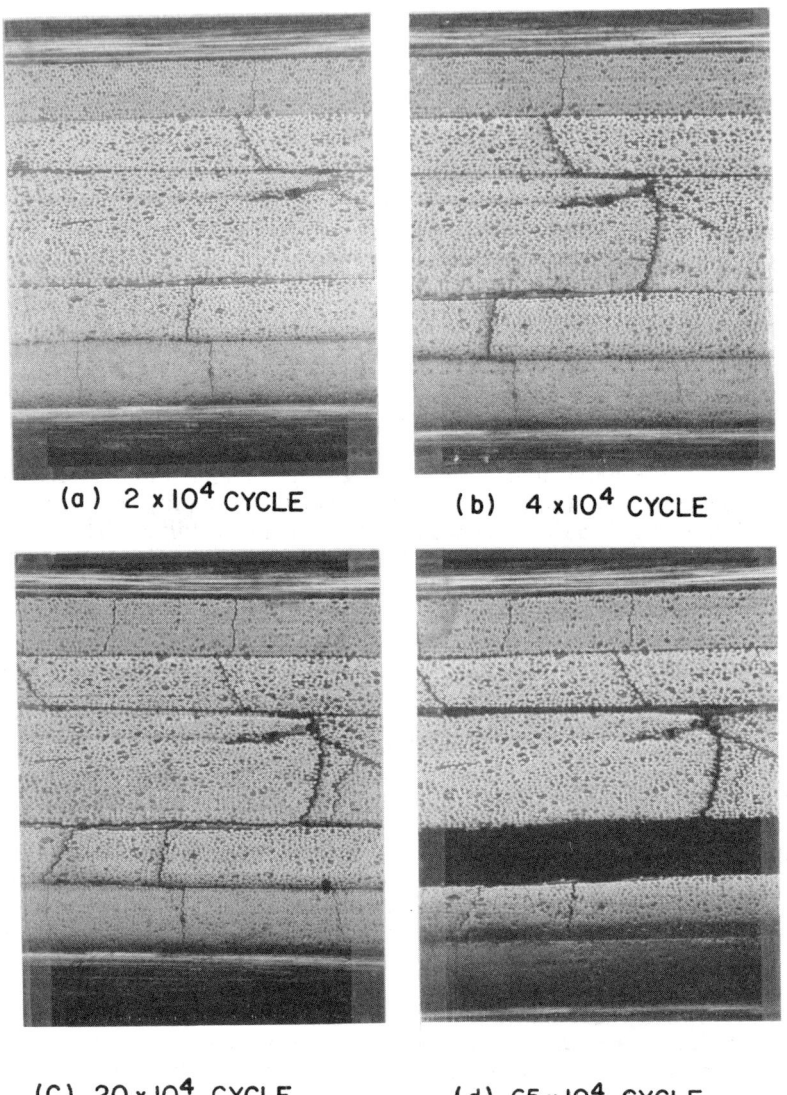

(a) 2×10^4 CYCLE   (b) 4×10^4 CYCLE

(C) 20×10^4 CYCLE   (d) 65×10^4 CYCLE

FIGURE 19.6   MICROGRAPHS SHOWING CRACK PATTERNS UNDER FATIGUE LOADING: $[0/90/\pm45]_s$, $\sigma max = 345$ MPa; N=793,300 CYCLES.

Figure 19.7 shows a micrograph of a free–edge and a x–ray picture of the specimen width showing delamination occurred in the [0/±45/90]$_s$ laminate under static tension. At about 350 MPa of the applied tension, delamination occurred and extended almost instantly over the entire length of the specimen taking irregular paths at the interfaces of the 90 degree/90 degree, 90 degree/–45 degree, and +45 degree/–45 degree plies. The change of the delamination path usually happened at transverse crack tips. The delamination also grew continuously toward the middle of the specimen from both free–edges as the load increased, Figure 19.7(b). In fatigue, the delamination at fatigue stress level smaller than static stress level at onset of delamination also occurs in the very early fatigue life and rapidly propagated

(a) 80X

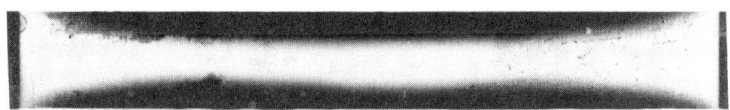

(b) 1X

FIGURE 19.7   A MICROGRAPH OF A FREE–EDGE (a) AND A X–RAY   PICTURE OF
THE WIDTH (b) SHOWING DELAMINATION OCCURRED IN CFRP
[0/±45/90]$_s$ SUBJECTED TO STATIC LOADING.

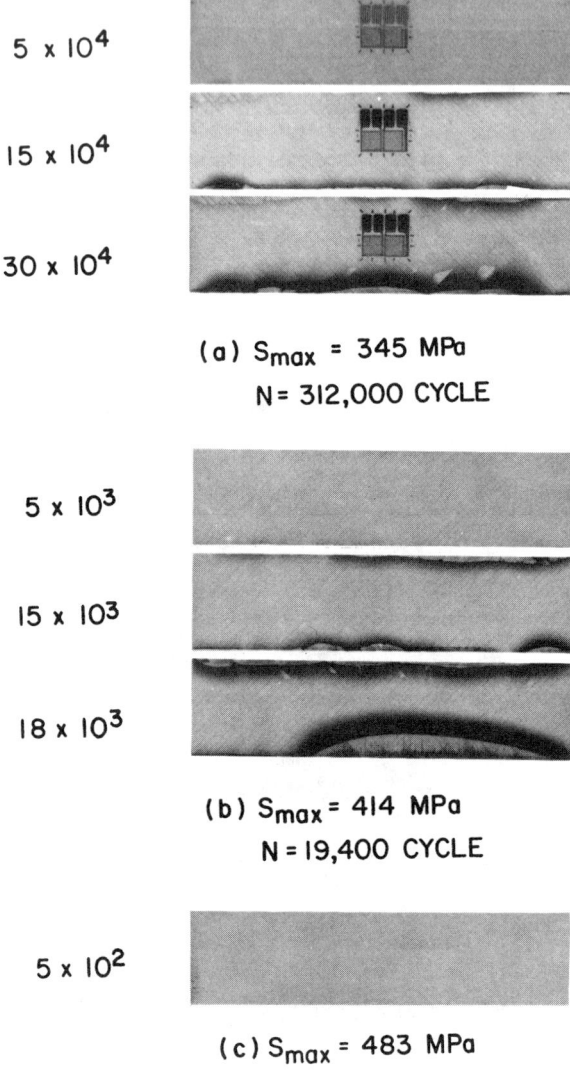

5 x 10⁴

15 x 10⁴

30 x 10⁴

(a) S_{max} = 345 MPa
N = 312,000 CYCLE

5 x 10³

15 x 10³

18 x 10³

(b) S_{max} = 414 MPa
N = 19,400 CYCLE

5 x 10²

(c) S_{max} = 483 MPa
N = 620 CYCLE

FIGURE 19.8. X–RAY PICTURES OF DELAMINATION GROWTH AS A FUNCTION OF FATIGUE CYCLES FOR A $[0/90/\pm45]_s$ CFRP T300/5208 LAMINATE

toward the middle of the specimen width as cycle increased. The lower bound of the delamination free stress level in fatigue expects to vary depending upon type of laminate for a predetermined life cycle.

In addition to interlaminar tensile stress, other mechanisms such as transverse cracking and interlaminar shearing appear to be significant in the onset and growth of delamination. The $[0/90/\pm45]_s$ laminate which has a compressive interlaminar normal stress does not show any delamination under static tension, but under tension fatigue shows a considerable delamination occurs at the interface between the +45 degree and –45 degree plies, Figure 19.6. The interlaminar shear stress at the +45 degree/–45 degree interface is not large enough to reach the interlaminar shear strength under static loading, but under fatigue loading, the shear stress becomes significant because of the high fatigue sensitivity of the epoxy matrix. Figure 19.8 shows x–ray pictures of delamination growth as a function of fatigue cycle for a $[0/90/\pm45]_s$ CFRP T300/5208 laminate. However, the growth of delamination in this case is much slower compared with the case of interlaminar tension.

19.4 FIBER BREAK AND INTERFACE DEBONDING

Fiber break and interface debonding differ widely depending on the properties of the constituent materials and defects of the fiber, shown in Figure 19.9. In most advanced composites, such as boron and graphite fiber with polymer matrix, the resistance to failure is greater in the matrix than in the fibers. Therefore, in longitudinal laminates, fibers are known to break before the interphase failure because of the presence of defects or weakness. The crack created by a fiber break tends to grow into the matrix at subsequent loading. The path of this growth depends mainly on matrix and interface properties. If bonding is strong, the crack tends to grow into the

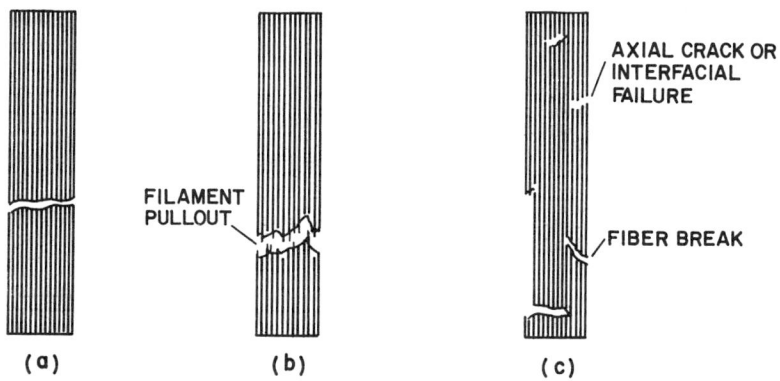

FIGURE 19.9 LONGITUDINAL TENSILE FAILURE MODES (a) BRITTLE, (b) BRITTLE WITH FILAMENT PULLOUT, (c) IRREGULAR.

matrix, exhibiting a fairly smooth surface across the section. Conversely, the crack is more likely to lead to interfacial debond than to extend into the matrix, exhibiting predominant fiber pullout for weak bond. The intermediate bond shows irregular failure surface with some fiber pullout. The foregoing failure mechanisms are applicable in static loading as well as in fatigue. However, discussion of fatigue failure requires consideration of the fatigue sensitivity of matrix, interface and fiber. Since the matrix is well within its failure strain up to the composite failure in most advanced composites, fatigue damage in the interface will be negligible except at the site of fiber breaks. Figure 19.10 shows fiber breaks under fatigue loading.

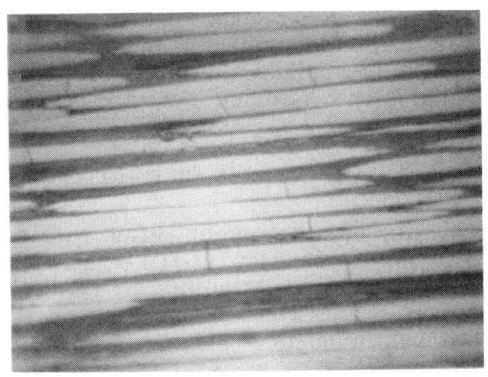

SPECIMEN 3–2–13, $\sigma_{min}/\sigma_{max} = -34/488$ MPa,
n = 5000 cycles

FIGURE 19.10 MICROGRAPHS SHOWING FIBER BREAKS IN THE 0 DEGREE PLY FOR [0/±45/90]$_{2s}$ CFRP T300/1034C LAMINATE.

TABLE 19.1 RESIDUAL STRENGTH DATA FOR [π/4] AT 10^6 CYCLE

Fatigue Loading	Specimen	$\sigma_{min}/\sigma_{max}$ (MPa)	Residual Strength (MPa) Tension	Compression
Tension– Tension	2–21–19	33/330	350	
	2–21–20	33/330		–200
	2–21–26	31/310	410	
	2–21–7	31/310		–227
Compression– Compression	2–21–78	–310/–31	582	
	2–21–79	–310/–31		–576
	2–21–71	–345/–35	572	
	2–21–76	–345/–35		–557
Tension– Compression	2–21–39	–190/190	506	
	2–21–38	–190/190		–428

19.5 CHANGE OF STRENGTH AND MODULUS

Fatigue damage often results in a significant reduction of strength and modulus of the composite laminates. The effect of the damage on the strength reduction varies widely, depending on the type of laminate, nature of loading, etc. A multidirectional laminate generally shows a gradual strength reduction until failure, whereas a longitudinal laminate (0 degree) shows hardly any strength change until immediately before failure. Table 19.1 shows the residual strength for $[0/45/90/-45]_{2s}$ after one million cycles of fatigue under three different fatigue loadings.

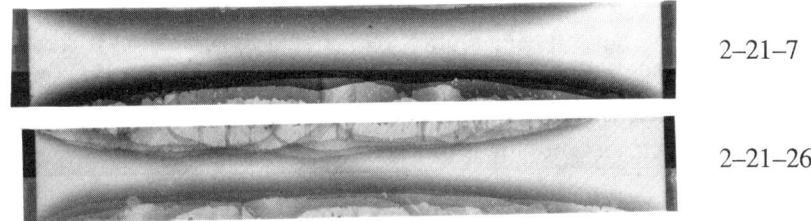

2–21–7

2–21–26

(a) TENSION–TENSION FATIGUE
$\sigma_{min}/\sigma_{max} = 31/310$ MPa

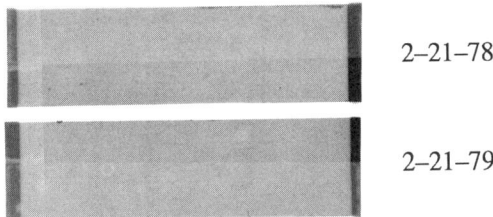

2–21–78

2–21–79

(b) COMPRESSION–COMPRESSION FATIGUE
$\sigma_{min}/\sigma_{max} = -310/-31$ MPa

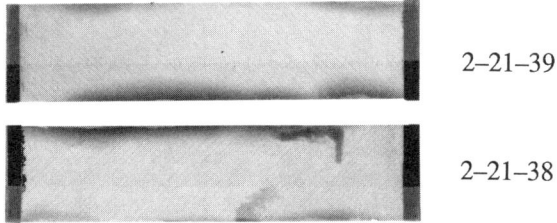

2–21–39

2–21–38

(c) TENSION–COMPRESSION FATIGUE
$\sigma_{min}/\sigma_{max} = -190/190$ MPa

FIGURE 19.11 X–RAY PHOTOGRAPHS SHOWING TYPICAL DAMAGE INCURRED AT ONE MILLION CYCLES, CFRP $[0/45/90/-45]_{2s}$.

Typical x–ray radiographs, indicating the extend of damage in each loading are shown in Figure 19.11. No damage under compression–compression fatigue has been detected by x–ray radiograph and this was confirmed by microscopic examination on the polished free edges. Extensive damages are exhibited by laminates subjected to tension–tension and tension–compression fatigue. The strength reduction appears to directly relate with the amount of damage incurred during fatigue, that is, the greatest strength reduction occurred in tension–tension fatigue.

Although the initial static tensile and compressive strengths are almost equal to each other, the residual strength is much greater in tension than in compression. All compression failures are characterized by compression buckling of the outer 0 degree plies. No strength degradation is shown in those specimens subjected to compression–compression fatigue. In most cases of compression–compression fatigue, no appreciable matrix damage was observed until final fatigue failure. Figure 19.12 shows the change of modulus in the course of fatigue cycles for various fatigue loadings.

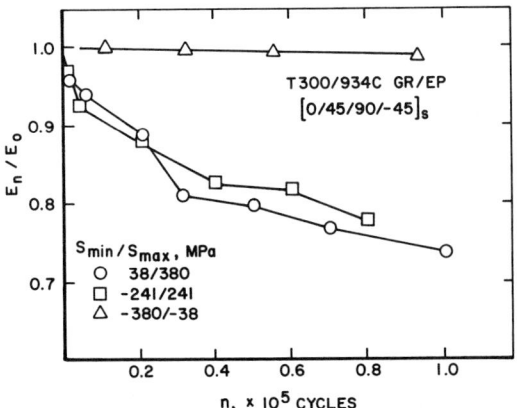

FIGURE 19.12 CHANGE IN MODULUS AS A FUNCTION OF FATIGUE LOADING.

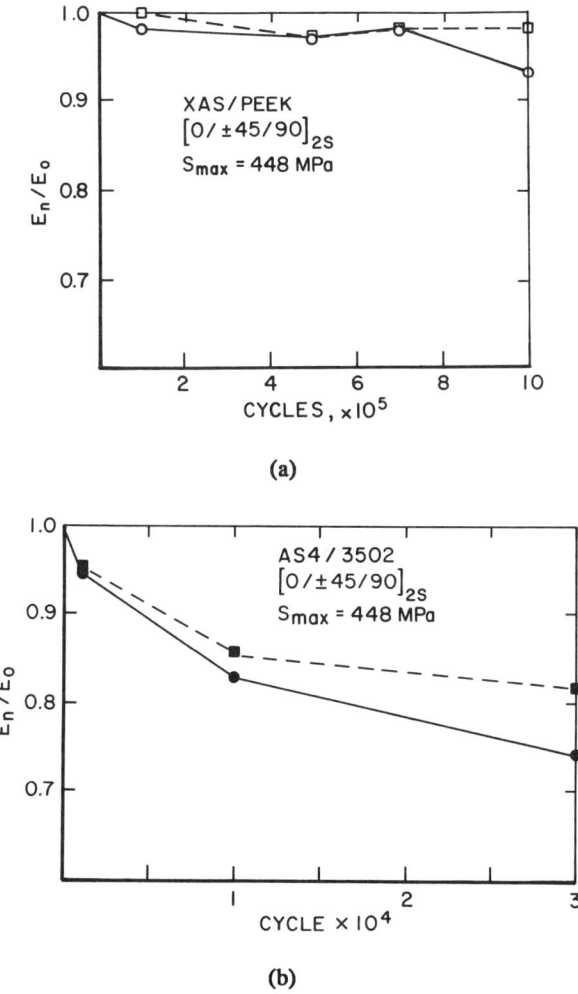

FIGURE 19.13   CHANGES IN MODULUS OF TWO FATIGUE TEST SPECIMENS FOR: (a) XAS/PEEK, (b) AS4/EPOXY.

A significant modulus change is obvious in the specimens subjected to tension–tension fatigue and tension–compression fatigue; whereas no modulus change is observed in compression–compression fatigue. Figure 19.13 (a) and (b), shows the modulus reduction as a function of the fatigue cycle for the graphite fiber reinforced PEEK and epoxy matrix composites. The PEEK system exhibits a very slight reduction in modulus up to one million cycles, but the epoxy system exhibits a very significant reduction at 30,000 cycles.

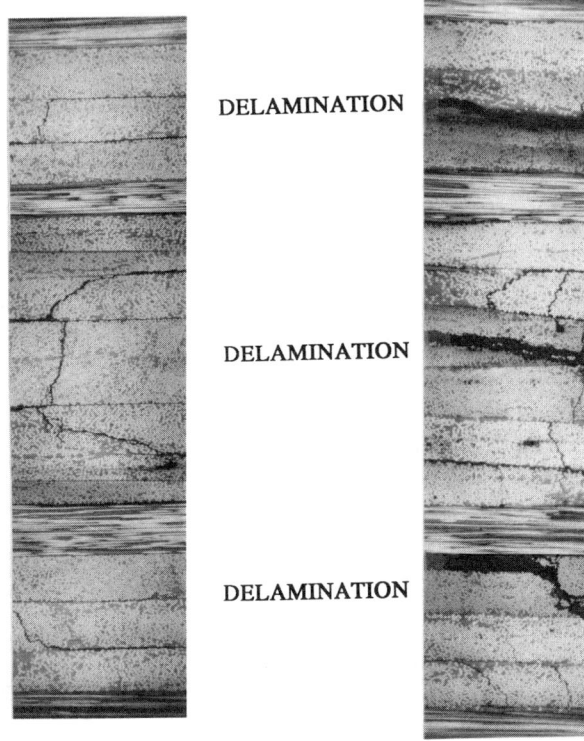

DELAMINATION

DELAMINATION

DELAMINATION

(a) XAS/PEEK, n = 10^6 (b) AS4/3502, n = 10^3

FIGURE 19.14   FATIGUE DAMAGE OF TWO MATERIALS AT DIFFERENT   CYCLES OF $[0/\pm45/90]_{2s}$, σ_{max}= 448 MPa.

Figure 19.14 shows the micrographs indicating damages in PEEK and epoxy composites, respectively. The epoxy system shows extensive ply cracks and delamination at only 1000 cycles, whereas the PEEK system shows much less damage even at one million cycles. The delamination is very extensive throughout the specimen in the epoxy system, but in the PEEK system, delamination is rather small and limited to a very local area.

Figure 19.15 (a) and (b) also show the crack density vs. fatigue cycles for PEEK and epoxy composites, respectively. A striking difference between the two composites is the crack density.

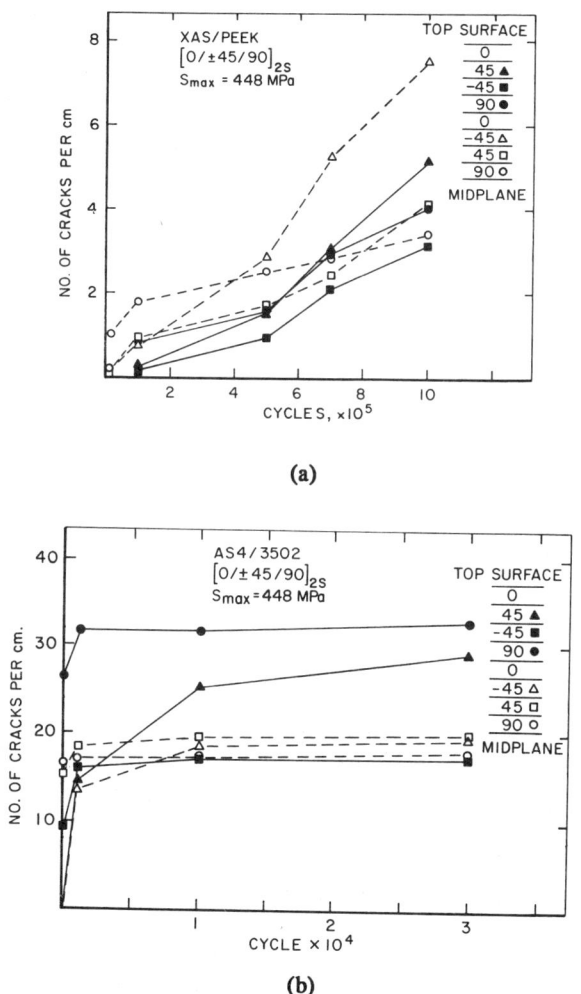

(a)

(b)

FIGURE 19.15   CRACK DENSITY VERSUS CYCLES FOR (a) PEEK AND (b) EPOXY COMPOSITES.

These observations indicate that the modulus reduction is mainly a result of ply cracks and delamination.

19.6 FATIGUE BEHAVIOR

In this and the following sections, the fatigue behavior of composite laminates is presented in the form of stress–life (S–N) relation and some important factors which affect the basic S–N relation are discussed.

The S–N relation in composite laminates is primarily dependent upon the constituent material properties. Most advanced fibers are very insensitive to fatigue and the resulting composites show good fatigue resistance. Figure 19.16 shows the S–N curves for CFRP AS4/3502 laminates.

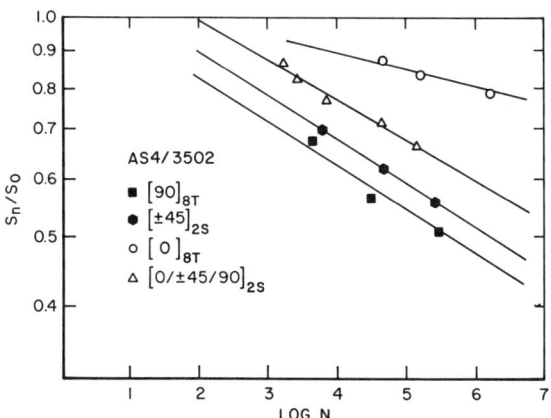

FIGURE 19.16 S–N CURVES FOR VARIOUS AS4/EPOXY LAMINATES.

The ordinate represents the fatigue strength ratio (ratio of fatigue stress to static strength). The laminates with matrix dominant failure modes exhibit a lower fatigue resistance than the laminates with fiber dominant failure modes. The slope of the S–N curve for the $[0]_{8T}$ laminate is relatively flat because of the fatigue insensitivity of the graphite fiber. Consequently the slope of the S–N curve tends to increase with the content of the 0 degree ply decreases, as shown in Figure 19.17. The fatigue strength of a $(\pm 45)_s$ laminate is frequently used to determine the longitudinal shear fatigue strength. The fatigue strength in compression–compression fatigue is slightly greater than that in tension–tension fatigue for the $[0/45/90/{-}45]_{2s}$ graphite/epoxy in Figure 19.18. The static tensile and compressive strengths for this laminate are practically identical.

Since the static strength of a laminate is mainly dependent upon the percentage of 0 degree ply and its strength, the fatigue strength of a multidirectional laminate can be estimated from the 0 degree fatigue strength unless the laminate undergoes extensive damaging processes during fatigue.

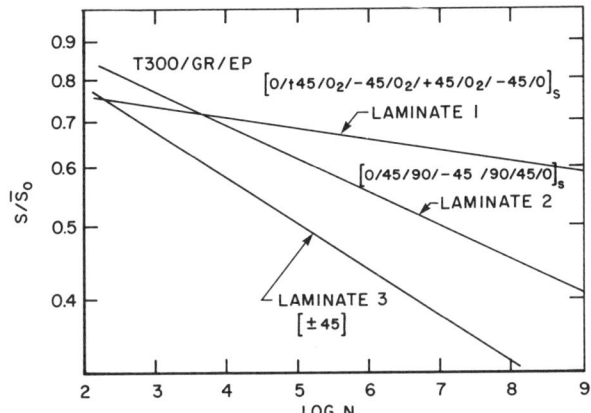

FIGURE 19.17   THE CORRELATION LINES OF S–N CURVES FOR THREE CFRP T300/EPOXY LAMINATES.

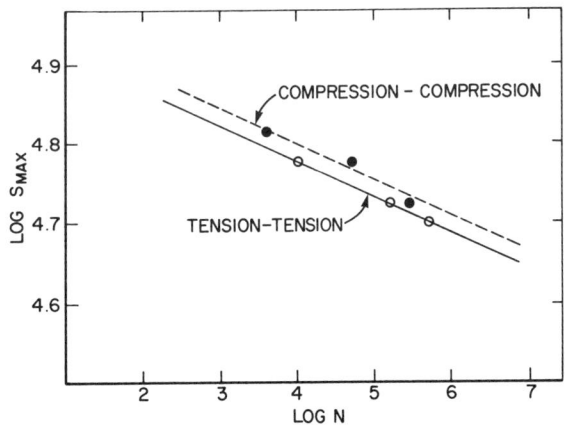

FIGURE 19.18   TENSION–TENSION AND COMPRESSION–COMPRESSION FATIGUE TESTS OF [0/45/90/–45]$_{2s}$ OF CFRP T300/5208.

Figure 19.19 shows the ratio of laminate fatigue strength to longitudinal fatigue strength vs. the ratio of laminate static strength to longitudinal static strength for various laminates of CFRP T300/5208. The ordinate axis reflects the fatigue strengths obtained from the tension–tension S–N curve of the respective laminate at 500,000 cycles and one million cycles.

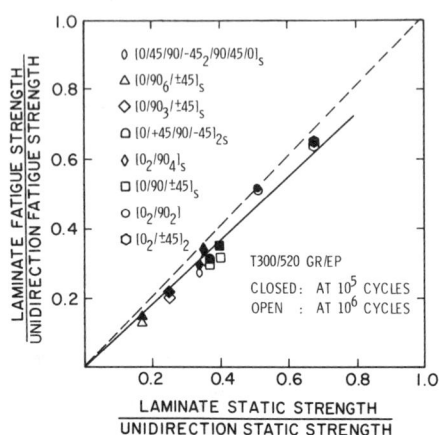

FIGURE 19.19   FATIGUE AND STATIC STRENGTHS NORMALIZED WITH RESPECT TO THE UNIDRECTIONAL TENSILE STRENGTHS.

19.7 MEAN STRESS

The general fatigue stress is considered a completely reversed stress upon which is superimposed a static mean stress S_m. The fatigue strength for this stress condition is expressed by the variable stress S_r for failure corresponding to various possible values of mean stress. The values of S_m and S_r are given by the following equations.

$$S_m = (S_{max}+S_{min})/2 \quad \text{and} \quad S_r = (S_{max}-S_{min})/2 \qquad (19.1)$$

where S_{max} and S_{min} are the maximum and minimum fatigue stresses, respectively.

Figure 19.20 shows the effect of mean stress on fatigue life in the form of a constant life diagram for $[0/45/90/-45]_{2s}$ graphite/epoxy laminates. This constant life diagram is practically symmetrical with respect to the alternating stress axis, S_r (or R= –1) although the peak of constant life curve representing maximum fatigue properties, slightly tends to lie in the tension–dominate fatigue region. This indicates that the S–N behavior of the composite is independent of the type of fatigue loading, that is, tension–tension, tension–compression and compression–compression fatigue as long as the tensile strength and compressive strength are equal. In tension–compression fatigue, the fatigue failure in the tension dominate region (T>|C|) was accompanied with severe matrix damages. Whereas, the fatigue failure in compression dominate region (T<|C|) was accompanied with less matrix damages. This effect on the S–N relation appears to be balanced out by the fact that the compressive stress is much more detrimental to the residual strength of damaged specimens than the tensile stress as is indicated in subsection 19.5. The peak of constant life curve for $(0/\pm30)_s$ CFRP lies in the positive mean stress due to the lower static compressive strength as shown in Figure 19.21.

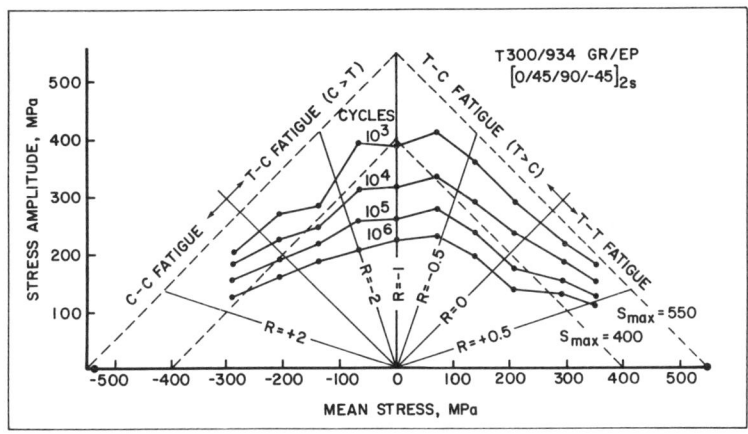

FIGURE 19.20   THE EFFECT OF MEAN STRESS ON FATIGUE LIFE OF CFRP
[0/45/90/–45]$_{2s}$ T300/5208.

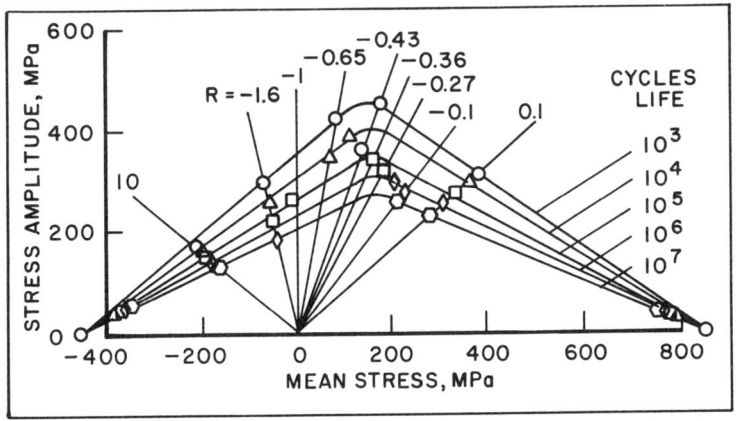

FIGURE 19.21   THE EFFECT OF MEAN STRESS ON FATIGUE LIFE OF CFRP [0/±30]$_{2s}$.

19.8 NOTCH

In metals, the problem of stress concentration resulting from various notches is complicated by the many factors which influence the behavior under cyclic stresses. In notched specimens, combined stresses are produced and vary widely in the region around the notch. When damages occur during the fatigue life of the specimen, change of magnitude and redistribution of stresses around the notch result. The foregoing factors have made it difficult to predict the fatigue strength of notched specimens from the fatigue strength of the unnotched specimens.

However, fatigue data in most composite laminates indicate that reduction in fatigue strength resulting from the presence of notches (circular hole and crack) is found to be insignificant. The value of fatigue notch factor (the ratio of the fatigue strength of unnotched specimens to the fatigue strength of notched specimens at n cycles) is much smaller than the static stress concentration factor and is close to unity in many cases. Figure 19.22 shows the net fatigue stress at the notch instead of gross stress vs. number of cycles to failure for unnotched and notched specimens under tension–compression fatigue with $R = -1$. The various symbols in Figure 19.22 represent the Weibull characteristic life, estimated from at least five specimens for each stress level. The S–N relations for notched specimens is almost identical to that for unnotched specimens over the range of fatigue life considered, indicating no notch effect in this laminate.

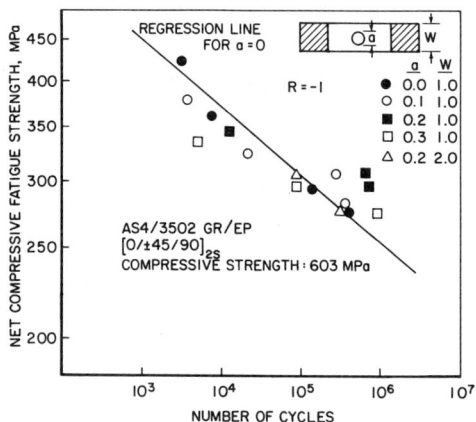

FIGURE 19.22   EFFECT OF CIRCULAR HOLE ON FATIGUE LIFE.

The residual strength after fatigue loading is usually greater than the static notch strength as shown in Figure 19.23.

The excellent fatigue resistance of the notched specimens is mainly due to the damage which relaxes the stress concentration around the notch tips.

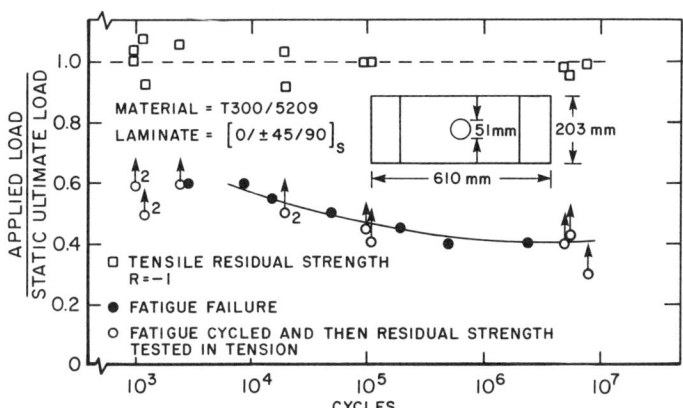

FIGURE 19.23   EFFECT OF CURCULAR HOLE ON RESIDUAL STRENGTH AND FATIGUE LIFE.

19.9 FREQUENCY

The effect of test frequency on the fatigue life appears to have some inconsistencies in various literatures. However, the frequency dependence of fatigue life is generally negligible in the range from 1 Hz to 30 Hz for most composites containing some portion of 0 degree ply. The matrix controlled laminates are expected to be susceptible to the test frequency because of the sensitivity of the matrix to loading rate and temperature. Figure 19.24 shows the significant life reduction (number of cycles to failure) at 0.1 Hz for the $(\pm 45)_{2S}$ specimens of AS/3501–6 graphite/epoxy. Note that the total time under load at 0.1 Hz is nearly twice that at 1 Hz.

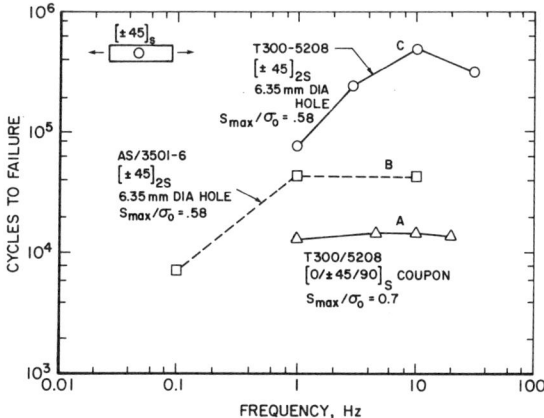

FIGURE 19.24   FREQUENCY EFFECT ON FATIGUE LIFE.

During fatigue, specimen temperature rises mainly due to the heat dissipation and failure processes within the specimen. The temperature increases with test frequency and fatigue stress level as shown in Figure 19.25.

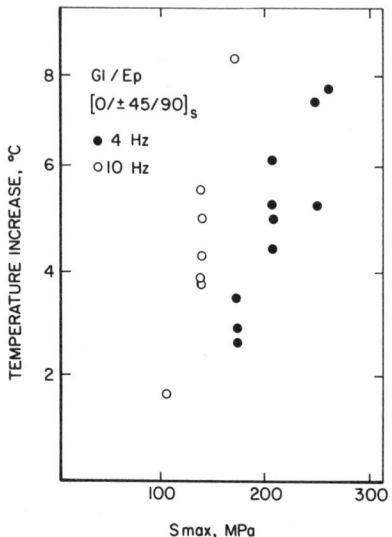

FIGURE 19.25 TEMPERATURE RISE DUE TO FREQUENCIES.

19.10 ENVIRONMENT

Among the various environmental factors which may influence the mechanical performance of composite materials, temperature and moisture have received great concerns. The change of temperature and moisture not only affects the intrinsic material strength, but also the state of residual stresses. Elevated temperature and high content of moisture usually lower the matrix dominant failure strength (transverse and shear strengths), but reduce the residual stresses. In addition, absorbed moisture lowers the glass transition temperature of the polymer matrix and affects the corrosion resistance of certain glass fibers.

Extensive published data indicate that the static tensile strength of these laminates exhibiting fiber dominant failure modes is relatively insensitive to temperature and moisture. Figures 19.26 and 19.27 show S–N data for angle–ply and multidirectional laminates for graphite/epoxy at elevated temperatures. The fatigue strength of angle–ply laminates (matrix dominant failure) slightly decreases with increasing temperature.

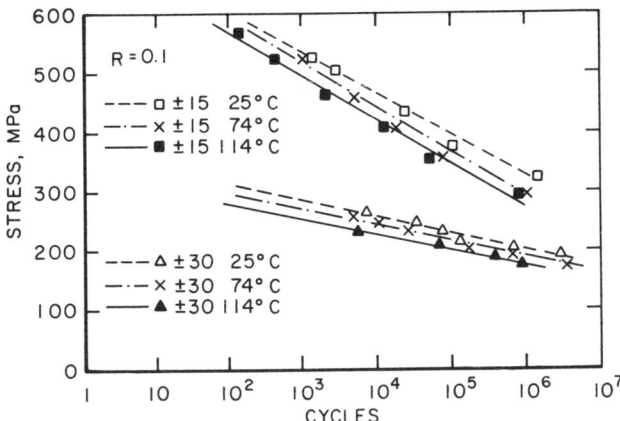

FIGURE 19.26   EFFECT OF TEMPERATURE ON FATIGUE LIFE OF ANGLE–PLY
LAMINATES.

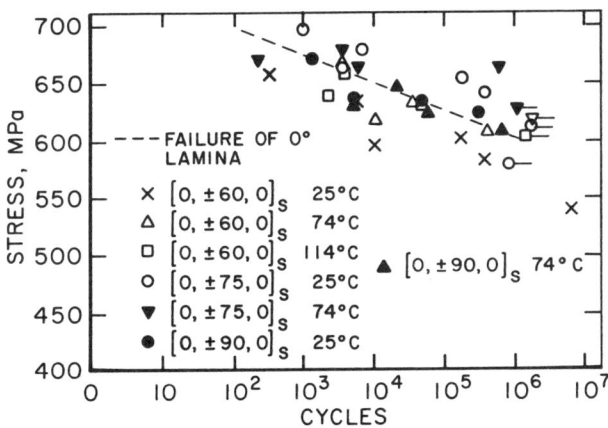

FIGURE 19.27   EFFECT OF TEMPERATURE ON FATIGUE LIFE OF
MULTIDIRECTIONAL LAMINATES CONTAINING 0–DEGREE PLIES.

The static compressive strengths of both coupons and 0.1 in diameter circular
hole specimens are appreciably decreased with increasing temperature, while
tensile strengths of circular hole specimens show increased strength in
Figure 19.28. Figure 19.29 shows the S–N relations of these specimens under
tension–compression fatigue for R = –1 at three temperatures. The ordinate
represents the ratio of the peak compressive fatigue stress to the compressive
strength at each case.

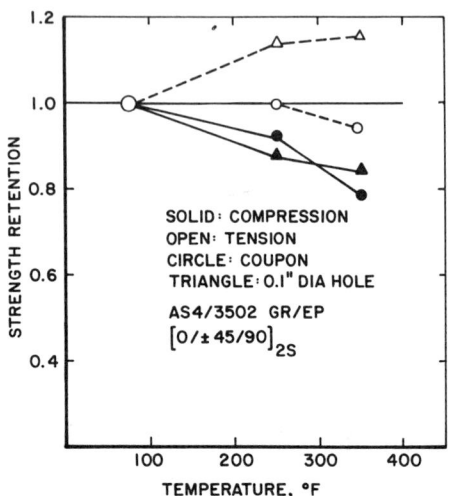

FIGURE 19.28   EFFECT OF TEMPERATURE ON THE STRENGTH RETENTION OF LAMINATES WITH AND WITHOUT HOLES.

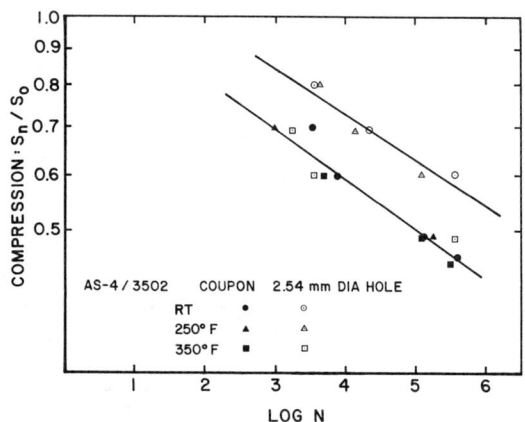

FIGURE 19.29   EFFECT OF TEMPERATURE ON THE LIFE OF TENSION–COMPRESSION FATIGUE.

The fatigue strength ratio appears to be independent of temperature for the coupon specimens. The higher strength ratio at RT and 250°F for the circular hole is attributed to the fact that the fatigue notch factor is smaller than the static stress concentration factor as discussed in Subsection 19.8. The reason for the smaller fatigue strength ratio for notched specimens at 350°F is not understood.

The effect of cryogenic temperature is almost negligible on fatigue life as shown in Figure 19.30.

Moisture does not seem to affect the fatigue life of CFRP laminates at room temperature as shown in Figures 19.31 and 19.32. Because of difficulty in testing under a combined environment of temperature and moisture, reliable fatigue data are nearly impossible to find. Consequently, an effort should be made to understand the combined effect of these variables on fatigue strengths of composite laminates.

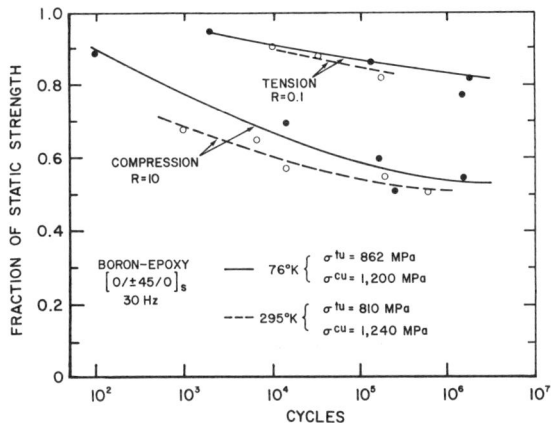

FIGURE 19.30   EFFECT OF CRYOGENIC TEMPERATURE ON THE FATIGUE OF BFRP.

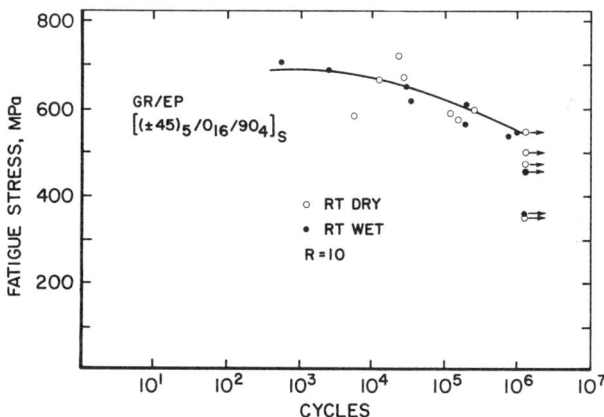

FIGURE 19.31   EFFECT OF MOISTURE ON THE FATIGUE LIFE OF CFRP.

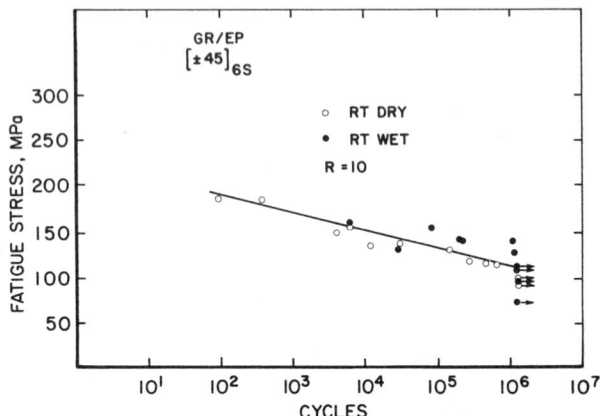

FIGURE 19.32 EFFECT OF MOISTURE ON THE FATIGUE LIFE OF [±45]$_{6s}$.

19.11 WEIBULL DISTRIBUTION AND PARAMETERS ESTIMATION

A random variable has a Weibull distribution with shape parameter α and scale parameter β if the cumulative distribution function $F(x)$ is

$$F(x) = \exp[-(x/\beta)^{\alpha}], \quad x>0 \tag{19.2}$$

$F(x)$ represents the probability of the survival for the random number x. On the other hand, the distribution at x_i, $1 < i < n$ for the data from n specimens $\{x_1 < x_2, \ldots < x_n\}$ experimentally is given by the medium rank

$$F(x) = 1 - (i-0.3)/(n+0.4) \tag{19.3}$$

The following relation exists

$$u = \text{Expected value of } X = \beta \Gamma(1+1/\alpha)$$

$$\sigma^2 \text{ Variance of } X = \beta^2 \{\Gamma(1+2/\alpha)-(\Gamma^2(1+1/\alpha)\} \tag{19.4}$$

where Γ is the Gamma function.

A maximum likelihood method is widely used for estimation of the Weibull parameters α and β. The maximum likelihood equations for estimating α and β are

$$\frac{\sum\limits_{i=1}^{n} x_i^{\tilde{\alpha}} \ln x_i}{\sum\limits_{i=1}^{n} x_i^{\tilde{\alpha}}} - \frac{1}{\tilde{\alpha}} - \frac{\sum\limits_{i=1}^{n} \ln x_i}{n} = 0 \tag{19.5}$$

and

$$\tilde{\beta} = [\frac{1}{n} \sum\limits_{i=1}^{n} x_i^{\tilde{\alpha}}]^{1/\tilde{\alpha}} \tag{19.6}$$

An efficient iterative technique for obtaining the solution of $f(\alpha) = 0$, is that of Newton–Raphson method in which the (j+1)st successive approximation, $\tilde{\alpha}_{j+1}$ to $\tilde{\alpha}_j$ is given by

$$\tilde{\alpha}_{j+1} = \tilde{\alpha}_j - f(\tilde{\alpha}_j)/f'(\tilde{\alpha}_j) \tag{19.7}$$

The maximum likelihood method has the advantage in that the confidence intervals for α and β can be computed and it can be applied to a life–test model in which censoring is progressive, that is, a model in which a portion of the survivors is withdrawn from life test several times during the test.

The 95 percent confidence interval (one–sided) for β_i can be obtained from Table 19.2 as follows

$$\Pr\{\tilde{\alpha} \ln(\tilde{\beta}_i/\beta_i) < 1^*_{0.95}\} = 0.95 \tag{19.8}$$

TABLE 19.2 PERCENTAGE POINTS $1^*_{0.95}$ SUCH THAT PR $\{\tilde{\alpha} \ln (\tilde{\beta}/\beta) < l_\gamma^*\} = \gamma$

n/γ	0.90	0.95	0.98
5	0.772	1.107	1.582
6	0.666	0.939	1.291
7	0.598	0.829	1.120
8	0.547	0.751	1.003
9	0.507	0.691	0.917
10	0.475	0.644	0.851
12	0.425	0.572	0.752
14	0.389	0.520	0.681
16	0.360	0.480	0.627
18	0.338	0.447	0.584
20	0.318	0.421	0.549
22	0.302	0.398	0.519
24	0.288	0.379	0.494
26	0.276	0.362	0.472
28	0.265	0.347	0.453
30	0.256	0.334	0.435
40	0.222	0.285	0.371
50	0.195	0.253	0.328

Let us denote the lower bound of 95 percent confidence interval for β_i by $\underline{\beta}_i$, then

$$\underline{\beta}_i = \tilde{\beta}_i \exp[-(l^*_{0.95} / \tilde{\alpha})] \tag{19.9}$$

where α is Weibull shape parameter estimated from fatigue data.

A–allowable (or B–allowable) as a material fatigue design value is defined by the probabilistic statement that we can be 95 percent confident of the assertion that the probability of surviving the A–allowable value is at least 0.99 (or 0.90 for B–allowable). Therefore A–allowable x_{Ai} under the stress level S_i, $i = 1,2,...,m$, can be obtained by solving the following equation

$$R(x_{Ai}) = \exp[-(x_{Ai}/\underline{\beta}_i)^{\tilde{\alpha}}] = 0.99 \tag{19.10}$$

where $\underline{\beta}_i$ is the 95 percent confidence lower limit for β_i. That is

$$x_{Ai} = \underline{\beta}_i [-\ln(0.99)]^{1/\tilde{\alpha}} \tag{19.11}$$

19.12 FATIGUE DATA POOLING

For obtaining the S–N relationship in fatigue test, m levels of stress are employed with n specimens tested at each m level of stress. The shape parameter and scale parameter (characteristic fatigue life) can be obtained from the pooled fatigue data $x_{i1}, x_{i2}, ..., x_{in}$ (under ith level of stress), $i=1,2,...m$. By assuming that the shape parameter α for each stress level is equal, the pooled estimation of α can be obtained by normalizing the data, i.e. by letting $Y_{ij} = X_{ij}/\beta_i$, for $i=1,2,..,n$. The maximum likelihood equation for the normalized data

$$\frac{\sum_{i=1}^{m} \sum_{j=1}^{n} y_{ij}^{\tilde{\alpha}} \ln y_{ij}}{\sum_{i=1}^{m} \sum_{j=1}^{n} y_{ij}^{\tilde{\alpha}}} - \frac{1}{\tilde{\alpha}} - \frac{\sum_{i=1}^{m} \sum_{j=1}^{n} \ln y_{ij}}{mn} = 0 \tag{19.12}$$

and

$$\tilde{\beta}_i = [\frac{1}{n} \sum_{j=1}^{n} x_{ij}^{\tilde{\alpha}}]^{1/\tilde{\alpha}}, \qquad i = 1,2,.........m \tag{19.13}$$

This pooled estimate is more efficient than the one introduced in the equation. As before, the solution of Equation 19.12 can be obtained by the iterative technique of the Newton–Raphson method. Table 19.3 is useful in computing the confidence interval of β.

TABLE 19.3 PERCENTAGE POINTS, l_γ^*, SUCH THAT $P_r(\tilde{\alpha}\ln(\tilde{\beta}/\beta) < l_\gamma^*) = \gamma$

m	γ	n					
		5	6	7	8	9	10
3	0.90	0.655	0.578	0.533	0.488	0.453	0.420
3	0.95	0.875	0.768	0.701	0.639	0.589	0.548
3	0.98	1.116	0.997	0.905	0.816	0.751	0.710
4	0.90	0.656	0.571	0.521	0.480	0.445	0.422
4	0.95	0.849	0.746	0.679	0.628	0.581	0.555
4	0.98	1.094	0.955	0.858	0.781	0.736	0.700
5	0.90	0.648	0.570	0.513	0.466	0.436	0.416
5	0.95	0.836	0.737	0.660	0.606	0.569	0.537
5	0.98	1.063	0.940	0.845	0.764	0.710	0.671

19.13 S–N CURVE CHARACTERIZATION

Traditionally the fatigue behavior of materials is expressed by the relationship between fatigue stress and fatigue life, cycle–to–failure. Although no general rules for S–N characterization are followed, the following is a general guide for this aspect. Constant amplitude fatigue tests are normally conducted under three to five different stress levels. The values of the extreme stress levels are approximately chosen so that the fatigue cycles under the extreme stress levels range between 10^4 and 10^6 cycles. The values of other intermediate stress levels are arbitrarily chosen. The number of specimens to be tested under each stress level depends on the size of scattering of the data and availability of the specimens and test time, but approximately four to ten specimens are common for the composite laminates. The large variation in fatigue life data is common in composites, and hence the S–N curve obtained from mean life is only considered an approximate curve which may be seriously in error depending upon the degree of the scatter for the material considered. In view of the foregoing variability in test results, a procedure developed for evaluating the fatigue strength more accurately is discussed.

Let us assume that the fatigue data follows classical power law and two–parameter Weibull distribution. The S–N curve takes the form

$$KS^bN = 1 \qquad (19.14)$$

where K and b are parameters.

The K and b can be estimated using least square linear regression since Equation 19.14 becomes a straight line after logarithm transformation. The fatigue life N_i for each stress level S_i can be replaced by Weibull fatigue characteristic life β_i. By taking natural logarithm transformation, we can obtain

$$\ln \beta_i = -b \ln S_i - \ln K \qquad (19.15)$$

The values of b and K can be easily determined by applying the least square linear regression analysis.

19.14 FATIGUE LIFE PREDICTION

Since composite laminates exhibit very complex failure processes, the analytical model accounting for all the failure processes has not been established. Consequently statistical life prediction methodologies have prevailed in the laminated composite materials. In this section we will describe the strength degradation model which is capable of predicting the statistical distribution of both the fatigue life and the residual strength.

The residual strength is chosen to describe the criticality of the damage instead of crack length because composite failure is characterized by a multitude of matrix cracks and fiber breaks rather than a single dominant crack growth.

In term of material age L, the change of the residual strength $X(n)$ after n fatigue cycles is assumed to be

$$dX(n)/dL = -(1/c)X^{-c+1}(n) \tag{19.16}$$

Upon integration Equation 19.16 yields the relation between the static strength, $X(o)$, and the residual strength, $X(n)$

$$X^c(n) = X^c(o) - L \tag{19.17}$$

If the material age L is related with test variables (e.g. stress level (S), frequency (w), stress ratio (R), and number of cycles incurred, then Equation 19.17 can be expressed as follows

$$X^c(n) = X^c(o) - f(S,\omega,R)n \tag{19.18}$$

For simplicity the test frequency ω and stress ratio R will be fixed so that $F(S,\omega,R) = f(S)$ and c is a constant.

The distribution of $X(o)$ is assumed to have a two–parameter Weibull distribution, with shape parameter α_o and scale parameter β_o. The distribution of residual strength obtained from Equations 19.2 and 19.17 as follows

$$R(x) = \exp[-\{(x/\beta_o)^c + n/(\beta_o{}^c/f(S))\}^{\alpha_o/c}] \tag{19.19}$$

Let N denote the number of cycles at which fatigue failure occurs under the applied stress level S. Then at the moment of fatigue fracture a relationship, $X(n) = S$ holds and the distribution of fatigue life N can be obtained from Equations 19.17 and 19.19 as

$$R(n) = \exp[-\{(n+(S^c/f(S)))/(\beta_o{}^c/f(S))\}^{\alpha_o/c}] \tag{19.20}$$

In general stress level is low such that $(S/\beta_o)^c \ll 1$ and Equation 19.20 is reduced to

$$R(n) = \exp\left[-\{n/(\beta_0{}^C/f(S))\}^{\alpha_0/c}\right] \tag{19.21}$$

It is noted that the fatigue life N has a two–parameter Weibull distribution with the characteristic life $\beta_0{}^C/f(S)$ and the shape parameter α_0/C, which is independent of the stress level S.

From the S–N curve relationship $K\ S^b N = 1$, an expression for $F(S)$ is obtained as $F(S) = \beta_0{}^C K S^b$ since the characteristic life is $N = 1/K S^b = \beta_0{}^C/f(S)$.

Note that Equations 19.19, 19.20, and 19.21 can be expressed as static strength and residual strength relations:

$$X(n)^C = X(o)^C - \beta_0{}^C K S^b n \tag{19.22}$$

Residual strength distribution:

$$R(x) = \exp\left[-\{(x/\beta_0)^C + n/(1/K S^b)\}^{\alpha_0/c}\right] \tag{19.23}$$

and fatigue life distribution:

$$R(n) = \exp\left[-(n/(1/K S^b))^{\alpha_0/c}\right]$$

or $\qquad = \exp\left[-(n/N)^{\alpha_f}\right] \tag{19.24}$

where $c = \alpha_0/\alpha_f$

Example: Static strength and fatigue life data of graphite/epoxy laminates are listed in Tables 19.4 and 19.5, respectively. The fatigue test was performed under tension–tension fatigue loading with $R = 0.1$ at 10 Hz.

TABLE 19.4 STATIC TENSILE STRENGTH DATA (MPA) FOR CFRP T300/5208 [0/90/±45]$_s$

496.7	499.5	528.2	532.2	533.4
547.2	554.9	562.1	565.2	566.8
566.9	568.9	574.7	578.5	586
590.9	591.5	595.9	597.2	598.3
606.5	610.5	612.7	617.8	621.7
630.5	632.5	636.9	643.5	

TABLE 19.5 FATIGUE DATA FOR CFRP T300/5208 [0/90/±45]$_s$

Stress Level (MPa)	Fatigue Failure Cycle (10 Hz)				
483	1150	1850	2436	3768	6898
448	2620	4920	6490	7000	9020
414	10300	21270	22550	28760	78720
375	71050	108550	168700	169480	325780
345	412000	614960	764680	1333390	1367890

The Weibull parameters of static strength were estimated by Equations 19.5 and 19.6 and are given by

$$\tilde{\alpha}_o = 18.0 \quad \text{and} \quad \tilde{\beta}_o = 598.4 \text{ MPa}$$

The pooled estimate α_f of the common parameter α_f is obtained from fatigue data by Equation 19.12 and is given by

$$\tilde{\alpha}_f = 1.95$$

The estimate $\tilde{\beta}_i$ of the characteristic life β_i is computed by Equation 19.13 with $\tilde{\alpha}_f = 1.95$ and the values are listed in Table 19.5.

The coefficient C in the residual strength degradation model is estimated by

$$c = \tilde{\alpha}_o/\tilde{\alpha}_f = 18.0/1.95 = 9.231$$

Equation 19.15 was estimated by the linear least square fitting from the data given in Table 19.5 and the resulting equation is

$$\ln \beta_i = -17.33 \ln S_i + 114.985 \tag{19.25}$$

and from this equation the constants b and K are obtained:

$$b = 17.33 \quad \text{and} \quad K = e^{-114.985} = 1.155 \times 10^{-50}$$

The critical value $l^*_{0.95} = 0.836$ was obtained from Table 19.3 (for m=5 and n=5) and the S–N curve relations for $N_i = \beta_i$ and $N_i = X_{Ai}$ are obtained from Equations 19.9 and 19.11 as follows:

$$\ln \beta_i = -17.33 \ln S_i + 114.555 \tag{19.26}$$

and

$$\ln X_{Ai} = -17.33 \ln S_i + 112.195 \tag{19.27}$$

The estimates β_i and the Equations 19.25, 19.26, and 19.27 are graphed in Figure 19.33 with experimental points denoted by open circles.

The residual strength distribution is plotted for the same composite material $[0/90/\pm45]_s$ CFRP T300/5208 laminate. Nine specimens were tested for residual strength after undertaking 10,000 cycles of tension–tension fatigue at the stress level of 414 MPa, and their values are given in Table 19.5. The theoretical distribution, Equation 19.23, is compared with the experimental data using Equation 19.3 in Figure 19.34. The comparison is fairly good.

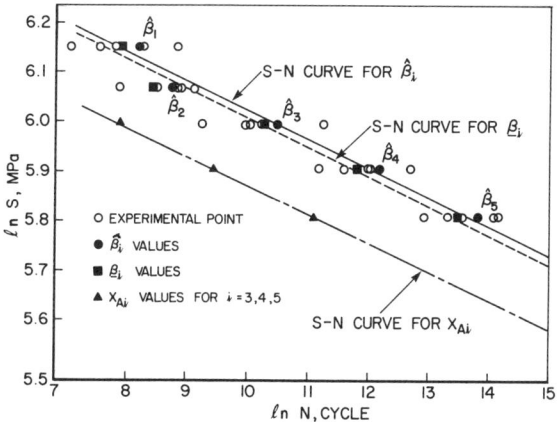

FIGURE 19.33   S–N CURVE FOR CFRP T300/5208 [0/90/±45]$_s$ LAMINATE.

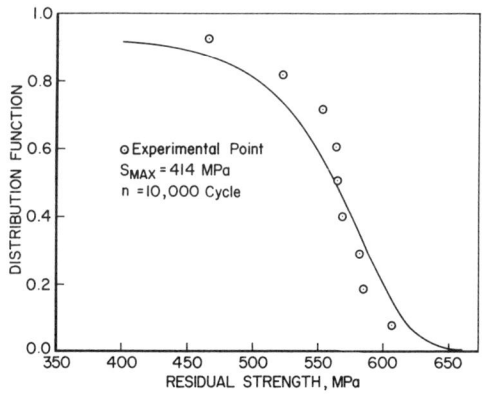

FIGURE 19.34   RESIDUAL STRENGTH DISTRIBUTION FOR CFRP T300/5208 [0/90/±45]$_{5s}$.

19.15 CONCLUSIONS

Fatigue of composite materials have been studied extensively in recent years. A great deal of confidence exists among the users of composite materials in terms of fatigue and environmental stability. There have been no surprises or glaring weaknesses of composite materials. We are confident that reliable design that will provide maintenance–free service during the life of a structure is now possible.

ACKNOWLEDGMENTS

The author wishes to acknowledge the following individuals for their work cited in various figures in this section: C. C. Chamis (Figure 19.9), J. M. Whitney (Figure 19.17), S. V. Ramani, and D. P. Williams (Figure 19.21), R. W. Walter, R. W. Johnson, R. R. June, and J. E. McCarty (Figure 19.23), C.R. Saff (Figure 19.24 B), C. T. Sun (Figure 19.24A), A. Rotem and H. G. Nelson (Figures 19.26 and 19.27), M. B. Kasen (Figure 19.30), and G. C. Grimes (Figures 19.31 and 19.32), H.T. Hahn and Y.J. Yang (Life prediction), D.R. Thomas, L.J. Bain and C.E. Amtle (Table 19.2), W.J. Park (Table 19.3).

Section 20

NOTCHED STRENGTH

Seng C. Tan and Stephen W. Tsai
U S AIR FORCE MATERIALS LABORATORY, DAYTON

20.1 INTRODUCTION

We will calculate the stresses and strains in a large symmetric laminate containing an elliptical opening. The in–plane load at infinity σ_i, the orientation of the major axes of the ellipse ψ, and its aspect ratio a/b are arbitrary inputs. The notation used in this section is shown in Figure 20.1.

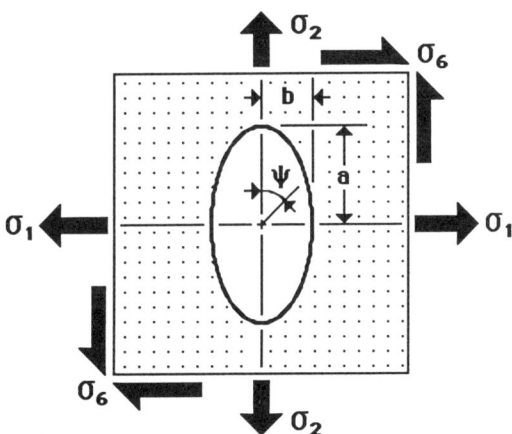

FIGURE 20.1 LAMINATED PLATE WITH AN ELLIPTIC OPENING, THE MAJOR AXIS OF WHICH CAN BE ROTATED BY AN ANGLE ψ.

20.2 GOVERNING EQUATIONS

The formulation of an anisotropic plate is based on the complex potential approach presented in Lekhnitskii's *Anisotropic Plates* [20–1]. The application of this approach to laminated composites discussed in this section is based in part on the work by Tan [20–2]. The stress distribution due to an opening is obtained from superposition of stresses

$$\{\sigma\} = \{\sigma^o\}+\{\sigma^*\} \tag{20.1}$$

where $\{\sigma^o\}$ = stress due to uniform stress field.

  $\{\sigma^*\}$ = stress due to the opening.

All the stress components refer to the major and minor axes of the ellipse. The relationship between the applied stress field at infinity in the laminate axes 1–2 and that in the axes of the ellipse is given by the following transformation equations

$$\sigma_1^o = \sigma_1\sin^2\psi+\sigma_2\cos^2\psi+\sigma_6\sin2\psi$$

$$\sigma_2^o = \sigma_1\cos^2\psi+\sigma_2\sin^2\psi-\sigma_6\sin2\psi \tag{20.2}$$

$$\sigma_6^o = -(\sigma_1-\sigma_2)\sin\psi\cos\psi-\sigma_6\cos2\psi$$

Using the complex potential technique of [20–1], the stress field due to the opening is

$$\sigma_1^* = Re[(\mu_1^2f_1g_2-\mu_2^2f_2g_1)/(\mu_1-\mu_2)]$$

$$\sigma_2^* = Re[(f_1g_2-f_2g_1)/(\mu_1-\mu_2)] \tag{20.3}$$

$$\sigma_6^* = Re[-(\mu_1f_1g_2-\mu_2f_2g_1)/(\mu_1-\mu_2)]$$

where $f_j = (1-i\mu_j\lambda)/[\beta\sqrt{\beta^2-1-\mu_j^2\lambda^2}+\beta^2-1-\mu_j^2\lambda^2]$ (20.4)

  $g_j = -(1-i\mu_j\lambda)\sigma_6^o-\mu_j\sigma_2^o+i\lambda\sigma_1^o$ (20.5)

  $j = 1,2$

  $\beta = (1+\alpha)\cos\theta+\mu_j(\lambda+\alpha)\sin\theta$ (20.6)

  $\lambda = b/a, \ \alpha = b_0/a$ (20.7)

where b_0 = characteristic dimension measured radially outward from the opening contour along the major and minor axes; see Figure 20.2.

The complex roots μ_j represent the solution of the following characteristic equation:

$$a_{11}\mu^4-2a_{16}\mu^3+(2a_{12}+a_{66})\mu^2-2a_{26}\mu+a_{22} = 0 \tag{20.8}$$

where a_{ij} = the in–plane compliance components of the laminated plate, defined in Equation 7.6.

For an orthotropic plate, $a_{16} = a_{26} = 0$, and Equation 20.8 becomes

$$a_{11}\mu^4+(2a_{12}+a_{66})\mu^2+a_{22} = 0 \tag{20.9}$$

For a square symmetric plate, $a_{11} = a_{22}$, and Equation 20.8 becomes

$$a_{11}\mu^4+(2a_{12}+a_{66})\mu^2+a_{11} = 0 \tag{20.10}$$

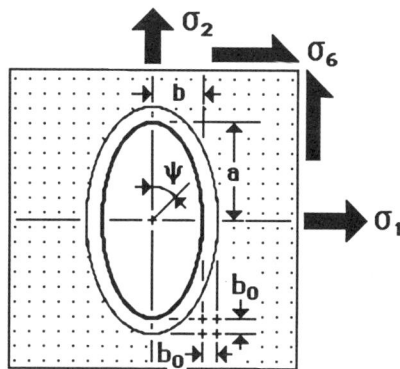

FIGURE 20.2 DEFINITION OF CHARACTERISTIC LENGTH, bo.

For an isotropic plate, Equation 20.8 becomes

$$\mu^4 + 2\mu^2 + 1 = 0 \tag{20.11}$$

because $a_{11} = a_{12} + a_{66}/2$, or

$$a_{66} = 2(a_{11} - a_{12}) \tag{20.12}$$

The last relation is analogous to Equation 3.7 for a homogeneous isotropic material.

20.3 NOTCHED STRENGTH PREDICTION

The strength prediction is based on first–ply–failure (FPF) along the elliptical contour with a radial displacement b_0 along both the 1– and 2–axes shown in Figure 20.2. The contour is described as

$$x^2/(a+b_0)^2 + y^2/(b+b_0)^2 = 1 \tag{20.13}$$

The aspect ratios of the inner and outer ellipses in Figure 20.2 are not the same. The notched strength is based on the lowest first–ply–failure strength/stress ratio **R** along this contour. Strength/stress ratio has been defined in section 11.3.

We can now define a strength reduction factor **SRF** as follows:

SRF = Notched Strength/Unnotched Strength

The unnotched strength is determined from a plate without holes using a quadratic failure criterion at FPF. If we assume that the strength reduction factor remains the same for the last–ply–failure or the experimentally measured ultimate strength, we can immediately find the corresponding notched strength.

20.4 NOTCHED STRENGTH DATA

Best fit curves and data are shown in Figure 20.3 for circular holes subjected to a uniaxial tensile load. The data are measured from $\pi/4$ CFRP and $\pi/4$ GFRP. The assumed characteristic length is $b_0 = 0.05$ inch. Similar data on the hole–size effects have been extensively reported by Awerbuch[20–3].

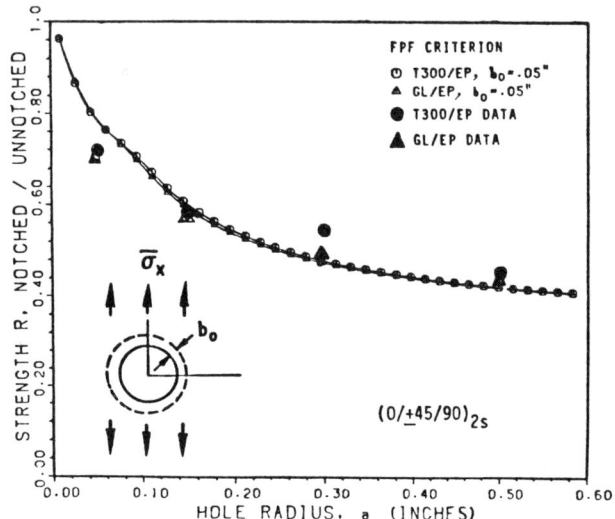

FIGURE 20.3   BEST FIT STRENGTH REDUCTION FACTOR AND DATA FOR CIRCULAR HOLES, UNDER UNIAXIAL TENSION, FOR CFRP AND GFRP.

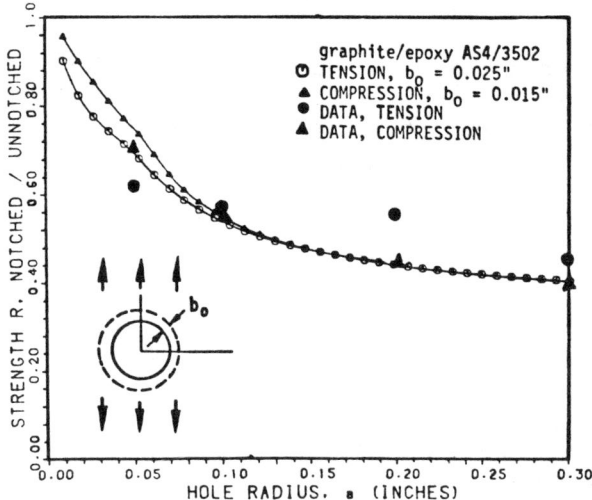

FIGURE 20.4   BEST FIT STRENGTH REDUCTION FACTOR AND DATA OF $\pi/4$ LAMINATES WITH CIRCULAR HOLES SUBJECTED TO UNIAXIAL TENSILE AND COMPRESSIVE LOADS, DOTS AND TRIANGLES, RESPECTIVELY.

For a plate with circular holes subjected to uniaxial compression, the best fit characteristic length is 0.015 inch for compression, as compared with 0.025 inch for tension. The material is CFRP AS4/3502. In Figure 20.4, we show the **SRF** (strength reduction factor) using those characteristic lengths. Experimental data from [20-4] are shown as solid dots for tensile data, and triangles, for compressive data.

For a laminate with slanted cracks under a uniaxial tensile load, a master curve can be drawn for all values of the slant angle ψ. Here a crack is defined as an elliptical opening with an aspect ratio **a/b** of 50.

In Figure 20.5, we compare data for CFRP T300/5208 and GFRP Scotchply π/4 laminates [20-5]. The best fit characteristic lengths are 0.14, and 0.08 inch, for carbon and glass, respectively. The data shown in Figure 20.5 are limited to laminates with cracks normal to the applied load. Data for slanted cracks can be found in [20-5].

The effect of the orientation of the crack on the notched strength of a laminate is simply the projected area on the axis perpendicular to the uniaxial tensile load. Thus the horizontal axis in Figure 20.5 is the product of the actual crack length and the cosine of the slant angle.

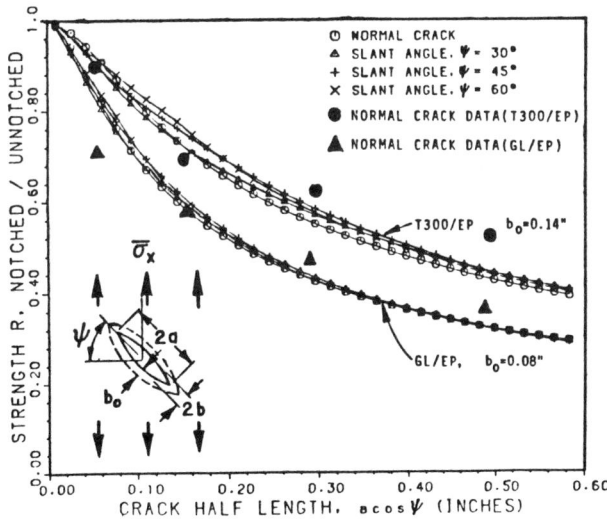

FIGURE 20.5   BEST FIT CURVES FOR STRENGTH REDUCTION FACTOR AND DATA FOR SLANTED CRACKS, UNDER UNIAXIAL TENSION, FOR CFRP(T300/5208) AND GFRP.

Based on the data reported by Morris and Hahn [20-5], the best fit characteristic length for cracks for a [0/±45] laminate is 0.075 inch. Note that this value for the [0/±45]$_s$ laminate is less than the 0.14 inch value for the π/4 laminate previously discussed.

If we assume a constant characteristic length for a given laminate and a fixed aspect ratio of the opening simulating a crack, we can easily generate theoretical curves for a slanted crack subjected to pure shear. The results are shown in Figure 20.6.

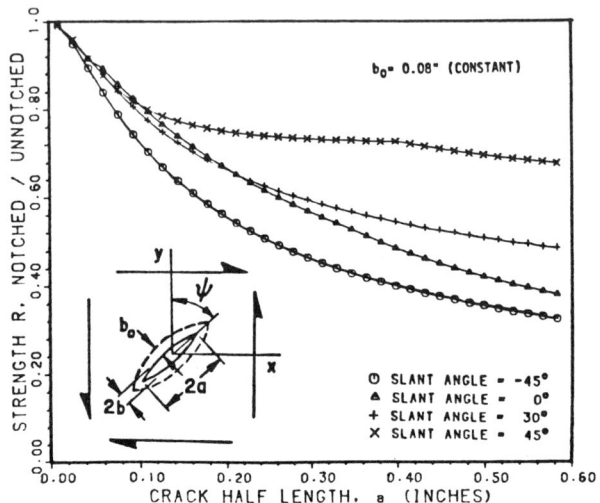

FIGURE 20.6   THEORETICAL STRENGTH REDUCTION FACTOR OF SLANTED CRACKS, UNDER PURE SHEAR, FOR GFRP.

Unlike the notched uniaxial tensile strength of slanted cracks in Figure 20.5, the notched shear strength of slanted cracks can not be collapsed to form one master curve. The shear strength varies with the angular orientation of the notch, where the ψ= +45 degree crack represents the upper bound and the –45 degree crack represents the lower bound. We are not aware of any data to compare with the predicted curves in Figure 20.6.

20.5 RANKING OF NOTCHED STRENGTHS

The key to our calculation of notched strength is the characteristic length. The characteristic length is determined empirically from measured strength of laminates with holes and cracks. We implicitly assume that the characteristic length is a function of the following parameters:

- The plies of composite used; e.g., CFRP, GFRP, etc.
- The layup of the plies.
- The aspect ratio of the opening; e.g., circular holes or cracks.
- The applied load at infinity; i.e., $\{\sigma_i\}$.

We also assume that the characteristic length does not vary significantly with:

- The absolute size of the opening.
- The absolute thickness of the laminate.

Kim's three–point bend test data [20–6] with edge and center cracks showed that damage zones remained reasonably equal in size. The measured crack extension for the 32–ply laminate was approximately the same as for the 64–ply laminate. The insensitivity of the notched strength to the laminate thickness was also demonstrated in [20–7].

The computed notched strength as a function of the characteristic length is shown in Figure 20.7 for circular holes subjected to a uniaxial tensile load. The laminates shown in Figures 20.7 through 20.9 represent those with the highest strength laminates determined by ranking 119   quadri– and tridirectional π/4 laminates.

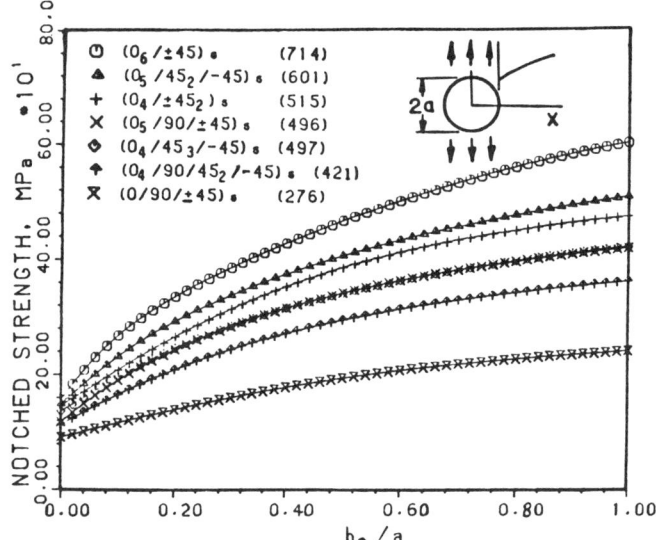

FIGURE 20.7   THE HIGHEST NOTCHED UNIAXIAL TENSILE STRENGTH OF π/4
FAMILY OF 119 LAMINATES WITH CIRCULAR HOLES OF CFRP. THE
NOTCHED STRENGTH ON THE VERTICAL AXIS MUST BE MULTIPLIED
BY A FACTOR OF TEN.

The characteristic length in Figures 20.7 is normalized with respect to the radius of the hole; i.e., b_0/a. For the same characteristic length, the larger normalized length implies smaller holes. This is the inverse of the SRF in Figure 20.3.   As the circular hole decreases in size, the notched strength increases and therefore the notch sensitivity will decrease. In the limit when hole size approaches zero, the unnotched strength is recovered.

If we assume that the characteristic length does not change with size and laminate thickness, the curves in Figure 20.7 may be used to aid design and damage assessment of laminates. The laminate with the highest notched strength is [6011] for the same characteristic length. The laminate code used in Sections 7 and 14 is also used here. A [6011] laminate implies a $[0_6/\pm45]_s$ laminate.   This laminate remains the strongest over a wide range of characteristic lengths.   It is substantially higher than [2222], the quasi–isotropic laminate—by nearly a factor of three.

The notched strength of CFRP T300/5208 laminates containing cracks transverse to the uniaxial tensile load is plotted in Figure 20.8 as a function of the normalized characteristic length b_0/a.

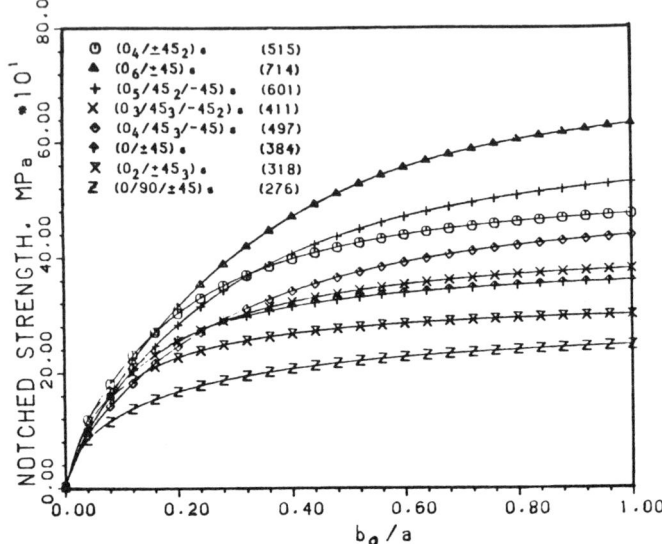

FIGURE 20.8   THE HIGHEST NOTCHED UNIAXIAL TENSILE STRENGTH OF $\pi/4$ FAMILY OF 119 CFRP LAMINATES WITH SMALL CRACKS.

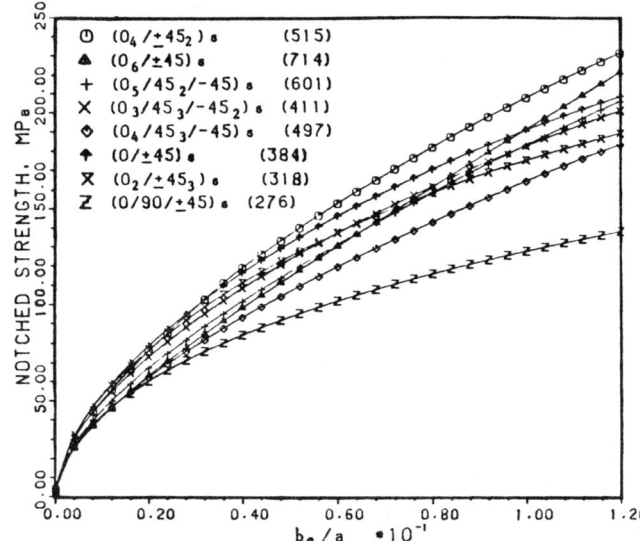

FIGURE 20.9   THE HIGHEST NOTCHED UNIAXIAL TENSILE STRENGTH OF $\pi/4$ FAMILY OF 119 CFRP LAMINATES WITH LARGE CRACKS.

Those shown in this Figure 20.9 are the laminates with the highest notched strength among the 119 $\pi/4$ laminates. The pattern is clear for the high values of the normalized characteristic length. Laminate [6011] is again the strongest laminate until the hole size becomes large. The effect of the absolute hole size can be easily estimated from Figure 20.9 once we have established one point on the curve. For example, in Figure 20.9

$$b_o/a = 0.20$$

and if we assume that $b_0 = 0.1$ inch, then from Equation 20.14 we can calculate that the half opening length: $a = 0.1/0.2 = 0.5$ inch.

We can expand the horizontal scale in Figure 20.8, resulting in Figure 20.9. The strongest laminate in this region, that with large holes, is [4022]. This laminate is stronger than [2222] by a factor of two.

20.6 LAMINATES WITH INCLUSIONS

In the previous sections, an anisotropic laminate containing an opening has been analyzed and the predicted notched strength agrees reasonably well with experimental data. It is of engineering interest to consider a laminate with inclusions. The stress distribution of an anisotropic laminate with an inclusion can be derived and modified using the open hole complex potential. The result of the stress analysis, the strength prediction and a guideline to choose an appropriate material for the inclusion are presented here.

For an infinite laminate containing an inclusion, the analysis can be proceeded by modifying the stress potential for a laminate with an open hole (Equation 20.1). The solution is given for the case that the principal axes of the elliptical inclusion coincide with the laminate axes; i.e., $\psi = 90°$. The relationships described by Equations 20.1 through 20.4 remain valid for determining the stress distribution for the base laminate. The function g_j of Equation (20.5) is modified to :

$$g_j = (\sigma_1{}^* - \sigma_1')\lambda i - (\sigma_2{}^* - \sigma_2')\mu_j - (\sigma_6{}^* - \sigma_6')(1 - i\mu_j\lambda) \qquad (20.15)$$

where j = 1,2; σ_1', σ_2', σ_6' are the stresses for the inclusion in the laminate axes.

The inclusion stresses can be written explicitly as

$$\sigma_1' = (\sigma_1{}^*/D1)[a_{11}a_{22}(k + n) + a_{11}a_{22}'k(1 + n) + a_{22}(a_{12} + a_{66} + a_{12}')]$$
$$+ (\sigma_2{}^*/D2)[a_{11}(a_{22} - a_{22}') + a_{22}(a_{12} - a_{12}')(n + k)/k^2]$$

$$\sigma_2' = (\sigma_1{}^*/D1)[a_{22}(a_{11} - a_{11}') + a_{11}(a_{12} - a_{12}')k(1 + n)]$$
$$+ (\sigma_2{}^*/D2)[a_{11}a_{22}(1 + n)/k + a_{22}a_{11}'(n + k)/k^2$$
$$+ a_{11}(a_{12} + a_{66} + a_{12}')]$$

$$\sigma_6' = (\sigma_6{}^*/D6)[a_{11}nk + (2a_{12} + a_{66})k + a_{22}(2 + n)]$$

$$(20.16)$$

where a_{ij} and a_{ij}', $i, j = 1, 2, 6$, are the compliances of the base laminate and the inclusion, respectively, and where

$$D1 = (a_{11}a_{22} + a_{11}'a_{22}')k + a_{22}(a_{66} + 2a_{12}') + (a_{11}a_{22}'k + a_{22}a_{11}')n \\ - (a_{12} - a_{12}')^2 k$$

$$D2 = (a_{11}a_{22} + a_{11}'a_{22}')/k + a_{11}(a_{66} + 2a_{12}') \\ + (a_{22}a_{11}'/k + a_{11}a_{22}')n/k - (a_{12} - a_{12}')^2/k \qquad (20.17)$$

$$D6 = a_{11}kn + (2a_{12} + a_{66}')k + a_{22}(2 + n)$$

where

$$k = -\mu_1\mu_2 = \sqrt{a_{22}/a_{11}} \qquad (20.18)$$

$$n = -i(\mu_1 + \mu_2) = \sqrt{(2a_{12} + a_{66})/a_{11} + 2\sqrt{a_{22}/a_{11}}} \qquad (20.19)$$

An example that utilizes the above equations is illustrated in Figure 20.10. The tangential stress at the base material/inclusion boundary is plotted for the CFRP T300/5208 $[0/\pm 45/90]_s$ laminate. The maximum positive tangential stress occurs on the axis normal to the applied load. The stress concentrations are shown for four cases in Figure 20.10 to equal (i) 3, in the absence of an any inclusion; (ii) 1.004, for an aluminum inclusion; (iii) 1, for a CFRP $\pi/4$ laminate inclusion; and (iv) 1.44, for a steel inclusion.

The strength of a laminate with an inclusion can be predicted using a characteristic length which is determined from a laminate with an open hole. An illustration is shown in Figure 20.11 for a CFRP T300/5208 $[0/\pm 45/90]_s$

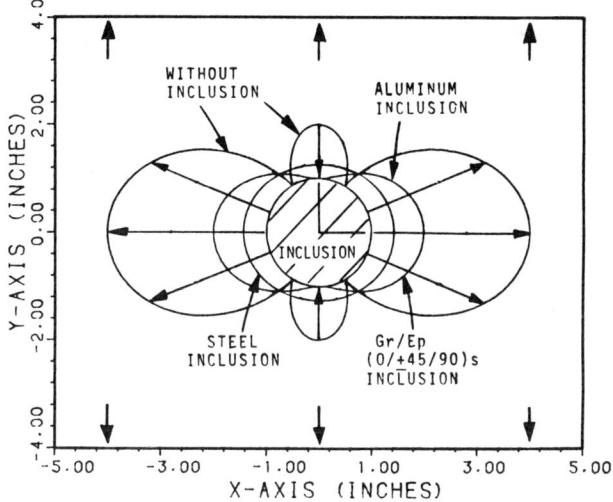

FIGURE 20.10   THE TANGENTIAL STRESS CONCENTRATION AT THE INTER–PHASE BOUNDARY OF THE GRAPHITE/EPOXY $[0/\pm45/90]_s$ LAMINATE CONTAINING A CIRCULAR INCLUSION.

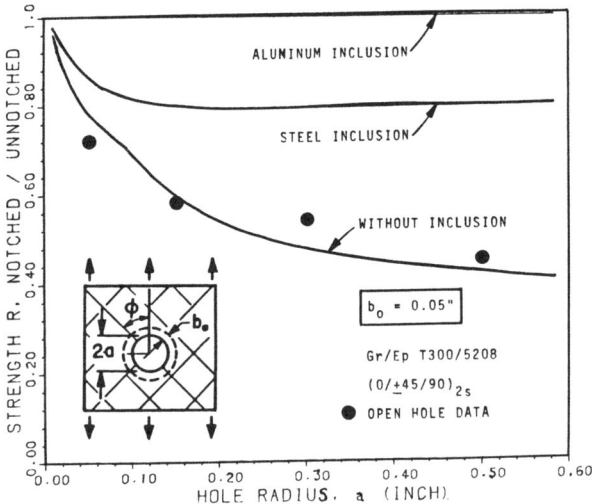

FIGURE 20.11   STRENGTH REDUCTION FACTOR FOR THE GR/EP T300/5208 $[0/\pm45/90]_{2s}$ LAMINATE WITH AN OPEN HOLE, AND INCLUSIONS OF ALUMINUM AND STEEl.

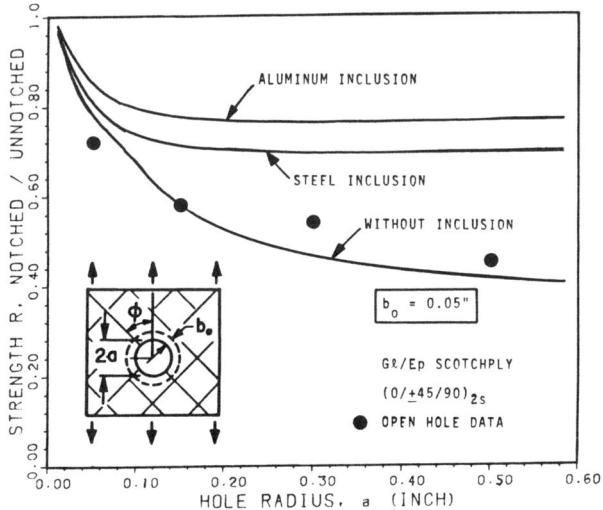

FIGURE 20.12   STRENGTH REDUCTION FACTOR FOR THE CFRP $[0/\pm45/90]_{2s}$ LAMINATE WITH AN OPEN HOLE, AND INCLUSIONS OF ALUMINUM AND STEEL.

laminate under tensile loading.   Using a characteristic length $b_0 = 0.05"$, which is best fit for the open hole case, the strength reduction for this laminate with an aluminum or a steel inclusion can also be predicted. The results show that the strength reduction for the laminate with an inclusion is significantly higher than that without an inclusion. For example, the strength reduction factor is about 0.4 for the π/4 laminate without an inclusion and 0.8 for the one with a steel inclusion and 0.996 for the one with an aluminum inclusion.

The strength predictions for the glass/epoxy $[0/\pm45/90]_s$ laminate with a circular hole, an aluminum core and a steel core are compared in Figure 20.12. The strength reduction factor for this π/4 laminate with a 1" open hole is about 0.4. For the one with an aluminum inclusion, the strength is recovered to 77 percent of that without any opening. The strength reduction factor of this GFRP π/4 laminate with a steel inclusion is about 0.7, which is lower than the one with an aluminum inclusion.

Two parametric studies for orthotropic laminates containing a circular inclusion are demonstrated in Figures 20.13–14. Three different inclusions

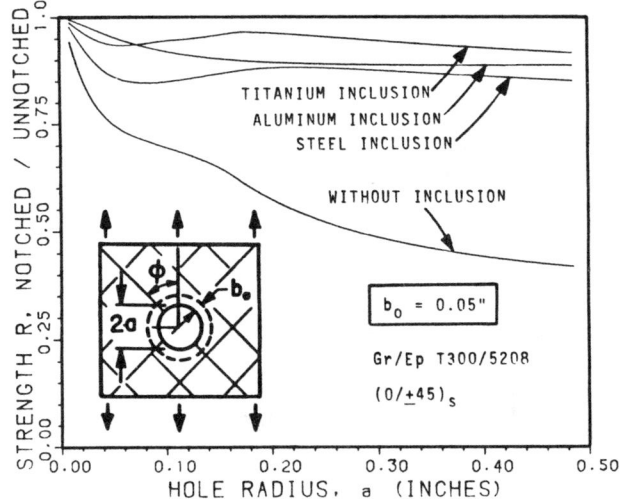

FIGURE 20.13   STRENGTH PREDICTION OF THE GR/EP T300/5208 $[0/\pm45]_s$ LAMINATE
CONTAINING A CIRCULAR OPEN HOLE AND INCLUSIONS.

are considered: aluminum, titanium and steel. In Figure 20.13 the strength reduction for a CFRP T300/5208 $[0/\pm45]_s$ laminate with an open hole is compared to one with an inclusion. A characteristic length, $b_o = 0.05"$, which is the best fit for the quasi–isotropic laminate, was used. The strength of the laminate with a titanium inclusion is the highest among the three materials. However, the laminate with any one of these inclusions is more than twice as strong as the one with an open hole for hole diameter larger than 0.6". In Figure 20.14 the T300/5208 $[0_2/90]_s$ laminate is chosen for the base material.

Again, the strength of this laminate, with any one of the inclusions, is significantly higher than of the one with an open hole. Among the three different inclusion materials, the laminate strength is the highest with the titanium inclusion and is the lowest with the aluminum inclusion.

At this moment, we have no experimental data for the strength a composite laminate with an inclusion under shear loading. The prediction in Figure 20.15 shows that the strength of a T300/5208 [0/90/±45]$_s$ laminate with an aluminum inclusion recovers to the unnotched strength. The strength reduction factors for this $\pi/4$ laminate with a titanium and a steel inclusion are about 0.9 and 0.8, respectively, for a wide range of inclusion sizes. These values are significantly higher than the one with an open hole.

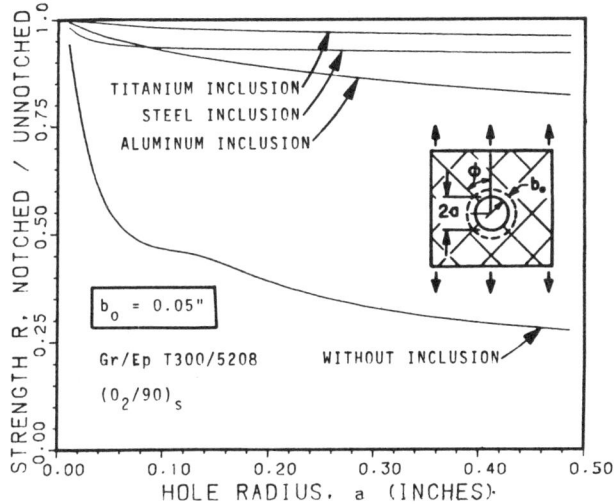

FIGURE 20.14   STRENGTH PREDICTION OF THE GR/EP T300/5208 [0$_2$/90]$_s$ LAMINATE CONTAINING A CIRCULAR OPEN HOLE AND INCLUSIONS.

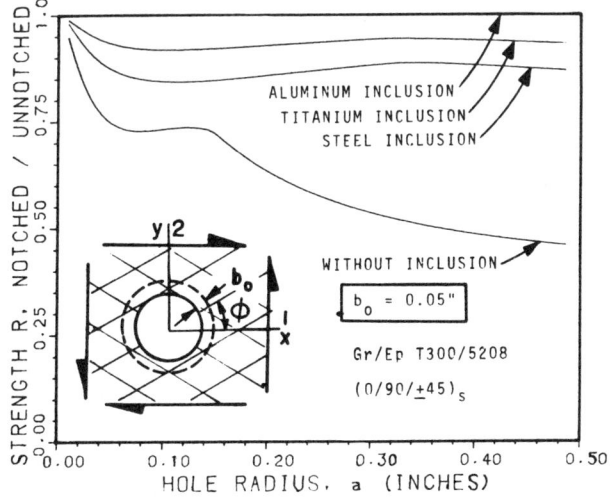

FIGURE 20.15   PREDICTED STRENGTH OF THE GR/EP T300/5208 [0/90/±45]$_s$ LAMINATE WITH AN OPENING AND INCLUSION UNDER SHEAR LOADING.

Although steel is stiffer than aluminum and titanium, the strength of the base laminate with a steel inclusion is either between or below the strength of the other two inclusion materials. This is because the mismatch in stiffnesses between the base plate and the steel inclusion is the highest among the three combinations. The distribution of the stresses and failure locations of the base plate are different for different inclusions. It can be concluded from this study that in the course of structural repair using inclusions, one should use an inclusion that has similar elastic properties to the base material in order to minimize the stress concentration in the base laminate.

The repairability and the design can be studied from the strength performance of a system of laminates with an inclusion of different materials. This task can be accomplished using a ranking method (same method used in the previous sections).

20.7 CONCLUSIONS

A method of estimating the notched strength of composite laminates is useful in design. The loss of strength is a function of material, laminate layup, the applied load, the size of holes and the size and orientation of cracks.

The laminate ranking method can also be applied to determine the laminates with the highest notched strength. The method here is identical to that used in Section 14 for single loads, and can be extended to the multiple loads.

The results here can also be applied to assess the severity of damage in composite laminates. A rational basis for repair is generated using this approach.

Fundamental to our method is the characteristic length. At this time, it is determined empirically by seeking the best fit of **SRF** curves from a set of test data. We would prefer to have a more generic constant. We believe that, as we learn more about notched strength, we will broaden our ability to estimate the strength of laminates.

REFERENCES

20–1   Lekhnitskii, S. G., *Anisotropic Plates*, 2nd edition. Translate from Russian by S. W. Tsai and T. Cheron, Gordon and Breach, 1968.

20–2   Tan, S. C., "Notched Strength Prediction and Design of Laminated Composites Under In–plane Loadings," to appear in *J. of Composite Materials*.

20–3   Awerbuch, J., and M. S. Madhukar, "Notched Strength of Composite Laminates: Prediction and Experiments – A Review," *J. Reinforced Plastics and Composites*, vol. 4, 1985.

20–4   Malik, B. U., "Strength and Failure Analysis of Composite Laminates with Holes at Room and Elevated Temperatures," master thesis of Air Force Institute of Technology, Dayton, 1984.

20–5   Morris, D. H., and H. T. Hahn, "Mixed–mode Fracture of Graphite/Epoxy Composites: Fracture Strength," *J. of Composite Materials*, vol. 11, 1977.

20–6   Kim, R. Y., "Fracture of Composite Laminates by Three–Point Bend,"
        Experimental Mechanics, vol. 19, 1979.

20–7   Harris, C. E., and D. H. Morris, "A Damage Tolerant Design Parameter for
        Graphite/Epoxy Laminated Composites," *J. Composites Technology and Research*,
        vol. 7, 1985.

Section 21

TEST METHODS

Ran Y. Kim
UNIVERSITY OF DAYTON RESEARCH INSTITUTE, DAYTON

21.1 TENSILE TESTS

The uniaxial tension test is the most fundamental method for the determination of data such as material specification, screening, research and development, and design of structural components.

For unidirectional and woven composites we can measure:

$$E_x, E_y, \nu_x, X, \text{ and } Y \tag{21.1}$$

For multidirectional, symmetric laminates we can measure:

$$E_1{}^\circ, \nu_{21}{}^\circ, \text{ and } X^\circ \text{ (tensile strength of laminates)} \tag{21.2}$$

TEST SPECIMEN

Straight–sided, constant cross section specimens with tabs bonded to the ends are widely accepted. Table 21.1 shows the recommended dimensions. Figure 21.1 shows the geometry of the specimen.

TABLE 21.1 RECOMMENDED SPECIMEN DIMENSIONS, mm

Orientation	Width	Length	Thickness
0 degree	12.7	127	1 to 2.54
90 degree	25.4	38	1 to 2.54
Multidirectional	25.4	127	1 to 2.54

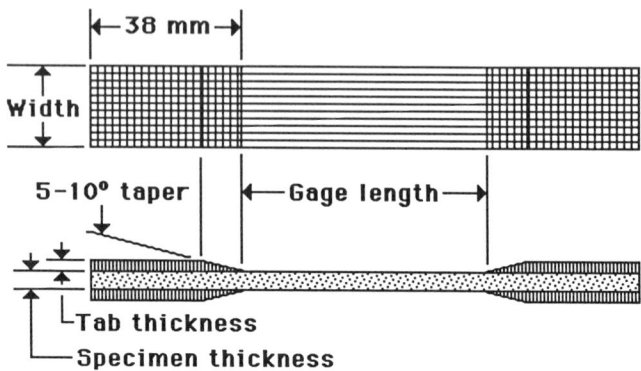

FIGURE 21.1 TENSILE TEST SPECIMEN WITH TAPERED TABS.

END TABS

- Fabric or cross–ply E–glass/epoxy and aluminum plates are widely used. The 90 degree specimen is often tested without end tabs.
- Length of tab is determined by the adhesive shear strength and the tensile strength of the composite. It should be about 25–38 mm.
- Tab thickness varies with specimen thickness, and can range between 1.5 to 2.5 mm.
- Use any high elongation adhesive that will meet the environmental conditions.
- Prepare bond surface by sanding and cleaning with an appropriate solvent.

SPECIMEN CUTTING

- Avoid rough or uneven cut edges, and surface scratches.
- Use diamond impregnated saw with water cooling.
- Specimen edges should be parallel to within 0.125 mm.

TEST PROCEDURE

- Measure width and thickness at several places, and take the minimum values to calculating the cross–sectional area.
- Apply load to the specimen through a set of wedge section grips in order to provide sufficient lateral pressure to prevent slippage.
- Serrated grip surface is desirable (always keep the serrated surface clean).
- Alignment of specimen axis to the line of load is extremely important. The bending due to misalignment can be checked by strain gages mounted as shown in Figure 21.2.
- A constant strain rate of 16.7×10^{-6} to 33.7×10^{-6} s^{-1} is recommended. A constant crosshead speed or loading rate corresponding to the strain rate is also acceptable.
- Strain measurement during test:

  – Extensometer with gage length 12.5 or 25 mm.
  – Electrical resistance strain gage: 350 or 120 ohm foil type gage with gage length in the range of 3.3 to 6.5 mm.
  – Follow manufacturer's recommendation for strain gage mounting technique and selection of adhesive. However, a precaution must be given for probable stiffening of test specimen by the strain gage and adhesive. This often occurs in certain composites such as the low density carbon–phenolic composites.

– Misalignment is a more serious problem with anisotropic material than the conventional material.

– Low voltage for the strain gage circuit is desirable to minimize heat generation. One volt is recommended.

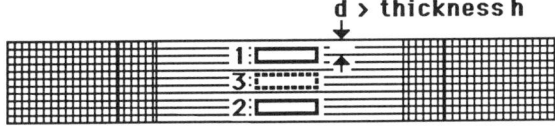

Note: Gage #3 is on the back side.

$$\left|[\epsilon_3-(\epsilon_1+\epsilon_2)/2]/\epsilon_1\right| \leq 0.05$$

$$\left|(\epsilon_1-\epsilon_2)/\epsilon_1\right| \leq 0.05$$

FIGURE 21.2   STRAIN GAGE LOCATIONS AND CALCULATIONS FOR MISALIGNMENT CHECK.

21.2 COMPRESSIVE TESTS

Compressive elastic constants and strengths are determined by these tests. Compressive strength is one of the most difficult properties to determine. A slight eccentric load will cause premature buckling failure rather than the intrinsic compressive failure. A number of test fixtures have been developed by various laboratories. The Celanese and the Illinois Institute of Technology Research Institute (IITRI) fixtures are designed for a specimen gage length less than 12.6 mm, and are primarily used for the 0 degree, 90 degree, and cross–ply laminates. Figure 21.3 illustrates the Celanese fixture and specimen.

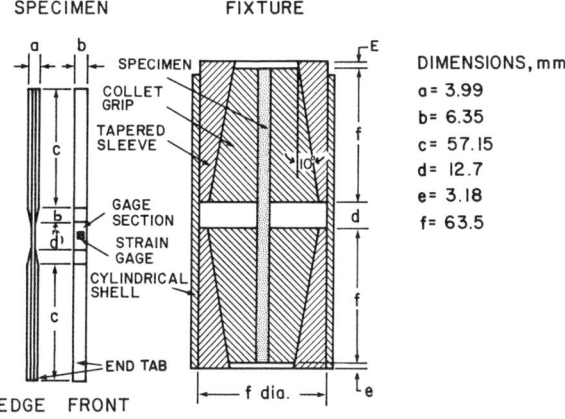

FIGURE 21.3 CELANESE FIXTURE AND SPECIMEN FOR COMPRESSION TESTS.

Recommended specimen thickness for various materials are:

Boron	1.5–2.0 mm
Graphite	1.5–3.0 mm
Glass	3.2–4.0 mm

Euler's column buckling formula can be used for the specimen thickness calculation. For pinned–end column with length L

$$P_{critical} = \pi^2 EI/L^2 \tag{21.3}$$

For a fixed–end column the buckling load is four times that for a pinned–end.

The test fixture is placed between two platens, and the compressive load is applied. One of the platens normally has a spherical seat to minimize the eccentricity in the load introduction.

The short gage length of this test has several undesirable features. Probable end effects for measuring elastic constants and strengths will be encountered. The test cannot be applied to laminates with off–axis angle, and cannot be used for tension–compression fatigue testing.

As an alternative to the Celanese fixture and specimen, a side–supported specimen is shown in Figure 21.4.

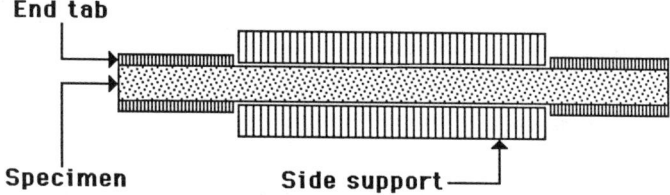

FIGURE 21.4   COMPRESSIVE SPECIMEN WITH SIDE SUPPORTS.

21.3 IN–PLANE SHEAR TESTS

This test determines the in–plane shear modulus, and in–plane shear strength. A number of tests are available:

[45/–45]₂ₛ COUPON

This is a simple test that follows the same procedure as the tensile test. Figure 21.5 shows the specimen and the locations of the two strain gages. From the measured longitudinal and transverse strain data, we can deduce the shear modulus, as follows:

$$\sigma_s = \sigma_1/2, \quad \varepsilon_s = \varepsilon_1 - \varepsilon_2$$

$$E_s = \sigma_s/\varepsilon_s = E_1/2(1+\nu_{21})$$

(21.4)

where $\nu_{21} = -\varepsilon_2/\varepsilon_1$

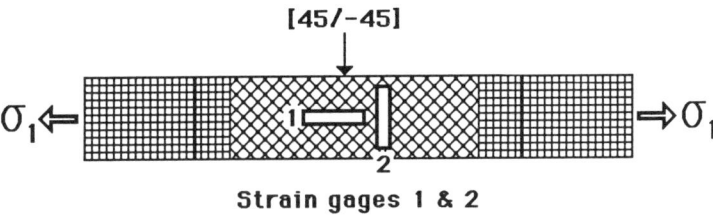

[45/-45]

$\sigma_1 \Leftarrow$ ... $\Rightarrow \sigma_1$

Strain gages 1 & 2

FIGURE 21.5   STRAIN GAGE LOCATIONS FOR MEASURING SHEAR PROPERTIES
FROM A $[45/-45]_{2s}$ TENSILE SPECIMEN.

A nonlinear stress–strain relation usually occurs in shear. Interpretation of shear strength requires care and judgement.

RAIL SHEAR TEST

A flat rectangular plate is tested in a two–rail or three–rail fixture. The latter is shown in Figure 21.6

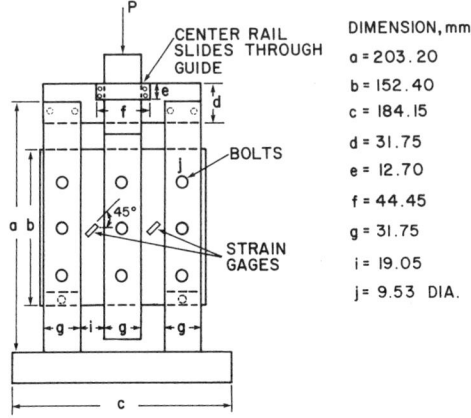

```
P
       CENTER RAIL          DIMENSION, mm
       SLIDES THROUGH
       GUIDE                a = 203.20
                            b = 152.40
                            c = 184.15
             BOLTS          d = 31.75
                            e = 12.70
                            f = 44.45
       STRAIN               g = 31.75
       GAGES                i = 19.05
                            j = 9.53  DIA.
```

FIGURE 21.6 THREE–RAIL SHEAR TEST FIXTURE.

An analysis of the load and strain gages data are, as follows:

$$\sigma_s = P/2A, \quad \varepsilon_s = 2\varepsilon_{45}$$

$$E_s = \sigma_s/\varepsilon_s$$

(21.5)

where **A = bh, b** = length, **h** = thickness

Special recommendations on the rail:

- Drill oversized holes to prevent stress risers when bolts are tightened.
- Abrasive paper or cloth should adhere to the rails for improved gripping.

On the specimen:

- Holes should be drilled and reamed. Use carbide tipped drill bit. Holes should be larger than the bolts.
- Apply torque of 7 to 70 Nm to each bolt. Tighten bolts evenly.
- A fixed pattern of tightening should follow finger tightening. The final level should be reached in two or three stages.

On testing:

- Unless otherwise specified, use a loading rate of 1 to 1.5 mm/min.
- Apply preload and release to align the heads and rails. Alignment can be improved by using a spherical seat between the load head and the center rail.

Others:

- For unidirectional laminates, the fiber orientation can be parallel or perpendicular to the longitudinal axis of the rails. The perpendicular orientation produces higher shear strength than the parallel orientation.
- Failure in the parallel orientation often starts in the corners of the rail caused by local stress concentration.

21.4 FLEXURAL TESTS

This is a quality control and material specifications test. It is not a data generation test. This test is used to determine the outer fiber strength and Young's modulus of homogeneous composite and polymeric materials. For flexural testing of multidirectional laminates, the strength and stiffness interpretations are not as simple.

Figures 21.8 and 21.9 show the most common three–point and four–point flexural tests, respectively. The three–point test is principally designed for materials that break at relatively small deflection.

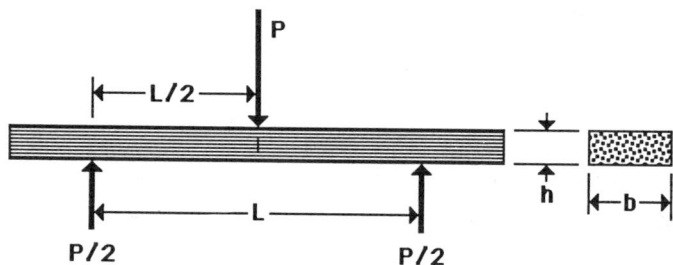

FIGURE 21.7 THREE–POINT FLEXURAL TEST.

The analysis for this test is:

$$\sigma_x = 3PL/2bh^2$$
$$E_x = PL^3/4bh^3\delta$$

(21.6)

where δ = deflection at the mid–point.

The four–point test is primarily designed for materials that undergo large deflection.

The analysis for this test is:

$$\sigma_x = 3PL/4bh^2$$
$$E_x = 11PL^3/64bh^3\delta$$

(21.7)

where δ = deflection at the mid–point.

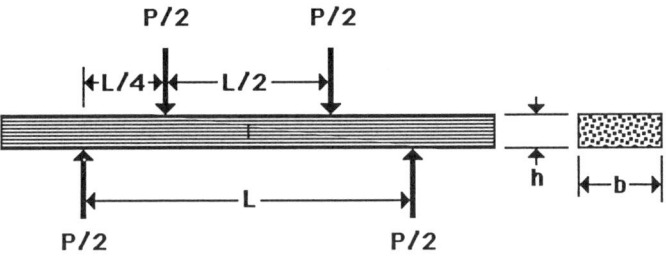

FIGURE 21.8 FOUR–POINT FLEXURAL TEST.

The specimen should be deflected until tensile or compressive rupture occurs, or the maximum fiber strain is reached in the outer fibers. Deflection should not exceed 10 percent of the span length. Correction factors for large deflection will be needed.

Dowel pins are widely used for loading and support points. Pin diameter larger than 6.4 mm will minimize local indentation and stress concentration.

Optimum span–to–depth ratio L/h depends on the ratio of the tensile to interlaminar shear strengths. Recommended ratios are: 16, 32, 40, and 60.

When a specimen is tested at low span–to–depth ratio, shear deflection can reduce the apparent modulus. The 60:1 ratio is recommended for modulus determination.

The specimen width b shall be greater than the depth h, but not to exceed one–fourth of the span.

21.5 INTERLAMINAR SHEAR TESTS

This test is for estimating the interlaminar shear strength only. The test is shown in Figure 21.9. The analysis for this test for the interlaminar shear strength S_I is:

$$S_I = 3P/4bh \tag{21.8}$$

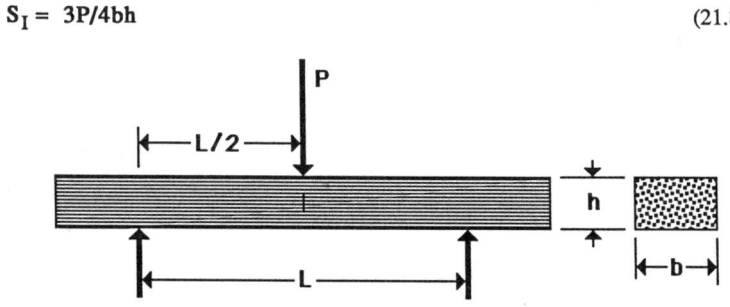

FIGURE 21.9 THREE–POINT INTERLAMINAR SHEAR TEST.

This test is not suitable for design data generation because failure often occurs at a location other than the expected neutral plane. It is therefore important to know the actual location of the fracture and the failure mode. The span–to–depth ratio should be selected so as to induce interlaminar shear fracture mode. The ratio between the maximum outer fiber stress and the interlaminar stress as a function of the span–to–depth ratio is shown in Figure 21.10.

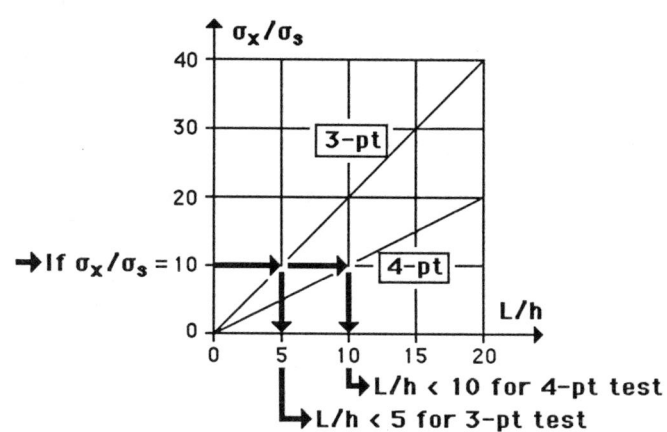

FIGURE 21.10 TENSILE/SHEAR STRENGTH RATIO VERSUS SPAN–TO–DEPTH RATIO. EXAMPLE SHOWS THE MAXIMUM L/h RATIO FOR A GIVEN STRENGTH RATIO OF 10 THAT WOULD LEAD TO SHEAR FAILURE. LARGER L/h WOULD LEAD TO TENSILE FAILURE.

21.6 MODE I FRACTURE TOUGHNESS TESTS

Double cantilever beam specimen has been used for the Mode I fracture toughness test of composite laminates. Figure 21.11 shows the geometry of this test specimen.

The starter crack can be made from a 0.025 mm thin film such as Teflon or Kapton film. This is accomplished by placing the film at the center plane before curing the specimen. Load tab (hinged or T type) shall be bonded to both surfaces of the top and bottom at one end of the beam.

TEST PROCEDURE

- Mark the edge of the specimen at 10 or 15 mm increments up to 60 or 90 mm beyond the tip of the starter crack.
- Specimen shall be mounted in the testing machine. An extensometer may be attached at the end of the specimen, or load tab if there is any doubt of the machine compliance.
- Load the specimen until the crack tip extends to the first mark then unload. Measure the total deflection of the specimen. Reload the specimen until the crack tip extends to the next mark and measure the total deflection. Repeat this procedure until crack tip has reached the last mark. It is virtually impossible in many cases to stop the crack tip exactly at the mark. Thus it is suggested that the actual crack length be measured each time.
- When the total deflection exceeds about 30 percent of the total crack length, test must be stopped because excessive deflection may produce mixed–mode fracture. It is suggested to increase the thickness of the specimen for the material with large deflection, such as glass/epoxy composites.

The fracture toughness value G_{IC} can be calculated from

$$G_{IC} = 3P_C\delta_C/WC \qquad\qquad (21.9)$$

where W = specimen width, C = crack length, P_C = applied load, δ_C = total deflection.

Three or four data points in one specimen are desirable in order to obtain an average.

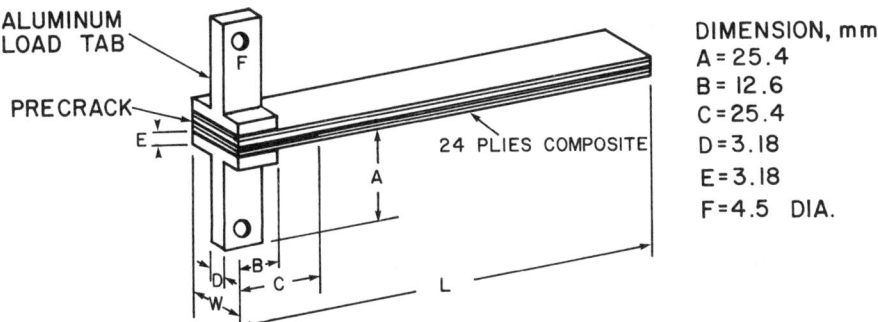

FIGURE 21.11   DOUBLE–CANTILEVER–BEAM (DCB) SPECIMEN WITH LOAD TABS ATTACHED.

21.7 MODE II FRACTURE TOUGHNESS TESTS

Mode II fracture toughness can be determined by testing an end–notch flexural specimen shown in Figure 21.12. Specimen fabrication, preparation, and test procedure for a mode II are not significantly different from those of mode I test.

Fracture toughness for mode II, G_{IIC}, is given

$$G_{IIC} = 9C^2P_C\delta_C/2W(2L^3+3C^3) \tag{21.10}$$

where δ_C = total deflection at center pin.

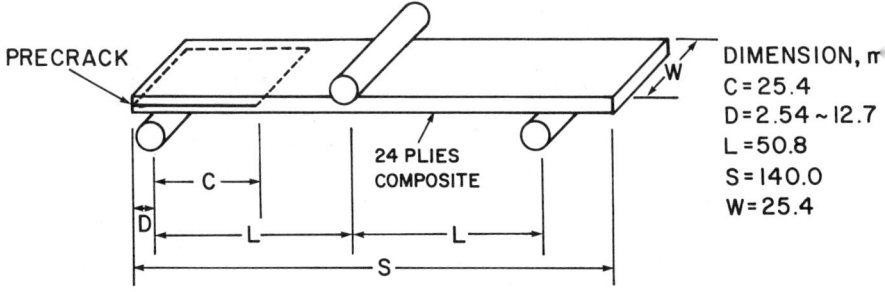

PRECRACK

24 PLIES
COMPOSITE

DIMENSION, m
C = 25.4
D = 2.54 ~ 12.7
L = 50.8
S = 140.0
W = 25.4

FIGURE 21.12 END–NOTCH FLEXURAL SPECIMEN FOR MODE II TESTS.

21.8 CONCLUSIONS

We have presented some of the most frequently used test methods in this section. Most of our experience in testing is in graphite/epoxy composites at room temperature. Other composite materials will require additional care in specimen preparation and testing. The information given here should be treated as guidelines.

In the case of fatigue loading, some of the techniques and experimental data have been discussed in Section 19. Other time– and history–dependent properties, such as creep and relaxation, will need special handling in specimen preparation, instrumentation, testing, and data reduction. Some of the necessary techniques can be found in the publications of the American Society of Testing and Materials (ASTM), the Society of Experimental Mechanics, and other engineering societies.

Test methods are by no means trivial and routine. Composite materials present special challenge to materials and design engineers because of directionally dependent properties. Fracture toughness data, for example, are often dependent on the test method. Many tests are performed which may only be useful for quality control, not for design data generation. Test methods will continue to draw the attention of researchers of composite materials for many years to come.

Section 22

INTERLAMINAR STRESSES

Ajit K. Roy and Stephen W. Tsai
U S AIR FORCE MATERIALS LABORATORY, DAYTON

22.1 ELASTICITY SOLUTION OF A LAYERED BEAM

The objective of this section is to determine the interlaminar stresses for the following problem from orthotropic elasticity theory:

- A cantilever beam with a concentrated load and a moment applied at the free end.
- The beam can have any number of plies of arbitrary isotropic or orthotropic materials. The beam can also be made of adjacent (±θ) angle off–axis plies so that the adjacent (±θ) angle off–axis plies can be assumed to act as orthotropic units. Finite stiffness honeycomb core, and soft interlayers can all be treated as plies.
- The laminate layup can be symmetric or unsymmetric about the mid–plane of the beam.

Presently our solution is limited to the following:

- It is a two–dimensional elasticity solution; i.e., plane stress or plane strain. The latter can be viewed as a plate under cylindrical bending subjected to a line load, and a distributed moment at the free edge.
- It assumes that the transverse (through the thickness) normal stress is identically zero. There are only longitudinal and shear stress components. The shear stress is also the interlaminar stress.

We have studied the stress, strain, and displacement as functions of the following material and geometric factors:

- Face sheet materials; we used [0°], [±15°], and [π/4] CFRP, T300/5208.
- Length–to–depth ratios, from 1 to 10.
- Fraction of core to total laminate thickness, from 0.1 (a beam with interlayer) to 0.9 (a thin wall sandwich beam).
- Core material: orthotropic and transversely isotropic, and isotropic material.
- Different core–to–face sheet stiffness ratios.
- One soft interlayer at the mid–plane, or two soft layers located symmetrically from the mid–plane.

22.2 MATHEMATICAL FORMULATION

The intent of this section is to determine the stress and strain field of an orthotropic layered beam as shown in Figure 22.1

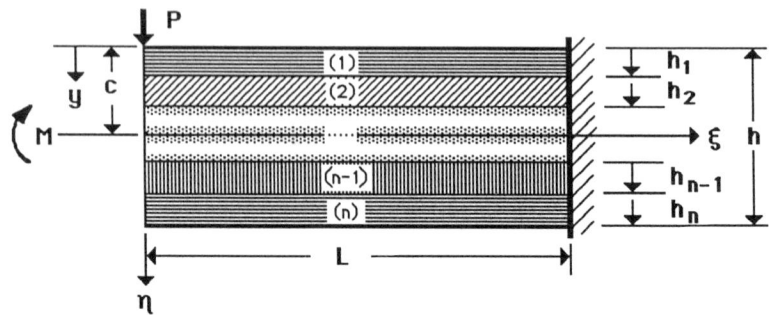

FIGURE 22.1 COORDINATES AND GEOMETRY OF A MULTILAYER CANTILEVER BEAM.

Beam Notation:

P = applied transverse force at the end of the beam
M = applied bending moment
n = number of plies
c = position of the neutral axis from the top face of the beam
h = total thickness of the beam
b = width of the beam
$\eta = y-c$

The position of the neutral axis, c , is calculated from the classical beam theory (CBT). According to CBT, the axial strain is:

$$\varepsilon_1 = \varepsilon_1{}^o + y k_1 \qquad (22.1)$$

where k_1 is the curvature along the axial direction.

At the neutral axis, $\varepsilon_1 = 0$. Thus,

$$c = -\varepsilon_1{}^o/k_1 \qquad (22.2)$$

Classical Beam Theory (CBT) solution:

Stress Field:

$$\sigma_1{}^{(j)}(\xi,\eta) = (M-P\xi)E^{(j)}\eta/(bD_{11})$$
$$\sigma_2{}^{(j)}(\xi,\eta) = 0 \qquad (22.3)$$
$$\sigma_6{}^{(j)}(\xi,\eta) = P \sum_{i=k+1}^{n} \left\{ E^{(i)}(h_i-c)^2-(h_{i-1}-c)^2 \right\} + E^{(j)}\left\{ (h_j-c)^2-\eta^2 \right\}$$

$$\text{for } h_{j-1} < \eta < h_j$$

where $\quad D_{11} = (1/3) \displaystyle\sum_{i=1}^{n} Q_{11}^{(i)} \left\{ (h_i - c)^3 - (h_{i-1} - c)^3 \right\}$ (22.4)

Strain Field:

$\varepsilon_1(\xi,\eta) = (M - P\xi)\eta/(bD_{11})$

$\varepsilon_2(\xi,\eta) = 0$ (22.5)

$\varepsilon_6(\xi,\eta) = 0$

Displacement Field:

$u(\xi,\eta) = (1/bD_{11}) \left[M(\xi - L) - (1/2)(\xi^2 - L^2) \right] \eta$

$v(\xi) = (1/bD_{11}) \left[P\xi^3/6 - M\xi^2/2 + (ML - PL^2/2)\xi - ML^2/2 + PL^3/3 \right]$

where $\quad v \neq v(\eta)$ (22.6)

Elasticity Solution:

Based on an assumed polynomial stress function the stress, strain, and displacement fields are obtained as follows:

Stress Field:

$\sigma_1^{(j)}(\xi,\eta) = E_j - B_j\xi + D_j\eta - 2C_j(\xi\eta + v_{61}^{(j)}\eta^2)$

$\sigma_2^{(j)}(\xi,\eta) = 0$ (22.7)

$\sigma_6^{(j)}(\xi,\eta) = A_j + B_j\eta + C_j\eta^2$

Strain Field:

$\varepsilon_1^{(j)}(\xi,\eta) = S_{11}^{(j)}\sigma_1^{(j)} + S_{16}^{(j)}\sigma_6^{(j)}$

$\varepsilon_2^{(j)}(\xi,\eta) = S_{12}^{(j)}\sigma_1^{(j)} + S_{26}^{(j)}\sigma_6^{(j)}$ (22.8)

$\varepsilon_6^{(j)}(\xi,\eta) = S_{16}^{(j)}\sigma_1^{(j)} + S_{66}^{(j)}\sigma_6^{(j)}$

Displacement Field:

$u^{(j)}(\xi,\eta) = A_j S_{16}^{(j)}\xi + B_j \left\{ -S_{11}^{(j)}\xi^2/2 + S_{16}^{(j)}\xi\eta + (S_{66}^{(j)} + S_{12}^{(j)})\eta^2 \right\}$

$\quad\quad + C_j \left\{ -S_{16}^{(j)}\xi\eta^2 - S_{11}^{(j)}\xi^2\eta + (S_{66}^{(j)} + S_{12}^{(j)} - 2S_{16}^{(j)}v_{61}^{(j)})\eta^3 \right\}$

$\quad\quad + D_j(S_{11}^{(j)}\xi\eta + S_{16}^{(j)}\eta^2) + E_j S_{11}^{(j)}\xi + Q_j\eta + R_j$

$$v^{(j)}(\xi,\eta) = A_j(S_{66}^{(j)}\xi+S_{26}^{(j)}\eta)+B_j(-S_{16}^{(j)}\xi^2-S_{12}^{(j)}\xi\eta+S_{26}^{(j)}\eta^2)$$

$$+C_j\left\{S_{11}^{(j)}\xi^3/3-S_{12}^{(j)}\xi\eta^2+(S_{26}^{(j)}-2S_{12}^{(j)}v_{61}^{(j)})\eta^3\right\}$$

$$+D_j(S_{12}^{(j)}\eta^2-S_{11}^{(j)}\xi^2)/2+E_j(S_{16}^{(j)}\xi+S_{12}^{(j)}\eta)-Q_j\xi+P_j \qquad (22.9)$$

The constants A_j, B_j, . . . , E_j, P_j, . . . , R_j, for the j–th ply are determined from the boundary conditions for the beam and contact conditions of the plies at each interface.

For ease of comparison, the stress and displacement fields can be normalized by (when $M=0$):

$$\sigma_1^{(j)} = \sigma_1^{(j)}(bh^2/(6PL))$$

$$\sigma_6^{(j)} = \sigma_6^{(j)}(bh/P) \qquad (22.10)$$

$$u^{(j)} = u^{(j)}(bD_{11}/(PL^2h))$$

$$v^{(j)} = v^{(j)}(bD_{11}/(PL^2h)) \qquad (22.11)$$

22.3 STRESS DISTRIBUTION

The normal stress along the axis of the beam, σ_1, and the shear or interlaminar stress, σ_6, are insensitive to many material and geometric changes. They deviate from the classical beam theory only when the length–to–span ratio of the beam is unity, implying a very short beam.

The normal stress of a sandwich construction, with 75 percent of honeycomb core is shown in Figure 22.2. The face sheet is [0°], CFRP T300/5208. The honeycomb is assumed to have zero longitudinal stiffness along the axis of the beam, and infinite transverse stiffness and shear rigidity. Beam theory agrees with the elasticity solution.

If [±15°] CFRP facing is used (i.e., each face has an adjacent ±15° CFRP), the normal stress distribution for the same sandwich beam is slightly different from the elasticity solution. But the difference vanishes when the span–to–depth ratio is increased from 1 to 5.

The interlaminar shear stress distribution for this beam is shown in Figure 22.3. Again there is no difference between the two theories.

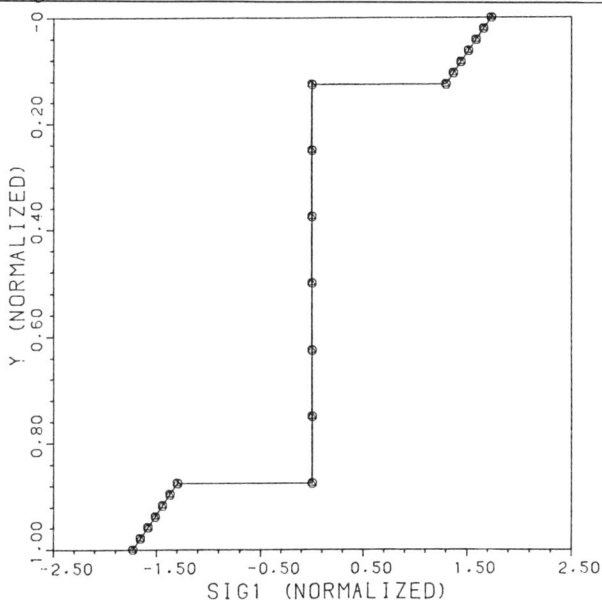

FIGURE 22.2   NORMAL STRESS DISTRIBUTION FOR A SHORT SANDWICH BEAM
(L/h = 1, c* = 0.75); CIRCLES ARE CLASSICAL BEAM THEORY, AND
TRIANGLES, THE ELASTICITY SOLUTION.

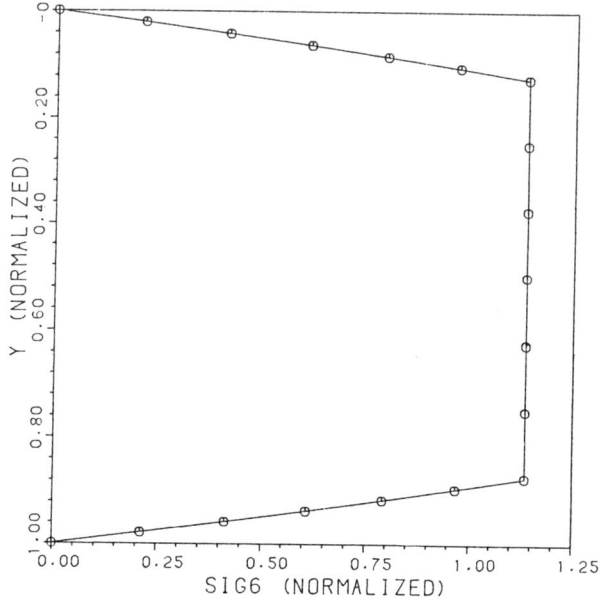

FIGURE 22.3   SHEAR STRESS DISTRIBUTION OF A SHORT SANDWICH BEAM, SAME
CONSTRUCTION AS THAT IN FIGURE 22.2, CIRCLES ARE FROM THE
CLASSICAL BEAM THEORY, AND THE SOLID LINE, ELASTICITY
SOLUTION.

The stress distribution of a beam with a soft interlayer can be seen in Figure 22.4. The core is accounts for ten percent of the depth and has the stiffness of an epoxy. The core has little effect on the normal stress. There is no difference between the beam and elasticity solutions. The interlaminar shear stress is not affected either. When the interlayer is located off the mid–plane, there is not a noticeable effect either. When orthotropic face is used, such as [±15°], there is some deviation from the beam theory. But for span–to–depth ratios of greater than five, the deviation becomes negligible.

It can be concluded from Figure 22.4 that, the stress distributions of a beam are insensitive to the presence of a sandwich core or interlayers. Furthermore, beam theory is accurate for span–to–depth ratios of greater than five.

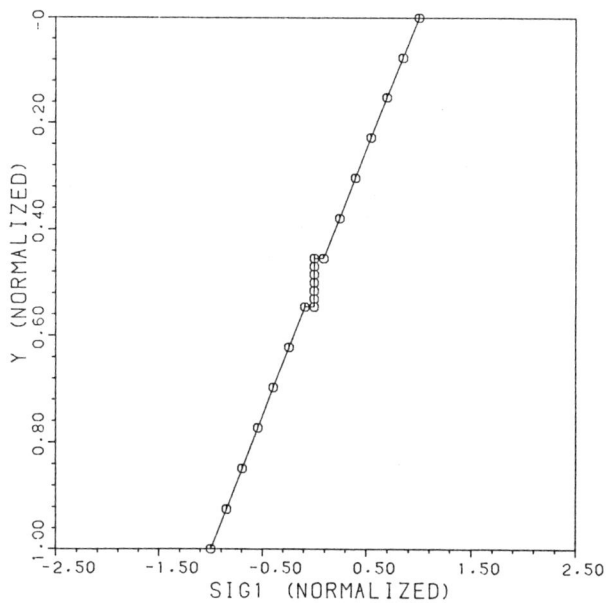

FIGURE 22.4   NORMAL STRESS DISTRIBUTION OF A SHORT BEAM WITH A SOFT INTERLAYER (L/h = 1, c* = 0.1); CIRCLES ARE FROM THE CLASSICAL BEAM THEORY, AND SOLID LINE, THE ELASTICITY SOLUTION.

22.4 STRAIN DISTRIBUTION

The strain distributions determined from the beam and elasticity solutions are different depending on the value of the ratio of shear modulus of the core to that of the face material. The normal strain along the beam axis ε_1 does not deviate until the shear modulus of the core is reduced to approximately 1 percent of that of the face. The dependence of the normal strain of the shear modulus ratio is shown in Figure 22.5 for a beam where the facing material is [±15°] CFRP T300/5208, the span–to–depth is unity, and the core is 70 percent.

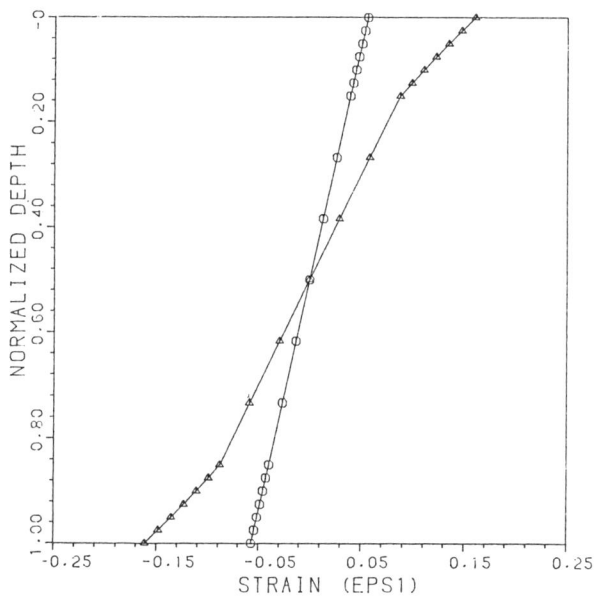

FIGURE 22.5 NORMAL STRAIN DISTRIBUTION OF A SHORT SANDWICH BEAM (L/h = 1, c^* = 0.7); THE FACING MATERIALS IS [±15°] CFRP, AND THE SHEAR MODULUS OF CORE IS 1 PERCENT THAT OF THE FACING; CIRCLES ARE FROM THE CLASSICAL BEAM THEORY, AND TRIANGLES, THE ELASTICITY SOLUTION.

The transverse strain ε_2 deviates from the elasticity solution. The beam theory predicts zero transverse strain. In Figure 22.6, the deviation from zero is shown as a function of the shear modulus ratio. Even for a beam with span–to–depth ratio of five, the deviation is significant.

The shear strain distribution is directly derivable from the shear stress across the beam. For example, for the sandwich beam shown in Figure 22.3, the corresponding shear strain will be parabolic across the top and bottom faces, and constant across the core. The shear stiffness of the core will determine the resulting shear strain.

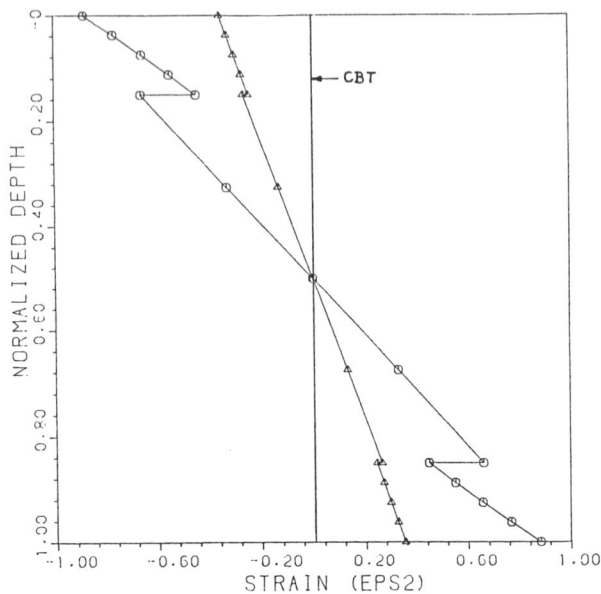

FIGURE 22.6   TRANSVERSE NORMAL STRAIN DISTRIBUTIONS FOR A MEDIUM
LENGTH SANDWICH BEAM (L/h=5,c*=0.7); SHEAR MODULI RATIO OF
0.01 ARE SHOWN AS CIRCLES, THAT OF 0.1 IN TRIANGLES, AND THE
CLASSICAL BEAM THEORY (CBT) SOLUTION IS IDENTICALLY ZERO
AND SHOWN AS A SOLID VERTICAL LINE.

22.5 DISPLACEMENT DISTRIBUTION

The displacement distribution is also highly dependent on the shear modulus
ratios.   Cassical beam theory is accurate when the ratio is near unity or when
the span–to–depth ratio is five or more.   Figure 22.7 shows the displacement
u in the 1–direction of a [0°] CFRP facing, with 70 percent honeycomb core,
and several shear modulus ratios.   Deviation becomes significant as the shear
modulus ratio is 0.1 or smaller.   At low shear modulus ratios (of value 0.1 or
less), the face sheets begin to act like two uncoupled separate sheets under
bending.

As the span–to–depth ratio is increased from unity to two, the displacements
predicted by the elasticity solution decreases by a factor of three to five.

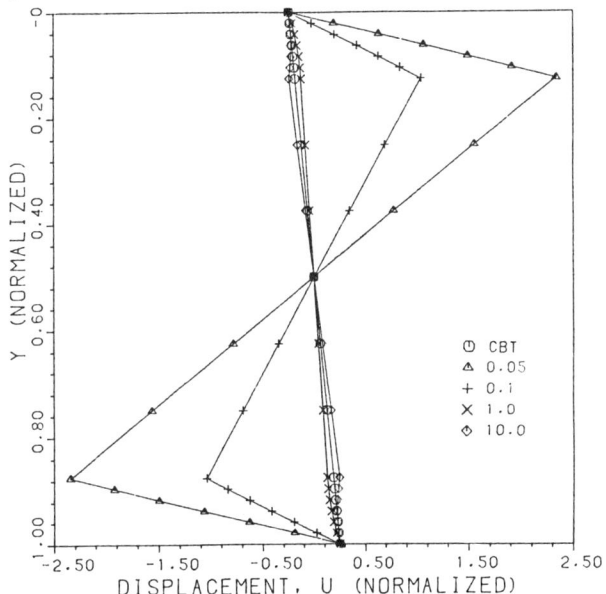

FIGURE 22.7   HORIZONTAL DISPLACEMENT OF A SHORT SANDWICH BEAM (L/h = 1, c* = 0.7); THE FACING MATERIALS IS [0°] CFRP; VARIOUS SHEAR MODULUS RATIOS ARE SHOWN.

Figure 22.8 shows the effect of the shear stiffness of the core on the average vertical displacement **v** at the end of the cantilever beam where the load is applied. As we may expect, as the shear modulus of the core decreases, the vertical displacement increases drastically. The beam in Figure 22.8 is of medium length (L/h = 5). The sandwich core fractions range from 0.1 (an interlayer) to 0.9 (almost a thin wall construction). The displacement **v** for a given core ratio is normalized by its classical beam theory (CBT) value. The normalized displacements for various core fractions do not follow the same order. The curves cross one another. Although, qualitatively, the effect of the softening core is the same for all core fractions.

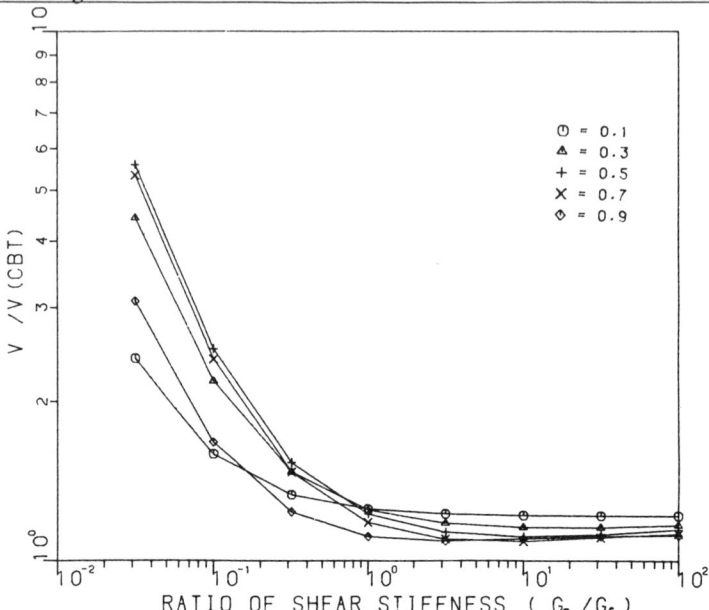

FIGURE 22.8   VERTICAL DISPLACEMENT AT THE END OF A MEDIUM LENGTH
CANTILEVER SANDWICH BEAM (L/h = 5) WITH [0°] CFRP FACING
MATERIAL; THE CORE FRACTIONS RANGE FROM 0.1 TO 0.9. THE
VERTICAL END DISPLACEMENT, v(CBT) IS OBTAINED FROM THE
CLASSICAL BEAM THEORY.

22.6 DISCUSSION

We have presented the stress, strain and displacement distributions of an
orthotropic layered cantilever beam.   A beam made up with adjacent ($\pm\alpha$)
angle plies is also treated as an orthotropic beam.   Our elasticity solution of
the problem can be extended directly to a three–point bend test by joining the
fixed ends of two cantilever beams.   The resulting distributions at the center
of the resulting three–point bend test will be the same as those at the fixed
end of the cantilever beam.   As mentioned earlier, the solution here can also
be extended to a plate under cylindrical bending by a line load and/or a
distributed moment.

Closed form solutions of interlaminar stresses are difficult to obtain for
plates with general loading and boundary conditions.   Our intent is to use
elasticity theory to solve the simplest problem first.   The next natural step
would be the inclusion of the nonzero transverse stress σ_2.

We have also examined the failure criterion that would be appropriate for the
present plane stress and plane strain solutions.   A three–dimensional failure
criterion was required because the interlaminar shears were acting in the
planes transverse to the axis of the beam.   Our results indicated that, due to
combined stresses, failure might occur not at the outermost fibers; e.g., this
occurs in short beams with L/h = 1.   We could conclude that the stress

distributions, as those shown in Figures 22.2 to 22.4, should yield sufficient information on the strength of a sandwich beam. The classical beam theory was found to be accurate for the strength analysis for long beams; i.e., those with span–to–depth ratios higher than five.

The soft interlayer had little effect on the shear stress distribution. The implication was that the strength would not be affected by the interlayer either. But the soft interlayer and soft sandwich core had profound effect on the strain and displacement of the beam. A many–fold increase in the end displacement was possible as the shear stiffness of the core decreases. The core fraction or percentage, however, did not qualitatively affect the increased end displacement of the cantilever beam.

22.7 CONCLUSIONS

We have discussed the progress of an ongoing effort to understand the interlaminar stresses in a layered composite. This is an important topic because the superior stiffness and strength of fiber–reinforced composites are not always extended to those related to the thickness direction of a laminate. Many problems of current interest are related to delamination. An improved understanding of the interlaminar stresses and the development of an appropriate failure criterion will be a correct step toward the solution of the delamination problem. Elasticity solution is reliable, consistent, and requires no additional assumption. We look forward to exploring further along this line.

REFERENCES

22–1. Lekhnitskii, S.G., *Anisotropic Plates*, 2nd edition; translated from Russian by S.W. Tsai and T. Cheron, Gordon and Breach Science Publication, 1968.

22–2. Tsai, S.W., 'A Survey of Macroscopic Failure Criteria for Composite Materials', *Journal of Reinforced Plastics and Composites*, Vol 3, Jan 1984, pp 40–62.

Section 23

PRESSURE VESSELS

Ajit K. Roy and Stephen W. Tsai

U S AIR FORCE MATERIALS LABORATORY, DAYTON

23.1 INTRODUCTION

Cylindrical pressure vessels are widely used, both in commercial and aerospace applications, ranging from small bottles of a few inches in diameter to large storage tanks. Its application is not only limited to the use of thin shells; in many of its applications thick shells with wall thickness ratio (ratio of the outer radius to the inner one of the cylindrical wall) of 2 or even higher are being used. For example, the wall thickness ratio of gun barrels can be of the order of two. Thick–walled vessels have also been considered for submersible vessels subjected to high external pressure, [23–1].

The emerging high modulus, high strength composite materials are being used in manufacturing pressure vessels for some time. It is now known that the use of composite materials improves performance and offers a significant amount of material savings over that of isotropic materials. However, to take the full advantage in the use of orthotropic properties of the composite materials, particularly in thick wall construction, a reliable design method based on an accurate stress analysis with the use of an appropriate failure criterion is required. In this section, the stress analysis of thick cylindrical vessels is based on a linear elasticity solution. Analysis based on elasticity solution is reliable and is not limited to any structural geometry, e.g., one such geometry can be wall thickness. For thick pressure vessels, the state of stress or strain is three dimensional. The use of maximum stress or strain criterion in 3–dimensional state of stress or strain of orthotropic materials, in particular, gives rise many vector equations, and none of these two criteria includes the interactions among the stress or strain components. Whereas a 3–dimensinal quadratic failure criterion yields only one scalar equation and it also includes the interactions among the stress or strain components. Thus, in this analysis, the quadratic failure criterion proposed by Tsai and Wu, [23–2], analogous to maximum distortional energy criterion has been used.

23.2 FORMULATION OF THE PROBLEM

The pressure vessel is assumed to be cylindrically orthotropic, i.e., one of the material symmetry axes is parallel to the longitudinal axis of the cylinder. The configuration of the vessel is given in Figure 23.1. In this analysis, filament wound pressure vessels are assumed to be have adjacent (±α) angle lay ups and that adjacent (±α) lay ups act as an orthotropic unit. A pressure vessel can be made up with several of such orthotropic units (Fig. 23.2) wound one over another. An orthotropic unit of (±α) angle lay ups will be referred, in this section, as an orthotropic layer of angle α.

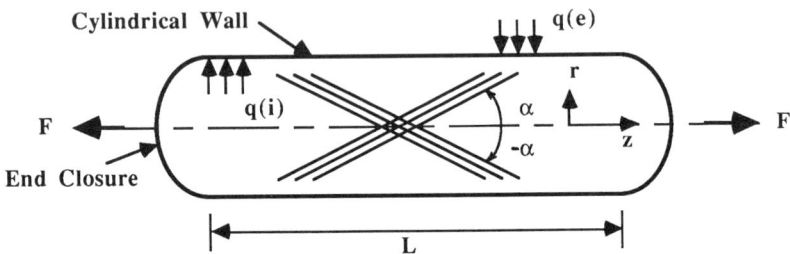

FIGURE 23.1 CONFIGURATION OF THE CLOSED END CYLINDER.

It is assumed that the length (L) of the vessel is such that the longitudinal bending deformation due to the end closures of the vessel is limited to only small end portions of the vessel compared to the overall length. The vessel is subject to axisymmetric internal ($q^{(i)}$) and external ($q^{(e)}$) pressures and axial force (F). Due to cylindrical orthotropy, axisymmetric loading, and ignoring the longitudinal bending deformation due to end closures, the problem can be treated as a generalized plane strain problem.

The strain–stress relations for an axisymmetric multi–layered cylinder in cylindrical coordinates are given by

$$\varepsilon_r^{(k)} = S_{rr}^{(k)}\sigma_r^{(k)}+S_{r\theta}^{(k)}\sigma_\theta^{(k)}+S_{rz}^{(k)}\sigma_z^{(k)}$$

$$\varepsilon_\theta^{(k)} = S_{r\theta}^{(k)}\sigma_r^{(k)}+S_{\theta\theta}^{(k)}\sigma_\theta^{(k)}+S_{\theta z}^{(k)}\sigma_z^{(k)} \qquad (23.1)$$

$$\varepsilon_z^{(k)} = S_{rz}^{(k)}\sigma_r^{(k)}+S_{\theta z}^{(k)}\sigma_\theta^{(k)}+S_{zz}^{(k)}\sigma_z^{(k)}$$

where $S_{ij}^{(k)}$ (i,j=r,θ,z) are components of the compliance matrix. The superscript k refers to the k–th layer.

The strain in z–direction is assumed to be constant, i.e. $\varepsilon_z^{(k)} = \varepsilon_z^{\bullet}$ (a constant). Using this generalized plane strain condition the above strain–stress relations modify to

$$\varepsilon_r^{(k)} = R_{rr}^{(k)}\sigma_r^{(k)}+R_{r\theta}^{(k)}\sigma_\theta^{(k)}+v_{rz}^{(k)}\varepsilon_z^{\bullet}$$

$$\varepsilon_\theta^{(k)} = R_{r\theta}^{(k)}\sigma_r^{(k)}+R_{\theta\theta}^{(k)}\sigma_\theta^{(k)}+v_{\theta z}^{(k)}\varepsilon_z^{\bullet} \qquad (23.2)$$

where $R_{ij}^{(k)} = S_{ij}^{(k)}-S_{iz}^{(k)}S_{jz}^{(k)}/S_{zz}^{(k)}$, (i,j=r,θ);

$v_{iz}^{(k)} = S_{iz}^{(k)}/S_{zz}^{(k)}$, (i=r,θ).

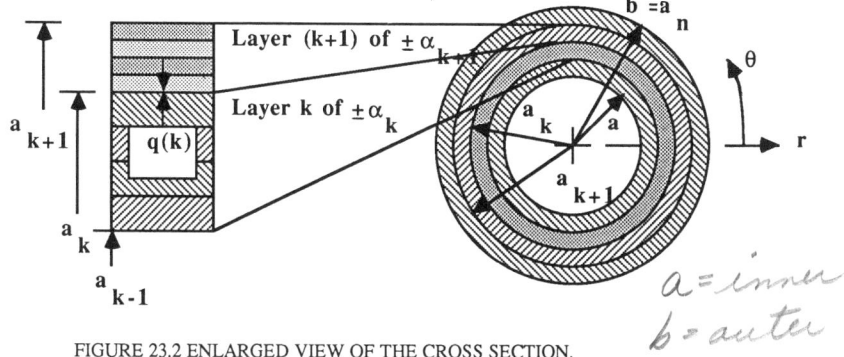

FIGURE 23.2 ENLARGED VIEW OF THE CROSS SECTION.

The normal traction acting on the interface between k–th and (k+1)th layers is denoted by $q^{(k)}$ (Figure 23.2). Then the radial, $\sigma_r^{(k)}$, and hoop, $\sigma_\theta^{(k)}$, stresses are, [23–3]:

$$\sigma_r^{(k)}=A_k[(r/a_k)^{g(k)-1}-(a_k/r)^{g(k)+1}]+B_k[-(r/a_k)^{g(k)-1}+c_k^{2g(k)}(r/a_k)^{g(k)+1}] \quad (23.3)$$

$$\sigma_\theta^{(k)}=A_k g(k)[(r/a_k)^{g(k)-1}+(a_k/r)^{g(k)+1}]-B_k g(k)[(r/a_k)^{g(k)-1}+c_k^{2g(k)}(a_k/r)^{g(k)+1}] \quad (23.4)$$

and

$$\sigma_z^{(k)} = (\varepsilon_z^{\bullet}-S_{rz}^{(k)}\sigma_r^{(k)}-S_{\theta z}^{(k)}\sigma_\theta^{(k)})/S_{zz}^{(k)}$$

$$\tau_{r\theta}^{(k)} = 0 \quad (23.5)$$

where

$$A_k = (q^{(k-1)}c_k^{g(k)+1})/(1-c_k^{2g(k)})$$

$$B_k = q^{(k)}/(1-c_k^{2g(k)})$$

$$c_k = a_{k-1}/a_k$$

$$g(k) = [R_{rr}^{(k)}/R_{\theta\theta}^{(k)}]^{1/2}$$

The expression g(k) is used to indicate that g is a function of k. The displacement components are

$$u^{(k)}(r) = [R_{r\theta}^{(k)}\sigma_r^{(k)}+R_{\theta\theta}^{(k)}\sigma_\theta^{(k)}+\nu_{\theta z}^{(k)}\varepsilon_z^{\bullet}]r$$

$$v^{(k)} = 0 \quad (23.6)$$

$$w^{(k)} = \varepsilon_z^{\bullet} L$$

To determine $\varepsilon_z^{\bullet}$, the axial stress, $\sigma_z^{(k)}$, is assumed to satisfy the axial traction on the average, i.e.

$$\sum_{k=1}^{n} 2\pi \int_{a_{k-1}}^{a_k} \sigma_z^{(k)} r dr = \pi(q^{(i)}-q^{(e)})a^2+F \qquad (23.7)$$

where $\mathbf{F}$ is the applied axial force and the first term on the right hand side of the above equation is the axial stress induced by the end closure due to internal, $\mathbf{q}^{(i)}$, and external, $\mathbf{q}^{(i)}$, pressures.

Substituting $\sigma_z^{(k)}$ from Equation 23.5 and the expressions for $\sigma_r^{(k)}$ and $\sigma_\theta^{(k)}$ from Equations 23.3 and 23.4 into equation 23.7 and performing the integration, the expression for ε_z° is given by

$$\varepsilon_z^\bullet = \left[(q^{(i)}-q^{(e)})a^2+F/\pi-\sum_{k=1}^{n} (q^{(k-1)}\delta_k + q^{(k)}\mu_k)\right]/\Delta \qquad (23.8)$$

where

$$\delta_k = -2[a_k c_k^{g(k)+1}(S_{rz}^{(k)}+g(k)S_{\theta z}^{(k)})(a_k-c_k^{g(k)}a_{k-1})/(1+g(k))-a_{k-1}(S_{rz}^{(k)}$$

$$-g(k)S_{\theta z}^{(k)})(a_k c_k^{g(k)}-a_{k-1})/(1-g(k))]/\{S_{zz}^{(k)}(1-c_k^{2g(k)})\} \qquad (23.9a)$$

$$\mu_k = -2[-a_k(S_{rz}^{(k)}+g(k)S_{\theta z}^{(k)})(a_k-c_k^{g(k)}a_{k-1})/(1+g(k))+a_k c_k^{g(k)}(S_{rz}^{(k)}$$

$$-g(k)S_{\theta z}^{(k)})(a_k c_k^{g(k)}-a_{k-1})/(1-g(k))]/\{S_{zz}^{(k)}(1-c_k^{2g(k)})\} \qquad (23.9b)$$

and

$$\Delta = \sum_{k=1}^{n} (a_k^2-a_{k-1}^2)/S_{zz}^{(k)}.$$

The interface normal tractions, $\mathbf{q}^{(k)}$'s, which are unknown, are to be determined by satisfying the contact condition of the interfaces,

$$u^{(k)} = u^{(k+1)} \qquad \text{at} \quad r=a_k \qquad (23.10)$$

which gives a set of simultaneous equations to determine $\mathbf{q}^{(k)}$'s:

$$q^{(k+1)}\phi^{(k+1)}a_{k+1}+q^{(k)}\gamma^{(k)}a_k+q^{(k-1)}\phi^{(k)}a_{k-1}$$

$$+(1/\Delta)(v_{\theta z}^{(k+1)}-v_{\theta z}^{(k)})\sum_{i=1}^{n}(q^{(i-1)}\delta_i+q^{(i)}\mu_i)a_i$$

$$= (1/\Delta)(v_{\theta z}^{(k+1)}-v_{\theta z}^{(k)})\left[(q^{(i)}-q^{(e)})a^2 +F/\pi\right]a_k; \qquad k=1,2,....,(n-1) \qquad (23.11)$$

where

$$\phi^{(k)} = 2g(k)R_{\theta\theta}^{(k)}c_k^{g(k)}/(1-c_k^{2g(k)})$$

and $$\gamma^{(k)} = -R_{r\theta}^{(k)}-g(k)R_{\theta\theta}^{(k)}(1+c_k^{2g(k)})/(1-c_k^{2g(k)})+R_{r\theta}^{(k+1)} \qquad (23.12)$$

$$-g(k+1)R_{\theta\theta}^{(k+1)}(1+c_{k+1}^{2g(k+1)})/(1-c_{k+1}^{2g(k+1)})$$

where $g(k+1) = [R_{rr}^{(k+1)}/R_{\theta\theta}^{(k+1)}]^{1/2}$.

The second term within the square parentheses of Equations 23.9a and 23.9b contain $(1-g(k))$ in the denominator. For winding angle $\alpha=0$, $g(k)=[R_{rr}^{(k)}/R_{\theta\theta}^{(k)}]^{1/2}=1$, then δ_k and μ_k become singular. In actual computation, this difficulty on singularity can be averted by assigning a very small number to α (=0.01) when $\alpha=0$.

23.3 PREDICTION OF BURST PRESSURE

The Last Ply Failure (LPF) is considered to be the burst pressure. The burst pressure of the vessel is calculated from Last–Ply–Failure (LPF) prediction by degrading the layer properties by a degradation factor (DF); DF<1 (see Section 12.12).

Material of a filament wound pressure vessel is transversely isotropic; the isotropic plane of the material is perpendicular to the fiber direction. Failure in pressure vessels is normally intra–laminar (due to matrix cracking, fiber breakage, etc.). Then the 3–dimensional intra–laminar quadratic failure criterion for the k–th layer in material symmetry coordinates is given by , [23–2]

$$F_{zz}^{(k)}\sigma_z^{(k)2}+F_{rr}^{(k)}(\sigma_r^{(k)2}+\sigma_\theta^{(k)2})+F_{ss}^{(k)}\tau_{\theta z}^{(k)2}+2F_{rz}^{(k)}(\sigma_r^{(k)}+\sigma_\theta^{(k)})\sigma_z^{(k)}$$

$$+2F_{r\theta}^{(k)}\sigma_r^{(k)}\sigma_\theta^{(k)}+F_r^{(k)}(\sigma_r^{(k)}+\sigma_\theta^{(k)})+F_z^{(k)}\sigma_z^{(k)}-1 = 0 \qquad (23.13)$$

where
$$F_{rr}^{(k)}=1/(Y^{(k)}Y'^{(k)})$$
$$F_{zz}^{(k)}=1/(X^{(k)}X'^{(k)})$$
$$F_{ss}^{(k)}=1/S^{(k)2}$$
$$F_r^{(k)}=1/Y^{(k)}-1/Y'^{(k)}$$
$$F_z^{(k)}=1/X^{(k)}-1/X'^{(k)}$$
$$F_{rz}^{(k)}=-0.5*[F_{rr}^{(k)}F_{zz}^{(k)}]^{1/2}$$
$$F_{r\theta}^{(k)}=-0.5*F_{rr}^{(k)}$$

and $X^{(k)},X'^{(k)}$ are respectively longitudinal tensile and compressive strengths, $Y^{(k)},Y'^{(k)}$ are those for transverse direction and $S^{(k)}$ is the shear strength of the k–th layer.

Although $\tau_{\theta z}^{(k)}$ in vessel coordinates (Figure 23.1) is zero, after taking stress transformation to material symmetry coordinates $\tau_{\theta z}^{(k)}$ will not be zero for winding angle, $\alpha\neq0°$, 90°. Since the failure criterion is used in material symmetry coordinates, the term containing $\tau_{\theta z}^{(k)}$ is included in the failure criterion.

The failure pressure can easily be calculated in terms of Strength Ratio, **R**, as suggested in section 11, such that

$$\{\sigma\}_{max} = R\,\{\sigma\}_{applied}. \qquad (23.14)$$

Substituting the above expression in the failure criterion, the expression for the positive root of **R** is given by

$$R = -(\xi/2\rho)+[(\xi/2\rho)^2+1/\rho]^{1/2} \tag{23.15}$$

where

$$\rho = F_{rr}^{(k)}(\sigma_r^{(k)2}+\sigma_\theta^{(k)2})+2F_{r\theta}^{(k)}\sigma_r^{(k)}\sigma_\theta^{(k)}+2F_{rz}^{(k)}(\sigma_r^{(k)}+\sigma_\theta^{(k)})\sigma_z^{(k)}$$

$$+F_{zz}^{(k)}\sigma_z^{(k)2}+ F_{ss}^{(k)}\tau_{\theta z}^{(k)2} \tag{23.16}$$

$$\xi = F_r^{(k)}\sigma_r^{(k)}+F_\theta^{(k)}\sigma_\theta^{(k)}+F_z^{(k)}\sigma_z^{(k)}$$

The negative root for **R** does not have any physical meaning, and thus omitted. When **R**=1, failure occurs. In burst pressure calculation, first the stresses are calculated after degrading the layer properties by DF, then those stress values are used in the failure criterion to calculate burst pressure. In point stress analysis (as in the case of elasticity solution) the point of minimum value of **R** dictates the failure point. When a unit load is applied the the minimum value of **R** is the burst pressure.

23.4 STRESS DISTRIBUTION

Except for Table 23.1 all the material data used are given in Appendix B at the back of the book. The results presented here are for pressure vessels subjected to internal pressure only. If not mentioned otherwise, the composite used to study the design parameters is CFRP T300/N5208.

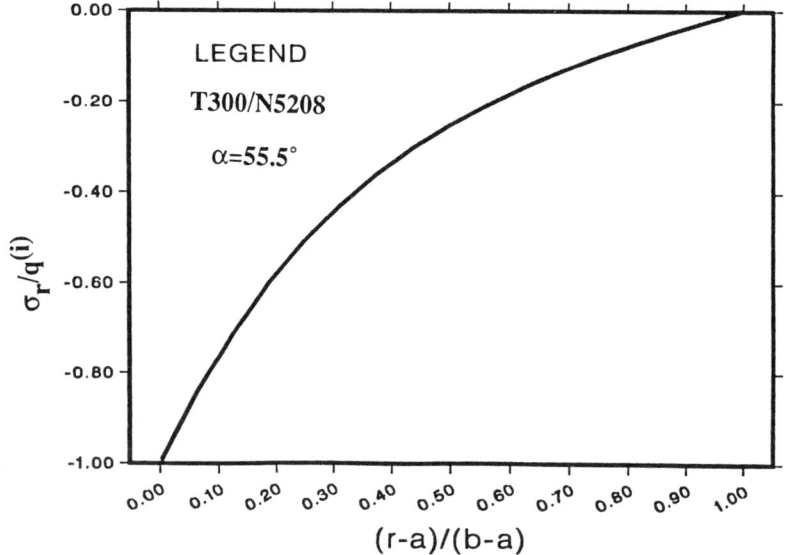

FIGURE 23.3   DISTRIBUTION OF RADIAL STRESS SUBJECTED TO INTERNAL PRESSURE. THE RADIAL STRESS IS NORMALIZED BY INTERNAL PRESSURE.

Figures 23.3 and 23.4 show the distribution of stresses through the thickness of a single layer cylinder of winding angle α=55.5° which happens to be the optimum angle for the maximum failure strength. Subjected to internal pressure, $q^{(i)}$, for all wall thickness ratio, b/a, the radial stress, σ_r, varies from $-q^{(i)}$ to 0 through the thickness, Figure 23.3. The thin wall solution, for a single layer, predicts hoop stress, σ_θ, and axial stress, σ_z, to be constant through the thickness and does not predict σ_r. Figure 23.4 shows the hoop stress distribution through the thickness. In this figure, σ_θ of thick wall solution (elasticity solution) is normalized by that of thin wall solution (membrane solution, see section 7.13). For a very thin wall, such as b/a=1.05, σ_θ predicted by the thick wall solution, as expected, is very close to that of predicted by the thin wall solution. The distribution of σ_θ through the thickness is nonlinear and with increasing wall thickness, b/a, the deviation of σ_θ increases from its thin wall value. The axial stress, σ_z, also shows a similar trend as that as in Figure 23.4 and thus is not shown separately.

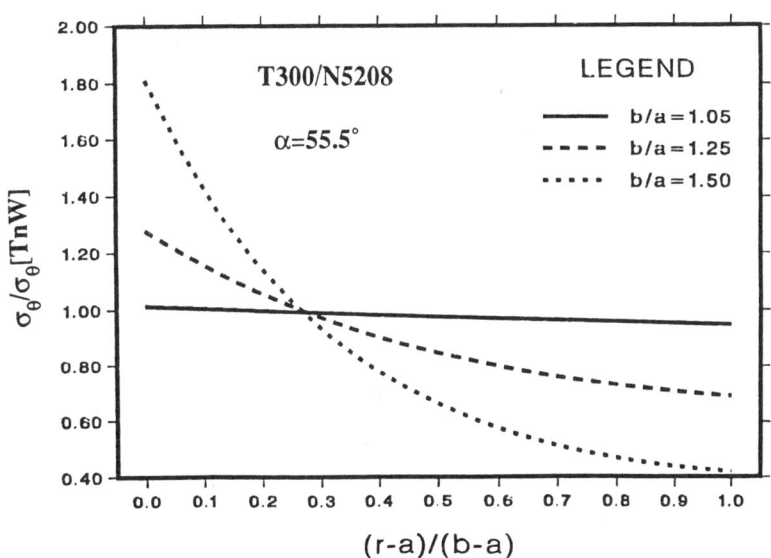

FIGURE 23.4   DISTRIBUTION OF HOOP STRESS THROUGH THE THICKNESS. HOOP STRESS IS NORMALIZED BY ITS THIN WALL SOLUTION VALUE. THREE DIFFERENT WALL THICKNESS RATIOS ARE SHOWN.

23.5 DISPLACEMENT DISTRIBUTION

The distribution of radial displacement, $u(r)$, through the thickness with increasing b/a is similar to that of either σ_θ or σ_z, and thus is not shown. However, the plot of outer displacement, $u(b)$, versus winding angle, α, shows some interesting results. In Figure 23.5, $u(b)$ is plotted versus α for b/a=1.25 (a moderately thick vessel), and for a given internal pressure. The displacement is normalized by that of zero winding angle. Although there is some disagreement between the thick and thin wall solution, however both the thin and thick wall solutions show that the radial displacement decreases monotonically with increasing winding angle until it becomes negative between 58° and 78°. The negative displacement is due to Poisson's effect at those winding angles. The same result is also observed for thin vessels. The **u(b)** for isotropic material, for instance, is not a function of winding angle and always positive, and does not show the above feature as observed in composite materials. The distribution of **u(b)** in Figure 23.5 is very interesting from the point of view of fastening the pressure vessel with other structural members. In other words, the radial displacement of the vessel can be made compatible with that of the fastening members by choosing a particular winding angle.

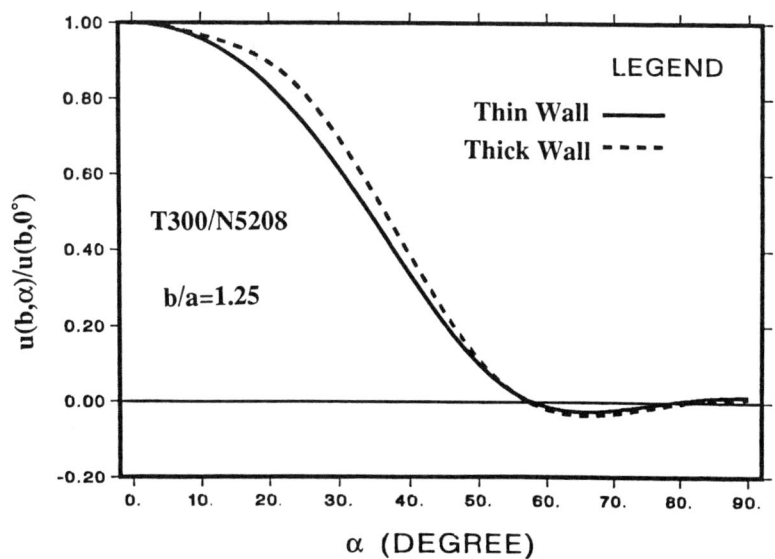

FIGURE 23.5   OUTER RADIAL DISPLACEMENT VERSUS WINDING ANGLE FOR A
MODERATELY THICK VESSEL. THE DISPLACEMENT IS NORMALIZED
BY ITS VALUE AT 0°.

23.6 DEGRADATION FACTOR (DF)

As mentioned in the analysis, to take the matrix cracking into account in predicting LPF, i.e., the burst pressure, macroscopically the properties of each layer is degraded by DF. Table 23.1 shows the comparison of the predicted burst pressure and failure strains with the available experimental results. The prediction is based on thick wall solution for two different DF values (0.3 and 0.1). For thin cylinders, it can be seen from the table that the predicted failure pressure is not very sensitive to the change in the values of DF. For a moderately thick cylinder, **b/a**=1.20, [Massard, Table 23.1] the failure pressure is somewhat sensitive to the value of DF. However, between the two values used, DF=0.3 gives overall a better prediction and thus is used for the rest of the results.

TABLE 23.1   COMPARISON OF EXPERIMENTAL AND PREDICTED FAILURE PRESSURES AND STRAINS.

Mat'l Liner	b/a	Layup#	Rep't. Fail. Press. (MPa)	Predicted Failure Pressure DF= 0.30	Predicted Failure Pressure DF= 0.10	Reported Failure Strains (10^{-2}) $\varepsilon(\theta)$	$\varepsilon(z)$	Predicted Failure* Strains (10^{-2}) $\varepsilon(\theta)$	$\varepsilon(z)$	Ref.
AS4/Ep Elastomer	1.03	$[\pm 24.5_{16}/\pm 89_{16}/$ $\pm 24.5_{34}/\pm 89_{16}/$ $\pm 24.5_{16}]T$	37.1	30.46	30.53	1.3	0.32	1.08	0.22	23–4
Kev49/Ep Rubber	1.01	$[0_{40}/90_{60}]T$	14.22	11.55	12.69	2	1.6	1.90	1.40	23–5
AS/Ep –	1.20	$[\pm 5_9/\pm 11_9/$ $\pm 18_7/\pm 24_{11}/$ $\pm 31_9/90_{52}]T$	103.9	107.5	96.00	–	–	0.65	0.44	23–6

*   Strain values for DF = 0.3
\#   Subscripts are the percentage thickness of respective angles

23.7 THICK AND THIN WALL SOLUTIONS

In Figure 23.6 the burst pressure, P_b , for both thick and thin walls is plotted versus increasing winding angle, α. The burst pressure is normalized by that of 0° winding angle.

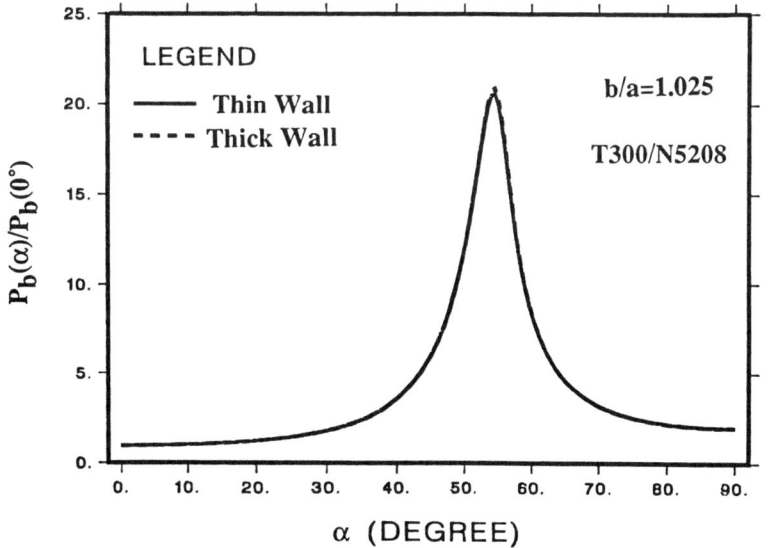

FIGURE 23.6   VARIATION OF BURST PRESSURE OF A THIN VESSEL WITH INCREASING WINDING ANGLE. BURST PRESSURE IS NORMALIZED BY ITS VALUE AT 0°.

For a thin wall, **b/a**=1.025, both thick and thin wall solutions predict 54.75° as the optimum angle for maximum burst pressure. The agreement between these two solutions is very good, except for the value of the burst pressure at α=54.75°, where the thick wall solution predicts the value a little higher than that of the thin wall solution. Figure 23.7 is a plot for a thick vessel, **b/a**=1.50. For a thick vessel there is a significant difference between the two predictions in the neighborhood of optimum winding angle, as can be seen from Figure 23.7.

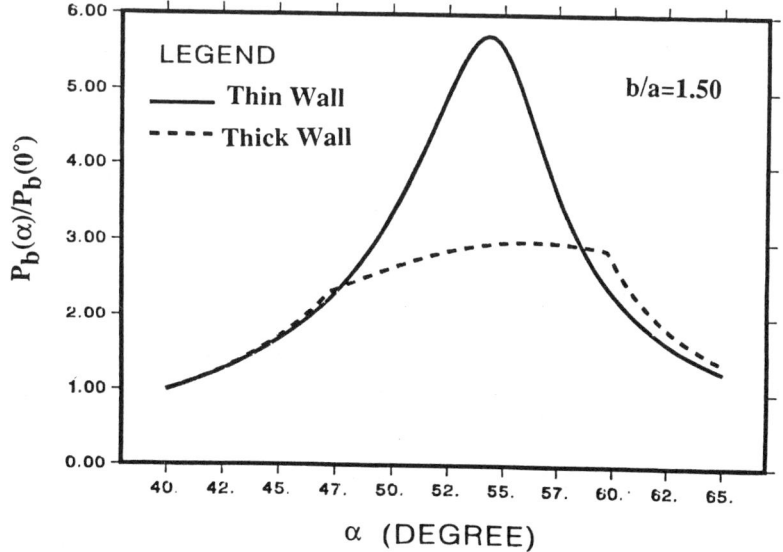

FIGURE 23.7   VARIATION OF BURST PRESSURE FOR A MODERATELY THICK
VESSEL WITH INCREASING WINDING ANGLE.

The thick wall solution predicts the optimum angle as about α=56° whereas the thi₁ wall solution prediction is the same as in Figure 23.6. Also thick wall predictio: (here **b/a**=1.50) of maximum failure pressure is significantly lower than that of th₁ thin wall and thus in this case the thin wall solution is no longer valid. It can als₁ be seen from the thick wall solution in Figure 23.7 that there is not much of penalt₁ in the loss of failure pressure due to some small error in optimum winding angle₁ Whereas in case of thin wall this penalty is significant, as can be seen from Figu₁₁ 23.6. To check the limitation of the thin wall solution on wall thickness P_b for bot₁ thin and thick wall is plotted for increasing wall thickness ratio in Figure 23.8. U₁ to **b/a**=1.10 the thin wall solution agrees well with that of the thick wall. Th₁ agreement differs significantly for **b/a**≥1.30. It is interesting to point out that th₁ thick wall solution does not predict any significant increase in failure pressure wit₁ increasing wall thickness for **b/a**>1.30. Physically this means that failure is not se₁ arresting. Once failure starts at a particular pressure, it will propagate through th₁ thickness and that can not be stopped by merely increasing the wall thickness.

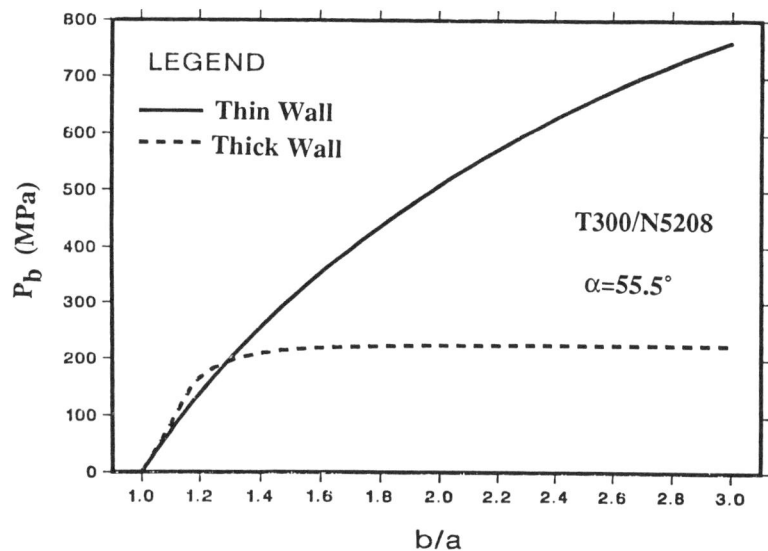

FIGURE 23.8   COMPARISON OF THICK AND THIN WALL BURST PRESSURE
PREDICTIONS WITH INCREASING WALL THICKNESS.

23.8 VESSEL PERFORMANCE OF SOME MATERIALS

The burst pressures, P_b, for T300, IM6, and KEV49 composites in Epoxy matrix with a layer of $\alpha=55.5°$ are compared with that of Aluminum (isotropic) in Figure 23.9. All three composites considered in this figure show limiting values of their respective failure pressures; the limiting values are 225, 174, and 70MPa for CFRP T300, IM6 and KFRP KEV49 composites respectively with $a=0.10$m. Whereas the isotropic material (Aluminum in this case) does not show this limiting pattern. Although IM6/Epoxy composite is longitudinally more than twice as strong as the T300/Epoxy composite, T300/Epoxy carries more internal pressure than IM6/Epoxy. However, for thin vessel, $b/a \leq 1.10$, IM6/Epoxy offers better performance than T300/Epoxy because IM6/Epoxy carries more internal pressure than T300/Epoxy. To compare the overall performance of the pressure vessels made of these materials, the pressure vessel performance efficiency, η, is plotted in Figure 23.10.

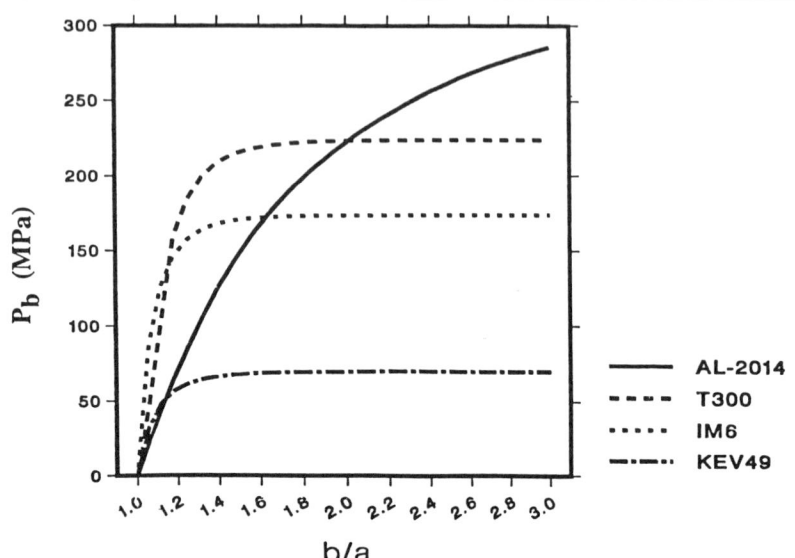

FIGURE 23.9   COMPARISON OF THICK WALL (ELASTICITY SOLUTION) BURST
PRESSURE PREDICTION FOR SOME MATERIALS.

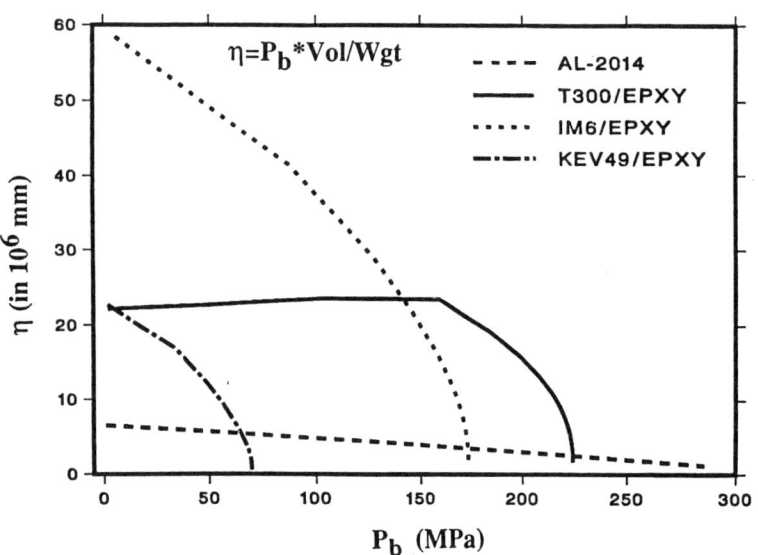

FIGURE 23.10 COMPARISON OF VESSEL PERFORMANCE EFFICIENCY OF SOME
MATERIALS. FOR COMPOSITES, WINDING ANGLE=55.5°.

The efficiency, η, is defined as the ratio of the product of burst pressure and
internal volume to the vessel weight and η has a dimension of length. As it

is known, and Figure 23.10 also reveals that the composite materials have much better efficiency than that of isotropic materials. As it was seen in Figure 23.9, in Figure 23.10 also it can be seen that at low pressure CFRP IM6/Epoxy has higher efficiency than that of other materials. However, near the limiting burst pressure the efficiency of all three composite materials drops very rapidly. Close to the limiting burst pressure, the increase of wall thickness (i.e. increase of material use) practically does not increase the burst pressure (Figure 23.9), and thus the performance efficiency drops drastically near the respective limiting burst pressures.

It has been observed so far that single layer (i.e. single winding angle) pressure vessels are not capable of carrying pressure beyond the limiting pressure irrespective of their wall thickness, and thus materials are also not used efficiently at the limiting pressures. The vessel pressure carrying capability can further be increased by considering hybrid construction having more than one layer. The layers can be of different materials or of same material with different winding angles. To simplify the study of design parameters multilayered vessels of same material are studied.

23.9 STUDY OF EFFICIENT MATERIAL USE

As discussed in section 23.2, the product of the Strength Ratio, **R**, and the applied load gives the strength (i.e. load carrying capacity) at any point. In Figure 23.11, it is observed that **R** is not constant through the thickness, thus the strength, which is proportional to the value of **R**, also varies through the thickness. This means, although the failure will first occur at the point where

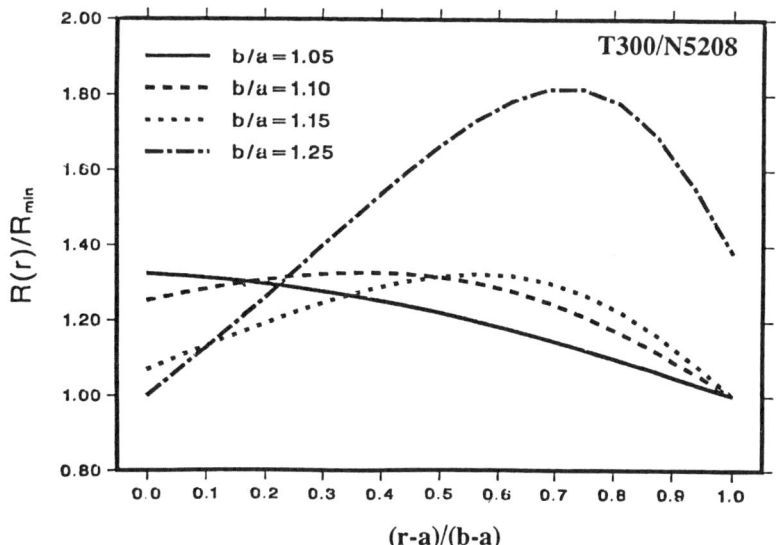

FIGURE 23.11 DISTRIBUTION OF STRENGTH RATIO THROUGTH THE THICKNESS FOR A SOME WALL THICKNESS RATIOS.

R is minimum, still other points have more strength than that of the failure point and thus an efficient material use is not achieved. A material is said to be used very efficiently when the ratio, R_{max}/R_{min}, is close to unity. Ideally, if the ratio is unity, i.e. if **R** has a constant value through the thickness, the material use efficiency is maximum. The deviation of the value of the above ratio from unity signifies non–efficient use of material. It is observed that, like R_{max}/R_{min}, the ratio, $R(a)/R(b)$ can also equally be used to study the material use efficiency. Here, **R(a)** and **R(b)** are the values of **R** at **r=a** and **r=b** respectively. Thus the ratio **R(a)/R(b)** is used to study the material use efficiency because this ratio is easy to calculate compared to that of R_{max}/R_{min}.

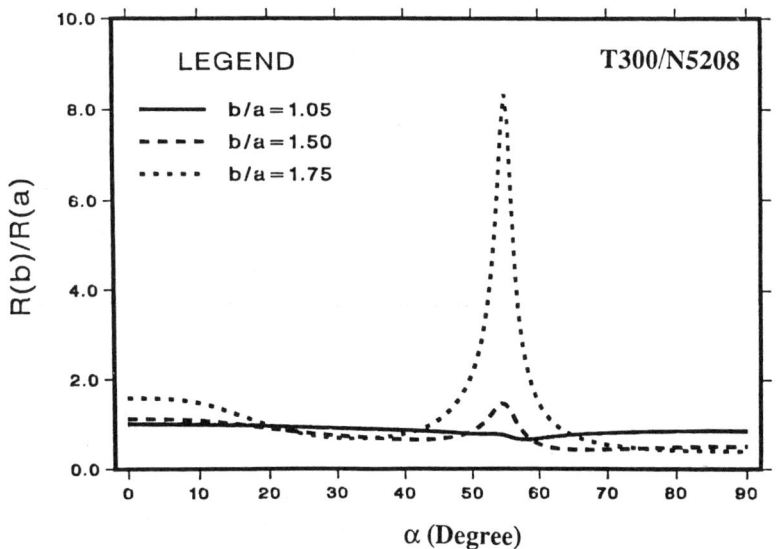

FIGURE 23.12 PLOT TO STUDY MATERIAL USE EFFICIENCY AS A FUCTION OF WINDING ANGLE. THREE THICKNESS RATIOS ARE SHOWN. FOR COMPOSITES α=55.5°.

It was shown in Figure 23.6 and 23.7 that winding angle of about 55° is about the optimum angle for maximum failure pressure. However, Figure 23.12 shows that around 55°, with increasing **b/a**, the ratio, **R(b)/R(a)** deviates significantly from unity. Thus, although about 55° happens to be the optimum winding angle, for thick vessels (high b/a ratio) this single winding angle does not offer efficient use of materials. This suggests, for thick vessels, one should go for hybrid construction or vessel of multiple winding angle to obtain an efficient material use.

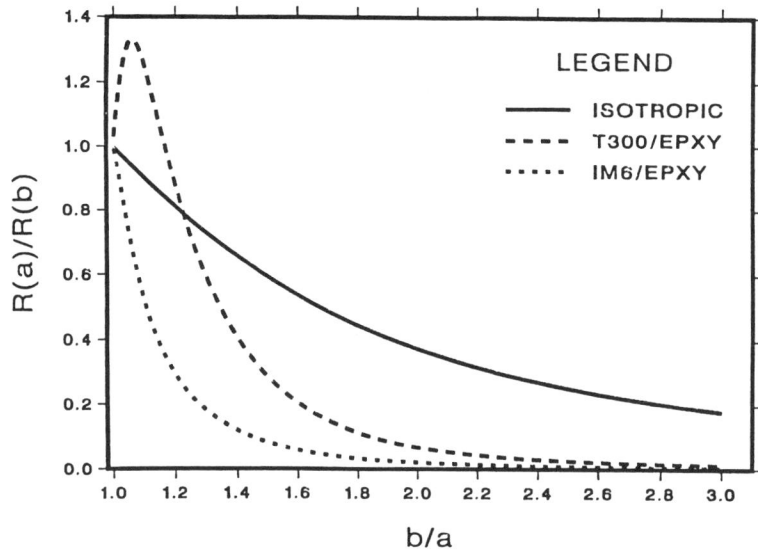

FIGURE 23.13 MATERIAL USE EFFICIENCY STUDY AS A FUNCTION OF WALL THICKNESS RATIO. FOR COMPOSITES, $\alpha=55.5°$.

In 23.10 it was shown that the orthotropic materials have better performance efficiency than that of isotropic materials. However, to compare qualitatively the material use efficiency of orthotropic materials with that of isotropic materials, the ratio, **R(a)/R(b)** is plotted versus **b/a** in Figure 23.13. This figure shows that with increasing wall thickness ratio, **b/a**, the material use efficiency in orthotropic materials drops drastically compared to that of the isotropic materials. Moreover, T300/Epoxy shows an interesting behavior. For **b/a≤1.15** the ratio, **R(a)/R(b)>1** and then for **b/a>1.15**, **R(a)/R(b)** becomes less than unity. That means for **b/a≤1.15** failure occurs on the outer surface and the failure shifts to the inner surface for **b/a>1.15**. The shift of failure point from outer to inner surface can also be confirmed from Figure 23.11. For **b/a** close to 1.15, the ratio **R(a)/R(b)** is very close to unity, and thus an efficient material use is already achieved. Any further significant improvement in material use is not possible, as is illustrated in Table 23.2 (for **b/a=1.15**).

23.10 MULTILAYER VESSELS

For a multilayer CFRP T300/N5208 vessel, results in Table 23.2 are obtained for layers of equal thickness and the thickness ratio of each layer is **(b/a−1)/n**; n is the number of layers. The multilayer optimum winding angle combinations are obtained within a resolution of one degree. The results of column E is plotted in Figure 23.14. For low **b/a**, an increase in number of layers increases burst pressure by very little, as observed in Figure 23.14.

TABLE 23.2   PREDICTION OF BURST PRESSURE OF SEVERAL MULTILAYER VESSELS. PREDICTION IS FROM ELASTICITY SOLUTION.

A	B	C	D	E
b/a	No of Layers n	Optimum Angle Combination (inside to outside)	Burst Pressure (MPa)	Percent Change in Burst Pressure
1.05	1	54.5	42.93	–
	2	60/48	45.38	5.71
	3	63/54/45	46.14	1.67
1.10	1	54.5	89.92	–
	2	66/42	95.56	6.27
	3	68/56/38	97.14	1.65
1.15	1	54.75	141.80	–
	2	84/34	142.27	0.33
	3	75/70/23	143.37	0.77
1.25	1	55.5	184.26	–
	2	40/66	211.19	14.61
	3	35/55/75	217.20	2.85
	4	36/48/67/65	224.80	3.49
1.50	1	55.75	216.25	–
	2	27/71	262.25	21.27
	3	23/41/81	284.48	8.48
	4	23/35/51/82	298.10	4.77
2.00	1	57.75	224.55	–
	2	0/73	272.50	21.34
	3	1/40/75	292.30	7.34
	4	2/32/66/52	316.90	8.42

From column F of Table 23.2 and Figure 23.15 it can be seen that percentage increase in burst pressure is significant only for thick vessels and limited to only two layers. Figure 23.15 also shows that there is some increase in percentage change in P_b for 4 layers than 3 layers for b/a=1.25 and 2.00. In other words, it reveals that the optimum angle combination for 3 layers at these two b/a's did not give the best burst pressure. In this conjecture, it is worth mentioning that the optimum angle combination in Table 23.2 is obtained by taking equal thickness of layers. Equal thickness consideration may not necessarily give the best burst pressure and this is evident here in 3 layer case. For a given number of layers, along with the angle optimization one should also optimize layer thicknesses, instead of taking equal thickness, to obtain the best burst pressure.

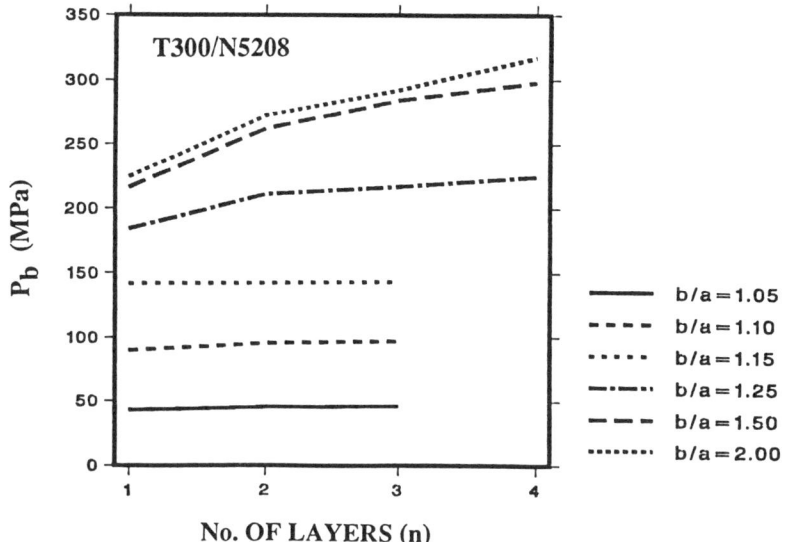

FIGURE 23.14 BURST PRESSURE FROM TABLE 23.2 WITH INCREASING NO. OF OPTIMIZED LAYERS.

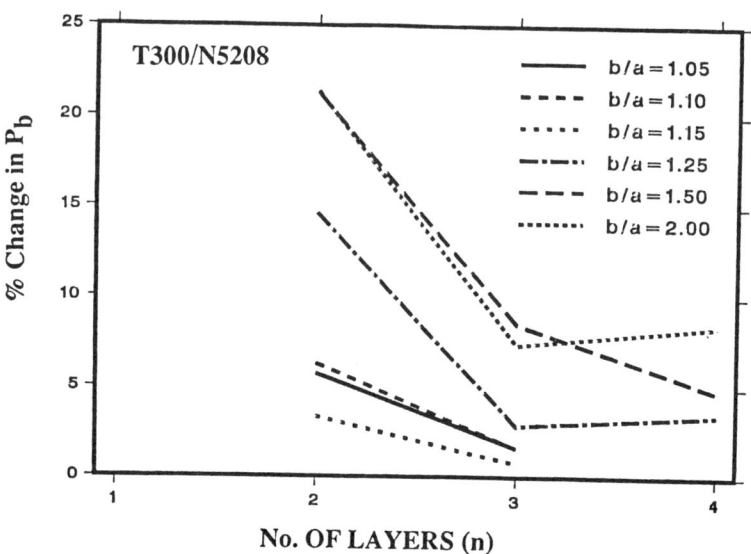

FIGURE 23.15 PERCENTACE CHANGE IN BURST PRESSURE FROM TABLE 23.2 WITH INCREASING NO. OF OPTIMIZED LAYERS.

As is discussed earlier, in case of CFRP T300/N5208, failure point shifts from outside surface to inside one as the wall thickness increases. At about

b/a=1.15, this transition occurs. Observation made on the multiple angle results in Table 23.2 reveals that the surface, where failure occurs, is to be softened by giving winding angle towards axial direction and the other surface is to be hardened by winding towards hoop direction. Thus, for **b/a**≤1.15 the optimum angle combinations in Table 23.2 shows angles close to hoop winding at inner layers and for higher **b/a**'s the hoop windings are on outer layers. Thus radial layer sequence is critical in optimizing, especially, multilayered thick cylinders. Such prediction of radial layer sequence is not possible to obtain by 2–dimensional analysis; because 2–dimensional analysis does not take into account radial stress or strain in the analysis.

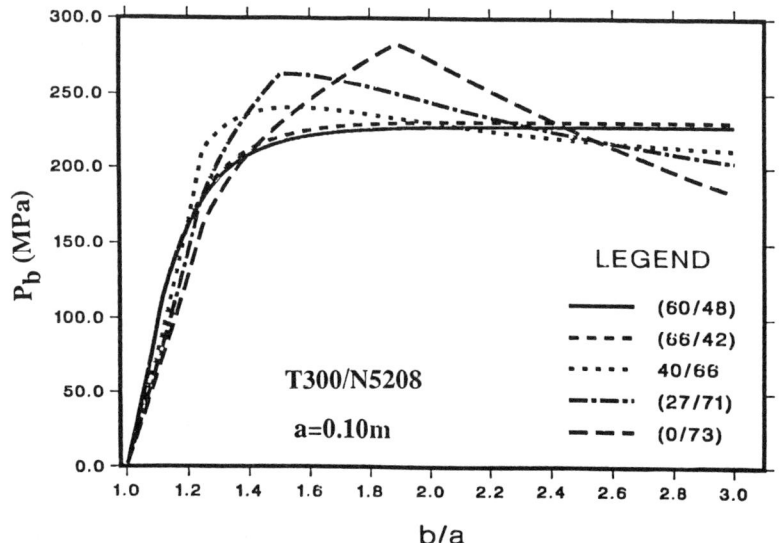

FIGURE 23.16   BURST PRESSURES FOR TWO LAYER VESSELS. ANGLE
COMBINATIONS ARE FROM TABLE 23.2.

It is indicated before that the optimization based on equal layer thickness may not always predict the best burst pressure. To justify that, the optimum angle combinations, for 2 layer case, are taken from Table 23.2 to calculate burst pressure with increasing **b/a** and are plotted in Figure 23.16 maintaining equal layer thickness for each layer. Although angle combinations (60/48) and (66/42) showed an increasing trend of burst pressure, however (40/66), (27/71), and (0/73) showed peaks in their respective curves. This means, the later three combinations are best for respective **b/a**'s where peaks occurred and the peak for (0/73) is most interesting. For (0/73), peak occurred at **b/a**=1.87 which is lower than the value for which this angle combination was optimized in Table 23.2. The optimization was done with equal thickness constraint; thus the above occurrence of the peak at lower **b/a** justifies the fact that, to obtain the best burst pressure one should optimize both layer thickness and winding angle simultaneously.

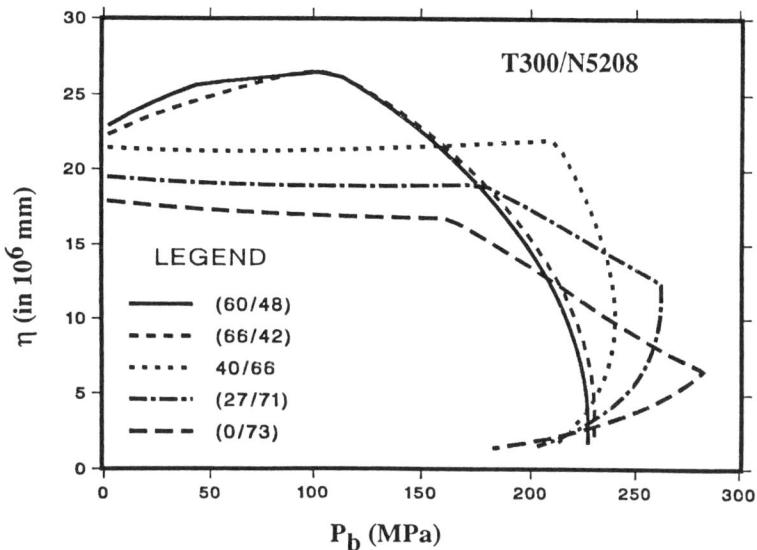

FIGURE 23.17 VESSEL PERFORMANCE EFFICIENCY FOR TWO LAYER VESSELS.
LAYER ANGLE COMBINATIONS ARE FROM TABLE 23.2.

A comparison is made in performance efficiency, η, of two layer vessels (layer combinations are from table 23.2) with that of a single layer vessel (T300/Epoxy of Figure 23.10).   The efficiency, η, for two layer vessels is plotted in Figure 23.17.   Angle combination (60/48) and (66/42) offer better efficiency than that of the single layer at lower pressure, however, did not improve in pressure carrying capacity because the efficiency for two layer cases dropped close to zero at 230 MPa which was almost the same for single layer case.   This is expected, because (60/48), (66/42) are optimized for lower pressures (45 and 95 MPa respectively).   Although angles (40/66), (27/71), and (0/73) do not show great promise on efficiency, but have more pressure carrying capability than earlier two angles.   In particular, the limiting pressure for (0/73) improved from 225 MPa (single layer) to 280 MPa (2 layer). The efficiency of the later three angles can also be improved by optimizing more layers instead of only two layers.

In section 23.3, it was inferred that a constant value of Strength Ratio, **R**, through the thickness will result in best material use. To justify that point, the distribution of **R** through the thickness is plotted in Figure 23.18 for all four optimized angles obtained for b/a=1.50 in Table 23.2. It can be seen from the plot that, with the increasing number optimized layers the value of R_{min} (i.e. the failure pressure) increases and the difference between the R_{max} and R_{min} decreases. With more number of optimized layers, the distribution of **R** can be brought more or less uniform through the thickness and a most efficient material use can be achieved. However, a comparison of rate of convergence of the distribution of **R** toward the uniform distribution of **R** and the values of P_b in Table 23.2, reveal that, for all practical purposes, pressure vessel with 2 or 3 optimized layers can offer very good performance.

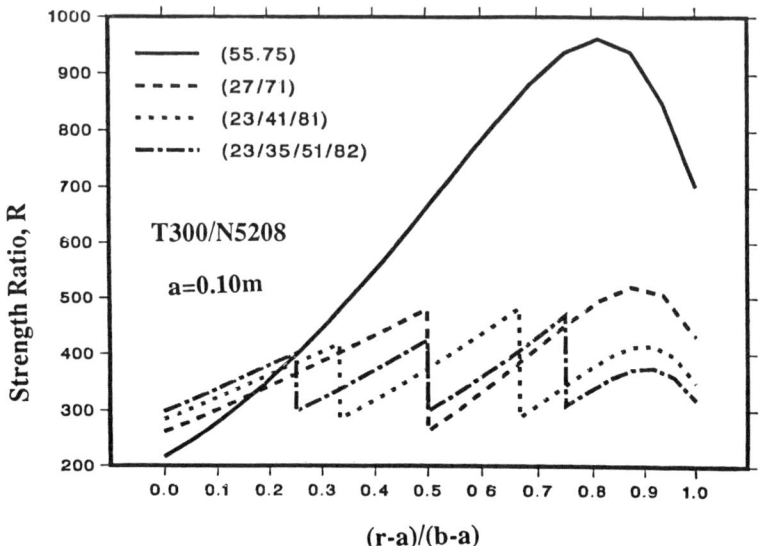

FIGURE 23.18 DISTRIBUTION OF STRENGTH RATIO THROUGTH THE THICKNESS FOR b/a=1.50. ANGLE COMBINATIONS ARE FROM TABLE 23.2.

23.11 CONCLUSIONS

Results of this study of design parameters, are presented for pressure vessels subjected to only internal pressure. Comparison of burst pressures calculated from thin wall and thick wall solutions reveals that the validity of the thin wall solution is limited to wall thickness ratio, **b/a**≤1.10 which in terms of radius to thickness ratio, **r/t**≥10.

The outer radial displacement of filament wound vessels decreases with increasing winding angle and becomes negative between 58° and 78°. This displacement property is very interesting from the point of view of fastening the vessel with other structural members. By choosing a proper winding angle the vessel displacement can be matched with that of the fastening members.

A single layer construction does not offer efficient material use, especially for thick vessels. A higher efficiency in material use can be obtained by minimizing the difference between the maximum and minimum value of Strength Ratio, **R**, through the thickness. It is observed that softening the part of the thickness of lower value of **R**, and hardening the part of higher value of **R** yields an efficient use of materials. The softening can be done

with layers of winding angle towards axial direction and the hardening can be done by winding towards hoop direction. Thus multilayer construction with optimized winding angles yields an efficient use of materials and increases pressure carrying capability. The optimization based on both layer thickness and winding angle will lead to best use of materials. For vessel wall thickness ratio up to 2, it is shown that vessel with optimized 2 or 3 layers practically yields a very good design within a reasonable computer time.

Optimization of thick multilayer cylinders reveals that radial layer sequence is very critical for maximumizing burst pressure. This radial layer sequence prediction can only be done by 3–dimensional analysis. 2–dimensional analysis does not differentiate one sequence from another composed of same layers. Therefore 2–dimensional analysis is not appropriate for optimizing thick cylinders.

In filament wound pressure vessel technology elastomeric (nonload bearing) or metallic (load bearing) liners are used to prevent leakage due to matrix cracking. The load bearing liners are designed to operate to be fully plastic throughout the operational life of the vessel. Although the analytical model discussed here does not include liner, the presence of load bearing liner will not alter the analysis because the liner always operate in plastic domain; only the amount of plastic load absorbed by the liner should be added to the predicted failure pressure to get the overall burst pressure. To keep the analysis simple, the effect of longitudinal bending deformation of the cylindrical wall due to the end closures is ignored. The vessel is assumed cylindrically orthotropic, i.e., the adjacent ($\pm\alpha$) angle wound plies are assumed to behave as an orthotropic unit. Even with these limitations, this model serves as an analytical tool to sort out important material parameters in the design of thick cylindrical vessels.

REFERENCES

23–1. Bert, C.W., Analysis of Radial Filament–Reinforced Spherical Shells Under Deep Submergence Conditions, *2nd Intl. Conference on Pressure Vessel Technology, Part I, Design and Analysis,* ASME, Oct 1973, pp. 529–534.

23–2. Tsai, S.W., A Survey of Macroscopic Failure Criteria for Composite Materials, *Journal of Reinforced Plastics and Composites,* Vol 3, Jan 1984, pp. 40–62.

23–3. Lekhnitskii, S.G., *Anisotropic Plates,* translated by S.W. Tsai and T. Cheron, Gordon and Breach, New York, 1968.

23–4. Beckwith,S.W., et.al., Filament Wound Case (FWC) Graphite/Epoxy Pressure Vessel Response to Environmental Conditioning, *31 Intl. SAMPE Symposium,* April 7–10, 1986, Las Vegas.

23–5. Lark, R.F., Recent Advances in Lightweight, Filament–Wound Composite Pressure Vessel Technology, in *Composites in Pressure Vessels and Piping,* ASME, PVP–PB–021, 1977.

23–6. Massard, T., Commission on Atomic Energy of France (CEA) – private communication.

Section 24

BUCKLING OF SANDWICH/STIFFENED PANELS

K. P. Rao

U S AIR FORCE MATERIALS LABORATORY, DAYTON
(ON LEAVE FROM INDIAN INSTITUTE OF SCIENCE, BANGALORE, INDIA)

24.1 INTRODUCTION

Laminated fiber reinforced sandwich/stiffened composite panels are increasingly being used in several engineering industries. For example in aerospace industry, typical components include wing skins, corrugated spar webs or interstages in rockets. These thin constructions are susceptible to buckling failure. Buckling studies are, thus, needed to achieve good structural performance with minimum weight. In this section we describe the procedure adopted for predicting the elastic buckling loads for simply supported sandwich/stiffened composite rectangular panels. The given panel is idealized as a homogeneous orthotropic plate whose stiffness properties are determined based on various parameters of the given panel. Critical buckling loads are obtained using conventional orthotropic plate theory derived on the basis of Kirchhoff–Love assumptions. The panels are assumed to have sinusoidally corrugated core, hat type corrugated core, or regular grid core. We consider uniaxial compression, biaxial loading and linearly varying loads. Present analysis is first applied to specific cases of CFRP sandwich plates subjected to uniaxial compression, for which experimental results are available. Fairly good agreement is found. Next is considered a large class of T300/5208 [0, 90, 45, −45] sandwich plates with quadri–directional, tridirectional and bidirectional layup schemes and the results are merit listed from buckling point of view. Such ranking of the lamination schemes based on critical buckling loads, does not only help in the choice of the optimum lamination scheme but also helps in assessing any ply drop scheme.

24.2 CONFIGURATIONS STUDIED

As shown in Figures 24.1, 24.2 and 24.3 the following configurations are studied:

- i) a sandwich plate with a sinusoidally corrugated core (Figure 24.1)
- ii) a sandwich plate with a hat type corrugated core (Figure 24.2)
- iii) a sandwich plate with regular grid as core (Figure 24.3)

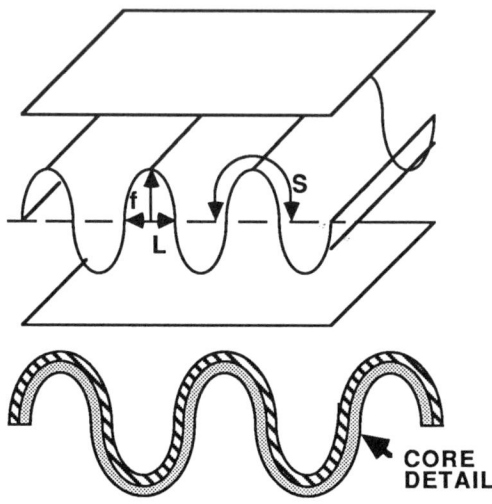

FIGURE 24.1   A LAMINATED COMPOSITE SANDWICH PLATE WITH SINUSOIDALLY
CORRUGATED CORE.

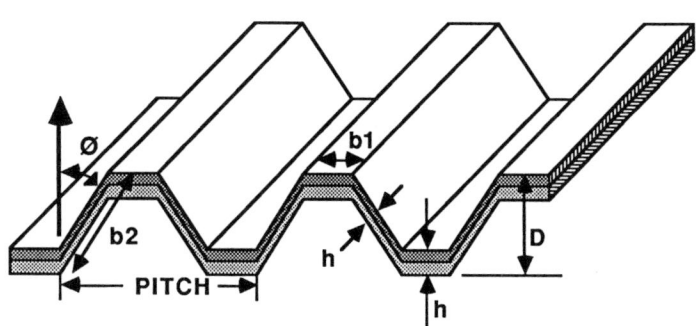

FIGURE. 24.2 HAT TYPE CORRUGATION.

While the analysis presented is general and applicable to any layup scheme
and material system, present numerical studies have been carried out for the
cases when core and face sheets are of laminated composite construction
using T300/5208 plies.

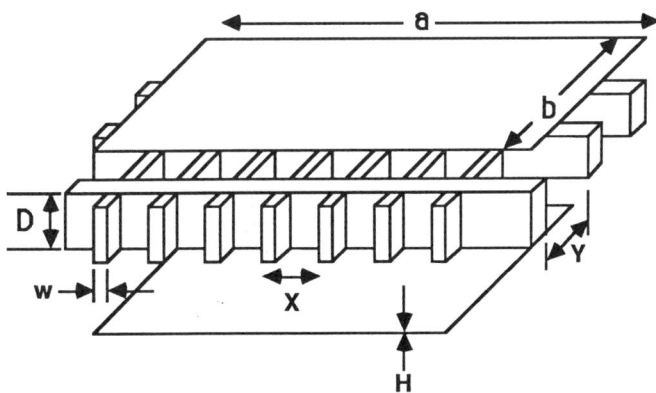

FIGURE 24.3   A LAMINATED COMPOSITE SANDWICH PLATE WITH REGULAR GRID
AS CORE.

24.3 GOVERNING EQUATIONS AND PROCEDURES USED

The equation governing the buckling behavior of an orthotropic plate [24–1]
is

$$D_{11}(\partial^4 w/\partial x^4)+2(D_{12}+2D_{66})(\partial^4 w/\partial x^2\partial y^2)$$

$$+D_{22}(\partial^4 w/\partial y^4)-N_x(\partial^2 w/\partial x^2)$$

$$-2N_{xy}(\partial^2 w/\partial x\partial y)-N_y(\partial^2 w/\partial y^2) = 0 \qquad (24.1)$$

where D_{11}, D_{12}, D_{22} and D_{66} are the plate flexural stiffnesses, N_x, N_y and
N_{xy} are the in–plane stress resultant components and w is the deflection
normal to the x, y plane.

The potential energy U is [24–1],

$$U = 1/2\int_0^a\int_0^b \{D_{11}(\partial^2 w/\partial x^2)^2$$

$$+2D_{12}(\partial^2 w/\partial x^2)(\partial^2 w/\partial y^2)+4D_{66}(\partial^2 w/\partial x\partial y)^2$$

$$+D_{22}(\partial^2 w/\partial y^2)^2+N_x(\partial w/\partial x)^2$$

$$+2N_{xy}(\partial w/\partial x)(\partial w/\partial y)+N_y(\partial w/\partial y)^2\}dxdy \qquad (24.2)$$

The object is to find first the flexural stiffnesses D_{11}, D_{12}, D_{22}, D_{66} (where
1, 2 refer to the laminate axes) of the homogeneous orthotropic plate which
is nearly equivalent to the given sandwich/stiffened panel and then use the

conventional procedures using Equations 24.1 and 24.2 to predict the buckling loads. The relevant formulas for homogeneous orthotropic plates are given in Reference [24–2].

24.4 SINUSOIDALLY CORRUGATED SHEET

In Figure 24.1 is shown a sinusoidal corrugation defining the notation used. The shape of the core can be expressed in terms of the geometric parameters as $z = f \sin \pi y/L$ where z is measured normal to the middle plane of the corrugation. Using Reference [24–3], we can express the stiffnesses of the homogeneous orthotropic plate equivalent to the corrugation (with reference to the middle plane) as,

$$[D_{11}]^{cor} = E_{equivalent}I, \quad [D_{12}]^{cor} = 0,$$

$$[D_{22}]^{cor} = L/S \; [D_{22}]^{lam}, \quad [D_{66}]^{cor} = S/L \; [D_{66}]^{lam},$$

$$[A_{11}]^{cor} = S/L \; [A_{11}]^{lam}, \quad\quad [A_{22}]^{cor} = 0, \; [A_{12}]^{cor} = 0,$$

$$[A_{66}]^{cor} = S/L \; [A_{66}]^{lam}$$

(24.3)

where $[\;]^{cor}$ refers to the property of the equivalent plate and $[\;]^{lam}$ refers to the laminate property of the corrugation. Lau [24–4] showed by evaluating complete elliptic integrals of the first and second kind, that

$$S = \{(2L/\pi)\sqrt{(1+\alpha^2)}\} E(k,\pi/2)$$

$$I = \left[\{(2hf^2)\sqrt{(1+\alpha^2)}\}/(3\pi k^2)\right]\left[(2k^2-1).\right.$$

$$\left. E(k,\pi/2)+(1-k^2)F(k,\pi/2)\right]$$

(24.4)

where

$$\alpha = f\pi/L, \quad \beta = \pi y/L, \quad k^2 = \alpha^2/(1+\alpha^2)$$

$$E(K,\pi/2) = \int_0^{\pi/2}\sqrt{(1-k^2\sin^2\beta)}d\beta = (\pi/2).$$

$$\left[1-(k^2/4)-(3k^4/64)-(45k^6/2304)\ \ldots\ldots\ \right]$$

$$F(k,\pi/2) = \int_0^{\pi/2}d\beta/\sqrt{(1-k^2\sin^2\beta)} = (\pi/2).$$

$$\left[1+(k^2/4)+(9k^4/64)+(225k^6/2304)\ \ldots\ldots\ \right]$$

$$E_{equivalent} = 1/(a_{11}h)$$

24.5 HAT TYPE CORRUGATED SHEET

Figure 24.2 shows a typical hat type corrugated sheet and the notation used. We can write equivalent properties as [24–5],

$$R = [b_1+b_2]/[b_1+b_2\sin\phi]$$

$$[A_{11}]^{hat} = [A_{11}]^{lam} R, \ [A_{12}]^{hat} = 0, \ [A_{66}]^{hat} = [A_{66}]^{lam} R \ ,$$

$$[A_{22}]^{hat} = 0,$$

$$[D_{12}]^{hat} = 0, \ [D_{22}]^{hat} = [D_{22}]^{lam}/R,$$

$$[D_{11}]^{hat} = E_{equivalent}[I_1+I_2]/[b_1+b_2\sin\phi]$$

$$[D_{66}]^{hat} = [D_{66}]^{lam}R$$

(24.5)

where $I_1=(b_2{}^2\cos^2\phi)b_1h/4$ and $I_2=b_2{}^3h(\cos^2\phi)/12$

24.6 LAMINATED COMPOSITE GRID

Figure 24.3 shows a typical grid with 'X' and 'Y' being uniform spacings between stiffeners in the x and y directions. Two possible layup schemes exist for the grid.

(a) the rib laminae are parallel to the grid middle plane (Figure 24.4a)
(b) the rib laminae are perpendicular to the grid middle plane (Figure 24.4b)

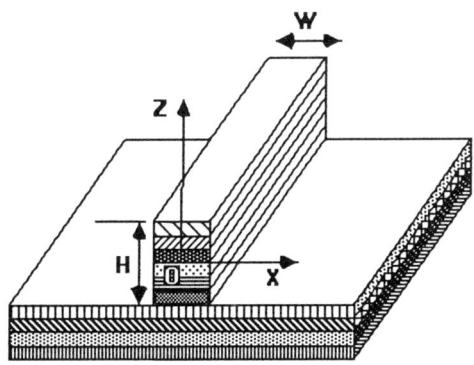

FIGURE 24.4a RIB WITH LAMINAE PARALLEL TO THE GRID MIDDLE PLANE

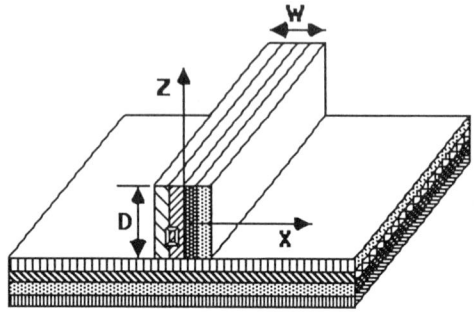

FIGURE. 24.4b RIB WITH LAMINAE PERPENDICULAR TO THE GRID MIDDLE PLANE

For case shown in Figure 24.4a, using Reference [24–3] , we can write with reference to the grid middle plane,

$$[D_{11}]^{Grid} = [D_{11}]^{lam}w/Y, \quad [D_{22}]^{Grid} = [D_{11}]^{lam}w/X,$$

$$[D_{12}]^{Grid} = 0, \quad [D_{66}]^{Grid} = 0,$$

$$[A_{11}]^{Grid} = [A_{11}]^{lam}w/Y,$$

$$[A_{12}]^{Grid} = 0, \quad [A_{22}]^{Grid} = [A_{11}]^{lam}w/X, \quad [A_{66}]^{Grid} = 0$$

(24.6)

Let us consider the behavior of the rib shown in Figure 24.4b. The object is to find the constitutive law for the rib corresponding to bending about 'x' axis and stretching along 'y' axis. The total strain due to these two components is,

$$\varepsilon_y = \varepsilon_y^{\,0} + z\kappa_y$$

(24.7a)

where $\varepsilon_y^{\,0}$ is the middle plane (x, y plane) strain, κ_y is the midplane change in curvature and z is measured normal to the grid middle plane. The stress is,

$$\sigma_y = Q_{11}[\varepsilon_y^{\,0} + z\kappa_y]$$

(24.7b)

$$WN_y = \sum_{i=1}^{N} \int_{-D/2}^{D/2} \int_{X_{i-1}}^{X_i} \sigma_y dz dx = A_{11}D\varepsilon_y^{\,0}$$

(24.8a)

Similarly

$$WM_y = \sum_{i=1}^{N} \int_{-D/2}^{D/2} \int_{X_{i-1}}^{X_i} \sigma_y z dz dx = A_{11}D^3\kappa_y/12$$

(24.8b)

where
      N = Number of Laminates
      $X_i - X_{i-1}$ = Thickness of the ith layer

Thus we can write the expressions for the equivalent stiffnesses of the grid construction shown in Figure 24.4b as,

$$[D_{11}]^{Grid} = [A_{11}]^{lam}D^3/(12Y), \quad [D_{12}]^{Grid} = [D_{66}]^{Grid} = 0,$$

$$[D_{22}]^{Grid} = [A_{11}]^{lam}D^3/(12X),$$

(24.9)

$$[A_{11}]^{Grid} = [A_{11}]^{lam} D/Y,$$

$$[A_{22}]^{Grid} = [A_{11}]^{lam}D/X, \quad [A_{12}]^{Grid} = [A_{66}]^{Grid} = 0$$

24.7 CONSTITUTIVE LAW FOR FACING SHEETS

The properties of the top and bottom laminated facing sheets are represented with reference to their respective middle planes as

$$\begin{vmatrix} N^i \\ M^i \end{vmatrix} = \begin{vmatrix} A^i & B^i \\ B^i & D^i \end{vmatrix} \begin{vmatrix} \epsilon^i \\ \kappa^i \end{vmatrix}$$

(24.10)

where i represents top or bottom face.

24.8 EQUIVALENT PROPERTIES OF SANDWICH PANELS

Having found the extensional and bending stiffnesses individually of the core and facing sheets, we now proceed to find the stiffnesses of the homogeneous anisotropic plate which is equivalent to the sandwich/stiffened panel. Figure 24.5 shows the middle planes of the facing sheets and core or grid and also the location of the neutral plane. In order to find **[A]**, **[B]**, **[D]** of the equivalent homogeneous plate with reference to the neutral plane, we use Reference [24–6].

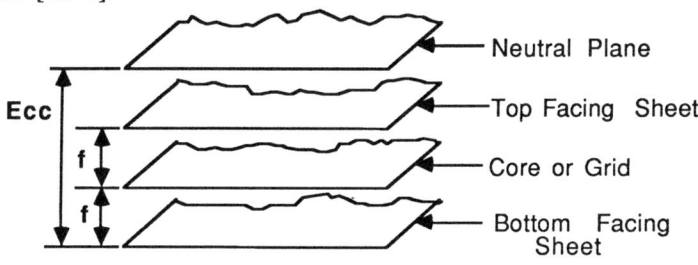

FIGURE 24.5 LOCATION OF THE NEUTRAL PLANE W.R.T. MID–PLANES OF FACING SHEETS AND CORE

Thus,

$$[A] = [A]^{top}+[A]^{core/Grid}+[A]^{bot}$$

$$[B] = [B]^{top}+[B]^{core/Grid}+[B]^{bot}-Ecc[A]^{bot}$$

$$-(Ecc-f)[A]^{core/Grid}-(Ecc-2f)[A]^{top}$$

$$[D] = [D]^{top}+[D]^{core/Grid}+[D]^{bot}-2Ecc[B]^{bot}$$

(24.11)

$$-2(Ecc-f)[B]^{core/Grid}-2(Ecc-2f)[B]^{top}$$

$$+(Ecc)^2[A]^{bot}+(Ecc-f)^2[A]^{core/Grid}+(Ecc-2f)^2[A]^{top}$$

where Ecc is yet to be determined.

In order to determine Ecc we make $B_{11} = 0$

$$Ecc = \{[B_{11}]^{top}+[B_{11}]^{core/Grid}+[B]^{bot}+2f[A_{11}]^{top}$$

$$+f[A_{11}]^{core/Grid}\}/\{[A_{11}]^{top}+[A_{11}]^{core/Grid}+[A_{11}]^{bot}\} \qquad (24.12)$$

Using the value of **Ecc** given by Equation 24.12, **[D]** is computed using Equation 24.11.

24.9 APPLICATION TO AN ISOTROPIC SANDWICH PLATE

The computer program based on the present analysis (see Figure 24.6 for flow chart) is first applied to the case of an Aluminum square sandwich plate subjected to uniaxial compression with the following parameters,

$a = 10"$, $H = 0.0394"$, $E = 10 \times 10^6$ psi , $\nu = 0.3$

i) sinusoidal core: $f = 0.25"$, $L = 1"$, $h = 0.0394"$

ii) hat type core: Pitch $= 2"$, $D = 0.5"$, $\phi = 30°$, $h = 0.0394"$

iii) grid core : $X = 2"$, $Y = 2"$, $D = 0.5"$, $w = 0.0394"$

The isotropic face sheets and the core are treated in the computer program as laminated plates consisting of 8 isotropic layers. The results are shown in Table 24.1. The results agree with those predicted by References [24–1, 24–2]. This problem is solved in order to check the correctness of the program.

TABLE 24.1 BUCKLING LOADS FOR THE ISOTROPIC SANDWICH PANEL UNDER UNIAXIAL COMPRESSION

CONFIGURATION	CRITICAL LOAD, Pc (1000 lb/in)		
	Sinusoidal Sheet Core	Grid Core	Hat Type Core
Top Face (only)	0.022	0.022	0.022
Bottom Face (only)	0.022	0.022	0.022
Core (only)	1.32	0.445	2.21
Top and Bottom Faces	21.4	21.4	21.4
Sandwich Plate	22.7	21.8	23.6

The advantage of using sandwich construction is clear from the Table 24.1. While the face sheets and the core individually have low critical buckling loads, sandwich construction using these sheets and core leads to manyfold increase in the loads at which buckling occures.

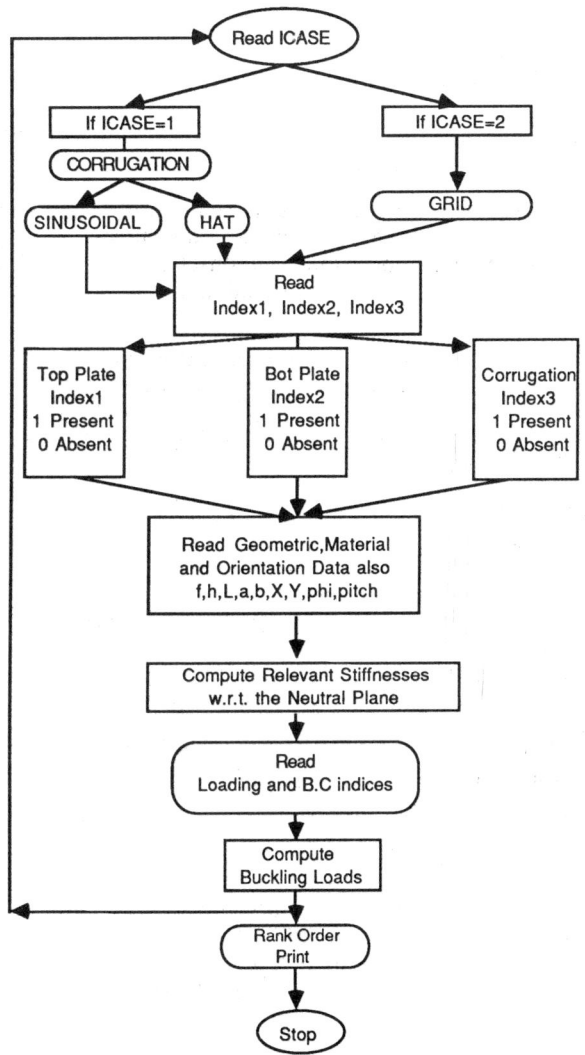

FIGURE 24.6 FLOW CHART FOR THE COMPUTER PROGRAM

24.10 COMPARISON WITH AVAILABLE EXPERIMENTAL RESULTS

Pearce and Webber [24–7] conducted experiments on simply supported square CFRP sandwich plates with the following parameters,

a = 228 mm, D = 5mm,

ply properties :

Thickness : 0.125 mm, E_L = 142000 N/mm^2, E_T = 9800N/mm^2,
G_{LT} = 4300 N/mm^2, v_{LT} = 0.34

Table 24.2 shows the comparison of results by the present analysis with the experimental and theoretical results obtained by Pearce and Webber. In the experiment, strain gages were attached to both facing sheets. The load at which the strain gage readings depart, due to one sheet experiencing tension and the other compression—the onset of buckling, is referred to as the experimental buckling load. The load at which the plate fails is defined as the failure load.

TABLE 24.2 COMPARISON WITH EXPERIMENTAL RESULTS OF [24–7]

Layup Scheme	3–ply [0/90/0]T	3–ply [45/0/45]T	4–ply [45/0/0/45]T	2–ply [0/90]T
Experimental Buckling [24.7] Load (N/mm)	185	161	262	—
Experimental Failure [24.7] Load (N/mm)	213	188	283	117
Theoretical Prediction [24.7] (N/mm)	152	199	238	105
Present Solution * (Orthotropic)	158	235	288	105
Modified Solution (Anisotropic)	158	187	240	105

* Solution assumes zero stiffness core.

Orthotropic solutions and also solutions modified to take into account the presence of bending–twisting coupling [24–8] are presented. Empirical formulas due to Fogg as given in reference [24–8] to take into account bending–twisting coupling in balanced symmetrical laminates (with $D_{16} > 0$) are,

$[Pc]^{anisotropic}/[Pc]^{orthotropic} =$

$1-5.585(D_{16}/D_z)^{k1}$ for m=1

$1-9.588(D_{16}/D_z)^{k2}$ for m=2   (24.13)

$1-9.766(D_{16}/D_z)^{k3}$ for m=3

where

k1 = 1.995, k2 = 2.135, k3 = 2.117,

$D_z = (D_{11}D_{22}{}^3)^{k4}+D_{12}+2D_{66}$, k4 = 0.25   (24.14)

These formulas have been arrived at by examining a large number of graphite/epoxy symmetric balanced laminates. Though these formulas are strictly applicable to symmetric balanced laminates, we apply them to sandwich panels considered in Reference [24–7] which are symmetric but not balanced (i.e. A_{16} and A_{26} of the equivalent homogeneous plate are not zero). It can be seen that there is a fairly good agreement between the modified solutions and the experimental results. Theoretical predictions of Reference [24–7] wherein the shear deformation effects are taken into account, are also presented in Table 24.2.

24.11 APPLICATION TO COMPOSITE SANDWICH PANELS

In this section are considered typical examples of sandwich/stiffened composite panels (see Figure 24.7) subjected to various types of loadings.

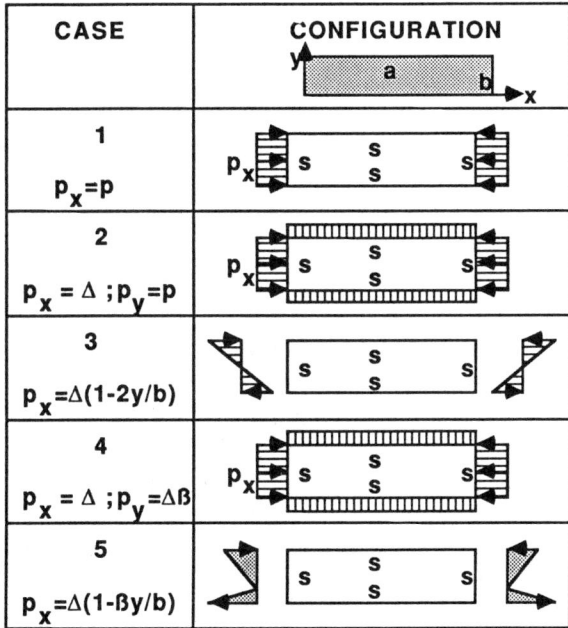

FIGURE 24.7   DIFFERENT LOADINGS FOR THE CASES STUDIED.

In all cases the material system chosen is T300/5208 with the following properties,

$$E_L = 26.3 \times 10^6 \text{psi}, \ E_T = 1.49 \times 10^6 \text{psi},$$
$$G_{LT} = 1.04 \times 10^6 \text{psi}, \ \nu_{LT} = 0.28, \tag{24.15}$$
$$\text{ply thickness} = 0.00492" \ (0.125 \text{ mm})$$

The computer code is so programmed that it can take into account different layup schemes, number of layers and materials for the top face, bottom face and the core or ribs individually. However, in the present exercise we assume the facing sheets and core to have the same lay up schemes and thicknesses. In addition the lay up angles chosen are 0, 90, 45, –45.

We examine

  i) **35, 8** ply, quadri–directional laminates starting with the code
  [5111],[4211],............[1115]

  ii) **40, 6** ply, tridirectional laminates starting with the code
  [4110],[3210].........[[0114]

  iii) **18, 4** ply, bidirectional laminates starting with the code
  [3100],[2200],.......[0013] and

  iv)**6, 2** ply, bidirectional laminates starting with the code
  [1100],.....[0011]

where the laminate code designates the number of plies in the order of 0, 90, 45, –45 degrees.

TABLE 24.3 CRITICAL LOADS FOR 8–, 6–, 4–, AND 2–PLY SCHEMES OF A 10" x 10" PANEL

No.	Code	Pc (1000 lb/in)	No.	Code	Pc (1000 lb/in)	No.	Code	Pc (1000 lb/in)	No.	Code	Pc (1000 lb/in)
1	1133	101.0	26	3221	85.7	51	222	72.1	76	31	55.5
2	1124	101.0	27	2312	84.7	52	3012	69.3	77	1410	55.4
3	1115	101.0	28	2321	84.7	53	3021	69.3	78	1401	55.4
4	1151	101.0	29	1412	83.7	54	2130	68.3	79	1030	50.9
5	1142	101.0	30	1421	83.7	55	2103	68.3	80	1003	50.9
6	2132	96.4	31	5111	81.8	56	1230	67.3	81	103	49.8
7	2123	96.4	32	4211	80.8	57	1203	67.3	82	130	49.8
8	2114	96.4	33	3311	79.8	58	321	66.3	83	2002	46.1
9	2141	96.4	34	2411	78.7	59	312	66.3	84	2020	46.1
10	1232	95.4	35	1014	78.7	60	4011	64.4	85	202	44.1
11	1223	95.4	36	1032	78.7	61	3120	63.4	86	220	44.1
12	1214	95.4	37	1023	78.7	62	3102	63.4	87	3010	41.2
13	1241	95.4	38	1041	78.7	63	2202	62.4	88	3001	41.2
14	3131	91.6	39	1511	77.7	64	2220	62.4	89	3100	35.2
15	3122	91.6	40	132	77.7	65	1302	61.4	90	2200	34.2
16	3113	91.6	41	123	77.7	66	1320	61.4	91	1300	33.2
17	2231	90.6	42	114	77.7	67	4110	58.4	92	301	32.3
18	2222	90.6	43	141	77.7	68	4101	58.4	93	310	32.3
19	2213	90.6	44	2022	74.1	69	3210	57.4	94	11	27.8
20	1322	89.6	45	2031	74.1	70	3201	57.4	95	1001	23.0
21	1313	89.6	46	2013	74.1	71	2310	56.4	96	1010	23.0
22	1331	89.6	47	1140	73.1	72	2301	56.4	97	101	22.0
23	4112	86.8	48	1104	73.1	73	411	56.2	98	110	22.0
24	4121	86.8	49	231	72.1	74	22	55.5	99	1100	17.1
25	3212	85.7	50	213	72.1	75	13	55.5			

For example, as presented in Section 7, [5111] designates [0$_5$/90/45/–45] There are altogether 99 laminates under this class. First we consider the sandwich plate (case 1 of Figure 24.7) with a grid core with the following parameters.

a = 10", b = 10", X = 2", Y = 2", D = 1"

We rank order the 99 laminates based on the buckling loads and the results are presented in Table 24.3.

We see that putting more ±45 degree layers compared to 0 degree layers leads to an improved performance. For example, [1115] gives a critical load which is 24 percent higher than that corresponding to [5111]. Also, the result is unaffected by the actual number of layers chosen of +45 and –45 orientation for a given total number of 45 degree layers (i.e. [1133], [1124], [1115], [1151]). Compared to [2222] laminate (quasi–isotropic) [1115] has 11.5 percent more buckling load. In many aerospace structures plies are dropped in zones of lower loads (for example, wing skin). Tables like the one presented here will help assess any ply drop scheme from buckling point of view.

Table 24.4 shows the effect of a/b ratio for case1 of Figure 24.7. Here we consider only 8 ply laminates.

TABLE 24.4   BUCKLING LOADS FOR THE CFRP SANDWICH PLATES (SIZE EFFECT)
(CASE 1 – FIGURE 24.7)

Plate Size	Top Five Laminates			Bottom Five Laminates		
	No.	Code	Crit. Load, Pc (1000 lb/in)	No.	Code	Crit. Load, Pc (1000 lb/in)
a = 10" b = 40"	1	5111	40.5	31	1313	19.5
	2	4121	36.3	32	1331	19.5
	3	4112	36.3	33	1412	17.2
	4	4211	33.9	34	1421	17.2
	5	3131	32.1	35	1511	14.9
a = 10" b=20"	1	5111	46.6	31	1313	29.5
	2	4121	44.0	32	2411	28.1
	3	4112	44.0	33	1412	25.9
	4	3122	41.5	34	1421	25.9
	5	3131	41.5	35	1511	22.2
a = 10" b = 5"	1	1133	404.0	31	5111	327.0
	2	1124	404.0	32	4211	323.0
	3	1115	404.0	33	3311	319.0
	4	1151	404.0	34	2411	315.0
	5	1142	404.0	35	1511	293.0
a = 10" b = 10"	1	1133	101.0	31	5111	81.8
	2	1124	101.0	32	4211	80.8
	3	1115	101.0	33	3311	79.8
	4	1151	101.0	34	2411	78.7
	5	1142	101.0	35	1511	77.7

It is found, for a given panel length 'a'(=10") if the panel length to width ratio a/b ≥ 1, that having more ±45 degree layers is more beneficial whereas if a/b < 1, having more 0 degree layers is more advantageous. For example, [5111] leads to 27 percent (for a/b = 0.5) and 69 percent (for a/b = 0.25) higher buckling loads compared to [1115]. The corresponding values by which [5111] is found to be superior to quasi–isotropic case [2222] are 32 percent (for a/b = 0.5) and 58 percent (for a/b = 0.25). For uniaxial compression, biaxial loading or linearly varying load, computations done for

the 10"x10" CFRP panel show that having ±45 degree layers is more beneficial (Table 24.5).

TABLE 24.5 BUCKLING LOADS FOR 10"X10" CFRP SANDWICH PLATE FOR DIFFERENT LOADING CASES

Case No. (Fig.24.7)	No.	Code	Crit. Load Pc (1000 lb/in)	No.	Code	Crit. Load Pc (1000 lb/in)
2 Py = 50000 (lb/in)	1	1133	151.0	31	3311	130.0
	2	1124	151.0	32	2411	125.0
	3	1115	151.0	33	1412	116.0
	4	1151	151.0	34	1421	116.0
	5	1142	151.0	35	1511	101.0
3	1	1133	675.0	31	2411	523.0
	2	1124	675.0	32	1421	517.0
	3	1115	675.0	33	1412	517.0
	4	1151	675.0	34	5111	501.0
	5	1142	675.0	35	1511	461.0
4 β =1.0	1	1133	50.5	31	5111	40.9
	2	1124	50.5	32	4211	40.4
	3	1115	50.5	33	3311	39.9
	4	1151	50.5	34	2411	39.4
	5	1142	50.5	35	1511	38.9
5 β =1.0	1	1133	197.0	31	5111	158.0
	2	1124	197.0	32	4211	158.0
	3	1115	197.0	33	3311	156.0
	4	1151	197.0	34	2411	155.0
	5	1142	197.0	35	1511	153.0

Maintaining all the parameters given in section 24.9 for the cases of sinusoidal core and hat type core, except the material and if T300/ 5208 is used, the highest and lowest buckling loads obtained for 8–ply, 6–ply,4–ply and 2–ply cases are given in Table 24.6.

TABLE 24.6   CFRP SANDWICH PLATE (10" x 10") WITH SINUSOIDAL OR HAT TYPE
CORRUGATED SHEET AS CORE

Number of Plies	Rank Order	Sinusoidal Corrugation		Hat Type Corrugation	
		Code	Crit. Load, Pc (1000 lb/in)	Code	Crit. Load, Pc (1000 lb/in)
8	Highest	1142	101.0	1142	101
	Lowest	1511	78.5	1511	79.4
6	Highest	1041	78.0	1041	78.7
	Lowest	1401	55.1	1401	55.5
4	Highest	22	55.1	22	55.4
	Lowest	1300	32.7	1300	32.9
2	Highest	11	27.5	11	27.7
	Lowest	1100	16.8	1100	17.1

24.12 CONCLUDING REMARKS

Present work deals with the prediction of elastic buckling loads for simply supported sandwich/stiffened composite rectangular panels under Kirchhoff–Love assumptions. The panels considered have sinusoidal core, hat type core or regular grid core and the loadings considered are uniaxial compression, biaxial loading and linearly varying loading. A large class of[0, 90, 45, –45] lamination schemes were examined. The results show that for a/b ≥1, having more 45 degree layers leads to increased buckling loads whereas for a/b <1, having more 0 degree layers is more advantageous.

Empirical formulas suggested by Fogg appear to give good predictions for symmetrical balanced laminates and sandwich panels. However, for sandwich panels with facings of general lay up scheme, the role of bending–stretching and bending–twisting couplings has yet to be investigated. Studies are also needed on the effect of finite shear stiffness of the core. In the case of a single composite sheet stiffened by a corrugation, by knowing the torsional rigidities of the individual components constituting the structure (the sheet and the corrugation), it is not possible to predict, accurately, the torsional rigidity of the assemblage. In the case of stiffened sheets, the neutral surface locations in 'x' and 'y' directions may be different. We are looking into these aspects currently and hope to include them in future.

ACKNOWLEDGMENTS

The author wishes to thank the U S National Research Council for providing the Research Associateship tenable at U S Air Force Materials Laboratory, WPAFB, Dayton.

REFERENCES

24–1.   Brunelle E. J., Oyibo G. A., "Generic Buckling Curves for Specially Orthotropic Rectangular Plates", *AIAA Jl*, vol. 21, no. 8, 1983, pp.1150–1156.

24–2.   Lekhnitskii S. G., *Anisotropic Plates*, translated by S. W. Tsai and T. Cheron, Gordon and Breach Science Publishers, 1968, pp. 445–526.

24–3.   Timoshenko S., Woinowski–Krieger S., *Th eory of Plates and Shells*, McGraw–Hill Book Company, 1959, pp. 367–368.

24–4.   Lau J., "Stiffness of Corrugated Plate", *Jl. of Engng. Mech. Div.*, ASCE, vol.107, no. EM1,1981, pp. 271–275.

24–5.   Van Zelst R. F. P., " Hand Calculation Method for Buckling of Composite Shell Structures" , Paper Presented at ESA Workshop on Composite Design for Space Applications, Oct15–18, 1985.

24–6.   Tsai S. W., *Composites Design–1986*, Think Composites,1986, pp. 9.6–9.7.

24–7.   Pearce T. R. A., Webber J. P. H., "Experimental Buckling Loads of Sandwich Panels with Carbon Fibre Face Plates", *Aero. Quarterly*, vol. 24, no. 4, 1973, pp. 295–312.

24–8.   Leissa Arthur W., *Buckling of Laminated Composite Plates and Shell Panels*, AFWAL–TR– 85–3069, June 1985.

Section 25

MANUAL FOR GENLAM

Jocelyn M. Patterson* and Peter O. Sjöblom**
*U S AIR FORCE MATERIALS LABORATORY, DAYTON
**UNIVERSITY OF DAYTON RESEARCH INSTITUTE, DAYTON

25.1 DESCRIPTION OF GENLAM PROGRAM

This section provides an overview of GENLAM, a GENeral purpose LAMinate program. GENLAM is a through–the–thickness point stress analysis computer program for composite laminates that computes the stiffness and strength of unsymmetric hybrid laminates subjected to complex, in–plane loads and bending moments applied to the edges of the plate. The user is prompted to input unit preference (SI or English), material selection, ply layup, hygrothermal conditions, loading and/or prescribed strains (mixed boundary conditions). The quickly obtained results are in the form of stiffness and compliance matrices in both absolute and normalized units, engineering constants, ply stresses and strains in both ply and laminate axes, and strength ratios (ratio of strength to applied stress) evaluated at the top and bottom of each ply group. The strength ratios, obained by analyzing the laminate twice—once with intact and once with completely degraded matrix material, are manipulated according to design rules (see Section 12) which then predict the limit and ultimate strengths. GENLAM is easy to use and fast. For example, a hybrid laminate under both mechanical and hygrothermal loads is analyzed in seconds.

This executable FORTRAN program is supported by the material data files MATRSI and MATRAM, presently containing a selection of 9 materials. Another executable FORTRAN program, MATFIX, allows easy modification and/or new material data entry to the material data files. At present, GENLAM–4 is dimensioned to handle a laminate consisting of up to: 5 materials, 10 ply angles, 40 angle–material combinations, 5 independent load cases and 200 plies. These limits can be altered by changing a few dimension statements in the source code and recompiling the routines. In fact, while GENLAM is a versatile main program, the intention was that this program should serve as an example of how to use the subroutine library FLEXCODE. We urge the users to read the symbolic code and tailor the program to fit their particular needs.

GENLAM is based on laminated plate theory (LPT), the analysis that describes the stiffness and strength at a point in a two dimensional plate. Laminated plate theory, an extension of the strength of materials formulation for plates, takes into account the possible anisotropy of the material and the layered structure of the plate. (For a review of the difference between ply stiffness and laminate stiffness, see Subsection 29.2 and Subsection 29.3.) The coefficients in the governing differential equation describing the behavior of a plate can be calculated using LPT. After the boundary value problem has been solved, LPT can be used to calculate the strain and stress state at a point. In the instances when the in–plane loads and moments are known, LPT can then be used directly to calculate the stresses in the plate.

As in all problems of design, a failure criterion is necessary. For homogeneous isotropic plates, the maximum allowable stress is constant throughout the entire plate. It is thus only necessary to search for the largest effective stress value to determine whether the plate is strong enough or not. A laminated composite plate is fundamentally different: the allowable stresses differ in different plies. Therefore, each ply must be examined separately. In GENLAM we calculate the stress values at the top and the bottom of each ply. We believe this procedure will reveal the most probable sites of failure. Instead of using the strength index directly, we use the strength/stress ratios, R–values; i.e., a value proportional to the safety factor. Applications of R–values can be found in Subsection 29.14. The quadratic failure criterion, the framework in which the R–values are calculated, is used for the many reasons elucidated in Section 11.

It should be noted that the results of doing identical problems in Mic–Mac and GenLam or LamRank may result in slightly different answers for the Last–Ply–Failure prediction. The cause of this disparity lies in the different implementation of the degraded ply model used to calculate Last–Ply–Failure. Unlike the use of the matrix degradation factor in the Mic–Macs based on micromechanics (Subsection 12.2), in GENLAM, we use an overall degradation factor DF applied directly to the plies as described in Subsection 12.12. Both are empirical methods and at this time it is debatable which is the better approach.

29.2 IBM PC VERSION OF GENLAM

The program requires the two material files MATRSI.DIR and MATRAM.DIR to be in the default directory. The program file is called GENLAM.EXE and is executed by typing its name, GENLAM<CR>. Questions appear as follows:

Do you want to send the output to a file or the printer (Y/N)?
Throughout the program *N* (No) is the default answer. A *N* or simply a *<CR>* will result in the output being displayed on the screen. If you answer *Yes* you will get another question:

Output file name (PRN = Printer)?
Here you can type any acceptable file name. On most systems *PRN* or *LPT1* is the file name for the printer. Should you change your mind, typing *CON* will give you the output on the screen.

SI (S) or English (E) units?
Answer with an *S* or an *E*. The SI system uses meter, Newton and °C. The English system uses inch, lbf and °F.

Is the laminate layup stored on file (Y/N)?
This is a convenient feature. You can store laminates as plain text in files, in ASCII format. You can use an editor or word processor to change them. Please remember that the file format should be ASCII; i.e., make sure that the word processor does not use control characters or a special format. Most word processors have the option to store text files in ASCII format. If you answer *Y* you will be asked for the file name. An *N* or just hitting the return key will give the following instructions and questions:

How many plies (total)?
Here you should answer with the total number of plies, including any core. A core is treated just like any other material. In the material file, material #9 is a 1/4 inch core. If you would like a 1/2 inch core you should count the core as 2 plies. For other thicknesses, other than even multiples of 1/4 inch, you just edit the material data files or introduce different cores as new materials.

Is the laminate symmetric (Y/N)?
If the laminate is symmetric you do not have to specify more than the lower half, or in the case of an odd number of plies, the lower part and the middle ply.

Enter the laminate from bottom to top; i.e., ply #1 is the bottom ply
We define positive z–direction from the bottom to the top of the laminate.

Angle (degree) and material number for ply #i:
You will get this question, with i indicating the ply number, for each ply in the laminate. For symmetric laminates, the number of questions is reduced of course. The angle should be given in degrees and the material number as an integer. The values can be separated with a blank (space), a <CR>, or a comma. Please remember that a core is treated just like any other material. Just specify a core material as one of your materials in the material data files. When the laminate has been specified you get a chance to change it.

Information about the materials in the data base can be obtained by executing the program MATFIX. Alternatively, the data can be examined directly by viewing the MATRSI.SYM or MATRAM.SYM files. Currently the material numbers (1–9) correspond to the materials in the data files as follows:

1	T300/5208	4	Scotchply 1002	7	IM6/Epoxy
2	B4/5505	5	Kev49/Epoxy	8	T300/F934
3	AS/3501	6	AS4/PEEK	9	6.35 mm Core

Change the laminate (Y/N)?
A *Y* or *y* will restart the laminate input process. A *N*, *n* or a *<CR>* will give you:

Do you want to store the laminate on a file (Y/N)?
We recommend that you save it. You never know when you will need it again. The program will then ask for the file name:

File name?
Any acceptable name will do.

How many Load Cases?
The program is dimensioned to handle 5 load cases. If you have need for more, just increase the dimensions of a few vectors and recompile the code. The number must be entered as an integer.

Safety Factor?
Here you define the factor of safety as any value greater than or equal to one (SF ≥ 1). The safety factor is defined as the desired minimum ratio between the ultimate and the limit loads. When SF = 1, the limit strength is equal to FPF. A common number used in the aircraft industry is 1.5; i.e., the structure should be able to withstand a 50 percent overload without failing. If design limit is used, the actual safety factor for some loads can be higher than specified. This is shown as a space between the limit and limit* strength envelopes in Section 12.

Prescribe any strains or curvatures for load case #i (Y/N)?
Most of the time, the stress resultants and moments are known, and the in–plane strains and curvatures are unknown. The system of equations consists of 6 knowns and 6 unknowns. We have a 6X6 matrix that describes the relationship between them. We can solve the problem for any combination of known and unknown variables as long as we do not prescribe both variables associated with a specific degree of freedom. For example, we cannot prescribe both the strain and the corresponding stress resultant; i.e., you cannot prescribe the N_1 and ε_1 simultaneously. If you know the value of any strain or curvature component you should answer *Y* to this question. The program will then print:

How many prescribed components?
You may enter any number from zero to six. The entry must be an integer. Thereafter you must give the component number and the corresponding prescribed value.

The prescribed components must be given in ascending order ! !
Eps1 : 1, Eps2 : 2, Eps6 : 3, k1 : 4, k2 : 5, k6 : 6
To avoid messy programming this restriction is applied to the entering of the values. It should not present any inconvenience. By checking the output results, it should be obvious whether the values had been entered correctly.

Component number and value?
The first value, the number of the prescribed component must be an integer. The values can be separated as before. For example, *4,0*, will force the laminate to stay flat in the 1–direction. The moment required will be calculated and stored in the mechanical load vector and the value is printed out in the output file. You will be asked this question until the total number of prescribed components you specified have been defined.

N1,N2,N6, [units], M1,M2,M6 [units], for Load Case #i
Here you should enter the stress resultants and moments. Please notice the units. The values can as before be separated by a blank (space), a <CR> or a comma. You can also use the backspace key to erase faulty inputs until you press the Return (<CR>) key. Also, by entering a non–number entity; i.e., a letter, the program will tell you that you have made a mistake and will repeat the question. The process is repeated until you have given all the loads for all load cases. If you wanted to prescribe any hygrothermal values, the next question happens to be:

Temperature difference, [units], and Moisture content, [units]
The temperature difference is defined as the difference between the operating temperature and the stress free temperature of the laminate. Normally the stress free temperature can be about 30°C below the cure temperature. This is an area of some uncertainty because of the time–dependent material properties and the solidification process. The model we use simply considers the linear thermoelasticity theory. Please note that the moisture content is always greater than zero and that the temperature difference is almost always negative.

We have now given all the necessary input data. The remaining questions are concerned with the output from the program. We have tried to keep the questions to a minimum while maintaining the option to minimize the amount of data being output. We strongly recommend that you try out the different options. By printing to a file instead of the printer, you can look at the results through an editor or word processor. You then also have the option to reformat the data to your liking before printing them.

29.3 APPLE MACINTOSH VERSION OF GENLAM

The dialog boxes that make up the GENLAM program are shown in this subsection with brief explanation. The program is intended to be user–friendly and has HELP information available in every major dialog box to explain the terminology used. At every dialog box, the option is also provided to EXIT the process, whereby the user is returned to the first screen and given the option to restart or QUIT the program. Default values are built in, enabling the first time user to easily proceed and learn the program by simply agreeing with the default values. The 4.0 version reflects the increased capability to calculate limit and limit* values for the laminate.

In analyzing a laminate, the first obvious input required is to specify the laminate configuration. The user is asked if a laminate already exists from a previous run and is stored on file, or if the laminate must be created from the beginning. Laminates with a large number of plies that require extensive sensitivity study may be stored in a file and called up instead of having to be input each time. Note that this program is especially useful for assessing the merits of repeated sublaminates and determining the significance of ply stacking sequence.

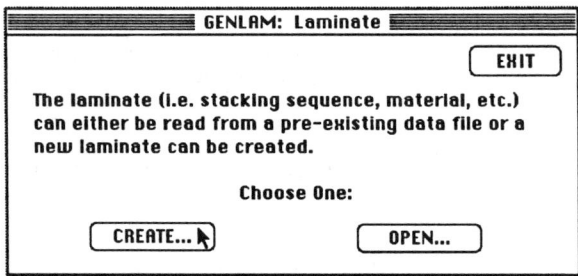

GENLAM is a complete point stress analysis program capable of analyzing unsymmetric laminates. If the laminate is symmetric, the user will only need to specify one half of the plies that make up the laminate. The user is queried initially for the total number of plies and subsequently is asked to describe each ply.

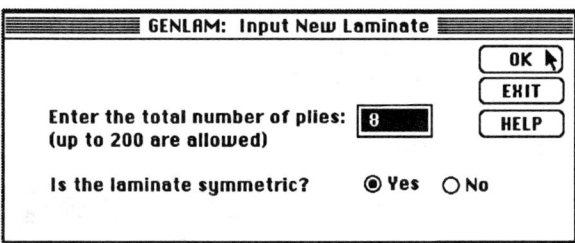

A laminate is specified by describing the angle of orientation and the material of each ply. Materials are identified by number. The laminate can be made of several materials. There are currently nine typical materials included in the data base, corresponding to those listed in Table 11.1. Revised and new materials can be easily added to the data file by using the support program called MATFIX. As the user inputs data in the lower half of the dialog window, the cumulative orientation and material of each ply of the laminate is displayed at the bottom of the top half of the dialog window.

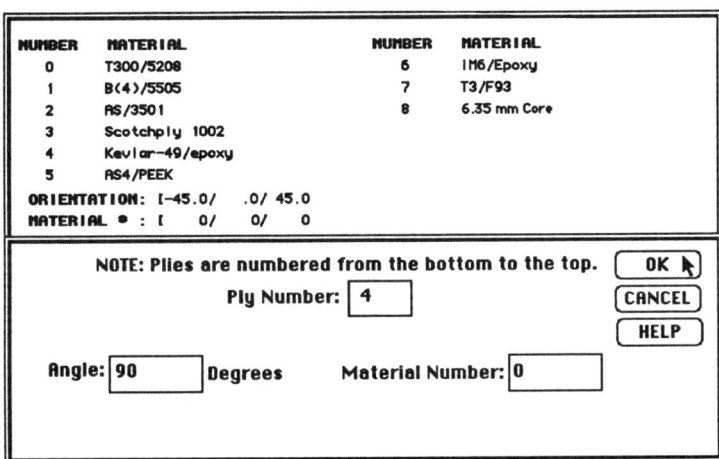

After the user has entered the angle and material information describing the necessary number of plies, a prompt window asks if any changes are necessary in case of input error.

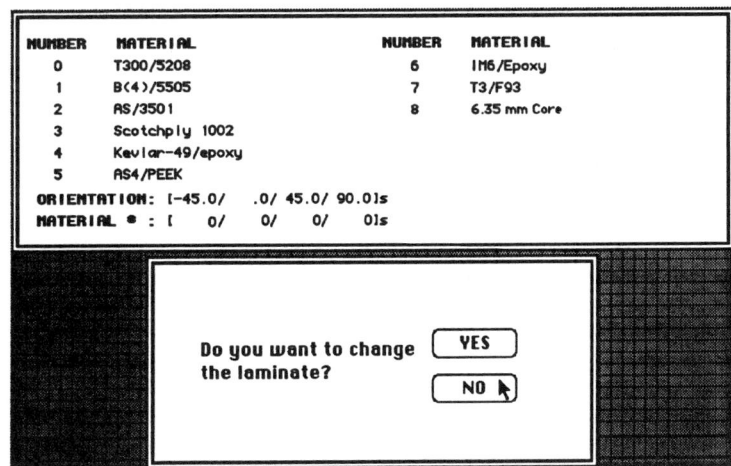

After the laminate has been successfully entered, a dialog box asks if the laminate data should be saved in a separate file.

```
========== GENLAM: Save New Laminate ==========

   Do you want to save              ┌──────────┐
   the laminate in a file?          │  OK    ▶ │
                                    └──────────┘
                                    ┌──────────┐
                                    │  EXIT    │
                                    └──────────┘

   ○ Don't Save    ⦿ Save As: ┌─────────────┐
                              │ T3-Quasi.Lam│
                              └─────────────┘
```

After the laminate has been specified, the loading conditions must be given. The total number of load cases must be specified and then each load case. Mixed boundary conditions can be considered. Only one variable per direction can be specified. If both load and deformation are specified for the same component, the program selects the load and ignores the displacement constraint.

```
========== GENLAM: Loads and Strains ==========

                                    ┌──────────┐
                                    │  OK    ▶ │
                                    └──────────┘
                                    ┌──────────┐
                                    │  EXIT    │
                                    └──────────┘

   Number of Load Cases: ┌──────────┐
   (up to 10 are allowed)│    1     │
                          └──────────┘
```

```
========== GENLAM: Loads & Displacements ==========

        Loads and/or Displacements        ┌──────────┐
                                           │  OK    ▶ │
              Load Case 1                  └──────────┘
                                           ┌──────────┐
                                           │  EXIT    │
                                           └──────────┘
                                           ┌──────────┐
                                           │  HELP    │
                                           └──────────┘

   N1: │ 0.1 │   [MN/m]   eps1: │        │
   N2: │ 0.2 │   [MN/m]   eps2: │        │
   N6: │     │   [MN/m]   eps6: │        │

   M1: │     │   [MN]     k1:  │        │   [1/m]
   M2: │     │   [MN]     k2:  │        │   [1/m]
   M6: │     │   [MN]     k6:  │        │   [1/m]
```

Residual stresses are calculated based on the difference in the hygrothermal expansion of a unidirectional ply along the longitudinal and transverse directions. Unlike the Mic–Macs (see Section 27), note that GENLAM does not consider changes of material properties due to changes in temperature and moisture.

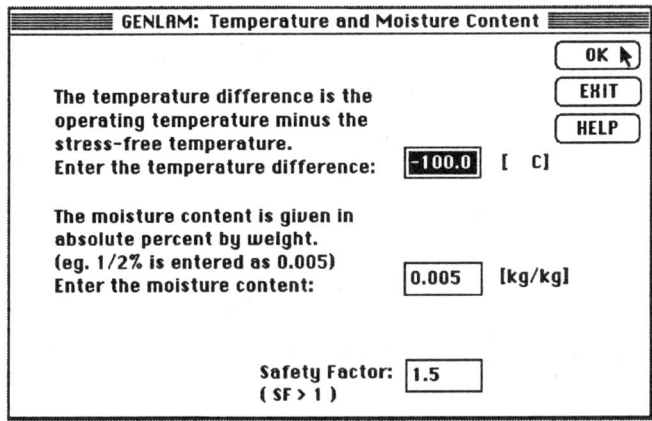

GENLAM provides the user with extensive information about the behavior of the specified laminate under the given loading conditions.

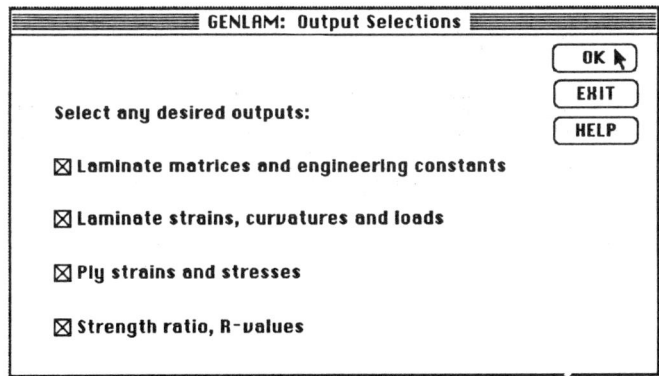

The effective laminate stiffness and compliance matrices will be displayed in both absolute and normalized forms. The normalized form is easier to read because of the fixed point display and because all the components have the same units (in GPa or msi). The relative importance of the components is then self–evident.

For symmetric laminates, the A matrix describes the in–plane behavior and the D matrix describes the flexural behavior of a laminate. The D matrix, unlike the A matrix, depends on the stacking sequence. Both the A and D matrices will always contain at least some nonzero terms. For unsymmetric laminates, the B matrices will contain nonzero terms. The B matrix reflects the coupling of the in–plane and flexural modes: the in–plane deformation due to bending loads and the flexural deformations due to in–plane loads. The stiffness components are for the intact plies only.

Factors of 3 and 1/3 are required in the process of normalization of the stiffness and compliance matrices, respectively, and in conjunction with normalized loads, moment and curvatures as shown in Equations 9.13 through 9.15.

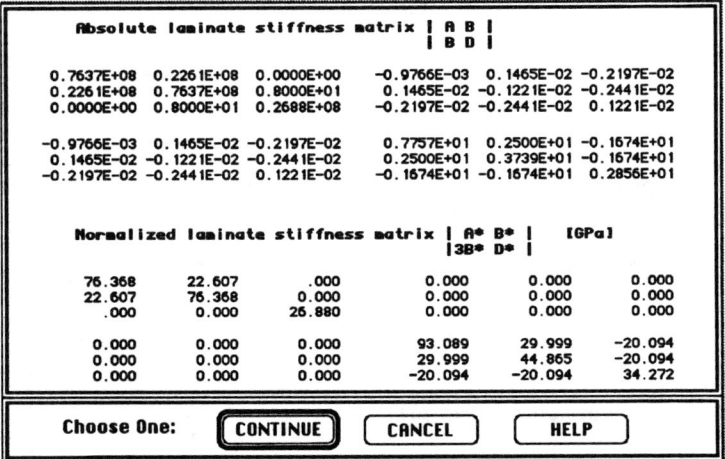

The compliance matrix is displayed similarly in the absolute and normalized forms. The compliance components are for the intact plies only.

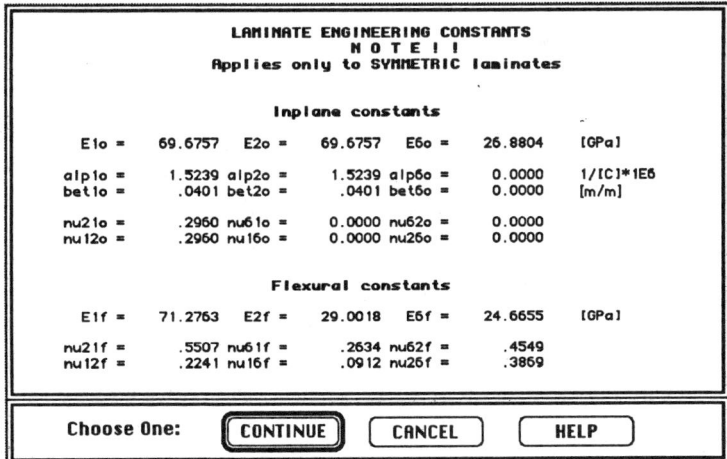

```
Absolute laminate compliance matrix | a b |
                                     | b d |

 0.1435E-07  -0.4249E-08   0.1264E-14    0.6776E-11  -0.8738E-11   0.6260E-11
-0.4249E-08   0.1435E-07  -0.4271E-14   -0.5299E-11   0.1700E-10   0.1586E-10
 0.1264E-14  -0.4271E-14   0.3720E-07    0.3328E-11   0.2145E-10  -0.1371E-11

 0.6776E-11  -0.5299E-11   0.3328E-11    0.1684E+00  -0.9271E-01   0.4435E-01
-0.8738E-11   0.1700E-10   0.2145E-10   -0.9271E-01   0.4138E+00   0.1882E+00
 0.6260E-11   0.1586E-10  -0.1371E-11    0.4435E-01   0.1882E+00   0.4865E+00


Normalized laminate compliance matrix | a*  b*/3| 1/[TPa]
                                       | b*t d*  |

   14.352      -4.249       0.000        0.000       0.000       0.000
   -4.249      14.352       0.000        0.000       0.000       0.000
    0.000       0.000      37.202        0.000       0.000       0.000

    0.000       0.000       0.000       14.030      -7.726       3.696
    0.000       0.000       0.000       -7.726      34.481      15.686
    0.000       0.000       0.000        3.696      15.686      40.542
```

Choose One: [CONTINUE] [CANCEL] [HELP]

Compliance is determined from stiffness matrix and in turn, the engineering constants are determined from the compliance matrix. The engineering constants describing in–plane and flexural stiffness, Poisson's ratios and shear coupling coefficients, and expansion coefficients are displayed. It should be emphasized that engineering constants are meaningful only for symmetric laminates. For unsymmetric laminates the results using Equations 9.24 et al cannot be used directly for design. The full 6 x 6 stiffness and compliance matrices should be used.

```
              LAMINATE ENGINEERING CONSTANTS
                        N O T E ! !
             Applies only to SYMMETRIC laminates


                      Inplane constants

   E1o =   69.6757   E2o =   69.6757   E6o =   26.8804   [GPa]

   alp1o =  1.5239  alp2o =   1.5239  alp6o =   0.0000   1/[C]*1E6
   bet1o =   .0401  bet2o =    .0401  bet6o =   0.0000   [m/m]

   nu21o =   .2960  nu61o =   0.0000  nu62o =   0.0000
   nu12o =   .2960  nu16o =   0.0000  nu26o =   0.0000


                      Flexural constants

   E1f =   71.2763   E2f =   29.0018   E6f =   24.6655   [GPa]

   nu21f =   .5507  nu61f =    .2634  nu62f =    .4549
   nu12f =   .2241  nu16f =    .0912  nu26f =    .3869
```

Choose One: [CONTINUE] [CANCEL] [HELP]

The laminate strains and stresses are calculated and displayed in both the absolute and normalized format. Again, the normalized quantities, introduced in Figure 9.1, are easier to understand.

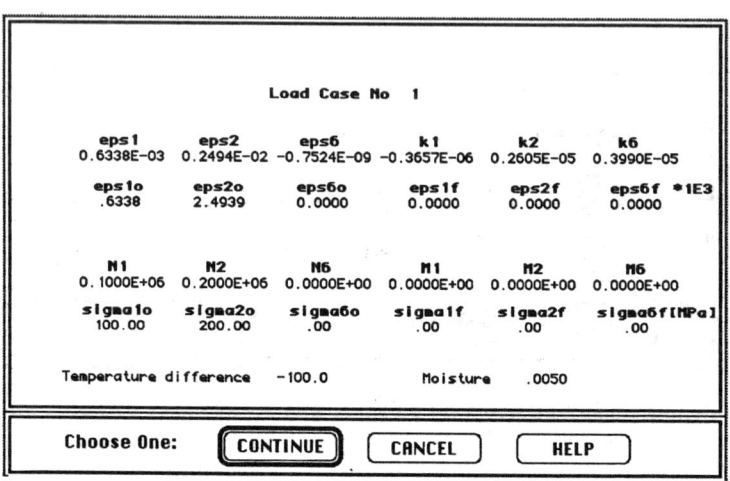

Ply strains, and ply stresses in the next dialog box, for both the laminate (1–2) and the ply (x–y) axes are displayed. The first ply is located at the bottom of the laminate. The stress and strain at the top and bottom of each ply are shown.

```
    Ply strains in 1000:s microstrains or E-3

Ply No    eps-1    eps-2    eps-6    eps-x    eps-y    eps-s

  8 Top    .6338   2.4939   0.0000   1.5638   1.5638   -1.8601
  8 Bot    .6338   2.4939   0.0000   1.5638   1.5638   -1.8601
  7 Top    .6338   2.4939   0.0000    .6338   2.4939    0.0000
  7 Bot    .6338   2.4939   0.0000    .6338   2.4939    0.0000
  6 Top    .6338   2.4939   0.0000   1.5638   1.5638    1.8601
  6 Bot    .6338   2.4939   0.0000   1.5638   1.5638    1.8601
  5 Top    .6338   2.4939   0.0000   2.4939    .6338    0.0000
  5 Bot    .6338   2.4939   0.0000   2.4939    .6338    0.0000
  4 Top    .6338   2.4939   0.0000   2.4939    .6338    0.0000
  4 Bot    .6338   2.4939   0.0000   2.4939    .6338    0.0000
  3 Top    .6338   2.4939   0.0000   1.5638   1.5638    1.8601
  3 Bot    .6338   2.4939   0.0000   1.5638   1.5638    1.8601
  2 Top    .6338   2.4939   0.0000    .6338   2.4939    0.0000
  2 Bot    .6338   2.4939   0.0000    .6338   2.4939    0.0000
  1 Top    .6338   2.4939   0.0000   1.5638   1.5638   -1.8601
  1 Bot    .6338   2.4939   0.0000   1.5638   1.5638   -1.8601
```

Choose One: [CONTINUE]   [CANCEL]   [HELP]

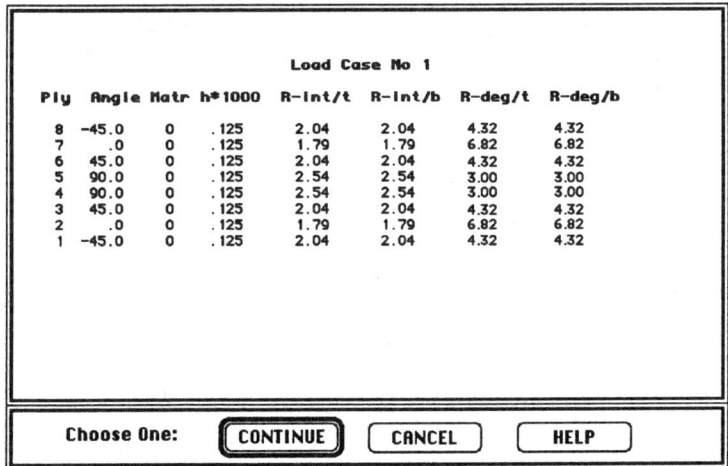

Ply No	sigma-1	sigma-2	sigma-6	sigma-x	sigma-y	sigma-s
8 Top	136.66	163.34	-137.04	287.04	12.96	-13.34
8 Bot	136.66	163.34	-137.04	287.04	12.96	-13.34
7 Top	120.65	19.88	0.00	120.65	19.88	0.00
7 Bot	120.65	19.88	0.00	120.65	19.88	0.00
6 Top	136.66	163.34	137.04	287.04	12.96	13.34
6 Bot	136.66	163.34	137.04	287.04	12.96	13.34
5 Top	6.03	453.44	0.00	453.44	6.03	0.00
5 Bot	6.03	453.44	0.00	453.44	6.03	0.00
4 Top	6.03	453.44	0.00	453.44	6.03	0.00
4 Bot	6.03	453.44	0.00	453.44	6.03	0.00
3 Top	136.66	163.34	137.04	287.04	12.96	13.34
3 Bot	136.66	163.34	137.04	287.04	12.96	13.34
2 Top	120.65	19.88	0.00	120.65	19.88	0.00
2 Bot	120.65	19.88	0.00	120.65	19.88	0.00
1 Top	136.66	163.34	-137.04	287.04	12.96	-13.34
1 Bot	136.66	163.34	-137.04	287.04	12.96	-13.34

Ply stresses in MPa

Choose One: CONTINUE   CANCEL   HELP

The final strength ratios are displayed in the following dialogue box, where, for example, **R–int/t** means strength ratio of the intact plies at the top layer.

Load Case No 1

Ply	Angle	Matr	h*1000	R-int/t	R-int/b	R-deg/t	R-deg/b
8	-45.0	0	.125	2.04	2.04	4.32	4.32
7	.0	0	.125	1.79	1.79	6.82	6.82
6	45.0	0	.125	2.04	2.04	4.32	4.32
5	90.0	0	.125	2.54	2.54	3.00	3.00
4	90.0	0	.125	2.54	2.54	3.00	3.00
3	45.0	0	.125	2.04	2.04	4.32	4.32
2	.0	0	.125	1.79	1.79	6.82	6.82
1	-45.0	0	.125	2.04	2.04	4.32	4.32

Choose One: CONTINUE   CANCEL   HELP

Ratios based on limit and ultimate strengths are given for each load case. The strength definitions can be found in Equations 12.1 through 12.3

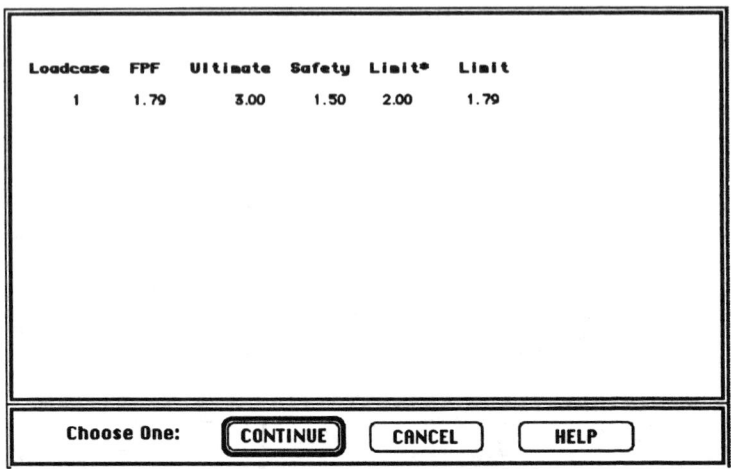

At the end of the program, the option is given to the user to cycle back and selectively change some of the parameters.

25.4 EXERCISES

Exercise 1. For a 1 mm CFRP T300/N5208 supporting a 1 MN/m in–plane longitudinal tensile load, compare the two orientations $[-45/0/45/90]_s$ and $[0/90/45/-45]_s$, and evaluate the differences exhibited in the following parameters. Assume standard operating conditions, namely, a safety factor of 1.5; temperature difference of −100C; and moisture content of 0.005 kg/kg.

a. What is the normalized in–plane longitudinal stiffness matrix element, A_{11}^*, in each laminate?

b. What is the flexural longitudinal modulus, E_1^f, in each laminate?

c. What is average in–plane laminate strain in the longitudinal direction in each laminate?

d. How much strain does the 90 degree ply undergo along its fiber axis?

e. What is the strength ratio at FPF for each laminate?

Answers.

a. $A_{11}*$: 76.4 GPa; 76.4 GPa
b. E_1^f : 71.3 GPa; 113.3 GPa
c. ε_1^o : 0.0144; 0.0144
d. $\varepsilon_x^{(90)}$: –0.0042; –0.0042
e. R_{FPF} : 0.325; 0.325 (The laminate can only support one third of the load, or else needs to be made three times thicker to support the given 1 MN/m in–plane load.)

Exercise 1 examines the effect of stacking sequence. For symmetric laminates, stacking sequence has no affect on the in–plane stiffness properties. Under in–plane loading, the stacking sequence has no effect on the strains, stresses or strength ratios. Stacking sequence does affect the flexural stiffness matrix. For unsymmetric laminates, stacking sequence affects both 6 x 6 stiffness and compliance matrices. From this problem, it can be observed that the largest flexural longitudinal modulus, E_1^f, is obtained when the outer fibers are aligned along the 1–axis.

Exercise 2. For a 0.5 mm E–glass/Epoxy laminate supporting a 0.1 MN/m in–plane longitudinal tensile load, assess the significance of an unsymmetric construction by comparing two laminates $[0_2/90_2]_T$ and $[0/90]_s$, and evaluating the differences exhibited in the following parameters. Assume standard operating conditions, namely, a safety factor of 1.5; temperature difference of –100C; and moisture content of 0.005 kg/kg.
a. What is the normalized in–plane transverse stiffness matrix element, $A_{22}*$, in each laminate?
b. What is the normalized flexural longitudinal compliance matrix element, $d_{11}*$, in each laminate?
c. What is average laminate strain in the longitudinal direction in each laminate?
d. What is the strength ratio for FPF for each laminate?

Answers.

a. $A_{22}*$: 23.8 GPa; 23.8 GPa (In–plane stiffness elements, A_{ij}, are independent of stacking sequence.)
b. $d_{11}*$: 62.1 1/TPa; 28.6 1/TPa (Compliance is stacking sequence dependent for unsymmetric laminates.)
c. ε_1^o : 0.1239; 0.0843 (Note that the laminate strain is equal to the ply strain in the symmetric laminate only.)
d. R_{FPF} : 0.153; 0.596

Exercise 3. For a 1 mm $[30]_{4s}$ Boron/Epoxy laminate supporting a 0.1 MN/m in–plane longitudinal tensile load, find the following. Assume standard operating conditions, namely, a safety factor of 1.5. (Note that the

temperature difference and moisture content are unspecified in this problem, because a unidirectional laminate is not constrained by any adjacent ply angles, there are no hygrothermal stresses due to lamination.)
a. What is the normalized in–plane shear stiffness matrix element, A_{66}*?
b. What is the normalized flexural longitudinal twisting stiffness matrix element, D_{16}*?
c. What is longitudinal thermal expansion coefficient?
d. How much strain does the 30 degree ply undergo along its fiber axis?
e. What is the strength ratio at ultimate?

Answers.

a. A_{66}* : 41.7 GPa
b. D_{16}* : 61.2 GPa
c. α_1 : 12.15 x 10^{-6} 1/C
d. $\varepsilon_x^{(30)}$: 0.038
e. R_{ult} : 1.17

Exercise 4. Assuming standard operating conditions, find the following for a 1 mm quasi–isotropic $[-45/0/45/90]_s$ E–Glass/Epoxy laminate supporting a multiple loading condition of
    i) 0.75 MN/m in–plane longitudinal tensile load,
    ii) 0.0001 MN moment, M_1,
    iii) –0.5 MN/m compressive hydrostatic load, i.e. $N_1=N_2=-0.5$, $N_6=0$,
    iv) 0.4 MN/m in–plane longitudinal tensile load and 0.003 imposed transverse in–plane strain.
a. What are the strength ratios at FPF?
b. Comparing the strength ratios at FPF, which of the four is the controlling load?

Answers

a. R_{FPF} : 0.130; 0.270; 0.595; 0.263
b. Loadcase 1

Exercise 5. For a 3 mm CFRP IM6/Epoxy supporting a 0.001 MN moment, M_1, compare the two orientations $[-45/0/45/90]_{3s}$ and $[-45/45/90/0/0/90/-45/45/45/-45/90/0]_s$, and evaluate the differences exhibited in the following parameters. Assume standard operating conditions, namely, a safety factor of 1.5; temperature difference of –100C; and moisture content of 0.005 kg/kg.
a. What is the flexural longitudinal modulus, E_1^f, in each laminate?
b. What is the strength ratio at limit* for each laminate?

Answers

a. E_1^f : 82.7 GPa; 74.3 GPa
b. R_{limit*} : 0.655; 0.768

Section 26

MANUAL FOR LAMRANK

Jocelyn M. Patterson* and Peter O. Sjöblom**

*U S AIR FORCE MATERIALS LABORATORY, DAYTON
**UNIVERSITY OF DAYTON RESEARCH INSTITUTE, DAYTON

26.1 DESCRIPTION OF LAMRANK PROGRAM

This section provides an overview of LAMRANK, a LAMinate RANKing program. LAMRANK is a laminate sizing computer program that identifies the optimum laminate orientation and required thickness to satisfy the given loads. Given the mechanical and hygrothermal loads, the program will calculate all the possible laminates of a family, constrained by the chosen layup angles and number of plies in the sublaminate, and size them according to laminated plate theory and the quadratic failure criterion. The output is provided as a list of laminates (with relevant information such as required thickness) that have been ranked according to the user's strength criterion preference between limit and limit*.

LAMRANK allows the user to define the material, possible layup angles and number of plies in the repeating sublaminate, multiple in-plane loads and the hygrothermal conditions. LAMRANK-4 is presently dimensioned to analyze a family of sublaminates consisting of 2 to 10 plies and 2 to 6 arbitrary ply angles. For example, when considering all the four angle sublaminates ranging in thickness from 2 to 10 plies, one thousand sublaminates are examined systematically (see Subsection 29.21). The program can consider up to five different mechanical load cases and one hygrothermal condition. The assumptions imposed by this program include: symmetric laminates, and only in-plane loads and deformations. LAMRANK can be extended to select laminates under flexural loads, however, if the laminate is nearly homogeneous, having many repeated sublaminates, or utilizes a thin wall construction (see Subsection 29.21).

The program ranks the laminates with respect to strength according to two different design criteria, limit or limit*. The difference between the two is that the limit criterion does not allow matrix cracking at the limit load. Both criteria guarantee the same safety factor; i.e., limit load $\leq$ ultimate load/sf, where sf stands for safety factor. In addition to the required number of plies to sustain the specified loads, the improvement over a quasi–isotropic laminate is computed. The run time is very short: the strength and stiffness of 165 laminates subjected to both mechanical and hygrothermal loads is analyzed and ranked in less than 15 seconds.

There could be excessive conservatism if the repeating index of the sublaminates, used to regulate the laminate thickness, is limited to an integer. The program therefore seeks discrete plies from the fractional sublaminate to form the best total laminate. This round–off feature makes it possible to more closely achieve the optimum laminate; i.e., the minimum number of plies.

It should be noted that the results of doing identical problems in Mic–Mac and GenLam or LamRank may result in slightly different answers for the Last–Ply–Failure prediction. The cause of this disparity lies in the different implementation of the degraded ply model used to calculate Last–Ply–Failure. Unlike the use of the matrix degradation factor in the Mic–Macs based on micromechanics (Subsection 12.2), in LAMRANK, we use an overall degradation factor DF applied directly to the plies as described in Subsection 12.12. Both are empirical methods and at this time it is debatable which is the better approach.

Like GENLAM, this program consists of a main program and a subroutine library, both written in FORTRAN. They are well documented in the source files. Batch files for recompiling, building the library file and linking the program are also supplied on the distribution disks.

The next two subsections are intended to explain the execution of LAMRANK on different computers. We recommend users to read both subsections, however, to obtain different views of the program.

26.2 IBM PC VERSION OF **LAMRANK**

The program is stored as an .EXE file. It can be started by typing its name. If the program is not in the default directory, the directory name must be included by either typing it or through a PATH command to DOS. Note that the material data files MATRSI.DIR and MATRAM.DIR **MUST** be in the default directory. The program will ask a number of questions. They are as follows:

SI (S) or English (E) units?
Answer with an *S* or an *E*. The SI system uses meter, Newton and °C. The English system uses inch, lbf and °F.

How many load cases (max 5)?

The program is dimensioned to handle 5 load cases. If you have need for more, just increase the dimensions of a few vectors and recompile the code. The number must be entered as an integer.

Give N1,N2,N6   [units] for load case No i.

Here you should enter the stress resultants. Please notice the units, in this question either MN/m or kip/in depending on how you answered the first question. The values can be separated by either a blank (space), a <CR>, or a comma. You can also use the backspace key to erase faulty inputs until you press the Return (<CR>) key. Also, by entering a non–number entity (e.g., a letter), the program will tell you that you have made a mistake and will repeat the question. No new questions will be asked until you have given all the loads for all load cases.

Temperature difference [units], and moisture content [units]

The temperature difference is defined as the difference between the operating temperature and the stress free temperature of the laminate. Normally the stress free temperature is about 30°C below the cure temperature. This is an area of some uncertainty because of the time–dependant material properties and the solidification process. The model we use simply considers the linear thermoelasticity theory. Please note that the moisture content is always greater than zero and that the temperature difference is almost always negative.

Give the number of different angles (/ = 4).

You may use between 2 and 6 different layup angles in your laminate. The default value is 4. By entering a slash, /, you will get the default value.

Give the N angles. / = (XX).

N is the number given in the previous question.
For N = 6: XX = 0,90,45,–45,60,–60
For N = 5: XX = 90,5,–5,55,–55
For N = 4: XX = 0,90,45,–45
For N = 3: XX = 0,60,–60
For N = 2: XX = 0,90

These are the default values, the values you get by entering a slash. You may of course enter any set of ply angles. Just remember to separate the numerical values with a blank (space), a carriage return <CR>, or a comma.

Material   Number?

Here you should enter the number, as defined in your material data file, of the material to be used.

Information about the materials in the data base can be obtained by executing the program MATFIX. Alternatively, the data can be examined directly by viewing the MATRSI.SYM or MATRAM.SYM files. Currently, the material numbers (1–9) correspond to the materials in the data files as follows:

1	T300/5208	4	Scotchply 1002	7	IM6/Epoxy
2	B4/5505	5	Kev49/Epoxy	8	T300/F934
3	AS/3501	6	AS4/PEEK	9	6.35 mm Core

Give the safety factor (SF ≥ 1.0).

The safety factor is defined as the desired minimum ratio between the ultimate and the limit loads. When SF = 1, the limit strength is equal to FPF. A common number used in the aircraft industry is 1.5; i.e., the structure should be able to withstand a 50 percent overload without failing. If design limit is used, the actual safety factor for some loads can be higher than specified. This is shown as a space between the limit and limit* strength envelopes in Section 12.

Number of plies in the repeating sublaminate (2–10)?

You can choose the number of plies in a sublaminate. The use of sublaminates will minimize layup errors, and design and analysis calculation. After you have entered a valid number, the program will start to calculate all the possible laminates. You will see the text **CALCULATING** on the display. The calculations will take from a few seconds to twenty minutes on an IBM PC equipped with an 8087 math coprocessor. The calculation time increases with increasing number of plies in the sublaminate, number of load cases, and number of angles. The time will also increase if you have specified any hygrothermal loads; i.e., if the temperature difference and the moisture content are not both zero.

Do you want the results on a file or the printer (Y/N)?

By printing to a file instead of the printer you can look at the results through an editor or word processor. You then also have the option to reformat the data to your liking before printing them. Throughout the program *N* (No) is the default answer. A *N* or simply a *<CR>* will give you the output on the screen. If you answer *Yes* you will get another question:

Output file name (PRN = Printer)?

Here you can type any acceptable file name. In most systems *PRN* or *LPT1* is the file name for the printer. Should you change your mind, typing *CON* will give you the output on the screen.

Ranking Limit (L) or Limit* (*)?

Answer with an *L* or an asterisk *.

We use the R–values, the strength/stress ratios, to calculate the necessary number of plies in the laminate. An R–value greater than one is required. The two different criteria are defined as follows:

$$R_{ult} = \text{maximum } (R_{FPF}, R_{LPF})$$
$$R_{limit} = \text{minimum } (R_{FPF}, R_{ult}/SF)$$
$$R_{limit*} = R_{ult}/SF$$

where SF denotes the safety factor.

The program will rank the laminates, according to the chosen criterion, in the order of descending strength; i.e., the strongest laminate will be number one. The time required for the computer to complete the ranking process ranges from being almost instantaneous up to a few seconds. If you choose not to print the results on a file or a printer they will be displayed on the screen five laminates at the time followed by the question: **More (Y/N)?**. A *Y* will give you five more laminates and another **More (Y/N)?** until you enter an *N*, a *<CR>*, or there are no more laminates to display. Then the program will once again ask you:

Ranking Limit (L) or Limit* (*)?

You can now choose to rank according to the other criterion or just enter a *<CR>* to go on.

Round–off (Y/N)?
As before, a *<CR>* is equivalent to an *N*. If you want to round–off the best laminates to try to save some additional weight answer with a *Y* and you will get the question:

How many layups do you want to round–off?
The program will use the last performed ranking criterion (limit or limit*) and the top laminates of that ranking. In other words, if you enter a *5* the program will round–off the five best repeating sublaminates. At present the program allows a maximum of 10 laminates to be rounded off. The round–off process will take from one second up to 30 seconds, again depending on the problem. When the output is ready the program prints:

Another run (Y/N)?
A *Y* will bring you back to the first question.

The Macintosh version of the program is very similar. It uses some special features of the Macintosh such as a mouse driven user interface.

26.3 APPLE MACINTOSH VERSION OF **LAMRANK**

Representative dialogue boxes for the LAMRANK program on the Apple Macintosh are shown below. The Macintosh version of the LAMRANK program is nearly identical to the IBM PC version. The initial choice is to select a system of units. Later inquiries for load values will be accompanied by appropriate units prompting the user, based on this initial choice.

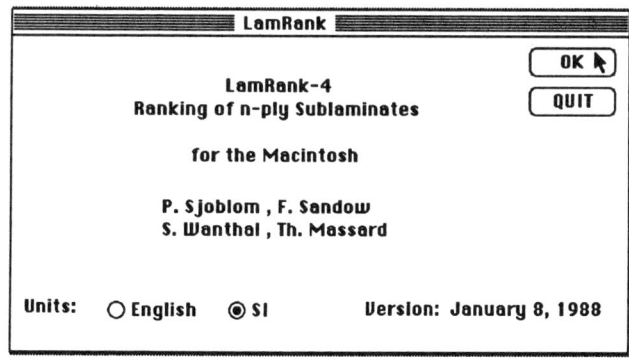

Up to five load cases can be specified. Hygrothermal conditions also must be specified. Default room temperature values are provided. The help button leads to an explanation of the terms requested in this dialog box. The exit button returns the user to the first screen, where the option is provided to restart the program or quit.

```
┌──────────────────────────────────────────────────────────────┐
│ ≡≡≡≡≡≡≡≡≡≡≡≡≡≡≡≡≡≡≡ LamRank: Loads ≡≡≡≡≡≡≡≡≡≡≡≡≡≡≡≡≡          │
│                                                  ┌─────────┐    │
│            N1 [MN/m]    N2 [MN/m]    N6 [MN/m]   │  OK  ▶   │    │
│                                                  └─────────┘    │
│  Load Case 1: │1│        │2│        │0.0│        ┌─────────┐    │
│                                                  │  EXIT    │    │
│  Load Case 2: │-1│       │2│        │0.0│        └─────────┘    │
│                                                  ┌─────────┐    │
│  Load Case 3: │0.0│      │1│        │0.5│        │  HELP    │    │
│                                                  └─────────┘    │
│  Load Case 4: │0.0│      │1│        │-0.5│                      │
│                                                                 │
│  Load Case 5: │0.0│      │0.0│      │0.0│                       │
│                                                                 │
│  Temperature              Moisture                             │
│  Difference:  │-100│ [deg C] Content: │0.005│  [kg/kg]         │
└──────────────────────────────────────────────────────────────┘
```

The sublaminate is defined in the Sublaminate and Safety dialog box by choosing the number of angles and the number of plies in the sublaminate. The range for the quantity of angles is 2 to 6; that for the plies, 2 to 10. The sensitivity of these parameters can be found in Section 14. In addition to the basic laminate parameters, the angles must be specified explicitly. Additionally, a material is selected by number. If the number is not known, the box can be left empty, and then a dialog box showing the material names and their numbers will appear and ask again for a choice. The remaining specification to be made is the safety factor, to determine the relationship of limit and ultimate values.

```
┌──────────────────────────────────────────────────────────────┐
│ □ ≡≡≡≡≡≡≡≡≡≡≡≡ LamRank: Sublaminate & Safety ≡≡≡≡≡≡≡           │
│                          Safety Factor: │1.5│   ┌─────────┐    │
│                          (SF > 1)               │  OK  ▶   │    │
│                                                  └─────────┘    │
│                                                  ┌─────────┐    │
│    Number of Angles in the Sublaminate: │4│     │  EXIT    │    │
│    (2 < N < 6)                                   └─────────┘    │
│                                                  ┌─────────┐    │
│    Number of Plies in the Sublaminate: │8│      │  HELP    │    │
│    ( 2 < M < 10)                                 └─────────┘    │
│                                                                 │
│                          Material Number: │  │                 │
│                          ( 0 < M.N. < 8 )                      │
│    Enter the                                                   │
│    Angles (deg): │0│  │90│  │45│  │-45│  │  │  │  │            │
└──────────────────────────────────────────────────────────────┘
```

The next box explains each material number and the material in the data base
to which it corresponds. The user must select a material by typing a number.

```
NUMBER    MATERIAL
   0      T300/5208
   1      B(4)/5505
   2      AS/3501
   3      Scotchply 1002
   4      Kevlar-49/epoxy
   5      AS4/PEEK
   6      IM6/Epoxy
   7      T3/F93
   8      1/4 inch Core

Select a material --> 0
```

LAMRANK will now evaluate every possible sublaminate in the family of
sublaminates that is generated based on the user inputs. The family is
generated by considering every possible distribution of the number of plies
amongst the different number of angles. See Section 14 for further
explanation.

Each sublaminate is evaluated based on laminated plate theory and the
quadratic failure criterion. From the quadratic failure criterion, the strength
ratios corresponding to first–ply–failure (FPF) and last–ply–failure (LPF)
can be calculated, from which then the strength ratios corresponding to
ultimate, limit and limit* are determined. See Section 12 for the exact
relationships and further explanation. The user must decide to design the
laminate to either limit or limit* capability and select in the next dialog box
either choice as the basis for establishing the required thickness. By clicking
on the RANK button, the program continues processing the output based on
the indicated ranking choice. From the strength ratio, R, corresponding to
either limit or limit* as specified, LAMRANK determines how many times
each sublaminate must be repeated to satisfy the given loading conditions.
The sublaminates are then ranked in order of increasing thickness. Note that
the thickness of a laminate designed to ultimate strength is by definition
simply the thickness divided by the safety factor of the same laminate
designed to limit* strength.

After the output has been viewed, the user is returned to this screen as the
juncture point in the program from which the user can choose to view the
output based on a different ranking or selectively choose to modify some of
the inputs. Again, this dialog box provides the user with the option to exit
this run and return to the initial dialog box of the program. Also, the help
button leads to another dialog box in which the terminology is explained.

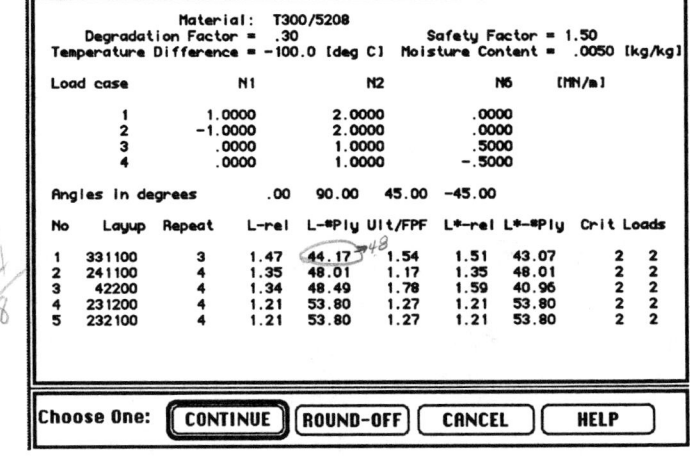

The next box is an example of the display of the ranking output based on the limit ranking. The inputs are reviewed in the top half of the screen. See Section 14 for an explanation of the output. The HELP button leads to an explanation of the information shown in this box. The CANCEL button leads to the LamRank:Ranking box shown above. The CONTINUE button provides the output information about the next five laminates in the ranking.

```
                      Material:  T300/5208
           Degradation Factor =  .30              Safety Factor = 1.50
   Temperature Difference = -100.0 [deg C]  Moisture Content =  .0050 [kg/kg]

   Load case            N1               N2              N6    [MN/m]

        1            1.0000          2.0000          .0000
        2           -1.0000          2.0000          .0000
        3             .0000          1.0000          .5000
        4             .0000          1.0000         -.5000

   Angles in degrees       .00    90.00    45.00   -45.00

   No   Layup   Repeat  L-rel  L-#Ply Ult/FPF  L*-rel L*-#Ply  Crit Loads

   1    331100    3     1.47   44.17   1.54    1.51   43.07      2    2
   2    241100    4     1.35   48.01   1.17    1.35   48.01      2    2
   3     42200    4     1.34   48.49   1.78    1.59   40.96      2    2
   4    231200    4     1.21   53.80   1.27    1.21   53.80      2    2
   5    232100    4     1.21   53.80   1.27    1.21   53.80      2    2

   Choose One:  [ CONTINUE ] [ ROUND-OFF ] [ CANCEL ] [ HELP ]
```

In this problem, the best laminate to satisfy the four complex loads is $[0_3/90_3/45_1/-45_1]_{3s}$ with a total of 48 plies, although theoretically only 44.17 plies are required as the minimum to insure that the stress does not exceed the limit* level. In order to obtain a laminate that more closely approaches the theoretical requirement, the ROUND–OFF button is selected and LAMRANK continues by computing a round–off laminate in place of one of the sublaminates. Notice also that for this particular laminate, the 1.47 value in the **L–rel** column indicates that, based on limit strength, a quasi–isotropic laminate, $[0_2/90_2/45_2/-45_2]$, is 47 percent thicker. Alternatively, it can be viewed that this best laminate, if made as thick as the quasi–isotropic laminate is required to be, would be 47 times thicker than necessary.

Looking at the round–off results for this problem, the best laminate to satisfy the four complex loads is $\{[0_3/90_3/45_1/-45_1]_2 + [0_2/90_3/45_0/-45_1]\}_s$ for a total of 44 plies.

Layup		#Ply	R–Limit	R–Limit*	Ult
[(331100) X	2 + (230100)]S	44	1.01	1.01	1.52
[(241100) X	3 + (100000)]S	50	1.10	1.10	1.64
[(42200) X	3 + (10000)]S	50	1.05	1.21	1.81
[(231200) X	3 + (200000)]S	52	1.04	1.04	1.57
[(232100) X	3 + (200000)]S	52	1.04	1.04	1.57
[(240200) X	3 + (110100)]S	54	1.00	1.00	1.50
[(242000) X	3 + (111000)]S	54	1.00	1.00	1.50
[(151100) X	3 + (120000)]S	54	1.01	1.01	1.52
[(330200) X	3 + (30100)]S	56	1.01	1.01	1.52
[(332000) X	3 + (31000)]S	56	1.01	1.01	1.52

Choose One: [CONTINUE]   [HELP]

The next box is an example of the display of the ranking output for the ranking based on limit* criterion. See Section 14 for an explanation of the output.

Material: T300/5208
Degradation Factor = .30   Safety Factor = 1.50
Temperature Difference = –100.0 [deg C]   Moisture Content = .0050 [kg/kg]

Load case	N1	N2	N6	[MN/m]
1	1.0000	2.0000	.0000	
2	–1.0000	2.0000	.0000	
3	.0000	1.0000	.5000	
4	.0000	1.0000	–.5000	

Angles in degrees   .00   90.00   45.00   –45.00

No	Layup	Repeat	L–rel	L–#Ply	Ult/FPF	L*–rel	L*–#Ply	Crit Loads	
1	42200	3	1.34	48.49	1.78	1.59	40.96	2	2
2	331100	3	1.47	44.17	1.54	1.51	43.07	2	2
3	33200	3	1.15	56.42	1.85	1.42	45.67	2	2
4	32300	3	1.15	56.42	1.85	1.42	45.67	2	2
5	241100	4	1.35	48.01	1.17	1.35	48.01	2	2

At the end of the program, the option is given to the user to cycle back and selectively change some of the parameters.

```
┌────────────────────────────────────────────────┐
│ ▓▓▓▓▓▓▓ GENLAM: Program Control ▓▓▓▓▓▓▓          │
│                                    ┌──────────┐  │
│        Make a Selection:           │    OK    │  │
│                                    └──────────┘  │
│                                    ┌──────────┐  │
│        ☐ Change Laminate           │   EXIT   │  │
│                                    └──────────┘  │
│                                                  │
│        ☐ Change Loads                            │
└────────────────────────────────────────────────┘
```

26.4 EXERCISES

Exercise 1. For CFRP T300/N5208, analyze a family of four angle, eight ply sublaminates that will best support a complex loading consisting of a 2 MN/m tensile load along the 1–axis of the laminate, –0.5 MN/m tensile load along the 2–axis of the laminate and –0.5 MN/m shear load. Assume standard operating conditions, namely a temperature difference of –100C, moisture content of 0.005, and a safety factor of 1.5.
a. Using the limit strength ranking, identify the best laminate before round–off. How many plies are required?
b. How much better is this laminate configuration than the quasi–isotropic laminate [2222]?
c. Identify the best laminate after round–off.
Answers.

a. $[0_5/90_0/45_2/-45_1]_{3s}$; 40.99 plies
b. 37 percent
c. $\{[5021]_2 + [2020]\}_s$ or rewritten explicitly $\{[0_5/45_2/-45_1]_2 + [0_2/45_2]\}_s$

Exercise 2. Analyze the family containing the CFRP T300/N5208 quasi–isotropic laminate $[0_2/60_2/-60_2]$ and supporting the following multiple loading conditions:
    i. uniaxial tensile load along the 1–axis (1,0,0)
    ii. hydrostatic compressive load (–0.5,–0.5,0)
    iii. compression along the 2–axis and negative shear (0,–0.4,–0.2)
a. Using the limit* ranking, what is the best directional laminate?
b. Identify which of the three is the controlling load?

Answers.
a. $\{[0_3/60_2/-60_1] + [0]\}_s$
b. Loadcase 1

Section 27

SPREADSHEET ANALYSIS OF MICRO–MACROMECHANICS

Jocelyn M. Patterson and Stephen W. Tsai
U S AIR FORCE MATERIALS LABORATORY, DAYTON

27.1 INTRODUCTION

The integrated micro–macromechanics analysis, or Mic–Mac for short, can be best performed using one of several spreadsheets now available for all personal computers. The Mic–Mac spreadsheets are templates that require a spreadsheet package as support software, namely Microsoft Excel for the Apple Macintosh computer, or Lotus 123 for the IBM PC computer. Computation times range from 30 to 90 seconds on an Apple Macintosh personal computer and from 10 to 20 seconds on an IBM PC or Macintosh II. The following discussion is illustrated using the Macintosh version.

Mic–Mac refers to the integrated micromechanics and macromechanics analysis of composite materials. The micromechanics analysis is based on modified rule–of–mixtures equations, outlined in Section 10 and Subsection 29.6. The macromechanics analysis is based on laminated plate theory and the quadratic failure criterion. The starting basis are baseline unidirectional ply data which include four stiffness constants, five strength constants, two thermal expansion coefficients, two moisture expansion coefficients, ply thickness, and specific gravity. There are several Mic–Mac spreadsheets available, differentiated by a specific structural application. These spreadsheets are useful for front end design calculations whenever a simple model can be considered. Additionally, these spreadsheets are useful as a teaching tool to aid the designer in understanding composites behavior. The format of this software coupled with the speed of computers results in a uniquely useful design tool. The engineer is empowered by a simple means to obtain reliable answers to the question "What if...?"

The current package of Mic–Macs includes the following programs:

- Mic-Mac Tutorials (subdivided or specialized Mic-Macs)

  EZ11   Unidirectional
  EZ12   In-plane stiffness
  EZ13   Hygrothermal
  EZ14   In-plane stress

    EZ15   In-plane strength

    EZ21   Flex stiffness
    EZ22   Flex stress
    EZ23   Flex strength

• Mic-Mac for one material

    Ply Data File
    Mic-Mac/In-plane
    Mic-Mac/Vessel
    Mic-Mac/Flex
    Mic-Mac/Beam
    Mic-Mac/Tubing
    Mic-Mac/Shaft

• Mic-Mac for one or two materials

    Dual Ply Data File
    Mic-Mac/Duplex
    Mic-Mac/Hybrid   *NOT LPF*
    Mic-Mac/Thin wall

The common features of all Mic–Macs will be explained in the next subsection. A brief description of the special features of each Mic–Mac will follow.

27.2 BASIC USER INFORMATION

The following common features are contained in each Mic–Mac program:

• A common system of units is used. Unless it is otherwise specified, the following units are implicit:

    Stiffness or modulus in GPa or msi (million psi)
    Stress in MPa or ksi
    Strain in E-3, or units of 0.001, 0.1 percent, or 1000 microstrain
    Force in MN or kip (1000 lbf)

• All inputs are labeled in brackets, and shown in boldfaced numerals.
• Many headings of rows or columns are explained or defined in the "Formula bar" which can be read by clicking or highlighting the cell that contains the heading.
• ##### appearing in the output cell of a Mic-Mac indicate an overflowing register due to unreasonable inputs which are generating extremely large answers.

The input and key output variables are located within the control module, the screen–full of cells that occupy the left uppermost section of the spreadsheet. The input parameters specify the design of the laminate (configured to accommodate up to four ply angles), the applied loads, and the micromechanical variables. The micromechanical variables include operating temperature, moisture content, fiber volume fraction, and stiffness and strength of each constituent material. The input variables also include specific geometric parameters as required in the analysis of either plates, pressure vessels, tubing, beams, thin wall constructions, hybrids, etc.

The input parameters can be varied for sensitivity studies. For example, the failure predictions, based on the quadratic criterion, can be modified directly in two ways. The quadratic interaction term can be altered. (Currently, the software is configured for what we recommend, namely –1/2.) Similarly, the matrix degradation constant can be altered. Note that all the Mic–Mac programs except for the last four, which consider two materials, are configured for LPF prediction (effectively the ultimate failure load), although the same information can be obtained in the last four by reducing the Em value by 0.3. More sensitivity studies can be found in Subsection 29.18–19.19.

Output parameters include the computation of the strength ratios (from which it can be inferred how thick a laminate must be to sustain the given loading conditions), average stresses, strains, and maximum stresses. Also within the control module, a comparison is provided to netting analysis predictions and to the relative performance of quasi–isotropic laminates.

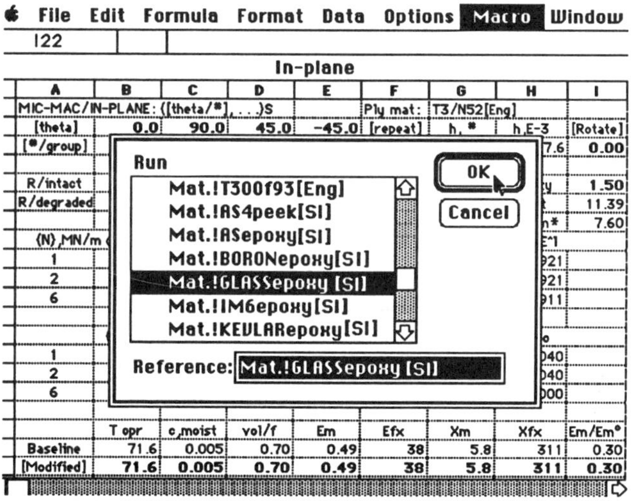

FIGURE 27.1   ILLUSTRATION TO SHOW MACRO COMMAND USED TO CHANGE MATERIAL

A material data spreadsheet, the Ply Data File, is linked to the structural Mic–Mac spreadsheets to allow easy selection of any of eight materials in either SI or English units. A typical composite material can be selected by running a built–in Macro. For the Macintosh version, when a one material Mic–Mac is opened, the Ply Data File and the Macro named MAT. should also be opened at the same time. Changing ply material can then be accomplished easily by selecting RUN under the MACRO and selecting one of the materials as shown in Figure 27.1. Units are determined at the time of material selection by selecting the material in the unit system desired. The unit system is indicated in brackets behind the material name, for example, Mat.!T3/N52[SI]. Note that the Macro name, Mat., precedes the material name. When changing material in a two material Mic–Mac, the Dual Ply Data File and the Macros named MatTop and MatBot should also be opened. Then to access Dual Ply Data File, the selected material should be preceded by MatTop or MatBot, referring to the relevant Macro of interest. The current data file can be easily expanded to accommodate new materials. New ply data must be entered following the same format in SI or English units.

27.3 UNDERLYING CONCEPTS

All Mic–Macs consist of several calculation modules as illustrated in Figure 27.2. The control module at the top left section represents a central location for key information, requiring user interface. The control module provides a simple format for input data and the display of desired output data. Note that just below the control module, the ply data are linked to the data file for one or two materials. To the right, the basic calculations are performed in the odd panels for the intact plies, and the same calculations, in the even panels for the degraded plies. Specifically, in the top row can be found the unidirectional material properties, laminate stiffness matrix calculations, ply strain calculations and strength ratio calculations. In the bottom row is the analogous sequence that evaluates a degraded laminate.

Control Module	Panel 1	Panel 3	Panel 5	Panel 7	Panel 9
	Ply data intact	Laminate stiffness intact	Ply strain intact	Strength ratios FPF	
Ply data link	Panel 2	Panel 4	Panel 6	Panel 8	Panel 10
	Ply data degrad	Laminate stiffness degrad	Ply strain degrad	Strength ratios LPF	

FIGURE 27.2   SCHEMATIC SHOWING CONTROL MODULE AND PANELS OF A TYPICAL MIC–MAC

The Mic–Macs for two materials are also performed in eight panels. The odd panels are for the first material, and the even panels for the second material. Either material can be either intact or degraded, but not both at the same time.

For reference, the essential flow of calculations made within the Mic–Macs can be summarized. The laminate stiffness is computed from the unidirectional ply properties and the given laminate orientation. The laminate strains, equivalent to the ply strains in the case of in–plane loading, are the sum of the mechanical ply strains calculated from the laminate stiffness and the given loads, and of the hygrothermal strains. The strength ratio of a ply group is calculated by applying the quadratic criterion to each set of ply strains. First–ply–failure (FPF) is defined by the ply group with the lowest strength ratio with plies intact. Next the entire process is repeated with a modified set of unidirectional ply properties that reflects a decrease in matrix modulus. This leads to a prediction of last–ply–failure (LPF), defined by the ply group of the degraded laminate with the lowest strength ratio. Finally, strength predictions lead to the derivation of definitions for limit and ultimate strengths, as explained in Figure 27.3. Ultimate strength is the largest value of either FPF and LPF. Limit* strength is the value of the ultimate strength divided by the given safety factor. Limit strength, a more conservative design criteria that does not permit matrix cracking, is the minimum of the limit strength* and FPF. It is up to the designer to evaluate the situation and select the appropriate design criteria: FPF, LPF, limit, limit*, or ultimate.

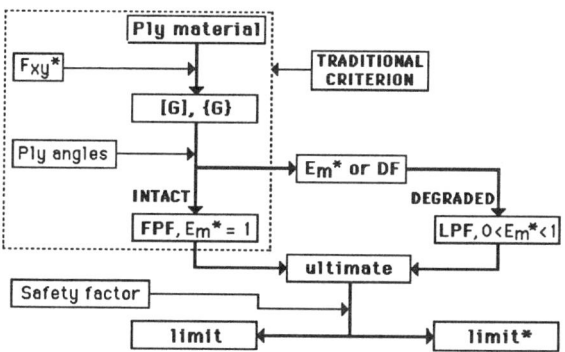

FIGURE 27.3   FLOW CHART SHOWING DERIVATION OF LAMINATE LIMIT AND
ULTIMATE STRENGTH DEFINITIONS

A more detailed explanation of each calculation module in a Mic–Mac is provided by the EZ series of Mic–Macs. Collectively referred to as the Mic–Mac Tutorials, the EZ series are subdivisions of the total Mic–Mac. For example, EZ11 Unidirectional shows the operation of Panel 1. EZ12 In–plane stiffness shows the operation of Panel 3 which requires the data from Panel 1 and the data link. EZ13 Hygrothermal shows the residual stress and effective expansion coefficients in the lower half of Panel 3. EZ14 In–plane stress shows the ply stress and ply strain calculations, portions of which are shown in Panel 5. EZ14 In–plane strength shows the operation of Panel 7.

27.4 EZ11 UNIDIRECTIONAL

This tutorial shows typical ply stiffness, strength, and hygrothermal data which are needed for the analysis and design of laminated composites. The baseline data follow the common flow shown in Figure 27.4.

Micro- mechanics	Ply stiff	Ply strength	Ply expansion	Hygro- thermal
E_m, E_f, v_f	E_x	X	$a°$	T_{cure}
	$Q_{ij} \rightarrow F_{ij}$		$\beta°$	T_{opr}
	$U_i \quad G_{ij}$			T_g
	E^{iso}			c

FIGURE 27.4 TYPICAL PLY AND MICROMECHANICAL VARIABLES.

	T3/N52[SI]				Strength	Base	Mod	Mod/B
Stiff	Baseline	Modified	Mod/B		X	1500	1500	1.00
E_x	181.00	181.00	1.00		X'	1500	1500	1.00
E_y	10.30	10.30	1.00		Y	40	40	1.00
v_x	0.28	0.28	1.00		Y'	246	246	1.00
Es	7.17	7.17	1.00		S	68	68	1.00
ho,E-6	125	125	1.00		$F_{xy}*$	-0.50	-0.50	1.00
Plane stress stiffness, GPa/msi					Gxx	12004	12004	1.00
Qxx	181.81	181.81	1.00		Gyy	10681	10681	1.00
Qyy	10.35	10.35	1.00		Gxy	-3069	-3069	1.00
Qxy	2.90	2.90	1.00		Gss	11118	11118	1.00
Qss	7.17	7.17	1.00		Gx	60.65	60.65	1.00
Quasi-isotropic constants					Gy	217	217	1.00
E^{iso}	69.68	69.68	1.00		Temperature and moisture			
v^{iso}	0.30	0.30	1.00		T opr	22	22	1.00
Linear combinations, GPa/msi					c,wet	0.005	0.005	1.00
U_1	76.37	76.37	1.00		T cure	122	122	1.00
U_2	85.73	85.73	1.00		T glass	160	160	1.00
U_3	19.71	19.71	1.00		T*	1.00	1.00	1.00
U_4	22.61	22.61	1.00		ΔT	-100	-100	1.00
$U_5 = G^{iso}$	26.88	26.88	1.00		Xfx	2143	2143	1.00
Micromechanics data					Xm	40	40	1.00
vol/f	0.70	0.70	1.00		Strength parameters, E-6			
Efx	259	259	1.00		Fxx	0.44	0.44	1.00
Em	3.40	3.40	1.00		Fyy	101.6	101.6	1.00
η/y	0.52	0.52	1.00		Fxy	-3.36	-3.36	1.00
v*/y	0.22	0.22	1.00		Fss	216.3	216.3	1.00
Efy	18.69	18.69	1.00		Fx,E-3	0.00	0.00	***
η/s	0.32	0.32	1.00		Fy,E-3	20.93	20.93	1.00
v*/s	0.14	0.14	1.00		Thermal expansion,E-6/deg			
Gfx	19.68	19.68	1.00		α_x	0.02	0.02	1.00
Density	1.60	1.60	1.00		α_y	22.50	22.50	1.00
ρ/m	1.20	1.20	1.00		Moisture expansion,/c			
ρ/f	1.77	1.77	1.00		β_x	0.00	0.00	1.00
					β_y	0.60	0.60	1.00

FIGURE 27.5 TYPICAL FORMAT OF PLY PROPERTIES OF A UNIDIRECTIONAL COMPOSITE MATERIAL.

The ply data are used to back–calculate the micromechanics variables such as the missing fiber moduli, and the implied hygrothermal exponents. With these empirically determined constants, we can forward–calculate the influence of the changes in the constituent properties and the temperature and moisture conditions.

In Figure 27.5, we show the format of this tutorial, which is based on Panel 1 with minor modifications. The boldfaced numbers that appear in the EZ11 Tutorial are inputs and can be changed to see "what if?" The ratio of modified over baseline data is useful in seeing the sensitivity of the changes due to the micromechanical inputs.

For beginners we recommend varying one input at a time. It should be apparent that the ply stiffness and strength will change when any one of the micromechanical variables is changed. The relations are nonlinear, and highly interlocked. It is futile trying to guess the sensitivity of these changes. The changes in the ply properties will be carried over to the laminate properties in an even more nonlinear and interactive manner. The power of the spreadsheet to properly take into account the complex relationships should become more obvious as we demand more calculations. A number of linear and nonlinear relations are also shown in Subsection 29.18.

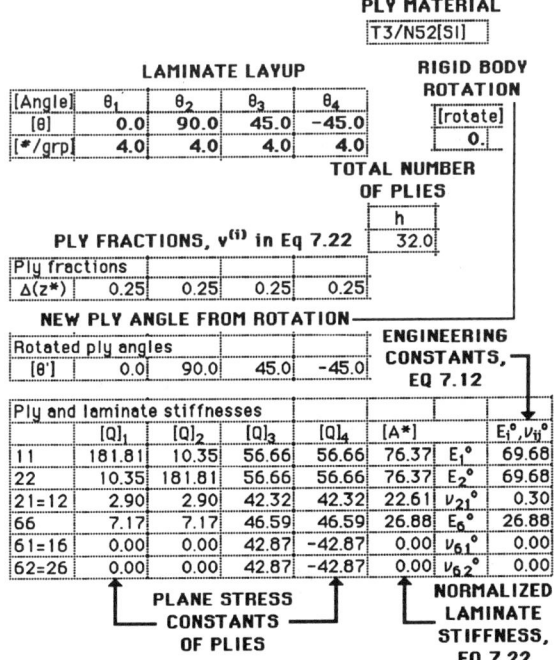

FIGURE 27.6 TYPICAL FORMAT OF IN–PLANE LAMINATE MODULI.

27.5 EZ12 IN–PLANE STIFFNESS

This tutorial consists of two parts: laminate layup, and in–plane moduli. The format for the laminate layup is shown in Figure 27.6. First, the ply material is identified. Up to four ply angles of any value can be selected. The number of plies in each ply group is arbitrary. Being limited to symmetric laminates, the total number of plies is twice the sum of the ply groups. Having four plies per angle, as an example in Figure 27.6, the top half of the laminate has 16 plies which makes the total 32 plies.

The ply fractions are easily calculated and they are needed for the rule of mixtures relation for the laminate stiffness [A*]. The entire laminate can be rotated as a rigid body. The rotated ply angles [θ'] are also shown. Finally the effective engineering constants are also calculated by inverting the stiffness matrix as per Section 6.4, followed by the definitions in Section 7.4.

27.6 EZ13 IN–PLANE RESIDUAL STRAINS AND EXPANSION COEFFICIENTS

This tutorial covers the calculation of the nonmechanical stresses and strains due to lamination (Equations 15.6 and 15.8), the traction–free ply expansions (Equation 15.1), laminate expansion coefficients (Equations 15.11 and 15.12), and residual stresses on the ply axes (Equations 15.10 and 7.13). The format is shown in Figure 27.7.

NONMECHANICAL STRESS AND STRAIN

LAMINATE LAYUP

	θ_1	θ_2	θ_3	θ_4
[θ]	0.0	90.0	45.0	-45.0
[*/grp]	4.0	0.0	0.0	0.0
[θ']	0.0	90.0	45.0	-45.0

PLY MATERIAL
T3/N52[SI]

RIGID BODY
ROTATION
[rotate]
0.0

TOTAL PLIES
h,*plies
8.0

NONMECHANICAL STRESSES, STRAINS, AND FREE EXPANSIONS

Laminate strains and expansions			
	$\{\sigma^{o(n)}\}$	$\{\epsilon^{o(n)}\}$	(e)
1	2E-03	-0.002	-0.002
2	8E-03	0.750	0.750
6	0E+00	0.000	0.000

THERMAL AND MOISTURE EXPANSIONS

(α^o)	(β^o)
0.02	0.00
22.50	0.60
0.00	0.00

RESIDUAL LAMINATION STRESSES ON THE PLY AXES

On-axis residual ply strains, $\{\epsilon'\}$				
	θ_1'	θ_2'	θ_3'	θ_4'
x	0.000	*DIV/0!	*DIV/0!	*DIV/0!
y	0.000	*DIV/0!	*DIV/0!	*DIV/0!
s	0.000	*DIV/0!	*DIV/0!	*DIV/0!

FIGURE 27.7 TYPICAL FORMAT OF IN–PLANE RESIDUAL STRESSES AND STRAINS, AND EXPANSION COEFFICIENTS.

27.7 EZ14 IN–PLANE PLY STRESSES AND PLY STRAINS

This tutorial provides the ply–by–ply analysis of stresses and strains in both the laminate and ply axes. All relevant formulas are shown in Equation 7.13, and examples in Section 7.12. The results are shown in Figure 27.8. The laminate stress and laminate strain are useful in comparing the relative strength between composite materials and isotropic materials. For isotropic materials, strength under combined stresses does not deviate significantly from the uniaxial strength.

Ply stresses and ply strains are useful in determining the strength of each ply in a laminate. These quantities, however, are functions of ply orientation. Each stress and strain has three components in the state of plane stress or plane strain. It is impossible to examine each component individually to assess the mode of failure and safety factor. It is simpler to consider the scalar products of the components to assess the magnitude of strength than to consider the components themselves. The scalar product approach leads to the quadratic failure criterion. The component by component approach leads to the maximum stress or maximum strain criterion.

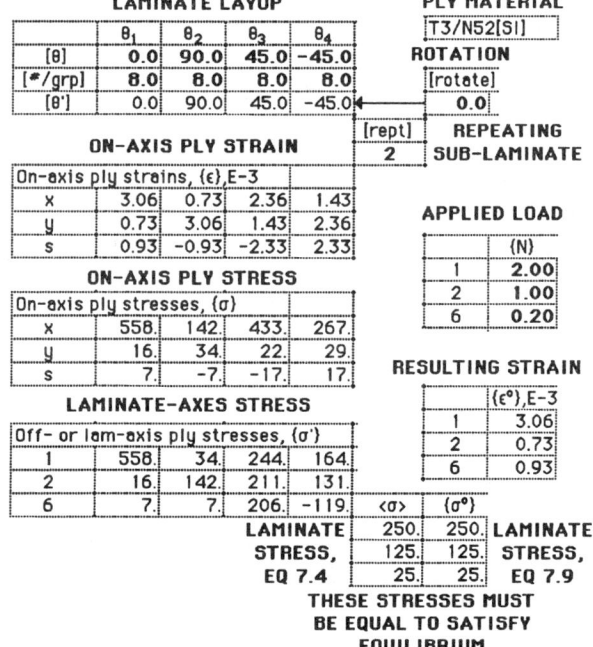

FIGURE 27.8 TYPICAL FORMAT OF IN–PLANE PLY STRESS AND PLY STRAIN CALCULATION AND THE EQUILIBRIUM CHECK.

The equilibrium check is made by comparing the applied stress to the summation of the resulting ply stresses. Such a check is necessary to verify the computation of the ply stress and ply strain.

27.8 EZ15 IN–PLANE LAMINATE STRENGTH

This tutorial shows the computation of the in–plane strength with and without considering the residual stresses resulting from the lamination of a multidirectional composite. The quadratic failure criterion is used. The residual stress is calculated using the results from Panel 3. The resulting mechanical ply strain is calculated in the last section. The maximum laminate stress and strain at FPF or LPF is simply the resulting laminate stress or strain multiplied by the strength ratio.

LAMINATE LAYUP   PLY MATERIAL

	θ_1	θ_2	θ_3	θ_4	T3/N52[SI]
[θ]	0.0	90.0	45.0	−45.0 [repeat][rotate]	
[*/grp]	4.0	4.0	0.0	0.0 2	0.0
[θ']	0.0	90.0	45.0	−45.0	

Laminate stress & strain analysis

	{N}	
1	1.00	APPLIED STRESS RESULTANT
2	0.00	
6	0.00	$\{\sigma^o\}$ $\{\epsilon^o\}$,E−3 RESULTING LAMINATE
		500.0 5.21 STRESS AND STRAIN
		0.0 −0.16
		0.0 0.00 $\{\sigma^o\}^{max}$ $\{\epsilon^o\}^{max}$, E−3

		440. 4.59
STRESS AND STRAIN	→	0. −0.14
AT FPF AND LPF		0. 0.00

STRENGTH RATIOS FOR EACH PLY   MIN R–VALUES

Ply-by-ply strength/stress ratios, w/ & w/o residual strains

	$\theta_1{}'$	$\theta_2{}'$	$\theta_3{}'$	$\theta_4{}'$		
R^{mech}	1.36	0.75	*****	*****	min R^{mech}	0.75
$R^{mech+res}$	1.45	0.88	*****	*****	min $R^{mech+res}$	0.88

RATIO OF R–VALUES
WITH AND WITHOUT | Margin: $R^{mech+res}/R^{mech}$ 1.18 |
RESIDUAL STRESSES

FIGURE 27.9   TYPICAL FORMAT OF IN–PLANE STRENGTH ANALYSIS INDICATING THE RESULTING STRENGTH WITH AND WITHOUT RESIDUAL STRESS.

We show in Figure 27.9 the results of ply by ply strength analysis. The lowest strength ratio determines the ply group that would fail first; i.e., the FPF of the laminate. The example in the figure shows that for the [0/90] laminate, subjected to uniaxial tensile load, the 90 degree ply would fail first for strength analysis with and without considering residual stress. The strength ratio including the effect of residual stress is 0.88. The laminate stress resulting from the applied load is 500 MPa. Therefore the stress at FPF is the product of 500 and 0.88; i.e., 440 MPa. If residual stress is ignored, the stress at FPF would be 500 times 0.75, or 375 MPa. It is therefore advantageous to have a more exact strength analysis because a margin of 18 percent exists for the FPF strength when the residual stress is considered. Of course, the margin can be less than unity if the load or laminate layup changes.

LAMINATE LAYUP					PLY MATERIAL T3/N52[SI]		
Angle	θ_1	θ_2	θ_3	θ_4			
[θ]	0.0	30.0	-30.0	-45.0	[rept]	[zc]	[Rotate
[#/grp]	3.0	0.0	0.0	0.0	4	0.0	0.0

└─CORE

Ply contributions				$2[z^{(i)}-z^{(i-1)}]/h$
$\Delta(z*)$	0.250	0.000	0.000	0.000 ◄─┘ (EQ 7.17)
$\Delta(z*^3)$	0.578	0.000	0.000	0.000 ◄─┐

$12[(z^{(i)})^3-(z^{(i+1)})^3]/h^3$

ROTATED LAMINATE   (EQ 8.19)

Rotated angles				
[θ']	0.0	30.0	-30.0	-45.0

PERCENT CORE

$c*$	0.00
$1-c*^3$	1.00

LAMINATE STIFFNESS & COMPLIANCE

Laminate constants					REDUCTION IN
	[A*]	[D*]	[a*]	[d*]	FLEX STIFFNESSS
11	181.81	181.81	0.006	0.006	
22	10.35	10.35	0.097	0.097	
21=12	2.90	2.90	-0.002	-0.002	
66	7.17	7.17	0.139	0.139	E_i^o,ν_{ij}^o E_i^f,ν_{ij}^f
61=16	0.00	0.00	0.000	0.000	E_1 181.0 181.0
62=26	0.00	0.00	0.000	0.000	E_2 10.3 10.3

ν_{21}	0.3	0.3
E_6	7.2	7.2
ν_{61}	0.0	0.0
ν_{62}	0.0	0.0

EFFECTIVE IN-PLANE AND FLEX CONSTANTS

FIGURE 27.10   TYPICAL FORMAT OF FLEXURAL RIGIDITY OF A SYMMETRIC LAMINATE.

27.9 EZ21 FLEXURAL RIGIDITY

This tutorial shows the calculation of flexural rigidity of a symmetric laminate with or without sandwich core. The in–plane stiffness is also calculated for comparison purposes. We show in Figure 27.10 the format of this tutorial.

We show in Figure 27.10 the principal results of the calculations. The use of repeated sublaminates is shown elsewhere in the spreadsheet, which can be found by scrolling. The contribution of each ply group to the total in–plane and flexural moduli is listed. The in–plane moduli are proportional to the difference between the z–coordinates; the flexural moduli, the difference between the cube of the z–coordinates. In the example in the figure, the 0 degree ply group is repeated four times. Thus the first sublaminate contributes 25 percent to the in–plane stiffness. Being the ply group located at the top of the laminate, this ply group contributes 57.8 percent of the laminate flexural rigidity.

As we increase the repeating index, the laminate becomes more homogenized. Then, the in–plane and flexural moduli will approach one another in value. The example in Figure 27.10 applies to a solid [0] laminate, for which the in–plane and flexural moduli are identically equal.

27.10 EZ22 FLEXURAL STRESS AND STRAIN

This tutorial shows the relative magnitudes of in–plane and flexural stresses. The former is inversely proportional to the laminate thickness; the latter, to the thickness squared. Thus the applied load and moment by themselves cannot be judged in terms of their relative magnitude. The normalized load (Equation 7.9) and moment (Equation 8.7) are the in–plane and flexural stresses. They have the same units, and can now be compared directly.

LAMINATE LAYUP					PLY MATERIAL		
	θ_1	θ_2	θ_3	θ_4	T3/N52[SI]		
[θ]	0.0	90.0	45.0	−45.0	[rept]	[zc]	[Rotate]
[#/grp]	4.0	4.0	4.0	4.0	1	0.0	0.0

Laminate loads & strain			
	(N)	(M)	APPLIED IN-PLANE
1	1.00	0.01	AND MOMENT
2	0.00	0.00	
6	0.00	0.00	

SANDWICH CORE

	(σ^o)	(σ^f)	RESULTING IN-PLANE AND FLEX STRESSES
	250.	3750	
	0.	0	
	0.	0	

	(ϵ^o),E-3	(ϵ^f),E-3	{k}
	3.59	33.10	16551.
	−1.06	−3.27	−1635.
	0.00	−9.91	−4955.

PLY-AXIS IN-PLANE AND FLEX STRAINS

On-axis in-plane and flex ply strains, (ϵ^o), (ϵ^f)				EFFECTIVE IN-PLANE, FLEX STRAINS AND CURVATURE
x^o	3.59	−1.06	1.26	1.26
y^o	−1.06	3.59	1.26	1.26
s^o	0.00	0.00	−4.65	4.65
x^f	33.10	−2.45	4.98	4.97
y^f	−3.27	24.83	9.94	2.49
s^f	−9.91	7.43	−18.19	9.09

PLY-AXIS STRAINS AT MAX PLY SURFACES

On-axis maximum ply strains, (ϵ^+), (ϵ^-)			
x^+	36.69	−3.51	6.24	6.23
y^+	−4.33	28.41	11.20	3.75
s^+	−9.91	7.43	−22.84	13.74
x^-	−29.51	1.39	−3.72	−3.70
y^-	2.21	−21.24	−8.67	−1.23
s^-	9.91	−7.43	13.54	−4.44

FIGURE 27.11 TYPICAL FORMAT OF FLEXURAL STRESS AND STRAIN IN A SYMMETRIC LAMINATE.

The laminate strains can also be compared directly. The in–plane strain is the strain at the mid–plane of the laminate; the flexural strain is the surface strain, defined by Equation 8.8. The surface strains have opposite signs at the outer surfaces. If the bending curvature is positive, the surface strain would be positive at the top surface; negative, at the bottom surface. This is seen in the example in Figure 27.11. The curvature along the 1–axis is positive; the 2–axis, negative, resulting from Poisson's contraction. Twisting is also induced because the twist and bending coupling coefficients are not zero.

The on–axis ply strains are also calculated. For the 0 degree ply group, the in–plane and flexural strains along the x–axis are 3.59 and 33.10, respectively. From Equation 9.17, the maximum strains at the top and bottom surfaces of the laminate is the sum and difference between the two strains; i.e., 3.59+33.10, and 3.59–33.10, respectively. The results are 36.69, and –29.51, which are shown in the last table in Figure 27.11.

LAMINATE LAYUP					PLY MATERIAL		
	θ_1	θ_2	θ_3	θ_4	T3/N52[SI]		
[θ]	0.0	90.0	45.0	-45.0	[rept]	[zc]	[Rotate
[#/group]	4.0	0.0	0.0	0.0	25	0.0	0.0
[θ']	0.0	90.0	45.0	-45.0			

Stress analysis					
	(N)	(M)	APPLIED IN-PLANE AND MOMENT		
1	20.00	0.10			
2	0.00	0.00			
6	0.00	0.00	(σ^o)	(σ^f)	IN-PLANE AND FLEX STRESSES
			800.	960.	
			0.	0.	
			0.	0.	$(\sigma^o)^{max}$ $(\sigma^f)^{max}$ $(\sigma)^{max}$
					682. 818. 1500.
					0. 0. 0.
					0. 0. 0.

MAXIMUM R-VALUES FOR EACH PLY AT OUT SURFACES

STRESSES AT FPF AND LPF, AND MAX FIBER STRESS

Strength analysis						
	θ_1'	θ_2'	θ_3'	θ_4'		
R_+^{mech}	0.85	*****	*****	*****	min R^{mech}	0.85
R_-^{mech}	9.38	*****	*****	*****		
$R_+^{mech+res}$	0.85	*****	*****	*****	min $R^{mech+res}$	0.85
$R_-^{mech+res}$	9.38	*****	*****	*****	MIN R-VALUES	

RATIO OF R-VALUES WITH AND WITHOUT RESIDUAL STRESSES   Margin: $R^{mech+res}/R^{mech}$ 1.00

FIGURE 27.12   TYPICAL FORMAT OF FLEXURAL STRENGTH IN A SYMMETRIC LAMINATE.

27.11 EZ23 FLEXURAL STRENGTH

We show in Figure 27.12 a 0 degree laminate subjected to both uniaxial tensile and bending along the ply axis. The resulting in–plane and flexural stresses are nearly equal for the 200–ply laminate. Because there is no multidirectional lamination, the residual stress is zero. Both strength ratios are equal to 0.85.

The maximum stress is the applied load and moment multiplied by the strength ratio; i.e., 800x0.85 = 682, and 960x0.85 = 818. Using Equation 9.18, the maximum fiber stress at the top surface is 682+818 = 1500 MPa, which is the longitudinal tensile strength of this CFRP. The bottom surface stress is equal to 682–818 = –136. If we have a multidirectional laminate, the outer surface stresses calculated in this manner will represent the laminate stresses, not the actual ply stresses. For the laminated composite case, the ply stress must be calculated from the ply strains shown in the last section, and also in Section 8.3.

27.12 PLY DATA FILE

The material properties data file that contains eight materials in both SI and English units is shown in Figure 27.13. The choice of units is made at the time of material selection and all the values subsequently obtained in the structural spreadsheets are determined consistent with these units. The Ply Data File is directly linked with Mic–Mac/In–plane, Mic–Mac/Vessel, Mic–Mac/Flex, Mic–Mac/Beam, Mic–Mac/Tubing and Mic–Mac/Shaft spreadsheets. Without ever directly interacting with the Ply Data File, a material can be selected by executing the MACRO RUN command, provided that the Ply Data File and Mat., a macro spreadsheet, are opened concurrently with the Mic–Mac spreadsheet.

	A	B	C	D	E	F	G	H
1	NAME[SI]	E_x,GPa	E_y,GPa	ν_x	Es,GPa	Em,GPa	T/cure	T/glass
2	X,MPa	X',MPa	Y,MPa	Y',MPa	S,MPa	ρ/m	T/opr	c,moist
3	F_{xy}*	ho,E-6m	Vf	ρ/ply	η/y	$^\circ a$,Em	$^\circ b$,eta	$^\circ c$,Xm
4	α_x,E-6	α_y,E-6	β_x	β_y	η/s	$^\circ f$,Ef	$^\circ h$,Xf	g,T shift
5	E^{iso},GPa	X^{iso},MPa	E^u/E^l	X^u/X^l	Em/Em$^\circ$			
6	Scotch[SI]	38.6	8.27	0.26	4.14	3.4	122	160
7	1062	610	31	118	72	1.2	22	0.005
8	-0.5	125	0.45	1.8	0.516	0.5	0.2	0.9
9	8.6	22.1	0	0.6	0.316	0.1	0.1	2000
10	18.96	97.83	0.78	1.76	0.007			
11	T3/N52[SI]	181	10.3	0.28	7.17	3.4	122	160
12	1500	1500	40	246	68	1.2	22	0.005

FIGURE 27.13   PORTION OF PLY DATA FILE SHOWING LINKED MATERIAL DATA BLOCK.

The data characterizing a material is summarized in a 40 cell block, contained within eight columns and five rows. The data directly linked with the structural Mic–Macs is located in rows 6 through 10 and columns A through H. A title block is provided in rows one through five, where symbols are given in each cell as reference labels of the content of a 40 cell block.

TABLE 27.1 Key to Symbol Notation Used in Title Block of the Ply Data File

Ex	0° elastic modulus	α_x	0° coefficient of thermal expansion
Ey	90° elastic modulus		
vx	Poisson's ratio	α_y	90° coefficient of thermal expansion
Es	Shear modulus		
Em	Matrix modulus		
T/cure	Cure temperature	β_x	0° moisture expansion
T/glass	Glass transition temperature	β_y	90° coefficient of moisture expansion
X	0° tensile strength		
X'	0° compressive strength	η/s	Stress partitioning parameter for the shear modulus
Y	90° tensile strength		
Y'	90° compressive strength		
S	shear strength	$^\wedge f, Ef$	Hygrothermal modulus of fiber
pm	Matrix density	$^\wedge h, Xf$	Hygrothermal exponent for fiber strength
T/opr	Operating temperature		
c	moisture content	$^\wedge g, T$	Temperature shift constant per unit moisture absorbed
F_{xy}^*	Normalized interaction term		
ho	Unit ply thickness		
vf	Fiber volume fraction	E^{Iso}	Quasi-isotropic stiffness
ρ/ply	Ply density	X^{Iso}	Quasi-isotropic uniaxial strength
η/y	Stress partitioning parameter for transverse stiffness	E^u/E^l	Ratio of elastic modulus at ultimate to elastic modulus at limit
$^\wedge a, Em$	Hygrothermal exponent for the matrix modulus	X^u/X^l	Ratio of uniaxial strength at ultimate to uniaxial strength at limit
$^\wedge b, \eta$	Hygrothermal exponent for stress partitioning parameter	Em/Em^o	Matrix modulus degradation constant
$^\wedge c, Xm$	Hygrothermal exponent for tensile strength		

The material data expressed in SI units are located in columns A through H. The material properties expressed in English units are located in columns J through Q. Additional materials can be easily added. Currently, the following materials are contained in the Ply Data File, starting in row 11:

TABLE 27.2 Materials Listed in Data File

T300/N5208	Graphite/Epoxy
B4/N5505	Boron/Epoxy
AS/3501	Graphite/Epoxy
Scotch/Ep	E–glass/Epoxy
Kev49/Ep	Kevlar 49/Epoxy
AS4/PEEK	Graphite/Epoxy
H–IM6/Ep	Graphite /Epoxy
T300/F934	Graphite cloth/Epoxy

27.13 MIC–MAC/IN–PLANE

This spreadsheet is used for the analysis of a symmetrically laminated plate under in–plane loading as shown in Figure 27.14. The analysis assumes that the skin is thin in comparison to the width and length dimensions of the plate. This is the most basic Mic–Mac. The other Mic–Macs have been adapted as required to satisfy other simple structural applications. Mic–Mac/In–plane includes LPF (last–ply–failure) analysis, leading to the ultimate strength predictions. Netting analysis predictions are also included for comparison.

FIGURE 27.14 SCHEMATIC OF PLATE MODEL SHOWING VARIABLES DEFINING IN–PLANE LOADING AND GEOMETRY CONDITIONS

The control module for Mic–Mac/In–plane is shown in Figure 27.15. The module can be divided into four parts:

- Lamination module
- Strength analysis module
- Stress analysis module: applied load, resulting stress and strain
- Micromechanics module

Only the stress analysis module differs among Mic–Macs. The other three modules remain almost identical.

LAMINATION MODULE

MIC-MAC/IN-PLANE: ([theta/*],...)S				Ply mat:	T3/N52[SI]		
[theta]	0.0	90.0	45.0	-45.0	[repeat]	h.*	h,E-3	[Rotate]
[*/group]	4.0	4.0	4.0	4.0	10.00	320.0	40.0	0.00

STRENGTH ANALYSIS MODULE

R/intact	1.12	1.79	1.64	1.14	R/FPF	1.12	safety	1.50
R/degraded	1.85	2.10	2.27	2.11	R/LPF	1.85	R/ult	1.85
					R/lim	1.12	R/lim*	1.24

APPLIED LOAD, RESULTING STRESS AND STRAIN

(N),MN/m or k/in	<sigma>	<sig>lim	<sig>lim*	<sig>ult	(E*)lim	E~u/E~1
1	0.00	0.	0.	0.	0.	69.7	0.921
2	10.00	250.	280.	309.	464.	69.7	0.921
6	4.00	100.	112.	124.	185.	26.9	0.911

(N) lim	<eps>E-3	<eps>lim	<eps>lim*	<eps>ult	alph o,E-6	beta o
1	0.00	-1.06	-1.19	-1.31	-1.97	1.524	0.040
2	11.21	3.59	4.02	4.44	6.65	1.524	0.040
6	4.48	3.72	4.17	4.60	6.90	0.000	0.000

MICROMECHANICS MODULE

	T opr	c,moist	vol/f	Em	Efx	Xm	Xfx	Em/Em*
Baseline	22.0	0.005	0.70	3.40	259	40.0	2143	0.30
[Modifed]	22.0	0.005	0.70	3.40	259	40.0	2143	0.30
Mod/Bsln	1.000	1.000	1.000	1.000	1.000	1.000	1.000	1.000

FIGURE 27.15 TYPICAL FORMAT OF IN–PLANE LOADING OF A SYMMETRIC LAMINATE.

The lamination module is the same as the Mic–Mac Tutorial EZ12, In–plane stiffness. The repeating index can have values other than integers. Such use can provide a basis for the round–off of a sublaminate, similar to the round–off procedure in Section 14 on laminate ranking.

The strength analysis module follows another Tutorial EZ15 In–plane strength. Both intact and degraded plies are calculated here. The degradation factor is 0.3, shown as the last column in the Micromechanics module.

As explained in Section 12, the lowest strength ratio of the intact model is the R/FPF, which is 1.12 in the example in Figure 27.15. The lowest strength ratio of the degraded model is the R/LPF, which is 1.85 here. For this laminate under the particular load, the 0 degree ply is controlling both the FPF and LPF.

The ultimate of the laminate is the higher of the FPF and LPF. This is valid if we limit loading to the monotonic, proportional type only; i.e., no unloading and reloading.

Safety factor, or SF for short, is an input. The example here shows SF=1.5.

As in Section 12, a design limit is defined as the lower FPF and LPF divided by safety factor. With this definition, limit is always equal to or lower than FPF; i.e., there is no matrix degradation at the design limit. This is a conservative criterion.

We can define another limit, called limit*. This is an ultimate–based limit without consideration of matrix degradation. Limit* simply equals ultimate divided by safety factor. At limit* matrix cracking is tolerated. Applications such as filament wound vessels utilize a inner rubber liner to prevent leaking and allow a design based on the ultimate fiber strength.

The applied in–plane load has no restriction. The resulting in–plane stress is simply the load divided by the total laminate thickness. The laminate stresses at limit, limit*, and ultimate are the resulting stress multiplied by the respective strength ratios.

The load at limit is also the applied load multiplied by the R/limit. The resulting in–plane strain is obtained from the stress–strain relation in Equation 7.6 in the absolute form or 7.10 in the normalized form. Like stresses, strains at limit, limit*, and ultimate are simply the resulting strain multiplied by the respective strength ratios. The utility of the strength ratios is also shown in Subsections 29.14 and 29.15.

We also listed the principal laminate stiffness component, and the loss of each component due to matrix degradation. If the degradation factor is lower than 0.3, the loss of laminate stiffness is expected to be lowered. In fact the loss of stiffness can be used to back–calculate the matrix degradation factor.

Also listed are the thermal and moisture expansion coefficients of the laminate. What output should appear in the control module is user's choice, and is easily done as one of the features of spreadsheets.

The micromechanics module is straightforward. We recommend that the values of each baseline cell be "Paste Special" into the corresponding modified cell before any parametric study is done. When the last row of this module shows unity, we have filled the baseline values in all modified cells. This action prevents the use of incorrect values in the Mic-Mac.

27.14 MIC-MAC/VESSEL *layup* *NOT* *filament* (23)

This spreadsheet is used for the analysis of a thin, cylindrical shell with closed ends, as shown in Figure 27.16. The analysis considers an unsymmetric laminate under any combination of axial, internal or external pressure, and torque loading. Having axial symmetry, the laminate that makes up the shell thickness does not have to be symmetrical. The analysis assumes a thin skin compared to the radius, to validate the membrane or strength of materials theory upon which it is based. The analysis employed in this and the other Mic-Macs does not consider buckling, or interlaminar fracture. To analyze an open ended pressure vessel, the inputs to the spreadsheet must include a fictitious axial load, $F = -\pi PD^2/4$.

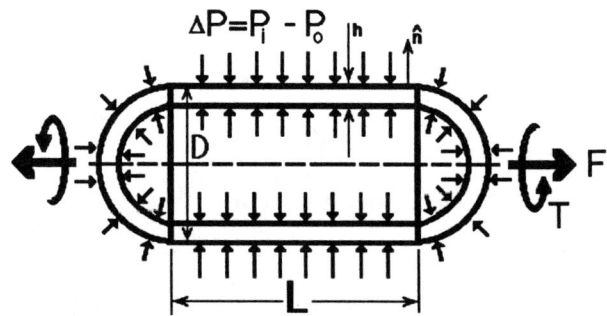

FIGURE 27.16   SCHEMATIC OF PRESSURE VESSEL MODEL SHOWING VARIABLES
DEFINING LOADING AND GEOMETRY CONDITIONS

We show in Figure 27.17 the control module of Mic-Mac/Vessel. Like Mic-Mac/In-plane there are four parts, of which only the third part contains distinguishing features. The laminate is a total laminate; e.g., a 20 repeat of a two-ply sublaminate leads to 40 total plies.

The strength analysis and micromechanics modules are identical to those for the in-plane case in the last section.

In the third part, the stress analysis module, we must input the length and diameter of the cylinder. There are three possible loads: an axial force in tension or compression, internal or external pressure, and a torque applied along the cylinder axis. All loads can be applied simultaneously. The changes in the length, diameter and angle of twist can be the result of mechanical and/or hygrothermal loads. The latter includes loads due to a temperature change.

LAMINATION MODULE

MIC-MAC/CYLIN VESSEL : ([theta/*] , . .)T					Ply mat :	T3/N52[SI]		
[theta]	0.0	90.0	45.0	-45.0	[repeat]	h,*	h,E-3	[rotate]
[*/group]	2.0	0.0	0.0	0.0	20	40.0	5.00	0.00

STRENGTH ANALYSIS MODULE

R/intact	23.56	******	******	******	R/FPF	23.56	safety	1.50
R/degraded	23.56	******	******	******	R/LPF	23.56	R/ult	23.56
					R/lim	15.71	R/lim*	15.71

SIZES, LOADS, STRESS, AND STRAIN

	size,m or in	ΔL,ΔD,E-3		<sigma>	<sig>lim	<sig>lim*	<sig>ult	(E°)lim
[Length]	10.00	3.52	1	64.	1000.	1000.	1500.	181.0
[Diameter]	1.00	-0.10	2	0.	0.	0.	0.	10.3
Angle of twist,deg	0.00	6		0.	0.	0.	0.	7.2

	[Load]	[Load] lim		<eps>E-3	<eps>lim	<eps>lim*	<eps>ult	E°u/E°l
Axial load F	1.00	23.56	1	0.35	5.52	5.52	8.29	1.00
Pressure P	0.00	0.00	2	-0.10	-1.55	-1.55	-2.32	0.44
Torque	0.00	0.00	6	0.00	0.00	0.00	0.00	0.39

MICROMECHANICS MODULE

	T opr	c,moist	vol/f	Em	Efx	Xm	Xfx	Em/Em°
Baseline	22.0	0.005	0.70	3.40	259	40.0	2143	0.30
[Modifd]	22.0	0.005	0.70	3.40	259	40.0	2143	0.30
Mod/Bl	1.000	1.000	1.000	1.000	1.000	1.000	1.000	1.000

FIGURE 27.17   TYPICAL FORMAT OF THE TOTAL LAMINATE FOR A THIN CYLINDRICAL SHELL SUBJECTED TO AXIAL LOAD, INTERNAL OR EXTERNAL PRESSURE, AND TORQUE.

The laminate stress induced from the combined loads can be calculated using Equation 7.60. The resulting strains are calculated from the usual in-plane stress-strain relation like that in Equation 7.61. The growths in length and diameter due to the applied loads can be found from using Equation 7.62; and the angle of twist, Equation 7.63. Finally the stresses and strains at limit, limit* and ultimate are simply the resulting stress and strain multiplied by the corresponding strength ratios.

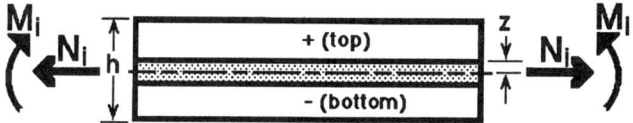

FIGURE 27.18   SCHEMATIC OF PLATE MODEL SHOWING VARIABLES DEFINING FLEXURAL AND IN-PLANE LOADING AND GEOMETRY CONDITIONS

27.15 MIC–MAC/FLEX

This spreadsheet is used for the flexural analysis of a symmetric laminate, as shown in Figure 27.18. A symmetric thick wall laminate construction under combined stresses due to in–plane and flexural loading is evaluated. The plus signs refer to the maximum values for positive z–coordinate for the ply group; those with minus signs, the negative z. This program is a slightly more elaborate version of Mic–Mac/In–plane, accommodating flexural loads, and the the computation time is slightly longer.

We show in Figure 27.19 the layout of Mic–Mac/Flex, which calculates the stiffness and strength of a symmetric laminate subjected to arbitrary in–plane and flexural loads. Again, of the four parts of this Mic–Mac, only the third part is unique for this application.

LAMINATE LAYUP MODULE

MIC-MAC/N&M(in-pl) & flex):([theta/*, . . .)r/zc)s					Ply mat:	T3/N52[SI]	
[theta]	0.0	90.0	45.0	-45.0 [repeat]	[z/core]	h,*	h, E-3
[*/group]	1	1	0	0 5	0.0	20	2.50

STRENGTH ANALYSIS MODULE

R+/FPF	1.81	1.10	******	******	[Rotate]	0.0	core, c*	0.00
R-/FPF	1.81	1.10	******	******	R/FPF	1.10	safety	1.50
R+/LPF	1.92	2.22	******	******	R/LPF	1.92	R/ult	1.92
R-/LPF	1.92	2.22	******	******	R/lim	1.10	R/lim*	1.28

LOAD, MOMENT, AND RESULTING STRESS AND STRAIN

(N) MN/m, k/in		<sig>o	<sig>o/lim	<sig>o/ult	<eps>o	<eps>o/lim	<eps>o/ult	(E)o
1	1.00	400.0	440.4	768.1	4.31	4.75	8.28	92.8
2	0.00	0.0	0.0	0.0	-0.02	-0.02	-0.03	92.8
6	0.00	0.0	0.0	0.0	0.00	0.00	0.00	2.8
(M) MN or kip		<sig>f	<sig>f/lim	<sig>f/ult	<eps>f	<eps>f/lim	<eps>f/ult	(E)f
1	0.00	0.0	0.0	0.0	0.00	0.00	0.00	106.0
2	0.00	0.0	0.0	0.0	0.00	0.00	0.00	79.5
6	0.00	0.0	0.0	0.0	0.00	0.00	0.00	2.8

MICROMECHANICS MODULE

	T opr	c,wet	vol/f	Em	Efx	Xm	Xfx	Em/Em°
Baseline	22.0	0.005	0.70	3.40	259	40.0	2143	0.30
[Modified]	22.0	0.005	0.70	3.40	259	40.0	2143	0.30
Mod/Base	1.000	1.000	1.000	1.000	1.000	1.000	1.000	1.000

FIGURE 27.19   TYPICAL FORMAT OF SYMMETRIC PLATE SUBJECTED TO   IN–PLANE AND BENDING LOADS

This Mic–Mac contains all the features of three Tutorials, EZ21, EZ22 and EZ23. In addition, the limit, limit* and ultimate of the laminate are also computed. The strength ratios with plus signs refer to those at the maximum positive z–coordinate for the ply group; those with minus signs, the maximum negative z.

If a sandwich core is present, the half–depth of which is expressed in equivalent number of plies, the percentage core, c*, is shown in the last column of the strength analysis module.

Mic–Mac/In–plane is a special case of Mic–Mac/Flex if the applied moment is kept to zero. But the former is slightly faster, and operationally simpler than the latter. Due to the lack of space in the control module, we do not show the laminate stress and strain at limit*. But they are easily calculated by using the strength ratio at limit*, or R/lim*, as the multiplier of the applied stress and resulting strain. In the example in Figure 27.13, the in–plane and flex stresses at limit* are 400x1.28, and 0, respectively.

27.16 MIC–MAC/BEAM

This spreadsheet is used for the analysis of a thick symmetric beam, as shown in Figure 27.20. Mic–Mac/Beam calculates the deflections and strength of a simple beam subjected to simple concentrated and distributed loads. Three different end fixities are considered: a cantilever beam, a simply supported–simply supported beam, or a fixed end – fixed end beam. The formulas for these beams are shown in Figure 8.3. The beam can be designed as a solid, thick wall structure or with a honeycomb core. The structural contribution of the core is assumed to be negligible and is only considered as a means of separating the supportive face skins.

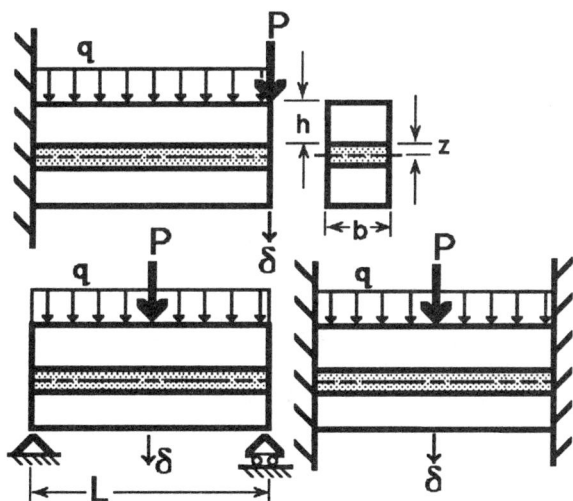

FIGURE 27.20 SCHEMATIC OF BEAM MODEL SHOWING VARIABLES DEFINING LOADING AND GEOMETRY CONDITIONS

The control module of the Mic–Mac/Beam is shown in Figure 27.21. In the stress analysis module, the length and width of the beam must be specified. The concentrated and distributed loads must also be specified. The strength ratios listed in the strength analysis module are for the cantilever beam. For the simply supported beam the strength ratios must be quadrupled because the moments are precise one fourth of that for the cantilever beam; see Figure 8.3 for more comparisons. The fixed/fixed beam cannot be analyzed by simple ratios. The moments resulting from the concentrated and distributed loads and the corresponding strength ratios must be calculated. The moments are calculated in Panel 5 in Figure 27.21, next to those for the cantilever beam. Strength ratios for the fixed/fixed beam are calculated in Panels 9 and 10.

MATERIAL AND LAMINATION MODULE

MIC-MAC/BEAM: ([theta/#],...)S				Ply mat:	T3/N52[SI]		
[theta]	0.0	90.0	90.0	0.0 [repeat]	[z/core]	h,#plies	h,E-3
[#/group]	1.0	1.0	0.0	0.0 4	72	160.	20

STRENGTH ANALYSIS MODULE

R/intact	1.32	0.81	******	******	R/FPF	0.81	safety	1.50
R/degraded	1.28	1.65	******	******	R/LPF	1.28	R/ult	1.28
					R/lim	0.81	R/lim*	0.85

STRESS ANALYSIS MODULE

size,m or in		m inertia,	CANTILVR	Δ,E-3	Δ/max	R	P/max	q/max
[Length L]	1.00	6.67E-08	limit	189.978	152.95	0.81	0.00	0.00
[Width b]	0.10	<sig>f	ultimate	196.417	250.93	1.28	0.00	0.00
applied loads		150.	SIMPLY SUPPORTED/SS					
[conc P]	0.00	<sig>lim	limit	11.8736	38.24	3.22	0.00	0.00
[distrib q]	0.00	121.	ultimate	12.2761	62.73	5.11	0.01	0.00
<E>f/intact	26.32	<sig>ult	FIXED/FIXED					
<E>f/degrad	25.46	192.	limit	2.96841	19.12	6.44	0.01	0.00
core,c*	0.900		ultimate	3.06902	28.68	10.22	0.01	0.00

MICROMECHANICS MODULE

	T opr	c,moist	vol/f	Em	Efx	Xm	Xfx	Em/Em*
Baseline	22.0	0.005	0.70	3.40	259	40.0	2143	0.30
[Modified]	22.0	0.005	0.70	3.40	259	40.0	2143	0.30
Mod/Bsln	1.000	1.000	1.000	1.000	1.000	1.000	1.000	1.000

FIGURE 27.21 TYPICAL FORMAT OF THREE SIMPLE, SYMMETRIC BEAM SUBJECTED TO CONCENTRATED AND DISTRIBUTED LOADS.

The Young's modulus in Figure 8.3, or that for any beam is simply the flexural modulus along the beam axis. Again this modulus is defined as an engineering constant in Equation 8.14, which is obtained from the matrix inversion of the flexural rigidity in Equation 8.5. In the stress analysis module, we show this modulus for both the intact and degraded laminate.

The moment of inertia is the same for all three beams. The flexural stress listed in the stress analysis module is that for the cantilever beam. But the flexural stresses at limit and ultimate are the same for all three beams because the increased moments for the simply supported and fixed/fixed beams are offset by the increased strength ratios. These flexural stresses are important for two reasons: 1. to compare the strength of a composite beam with other composite or isotropic beams; 2. to recover the uniaxial strength of a unidirectional composite as a quick way of verifying the accuracy of this Mic–Mac.

The deflections, in mm or mil, resulting from the applied loads are listed for all three beams; so are those at limit and ultimate strengths. The latter are obtained by multiplying the resulting deflections by the strength ratios at limit and ultimate.

The loads at limit and ultimate are simply the applied loads multiplied by the corresponding strength ratios. In the example shown in Figure 27.21, the applied load is invisible in the particular fixed point display. There is only a concentrated load of 0.001 MN. For the case of the fixed/fixed beam the maximum allowable loads at limit and ultimate would be the applied load multiplied by strength ratios of 6.44 and 10.22, respectively. This would lead to the P/max of 0.01 for both limit and ultimate strength, which is the rounded results of 0.00644, and 0.01022.

27.17 MIC–MAC/TUBING

This spreadsheet is used for the analysis of a tube with symmetric thin wall laminate construction of rectangular or elliptical cross section, as shown in Figure 27.22. The analysis considers the same end fixities and loading as Mic–Mac/Beam, namely that the tube can be constrained by three different cases of end fixities (cantilever, simply supported – simply supported, fixed end – fixed end) and can support a concentrated load and/or a uniformly distributed load.

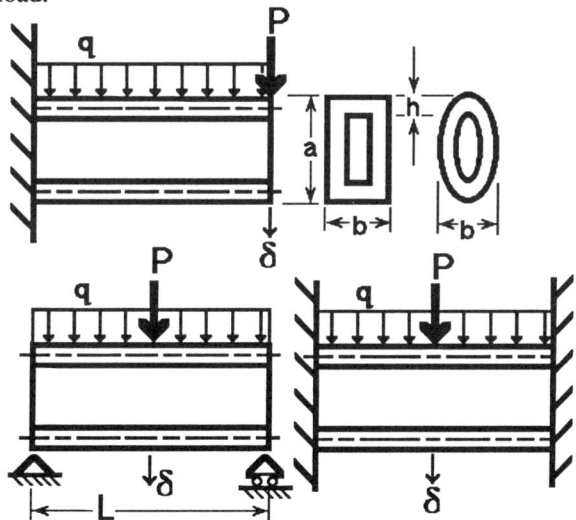

FIGURE 27.22   SCHEMATIC OF TUBING MODEL SHOWING VARIABLES DEFINING
LOADING AND GEOMETRY CONDITIONS

The control panel of the Mic–Mac/Tube is shown in Figure 27.23. Again, only the third part of this Mic–Mac is unique. The key feature of a thin wall tubing is the use of in–plane stiffness along the tube axis, as stated in Equation 8.44. The cross sections, their moments of inertia, and the equivalent widths are shown in Figure 8.5.

The principal difference between Mic–Mac/Beam and Mic–Mac/Tubing is that the former uses the effective flexural modulus, and the latter, the in–plane modulus, shown in Equation 8.45. From the maximum moment in Figure 8.3, we can compute the maximum curvatures using Equations 8.45 and 8.46. From the strength analysis, the maximum in–plane strains are computed using Equation 8.48. The explanation for the remaining part of the stress analysis module is the same as that for the beam, in the last section, and will not be repeated here.

In the example in Figure 27.23, we have a [0] tubing, subjected to a uniformly distributed load. We recover that longitudinal strength of the composite at 1500 MPa shown as <sig>°ult. Having a safety margin of 1.5, the stress at limit should be 1000 MPa, which again agrees with the value in cell below <sig>°lim.

Although we did not show the maximum allowable loads, they can be obtained by multiplying the applied loads by the corresponding strength ratios. Again the analysis here does not take into account buckling.

LAMINATION MODULE

MIC–MAC/RECT[ ] & ELLIP() TUBING: ([theta/*], . . .)S					Ply mat:	T3/N52[SI]		
[theta]	0.0	90.0	45.0	−45.0	[repeat]	h,*plies	h,E-3	[Rotate]
[*/group]	1.0	0.0	0.0	0.0	20	40.0	5.0	0.0

STRENGTH ANALYSIS MODULE

R/intact	0.80	*****	******	*****	R/FPF	0.80	safety	1.50
R/degrad	0.66	*****	******	*****	R/LPF	0.66	R/ult	0.80
					R/lim	0.53	R/lim	0.53

DIMENSIONS, LOADS, DEFLECTIONS AND R-VALUES

	Size, m or in	m inertia	CANTILVR	Δ[ ],E-3	Δ[]/max	R[]	ΔO,E-3	ΔO/max	RO
[Length L]	0.50	[rect]	limit	12.949	6.91	0.53	21.98	4.07	0.31
[Depth a]	0.10	3.3E-06	ultimate	12.949	10.36	0.80	21.98	6.10	0.47
[Width b]	0.10	(ellip)	SIMPLY SUPPORTED/SS						
a/b	1.00	2.0E-06	limit	1.3488	2.88	2.13	2.29	1.70	1.26
[conc P]	0.0	<sig>°lim	ultimate	1.3488	4.32	3.20	2.29	2.54	1.88
[distrib q]	1.0	1000.0	FIXED/FIXED						
<E>°intact	181.0	<sig>°ult	limit	0.2698	0.86	3.20	0.458	0.51	1.88
<E>°degrad	181.0	1500.0	ultimate	0.2698	1.29	4.80	0.458	0.76	2.83

MICROMECHANICS MODULE

	T opr	c,moist	vol/f	Em	Efx	Xm	Xfx	Em/Em°
Baseline	22.0	0.005	0.70	3.40	259	40.0	2143	0.30
[Modified]	22.0	0.005	0.70	3.40	259	40.0	2143	0.30
Mod/Bsln	1.000	1.000	1.000	1.000	1.000	1.000	1.000	1.000

FIGURE 27.23 TYPICAL FORMAT OF RECTANGULAR AND ELLIPTIC TUBING SUBJECTED TO CONCENTRATED AND DISTRIBUTED LOADS.

27.18 MIC–MAC/SHAFT

This spreadsheet is used for the analysis of a cantilevered shaft with a symmetric thin wall laminate construction of circular cross section, as shown in Figure 27.24. The shaft can support a concentrated load, a uniformly distributed load and/or a torque.

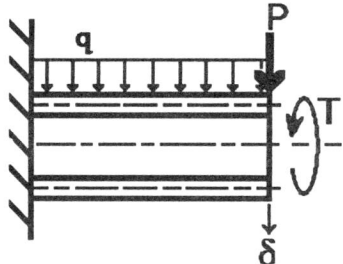

FIGURE 27.24   SCHEMATIC OF SHAFT MODEL SHOWING VARIABLES DEFINING LOADINGCONDITIONS

The control panel of the Mic–Mac/Shaft is shown in Figure 27.25. Again, only the third part of this Mic–Mac is unique. The key feature of Mic–Mac/Shaft, distinguishing it from the Mic–Mac/Beam and Mic–Mac/Tubing, is the capability to support a torque loading, for which the membrane stress on a circular section is known.

The explanation for the stress analysis module is similar to that for the pressure vessel and will not be repeated here. Again the analysis here does not take into account buckling.

MATERIAL AND LAMINATION MODULE

MIC-MAC/Cantilever tube: ([Δ/*], ...)symm								
READ ME	Theta 1	Theta 2	Theta 3	Theta 4	Ply mat :T3/N52[SI]			
[ply angle]	0.0	90.0	45.0	–45.0	[repeat]	h, *	h, E-3	[Rotate]
[ply #]	1	0	0	0	40.0	80.0	10.0	0.00

STRENGTH ANALYSIS MODULE

R/intact	1.07	****	*****	*****	R/FPF	1.07	safety	1.50
R/degraded	1.07	****	*****	*****	R/LPF	1.07	R/lim*	0.71
					R/ult	1.07	R/lim	0.71

STRESS ANALYSIS MODULE

size, m or in	inertia,I							
[Length]	0.50	4.E-06		<sig>	<sig>lim	<sig>lim	<sig>ult	(E°)lim
[Diameter]	0.10		1	0.0	0.	0.	0.	181.0
δ, E-3		0	2	0.0	0.	0.	0.	10.3
Angle of twist,deg	5.09		6	63.7	45.	45.	68.	7.2

	[Load]	[Load] lim		<eps>,E-	<eps>lim	<eps>lim	<eps>ult	E"u/E"l
[conc P]	0	0.00	1	0.00	0.00	0.00	0.00	1.00
[distrib q]	0	0.00	2	0.00	0.00	0.00	0.00	0.44
Torque	0.01	0.01	6	8.88	6.32	6.32	24.51	0.39

MICROMECHANICS MODULE

	T opr	c,moist	vol/f	Em	Efx	Xm	Xfx	Em/Em°
Baseline	22.0	0.005	0.70	3.40	259	40.0	2143	0.30
[Modified]	22.0	0.005	0.70	3.40	259	40.0	2143	0.30
Mod/Base	1.000	1.000	1.000	1.000	1.000	1.000	1.000	1.000

FIGURE 27.25   TYPICAL FORMAT OF A SHAFT SUBJECTED TO CONCENTRATED AND DISTRIBUTED LOADS AND TORQUE LOADING.

27.19 DUAL PLY DATA FILE

As shown in Figure 27.26, this is the material properties data file that is linked to the Mic–Mac/Duplex, Mic–Mac/Hybrid and Mic–Mac/Thin Wall spreadsheets. MatTop and MatBot are the appropriate Macro programs that access the Dual Ply Data File and link two selected materials with the Mic–Mac spreadsheets. Without ever directly interacting with the Dual Ply Data File, the two materials can be selected by twice executing the MACRO RUN command, provided that the Ply Data File, MatTop and MatBot are opened simultaneously with the Mic–Mac spreadsheet.

	A	B	C	D	E	F	G	H
1	NAME[SI]	Ex,GPa	Ey,GPa	nu/x	Es,GPa	Em,GPa	T/cure	T/glass
2	X,MPa	X',MPa	Y,MPa	Y',MPa	S,MPa	rho/m	T/opr	c,moist
3	Fxy *	ho,E-6m	Vf	rho/ply	eta/y	a,Em	b,eta	c,Xm
4	alph/x,E-6	alph/y,E-6	beta/x	beta/y	eta/s	f,Ef	h,Xf	g,T shift
5	E~iso,GPa	X~iso,MPa	E~u/E^1	X~u/X^1	Em/Em°			
6	T3/N52[SI]	181	10.3	0.28	7.17	3.4	122	160
7	1500	1500	40	246	68	1.2	22	0.005
8	-0.5	125	0.7	1.6	0.516	0.5	0.2	0.9
9	0.02	22.5	0.0	0.6	0.316	0.004	0.004	2000
10	69.7	325	0.916	1.56	0.3			
11	Scotch[SI]	38.6	8.27	0.26	4.14	3.4	122	160
12	1062	610	31	118	72	1.2	22	0.005
13	-0.5	125	0.45	1.8	0.516	0.5	0.2	0.9
14	8.6	22.1	0.0	0.6	0.316	0.01	0.01	2000
15	18.96	97.7	0.775	1.76	0.1			
16	T3/N52[SI]	181	10.3	0.28	7.17	3.4	122	160
17	1500	1500	40	246	68	1.2	22	0.005

FIGURE 27.26 PORTION OF DUAL PLY DATA FILE SHOWING LINKED MATERIAL DATA BLOCK.

The major difference between the Dual Data File and the Ply Data File is that *two* materials are linked to the Mic–Mac spreadsheets. The data directly linked with the structural Mic–Macs is located in columns A through H and rows 6 through 10 for the top material, and columns A through H and rows 11 through 15 for the bottom material.

In other respects, the Dual Ply Data File is similar to the Ply Data File. The data characterizing a material is summarized in a 40 cell block, contained within eight columns and five rows. A title block is provided in rows one through five, where symbols are given in each cell as reference labels of the content of a 40 cell block. Eight materials are provided in both SI and English units. The choice of units is made at the time of material selection and all the values subsequently obtained in the structural spreadsheets are determined consistent with these units.

27.20 MIC–MAC/DUPLEX

This spreadsheet is used for the analysis of two different symmetric laminates with an applied in–plane load, as shown in Figure 17.27. Mic–Mac/Duplex is especially useful in tradeoff studies when making comparisons to understand the effects of material and geometric variables. In addition to comparing different materials, it is also useful for examining the same material under different conditions.

The control module of the Mic–Mac/Duplex is shown in Figure 27.28. This is limited to in–plane loading of symmetric laminates. The first and second materials are identified with plus and minus signs, respectively. The Mic–Mac/Duplex treats the two materials acting independently. The layups and ply materials are separate. The applied loads are separate. And the micromechanics variables are separate. All Mic–Macs with two materials can handle either intact or degraded plies, but not both at the same time. The degradation factor in the Micromechanics module can control the analysis using the intact or degraded material. Since the results pertaining to the intact and degraded plies do not appear in the spreadsheet simultaneously, the strength at limit, limit*, and ultimate must be calculated by hand. The same restriction applies to Mic–Mac/Hybrid and Mic–Mac/Thin Wall.

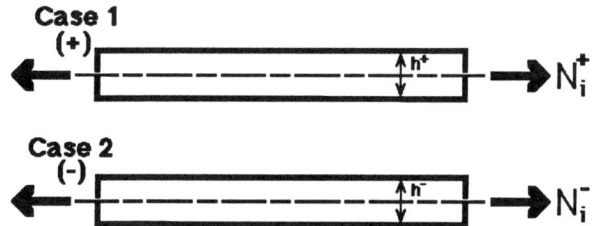

FIGURE 27.27   SCHEMATIC OF TWO PLATE MODELS SHOWING VARIABLES
DEFINING LOADING AND GEOMETRY CONDITIONS

If the same material is installed, this Mic/Mac is useful in comparing the changes resulting from one or more variables. Such display of comparative results can lead to information not readily achieved in Mic–Macs for one material. Of course when two materials are installed, comparative information is readily generated.

SEPARATE LAYUPS AND MATERIALS MODULE

MIC-MAC/DUPLEX: ([theta/#]+, . . .)S						T3/N52[SI]	Scotch[SI]
[theta]+	0.0	90.0	45.0	-45.0	[repeat]+	h+,#	h+,E-3
[#/group]+	4	0	0	0	1	8	1.00
[theta]-	0.0	90.0	45.0	-45.0	[repeat]-	h-,#	h-,E-3
[#/group]-	4	0	0	0	1	8	1.00

SEPARATE STRENGTH ANALYSIS MODULE

R+	1.50	******	******	******	R+/FPF	1.50	
R-	1.06	******	******	******	R-/FPF	1.06	

SEPARATE LOADS, AND RESULTING STRESS AND STRAIN

{N}+ MN/m or kip/in	<sig>+	<sig>+FPF	<eps>+E-3	<eps>+FPF	(E)+
1	1.00	1000.0	1500.0	5.52	8.29	181.00
2	0.00	0.0	0.0	-1.55	-2.32	10.30
6	0.00	0.0	0.0	0.00	0.00	7.17
{N}- MN/m or kip/in	<sig>-	<sig>-FPF	<eps>-E-3	<eps>-FPF	(E)-
1	1.00	1000.0	1062.0	25.91	27.51	38.60
2	0.00	0.0	0.0	-6.74	-7.15	1.26
6	0.00	0.0	0.0	0.00	0.00	0.64

SEPARATE MICROMECHANICS MODULE

	T opr,	c, moist	vol/f	Em	Efx	Xm	Xfx	Em/Em*
Baseline+	22.0	0.005	0.70	3.40	259	40.0	2143	1.00
[Modified]+	22.0	0.005	0.70	3.40	259	40.0	2143	1.00
Baseline-	22.0	0.005	0.45	3.40	86	31.0	2360	1.00
[Modified]-	22.0	0.005	0.45	0.49	86	31.0	2360	1.00

USE LOWER DEGRADATION FACTORS FOR LPF—↑

FIGURE 27.28   TYPICAL FORMAT OF TWO MATERIALS SUBJECTED TO DIFFERENT IN–PLANE LOADS.

27.21 MIC–MAC/HYBRID

This spreadsheet is used for the analysis of a symmetric laminate made with two different materials and under in–plane loading, as shown in Figure 27.29. The order of the ply groups is irrelevant to the analysis, since only in–plane loads are considered.

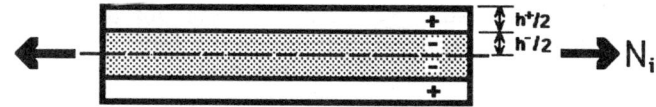

FIGURE 27.29   SCHEMATIC OF IN–PLANE MODEL SHOWING VARIABLES DEFINING LOADING AND GEOMETRY CONDITIONS

The control module of the Mic–Mac/Hybrid is shown in Figure 27.30. The format is similar to the Mic–Mac/Duplex of the last section except that the applied load must be shared by the combined laminate. The only new term is the effective quasi–isotropic Young's and shear moduli of the hybrid, which is obtained by applying the rule–of–mixtures equations to the quasi–isotropic moduli of the two laminates.

DUAL LAYUPS AND MATERIALS MODULE

MIC-MAC/HYBRID: {[theta/*]+ , ...)S					T3/N52[SI]	Scotch[SI]
[theta]+	0.0	90.0	45.0	-45.0 [repeat]+	h+, *	h, E-3
[*/group]+	4	0	0	0 1	8	2.00
[theta]-	0.0	90.0	45.0	-45.0 [repeat]-	h-, *	[Rotate]
[*/group]-	4	0	0	0 1	8	0.00

DUAL STRENGTH ANALYSIS MODULE

R+	1.85	******	******	******	R+/FPF	1.85	
R-	5.89	******	******	******	R-/FPF	5.89	

APPLIED LOAD, AND RESULTING STRESS AND STRAIN

(N) MN/m,kip/in	<sigma>	<sig>FPF	<eps>E-3	<eps>FPF		(E)	(E),Q-i
1	1.00	500.0	926.9	4.55	8.44	109.80	44.33
2	0.00	0.0	0.0	-1.23	-2.29	9.31	44.33
6	0.00	0.0	0.0	0.00	0.00	5.66	17.17

DUAL MICROMECHANICS MODULE

	T opr	c,moist	vol/f	Em	Efx	Xm	Xfx	Em/Em*
Baseline+	22.0	0.005	0.70	3.40	258.6	40.0	2142.9	1.00
[Modified]+	22.0	0.005	0.70	3.40	258.6	40.0	2142.9	1.00
Baseline-	22.0	0.005	0.45	3.40	85.8	31.0	2360.0	1.00
[Modified]-	22.0	0.005	0.45	3.40	85.8	31.0	2360.0	1.00

USE LOWER DEGRADATION FACTORS FOR LPF⏋

FIGURE 27.30   TYPICAL FORMAT OF A HYBRID OF TWO MATERIALS SUBJECTED TO A COMMON IN–PLANE LOAD.

27.22 MIC–MAC/THIN WALL

This spreadsheet is used for the analysis of a symmetric thin wall laminate, as shown in Figure 27.31. By specifying the total depth of the thin wall laminate, the percentage of core is determined. The loading consists of a moment and in–plane load applied to the entire assemblage.

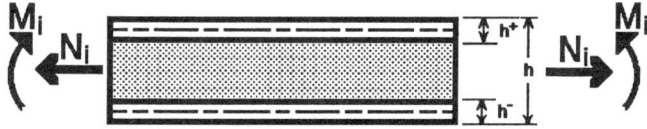

FIGURE 27.31   SCHEMATIC OF THIN WALLED PLATE MODEL SHOWING VARIABLES DEFINING LOADING AND GEOMETRY CONDITIONS

The control module of the Mic–Mac/Thin Wall is shown in Figure 27.32. The unique feature of this Mic/Mac is the resolution of the applied in–plane load and moment into in–plane load acting on the top and bottom face laminate, following Equation 9.41. Each face laminate must be symmetric. The total construction, however, can be unsymmetric. The total depth of the construction h is an input. It is assumed that the thickness of the face laminates are small compared with this total depth.

The resulting laminate stresses and strains are calculated using Equation 9.43. The other strains and effective stiffness of the total construction also follow the formulas in Section 9.9.

LAMINATE LAYUP AND STRENGTH ANALYSIS MODULE

MIC-MAC/THIN WALL: ([theta/*]+, . .S)T					T3/N52[SI]	Scotch[SI]	
[theta]+	0.0	90.0	45.0	-45.0	[rept]+	h+,*	
[*/group]+	1	0	0	0	1	2	
[theta]-	0.0	90.0	45.0	-45.0	[rept]-	h-,*	
[*/group]-	1	0	0	0	1	2	
R+	0.75	******	******	******	R+/FPF	0.75	
R-	0.53	******	******	******	R-/FPF	0.53	

		[Total h]	[Rotate]
		1.000	0.00
STRESS ANALYSIS MODULE		core,c*	
		0.9995	

(N) MN/m or kip/in	<sig>+	<sig>+FPF	<eps>+E-3	<eps>+FPF	<eps>°	<eps>°FPF	(E)+
1	1.00	2000.0	1500.0	11.05	8.29	31.43	17.90	181.00
2	0.00	0.0	0.0	-3.09	-2.32	-8.28	-4.74	10.30
6	0.00	0.0	0.0	0.00	0.00	0.00	0.00	7.17
(M) MN or kip	<sig>-	<sig>-FPF	<eps>-E-3	<eps>-FPF	<eps>f	<eps>f/FPF	(E)-
1	0.00	2000.0	1062.0	51.81	27.51	-20.38	-9.61	38.60
2	0.00	0.0	0.0	-13.47	-7.15	5.19	2.42	8.27
6	0.00	0.0	0.0	0.00	0.00	0.00	0.00	4.14

MICROMECHANICS MODULE

	T opr	c,moist	vol/f	Em	Efx	Xm	Xfx	Em/Em°
Baseline+	22.0	0.005	0.70	3.40	259	40.0	2143	1.00
[Modified]+	22.0	0.005	0.70	3.40	259	40.0	2143	1.00
Baseline-	22.0	0.005	0.45	3.40	86	40.0	2360	1.00
[Modified]-	22.0	0.005	0.45	3.40	86	40.0	2360	1.00

FIGURE 27.32   TYPICAL FORMAT OF A THIN WALL CONSTRUCTION OF ONE OR TWO
MATERIALS SUBJECTED TO IN–PLANE AND BENDING LOADS.

27.23 CHART–QUICK

Chart–quick is a macro spreadsheet useful for conducting sensitivity studies
with the Mic–Mac spreadsheets on the Apple Macintosh. A Mic–Mac
spreadsheet should be opened and have input values consistent with the
problem that is to be evaluated. Chart–quick must also be opened. The user
must input four values into column G, rows 2 through 5, as defined by
Column F, rows 2 through 5. Chart–quick is executed by selecting RUN
from the MACRO menu, and then selecting Chart–quick from the list of
macros.

For example, the sensitivity of the in–plane and flexural moduli of a [0/90]
laminate can be examined due to the effect of increasing the repeat index, i.e.
the number of sublaminates. The Mic–Mac/Flex spreadsheet must be opened
and a [0/90] laminate must be specified. Since the load conditions have no
effect on the moduli, their input values are arbitrary. Since the
micromechanics inputs and the safety factor are not the focus of this study,
their default values are suitable.

In the Chart–quick spreadsheet, the range of the repeat index is chosen to be
from 1 to 10, with a total of 10 equally spaced points examined in that range.
The START FLAG should be set to 0 to indicate that this will be the initial
run of a new problem. Having set the scenario, the macro is ready to be
executed.

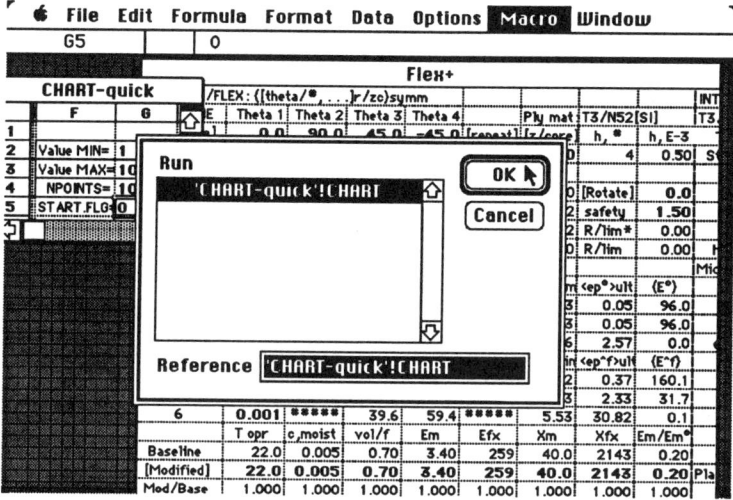

Once the Chart–quick macro is selected, the macro begins by asking which Mic–Mac spreadsheet should be used for the calculations. The user must type in exactly the name of the spreadsheet.

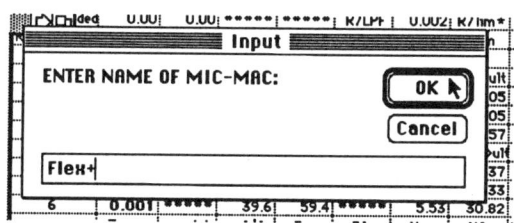

Next, the user must specify the independent variable. This is most simply accomplished by clicking on the cell displaying the independent variable in the Mic–Mac, as opposed to explicitly typing out the cell location. Note that the macro's INPUT dialog box can be moved by dragging the title bar, if it is in a bad location on the screen and covering a pertinent part of the Mic–Mac. Similarly, the scroll bars on the Mic–Mac are functional and can be used to select an independent variable not necessarily located in the control module of the Mic–Mac. In the example being considered, the repeat index, located in row F, column 4, is selected.

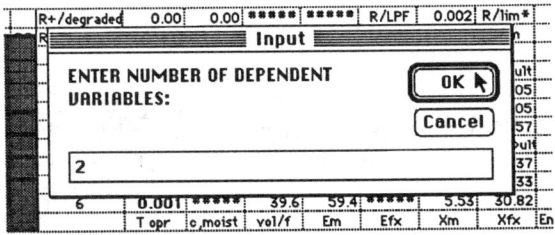

A number of dependent variables, up to three, must be specified. In this example, two dependent variables will be examined, namely the flexural modulus and the in–plane modulus both along the 1–axis, and is so indicated.

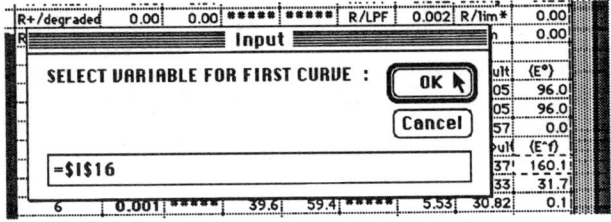

Similar to the identification process for the independent variable, the dependent variable can be selected by clicking on the cell in the Mic–Mac spreadsheet that shows its value. In this example, the data cell in Mic–Mac/Flex showing the flexural modulus, E1f is selected.

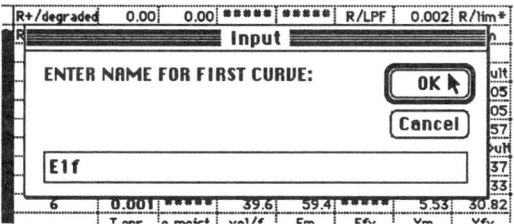

Similar requests to select a variable and enter a name for the curve follow for the remaining dependent variables. Up to three dependent variables can be specified.

After all the inputs have been made, the macro proceeds through an iterative process of changing the independent variable in the spreadsheet, allowing it to recalculate, and then reading and storing the values of the dependent variables. When the iterations are complete, the collected data are used to generate an x–y chart, complete with a legend. There are many sensitivity charts in Section 29 generated in this manner. This chart showing flexural stiffnesses versus repeating index for a [0/90] laminate, in fact, is the basis of one shown in Subsection 29.5.

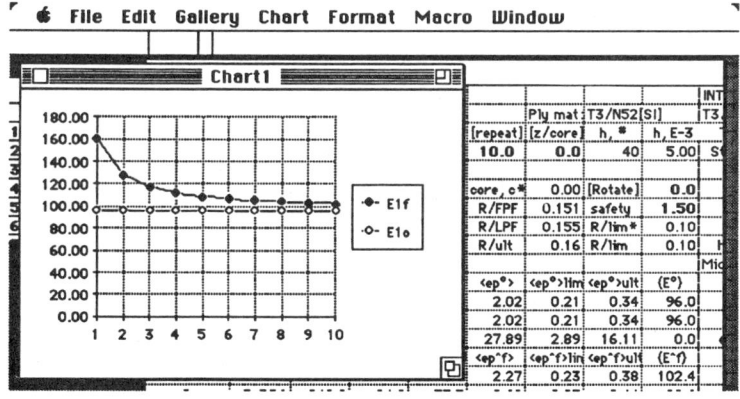

27.24 CONCLUSIONS

We have described briefly the use of spreadsheets for performing integrated micro–macromechanics analysis. We have found that the most important feature of this approach includes the accessibility of inputs without being constrained by a prescribed sequence. Programming is easy because only algebra is used. Calculations can be easily changed. Calculation is fast. Above all, spreadsheets are easy to learn. We therefore recommend users to consider spreadsheets as an alternative method of computation. While we all can program our own spreadsheet, we recommend purchasing ready–made software as a cost–effective, if not less frustrating, way to rationally analyze and design composite materials. In addition, data generated from spreadsheets are easily plotted, and macros are available for sensitivity studies.

27.25 EXERCISES FOR MIC-MAC SPREADSHEETS

The following is a set of simple exercises designed to aid the user in becoming acquainted with the use and format of the Mic-Mac spreadsheets. The attached answers include a printout of the appropriate control module section of the spreadsheet used to solve the problems. Before working these problems, the user should have read the general documentation at the beginning of Section 27 to become acquainted with the capability of each spreadsheet and how to vary the material being analyzed. For all the exercises a safety factor of $SF = 1.5$ is used.

Exercise 1. Plate Under In-Plane Loading. For a $[0_2/90/\pm45]_s$ laminate of T300/N5208 Graphite/Epoxy supporting an in-plane load of 0.175 MN/m under baseline hygrothermal conditions (Operating temperature $T_0=122°C$, moisture content c=0.5 percent by weight), find the following.
a) What is the thickness of the laminate?
b) Which ply group fails first?
c) What is the average longitudinal stress?
d) What is the average transverse strain?

Solution.

1. The problem calls for the analysis of a laminated plate with an in-plane load. This type of analysis is covered in the **In-Plane** MIC-MAC Module. After opening the in-plane analysis module, make T300/N5208 the linked material by running the macro "Mat!:T3/N52[SI]". Row 2, column H should indicate **T3/N52[SI]** as shown below.
2. The next step is to enter the ply angles of the layup, $[0_2/90/\pm45]_s$, of the laminate into row 3, columns B through E.
3. Next the number of plies in each repeating laminate is entered into row 4, columns B through E. The number of plies is entered directly below its associated layup, with a zero entered below any column which is not used. A one is entered into row 4, column F to signify one repeat of the symmetric laminate.
4. The next step is to enter the required loads. These are input in column B, rows 10 through 12. Column A, rows 10 through 12 show the references for the loads. For this problem, 0.175 is entered into row 10, column B and zeros are entered into the remaining locations.

	A	B	C	D	E	F	G	H	I
1	MIC-MAC/IN-PLANE: ([theta/#],...)symm								
2	READ ME	Theta 1	Theta 2	Theta 3	Theta 4		Ply mat	T3/N52[SI]	
3	[ply angle]	0.0	90.0	45.0	-45.0	[repeat]	h, #	h, E-3	[Rotate]
4	[ply #]	2.0	1.0	1.0	1.0	1.0	10.0	1.3	0.00
5									
6	R/intact	5.64	3.08	3.62	3.62	R/FPF	3.08	safety	1.50
7	R/degrade	5.49	6.10	9.55	9.55	R/LPF	5.49	R/lim*	3.66
8						R/ult	5.49	R/lim	3.08
9	(N), MN/m or k/in	(N)	(N)lim	(N)lim*	(N)ult	(E°)lim	E^ul/E^lr	<alph>E-6	<beta>
10	1	0.175	0.539	0.641	0.961	91.941	0.943	0.925	0.0241
11	2	0.000	0.000	0.000	0.000	59.589	0.894	2.374	0.0628
12	6	0.000	0.000	0.000	0.000	22.938	0.852	0.000	0.0000
13									
14		<sq°>	<sq°>lim	<sq°>lim	<sq°>ult	<ep°>E-3	<ep°>lim	<ep°>lim*	<ep°>ult
15	1	140.	431.	513.	769.	1.52	4.69	5.91	8.87
16	2	0.	0.	0.	0.	-0.45	-1.39	-1.86	-2.78
17	6	0.	0.	0.	0.	0.00	0.00	0.00	0.00
18				<sq°>netting	1.28				
19		T opr	c,moist	vol/f	Em	Efx	Xm	Xfx	Em/Em°
20	Baseline	22.0	0.005	0.70	3.40	259	40.0	2143	0.20
21	[Modified]	22.0	0.005	0.70	3.40	259	40.0	2143	0.20

5. This completes the input of the data for this case. After the spreadsheet completes its calculations the following answers are read.
   a. The laminate is **1.3 x 10⁻³ m** thick as indicated in row 4 column H. Note that thickness on the spreadsheet is given in mils.
   b. The **90° plies** will fail first. The information on first ply failure can be found by comparing the first ply failure R values shown in row 6, columns B through E, directly below the layup information. The laminate with the lowest values will fail first.
   c. The average longitudinal stress is **140 MPa.** The longitudinal information is in row 15, with the average stress in column B.
   d. The average strain in the transverse direction is **–0.45 x 10⁻³ m/m.** The transverse information is in row 16 with the average strain in column F.

Exercise 2.   Plate Under In–Plane and Hygrothermal Loading.
Repeat Exercise 1, but assume an operating temperature of 122°C and 1 percent moisture content.

Solution.

1. All conditions except moisture and temperature are the same for this and Exercise 1. Therefore follow the first 4 steps of the previous exercise to start.
2. The information on baseline properties is listed in row 20 with labels of the property directly above. Changes from the baseline are input in row 21 as [modified]. For this problem, 122 is entered into row 21, column B for temperature and 0.01 is entered into row 21, column C for 1 percent moisture content.

	A	B	C	D	E	F	G	H	I
1	MIC-MAC/IN-PLANE: [(theta/#], . . .]symm								
2	READ ME	Theta 1	Theta 2	Theta 3	Theta 4		Ply mat:	T3/N52[SI]	
3	[ply angle]	0.0	90.0	45.0	-45.0	[repeat]	h, #	h, E-3	[Rotate]
4	[ply#]	2.0	1.0	1.0	1.0	1.0	10.0	1.3	0.00
5									
6	R/intact	3.64	4.80	2.43	2.43	R/FPF	2.43	safety	1.50
7	R/degrade	6.40	5.42	6.12	6.12	R/LPF	5.42	R/lim*	3.62
8						R/ult	5.42	R/lim	2.43
9	(N), MN/m	or k/in	(N)lim	(N)lim*	(N]ult	[(E°)lim	E^ul/E^lr	<alph>E-6	<beta>
10	1	0.175	0.42	0.63	0.95	89.2	0.954	0.677	0.018
11	2	0.000	0.00	0.00	0.00	56.7	0.914	1.799	0.047
12	6	0.000	0.00	0.00	0.00	21.4	0.879	0.000	0.000
13									
14		<sg°>	<sg°>lim	<sg°>lim	<sg°>ult	<ep°>E-3	<ep°>lim	<ep°>lim*	<ep°>ult
15	1	140.	340.	506.	759.	1.57	3.81	5.95	8.92
16	2	0.	0.	0.	0.	-0.48	-1.17	-1.91	-2.87
17	6	0.	0.	0.	0.	0.00	0.00	0.00	0.00
18				<sg°>net	1.27				
19		T opr	c,moist	vol/f	Em	Efx	Xm	Xfx	Em/Em°
20	Baseline	22.0	0.005	0.70	3.40	259	40.0	2143	0.20
21	[Modified]	122.0	0.010	0.70	3.40	259	40.0	2143	0.20

3. After the spreadsheet completes calculation, the results are read as follows:

   a. The laminate is **1.3 x 10⁻³ m** thick as indicated in row 4 column H. Note that thickness on the spreadsheet is given in mils.
   b. The **±45° plies** will now fail first. The information on first ply failure can be found by comparing the first ply failure R values shown in row 6 directly below the layup information. The ply with the lowest values will fail first.
   c. The average longitudinal stress is **140 MPa**. The longitudinal information is in row 15, with the average stress in column B.
   d. The average strain in the transverse direction is **–0.48 x 10⁻³ m/m**. The transverse strain information is in row 16 with the ultimate in column F.

Exercise 3. Circular Tubing. For an 0.457 m long, 0.0254 m outer diameter *round* thin walled tube supported as a cantilever beam under a 0.00175 MN/m distributed load, find the following items. Assume baseline hygrothermal conditions and a [0₆/±60]₂ₛ layup of Kevlar 49/Epoxy.
a) Which ply group fails first?
b) What is the area moment of inertia of the cross-section?
c) What is the end deflection at the ultimate load?

Solution.

1. The problem calls for the analysis of a thin walled tube. This type of analysis is covered in the **Tubing** MIC–MAC Module. After opening the Tubing analysis module, make Kevlar49/Epoxy the linked material by running the macro "Mat!:Kev/ep[SI]". Row 2, column H should indicate **Kev/ep[SI]** as shown below.

	A	B	C	D	E	F	G	H	I	J
1	MIC-MAC/RECT[ ] & ELLIP( ) TUBING: ([theta/#]...)symm									
2	READ ME	Theta 1	Theta 2	Theta 3	Theta 4		Ply mat	Kev/ep[SI]		
3	[ply angle]	0.0	60.0	-60.0	90.0	[repeat]	h, *	h, E-3	[Rotate]	
4	[ply #]	6	1	1	0	2.0	32.00	4.0	0.0	
5										
6	R/intact	3.05	2.88	2.88	*****	R/FPF	2.88	safety	1.50	
7	R/degraded	1.67	67.93	67.93	*****	R/LPF	1.67	R/lim*	1.92	
8	Size, m or in	inertia,I				R/ult	2.88	R/lim	1.92	
9	[Length L]	0.457	[rect]		$\partial[\ ]$,E-3	$\partial[]$/max	R[ ]	$\partial()$,E-3	$\partial()$/max	R( )
10	[Depth a]	0.025	4.2E-08	CANTILEVER						
11	[Width b]	0.025	(ellip)	limit	3.9223	7.52	1.92	6.6587	7.52	1.13
12	a/b	1.00	2.5E-08	ult	4.0108	11.53	2.88	6.8089	11.53	1.69
13	Applied loads		SIMPLY SUPPORTED/SS							
14	[conc P]	0.0		limit	0.4086	3.13	7.67	0.6936	3.13	4.52
15	[distrib q]	1.8E-3	<sg°>lim	ult	0.4178	4.81	11.50	0.7093	4.81	6.78
16			105.1	FIXED/FIXED						
17	<E°>intact	58.4	<sg°>ult	limit	0.0817	0.94	11.50	0.139	0.94	6.78
18	<E°>degrade	57.1	157.7	ult	0.0836	1.44	17.25	0.142	1.44	10.16
19		T opr	c,moist	vol/f	Em	Efx	Xm	Xfx	Em/Em°	
20	Baseline	22.0	0.005	0.60	3.40	127	12.0	2333	0.02	
21	[Modified]	22.0	0.005	0.60	3.40	127	12.0	2333	0.02	

2. The next step is to enter the layup, $[0_6/\pm60]_{2s}$, of the laminate into row 3, columns B through E. Note that it does not matter what is entered in the column for the fourth possible laminate when less than four ply angles are used.

3. Next, the number of plies is entered into row 4, columns B through E. The number of plies is entered directly below its associated layup, with a zero entered below the column which is not used. A two is entered into row 4 column F, to signify the 2 repeats of the layup.

4. The next step is to enter the tubes dimensions. These are input in column B, rows 9 through 11. Column A, rows 9 through 11 show the reference for the dimensions. For this problem 0.457 is entered into row 9, column B for the length of the tube. The program is setup for an elliptical tube with a being the depth and b being the width. For the round tube, 0.0254 is entered for both dimensions in column B, rows 10 and 11.

5. Next the distributed load of 0.00175 MN/m is entered into column B, row 15. A zero is entered into column B, row 14 because there is no concentrated end load on the tube.

6. This completes the input of the data for this case. After the spreadsheet completes its calculations the answers are read directly.

    a. The **±60° plies** will now fail first. The information on first ply failure can be found by comparing the first ply failure R values shown in row 6 directly below the layup information. The ply with the lowest values will fail first.

    b. The area moment of inertia of the cross section is **2.5 x 10^{-4} m^4**. This can be read from row 12, column C. The notational reference is above. The normal parentheses () signify the elliptical cross section. Note that the square brackets [] signify the results from calculations for a rectangular cross section.

    c. The tube will deflect **6.8089 x 10^{-3} m** at ultimate load. This information is in row 12, column H.

Exercise 4.   Rectangular Tubing. For a 0.457 m long, 0.0254 m *square* thin walled tube supported as a cantilever beam under a 0.00175 MN/m distributed load, find the following items. Assume baseline hygrothermal conditions and a $[0_6/\pm60]_{2s}$ layup of Kevlar 49/Epoxy.

a) Which ply group fails first?
b) What is the area moment of inertia of the cross–section?
c) What is the end deflection at the ultimate load?

Solution.

1. The inputs for this problem are exactly the same as Exercise 4. The only difference is how you think about them. Ply layups, number of plies, material and tube length are the same. For depth and width in this case, *a* and *b* correspond to the sides of the rectangular tube.

	A	B	C	D	E	F	G	H	I	J
1	MIC-MAC/RECT[ ] & ELLIP( ) TUBING : ([theta/#]...)symm									
2	READ ME	Theta 1	Theta 2	Theta 3	Theta 4		Ply mat	Kev/ep[SI]		
3	[ply angle]	0.0	60.0	-60.0	90.0	[repeat]	h, *	32.00	h, E-3	[Rotate]
4	[ply #]	6	1	1	0	2.0	32.00	4.0	0.0	
5										
6	R/intact	3.05	2.88	2.88	*****	R/FPF	2.88	safety	1.50	
7	R/degraded	1.67	67.93	67.93	*****	R/LPF	1.67	R/lim*	1.92	
8	Size, m or in		inertia,I			R/ult	2.88	R/lim	1.92	
9	[Length L]	0.457	[rect]		∂[ ],E-3	∂[]/max	R[ ]	∂() E-3	∂()/max	R( )
10	[Depth a]	0.025	4.2E-08	CANTILEVER						
11	[Width b]	0.025	(ellip)	limit	3.9223	7.52	1.92	6.6587	7.52	1.13
12	a/b	1.00	2.5E-08	ult	4.0108	11.53	2.88	6.8089	11.53	1.69
13	Applied loads			SIMPLY SUPPORTED/SS						
14	[conc P]	0.0		limit	0.4086	3.13	7.67	0.6936	3.13	4.52
15	[distrib q]	1.8E-3	<sq°>lim	ult	0.4178	4.81	11.50	0.7093	4.81	6.78
16			105.1	FIXED/FIXED						
17	<E°>intact	58.4	<sq°>ult	limit	0.0817	0.94	11.50	0.139	0.94	6.78
18	<E°>degrade	57.1	157.7	ult	0.0836	1.44	17.25	0.142	1.44	10.16
19		T opr	c,moist	vol/f	Em	Efx	Xm	Xfx	Em/Em°	
20	Baseline	22.0	0.005	0.60	3.40	127	12.0	2333	0.02	
21	[Modified]	22.0	0.005	0.60	3.40	127	12.0	2333	0.02	

2. This completes the input of the data for this case. After the spreadsheet completes its calculations the answers are read directly. For the rectangular cross section, the data with the square brackets [] are read.

   a. The ±60° **plies** will fail first. The information on first ply failure can be found by comparing the first ply failure R values shown in row 6 directly below the layup information. The ply with the lowest values will fail first.

   b. The area moment of inertia of the cross section is **4.2 x 10⁻⁸ m⁴.** This can be read from row 10, column C. The notational reference is directly above the answer. The square brackets [] signify the results for a rectangular cross section. Note that the normal parentheses () signify the results from the same calculation for an elliptical cross section.

   c. The tube will deflect **4.0108 x 10⁻³ m** at ultimate load. This information is in row 12, column E.

Exercise 5.   Pressure Vessel. For a pressure vessel 0.610 m long and 0.152 m in diameter, under axial loading of 0.002225 MN, internal pressure of 3.445 MPa and an applied torque of 0.000056 MNm, find the following. Assume baseline hygrothermal conditions and a $[0_7/90/\pm45]_{5T}$ layup of E–Glass/Epoxy.

a) Which ply group fails first?
b) Which ply group precipitates final laminate failure?
d) How much will the diameter increase under these loading conditions?
c) What is the angle of twist of the pressure vessel?
e) In the hoop direction, what is the average strain due to the given loading, and the maximum possible strains for this laminate according to the rules governing limit, limit* and ultimate?

Solution.

1. The problem calls for the analysis of a pressure vessel. This type of analysis is covered in the **Vessel** MIC–MAC Module. After opening the Vessel analysis module, make E–glass/Epoxy the linked material by running the macro "Mat!:Scotch[SI]". Row 2, column H should indicate **Scotch[SI]** as shown below.

	A	B	C	D	E	F	G	H	I
1	MIC-MAC/CYLIN VESSEL : {[theta/*], . . .}total								
2	READ ME	Theta 1	Theta 2	Theta 3	Theta 4		Ply mat:	Scotch[SI]	
3	[ply angle]	0.0	90.0	45.0	-45.0	[repeat]	h,*	h, E-3	[Rotate]
4	[ply*]	7	1	1	1	5.0	50.0	6.3	0.00
5									
6	R/intact	1.44	5.16	2.26	2.22	R/FPF	1.44	safety	1.50
7	R/degraded	9.01	4.18	7.02	7.18	R/LPF	4.18	R/lim*	2.79
8						R/ult	4.18	R/lim	1.44
9	size, m or in	ΔL,ΔD,E-3			<sq>	<sq>lim	<sq>lim*	<sq>ult	(E°)lim
10	[Length]	0.61	0.21	1	22.	31.	61.	91.	30.7
11	[Diameter]	0.15	0.47	2	42.	60.	117.	175.	12.8
12	Angle of twist,deg	0.02		6	0.	0.	1.	1.	5.5
13									
14		[Load]	[Load] lim		<ep>E-3	<ep>lim	<ep>lim*	<ep>ult	E"u/E"l
15	Axial load F	2.2E-3	0.00	1	0.34	0.49	0.88	1.32	0.93
16	Pressure P	3.445	4.97	2	3.08	4.44	18.24	27.37	0.48
17	Torque	5.6E-5	0.00	6	0.05	0.07	0.31	0.47	0.40
18									
19		T opr	o,moist	vol/f	Em	Efx	Xm	Xfx	Em/Em°
20	Baseline	22.0	0.005	0.45	3.40	86	31.0	2360	0.07
21	[Modified]	22.0	0.005	0.45	3.40	86	31.0	2360	0.07

2. The next step is to enter the plies of each repeating laminate, $[0_7/90/\pm45]_{5T}$, into row 3, columns B through E.
3. Next the number of plies is entered into row 4, columns B through E. The number of plies is entered directly below its associated layup. A 5 is input into row 4, column F for the five repeats of the laminate
4. The next step is to enter the dimensions of the vessel. These are input in column B, rows 10 and 11.
5. Next, the loads are input into column B, with the longitudinal load in row 15, the pressure load in row 16 and the torque in row 17.
6. This completes the input of the data for this case. After the spreadsheet completes its calculations the answers are read.

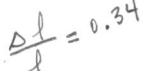

$$\frac{\Delta l}{l} = 0.34$$

a. The **0° plies** will fail first. The information on first ply failure can be found by comparing the first ply failure R values shown in row 6 directly below the layup information. The ply with the lowest values will fail first, and for easy reference is shown as the FPF strength ratio in row 6, column G..

b. The **90° plies** fail first in LPF. This is obtained by comparing the R values in row 7. The lowest indicates the first to fail and for easy reference is shown as the LPF strength ratio in row 7, column G.

c. The increase in diameter is **0.47 x 10⁻³ m** (row 11, column C).

d. The twist/angle is **0.02 degrees** (row 12, column C).

e. The transverse strains are ε_o = **0.00308 m/m**, ε_{lim} = **0.00444 m/m**, ε_{lim*} = **0.01824 m/m** and ε_{ult} = **0.02737 m/m**. These are found in row 17, columns E through H.

Exercise 6. Beam. For a honeycomb sandwich beam 0.305 m long and 0.0254 m wide, with a distributed load of 0.000875 MN/m, find the following. Assume baseline hygrothermal conditions and a $[0/90]_{3s}$ layup of Boron/Epoxy B4/N5505. The total core thickness is 0.005 m, the equivalent thickness of 40 plies.

a) Which ply group fails first?

b) If the beam is simply–supported at both ends under the given loading, what is the maximum mid–span displacement of the beam at the first sign of failure?

c) If the beam is fixed at both ends, how much can the current loading be increased before the ultimate strength of the laminate is attained?

d) If the beam is fixed at both ends and evaluated under the ultimate load supportable by this laminate, what then is the maximum mid–span displacement ?

Solution.

1. The problem calls for the analysis of a loaded beam. This type of analysis is covered in the **Beam** MIC–MAC Module. After opening the beam analysis module, make Boron/Epoxy the linked material by running the macro "Mat!:B4/N55[SI]". Row 2, column H should indicate **B4/N55[SI]** as shown below.

2. The next step is to enter the layup of each repeating laminate, $[0/90]_{3s}$, into row 3, columns B and C. Note that is does not matter what is input into columns D and E when two layups are used.

3. Next the number of plies is entered into row 4, columns B through E. The number of plies is entered directly below its associated layup, with a zero entered in columns which are not used. A three in then entered into row 4, column F to signify the 3 repeats of the laminate.

4. A 20 is entered into row 4, column G for the core thickness. The value entered represents the half core thickness in terms of equivalent ply thickness. In this case the desired total core thickness is 0.005 m.

5. The next step is to enter the dimensions of the beam. 0.305 is entered into column B, row 9 for the length and 0.0254 is entered into column B, row 10 for the width.
6. Finally, the 0.000875 distributed load is input into row 13, column B.

	A	B	C	D	E	F	G	H	I
1	MIC-MAC/BEAM: ([theta/*], . . .)symm								
2	READ ME	Theta 1	Theta 2	Theta 3	Theta 4		Ply mat	B4/N55[SI]	
3	[ply angle]	0.0	90.0	45.0	-45.0	[repeat]	[z/core]	h, *	h, E-3
4	[ply *]	1	1	0	0	3.0	20.0	52.0	6.5
5									
6	R/intact	1.59	1.04	*****	*****	R/FPF	1.04	safety	1.50
7	R/degraded	1.59	3.02	*****	*****	R/LPF	1.59	R/lim*	1.06
8	size, m or in	Inertia, I				R/ult	1.59	R/lim	1.04
9	[Length L]	0.305	6E-10		b, E-3	b/max	R	P/max	q/max
10	[Width b]	0.025		CANTILEVER					
11	applied loads	<sig>f	limit	26.256	27.39	1.04	0.000	0.001
12	[conc P]	0.000	231.	ult	27.819	44.30	1.59	0.000	0.001
13	[distrib q]	8.8E-4	<sig>lim	SIMPLY SUPPORTED/SS					
14			241.	limit	2.735	11.41	4.17	0.000	0.004
15	<E>f/intact	63.01	<sig>ult	ult	2.8978	18.46	6.37	0.000	0.006
16	<E>f/degrad	59.47	368.	FIXED/FIXED					
17	% core, c*	0.77		limit	0.547	3.42	6.26	0.000	0.005
18				ult	0.5796	5.14	9.56	0.000	0.008
19		T opr	c,moist	vol/f	Em	Efx	Xm	Xfx	Em/Em*
20	Baseline	22.0	0.005	0.50	3.40	408	61.0	2520	0.30
21	[Modified]	22.0	0.005	0.50	3.40	408	61.0	2520	0.30

7. This completes the input of the data for this case. After the spreadsheet completes its calculations the answers are read.
   a. For cantilever loading, the **90° ply** will fail first. This is again found by comparing the R values in row 6. In this case the R value is marginally greater than one, which indicates the beam will fail at just more than the specified load for the cantilevered beam case.
   b. The mid-span displacement for the simply supported case is **2.735 x 10⁻³ m** (row 14, column E).
   c. The strength ratio, as indicated by the heading in row 9 column G, at ultimate load, as indicated by the heading in row 18 column D, for the fixed/fixed case is **9.56** (row 18, column G).
   d. For the fixed/fixed case, the maximum deflection at ultimate is **5.14 x 10⁻³ m** (row 18, column F).

Exercise 7.   Plate in Bending.   For a honeycomb sandwich laminate subjected to an in-plane load of 0.175 MN/m each in the transverse and longitudinal directions, and an additional flexural load of 0.00445 MPa in the longitudinal direction, find the following.   Assume baseline hygrothermal conditions and a $[0/90/\pm45]_{8s}$ layup of Kevlar49/Epoxy for each laminate skin. The core thickness is 0.025 m, the equivalent thickness of 200 plies.
a) Which ply group will fail first?
b) What are the average values of in-plane transverse stress and strain due to the applied loads?
c) What are the longitudinal flexural stress and strain due to the applied loads? What is the longitudinal flexural modulus?

Solution.

1. The problem calls for the analysis of a laminated plate with an in–plane load and a flexural load. This type of analysis is covered in the **Flex** MIC–MAC Module. After opening the Flex analysis module, make Kevlar49/Epoxy the linked material by running the macro "Mat!:Kev/ep[SI]". Row 2, column H should indicate **Kev49/ep[SI]** as shown below.

	A	B	C	D	E	F	G	H	I
1	MIC-MAC/FLEX: ([theta/*₁....)r/zc)symm								
2	READ ME	Theta 1	Theta 2	Theta 3	Theta 4		Ply mat	Kev/ep[SI]	
3	[ply angle]	0.0	90.0	45.0	-45.0	[repeat]	[z/core]	h, *	h, E-3
4	[ply *]	1	1	1	1	8.0	100.0	264	33.00
5									
6	R+/intact	7.49	0.96	2.15	2.18	core, c*	0.76	[Rotate]	0.0
7	R-/intact	1.48	11.02	7.18	7.10	R/FPF	0.958	safety	1.50
8	R+/degraded	8.13	26.74	15.78	15.72	R/LPF	1.531	R/lim*	1.02
9	R-/degraded	1.53	16.84	162.68	146.94	R/ult	1.53	R/lim	0.96
10									
11	(N) MN/m or kip/in	<sg°>	<sg°>lim	<sg°>ult	<ep°>	<ep°>lim	<ep°>ult	{E°}	
12	1	0.175	5.3	5.1	8.1	0.51	0.49	0.88	7.0
13	2	0.175	5.3	5.1	8.1	0.51	0.49	0.88	7.0
14	6	0.000	0.0	0.0	0.0	0.00	0.00	0.00	0.3
15	(M) MN or kip	<sg^f>	<sg^f>lim	<sg^f>ult	<ep^f>	<ep^f>lim	<ep^f>ult	{E^f}	
16	1	4.5E-3	24.8	23.7	38.0	1.49	1.43	2.59	16.6
17	2	0	0.0	0.0	0.0	-0.48	-0.46	-0.84	16.5
18	6	0	0.0	0.0	0.0	-0.01	-0.01	-0.01	0.3
19		T opr	o,moist	vol/f	Em	Efx	Xm	Xfx	Em/Em°
20	Baseline	22.0	0.005	0.60	3.40	127	12.0	2333	0.02
21	[Modified]	22.0	0.005	0.60	3.40	127	12.0	2333	0.02

2. The next step is to enter the layup of each repeating laminate, $[0/90/\pm45]_{8s}$, into row 3, columns B through E.
3. Next the number of plies is entered into row 4, columns B through E. The number of plies is entered directly below its associated layup. An 8 is then entered into row 4, column F to signify the 8 repeats of the laminate.
4. A 100 is entered into row 4, column G for the core thickness. Each unit entered into this location adds a core thickness equivalent to twice the nominal ply thickness of the composite material. In this case, a 100 is entered as the half core thickness which equates to the desired 0.025 m total core thickness, 200 times the nominal ply thickness.
5. The next step is to enter the required loads. The in–plane loads are input in column B, rows 12 through 14. Column A, rows 12 through 14 show the references for the loads. The flexural loads are input in column B, rows 16 through 18. Column A, rows 16 through 18 show the references for the loads.
6. This completes the input of the data for this case. After the spreadsheet completes its calculations, the answers are read.
   a. For cantilever loading the **90° ply in the upper skin of the honeycomb laminate** will fail first. This is found by comparing the R values in row 6 and 7. The R+ values are for the upper skin and the R− values are for the lower. The lowest value will fail first and defines the strength ratio at FPF, indicated in row 7, column G.

b. The average transverse in–plane stress is **5.3 MPa** (row 13, column C) and the transverse in–plane strain is **0.00051 in/in** (row 13, column F).

c. The longitudinal flexural stress is **24.8 MPa** (row 16, column C) and the longitudinal flexural strain is **0.00149 m/m** (row 16, column F). The longitudinal flexural modulus is **16.6 GPa** (row 16, column I).

Exercise 8. Hybrid Plate. For a Hybrid laminate with the outer plies consisting of AS4/PEEK in a $[0_2/90/\pm45]_{2s}$ layup and the inner plies consisting of T300/N5208 in a $[0/90]_{2s}$ layup, find the following. Consider that transverse and longitudinal loads of 0.00445 MPa each are applied under baseline hygrothermal conditions.
a) What is the thickness of the laminate?
b) Which ply group will fail first?
c) What are the average stress and strain in the transverse and longitudinal directions?
d) What are the longitudinal and transverse moduli?

Solution.

1. The problem calls for the analysis of a hybrid laminated plate with an in–plane load. This type of analysis is covered in the **Hybrid** MIC–MAC Module. After opening the Hybrid analysis module, make Kevlar49/Epoxy the linked material by running the macro "MatTop!:AS4/PK[SI] and "MatBot!:T3/N52[SI]". Row 1, columns G and I should indicate **AS4/PK[SI]** and **T3/N52[SI]**, respectively, as shown below.

	A	B	C	D	E	F	G	H	I
1	MIC-MAC/HYBRID :([theta/●...]+, [theta/●...]-)symn					Ply mat+	AS4/PK[S	Ply mat-	T3/N52[S
2	READ ME	Theta 1	Theta 2	Theta 3	Theta 4				
3	[ply angle]+	0.0	90.0	45.0	-45.0	[repeat]+	h+, ●	h, E-3	[rotate]+
4	[ply ●]+	2	1	1	1	2.0	20.00	3.50	0.00
5	[ply angle]-	0.0	90.0	45.0	-45.0	[repeat]-	h- ●	[rotate]tot	[rotate]-
6	[ply ●]-	1	1	0	0	2.0	8.00	0.00	0.00
7									
8	R+	25.06	18.78	21.49	21.49	min R+	18.78	min R	8.87
9	R-	10.36	8.87	●●●●●●	●●●●●●	min R-	8.87		
10									
11	(N) MN/m, kip/in		<sq●>	<sq●>Fail	<ep●>E-3	<ep●>Fail	(E●)	(E●), Q-iso	(alph)E-6
12	1	0.175	50.0	443.6	0.57	5.03	73.12	50.80	0.05
13	2	0.175	50.0	443.6	0.80	7.09	54.60	50.80	0.32
14	6	0	0.0	0.0	0.00	0.00	10.58	19.23	0.00
15									
16		T opr	c, moist	vol/f	Em	Efx	Xm	Xfx	Em/Em●
17	Baseline+	22.0	0.000	0.66	3.40	203.0	80.0	3227	0.10
18	[Modified]+	22.0	0.000	0.66	3.40	203.0	80.0	3227	0.10
19	Baseline-	22.0	0.005	0.70	3.40	258.6	40.0	2143	0.20
20	[Modified]-	22.0	0.005	0.70	3.40	258.6	40.0	2143	0.20

2. The next step is to enter the layups. Row 3, columns B through E contains the information of the first material and row 5, columns B through E contains the information for the second material. The

$[0_2/90/\pm45]_{2s}$ is entered for the first material and $[0/90]_{2s}$ is entered for the second.

3. Next the number of plies is entered into row 4, columns B through E and row 6, columns B through E. The number of plies is entered directly below its associated layup, with a zero entered below any column which is not used. Finally a 2 is entered into column F, rows 4 and 6 for the two repeats of each laminate in the layup.

4. The next step is to enter the required loads. These are input in column B, rows 12 through 14. Column A, rows 12 through 14 show the references for the loads. For this problem, 0.175 is entered into row 12, column B; 0.175 is entered into row 13, column B; and a zero is entered into row 14, column B.

5. This completes the input of the data for this case. After the spreadsheet completes its calculations the answers are read directly.

   a. The laminate is **3.5 x 10⁻³ m** thick (refer to row 4, column H).

   b. The **0° ply in the AS4/PK** will fail first. The information on first ply failure can be found by comparing the first ply failure R values shown in row 8 and 9 directly below the layup information. Row 8 contains the information for the first laminate and row 9 contains the information for the second. The laminate layer with the lowest value will fail first.

   c. The longitudinal stress is **50 MPa** (row 12, column C) and the longitudinal strain is **0.00057 m/m** (row 12, column E). The transverse stress is **50 MPa** (row 13, column C) and the transverse strain is **0.00080 m/m** (row 13, column E).

   d. The longitudinal modulus is **73.12 GPa** (row 12, column G) and the transverse modulus is **54.60 GPa** (row 13, column G).

Section 28

INTERNATIONAL OUTLINE

28.1 ENGLISH OUTLINE

1

SIMPLIFIED DESIGN OF COMPOSITE MATERIALS

A set of working tools for designers

Stephen W. Tsai
USAF Materials Laboratory
AFWAL/MLBM, WPAFB, OH 45433–6533
Telephone: (513) 255–3068

REFERENCES

Stephen W. Tsai
Composites Design–1987
Think Composites, Dayton, Ohio (1987)

Stephen W. Tsai and H. Thomas Hahn
Introduction to Composite Materials
Technomic, Lancaster, Pa. (1985)

2

APPROACHES AND METHODS

• Simplest possible theory and models
• Integrated micro–macromechanics analysis
• Repeating sublaminates to simplify design
• Thin wall theory for unsymmetric construction
• Quadractic criterion, and design limit/ultimate
• Hygrothermal–dependent properties
• Curing stresses from lamination
• Generalized laminate ranking

QUESTIONABLE TOOLS

• Models based on simple states of stress
• Carpet plots for strength
• Noninteracting failure modes analysis
• Shear lag analysis of fiber pullout
• Netting analysis for pressure vessels
• Max stress and max strain criteria
• Ply angle fraction optimization
• Balanced laminate and 10 percent rule

3

PACKAGING OF TOOLS

• User–friendly packages
• Spreadsheets: Excel or Lotus 123
• Integrated graphics and macros
• Answers to "What if?" and "What's best?"
• Self–teaching tutorials

READY–TO–GO SOFTWARE

• Verified and error free
• Savings in time and effort
• New documentation
• Continual updating
• Easy self– and cross–training
• Costs less than one man–day
• Time for more design iteration

4

SIMPLE OR COMPLEX STRESSES

• Simple stresses:
  Uniaxial, pure shear, hydrostatic
• Complex stresses:
  Biaxial, complex

*Behavior under complex stresses
cannot be predicted directly
from that under simple stresses.*

STATES OF STRESS

	Uniaxial	Shear	Hydro	Biaxial	Complex
σ_1	1.0	0.0	1.0	1.0	−3.0
σ_2	0.0	0.0	1.0	2.0	−2.0
σ_6	0.0	1.0	0.0	0.0	1.0

5

SINGLE OR MULTIPLE LOADS

Multiple loads represent the different conditions that a structure will encounter during its expected life.

For composites design, multiple loads must be included initially because ply number and ply angles together dictate the controlling design load.

MULTIPLE LOADS

	#1	#2	#3	#4
σ_1	1.0	2.0	–1.0	2.0
σ_2	0.0	0.0	–2.0	–1.0
σ_6	0.0	1.0	–1.0	1.0

6

AVERAGED STRESS IN UNIDIRECTIONAL COMPOSITES

• Off–axis ply stress: simple or complex
• On–axis ply stress: simple or complex
• Constituent stress: always complex
• Interfacial stress: always complex

For composites design, complex stresses must be included in almost all cases

AVERAGED STRESS IN LAMINATED COMPOSITES

• Laminate stress: simple or complex
• Off–axis ply stress: always complex
• On–axis ply stress: always complex
• Interlaminar stress: always complex

Complex stresses are present in all levels

7

STRESSES
Eq 5.1 and 5.16

$\sigma_1' = m^2\sigma_1 + n^2\sigma_2 + 2mn\sigma_6$
$\sigma_2' = n^2\sigma_1 + m^2\sigma_2 - 2mn\sigma_6$
$\sigma_6' = mn(-\sigma_1 + \sigma_2) + (m^2 - n^2)\sigma_6$
$\qquad m = \cos\theta, \ n = \sin\theta$

$\tan 2\theta_0 = 2\sigma_6/(\sigma_1 - \sigma_2)$
$\qquad \theta_0 = $ principal axes orientation
$\qquad \theta_0 + \pi/4 = $ max shear orientation

STRESS TRANSFORMATION

	Refer–ence	Any angle	Princ θ_0	Max shear	Invar–iants
θ	0.0	*10.0*	10.9	+π/4	p, q, R
σ_1	*–2.0*	–2.2	–2.2	0.5	0.5
σ_2	*3.0*	3.2	3.2	0.5	–2.5
σ_6	*–1.0*	–0.1	0.0	–2.7	2.7

Bold faced italics are inputs

8

STRAINS
Eq 5.1 and 5.18

$\varepsilon_1' = m^2\varepsilon_1 + n^2\varepsilon_2 + mn\varepsilon_6$
$\varepsilon_2' = n^2\varepsilon_1 + m^2\varepsilon_2 - mn\varepsilon_6$
$\varepsilon_6' = 2mn(-\varepsilon_1 + \varepsilon_2) + (m^2 - n^2)\varepsilon_6$
$\qquad m = \cos\theta, \ n = \sin\theta$

$\tan 2\theta_0 = \varepsilon_6/(\varepsilon_1 - \varepsilon_2)$
$\qquad \theta_0 = $ principal axes orientation
$\qquad \theta_0 + \pi/4 = $ max shear orientation

STRAIN TRANSFORMATION

	Refer–ence	Any angle	Princ θ_0	Max shear	Invar–iants
θ	0.0	*10.0*	5.7	+π/4	p,q,R
ε_1	*–2.0*	–2.0	–2.0	0.5	0.5
ε_2	*3.0*	3.0	3.0	0.5	–2.5
ε_6	*–1.0*	0.8	0.0	–2.5	2.5

Bold faced italics are inputs

9

LAMINATED PLATE THEORY
Sect 7–9,11

• Effective in–plane constants: {E°}, [v°]
• Average stress and strain: {σ°}, {ε°}
• Effective expansions: {α°}, {β°}
• Effective flex constants: {Eᶠ}, [vᶠ]
• Effective surface stress and strain: {σᵗ}, {εᵗ}

• Ply strength/stress ratio: R
• Laminate strength at limit and ultimate

BASIC ASSUMPTIONS

• Thin laminates
• Nondeforming normals
• Linear stress–strain relations
• Linear strain–displacement relations
• Quadratic failure criteria for FPF and LPF
• Linear hygrothermoelasticity
• Back–calculation of micromechanics
• Data fit by power–laws

10

ON–AXIS PLY STIFFNESS
Sect 6.1
Four orthotropic constants:
- Longitudinal stiffness: E_x
- Transverse stiffness: E_y
- Major Poisson's ratio: v_x
- Shear modulus: E_s

Only two constants for isotropic materials:
$E_x = E_y = E$, $v_x = v_y = v$, $E_s = E/2(1+v)$

11

ON–AXIS STRESS–STRAIN LAW
Sect 6.1
$\{\sigma\} = [Q]\{\varepsilon\}$
$\{\varepsilon\} = [S]\{\sigma\}$
Stiffness: $Q_{xx} = E_x/(1-v_x v_y)$
Compliance: $S_{xx} = Q_{yy}/(Q_{xx}Q_{yy}-Q_{xy}^2)$
Engineering const: $E_x = 1/S_{xx}$

For isotropic materials:
$Q_{xx} = E/(1-v^2)$, $S_{xx} = 1/E$

12

OFF–AXIS PLY STIFFNESS
Sect 6.1 and 6.2
$Q_{11} = m^4 Q_{xx} + n^4 Q_{yy} + 2m^2 n^2 Q_{xy} + 4m^2 n^2 Q_{ss}$
$m = \cos\theta$, $n = \sin\theta$, θ = ply angle

$Q_{11} = U_1 + U_2\cos2\theta + U_3\cos4\theta$
U_i = linear combo of on–axis [Q]
$U_1 = (3Q_{xx} + 3Q_{yy} + 2Q_{xy} + 4Q_{ss})/8$
$U_2 = (Q_{xx} - Q_{yy})/2$

13

QUASI–ISOTROPIC CONSTANTS
Sect 6.3
Linear invariants:
$U_1 = (3Q_{11} + 3Q_{22} + 2Q_{12} + 4Q_{66})/8$
$U_4 = (Q_{11} + Q_{22} + 6Q_{12} - 4Q_{66})/8$

$E^{iso} = (U_1^2 - U_4^2)/U_1$
$v^{iso} = U_4/U_1$
$G^{iso} = (U_1 - U_4)/2$

14

EFFECTIVE IN–PLANE STIFFNESS
Sect 7.2
$[A^*] = 1/h \int [Q]dz$
$[a^*] = [A^*]^{-1}$

$\{\sigma^o\} = [A^*]\{\varepsilon^o\}$
$\{\varepsilon^o\} = [a^*]\{\sigma^o\}$

$\{\sigma^o\} = 1/h \int\{\sigma\}dz$,
$\{\varepsilon^o\} \neq f(z)$

ENGINEERING CONSTANT (GPa)
TABLE 6.4

[Q]	CFRP T300	GFRP Scotch	KFRP Kevlar	CCRP Fabric	Metal Alum
E_x	181.0	38.6	76.0	74.0	69.0
E_y	10.3	8.3	5.5	74.0	69.0
v_x	0.28	0.26	0.34	0.05	0.30
E_s	7.2	4.1	2.3	4.6	26.5

ON–AXIS DATA (GPa)
TABLE 6.4

[Q]	CFRP T300	GFRP Scotch	KFRP Kevlar	CCRP Fabric	Metal Alum
Q_{xx}	181.8	39.2	76.6	74.0	75.8
Q_{yy}	10.4	8.4	5.6	74.0	75.8
Q_{xy}	2.9	2.2	1.9	0.1	22.7
Q_{ss}	7.2	4.1	2.3	4.6	26.5

OFF–AXIS DATA (GPa)
T300

θ	0°	15°	30°	45°	60°	90°
Q_{11}	181.8	160.4	109.3	56.7	23.6	10.
Q_{22}	10.3	11.9	23.6	56.7	109.3	182.
Q_{12}	2.9	12.8	32.4	42.3	32.4	3.
Q_{66}	7.2	17.0	36.7	46.6	36.8	7.
Q_{16}	0.0	38.5	54.2	42.9	20.1	0.
Q_{26}	0.0	4.4	20.1	42.9	54.2	0.

QUASI–ISOTROPIC (GPa)
TABLE 6.4

	CFRP T300	GFRP Scotch	KFRP Kevlar	CCRP Fabric	Metal Alum
E^{iso}	69.7	19.0	29.0	52.7	69.0
v^{iso}	0.30	0.27	0.32	0.32	0.30
ρ	1.6	1.8	1.5	1.5	2.6
E^{iso}/ρ	43.1	10.5	19.8	35.1	26.5

IN–PLANE STIFF (GPa)
T300

	[0]	[π/4]	[0/90]	[+/–45]	[0/±45]	Alum
$A_{11}{}^*$	181.8	76.4	96.0	56.7	98.4	75.8
$A_{22}{}^*$	10.4	76.4	96.0	56.7	41.2	75.8
$A_{12}{}^*$	2.9	22.6	2.9	42.3	29.2	22.7
$A_{66}{}^*$	7.2	26.9	7.2	46.6	33.4	26.5
$A_{16}{}^*$	0.0	0.0	0.0	0.0	0.0	0.0
$A_{26}{}^*$	0.0	0.0	0.0	0.0	0.0	0.0

15
IN-PLANE ENGINEERING CONST
Sect 7.3 and 7.4

$[a^*] = [A^*]^{-1} \neq \int[S]dz$

$E_1^{\,o} = 1/a_{11}{}^* \neq \int E_1 dz$

$E_2^{\,o} = 1/a_{22}{}^*, \; E_6^{\,o} = 1/a_{66}{}^*$

$v_{21}^{\,o} = -a_{21}/a_{11}$

$v_{61}^{\,o} = a_{61}/a_{11}$

IN-PLANE CONSTANT, GPa
T300

	[0]	[π/4]	[0/90]	[+/–45]	[0/±45]	Alur
$E_1^{\,o}$	181.0	69.7	96.0	25.0	77.7	69.
$E_2^{\,o}$	10.3	69.7	96.0	25.0	32.6	69.
$E_6^{\,o}$	7.2	26.9	7.2	46.6	33.5	26.
$v_{21}^{\,o}$	0.28	0.30	0.03	0.75	0.71	0.3
$v_{61}^{\,o}$	0.0	0.0	0.0	0.0	0.0	0.

16
PRESSURE VESSELS
Sect 7.13

P = press,   F = axial force
D = diameter,   h = wall thickness

$\sigma_1^{\,o} = PD/4h + F/\pi Dh$

$\sigma_2^{\,o} = PD/2h$

$\varepsilon_1^{\,o} = a_{11}{}^*\sigma_1^{\,o} + a_{12}{}^*\sigma_2^{\,o} = (\sigma_1^{\,o} - v_{12}^{\,o}\sigma_2^{\,o})/E_1^{\,o}$

$\varepsilon_2^{\,o} = a_{21}{}^*\sigma_1^{\,o} + a_{22}{}^*\sigma_2^{\,o} = (\sigma_2^{\,o} - v_{21}^{\,o}\sigma_1^{\,o})/E_2^{\,o}$

EXAMPLE: PRESSURE VESSEL
T300/5208, [0/45/±45]T

F, MN =	**10**	$\sigma_1^{\,o} =$ 849. $E_1^{\,o} = 78$
P,MPa=	**0**	$\sigma_2^{\,o} =$ 0. $E_2^{\,o} = 33$
D, m =	**1**	$\varepsilon_1^{\,o} =$ 10.92 $v_{21}^{\,o} = 0.7$
n, plies =	**30**	$\varepsilon_2^{\,o} =$ –7.76 $v_{12}^{\,o} = 0.3$
h, mm =	3.75	

Bold face italics are inputs

17
TORQUE TUBES
Sect 7.13

T = torque,   D = diameter
h = wall thickness   L = length

$\sigma_6^{\,o} = 2T/\pi D^2 h$

$\varepsilon_6^{\,o} = \sigma_6^{\,o}/E_6^{\,o}$

$\theta = 2(L/D)\varepsilon_6^{\,o}(180/\pi)$

EXAMPLE: TORQUE TUBE
T300/5208, [+/–45]T

T, MNm =	**1**	$\sigma_6^{\,o} =$ 127.
D, m =	**1**	$E_6^{\,o} =$ 46.60
L, m =	**10**	$\varepsilon_6^{\,o} =$ 2.73
n, plies =	**40**	$\theta =$ 3.13
h, mm =	5.00	

Bold face italics are inputs

18
FLEX STIFFNESS CONSTANTS
Sect 8.1

$[D] = \int[Q]z^2 dz$

$[d] = [D]^{-1} \neq \int[S]z^2 dz$

{M} = moment,   {k} = curvature

$\{M\} = [D]\{k\}$

$\{k\} = [d]\{M\}$

ABSOLUTE 8-PLY FLEX (MNm)
T300

	[0]	[π/4]	[0/90]	[+/–45]	Alum
D_{11}	15.2	9.6	10.7	4.7	6.3
D_{22}	0.9	5.6	5.3	4.7	6.3
D_{12}	0.2	0.7	0.2	3.5	1.9
D_{66}	0.6	1.0	0.6	3.9	2.2
D_{16}	0.0	0.3	0.0	1.3	0.0
D_{26}	0.0	0.3	0.0	1.3	0.0

h = 8x0.125 = 1 mm, $h^3/12 = 0.0833$

19
NORMALIZED FLEX CONST
Sect 8.1

$[D^*] = 12/h^3 \int[Q]z^2 dz$

$I^* = h^3/12, \quad [d^*] = [D^*]^{-1}$

$\{\sigma^f\} = [D^*]\{\varepsilon^f\}$

$\{\varepsilon^f\} = [d^*]\{\sigma^f\}$

$\{\sigma^f\} = 6/h^2 \int\{\sigma\}z dz$

$\{\varepsilon^f\} = h\{k\}/2$

NORMALIZED 8-PLY FLEX (GPa)
T300

	[0]	[π/4]	[0/90]	[+/–45]	Alum
$D_{11}{}^*$	181.8	115.2	128.2	56.7	75.8
$D_{22}{}^*$	10.4	67.0	63.9	56.7	75.8
$D_{12}{}^*$	2.9	7.8	2.9	42.3	22.7
$D_{66}{}^*$	7.2	12.1	7.2	45.6	26.5
$D_{16}{}^*$	0.0	4.0	0.0	16.0	0.0
$D_{26}{}^*$	0.0	4.0	0.0	16.0	0.0

20

FLEX ENG'G CONSTANTS
Sect 8.2

$[d^*] = [D^*]^{-1}$

$E_1^f = 1/d_{11}^*$

$E_2^f = 1/d_{22}^*, \quad E_6^f = 1/d_{66}^*$

$v_{21}^f = -d_{21}/d_{11}$

$v_{61}^f = d_{61}/d_{11}$

8–PLY ENG'G FLEX (GPa)
T300

	[0]	[π/4]	[0/90]	[+/–45]	Alum
E_1^f	181.0	113.3	128.1	24.7	69.0
E_2^f	10.3	65.3	63.9	24.7	69.0
E_6^f	7.2	11.7	7.2	41.4	26.5
v_{21}^f	0.28	0.10	0.05	0.72	0.30
v_{61}^f	0.00	–0.30	0.00	–0.10	0.0

21

SANDWICH PLATES
Sect 8.5

$$[D] = 2 \int_{zc}^{h/2} [Q]z^2 dz$$

$[D^*] = 12/h^3 [D]$

Percentage core $= c^* = 2zc/h$

$[d^*] = [D^*]^{-1}$

$E_1^f = 1/d_{11}^*$

FLEX: $\{[0/90]_i/zc\}$s, T300, GPa
Alum

i	2	2	2	8	8
zc	0	4	36	144	144
h	8	16	80	320	320
c*	0.0	0.5	0.9	0.9	0.9
E_1^f	128.1	96.0	26.6	26.2	18.7
E_2^f	63.9	71.9	25.4	25.9	18.7

For homogeneous materials: $E^t = (1-c^{*3})E$

22

CANTILEVER BEAMS
Sect 8.6

P = end load, L = length, b = width

$M^{max} = PL$

$k_1 = d_{11}M_1 = d_{11}PL/b$

or $= d_{11}^*PL/I = PL/E_1^fI$

$\delta^{max} = PL^3/3E_1^fbI^*$

CANTILEVER SANDWICH BEAM
T300/5208, $\{[0/90]_4/zc_{72}\}$s

P, kN =	*1*	I, m⁴ =	7E–08
L, m =	*1*	E_1^f =	26.3
b, m =	*0.1*	k_1,1/m =	0.57
n, plies =	160	ε_1^t, E–3 =	5.70
h, mm =	20.0	δ, mm =	190.

Bold faced italics are inputs

23

CANTILEVER CIRCULAR TUBINGS
Sect 8.7

a = diameter, h = wall thickness

$M^{max} = PL, \quad I = \pi a^3 h/8$

$k_1 = d_{11}M_1 = PL/E_1^\circ I$

$\delta^{max} = PL^3/3E_1^\circ I$

CANTILEVER CIRCULAR TUBE
T300/5208, $\{[0/90]_2\}$s

P, MN =	*1*	I, m⁴ =	4E–07
L, m =	*1*	E_1° =	96.0
a, m =	*0.1*	k_1,1/m =	0.03
n, plies =	8	ε_1^t, E–3 =	1.33
h, mm =	1.0	δ, mm =	8.8

Bold faced italics are inputs

24

UNSYMMETRIC LAMINATES
Sect 9

$\{\varepsilon\} = \{\varepsilon^\circ\} + z\{k\}$

$\{N\} = [A]\{\varepsilon^\circ\} + [B]\{k\}$

$\{M\} = [B]\{\varepsilon^\circ\} + [D]\{k\}$

$[B] = \int[Q]zdz = $ In–plane flex coupling

$[B] = 0$ for symmetric laminates

UNUSUAL CHARACTERISTICS

Disadvantages:
• Cured laminates are warped
• Behavior difficult to predict

Advantages:
• Natural curvature to prevent delamination
• Complex curvature from simple molds
• Potential use of prestressing

25

NORMALIZED CONSTANTS
Sect 9.4

$\{\sigma^o\} = [A^*]\{\epsilon^o\}+[B^*]\{\epsilon^f\}$
$\{\sigma^f\} = 3[B^*]\{\epsilon^o\}+[D^*]\{\epsilon^f\}$

$\{\epsilon^o\} = [\alpha^*]\{\sigma^o\}+[\beta^*]\{\sigma^f\}/3$
$\{\epsilon^f\} = [\beta^*]^t\{\sigma^o\}+[\delta^*]\{\sigma^f\}$

$[B^*] = 2[B]/h^2, \quad [\beta^*] = h^2[\beta]/2$

ENGINEERING CONSTANTS
Sect 9.5

$\{\epsilon^o\} = (\{\epsilon^+\}+\{\epsilon^-\})/2$
$\{\epsilon^f\} = (\{\epsilon^+\}-\{\epsilon^-\})/2$

$E_1^o = 1/\alpha_{11}^*, \quad \nu_{21}^o = -\alpha_{21}/\alpha_{11}, \ldots$
$E_1^t = 1/\delta_{11}^*, \quad \nu_{21}^t = -\delta_{21}/\delta_{11}, \ldots$

Not valid for statically determinant
structures due to coupled behavior

26

THE PARALLEL AXIS THEOREM
Sect 9.7

$\{N'\} = \{N\}$
$\{M'\} = \{M\}+d\{N\}$

$d = $ transfer distance $= z'-z$

$[A'] = [A]$
$[B'] = [B]+d[A]$
$[D'] = [D]+2d[B]+d^2[A]$

OLD AND NEW AXES

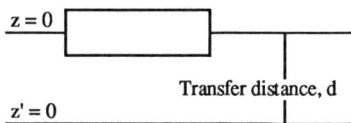

$z = 0$

$z' = 0$ Transfer distance, d

27

REPEATING SUB-LAMINATES
Sect 9.8

Laminate code: $\{[\theta_1/\theta_2/\theta_3/\theta_4]r/zc\}s$

$[A] = 2r[A^o]$
$[B] = 0$
$[D] = 2r\{[D^o]-(r-1)u[B^o]$
        $+(r-1)(2r-1)u^2[A^o]/6\}$
$r = $ repeat, $u = $ sub-laminate thickness
$[A^o, B^o, D^o] = $ sub-laminate stiffness

ADVANTAGES

• Simpler analysis for flexure
• Easier optimization of angles
• Higher laminate toughness due to
  finer ply dispersion (splicing)
• Simpler layup reduces errors,
  and lowers cost of fabrication

28

THIN WALL CONSTRUCTION
Sect 9.9

$\{N^+\} = \{N\}/2+\{M\}/h$
$\{N^-\} = \{N\}/2-\{M\}/h$

$[A^*, D^*] = [1, 3][A^++A^-]/h$
$[B^*] = [A^+-A^-]/h$

$[\alpha^*, \delta^*] = [1, 1/3][a^++a^-]h/4$
$[\beta^*] = [a^+-a^-]h/4$

ADVANTAGES

• Uses 3x3, instead of 6x6, matrices
  for unsymmetric construction
• Simpler laminate optimization
• Easier incorporation of hybrids
• Error equal to facing-depth ratio

29

MICROMECHANICS
Sect 10

Opportunities offered:
    • Degraded matrix model for LPF
    • Hygrothermal dependent data
    • Materials optimization
    • Failure modes

COMMON MODELS

• Parallel model (upper bound)
• Series model (lower bound)
• Modified rule-of-mixtures
• Other strength-of-materials models
• Concentric cylinders model
• Square packing model
• Self-consistent model

30

LIMITATIONS OF MICROMECHANICS

- Idealized fiber cross sectional shape
- Idealized fiber packing symmetry
- Assumed continuity at interface
- Approximations in stress analysis
- Unmeasurable fiber properties
- Overlooked shrinkage stresses
- Undefined failure modes

RECOMMENDED USE OF MICROMECHANICS

Apply back–calculation to determine missing constituent properties and empirical constants

Then, apply forward–calculation to determine sensitivities of various micromechanics variables

31

MODIFIED RULE–OF–MIXTURES
Sect 10.2–5

Rule of mixtures:
$$E_x = v_f E_f + v_m E_m$$
$$v_x = v_f v_f + v_m v_m$$

Modified rule of mixtures:
$$(1+v_y^*)/E_y = 1/E_{fx} + v_y^*/E_m$$
$$(1+v_s^*)/E_s = 1/G_{fs} + v_s^*/G_m$$
$$v_y^* = \eta_y v_m/v_f, \quad v_s^* = \eta_s v_m/v_f$$

STRESS PARTITIONING PARAMETERS
Eq 10.9
$$\eta_y = [<\sigma_m>/<\sigma_f>]_y$$
$$\eta_s = [<\sigma_m>/<\sigma_f>]_s$$
From the stiffnesses of a unidirect GFRP ply, and the moduli of an isotropic glass fiber, back–calculate the partitioning parameters:
$$\eta_y = 0.5161$$
$$\eta_s = 0.3162$$

32

TRANSVERSE PLY STIFFNESS
Eq 10.28 and 10.25
$\eta_y = 0.516$ (back–calc from GFRP)

Back–calc transverse fiber stiff:
$$E_{fy} = [(1 + v_y^*)/E_y - v_y^*/E_m]^{-1}$$

Forward–calc transverse ply stiffness:
$$E_y' = (1+v_y^*)/[1/E_{fy}' + v_y^*/E_m]$$

BACK– AND FORWARD–CALC TRANSVERSE STIFFNESS

$E_y =$	**10.3**	$v_y^* =$	0.22
$E_m =$	**3.40**	$E_{fy} =$	18.69 Back–calculated
$v_f =$	**0.70**	$E_{fy}' =$	18.69 Fixed value
$\eta_y =$	**0.52**	$E_y' =$	10.30 Forward–calc
$E_m{}^o =$	3.40	$E_y'/E_y =$	1.00
$E_m/E_m{}^o=$	1.00		

Bold faced italics are inputs

33

SHEAR MODULUS OF PLY
Eq 10.19 and 10.10
$\eta_s = 0.316$ (back–calc from GFRP)

Back–calc fiber shear modulus:
$$G_{fx} = [(1+v_s^*)/E_s - v_s^*/G_m]^{-1}$$

Forward–calc ply shear modulus:
$$E_s' = (1+v_s^*)/[1/G_{fx} + v_s^*/G_m]$$

BACK– AND FORWARD–CALC SHEAR MODULUS

$E_s =$	**7.17**	$v_s^* =$	0.14
$E_m =$	**3.40**	$G_{fx} =$	19.70 Back–calculated
$v_f =$	**0.70**	$G_{fx}' =$	19.70 Fixed value
$\eta_s =$	**0.32**	$E_s' =$	7.17 Forward–calc
$E_m{}^o =$	3.40	$E_s'/E_s =$	1.00
$E_m/E_m{}^o =$	1.00		

Bold faced italics are inputs

34

ORTHOTROPIC STRENGTHS
Sect 11.2
$\sigma_x \leq X$: longitudinal tensile
$-\sigma_x \leq X'$: longitudinal compress
$\sigma_y \leq Y$: transverse tensile
$-\sigma_y \leq Y'$: transverse compress
$\sigma/s \leq S$: longitudinal shear

von Mises: $X = X' = Y = Y', S = 0.57X$
Tresca: $X = X' = Y = Y', S = 0.50X$

STRENGTHS (MPa)
Table 11.1

	CFRP T300	GFRP Scotch	KFRP Kevlar	CCRP Fabric	Metal Alum
X	1500	1062	1400	499	400
X'	1500	610	235	352	400
Y	40	31	12	458	400
Y'	246	118	53	352	400
S	68	72	34	46	228

35

MAXIMUM STRAINS
Sect 11.5

$\varepsilon_x^* = X/E_x$
$\varepsilon_x'^* = X'/E_x$
$\varepsilon_y^* = Y/E_y$
$\varepsilon_y'^* = Y'/E_y$
$\varepsilon_s^* = S/E_s$, based on tangent modulus

Maximum strain criterion compares
strains, component by component.

MAXIMUM STRAINS (E-3)
Table 11.1

ε^*	CFRP T300	GFRP Scotch	KFRP Kevlar	CCRP Fabric	Metal Alum
x	8.3	27.5	18.4	6.5	5.8
x'	8.3	15.8	3.1	4.8	5.8
y	3.9	3.8	2.2	6.2	5.8
y'	23.9	14.3	9.6	4.8	5.8
s	9.5	17.4	14.8	10.1	8.6

36

STRENGTH/STRESS RATIOS
Sect 11.3

$\{\sigma\}^{max} = R\{\sigma\}^{appl}$
$\{\varepsilon\}^{max} = R\{\varepsilon\}^{appl}$

$R = 1$, failure occurs
$R = 2$, safety margin is 2

R = strength, if unit $\{\sigma\}$ is applied

EXAMPLES

	Given data	Change h FPF	LPF	Change {N} FPF	LPF
h, plies =	*10.*	8.33	10.71	10.00	10.00
{N} =	*2.00*	2.00	2.00	2.40	1.87
R/FPF =	*1.20*	1.00	1.29	1.00	1.29
R/LPF =	*1.40*	1.17	1.50	1.17	1.50

Bold faced italics are inputs

37

QUADRATIC STRESS CRITERIA
Sect 11.6

$F_{ij}\sigma_i\sigma_j + F_i\sigma_i = 1$

$F_{xx} = 1/XX'$, $F_{yy} = 1/YY'$, $F_{ss} = 1/S^2$
$F_{xy} = F_{xy}^*\sqrt{[F_{xx}F_{yy}]}$, $-1/2 \leq F_{xy}^* \leq 0$
$F_x = 1/X - 1/X'$, $F_y = 1/Y - 1/Y'$

$aR^2 + bR - 1 = 0$
Scalar products: $a = F_{ij}\sigma_i\sigma_j$, $b = F_i\sigma_i$

STRESS PARAMETERS
Table 11.1

F_{ij} F_i	CFRP T300	GFRP Scotch	KFRP Kevlar
F_{xx}	4E-19	2E-18	3E-18
F_{yy}	1E-16	3E-16	2E-15
F_{xy}	-3E-18	-1E-17	-3E-17
F_{ss}	2E-16	2E-16	9E-16
F_x	0E+0	-7E-10	-4E-9
F_y	2E-16	2E-08	6E-08

38

QUADRATIC STRAIN CRITERIA
Sect 11.7

$G_{ij}\varepsilon_i\varepsilon_j + G_i\varepsilon_i = 1$

$G_{xx} = F_{xx}Q_{xx}^2 + 2F_{xy}Q_{xx}Q_{xy} + F_{yy}Q_{xy}^2$
$G_x = F_xQ_{xx} + F_yQ_{xy}$

$aR^2 + bR - 1 = 0$
Scalar products: $a = G_{ij}\varepsilon_i\varepsilon_j$, $b = G_i\varepsilon_i$

STRAIN PARAMETERS
Table 11.1

G_{ij} G_i	CFRP T300	GFRP Scotch	KFRP Kevlar
G_{xx}	12004	1914	13454
G_{yy}	10681	18882	47657
G_{xy}	-3069	1712	2068
G_{ss}	11118	3306	4576
G_x	61	25	-150
G_y	217	198	351

39

ADVANTAGES OF QUADRATIC
FAILURE CRITERIA

• Analytically sound and simple
• Strength interactions included
• A scalar, not tensorial, criterion
• Single-valued, well behaved functions
• Simple to understand, to use, and to plot
• Conjugate roots make flex strength easy

ADVANTAGES OF STRAIN SPACE
(OVER STRESS SPACE)
Sect 11.7

• Dimensionless; same for all units
• Envelopes fixed for all laminates
• Easy to define limit and ultimate
• Rigid body rotation in p=0 plane
Pi/4 envelopes in principal strain space
give bounds for all balanced ply angles.

40

FAILURE MODES

Fiber tensile:	X
Fiber compressive:	X'
Matrix/interface tensile:	Y
Matrix compressive:	Y'
Matrix/interface shear:	S

Delamination occurs at free edge, or resulting from transverse impact or nonuniform curing.

41

FIRST–PLY–FAILURE

- Inner failure envelope of a laminate
- **Failure modes are mixed**
- Simplest type: matrix/interface cracks
- Cracks run parallel to fibers, are evenly spaced, and are saturated when ultimate is reached.
- Laminated plate theory must be modified when plies contain cracks.

42

MATRIX DEGRADATION MODEL
Sect 12

To extend laminated plate theory beyond FPF, plies with cracks are mathematically replaced by continuous plies having lower matrix modulus; i.e. reduced stiffness and Poisson's ratio:

$$0 < (E_m/E_m{}^\circ) < 1$$
$$v_x/v_x{}^\circ = E_m/E_m{}^\circ$$

Approx model: $E_y/E_y{}^\circ = E_s/E_s{}^\circ = E_m/E_m{}^\circ$

43

DEGRADED MATRIX MODULUS

To be determined empirically from:

- Laminate strains at FPF, and LPF
- Stiffness loss as cracks increase under static or fatigue loads
- Observed ultimate strength

44

ULTIMATE LAMINATE STRENGTH
SECT 12
The larger of the LPF and FPF

- LPF > FPF in tension–tension quadrant
- LPF = FPF when plies fail simultaneously
- LPF < FPF in compress–compress quadrant

MODE INTERACTIONS

- Interactions cannot be ignored
- Beneficial in 1st and 3rd quadrants
- Detrimental in 2nd and 4th quadrants
- Delamination lowers stiffness, ultimate strength, and buckling load
- Mode identification is difficult

CRACK DENSITY DATA, T300
Fig 19.2 to 19.5

Shear lag analysis predicts crack spacing of seven ply group thickness, or a density of 10 to 15 cracks per centimeter.

Data agree with predicted density in 45–degree plies, but is higher in 90–plies by almost a factor of 3; i.e., 40 cracks/cm.

DEGRADED T300 STIFFNESS
Figure 12.2

$E_m/E_m{}^\circ$	$E_y/E_y{}^\circ$	$E_s/E_s{}^\circ$	$v_x/v_x{}^\circ$	$E_x/E_x{}^\circ$
0.40	0.55	0.50	0.112	1.00
0.30	0.44	0.39	0.084	1.00
0.20	0.32	0.27	0.056	1.00
0.10	0.17	0.14	0.028	1.00
0.01	0.01	0.01	0.003	1.00

Recommended degradation is between 0.1 to 0.3

LAST–PLY–FAILURE

- Plies remain intact below the FPF, or the endurance limit under fatigue
- Beyond FPF, plies begin to degrade
- LPF is the lowest ply failure load after all plies are degraded, or the inner envelope of a degraded laminate
- For some laminates LPF ≤ FPF

ULTIMATE STRENGTHS

FPF =	*1.00*
LPF =	*1.60*

Ultimate = MAX(FPF,LPF)
    =   1.60

Bold faced italics are inputs

45

LIMIT STRENGTH

A recommended conservative limit can be
defined by the following rules:
Rule 1:
No matrix degradtion at limit
(To avoid detrimental mode interactions)
Rule 2:
A minimum safety margin: ult/lim≥sm

$$lim = MIN(FPF, ult/sm)$$

46

ALTERNATIVE LIMIT OF LAMINATES

Matrix degrdation allowed:
Ultimate divided by safety margin

$$lim^* = MAX(FPF, LPF)/sm$$
$$or = ult/sm$$

If LPF/FPF > safety margin, degradation
is harmless when load remains tensile, such
as that in pressure vessels with rubber liners.

47

RESIDUAL LAM STRESSES
Sect 15

Based on linear thermoelastic model

• Nonmechanical stresses and strains
• Residual stresses and strains
• Free orthotropic expansions
• Quadratic failure criteria

48

NONMECHANICAL STRESSES
Eq 15.6 and 15.8

Nonmechanical stresses:
$$\{\sigma\}^n = [Q]\{e\}$$

$$\{\sigma\}^{(o)n} = 1/h \int \{\sigma\}^n dz$$

Nonmechanical strains:
$$\{\varepsilon\}^{(o)n} = [a]\{\sigma\}^{(o)n}$$

49

EFFECTIVE EXPANSIONS
Eq 15.11 and 15.12

$$\{\varepsilon\}^{(o)n} = \{\alpha\}^o \Delta T + \{\beta\}^o c$$

$$\{\alpha\}^o = [a] \int [Q]\{\alpha\} dz$$

$$\{\beta\}^o = [a] \int [Q]\{\beta\} dz$$

LIMIT AND ULTIMATE OF LAMINATES

FPF =	**_1.00_**
LPF =	**_1.60_**
Safety margin =	**_1.50_**
ultimate =	1.60
limit =	1.00
ult/lim =	1.60

Bold faced italics are inputs

LAMINATE DESIGN CRITERIA

FPF =	**_1.00_**
LPF =	**_1.60_**
Safety margin =	**_1.20_**
ultimate =	1.60

		Matrix degradation
lim =	1.00	Not allowed
lim* =	1.33	Allowed

TRACTION–FREE EXPANSIONS
Eq 15.1

$$e_x = \alpha_x \Delta T + \beta_x c$$
$$e_y = \alpha_y \Delta T + \beta_y c$$

$\{\alpha\}$ = thermal expansion
$\{\beta\}$ = moisture expansion
$\Delta T = T/opr - T/cure$
c = moisture

RESIDUAL STRAINS
Eq 15.10

$$\{\varepsilon\}^{(o)r} = \{\varepsilon\}^{(o)n} - \{e\}$$

Resolved components:
$$\varepsilon_x^{(o)r} = \varepsilon_x^{(o)n} - e_x$$
$$\varepsilon_y^{(o)r} = \varepsilon_y^{(o)n} - e_y$$
$$\varepsilon_s^{(o)r} = \varepsilon_s^{(o)n}$$

QUADRATIC CRITERION WITH RESIDUAL STRESSES
Eq 15.14 to 15.18

$$\{\varepsilon\}^* = R^m \{\varepsilon\}^m + \{\varepsilon\}^r$$
$$or = R^m \{\varepsilon\}^m + \{\varepsilon\}^n - \{e\}$$

$$\{\varepsilon\}^*[G]\{\varepsilon\}^* + \{G\}\{\varepsilon\}^* = 1$$

$$a(R^m)^2 + bR^m - 1 = 0$$

50

NONDIMENSIONAL TEMPERATURE
Sect 17.2

$T^* = [T/g - T/opr]/[T/g - T/rm]$
$T^* = 1$ at room temperature
$T^* = 0$ at glass transition temp

$T/g = T/g^o - gc$
g = temp shift per moisture

POWER–LAW HYGRO DATA
Eq 17.3 to 17.7
Matrix data:
$E_m^* = (T^*)^a$
$\eta_y^* = \eta_s^* = (T^*)^b$
$X_m^* = (T^*)^c$

Fiber data:
$E_{fx}^* = E_{fy}^* = G_{fx}^* = (T^*)^t$
$X_f^* = (T^*)^h$

51

POWER–LAW STIFFNESS DATA
Eq 17.8 to 17.11

$E_x/E_x^o = (v_f/v_f^o)(T^*)^f$

$v_x/v_x^o = 1$ (constant)

E_y/E_y^o = nonlinear function (T^*, v_f)

E_s/E_s^o = nonlinear function (T^*, v_f)

POWER–LAW STRENGTH DATA
Eq 17.12 to 17.14

$X^* = (v_f/v_f^o)(T^*)^h$
$X'^* = (v_f/v_f^o)(T^*)^h(E_s/E_s^o)^a$
Microbuckling effect is included

$Y^* = Y'^* = S^* = (T^*)^c$
Effects of interfacial strength and residual
stress $<\sigma>^r$ are imbedded in these data

52

LAMINATE RANKING
Sect 14
In–plane symmetric laminates only
Analysis include:
    Multiple, complex loads
    Residual stresses
    FPF, LPF, limit, limit*, and ultimate
Ranking families based on choice of:
    2 to10 ply sub–laminates
    2 to 4 arbitrary ply angles

RANKING CRITERIA

Options for strength:
lim = limit without degradation
lim* = limit with degradation

Limits are based on specific values of:
Matrix degradation factor, about 0.3
A minimum safety margin

53

SUB AND ROUND–OFF LAMINATES
• Sub–laminate code:
    $\{[a\ b\ c\ d]r\}_s$
    (a plies in θ_1, b plies in θ_2, etc)
• Round–off laminate code:
    $[A\ B\ C\ D]_s$
    (A plies in θ_1, B plies in θ_2, etc)
• Total laminate code:
    $\{[a\ b\ c\ d]r \pm [A\ B\ C\ D]\}_s$

LAMINATE FAMILIES

Plies in	No ply angles			
Sub–lam	2	3	4	Total
6	7	28	84	119
7	8	36	120	164
8	9	45	165	219
9	10	55	220	285
10	11	66	286	363
				1150

54

INTEGRATED MICRO–MACRO MECHANICS ANALYSIS

Stiffness and strength analysis:
    • Fiber material and geometry
    • Matrix material and geometry
    • Laminate layup and applied loads
    • Cure temp and hygrothermal conditions
    • Simple statically determinant structures
    • Hybrids, thin wall construction and duplex

MIC–MAC FLOW DIAGRAM

Hygro		Point str	>>>	Comp
Micro	>>>	Macro		Struct
T/cure	>>>	Loads		

Composites Design

28–12

INTERNATIONAL OUTLINE

55

CONCLUSIONS

Composites design is:
- Simple
- Straightforward
- Internally consistent
- On par with isotropic theories
- Novice can learn quickly
- Even experts can improve
- We are ready when you are

56

A FEW DON'TS
- Don't use carpet plots
- Don't believe in pullouts
- Don't trust netting analysis
- Don't outguess matrix inversions
- Don't be limited to balanced laminates
- Don't use scalars to describe composites
- Don't use uniaxial data to explain composites
- Don't use simple modes to explain mixed modes
- Don't let expert say that you don't understand

A FEW DO'S
- Always calculate
- Use laminate plate theory
- Use quadratic failure criterion
- Include curing stresses from lamination
- Use micro–macromechanics to gain insight
- Use simplified theory to allow design iterations
- Use laminate ranking together with optimization
- Have fun with the magic of composite materials

FUTURE OF COMPOSITES
- Low material cost
- Low processing cost
- Precise and rational design
- Combined functions
- Innovative concepts
- Rigorous theory
- New workers
- Be positive

28.2 FRENCH OUTLINE

1

CONCEPTION SIMPLIFIEE DES MATERIAUX COMPOSITES

Un ensemble d'outils pour le bureau d'études

Thierry N. Massard
Think Composites–France
155 Bd Brune – 75014 Paris – France
Telephone: (33) 1 – 64 90 57 62

REFERENCES

Stephen W. Tsai
Composites Design–1987
Think Composites, Dayton, Ohio (1987)

Stephen W. Tsai and H. Thomas Hahn
Introduction to Composite Materials
Technomic, Lancaster, Pa. (1985)

2

APPROCHES ET METHODES

- Théorie et modèles les plus simples possibles
- Analyse micro–macromécanique intégrée
- Sous stratifiés : une conception plus simple
- Th. des parois minces : struct. non symétriques
- Critère quadratique avec valeur limite et ultime
- Propriétés à dépendance hygrothermique
- Contraintes de cuisson
- Méthode de classement généralisée

DES OUTILS DISCUTABLES

- Modèles avec des états de contraintes simples
- Abaques "tapis" pour le calcul de résistance
- Analyse de la rupture sans terme d'interaction
- Analyse du transfert de charge par extraction d'un monofilament
- Théorie du filet pour les réservoirs sous pression
- Crit. de contrainte ou de déformation max
- Optimisation par fraction de chaque orientation

3

CONDITIONNEMENT DES OUTILS

- Logiciels conviviaux
- Tableurs: Excel ou Lotus 123
- Graphismes et macro–commandes intégrées
- Réponses à "Et si?" et "Quel est le meilleur?"
- Auto–apprentissage

DES LOGICIELS PRET A L'EMPLOI

- Testés et validés
- Economie de temps et d'efforts
- Nouvelle documentation
- Mise à jour continue
- Apprentissage simple par recoupements
- Coût inférieur à une journée d'ingénieur

4

CONTRAINTES SIMPLES/COMPLEXES

- Contraintes simples: Uniaxiales, cisaillement pur, hydrostatiques
- Contraintes complexes: Biaxiales, complexes

Le comportement sous contraintes complexes ne peut être prédit directement à partir de celui sous contraintes simples

ETATS DE CONTRAINTES

	Uniaxial	Cisail.	Hydro	Biaxial	Complex
σ_1	1.0	0.0	1.0	1.0	–3.0
σ_2	0.0	0.0	1.0	2.0	–2.0
σ_6	0.0	1.0	0.0	0.0	1.0

5
CHARGEMENT SIMPLE OU MULTIPLE

Les chargements multiples représentent les différentes conditions qu'une structure rencontrera au cours de sa vie potentielle.

Dans la conception des composites, les chargements multiples doivent être considérés car le nombre et l'orientation des couches déterminent a posteriori le chargement critique

6
CONTRAINTES MOYENNES DANS UN COMPOSITE UNIDIRECTIONEL

• σ_i dans les axes: simples ou complexes
• σ_i hors des axes: simples ou complexes
• σ_i dans les constituants: toujours complexes
• σ_i interfaciales: toujours complexes

Les contraintes complexes doivent être utilisées dans presque tous les cas

7
CONTRAINTES
Eq 5.1 et 5.16

$\sigma_1' = m^2\sigma_1 + n^2\sigma_2 + 2mn\sigma_6$
$\sigma_2' = n^2\sigma_1 + m^2\sigma_2 - 2mn\sigma_6$
$\sigma_6' = mn(-\sigma_1+\sigma_2) + (m^2-n^2)\sigma_6$
$m = \cos\theta, \ n = \sin\theta$

$\tan 2\theta_0 = 2\sigma_6/(\sigma_1-\sigma_2)$
θ_0 = orientation des axes principaux
$\theta_0+\pi/4$ = orientation du cisaillement maximum

8
DEFORMATIONS
Eq 5.1 et 5.18

$\varepsilon_1' = m^2\varepsilon_1 + n^2\varepsilon_2 + mn\varepsilon_6$
$\varepsilon_2' = n^2\varepsilon_1 + m^2\varepsilon_2 - mn\varepsilon_6$
$\varepsilon_6' = 2mn(-\varepsilon_1+\varepsilon_2) + (m^2-n^2)\varepsilon_6$
$m = \cos\theta, \ n = \sin\theta$

$\tan 2\theta_0 = \varepsilon_6/(\varepsilon_1-\varepsilon_2)$
θ_0 = orientation des axes principaux
$\theta_0+\pi/4$ = orientation du cisaillement maximum

9
THEORIE DES STRATIFIES
Sect 7–9

• Constantes d'ingénieur en membrane: $\{E^o\}$, $[v^o]$
• Contrainte et déformation moyennes: $\{\sigma^o\}$, $\{\varepsilon^o\}$
• Coefficients de dilatation apparents: $\{\alpha^o\}$, $\{\beta^o\}$

• Constantes d'ingénieur en flexion: $\{E^f\}$, $[v^f]$
• σ_j et ε_j apparentes en surface: $\{\sigma^f\}$, $\{\varepsilon^f\}$

• Rapport contrainte/résistance: R

CHARGEMENTS MULTIPLES

	#1	#2	#3	#4
σ_1	1.0	2.0	-1.0	2.0
σ_2	0.0	0.0	-2.0	-1.0
σ_6	0.0	1.0	-1.0	1.0

Un chargement secondaire est tel que $\sigma'_i<\sigma_i$
Il n'est pas critique pour un matériau isotrope
mais il peut l'être pour un matériau stratifié

CONTRAINTES MOYENNES DANS UN COMPOSITE STRATIFIE

• σ du stratifié : simples ou complexes
• σ hors axes de la couche: tjrs complexes
• σ ds les axes de la couche: tjrs complexes
• σ interlaminaires: tjrs complexes

Les σ_j sont complexes à tous les niveaux

TRANSFORM. DES CONTRAINTES

	Réfer-ence	Un angle	Princ θ_0	Cis. Max	Invar-iants
θ	0.0	10.0	10.9	+π/4	p, q, R
σ_1	-2.0	-2.2	-2.2	0.5	0.5
σ_2	3.0	3.2	3.2	0.5	-2.5
σ_6	-1.0	-0.1	0.0	-2.7	2.7

Données : caract. italiques gras

TRANSFORM. DES DEFORMATIONS

	Réfer-ence	Un angle	Princ θ_0	Cis. Max	Invar-iants
θ	0.0	10.0	5.7	+π/4	p,q,R
ε_1	-2.0	-2.0	-2.0	0.5	0.5
ε_2	3.0	3.0	3.0	0.5	-2.5
ε_6	-1.0	0.8	0.0	-2.5	2.5

Données : caract. italiques gras

HYPOTHESES DE BASE

• Stratifiés minces
• La normale reste normale
• Relations σ_i–ε_i linéaires
• Relations ε_i–u_i linéaires
• Critère de rupture quadratique
• Hygrothermoélasticité linéaire
• Micromécanique calculée en retour
• Données repr. par des lois puissances

10
RIGIDITE D'UN PLI DANS SES AXES
Sect 6.1
Quatre constantes orthotropes:
- Rigidité longitudinale: E_x
- Rigidité transverse E_y
- Coefficient de Poisson principal: v_x
- Module de cisaillement: E_s

Seulement deux const. pour un matériau isotrope:
$E_x = E_y = E, \quad v_x = v_y = v, \quad E_s = E/2(1+v)$

11
REL. CONTRAINTE/DEFORMATION
Sect 6.1

$\{\sigma\} = [Q]\{\varepsilon\}$
$\{\varepsilon\} = [S]\{\sigma\}$
Rigidité: $Q_{xx} = E_x/(1-v_x v_y)$
Souplesse $S_{xx} = Q_{yy}/(Q_{xx}Q_{yy}-Q_{xy}^2)$
Constantes d'ingénieur: $E_x = 1/S_{xx}$

Pour un matériau isotrope:
$Q_{xx} = E/(1-v^2), \quad S_{xx} = 1/E$

12
RIGIDITE HORS-AXES
Sect 6.1 et 6.2
$Q_{11} = m^4 Q_{xx}+n^4 Q_{yy}+2m^2 n^2 Q_{xy}$
$+4m^2 n^2 Q_{ss}$
$m = \cos\theta, \quad n = \sin\theta, \quad \theta = $ ply angle

$Q_{11} = U_1+U_2\cos2\theta+U_3\cos4\theta$
$U_i = $ combi. linéaire des [Q]
$U_1 = (3Q_{xx}+3Q_{yy}+2Q_{xy}+4Q_{ss})/8$
$U_2 = (Q_{xx}-Q_{yy})/2$

13
CONSTANTES QUASI-ISOTROPES
Sect 6.3
Invariants linéaires :
$U_1 = (3Q_{11}+3Q_{22}+2Q_{12}+4Q_{66})/8$
$U_4 = (Q_{11}+Q_{22}+6Q_{12}-4Q_{66})/8$

$E^{iso} = (U_1^2-U_4^2)/U_1$
$v^{iso} = U_4/U_1$
$G^{iso} = (U_1-U_4)/2$

14
RIGIDITE DE MEMBRANE
Sect 7.2
$[A^*] = 1/h \int[Q]dz$
$[a^*] = [A^*]^{-1}$

$\{\sigma^0\} = [A^*]\{\varepsilon^0\}$
$\{\varepsilon^0\} = [a^*]\{\sigma^0\}$

$\{\sigma^0\} = 1/h \int\{\sigma\}dz,$
$\{\varepsilon^0\} \neq f(z)$

CONSTANTES D'INGENIEUR (GPa)
Table 6.4

	CFRP T300	GFRP Scotch	KFRP Kevlar	CCRP Tissu	Métal Alum
E_x	181.0	38.6	76.0	74.0	69.0
E_y	10.3	8.3	5.5	74.0	69.0
v_x	0.28	0.26	0.34	0.05	0.30
E_s	7.2	4.1	2.3	4.6	26.5

RIGIDITE DANS LES AXES (GPa)
Table 6.4

[Q]	CFRP T300	GFRP Scotch	KFRP Kevlar	CCRP Tissu	Métal Alum
Q_{xx}	181.8	39.2	76.6	74.0	75.8
Q_{yy}	10.4	8.4	5.6	74.0	75.8
Q_{xy}	2.9	2.2	1.9	0.1	22.7
Q_{ss}	7.2	4.1	2.3	4.6	26.5

RIGIDITES HORS AXES (GPa)
T300/5208

θ	0°	15°	30°	45°	60°	90°
Q_{11}	181.8	160.4	109.4	56.7	23.6	10.3
Q_{22}	10.3	11.9	23.6	56.7	160.4	181.8
Q_{12}	2.9	12.8	32.4	42.3	32.4	2.9
Q_{66}	7.2	17.0	36.7	46.6	17.0	7.2
Q_{16}	0.0	38.5	54.2	42.9	20.1	0.0
Q_{26}	0.0	4.4	20.1	42.9	54.2	0.0

QUASI-ISOTROPE (GPa)
Table 6.4

	CFRP T300	GFRP Scotch	KFRP Kevlar	CCRP Tissu	Métal Alum
E^{iso}	69.7	19.0	29.0	52.7	69.0
v^{iso}	0.30	0.27	0.32	0.32	0.30
ρ	1.6	1.8	1.5	1.5	2.6
E^{iso}/ρ	43.1	10.5	19.8	35.1	26.5

RIGIDITE DE MEMBRANE (GPa)
T300/5208

	[0]	[π/4] [0/90][+/−45][0/±45]				Alum
A_{11}^*	181.8	76.4	96.0	56.7	98.4	75.8
A_{22}^*	10.4	76.4	96.0	56.7	41.2	75.8
A_{12}^*	2.9	22.6	2.9	42.3	29.2	22.7
A_{66}^*	7.2	26.9	7.2	46.6	33.4	26.5
A_{16}^*	0.0	0.0	0.0	0.0	0.0	0.0
A_{26}^*	0.0	0.0	0.0	0.0	0.0	0.0

15

CONST. D'ING. EN MEMBRANE
Sect 7.3 et 7.4

$[a^*] = [A^*]^{-1} \neq \int [S]dz$

$E_1^{\,o} = 1/a_{11}^* \neq \int E_1 dz$

$E_2^{\,o} = 1/a_{22}^*, \quad E_6^{\,o} = 1/a_{66}^*$

$\nu_{21}^{\,o} = -a_{21}/a_{11}$

$\nu_{61}^{\,o} = a_{61}/a_{11}$

CONSTANTES DE MEMBRANE, GPa
T300/5208

	[0]	[π/4]	[0/90]	[+/–45]	[0/±45]	Alum
$E_1^{\,o}$	181.0	69.7	96.0	25.0	77.7	69.0
$E_2^{\,o}$	10.3	69.7	96.0	25.0	32.6	69.0
$E_6^{\,o}$	7.2	26.9	7.2	46.6	33.5	26.5
$\nu_{21}^{\,o}$	0.28	0.30	0.03	0.75	0.71	0.30
$\nu_{61}^{\,o}$	0.0	0.0	0.0	0.0	0.0	0.0

16

RESERVOIRS SOUS PRESSION
Sect 7.13

P = pression,   F = force axiale
D = diamètre,   h = épaisseur de paroi

$\sigma_1^{\,o} = PD/4h + F/\pi Dh$

$\sigma_2^{\,o} = PD/2h$

$\varepsilon_1^{\,o} = a_{11}^*\sigma_1^{\,o} + a_{12}^*\sigma_2^{\,o} = (\sigma_1^{\,o} - \nu_{12}^{\,o}\sigma_2^{\,o})/E_1^{\,o}$

$\varepsilon_2^{\,o} = a_{21}^*\sigma_1^{\,o} + a_{22}^*\sigma_2^{\,o} = (\sigma_2^{\,o} - \nu_{21}^{\,o}\sigma_1^{\,o})/E_2^{\,o}$

17

TORSION DE TUBES
Sect 7.13

T = couple,   D = diamètre
h = épaisseur de parois   L = longueur

$\sigma_6^{\,o} = 2T/\pi D^2 h$

$\varepsilon_6^{\,o} = \sigma_6^{\,o}/E_6^{\,o}$

$\theta = 2(L/D)\varepsilon_6^{\,o}(180/\pi)$

EXEMPLE: RESERVOIR SOUS PRESSION
T300/5208, [0/45/±45]T

F, kN =	**10**	$\sigma_1^{\,o} =$	849.	$E_1^{\,o} = 77.7$
P,MPa=	**0**	$\sigma_2^{\,o} =$	0.	$E_2^{\,o} = 32.6$
D, m =	**1**	$\varepsilon_1^{\,o} =$	10.92	$\nu_{21}^{\,o} = 0.71$
n, plis =	**30**	$\varepsilon_2^{\,o} =$	–7.76	$\nu_{12}^{\,o} = 0.30$
h, mm =	3.75			

Données : caract. italiques gras

EXEMPLE: TUBE DE TORSION
T300/5208, [+/–45]T

T, MNm =	**1**	$\sigma_6^{\,o} =$	127.
D, m =	**1**	$E_6^{\,o} =$	46.60
L, m =	**10**	$\varepsilon_6^{\,o} =$	2.73
n, plis =	**40**	$\theta =$	3.13
h, mm =	5.00		

Données : caract. italiques gras

18

RIGIDITE DE FLEXION
Sect 8.1

$[D] = \int [Q]z^2 dz$

$[d] = [D]^{-1} \neq \int [S]z^2 dz$

{M} = moment,   {k} = courbure

$\{M\} = [D]\{k\}$

$\{k\} = [d]\{M\}$

RIGIDITE DE FLEXION – 8 PLIS (MNm)
T300/5208

	[0]	[π/4]	[0/90]	[+/–45]	Alum
D_{11}	15.2	9.6	10.7	4.7	6.3
D_{22}	0.9	5.6	5.3	4.7	6.3
D_{12}	0.2	0.7	0.2	3.5	1.9
D_{66}	0.6	1.0	0.6	3.9	2.2
D_{16}	0.0	0.3	0.0	1.3	0.0
D_{26}	0.0	0.3	0.0	1.3	0.0

h = 8x0.125 = 1 mm, $h^3/12 = 0.0833$

19

CONST. NORM. DE FLEXION
Sect 8.1

$[D^*] = 12/h^3 \int [Q]z^2 dz$

$I^* = h^3/12, \quad [d^*] = [D^*]^{-1}$

$\{\sigma^f\} = [D^*]\{\varepsilon^f\}$

$\{\varepsilon^f\} = [d^*]\{\sigma^f\}$

$\{\sigma^f\} = 6/h^2 \int \{\sigma\}z dz$

$\{\varepsilon^f\} = h\{k\}/2$

RIGIDITE FLEXION NORM– 8 PLIS (MPa)
T300/5208

	[0]	[π/4]	[0/90]	[+/–45]	Alum
D_{11}^*	181.8	115.2	128.2	56.7	75.8
D_{22}^*	10.4	67.0	63.9	56.7	75.8
D_{12}^*	2.9	7.8	2.9	42.3	22.7
D_{66}^*	7.2	12.1	7.2	45.6	26.5
D_{16}^*	0.0	4.0	0.0	16.0	0.0
D_{26}^*	0.0	4.0	0.0	16.0	0.0

20

CONST. D'ING. EN FLEXION
Sect 8.2

$[d^*] = [D^*]^{-1}$

$E_1^f = 1/d_{11}^*$
$E_2^f = 1/d_{22}^*$, $E_6^f = 1/d_{66}^*$

$v_{21}^f = -d_{21}/d_{11}$
$v_{61}^f = d_{61}/d_{11}$

CONST. D'ING. FLEXION –8 PLIS (GPa)
T300/5208

	[0]	[π/4]	[0/90]	[+/–45]	Alum
E_1^f	181.0	113.3	128.1	24.7	69.0
E_2^f	10.3	65.3	63.9	24.7	69.0
E_6^f	7.2	11.7	7.2	41.4	26.5
v_{21}^f	0.28	0.10	0.05	0.72	0.30
v_{61}^f	0.00	–0.30	0.00	–0.10	0.0

21

PLAQUES SANDWICHES
Sect 8.5

$$[D] = 2 \int_{zc}^{h/2} [Q]z^2 dz$$

$[D^*] = 12/h^3 [D]$
Pourcentage de l'âme = $c^* = 2zc/h$
$[d^*] = [D^*]^{-1}$
$E_1^f = 1/d_{11}^*$

FLEX: {[0/90]ᵢ/zc}s, T300/5208, GPa

					Alum
i	2	2	2	8	8
zc	0	4	36	144	144
h	8	16	80	320	320
c*	0.0	0.5	0.9	0.9	0.9
E_1^f	128.1	96.0	26.6	26.2	18.7
E_2^f	63.9	71.9	25.4	25.9	18.7

Pour un matériau homogène : $E^t = (1-c^{*3})E$

22

POUTRE CONSOLE
Sect 8.6

P = charge,   L = long.,   b = larg.
$\quad M^{max} = PL$

$k_1 = d_{11}M_1 = d_{11}PL/b$
ou $= d_{11}^*PL/I = PL/E_1^f I$

$\delta^{max} = PL^3/3E_1^f bI^*$

POUTRE SANDWICH CONSOLE
T300/5208, {[0/90]₄/zc₇₂}s

P, kN =	*1*	I, m⁴ =	7E–08
L, m =	*1*	E_1^f =	26.60
b, m =	*0.1*	k_1,1/m =	0.56
n, plis =	160	ε_1^t, E–3 =	5.64
h, mm =	20.0	δ, mm =	188.0

Données : caract. italiques gras

23

POUTRE CAISSON CONSOLE
Sect 8.7

a = diamètre,   h = épais. de parois
$M^{max} = PL, \quad I = \pi a^3 h/8$

$k_1 = d_{11}M_1 = PL/E_1°I$

$\delta^{max} = PL^3/3E_1°I$

TUBE CIRCULAIRE CONSOLE
T300/5208, {[0/90]₂}s

P, kN =	*1*	I, m⁴ =	1E–07
L, m =	*1*	$E_1°$ =	96.00
a, m =	*0.1*	k_1,1/m =	0.11
n, plis =	8	ε_1^t, E–3 =	5.31
h, mm =	1.0	δ, mm =	35.37

Données : caract. italiques gras

24

STRATIFIES NON SYMETRIQUES
Sect 9

$\{\varepsilon\} = \{\varepsilon°\} + z\{k\}$

$\{N\} = [A]\{\varepsilon°\} + [B]\{k\}$
$\{M\} = [B]\{\varepsilon°\} + [D]\{k\}$

$[B] = \frac{1}{2}\int[Q]z dz$ = couplage membrane flexion

$[B] = 0$ pour un stratifié symétrique

CARACTERISTIQUES INHABITUELLES

Désavantages:
- Les stratifiés sont courbés
- Comportement difficile à prédire

Avantages:
- Courbure naturelle pour éviter les délaminages.
- Courbures compl. à partir de moules simples
- Utilisation potentielle pour précontrainte

25

CONSTANTES NORMALISEES
Sect 9.4

$\{\sigma^o\} = [A^*]\{\varepsilon^o\} + [B^*]\{\varepsilon^f\}$
$\{\sigma^f\} = 3[B^*]\{\varepsilon^o\} + [D^*]\{\varepsilon^f\}$

$\{\varepsilon^o\} = [\alpha^*]\{\sigma^o\} + [\beta^*]\{\sigma^f\}/3$
$\{\varepsilon^f\} = [\beta^*]^t\{\sigma^o\} + [\delta^*]\{\sigma^f\}$

$[B^*] = 2[B]/h^2, \quad [\beta^*] = h^2[\beta]/2$

CONSTANTES D'INGENIEUR
Sect 9.5

$\{\varepsilon^o\} = (\{\varepsilon^+\}+\{\varepsilon^-\})/2$
$\{\varepsilon^f\} = (\{\varepsilon^+\}-\{\varepsilon^-\})/2$

$E_1{}^o = 1/\alpha_{11}{}^*, \quad \nu_{21}{}^o = -\alpha_{21}/\alpha_{11}, \ldots$
$E_1{}^f = 1/\delta_{11}{}^*, \quad \nu_{21}{}^f = -\delta_{21}/\delta_{11}, \ldots$

26

LE THEOREME DES AXES PARALLELES
Sect 9.7

$\{N'\} = \{N\}$
$\{M'\} = \{M\} + d\{N\}$
d = distance de transfert = $z'-z$

$[A'] = [A]$
$[B'] = [B] + d[A]$
$[D'] = [D] + 2d[B] + d^2[A]$

ANCIENS ET NOUVEAUX AXES

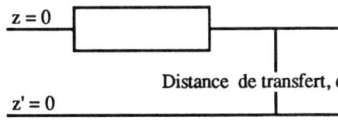

27

SOUS-STRATIFIES
Sect 9.8

$\{[\theta_1/\theta_2/\theta_3/\theta_4]r/zc\}s$

r = répét., u = épais. du sous–stratifié

$[A] = 2r[A^o]$
$[B] = 0$
$[D] = 2r\{[D^o] - (r-1)u[B^o]$
$\quad\quad + (r-1)(2r-1)u^2[A^o]/6\}$

AVANTAGES

• Analyse plus simple en flexion
•Optimisation plus simple
• Plus grande tenacité des stratifiés :
  meilleure dispersion des plis
• Stratification plus simple donc plus sure,
  et coûts de fabrication plus faibles.

28

CONSTRUCTION A PAROIS MINCES
Sect 9.9

$\{N^+\} = \{N\}/2 + \{M\}/h$
$\{N^-\} = \{N\}/2 - \{M\}/h$

$[A^*, D^*] = [1,3][A^+ + A^-]/h$
$[B^*] = [A^+ - A^-]/h$

$[\alpha^*, \delta^*] = [1, 1/3][a^+ + a^-]h/4$
$[\beta^*] = [a^+ - a^-]h/4$

AVANTAGES

• Matrices 3x3, au lieu de 6x6
  pour les constructions non symétriques
• Optimisation plus simple des stratifiés
• Incorporation plus facile des hybrides
• Ordre de grand. de l'approximation connu.

29

MICROMECANIQUE
Sect 10

Possibilités offertes:
  • Modèle de dégradation de matrice pour LPF
  • Données fonction de l'hygrothermie
  • Optimisation des matériaux
  • Modes de rupture

MODELES CLASSIQUES

• Modèle parallèle (borne sup.)
• Modèle série (borne inf.)
• Loi des mélanges modifiée
• Autres modèles de résistance
• Modèle des cylindres concentriques
• Modèle d'arrangement carré
• Modèle auto–consistant

30

LIMITATIONS DE LA MICROMECANIQUE

- Section des fibres idéalisée
- Arrangement idéalisé des fibres
- Hypothèses de continuité à l'interface
- Approximations dans l'analyse des contraintes
- Propriétés des fibres impossibles à mesurer
- Contraintes internes globalisées
- Modes de ruptures indéfinis

RECOMMENDATIONS SUR L'USAGE DE LA MICROMECANIQUE

Utiliser le calcul en retour pour déterminer les propriétés inconnues des constituants et les constantes empiriques

Ensuite, utiliser le calcul direct pour étudier l'influence des variables micromécaniques

31

LOI DES MELANGES MODIFIEE
Sect 10.2–5

Loi des mélanges:

$$E_x = v_f E_f + v_m E_m$$
$$v_x = v_f v_f + v_m v_m$$

Loi des mélanges modifiée:

$$(1 + v_y^*)/E_y = 1/E_{fx} + v_y^*/E_m$$
$$(1 + v_s^*)/E_s = 1/G_{fs} + v_s^*/G_m$$
$$v_y^* = \eta_y v_m/v_f, \quad v_s^* = \eta_s v_m/v_f$$

PARAMETRES DE REPARTITION DE CONTRAINTE
Eq 10.9

$$\eta = <\sigma_2>/<\sigma_1>$$

Paramètres calculés pour une fibre de carbone :

$$\eta_y = 0.5161$$
$$\eta_s = 0.3162$$

32

RIGIDITE TRANSVERSE DE LA COUCHE

$\eta_y = 0.516$ (calculé à partir du GFRP)
Rigidité transverse de la fibre:
$$E_{fy} = [(1 + v_y^*)/E_y - v_y^*/E_m]^{-1}$$

Rigidité transverse de la couche:
$$E_y' = (1 + v_y^*)/[1/E_{fx}' + v_y^*/E_m]$$

CALCUL DIRECT ET EN RETOUR DE LA RIGIDITE TRANSVERSE

$E_y =$	*10.3*	$v_y^* =$	0.22
$E_m =$	*3.40*	$E_{fx} =$	18.69 En retour
$v_f =$	*0.70*	$E_{fx}' =$	18.69 Valeur fixe
$\eta_y =$	*0.52*	$E_y' =$	10.30 Direct
$E_m^o =$	3.40	$E_y'/E_y =$	1.00
$E_m/E_m^o =$	1.00		

Données : caract. italiques gras

33

MODULE DE CISAILLEMENT DE LA COUCHE

$\eta_s = 0.316$ (calculé à partir du GFRP)
Module de cisaillement de la fibre:
$$G_{fx} = [(1+v_s^*)/E_s - v_s^*/G_m]^{-1}$$

Module de cisaillement de la couche:
$$E_s' = (1+v_s^*)/[1/G_{fx}+v_s^*/G_m]$$

CALCUL DIRECT ET EN RETOUR DU MODULE DE CISAILLEMENT

$E_s =$	*7.17*	$v_s^* =$	0.14
$E_m =$	*3.40*	$G_{fx} =$	19.70 En retour
$v_f =$	*0.70*	$G_{fx}' =$	19.70 Valeur fixe
$\eta_s =$	*0.32*	$E_s' =$	7.17 Direct
$E_m^o =$	3.40	$E_s'/E_s =$	1.00
$E_m/E_m^o =$	1.00		

Données : caract. italiques gras

34

RESISTANCES ORTHOTROPES
Sect 11.2

$\sigma_x \leq X$: longitudinale traction
$-\sigma_x \leq X'$: longitudinale compression
$\sigma_y \leq Y$: transverse traction
$-\sigma_y \leq Y'$: transverse compression
$\sigma/s \leq S$: cisaillement intralaminaire

von Mises: $X = X' = Y = Y', S = 0.57X$
Tresca: $X = X' = Y = Y', S = 0.50X$

RESISTANCES (MPa)
Table 11.1

	CFRP T300	GFRP Scotch	KFRP Kevlar	CCRP Tissu	Métal Alum
X	1500	1062	1400	499	400
X'	1500	610	235	352	400
Y	40	31	12	458	400
Y'	246	118	53	352	400
S	68	72	34	46	228

35
DEFORMATIONS MAXIMALES
Sect 11.5

$\varepsilon_x^* = X/E_x$
$\varepsilon_x'^* = X'/E_x$
$\varepsilon_y^* = Y/E_y$
$\varepsilon_y'^* = Y'/E_y$
$\varepsilon_s^* = S/E_s$, basé sur le module tangent

Le critère de déformation maximale compare
les déformations composante par composante

36
RAPPORTS CONTRAINTES/ /RESISTANCE
Sect 11.3

$\{\sigma\}^{max} = R\{\sigma\}^{appl}$
$\{\varepsilon\}^{max} = R\{\varepsilon\}^{appl}$

$R = 1$, rupture
$R = 2$, coefficient de sécurité de 2

R = résistance, si $\{\sigma\}$ unité est appliquée

37
CRITERE QUADRATIQUES DES CONTRAINTES
Sect 11.6

$F_{ij}\sigma_i\sigma_j + F_i\sigma_i = 1$
$F_{xx} = 1/XX'$, $F_{yy} = 1/YY'$, $F_{ss} = 1/S^2$
$F_{xy} = F_{xy}^*\sqrt{[F_{xx}F_{yy}]}$, $-1/2 \leq F_{xy}^* \leq 0$
$F_x = 1/X - 1/X'$, $F_y = 1/Y - 1/Y'$

$aR^2 + bR - 1 = 0$
Produits scalaires: $a = F_{ij}\sigma_i\sigma_j$, $b = F_i\sigma_i$

38
CRITERE QUADRTIQUES DES DEFORMATIONS
Sect 11.7

$G_{ij}\varepsilon_i\varepsilon_j + G_i\varepsilon_i = 1$

$G_{xx} = F_{xx}Q_{xx}^2 + 2F_{xy}Q_{xx}Q_{xy} + F_{yy}Q_{xy}^2$
$G_x = F_xQ_{xx} + F_yQ_{xy}$

$aR^2 + bR - 1 = 0$
Produits scalaires: $a = G_{ij}\varepsilon_i\varepsilon_j$, $b = G_i\varepsilon_i$

39
AVANTAGES DES CRITERES DE RUPTURE QUADRATIQUES

- Analytiquement simple
- Termes d'interaction inclus
- Critère scalaire et non tensoriel
- Fonctions bijectives
- Simple à mettre en oeuvre
- Racines conjuguées pour flexion

DEFORMATIONS MAXIMALES (E–3)
Table 11.1

ε^*	CFRP T300	GFRP Scotch	KFRP Kevlar	CCRP Tissu	Métal Alum
x	8.3	27.5	18.4	6.5	5.8
x'	8.3	15.8	3.1	4.8	5.8
y	3.9	3.8	2.2	6.2	5.8
y'	23.9	14.3	9.6	4.8	5.8
s	9.5	17.4	14.8	10.1	8.6

EXEMPLES

	Donnée	Modif. h FPF	Modif. h LPF	Modif. {N} FPF	Modif. {N} LPF
h, plis =	*8.*	6.67	8.57	8.00	8.00
{N} =	*2.00*	2.00	2.00	2.40	1.87
R/FPF =	*1.20*	1.00	1.29	1.00	1.29
R/LPF =	*1.40*	1.17	1.50	1.17	1.50
coef. de sécu	*1.5*				

Données : caract. italiques gras

PARAMETRES DE CONTRAINTES
Table 11.1

F_{ij} / F_i	CFRP T300	GFRP Scotch	KFRP Kevlar
F_{xx}	4E–19	2E–18	3E–18
F_{yy}	1E–16	3E–16	2E–15
F_{xy}	–3E–18	–1E–17	–3E–17
F_{ss}	2E–16	2E–16	9E–16
F_x	0E+0	–7E–10	–4E–9
F_y	2E–16	2E–08	6E–08

PARAMETRES DE DEFORMATIONS
Table 11.1

G_{ij} / G_i	CFRP T300	GFRP Scotch	KFRP Kevlar
G_{xx}	12004	1914	13454
G_{yy}	10681	18882	47657
G_{xy}	–3069	1712	2068
G_{ss}	11118	3306	4576
G_x	61	25	–150
G_y	217	198	351

AVANTAGES DES DEFORMATIONS (SUR LES CONTRAINTES)
Sect 11.7

- Grandeur adimensionnelle (unités)
- Enveloppes fixes pour tous les stratifiés
- Limite et ultime faciles à définir

Les enveloppes π/4 en ε donnent les limites pour les stratifiés équilibrés

40

MODES DE RUPTURE

Traction fibre:	X
Compression fibre:	X'
Traction matrice/interface:	Y
Compression matrice:	Y'
Cisaillement matrice/interface:	S

Delaminage aux bords libres ou par impact transverse ou par cuisson non uniforme.

41

RUPTURE DE PREMIERE COUCHE

• **Les modes de rupture sont mixtes**
• Type le + simple : rupt. matrice/interface
• Fissures // aux fibres, régulièrement espacées, saturées à la valeur ultime.
• La théorie des stratifiés doit être modifiée si les couches sont fissurées.

42

MODELE DE DEGRADATION DE MATRICE
Sect 12

Permet d'étendre la théorie des stratifiés au delà de la FPF. Les couches fissurées sont modélisées par des couches continues ayant un module de matrice plus faible soit :

$$0 < (E_m/E_m^o) < 1$$
$$v_x/v_x^o = E_m/E_m^o$$

43

MODULE DEGRADE DE LA MATRICE

Détermination empirique à partir de:

• Déformations du stratifié à FPF, et LPF
• Perte de rigidité lorsque les fissures augmentent sous chargement statique ou alterné
• Limite de rupture constatée

44

RESISTANCE ULTIME DU STRATIFIE

Le plus grand de LPF et FPF

• LPF > FPF dans le quadrant traction–traction
• LPF = FPF rupture simultanée des couches
• LPF < FPF dans le quadrant compres.–compres.

INTERACTIONS DES MODES

• Ne pas négliger les interactions.
• Bénéfiques dans les 1er et 3ème quadrants
• Pénalisantes dans les 2ème et 4ème quad.
• Le délaminage abaisse les valeurs limites
• Modèles d'identification délicats

DENSITE DE FISSURES, T300
Fig 19.2 à 19.5

L'analyse de transfert de charge prédit un espacement de 7 couches en épaisseur, soit une densité de 10 à 15 fissures par cm.

Résultat en accord pour un stratifié 45–degrés, mais plus fort pour un 90–degrés d'un facteur 3 soit 40 fissures/cm.

RIGIDITE DEGRADEE T300
Figure 12.3

E_m/E_m^o	E_y/E_y^o	E_s/E_s^o	v_x/v_x^o	E_x/E_x^o
0.4	0.55	0.50	0.112	1.00
0.3	0.44	0.39	0.084	1.00
0.2	0.32	0.27	0.056	1.00
0.1	0.17	0.14	0.028	1.00
0.01	0.01	0.01	0.003	1.00

Valeur recommandée : entre 0.1 et 0.3

RUPTURE DE DERNIERE COUCHE

• Plis intacts avant FPF
  ou la limite d'endurance
• Au delà, les plis se dégradent
• **LPF est la plus basse rupture de pli après dégradation de tous les plis**
• Dans certains cas : LPF ≤ FPF

RESISTANCE ULTIMES

FPF = $\boxed{1.00}$
LPF = $\boxed{1.40}$

Ultime = 1.40
Ultime = MAX(FPF,LPF)

Données : caract. italiques gras

45

RESISTANCE LIMITE

Une limite conservative peut être définie
par la règle suivante:
Règle 1:
Pas de dégradation de la matrice
(Afin d'éviter des modes de détérioration)
Règle 2 :
Une marge minimale entre ult. et lim.
(Coefficient de sécurité)
limite = MIN(FPF,ultim/coef. séc)

DIMENSIONNEMENT LIMITE ET ULTIME

FPF =	*1.00*
LPF =	*1.40*
Coefficient de sécurité =	*1.50*
ultime =	1.40
limite =	0.93
ult/lim =	1.50

Données : caract. italiques gras

46

AUTRE LIMITE DE DIMENSIONNEMENT

Dégradation de la matrice admissible
Ultime divisé par le coefficient de sécurité
lim* = MAX(FPF,LPF)/coef. sécurité
lim* = ultime/ coef. sécurité
Si LPF/FPF > Coef. sécurité, l'endommagement
peut être justifié s'il n'en résulte pas une perte
de capacité.(par l'utilisation d'une vessie dans
un réservoir par ex.)

CRITERES DE DIM. LIMITE D'UN STRATIFIE

FPF =	*1.00*
LPF =	*1.80*
Coefficient de sécurité =	*1.50*
ultime =	1.80

Dégradation de la matrice :

limite =	1.00	Interdite
lim* =	1.20	Admissible

47

CONTRAINTES RESIDUELLES
Sect 15

Basé sur un modèle thermoélastique linéaire

• Contraintes et déform. non mécaniques
• Contraintes et déform. résiduelles
• Expansion libre orthotrope
• Critère de rupture quadratique

DILATATION LIBRE
Eq 15.1

$$e_x = \alpha_x \Delta T + \beta_x c$$
$$e_y = \alpha_y \Delta T + \beta_y c$$

$\{\alpha\}$ = dilatation thermique
$\{\beta\}$ = dilatation humide
$\Delta T = T/oper - T/cuisson$
c = humidité

48

CONTRAINTES NON MECANIQUES
Eq 15.6 et 15.8

Contraintes non mécaniques:
$$\{\sigma\}^n = [Q]\{e\}$$

$$\{\sigma\}^{(o)n} = 1/h \int \{\sigma\}^n dz$$

Déformations non mécaniques:
$$\{\varepsilon\}^{(o)n} = [a]\{\sigma\}^{(o)n}$$

DEFORMATIONS RESIDUELLES
Eq 15.10

$$\{\varepsilon\}^{(o)r} = \{\varepsilon\}^{(o)n} - \{e\}$$

composantes:
$$\varepsilon_x^{(o)r} = \varepsilon_x^{(o)n} - e_x$$
$$\varepsilon_y^{(o)r} = \varepsilon_y^{(o)n} - e_y$$
$$\varepsilon_s^{(o)r} = \varepsilon_s^{(o)n}$$

49

DILATATIONS EFFECTIVES
Eq 15.11 et 15.12

$$\{\varepsilon\}^{(o)n} = \{\alpha\}^o \Delta T + \{\beta\}^o c$$

$$\{\alpha\}^o = [a]\int [Q]\{\alpha\} dz$$

$$\{\beta\}^o = [a]\int [Q]\{\beta\} dz$$

CRITERE QUADRATIQUE AVEC CONTRAINTES RESIDUELLES
Eq 15.14 à 15.18

$$\{\varepsilon\}^* = R^m\{\varepsilon\}^m + \{\varepsilon\}^r$$
ou $$= R^m\{\varepsilon\}^m + \{\varepsilon\}^n - \{e\}$$

$$\{\varepsilon\}^*[G]\{\varepsilon\}^{*t} + \{G\}\{\varepsilon\}^* = 1$$

$$a(R^m)^2 + bR^m - 1 = 0$$

50
TEMPERATURE REDUITE
Sect 17.2

$T^* = [T/g - T/opr]/[T/g - T/rm]$
$T^* = 1$ à l'ambiante
$T^* = 0$ à la temp. de transition vitreuse

$T/g = T/g^o - gc$
g = glissement en température dû à l'humidité

51
LOI PUISSANCE POUR LES RIGIDITES
Eq 17.8 à17.11

$E_x/E_x^o = (v_f/v_f^o)(T^*)^f$
$v_x/v_x^o = 1$ (constant)
$E_y/E_y^o =$ fonction non linéaire (T*, v_f)
$E_s/E_s^o =$ fonction non linéaire (T*, v_f)

52
METHODE DE CLASSEMENT
Sect 13
Stratifiés sym. / efforts de membrane
L'analyse prend en compte:
Les chargements complexes et multiples
Les contraintes résiduelles
Les critères limites FPF, LPF
Base de données générée par:
Sous–stratifiés de 2 à10 couches
2 à 4 orientations quelconques

53
SOUS–STRATIFIES ET ARRONDIS
• Code du sous stratifié:
{[a b c d]r}$_s$
(a plis à θ_1, b plis à θ_2, etc)
• Code du stratifié d'arrondi:
[A B C D]$_s$
(A plis à θ_1, etc)
• Code complet du stratifié:
{[a b c d]r ± [A B C D]}$_s$

54
ANALYSE MICRO–MACRO MECANIQUE INTEGREE

Analyse de la résistance et de la rigidité:
• Matière et géométrie de la fibre
• Matière et géométrie de la matrice
• Séq. d'empilement et chargements
• Temp. de cuisson et cond. hyhrothermiques
• Structures simples statiques
• Hybrides, parois minces et duplex

LOI PUISSANCE POUR DONNEES HYGRO
Eq 17.3 à 17.7
Matrice:
$E_m^* = (T^*)^a$
$\eta_v^* = \eta_s^* = (T^*)^b$
$X_m^* = (T^*)^c$

Fibre:
$E_{fx}^* = E_{fy}^* = G_{fx}^* = (T^*)^f$
$X_f^* = (T^*)^h$

LOI PUISSANCE POUR RESISTANCE
Eq 17.12 à 17.14

$X^* = (v_f/v_f^o)(T^*)^h$
$X'^* = (v_f/v_f^o)(T^*)^h(E_s/E_s^o)^a$

Le micro–flambement est pris en compte
$Y^* = Y'^* = S^* = (T^*)^c$

Effets d'interface compris

CRITERES DE CLASSEMENT

Options en résistance :
lim = limite sans dégradation possible
lim* = limite avec dégradation possible

Les limites sont fonction des valeurs :
du coef. de dégradation de la matrice, environ 0.3
du coefficient de sécurité , 1.5 ou plus

FAMILLES DE STRATIFIES

Sous–str. Plis	No orientations 2	3	4	Total
6	7	28	84	119
7	8	36	120	164
8	9	45	165	219
9	10	55	220	285
10	11	66	286	363
				1150

ORGANIGRAMME D'UN MIC–MAC

Hygro		Contr.	>>>	Comp
Micro	>>>	Macro		Struct
T/cuisson	>>>	Charges		

55

CONCLUSIONS

Le dimensionnement des composites c'est:
- Simple
- Direct
- Consistant
- Compatible avec les théories isotropes
- Facile d'abord pour les novices
- Perfectible même pour les experts
- Quand vous voulez, nous sommes prêts.

56

NE FAITES PAS ...

- N'utilisez pas les abaques
- Ne croyez pas au déchaussement des fibres
- N'utilisez pas la théorie du filet
- Ne devinez pas l'inversion d'une matrice
- N'utilisez pas des scalaires pour les composites
- N'utilisez pas les contraintes uniaxiales
- N'utilisez pas les modes simples pour décrire les modes mixtes
- Ne laissez pas les experts vous dire que vous ne comprenez pas.

FAITES...

- Toujours calculer
- Utiliser la théorie des stratifiés
- Utiliser les critère de rupture quadratiques
- Inclure les contraintes de cuisson
- Utiliser la micro–macromécanique
- Utiliser la théorie simplifiée dans les itérations
- Combiner la méthode du classement et l'optimisation
- Prenez du plaisir avec les composites

LE FUTUR DES COMPOSITES

- Coût des matériaux plus bas
- Coût de fabrication plus bas
- Conception précise et rationnelle
- Théories rationnelles et rigoureuses
- Vision positive et constructive
- Concepts nouveaux et audacieux
- Fonctions multiples et intégrées
- Spécialistes jeunes et bien formés

28.3 GERMAN OUTLINE

VEREINFACHTE BERECHNUNG VON FASERVERBUNDWERKSTOFFEN (FVW)

Grundlagen für den Entwicklungsingenieur

R.M.Aoki
DFVLR-Stuttgart
Inst.f.Bauweisen-u.Konstruktionsforschung
Telefon: (0711)-6862-470

ANNAHMEN UND METHODEN

* Möglichst einfache Theorien u. Modelle
* Integrierte mikro-makromechanische Rechenverfahren
* Wiederholung v.Sublaminaten z.Lösungsvereinfachung
* Für unsym.Bauteile Theorie d.dünnwandige Schalen
* Quadratisches Kriterium u.Versagens-/Festigkeitsgrenze
* Hygrothermisch-abhängige Eigenschaften
* Eingefrorene Spannungen
* Verallgemeinerte Rangfolge von Laminaten

RÜSTZEUG

* Benutzerfreundliche Pakete
* Tabellenkalkulationsprogramme:Excel od. Lotus 123
* Integrierte Graphik und Makros
* Antworten auf:Was wenn? und:Was ist das Beste?
* Selbsterlernbare Anweisungen

EINFACHE OD. KOMPLEXE SPANNUNGSZUSTÄNDE

* Einfache Spannungszustände: uniaxial, reiner Schub, hydrostatisch
* Komplexe Spannungszustände: zweiachsig od. komplexer

Komplexe Spannungszustände lassen sich nicht aus einfachen Spannungszuständen vorhersagen.

LITERATURHINWEISE

Stephen W. Tsai
Composites Design-1987
Think Composites,Dayton,Ohio (1987)

Stephen W. Tsai und H.Thomas Hahn
Introduction to Composite Materials
Technomic, Lancaster, Pa. (1985)

FRAGLICHE HILFSMITTEL

* Modelle mit einfachen Spannungszuständen
* Nomogramme für Spannungen
* Nichtinteraktive Versagensanalyse
* Shear lag Analyse für Faserauszug
* Netzanalyse für Druckgefäße
* Max.Spannungs- bzw. Dehnungskriterien
* Optimierung des Winkellaminatanteils

FERTIGE SOFTWARE

* Geprüft und fehlerfrei
* Geringer Aufwand
* Neue Dokumentation
* Ständig auf dem neuesten Stand
* Einfaches Selbst-und Dialogtraining
* Kostet weniger als ein Mann-Tag

SPANNUNGSZUSTÄNDE

	Uniaxial	Schub	Hydro	Biaxial	Komplex
σ_1	1.0	0.0	1.0	1.0	-3.0
σ_2	0.0	0.0	1.0	2.0	-2.0
σ_6	0.0	1.0	0.0	0.0	1.0

5
EINZELNE OD. MEHRFACHE LASTEN

Mehrfache Lasten stellen die verschiedenen Belastungszustände während der Lebensdauer einer Struktur dar.

Bei dem Entwurf von FVW müssen merfache Lasten von Anfang an berücksicht werden, da Schichtanzahl und -orientierung die Entwurfslast bestimmen.

MEHRFACHE LASTEN

	#1	#2	#3	#4
σ_1	1.0	2.0	–1.0	2.0
σ_2	0.0	0.0	–2.0	–1.0
σ_6	0.0	1.0	–1.0	1.0

6
MITTLERE SPANNUNGEN IN UNIDIREKTIONALEN FVW

* Off-axis Schichtspannungen:einfach od. komplex
* On-axis Schispannungen:einfach oder komplex
* Spannungen der Komponente:immer komplex
* Grenzflächenspannungen:immer komplex

Bei FVW-Entwürfen müssen komplexe Spannungen in fast allen Fällen berücksichtigt werden.

MITTLERE SPANNUNGEN IN LAMINIERTEN FVW

* Laminatspannung:einfach od.komplex
* Off-axis Schichtspannung:immer komplex
* On-axis Schichtspannung:immer komplex
* Interlaminare Spannung:immer komplex

In allen Fällen treten komplexe Spannungen auf

7
SPANNUNGEN

Gl.5.1 und Gl.5.16

$$\sigma_1' = m^2\sigma_1 + n^2\sigma_2 + 2mn\sigma_6$$
$$\sigma_2' = n^2\sigma_1 + m^2\sigma_2 - 2mn\sigma_6$$
$$\sigma_6' = mn(-\sigma_1+\sigma_2) + (m^2-n^2)\sigma_6$$
$$m = \cos\theta, \ n = \sin\theta$$

$$\tan2\theta_0 = 2\sigma_6/(\sigma_1-\sigma_2)$$

θ_0 = Orientierung der Hauptachsen
$\theta_0+\pi/4$ = Orientierung des max. Schubs

SPANNUNGSTRANSFORMATIONEN

Bezug	Belieb.	Haupt.	Max.	Invarian-
Winkel θ		θ_0	Schub	ten

θ	0.0	10.0	10.9	+π/4	p, q, R
σ_1	–2.0	–2.2	–2.2	0.5	0.5
σ_2	3.0	3.2	3.2	0.5	–2.5
σ_6	–1.0	–0.1	0.0	–2.7	2.7

Eingaben sind fettgedruckt

8
VERZERRUNGEN

Gl.5.1 und 5.18

$$\epsilon_1' = m^2\epsilon_1 + n^2\epsilon_2 + mn\epsilon_6$$
$$\epsilon_2' = n^2\epsilon_1 + m^2\epsilon_2 - mn\epsilon_6$$
$$\epsilon_6' = 2mn(-\epsilon_1+\epsilon_2) + (m^2-n^2)\epsilon_6$$
$$m = \cos\theta, \ n = \sin\theta$$

$$\tan2\theta_0 = \epsilon_6/(\epsilon_1-\epsilon_2)$$

θ_0 = Orientierung der Hauptachsen
$\theta_0+\pi/4$ = Orientierung des max.Schubs

VERZERRUNGSTRANSFORMATIONEN

Bezug	Belieb.	Haupt.	Max.	Invarian-
Winkel θ		θ_0	Schub	ten

θ	0.0	10.0	5.7	+π/4	p,q,R
ϵ_1	–2.0	–2.0	–2.0	0.5	0.5
ϵ_2	3.0	3.0	3.0	0.5	–2.5
ϵ_6	–1.0	0.8	0.0	–2.5	2.5

Eingaben sind fettgedruckt

9
KLASSISCHE LAMINAT-THEORIE
Abschnitt 7-9
* Effektive Konstanten in der Ebene $[E^0],[v^0]$
* Spannungs-u.Verzerrungsmittelwert:$[\sigma^0],[\epsilon^0]$
* Effektive Ausdehnung: $[\alpha^0]$, $[\beta^0]$

* Effektive Ausdehnungen: $[E^f]$, $[v^f]$
* Effektive Oberflächenspannung u.Verzerrung $[\sigma^f]$, $[\epsilon^f]$
* Schichtfestigkeit/Spannungsverhältnis: R

GRUNDANNAHMEN
* Dünne Laminate
* Querschnitte bleiben eben
* Lineare Spannungs-Verzerrungsbeziehung
* Lineare Verzerrungs-Verschiebungsbezieh.
* Quadratisches Versagenskriterium f.FPFu.LPF
* Lineare Hygrothermoelastizität
* Mikromechanische Rückrechnung
* Nichtlineare Regressionskurven

10
ON-AXIS SCHICHTSTEIFIGKEIT
Abschnitt 6.1
Vier Orthotropiekonstanten:
* Längssteifigkeit: E_x
* Quersteifigkeit: E_y
* Querkontraktionszahl: v_x
* Schubmodul: E_s

INGENIEURKONSTANTEN (GPa)
Tabelle 6.4

[Q]	CFK	GFK	SFK	CFK	METALL
	T300	Scotch	Kevlar	Gewebe	Al
E_x	181.0	38.6	76.0	74.0	69.0
E_y	10.3	8.3	5.5	74.0	69.0
v_x	0.28	0.26	0.34	0.05	0.30
E_s	7.2	4.1	2.3	4.6	26.5

Für isotrope Werkstoffe nur zwei
Konstanten:
$E_x = E_y = E$, $v_x = v_y = v$, $E_s = E/2(1+v)$

11
ON-AXIS SPANNUNGS-VERZERRUNGS-GESETZ
Abschnitt 6.1
$\{\sigma\} = [Q]\{\epsilon\}$
$\{\epsilon\} = [S]\{\sigma\}$
Steifigkeit: $Q_{xx} = E_x/(1-v_xv_y)$
Nachgiebigkeit: $S_{xx} = Q_{yy}/(Q_{xx}Q_{yy}-Q_{xy}^2)$
Ingenieurkonstanten: $E_x = 1/S_{xx}$

Für isotrope Werkstoffe:
$Q_{xx} = E/(1-v^2)$, $S_{xx} = 1/E$

ON-AXIS WERTE (GPa)
Tabelle 6.4

[Q]	CFK	GFK	SFK	CFK	METALL
	T300	Scotch	Kevlar	Gewebe	Al
Q_{xx}	181.8	39.2	76.6	74.0	75.8
Q_{yy}	10.4	8.4	5.6	74.0	75.8
Q_{xy}	2.9	2.2	1.9	0.1	22.7
Q_{ss}	7.2	4.1	2.3	4.6	26.5

12
OFF-AXIS SCHICHTSTEIFIGKEIT
Abschnitt 6.1 u. 6.2
$Q_{11} = m^4Q_{xx}+n^4Q_{yy}+2m^2n^2Q_{xy}+4m^2n^2Q_{ss}$
$m = \cos\theta$, $n = \sin\theta$, θ = ply angle

$Q_{11} = U_1+U_2\cos2\theta+U_3\cos4\theta$
U_i= lineare Kombination von on-axis [Q]
$U_1 = (3Q_{xx}+3Q_{yy}+2Q_{xy}+4Q_{ss})/8$
$U_2 = (Q_{xx}-Q_{yy})/2$

OFF-AXIS WERTE (GPa)
T300

θ	0°	15°	30°	45°	60°	90°
Q_{11}	181.8	160.4	109.4	56.7	23.6	10.3
Q_{22}	10.3	11.9	23.6	56.7	160.4	181.8
Q_{12}	2.9	12.8	32.4	42.3	32.4	2.9
Q_{66}	7.2	17.0	36.7	46.6	17.0	7.2
Q_{16}	0.0	38.5	54.2	42.9	20.1	0.0
Q_{26}	0.0	4.4	20.1	42.9	54.2	0.0

13

QUASI-ISOTROPE KONSTANTEN
Abschnitt 6.3

Lineare Invarianten:

$U_1 = (3Q_{11}+3Q_{22}+2Q_{12}+4Q_{66})/8$
$U_4 = (Q_{11}+Q_{22}+6Q_{12}-4Q_{66})/8$

$E^{iso} = (U_1{}^2-U_4{}^2)/U_1$
$v^{iso} = U_4/U_1$
$G^{iso} = (U_1-U_4)/2$

QUASI-ISOTROPISCH (GPa)
Tabelle 6.4

T300 Scotch Kevlar Gewebe Al

	CFK	GFK	SFK	CFK	METALL
E^{iso}	69.7	19.0	29.0	52.7	69.0
v^{iso}	0.30	0.27	0.32	0.32	0.30
ρ	1.6	1.8	1.5	1.5	2.6
E^{iso}/ρ	43.1	10.5	19.8	35.1	26.5

EFFEKTIVE SCHEIBENSTEIFIGKEITEN
Abschnitt 7.2

$[A^*] = 1/h \int[Q]dz$
$[a^*] = [A^*]^{-1}$

$\{\sigma^o\} = [A^*]\{\epsilon^o\}$
$\{\epsilon^o\} = [a^*]\{\sigma^o\}$

$\{\sigma^o\} = 1/h \int\{\sigma\}dz,$
$\{\epsilon^o\} \neq f(z)$

SCHEIBENSTEIFIGKEIT (GPa)
T300

	[0]	[π/4]	[0/90]	[+/-45]	[0/±45]	Alum
A_{11}^*	181.8	76.4	96.0	56.7	98.4	75.8
A_{22}^*	10.4	76.4	96.0	56.7	41.2	75.8
A_{12}^*	2.9	22.6	2.9	42.3	29.2	22.7
A_{66}^*	7.2	26.9	7.2	46.6	33.4	26.5
A_{16}^*	0.0	0.0	0.0	0.0	0.0	0.0
A_{26}^*	0.0	0.0	0.0	0.0	0.0	0.0

INGENIEUR-SCHEIBENKONSTANTEN
Abschnitte 7.3 u.7.4

$[a^*] = [A^*]^{-1} \neq \int[S]dz$

$E_1{}^o = 1/a_{11}^* \neq \int E_1 dz$
$E_2{}^o = 1/a_{22}^*, E_6{}^o = 1/a_{66}^*$

$v_{21}{}^o = -a_{21}/a_{11}$
$v_{61}{}^o = a_{61}/a_{11}$

SCHEIBEN-KONSTANTEN GPa
T300

	[0]	[π/4]	[0/90]	[+/-45]	[0/±45]	Alum
$E_1{}^o$	181.0	69.7	96.0	25.0	77.7	69.0
$E_2{}^o$	10.3	69.7	96.0	25.0	32.6	69.0
$E_6{}^o$	7.2	26.9	7.2	46.6	33.5	26.5
$v_{21}{}^o$	0.28	0.30	0.03	0.75	0.71	0.30
$v_{61}{}^o$	0.0	0.0	0.0	0.0	0.0	0.0

16

DRUCKGEFÄBE
Abschnitt 7.13

P = Innendruck   F = axiale Kraft
D = Durchmesser h = Wanddicke

$\sigma_1{}^o = PD/4h + F/\pi Dh$
$\sigma_2{}^o = PD/2h$

$\epsilon_1{}^o = a_{11}^*\sigma_1{}^o + a_{12}^*\sigma_2{}^o = (\sigma_1{}^o - v_{12}{}^o\sigma_2{}^o)/E_1{}^o$
$\epsilon_2{}^o = a_{21}^*\sigma_1{}^o + a_{22}^*\sigma_2{}^o = (\sigma_2{}^o - v_{21}\sigma_1{}^o)/E_2{}^o$

BEISPIEL: DRUCKGEFÄB
T300/5208, [0/45/±45]T

F, kN =	10	$\sigma_1{}^o =$	849.	$E_1{}^o = 77.7$
P,MPa=	0	$\sigma_2{}^o =$	0.	$E_2{}^o = 32.6$
D, m =	1	$\epsilon_1{}^o =$	10.92	$v_{21}{}^o = 0.71$
n,Lagen =	30	$\epsilon_2{}^o =$	-7.76	$v_{12}{}^o = 0.30$
h, mm =	3.75			

17

ROHRE UNTER TORSION
Abschnitt 7.13

T = Torsionsmoment   D = Durchmesser
h = Wanddicke   L = Länge

$\sigma_6^{\,0} = 2T/\pi D^2 h$
$\varepsilon_6^{\,0} = \sigma_6^{\,0}/E_6^{\,0}$
$\theta = 2(L/D)\varepsilon_6^{\,0}(180/\pi)$

18

BIEGESTEIFIGKEITSKONSTANTEN
Abschnitt 8.1

$[D] = \int[Q]z^2 dz$
$[d] = [D]^{-1} \neq \int[S]z^2 dz$

$\{M\}$ = moment, $\{k\}$ = curvature

$\{M\} = [D]\{k\}$
$\{k\} = [d]\{M\}$

19

NORMIERTE BIEGEKONSTANTEN
Abschnitt 8.1

$[D^*] = 12/h^3 \int[Q]z^2 dz$
$I^* = h^3/12,\quad [d^*] = [D^*]^{-1}$

$\{\sigma^f\} = [D^*]\{\varepsilon^f\}$
$\{\varepsilon^f\} = [d^*]\{\sigma^f\}$

$\{\sigma^f\} = 6/h^2 \int\{\sigma\}z dz$
$\{\varepsilon^f\} = h\{k\}/2$

20

INGENIEUR-BIEGEKONSTANTEN
Abschnitt 8.2

$[d^*] = [D^*]^{-1}$

$E_1^{\,f} = 1/d_{11}^{\,*}$
$E_2^{\,f} = 1/d_{22}^{\,*},\quad E_6^{\,f} = 1/d_{66}^{\,*}$

$v_{21}^{\,f} = -d_{21}/d_{11}$
$v_{61}^{\,f} = d_{61}/d_{11}$

BEISPIEL: ROHR UNTER TORSION
T300/5208, [+/–45]T

T, MNm =	1		$\sigma_6^{\,0}$ =	127.
D, m =	1		$E_6^{\,0}$ =	46.60
L, m =	10		$\varepsilon_6^{\,0}$ =	2.73
n,Lagen =	40		θ =	3.13
h, mm =	5.00			

ABSOLUTE BIEGEWERTE BEI 8-LAGEN
(MNm)   T300

	[0]	[π/4]	[0/90]	[+/–45]	Alum
D_{11}	15.2	9.6	10.7	4.7	6.3
D_{22}	0.9	5.6	5.3	4.7	6.3
D_{12}	0.2	0.7	0.2	3.5	1.9
D_{66}	0.6	1.0	0.6	3.9	2.2
D_{16}	0.0	0.3	0.0	1.3	0.0
D_{26}	0.0	0.3	0.0	1.3	0.0

$h = 8 \times 0.125 = 1$ mm, $h^3/12 = 0.0833$

NORMIERTE BIEGEWERTE BEI 8-LAGEN
(GPa)   T300

	[0]	[π/4]	[0/90]	[+/–45]	Alum
$D_{11}^{\,*}$	181.8	115.2	128.2	56.7	75.8
$D_{22}^{\,*}$	10.4	67.0	63.9	56.7	75.8
$D_{12}^{\,*}$	2.9	7.8	2.9	42.3	22.7
$D_{66}^{\,*}$	7.2	12.1	7.2	45.6	26.5
$D_{16}^{\,*}$	0.0	4.0	0.0	16.0	0.0
$D_{26}^{\,*}$	0.0	4.0	0.0	16.0	0.0

ING.-BIEGEKONSTANTEN BEI 8-LAGEN
(GPa)   T300

	[0]	[π/4]	[0/90]	[+/–45]	Alum
$E_1^{\,f}$	181.0	113.3	128.1	24.7	69.0
$E_2^{\,f}$	10.3	65.3	63.9	24.7	69.0
$E_6^{\,f}$	7.2	11.7	7.2	41.4	26.5
$v_{21}^{\,f}$	0.28	0.10	0.05	0.72	0.30
$v_{61}^{\,f}$	0.00	–0.30	0.00	–0.10	0.0

21

SANDWICH PLATTEN
Abschnitt 8.5

$$[D] = 2 \int_{zc}^{h/2} [Q]z^2 dz$$

$[D^*] = 12/h^3 \, [D]$

Prozentualer Kernanteil = $c^* = 2zc/h$

$[d^*] = [D^*]^{-1}$

$E_1^f = 1/d_{11}^*$

22

EINSEITIG-EINGESP.BALKEN
Abschnitt 8.6

P= Endlast, L =Länge, b =Breite

$$M^{max} = PL$$

$k_1 = d_{11}M_1 = d_{11}PL/b$
or $= d_{11}^* PL/I = PL/E_1^f I$

$$\delta^{max} = PL^3/3E_1^f bI^*$$

23

EINSEITIG-EINGESP. ROHR
Abschnitt 8.7

a = Durchmesser, h =Wanddicke

$$M^{max} = PL, \quad I = \pi a^3 h/8$$

$k_1 = d_{11}M_1 = PL/E_1^o I$

$$\delta^{max} = PL^3/3E_1^o I$$

24

UNSYMMETRISCHE LAMINATE
Abschnitt 9

$$\{\varepsilon\} = \{\varepsilon^o\} + z\{k\}$$

$\{N\} = [A]\{\varepsilon^o\} + [B]\{k\}$
$\{M\} = [B]\{\varepsilon^o\} + [D]\{k\}$

$[B] = \int [Q]z dz = $ Kopplung Scheibe-Platte

$[B] = 0$ für sym. Laminate

BIEGUNG: $\{[0/90]_i/zc\}s$, T300, GPa

i	2	2	2	8	8 Alum
zc	0	4	36	144	144
h	8	16	80	320	320
c^*	0.0	0.5	0.9	0.9	0.9
E_1^f	128.1	96.0	26.6	26.2	18.7
E_2^f	63.9	71.9	25.4	25.9	18.7

Für homogene Werkstoffe: $E^f = (1 - c^{*3})E$

EINSEITIG-EINGESP.SANDWICHBALKEN
T300/5208, $\{[0/90]_4/zc_{72}\}s$

P, kN =	1	I, m⁴ = 7E–08
L, m =	1	E_1^f = 26.60
b, m =	0.1	k_1,1/m = 0.56
n,Lagen =	160	ε_1^t, E–3 = 5.64
h, mm =	20.0	δ, mm = 188.0

EINSEITIG-EINGESP. ROHR
T300/5208, $\{[0/90]_2\}s$

P, kN =	1	I, m⁴ = 1E–07
L, m =	1	E_1^o = 96.00
a, m =	0.1	k_1,1/m = 0.11
n,Lagen =	8	ε_1^t, E–3 = 5.31
h, mm =	1.0	δ, mm = 35.37

BESONDERE EIGENSCHAFTEN

Nachteile:
* Laminate sind deformiert
* Verhalten schwer vorherzusagen

Vorteile:
* Natürliche Krümmungen um Delaminationen zu vermeiden
* Komplexe Krümmungen aus einfachen Formen
* Potentielle Anwendung von Vorlasten

25

NORMIERTE KONSTANTEN
Abschnitt 9.4

$\{\sigma^o\} = [A^*]\{\epsilon^o\} + [B^*]\{\epsilon^f\}$
$\{\sigma^f\} = 3[B^*]\{\epsilon^o\} + [D^*]\{\epsilon^f\}$

$\{\epsilon^o\} = [\alpha^*]\{\sigma^o\} + [\beta^*]\{\sigma^f\}/3$
$\{\epsilon^f\} = [\beta^*]^t\{\sigma^o\} + [\delta^*]\{\sigma^f\}$

$[B^*] = 2[B]/h^2, \quad [\beta^*] = h^2[\beta]/2$

26

PARALLELES ACHSEN THEOREM
Abschnitt 9.7

$\{N'\} = \{N\}$
$\{M'\} = \{M\} + d\{N\}$

$d = $ Versetzungsabstand $= z'-z$

$[A'] = [A]$
$[B'] = [B] + d[A]$
$[D'] = [D] + 2d[B] + d^2[A]$

27

WIEDERHOLUNG VON SUBLAMINATEN
Abschnitt 9.8

$\{[\theta_1/\theta_2/\theta_3/\theta_4]r/zc\}s$

r=wiederholen, u=Dicke des Sublaminates

$[A] = 2r[A^o]$
$[B] = 0$
$[D] = 2r\{[D^o] - (r-1)u[B^o]$
$\quad\quad\quad + (r-1)(2r-1)u^2[A^o]/6\}$

28

DÜNNWANDIGE KONSTRUKTION
Abschnitt 9.9

$\{N^+\} = \{N\}/2 + \{M\}/h$
$\{N^-\} = \{N\}/2 - \{M\}/h$

$[A^*, D^*] = [1,3][A^+ + A^-]/h$
$[B^*] = [A^+ - A^-]/h$

$[\alpha^*, \delta^*] = [1, 1/3][a^+ + a^-]h/4$
$[\beta^*] = [a^+ - a^-]h/4$

INGENIEURKONSTANTEN
Abschnitt 9.5

$\{\epsilon^o\} = (\{\epsilon^+\} + \{\epsilon^-\})/2$
$\{\epsilon^1\} = (\{\epsilon^+\} - \{\epsilon^-\})/2$

$E_1^o = 1/\alpha_{11}^*, \quad v_{21}^o = -\alpha_{21}/\alpha_{11}, \ldots$
$E_1^1 = 1/\delta_{11}^*, \quad v_{21}^1 = -\delta_{21}/\delta_{11}, \ldots$

Nicht gültig für statisch bestimmte
Strukturen wegen Koppelung

ALTE UND NEUE ACHSEN

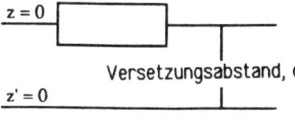

Versetzungsabstand, d

VORTEILE
* Vereinfachte Biegetheorie
* Einfachere Winkeloptimierung
* Höhere Laminatzähigkeit wegen
  feinerer Schichtdispersion (Spleissung)
* Einfacher Lagenaufbau reduziert Fehler
  und mindert Herstellungskosten

VORTEILE
* 3X3 Matrizen anstatt 6x6 Matrizen
  für unsymmetrische Aufbauten
* Einfachere Laminatoptimierung
* Leichtere Berücksichtigung von Hybriden
* Fehler entspricht dem Flächen-Tiefen-
  verhältnis

29 MIKROMECHANIK

Möglichkeiten:
* Für LPF Matrixdegradationsmodell
* Hygrothermisch abhängige Daten
* Werkstoffoptimierung
* Versagensformen

30 GRENZEN DER MIKROMECHANIK
* Idealisierte Faserquerschnitte
* Idealisierte Symmetrie der Faser-
  verteilung
* Angenommene Kontinuität an der
  Grenzschicht (interface)
* Näherungen in der Spannungsanalyse
* Nicht meßbare Fasereigenschaften
* Nichtberücksichtigung v. Schrumpf-
  spannungen
* Nichtdefinierte Versagensformen

ÜBLICHE MODELLE
* Parallel-Modell (obere Grenze)
* Reihen-Modell (untere Grenze)
* Modifizierte Mischungsregel
* Andere Werkstoffestigkeitsmodelle
* Konzentrisches Zylindermodell
* Quadratisches Verteilungsmodell
* Selbstvertägliches Modell

EMPFOHLENE ANWENDUNG DER MIKROMECHANIK
Rückrechnung zur Bestimmung der
unbekannten Komponenteneigenschaften
und empirischen Konstanten

Dann Vorausrechnung zur Bestimmung der
Empfindlichkeit der verschiedenen mikro-
mechanischen Variablen

31 MODIFIZIERTE MISCHUNGSREGEL

Mischungsregel:
$$E_x = v_f E_f + v_m E_m$$
$$v_x = v_f v_f + v_m v_m$$

Modifizierte Mischungsregel
$$(1 + v_y^*)/E_y = 1/E_{fx} + v_y^*/E_m$$
$$(1 + v_s^*)/E_s = 1/G_{fs} + v_s^*/G_m$$
$$v_y^* = \eta_y v_m/v_f, \quad v_s^* = \eta_s v_m/v_f$$

32 QUERSTEIFIGKEIT DER SCHICHT

η_y = 0.516 (Rückrechnung von GFK)

Rückr.Faserquersteifigkeit
$$E_{fy} = [(1 + v_y^*)/E_y - v_y^*/E_m]^{-1}$$

Berechnung Schichtquersteifigkeit
$$E_y' = (1 + v_y^*)/[1/E_{fx}' + v_y^*/E_m]$$

PARAMETER DER SPANNUNGS-AUFTEILUNG

$$\eta = <\sigma_2>/<\sigma_1>$$
Für Schicht-Quersteifigkeit und isotrope
Fasern in GFK Rückrechnung der Spannungs-
parameter:
$$\eta_y = 0.5161$$
$$\eta_s = 0.3162$$

RÜCK- UND VORAUSRECHNUNG QUERSTEIFIGKEIT

E_y =	**10.3**	
E_m =	**3.40**	
v_f =	**0.70**	
η_y =	**0.52**	
E_m^o =	3.40	
E_m/E_m^o =	1.00	

v_y^* =	0.22
E_{fx} =	18.69 Rückrechnung
E_{fx}' =	18.69 fester Wert
E_y' =	10.30 Vorausrechnung
E_y'/E_y =	1.00

33

SCHUBMODUL DER SCHICHT

$\eta_S = 0.316$ (Rückrechnung aus GFK)

Rückrechnung des Faserschubmoduls
$G_{fx} = [(1+v_s{}^*)/E_s - v_s{}^*/G_m]^{-1}$

Vorausberechn. des Schichtschubmoduls
$E_s{}' = (1+v_s{}^*)/[1/G_{fx} + v_s{}^*/G_m]$

RÜCK- UND VORAUSRECHNUNG SCHUBMODUL

$E_s =$	7.17	$v_s{}^* =$	0.14
$E_m =$	3.40	$G_{fx} =$	19.70 Rückrechn.
$v_f =$	0.70	$G_{fx}{}' =$	19.70 fester Wert
$\eta_s =$	0.32	$E_s{}' =$	7.17 Vorausrechn.
$E_m{}^o =$	3.40	$E_s{}'/E_s =$	1.00
$E_m/E_m{}^o =$	1.00		

34

ORTHOTROPIE FESTIGKEITEN

$\sigma_x \leq X$: Längszugfestigkeit
$-\sigma_x \leq X'$: Längsdruckfestigkeit
$\sigma_y \leq Y$: Querzugfestigkeit
$-\sigma_y \leq Y'$: Querdruckfestigkeit
$\sigma/s \leq S$: Schubfestigkeit

von Mises: $X = X' = Y = Y'$, $S = 0.57X$
Tresca: $X = X' = Y = Y'$, $S = 0.50X$

FESTIGKEITEN (MPa)

	CFK	GFK	SFK	CFK	Metal
	T300	Scotch	Kevlar	Gewebe	Al
X	1500	1062	1400	499	400
X'	1500	610	235	352	400
Y	40	31	12	458	400
Y'	246	118	53	352	400
S	68	72	34	46	228

35

MAXIMALE DEHNUNGEN

$$\varepsilon_x{}^* = X/E_x$$
$$\varepsilon_x{}'^* = X'/E_x$$
$$\varepsilon_y{}^* = Y/E_y$$
$$\varepsilon_y{}'^* = Y'/E_y$$
$$\varepsilon_s{}^* = S/E_s, \text{ bezogen auf Tangentenmodul}$$

Kriterium der maximalen Verzerrung
vergleicht Dehnungen jeder Komponente

MAXIMALE DEHNUNGEN (E-3)

	CFK	GFK	SFK	CFK	Metal
ε^*	T300	Scotch	Kevlar	Gewebe	Al
x	8.3	27.5	18.4	6.5	5.8
x'	8.3	15.8	3.1	4.8	5.8
y	3.9	3.8	2.2	6.2	5.8
y'	23.9	14.3	9.6	4.8	5.8
s	9.5	17.4	14.8	10.1	8.6

36

VERHÄLTNIS FESTIGKEIT/SPANNUNG

$$\{\sigma\}^{max} = R\{\sigma\}^{appl}$$
$$\{\varepsilon\}^{max} = R\{\varepsilon\}^{appl}$$

R = 1, Versagen
R = 2, Sicherheitsfaktor 2
R = Festigkeit, wenn Einheits(σ) wirkt

BEISPIELE

	Gegebene	Ändere h		Ändere (N)	
	Daten	FPF	LPF	FPF	LPF
h, Lagen =	10.	8.33	10.71	10.00	10.00
(N) =	2.00	2.00	2.00	2.40	1.87
R/FPF =	1.20	1.00	1.29	1.00	1.29
R/LPF =	1.40	1.17	1.50	1.17	1.50

37 QUADRATISCHES SPANNUNGS-KRITERIUM

$$F_{ij}\sigma_i\sigma_j + F_i\sigma_i = 1$$

$$F_{xx} = 1/XX', \quad F_{yy} = 1/YY', \quad F_{ss} = 1/S^2$$
$$F_{xy} = F_{xy}^*\sqrt{[F_{xx}F_{yy}]}, \quad -1/2 \le F_{xy}^* \le 0$$
$$F_x = 1/X - 1/X', \quad F_y = 1/Y - 1/Y'$$

$$aR^2 + bR - 1 = 0$$

Skalare Produkte: $a = F_{ij}\sigma_i\sigma_j$, $\quad b = F_i\sigma_i$

38 QUADRATISCHES VERZERRUNGS-KRITERIUM

$$G_{ij}\epsilon_i\epsilon_j + G_i\epsilon_i = 1$$

$$G_{xx} = F_{xx}Q_{xx}^2 + 2F_{xy}Q_{xx}Q_{xy} + F_{yy}Q_{xy}^2$$
$$G_x = F_xQ_{xx} + F_yQ_{xy}$$

$$aR^2 + bR - 1 = 0$$

Skalare Produkte: $a = G_{ij}\epsilon_i\epsilon_j$, $\quad b = G_i\epsilon_i$

39 VORTEILE VON QUADRATISCHEN VERSAGENSKRITERIEN

* Analytisch zuverlässig und einfach
* Festigkeitsinteraktion berücksichtigt
* Ein skalares und nicht tensorielles Kriterium
* Eindeutig, einfache Funktionen
* Leicht zu verstehen,zu benützen und darzustellen
* Konjugierte Wurzeln für Biegefestigkeit

40 VERSAGENSFORMEN

Faser Zug   : X
Faser Druck : X'
Matrixgrenzschicht Zug : Y
Matrix Druck   : Y'
Matrixgrenzschicht Schub : S
Delaminationen an freien Rändern, oder durch transversalen Impact oder ungleichmäßige Härtung

SPANNUNGSPARAMETER

F_{ij} F_i	CFK T300	GFK Scotch	SFK Kevlar
F_{xx}	4E–19	2E–18	3E–18
F_{yy}	1E–16	3E–16	2E–15
F_{xy}	#####	#####	#####
F_{ss}	2E–16	2E–16	9E–16
F_x	0E+0	#####	–4E–9
F_y	2E–16	2E–08	6E–08

DEHNUNGSPARAMETER

G_{ij} G_i	CFK T300	GFK Scotch	SFK Kevlar
G_{xx}	12004	1914	13454
G_{yy}	10681	18882	47657
G_{xy}	–3069	1712	2068
G_{ss}	11118	3306	4576
G_x	61	25	–150
G_y	217	198	351

VORTEILE DES DEHNUNGSRAUMS (GEGENÜBER SPANNUNGSRAUM)

* Dimensionlos
* Feste Einhüllenden für alle Laminate
* Leicht zu definierende Gültigkeitsgrenzen

Pi/4 Einhüllenden im Hauptdehnungsraum begrenzen den Bereich aller symmetrischen Winkellaminate

ZUSAMMENWIRKEN VON VERSAGENSFORMEN

* Interaktionen müssen berücksichtigt werden
* Vorteilhaft im 1. und 3. Quadrant
* Nachteilig im 2. und 4. Quadrant
* Delaminationen erniedrigen die Festigkeits- u. Stabilitätsgrenzen
* Versagensform schwer zu identifizieren

41

VERSAGEN DER ERSTEN SCHICHT(FPF)

* Zusammengesetzte Versagensformen
* Einfachste Art: Matrix/Interface Risse
* Risse verlaufen parallel zu den Fasern, sind gleichmäßig verteilt und zeigen einen Endzustand wenn die Festigkeitsgrenze erreicht wird
* Klassische Laminat-Theorie muß modifiziert werden,wenn die Lagen Risse enthalten.

42

MODELL DER MATRIX-DEGRADATION

Um die klassische Laminat-Theorie auch nach dem Versagen der 1.Schicht anwenden zu können,werden die Lagen mit Rissen mathematisch durch Lagen mit kleineren Matrixmoduli,d.h.Steifigkeit und Querkontraktionszahl,ersetzt.

$$0 < (E_m/E_m^{\,o}) < 1$$
$$v_x/v_x^{\,o} = E_m/E_m^{\,o}$$

43 ABMINDERUNG DES MATRIX-MODULS

Wird empirisch bestimmt aus:

* Laminatdehnungen bei FPF u. LPF
* Steifigkeitsabminderung infolge von Rissen bei stat. od. dyn.Belastung
* Ermittelte Grenzfestigkeit

44

MODIFIZIERTES VERSAGEN DER LETZTEN SCHICHT (LPF)

Den größeren von LPF oder FPF

* LPF > FPF Quadrant Zug-Zug
* LPF = FPF bei gleichzeitigem Schichtversagen
* LPF < FPF Quadrant Druck-Druck

DATEN ZUR RIßDICHTE, T300

Abbildungen 19.2 bis 19.5
Die Shear lag-Analyse ergibt einen Rißabstand von sieben Gruppen-Schichtdicken oder eine Dichte von 10 bis 15 Rissen pro Zentimeter.
Die analytisch ermittelten Rißdichten stimmen für die 45°-Lagen mit den experimentell ermittelten überein,sind aber für die 90°-Lagen fast um den Faktor 3 zu groß, d.h. 40 Risse/cm.

DEGRADIERTE STEIFIGKEIT T300

$E_m/E_m^{\,o}$	$E_x/E_x^{\,o}$	$E_y/E_y^{\,o}$	$v_x/v_x^{\,o}$	$E_s/E_s^{\,o}$
0.4	0.55	0.50	0.112	1.00
0.3	0.44	0.39	0.084	1.00
0.2	0.32	0.27	0.056	1.00
0.1	0.17	0.14	0.028	1.00
0.01	0.01	0.01	0.003	1.00

Empfohlene Degradation zwischen
0.1 und 0.3

VERSAGEN DER LETZTEN SCHICHT(LPF)

* Lagen bleiben intakt unterhalb von FPF oder Dauerfestigkeit
* Nach FPF degradieren die Schichten
* **LPF ist die niedrigste Schichtversagensgrenze,nachdem alle Schichten degradiert sind**
* Für einige Laminate: LPF ≤ FPF

FESTIGKEITEN

FPF = ☐ 1.00 ☐
LPF = ☐ 0.90 ☐

LPF modifiziert = 1.00

45
ENTWURFSGRENZEN BZGL. FESTIGKEIT
Eine sichere Grenze kann nach
folgenden Regeln definiert werden:
Regel 1 :
Keine Matrixdegradation an Auslegungsgrenze
(Um schädliche Interaktionen zu vermeiden)
Regel 2 :
Fester Sicherheitsfaktor für Versagen/Auslegung

AUSLEGUNGSGRENZE UND BRUCH

$$FPF = \boxed{1.00}$$
$$LPF = \boxed{1.50}$$
$$Sicherheitsfaktor = \boxed{1.50}$$
$$LPF\ mod = 1.50$$

$$Grenze = 1.00$$
$$Bruch = 1.50$$

46
ALTERNATIVE AUSLEGUNGSGRENZE
LPF geteilt durch Sicherheitsfaktor
Wenn LPF/FPF>Sicherheitsfaktor kann
Degradation in Kauf genommen werden,
falls Lastumkehr vermieden wird,wie
bei Druckgefäßen durch Benützung von
Verstärkung.
Wenn LPF/FPF≤Sicherheitsfaktor,keine
Degradation, d.h. Grenzen wie vorher.

ALTERNATIVE AUSLEGUNGSGRENZEN

$$FPF = \boxed{1.00}$$
$$LPF = \boxed{2.00}$$
$$Sicherheitsfaktor = \boxed{1.50}$$
$$LPF\ mod = \boxed{2.00}$$

	Sicher	Alternativ
Grenze =	1.00	1.33
Bruch =	1.50	2.00

47
EINGEFRORENE SPANNUNGEN
Abschnitt 15
Beruhend auf linear-thermoelastischem Modell
* Nichtmechanische Spannungen u.Verzerrungen
* Eingefrorene Spannungen u.Verzerrungen
* Freie orthotrope Ausdehnungen
* Quadratische Versagenskriterien

ZUGFREIE AUSDEHNUNGEN
Gl. 15.1
$$e_x = \alpha_x \Delta T + \beta_x c$$
$$e_y = \alpha_y \Delta T + \beta_y c$$
(α) = Wärmeausdehnungskoeffizient
(β) = Feuchtekoeffizient
λT = T/Betrieb - T/Härtung
c = Feuchte

48
NICHTMECHANISCHE SPANNUNGEN
Gl. 15.6 und 15.8
Nichtmechan. Spannungen
$$\{\sigma\}^n = [Q]\{e\}$$
$$\{\sigma\}^{(o)n} = 1/h \int \{\sigma\}^n dz$$
Nichtmechan. Verzerrungen
$$\{\varepsilon\}^{(o)n} = [a]\{\sigma\}^{(o)n}$$

EINGEFRORENE VERZERRUNGEN
Gl.15.10
$$\{\varepsilon\}^{(o)r} = \{\varepsilon\}^{(o)n} - \{e\}$$
Einzelkomponenten:
$$\varepsilon_x^{(o)r} = \varepsilon_x^{(o)n} - e_x$$
$$\varepsilon_y^{(o)r} = \varepsilon_y^{(o)n} - e_y$$
$$\varepsilon_s^{(o)r} = \varepsilon_s^{(o)n}$$

49 TATSÄCHLICHE AUSDEHNUNGEN
Gl. 15.11 und 15.12

$$\{\epsilon\}^{(o)n} = \{\alpha\}^\circ\Delta T + \{\beta\}^\circ c$$

$$\{\alpha\}^\circ = [a]\int[Q]\{\alpha\}dz$$

$$\{\beta\}^\circ = [a]\int[Q]\{\beta\}dz$$

50 DIMENSIONSLOSE TEMPERATUR
Abschnitt 17.2

$T^* = [T/g - T/opr]/[T/g - T/rm]$
$T^* = 1$ Raumtemp.
$T^* = 0$ Glasumwandlungstemp.

$T/g = T/g^\circ - gc$
$g =$ Temp. Verschiebung d. Feuchte

51 NICHTLINEARE STEIFIGKEITSZAHLEN
Gl. 17.8 bis 17.11

$E_x/E_x^\circ = (v_f/v_f^\circ)(T^*)^f$
$v_x/v_x^\circ = 1$ Konstante
$E_y/E_y^\circ =$ nichtlineare Funkt. (T^*, ν_f)
$E_s/E_s^\circ =$ nichtlineare Funkt. (T^*, ν_f)

52 RANGORDNUNG DER LAMINATE
Abschnitt 13
Nur für ebene, symmetrische Laminate
Analyse beinhaltet:
Mehrfache, komplexe Lasten
Eingefrorene Spannungen
Auslegungsgrenze FPF, LPF
Rangordnungsgruppen basieren
auf der Auswahl von:
2-10 Lagen Sublaminate
2-4 beliebigen Lagewinkeln

QUADRATISCHES KRITERIUM MIT BERÜCKS. D.EINGEFRORENEN SPANNUNGEN
Gl.15.14 bis 15.18
$\{\epsilon\}^* = R^m\{\epsilon\}^m + \{\epsilon\}^r$
oder $= R^m\{\epsilon\}^m + \{\epsilon\}^n - \{e\}$

$$\{\epsilon\}^*[G]\{\epsilon\}^{*t} + \{G\}\{\epsilon\}^* = 1$$

$$a(R^m)^2 + bR^m - 1 = 0$$

NICHTLINEARE HYGROTHERMISCHE WERTE
Gl.17.3 bis 17.7
Matrixwerte :
$E_m^* = (T^*)^a$
$\eta_y^* = \eta_s^* = (T^*)^b$
$X_m^* = (T^*)^c$

Faserwerte:
$E_{fx}^* = E_{fy}^* = G_{fx}^* = (T^*)^t$
$X_f^* = (T^*)^h$

NICHTLINEARE FESTIGKEITSWERTE
Gl.17.12 bis 17.14

$X^* = (v_f/v_f^\circ)(T^*)^h$
$X'^* = (v_f/v_f^\circ)(T^*)^h(E_x/E_x^\circ)^a$

Mikroinstabilitätseffekt berücksichtigt
$Y^* = Y'^* = S^* = (T^*)^c$
Interface-Effekte und $\langle\sigma\rangle^r$ sind
eingeschlossen

KRITERIEN FÜR DIE RANGORDNUNG
Optionen für Festigkeit:
Grenze basierend auf FPF, oder
Grenze basierend auf Bruchwert
Optionen für Steifigkeit:
Quadratische, normale oder
hygrothermische Dehnungen

53

SUB-UND ERGÄNZUNGSLAMINATE

* Code für Sublaminate:
  {[a b c d]r}$_s$
  (a Lagen in θ_1, b Lagen in θ_2,etc)
* Ergänzungslaminate:
  [A B C D]$_s$
  (A Lagen in θ_1, etc)
* Gesamtlaminat Code
  {[a b c d]r ± [A B C D]}$_s$

54

INTEGRIERTE MIKRO-MAKRO-MECHANISCHE ANALYSE

Steifigkeits- und Festigkeitsanalyse
* Faserwerkstoff und geometrie
* Matrixwerkstoff und geometrie
* Laminataufbau u.aufgebrachte Last
* Härtungstemp. u. hygrotherm.Bedingugen
* Einfache statisch bestimmte Strukturen
* Hybride,dünnwandige Konstruktionen oder
  beides

55

ZUSAMMENFASSUNG

Entwerfen mit FVW ist:
* Einfach
* Unkompliziert
* Folgerichtig
* Gleichwertig isotrop.Theorien
* Neulinge können sich schnell
  einarbeiten
* Auch Experten lernen dazu
* Wir sind bereit, wenn Sie es sind

56

EINIGE VERBOTE

* Benütze keine Nomogramme
* Glaube nicht an pullout
* Benütze keine Netzanalyse
* Errate nicht Matrixinversionen
* Benütze keine Skalare um FVW
  zu beschreiben
* Verwende nicht einachsige Spannun-
  gen,um FVW zu beschreiben
* Wende nicht einfache Modes,um
  gemischte Modes zu erklären
* Lass Dir nicht von Experten sagen,
  daß Du nichts verstehst.

LAMINATGRUPPEN

Sublam. keine Winkellagen

Lagen	2	3	4	Gesamt
6	7	28	84	119
7	8	36	120	164
8	9	45	165	219
9	10	55	220	285
10	11	66	286	363
				1150

MIC-MAC FLUßDIAGRAMM

Hygro		Pt str	>>>	FVW
Micro	>>>	Makro		Strukt
T/Här.	>>>	Lasten		

EINIGE EMPFEHLUNGEN

* Rechne stets
* Wende die Laminat-Theorie an
* Verwende ein quadratisches
  Versagenskriterium
* Berücksichtige eingefrorene
  Spannungen
* Benütze die Mikro-Makromechanik,
  um einen Einblick zu bekommen
* Benütze vereinfachte Theorien, um
  Auslegungsvarianten durchzurechnen
* Benütze die Laminatrangordnung
  zusammen mit der Optimierung
* Hab' Spaß am Zauber der FVW

ZUKUNFT VON FVW

* Niedrigere Materialkosten
* Niedrigere Verarbeitungskosten
* Präzise u. vernünftige Auslegung
* Kombinierte Funktionen
* Innovative Konzepte
* Genaue Theorien
* Neue Mitarbeiter
* Sei optimistisch

28.4 JAPANESE OUTLINE

わかりやすい複合材料設計法
設計技術者に贈るツール・ボックス

Stephen W. Tsai ／薄 一平
USAF Material Laboratory
AFWAL/MLBM,WPAFB,OH 45433-6533,USA
航空宇宙技術研究所
〒182 調布市深大寺東町7-44-1

2

参考図書

Stephen W. Tsai
Composites Design–1987
Think Composites, Dayton, Ohio (1987)

Stephen W. Tsai and H. Thomas Hahn
Introduction to Composite Materials
Technomic, Lancaster, Pa. (1985)

解析方法と設計手順
- 明快な理論と解析モデル
- 微視的機構と巨視的解析の結合
- 繰り返し部分積層を用いた簡略設計
- 非対称薄肉構造解析
- 2次形式破壊基準と設計限界
- 温湿度環境を考慮した材料特性
- 積層板の成形応力
- 積層板ランキング手法

3

信頼できないツール
- 単純応力に基づく解析モデル
- カーペット・プロット強度解析法
- 相互作用を無視した破壊基準
- 繊維引抜けのシアラグ解析
- 圧力容器設計における網目理論
- 最大応力,最大歪破壊基準
- 繊維配向角微調整最適化

ツール・ボックス

- 使う人の立場に立った工具一式
- 作表プログラム: ExcelまたはLotus123
- マクロ機能や作図機能の一体化
- 「もしこうなら?」「何が一番?」
  に答えるプログラム
- 充実している自習教材

4

即戦力ソフトウェア

- 信頼されているソフトウェア
- 無駄な時間と苦労を省く
- 新版説明書
- 絶え間ないアップデイト
- 使いやすい自己啓発,相互教育の道具
- 日給一人分より安い価格

単純応力、組合せ応力

- 単純応力:
  1軸、純せん断、静水圧
- 組合せ応力:
  2軸応力、組合せ応力

  組合せ応力下の挙動を
  単一応力下の挙動の組合せとして
  直接推定は出来ない

応力状態

	一軸	せん断	静水圧	2軸	組合せ応力
σ_1	1.0	0.0	1.0	1.0	–3.0
σ_2	0.0	0.0	1.0	2.0	–2.0
σ_6	0.0	1.0	0.0	0.0	1.0

5

単一荷重と多重荷重

多重荷重とは構造物が使用期間中に
出会う種々の条件を表している

複合材料設計では多重荷重は設計段階
初期から考慮する必要がある
　クリティカルになる支配荷重に対して
積層数と配向角を同時に考えなくては
ならない

6

一方向複合材料の応力平均化

・斜向軸系応力：単純応力、組合せ応力
・繊維軸系応力：単純応力、組合せ応力
・微視的応力　：常に組合せ応力
・境界応力　　：常に組合せ応力

複合材料設計ではほとんどすべての場合に
組合せ応力下となる

7

応力成分

Eq 5.1 and 5.16

$\sigma_1' = m^2\sigma_1 + n^2\sigma_2 + 2mn\sigma_6$
$\sigma_2' = n^2\sigma_1 + m^2\sigma_2 - 2mn\sigma_6$
$\sigma_6' = mn(-\sigma_1+\sigma_2) + (m^2-n^2)\sigma_6$
　　$m = \cos\theta, \; n = \sin\theta$

$\tan2\theta_0 = 2\sigma_6/(\sigma_1-\sigma_2)$
　$\theta_0 = $ 主応力方向
　$\theta_0 + \pi/4 = $ 最大せん断方向

8

歪み成分

Eq 5.1 and 5.18

$\varepsilon_1' = m^2\varepsilon_1 + n^2\varepsilon_2 + mn\varepsilon_6$
$\varepsilon_2' = n^2\varepsilon_1 + m^2\varepsilon_2 - mn\varepsilon_6$
$\varepsilon_6' = 2mn(-\varepsilon_1+\varepsilon_2) + (m^2-n^2)\varepsilon_6$
　　$m = \cos\theta, \; n = \sin\theta$

$\tan2\theta_0 = \varepsilon_6/(\varepsilon_1-\varepsilon_2)$
　$\theta_0 = $ 主歪み方向
　$\theta_0 + \pi/4 = $ 最大せん断歪み方向

多重荷重

	#1	#2	#3	#4
σ_1	1.0	2.0	−1.0	2.0
σ_2	0.0	0.0	−2.0	−1.0
σ_6	0.0	1.0	−1.0	1.0

積層複合材料の応力平均化

・積層板応力　：単純応力、組合せ応力
・斜向軸層応力：常に組合せ応力
・繊維軸層応力：常に組合せ応力
・層間応力　　：常に組合せ応力

すべての範囲で組合せ応力下となる

応力変換

	基準 座標	任意 方向	主応力 方向θ_0	最大せん断 方向	不変量
θ	0.0	*10.0*	10.9	$+\pi/4$	p, q, R
σ_1	*−2.0*	−2.2	−2.2	0.5	0.5
σ_2	*3.0*	3.2	3.2	0.5	−2.5
σ_6	*−1.0*	−0.1	0.0	−2.7	2.7

太字イタリックは入力値

歪み変換

	基準 座標	任意 方向	主応力 方向θ_0	最大せん断 方向	不変量
θ	0.0	*10.0*	5.7	$+\pi/4$	p,q,R
ε_1	*−2.0*	−2.0	−2.0	0.5	0.5
ε_2	*3.0*	3.0	3.0	0.5	−2.5
ε_6	*−1.0*	0.8	0.0	−2.5	2.5

太字イタリックは入力値

9

積層板理論
第7-9,11章
- 等価面内工学定数 : $[E^o]$, $[\nu^o]$
- 平均化応力及び歪み : $\{\sigma^o\}$, $\{\varepsilon^o\}$
- 等価膨張係数 : $\{\alpha^o\}$, $\{\beta^o\}$
- 等価曲げ工学定数 : $[E^f]$, $[\nu^f]$
- 等価表面応力歪み : $\{\sigma^f\}$, $\{\varepsilon^f\}$

- プライの強度／応力比: R

10

繊維軸方向の剛性
第6.1章
4つの直交異方性材料定数:
- 繊維軸方向弾性率: E_x
- 直角方向弾性率 : E_y
- 主ポアッソン比 : ν_x
- せん断弾性率 : E_s

等方性材料の材料定数は2つ:
$$E_x = E_y = E, \ \nu_x = \nu_y = \nu, \ E_s = E/2(1+\nu)$$

11

繊維軸上の応力-歪み関係
第6.1章
$$\{\sigma\} = [Q]\{\varepsilon\}$$
$$\{\varepsilon\} = [S]\{\sigma\}$$

剛性 : $Q_{xx} = E_x/(1-\nu_x\nu_y)$

コンプライアンス:$S_{xx} = Q_{yy}/(Q_{xx}Q_{yy}-Q_{xy}^2)$

工学定数 : $E_x = 1/S_{xx}$

等方性材料の場合:
$$Q_{xx} = E/(1-\nu^2), \ S_{xx} = 1/E$$

12

斜向軸上の応力-歪み関係
第6.1,6.2章
$$Q_{11} = m^4 Q_{xx}+n^4 Q_{yy}+2m^2n^2 Q_{xy}+4m^2n^2 Q_{ss}$$
$m = \cos\theta$, $n = \sin\theta$, θ = ply angle

$$Q_{11} = U_1+U_2\cos2\theta+U_3\cos4\theta$$
U_i = linear combo of on-axis [Q]
$$U_1 = (3Q_{xx}+3Q_{yy}+2Q_{xy}+4Q_{ss})/8$$
$$U_2 = (Q_{xx}-Q_{yy})/2$$

基本仮定
- 薄板積層板
- 断面の平面保持
- 線形応力-歪み関係
- 線形歪み-変位関係
- 2次形式破壊基準による
  最弱層(FPF)及び最強層(LPF)
- 線形温度湿度弾性率
- 微視機構の逆算出
- 2次則によるデータ最適化

工学定数 (GPa)
表6.4

[Q]	CFRP T300	GFRP Scotch	KFRP Kevlar	CCRP Fabric	Metal Alum
E_x	181.0	38.6	76.0	74.0	69.0
E_y	10.3	8.3	5.5	74.0	69.0
ν_x	0.28	0.26	0.34	0.05	0.30
E_s	7.2	4.1	2.3	4.6	26.5

繊維軸上の値 (GPa)
表6.4

[Q]	CFRP T300	GFRP Scotch	KFRP Kevlar	CCRP Fabric	Metal Alum
Q_{xx}	181.0	39.2	76.6	74.0	75.8
Q_{yy}	10.4	8.4	5.6	74.0	75.8
Q_{xy}	2.9	2.2	1.9	0.1	22.7
Q_{ss}	7.2	4.1	2.3	4.6	26.5

斜向軸上の値 (GPa)
T300

θ	0°	15°	30°	45°	60°	90°
Q_{11}	181.8	160.4	109.4	56.7	23.6	10.3
Q_{22}	10.3	11.9	23.6	56.7	109.3	181.8
Q_{12}	2.9	12.8	32.4	42.3	32.4	2.9
Q_{66}	7.2	17.0	36.7	46.6	36.8	7.2
Q_{16}	0.0	38.5	54.2	42.9	20.1	0.0
Q_{26}	0.0	4.4	20.1	42.9	54.2	0.0

13

疑似等方性積層板の工学定数
第6.3章

一次不変量:

$U_1 = (3Q_{11}+3Q_{22}+2Q_{12}+4Q_{66})/8$

$U_4 = (Q_{11}+Q_{22}+6Q_{12}-4Q_{66})/8$

$E^{iso} = (U_1{}^2-U_4{}^2)/U_1$

$\nu^{iso} = U_4/U_1$

$G^{iso} = (U_1-U_4)/2$

疑似等方性積層板 (GPa)
表6.4

	CFRP T300	GFRP Scotch	KFRP Kevlar	CCRP Fabric	Metal Alum
E^{iso}	69.7	19.0	29.0	52.7	69.0
ν^{iso}	0.30	0.27	0.32	0.32	0.30
ρ	1.6	1.8	1.5	1.5	2.6
E^{iso}/ρ	43.1	10.5	19.8	35.1	26.5

14

等価面内剛性
第7.2章

$[A^*] = 1/h \int [Q]dz$

$[a^*] = [A^*]^{-1}$

$\{\sigma^o\} = [A^*]\{\varepsilon^o\}$

$\{\varepsilon^o\} = [a^*]\{\sigma^o\}$

$\{\sigma^o\} = 1/h \int \{\sigma\}dz,$

$\{\varepsilon^o\} \neq f(z)$

等価面内剛性 (GPa)
T300

	[0]	[π/4]	[0/90]	[+/–45]	[0/±45]	Alum
$A_{11}{}^*$	181.8	76.4	96.0	56.7	98.4	75.8
$A_{22}{}^*$	10.4	76.4	96.0	56.7	41.2	75.8
$A_{12}{}^*$	2.9	22.6	2.9	42.3	29.2	22.7
$A_{66}{}^*$	7.2	26.9	7.2	46.6	33.4	26.5
$A_{16}{}^*$	0.0	0.0	0.0	0.0	0.0	0.0
$A_{26}{}^*$	0.0	0.0	0.0	0.0	0.0	0.0

15

面内工学定数
第7.3, 7.4章

$[a^*] = [A^*]^{-1} \neq \int [S]dz$

$E_1{}^o = 1/a_{11}{}^* \neq \int E_1 dz$

$E_2{}^o = 1/a_{22}{}^*, E_6{}^o = 1/a_{66}{}^*$

$\nu_{21}{}^o = -a_{21}/a_{11}$

$\nu_{61}{}^o = a_{61}/a_{11}$

面内工学定数 (GPa)
T300

	[0]	[π/4]	[0/90]	[+/–45]	[0/±45]	Alum
$E_1{}^o$	181.0	69.7	96.0	25.0	77.7	69.0
$E_2{}^o$	10.3	69.7	96.0	25.0	32.6	69.0
$E_6{}^o$	7.2	26.9	7.2	46.6	33.5	26.5
$\nu_{21}{}^o$	0.28	0.30	0.03	0.75	0.71	0.30
$\nu_{61}{}^o$	0.0	0.0	0.0	0.0	0.0	0.0

16

圧力容器
第7.13章

P = 圧力   F = 軸力

D = 直径   h = 厚さ

$\sigma_1{}^o = PD/4h + F/\pi Dh$

$\sigma_2{}^o = PD/2h$

$\varepsilon_1{}^o = a_{11}{}^*\sigma_1{}^o + a_{12}{}^*\sigma_2{}^o = (\sigma_1{}^o - \nu_{12}{}^o\sigma_2{}^o)/E_1{}^o$

$\varepsilon_2{}^o = a_{21}{}^*\sigma_1{}^o + a_{22}{}^*\sigma_2{}^o = (\sigma_2{}^o - \nu_{21}{}^o\sigma_1{}^o)/E_2{}^o$

圧力容器の解析例
T300/5208, [0/±45]45]T

F, kN =	**10**	$\sigma_1{}^o =$	849.	$E_1{}^o = 77.7$
P,MPa=	**0**	$\sigma_2{}^o =$	0.	$E_2{}^o = 32.6$
D, m =	**1**	$\varepsilon_1{}^o =$	10.92	$\nu_{21}{}^o = 0.71$
n, plies =	**30**	$\varepsilon_2{}^o =$	–7.76	$\nu_{12}{}^o = 0.30$
h, mm =	3.75			

太字イタリックは入力値

17

薄肉円筒のねじり
第7.13章

T =トルク   D = 直径
h = 厚さ   L = 長さ

$$\sigma_6^o = 2T/\pi D^2 h$$

$$\varepsilon_6^o = \sigma_6^o/E_6^o$$

$$\theta = 2(L/D)\varepsilon_6^o(180/\pi)$$

18

曲げ剛性定数
第8.1章

$[D] = \int[Q]z^2dz$
$[d] = [D]^{-1} \neq \int[S]z^2dz$

$\{M\}$ = moment, $\{k\}$ = curvature

$\{M\} = [D]\{k\}$
$\{k\} = [d]\{M\}$

19

曲げ剛性定数の基準化
第8.1章

$[D^*] = 12/h^3 \int[Q]z^2dz$
$I^* = h^3/12,$ $[d^*] = [D^*]^{-1}$

$\{\sigma^f\} = [D^*]\{\varepsilon^f\}$
$\{\varepsilon^f\} = [d^*]\{\sigma^f\}$

$\{\sigma^f\} = 6/h^2 \int\{\sigma\}zdz$
$\{\varepsilon^f\} = h\{k\}/2$

20

曲げの工学定数
第8.2章

$[d^*] = [D^*]^{-1}$

$E_1^f = 1/d_{11}^*$
$E_2^f = 1/d_{22}^*,$ $E_6^f = 1/d_{66}^*$

$\nu_{21}^f = -d_{21}/d_{11}$
$\nu_{61}^f = d_{61}/d_{11}$

薄肉円筒のねじりの解析例
T300/5208, [+/−45]T

T, MNm =	*1*	σ_6^o =	127.
D, m =	*1*	E_6^o =	46.60
L, m =	*10*	ε_6^o =	2.73
n, plies =	*40*	θ =	3.13
h, mm =	5.00		

太字イタリックは入力値

8層積層材の曲げ剛性値 (MNm)
T300

	[0]	[π/4]	[0/90]	[+/−45]	Alum
D_{11}	15.2	9.6	10.7	4.7	6.3
D_{22}	0.9	5.6	5.3	4.7	6.3
D_{12}	0.2	0.7	0.2	3.5	1.9
D_{66}	0.6	1.0	0.6	3.9	2.2
D_{16}	0.0	0.3	0.0	1.3	0.0
D_{26}	0.0	0.3	0.0	1.3	0.0

h = 8x0.125 = 1 mm, $h^3/12 = 0.0833$

8層積層材の曲げ剛性値 (GPa)
T300

	[0]	[π/4]	[0/90]	[+/−45]	Alum
D_{11}^*	181.8	115.2	128.2	56.7	75.8
D_{22}^*	10.4	67.0	63.9	56.7	75.8
D_{12}^*	2.9	7.8	2.9	42.3	22.7
D_{66}^*	7.2	12.1	7.2	45.6	26.5
D_{16}^*	0.0	4.0	0.0	16.0	0.0
D_{26}^*	0.0	4.0	0.0	16.0	0.0

8層積層材の曲げ定数値 (GPa)
T300

	[0]	[π/4]	[0/90]	[+/−45]	Alum
E_1^f	181.0	113.3	128.1	24.7	69.0
E_2^f	10.3	65.3	63.9	24.7	69.0
E_6^f	7.2	11.7	7.2	41.4	26.5
ν_{21}^f	0.28	0.10	0.05	0.72	0.30
ν_{61}^f	0.00	−0.30	0.00	−0.10	0.00

21

サンドイッチ板
第8.5章

$$[D] = 2 \int_{zc}^{h/2} [Q]z^2 dz$$

$[D^*] = 12/h^3 [D]$

コア比 $= c^* = 2zc/h$

$[d^*] = [D^*]^{-1}$

$E_1^f = 1/d_{11}^*$

22

片持ち梁
第8.6章

$P =$ 自由端に $L =$ 長さ $b =$ 幅
おける荷重 $M^{max} = PL$

$k_1 = d_{11}M_1 = d_{11}PL/b$
or $= d_{11}*PL/I = PL/E_1^f I$

$$\delta^{max} = PL^3/3E_1^f bI^*$$

23

片持ち中空円筒梁
第8.7章

$a =$ 直径 $h =$ 厚さ
$M^{max} = PL$, $I = \pi a^3 h/8$

$k_1 = d_{11}M_1 = PL/E_1^o I$

$$\delta^{max} = PL^3/3E_1^o I$$

24

非対称積層板
第9章
$\{\varepsilon\} = \{\varepsilon^o\} + z\{k\}$

$\{N\} = [A]\{\varepsilon^o\} + [B]\{k\}$
$\{M\} = [B]\{\varepsilon^o\} + [D]\{k\}$

$[B] = \int [Q]z dz =$ 面内曲げカップリング

$[B] = 0$ 対称積層板の場合

曲げ問題: $\{[0/90]_i/zc\}s$, T300, GPa

i	2	2	2	8	Alum 8
zc	0	4	36	144	144
h	8	16	80	320	320
c*	0.0	0.5	0.9	0.9	0.9
E_1^f	128.1	96.0	26.6	26.2	18.7
E_2^f	63.9	71.9	25.4	25.9	18.7

等方性材料の場合は: $E^t = (1-c^{*3})E$

片持ちサンドイッチ梁
T300/5208, $\{[0/90]_4/zc_{72}\}s$

P, kN =	**1**	I, m⁴ =	7E–08
L, m =	**1**	E_1^f =	26.60
b, m =	**0.1**	k_1,1/m =	0.56
n, plies =	160	ε_1^t, E–3 =	5.64
h, mm =	20.0	δ, mm =	188.0

太字イタリックは入力値

片持ち中空円筒梁解析例
T300/5208, $\{[0/90]_2\}s$

P, kN =	**1**	I, m⁴ =	4E–07
L, m =	**1**	E_1^o =	96.0
a, m =	**0.1**	k_1,1/m =	0.03
n, plies =	8	ε_1^t, E–3 =	1.33
h, mm =	1.0	δ, mm =	8.8

太字イタリックは入力値

特異な性質
欠 点
・積層板成形時のねじれ
・予測困難な挙動

利 点
・層間剥離を妨げる自然な曲面
・簡単なモールドで複雑な曲面形成
・予荷重の積極的な活用

25

工学定数の基準化表示
第9.4章

$$\{\sigma^o\} = [A^*]\{\varepsilon^o\}+[B^*]\{\varepsilon^f\}$$
$$\{\sigma^f\} = 3[B^*]\{\varepsilon^o\}+[D^*]\{\varepsilon^f\}$$

$$\{\varepsilon^o\} = [\alpha^*]\{\sigma^o\}+[\beta^*]\{\sigma^f\}/3$$
$$\{\varepsilon^f\} = [\beta^*]^t\{\sigma^o\}+[\delta^*]\{\sigma^f\}$$

$$[B^*] = 2[B]/h^2, \quad [\beta^*] = h^2[\beta]/2$$

工学定数
第9.5章

$$\{\varepsilon^o\} = (\{\varepsilon^+\}+\{\varepsilon^-\})/2$$
$$\{\varepsilon^f\} = (\{\varepsilon^+\}-\{\varepsilon^-\})/2$$

$$E_1^o = 1/\alpha_{11}^*, \quad \nu_{21}^o = -\alpha_{21}/\alpha_{11}, \ldots$$
$$E_1^f = 1/\delta_{11}, \quad \nu_{21}^f = -\delta_{21}/\delta_{11}, \ldots$$

カップリング挙動で決定する
静定構造には適用出来ない

26

平行軸理論
第9.7章

$$\{N'\} = \{N\}$$
$$\{M'\} = \{M\}+d\{N\}$$

$$d = 移動距離 \quad = z'-z$$

$$[A'] = [A]$$
$$[B'] = [B]+d[A]$$
$$[D'] = [D]+2d[B]+d^2[A]$$

新旧の座標表示

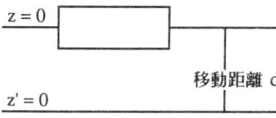

z = 0

移動距離 d

z' = 0

27

繰り返し積層板
第9.8章
積層コード: $\{[\theta_1/\theta_2/\theta_3/\theta_4]r/zc\}s$

$$[A] = 2r[A^o]$$
$$[B] = 0$$
$$[D] = 2r\{[D^o]-(r-1)u[B^o]$$
$$+(r-1)(2r-1)u^2[A^o]/6\}$$
r = 繰返数   u = 副積層板厚さ
$[A^o, B^o, D^o]$ = 副積層板の剛性

利 点

・曲げ解析が簡素化される
・繊維配向角の最適化が容易になる
・きめ細かな積層により全体的な
　剛性が向上
・積層工程の単純化によりミスを
　減らし、コスト低減に役立つ

28

薄肉構造
第9.9章

$$\{N^+\} = \{N\}/2+\{M\}/h$$
$$\{N^-\} = \{N\}/2-\{M\}/h$$

$$[A^*, D^*] = [1, 3][A^++A^-]/h$$
$$[B^*] = [A^+-A^-]/h$$

$$[\alpha^*, \delta^*] = [1, 1/3][a^++a^-]h/4$$
$$[\beta^*] = [a^+-a^-]h/4$$

利 点

・非対称構造のマトリックスが
　6＊6ではなく3＊3になる
・積層板の最適化が簡単になる
・ハイブリッド構造を容易に扱える
・誤差は表面厚さ／深さ比で決まる

29

マイクロ・メカニックス
微視材料力学
第10章
扱う項目
- LPF算定に対する母材劣化
- 温度湿度依存データ
- 材料最適化
- 種々の破壊モード

通常用いられるモデル
- 並列モデル（上限モデル）
- 直列モデル（下限モデル）
- 修正複合則
- いろいろな材料力学モデル
- 同心円筒モデル
- 方陣バックモデル
- 自己調和モデル

30

マイクロ・メカニックスの
適用限界
- 理想化繊維断面形状
- 理想化繊維配列対称性
- 境界面に於ける連続性仮定
- 繊維特性の計測不能部分
- 縮体応力算出
- 未確立の破壊モード

マイクロ・メカニックスの
適用方法

未知の要素特性や実験定数を逆算出
によって求める

次に種々のマイクロ・メカニックスの変数
について感度解析を行う

31

修正複合則
第10.2-5章
複合則
$$E_x = v_f E_f + v_m E_m$$
$$v_x = v_f v_f + v_m v_m$$

修正複合則
$$(1+v_y^*)/E_y = 1/E_{fx} + v_y^*/E_m$$
$$(1+v_s^*)/E_s = 1/G_{fs} + v_s^*/G_m$$
$$v_y^* = \eta_y v_m/v_f, \quad v_s^* = \eta_s v_m/v_f$$

応力配分パラメータ
PARAMETERS
式10.9
$$\eta_y = [<\sigma_m>/<\sigma_f>]_y$$
$$\eta_s = [<\sigma_m>/<\sigma_f>]_s$$
一方向GFRP材の剛性とガラス繊維を等方性
と仮定した弾性係数から逆演算で求めた
応力配分パラメータは
$$\eta_y = 0.5161$$
$$\eta_s = 0.3162$$

32

直角方向プライ剛性
式10.28, 10.25
$\eta_y = 0.516$（GFRPからの逆演算）

逆演算による直角方向繊維剛性:
$$E_{fy} = [(1 + v_y^*)/E_y - v_y^*/E_m]^{-1}$$

順演算による直角方向プライ剛性:
$$E_y' = (1+v_y^*)/[1/E_{fy}' + v_y^*/E_m]$$

逆／順演算による
直角方向の剛性計算例

E_y =	**10.3**	v_y^* =	0.22	
E_m =	**3.40**	E_{fy} =	18.69	逆演算
v_f =	**0.70**	E_{fy}' =	18.69	固定値
η_y =	**0.52**	E_y' =	10.30	順演算
E_m^o =	3.40	E_y/E_y =	1.00	
E_m/E_m^o=	1.00			

太字イタリックは入力値を示す

33

ブライのせん断弾性係数
式10.19, 10.10

$\eta_s = 0.316$ （GFRPからの逆演算）

逆演算による繊維のせん断弾性係数:
$$G_{fx} = [(1+v_s{}^*)/E_s - v_s{}^*/G_m]^{-1}$$

順演算によるプライのせん断弾性係数:
$$E_s{}' = (1+v_s{}^*)/[1/G_{fx} + v_s{}^*/G_m]$$

逆／順演算による せん断弾性係数の計算例

$E_s =$	**7.17**	$v_s{}^* =$	0.14
$E_m =$	**3.40**	$G_{fx} =$	19.70 逆演算
$v_f =$	**0.70**	$G_{fx}{}' =$	19.70 固定値
$\eta_s =$	**0.32**	$E_s{}' =$	7.17 順演算
$E_m{}^o =$	3.40	$E_s{}'/E_s =$	1.00
$E_m/E_m{}^o =$	1.00		

太字イタリックは入力値を示す

34

各軸方向の強度
第11.2章

$\sigma_x \le X$: 繊維軸方向引張強度
$-\sigma_x \le X'$: 繊維軸方向圧縮強度
$\sigma_y \le Y$: 直角軸方向引張強度
$-\sigma_y \le Y'$: 直角軸方向圧縮強度
$\sigma/s \le S$: 繊維軸方向せん断強度

von Mises: $X = X' = Y = Y'$, $S = 0.57X$
Tresca: $X = X' = Y = Y'$, $S = 0.50X$

各軸方向の強度 (MPa)
表11.1

	CFRP T300	GFRP Scotch	KFRP Kevlar	CCRP Fabric	Metal Alum
X	1500	1062	1400	499	400
X'	1500	610	235	352	400
Y	40	31	12	458	400
Y'	246	118	53	352	400
S	68	72	34	46	228

35

最大歪み
第11.5章

$\varepsilon_x{}^* = X/E_x$
$\varepsilon_x{}'^* = X'/E_x$
$\varepsilon_y{}^* = Y/E_y$
$\varepsilon_y{}'^* = Y'/E_y$
$\varepsilon_s{}^* = S/E_s$, 接線弾性率による値

最大歪み破壊基準では
歪みを成分毎に比較する

最大歪み計算例 (10^{-3})
Table 11.1

ε^*	CFRP T300	GFRP Scotch	KFRP Kevlar	CCRP Fabric	Metal Alum
x	8.3	27.5	18.4	6.5	5.8
x'	8.3	15.8	3.1	4.8	5.8
y	3.9	8.8	2.2	6.8	5.8
y'	23.9	14.3	9.6	4.8	5.8
s	9.5	17.4	14.8	10.1	8.6

36

強度／応力比
第11.3章

$$\{\sigma\}^{max} = R\{\sigma\}^{appl}$$
$$\{\varepsilon\}^{max} = R\{\varepsilon\}^{appl}$$

R = 1, 破壊発生
R = 2, 安全率は2
R = 単位 $\{\sigma\}$が負荷されている場合は
強度値

例題

	Given data	Change h FPF	Change h LPF	Change {N} FPF	Change {N} LPF
h, plies =	**10.**	8.33	10.71	10.00	10.00
{N} =	**2.00**	2.00	2.00	2.40	1.87
R/FPF =	**1.20**	1.00	1.29	1.00	1.29
R/LPF =	**1.40**	1.17	1.50	1.17	1.50

太字イタリックは入力値を示す

37

2 次形式破壊基準の応力成分による表示

第１１.６章 $F_{ij}\sigma_i\sigma_j+F_i\sigma_i = 1$

$F_{xx} = 1/XX'$, $F_{yy} = 1/YY'$, $F_{ss} = 1/S^2$
$F_{xy} = F_{xy}^*\sqrt{[F_{xx}F_{yy}]}$, $-1/2 \leq F_{xy}^* \leq 0$
$F_x = 1/X - 1/X'$, $F_y = 1/Y - 1/Y'$

$$aR^2+bR-1 = 0$$
スカラー積 $a = F_{ij}\sigma_i\sigma_j$, $b = F_i\sigma_i$

38

2 次形式破壊基準の歪み成分による表示

第１１.７章 $G_{ij}\varepsilon_i\varepsilon_j+G_i\varepsilon_i = 1$

$G_{xx} = F_{xx}Q_{xx}^2+2F_{xy}Q_{xx}Q_{xy}+F_{yy}Q_{xy}^2$
$G_x = F_xQ_{xx}+F_yQ_{xy}$

$$aR^2+bR-1 = 0$$
スカラー積 $a = G_{ij}\varepsilon_i\varepsilon_j$, $b = G_i\varepsilon_i$

39

2 次形式破壊基準の特長

- 解析的であり明快である
- 強度干渉効果が含まれている
- テンソルではなくスカラー基準である
- 簡単な一価関数で表される
- 理解し易い、使い易い、書き易い
- 共役根から容易に曲げ強度を計算出来る

40

破壊モード

繊維引張り： X
繊維圧縮： X'
母材／境界 引張り： Y
母材／境界圧縮： Y'
母材／境界 せん断： S

自由端における層間剝離、直角方向インパクト
不均一成形に起因するもの

応力パラメータ
表11.1

F_{ij} F_i	CFRP GFRP KFRP T300 Scotch Kevlar		
F_{xx}	4E–19	2E–18	3E–18
F_{yy}	1E–16	3E–16	2E–15
F_{xy}	#####	#####	#####
F_{ss}	2E–16	2E–16	9E–16
F_x	0E+0	#####	–4E–9
F_y	2E–16	2E–08	6E–08

歪みパラメータ
表11.1

G_{ij} G_i	CFRP GFRP KFRP T300 Scotch Kevlar		
G_{xx}	12004	1914	13454
G_{yy}	10681	18882	47657
G_{xy}	–3069	1712	2068
G_{ss}	11118	3306	4576
G_x	61	25	–150
G_y	217	198	351

歪み空間表示の優位性
（応力空間に対して）
第１１.７章

- 無次元表示、用いる単位によらない
- 総ての積層にたいして不変
- 上限／極限を容易に計算出来る

主歪み空間におけるPi/4（π/4）包絡面
は任意のバランス積層の限界値を与える

モード干渉

- 干渉は無視出来ない
- 第１、第３限では有利になる
- 第２、第４象限では有害
- 層間剝離は極限応力、不安定破壊強度を低下させる
- モードの特定は困難

41
最弱層の初期破壊（ＦＰＦ）
FIRST–PLY–FAILURE

- 積層板の内側破壊包絡面
- 破壊モードは複合している
- 最も単純なタイプ：母材／境界クラック
- 繊維軸に平行するクラックは一様に
  分布する。極限値で飽和する。
- 積層板理論はプライにクラックが
  含まれる時は修正されなければならない

42
母材劣化モデル
第１２.１１章

ＦＰＦ以降に対しても積層板理論を拡張するた
めには、クラックを生じた層についてその母材
の弾性係数を連続的に低下させていく計算モデ
ルが必要である。即ち剛性とポアッソン比を減
少させていくモデルである。

$$0 < (E_m/E_m^o) < 1$$
$$\nu_x/\nu_x^o = E_m/E_m^o$$

43
劣化した母材の弾性係数
実験データから決める

- ＦＰＦ、ＬＰＦの積層板歪み
- 静的／疲労荷重下でのクラック増加
  に伴う剛性低下
- 極限強さデータ値

44
積層板の極限強さ
第１２章

ＬＰＦ荷重とＦＰＦ荷重の大きい方を選ぶ

- ＬＰＦ＞ＦＰＦ　　引張-引張り領域
- ＬＰＦ＝ＦＰＦ　　各層同時破壊
- ＬＰＦ＜ＦＰＦ　　圧縮-圧縮領域

Ｔ３００のクラック密度
図19.2～図19.5

シア・ラグ解析によれば、7プライ・グループ
厚さでのクラック配置あるいはクラック密度は
1cm当り10ないし15個である

　解析結果は45度層での実測結果と良く一致
したが、90度層での実測データはおよそ3倍
程度（40個/cm）上回った。

Ｔ３００の剛性劣化計算例
図12.2

E_m/E_m^o	E_y/E_y^o	E_s/E_s^o	ν_x/ν_x^o	E_x/E_x^o
0.4	0.55	0.50	0.112	1.00
0.3	0.44	0.39	0.084	1.00
0.2	0.32	0.27	0.056	1.00
0.1	0.17	0.14	0.028	1.00
0.01	0.01	0.01	0.003	1.00

劣化の適用範囲は0.1～0.3程度を考える

層の最終破壊（ＬＰＦ）
LAST–PLY–FAILURE

- ＦＰＦ以下あるいは疲労限以下では
  各層の強度低下なし
- ＦＰＦを超えると各層の劣化が始まる
- ＬＰＦは劣化後のすべての層のうち
  破壊荷重の最も低い層、あるいは劣化後の
  積層板の内側破壊包絡面のこと
- ＬＰＦ≦ＦＰＦの場合もある

極限強さ

ＦＰＦ＝ $\boxed{\mathit{1.00}}$
ＬＰＦ＝ $\boxed{\mathit{1.60}}$

極限強さ＝ MAX(FPF,LPF)
　　　　＝　1.60

太字イタリックは入力値

45

設計限界強度の求め方（その1）

下記のルールによって安全側限界強度を
算出する

ルール1
限界値において母材劣化は生じない
（有害なモード干渉をさけるため）

ルール2
最小安全率（極限強さ／設計限界）を用いる

lim = MIN(FPF,LPF)/sm

46

設計限界強度の求め方（その2）

母材劣化の許容
極限強さを安全率で除す

lim* = MAX(FPF,LPF)/sm

例えば圧力容器をゴムライナーで補強する例
の様に荷重が引張側に限られている場合は
（LPF／FPF）＞（安全率）であっても
劣化は許され得る

47

積層板の残留応力
第15章

線形熱弾性モデルに基づく

・非力学的応力と歪み
・残留応力と歪み
・各軸方向の自由膨張
・2次形式破壊基準

48

非力学的応力
式15.6, and 15.8

非力学的応力

$$\{\sigma\}^n = [Q]\{e\}$$

$$\{\sigma\}^{(o)n} = 1/h \int \{\sigma\}^n dz$$

非力学的歪み

$$\{\varepsilon\}^{(o)n} = [a]\{\sigma\}^{(o)n}$$

極限強さと設計限界強度の算出

FPF =	*1.00*
LPF =	*1.60*
安全率 =	*1.20*

設計限界強度 = 1.00
極限強さ = 1.60

太字イタリックは入力値

設計限界強度値の比較

FPF =	*1.00*
LPF =	*1.60*
安全率 =	*1.20*
極限強さ =	1.60

設計限界強度値　　　　母材の劣化
lim = 1.00 許されない場合
lim* = 1.33 許される場合

自由膨張
式15.1

$$e_x = \alpha_x \Delta T + \beta_x c$$
$$e_y = \alpha_y \Delta T + \beta_y c$$

$\{\alpha\}$ = 熱膨張係数
$\{\beta\}$ = 湿度膨張係数
ΔT = 運用温度 − 成形温度
c = 湿度

残留歪み
式15.10

$$\{\varepsilon\}^{(o)r} = \{\varepsilon\}^{(o)n} - \{e\}$$

成分表示
$$\varepsilon_x^{(o)r} = \varepsilon_x^{(o)n} - e_x$$
$$\varepsilon_y^{(o)r} = \varepsilon_y^{(o)n} - e_y$$
$$\varepsilon_s^{(o)r} = \varepsilon_s^{(o)n}$$

49

等価膨張係数
式15.11,15.12

$$\{\varepsilon\}^{(o)n} = \{\alpha\}^o \Delta T + \{\beta\}^o c$$

$$\{\alpha\}^o = [a]\int[Q]\{\alpha\}dz$$

$$\{\beta\}^o = [a]\int[Q]\{\beta\}dz$$

50

温度の無次元化表示
第17.2章

$$T^* = [T/g - T/opr]/[T/g - T/rm]$$
$T^* = 1$ 室温
$T^* = 0$ ガラス転移温度

$$T/g = T/g^o - gc$$
$g =$ 単位吸湿による温度変化

51

ベキ乗則を用いた剛性データ
式17.8～17.11

$$E_x/E_x{}^o = (v_f/v_f{}^o)(T^*)^f$$

$$v_x/v_x{}^o = 1 \text{ (constant)}$$

$$E_y/E_y{}^o = \text{nonlinear function } (T^*, v_f)$$

$$E_s/E_s{}^o = \text{nonlinear function } (T^*, v_f)$$

52

積層板ランキング　第14章
面内荷重を受ける対称積層板に限定する
解析に考慮されている点
　多重、組合せ荷重
　残留応力
　設計限界、ＦＰＦ、ＬＰＦ
ランキングの母集団の選択
　２-１０層の副積層
　２-４方向の任意の繊維配向角

残留応力を考慮した
2次形式破壊基準
式15.14～15.18

$$\{\varepsilon\}^* = R^m\{\varepsilon\}^m + \{\varepsilon\}^r$$
or $\quad = R^m\{\varepsilon\}^m + \{\varepsilon\}^n - \{e\}$

$$\{\varepsilon\}^*[G]\{\varepsilon\}^{*t} + \{G\}\{\varepsilon\}^* = 1$$

$$a(R^m)^2 + bR^m - 1 = 0$$

ベキ乗則を用いた温度湿度データ
式17.3～17.7
母材データ
$$E_m{}^* = (T^*)^a$$
$$\eta_y{}^* = \eta_s{}^* = (T^*)^b$$
$$X_m{}^* = (T^*)^c$$

繊維データ
$$E_{fx}{}^* = E_{fy}{}^* = G_{fx}{}^* = (T^*)^f$$
$$X_f{}^* = (T^*)^h$$

ベキ乗則を用いた強度データ
式17.12～17.14

$$X^* = (v_f/v_f{}^o)(T^*)^h$$
$$X'^* = (v_f/v_f{}^o)(T^*)^h(E_s/E_s{}^o)^a$$
マイクロ・バックリング効果は含まれる

$$Y^* = Y'^* = S^* = (T^*)^c$$
境界面強度及び残留応力 $<\sigma>^r$ の影響は
これらのデータに含まれている

ランキングの基準

強度評定の場合
lim = 母材劣化を許容しない限界強度基準
lim* =母材劣化を許容する　限界強度基準

次の値に基づくものとする
　母材劣化ファクターはおよそ0.3
　安全率は1.5またはそれ以上

53

副積層とラウンド・オフ積層板
- 副積層板コード
  {[a b c d]r}ₛ
  (θ₁方向にa層、θ₂方向にb層、等)
- ラウンド・オフ積層板コード
  [A B C D]ₛ
  (θ₁方向にA層、等)
- 全積層板コード
  {[a b c d]r ± [A B C D]}ₛ

積層板母集団

| 積層板母集団 | 繊維配向角の数 | | | |
副積層数	2	3	4	合計
6	7	28	84	119
7	8	36	120	164
8	9	45	165	219
9	10	55	220	285
10	11	66	286	363
				1150

54

微視的／巨視的材料力学の統合化解析

剛性及び強度解析
- 繊維の材質と形状
- 母材の材質と形状
- 積層構成と負荷荷重
- 成形温度と温度湿度条件
- 単純静定構造
- ハイブリッド、繰返し積層を含む薄肉構造

微視的／巨視的材料力学の解析流れ図

Hygro		Pt str	>>>	Comp
Micro	>>>	Macro		Struct
T/cure	>>>	Loads		

55

結 論

複合材料設計は
- 単純明快
- 流れが理解容易
- 首尾一貫して矛盾がない
- 等方性材料と同程度の理論的根拠
- 初めての設計者は短時間で熟練域へ
- 熟練設計者はより優れた設計を求めて
- 我々は常に支援態勢にあります

実践のすすめ
- 常に計算をして確認
- 積層板理論を用いる
- 2次形式破壊基準を用いる
- 積層による成形応力を考慮にいれる
- 直感力を微視/巨視材料力学で養う
- 反復設計が容易な簡易化理論を用いる
- 積層板ランキング法を最適化法と共に使う
- 複合材料のマジックを楽しむ

56

べからず集
- カーペット・プロット法を使わない
- 繊維引抜けを信じない
- ネッティング理論を使わない
- 逆マトリックスを当て推量しない
- 複合材料をスカラーで論じない
- 複合材料を一軸応力で説明しない
- 単モードの和集合で混合モードを説明しない
- 専門家に「君はわかってない」と言わせない

複合材料の将来
- 原材料費用の低下
- 製造コストの低下
- 正確で合理的な設計
- 多機能多目的
- 革新的概念
- 精密な理論
- 新しい働き手
- 積極的であれ

Section 29

HYPERCOMPOSITES

29.0 COMPOSITES DESIGN HOME CARD

This section consists of a number of cards arranged in stacks within the framework of Apple Computer's HyperCard software. Each card contains word/graphic information relevant to composite materials. Although a few of the cards contain nearly identical information as that in the text portion of this book, most cards are complementary as well as supplementary to the basic text. This section is for more advanced readers and provides only cursory explanation. Just as the home card acts as the central starting point from which the HyperComposites user branches out to the topic of interest, the home card is shown below as a table of contents to this section.

We are presenting this section as an experiment in communication. Although only the hardcopies are shown here, the software provides the opportunity of incorporating additional features such as speech, music, animation, and smart cards (ones that calcuate and give answers to questions). We hope to develop a training package. Electronic transmission, and instant updates are two immediate benefits of this package.

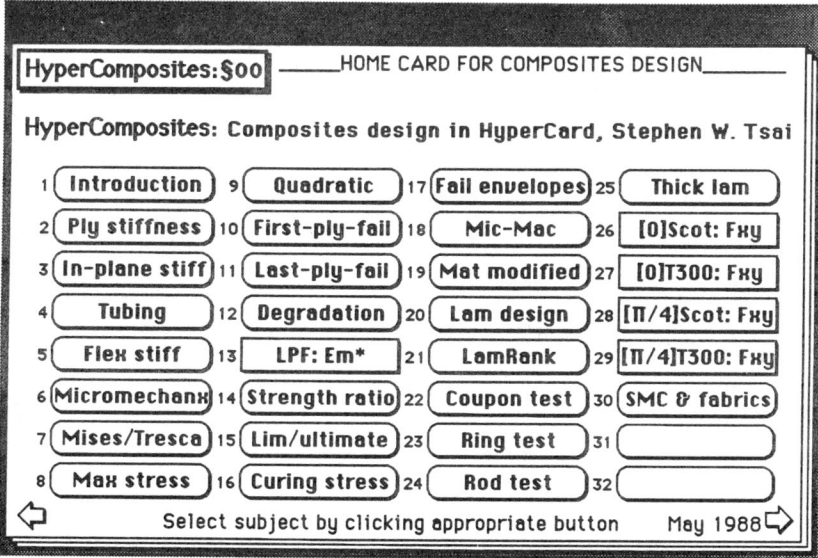

29.0 COMPOSITES DESIGN HOME CARD (continued)

HyperComposites:§00 ········· TOPICS OF HYPERCOMPOSITES ·········

- Relations among stiffness, compliance, and engineering constants are similar for unidirectional, and laminates under in-plane and flex.
- Repeating sub-laminates lead to stronger laminates, and simpler laminate selection, including designing for flexural loads.
- Micromechanics for nonisotropic fibers is simpler using modified rule-of-mixtures relations.
- Failure envelopes anchored by uniaixal test data are illustrated. Quadratic criteria are flexible to include interaction among mixed modes of failure, and can recover max stress and strain in the limit.
- Differences between stress- and strain-space representation of failure envelopes are shown. The latter is preferred.
- Matrix degradation model provides a continuous parameter to estimate the last-ply-failure (LPF) of a laminate. A semi-empirical method of determining the degradation factor is indicated.
- Strength ratios are more useful than strength index. The former can be readily applied to FPF, FPF and others with internal consistency.

HyperComposites:§00 ········· TOPICS OF HYPERCOMPOSITES ·········

- Illustrations of the sensitivity of the strength interaction term, the matrix degradation factor, the hygrothermal and residual stresses, and the safety factor are shown for several composites.
- Integrated micro-macromechanics analysis model (Mic-Mac) shows the power of "what if" and "what's best?" derived from spreadsheets.
- Optimization of constituent materials, including the interfacial strength and fiber strength, is a new option in materials engineering.
- LamRank can be extended to select laminates under flexural loads.
- Several tests for the strength interaction term are proposed. Bi-axial stresses can be induced without the use of tubular specimens.
- The out-of-plane elastic moduli can be estimated using models of minimechanics. 3-D intralaminar and traction-based interlaminar failure criteria can form a rational basis for thick laminate analysis.
- Prediction of the strength of SMC and whisker composites based on the [π/3] laminate is added to that of the elastic moduli.

29.1 INTRODUCTION

HyperComposites:§01 ............INTRODUCTION TO COMPOSITES DESIGN............
.................Ever expanding opportunities..............

As composite materials for structural applications enter the third decade of development, opportunities abound:

Aerospace applications continue to expand for numerous reasons: high specific stiffness, high specific strength, corrosion and fatigue resistance, reduction in part and fastener count, etc.

Automotive applications have been limited to lightly loaded structures. The percentage of composites utilization, however, has increased from a very low base to a significant proportion.

Sporting goods have always associated composites with high performance, and have popularized composites better than all others.

There is no stopping now. Are we doing the right thing?

HyperComposites:§01 ....ADVANCES IN COMPOSITE MATERIALS............
.................Basic understanding is still lacking..............

What are some of the milestones?

After E– and S–glass, we have seen boron, graphite, Kevlar, pitch, silicon nitride, polyethelene, and other organic and inorganic fibers.

Equally giant steps have occurred in the development of matrix materials, starting with polyester and phenolic, and followed by epoxy, high temperature organic matrices, metal matrix, and ceramic matrix.

The theory of composites has not successfully explained some of the fundamental mechanisms of reinforcement and those of failures. The role of the interface or interphase, the truth about fiber pullout, synergism between hybrids, interlaminar failure, compressive failure (unusually low in many new composites), and others still await rational explanations.

29.1 INTRODUCTION (continued)

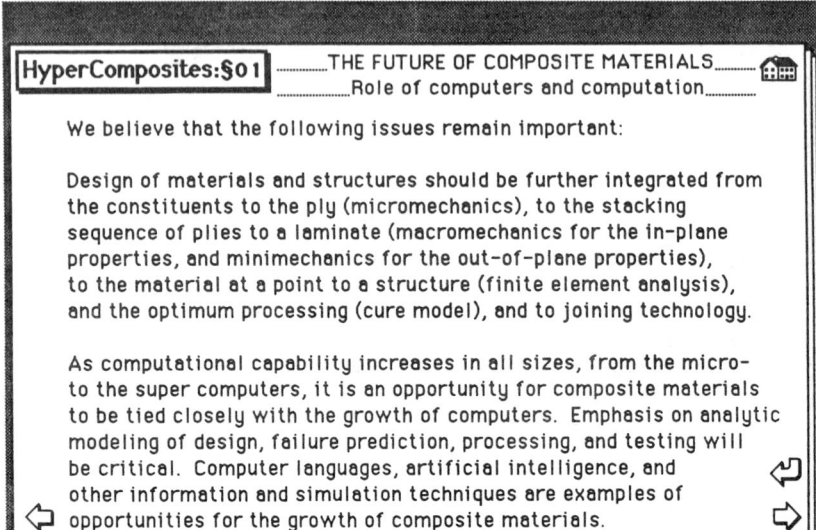

HyperComposites:§01 ....THE FUTURE OF COMPOSITE MATERIALS.............
.............Role of computers and computation.............

We believe that the following issues remain important:

Design of materials and structures should be further integrated from the constituents to the ply (micromechanics), to the stacking sequence of plies to a laminate (macromechanics for the in-plane properties, and minimechanics for the out-of-plane properties), to the material at a point to a structure (finite element analysis), and the optimum processing (cure model), and to joining technology.

As computational capability increases in all sizes, from the micro- to the super computers, it is an opportunity for composite materials to be tied closely with the growth of computers. Emphasis on analytic modeling of design, failure prediction, processing, and testing will be critical. Computer languages, artificial intelligence, and other information and simulation techniques are examples of opportunities for the growth of composite materials.

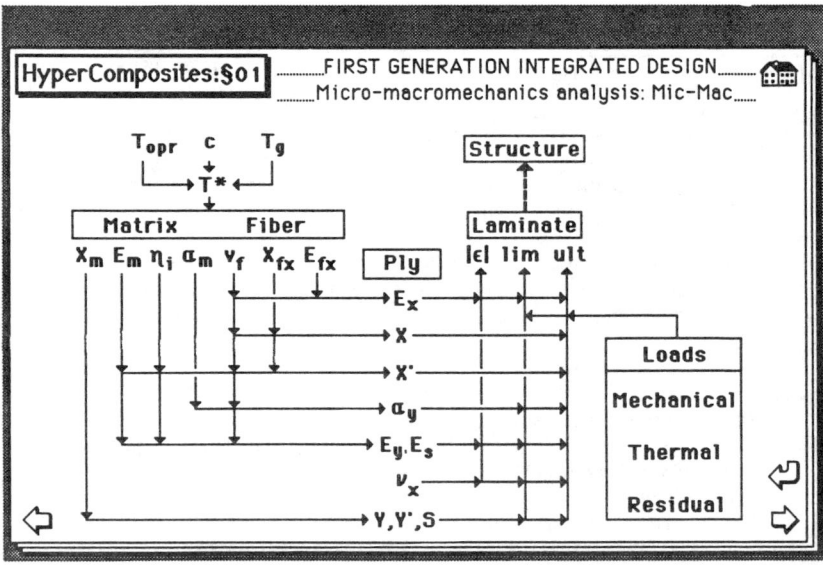

HyperComposites:§01 ....FIRST GENERATION INTEGRATED DESIGN.............
.............Micro-macromechanics analysis: Mic-Mac.............

29.2 PLY STIFFNESS

HyperComposites:§02 ......STIFFNESS OF UNIDIRECTIONAL COMPOSITES

The most important difference between the stiffness of isotropic materials and that of orthotropic materials lies in the number of independent components of the elastic modulus. Isotropic materials have two independent moduli; orthotropic materials have nine. The same linear stress and strain relations are shared by all elastic materials; i.e., the generalized Hooke's law.

The analysis and design of composite materials must include the nonisotropic nature. Many rules and practices based on isotropic materials must be modified to reflect the directionality of the stiffness as well as the strength of composite materials. The unique features resulting from directionality provide exciting opportunities to exploit composite materials which have no counterpart in the conventional isotropic materials.

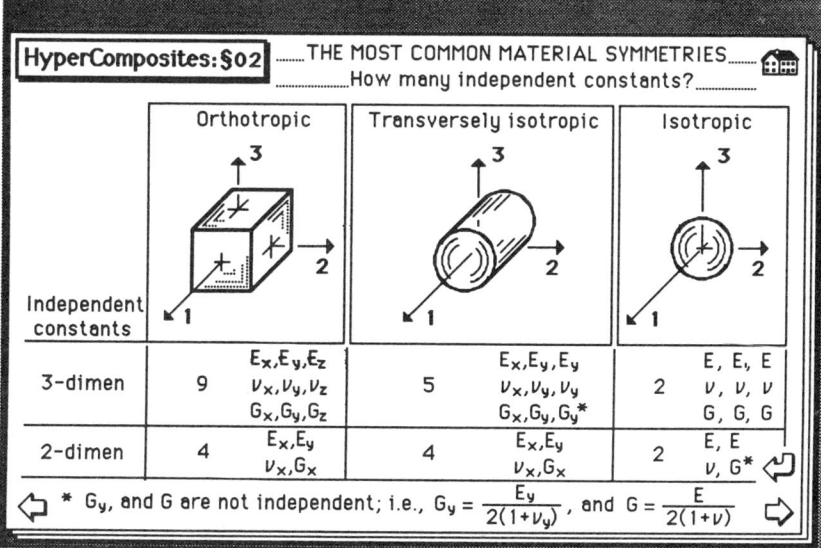

HyperComposites:§02 ......THE MOST COMMON MATERIAL SYMMETRIES......
......How many independent constants?......

Independent constants	Orthotropic		Transversely isotropic		Isotropic	
3-dimen	9	E_x, E_y, E_z ν_x, ν_y, ν_z G_x, G_y, G_z	5	E_x, E_y, E_y ν_x, ν_y, ν_y G_x, G_y, G_y^*	2	E, E, E ν, ν, ν G, G, G
2-dimen	4	E_x, E_y ν_x, G_x	4	E_x, E_y ν_x, G_x	2	E, E ν, G^*

* G_y, and G are not independent; i.e., $G_y = \dfrac{E_y}{2(1+\nu_y)}$, and $G = \dfrac{E}{2(1+\nu)}$

29.2 PLY STIFFNESS (continued)

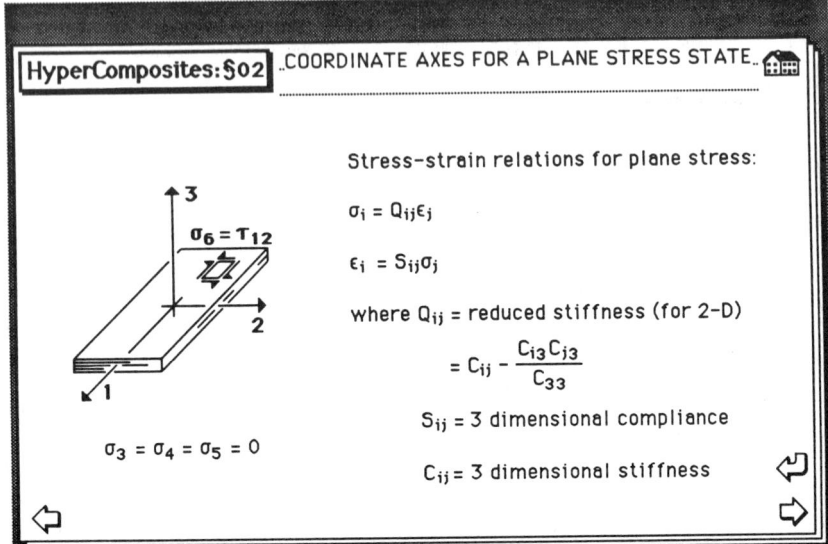

HyperComposites:§02   ..COORDINATE AXES FOR A PLANE STRESS STATE..

Stress-strain relations for plane stress:

$$\sigma_i = Q_{ij}\epsilon_j$$

$$\epsilon_i = S_{ij}\sigma_j$$

where Q_{ij} = reduced stiffness (for 2-D)

$$= C_{ij} - \frac{C_{i3}C_{j3}}{C_{33}}$$

S_{ij} = 3 dimensional compliance

C_{ij} = 3 dimensional stiffness

$\sigma_6 = \tau_{12}$

$\sigma_3 = \sigma_4 = \sigma_5 = 0$

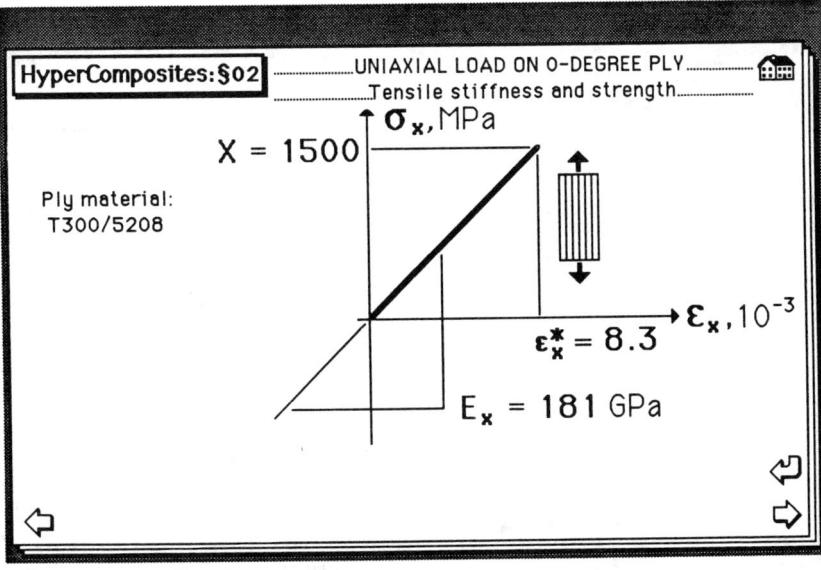

HyperComposites:§02   ....UNIAXIAL LOAD ON 0-DEGREE PLY............
............Tensile stiffness and strength............

Ply material:
T300/5208

σ_x, MPa

X = 1500

$\epsilon_x^* = 8.3$

$\epsilon_x, 10^{-3}$

$E_x = 181$ GPa

29.2 PLY STIFFNESS (continued)

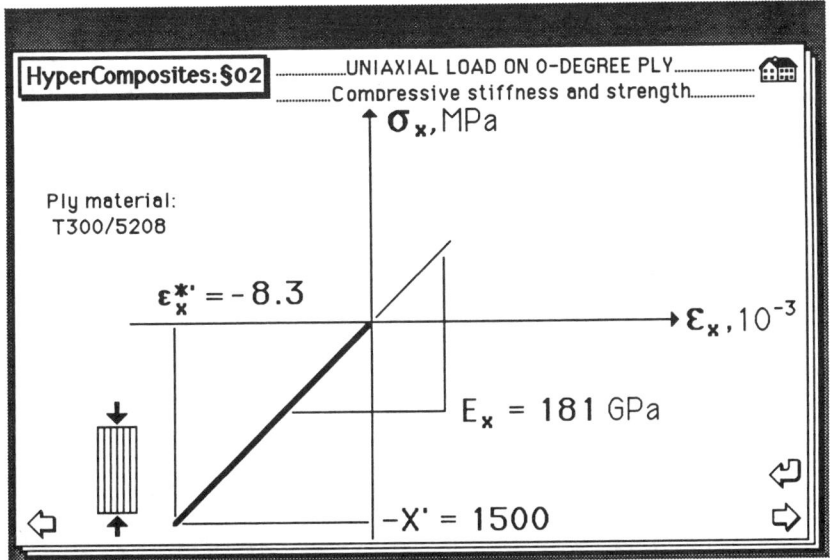

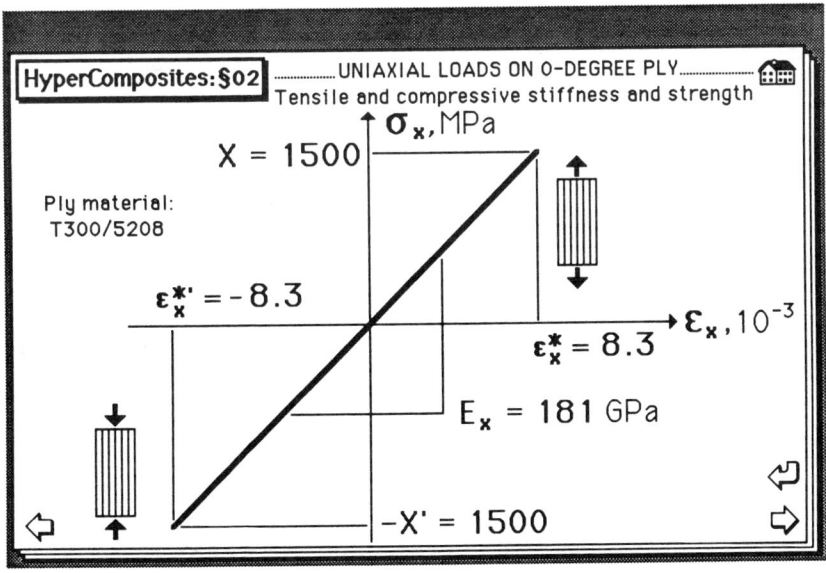

29.2 PLY STIFFNESS (continued)

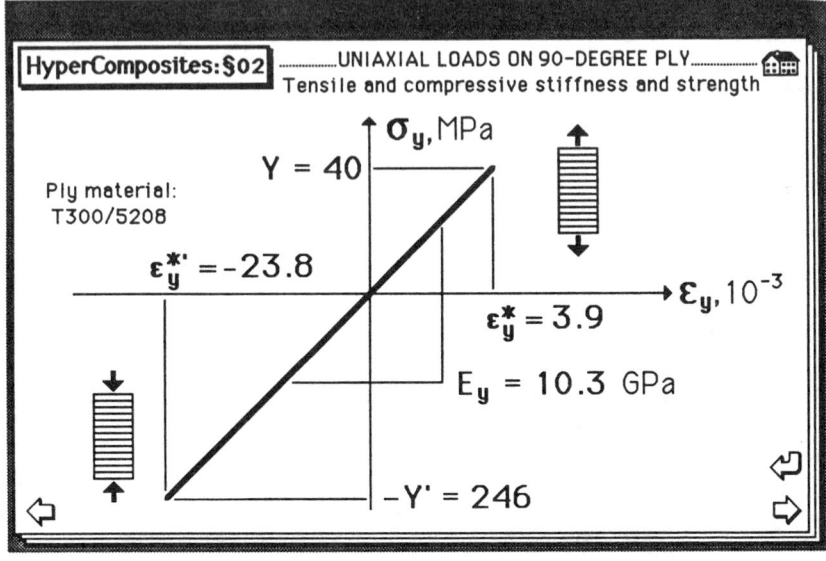

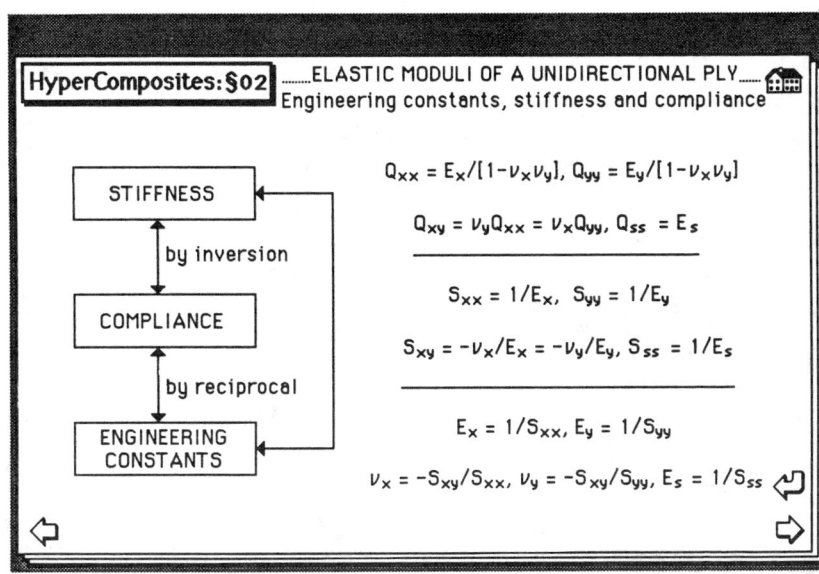

29.2 PLY STIFFNESS (continued)

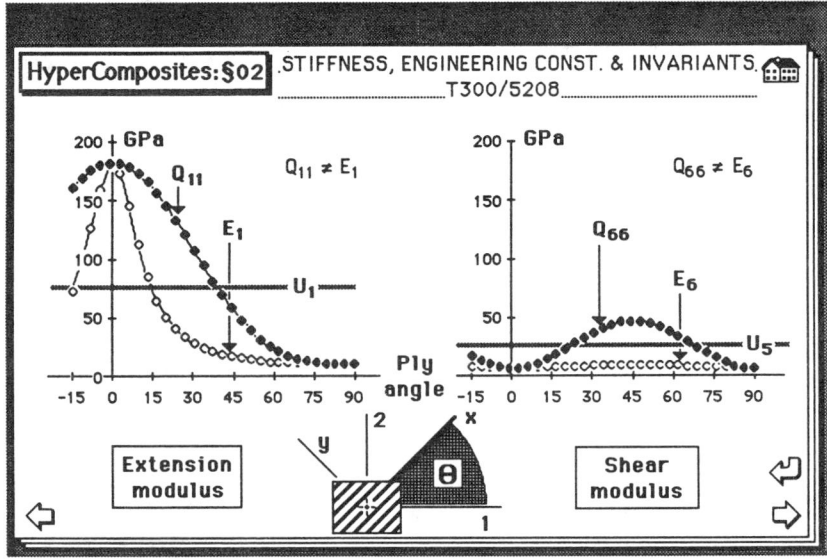

HyperComposites:§02   STIFFNESS, ENGINEERING CONST. & INVARIANTS. T300/5208

$Q_{11} \neq E_1$

$Q_{66} \neq E_6$

Ply angle

Extension modulus

Shear modulus

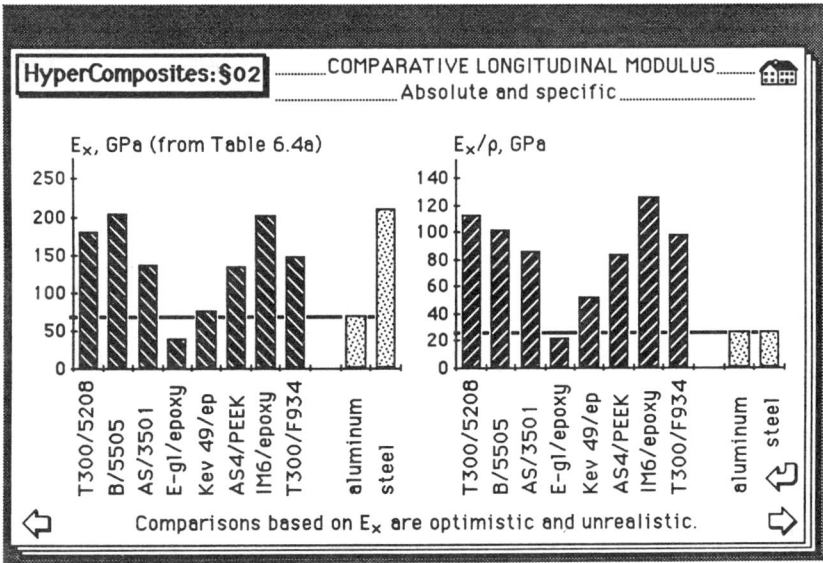

HyperComposites:§02   COMPARATIVE LONGITUDINAL MODULUS. Absolute and specific

E_x, GPa (from Table 6.4a)

E_x/ρ, GPa

T300/5208, B/5505, AS/3501, E-gl/epoxy, Kev 49/ep, AS4/PEEK, IM6/epoxy, T300/F934, aluminum, steel

Comparisons based on E_x are optimistic and unrealistic.

29.2 PLY STIFFNESS (continued)

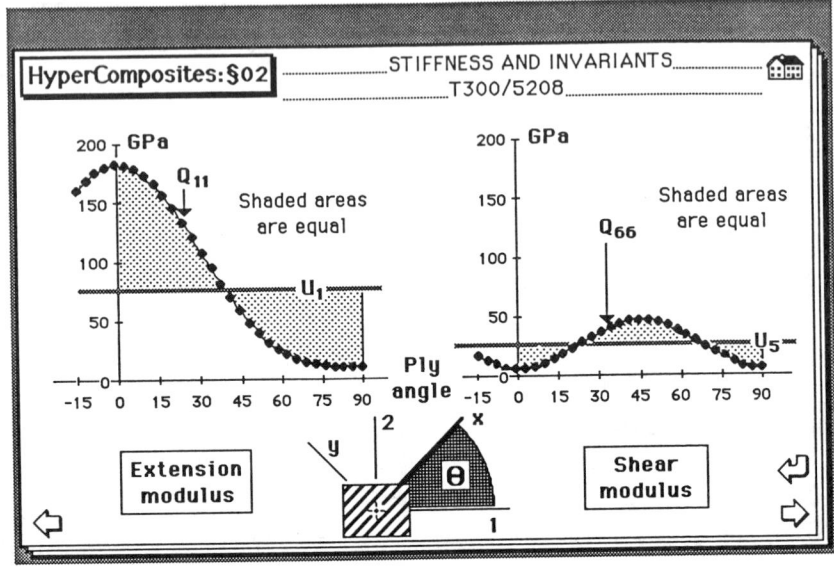

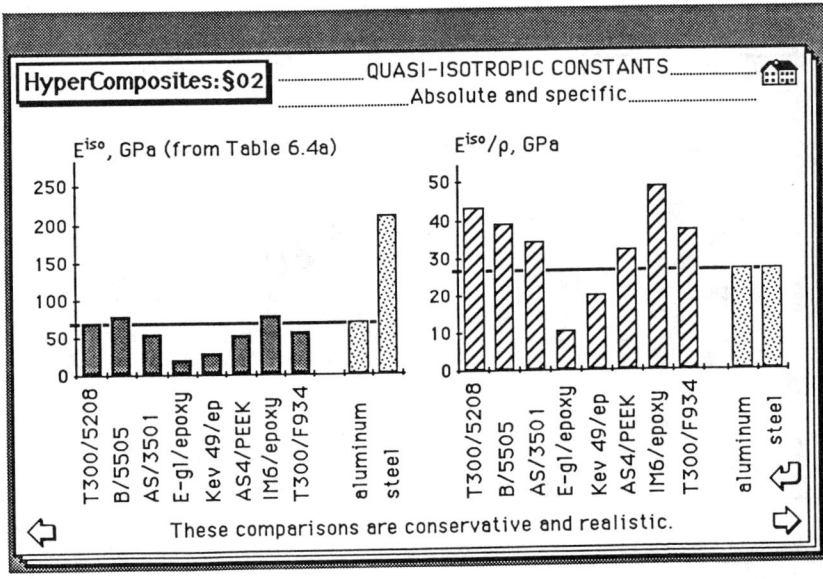

29.3 IN–PLANE STIFFNESS

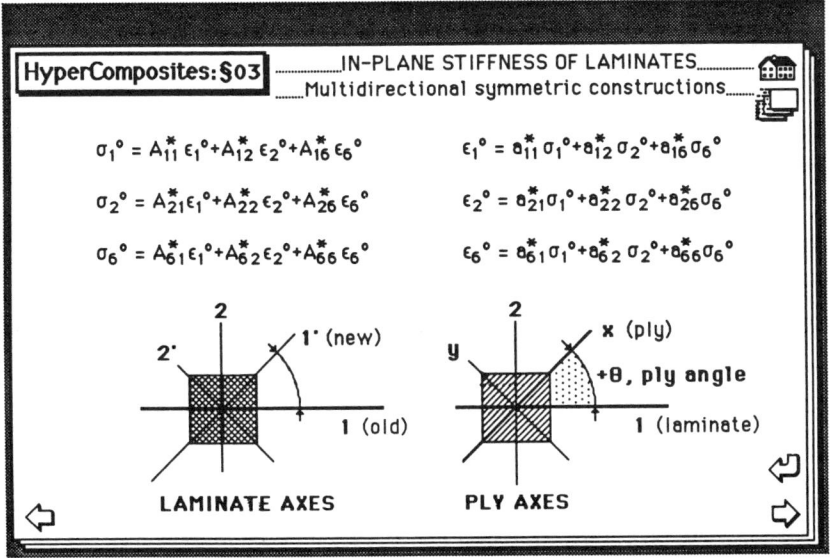

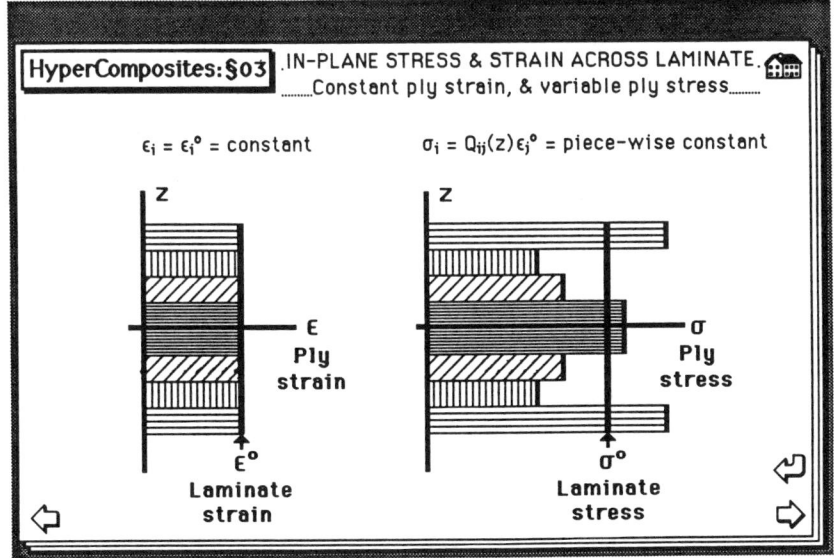

29.3 IN–PLANE STIFFNESS (continued)

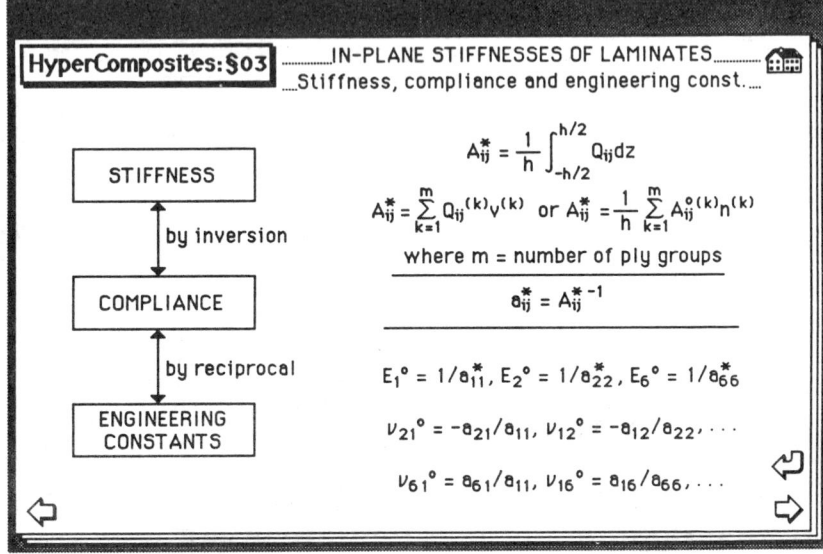

HyperComposites:§03 — IN-PLANE STIFFNESSES OF LAMINATES — Stiffness, compliance and engineering const. —

STIFFNESS

by inversion

COMPLIANCE

by reciprocal

ENGINEERING CONSTANTS

$$A_{ij}^* = \frac{1}{h} \int_{-h/2}^{h/2} Q_{ij} dz$$

$$A_{ij}^* = \sum_{k=1}^{m} Q_{ij}^{(k)} v^{(k)} \quad \text{or} \quad A_{ij}^* = \frac{1}{h} \sum_{k=1}^{m} A_{ij}^{o(k)} n^{(k)}$$

where m = number of ply groups

$$a_{ij}^* = A_{ij}^{*-1}$$

$$E_1^o = 1/a_{11}^*, \quad E_2^o = 1/a_{22}^*, \quad E_6^o = 1/a_{66}^*$$

$$\nu_{21}^o = -a_{21}/a_{11}, \quad \nu_{12}^o = -a_{12}/a_{22}, \dots$$

$$\nu_{61}^o = a_{61}/a_{11}, \quad \nu_{16}^o = a_{16}/a_{66}, \dots$$

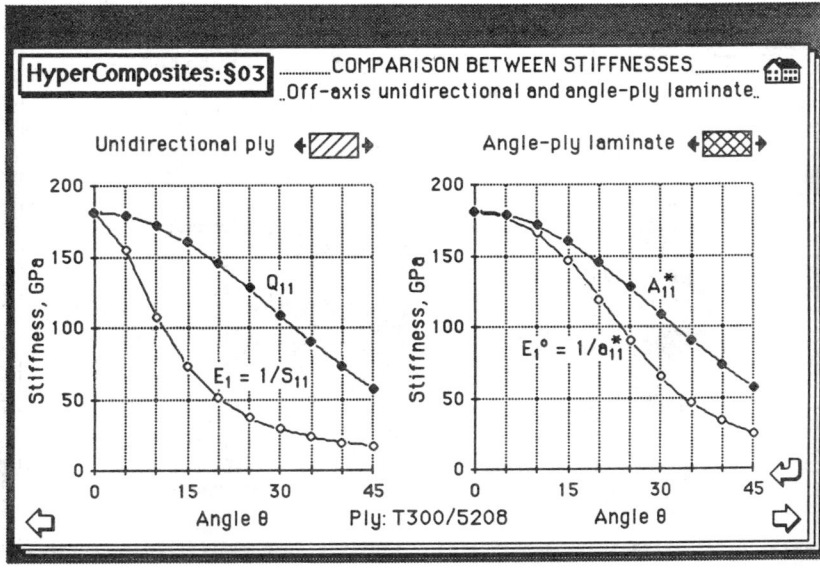

HyperComposites:§03 — COMPARISON BETWEEN STIFFNESSES — Off-axis unidirectional and angle-ply laminate.

Unidirectional ply   Angle-ply laminate

Stiffness, GPa — Angle θ   Ply: T300/5208 — Angle θ

Q_{11}

$E_1 = 1/S_{11}$

A_{11}^*

$E_1^o = 1/a_{11}^*$

29.3 IN–PLANE STIFFNESS (continued)

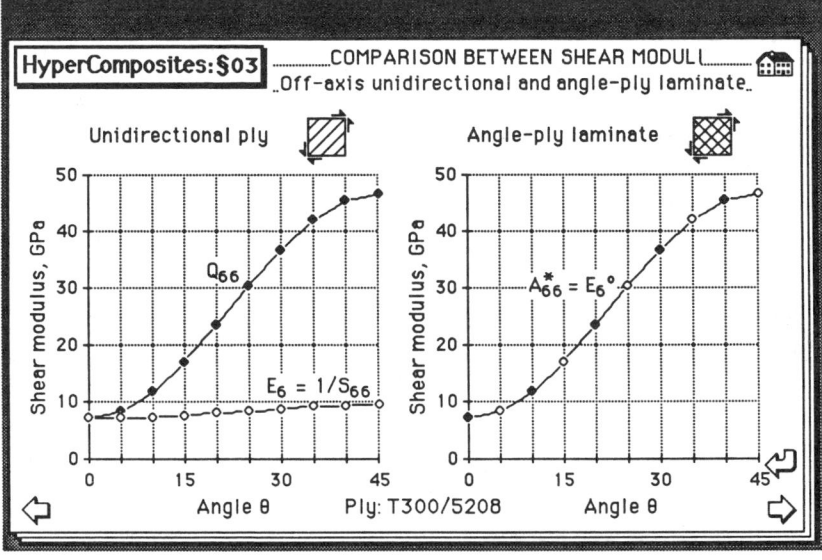

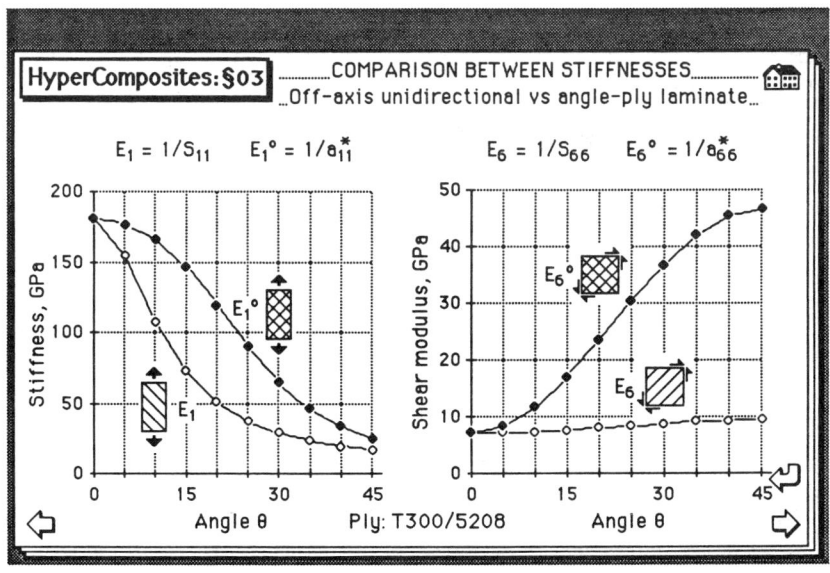

29.3 IN–PLANE STIFFNESS (continued)

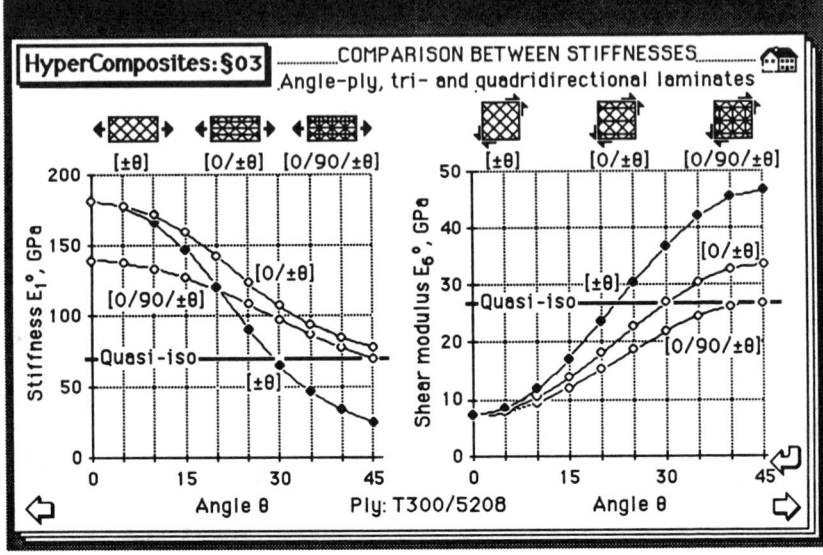

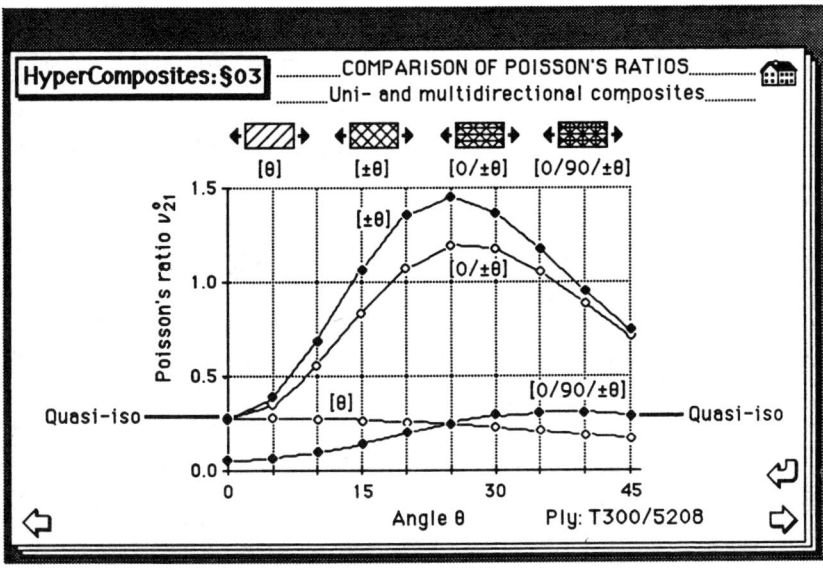

29.4 TUBING

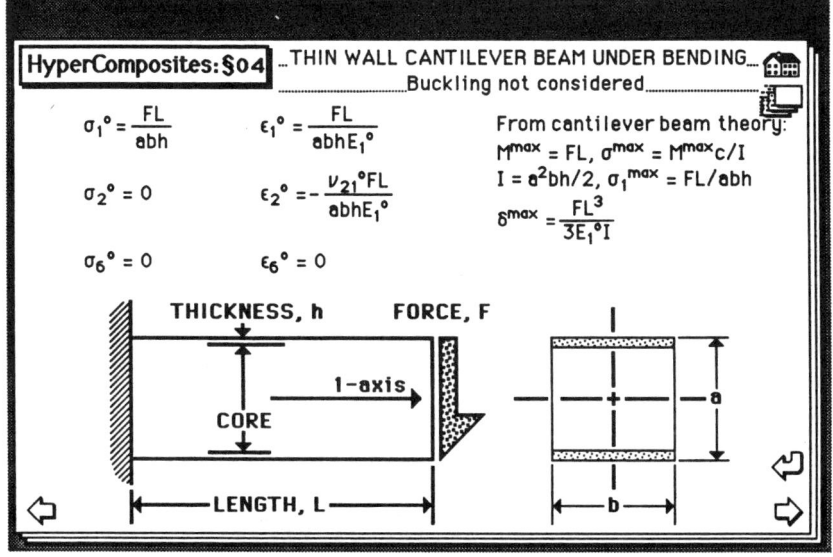

HyperComposites: §04 ....THIN WALL CANTILEVER BEAM UNDER BENDING....
....................................Buckling not considered....................

$$\sigma_1^{\,0} = \frac{FL}{abh}$$

$$\epsilon_1^{\,0} = \frac{FL}{abhE_1^{\,0}}$$

$$\sigma_2^{\,0} = 0$$

$$\epsilon_2^{\,0} = -\frac{\nu_{21}^{\,0}FL}{abhE_1^{\,0}}$$

$$\sigma_6^{\,0} = 0$$

$$\epsilon_6^{\,0} = 0$$

From cantilever beam theory:
$$M^{max} = FL, \quad \sigma^{max} = M^{max}c/I$$
$$I = a^2bh/2, \quad \sigma_1^{max} = FL/abh$$
$$\delta^{max} = \frac{FL^3}{3E_1^{\,0}I}$$

THICKNESS, h   FORCE, F

1-axis

CORE

LENGTH, L

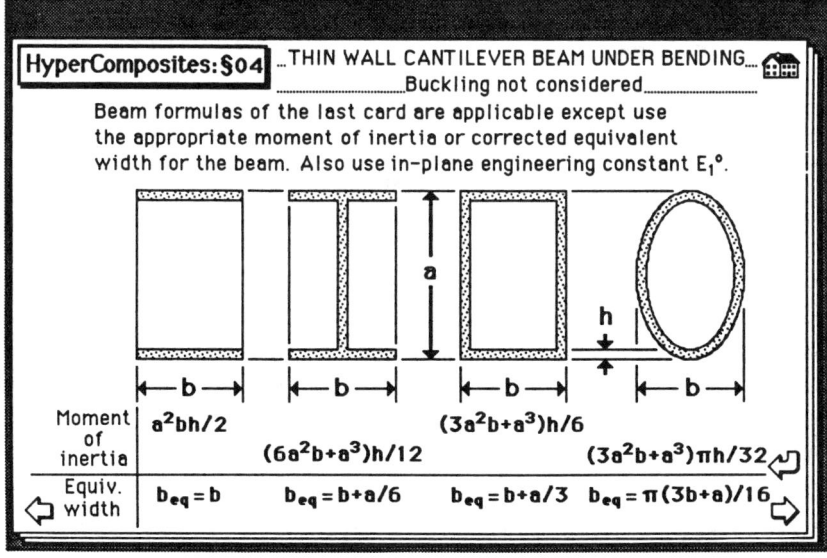

HyperComposites: §04 ....THIN WALL CANTILEVER BEAM UNDER BENDING....
....................................Buckling not considered....................

Beam formulas of the last card are applicable except use the appropriate moment of inertia or corrected equivalent width for the beam. Also use in-plane engineering constant $E_1^{\,0}$.

Moment of inertia	$a^2bh/2$	$(6a^2b+a^3)h/12$	$(3a^2b+a^3)h/6$ $(3a^2b+a^3)\pi h/32$
Equiv. width	$b_{eq}=b$	$b_{eq}=b+a/6$	$b_{eq}=b+a/3$ $b_{eq}=\pi(3b+a)/16$

29.4 TUBING (continued)

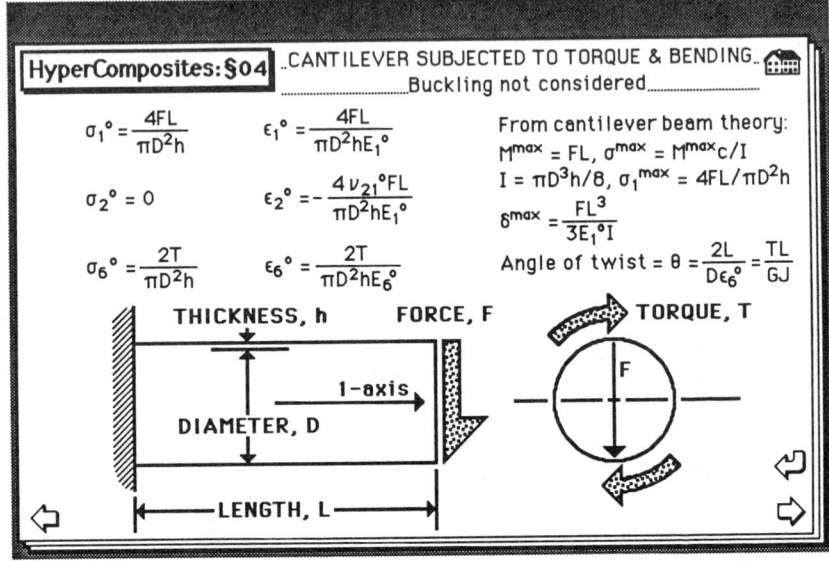

HyperComposites: §04   CANTILEVER SUBJECTED TO TORQUE & BENDING

Buckling not considered

$$\sigma_1^\circ = \frac{4FL}{\pi D^2 h}$$

$$\epsilon_1^\circ = \frac{4FL}{\pi D^2 h E_1^\circ}$$

From cantilever beam theory:
$$M^{max} = FL, \quad \sigma^{max} = M^{max}c/I$$

$$\sigma_2^\circ = 0$$

$$\epsilon_2^\circ = -\frac{4\nu_{21}^\circ FL}{\pi D^2 h E_1^\circ}$$

$$I = \pi D^3 h/8, \quad \sigma_1^{max} = 4FL/\pi D^2 h$$

$$\delta^{max} = \frac{FL^3}{3E_1^\circ I}$$

$$\sigma_6^\circ = \frac{2T}{\pi D^2 h}$$

$$\epsilon_6^\circ = \frac{2T}{\pi D^2 h E_6^\circ}$$

Angle of twist $= \theta = \frac{2L}{D\epsilon_6^\circ} = \frac{TL}{GJ}$

THICKNESS, h   FORCE, F   TORQUE, T

1-axis

DIAMETER, D

LENGTH, L

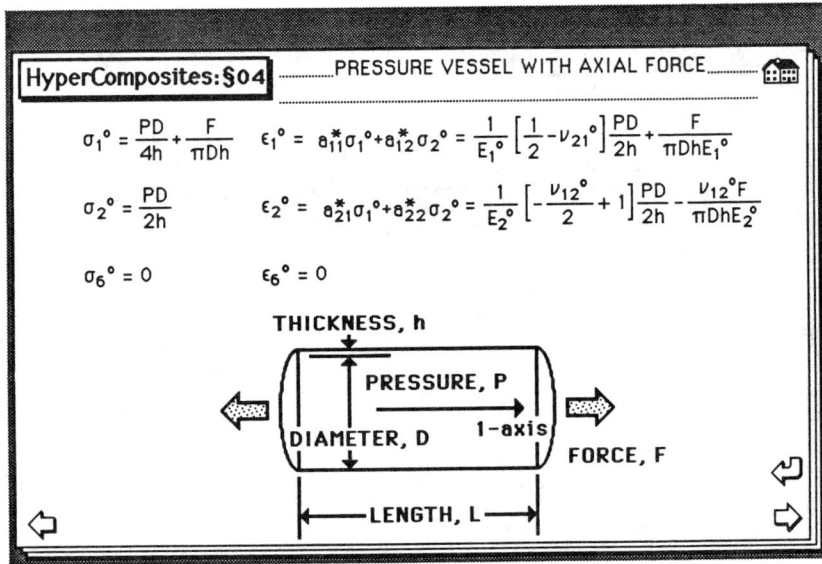

HyperComposites: §04   PRESSURE VESSEL WITH AXIAL FORCE

$$\sigma_1^\circ = \frac{PD}{4h} + \frac{F}{\pi Dh}$$

$$\epsilon_1^\circ = a_{11}^* \sigma_1^\circ + a_{12}^* \sigma_2^\circ = \frac{1}{E_1^\circ}\left[\frac{1}{2} - \nu_{21}^\circ\right]\frac{PD}{2h} + \frac{F}{\pi DhE_1^\circ}$$

$$\sigma_2^\circ = \frac{PD}{2h}$$

$$\epsilon_2^\circ = a_{21}^* \sigma_1^\circ + a_{22}^* \sigma_2^\circ = \frac{1}{E_2^\circ}\left[-\frac{\nu_{12}^\circ}{2} + 1\right]\frac{PD}{2h} - \frac{\nu_{12}^\circ F}{\pi DhE_2^\circ}$$

$$\sigma_6^\circ = 0$$

$$\epsilon_6^\circ = 0$$

THICKNESS, h

PRESSURE, P

DIAMETER, D   1-axis

FORCE, F

LENGTH, L

29.5 FLEXURAL STIFFNESS

HyperComposites: §05 FLEXURAL STIFFNESS OF COMPOSITE LAMINATES
........Multidirectional symmetric constructions......

Symmetric laminates consisting of unidirectional plies or fabrics
having multiple ply orientations can be characterized by the same
linear elastic stress-strain relation under flexural load as
that for the in-plane load. The key difference for the flexural
constants is their dependence on the stacking sequence of the plies.

The relations between stiffness, compliance and engineering
constants under flexure are precisely the same as those for the
in-plane. Sandwich core can be added to increase the flexural
stiffness per unit weight. Effective flexural moduli can replace those
for isotropic materials for statically determinate structures.

Other features that can simplify design include the use of thin wall
construction where 3x3 can replace 6x6 matrices. Repeated sublaminates are easy to design, and make stronger laminates as well.

HyperComposites: §05 ....LAMINATE STRESS-STRAIN RELATIONS........

$$\sigma_1^f = D_{11}^* \epsilon_1^f + D_{12}^* \epsilon_2^f + D_{16}^* \epsilon_6^f$$

$$\sigma_2^f = D_{21}^* \epsilon_1^f + D_{22}^* \epsilon_2^f + D_{26}^* \epsilon_6^f$$

$$\sigma_6^f = D_{61}^* \epsilon_1^f + D_{62}^* \epsilon_2^f + D_{66}^* \epsilon_6^f$$

$$\epsilon_1^f = d_{11}^* \sigma_1^f + d_{12}^* \sigma_2^f + d_{16}^* \sigma_6^f$$

$$\epsilon_2^f = d_{21}^* \sigma_1^f + d_{22}^* \sigma_2^f + d_{26}^* \sigma_6^f$$

$$\epsilon_6^f = d_{61}^* \sigma_1^f + d_{62}^* \sigma_2^f + d_{66}^* \sigma_6^f$$

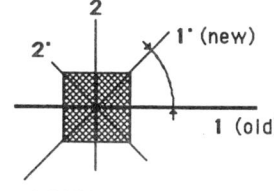

LAMINATE AXES

2
2·
1· (new)
1 (old)

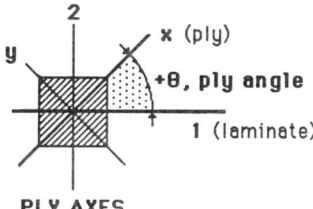

PLY AXES

2
y
x (ply)
+θ, ply angle
1 (laminate)

29.5 FLEXURAL STIFFNESS (continued)

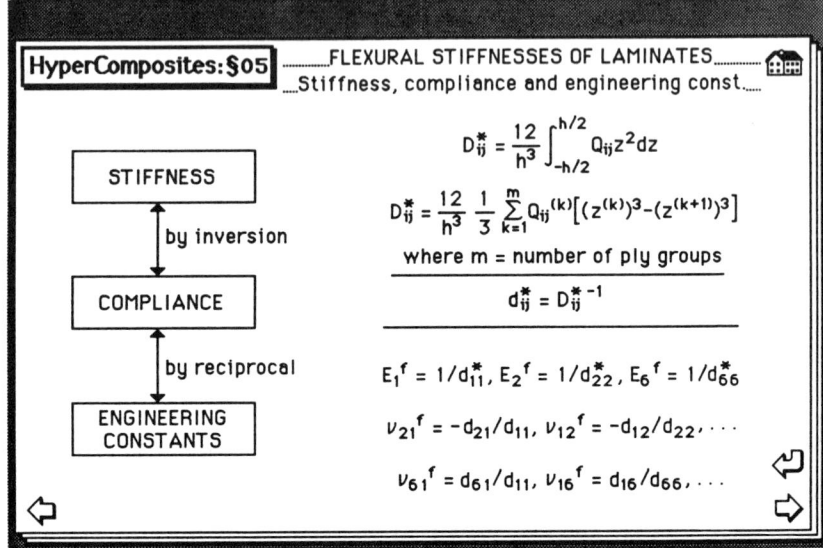

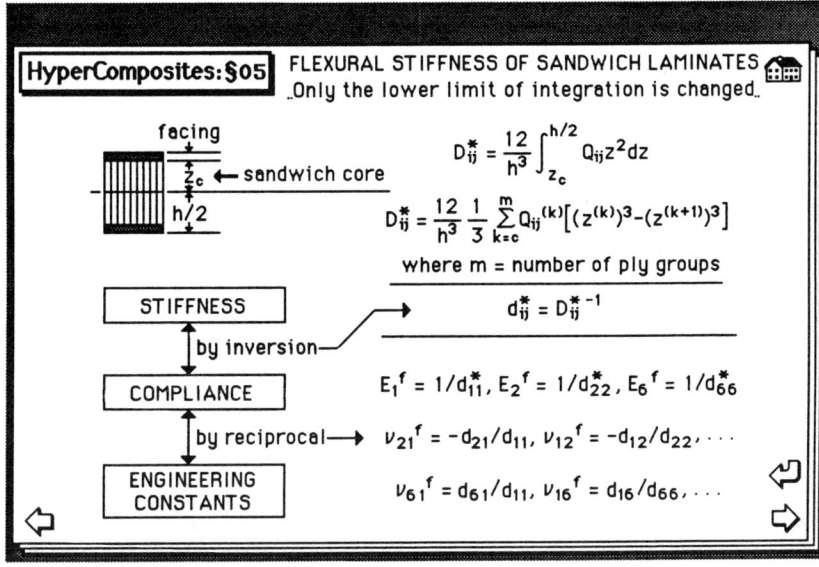

29.5 FLEXURAL STIFFNESS (continued)

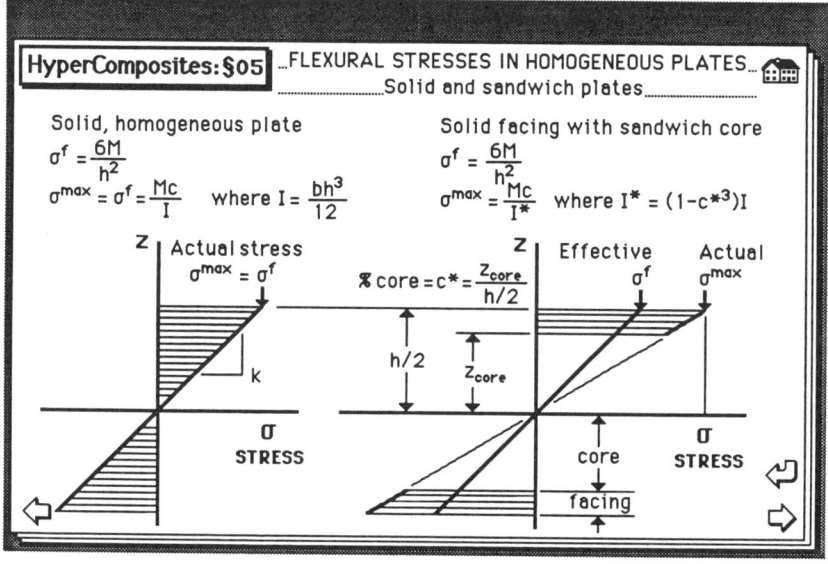

HyperComposites: §05 ...FLEXURAL STRESSES IN HOMOGENEOUS PLATES...
........................Solid and sandwich plates........................

Solid, homogeneous plate

$$\sigma^f = \frac{6M}{h^2}$$

$$\sigma^{max} = \sigma^f = \frac{Mc}{I} \quad \text{where } I = \frac{bh^3}{12}$$

Solid facing with sandwich core

$$\sigma^f = \frac{6M}{h^2}$$

$$\sigma^{max} = \frac{Mc}{I^*} \quad \text{where } I^* = (1 - c^{*3})I$$

$\%\text{ core} = c^* = \dfrac{z_{core}}{h/2}$

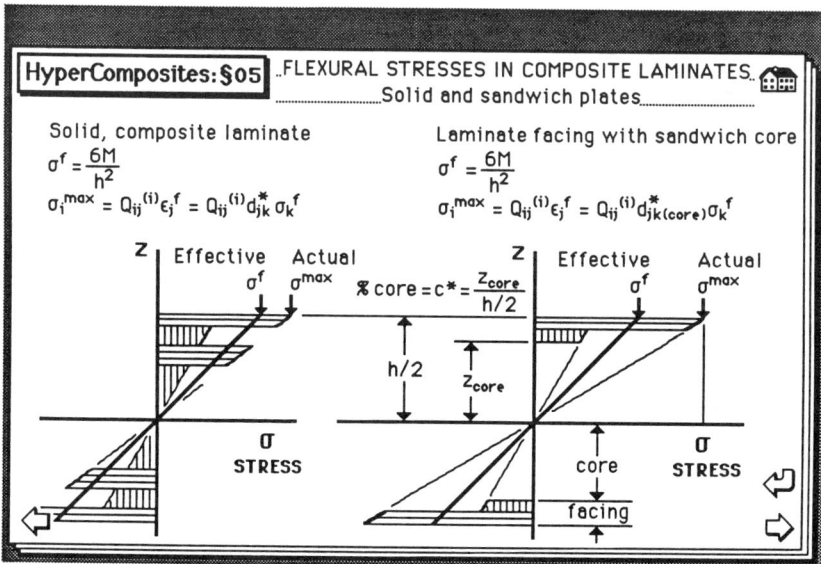

HyperComposites: §05 ...FLEXURAL STRESSES IN COMPOSITE LAMINATES...
........................Solid and sandwich plates........................

Solid, composite laminate

$$\sigma^f = \frac{6M}{h^2}$$

$$\sigma_i^{max} = Q_{ij}^{(i)}\epsilon_j^f = Q_{ij}^{(i)}d_{jk}^*\sigma_k^f$$

Laminate facing with sandwich core

$$\sigma^f = \frac{6M}{h^2}$$

$$\sigma_i^{max} = Q_{ij}^{(i)}\epsilon_j^f = Q_{ij}^{(i)}d_{jk(core)}^*\sigma_k^f$$

$\%\text{ core} = c^* = \dfrac{z_{core}}{h/2}$

29.5 FLEXURAL STIFFNESS (continued)

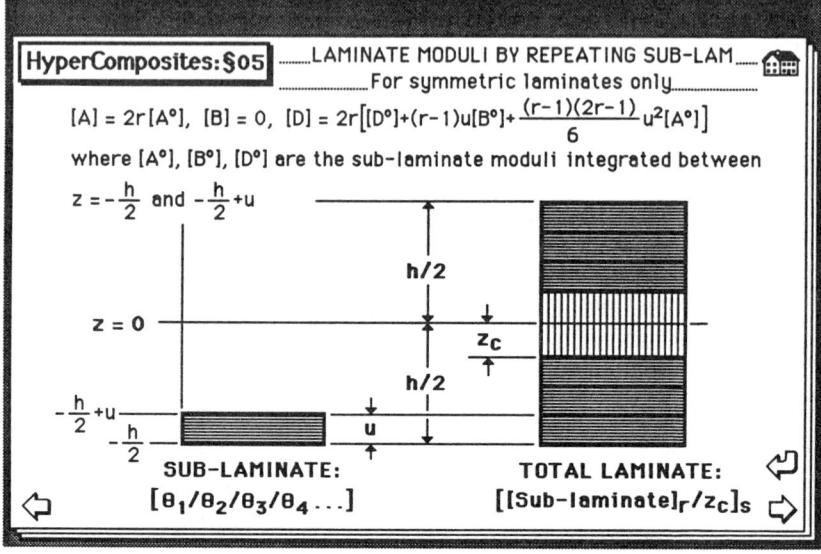

HyperComposites:§05 ....LAMINATE MODULI BY REPEATING SUB-LAM......

........................For symmetric laminates only........................

$$[A] = 2r[A^\circ], \quad [B] = 0, \quad [D] = 2r\left[[D^\circ]+(r-1)u[B^\circ]+\frac{(r-1)(2r-1)}{6}u^2[A^\circ]\right]$$

where $[A^\circ]$, $[B^\circ]$, $[D^\circ]$ are the sub-laminate moduli integrated between

$z = -\dfrac{h}{2}$ and $-\dfrac{h}{2}+u$

SUB-LAMINATE:
$[\theta_1/\theta_2/\theta_3/\theta_4 \ldots]$

TOTAL LAMINATE:
$[[\text{Sub-laminate}]_r/z_c]_s$

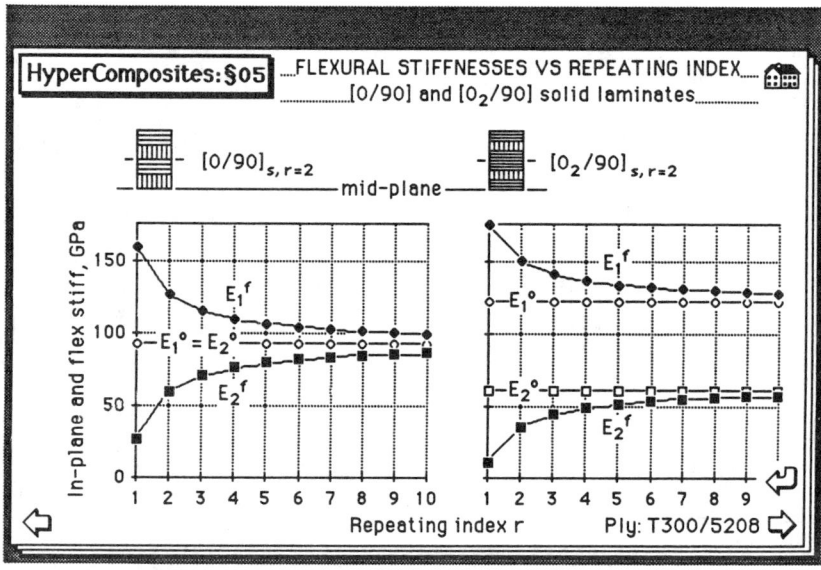

HyperComposites:§05 ....FLEXURAL STIFFNESSES VS REPEATING INDEX......

........................$[0/90]$ and $[0_2/90]$ solid laminates........................

$[0/90]_{s,\,r=2}$ $[0_2/90]_{s,\,r=2}$

_____ mid-plane _____

In-plane and flex stiff, GPa

E_1^f

$E_1^\circ = E_2^\circ$

E_2^f

E_1^f

E_1°

E_2°

E_2^f

Repeating index r   Ply: T300/5208

29.5 FLEXURAL STIFFNESS (continued)

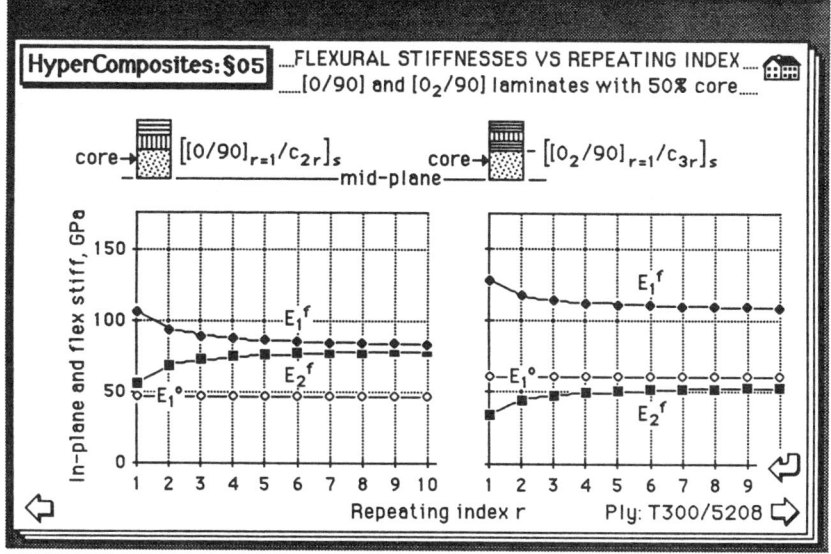

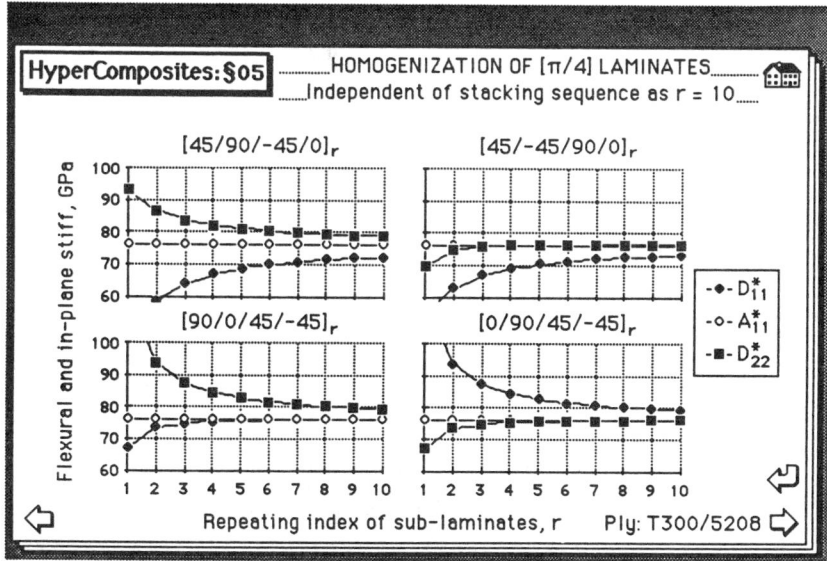

29.5 FLEXURAL STIFFNESS (continued)

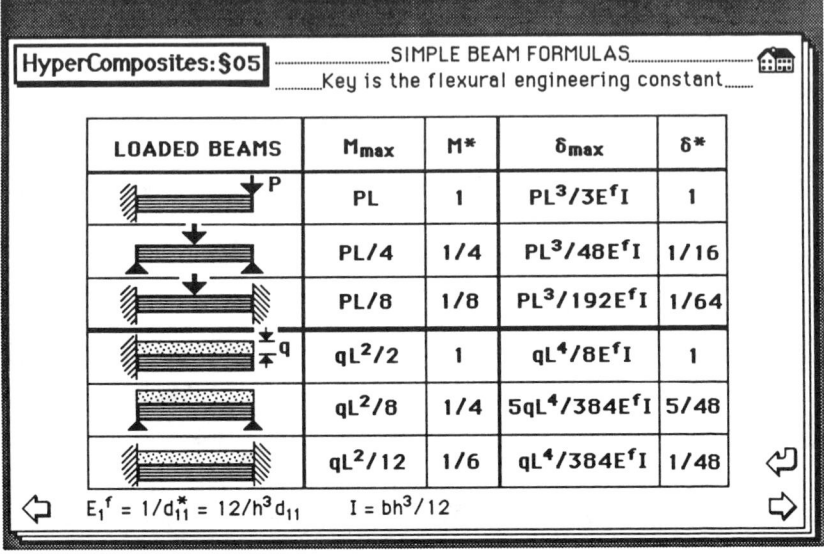

HyperComposites: §05 ....SIMPLE BEAM FORMULAS.........
.........Key is the flexural engineering constant.........

LOADED BEAMS	M_{max}	M^*	δ_{max}	δ^*
	PL	1	$PL^3/3E^fI$	1
	$PL/4$	1/4	$PL^3/48E^fI$	1/16
	$PL/8$	1/8	$PL^3/192E^fI$	1/64
	$qL^2/2$	1	$qL^4/8E^fI$	1
	$qL^2/8$	1/4	$5qL^4/384E^fI$	5/48
	$qL^2/12$	1/6	$qL^4/384E^fI$	1/48

$E_1^f = 1/d_{11}^* = 12/h^3 d_{11}$ $I = bh^3/12$

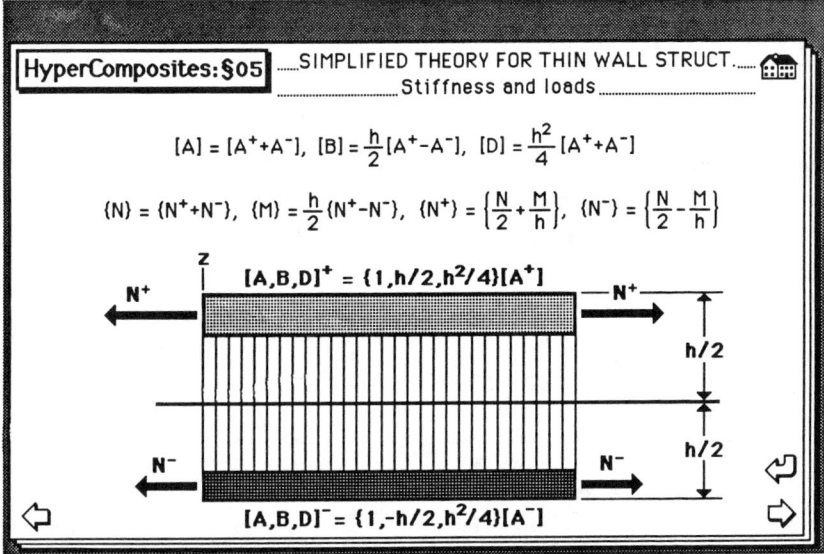

HyperComposites: §05 ....SIMPLIFIED THEORY FOR THIN WALL STRUCT.......
.........Stiffness and loads.........

$$[A] = [A^+ + A^-], \quad [B] = \frac{h}{2}[A^+ - A^-], \quad [D] = \frac{h^2}{4}[A^+ + A^-]$$

$$\{N\} = \{N^+ + N^-\}, \quad \{M\} = \frac{h}{2}\{N^+ - N^-\}, \quad \{N^+\} = \left\{\frac{N}{2} + \frac{M}{h}\right\}, \quad \{N^-\} = \left\{\frac{N}{2} - \frac{M}{h}\right\}$$

$$[A,B,D]^+ = \{1, h/2, h^2/4\}[A^+]$$

$$[A,B,D]^- = \{1, -h/2, h^2/4\}[A^-]$$

29.6 MICROMECHANICS

Micromechanics relates the properties of the constituents to those of unidirectional ply. Numerous approaches can be found in the literature. We propose the use of a modified rule-of-mixtures relation, using the stress partitioning parameter as a back calculated constant. We use E-glass/epoxy composite for this calculation assuming that glass fiber is homogeneous and isotropic. With the partitioning parameters obtained from this composite, we apply the same values for graphite and Kevlar composites.

This approach is easy to use, and eliminates the need to estimate the transverse and shear moduli of nonisotropic fibers.

With simplified micromechanics, an integrated micro- and macro-mechanics analysis is easy to perform. The use of spreadsheet is particularly useful in optimizing laminates from constituents.

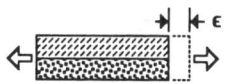   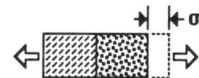

PARALLEL MODEL   **SERIES MODEL**
Equal strain   **Equal stress**

$$p = v_f p_f + v_m p_m \qquad\qquad \frac{1}{p} = \frac{v_f}{p_f} + \frac{v_m}{p_m}$$

where p = property, $v_f + v_m = 1$

Example: $v_f = v_m = 0.5$, $p_f = 10$, $p_m = 1$

$$p^{para} = 11 \times 0.5 = 5.5 \qquad\qquad p^{series} = \frac{1}{[0.5 \times 1.1]} = 1.82$$

29.6 MICROMECHANICS (continued)

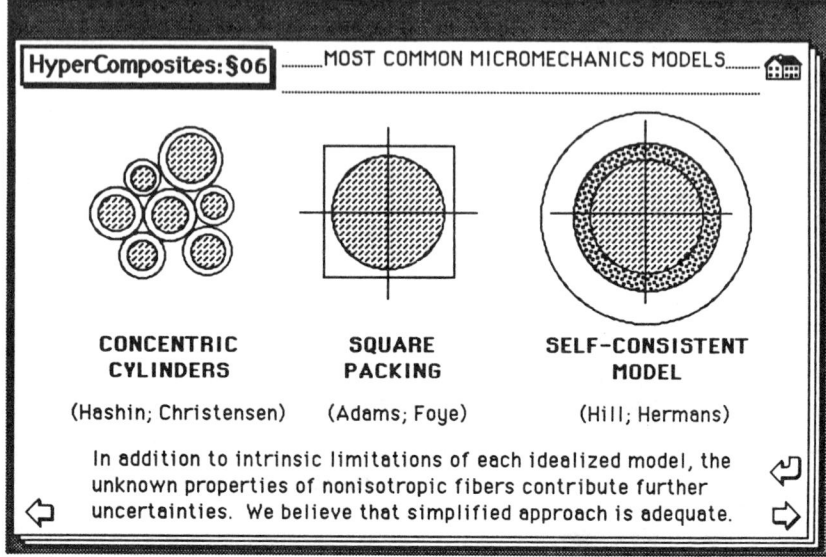

HyperComposites: §06 ....MOST COMMON MICROMECHANICS MODELS.........

CONCENTRIC CYLINDERS   **SQUARE PACKING**   **SELF-CONSISTENT MODEL**

(Hashin; Christensen)   (Adams; Foye)   (Hill; Hermans)

In addition to intrinsic limitations of each idealized model, the unknown properties of nonisotropic fibers contribute further uncertainties. We believe that simplified approach is adequate.

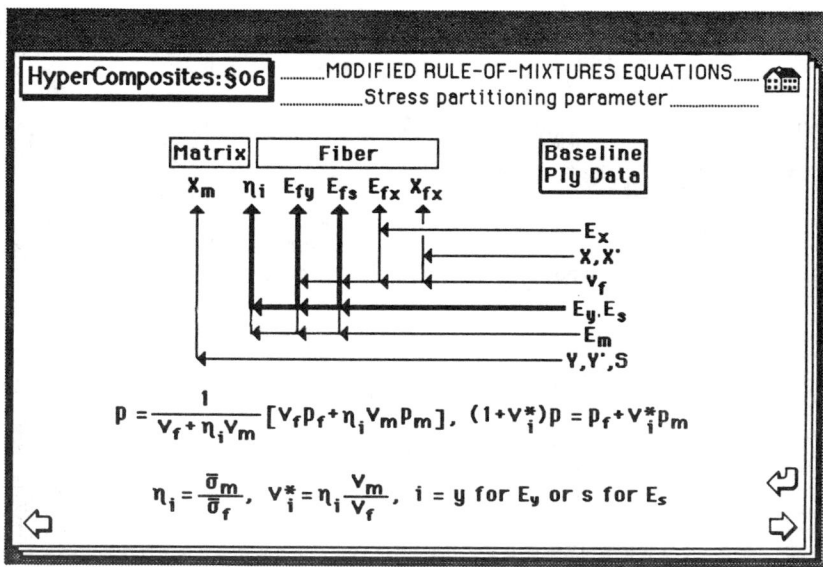

HyperComposites: §06 ....MODIFIED RULE-OF-MIXTURES EQUATIONS.........
.........Stress partitioning parameter.........

| Matrix | Fiber | | | | | Baseline Ply Data |

X_m η_i E_{fy} E_{fs} E_{fx} X_{fx}

E_x
X, X'
ν_f
E_y, E_s
E_m
Y, Y', S

$$p = \frac{1}{v_f + \eta_i v_m}[v_f p_f + \eta_i v_m p_m], \quad (1 + v_i^*)p = p_f + v_i^* p_m$$

$$\eta_i = \frac{\bar{\sigma}_m}{\bar{\sigma}_f}, \quad v_i^* = \eta_i \frac{v_m}{v_f}, \quad i = y \text{ for } E_y \text{ or } s \text{ for } E_s$$

29.6 MICROMECHANICS (continued)

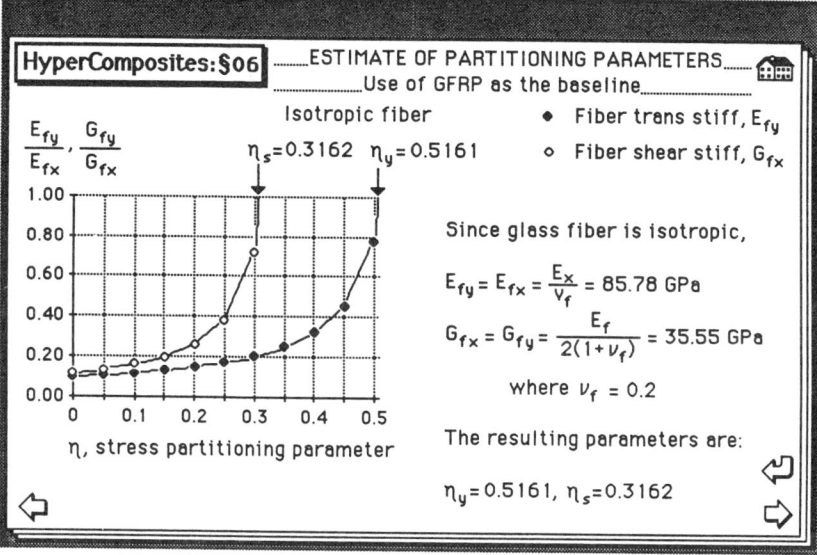

HyperComposites:§06 ....ESTIMATE OF PARTITIONING PARAMETERS........
................Use of GFRP as the baseline.................

$\dfrac{E_{fy}}{E_{fx}}, \dfrac{G_{fy}}{G_{fx}}$

Isotropic fiber

$\eta_s = 0.3162 \quad \eta_y = 0.5161$

- Fiber trans stiff, E_{fy}
- Fiber shear stiff, G_{fx}

η, stress partitioning parameter

Since glass fiber is isotropic,

$$E_{fy} = E_{fx} = \frac{E_x}{v_f} = 85.78 \text{ GPa}$$

$$G_{fx} = G_{fy} = \frac{E_f}{2(1+v_f)} = 35.55 \text{ GPa}$$

where $v_f = 0.2$

The resulting parameters are:

$$\eta_y = 0.5161, \quad \eta_s = 0.3162$$

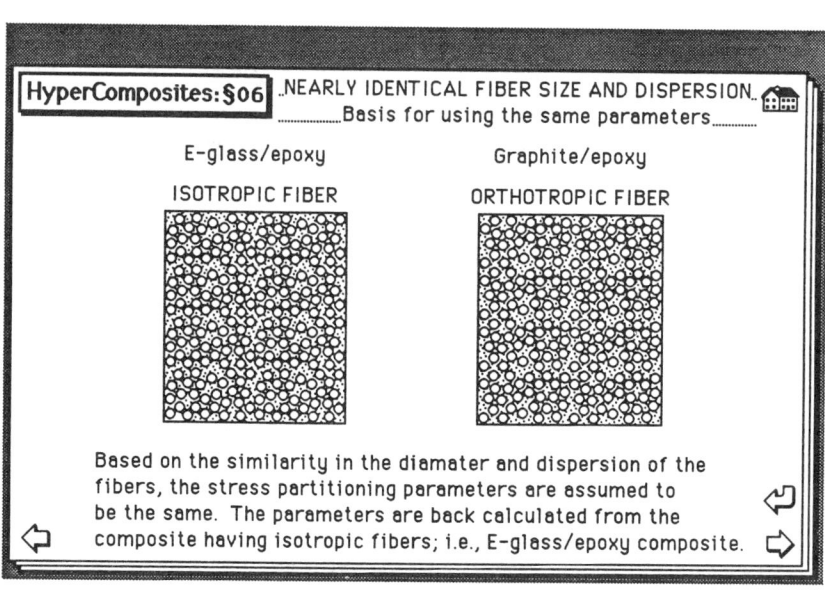

HyperComposites:§06 ..NEARLY IDENTICAL FIBER SIZE AND DISPERSION..
................Basis for using the same parameters.................

E-glass/epoxy   Graphite/epoxy

ISOTROPIC FIBER   ORTHOTROPIC FIBER

Based on the similarity in the diameter and dispersion of the fibers, the stress partitioning parameters are assumed to be the same. The parameters are back calculated from the composite having isotropic fibers; i.e., E-glass/epoxy composite.

29.6 MICROMECHANICS (continued)

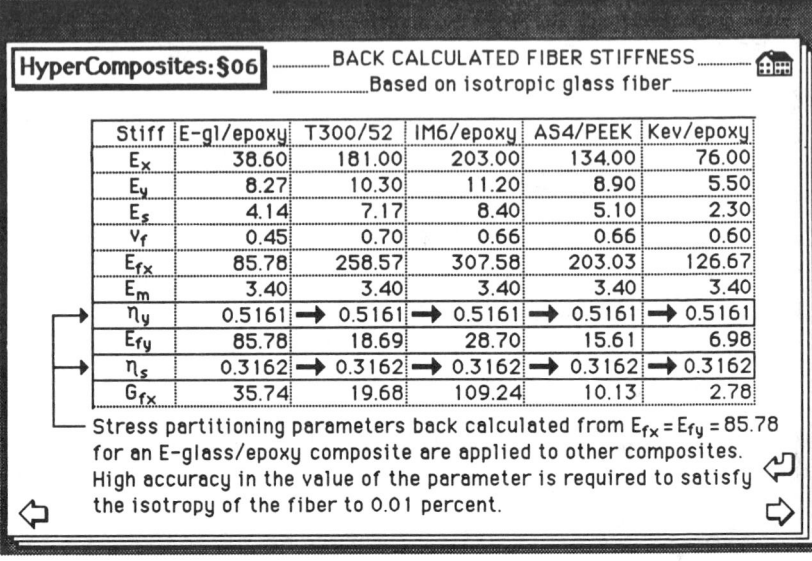

HyperComposites: §06   ········ BACK CALCULATED FIBER STIFFNESS ········
········ Based on isotropic glass fiber ········

Stiff	E-gl/epoxy	T300/52	IM6/epoxy	AS4/PEEK	Kev/epoxy
E_x	38.60	181.00	203.00	134.00	76.00
E_y	8.27	10.30	11.20	8.90	5.50
E_s	4.14	7.17	8.40	5.10	2.30
v_f	0.45	0.70	0.66	0.66	0.60
E_{fx}	85.78	258.57	307.58	203.03	126.67
E_m	3.40	3.40	3.40	3.40	3.40
η_y	0.5161 ➔	0.5161 ➔	0.5161 ➔	0.5161 ➔	0.5161
E_{fy}	85.78	18.69	28.70	15.61	6.98
η_s	0.3162 ➔	0.3162 ➔	0.3162 ➔	0.3162 ➔	0.3162
G_{fx}	35.74	19.68	109.24	10.13	2.78

Stress partitioning parameters back calculated from $E_{fx} = E_{fy} = 85.78$ for an E-glass/epoxy composite are applied to other composites. High accuracy in the value of the parameter is required to satisfy the isotropy of the fiber to 0.01 percent.

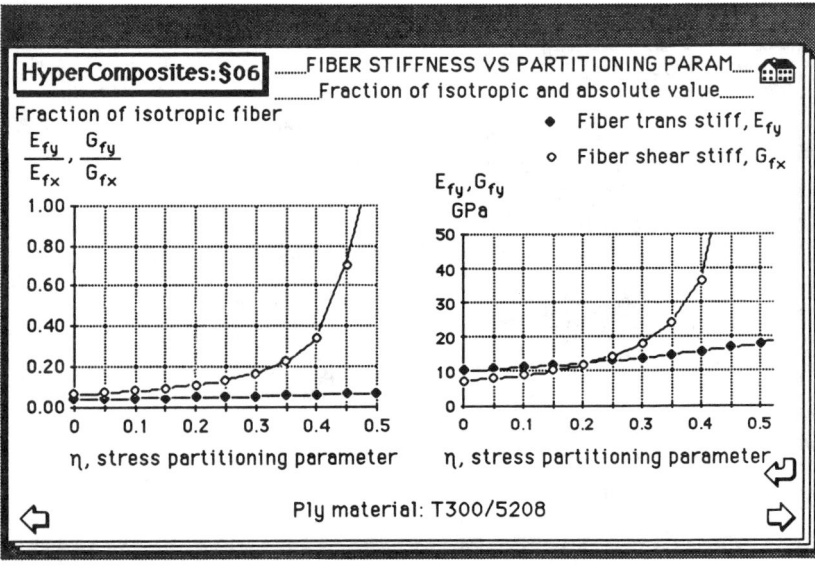

HyperComposites: §06   ········ FIBER STIFFNESS VS PARTITIONING PARAM ········
········ Fraction of isotropic and absolute value ········

Fraction of isotropic fiber

$\dfrac{E_{fy}}{E_{fx}}, \dfrac{G_{fy}}{G_{fx}}$

● Fiber trans stiff, E_{fy}
○ Fiber shear stiff, G_{fx}

η, stress partitioning parameter η, stress partitioning parameter

Ply material: T300/5208

29.6 MICROMECHANICS (continued)

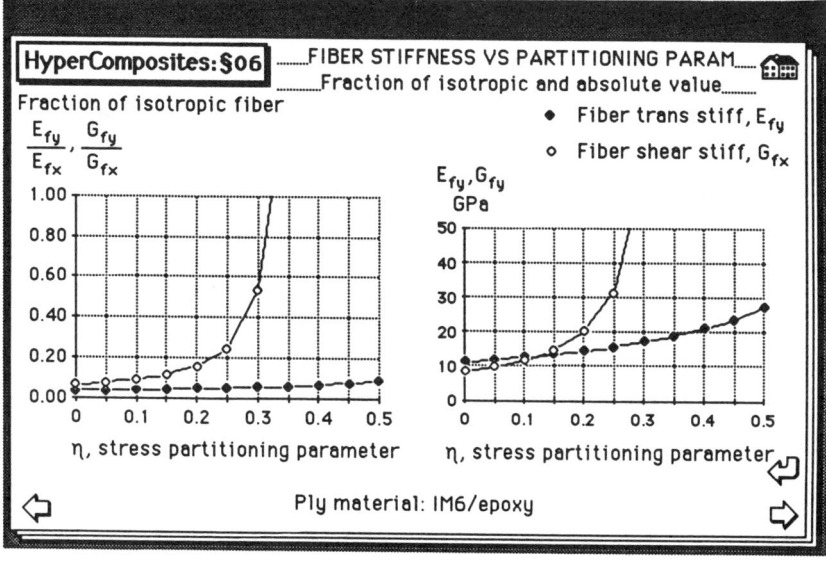

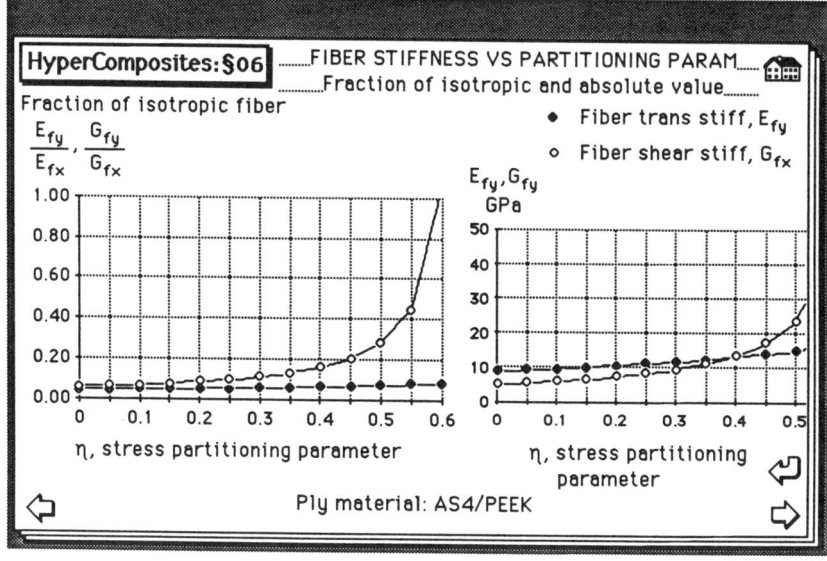

29.6 MICROMECHANICS (continued)

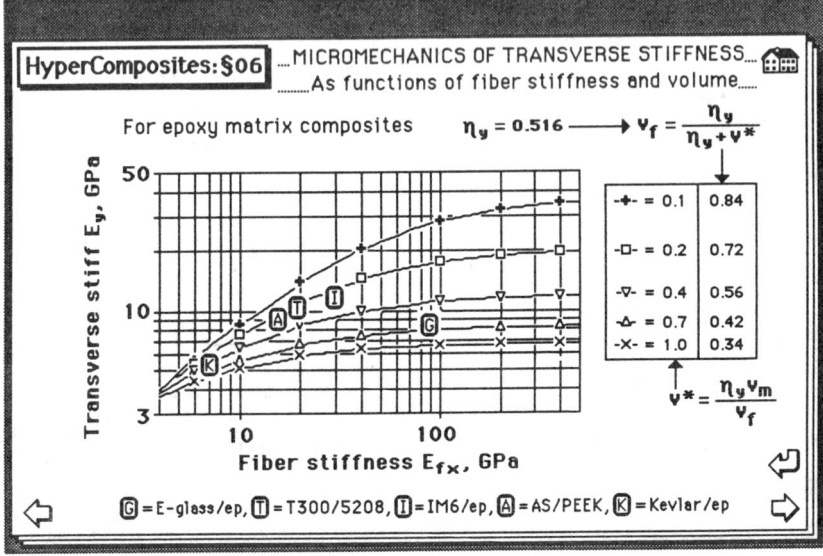

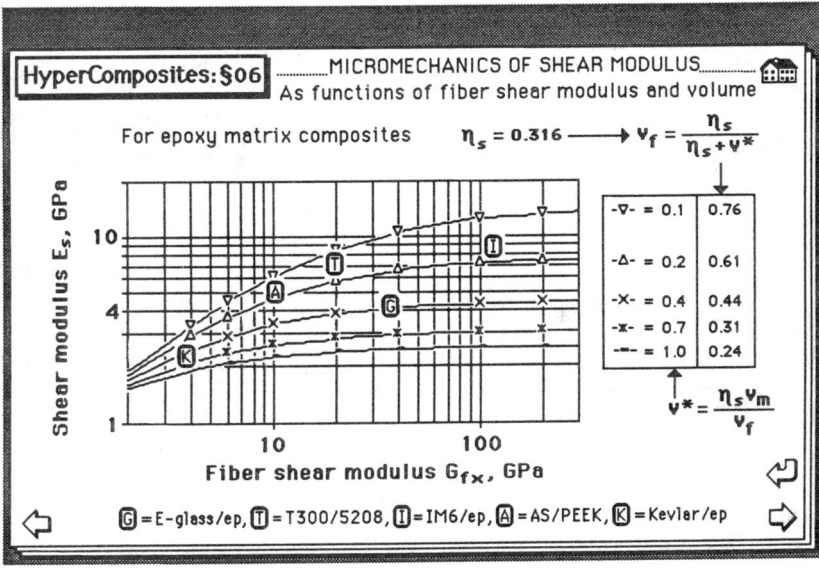

29.7 MISES/TRESCA FAILURE CRITERIA

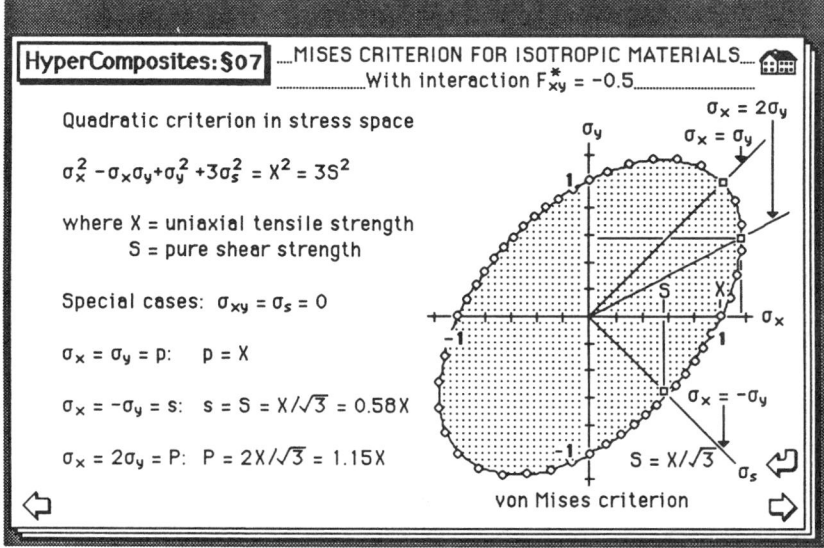

HyperComposites:§07 ⸺MISES CRITERION FOR ISOTROPIC MATERIALS⸺
⸺With interaction $F^*_{xy} = -0.5$⸺

Quadratic criterion in stress space

$$\sigma_x^2 - \sigma_x\sigma_y + \sigma_y^2 + 3\sigma_s^2 = X^2 = 3S^2$$

where X = uniaxial tensile strength
S = pure shear strength

Special cases: $\sigma_{xy} = \sigma_s = 0$

$\sigma_x = \sigma_y = p$: $p = X$

$\sigma_x = -\sigma_y = s$: $s = S = X/\sqrt{3} = 0.58X$

$\sigma_x = 2\sigma_y = P$: $P = 2X/\sqrt{3} = 1.15X$

von Mises criterion

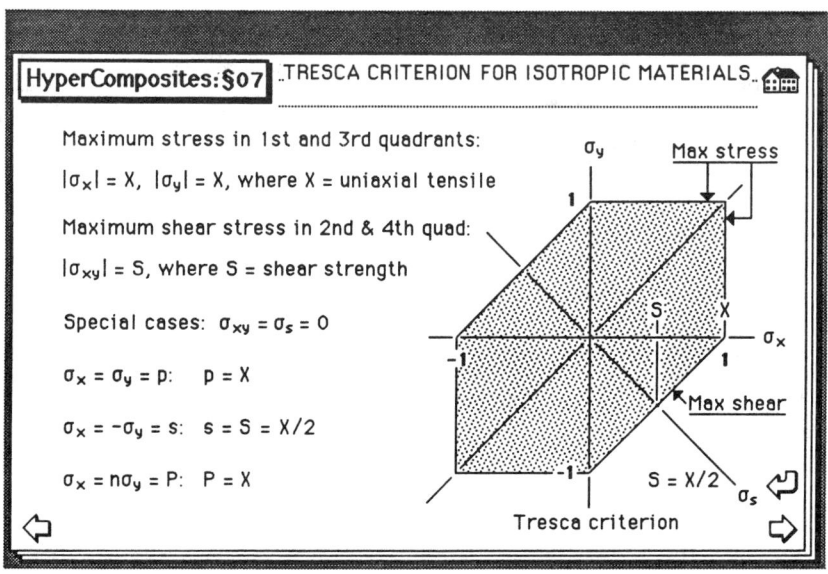

HyperComposites:§07 ⸺TRESCA CRITERION FOR ISOTROPIC MATERIALS⸺

Maximum stress in 1st and 3rd quadrants:

$|\sigma_x| = X$, $|\sigma_y| = X$, where X = uniaxial tensile

Maximum shear stress in 2nd & 4th quad:

$|\sigma_{xy}| = S$, where S = shear strength

Special cases: $\sigma_{xy} = \sigma_s = 0$

$\sigma_x = \sigma_y = p$: $p = X$

$\sigma_x = -\sigma_y = s$: $s = S = X/2$

$\sigma_x = n\sigma_y = P$: $P = X$

Tresca criterion

29.7 MISES/TRESCA FAILURE CRITERIA (continued)

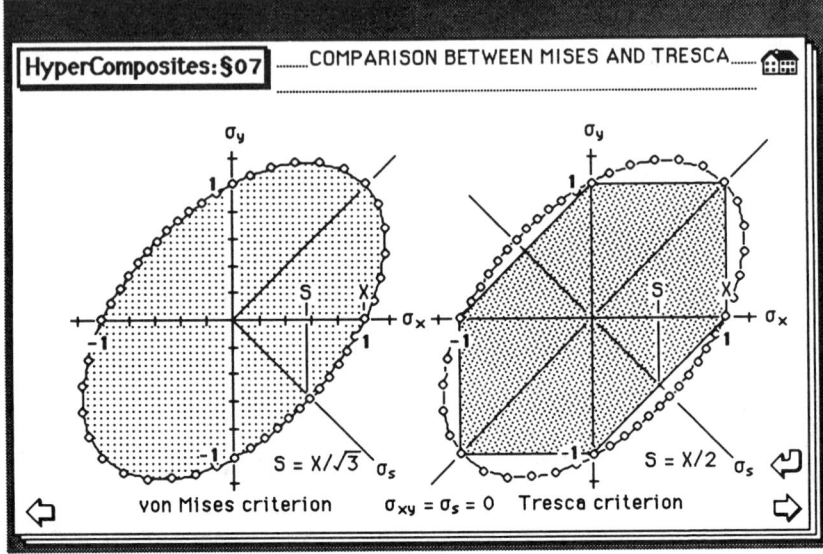

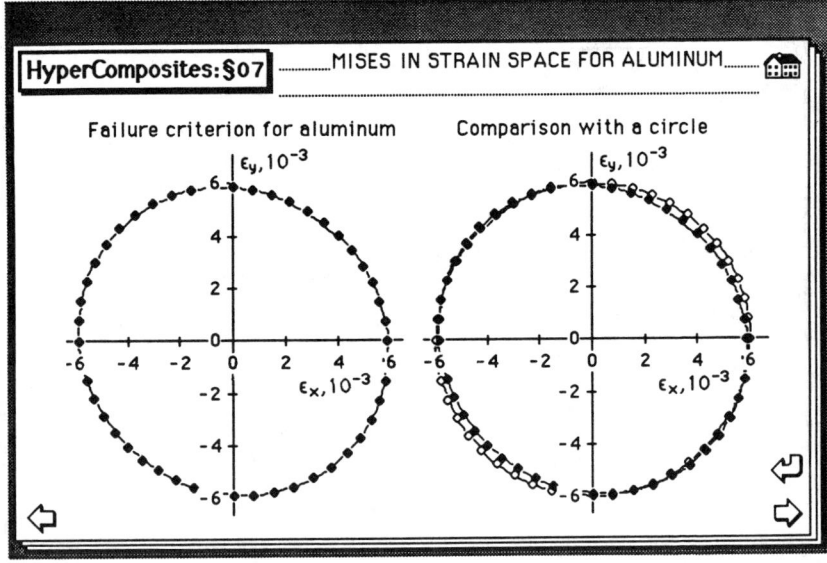

29.8 MAXIMUM STRESS CRITERION

HyperComposites: §08 ....STRENGTH OF UNIDIRECTIONAL PLIES........

The strength of orthotropic plies is defined by at least five data points: X, X', Y, Y', and S. Each ply in a laminate is subjected to combined stresses. Thus, failure envelopes of orthotropic ply materials are the critical starting points in determining the strength of laminates.

We recommend the use of quadratic failure criteria because they are easy to use, and are flexible to include failure mode interactions. Being more versatile, we can easily recover the maximum stress and maximum strain criteria as limiting cases. We need reliable data! The shape of failure envelopes depends on the particular orthotropic strengths of each material, and the interaction term.

Extensions of quadratic criteria to three dimensional stresses for intralaminar failure, and to a failure criterion based on interlaminar tractions are covered in "Thick laminates."

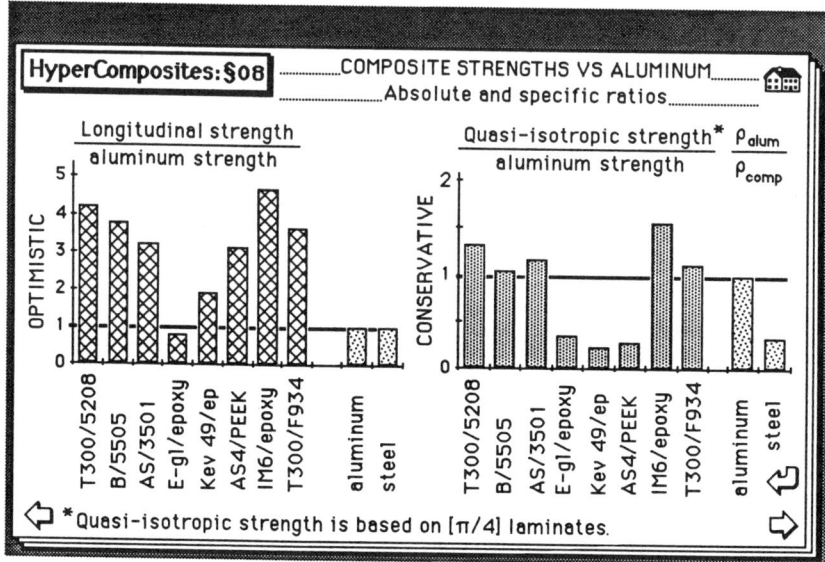

HyperComposites: §08 ....COMPOSITE STRENGTHS VS ALUMINUM........
........Absolute and specific ratios........

$* $Quasi-isotropic strength is based on $[\pi/4]$ laminates.

29.8 MAXIMUM STRESS CRITERION (continued)

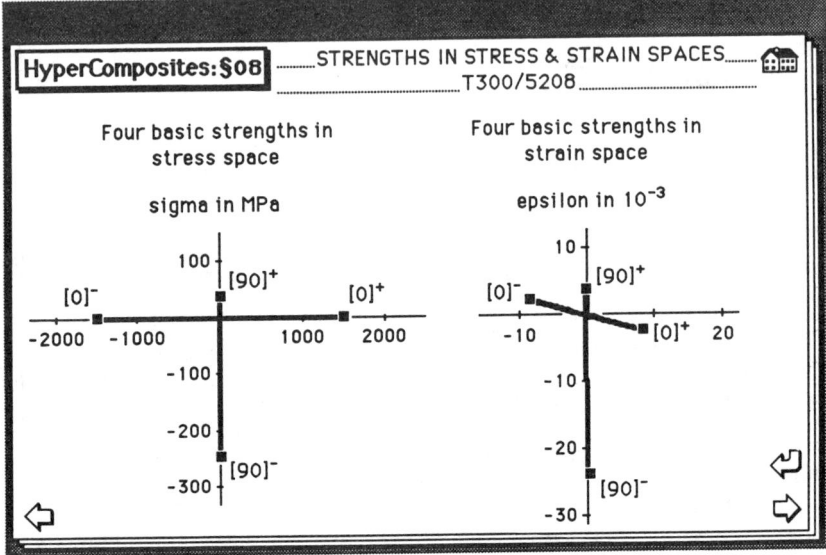

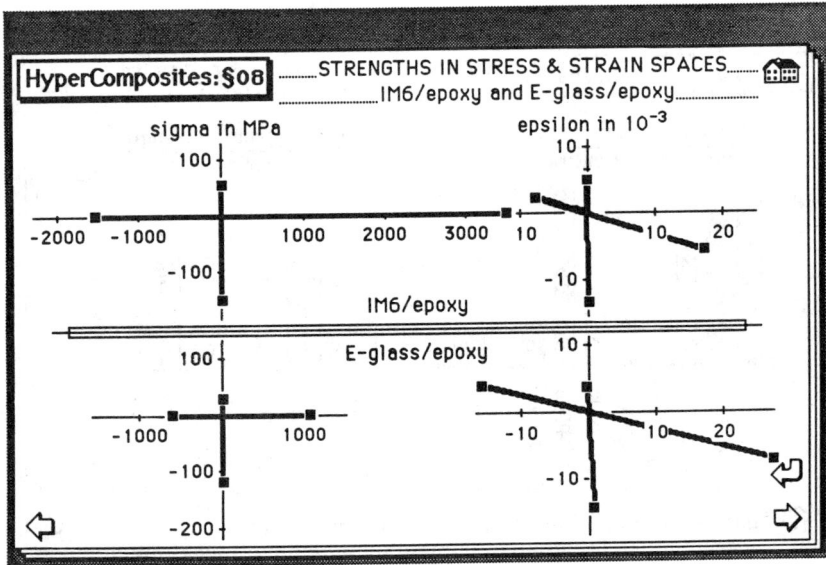

29.8 MAXIMUM STRESS CRITERION (continued)

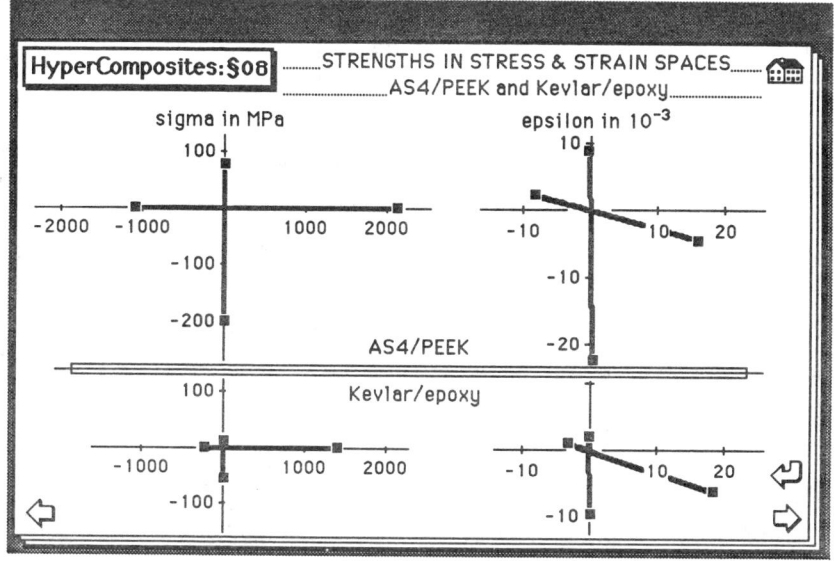

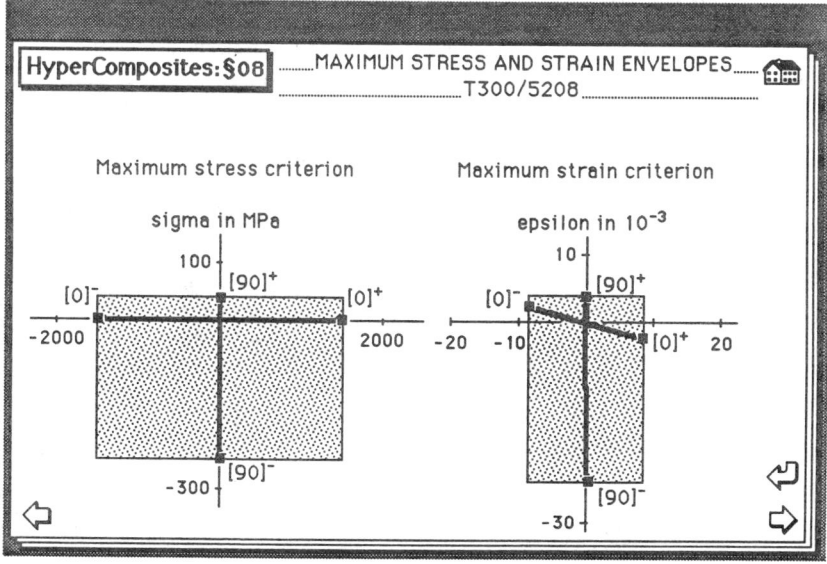

29.8 MAXIMUM STRESS CRITERION (continued)

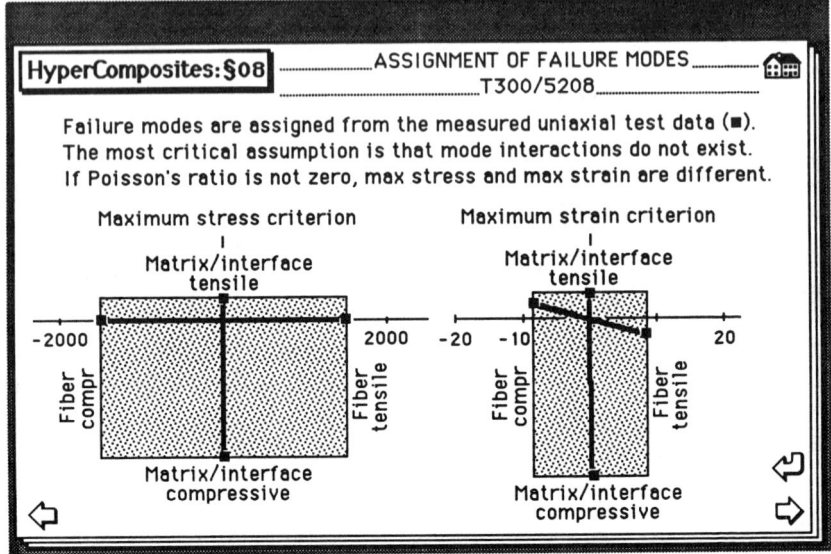

HyperComposites: §08 — ASSIGNMENT OF FAILURE MODES — T300/5208

Failure modes are assigned from the measured uniaxial test data (■).
The most critical assumption is that mode interactions do not exist.
If Poisson's ratio is not zero, max stress and max strain are different.

Maximum stress criterion

Matrix/interface tensile

−2000   2000

Fiber compr

Fiber tensile

Matrix/interface compressive

Maximum strain criterion

Matrix/interface tensile

−20   −10   20

Fiber compr

Fiber tensile

Matrix/interface compressive

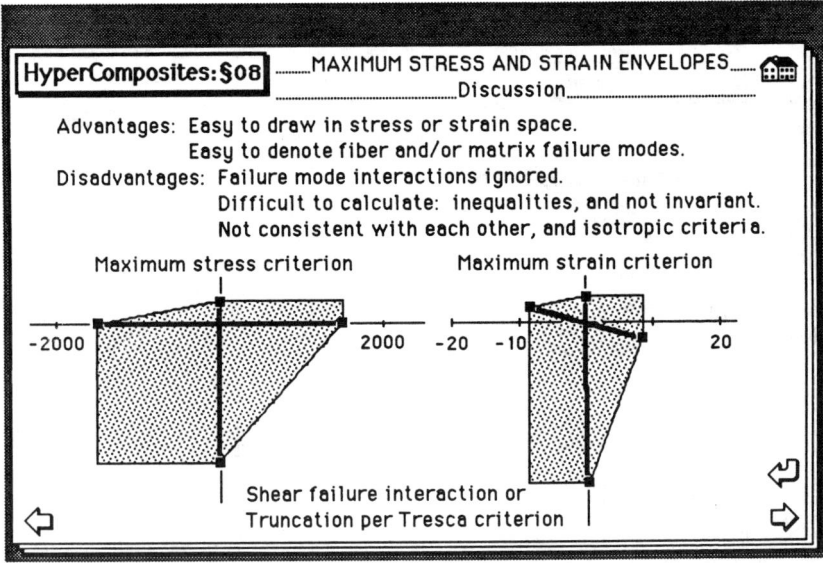

HyperComposites: §08 — MAXIMUM STRESS AND STRAIN ENVELOPES — Discussion

Advantages: Easy to draw in stress or strain space.
            Easy to denote fiber and/or matrix failure modes.
Disadvantages: Failure mode interactions ignored.
               Difficult to calculate: inequalities, and not invariant.
               Not consistent with each other, and isotropic criteria.

Maximum stress criterion

−2000   2000

Maximum strain criterion

−20   −10   20

Shear failure interaction or
Truncation per Tresca criterion

29.9 QUADRATIC FAILURE CRITERION

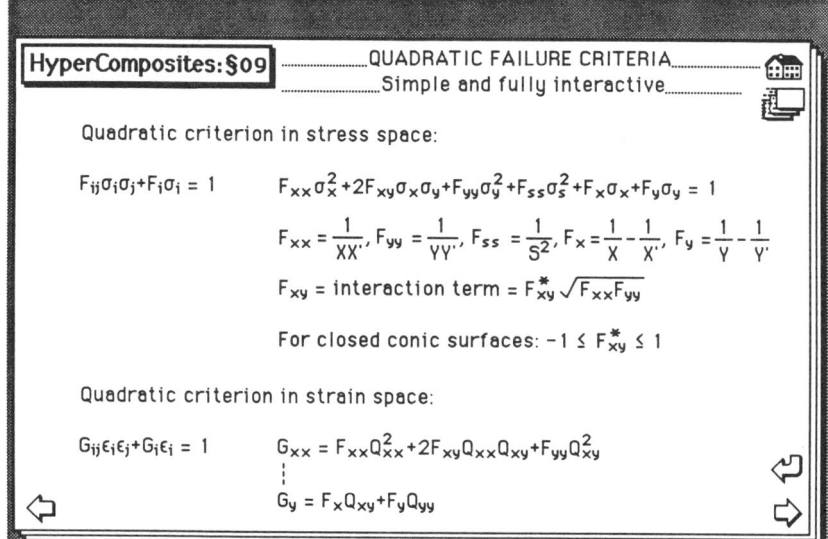

HyperComposites:§09 ....QUADRATIC FAILURE CRITERIA............
............Simple and fully interactive............

Quadratic criterion in stress space:

$$F_{ij}\sigma_i\sigma_j + F_i\sigma_i = 1 \qquad F_{xx}\sigma_x^2 + 2F_{xy}\sigma_x\sigma_y + F_{yy}\sigma_y^2 + F_{ss}\sigma_s^2 + F_x\sigma_x + F_y\sigma_y = 1$$

$$F_{xx} = \frac{1}{XX'}, \; F_{yy} = \frac{1}{YY'}, \; F_{ss} = \frac{1}{S^2}, \; F_x = \frac{1}{X} - \frac{1}{X'}, \; F_y = \frac{1}{Y} - \frac{1}{Y'}$$

$$F_{xy} = \text{interaction term} = F_{xy}^* \sqrt{F_{xx}F_{yy}}$$

For closed conic surfaces: $-1 \leq F_{xy}^* \leq 1$

Quadratic criterion in strain space:

$$G_{ij}\epsilon_i\epsilon_j + G_i\epsilon_i = 1 \qquad G_{xx} = F_{xx}Q_{xx}^2 + 2F_{xy}Q_{xx}Q_{xy} + F_{yy}Q_{xy}^2$$

$$\vdots$$

$$G_y = F_xQ_{xy} + F_yQ_{yy}$$

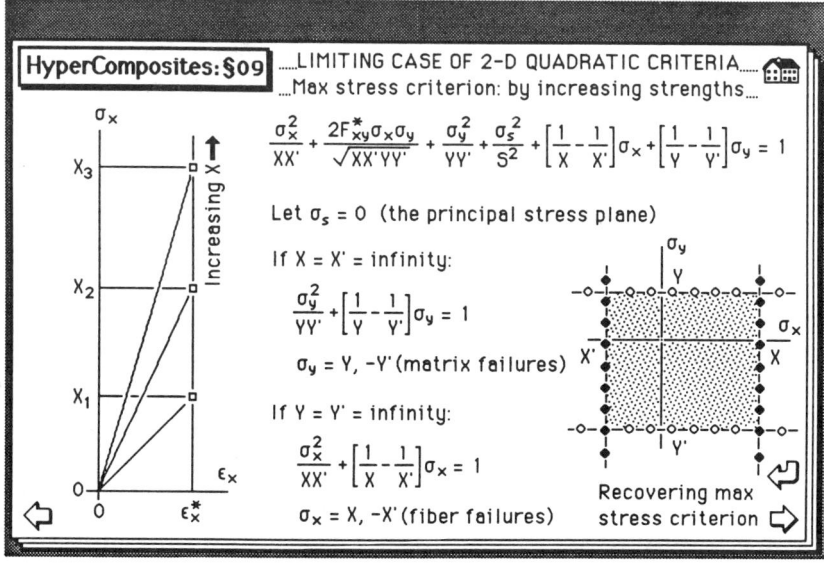

HyperComposites:§09 ....LIMITING CASE OF 2-D QUADRATIC CRITERIA....
....Max stress criterion: by increasing strengths....

$$\frac{\sigma_x^2}{XX'} + \frac{2F_{xy}^*\sigma_x\sigma_y}{\sqrt{XX'YY'}} + \frac{\sigma_y^2}{YY'} + \frac{\sigma_s^2}{S^2} + \left[\frac{1}{X} - \frac{1}{X'}\right]\sigma_x + \left[\frac{1}{Y} - \frac{1}{Y'}\right]\sigma_y = 1$$

Let $\sigma_s = 0$ (the principal stress plane)

If $X = X' = $ infinity:

$$\frac{\sigma_y^2}{YY'} + \left[\frac{1}{Y} - \frac{1}{Y'}\right]\sigma_y = 1$$

$$\sigma_y = Y, -Y' \text{(matrix failures)}$$

If $Y = Y' = $ infinity:

$$\frac{\sigma_x^2}{XX'} + \left[\frac{1}{X} - \frac{1}{X'}\right]\sigma_x = 1$$

$$\sigma_x = X, -X' \text{(fiber failures)}$$

Recovering max stress criterion

29.9 QUADRATIC FAILURE CRITERION (continued)

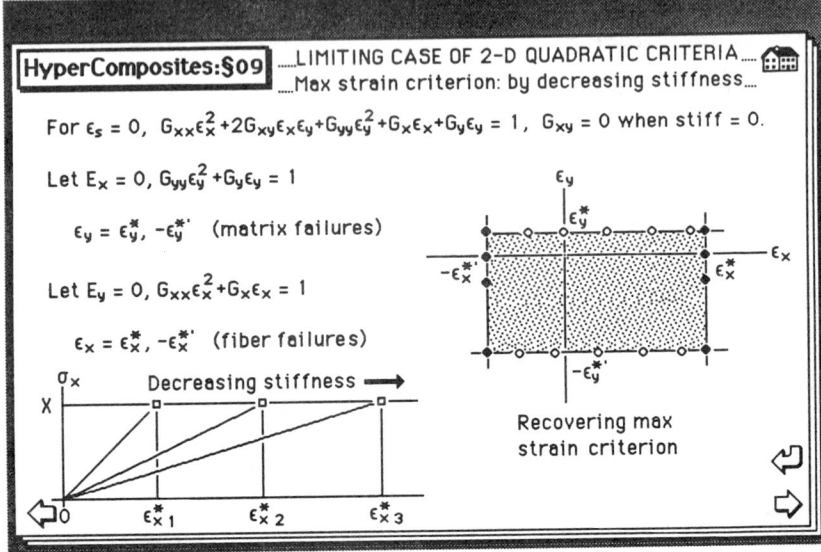

HyperComposites:§09   ....LIMITING CASE OF 2-D QUADRATIC CRITERIA....
                       ....Max strain criterion: by decreasing stiffness....

For $\epsilon_s = 0$, $G_{xx}\epsilon_x^2 + 2G_{xy}\epsilon_x\epsilon_y + G_{yy}\epsilon_y^2 + G_x\epsilon_x + G_y\epsilon_y = 1$, $G_{xy} = 0$ when stiff = 0.

Let $E_x = 0$, $G_{yy}\epsilon_y^2 + G_y\epsilon_y = 1$

$\epsilon_y = \epsilon_y^*, -\epsilon_y^{*'}$ (matrix failures)

Let $E_y = 0$, $G_{xx}\epsilon_x^2 + G_x\epsilon_x = 1$

$\epsilon_x = \epsilon_x^*, -\epsilon_x^{*'}$ (fiber failures)

Decreasing stiffness ⟶

Recovering max strain criterion

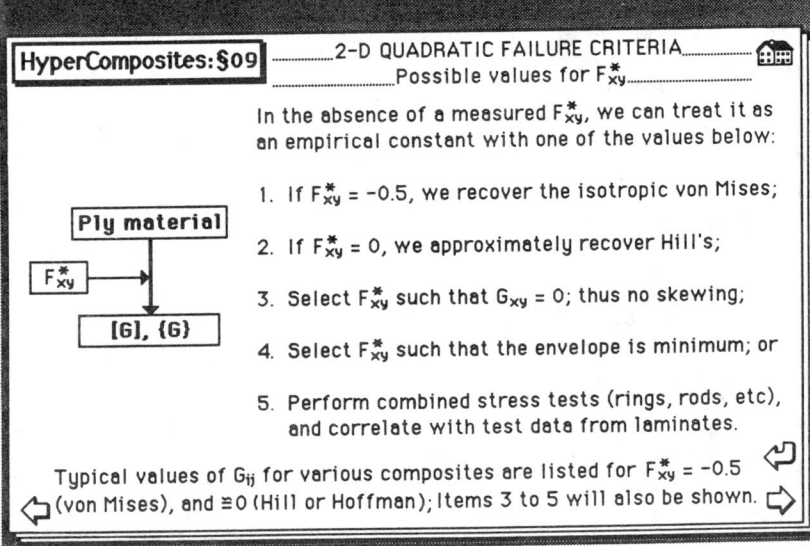

HyperComposites:§09   ....2-D QUADRATIC FAILURE CRITERIA..........
                       ....Possible values for F_{xy}^*..........

In the absence of a measured F_{xy}^*, we can treat it as an empirical constant with one of the values below:

1. If $F_{xy}^* = -0.5$, we recover the isotropic von Mises;

2. If $F_{xy}^* = 0$, we approximately recover Hill's;

3. Select F_{xy}^* such that $G_{xy} = 0$; thus no skewing;

4. Select F_{xy}^* such that the envelope is minimum; or

5. Perform combined stress tests (rings, rods, etc), and correlate with test data from laminates.

Ply material

F_{xy}^*

[G], {G}

Typical values of G_{ij} for various composites are listed for $F_{xy}^* = -0.5$ (von Mises), and $\cong 0$ (Hill or Hoffman); Items 3 to 5 will also be shown.

29.9 QUADRATIC FAILURE CRITERION (continued)

HyperComposites: §09 ....ADVANTAGES OF QUADRATIC CRITERIA..........

Quadratic failure criterion has the following desirable features:

1. Mathematically simple: single valued, invariant, and easy to plot.

2. Flexibility in selection of the desired or measured interactions, and degradation to provide a continuous variation from FPF to LPF.

3. Identification of combined stress effects in quadrants of tens-tens (1st), compr-compr (3rd), and tens-compr (2nd and 4th).

4. Easy recovery of the Mises and Hill criteria when orthotropy is reduced to isotropy.

5. Recovery of netting analysis for a laminate as well as the non-interacting criterion of max stress or max strain as limiting cases. A continuous variation of matrix degradation is possible.

HyperComposites: §09 ....QUADRATIC CRITERIA IN STRAIN SPACE...........
...................................Advantages...............

1. Not affected by the presence of ply angles and materials (hybrids). Laminate failure envelopes can be obtained by superposition. Envelopes in stress space changes with ply angles or sequencing. This will be illustrated in the stack entitled "Laminate strength."

2. Less difference between longitudinal and transverse failure strains.

3. Easy to obtain off-axis failure envelopes by rigid-body rotation the q-r space.

4. Easy to extend the criteria to include last-ply-failure, hygrothermal effects, and sensitivity studies.

5. Strain is dimensionless, and has the same values for all units.

 6. Easy to plot envelopes, including limiting cases of max strain, etc.

29.9 QUADRATIC FAILURE CRITERION (continued)

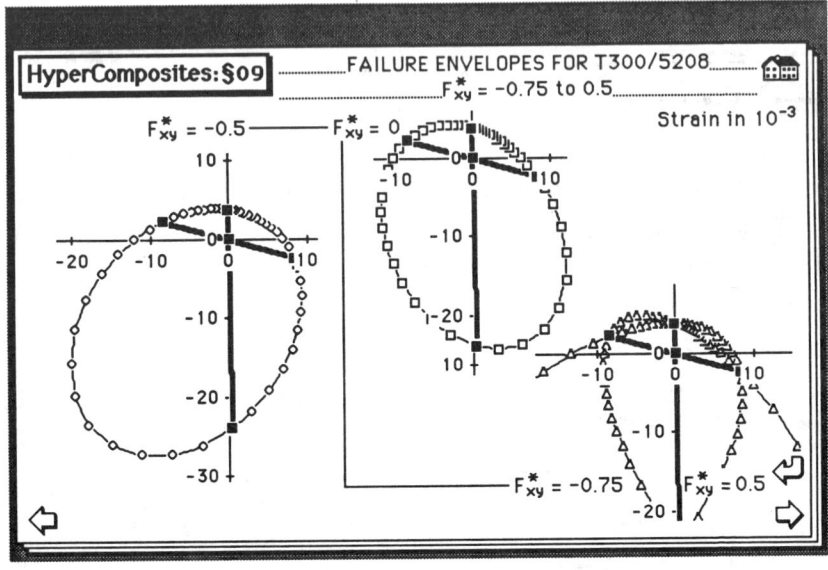

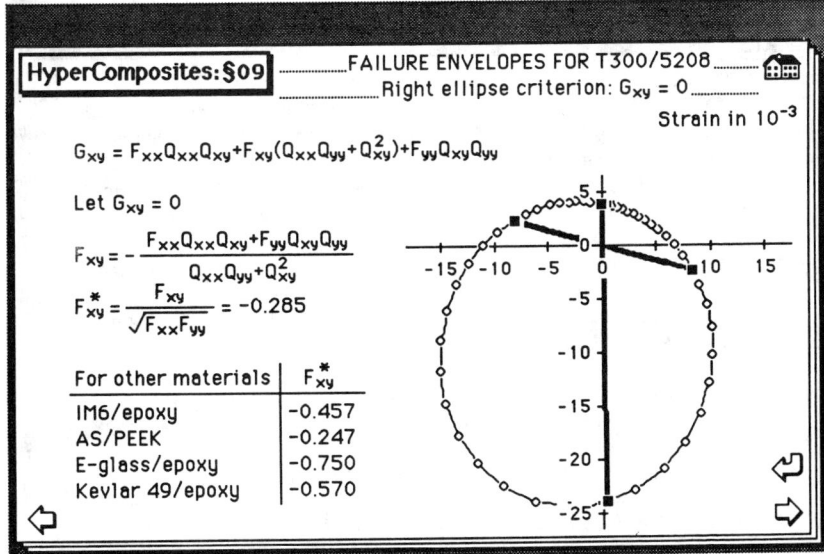

29.9 QUADRATIC FAILURE CRITERION (continued)

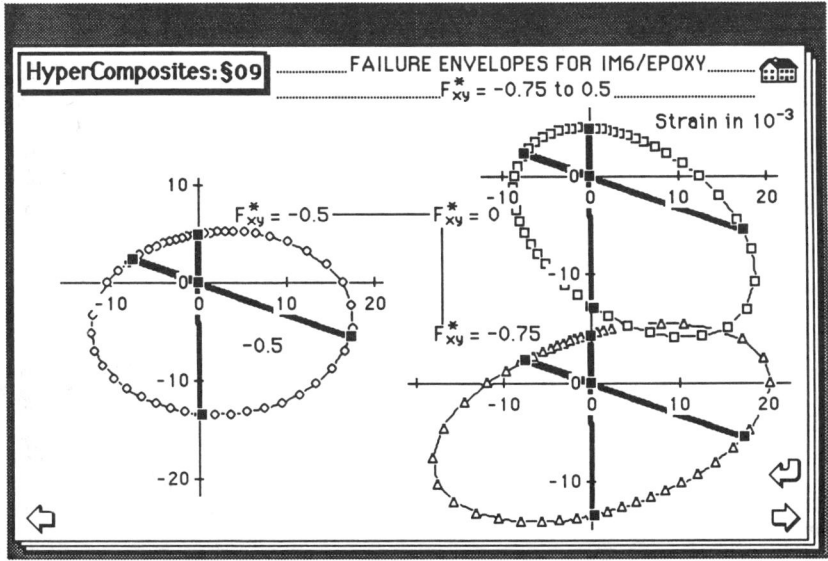

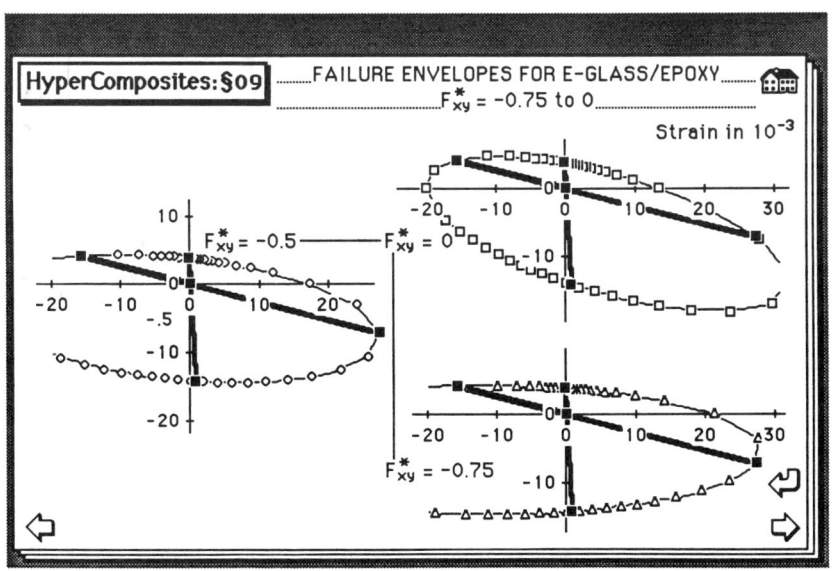

29.9 QUADRATIC FAILURE CRITERION (continued)

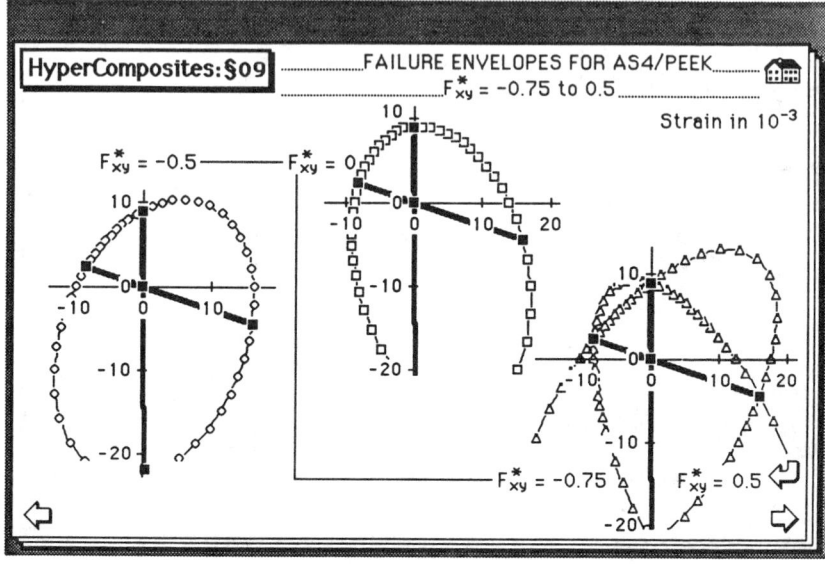

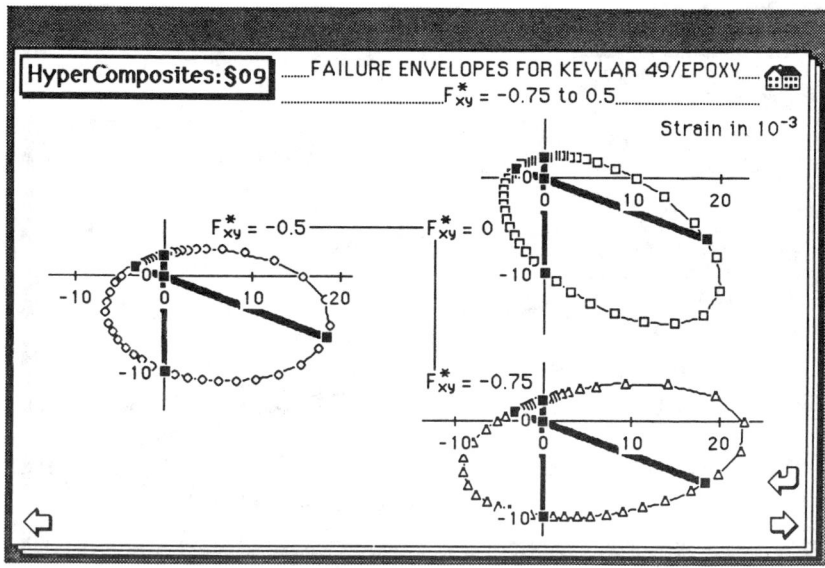

29.10 FIRST–PLY–FAILURE

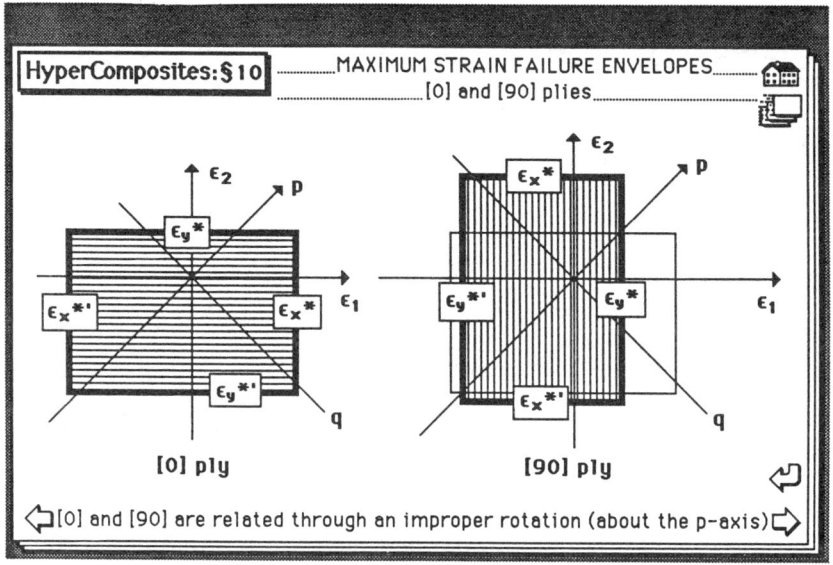

HyperComposites:§10 ....MAXIMUM STRAIN FAILURE ENVELOPES............ ....[0] and [90] plies..........................

[0] ply   **[90] ply**

◁[0] and [90] are related through an improper rotation (about the p-axis)▷

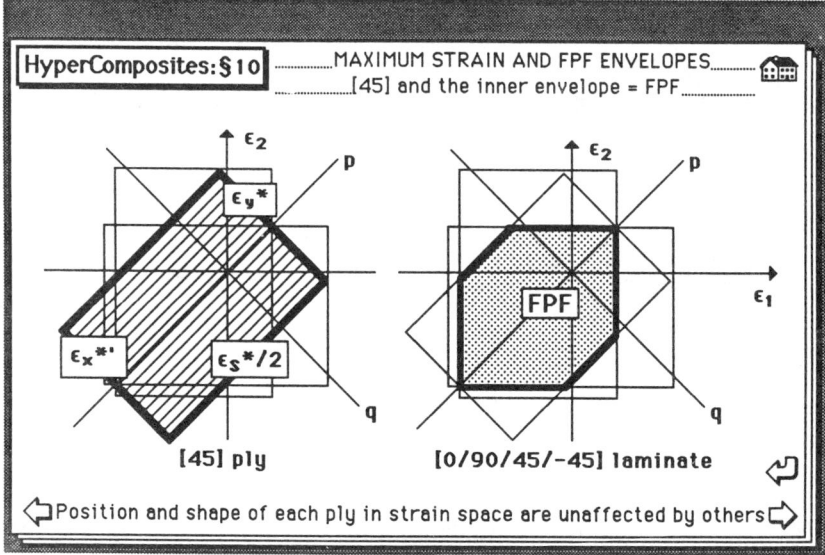

HyperComposites:§10 ....MAXIMUM STRAIN AND FPF ENVELOPES............ ....[45] and the inner envelope = FPF....................

[45] ply   **[0/90/45/−45] laminate**

◁Position and shape of each ply in strain space are unaffected by others▷

29.10 FIRST–PLY–FAILURE (continued)

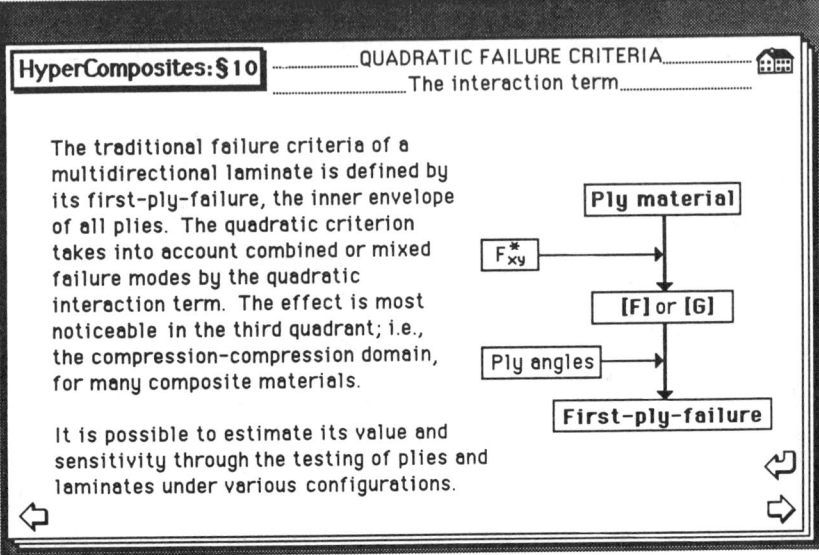

HyperComposites: §10 ....QUADRATIC FAILURE CRITERIA.................... 🏠
........................The interaction term.....................

The traditional failure criteria of a multidirectional laminate is defined by its first-ply-failure, the inner envelope of all plies. The quadratic criterion takes into account combined or mixed failure modes by the quadratic interaction term. The effect is most noticeable in the third quadrant; i.e., the compression-compression domain, for many composite materials.

It is possible to estimate its value and sensitivity through the testing of plies and laminates under various configurations.

Ply material

F^*_{xy}

[F] or [G]

Ply angles

First-ply-failure

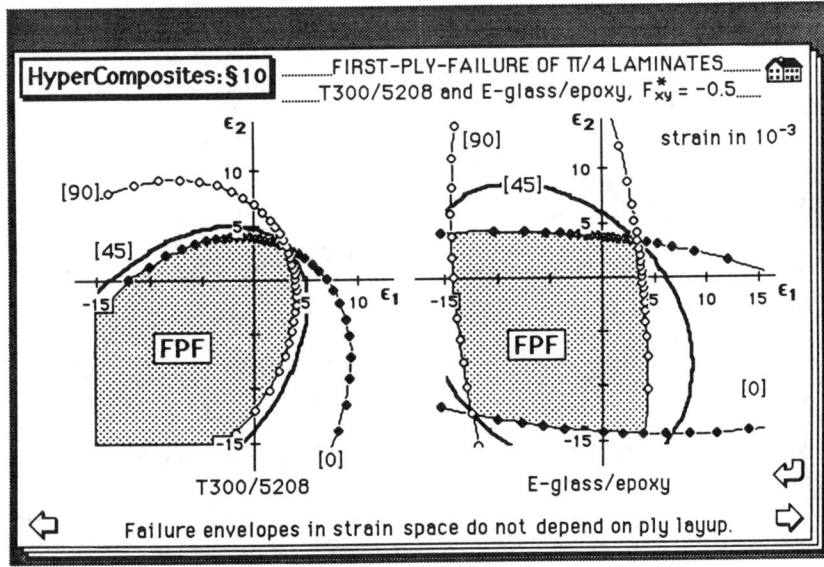

HyperComposites: §10 ....FIRST-PLY-FAILURE OF π/4 LAMINATES........... 🏠
...............T300/5208 and E-glass/epoxy, $F^*_{xy} = -0.5$......

ε_2 [90] ε_2 strain in 10^{-3}

[90] 10 [45] 10

[45] 5 5

-15 5 10 ε_1 -15 5 10 15 ε_1

FPF FPF [0]

-15 [0] -15

T300/5208 E-glass/epoxy

Failure envelopes in strain space do not depend on ply layup.

29.10 FIRST–PLY–FAILURE (continued)

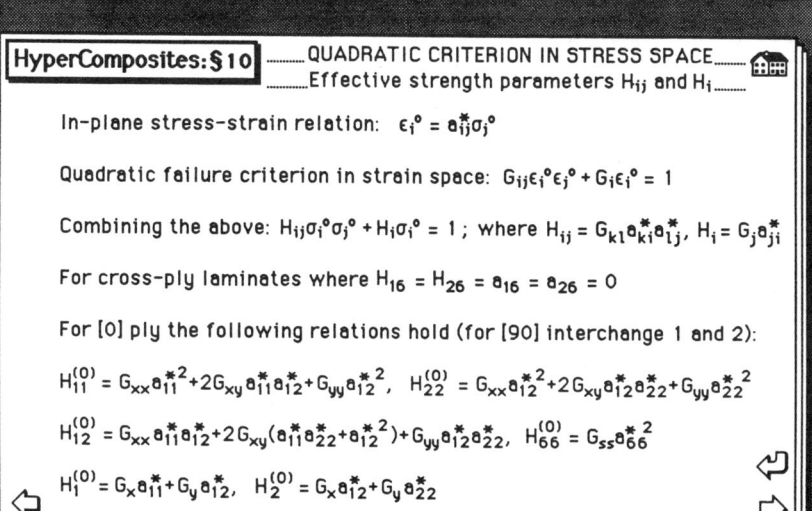

HyperComposites: §10 ········ QUADRATIC CRITERION IN STRESS SPACE········
········Effective strength parameters H_{ij} and H_i········

In-plane stress-strain relation: $\epsilon_i^\circ = a_{ij}^* \sigma_j^\circ$

Quadratic failure criterion in strain space: $G_{ij}\epsilon_i^\circ \epsilon_j^\circ + G_i \epsilon_i^\circ = 1$

Combining the above: $H_{ij}\sigma_i^\circ \sigma_j^\circ + H_i \sigma_i^\circ = 1$; where $H_{ij} = G_{kl}a_{ki}^* a_{1j}^*$, $H_i = G_j a_{ji}^*$

For cross-ply laminates where $H_{16} = H_{26} = a_{16} = a_{26} = 0$

For [0] ply the following relations hold (for [90] interchange 1 and 2):

$$H_{11}^{(0)} = G_{xx}a_{11}^{*2} + 2G_{xy}a_{11}^* a_{12}^* + G_{yy}a_{12}^{*2}, \quad H_{22}^{(0)} = G_{xx}a_{12}^{*2} + 2G_{xy}a_{12}^* a_{22}^* + G_{yy}a_{22}^{*2}$$

$$H_{12}^{(0)} = G_{xx}a_{11}^* a_{12}^* + 2G_{xy}(a_{11}^* a_{22}^* + a_{12}^{*2}) + G_{yy}a_{12}^* a_{22}^*, \quad H_{66}^{(0)} = G_{ss}a_{66}^{*2}$$

$$H_1^{(0)} = G_x a_{11}^* + G_y a_{12}^*, \quad H_2^{(0)} = G_x a_{12}^* + G_y a_{22}^*$$

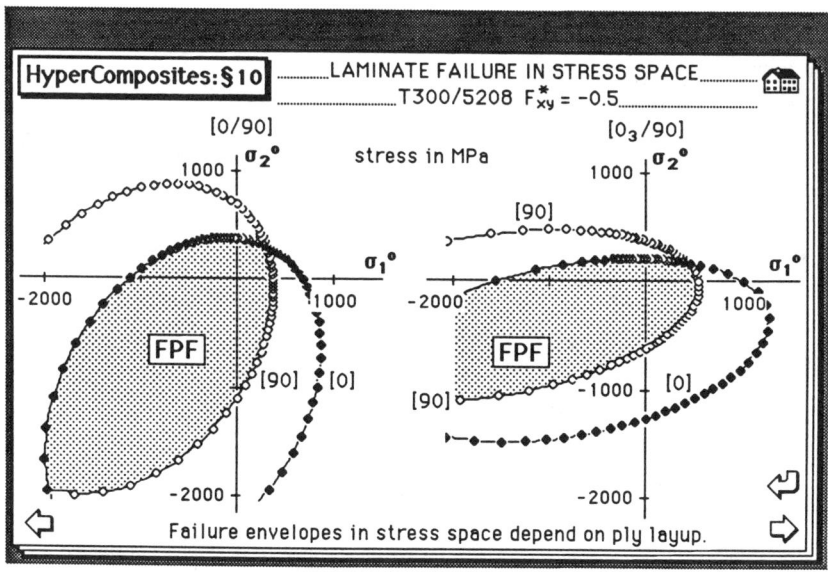

HyperComposites: §10 ········ LAMINATE FAILURE IN STRESS SPACE········
········T300/5208 $F_{xy}^* = -0.5$········

[0/90]   [0_3/90]

σ_2° stress in MPa σ_2°

1000   1000

[90]

σ_1° σ_1°

-2000   1000   -2000   1000

FPF   FPF

[90] [0]   [90]   -1000   [0]

-2000   -2000

Failure envelopes in stress space depend on ply layup.

29.10 FIRST–PLY–FAILURE (continued)

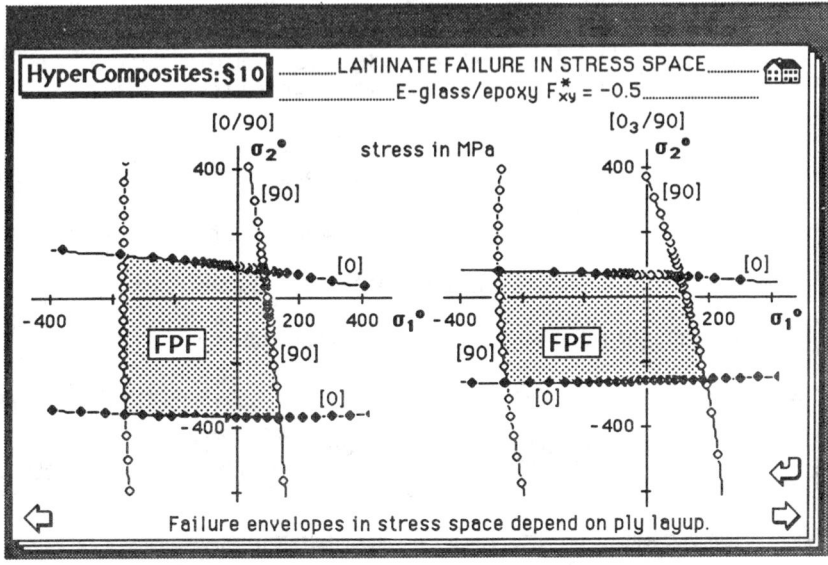

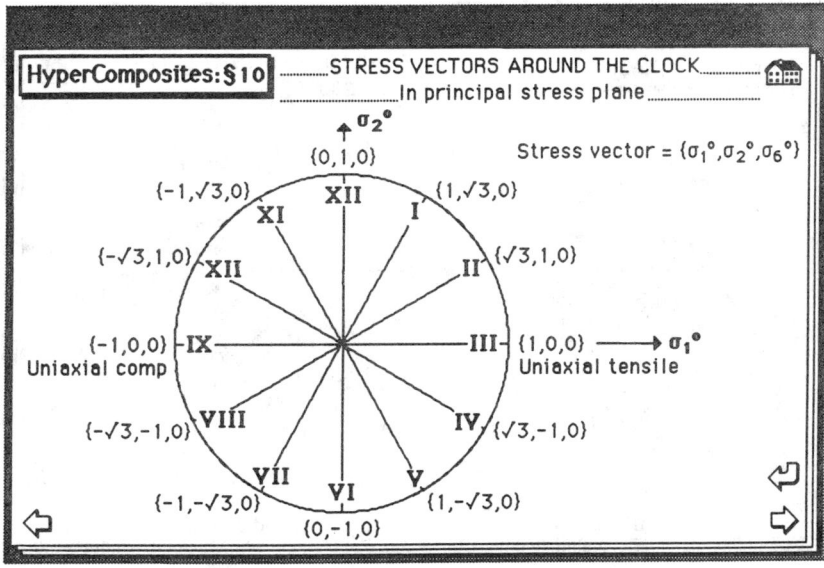

29.10 FIRST–PLY–FAILURE (continued)

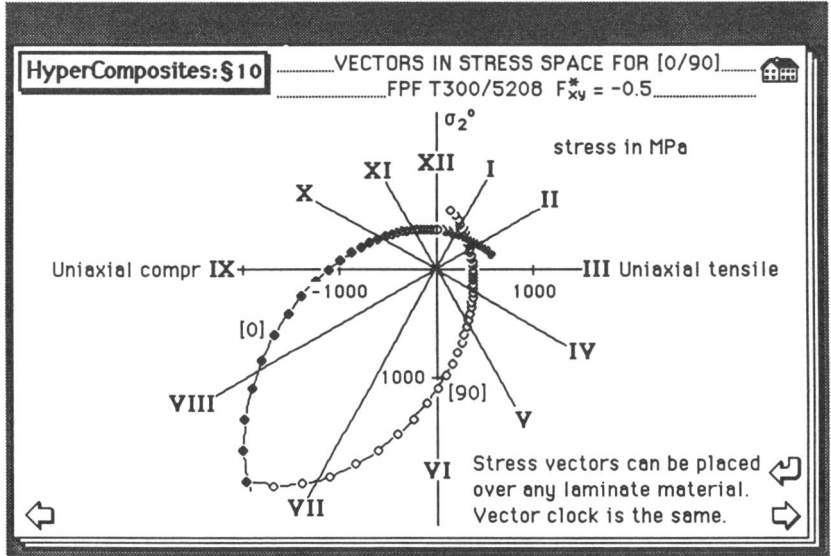

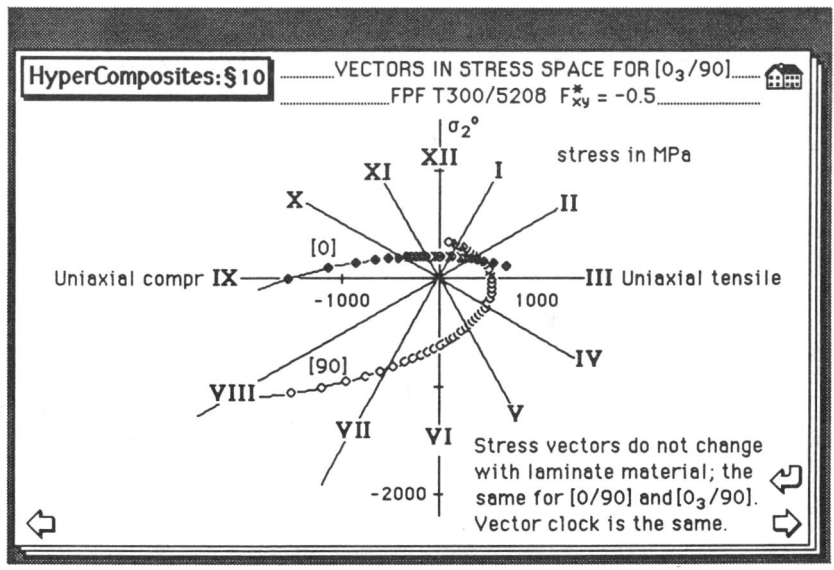

29.10 FIRST–PLY–FAILURE (continued)

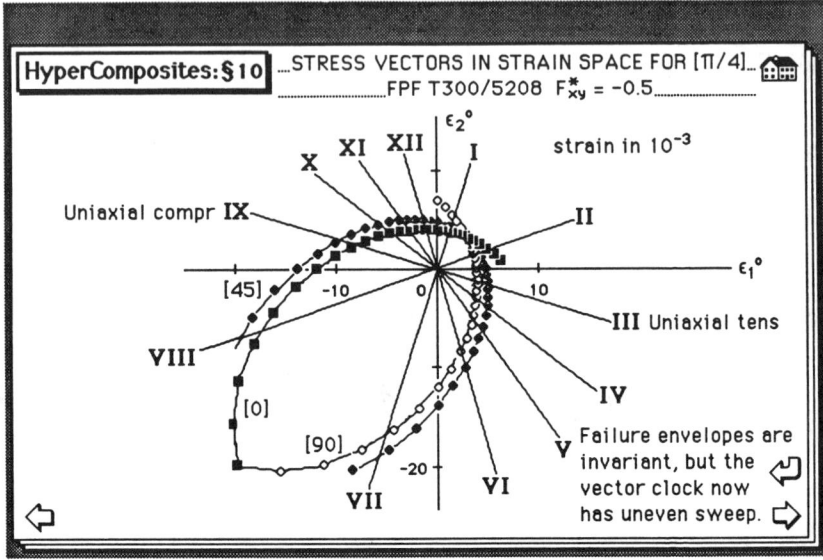

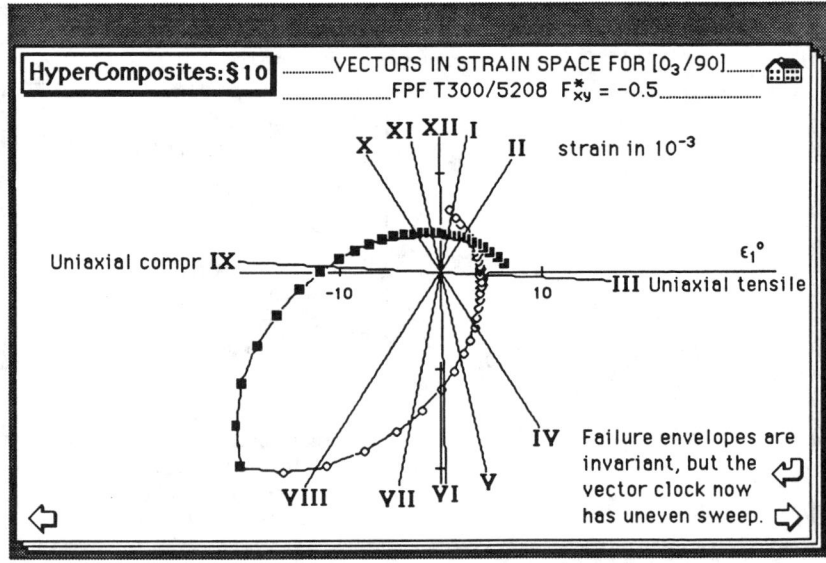

29.11 LAST–PLY–FAILURE

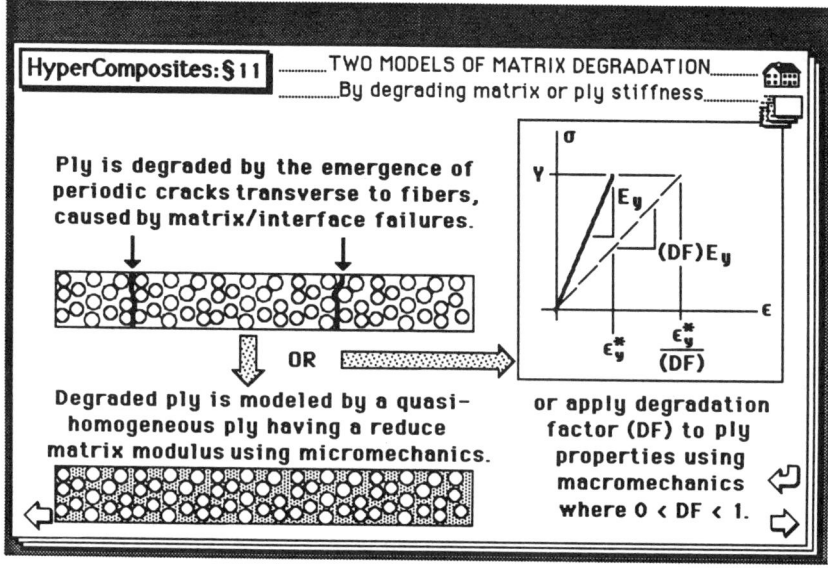

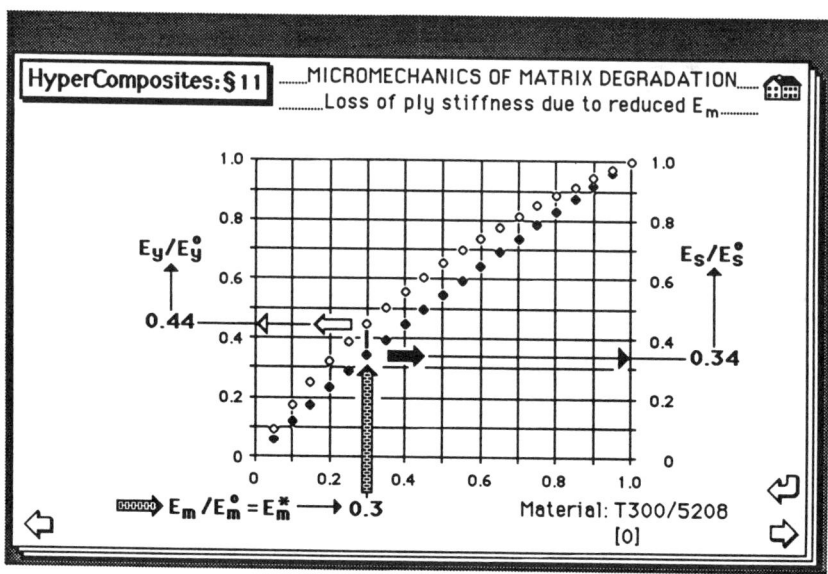

29.11 LAST–PLY–FAILURE (continued)

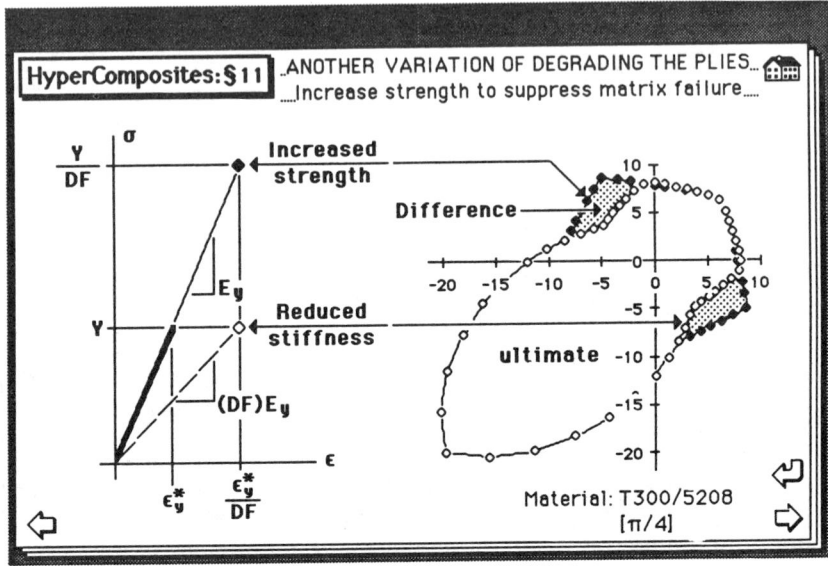

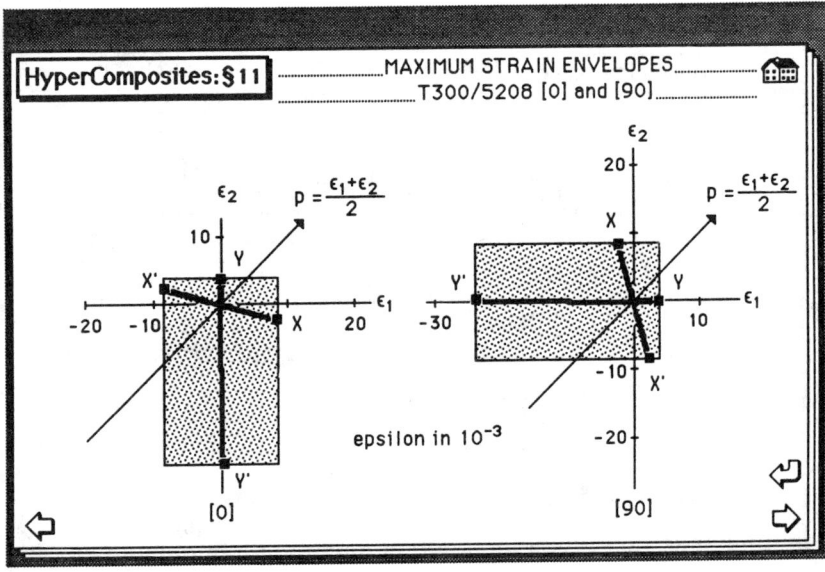

29.11 LAST–PLY–FAILURE (continued)

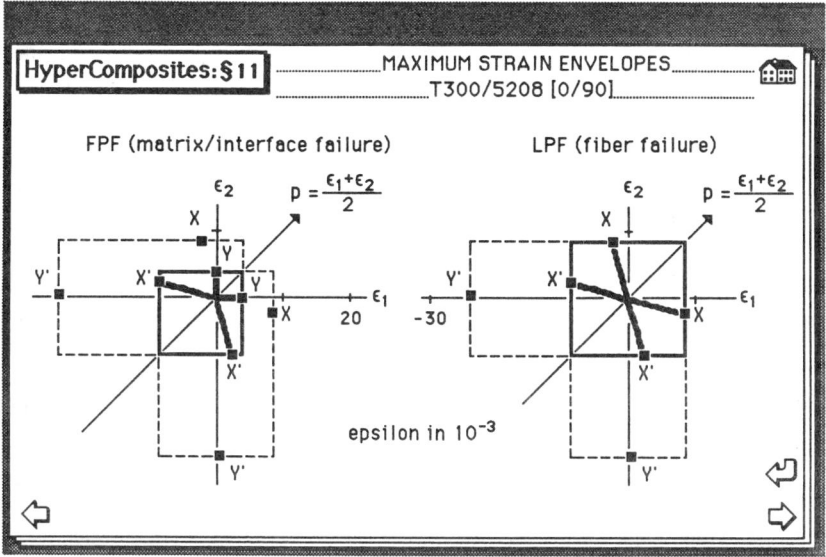

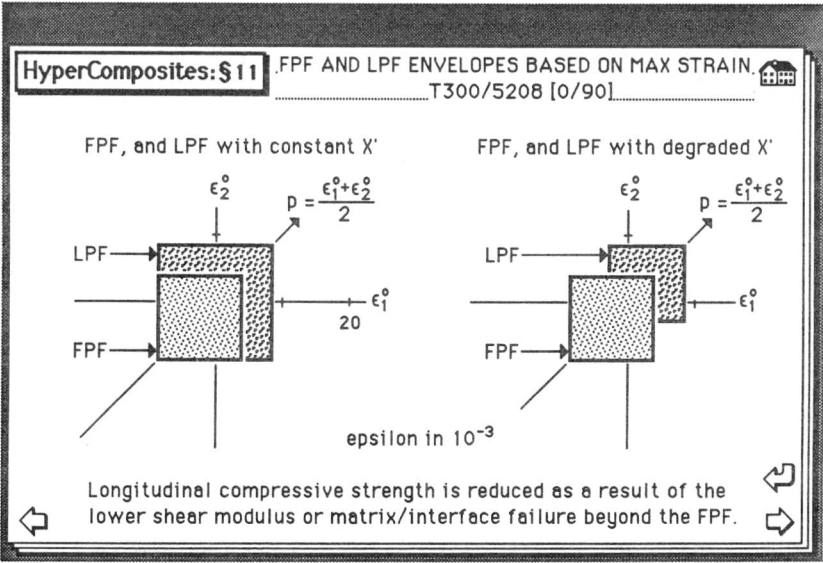

Longitudinal compressive strength is reduced as a result of the lower shear modulus or matrix/interface failure beyond the FPF.

29.11 LAST–PLY–FAILURE (continued)

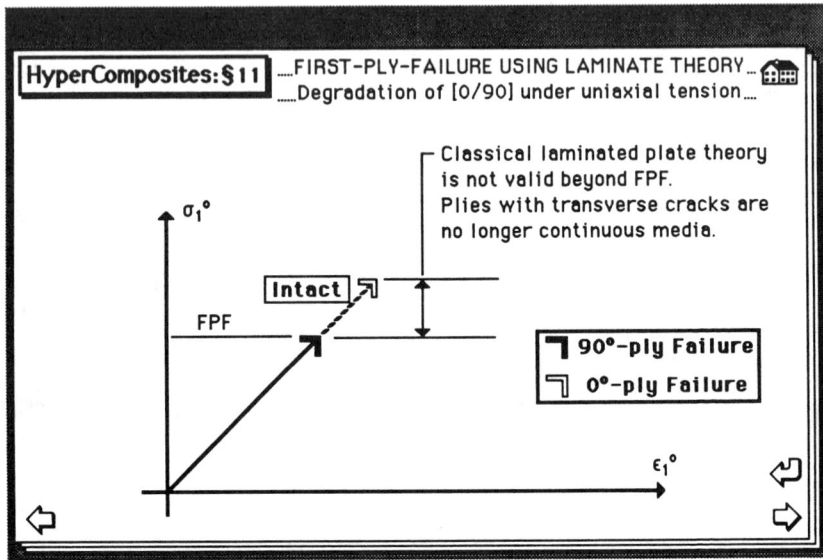

HyperComposites: §11 ....FIRST-PLY-FAILURE USING LAMINATE THEORY...
.....Degradation of [0/90] under uniaxial tension....

Classical laminated plate theory is not valid beyond FPF.
Plies with transverse cracks are no longer continuous media.

Intact

FPF

90°-ply Failure
0°-ply Failure

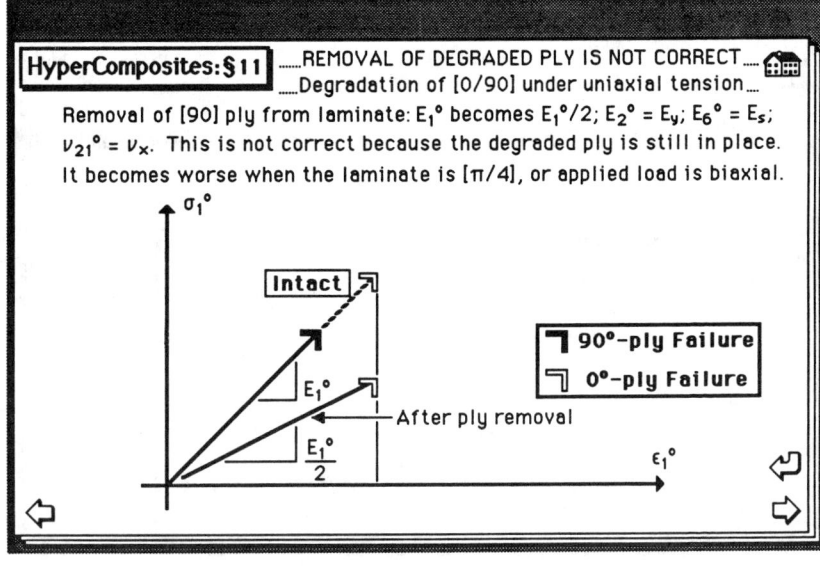

HyperComposites: §11 ......REMOVAL OF DEGRADED PLY IS NOT CORRECT....
.....Degradation of [0/90] under uniaxial tension....

Removal of [90] ply from laminate: E_1° becomes $E_1^\circ/2$; $E_2^\circ = E_y$; $E_6^\circ = E_s$; $\nu_{21}^\circ = \nu_x$. This is not correct because the degraded ply is still in place. It becomes worse when the laminate is $[\pi/4]$, or applied load is biaxial.

Intact

E_1°

$\dfrac{E_1^\circ}{2}$

After ply removal

90°-ply Failure
0°-ply Failure

29.11 LAST–PLY–FAILURE (continued)

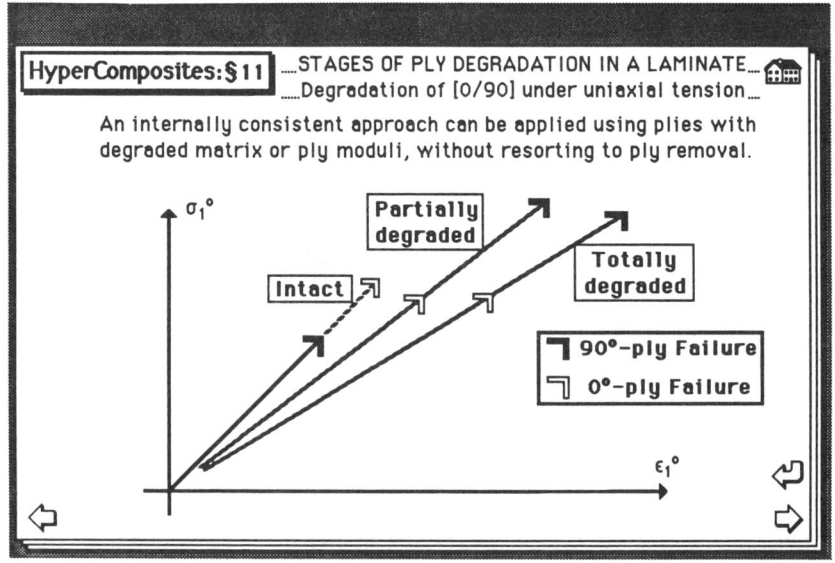

HyperComposites:§11   ....STAGES OF PLY DEGRADATION IN A LAMINATE....
....Degradation of [0/90] under uniaxial tension....

An internally consistent approach can be applied using plies with degraded matrix or ply moduli, without resorting to ply removal.

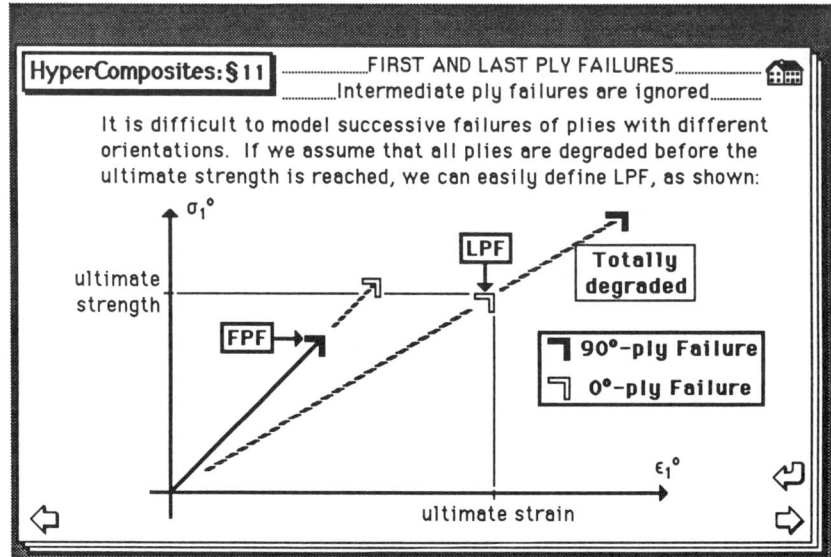

HyperComposites:§11   ....FIRST AND LAST PLY FAILURES............
............Intermediate ply failures are ignored............

It is difficult to model successive failures of plies with different orientations. If we assume that all plies are degraded before the ultimate strength is reached, we can easily define LPF, as shown:

29.11 LAST–PLY–FAILURE (continued)

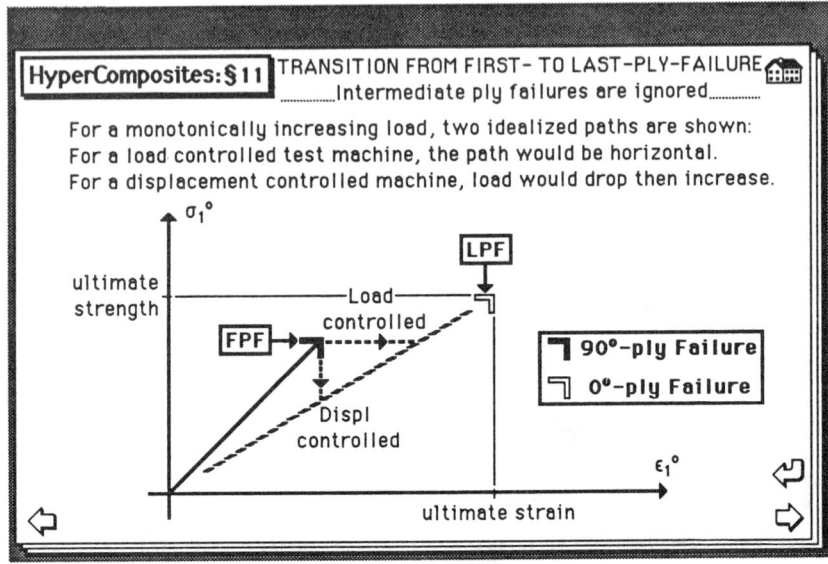

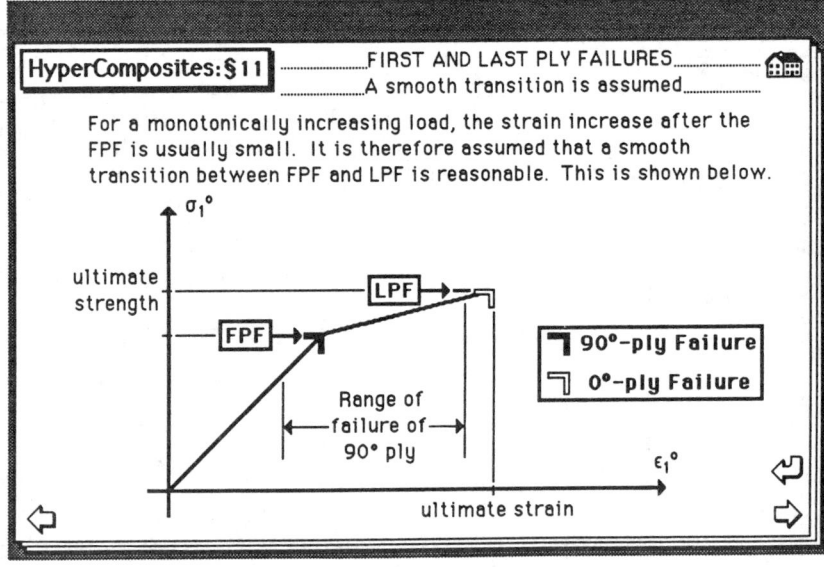

29.12 DEGRADATION

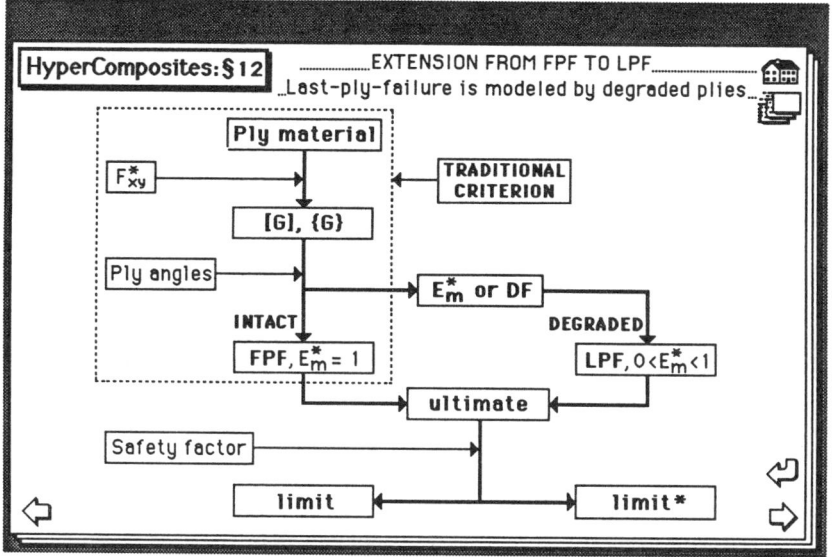

HyperComposites:§12 ....EXTENSION FROM FPF TO LPF........
.....Last-ply-failure is modeled by degraded plies....

Ply material

F^*_{xy}

TRADITIONAL CRITERION

[G], {G}

Ply angles

E^*_m or DF

INTACT   DEGRADED

FPF, $E^*_m = 1$ LPF, $0 < E^*_m < 1$

ultimate

Safety factor

limit   limit*

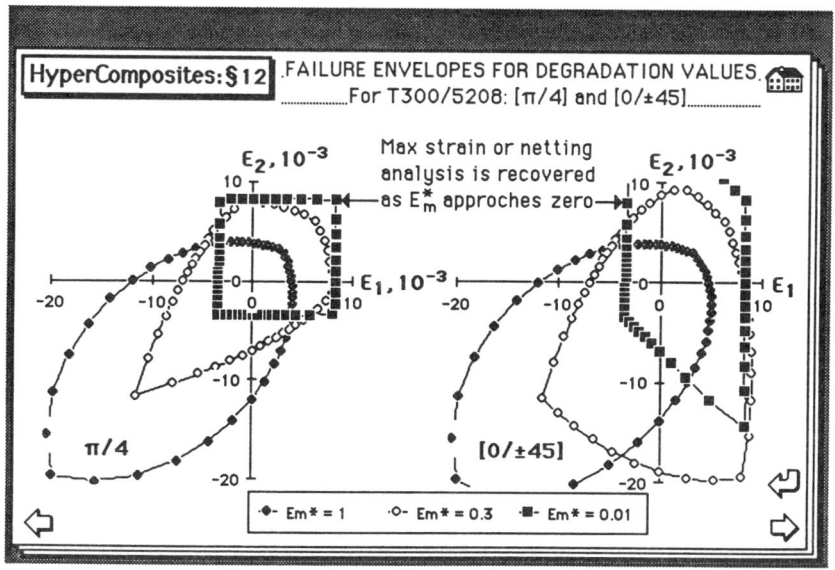

HyperComposites:§12 ..FAILURE ENVELOPES FOR DEGRADATION VALUES..
.............For T300/5208: [π/4] and [0/±45]..............

$\epsilon_2, 10^{-3}$

Max strain or netting analysis is recovered as E^*_m approaches zero→

$\epsilon_2, 10^{-3}$

$\epsilon_1, 10^{-3}$

ϵ_1

π/4

[0/±45]

●- Em* = 1   -○- Em* = 0.3   ■- Em* = 0.01

29.12 DEGRADATION (continued)

HyperComposites: §12 DETERMINATION OF MATRIX DEGRADTION FACTOR 🏠

In a fully degraded laminate, it is assumed that the ultimate tensile strength is equal to or higher than the tensile strength corrected by the fraction of [0] in the laminate. This is the implication of netting analysis shown in the last card when the degradation factor approaches zero.

$$\sigma_1^{netting} = v^{(0)}X = (\text{fraction of } [0])(\text{longitudinal tensile})$$

Using laminated plate theory we can compute the uniaxial tensile strength of a laminate as a function of the degradation factor that varies between zero and unity; the fully degraded and the intact, respectively. This computed strength can be normalized with respect to the strength based on netting analysis above. Then, from this normalized strength as a function of degradation factor and tensile test data, we can establish the value or the range of values for the degradation factor. The value should be equal to or higher than unity. ↵ ⇦ ⇨

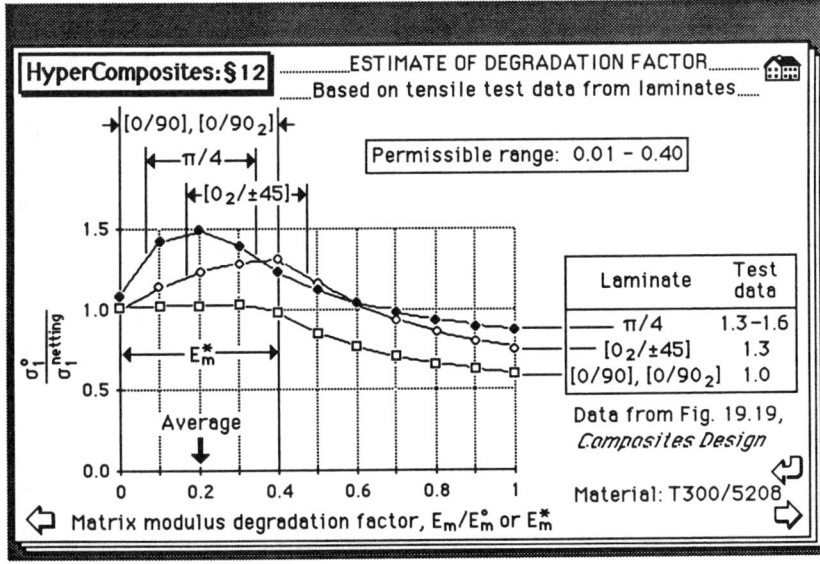

HyperComposites: §12 ....ESTIMATE OF DEGRADATION FACTOR........ 🏠
........Based on tensile test data from laminates........

→[0/90], [0/90₂]←
|←π/4→|
|←[0₂/±45]→|

Permissible range: 0.01 – 0.40

Laminate	Test data
── π/4	1.3–1.6
── [0₂/±45]	1.3
[0/90], [0/90₂]	1.0

Data from Fig. 19.19, *Composites Design*

Material: T300/5208

⇦ Matrix modulus degradation factor, E_m/E_m° or E_m^* ⇨

29.12 DEGRADATION (continued)

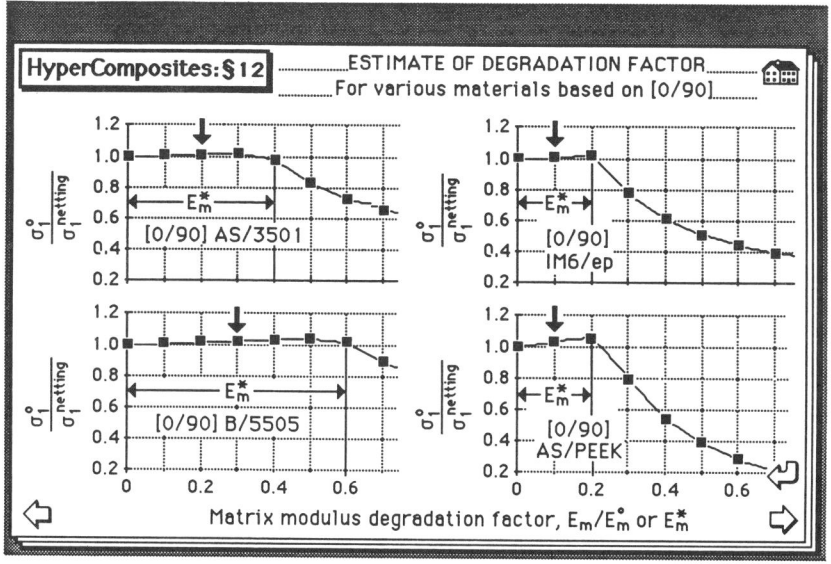

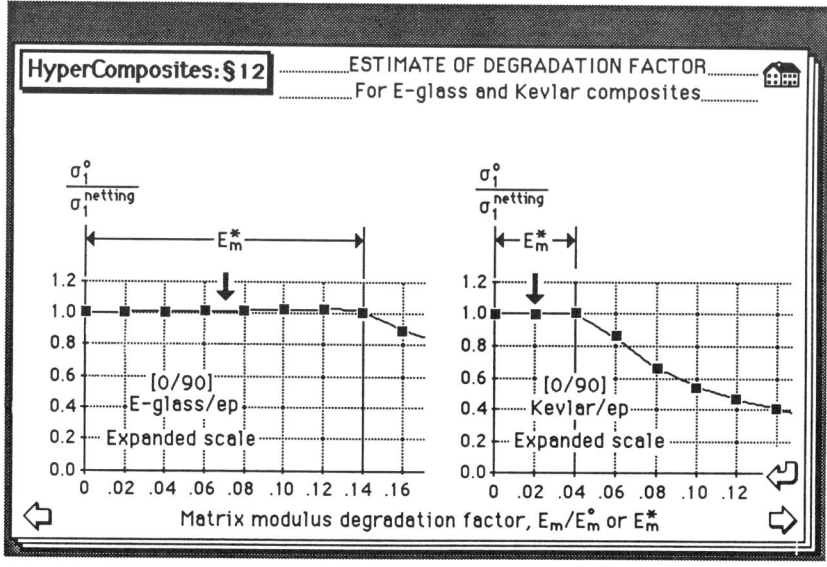

29.12 DEGRADATION (continued)

HyperComposites:§12 — DEGRADATION OF STIFFNESS AND STRENGTH — Based on matrix degradation

Degrade	T300/52	IM6/epoxy	AS4/PEEK	E-gl/epoxy	Kev/epoxy
E_m	3.40	3.40	3.40	3.40	3.40
E_m^*	0.20	0.10	0.10	0.07	0.02
E_y	10.30	11.20	8.90	8.27	5.50
E_y^*	0.31	0.14	0.17	0.07	0.05
E_s	7.17	8.40	5.10	4.14	2.30
E_s^*	0.27	0.11	0.16	0.08	0.06
X'	1500	1540	1100	610	235
X'^*	0.77	0.64	0.70	0.60	0.57
ν_x^*	0.20	0.10	0.10	0.07	0.02
$(F_{xy}^*)^*$	0.20	0.10	0.10	0.07	0.02

$*$ means percent degradation from intact to degraded matrix.
Longitudinal compressive strength are degraded, not linearly,
but to the 0.2th power; i.e., $X'^* = [E_s^*]^{0.2}$.
Poisson's ratio and interaction term in the quadratic failure
criterion are linearly degraded with the matrix stiffness.

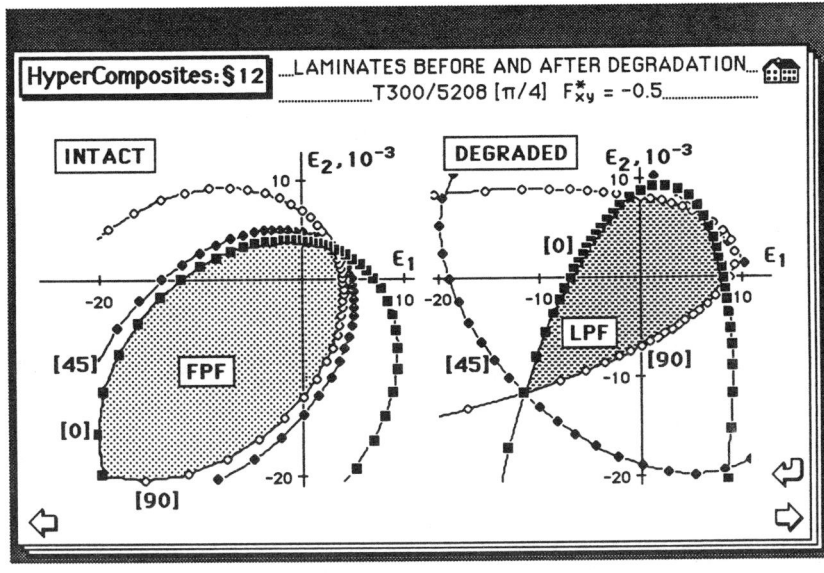

HyperComposites:§12 — LAMINATES BEFORE AND AFTER DEGRADATION — T300/5208 [π/4] $F_{xy}^* = -0.5$

29.13 LAST–PLY–FAILURE VERSUS Em*

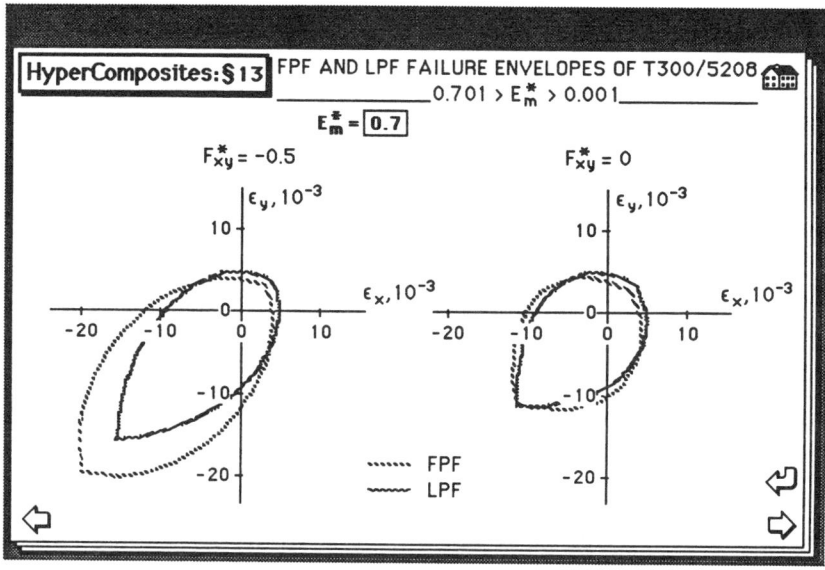

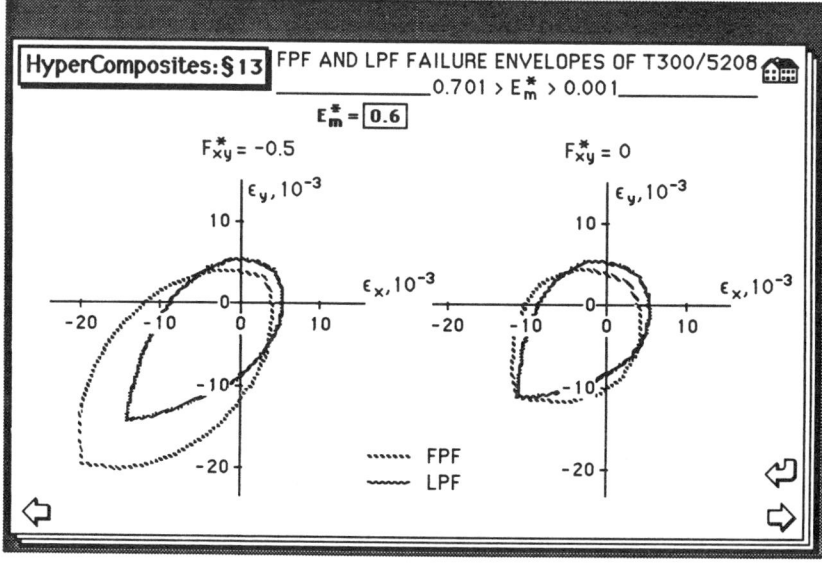

29.13 LAST–PLY–FAILURE VERSUS Em* (continued)

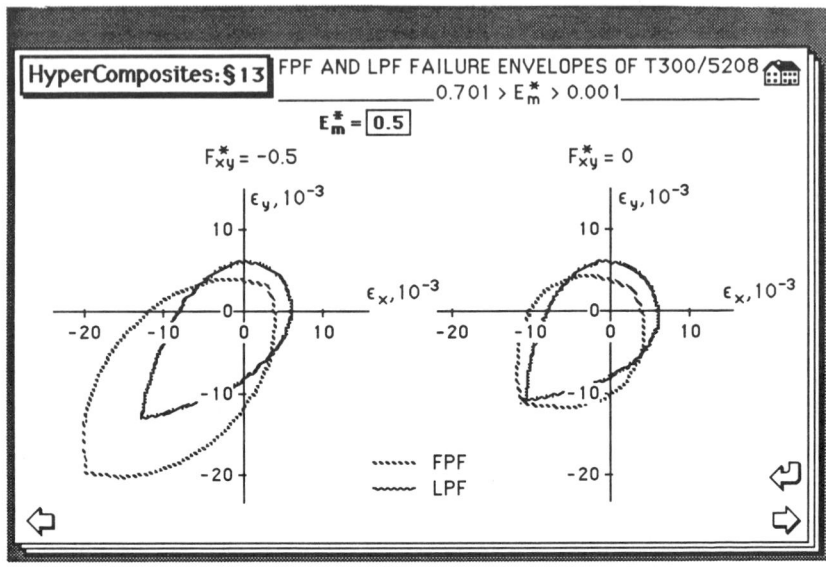

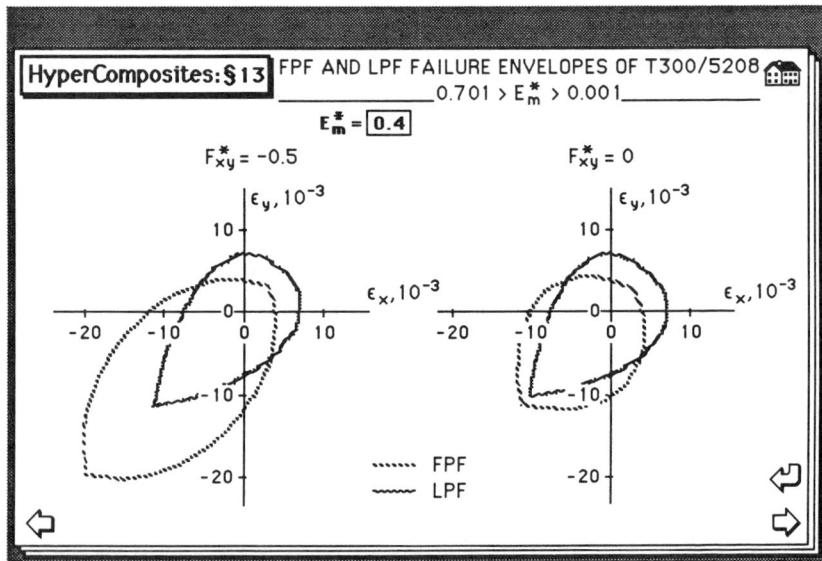

29.13 LAST–PLY–FAILURE VERSUS Em* (continued)

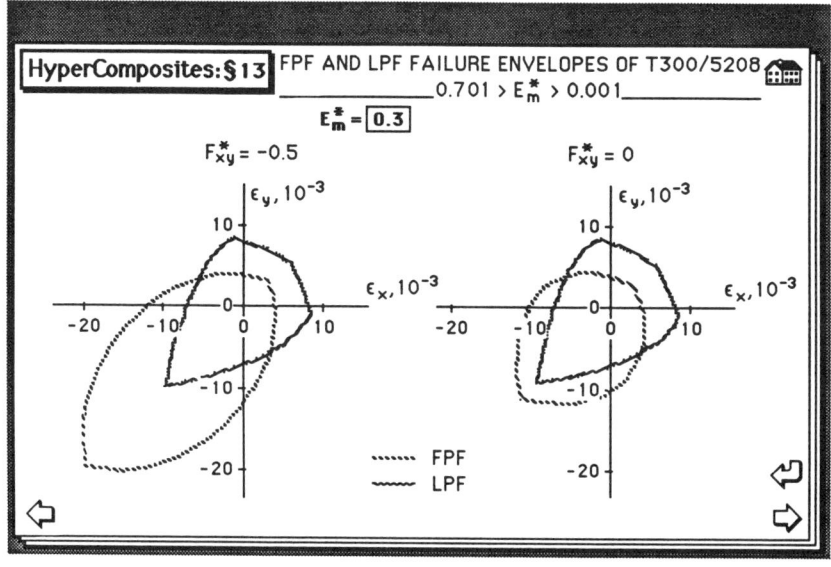

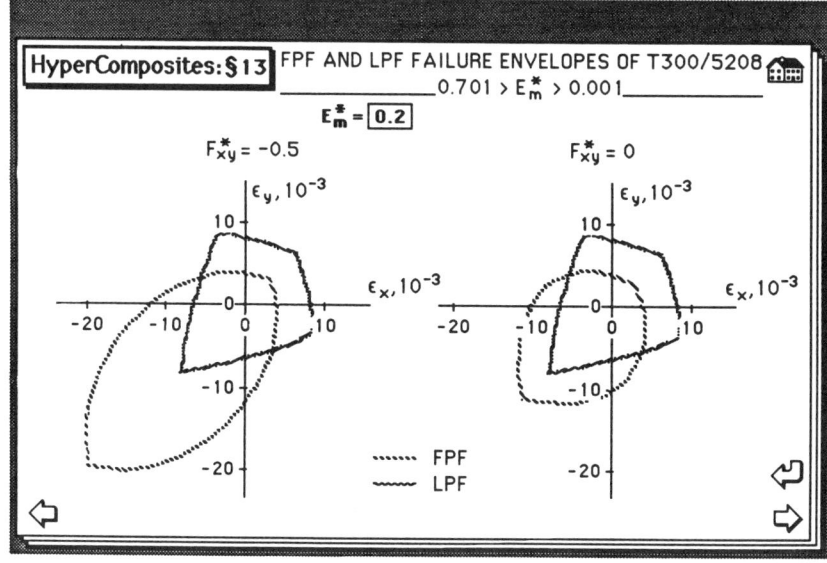

29.13 LAST–PLY–FAILURE VERSUS Em* (continued)

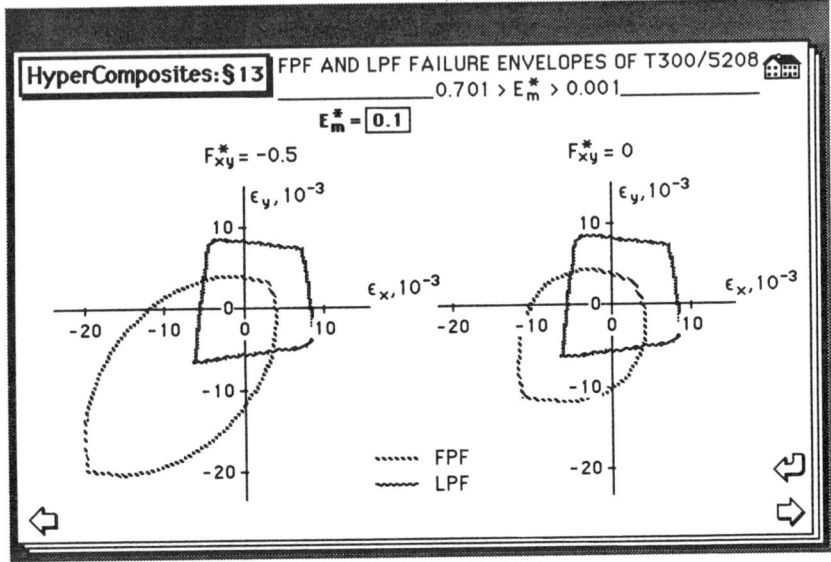

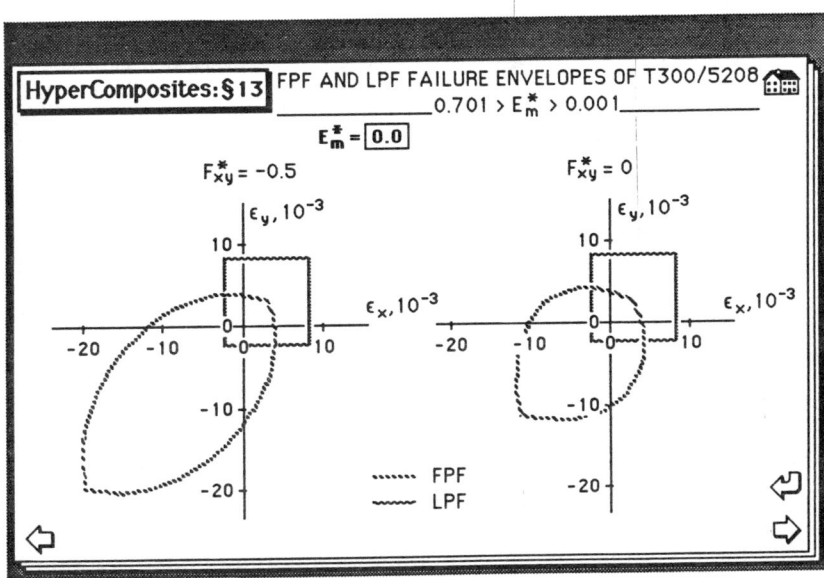

29.14 STRENGTH RATIO

HyperComposites:§14 ⸺STRENGTH RATIO AND STRENGTH INDEX⸺

Strength ratios and strength indices are useful extensions of failure criteria. Such measures can determine not only imminent failures but also the factor of safety of a laminate under an applied load.

When strength ratio is unity, failure occurs. When it has a value of two the factor of safety is two; i.e., the load can be doubled or the plies reduced to a half before failure occurs.

When strength index is unity, failure occurs. When it is less than unity, it is safe. But the value is not proportional to the factor of safety. Some finite element programs still use this index for strength analysis.

For most composite materials where the tensile and compressive strengths can be markedly different, the use of strength ratio is preferred over that of the strength index. We will see the difference.

HyperComposites:§14 ⸺GENERAL QUADRATIC STRENGTH ENVELOPES⸺

Strength ratio R: $[F_{ij}\sigma_i\sigma_j]R^2+[F_i\sigma_i]R-1 = 0$ $R = -b/2a+\sqrt{(b/2a)^2+1/a}$

Strength index k: $F_{ij}\sigma_i\sigma_j+F_i\sigma_i = k^2$ $k = \sqrt{a+b}$

where $a = F_{ij}\sigma_i\sigma_j$; $b = F_i\sigma_i$

In general $R \neq 1/k$, except when $F_i = 0$ or $b = 0$, or

when $X = X'$, and $Y = Y'$

(uniaxial tensile and compressive strengths are equal)

$R = 1/\sqrt{a} = 1/k$

$k = \sqrt{a} = 1/R = $ von Mises index for isotropic materials

29.14 STRENGTH RATIO (continued)

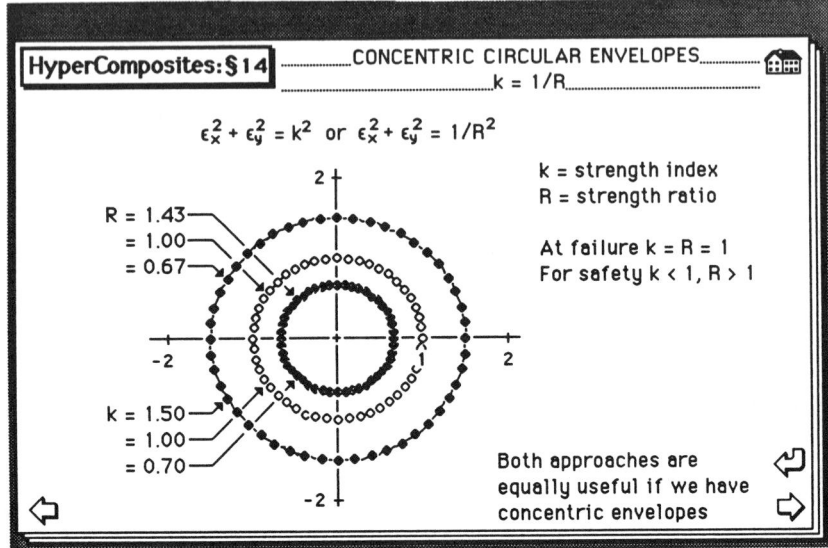

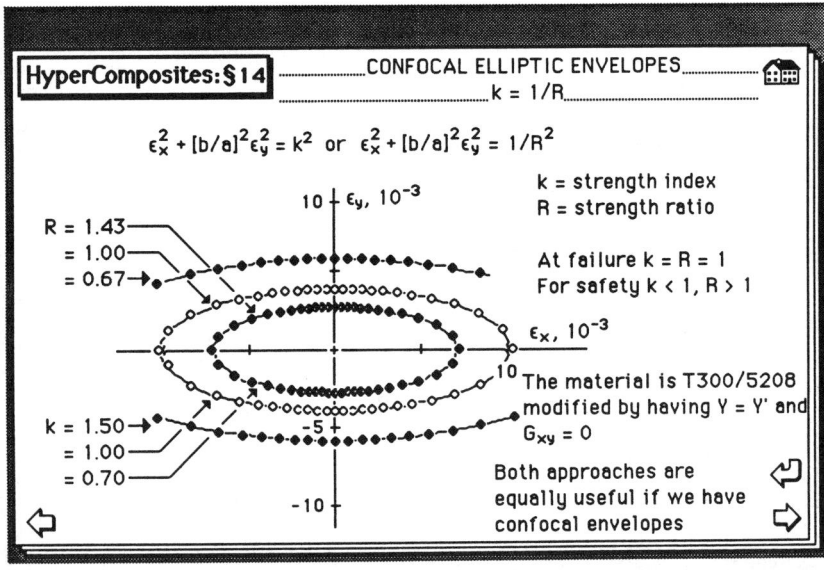

29.14 STRENGTH RATIO (continued)

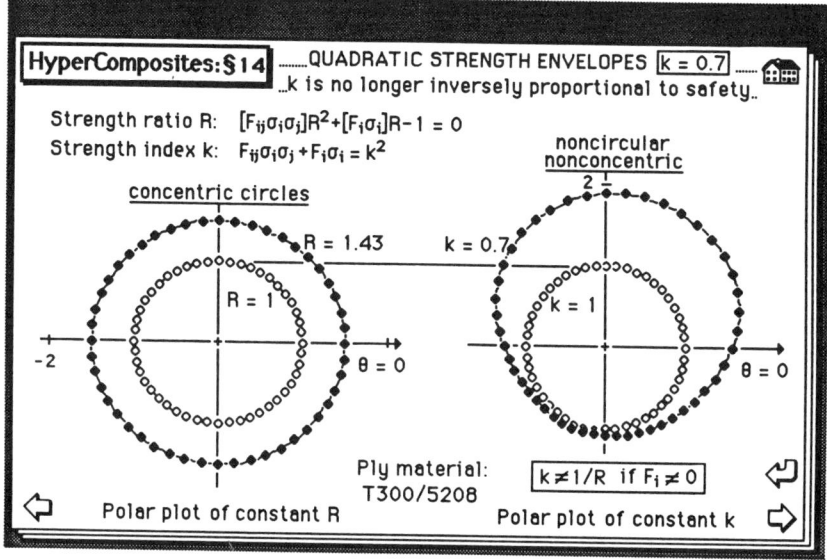

HyperComposites:§14 ......QUADRATIC STRENGTH ENVELOPES k = 0.7 ...... 🏠
..k is no longer inversely proportional to safety..

Strength ratio R: $[F_{ij}\sigma_i\sigma_j]R^2+[F_i\sigma_i]R-1 = 0$
Strength index k: $F_{ij}\sigma_i\sigma_j+F_i\sigma_i = k^2$

noncircular
nonconcentric

concentric circles

R = 1.43   k = 0.7

R = 1   k = 1

-2   θ = 0   θ = 0

Ply material:
T300/5208 $k \neq 1/R$ if $F_i \neq 0$

Polar plot of constant R   Polar plot of constant k

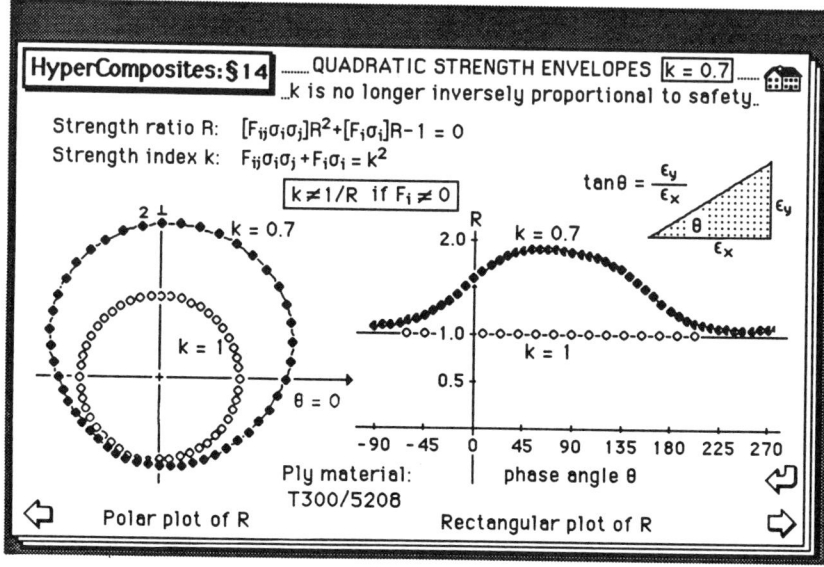

HyperComposites:§14 ......QUADRATIC STRENGTH ENVELOPES k = 0.7 ...... 🏠
..k is no longer inversely proportional to safety..

Strength ratio R: $[F_{ij}\sigma_i\sigma_j]R^2+[F_i\sigma_i]R-1 = 0$
Strength index k: $F_{ij}\sigma_i\sigma_j+F_i\sigma_i = k^2$

$k \neq 1/R$ if $F_i \neq 0$ $\tan\theta = \dfrac{\epsilon_y}{\epsilon_x}$

2   k = 0.7   R
                                  2.0   k = 0.7

k = 1   -1.0   k = 1

θ = 0   0.5

-90 -45   0   45   90 135 180 225 270

Ply material:
T300/5208   phase angle θ

Polar plot of R   Rectangular plot of R

29.14 STRENGTH RATIO (continued)

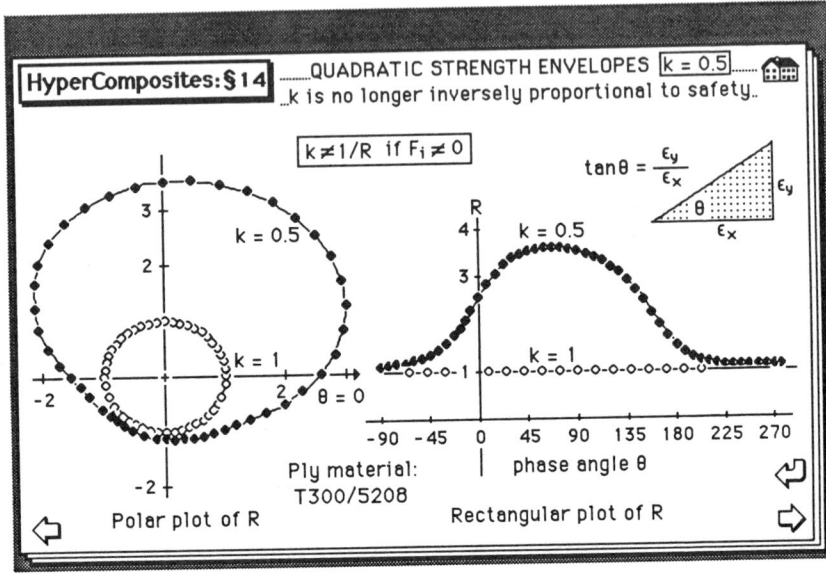

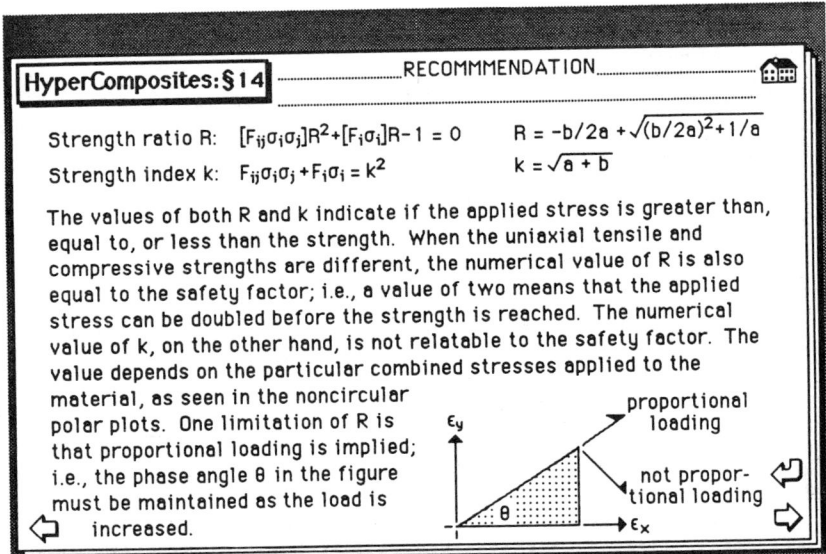

29.15 LIMIT AND ULTIMATE STRENGTHS

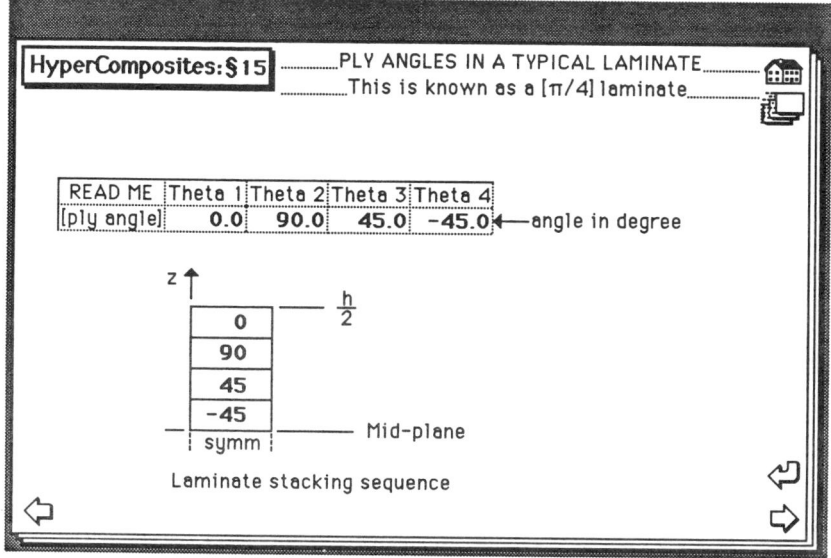

HyperComposites: §15 .... PLY ANGLES IN A TYPICAL LAMINATE ....
.... This is known as a [π/4] laminate ....

READ ME	Theta 1	Theta 2	Theta 3	Theta 4	
[ply angle]	0.0	90.0	45.0	−45.0	←— angle in degree

Laminate stacking sequence

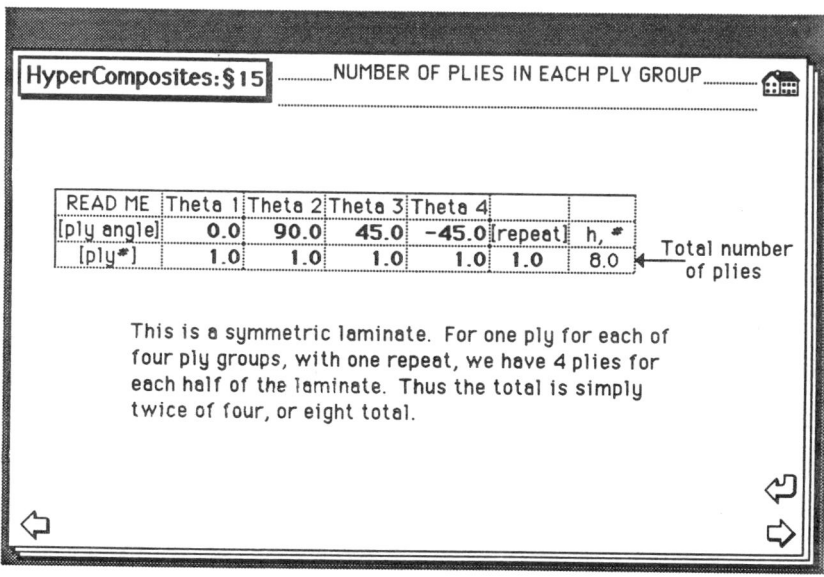

HyperComposites: §15 .... NUMBER OF PLIES IN EACH PLY GROUP ....

READ ME	Theta 1	Theta 2	Theta 3	Theta 4			
[ply angle]	0.0	90.0	45.0	−45.0	[repeat]	h, #	Total number
[ply#]	1.0	1.0	1.0	1.0	1.0	8.0	←— of plies

This is a symmetric laminate. For one ply for each of
four ply groups, with one repeat, we have 4 plies for
each half of the laminate. Thus the total is simply
twice of four, or eight total.

29.15 LIMIT AND ULTIMATE STRENGTHS (continued)

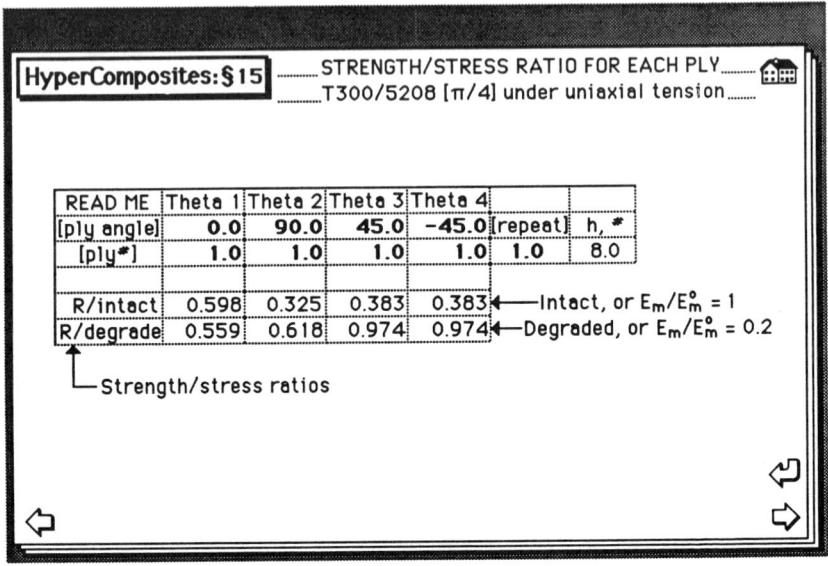

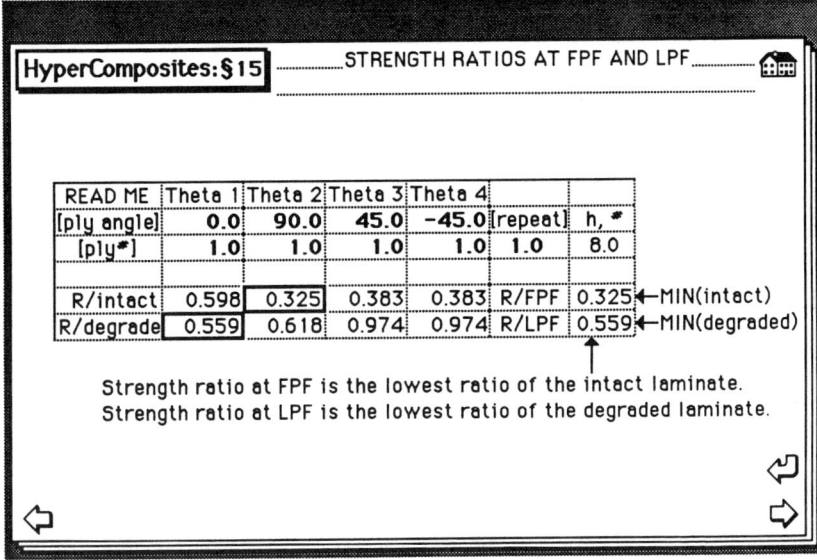

29.15 LIMIT AND ULTIMATE STRENGTHS (continued)

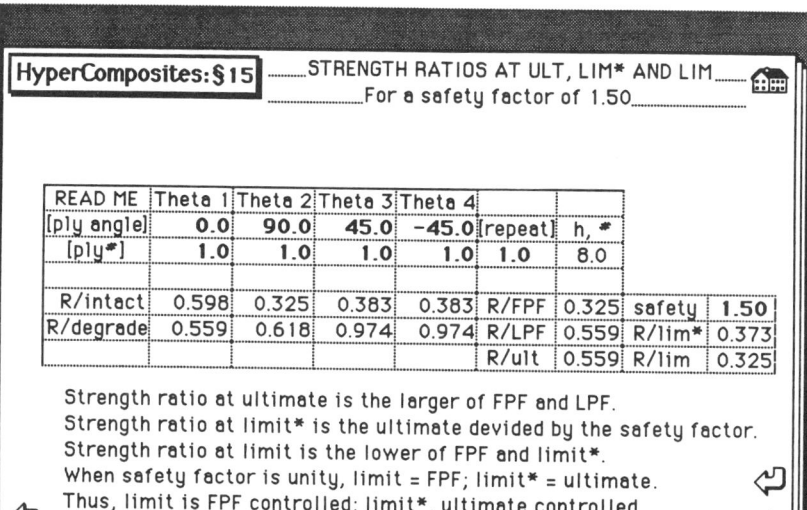

HyperComposites: §15 ....STRENGTH RATIOS AT ULT, LIM* AND LIM........
.........For a safety factor of 1.50........

READ ME	Theta 1	Theta 2	Theta 3	Theta 4				
[ply angle]	0.0	90.0	45.0	−45.0	[repeat]	h, #		
[ply#]	1.0	1.0	1.0	1.0	1.0	8.0		
R/intact	0.598	0.325	0.383	0.383	R/FPF	0.325	safety	1.50
R/degrade	0.559	0.618	0.974	0.974	R/LPF	0.559	R/lim*	0.373
					R/ult	0.559	R/lim	0.325

Strength ratio at ultimate is the larger of FPF and LPF.
Strength ratio at limit* is the ultimate devided by the safety factor.
Strength ratio at limit is the lower of FPF and limit*.
When safety factor is unity, limit = FPF; limit* = ultimate.
Thus, limit is FPF controlled; limit*, ultimate controlled.

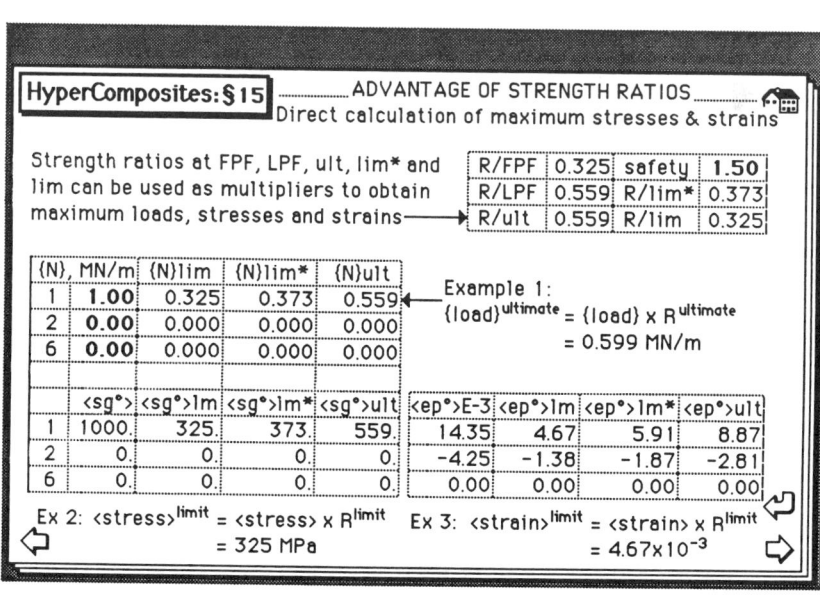

HyperComposites: §15 ....ADVANTAGE OF STRENGTH RATIOS........
Direct calculation of maximum stresses & strains

Strength ratios at FPF, LPF, ult, lim* and lim can be used as multipliers to obtain maximum loads, stresses and strains——▸

R/FPF	0.325	safety	1.50
R/LPF	0.559	R/lim*	0.373
R/ult	0.559	R/lim	0.325

{N}, MN/m	{N}lim	{N}lim*	{N}ult
1	1.00	0.325	0.373	0.559
2	0.00	0.000	0.000	0.000
6	0.00	0.000	0.000	0.000

Example 1:
$$\{load\}^{ultimate} = \{load\} \times R^{ultimate}$$
$$= 0.599 \text{ MN/m}$$

	<sg°>	<sg°>lm	<sg°>lm*	<sg°>ult	<ep°>E-3	<ep°>lm	<ep°>lm*	<ep°>ult
1	1000.	325.	373.	559.	14.35	4.67	5.91	8.87
2	0.	0.	0.	0.	−4.25	−1.38	−1.87	−2.81
6	0.	0.	0.	0.	0.00	0.00	0.00	0.00

Ex 2: $\langle stress \rangle^{limit} = \langle stress \rangle \times R^{limit}$
$$= 325 \text{ MPa}$$

Ex 3: $\langle strain \rangle^{limit} = \langle strain \rangle \times R^{limit}$
$$= 4.67 \times 10^{-3}$$

29.15 LIMIT AND ULTIMATE STRENGTHS (continued)

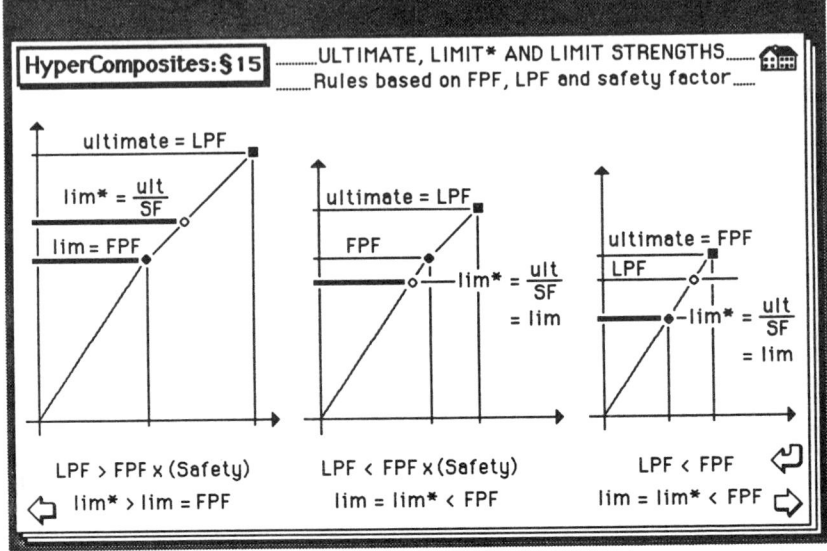

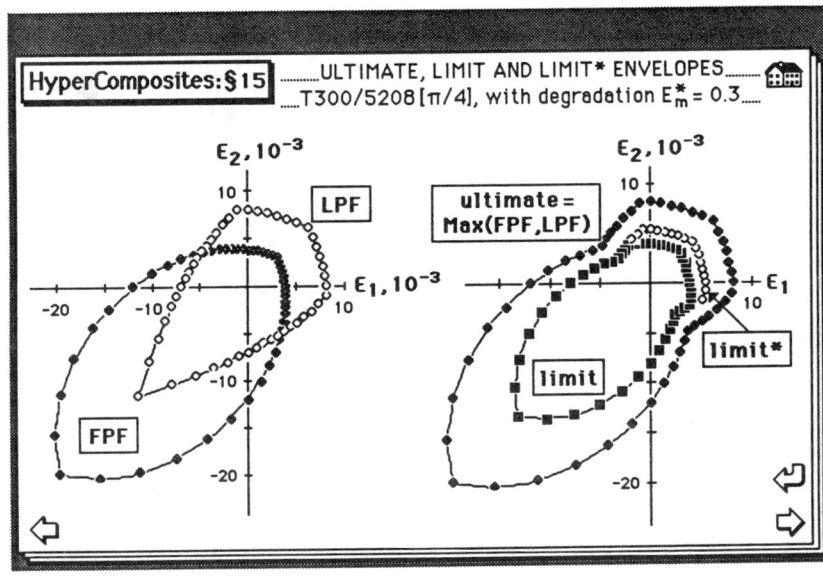

29.15 LIMIT AND ULTIMATE STRENGTHS (continued)

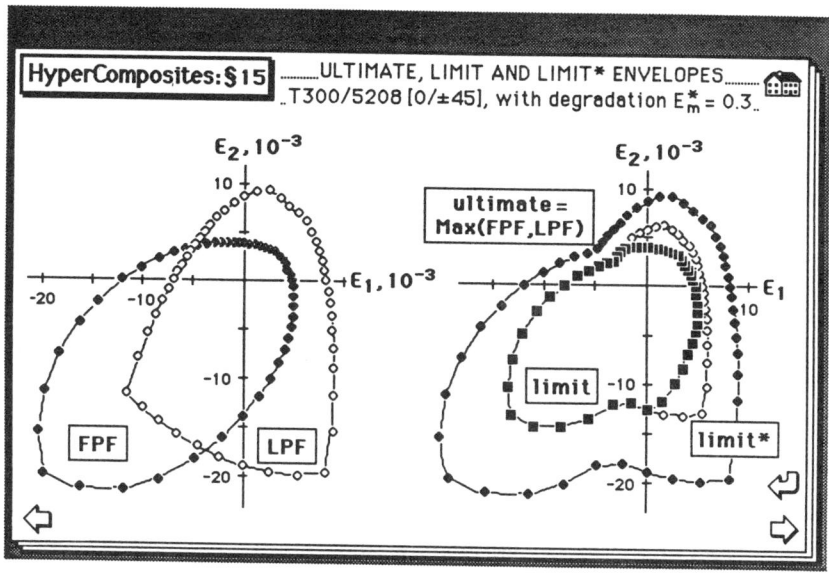

HyperComposites: §15 ....ULTIMATE, LIMIT AND LIMIT* ENVELOPES.........

.T300/5208 [0/±45], with degradation $E_m^* = 0.3$.

ultimate = Max(FPF,LPF)

FPF   LPF

limit

limit*

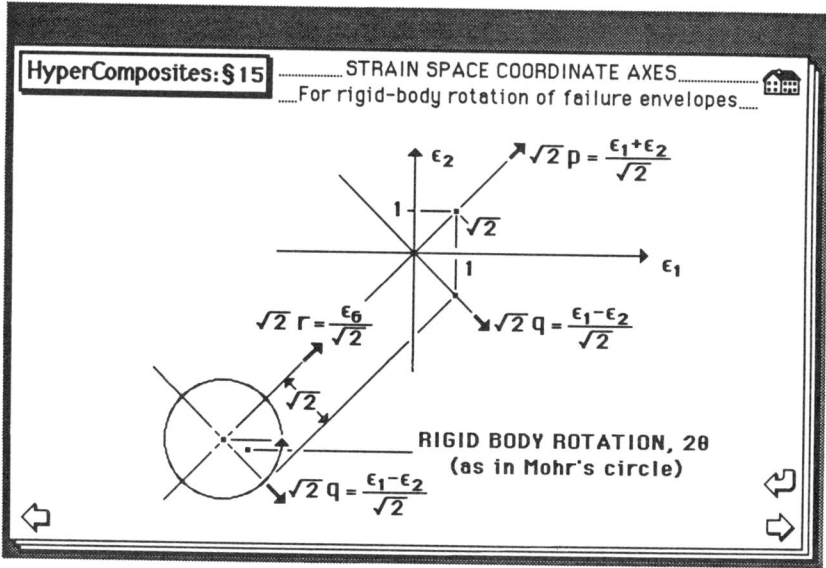

HyperComposites: §15 ....STRAIN SPACE COORDINATE AXES............

.....For rigid-body rotation of failure envelopes.....

$$\sqrt{2}\, p = \frac{\varepsilon_1 + \varepsilon_2}{\sqrt{2}}$$

$$\sqrt{2}\, r = \frac{\varepsilon_6}{\sqrt{2}}$$

$$\sqrt{2}\, q = \frac{\varepsilon_1 - \varepsilon_2}{\sqrt{2}}$$

$$\sqrt{2}\, q = \frac{\varepsilon_1 - \varepsilon_2}{\sqrt{2}}$$

RIGID BODY ROTATION, 2θ
(as in Mohr's circle)

29.15 LIMIT AND ULTIMATE STRENGTHS (continued)

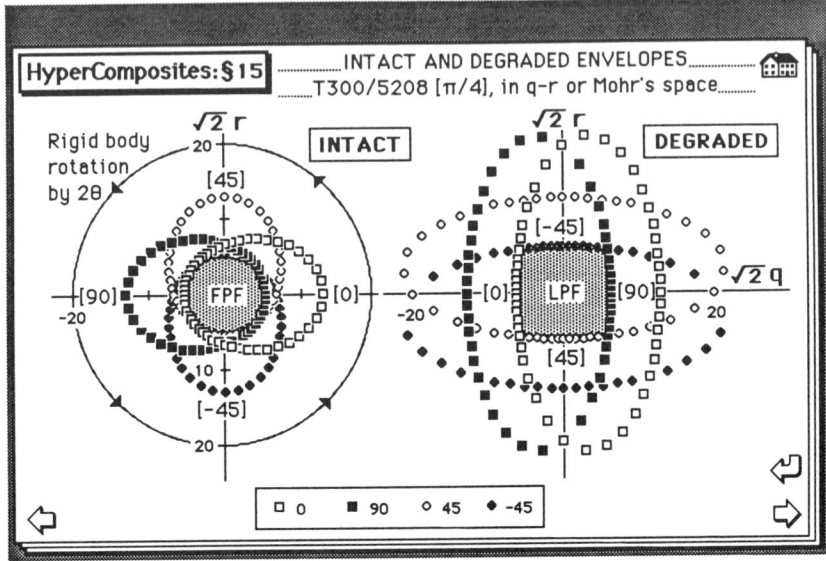

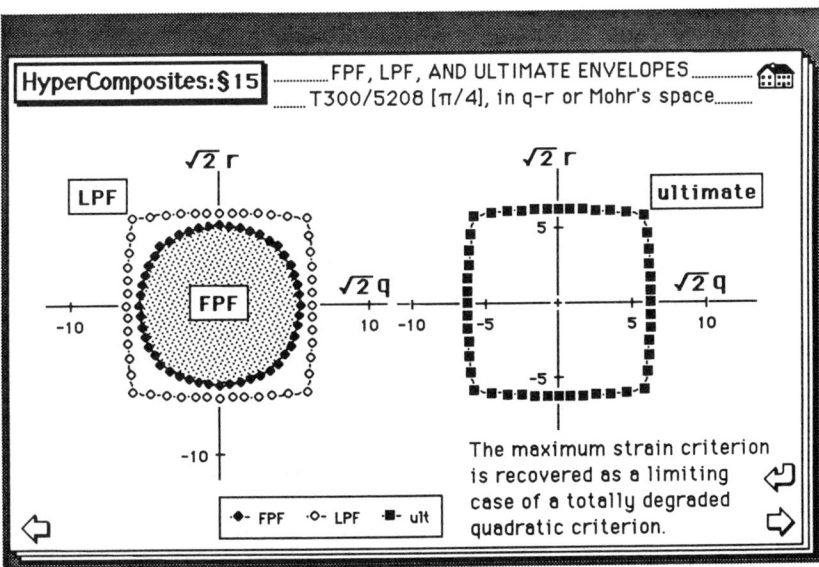

29.16 CURING STRESSES

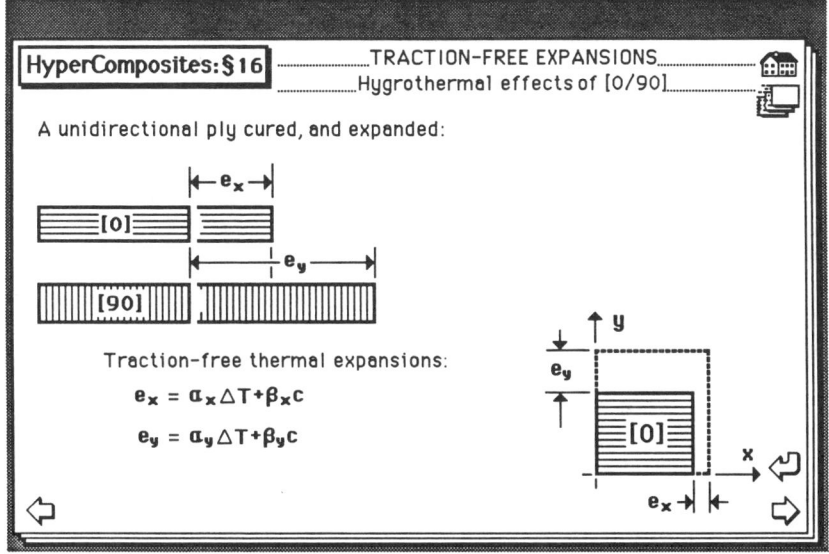

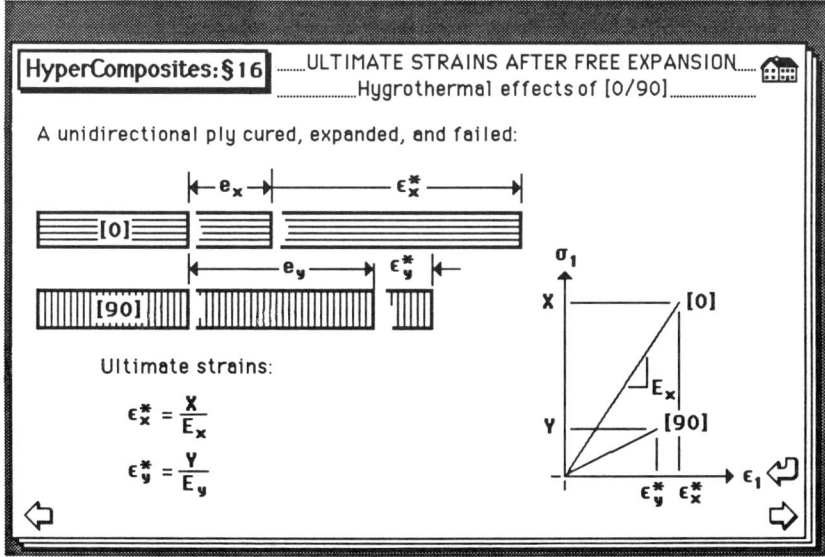

29.16 CURING STRESSES (continued)

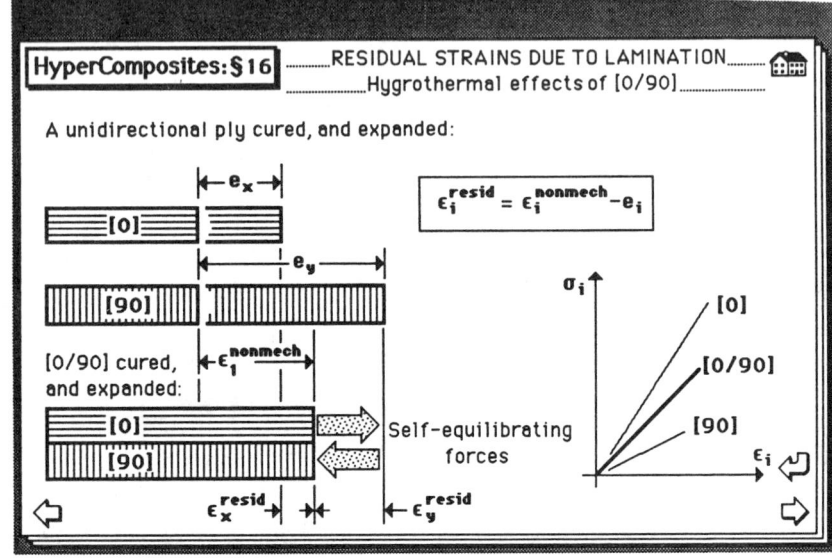

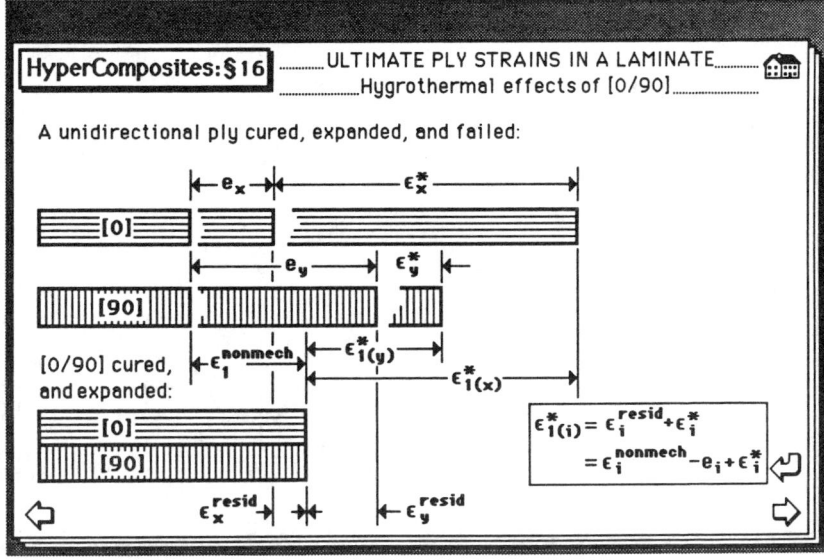

29.16 CURING STRESSES (continued)

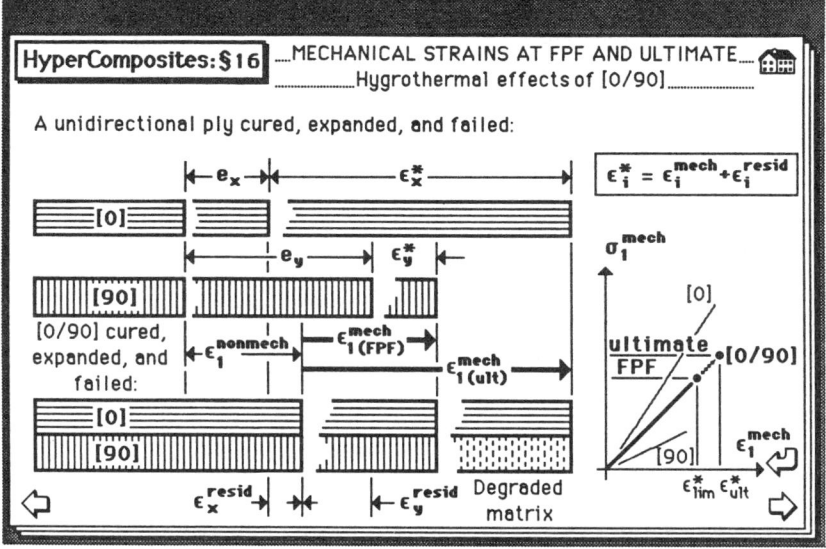

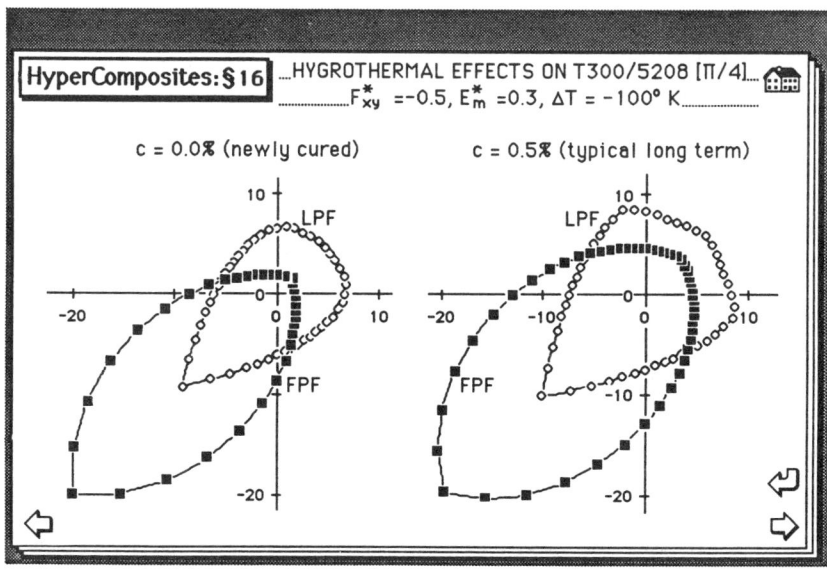

29.16 CURING STRESSES (continued)

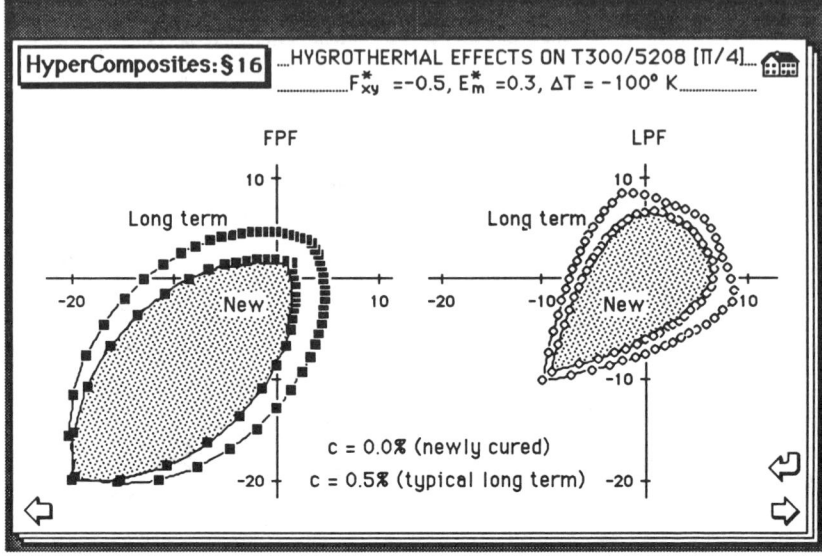

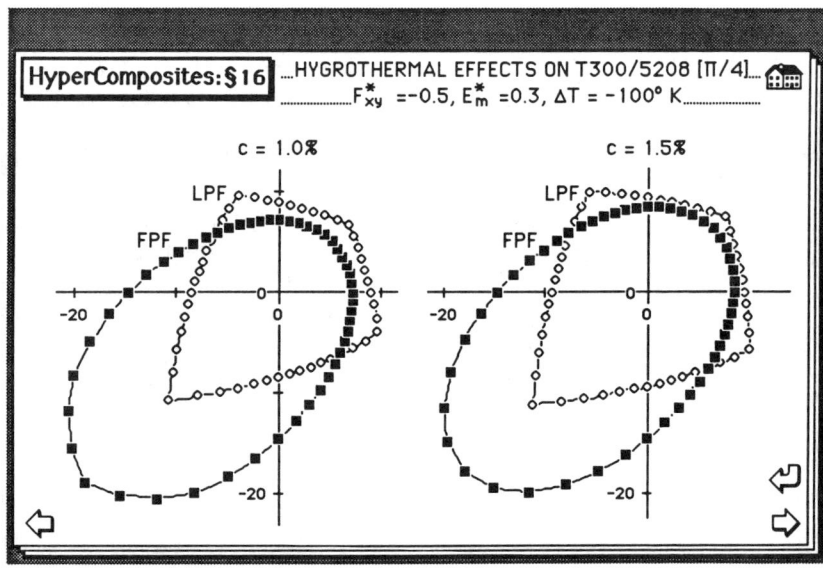

29.17 FAILURE ENVELOPES

HyperComposites:§17 ....TYPICAL FAILURE ENVELOPES................

Variations of the quadratic failure envelopes for typical composite materials are shown.

The sensitivity of the interaction term F_{xy}^* is more pronounced for the intact plies than the degraded ones. Thus it is most noticeable for the FPF envelopes. This interaction term is reduced by the same degradation factor. As matrix or ply degradation proceeds, the interaction is proportionally reduced. Mode interaction approaches zero in a fully degraded laminate. This is consistent with the implication of the netting analysis.

The LPF envelopes, on the other hand, are governed by the degradation factor. In the limit, as the degradation factor approaches zero, the LPF coincides with the netting analysis. The loss of longitudinal compressive strength due to degradation is also included. The precise magnitude must be determined experimentally.

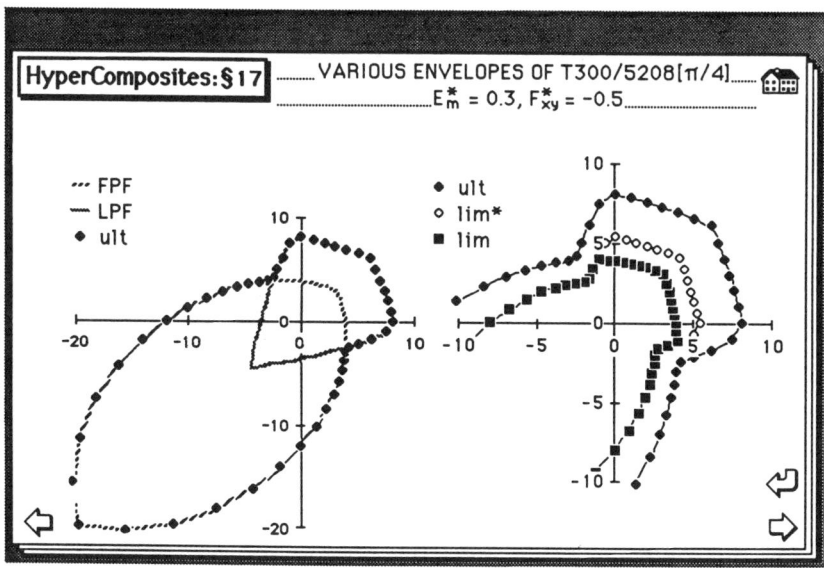

HyperComposites:§17 ....VARIOUS ENVELOPES OF T300/5208[π/4]..........
$E_m^* = 0.3, F_{xy}^* = -0.5$

- ⋯ FPF
- — LPF
- • ult

- • ult
- ○ lim*
- ■ lim

29.17 FAILURE ENVELOPES (continued)

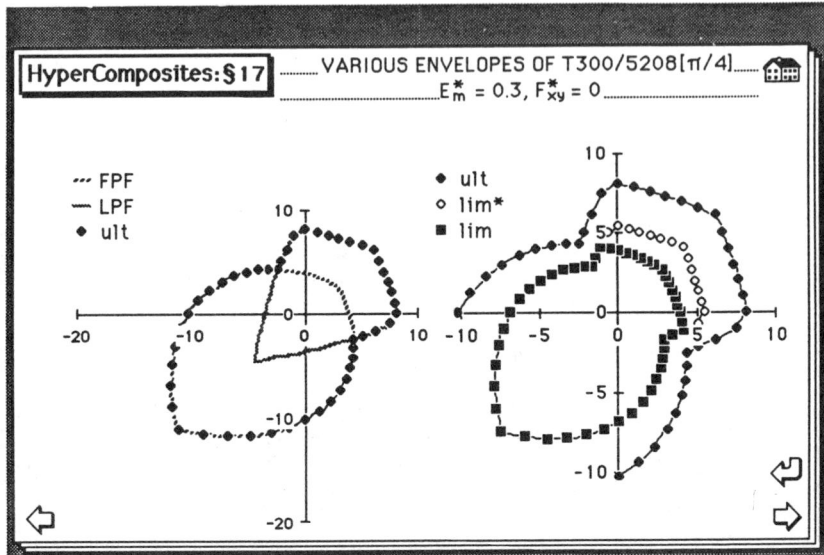

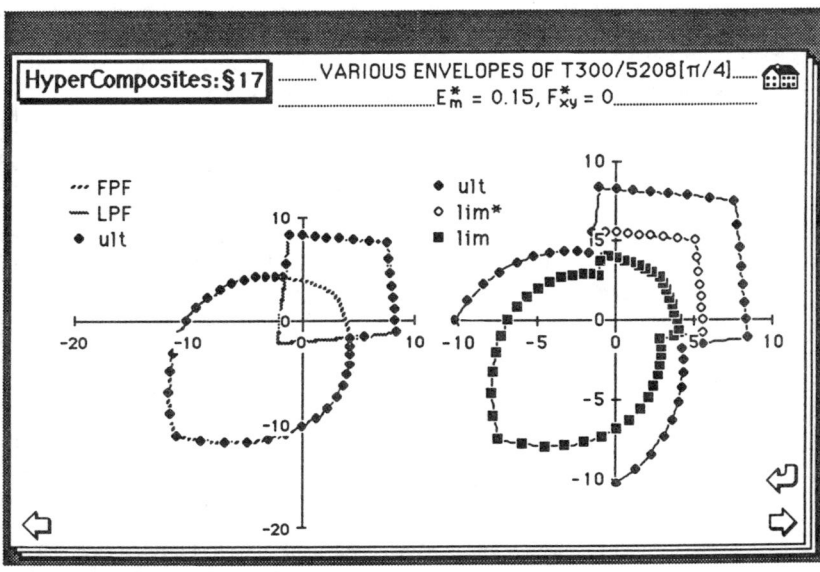

29.17 FAILURE ENVELOPES (continued)

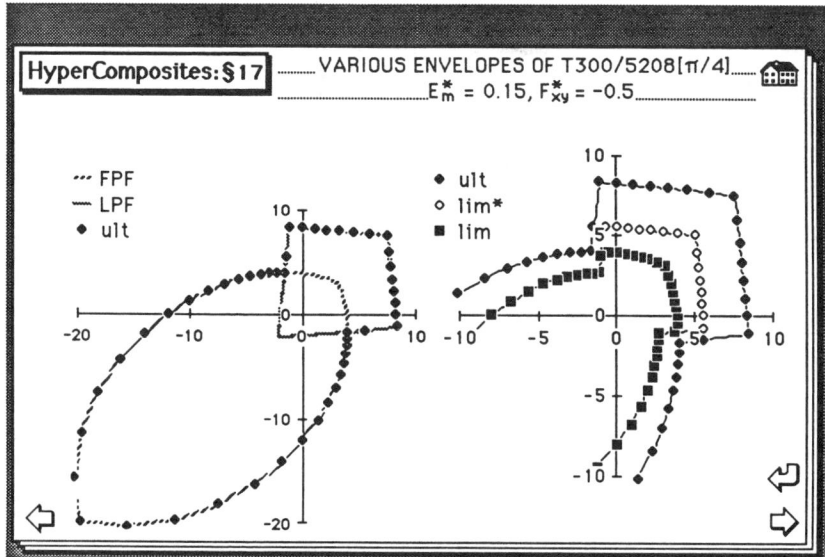

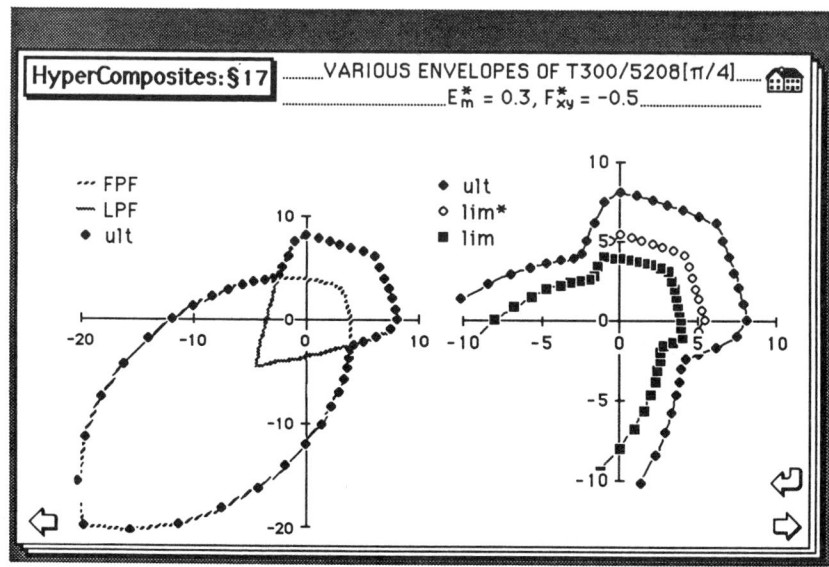

29.17 FAILURE ENVELOPES (continued)

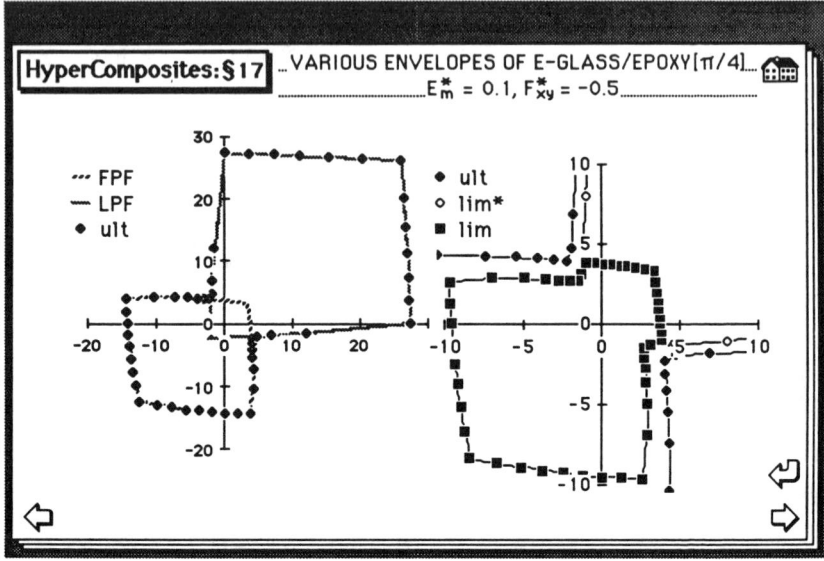

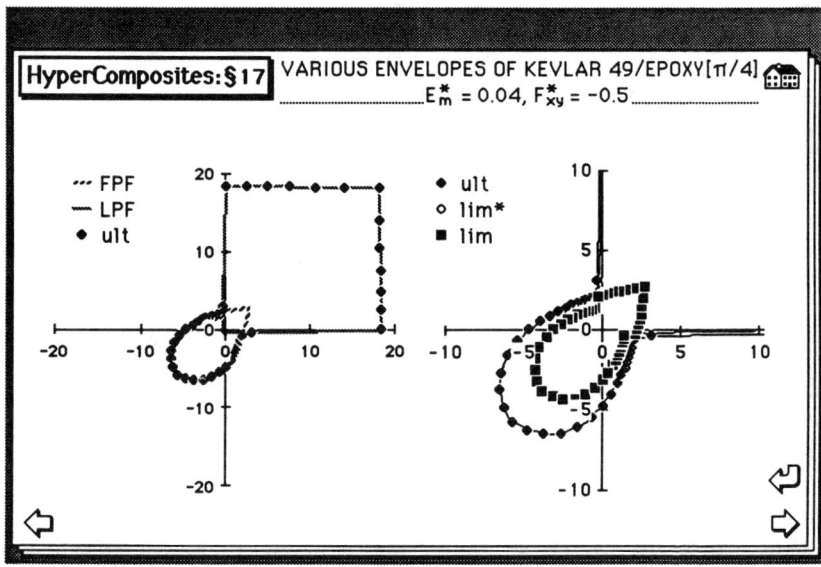

29.17 FAILURE ENVELOPES (continued)

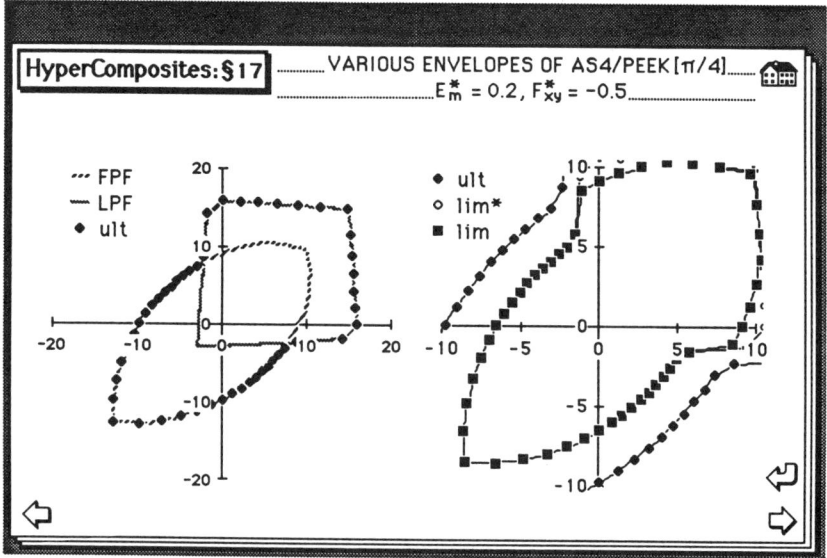

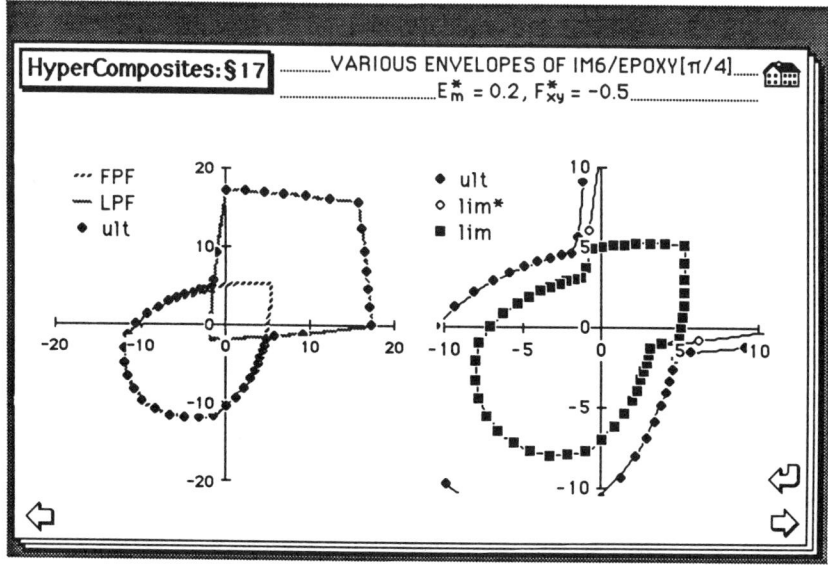

29.17 FAILURE ENVELOPES (continued)

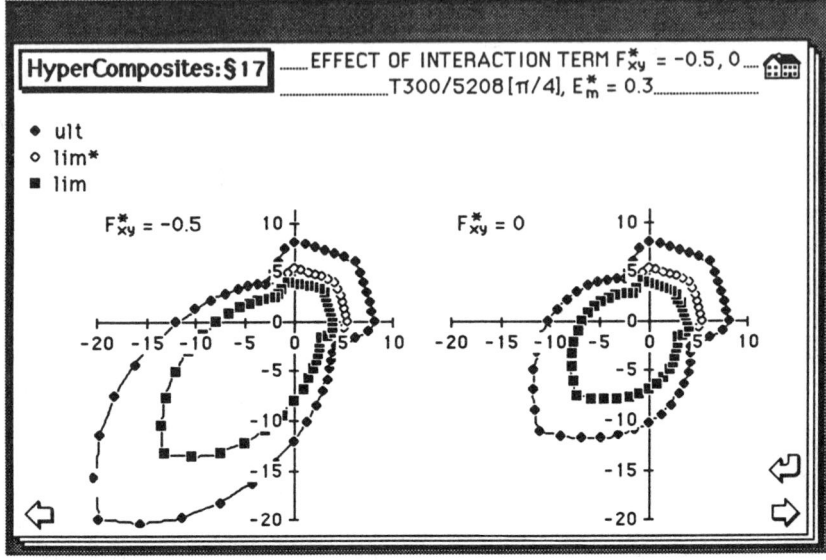

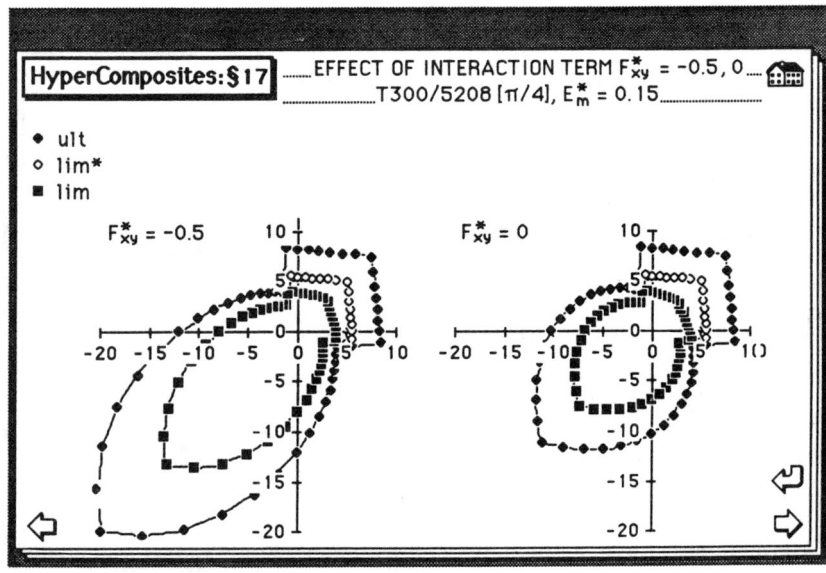

29.17 FAILURE ENVELOPES (continued)

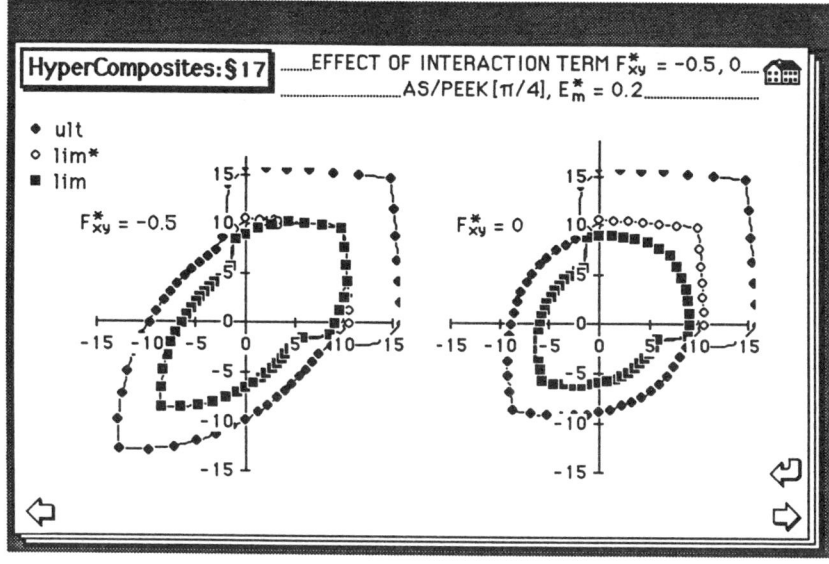

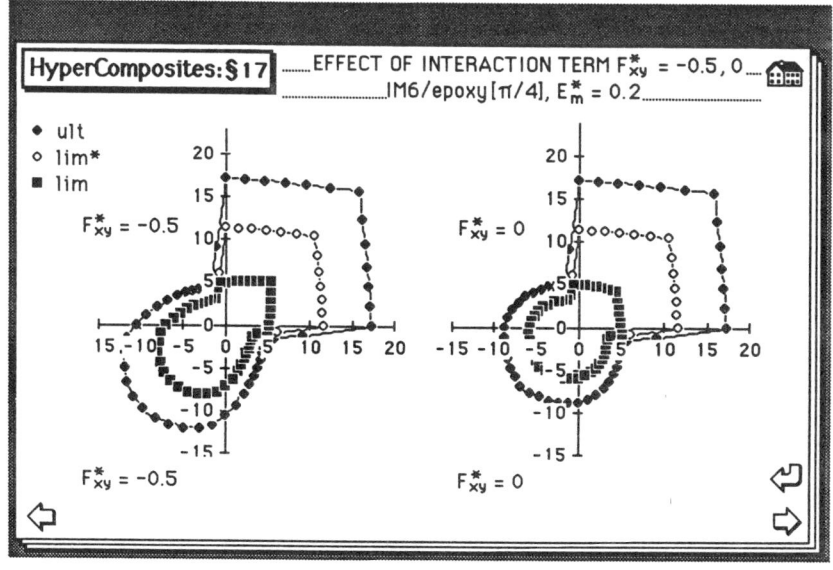

29.17 FAILURE ENVELOPES (continued)

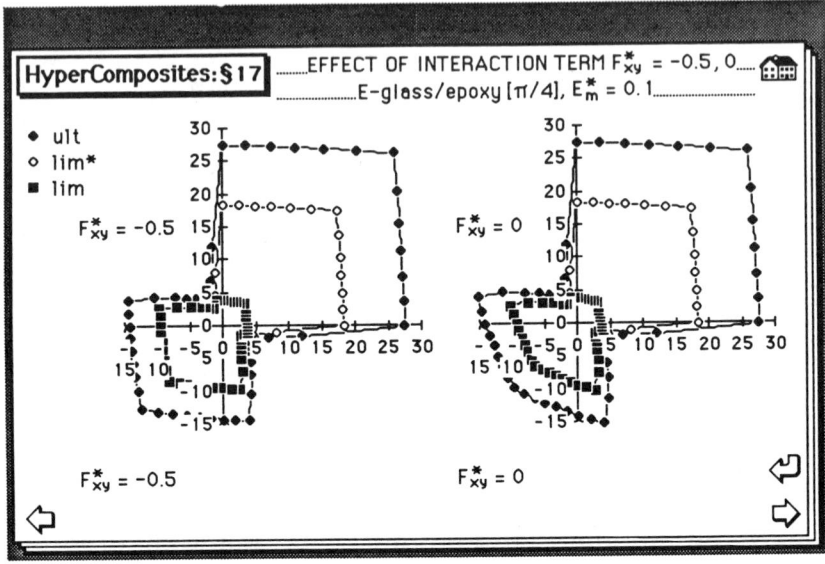

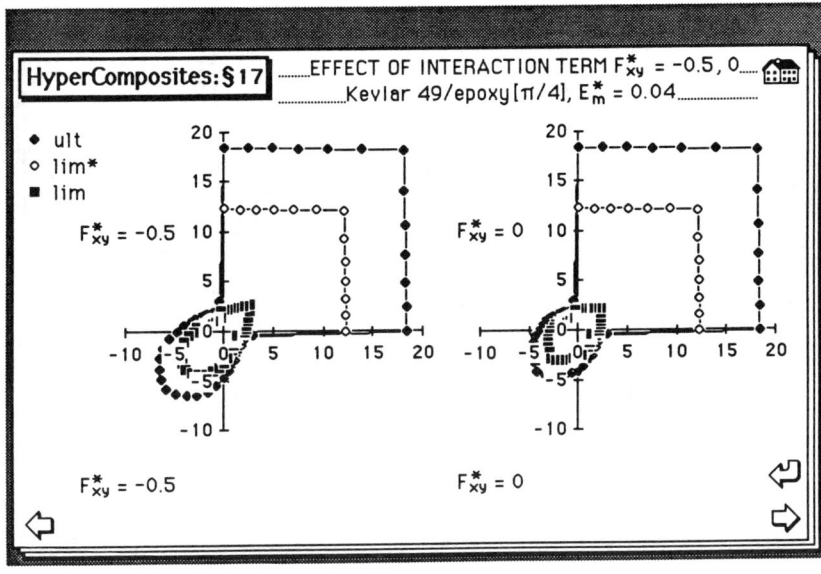

29.18 MIC–MAC

HyperComposites:§18 ·········SENSITIVITY OF INTEGRATED MIC-MAC·········

The contribution of the constituents to that of a laminate can best be illustrated by an integrated micro-macromechanics analysis model. One approach is shown in the flow chart in the following card.

It is fairly easy to use spreadsheets to perform the necessary linking of data and formulas. This is done in the Mic-Mac. We can not only find out "what if" but also "what's best?" The latter is achieved using the macros associated with the spreadsheets.

The sensitivity of each input on all the outputs related to the stiffness and strength of a laminate will be shown in the following cards. We limit our study to the in-plane deformation of a symmetric laminate. From the examples here, we can extend the sensitivity study to other Mic-Mac's, including simple structures like beams, tubings, etc. An understanding of the nonlinear and coupleing effects of Mic-Mac's will contribute to the confident and effective use of composites.

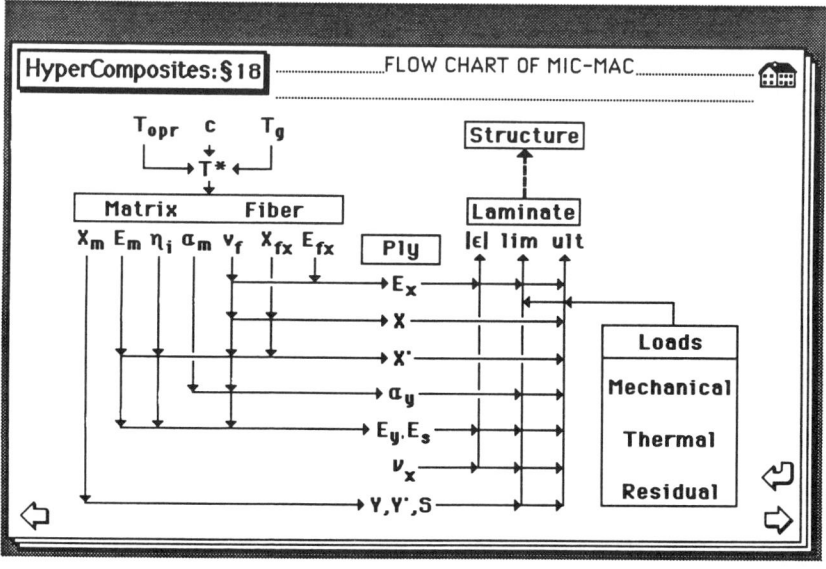

HyperComposites:§18 ·········FLOW CHART OF MIC-MAC·········

29.18 MIC–MAC (continued)

HyperComposites:§18 ....MIC–MAC FOR IN-PLANE LOADING.........🏠
..Uniaixal tensile applied to quasi-iso laminate..

	READ ME	Theta 1	Theta 2	Theta 3	Theta 4		Ply mat	T3/N52[SI]	
stacking	[ply angle]	0.0	90.0	45.0	-45.0	[repeat]	h, *	h, E-3	[Rotate]
	[ply #]	1.0	1.0	1.0	1.0	1.0	8.0	1.0	0.00
strength	R/intact	0.598	0.325	0.383	0.383	R/FPF	0.325	safety	1.50
ratios	R/degrade	0.559	0.618	0.974	0.974	R/LPF	0.559	R/lim*	0.373
						R/ult	0.559	R/lim	0.325
loads &	(N), MN/m or k/in	(N)lim	(N)lim*	(N)ult	(E°)lim	E"ul/E"lr	<alph>E-6	<beta>
laminate	compon't 1	1.00	0.325	0.373	0.559	69.68	0.91	1.52	0.0401
moduli	compon't 2	0.00	0.000	0.000	0.000	69.68	0.91	1.52	0.0401
	compon't 6	0.00	0.000	0.000	0.000	26.88	0.89	0.00	0.0000
stresses &		<sg°>	<sg°>lim	<sg°>lim*	<sg°>ult	<ep°>E-3	<ep°>lim	<ep°>lim*	<ep°>ult
strains at	compon't 1	1000	325	373	559	14.35	4.67	5.91	8.87
limit, et al.	compon't 2	0	0	0	0	-4.25	-1.38	-1.87	-2.81
	compon't 6	0	0	0	0	0.00	0.00	0.00	0.00
		T opr	c,moist	vol/f	Em	Efx	Xm	Xfx	Em/Em°
micromech	Baseline	22.0	0.005	0.70	3.40	259	40.0	2143	0.20
variables	[Modified]	22.0	0.005	0.70	3.40	259	40.0	2143	0.20
⇦	Mod/Base	1.000	1.000	1.000	1.000	1.000	1.000	1.000	1.000	⇨

HyperComposites:§18 .....NORMALIZED SENSITIVITY OF BASELINE CASE.... 🏠
....Note all bold-face inputs/outputs are unity...

BASELINE CASE: QUASI-ISOTROPIC, UNIAIXAL TENSILE LOAD									
READ ME	Theta 1	Theta 2	Theta 3	Theta 4		Ply mat	T3/N52[SI]	
[ply angle]	0.0	90.0	45.0	-45.0	[repeat]	h, *	h, E-3	[Rotate]
[ply #]	1.00	1.00	1.00	1.00	1.00	1.00	1.00	0.00
R/intact	1.00	1.00	1.00	1.00	R/FPF	1.00	safety	1.00
R/degrade	1.00	1.00	1.00	1.00	R/LPF	1.00	R/lim*	1.00
					R/ult	1.00	R/lim	1.00
(N), MN/m or k/in	(N)lim	(N)lim*	(N)ult	(E°)lim	E"ul/E"lr	<alph>E-6	<beta>
compon't 1	1.00	1.00	1.00	1.00	1.00	1.00	1.00	1.00
	<sg°>	<sg°>lm	<sg°>lm*	<sg°>ult	<ep°>E-3	<ep°>lm	<ep°>lm*	<ep°>ult
compon't 1	1.00	1.00	1.00	1.00	1.00	1.00	1.00	1.00
	T opr	c,moist	vol/f	Em	Efx	Xm	Xfx	Em/Em°
[Modified]	22.0	0.005	0.70	3.40	259.	40.	2143.	0.20
Mod/Base	1.00	1.00	1.00	1.00	1.00	1.00	1.00	1.00

The ratios are obtained by the actual input/outputs normalized by
the baseline number in the previous card; i.e., when ratios equal to
unity, there is no change; when two, they are twice of the baseline.
⇦ Only the first component is shown for stress, strain, modulus, etc.

Ratios are relative to baseline values; cannot be compared with one another.

29.18 MIC–MAC (continued)

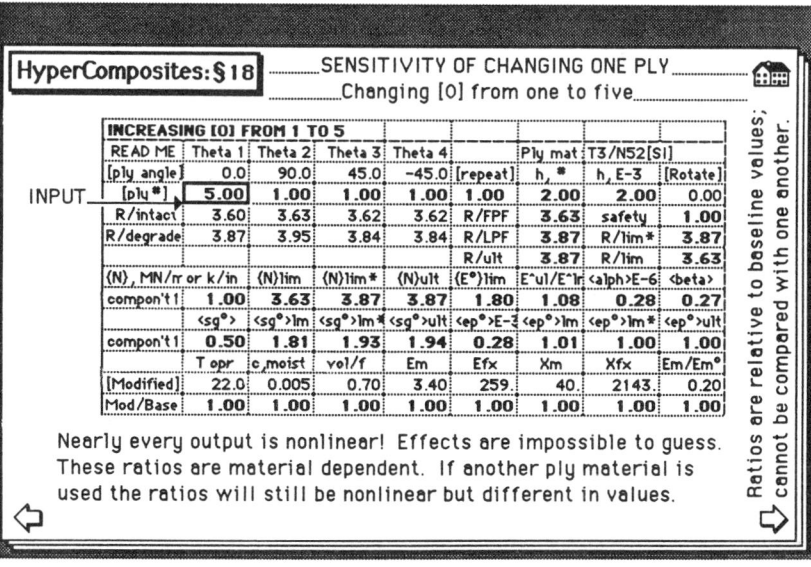

HyperComposites: §18 _____SENSITIVITY OF NUMBER OF PLIES_____ ___Increasing all ply groups by a factor of two___

DOUBLING PLIES IN EACH PLY GROUP								
READ ME	Theta 1	Theta 2	Theta 3	Theta 4		Ply mat	T3/N52[SI]	
[ply angle]	0.0	90.0	45.0	-45.0	[repeat]	h, *	h, E-3	[Rotate]
[ply *]	2.00	2.00	2.00	2.00	1.00	2.00	2.00	0.00
R/intact	2.00	2.00	2.00	2.00	R/FPF	2.00	safety	1.00
R/degrade	2.00	2.00	2.00	2.00	R/LPF	2.00	R/lim*	2.00
					R/ult	2.00	R/lim	2.00
(N), MN/m or k/in	(N)lim	(N)lim*	(N)ult	(E°)lim	E~ul/E~lr	<alph>E-6	<beta>
compon't 1	1.00	2.00	2.00	2.00	1.00	1.00	1.00	1.00
	<sg°>	<sg°>lm	<sg°>lm*	<sg°>ult	<ep°>E-3	<ep°>lm	<ep°>lm*	<ep°>ult
compon't 1	0.50	1.00	1.00	1.00	0.50	1.00	1.00	1.00
	T opr	c,moist	vol/f	Em	Efx	Xm	Xfx	Em/Em°
[Modified]	22.0	0.005	0.70	3.40	259.	40.	2143.	0.20
Mod/Base	1.00	1.00	1.00	1.00	1.00	1.00	1.00	1.00

Doubled: thickness, FPF, LPF, allowable loads.
Unchanged: laminate moduli, stress and strain at lim, lim* and ult.
Halved: stress and strain due to applied load (thickness is doubled).
These ratios remain the same for other ply materials.

Ratios are relative to baseline values; cannot be compared with one another.

HyperComposites: §18 _____SENSITIVITY OF CHANGING ONE PLY_____ ___Changing [0] from one to five___

INCREASING [0] FROM 1 TO 5								
READ ME	Theta 1	Theta 2	Theta 3	Theta 4		Ply mat	T3/N52[SI]	
[ply angle]	0.0	90.0	45.0	-45.0	[repeat]	h, *	h, E-3	[Rotate]
[ply *]	5.00	1.00	1.00	1.00	1.00	2.00	2.00	0.00
R/intact	3.60	3.63	3.62	3.62	R/FPF	3.63	safety	1.00
R/degrade	3.87	3.95	3.84	3.84	R/LPF	3.87	R/lim*	3.87
					R/ult	3.87	R/lim	3.63
(N), MN/m or k/in	(N)lim	(N)lim*	(N)ult	(E°)lim	E~ul/E~lr	<alph>E-6	<beta>
compon't 1	1.00	3.63	3.87	1.80	1.08	0.28	0.27
	<sg°>	<sg°>lm	<sg°>lm*	<sg°>ult	<ep°>E-3	<ep°>lm	<ep°>lm*	<ep°>ult
compon't 1	0.50	1.81	1.93	1.94	0.28	1.01	1.00	1.00
	T opr	c,moist	vol/f	Em	Efx	Xm	Xfx	Em/Em°
[Modified]	22.0	0.005	0.70	3.40	259.	40.	2143.	0.20
Mod/Base	1.00	1.00	1.00	1.00	1.00	1.00	1.00	1.00

Nearly every output is nonlinear! Effects are impossible to guess.
These ratios are material dependent. If another ply material is
used the ratios will still be nonlinear but different in values.

Ratios are relative to baseline values; cannot be compared with one another.

29.18 MIC–MAC (continued)

HyperComposites: §18 — SENSITIVITY OF RIGID BODY ROTATION — An in-plane rotation of 30 degrees

INPUT

RIGID BODY ROTATION OF LAMINATE BY 30 DEGREE							
READ ME	Theta 1	Theta 2	Theta 3	Theta 4		Ply mat	T3/N52[SI]
[ply angle]	0.0	90.0	45.0	−45.0	[repeat]	h, *	h, E-3	[Rotate→
[ply *]	1.00	1.00	1.00	1.00	1.00	1.00	1.00	30.00
R/intact	0.76	1.06	0.86	1.42	R/FPF	1.01	safety	1.00
R/degrade	1.31	1.59	0.72	0.61	R/LPF	1.07	R/lim*	1.07
					R/ult	1.07	R/lim	1.01
(N), MN/m or k/in	(N)lim	(N)lim*	(N)ult	(E°)lim	E°ul/E°lr	<alph>E-6	<beta>
compon't 1	1.00	1.01	1.07	1.00	1.00	1.00	1.00	1.00
	<sq°>	<sq°>lm	<sq°>lm*	<sq°>ult	<ep°>E-3	<ep°>lm	<ep°>lm*	<ep°>ult
compon't 1	1.00	1.01	1.07	1.07	1.00	1.01	1.07	1.07
	T opr	c moist	vol/f	Em	Efx	Xm	Xfx	Em/Em°
[Modified]	22.0	0.005	0.70	3.40	259.	40.	2143.	0.20
Mod/Base	1.00	1.00	1.00	1.00	1.00	1.00	1.00	1.00

Stiffnesses remain unchanged because the laminate is elastically isotropic. But strengths change slightly because ply stresses and strains are no longer the same.

HyperComposites: §18 — SENSITIVITY OF SAFETY FACTOR — Changing from 1.5 to 3.0

INPUT

DOUBLING SAFETY FACTOR							
READ ME	Theta 1	Theta 2	Theta 3	Theta 4		Ply mat	T3/N52[SI]
[ply angle]	0.0	90.0	45.0	−45.0	[repeat]	h, *	h, E-3	[Rotate
[ply *]	1.00	1.00	1.00	1.00	1.00	1.00	1.00	0.00
R/intact	1.00	1.00	1.00	1.00	R/FPF	1.00	safety	2.00
R/degrade	1.00	1.00	1.00	1.00	R/LPF	1.00	R/lim*	0.50
					R/ult	1.00	R/lim	0.57
(N), MN/m or k/in	(N)lim	(N)lim*	(N)ult	(E°)lim	E°ul/E°lr	<alph>E-6	<beta>
compon't 1	1.00	0.57	0.50	1.00	1.00	1.00	1.00	1.00
	<sq°>	<sq°>lm	<sq°>lm*	<sq°>ult	<ep°>E-3	<ep°>lm	<ep°>lm*	<ep°>ult
compon't 1	1.00	0.57	0.50	1.00	1.00	0.52	0.45	1.00
	T opr	c moist	vol/f	Em	Efx	Xm	Xfx	Em/Em°
[Modified]	22.0	0.005	0.70	3.40	259.	40.	2143.	0.20
Mod/Base	1.00	1.00	1.00	1.00	1.00	1.00	1.00	1.00

Safety factor affects strength at limit and limit*, but not that at ultimate. The normalized strengths at limit and limit* are different but the absolute values are equal.

Ratios are relative to baseline values; cannot be compared with one another.

29.18 MIC–MAC (continued)

HyperComposites:§18 .... SENSITIVITY OF APPLIED LOAD .... 🏠
.... Changing tensile load by a factor of two ....

DOUBLING APPLIED UNIAXIAL LOAD

READ ME	Theta 1	Theta 2	Theta 3	Theta 4		Ply mat	T3/N52[SI]	
[ply angle]	0.0	90.0	45.0	-45.0	[repeat]	h, *	h, E-3	[Rotate]
[ply *]	1.00	1.00	1.00	1.00	1.00	1.00	1.00	0.00
R/intact	0.50	0.50	0.50	0.50	R/FPF	0.50	safety	1.00
R/degrade	0.50	0.50	0.50	0.50	R/LPF	0.50	R/lim*	0.50
					R/ult	0.50	R/lim	0.50
(N), MN/m or k/in	(N)lim	(N)lim*	(N)ult	(E°)lim	E~ul/E~lr	⟨alph⟩E-6	⟨beta⟩
compon't1	**2.00**	1.00	1.00	1.00	1.00	1.00	1.00	1.00
	⟨sg°⟩	⟨sg°⟩lm	⟨sg°⟩lm*	⟨sg°⟩ult	⟨ep°⟩E-3	⟨ep°⟩lm	⟨ep°⟩lm*	⟨ep°⟩ult
compon't1	2.00	1.00	1.00	1.00	2.00	1.00	1.00	1.00
	T opr	c,moist	vol/f	Em	Efx	Xm	Xfx	Em/Em°
[Modified]	22.0	0.005	0.70	3.40	259.	40.	2143.	0.20
Mod/Base	1.00	1.00	1.00	1.00	1.00	1.00	1.00	1.00

INPUT ⟶ compon't1

When load is doubled, the resulting stress and strain will double.
The strength ratios at limit, limit* and ultimate will be one half.
◁ Moduli, and stress and strain at failure remain the same. ⇨

Ratios are relative to baseline values; cannot be compared with one another.

HyperComposites:§18 .... SENSITIVITY OF OPERATING TEMPERATURE .... 🏠
.... Temperature increase from 22 to 88 ....

Changes in strengths due to temperature are all nonlinear. The
effects are different for different output. Do not try to guess.

QUADRUPLING OPERATING TEMPERATURE

READ ME	Theta 1	Theta 2	Theta 3	Theta 4		Ply mat	T3/N52[SI]	
[ply angle]	0.0	90.0	45.0	-45.0	[repeat]	h, *	h, E-3	[Rotate]
[ply *]	1.00	1.00	1.00	1.00	1.00	1.00	1.00	0.00
R/intact	1.03	1.00	0.82	0.82	R/FPF	0.97	safety	1.00
R/degrade	1.06	0.85	0.82	0.82	R/LPF	0.94	R/lim*	0.94
					R/ult	0.94	R/lim	0.97
(N), MN/m or k/in	(N)lim	(N)lim*	(N)ult	(E°)lim	E~ul/E~lr	⟨alph⟩E-6	⟨beta⟩
compon't1	1.00	0.97	0.94	0.94	0.98	1.01	0.89	0.89
	⟨sg°⟩	⟨sg°⟩lm	⟨sg°⟩lm*	⟨sg°⟩ult	⟨ep°⟩E-3	⟨ep°⟩lm	⟨ep°⟩lm*	⟨ep°⟩ult
compon't1	1.00	0.97	0.94	0.94	1.02	0.99	0.95	0.95
	T opr	c,moist	vol/f	Em	Efx	Xm	Xfx	Em/Em°
[Modified]	88.0	0.005	0.70	3.40	259	40.	2143	0.20
Mod/Base	4.00	1.00	1.00	1.00	1.00	1.00	1.00	1.00

◁   INPUT ⟶ [Modified]

⇨

Ratios are relative to baseline values; cannot be compared with one another.

29.18 MIC–MAC (continued)

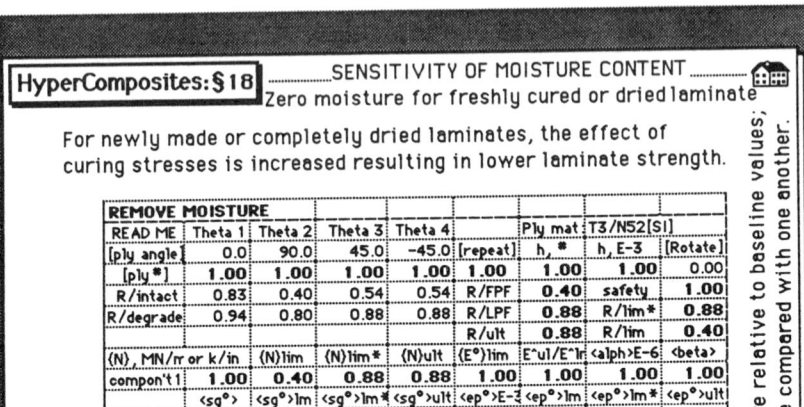

HyperComposites: §18 — SENSITIVITY OF MOISTURE CONTENT
Zero moisture for freshly cured or dried laminate

For newly made or completely dried laminates, the effect of
curing stresses is increased resulting in lower laminate strength.

Ratios are relative to baseline values;
cannot be compared with one another.

REMOVE MOISTURE								
READ ME	Theta 1	Theta 2	Theta 3	Theta 4		Ply mat	T3/N52[SI]	
[ply angle]	0.0	90.0	45.0	-45.0	[repeat]	h_*	h, E-3	[Rotate]
[ply *]	1.00	1.00	1.00	1.00	1.00	1.00	1.00	0.00
R/intact	0.83	0.40	0.54	0.54	R/FPF	0.40	safety	1.00
R/degrade	0.94	0.80	0.88	0.88	R/LPF	0.88	R/lim*	0.88
					R/ult	0.88	R/lim	0.40
(N), MN/π or k/in	(N)lim	(N)lim*	(N)ult	(E°)lim	E^ul/E^lr	<alph>E-6	<beta>	
compon't 1	1.00	0.40	0.88	0.88	1.00	1.00	1.00	1.00
	<sg°>	<sg°>lm	<sg°>lm*	<sg°>ult	<ep°>E-3	<ep°>lm	<ep°>lm*	<ep°>ult
compon't 1	1.00	0.40	0.88	0.88	1.00	0.39	0.88	0.88
	T opr	c moist	vol/f	Em	Efx	Xm	Xfx	Em/Em°
[Modified]	22.0	0.000	0.70	3.40	259.	40.	2143.	0.20
Mod/Base	1.00	0.00	1.00	1.00	1.00	1.00	1.00	1.00

INPUT

HyperComposites: §18 — SENSITIVITY OF FIBER VOLUME FRACTION
A reduction from 0.7 to 0.5, or 71 percent

All strengths are changed due to the change in fiber volume.
The thickness is increased to make up the lower fiber content.

Ratios are relative to baseline values;
cannot be compared with one another.

REDUCE FIBER VOLUME TO 50 PERCENT								
READ ME	Theta 1	Theta 2	Theta 3	Theta 4		Ply mat	T3/N52[SI]	
[ply angle]	0.0	90.0	45.0	-45.0	[repeat]	h_*	h, E-3	[Rotate]
[ply *]	1.00	1.00	1.00	1.00	1.00	1.00	1.40	0.00
R/intact	0.99	1.35	1.53	1.53	R/FPF	1.35	safety	1.00
R/degrade	0.97	1.20	1.29	1.29	R/LPF	0.97	R/lim*	0.97
					R/ult	0.97	R/lim	1.11
(N), MN/π or k/in	(N)lim	(N)lim*	(N)ult	(E°)lim	E^ul/E^lr	<alph>E-6	<beta>	
compon't 1	1.00	1.11	0.97	0.97	0.71	1.00	1.66	1.67
	<sg°>	<sg°>lm	<sg°>lm*	<sg°>ult	<ep°>E-3	<ep°>lm	<ep°>lm*	<ep°>ult
compon't 1	0.71	0.79	0.69	0.69	1.01	1.12	0.89	0.98
	T opr	c moist	vol/f	Em	Efx	Xm	Xfx	Em/Em°
[Modified]	22.0	0.005	0.50	3.40	259.	40.	2143.	0.20
Mod/Base	1.00	1.00	0.71	1.00	1.00	1.00	1.00	1.00

INPUT

29.19 MATERIAL MODIFIED

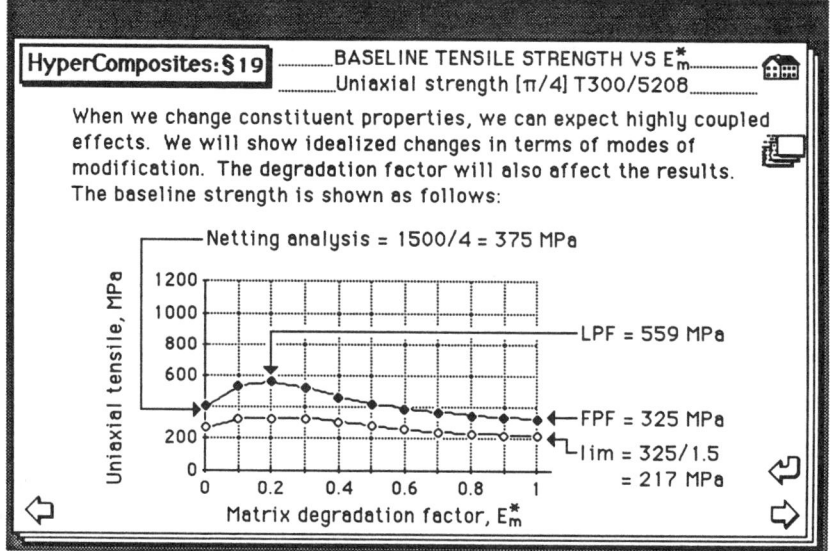

HyperComposites: §19 — BASELINE TENSILE STRENGTH VS E_m^*
Uniaxial strength [π/4] T300/5208

When we change constituent properties, we can expect highly coupled effects. We will show idealized changes in terms of modes of modification. The degradation factor will also affect the results. The baseline strength is shown as follows:

Netting analysis = 1500/4 = 375 MPa

LPF = 559 MPa
FPF = 325 MPa
lim = 325/1.5 = 217 MPa

Uniaxial tensile, MPa

Matrix degradation factor, E_m^*

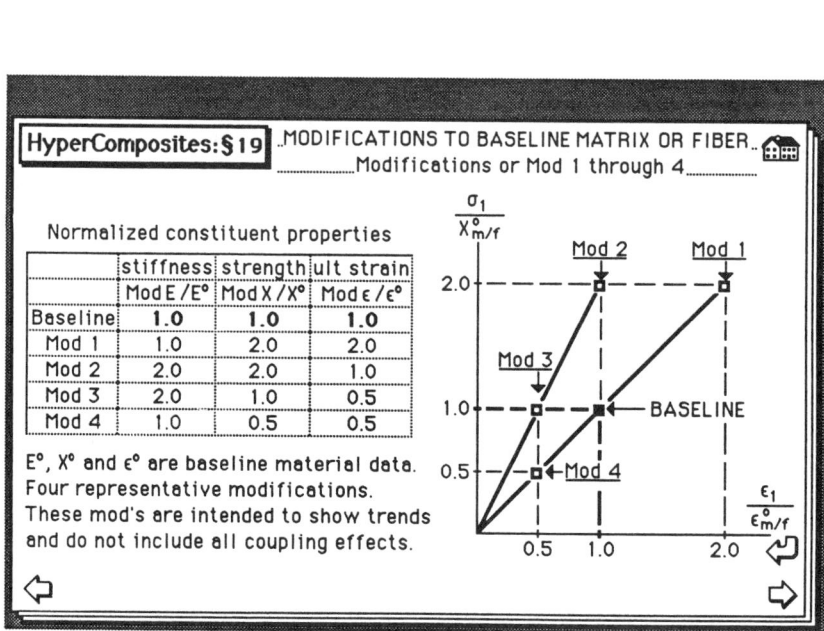

HyperComposites: §19 — MODIFICATIONS TO BASELINE MATRIX OR FIBER
Modifications or Mod 1 through 4

Normalized constituent properties

	stiffness	strength	ult strain
	Mod $E/E°$	Mod $X/X°$	Mod $\epsilon/\epsilon°$
Baseline	1.0	1.0	1.0
Mod 1	1.0	2.0	2.0
Mod 2	2.0	2.0	1.0
Mod 3	2.0	1.0	0.5
Mod 4	1.0	0.5	0.5

$E°$, $X°$ and $\epsilon°$ are baseline material data.
Four representative modifications.
These mod's are intended to show trends
and do not include all coupling effects.

$\frac{\sigma_1}{X_{m/f}^°}$

Mod 2   Mod 1
Mod 3
BASELINE
Mod 4

$\frac{\epsilon_1}{\epsilon_{m/f}^°}$

29.19 MATERIAL MODIFIED (continued)

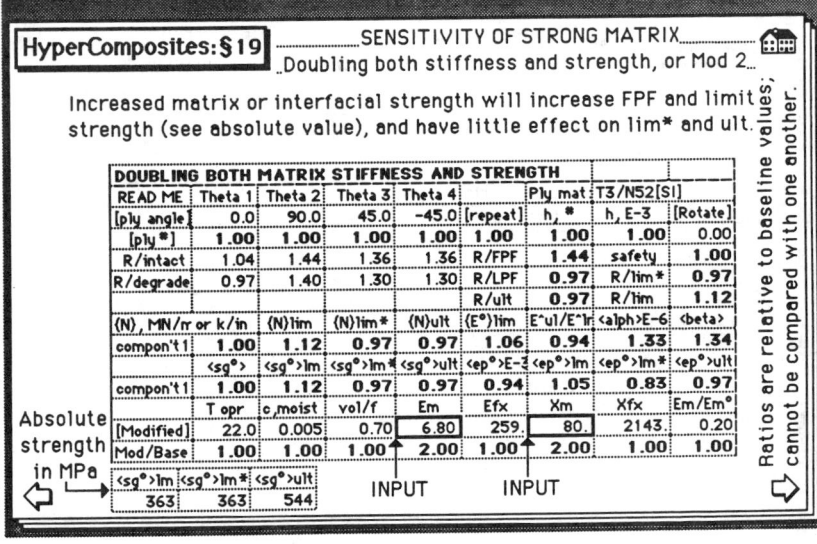

HyperComposites: §19 ....SENSITIVITY OF MATRIX STRENGTH...........
....Changing strength from 40 to 80, or Mod 1....

Increase in matrix strength with the same stiffness will suppress matrix/interfacial failure, with small change in laminate strength.

Ratios are relative to baseline values; cannot be compared with one another.

DOUBLING MATRIX STRENGTH

READ ME	Theta 1	Theta 2	Theta 3	Theta 4		Ply mat	T3/N52[SI]	
[ply angle]	0.0	90.0	45.0	−45.0	[repeat]	h, *	h, E-3	[Rotate]
[ply *]	1.00	1.00	1.00	1.00	1.00	1.00	1.00	0.00
R/intact	0.98	1.71	1.79	1.79	R/FPF	1.71	safety	1.00
R/degrade	0.97	1.39	1.30	1.30	R/LPF	0.97	R/lim*	0.99
					R/ult	0.99	R/lim	1.14
(N), MN/m or k/in	(N)lim	(N)lim*	(N)ult	(E°)lim	E¯ul/E¯lr	⟨alph⟩E-6	⟨beta⟩	
compon't 1	1.00	1.14	0.99	0.99	1.00	1.00	1.00	1.00
	⟨sg°⟩	⟨sg°⟩lm	⟨sg°⟩lm*	⟨sg°⟩ult	⟨ep°⟩E-3	⟨ep°⟩lm	⟨ep°⟩lm*	⟨ep°⟩ult
compon't 1	1.00	1.14	0.99	0.99	1.00	1.14	0.90	0.99
	T opr	c,moist	vol/f	Em	Efx	Xm	Xfx	Em/Em°
[Modified]	22.0	0.005	0.70	3.40	259.	80.	2143.	0.20
Mod/Base	1.00	1.00	1.00	1.00	1.00	2.00	1.00	1.00
⟨sg°⟩lm	⟨sg°⟩lm*	⟨sg°⟩ult			INPUT			
371	371	556						

Absolute strength in MPa

HyperComposites: §19 ....SENSITIVITY OF STRONG MATRIX...........
.Doubling both stiffness and strength, or Mod 2..

Increased matrix or interfacial strength will increase FPF and limit strength (see absolute value), and have little effect on lim* and ult.

Ratios are relative to baseline values; cannot be compared with one another.

DOUBLING BOTH MATRIX STIFFNESS AND STRENGTH

READ ME	Theta 1	Theta 2	Theta 3	Theta 4		Ply mat	T3/N52[SI]	
[ply angle]	0.0	90.0	45.0	−45.0	[repeat]	h, *	h, E-3	[Rotate]
[ply *]	1.00	1.00	1.00	1.00	1.00	1.00	1.00	0.00
R/intact	1.04	1.44	1.36	1.36	R/FPF	1.44	safety	1.00
R/degrade	0.97	1.40	1.30	1.30	R/LPF	0.97	R/lim*	0.97
					R/ult	0.97	R/lim	1.12
(N), MN/m or k/in	(N)lim	(N)lim*	(N)ult	(E°)lim	E¯ul/E¯lr	⟨alph⟩E-6	⟨beta⟩	
compon't 1	1.00	1.12	0.97	0.97	1.06	0.94	1.33	1.34
	⟨sg°⟩	⟨sg°⟩lm	⟨sg°⟩lm*	⟨sg°⟩ult	⟨ep°⟩E-3	⟨ep°⟩lm	⟨ep°⟩lm*	⟨ep°⟩ult
compon't 1	1.00	1.12	0.97	0.97	0.94	1.05	0.83	0.97
	T opr	c,moist	vol/f	Em	Efx	Xm	Xfx	Em/Em°
[Modified]	22.0	0.005	0.70	6.80	259.	80.	2143.	0.20
Mod/Base	1.00	1.00	1.00	2.00	1.00	2.00	1.00	1.00
⟨sg°⟩lm	⟨sg°⟩lm*	⟨sg°⟩ult		INPUT		INPUT		
363	363	544						

Absolute strength in MPa

29.19 MATERIAL MODIFIED (continued)

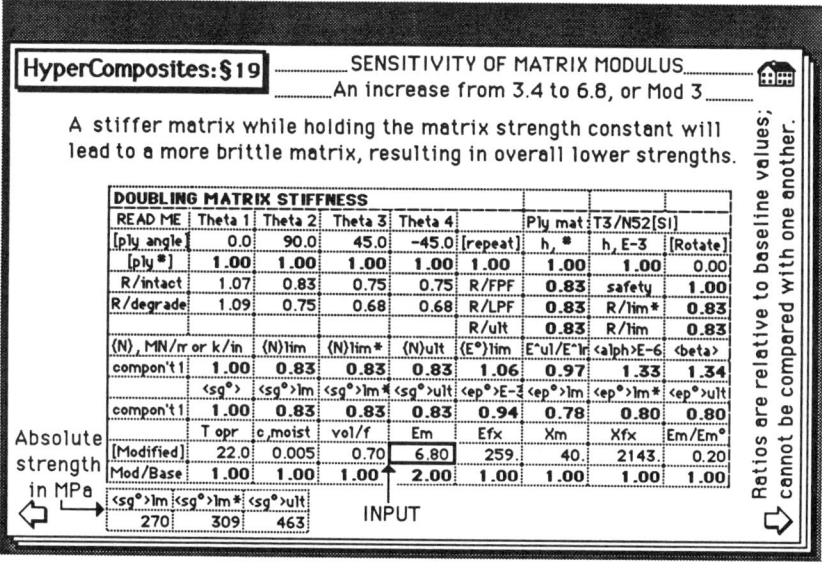

HyperComposites: §19 ....SENSITIVITY OF MATRIX MODULUS.............
............An increase from 3.4 to 6.8, or Mod 3.........

A stiffer matrix while holding the matrix strength constant will lead to a more brittle matrix, resulting in overall lower strengths.

Ratios are relative to baseline values; cannot be compared with one another.

DOUBLING MATRIX STIFFNESS								
READ ME	Theta 1	Theta 2	Theta 3	Theta 4		Ply mat	T3/N52[SI]	
[ply angle]	0.0	90.0	45.0	−45.0	[repeat]	h, #	h, E-3	[Rotate]
[ply #]	1.00	1.00	1.00	1.00	1.00	1.00	1.00	0.00
R/intact	1.07	0.83	0.75	0.75	R/FPF	0.83	safety	1.00
R/degrade	1.09	0.75	0.68	0.68	R/LPF	0.83	R/lim*	0.83
					R/ult	0.83	R/lim	0.83
(N), MN/π or k/in	(N)lim	(N)lim*	(N)ult	(E°)lim	E˜ul/E˜lr	⟨alph⟩E-6	⟨beta⟩
compon't 1	1.00	0.83	0.83	0.83	1.06	0.97	1.33	1.34
	⟨sq°⟩	⟨sq°⟩lm	⟨sq°⟩lm*	⟨sq°⟩ult	⟨ep°⟩E-3	⟨ep°⟩lm	⟨ep°⟩lm*	⟨ep°⟩ult
compon't 1	1.00	0.83	0.83	0.83	0.94	0.78	0.80	0.80
	T opr	c,moist	vol/f	Em	Efx	Xm	Xfx	Em/Em°
[Modified]	22.0	0.005	0.70	**6.80**	259.	40.	2143.	0.20
Mod/Base	1.00	1.00	1.00	2.00	1.00	1.00	1.00	1.00
⟨sq°⟩lm	⟨sq°⟩lm*	⟨sq°⟩ult		INPUT				
270	309	463						

Absolute strength in MPa

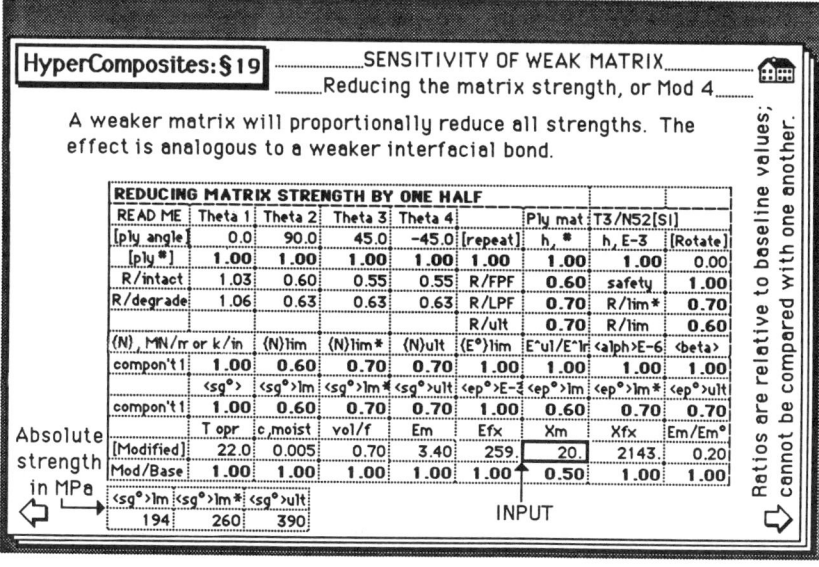

HyperComposites: §19 ....SENSITIVITY OF WEAK MATRIX............
............Reducing the matrix strength, or Mod 4.........

A weaker matrix will proportionally reduce all strengths. The effect is analogous to a weaker interfacial bond.

Ratios are relative to baseline values; cannot be compared with one another.

REDUCING MATRIX STRENGTH BY ONE HALF								
READ ME	Theta 1	Theta 2	Theta 3	Theta 4		Ply mat	T3/N52[SI]	
[ply angle]	0.0	90.0	45.0	−45.0	[repeat]	h, #	h, E-3	[Rotate]
[ply #]	1.00	1.00	1.00	1.00	1.00	1.00	1.00	0.00
R/intact	1.03	0.60	0.55	0.55	R/FPF	0.60	safety	1.00
R/degrade	1.06	0.63	0.63	0.63	R/LPF	0.70	R/lim*	0.70
					R/ult	0.70	R/lim	0.60
(N), MN/π or k/in	(N)lim	(N)lim*	(N)ult	(E°)lim	E˜ul/E˜lr	⟨alph⟩E-6	⟨beta⟩
compon't 1	1.00	0.60	0.70	0.70	1.00	1.00	1.00	1.00
	⟨sq°⟩	⟨sq°⟩lm	⟨sq°⟩lm*	⟨sq°⟩ult	⟨ep°⟩E-3	⟨ep°⟩lm	⟨ep°⟩lm*	⟨ep°⟩ult
compon't 1	1.00	0.60	0.70	0.70	1.00	0.60	0.70	0.70
	T opr	c,moist	vol/f	Em	Efx	Xm	Xfx	Em/Em°
[Modified]	22.0	0.005	0.70	3.40	259.	**20.**	2143.	0.20
Mod/Base	1.00	1.00	1.00	1.00	1.00	0.50	1.00	1.00
⟨sq°⟩lm	⟨sq°⟩lm*	⟨sq°⟩ult		INPUT				
194	260	390						

Absolute strength in MPa

29.19 MATERIAL MODIFIED (continued)

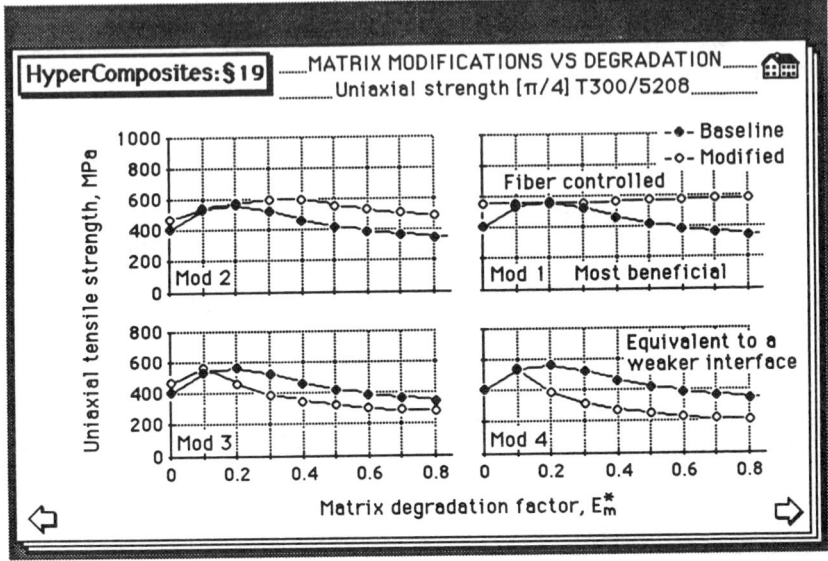

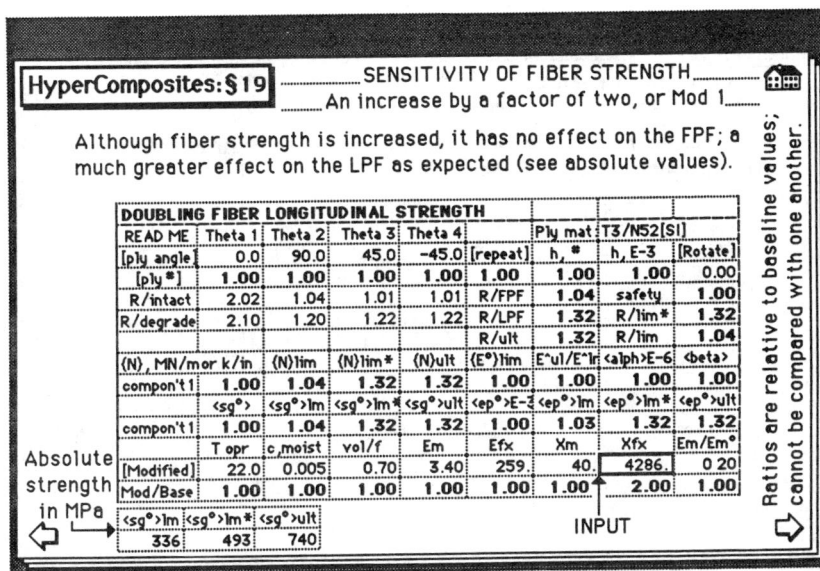

29.19 MATERIAL MODIFIED (continued)

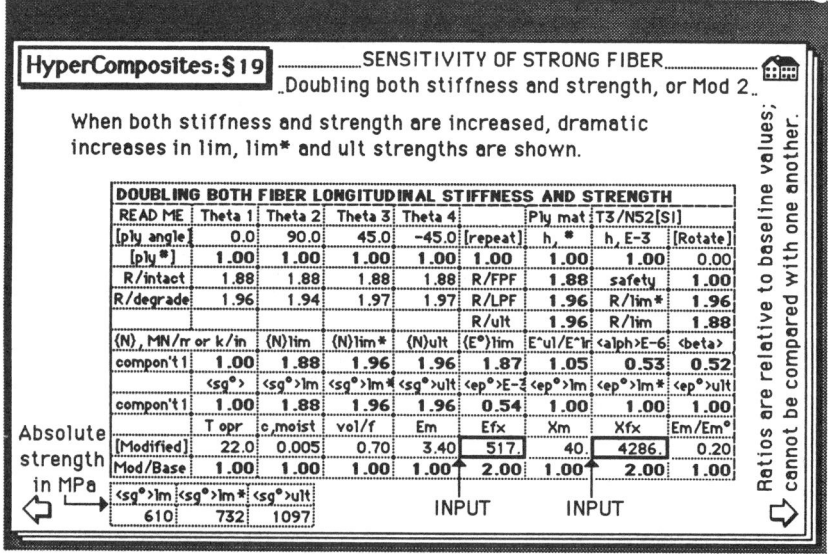

HyperComposites:§19 _____ SENSITIVITY OF STRONG FIBER _____
Doubling both stiffness and strength, or Mod 2.

When both stiffness and strength are increased, dramatic increases in lim, lim* and ult strengths are shown.

DOUBLING BOTH FIBER LONGITUDINAL STIFFNESS AND STRENGTH

READ ME	Theta 1	Theta 2	Theta 3	Theta 4		Ply mat	T3/N52[SI]	
[ply angle]	0.0	90.0	45.0	-45.0	[repeat]	h, *	h, E-3	[Rotate]
[ply*]	1.00	1.00	1.00	1.00	1.00	1.00	1.00	0.00
R/intact	1.88	1.88	1.88	1.88	R/FPF	1.88	safety	1.00
R/degrade	1.96	1.94	1.97	1.97	R/LPF	1.96	R/lim*	1.96
					R/ult	1.96	R/lim	1.88

(N), MN/m or k/in	(N)lim	(N)lim*	(N)ult	(E°)lim	E^ul/E^lr	<alph>E-6	<beta>
compon't 1	1.00	1.88	1.96	1.96	1.87	1.05	0.53	0.52
	<sg°>	<sg°>lm	<sg°>lm*	<sg°>ult	<ep°>E-3	<ep°>lm	<ep°>lm*	<ep°>ult
compon't 1	1.00	1.88	1.96	1.96	0.54	1.00	1.00	1.00

	T opr	c,moist	vol/f	Em	Efx	Xm	Xfx	Em/Em°
[Modified]	22.0	0.005	0.70	3.40	517.	40.	4286.	0.20
Mod/Base	1.00	1.00	1.00	1.00	2.00	1.00	2.00	1.00

<sg°>lm	<sg°>lm*	<sg°>ult
610	732	1097

INPUT   INPUT

Absolute strength in MPa

Ratios are relative to baseline values; cannot be compared with one another.

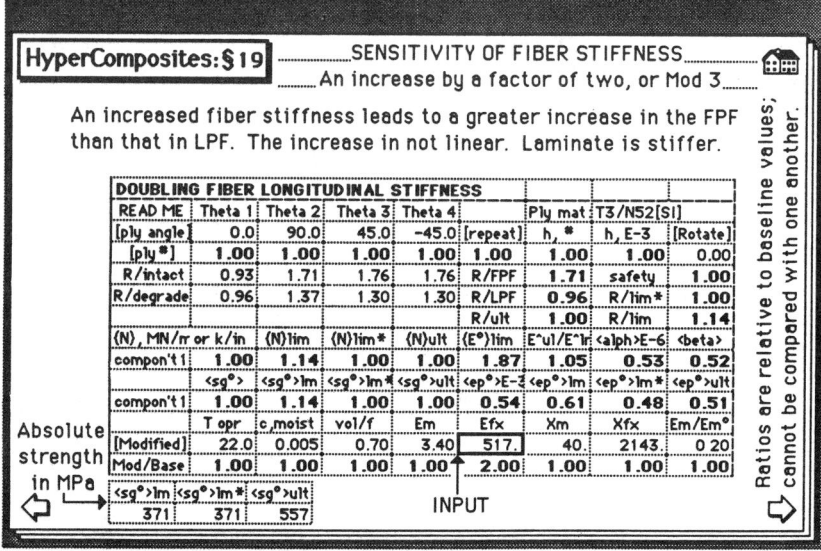

HyperComposites:§19 _____ SENSITIVITY OF FIBER STIFFNESS _____
An increase by a factor of two, or Mod 3

An increased fiber stiffness leads to a greater increase in the FPF than that in LPF. The increase in not linear. Laminate is stiffer.

DOUBLING FIBER LONGITUDINAL STIFFNESS

READ ME	Theta 1	Theta 2	Theta 3	Theta 4		Ply mat	T3/N52[SI]	
[ply angle]	0.0	90.0	45.0	-45.0	[repeat]	h, *	h, E-3	[Rotate]
[ply*]	1.00	1.00	1.00	1.00	1.00	1.00	1.00	0.00
R/intact	0.93	1.71	1.76	1.76	R/FPF	1.71	safety	1.00
R/degrade	0.96	1.37	1.30	1.30	R/LPF	0.96	R/lim*	1.00
					R/ult	1.00	R/lim	1.14

(N), MN/m or k/in	(N)lim	(N)lim*	(N)ult	(E°)lim	E^ul/E^lr	<alph>E-6	<beta>
compon't 1	1.00	1.14	1.00	1.00	1.87	1.05	0.53	0.52
	<sg°>	<sg°>lm	<sg°>lm*	<sg°>ult	<ep°>E-3	<ep°>lm	<ep°>lm*	<ep°>ult
compon't 1	1.00	1.14	1.00	1.00	0.54	0.61	0.48	0.51

	T opr	c,moist	vol/f	Em	Efx	Xm	Xfx	Em/Em°
[Modified]	22.0	0.005	0.70	3.40	517.	40.	2143.	0.20
Mod/Base	1.00	1.00	1.00	1.00	2.00	1.00	1.00	1.00

<sg°>lm	<sg°>lm*	<sg°>ult
371	371	557

INPUT

Absolute strength in MPa

Ratios are relative to baseline values; cannot be compared with one another.

29.19 MATERIAL MODIFIED (continued)

HyperComposites:§19   SENSITIVITY OF WEAK FIBER
..........Reducing fiber strength of one half, or Mod 4....

Having a lower strength fiber drastically reduced lim, lim* and ult strengths. This is clearly shown in the reduced absolute values.

Ratios are relative to baseline values; cannot be compared with one another.

REDUCING FIBER LONGITUDINAL STRENGTH BY ONE HALF									
READ ME	Theta 1	Theta 2	Theta 3	Theta 4		Ply mat	T3/N52[SI]		
[ply angle]	0.0	90.0	45.0	–45.0	[repeat]	h, *	h, E-3	[Rotate]	
[ply*]	1.00	1.00	1.00	1.00	1.00	1.00	1.00	0.00	
R/intact	0.50	0.92	0.93	0.93	R/FPF	0.91	safety	1.00	
R/degrade	0.49	0.71	0.66	0.66	R/LPF	0.49	R/lim*	0.53	
					R/ult	0.53	R/lim	0.61	
(N), MN/r or k/in	(N)lim	(N)lim*	(N)ult	(E°)lim	E°ul/E°lr	\<alph\>E-6	\<beta\>		
compon't 1	1.00	0.61	0.53	0.53	1.00	1.00	1.00	1.00	
	\<sq°\>	\<sq°\>lm	\<sq°\>lm*	\<sq°\>ult	\<ep°\>E-3	\<ep°\>lm	\<ep°\>lm*	\<ep°\>ult	
compon't 1	1.00	0.61	0.53	0.53	1.00	0.61	0.48	0.53	
	T opr	c,moist	vol/f	Em	Efx	Xm	Xfx	Em/Em°	
[Modified]	22.0	0.005	0.70	3.40	259.	40.	1071.	0.20	
Mod/Base	1.00	1.00	1.00	1.00	1.00	1.00	0.50	1.00	
\<sq°\>lm	\<sq°\>lm*	\<sq°\>ult							
198	198	297							

Absolute strength in MPa

INPUT

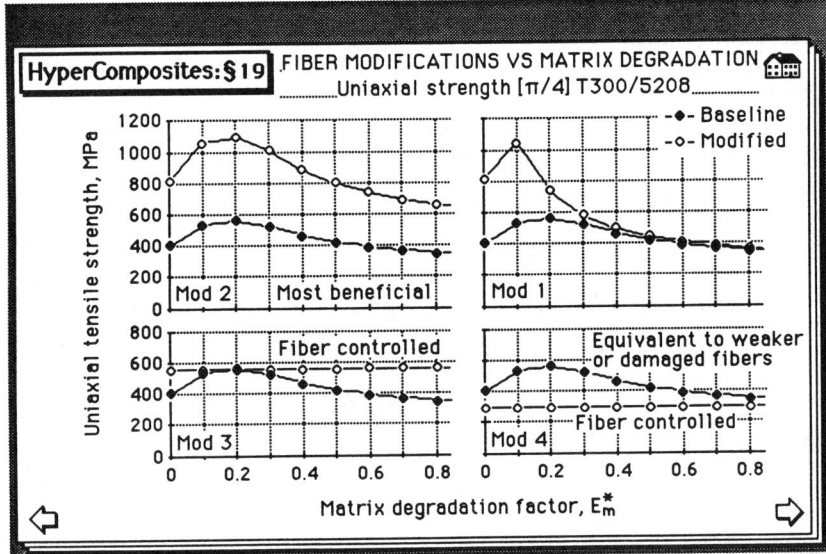

HyperComposites:§19 FIBER MODIFICATIONS VS MATRIX DEGRADATION
..........Uniaxial strength [π/4] T300/5208..........

-•- Baseline
-o- Modified

Uniaxial tensile strength, MPa

Mod 2   Most beneficial

Mod 1

Mod 3   Fiber controlled

Mod 4   Equivalent to weaker or damaged fibers   Fiber controlled

Matrix degradation factor, E_m^*

29.20 LAMINATE DESIGN

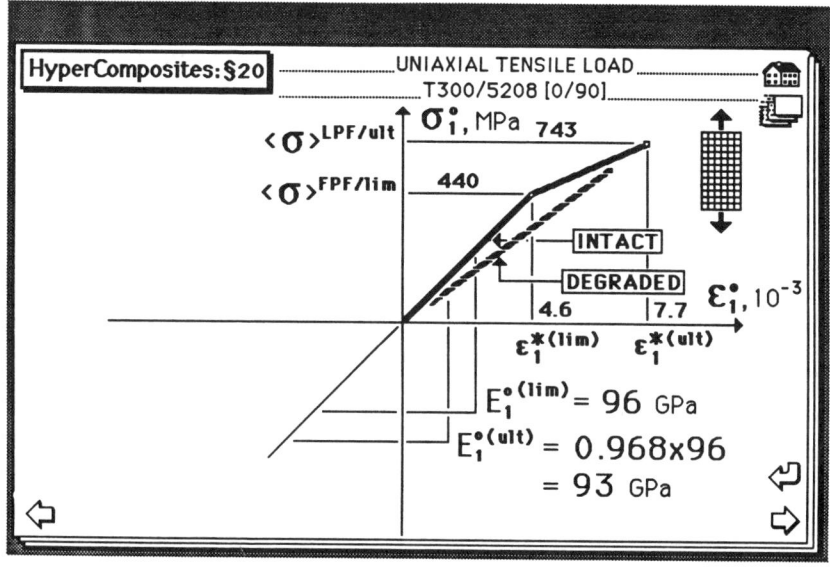

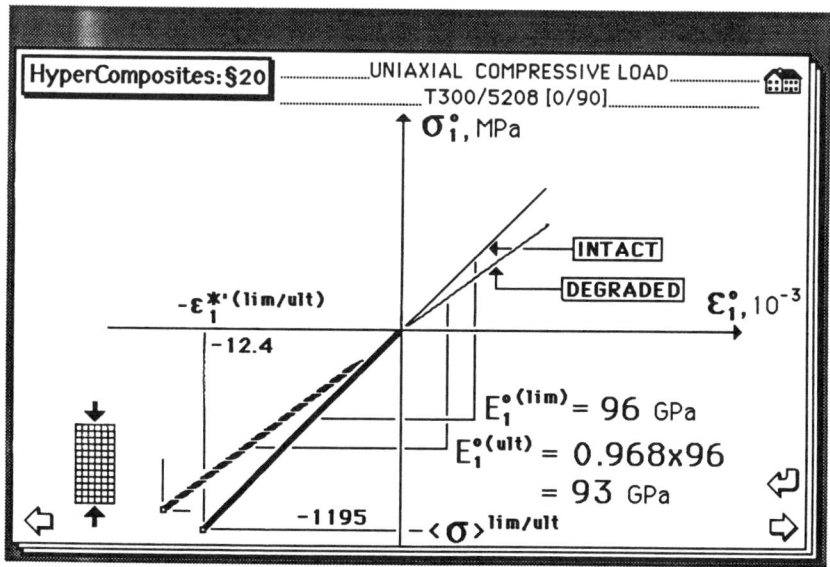

29.20 LAMINATE DESIGN (continued)

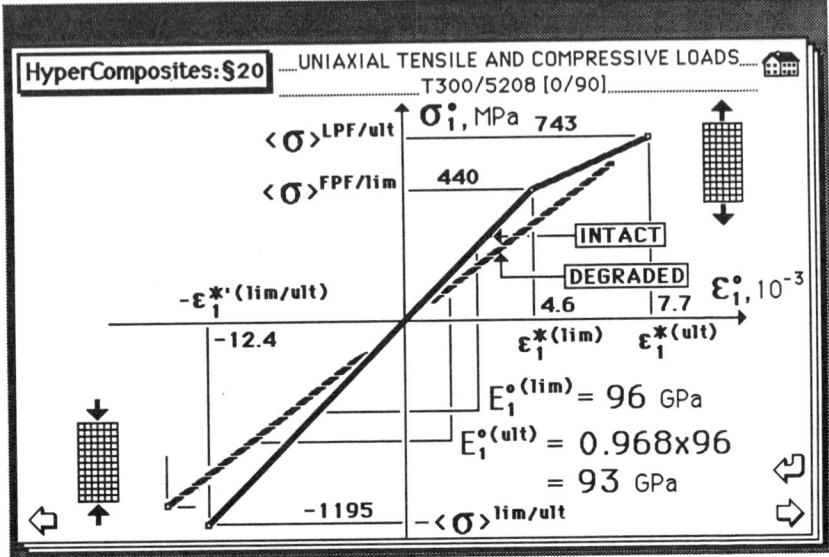

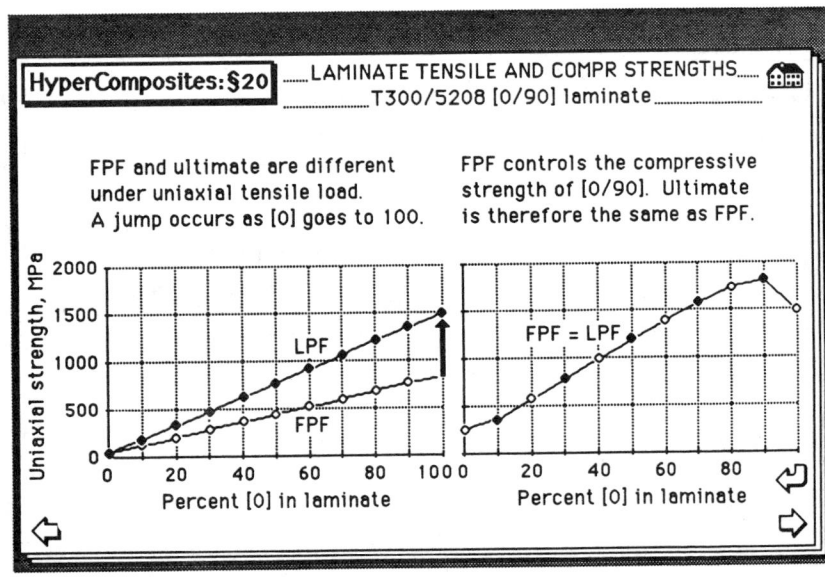

29.20 LAMINATE DESIGN (continued)

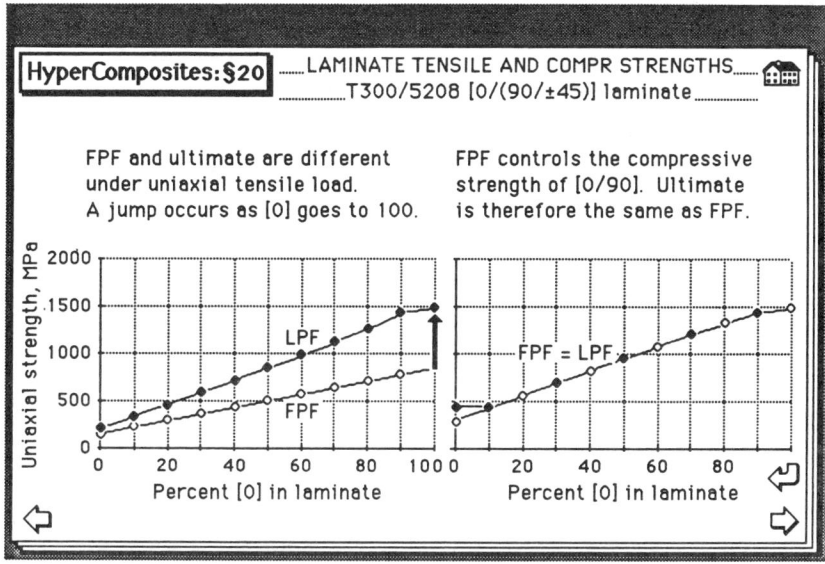

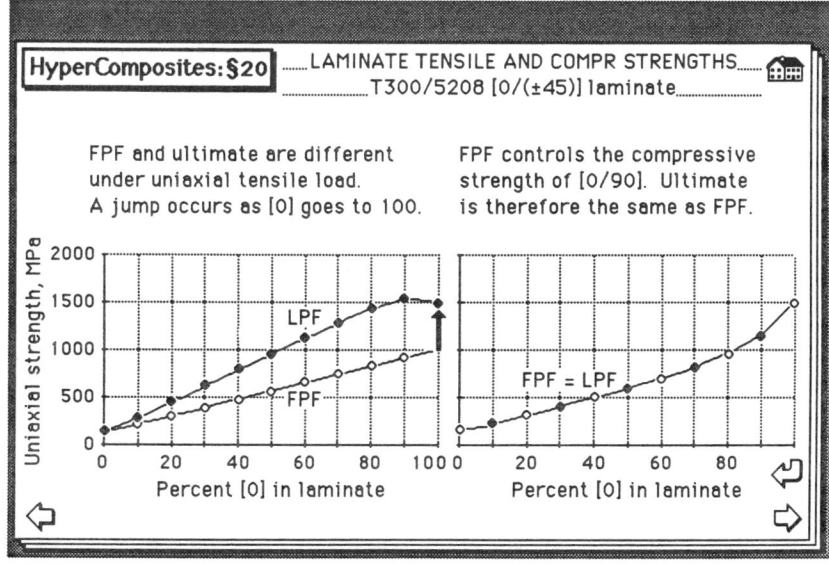

29.20 LAMINATE DESIGN (continued)

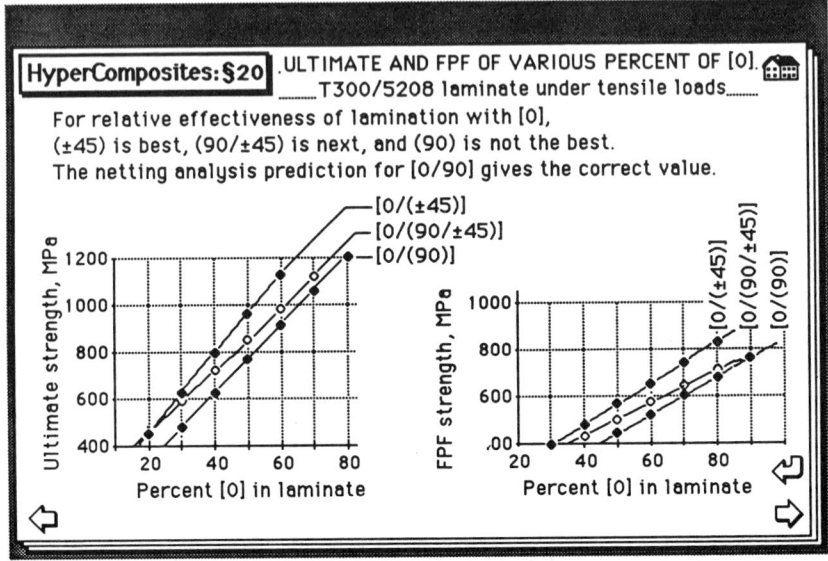

HyperComposites: §20 ULTIMATE AND FPF OF VARIOUS PERCENT OF [0].
T300/5208 laminate under tensile loads

For relative effectiveness of lamination with [0],
(±45) is best, (90/±45) is next, and (90) is not the best.
The netting analysis prediction for [0/90] gives the correct value.

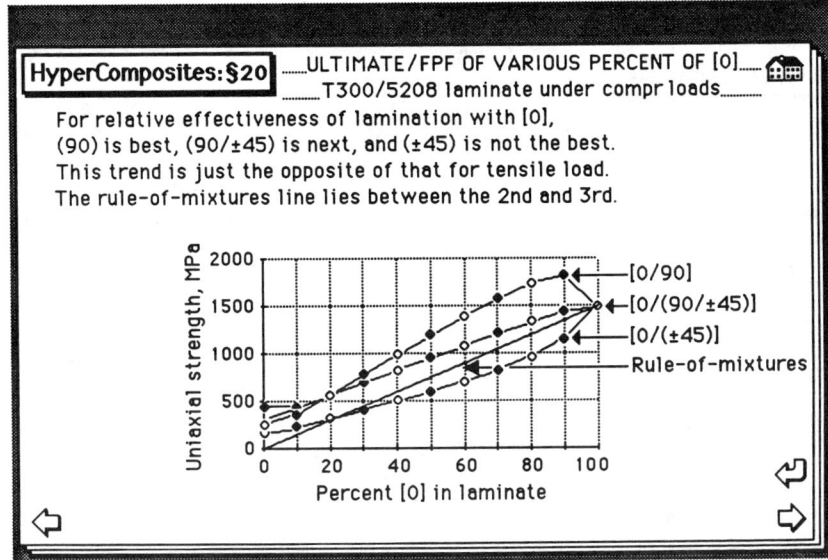

HyperComposites: §20 ULTIMATE/FPF OF VARIOUS PERCENT OF [0].
T300/5208 laminate under compr loads

For relative effectiveness of lamination with [0],
(90) is best, (90/±45) is next, and (±45) is not the best.
This trend is just the opposite of that for tensile load.
The rule-of-mixtures line lies between the 2nd and 3rd.

29.21 LAMRANK

HyperComposites: §21   ....LAMINATE RANKING METHOD..........
..........An effective laminate design procedure..........

Ranking of all memebers of each laminate family.

A family is defined by the number of ply angles, and
and the number of plies in the sub-laminate; see table:

Number of Plies	Family of 2 orientations	Family of 3 orientations	Family of 4 orientations	
2	3	6	10	
3	4	10	20	
4	5	15	35	
5	6	21	56	
6	7	28	84	
7	8	36	120	
8	9	45	165	
9	10	55	220	
10	11	66	286	Grand total
Total	65	285	1000	1350

Ranking can be based on FPF, limit, limit*, or ultimate.

HyperComposites: §21   ....STACKING SEQUENCE DEPENDENCE VS REPEAT....
..........LamRank is applicable for flex if r is high..........

LamRank is limited to in-plane stresses only. When applied to flexure,
the error is equal to the degree of homogenization of the laminate; i.e.,
the values of the normalized flex stiffness that deviate from unity. For
10 percent error, use $r > 6$; for 5 percent, $r > 10$.

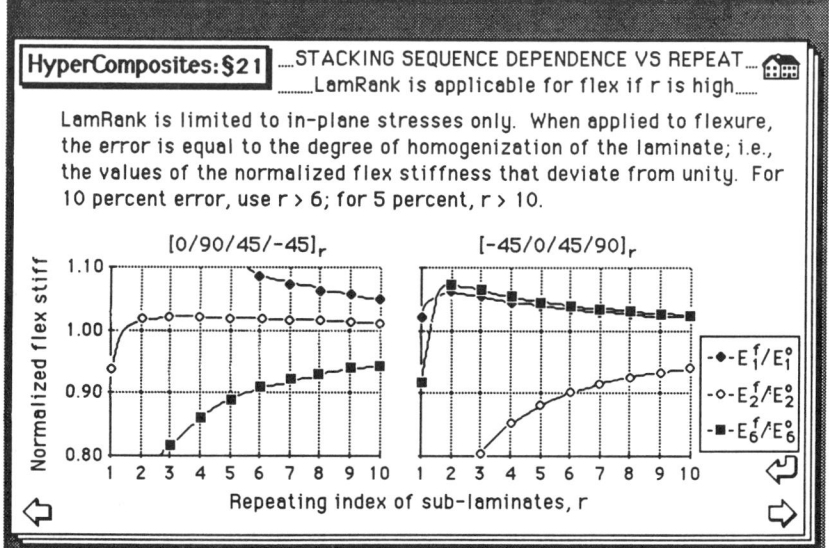

$[0/90/45/-45]_r$ $[-45/0/45/90]_r$

Normalized flex stiff

Repeating index of sub-laminates, r

- ◆ - E_1^f/E_1^o
- ○ - E_2^f/E_2^o
- ■ - E_6^f/E_6^o

29.21 LAMRANK (continued)

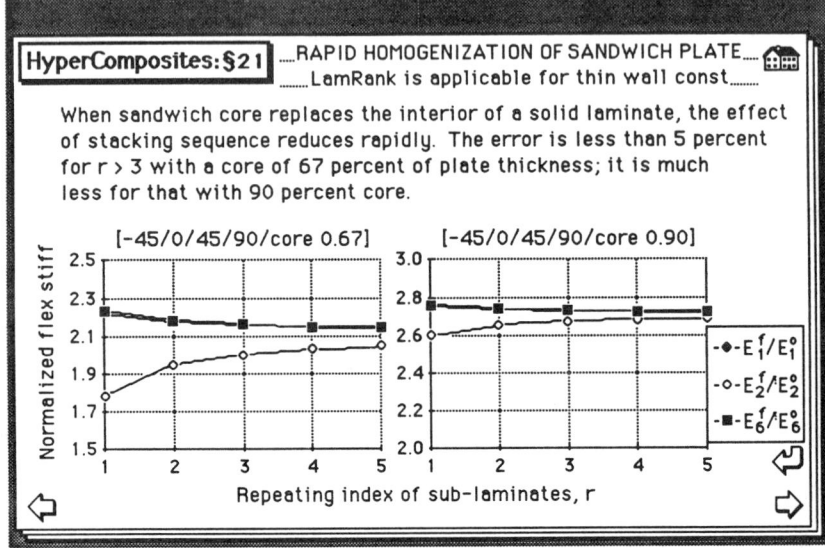

HyperComposites:§21   ......RAPID HOMOGENIZATION OF SANDWICH PLATE......
      ......LamRank is applicable for thin wall const......

When sandwich core replaces the interior of a solid laminate, the effect of stacking sequence reduces rapidly. The error is less than 5 percent for r > 3 with a core of 67 percent of plate thickness; it is much less for that with 90 percent core.

[-45/0/45/90/core 0.67]   [-45/0/45/90/core 0.90]

Normalized flex stiff

Repeating index of sub-laminates, r

$-\bullet-E_1^f/E_1^o$
$-\circ-E_2^f/E_2^o$
$-\blacksquare-E_6^f/E_6^o$

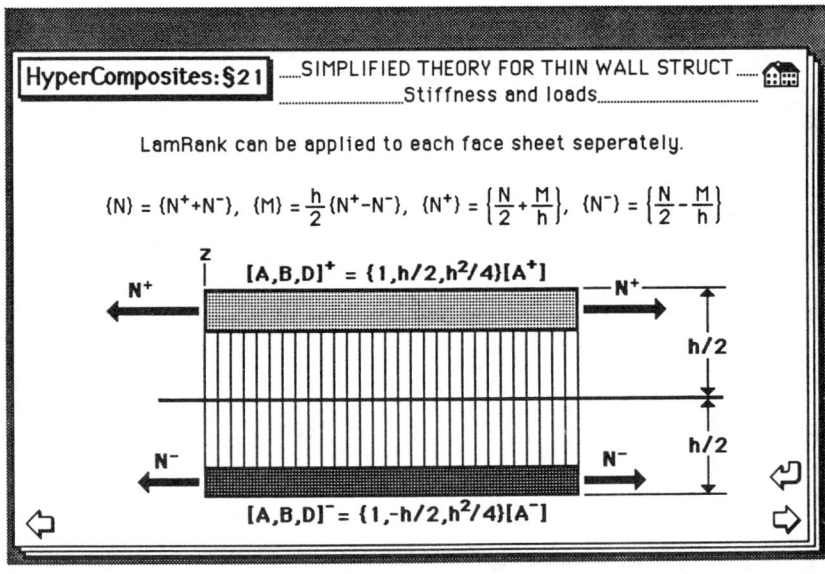

HyperComposites:§21   ......SIMPLIFIED THEORY FOR THIN WALL STRUCT ......
      ......Stiffness and loads......

LamRank can be applied to each face sheet seperately.

$$\{N\} = \{N^+ + N^-\}, \quad \{M\} = \frac{h}{2}\{N^+ - N^-\}, \quad \{N^+\} = \left\{\frac{N}{2} + \frac{M}{h}\right\}, \quad \{N^-\} = \left\{\frac{N}{2} - \frac{M}{h}\right\}$$

$$[A,B,D]^+ = \{1, h/2, h^2/4\}[A^+]$$

N^+ N^+

$h/2$

$h/2$

N^- N^-

$$[A,B,D]^- = \{1, -h/2, h^2/4\}[A^-]$$

29.21 LAMRANK (continued)

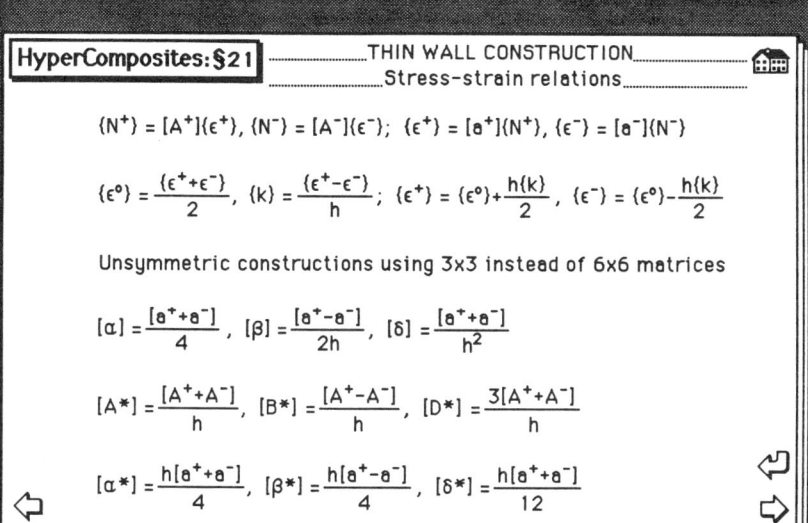

HyperComposites:§21 ....THIN WALL CONSTRUCTION........
........Stress-strain relations........

$$\{N^+\} = [A^+]\{\epsilon^+\}, \ \{N^-\} = [A^-]\{\epsilon^-\}; \ \{\epsilon^+\} = [a^+]\{N^+\}, \ \{\epsilon^-\} = [a^-]\{N^-\}$$

$$\{\epsilon^\circ\} = \frac{\{\epsilon^+ + \epsilon^-\}}{2}, \ \{k\} = \frac{\{\epsilon^+ - \epsilon^-\}}{h}; \ \{\epsilon^+\} = \{\epsilon^\circ\} + \frac{h\{k\}}{2}, \ \{\epsilon^-\} = \{\epsilon^\circ\} - \frac{h\{k\}}{2}$$

Unsymmetric constructions using 3x3 instead of 6x6 matrices

$$[\alpha] = \frac{[a^+ + a^-]}{4}, \ [\beta] = \frac{[a^+ - a^-]}{2h}, \ [\delta] = \frac{[a^+ + a^-]}{h^2}$$

$$[A^*] = \frac{[A^+ + A^-]}{h}, \ [B^*] = \frac{[A^+ - A^-]}{h}, \ [D^*] = \frac{3[A^+ + A^-]}{h}$$

$$[\alpha^*] = \frac{h[a^+ + a^-]}{4}, \ [\beta^*] = \frac{h[a^+ - a^-]}{4}, \ [\delta^*] = \frac{h[a^+ + a^-]}{12}$$

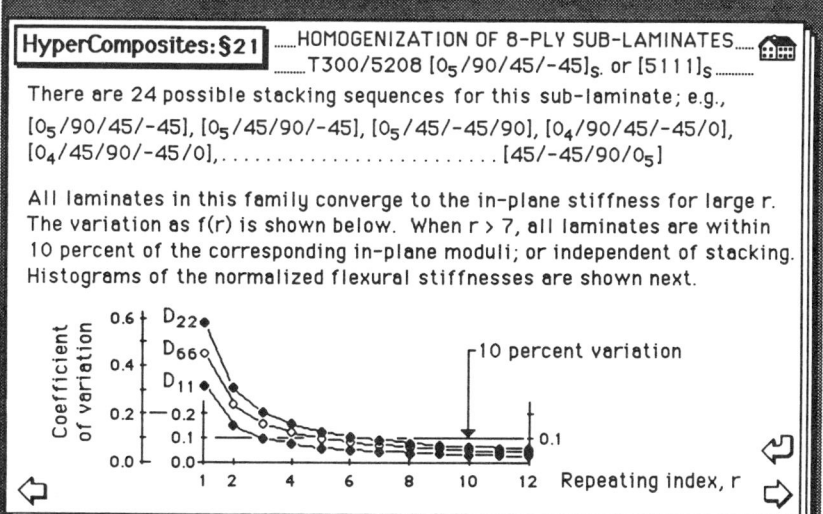

HyperComposites:§21 ........HOMOGENIZATION OF 8-PLY SUB-LAMINATES........
........T300/5208 $[0_5/90/45/-45]_s$. or $[5111]_s$........

There are 24 possible stacking sequences for this sub-laminate; e.g.,
$[0_5/90/45/-45]$, $[0_5/45/90/-45]$, $[0_5/45/-45/90]$, $[0_4/90/45/-45/0]$,
$[0_4/45/90/-45/0]$,........................ $[45/-45/90/0_5]$

All laminates in this family converge to the in-plane stiffness for large r.
The variation as f(r) is shown below. When r > 7, all laminates are within
10 percent of the corresponding in-plane moduli; or independent of stacking.
Histograms of the normalized flexural stiffnesses are shown next.

29.21 LAMRANK (continued)

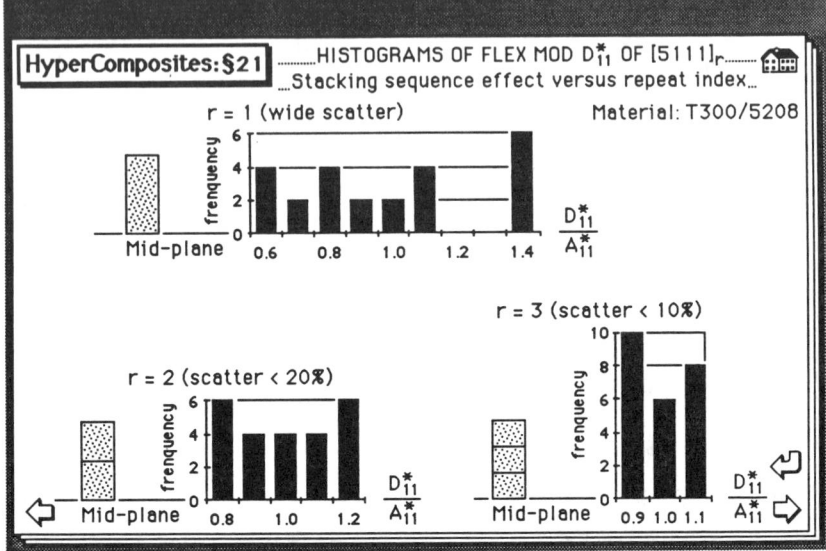

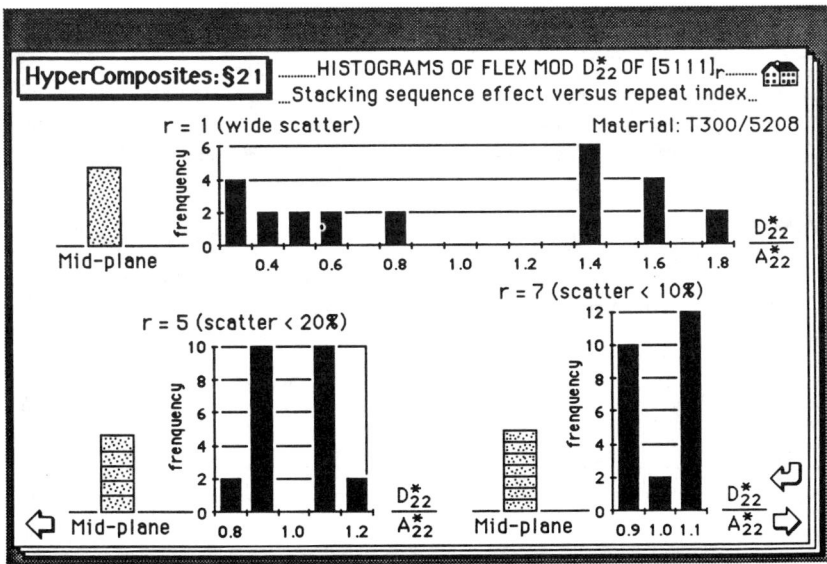

29.21 LAMRANK (continued)

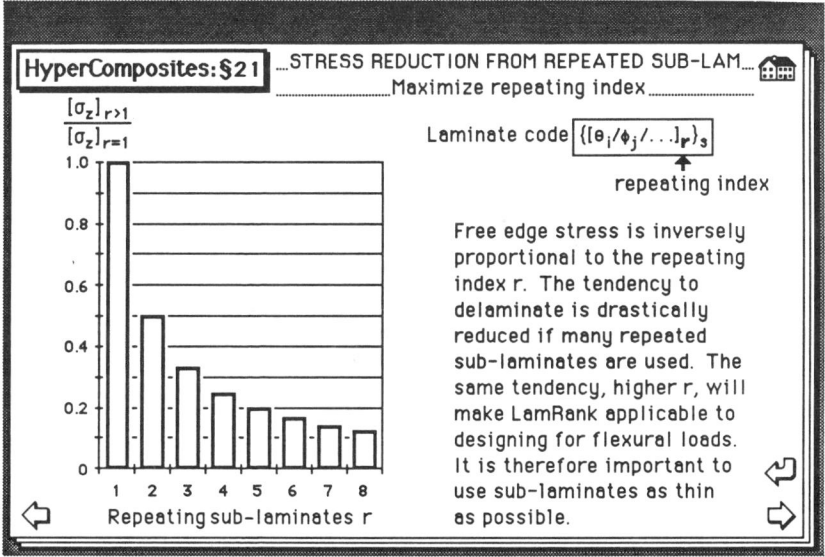

HyperComposites: §21 — STRESS REDUCTION FROM REPEATED SUB-LAM.
Maximize repeating index

$$\frac{[\sigma_z]_{r>1}}{[\sigma_z]_{r=1}}$$

Laminate code $\{[\theta_i/\phi_j/\dots]_r\}_s$

↑ repeating index

Free edge stress is inversely proportional to the repeating index r. The tendency to delaminate is drastically reduced if many repeated sub-laminates are used. The same tendency, higher r, will make LamRank applicable to designing for flexural loads. It is therefore important to use sub-laminates as thin as possible.

Repeating sub-laminates r

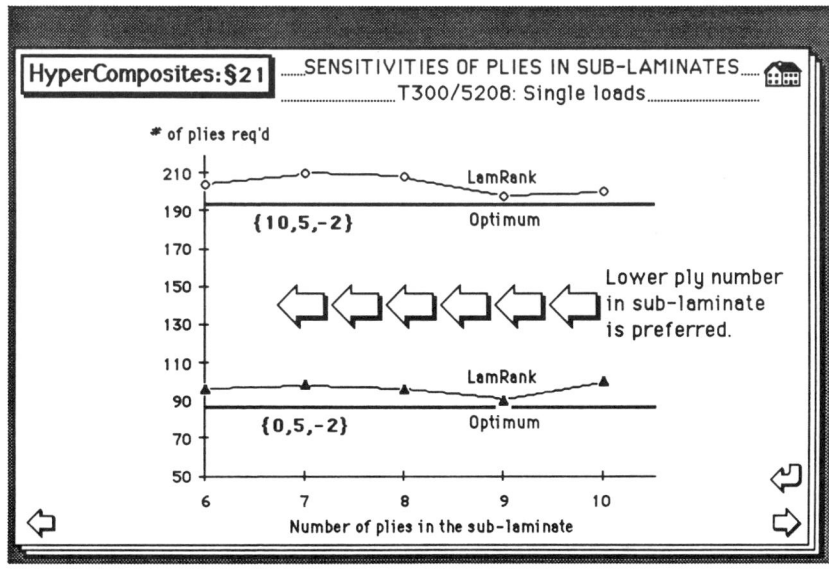

HyperComposites: §21 — SENSITIVITIES OF PLIES IN SUB-LAMINATES
T300/5208: Single loads

# of plies req'd

{10,5,-2}   LamRank   Optimum

{0,5,-2}   LamRank   Optimum

Lower ply number in sub-laminate is preferred.

Number of plies in the sub-laminate

29.21 LAMRANK (continued)

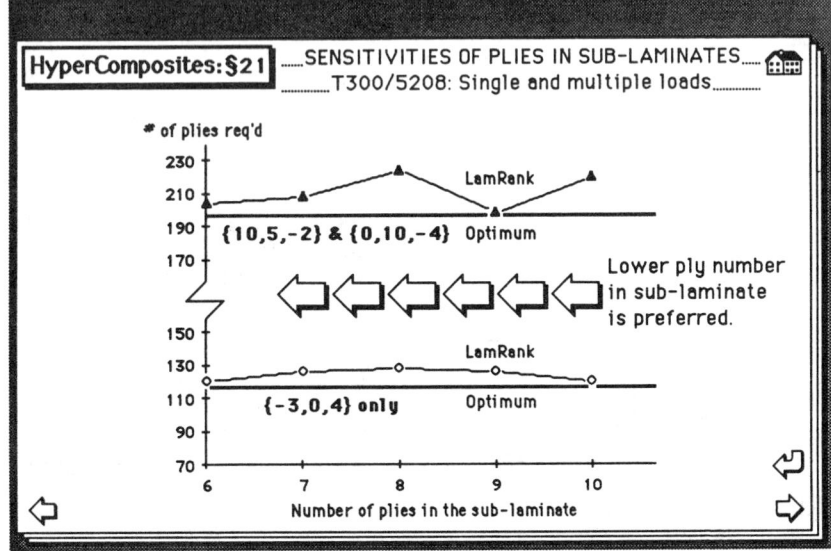

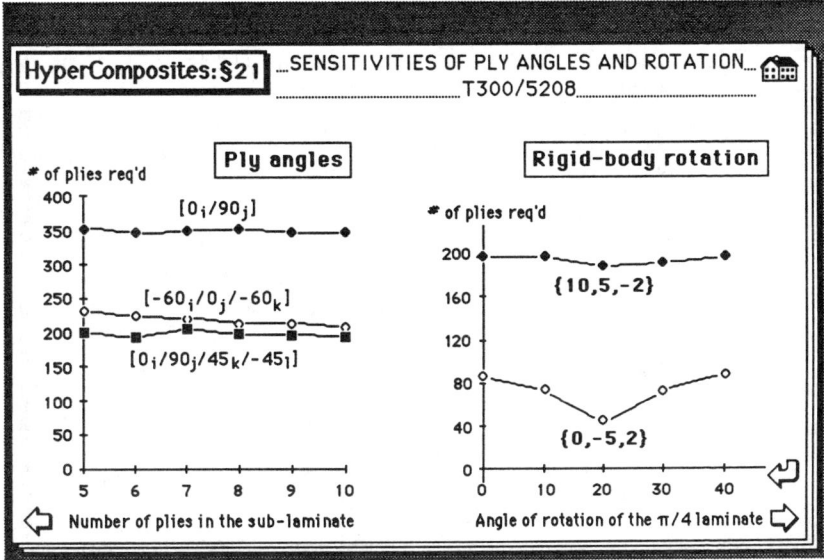

29.22 COUPON TEST

HyperComposites: §22 ........EXPERIMENTAL DETERMINATION OF F_{xy}^*........
........The missing link in the quadratic criterion........

Quadratic criterion in stress space: $F_{ij}\sigma_i\sigma_j + F_i\sigma_i = 1$

Easy to measure: $F_{xx} = \frac{1}{XX'}$, $F_{yy} = \frac{1}{YY'}$, $F_{ss} = \frac{1}{S^2}$, $F_x = \frac{1}{X} - \frac{1}{X'}$, $F_y = \frac{1}{Y} - \frac{1}{Y'}$

Not so easy: F_{xy} = interaction term = $F_{xy}^* \sqrt{F_{xx}F_{yy}}$

For closed conic surface: $-1 \le F_{xy}^* \le 1$

F_{xy} can only be measured with combined stresses: for simple examples:

1. Cross-ply laminates subjected to uniaxial compressive loads.

2. Unidirectional rings tested under external or internal pressure.

3. Unidirectional rods subjected to confined compressive loads.

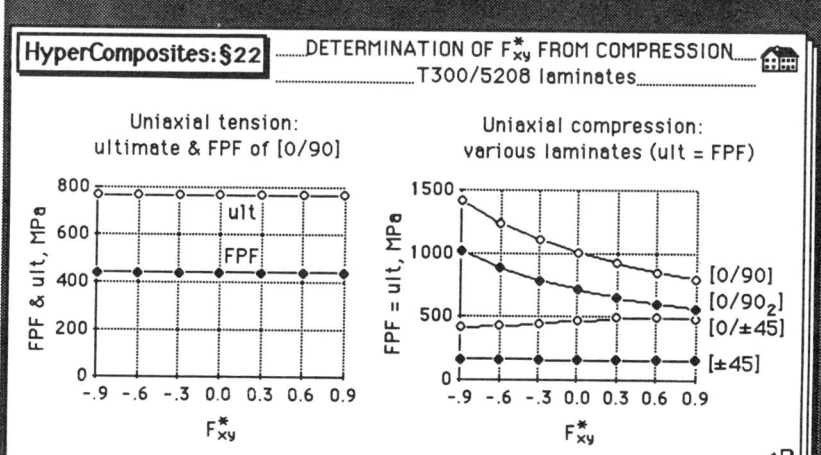

HyperComposites: §22 ........DETERMINATION OF F_{xy}^* FROM COMPRESSION........
........T300/5208 laminates........

Uniaxial tension: ultimate & FPF of [0/90]

Uniaxial compression: various laminates (ult = FPF)

[0/90]
[0/90₂]
[0/±45]
[±45]

Recommendation: Use [0/90] and [0/90₂] subjected to uniaxial compression to experimentally determine F_{xy}^*.

29.22 COUPON TEST (continued)

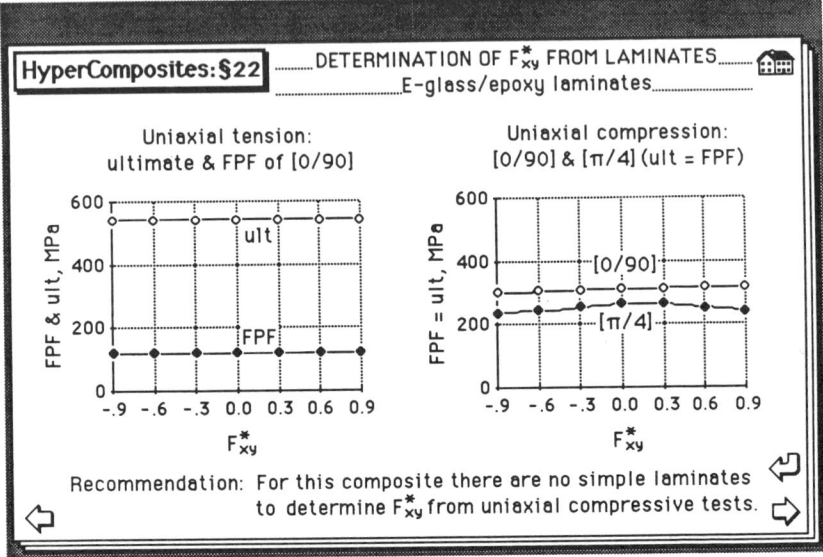

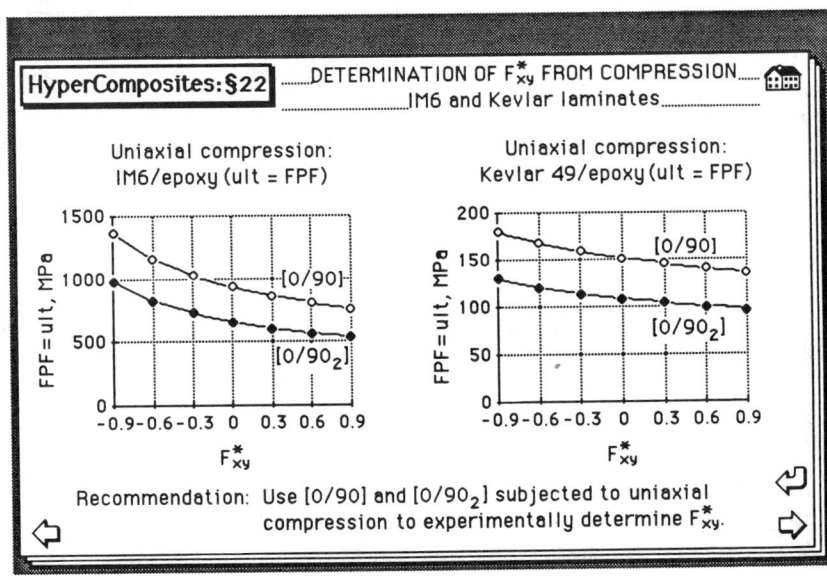

29.23 RING TEST

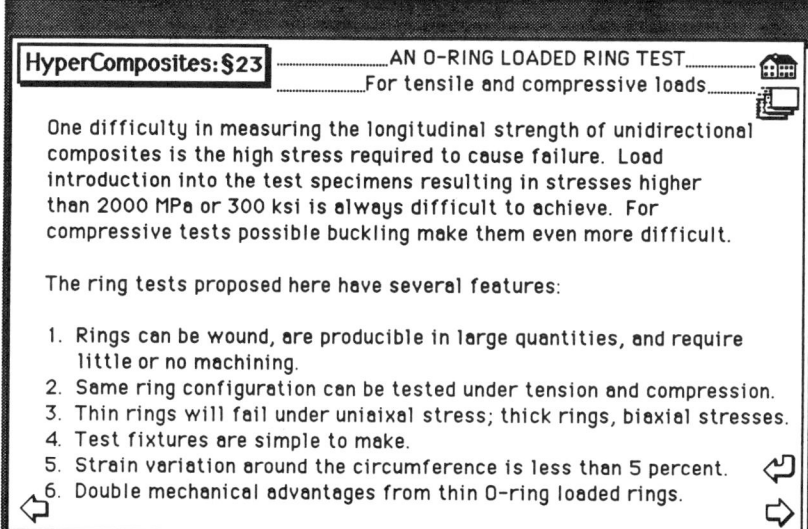

HyperComposites:§23 ················AN O-RING LOADED RING TEST·············
·······················For tensile and compressive loads··········

One difficulty in measuring the longitudinal strength of unidirectional composites is the high stress required to cause failure. Load introduction into the test specimens resulting in stresses higher than 2000 MPa or 300 ksi is always difficult to achieve. For compressive tests possible buckling make them even more difficult.

The ring tests proposed here have several features:

1. Rings can be wound, are producible in large quantities, and require little or no machining.
2. Same ring configuration can be tested under tension and compression.
3. Thin rings will fail under uniaxal stress; thick rings, biaxial stresses.
4. Test fixtures are simple to make.
5. Strain variation around the circumference is less than 5 percent.
6. Double mechanical advantages from thin O-ring loaded rings.

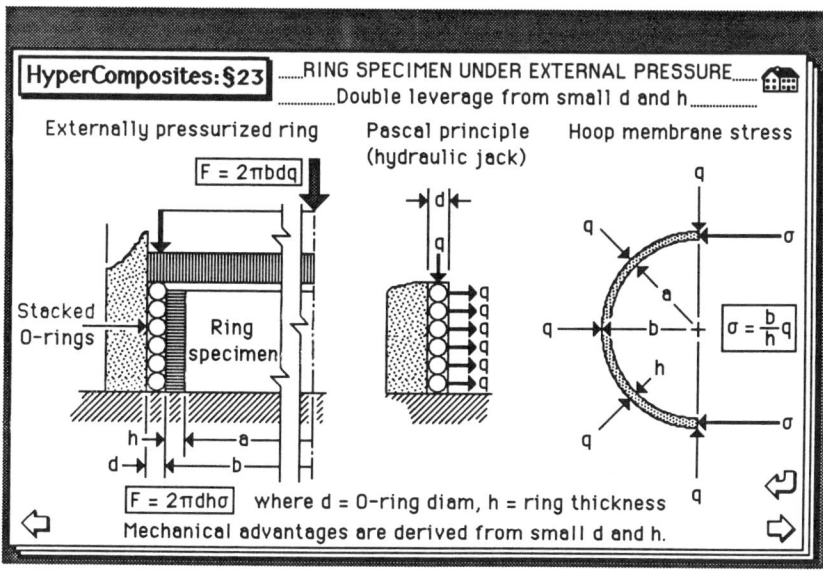

HyperComposites:§23 ·······RING SPECIMEN UNDER EXTERNAL PRESSURE·······
·················Double leverage from small d and h·················

Externally pressurized ring   Pascal principle   Hoop membrane stress
                                    (hydraulic jack)

$F = 2\pi bdq$

Stacked O-rings   Ring specimen

$\sigma = \frac{b}{h}q$

$F = 2\pi dh\sigma$ where d = O-ring diam, h = ring thickness
Mechanical advantages are derived from small d and h.

29.23 RING TEST (continued)

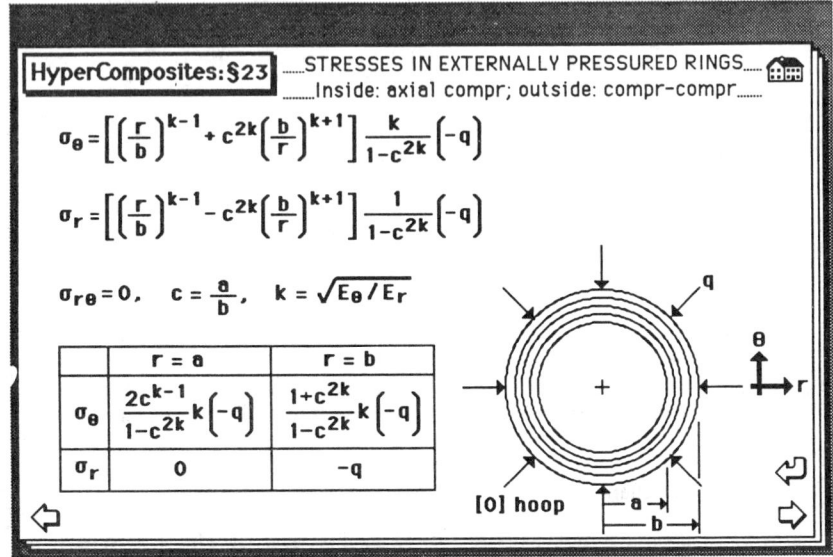

HyperComposites:§23 ....STRESSES IN EXTERNALLY PRESSURED RINGS.......
........Inside: axial compr; outside: compr-compr.......

$$\sigma_\theta = \left[\left(\frac{r}{b}\right)^{k-1} + c^{2k}\left(\frac{b}{r}\right)^{k+1}\right]\frac{k}{1-c^{2k}}(-q)$$

$$\sigma_r = \left[\left(\frac{r}{b}\right)^{k-1} - c^{2k}\left(\frac{b}{r}\right)^{k+1}\right]\frac{1}{1-c^{2k}}(-q)$$

$$\sigma_{r\theta} = 0, \quad c = \frac{a}{b}, \quad k = \sqrt{E_\theta/E_r}$$

	$r = a$	$r = b$
σ_θ	$\dfrac{2c^{k-1}}{1-c^{2k}}k(-q)$	$\dfrac{1+c^{2k}}{1-c^{2k}}k(-q)$
σ_r	0	$-q$

[0] hoop

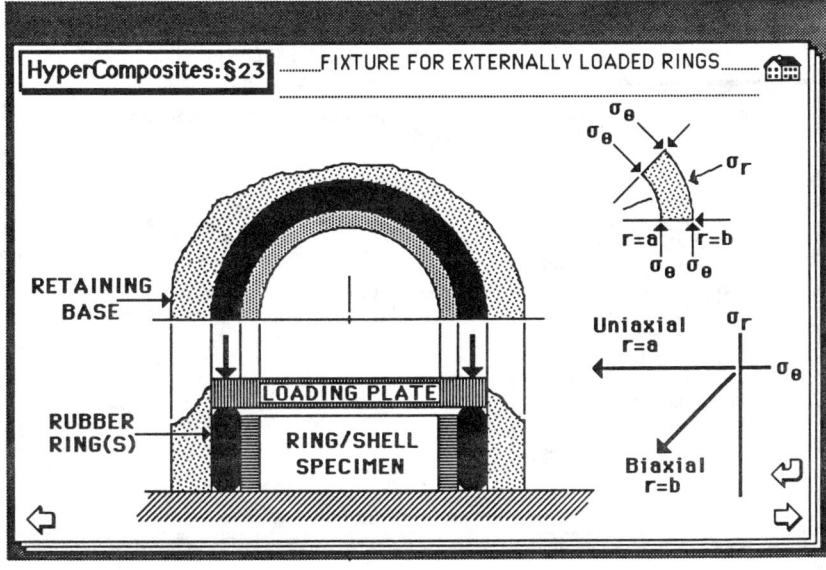

HyperComposites:§23 ....FIXTURE FOR EXTERNALLY LOADED RINGS.......

RETAINING BASE

RUBBER RING(S)

LOADING PLATE

RING/SHELL SPECIMEN

$r=a$ $r=b$

Uniaxial $r=a$

Biaxial $r=b$

29.23 RING TEST (continued)

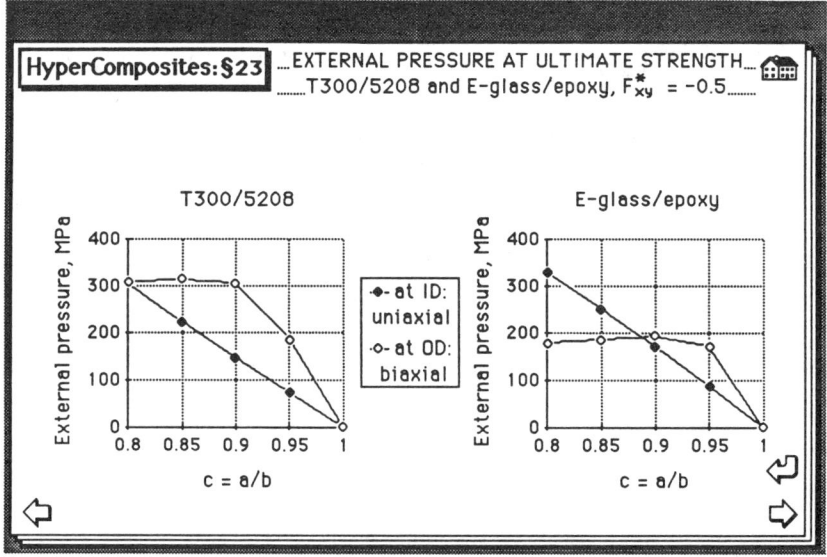

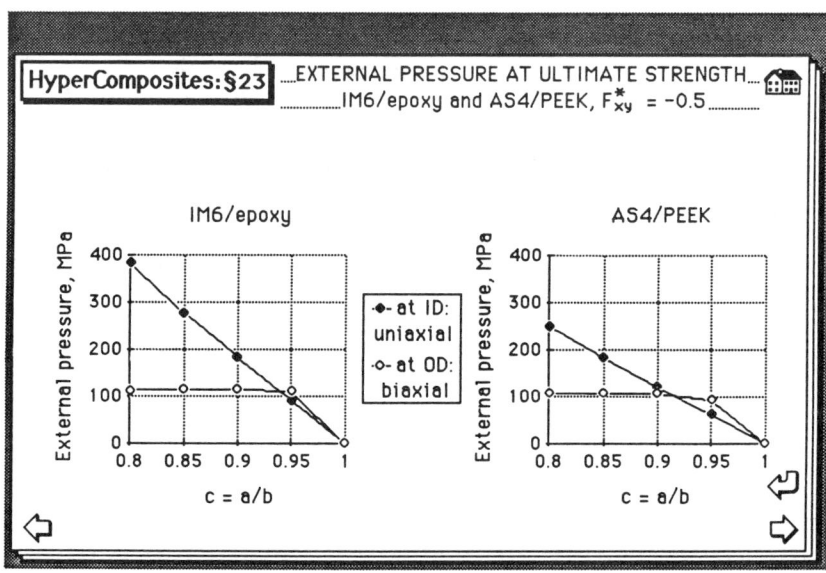

29.23 RING TEST (continued)

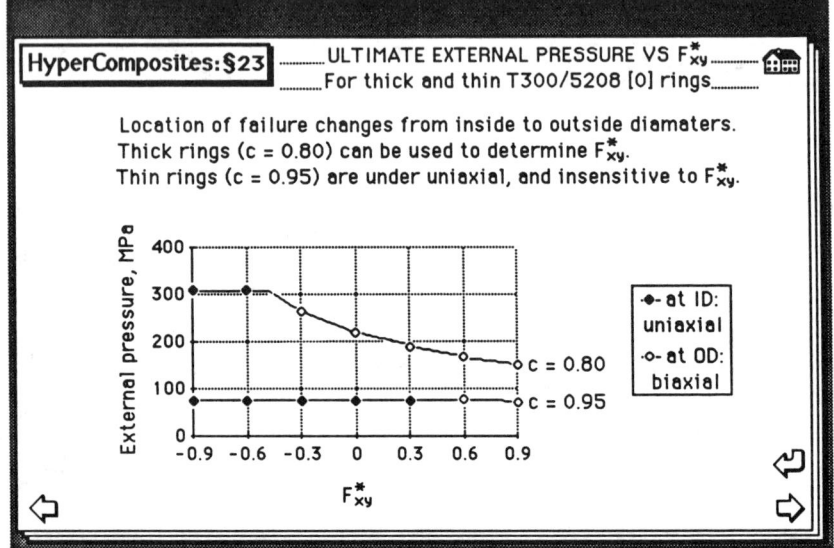

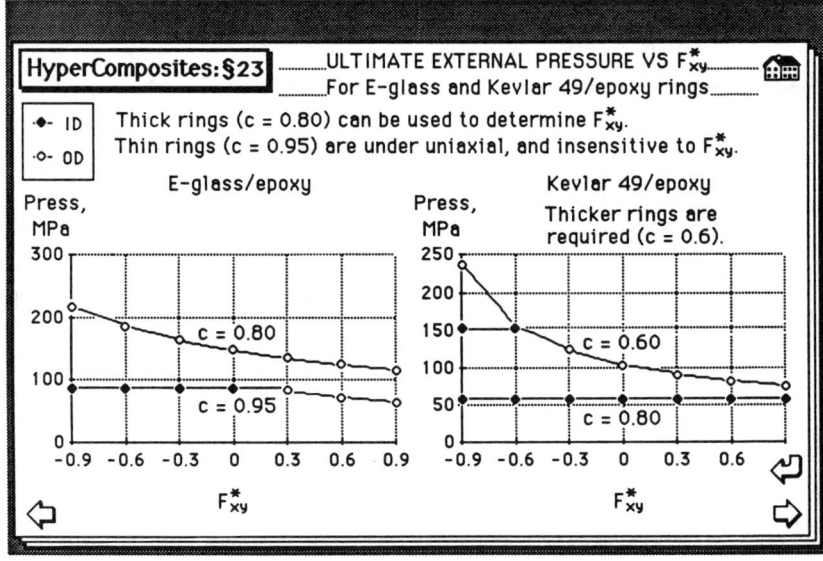

29.23 RING TEST (continued)

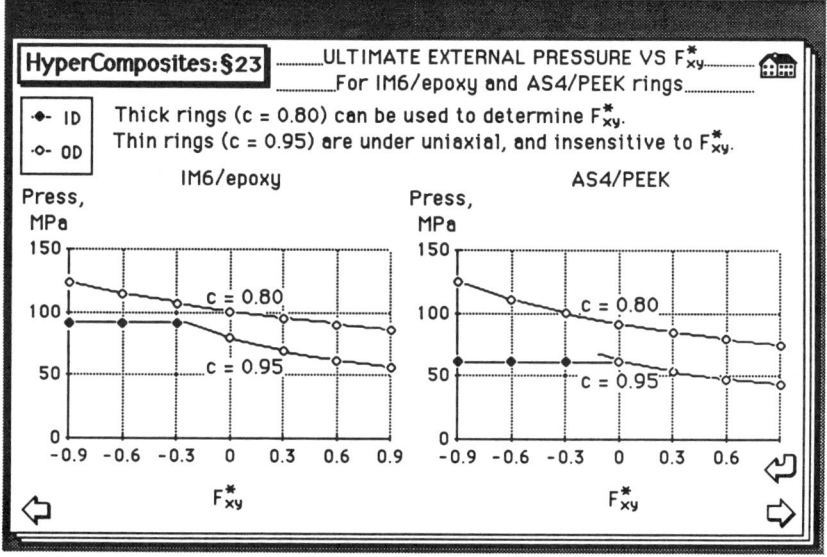

HyperComposites:§23 ....ULTIMATE EXTERNAL PRESSURE VS F_{xy}^*........

........For IM6/epoxy and AS4/PEEK rings........

- ID
- OD

Thick rings (c = 0.80) can be used to determine F_{xy}^*.
Thin rings (c = 0.95) are under uniaxial, and insensitive to F_{xy}^*.

IM6/epoxy   AS4/PEEK

Press, MPa

c = 0.80
c = 0.95

F_{xy}^*

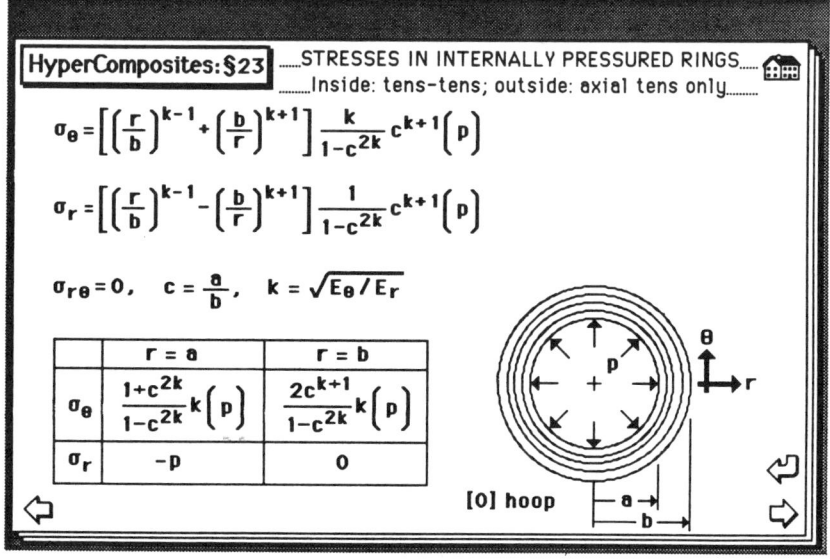

HyperComposites:§23 ......STRESSES IN INTERNALLY PRESSURED RINGS......

......Inside: tens-tens; outside: axial tens only......

$$\sigma_\theta = \left[\left(\frac{r}{b}\right)^{k-1} + \left(\frac{b}{r}\right)^{k+1}\right]\frac{k}{1-c^{2k}}c^{k+1}\left(p\right)$$

$$\sigma_r = \left[\left(\frac{r}{b}\right)^{k-1} - \left(\frac{b}{r}\right)^{k+1}\right]\frac{1}{1-c^{2k}}c^{k+1}\left(p\right)$$

$$\sigma_{r\theta} = 0, \quad c = \frac{a}{b}, \quad k = \sqrt{E_\theta/E_r}$$

	r = a	r = b
σ_θ	$\dfrac{1+c^{2k}}{1-c^{2k}}k\left(p\right)$	$\dfrac{2c^{k+1}}{1-c^{2k}}k\left(p\right)$
σ_r	-p	0

[0] hoop

29.23 RING TEST (continued)

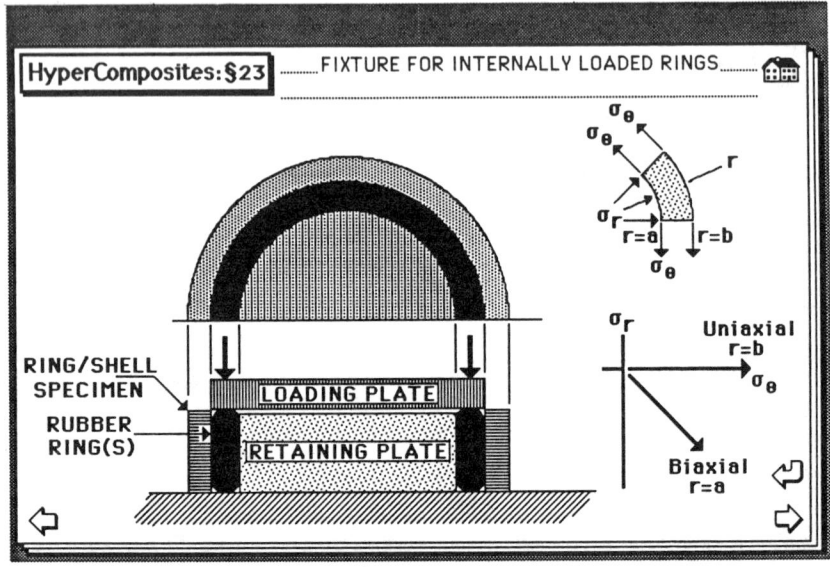

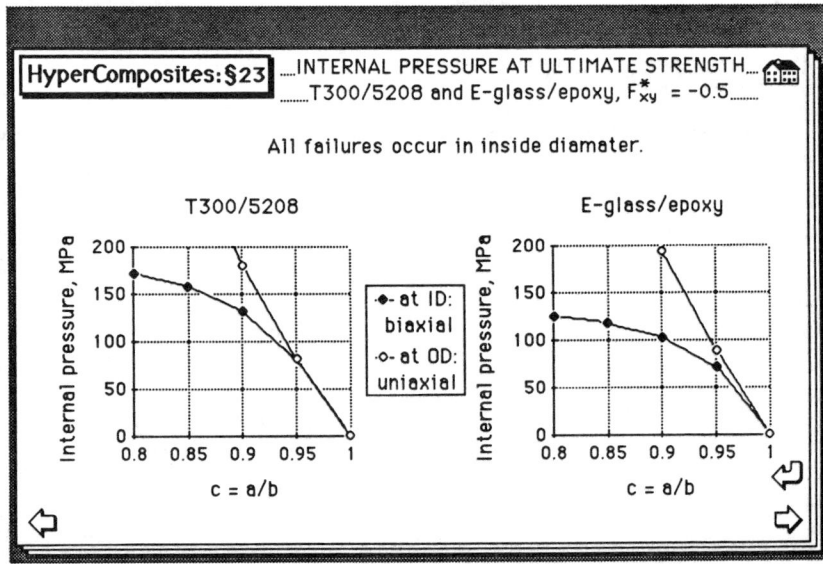

29.23 RING TEST (continued)

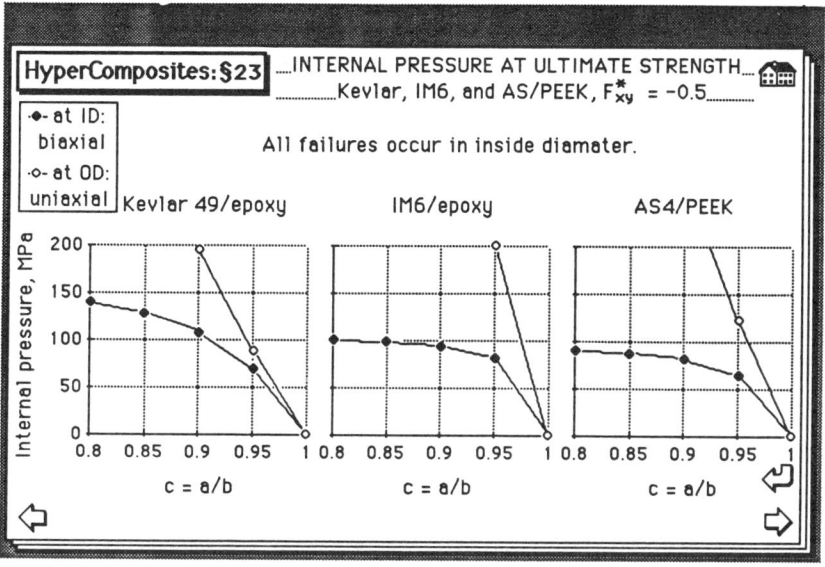

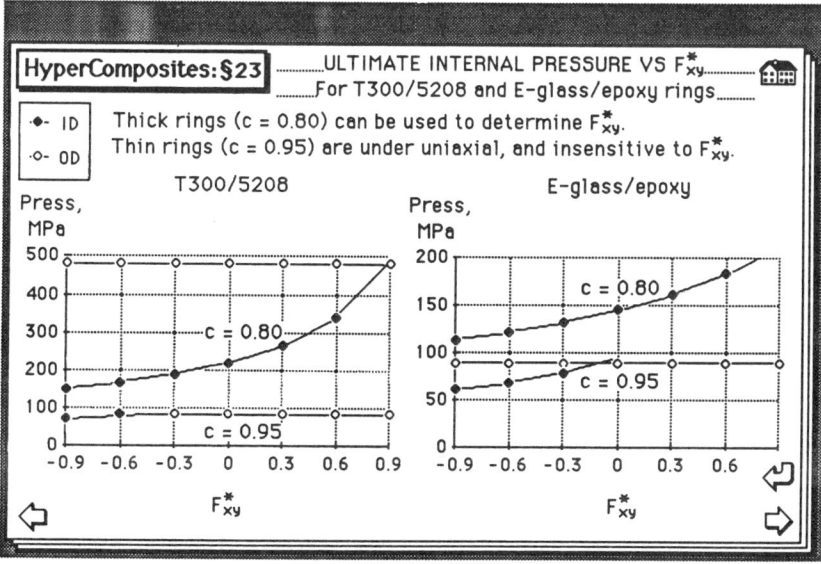

29.23 RING TEST (continued)

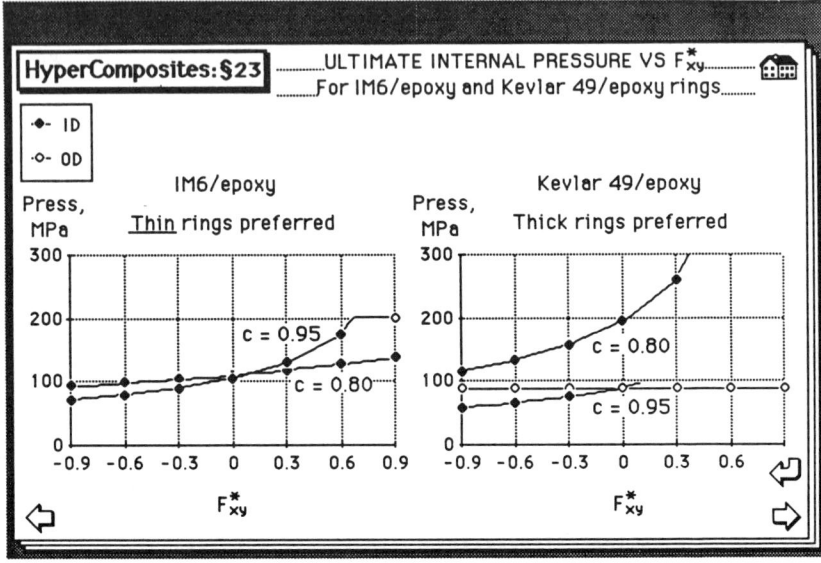

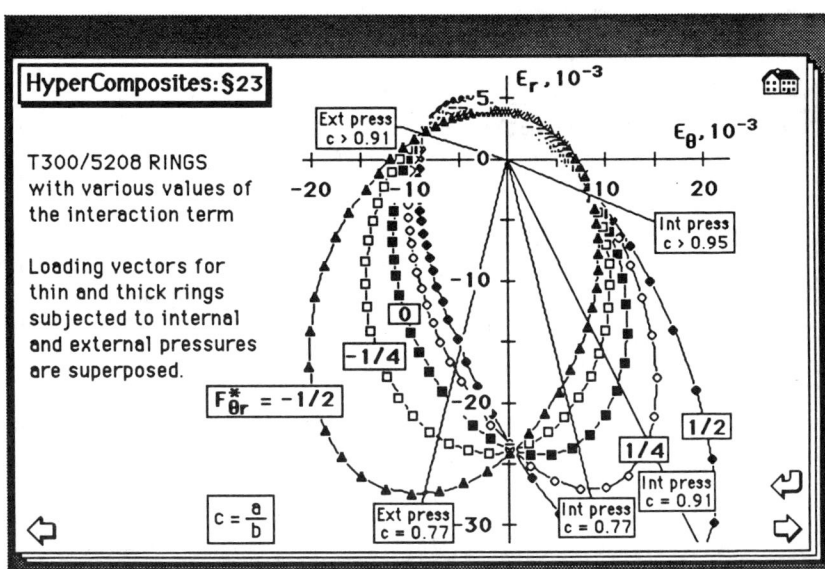

29.24 ROD TEST

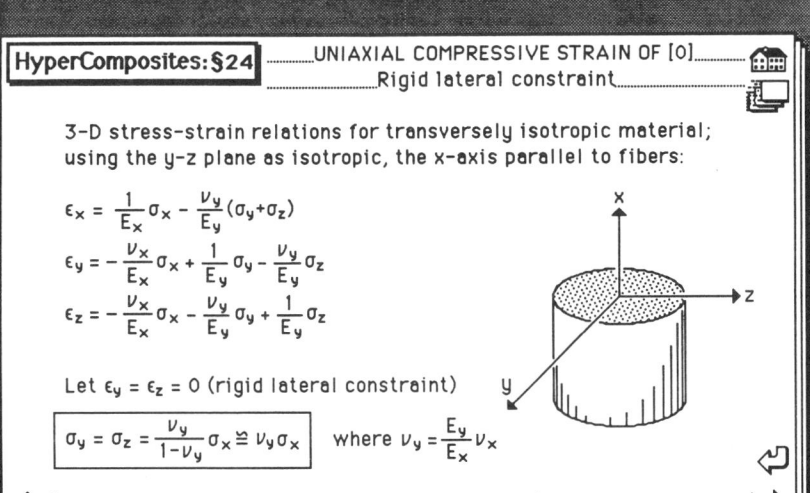

HyperComposites: §24 ....UNIAXIAL COMPRESSIVE STRAIN OF [0]............
............Rigid lateral constraint............

3-D stress-strain relations for transversely isotropic material; using the y-z plane as isotropic, the x-axis parallel to fibers:

$$\epsilon_x = \frac{1}{E_x}\sigma_x - \frac{\nu_y}{E_y}(\sigma_y+\sigma_z)$$

$$\epsilon_y = -\frac{\nu_x}{E_x}\sigma_x + \frac{1}{E_y}\sigma_y - \frac{\nu_y}{E_y}\sigma_z$$

$$\epsilon_z = -\frac{\nu_x}{E_x}\sigma_x - \frac{\nu_y}{E_y}\sigma_y + \frac{1}{E_y}\sigma_z$$

Let $\epsilon_y = \epsilon_z = 0$ (rigid lateral constraint)

$$\boxed{\sigma_y = \sigma_z = \frac{\nu_y}{1-\nu_y}\sigma_x \cong \nu_y\sigma_x} \quad \text{where } \nu_y = \frac{E_y}{E_x}\nu_x$$

(We use special subscripts for Poisson's ratios; i.e., $\nu_x = \nu_{yx}$, $\nu_y = \nu_{xy}$.)

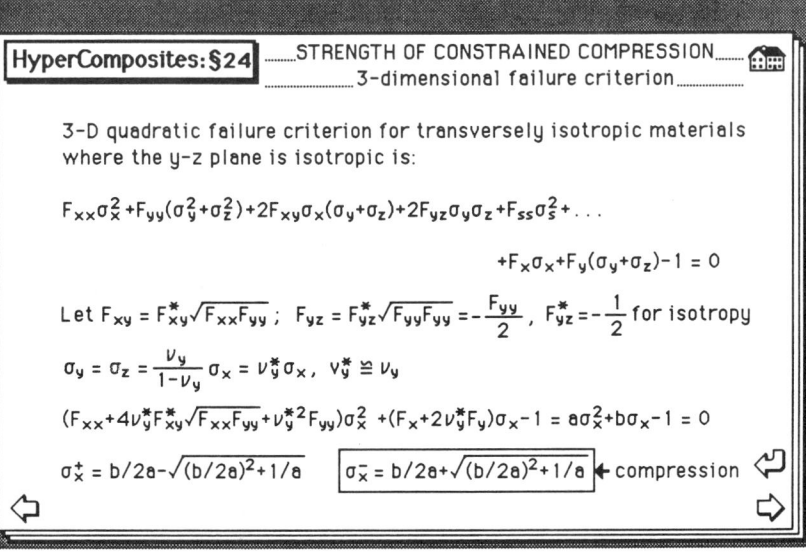

HyperComposites: §24 ....STRENGTH OF CONSTRAINED COMPRESSION............
............3-dimensional failure criterion............

3-D quadratic failure criterion for transversely isotropic materials where the y-z plane is isotropic is:

$$F_{xx}\sigma_x^2 + F_{yy}(\sigma_y^2+\sigma_z^2) + 2F_{xy}\sigma_x(\sigma_y+\sigma_z) + 2F_{yz}\sigma_y\sigma_z + F_{ss}\sigma_s^2 + \ldots$$

$$+ F_x\sigma_x + F_y(\sigma_y+\sigma_z) - 1 = 0$$

Let $F_{xy} = F_{xy}^*\sqrt{F_{xx}F_{yy}}$; $F_{yz} = F_{yz}^*\sqrt{F_{yy}F_{yy}} = -\frac{F_{yy}}{2}$, $F_{yz}^* = -\frac{1}{2}$ for isotropy

$$\sigma_y = \sigma_z = \frac{\nu_y}{1-\nu_y}\sigma_x = \nu_y^*\sigma_x, \quad \nu_y^* \cong \nu_y$$

$$(F_{xx} + 4\nu_y^* F_{xy}^*\sqrt{F_{xx}F_{yy}} + \nu_y^{*2}F_{yy})\sigma_x^2 + (F_x + 2\nu_y^*F_y)\sigma_x - 1 = a\sigma_x^2 + b\sigma_x - 1 = 0$$

$$\sigma_x^+ = b/2a - \sqrt{(b/2a)^2 + 1/a} \quad \boxed{\sigma_x^- = b/2a + \sqrt{(b/2a)^2 + 1/a}} \leftarrow \text{compression}$$

29.24 ROD TEST (continued)

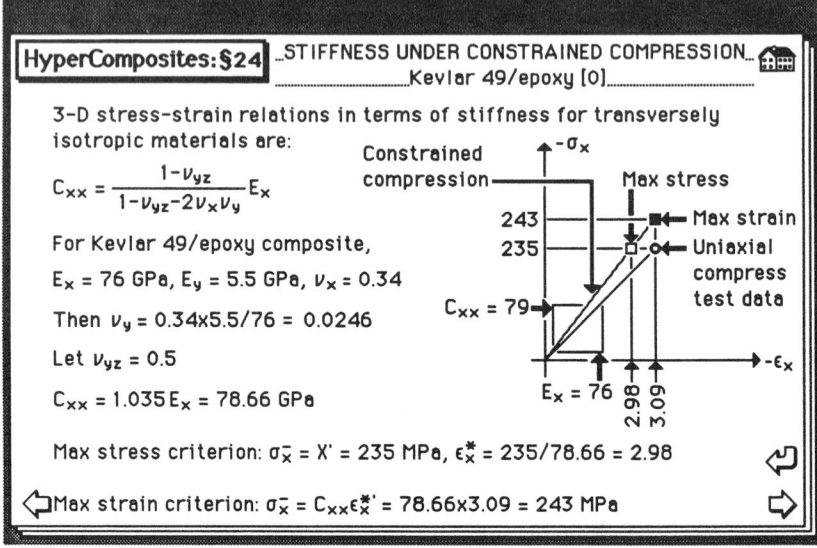

HyperComposites:§24 ....STIFFNESS UNDER CONSTRAINED COMPRESSION.. 🏠
......................Kevlar 49/epoxy [0]................

3-D stress-strain relations in terms of stiffness for transversely isotropic materials are:

$$C_{xx} = \frac{1-\nu_{yz}}{1-\nu_{yz}-2\nu_x\nu_y}E_x$$

For Kevlar 49/epoxy composite,

E_x = 76 GPa, E_y = 5.5 GPa, ν_x = 0.34

Then ν_y = 0.34x5.5/76 = 0.0246

Let ν_{yz} = 0.5

C_{xx} = 1.035E_x = 78.66 GPa

Constrained compression — Max stress, Max strain, Uniaxial compress test data

243, 235, C_{xx} = 79, E_x = 76, 2.98, 3.09

Max stress criterion: σ_x^- = X' = 235 MPa, ϵ_x^* = 235/78.66 = 2.98

Max strain criterion: σ_x^- = $C_{xx}\epsilon_x^*$' = 78.66x3.09 = 243 MPa

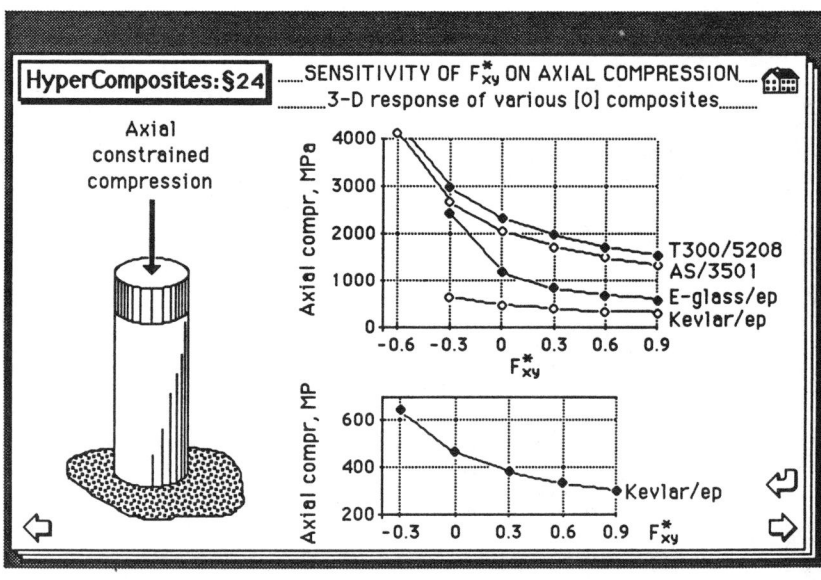

HyperComposites:§24 ......SENSITIVITY OF F_{xy}^* ON AXIAL COMPRESSION...... 🏠
.........3-D response of various [0] composites.........

Axial constrained compression

Axial compr, MPa — 4000, 3000, 2000, 1000, 0

-0.6 -0.3 0 0.3 0.6 0.9 F_{xy}^*

T300/5208
AS/3501
E-glass/ep
Kevlar/ep

Axial compr, MP — 600, 400, 200

-0.3 0 0.3 0.6 0.9 F_{xy}^*

Kevlar/ep

29.24 ROD TEST (continued)

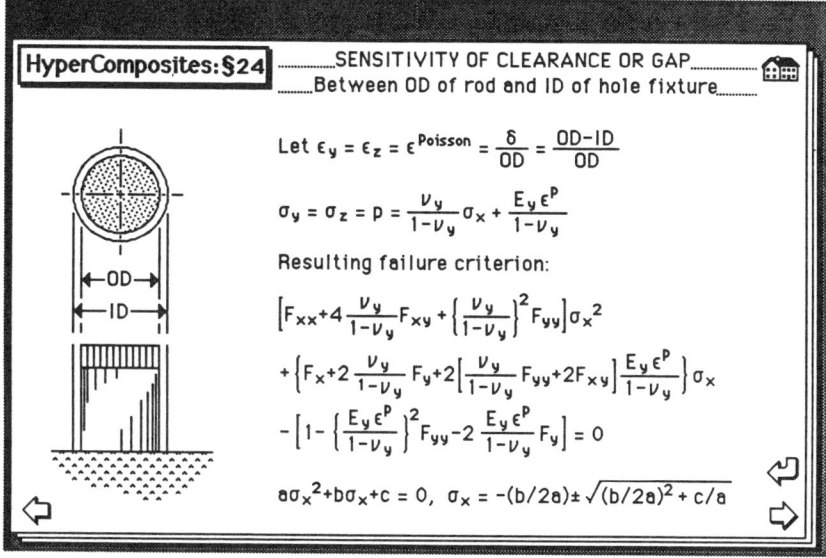

HyperComposites: §24 ....SENSITIVITY OF CLEARANCE OR GAP.........
.........Between OD of rod and ID of hole fixture.........

Let $\epsilon_y = \epsilon_z = \epsilon^{Poisson} = \dfrac{\delta}{OD} = \dfrac{OD-ID}{OD}$

$\sigma_y = \sigma_z = p = \dfrac{\nu_y}{1-\nu_y}\sigma_x + \dfrac{E_y \epsilon^p}{1-\nu_y}$

Resulting failure criterion:

$$\left[F_{xx}+4\frac{\nu_y}{1-\nu_y}F_{xy}+\left\{\frac{\nu_y}{1-\nu_y}\right\}^2 F_{yy}\right]\sigma_x^2$$

$$+\left\{F_x+2\frac{\nu_y}{1-\nu_y}F_y+2\left[\frac{\nu_y}{1-\nu_y}F_{yy}+2F_{xy}\right]\frac{E_y\epsilon^p}{1-\nu_y}\right\}\sigma_x$$

$$-\left[1-\left\{\frac{E_y\epsilon^p}{1-\nu_y}\right\}^2 F_{yy}-2\frac{E_y\epsilon^p}{1-\nu_y}F_y\right] = 0$$

$$a\sigma_x^2+b\sigma_x+c = 0, \quad \sigma_x = -(b/2a)\pm\sqrt{(b/2a)^2 + c/a}$$

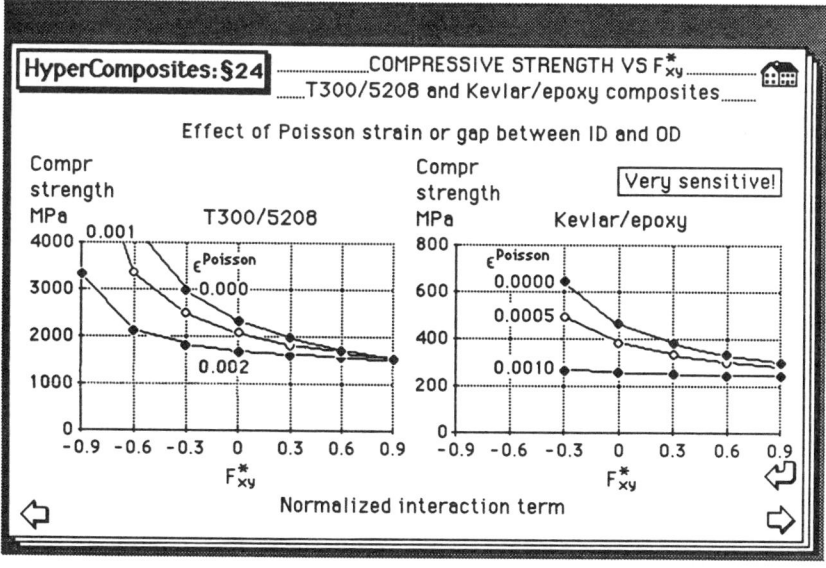

HyperComposites: §24 ....COMPRESSIVE STRENGTH VS F_{xy}^*.........
.........T300/5208 and Kevlar/epoxy composites.........

Effect of Poisson strain or gap between ID and OD

Very sensitive!

T300/5208

Compr strength MPa

$\epsilon^{Poisson}$
0.001
0.000
0.002

Kevlar/epoxy

Compr strength MPa

$\epsilon^{Poisson}$
0.0000
0.0005
0.0010

F_{xy}^*

Normalized interaction term

29.24 ROD TEST (continued)

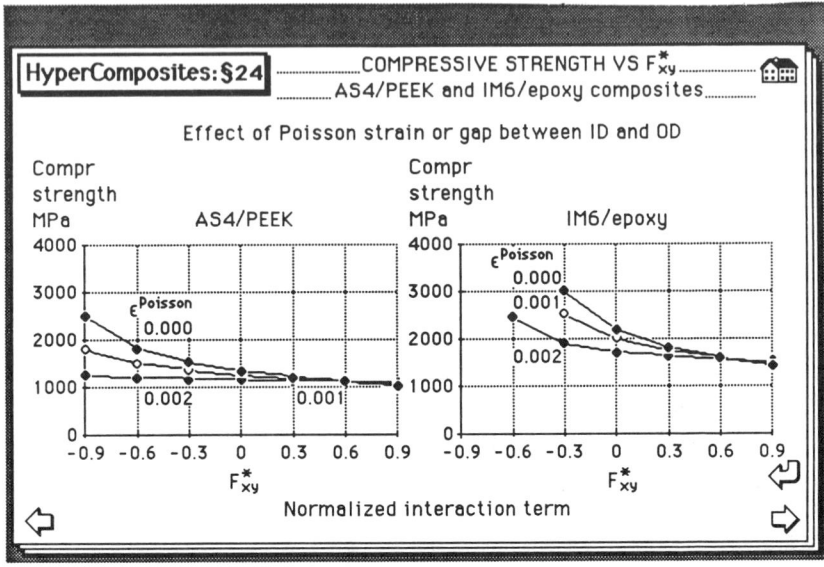

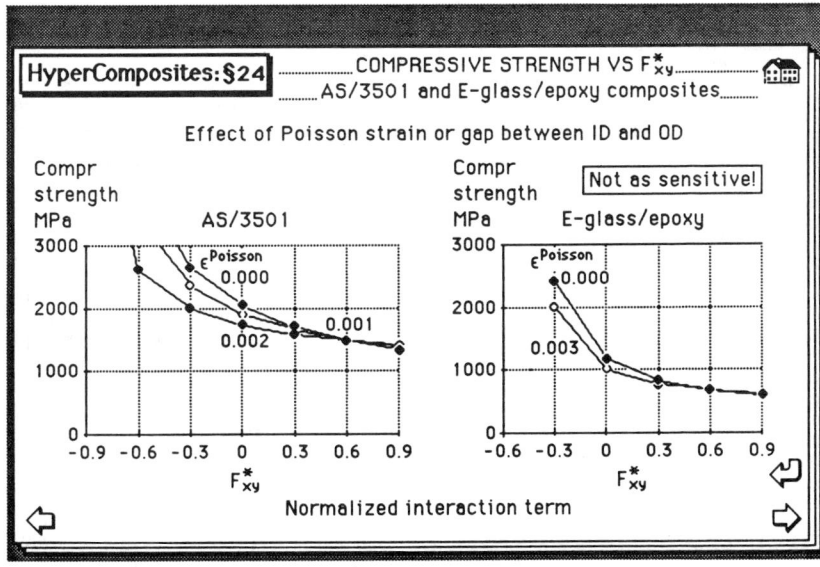

29.25 THICK LAMINATES

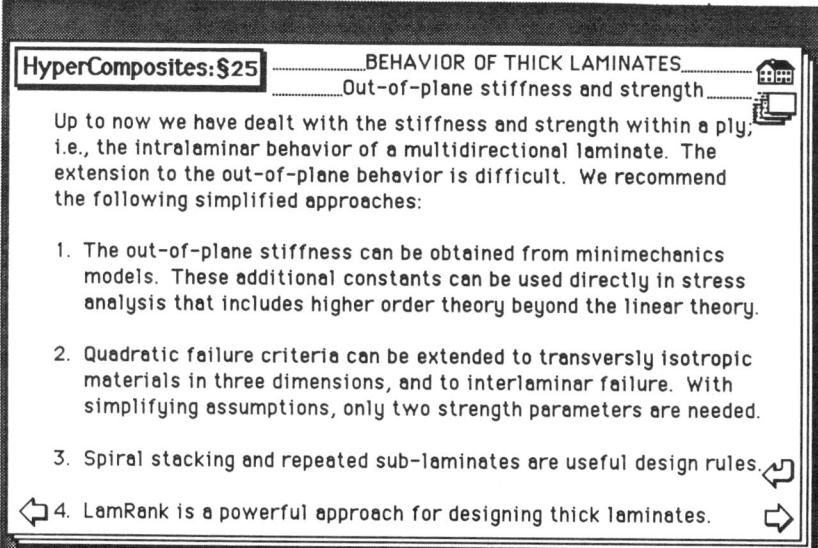

HyperComposites: §25 ....BEHAVIOR OF THICK LAMINATES..............
.............Out-of-plane stiffness and strength ....

Up to now we have dealt with the stiffness and strength within a ply, i.e., the intralaminar behavior of a multidirectional laminate. The extension to the out-of-plane behavior is difficult. We recommend the following simplified approaches:

1. The out-of-plane stiffness can be obtained from minimechanics models. These additional constants can be used directly in stress analysis that includes higher order theory beyond the linear theory.

2. Quadratic failure criteria can be extended to transversely isotropic materials in three dimensions, and to interlaminar failure. With simplifying assumptions, only two strength parameters are needed.

3. Spiral stacking and repeated sub-laminates are useful design rules.

4. LamRank is a powerful approach for designing thick laminates.

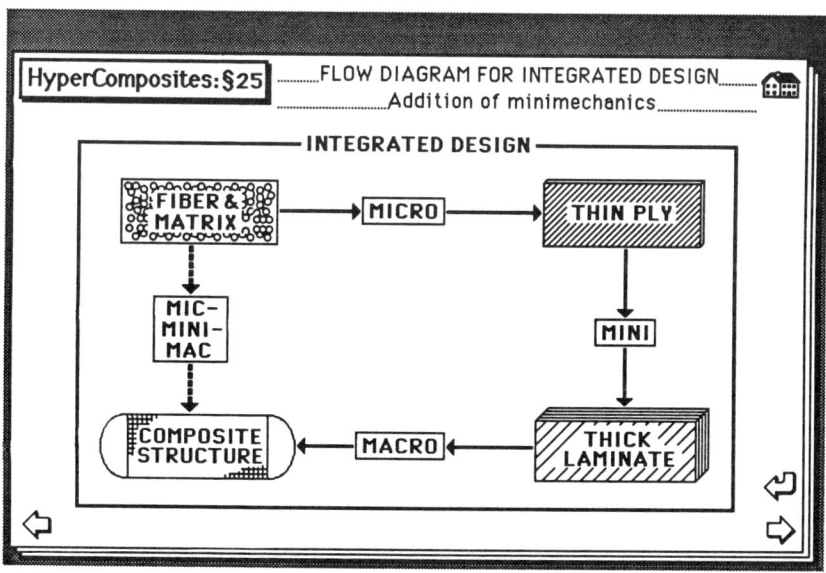

HyperComposites: §25 ....FLOW DIAGRAM FOR INTEGRATED DESIGN...........
.............Addition of minimechanics...........

━ INTEGRATED DESIGN ━

FIBER & MATRIX → MICRO → THIN PLY

MIC-MINI-MAC

MINI

COMPOSITE STRUCTURE ← MACRO ← THICK LAMINATE

29.25 THICK LAMINATES (continued)

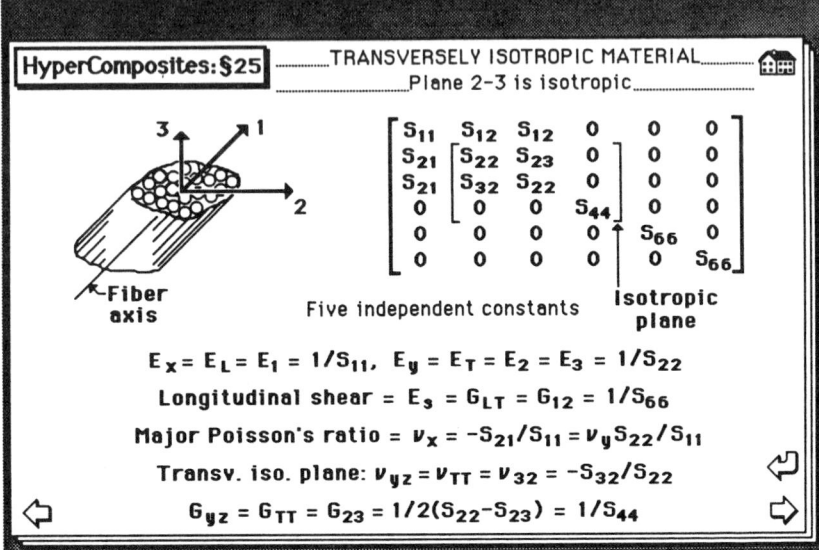

HyperComposites:§25 ............TRANSVERSELY ISOTROPIC MATERIAL............ 🏠

...................................Plane 2-3 is isotropic...................................

$$\begin{bmatrix} S_{11} & S_{12} & S_{12} & 0 & 0 & 0 \\ S_{21} & S_{22} & S_{23} & 0 & 0 & 0 \\ S_{21} & S_{32} & S_{22} & 0 & 0 & 0 \\ 0 & 0 & 0 & S_{44} & 0 & 0 \\ 0 & 0 & 0 & 0 & S_{66} & 0 \\ 0 & 0 & 0 & 0 & 0 & S_{66} \end{bmatrix}$$

Fiber axis   Five independent constants   Isotropic plane

$$E_x = E_L = E_1 = 1/S_{11}, \quad E_y = E_T = E_2 = E_3 = 1/S_{22}$$

Longitudinal shear $= E_s = G_{LT} = G_{12} = 1/S_{66}$

Major Poisson's ratio $= \nu_x = -S_{21}/S_{11} = \nu_y S_{22}/S_{11}$

Transv. iso. plane: $\nu_{yz} = \nu_{TT} = \nu_{32} = -S_{32}/S_{22}$

$$G_{yz} = G_{TT} = G_{23} = 1/2(S_{22}-S_{23}) = 1/S_{44}$$

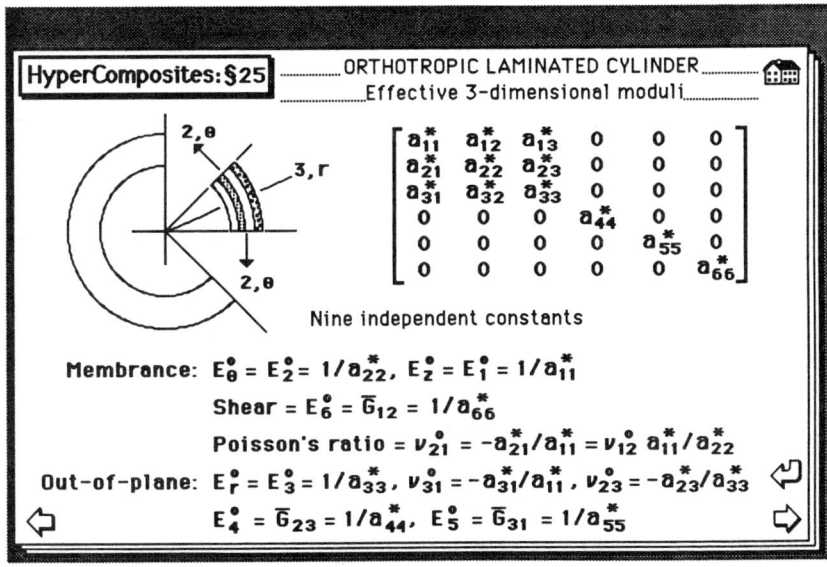

HyperComposites:§25 ....ORTHOTROPIC LAMINATED CYLINDER............ 🏠

...................................Effective 3-dimensional moduli...................................

$$\begin{bmatrix} a_{11}^* & a_{12}^* & a_{13}^* & 0 & 0 & 0 \\ a_{21}^* & a_{22}^* & a_{23}^* & 0 & 0 & 0 \\ a_{31}^* & a_{32}^* & a_{33}^* & 0 & 0 & 0 \\ 0 & 0 & 0 & a_{44}^* & 0 & 0 \\ 0 & 0 & 0 & 0 & a_{55}^* & 0 \\ 0 & 0 & 0 & 0 & 0 & a_{66}^* \end{bmatrix}$$

Nine independent constants

Membrance: $E_\theta^\circ = E_2^\circ = 1/a_{22}^*, \quad E_z^\circ = E_1^\circ = 1/a_{11}^*$

Shear $= E_6^\circ = \overline{G}_{12} = 1/a_{66}^*$

Poisson's ratio $= \nu_{21}^\circ = -a_{21}^*/a_{11}^* = \nu_{12}^\circ \, a_{11}^*/a_{22}^*$

Out-of-plane: $E_r^\circ = E_3^\circ = 1/a_{33}^*, \quad \nu_{31}^\circ = -a_{31}^*/a_{11}^*, \quad \nu_{23}^\circ = -a_{23}^*/a_{33}^*$

$$E_4^\circ = \overline{G}_{23} = 1/a_{44}^*, \quad E_5^\circ = \overline{G}_{31} = 1/a_{55}^*$$

29.25 THICK LAMINATES (continued)

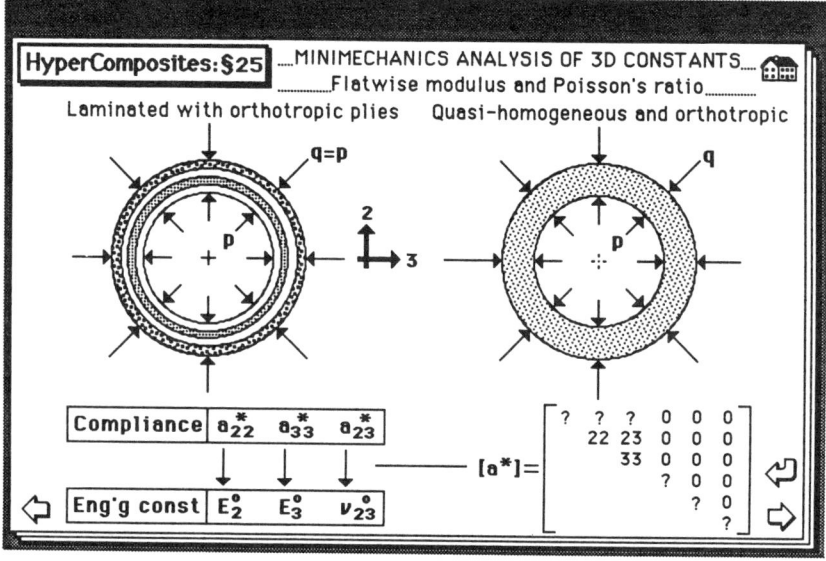

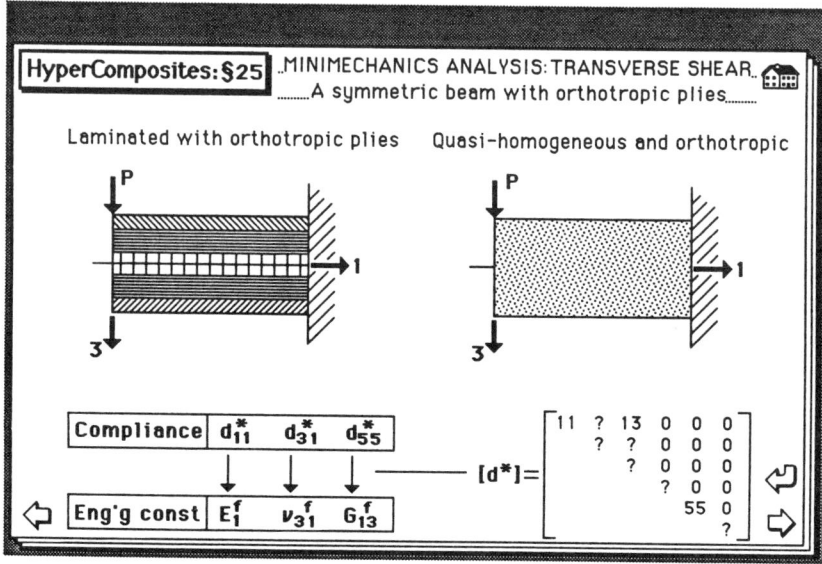

29.25 THICK LAMINATES (continued)

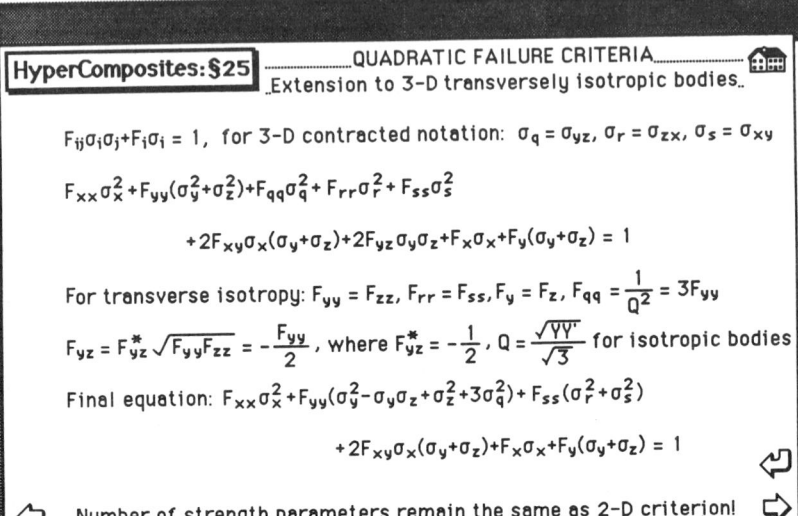

HyperComposites:§25 ....QUADRATIC FAILURE CRITERIA............ 🏠⊞

................Extension to 3-D transversely isotropic bodies...

$F_{ij}\sigma_i\sigma_j + F_i\sigma_i = 1$, for 3-D contracted notation: $\sigma_q = \sigma_{yz}$, $\sigma_r = \sigma_{zx}$, $\sigma_s = \sigma_{xy}$

$F_{xx}\sigma_x^2 + F_{yy}(\sigma_y^2 + \sigma_z^2) + F_{qq}\sigma_q^2 + F_{rr}\sigma_r^2 + F_{ss}\sigma_s^2$

$\qquad + 2F_{xy}\sigma_x(\sigma_y + \sigma_z) + 2F_{yz}\sigma_y\sigma_z + F_x\sigma_x + F_y(\sigma_y + \sigma_z) = 1$

For transverse isotropy: $F_{yy} = F_{zz}$, $F_{rr} = F_{ss}$, $F_y = F_z$, $F_{qq} = \dfrac{1}{Q^2} = 3F_{yy}$

$F_{yz} = F_{yz}^* \sqrt{F_{yy}F_{zz}} = -\dfrac{F_{yy}}{2}$, where $F_{yz}^* = -\dfrac{1}{2}$, $Q = \dfrac{\sqrt{YY'}}{\sqrt{3}}$ for isotropic bodies

Final equation: $F_{xx}\sigma_x^2 + F_{yy}(\sigma_y^2 - \sigma_y\sigma_z + \sigma_z^2 + 3\sigma_q^2) + F_{ss}(\sigma_r^2 + \sigma_s^2)$

$\qquad + 2F_{xy}\sigma_x(\sigma_y + \sigma_z) + F_x\sigma_x + F_y(\sigma_y + \sigma_z) = 1$ ↵

⇦   Number of strength parameters remain the same as 2-D criterion!   ⇨

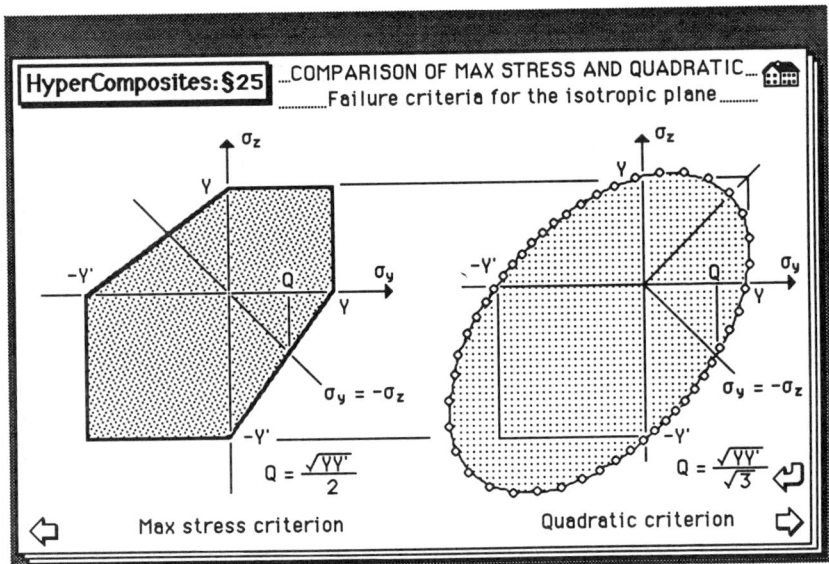

HyperComposites:§25 .....COMPARISON OF MAX STRESS AND QUADRATIC.... 🏠⊞

............Failure criteria for the isotropic plane............

$Q = \dfrac{\sqrt{YY'}}{2}$ $Q = \dfrac{\sqrt{YY'}}{\sqrt{3}}$ ↵

⇦   Max stress criterion   Quadratic criterion   ⇨

29.25 THICK LAMINATES (continued)

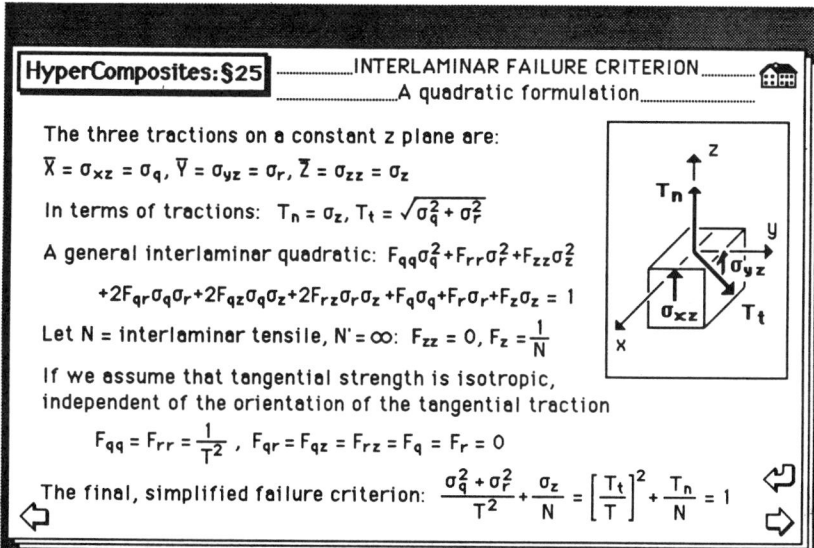

HyperComposites:§25 ............INTERLAMINAR FAILURE CRITERION............
.............A quadratic formulation.............

The three tractions on a constant z plane are:

$\overline{X} = \sigma_{xz} = \sigma_q$, $\overline{Y} = \sigma_{yz} = \sigma_r$, $\overline{Z} = \sigma_{zz} = \sigma_z$

In terms of tractions: $T_n = \sigma_z$, $T_t = \sqrt{\sigma_q^2 + \sigma_r^2}$

A general interlaminar quadratic: $F_{qq}\sigma_q^2 + F_{rr}\sigma_r^2 + F_{zz}\sigma_z^2$

$+ 2F_{qr}\sigma_q\sigma_r + 2F_{qz}\sigma_q\sigma_z + 2F_{rz}\sigma_r\sigma_z + F_q\sigma_q + F_r\sigma_r + F_z\sigma_z = 1$

Let N = interlaminar tensile, N' = ∞: $F_{zz} = 0$, $F_z = \dfrac{1}{N}$

If we assume that tangential strength is isotropic,
independent of the orientation of the tangential traction

$F_{qq} = F_{rr} = \dfrac{1}{T^2}$, $F_{qr} = F_{qz} = F_{rz} = F_q = F_r = 0$

The final, simplified failure criterion: $\dfrac{\sigma_q^2 + \sigma_r^2}{T^2} + \dfrac{\sigma_z}{N} = \left[\dfrac{T_t}{T}\right]^2 + \dfrac{T_n}{N} = 1$

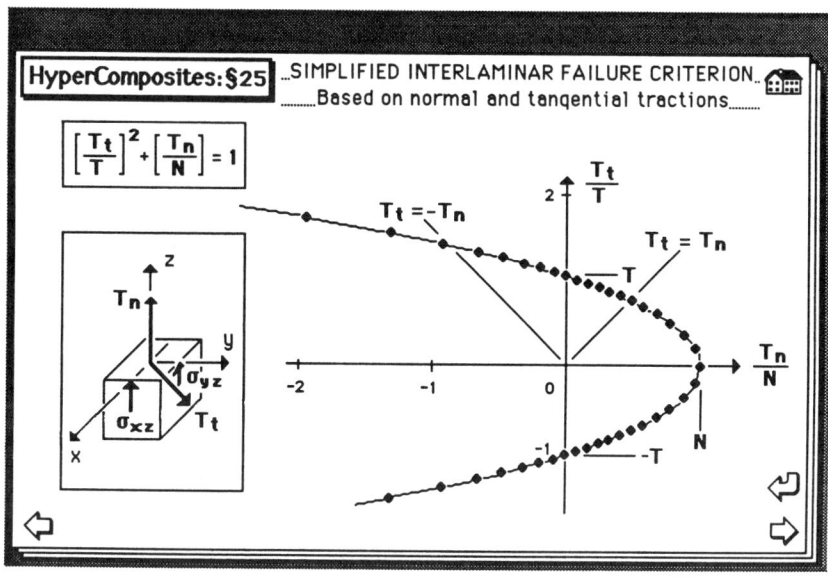

HyperComposites:§25 ...SIMPLIFIED INTERLAMINAR FAILURE CRITERION.
..........Based on normal and tangential tractions..........

$\left[\dfrac{T_t}{T}\right]^2 + \left[\dfrac{T_n}{N}\right] = 1$

29.25 THICK LAMINATES (continued)

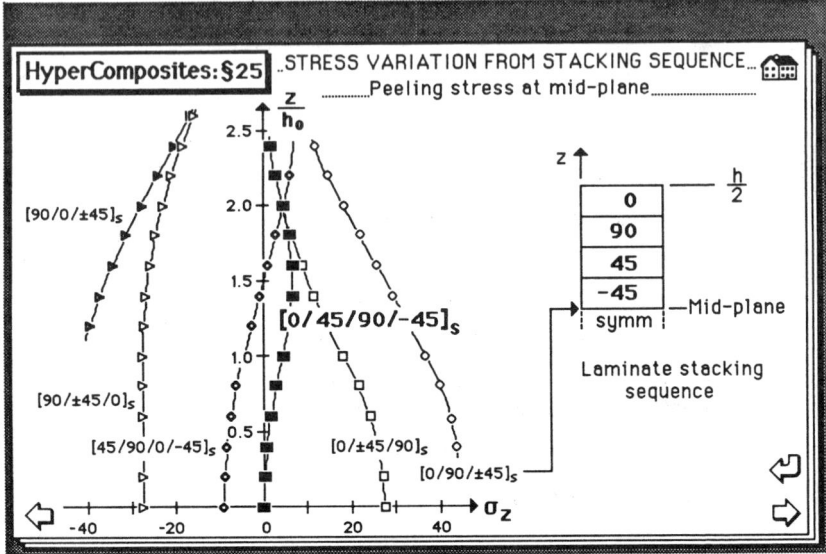

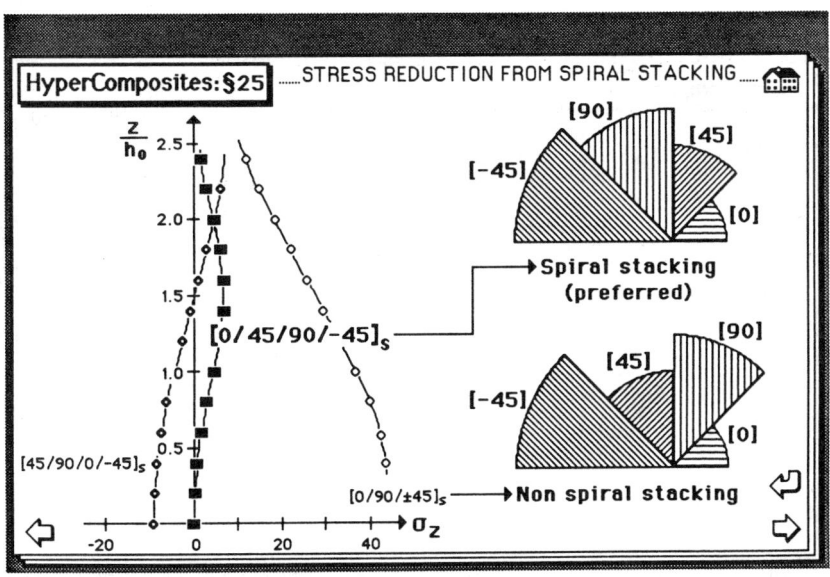

29.26 [0] SCOTCH VERSUS Fxy

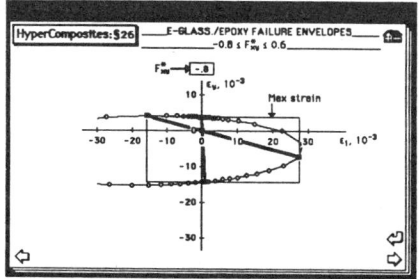 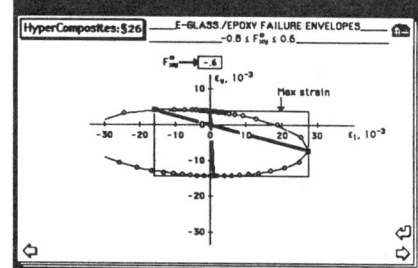

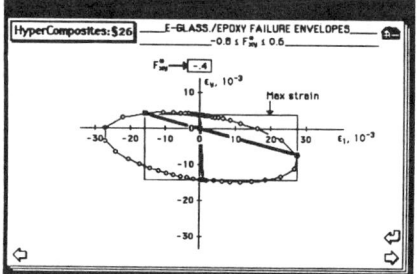 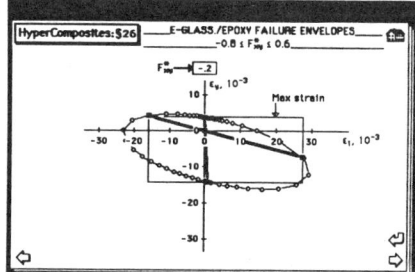

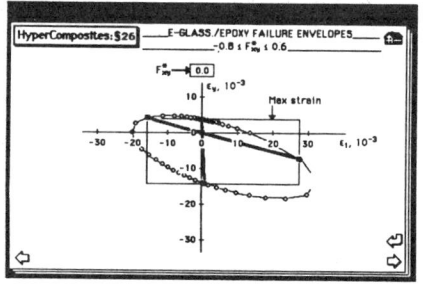 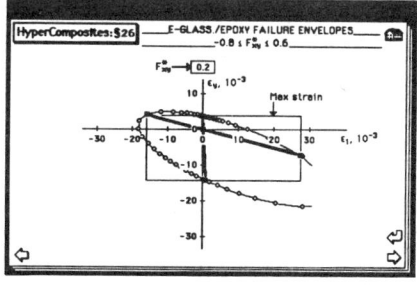

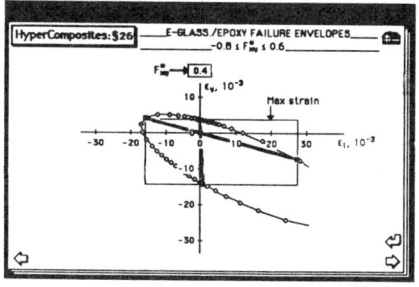 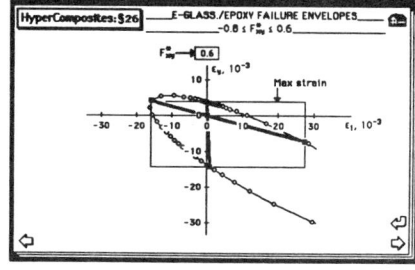

29.27 [0] T300 VERSUS Fxy

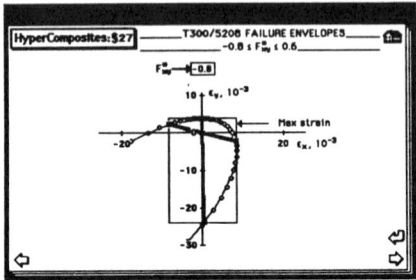
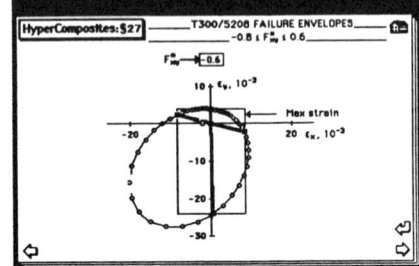

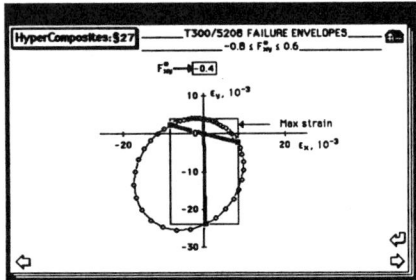
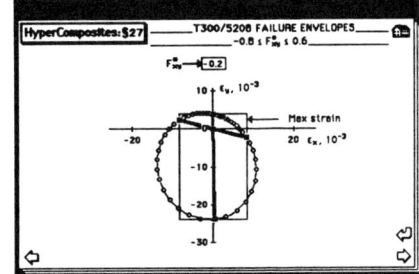

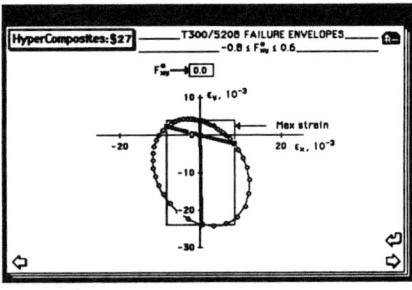
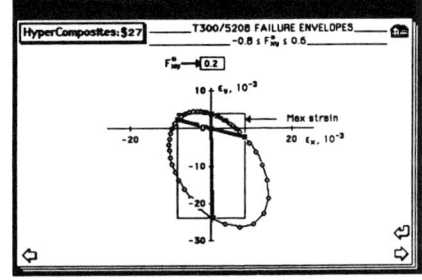

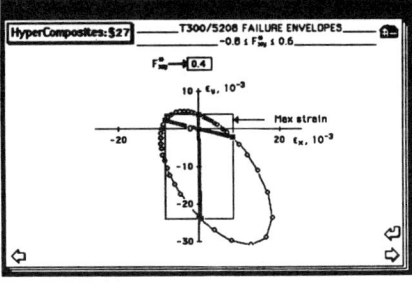
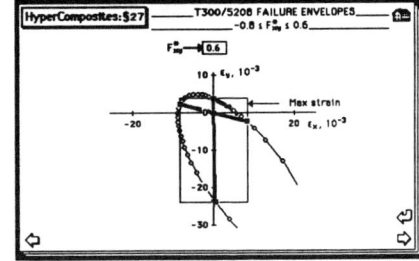

29.28 [Pi/4] SCOTCH VERSUS Fxy

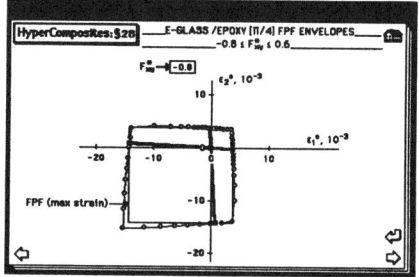
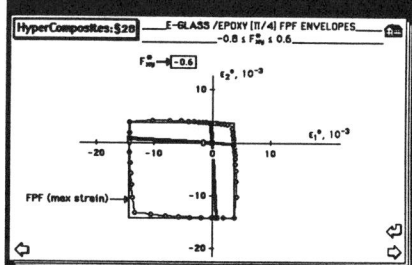
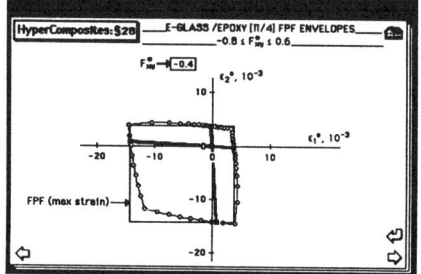
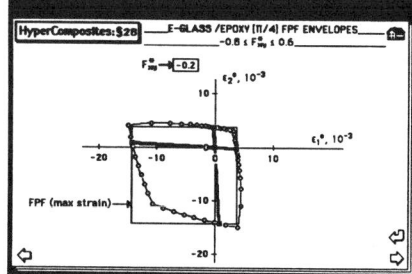
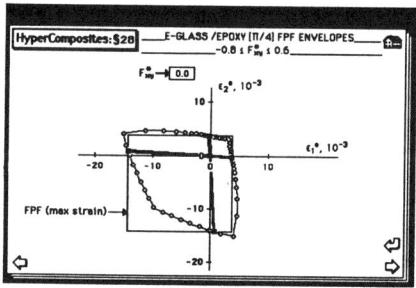
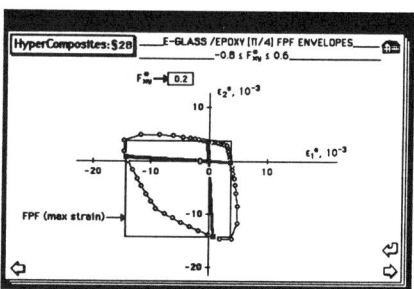
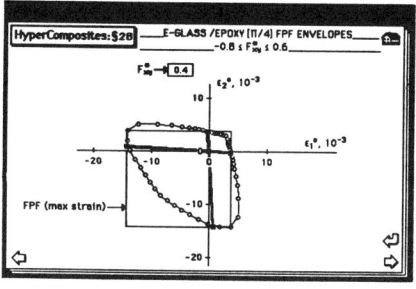
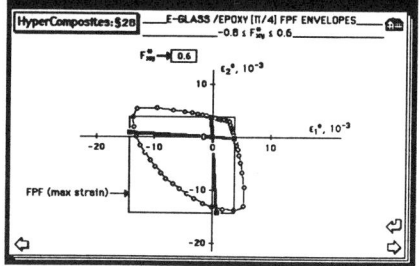

29.29 [Pi/4] T300 VERSUS Fxy

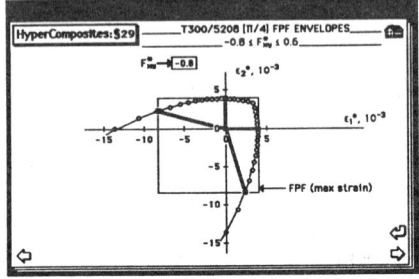
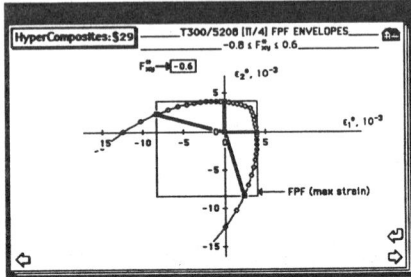
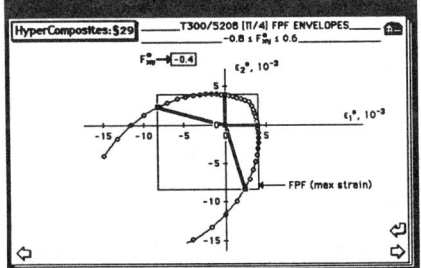
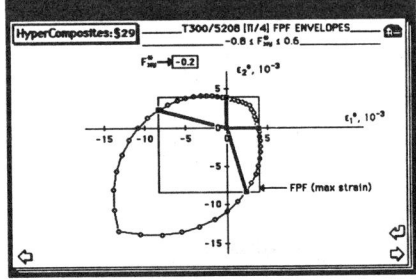
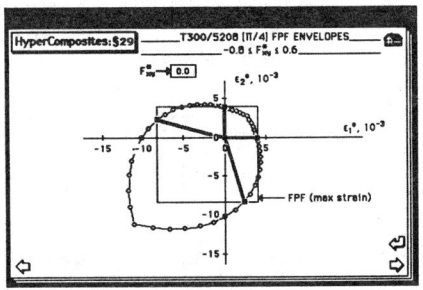
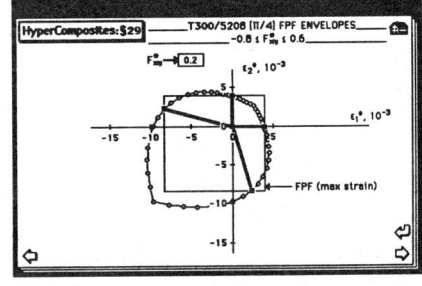
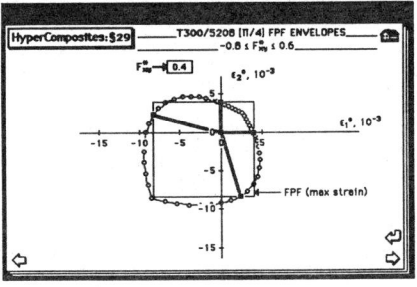
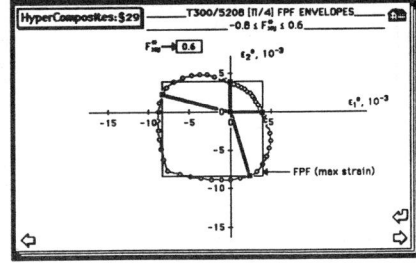

29.30 SMC AND FABRICS

HyperComposites:§30 ·······················SHORT FIBER COMPOSITES···················

·······················Stiffness and strength···············

Short fiber composites include sheet molding composites (SMC) and whisker composites. Using laminated plate theory, we can derive:

The quasi-isotropic constants for randomly oriented fibers in the plane can be obtained using the plane stress constants mentioned before.

The quasi-isotropic strengths can be obtained using the [π/3] quasi-isotropic laminates subjected to uniaxial tensile and compressive stresses, and pure shear, together with the quadratic failure criterion.

The strength is based on the first-ply-failure on the assumption that the SMC strength reaches its ultimate at FPF. The Tresca and Mises criteria can be modified to predict the shear strength. Sensitivity of the fiber volume on the SMC strength will also be shown. The cost effectiveness in terms of fiber volume can then be predicted accordingly.

HyperComposites:§30 ·······················ISOTROPIC STIFFNESS OF SMC···················

The quasi-isotropic constants in plane stress can be used for randomly oriented SMC in the plane:

	1	2	3	4	5	6	7	8	9	10	11
1	Type	CFRP	BFRP	CFRP	GFRP	KFRP	CFRTP	CFRP	CFRP	CCRP	CCRP
2	Fiber/cloth	T300	B(4)	AS	E-glass	Kev 49	AS 4	IM6	T300	T300	T300
3	Matrix	N5208	N5505	H3501	epoxy	epoxy	PEEK	epoxy	Fbrt 934	Fbrt 934	Fbrt 934
4							APC2		4-mil tp	13-mil c	7-mil c
27	Linear combinations of [Q],GPa										
28	U1 *	76.37	87.70	59.66	20.45	32.44	57.04	85.88	62.47	58.84	52.37
31	U4 *	22.61	28.36	16.96	5.51	10.54	17.28	25.43	19.73	19.05	16.66
32	U5 *	26.88	29.67	21.35	7.47	10.95	19.88	30.23	21.37	19.89	17.85
33	* invariant										
34	Quasi-isotropic constants										
35	E,GPa	69.68	78.53	54.84	18.96	29.02	51.81	78.35	56.24	52.67	47.0
35	nu	0.30	0.32	0.28	0.27	0.32	0.30	0.30	0.32	0.32	0.32
37	G,GPa	26.88	29.67	21.35	7.47	10.95	19.88	30.23	21.37	19.89	17.8

$$E^{iso} = \left[1 - \nu^{iso\,2}\right]U_1, \quad \nu^{iso} = \frac{U_4}{U_1}, \quad G^{iso} = U_5$$

29.30 SMC AND FABRICS (continued)

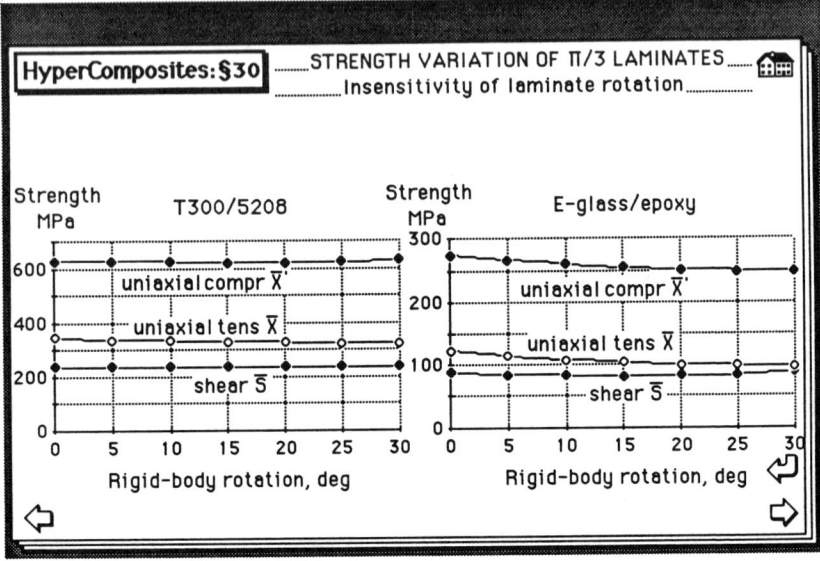

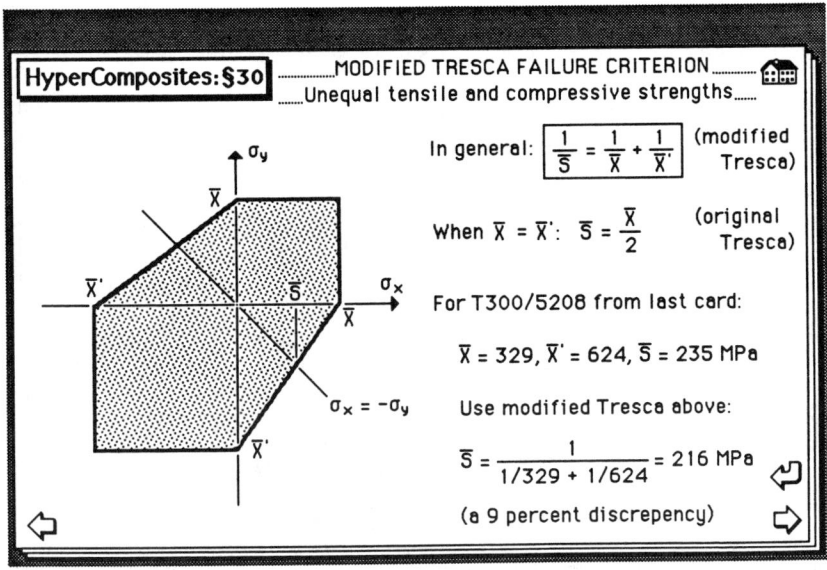

29.30 SMC AND FABRICS (continued)

HyperComposites:§30   MODIFIED MISES FAILURE CRITERION
For unequal tensile and compressive strengths

$$F_{xx}\sigma_x{}^2 + 2F_{xy}\sigma_x\sigma_y + F_{yy}\sigma_y{}^2 + F_x\sigma_x + F_y\sigma_y = 1$$

For isotropic materials, $F_{xx} = F_{yy} = \dfrac{1}{XX'}$, $F_x = F_y = \dfrac{1}{X} - \dfrac{1}{X'}$, $F_{xy}^* = -0.5$

Let $\sigma_x = -\sigma_y = S$

$$\boxed{S = \dfrac{\sqrt{XX'}}{\sqrt{3}}}$$ (Note: when $X = X'$, $S = X/\sqrt{3} = 0.57\,X$)

For T300/5208 SMC, X = 329, X' = 624 MPa

S = 261 MPa

This is higher than the modified Tresca criterion, where S = 216.

The value from laminated plate theory (S = 235) is in between.

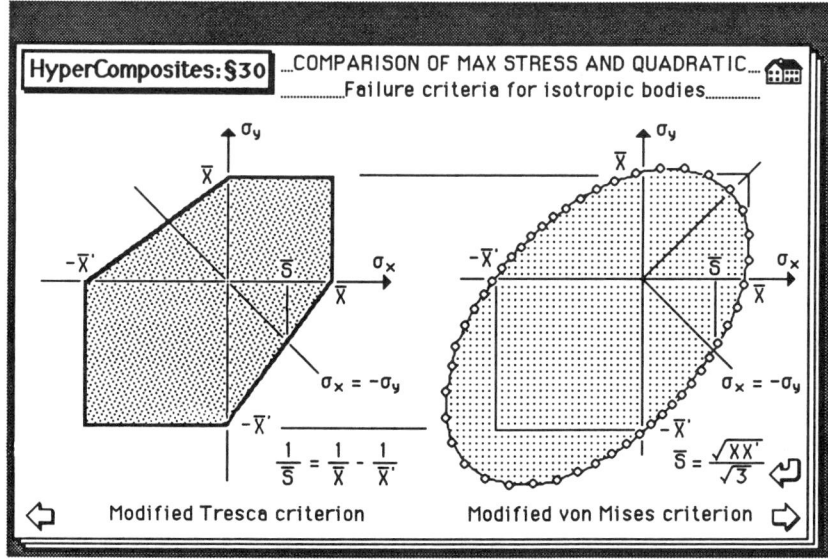

HyperComposites:§30   COMPARISON OF MAX STRESS AND QUADRATIC
Failure criteria for isotropic bodies

$$\frac{1}{\overline{S}} = \frac{1}{\overline{X}} - \frac{1}{\overline{X}'}$$

Modified Tresca criterion

$$\overline{S} = \frac{\sqrt{XX'}}{\sqrt{3}}$$

Modified von Mises criterion

29.30 SMC AND FABRICS (continued)

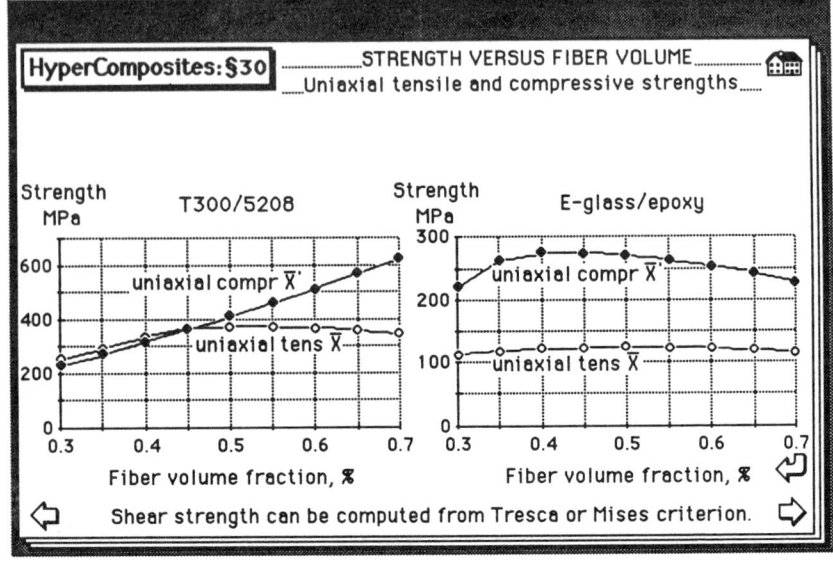

HyperComposites:§30 ....STRENGTH VERSUS FIBER VOLUME....
....Uniaxial tensile and compressive strengths....

T300/5208 — Strength MPa — E-glass/epoxy — Strength MPa

uniaxial compr $\overline{X}'$

uniaxial tens $\overline{X}$

Fiber volume fraction, %

Shear strength can be computed from Tresca or Mises criterion.

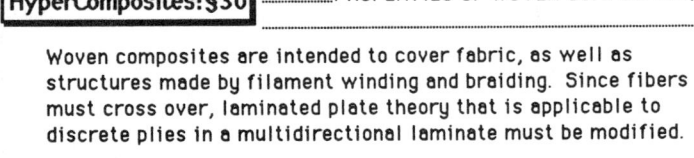

HyperComposites:§30 ....PROPERTIES OF WOVEN COMPOSITES....

Woven composites are intended to cover fabric, as well as structures made by filament winding and braiding. Since fibers must cross over, laminated plate theory that is applicable to discrete plies in a multidirectional laminate must be modified.

We are not aware of any simple theory that can predict the stiffness and strength of woven composites. The simplest is to use a [0/90] laminate of the same ply material to model a balanced woven fabric. For unbalanced fabrics, the ratio between the 0- and 90-degree plies can match that between the warp and fill yarns.

The difficulties in taking into account of the fiber cross over arise from the loss of stiffness and strength along the fibers. When fibers are not straight their effective stiffness will reduce. Their tensile strength will reduce because of the additional bending stress and contact stress at cross over points. The compressive strength

29.30 SMC AND FABRICS (continued)

HyperComposites: §30 ⸺⸺ PROPERTIES OF WOVEN COMPOSITES⸺⸺
⸺⸺Micro-macromechanics modeling⸺⸺

will also reduce because fibers are more prone to buckling. Another factor that causes difficulty is the fiber volume fraction, which is not likely to be as uniform as that for cross ply composites. Voids are also more likely to occur near the cross over points.

In the next card, we show the comparison between the stiffness and strength of a [0/90] composite and those of a balanced fabric made from the same composite material. While the fiber volume fractions are only comparable, the use of cross ply to model fabric is accurate within 20 percent for glass and Kevlar composites. But for graphite composites which have stiff fibers the model is not as accurate.

For purpose of design, it is best to use the experimentally measured fabric data directly, replacing the ply data of a unidirectional composite. Further development of the model for the fiber cross over will include the degraded fiber stiffness and strength.

HyperComposites: §30 ⸺COMPARISON OF [0], [0/90] AND WOVEN FABRIC⸺
⸺⸺Stiffness and strength properties⸺⸺

| | A | Graphite/epoxy | | | E-glass/epoxy | | | Kevlar 49/epoxy | | |
		I	J	K	L	M	N	O	P	Q
1	Type	CFRP	CCRP	CCRP	GFRP	GFRP	GCRP	KFRP	KFRP	KCRP
2	Fiber	T300	T300	T300	E-glass	E-glass	F161	Kev 49	Kev 49	Kev 49
3	Matrix	F934	F934	F934	epoxy	epoxy	6581	epoxy	epoxy	N5209
4		[0]	[0/90]		[0]	[0/90]		[0]	[0/90]	
5		tape	laminate	cloth	tape	laminate	cloth	tape	laminate	cloth
6	Stiffness									
7	Ex	148.00	79.2	66.00	38.60	23.6	29.6	76.00	41.0	35.8
8	Ey	9.65	79.2	66.00	8.27	23.6	26.9	5.50	41.0	35.8
9	nu/x	0.30	0.04	0.04	0.26	0.09	0.12	0.34	0.05	0.09
10	Es	4.55	4.6	4.10	4.14	4.1	6.24	2.30	2.3	1.79
17	Strengths									
18	X	1314	664	375	1062	545	489	1400	704	582
19	X'	1220	899	279	610	306	390	235	165	189
20	Y	43	664	368	31	545	444	12	704	582
21	Y'	168	899	278	118	306	305	53	165	189
22	S	48	49	46	72	80	133	34	34	84

Boxed [0/90] predictions are within 20 percent of woven fabric data.

Section 30

GLOSSARY

ADHEREND – Plate adhesively bonded to another plate.

ADHESIVE – Substance capable of holding two surfaces together.

ADVANCED COMPOSITES – Composite materials with structural properties comparable to or better than aluminum; e.g., boron, graphite and Kevlar composites.

AGING – Loss of properties through time–exposure of elevated temperature, ultra–violet radiation, moisture or other hostile environments.

ALLOWABLES – Property values used for design with a 95 percent confidence interval: the "A" allowable is the minimum value for 99 percent of the population; and the "B" allowable, 90 percent.

AMBIENT CONDITIONS – Prevailing environmental conditions such as the surrounding temperature, pressure, and relative humidity.

ANISOTROPY – Material properties that vary with the orientation or direction of the reference coordinates. Composite materials, like wood, are anisotropic.

ASPECT RATIO – Length–to–width ratio of a rectangular plate, the length–to–diameter ratio of a discontinuous fiber, or the length–to–bundle diameter ratio of a bundle of parallel fibers.

ANGLE–PLY LAMINATE – Possessing equal plies with positive and negative angles. This bi–directional laminate is simple because it is orthotropic, not anisotropic. A [±45] is a very common angle–ply laminate. A cross–ply laminate is another simple laminate.

ANTISYMMETRY – Special symmetry with sign change between off–diagonal components; e.g., an unsymmetric angle–ply laminate.

AUTOCLAVE – Pressure vessel that can maintain temperature and pressure of a desired air or gas for the curing of organic–matrix composite materials.

AXISYMMETRY – Symmetry about an axis; i.e., isotropic in the plane normal to the axis, and this material is called transversely isotropic.

BFRA – Boron fiber reinforced aluminum.

BFRP – Boron fiber reinforced plastic.

B–STAGE – Intermediate or precured stage of a thermosetting resin. This stage provides easier handling and processing.

BALANCED LAMINATE – Where plies with positive angles are balanced by equal plies with negative angles. While angle–ply laminates have only one pair of matched angles, balanced laminates can have many pairs, plus 0 and 90 degrees. A balanced laminate is orthotropic in in–plane behavior, but anisotropic in flexural behavior.

BALANCED SYMMETRIC LAMINATE – A laminate which is symmetric and balanced.

BENDING: STRETCHING COUPLING – Coupling brought into play in a laminate due to the presence of **[B]**.

BENDING: TWISTING COUPLING – Coupling brought into play in a laminate due to the presence of D_{16}, D_{26}.

BENDING MOMENT – Stress couple that changes curvature of a beam or plate.

BI–AXIAL – Having both normal components of stress or strain acting.

BLEEDER CLOTH – Nonstructural, fiber glass cloth placed adjacent to the composite material part to absorb excess resin during cure, and is removed from the part after cure.

BONDED JOINT – Location where two adherends are bonded together with a layer of adhesive in between. A lap joint positions the adherends with an overlap; a scarf joint, with matched tapered sections; a stepped joint, through steps.

BORON FILAMENT – Made by vapor deposition of B_4C onto a tungsten substrate. Two filament diameters, 0.1 and 0.2 mm, are made. Two outstanding features of boron are: the high longitudinal compressive strength, and the relative ease of fabrication of boron/aluminum composite material.

BOUNDARY CONDITIONS – Load and environmental conditions that exist at the boundaries. Conditions must be specified to perform stress analysis.

BRAIDING – A mechanized weaving of fibers into a structural foam such as tube, square box, or u–shapped channel.

BREATHER – Porous material, such as a fabric or mat, placed inside the vacuum bag to facilitate removal of air, moisture, and volatiles during cure.

BUCKLING – Unstable lateral displacement of a structural part such as a panel caused by excessive compression and shear. Microbuckling of fibers in a composite material can also occur under axial compression.

BUNDLE STRENGTH – Strength obtained from a test of parallel filaments, with or without organic matrix. The bundle test is often used in place of the tedious monofilament test.

BURST PRESSURE – Pressure corresponding to the final failure of a pressure vessel.

CARPET PLOT – A design chart showing the uniaxial stiffness or strength as a function of arbitrary ratios of 0, 90, and ±45 degree plies.

CAUL PLATE – Smooth, metallic plate that is placed in contact with the laminate to insure uniform pressure and temperature during cure, and smooth finish after cure.

CCRP – Carbon or graphite cloth reinforced plastic.

CFRP – Carbon or graphite fiber reinforced plastic. Letter G in GFRP is for glass, not graphite.

CFRTP – Carbon or graphite fiber reinforced thermoplastic.

CHARACTERISTIC LENGTH – A dimension measured between the opening and a characteristic curve of the laminate.

COCURE – Simultaneous curing and bonding of a composite laminate to another material or parts like honeycomb core, and stiffeners. Cocuring can reduce fabrication cost.

COLLIMATED – Rendered parallel, such as fibers in unidirectional tapes.

COMBINED STRESSES – State of stress with all possible components of active. In case of plane stress, all three components are present.

COMPLEX ROOTS – The solutions of a characteristic equatuion are obtained in a complex form, i.e., real plus imaginary parts.

COMPLIANCE – Measurement of softness as opposed to stiffness of a material. It is a reciprocal of the Young's modulus, or an inverse of the stiffness matrix.

COMPOSITE OR COMPOSITE MATERIAL – Material that is made of two or more constituent materials. Although most natural and man–made materials are composites, our current interest covers only fiber–reinforced materials; e.g., uni and multidirectional filamentary composites in woven and nonwoven forms.

CONFIDENCE INTERVAL – A range within which a population parameter can be expected to lie.

CONSTANT LIFE DIAGRAM – A plot of family of curves used in fatigue analysis, each of which is for a single fatigue life relating alternating stress and mean stress. The constant life diagram is usually obtained from a family of S–N curves.

CONSTITUENT MATERIALS – Individual materials that make up the composite material; e.g., graphite and epoxy are the constituent materials of a graphite/epoxy composite material.

CONTRACTED NOTATION – A short–hand notation for stress, strain and material constants such as elastic moduli and strength parameters.

CORE – Inner, light weight material used in a sandwich panel. Metallic or composite facing materials are bonded to the core to form a sandwich panel.

COUNT – Number of warp and fill yarns per unit length; e.g., a fabric count of 24x26 in the English unit means 24 yarns per inch in the warp, and 26 in the fill.

COUPLING – Linking a side effect to a principal effect. Poisson coupling links the lateral contraction to an axial extension. For composite materials, an anisotropic laminate couples the shear to normal components; an unsymmetric laminate couples curvature with extension. These couplings are unique with composites and provide opportunity to perform extraordinary functions.

CRACK DENSITY – Number of distinctive cracks per unit length.

CRAZING – Formation of fine cracks in an organic matrix material. Cracks in composite laminates are also referred to as crazing even though the cracks could be in the matrix material as well as at the interface between the constituent materials.

CRITICAL BUCKLING LOADS – Lowest loads at which buckling occurs.

CROSS–PLY LAMINATE – Special laminate that contains only 0 and 90 degree plies. This bi–directional laminate is orthotropic, and has nearly zero Poisson's ratio. The other simple bi–directional laminate is the angle–ply, which possesses one pair of balanced off–axis plies.

CUMMULATIVE DISTRIBUTION FUNCTION – A probability distribution function obtained by integrating the density function from negative infinity to an arbitrary point x. It identifies the percentage of a population that lies below the value x.

CURE – To change the properties of a thermosetting resin irreversibly by chemical reaction. Cure may be accomplished by addition of curing agents, with or without catalyst, and with or without heat.

CURVATURE – Geometric measure of the bending and twisting of a plate.

DAM – Ridge circumventing a mold to prevent resin runout during cure.

DEBOND – Area of separation within or between plies in a laminate, or between a bonded joint caused by contamination, improper adhesion during processing, or damaging interlaminar stresses.

DEBULK – To reduce laminate thickness by application of pressure. The compaction is achieved by removing trapped air, vapor, and volatiles between plies.

DEFORMATION – Changes in size and shape of a body resulting from externally applied stresses, temperature change, and moisture absorption. Deformation in size is measured by the normal strain components; that in shape, by shear component.

DEFLECTION – Displacement of a structure such as a beam.

DEGRADATION – Loss of property due to aging, corrosion, and repeated or sustained stress (fatigue or stress rupture). Composite materials are insensitive to any form of degradation.

DELAMINATION – Debonding process primarily resulting from unfavorable interlaminar stresses. Edge delamination however can be effectively prevented by a wrap–around reinforcement.

DESIGN – To select optimum ply number and orientations for a given composite laminate subjected to one or more sets of applied stresses. This is the antithesis of stress analysis.

DIMENSIONAL STABILITY – Zero or nearly zero deformation due to change in temperature and moisture content. This unique property of graphite/epoxy composite material is utilized for antennas in space.

DISPLACEMENT – Measure of the movement of a point on the surface and in the interior of a body.

DOUBLER – Locally built–up reinforcement or repair.

DRAPE – Ability of woven and nonwoven composite materials to conform to complex curvature.

DWELL TIME – Period of time during cure that a laminate is held at elevated temperature prior to application of pressure.

EFFECTIVE PROPERTIES – The volumetric average of the properties of the constituents within a material system, or plies within a multidirectional laminate. For example, effective moduli, stress, and stain.

ELASTIC RELATION – Fully reversible, single–valued stress–strain relation. Loading and unloading follow the same path; there is no hysteresis, or residual strain. Although nonlinear relation is admissible, the relation for composite materials is essentially linear.

ELEMENTARY THEORY – Theory based on strength of materials.

ELLIPTIC INTEGRALS – $E(k,\pi/2)$, $F(k,\pi/2)$ defined in Equation 24.4.

ELLIPTIC OPENING – An opening whose shape resembles an ellipse.

END – Individual warp yarn, thread, monofilament, or roving. For glass fibers, an end contains 206 filaments.

ENGINEERING CONSTANTS – Measured directly from uniaxial tensile and compressive, and pure shear tests applied to unidirectional as well as laminated composites. Typical constants are the effective Young's modulus, Poisson's ratio, and shear modulus. Each constant is accompanied by letter or numeric subscripts designating the direction associated with the property.

ENVIRONMENTAL CONDITIONS – Prevailing temperature and humidity.

EPOXY – Thermosetting resin made by polymerization of an epoxide.

EXPANSION COEFFICIENT – Measurement of swelling or expansion of composite materials due to temperature change and moisture absorption.

EXTENSOMETER – A device for measuring the change in length over a given gage length.

FABRIC – Planar, woven material constructed by interlacing yarns, fibers or filaments.

FACE – Outer ply of a laminate.

FAILURE CRITERION – Empirical description of the failure of composite materials subjected to complex state of stresses or strains. The most commonly used are the maximum stress, the maximum strain, and the quadratic criteria.

FAILURE ENVELOPE – Ultimate limit in combined stress or strain state defined by a failure criterion.

FATIGUE LIFE – The number of cycles of stress or strain at fatigue failure.

FATIGUE NOTCH FACTOR – The ratio of fatigue strength of unnotched specimens at N cycles to the fatigue strength of notched specimens at N cycles.

FATIGUE NOTCH SENSITIVITY – An estimate of the effect of a notch on the fatigue strength or life of a material. It is expressed as $q=(k_f-1)/(k_t-1)$ where k_f is the fatigue notch factor and k_t is the static theoretical stress concentration factor.

FATIGUE STRESSES – Stresses that vary with time in manner such as the sinusoidal form.

FATIGUE STRESS RATIO – The ratio of the minimum fatigue stress to the maximum fatigue stress, usually denoted by R.

FATIGUE STRENGTH – Maximum fatigue stress where the material can withstand without undergoing failure.

FATIGUE STRENGTH RATIO – The ratio of fatigue strength to the static strength.

FIBER – Single filament, rolled or formed in one direction, and used as the principal constituent of woven and nonwoven composite materials. Most common fibers are glass, boron, graphite and Kevlar.

FIBER CONTENT – Percent volume of fiber in a composite material. Most common composites in use today have fiber content between 45 and 70 percent. Percent weight or mass of fiber is also used.

FICK'S EQUATION – Diffusion equation for moisture migration. This is analogous to the Fourier's equation of heat conduction.

FILAMENT – Continuous fiber with exceptionally high specific stiffness and strength, and is the principal constituent of advanced composites.

FILAMENT WINDING – Automated process of placing filament onto a mandrel in prescribed patterns. The resin impregnation can be before or during the winding, known as prepreg or wet winding, respectively. The mandrel can subsequently be removed after curing of the composite material. Filament winding is most advantageous in building pressure vessels, pipes, drive shafts, or any device that is axisymmetrical.

FILL – Yarn oriented at right angles to the warp in a woven fabric.

FINISH – Material and process used to treat fibers to improve the interfacial bond between fiber and matrix.

FIRST PLY FAILURE – The failure of the ply or ply group in a multidirectional laminate that occurs at first. The load corresponding to this failure can be the design limit load.

FLASH – Excess material that is formed at the parting line of a mold or die, or that is extruded from a closed mold.

FLOW CHART – Chart showing the salient steps of a computer program.

FOURIER'S EQUATION – Diffusion equation commonly associated with the heat conduction in a body. Fick's equation is a special case, applied to the moisture migration and accumulation.

FREE EXPANSION – Thermal or moisture expansion without external stress.

FREQUENCY – Number of fatigue cycles per second, expressed in Hertz.

GELCOAT – Quick–setting resin used in the molding process to provide an improved surface for the composite; it is the first resin applied to the mold after the mold–release agent.

GENERALIZED HOOKE'S LAW – The most general linear elastic stress–strain relation for an anisotropic material from which materials with various types of symmetries can be derived.

GENERALIZED PLANE STRAIN – A modified state of plane strain with a nonzero constant strain perpendicular to the plane containing the state of plane strain.

GENLAM – Analysis of stress, strain, and failure of a general, unsymmetric laminate.

GFRP – Glass fiber reinforced plastic. Graphite fiber reinforced plastic is called CFRP.

GLASS FILAMENT – Drawn from molten glass through platnium bushings. Most widely used filament in composite materials. Glass filament can be made into unidirectional plies, woven fabric, mats, and short–fiber composites like the sheet molding compound.

GLASSY TEMPERATURE – When the stiffness and strength of an organic resin undergo drastic reduction. This is also known as the glass transition temperature and can be the maximum use temperature.

GRAPHITE FILAMENT – Made from poly–acrylic–nitrile (PAN) filament after high temperature exposure and mechanical stretching. Other materials and processes are available but not as common.

HAT TYPE CORRUGATED CORE – Corrugated sheet of repeating hat sections.

HETEROGENEITY – On the micro level, local variation of constituent materials. On the macro level, ply by ply variation of materials or orientations.

HOMOGENEITY – Material uniformity within a body. In the mechanics of composite materials, micro and macro homogeneity is achieved by smearing the actual heterogeneity.

HONEYCOMB CORE – Made from metallic and nonmetallic materials, and when bonded with face sheets form a sandwich panel. The core is assumed to have no stiffness in the plane of the sandwich panel, and infinite stiffness normal to the panel.

HOOKE'S LAW – A linear relationship between stress and strain.

HOOP WINDING – The placing of fibers (filament) perpendicular to the longitudinal axis of a cylinder or a pressure vessel.

HORIZONTAL SHEAR STRENGTH – Estimated from a short–beam–shear test. This test is approximate because the stresses calculated from the simple beam theory is not exact.

HYBRID – Composite with more than two constituents; e.g., a graphite/glass/epoxy hybrid. An intralaminar hybrid has hybrid plies made from graphite and glass filaments. An interlaminar hybrid has laminates made from two or more different ply materials.

HYGROTHERMAL EFFECT – Change in properties due to moisture absorption and temperature change.

INCLUSION – A plug which is inserted into the opening of a plate.

INDICIAL NOTATION – Sub or superscript notation for matrices and tensors.

INTERACTION – Same as coupling. For example, longitudinal tensile strength is affected by the presence of transverse stress. Similar interaction exists between the longitudinal buckling stress and the transverse or shear stress. As a rule, the interaction effects for composite materials are greater than the conventional isotropic material. All anticipated stresses should be considered simultaneously.

INTERFACE – Boundary or transition zone between constituent materials, such as the fiber/matrix interface, or the boundary between plies of a laminate. Debond at the microscopic or fiber/matrix interface can lead to fiber breakage and matrix cracking. Debond at the macroscopic or interlaminar interface can lead to delamination.

INTERLAMINAR STRESSES – Three stress components associated with the thickness direction of a plate. The remaining three are the in–plane components of the plate. Interlaminar stresses are significant only if the thickness is greater than 10 percent of the length or width of the plate. These stresses can also be significant in areas of concentrated loads, and abrupt change in material and geometry. The effects of these stresses are not easy to assess because 3–dimensional stress analysis and failure criterion are not well understood.

INVARIANT – Constant values for all orientations of the coordinate axes. Components of stress, strain, stiffness and compliance all have linear and quadratic invariants. For composite materials they represent directionally independent properties, and the bounds of stiffness and strength of multidirectional laminates.

ISOTROPY – Property that is not directionally dependent. Stiffness and strength of aluminum, for example, are isotropic and remain the same for all orientations of the coordinate axes. Composite laminates can be made isotropic in its in–plane stiffness; e.g., any [π/n] laminate with n greater than 2, which is referred to as quasi–isotropic.

KEVLAR FIBER – DuPont company trade name for an aramid fiber.

KFRP – Kevlar fiber reinforced plastic.

KIRCHHOFF–LOVE ASSUMPTION –It is assumed that the normals to the middle plane of a plate remain normal and unstretched after deformation.

LAMINA – Ply or layer of unidirectional composite or fabric.

LAMINATE – Plate consisting of layers of uni or multidirectional plies of one or more composite materials. A laminate is usually thin.

LAMINATE FAMILY – Laminates sharing the same ply number and angles.

LAMINATED PLATE THEORY – The most common method for the analysis and design of composite laminates. Each ply or ply group is treated as a quasi–homogeneous material. Linear strain across the thickness is assumed. This is also called the lamination theory.

LAMRANK – Design of an optimum laminate for a given loading conditions by a laminate ranking method.

LAST PLY FAILURE – The failure of the ply or ply group in a multidirectional laminate that occurs at last. The load corresponding to this failure can be the ultimate load.

LAYUP – Hand or machine–operated process of ply by ply laying of a multidirectional laminate.

LAYUP – Ply stacking sequence or ply orientations of a laminate.

LINEAR RELATION – straight line relation between variables; i.e., each output variable is unique and linearly proportional to an input variable.

LOAD – Force, or generalized force, such as in–plane or flexural stress.

LOADING PATH – Locus of increasing load in stress or strain space.

LOADING RATE – The change in load per unit time in mechanical testing.

LONGITUDINAL MODULUS – Elastic constant along the fiber direction in a unidirectional composite; e.g., longitudinal Young's and shear moduli.

MACROMECHANICS – Structural behavior of composite laminates using the laminated plate theory. The fiber and matrix within each ply are smeared and no longer identifiable.

MANDREL – Male mold used for filament winding. For pressure vessels, the mandrel is made of salt, styroform or plaster, supported by a collapsable framing.

MASS FRACTION – Fraction of a constituent material based on its mass.

MATERIAL USE EFFICIENCY – Defined to study qualitatively the best use of material from strength point of view.

MATRIX – Material that binds the filaments or fabric to form a composite material. The most common matrices for organic composites are polyester and epoxy; for metal–matrix composites, alunimum.

MATRIX – Mathematical entity, consisting of rows and columns of numbers. In two dimensions, stress and strain are 1x3 matrices; and stiffness and compliance, 3x3 matrices.

MATRIX DEGRADATION FACTOR (MDF) – Factor to reduce the stiffness of matrix material to include the effect of transverse cracking of plies.

MATRIX INVERSION – Algebraic operation to obtain compliance matrix from stiffness matrix, or vice versa. It is analogous to obtaining the reciprocal of a number.

MAXIMUM FATIGUE STRESS – The stress having the largest algebraic value in a cycle.

MAXIMUM STRAIN – Failure criterion based on the maximum strains.

MAXIMUM STRESS – Failure criterion based on the maximum stresses.

MEAN STRESS – The algebraic average of the minimum and maximum stresses in a cycle of fatigue loading.

MECHANICAL LOAD – Mechanically applied load as distinguished from cure– or environment–induced load.

MIC–MAC – The integration of micromechanics and macromechanics in the design of composites.

MICROMECHANICS – Calculation of the effective ply properties as functions of the fiber and matrix properties. Some numerical approaches also provide the stress and strain within each constituent and those at the interface.

MIDDLE PLANE – Plane cutting a plate into two halves in the thickness direction.

MID–PLANE – Middle surface of a laminate; usually the $z = 0$ plane.

MINIMUM FATIGUE STRESS – The stress having the smallest algebraic value in a cycle.

MODULUS – Elastic constants such as the Young's modulus, shear modulus, or stiffness moduli in general.

MOHR'S CIRCLE – Graphical representation of the variation of the stress and strain components resulting from rotating coordinate axes. Analogous representations for material property such as the stiffness and compliance of composite laminates can also be made.

MOISTURE ABSORPTION – Property of epoxy changes due to moisture absorption; it is detrimental because the glassy temperature of the epoxy is suppressed, and beneficial because swelling counteracts curing stresses.

MOISTURE DISTRIBUTION – Transient moisture profile changes very slowly with time. For temperature, a steady–state distribution can be attained in a short time. But for moisture concentration, only the first few plies from the exposed surface can change significantly with time. For the interior plies, months if not years will elapse before change takes place. This nonuniform distribution must be considered in the assessment of the effect of moisture on the properties of composite materials.

MOLD – Cavity on which a composite part is placed, and from which it takes its shape after curing.

MOLD RELEASE AGENT – Lubricant applied to mold surfaces to facilitate release of the molded part.

MOMENT – Stress couple that causes a plate to bend or twist.

MONOCLINIC MATERIAL – Material with only one symmetric plane and 13 independent elastic constants.

MULTIDIRECTIONAL – Having multiple ply orientations in a laminate.

MULTIPLE LOADS – Stress applied to a body in many directions.

NETTING ANALYSIS – Treating composites like fibers without matrix. It is not a mechanics analysis, and is not applicable to composites.

NEUTRAL PLANE – Plane which experiences no stretching.

NONMECHANICAL STRESS – Originated from curing and hygrothermal stress.

NOTCHED STRENGTH – The effective strength of a plate with stress raisers like holes, notches and cracks.

OFF–AXIS – Not coincident with the symmetry axis; also called off–angle.

ON–AXIS – Coincident with the symmetry axis; also called on–angle.

OPEN HOLE – A through–the–thickness opening without constraints at the hole boundary.

OPTIMUM LAMINATE – Having the highest stiffness or strength per unit mass or cost.

ORTHOTROPIC LAYER – Layer having three perpendicular planes of symmetry. The adjacent ($\pm\alpha$) off–axis plies together are assumed to behave as an orthotropic layer.

ORTHOTROPY – Having three mutually perpendicular planes of symmetry. Unidirectional plies, fabric, cross–ply and angle–ply laminates are all orthotropic.

ORTHOTROPIC PLATE THEORY – Theory of bending of an homogeneous orthotropic plate.

PARALLEL–AXIS THEOREM – Formula for elastic moduli relative to a displaced reference coordinate frame; analogous to that for moments of inertia.

PEEL PLY – Fabric material applied to a laminate to protect the clean, ready–to–use bonding surface and peeled off prior to curing.

PHENOLIC – Thermosetting resin for elevated temperature.

PICK – Individual fill yarn or roving in a fabric.

PLANE STRAIN – Two–dimensional simplification for stress analysis, applicable to the cross–section of long cylinders.

PLANE STRESS – Two–dimensional simplification for stress analysis, applicable to thin homogeneous and laminated plates.

PLATEN – Mounting plates of a press to which the mold assembly is fastened.

PLY DROP – Laminate thickness reduction in zones of lower loads by dropping some plies.

PLY GROUP – Group formed by continuous plies with the same angle.

PLY STRAIN – Those components in a ply which, by the laminated plate theory, are the same as those of the laminate.

PLY STRESS – Those components in a ply, which vary from ply to ply depending on the materials and angles in the laminate.

POISSON'S RATIO – The ratio of transverse strain to the corresponding axial strain resulting from the applied axial load below the elastic limit of the material.

POROSITY – Having voids; i.e., containing pockets of trapped air and gas after cure. Its measurement is the same as void content. It is commonly assumed that porosity is finely and uniformily distributed throughout the laminate.

POST CURE – Additional exposure to temperature after initial cure. The post cure temperature may be higher than the cure temperature.

PREFORM – Layup made on a mandrel or mockup that is subsequently transferred to the curing tool or mold.

PREPREG – Short for preimpregnated; a woven or unidirectional ply, or roving impregnated with resin, usually advanced to B–stage, and ready for layup or winding.

PRINCIPAL DIRECTION – Specific coordinate axes orientation when stress and strain components reach maximum and minimum for the normal components, and zero for the shear.

QUASI–ISOTROPIC LAMINATE – A laminate with only two equivalent elastic constants.

RANKING – Ordering of laminates by strength, stiffness or others.

REGULAR GRID CORE – Sandwich plate core in the form of a grid with periodically placed members.

REPAIR (COMPOSITE) – Fixing the damage such as holes and cracks in (composite) structures.

REPEATING INDEX – Used in laminate code to represent the number of repeating sub–laminates.

RESIDUAL STRESS – Resulting from cooldown after cure and moisture content. On the micromechanical level, stress is tensile in the resin and compressive in the fiber. On the macromecahnical level, it is tensile in the transverse direction to the unidirectional fibers, and compressive in the longitudinal direction, resulting in a lowered first–ply–failure load. Moisture absorption offsets this detrimental thermal effect in both micro and macro levels.

RESIDUAL FATIGUE STRENGTH – The retention of static strength after subjected to a certain fatigue load history.

RESIDUAL STRENGTH –The retention of static strength after subjected to a load history and/or environment.

RESIN – Organic material with high molecular weight, insoluble in water, with no definite melting point and no tendency to crystallize.

RESIN CONTENT – Percent resin in a composite material.

RESIN–RICH AREA – Where local resin content is higher than the average of a laminate due to improper compaction or curing. It may be detrimental because every resin–rich area may mean a resin–starved area somewhere else.

RESIN–STARVED AREA – Where local resin content is lower than the average. It has a dry appearance where filaments or fabric is not completely wetted. This is probably more detrimental than the resin–rich area.

RIB LAMINAE – Laminae of the individual members of a grid core.

RIGID–BODY ROTATION – Rotation without change in shape; occurs in the relation between the off– and on–axis failure envelopes if rotation is carried out in the Mohr's circle or the q–r plane.

ROSIN – Specific natural resin, not to be confused with resin for composite materials.

ROVING – Loose assemblage of filaments. Roving can be impregnated for use in filament winding, in braiding, and in unidirectional tapes.

RULE–OF–MIXTURES – Linear volume fraction relation between the composite and the corresponding constituent properties.

SAFETY FACTOR – The ratio of the ultimate strength to the design or allowable stress.

SANDWICH PANEL – Consisting of two thin face sheets bonded to a thick, lightweight, honeycomb or foam core. Or, sinusoidal, hat type, or grid type core.

SCRIM – Reinforcing fabric woven into an open mesh construction, used in processing of tape and other B–staged material to facilitate handling.

SECANT MODULUS – Idealized Young's modulus derived from a secant drawn between the origin and any point on a nonlinear stress–strain curve. Tangent modulus is the other idealized Young's modulus derived from the tangent to the stress–strain curve.

SECONDARY BONDING – Joining by adhesive bonding parts which have already been cured. This is different from cocuring.

SELF–CONSISTENT MODEL – A micromechanics model to estimate the effective properties of composites. The fiber is modeled as an inclusion embedded in an infinite medium having a stiffness equal to that of the composite.

SELF–DESTRUCT – Failure due to the stress induced by temperature or moisture, without applied mechanical stress.

SHEAR COUPLING – Induced shear strain from normal stress. This coupling is unique with anisotropic materials.

SHEAR MODULUS RATIO – Ratio of the shear modulus of core material to that of the face material of a sandwich beam.

SHEAR STRESS – Component that results in distortion; different from normal components that results in extension or contraction. For multidirectional laminates, in–plane shear is present in every ply. The shear as well as the in–plane normal components exhibit a discontinuous dependence on ply orientation, although the discontinuity should cause no concern. Note that transverse shear stresses are associated with the thickness direction and are not in the plane of the laminate. They are difficult to calculate, and equally difficult to observe experimentally, but fortunately only become important when the laminate thickness is greater than 10 percent of the length or width.

SHEET MOLDING COMPOUND (SMC) – Short fiber reinforced composite.

SHELF LIFE – Length of time that a material can be stored under specified environmental conditions without failure to meet specifications.

SHRINKAGE – Contraction of a molded part during and after cure. Parts can meet dimensional tolerance if the dimensional changes due to temperature of the part and the mold are properly considered.

SIMPLY SUPPORTED STRUCTURE – A structure with supports which give zero displacements and zero moments.

SINGLE LOAD – Stress applied to a body in one direction only.

SINUSOIDALLY CORRUGATED CORE – Sandwich plate core in the form of a sine wave.

SIZING – To select by design the ply number and angles of a laminate subjected to one or more sets of applied stresses. Sizing of isotropic materials is easy because there is one thickness required for each load. Sizing of composite laminates is fundamentally different because both ply number and angles must be considered. It is a nonlinear process; i.e., 10 percent ply addition does not mean 10 percent increase in strength.

S–N CURVE – A plot of fatigue stress, fatigue strain, or fatigue stress ratio vs. number of cycles to failure.

SPAN–TO–DEPTH RATIO – The ratio of the depth of a beam to the loading span of the beam.

SQUARE PACKING OR ARRAY – An idealized fiber position in the center of a square shapped matrix.

SQUARE–SYMMETRY – An orthotropic material with equal stiffness or strength properties in two orthogonal axes. A balanced weave is a square symmetric.

SRF – The strength reduction factor which is defined as the ratio of notched strength to the unnotched strength.

STABILITY – Buckling.

STACKING SEQUENCE – Ply ordering in a laminate. Stacking sequence does not affect the in–plane properties of a symmetric laminate. Only the ply number and angles are important. But stacking sequence becomes critical for the flexural properties, and the interlaminar stresses for any laminate, symmetric or not.

STIFFENED PANEL – Panel reinforced with members in principal directions.

STIFFNESS – Ratio between the applied stress and the resulting strain. Young's modulus is the stiffness of a material subjected to uniaxial stress; shear modulus, to shear stress. For composite materials, stiffness and other properties are dependent on the orientation of the material.

STRAIN – Geometric measurement of deformation.

STRAIN INVARIANT – Scalar combination of strain components.

STRAIN RATE – Change in strain per unit time in mechanical testing.

STRENGTH – Maximum stress that a material can sustain. Like the stiffness of a composite material, strength is highly dependent on the direction as well as the sign of the applied stress; e.g., axial tensile, transverse compressive, and others.

STRENGTH PARAMETER – Strength coefficient of a quadratic failure criterion in stress or strain space; tensors F and G, respectively.

STRENGTH RATIO OR STRENGTH/STRESS RATIO – Useful measure related to margin of safety. Failure occurs when the ratio is unity; safety is assured for example by a factor of 2 if the ratio is 2. The ratio is particularly easy to obtain if the quadratic failure criterion is used.

STRESS – Intensity of forces within a body. The normal components induces length or volume change; the shear component, shape change. The numerical value of each component changes as the reference coordinate system rotates. For every stress state there exists a principal direction, a unique direction when the normal components reach maximum and minimum, and the shear component vanishes.

STRESS CONCENTRATION – Increased ratio of a local stress over the average stress. On the micromechanical level, concentration occurs at the fiber/matrix interface. On the macromechanical level, concentration occurs at notches, ply termination points, joints, etc.

STRESS RELAXATION – Decrease of stress in a solid with time under constant constaints (strain or deformation) at a constant temperature.

STRESS–STRAIN RELATION – Linear relation is usually assumed for calculating stress from strain, or from strain to stress. For multidirectional laminates, it can be generalized to include in–plane stress–strain, and flexural stress–strain relations. All anisotropic relations are simple extensions of the isotropic relation.

SUB–LAMINATE – Repeating multidirectional assemblage within a laminate.

SUCCESSIVE PLY FAILURE – Sequential failures of plies in a multidirectional laminate due to increasing loads.

SWELLING – Volumetric increasing due to temperature increase or moisture absorption.

SYMMETRIC LAMINATE – Possessing midplane symmetry. This is the most common construction because the curing stresses are also symmetric. The laminate does not twist when the temperature and moisture content change. An unsymmetric laminate on the other hand twists upon cooldown and untwists after moisture absorption.

SYMMETRIC MATRIX – Equal off–diagonal components in a matrix; i.e., components "12" is equal to "21"; or "ij" equal to "ji" for the entire range of values of the i and j subscripts. The stiffness and compliance matrices for all materials including composite materials are always symmetric. This symmetry is also known as the reciprocal relation.

SYMMETRY IN MATERIAL – Repeating material property; four common symmetries for composite materials are: orthotropy, transverse isotropy, square symmetry, and, ultimately, isotropy. For these cases the functional relations between stress and strain remain the same, only the independent material constants decrease from 9, 5, 3, to 2, respectively.

SYMMETRY IN PLY STACKING – Midplane symmetry in ply stacking or layup of a laminate; resulting in a symmetric laminate.

SYMMETRY IN TRANSFORMED PROPERTIES – Transformed stiffness and compliance components of an orthotropic material have even and odd symmetries. The diagonal components are even; i.e., components 11, 22 and 66 are always positive and symmetrical with respect to the 0 and 90 degree axes. The Poisson coupling component is positive for the stiffness matrix; negative, for the compliance. Remaining components 16 and 26 are odd; i.e., their value can be either positive or negative.

TACK – Stickiness of a prepreg; an important handling characteristic.

TANGENT MODULUS – Idealized Young's modulus derived from the tangent drawn at the origin or any point on a nonlinear stress–strain curve. Secant modulus is the other idealized Young's modulus between the origin and same point on the stress–strain curve.

TANGENTIAL STRESS – The normal stress along the tangent of the opening.

TEMPLATE – Pattern used as a guide for cutting and laying plies.

THERMAL LOAD – One component of the hygrothermal load. The difference between the cure and operating temperature gives rise to in–plane thermal load for symmetric laminates; and both in–plane and flexural thermal loads for unsymmetric laminates. The presence of the flexural load causes twisting of unsymmetric laminates after cure.

THERMOPLASTIC – Organic material that can reversibly change its stiffness by temperature change. One unique property of this material is its large strain capability. But processing requires high temperature and pressure, compared with thermosetting plastics.

THERMOSETTING PLASTIC – Organic material that can be converted to a solid body by cross–linking, accelerated by heat, catalyst, ultraviolet light, and others. This is the most popular matrix material for composite materials.

TOW – A loose, untwisted bundle of filaments. Graphite fibers are typically available in multiples of 3000–filament tows.

TRANSFORMATION – Variation of stiffness, strength, hygrothermal expansion, stress, strain and others due to the coordinate transformation or, simply, the rotation of the reference coordinate axes. Transformation follows strict mathematical equations. The study of composite materials relies heavily these transformation equations to correctly describe the directional dependency of the materials. Mohr's circles are geometric representation of the transformation equations. Associated with each transformation are several invariants which are useful design parameters.

TRANSVERSE CRACK – Matrix and interfacial failure caused by excessive tensile stress applied transversely to the fibers in a unidirectional ply of a laminate. This cracking is normally the source of the first–ply–failure.

TRANSVERSE ISOTROPY – Material symmetry that possesses an isotropic plane; e.g., a unidirectional composite.

TRICLINIC MATERIAL – Material without any symmetric plane and with 21 independent elastic constants.

UNBALANCED LAMINATE – See balanced.

UNIDIRECTIONAL COMPOSITE – Having parallel fibers in a composite.

UNNOTCHED STRENGTH – The strength of a laminate without an opening.

UNSYMMETRIC LAMINATE – One without mid–plane symmetry.

VACUUM BAG – Flexible nylon, Mylar or elastomeric film that provides the outer cover of composite material cure assemblage, which can be sealed and evacuated to provide compaction pressure. The entire assemblage with the bag can be placed in an oven or autoclave for curing at desired temperature and additional pressure.

VESSEL PERFORMANCE EFFICIENCY – Defined as the ratio of the product of burst pressure and internal volume to the vessel weight. It has a dimension of length. It is used to study relative performance of pressure vessels.

VOLUME FRACTION – Fraction of a constituent material based on its volume.

VOID – The space occuppied by air or gas trapped in a composite material.

VOID CONTENT – Volume percentage of voids, usually less than 1 percent. The experimental determination is however only indirect; i.e., calculated from the measured density of a cured composite and the "theoretical" density of the starting material. Such determination also implies that voids are uniformily distributed throughout the body.

WALL THICKNESS RATIO – Ratio of outer radius to inner radius of a pressure vessel or a cylinder.

WARP – The direction along which yarn is oriented longitudinally in a fabric and perpendicularly to the fill yarn.

WEIBULL PARAMETERS – Frequently used statistical measures for the static and fatigue strengths of composite materials. Shape parameter a is proportional to the coefficient of variation; scale parameter b, to the mean.

WEIGHT FRACTION – Faction of a constituent material based on its weight.

WET – Having absorbed moisture. Like having voids, a uniform moisture distribution is implied which is unlikely to attain in real life. Most absorbed moisture is located near the exposed surface. The interpretation of the effect of being wet must take into account the realistic, highly nonuniform moisture distribution.

WINDING ANGLE – The angular measure between fiber (filament) direction and a reference axis (longitudinal axis or axis of rotation of a cylinder or a pressure vessel).

YOUNG'S MODULUS – The slope of a stress–strain curve under uniaxial test.

Appendix A

LIST OF PRINCIPAL SYMBOLS

A	Surface area exposed to the ambient temperature and humidity conditions
[A], [a]	In–plane stiffness and compliance matrices, respectively
[A*], [a*]	Normalized [A] and [a], respectively; $[A*] = [A]/h$, $[a*] = h[a]$
[A'], [A*]	Absolute and normalied in–plane striffness matrices with respect to the new or z'–axis, respectively
$[A^O]$	In–plane stiffness sub–matrix of a sub–laminate
$[A^+]$, $[A^-]$	In–plane stiffness matrices at the top and the bottom faces of a thin wall construction, respectively
$[A]^p$, $[A]^r$	In–plane stiffness matrices of the base plate and the rib of a stiffened panel, respectively
|A|	Determinant of [A]
a	Length of a plate; Width of the rib in a stiffened panel; or Major radius of an ellipse
a_{ij}	Compliance matrix
$[a^+]$, $[a^-]$	In–plane compliance matrices at the top and the bottom faces of a thin wall construction, respectively
a, b, c	Coefficients in the quadratic equation, i.e., $ax^2+bx+c = 0$. This is used in the quadratic failure criterion; or Exponents for the hygrothermal effects on matrix related properties; exponents f and h, for fiber related properties
[B]	In–plane/flexural coupling sub–matrix of the stiffness matrix of an unsymmetric laminate
[B*]	Normalized [B]; $[B*] = 2[B]/h^2$
$[B^O]$	In–plane/flexural coupling sub–matrix of a sub–laminate

$[B]^p, [B]^r$	In–plane/flexural coupling stiffness matrices of the base plate and the rib of a stiffened panel, respectively
b	Width of a beam or stiffened panel; or Minor radius of an ellipse
b_1	Flat side length of the hat type corrugation
b_2	Inclined length of the hat type corrugation
b^{mix}	Cross products of mechanical and residual strains in the evaluation of the quadratic failure criterion
b_0	Characteristic length applied to a laminate with an opening
b_{eq}	Equivalent width or radius of a tubing
C	Crack length in a fracture toughness test
C_{pqst}	Stiffness components in the generalized Hooke's law; p,q,r,s = 1,2,3 in uncontracted notation
$[C], C_{ij}$	Stiffness matrix in the generalized Hooke's law; in contracted notation, i,j = 1,2,3,4,5,6
c	Designate sandwich core; Half–depth of a beam; Ratio of the inner radius to the outer radius of a ring; or Moisture concentration in a composite or matrix
c_a	Ambient moisture concentration
c_i, c_m	Initial, and maximum or saturation moisture concentrations, respectively
c^*	Percent core thickness in a sandwich plate; $c^* = 2z_c/h = z_c^*$
D	Diamter of a pressure vessel; Diffusivity; when subscripts o, x, y, m and f are appended, they refer to the base line condition, along the x–axis, along the y–axis, that of the matrix, and that of the fiber,respectively; or Thickness of a sandwich plate
$[D], [d]$	Flexural stiffness and compliance matrices
$[D^*], [d^*]$	Normalized [D] and [d], respectively; $[D^*] = 12[D]/h^3$, and $[d^*] = h^3[d]/12$
$[D^o]$	Flexural stiffness sub–matrix of a sub–laminate
$[D]^p, [D]^r$	Flexural stiffness matrices of the base plate and the rib of a stiffened panel, respectively

DF	Matrix degradation factor
d	Transfer distance in the parallel axis theorem; or Bolt diameter
d^*	Normalized d; $d^* = d/h$
d^+, d^-	Transfer distances of the top and the bottom faces of a thin wall construction, respectively
d^p, d^r	Transfer distances of the base plate and the rib of a stiffened panel, respectively
E	Young's modulus
$E(k,\pi/2)$	Elliptic integral of the second kind
E_{cc}	Distance between the neutral plane and the bottom facing sheet of a panel
$E_{equivalent}$	Equivalent Young's Modulus in the direction transverse to the corrugation plane
E_i	Young's modulus in the i–th direction; i = x,y,s
E_i^0	Young's modulus of the ply material in the base line conditions; i.e., at room temperature (22°C), and having 0.005 moisture content; i = x,y,s (on–axis of a ply)
E_i^0, E_i^f	Effective in–plane and flexural stiffness in the i–th direction of a laminate, respectively; i = 1,2,6 (Note: i = x,y,s in last entry)
E_{fx}, E_{fx}^0	Longitudinal Young's modulus of the fiber in modified and the base line states, respectively. The base line is at room temperature and having 0.005 moisture content
E_L	Young's Modulus in fiber direction
E_T	Young's Modulus in the transverse direction
E_m, E_m^0	Young's modulus of the matrix in modified and the base line states, respectively. The base line is at room temperature and having 0.005 moisture content
E_n/E_0	Ratio of stiffness after n fatigue cycles and that at 0 cycle
e	End distance between the center of bolt to the end of bolted joint (see Figure 18.2)
e_i	Free (traction–free) hygrothermal expansions; i = x,y,s

F	Axial force applied to a pressure vessel
$F(k,\pi/2)$	Elliptic integral of the first kind
$F(x)$	Cummulative distribution function
$F_{critical}$	Critical buckling load, same as $P_{critical}$
F_{ij}, F_i	Strength parameters in stress formulation of the quadratic failure criterion
$F_{xy}*$	Normalized interaction term in the quadratic failure criterion of an orthotropic ply
f	Designates flexure, usually as a superscript; Designates fiber, usually as a subscript; Exponent f designates hygrothermal effect on fiber stiffness; or Amplitude of the sinusoidal corrugation
f_i	Function drived from the complex potential for plane elasticity solution
FPF	First–Ply–Failure
G	Shear modulus; Prefix for giga (10^9); or Mass fractrion of moisture absorbed
G_{ij}, G_i	Strength parameters in strain formulation of the quadratic failure criterion; or Shear moduli of an anisotropic material
G_{IC}, G_{IIC}	Energy release rate for mode I and mode II fracture toughness tests, respectively
G_{LT}	Shear modulus of an unidirectional ply
G_x, G_y, G_z	Shear stiffness components, the subscripts x,y, and z are the contracted notations for xy, yx, and yz respectively
g	Temperature shift constant per unit moisture absorbed
g_i	Function drived from the complex potential for plane elasticity solution
H_{ij}, H_i	Strength parameters in laminate stress formulation of the quadratic failure criterion
h	Total thickness of laminate, solid or sandwich beam, and thin wall construction; Total wall thickness of pressure vessel, and tubing; or Exponent h designates hygrothermal effects on fiber strength

h_i	Thickness of the i–th ply group
h_o	Thickness of unit ply
$h^{(i)}$	Thickness of the i–th ply group
h', h"	Thickness of the base plate and the rib of a stiffened panel, respectively
I	Moment of inertia
I, I*	Absolute and normalized area moment of inertia, respectively; $I* = I/b$
i	Interface index; or Exponent index for hygrothermal dependent properties
iso	Designates isotropy, usually as a super– or subscript
J	Polar moment of intertia
[J]	Coordinate transformation matrix; q is positive
$[J]^{-1}$	Inverse transformation of [J]; i.e., q is negative
$[J^T]$	Transposed [J]
K	Strength reduction factor in a bolted joint; or Degrees in Kelvin
K_i	Thermal conductivity of the i–th ply, or ply group
[K]	Rigid–body rotation matrix
$[K]^{-1}$	Inverse transformation of [K], i.e., q is negative
$[K^T]$	Transposed [K]
{k}, {k*}	Absolute and normalized curvature, respectively; $\{k*\} = h\{k\}/2$
L	Length of a beam, pressure vessel or tubing; or Half length of a a sinusoidal corrugation
LPF	Last–Ply–Failure
lim	MIN(FPF,ultimate); denotes a conservative design limit
lim*	Ultimate/safety
M	Weight gain of a composite or matrix due to moisture absorbed; when subscripts i and m are appended, they refer to the initial and maximum levels of absorption

$\{M\}, \{M^*\}$	Absolute and normalized moment components, respectively; $\{M^*\} = 6\{M\}/h^2 = \{\sigma^f\}$
m	Designates mechanical, usually as a superscript; Designates matrix, usually as a subscript; Number of ply groups; Total mass of a composite or matrix, and moisture absorbed; when superscript o is appended, it refers to the mass at dry state; Prefix for mega (10^6); or $= \cos\theta$
m_i, m_m	Initial, and maximum total mass of a composite or matrix with absorbed moisture, respectively
N	Number of fatigue cycles to failure; Number of layers; or Interlaminar normal strength
$\{N\}, \{N^*\}$	Absolute and normalized in-plane stress resultant components, respectively; $\{N^*\} = \{N\}/h = \{\sigma^0\}$
$\{N^+\}, \{N^-\}$	Stress resultant components at top and bottom faces of a thin wall construction, respectively;
n	Designates nonmechanical, usually as a superscript; Number of plies in a laminate; Number of bolts in a bolted joint; Number of fatigue cycles without failure; Number of plies; or $= \sin\theta$
$n^{(i)}$	Number of plies in the i-th ply group
P	Internal or external pressure applied to a pressure vessel; Concentrated load applied to a beam; or Failure load in a bolted joint
P_b	Burst pressure of a pressure vessel
P_c	Applied load to a fracture toughness test; or Critical load at which buckling occurs
p, p^o	Hygrothermal dependent properties at specified and base line conditions, respectively
$P_{critical}$	Critical buckling load; same as $F_{critical}$
P_{min}	Minimum strength of a bolted joint
Pa	Pascal (N/m^2)
p	Pitch between bolts of a multi-bolt joint

p, q, r	Linear combinations of stress or strain components; defined in Equations 5.10 and 5.11
princ	Designates principal stress or strain, as a superscript
[Q]	Reduced stiffness matrix for plane stress
|Q|	Determinant of [Q]
q	Second linear combination of stress or strain components
R	Radius of Mohr's circle; or Strength/stress ratio or strength ratio; or Ratio of the maximum stress to the minimum stress in fatigue
R^m, R^r	Strength/stress ratio based on mechanical and residual loads, respectively
R^t, R^c	Strength/stress ratio based on thermal load and moisture respectively
R^+, R^-	Conjugate strength/stress ratios, derived from the conjugate roots of the quadratic failure criterion; or Strength/stress ratios of the top and bottom faces of a thin wall construction, respectively
R_x, R_x'	Tensile and compresive strength/stress ratios in the longitudinal direction of a unidirectional composite, respectively
R_y, R_y'	Tensile and compresive strength/stress ratios in the transverse direction of a unidirectional composite, respectively
R_i	Thermal conductance of the i–th ply or ply group
R_s	Shear strength/stress ratio of a unidirectional composite
[R]	Reduced compliance matrix for plane strain
r	Third linear combination of stress or strain components; or Index for a repeating sub–laminate
r^+, r^-	Repeating indices for the top and bottom faces of a sandwich or thin wall construction, respectively
S	Shear strength in the xy– or 12–plane of a ply; Designates symmetric laminate in the laminate code; usually as a subscript; or Length of a half sine wave
S_I	Interlaminar shear strength from a three point bend test
S_{pqrs}	Compliance components of the generalized Hooke's law; p,q,r,s = 1,2,3 in the tensorial, uncontracted notation

S_r Ratio of the maximum stress to the minimum stress in fatigue

$[S], S_{ij}$ Compliance matrix of the generalized Hooke's law;
          $i,j = 1,2,3,4,5,6$ in contracted notation

SL   Sub–Laminate; when superscripts + and – are appended, the
          symbols refer to the top and bottom faces of a thin wall
          construction, respectively

SRF   Strength Reduction Factor to describe notched strength

s   Designates shear component in the xy– or the 12–plane,
          usually as a subscript; or
       Designates symmetric laminate in the laminate code, usually as
          a subscript, or regular lower case letter of reduced size

T   Temperature;
       Torque applied to a vessel, rod or tubing;
       Designate total laminate in the laminate code, usually as a
          subscript;
       Shear strength in the yz– or 23–plane;
       Interlaminar tangential strength; or
       Designate tetra (10^{12})

T_a Ambient temperature

T_g Glass transition temperature; when superscript o, and
          subscripts m and f are appended, they refer to the dry
          state, and matrix and fiber, respectively

T_i Temperature of the i–th ply or ply group

T_n, T_t Interlaminar normal and shear tractions respectively

T^* Nondimensional temperature parameter for fitting empirically
          the measured hygrothermal data

t   Summation index;
       Designate the shear component in the yz– or 23–plane, usually
          as a subscript;
       Time; or
       Thickness of the plate in a bolted joint

t_1, t_2 Time at point 1 and point 2, respectively

U   Shear strength in the zx– or 31–plane; or
       Potential energy

U_i Linear combinations of [Q], $i = 1,2,3,4,5$

u   Thickness of a sub–laminate;
       Designates the shear component in the zx– or 31–plane,
          usually as a subscript; or
       Horizontal or the x–axis displacement

u_i	Displacement in the i–th direction
ult	Denotes ultimate failure, usually appears as a subscript or superscript
V_i	Integrated trignometric functions of ply angles for the in–plane stiffness of a symmetric laminate, i = 1,2,3,4
V_i^*	Normalized V_i; i.e., $V_i^* = V_i/h$
v	Volume fractions in rule–of–mixtures equations; or Vertical or the h–axis displacement
$v^{(i)}$	Volume fractions of the i–th ply group
v_q	Volume fractions of the ply group of q ply angle
v_v	Void volume fraction
v^*	Reduced matrix/fiber volume ratio, used in micromechanics formulas for transverse and shear moduli calculations
W	Normal displacement; or Width of a rib
W, W^o	Weight of moist and dry material, respectively
W_i	Integrated trignometric functions of ply angles for the flexural stiffness of a symmetric laminate, i = 1,2,3,4
W_i^*	Normalized W_i; i.e., $W_i^* = 12W_i/h^3 = W_i/I^*$
w	Displacement along the z–axis; or Width of a bolted joint
X	Longitudinal tensile strength of a ply along the x–axis; or Uniaxial tensile strength of an isotropic medium
X'	Longitudinal compressive strength of a ply along the x–axis
X_m, X_f	Tensile strength of the matrix and the fiber, respectively; when superscript o is appended, the symbols refer to the base line states: at room temperature and having 0.005 moisture content
x	Longitudinal axis of an orthotropic ply, usually along the fiber in a unidirectional material
x^*	Normalized x–axis; e.g., $x^* = x/h$
Y	Transverse tensile strength along the y–axis
Y'	Transverse compressive strength along the y–axis

y	The transverse axis of an orthotropic ply, usually transverse to the fiber in a unidirectional material
y^*	Normalized y–axis; e.g., $y^* = y/h$
z	Axis transverse to the plane of a laminate; or Thickness direction of a laminate
z^*	Normalized z; $z^* = 2z/h$
z_c	Half–depth of sandwich core; same as c^*
α	Normalized characteristic length; equal to b_0/a; Wrap angle in pressure vessel; or Weibull shape parameter
$\{\alpha\}$	Anisotropic thermal expansion components of a ply
$\{\alpha^0\}$	Anisotropic thermal expansion components of a laminate
$[\alpha], [\alpha^*]$	Absolute and normalized in–plane sub–matrix of the compliance components of an unsymmetric laminate; $[\alpha^*] = h[\alpha]$
β	Weibull scale parameter
β_m, β_f	Moisture expansion coefficients of matrix and fiber, respectively
$\{\beta\}$	Anisotropic moisture expansion components of a ply
$\{\beta^0\}$	Anisotropic moisture expansion components of a laminate
$[\beta], [\beta^*]$	Absolute and normalized in–plane/flexure coupling sub–matrices of the compliance matrix of an unsymmetric laminate, respectively; $[\beta^*] = h^2[\beta]/2$
$[\beta^T]$	Transposed $[\beta]$
γ	Rigid–body rotation of a laminate
δ	Incremental displacement, like δL or δD to designate the change in length or diameter of a vessel, respectively
δT	One half of the temperature difference between the top and bottom faces of a laminate
δ_c	Total deflection of a fracture toughness test
ΔT	Difference between the operating temperature and the cure temperature; usually negative because operating temperature is lower than the cure temperature

$[\delta]$, $[\delta^*]$	Absolute and normalized flexural sub–matrix of the compliance matrix of an unsymmetric laminate, respectively; $[\delta^*] = h^3[\delta]/12$
$\{\varepsilon\}$	Strain components
$\{\varepsilon^+\}$, $\{\varepsilon^-\}$	Strain at the top and bottom faces of a thin wall construction, respectively
$|\varepsilon|$	Effective or invariant strain
ε_I, ε_{II}	Principal strain components
ε_q, ε_r, ε_s	Shear strain components; the subscript q for (2–3) plane, r for (3–1) plane, and s for (1–2) plane
$\{\varepsilon^0\}$	In–plane strain components
$\{\varepsilon^f\}$	Flexural strain components
$\{\varepsilon^*\}$	Maximum, ultimate or failure strain components
$\{\varepsilon^m\}$	Mechanical strain components
$\{\varepsilon^n\}$	Nonmechanical strain components
$\{\varepsilon^r\}$	Residual strain components
$\varepsilon_i{}^{(0)n}$	Nonmechanical in–plane strain components; same as $\{\varepsilon^0\}^n$
$\varepsilon_i{}^{(0)r}$	Residual in–plane strain components; same as $\{\varepsilon^0\}^r$
η	Pressure vessel efficiency which is the ratio of the product of burst pressure and internal volume to the vessel weight
η_y	Stress partitioning parameter for transverse stiffness modulus formula in micromechanics
η_s	Stress partitioning parameter for shear modulus formula in micromechanics
λ	Aspect ratio of an ellipse; equal to b/a
ν	Poisson's ratio of an isotropic material
ν_x, ν_y	Major, and minor Poisson's ratios an anisotropic material, respectively

v_x^0, v_y^0	Major, and minor Poisson's ratios in the base line conditions, respectively; i.e., at room temperature and having 0.005 moisture content; or Poisson's ratios for in–plane deformation
v_z^0	Poisson's ratio in (y–z) plane due to in–plane deformation, superscript o denotes in–plane deformation and subscript z is the contracted notation for yz
v_x^f, v_y^f, v_z^f	Poisson's ratios due to flexural deformation
v_{yz}	same as v_z
v_{ij}	Poisson's ratio and shear coupling coefficients; i,j = 1,2,6 for plane stress in the 1–2 plane
v_{LT}	Major Poisson's ratio of a unidirectional ply
μ_i	Complex roots of the characteristic equation, Equation 20.8
ρ	Density
ϕ	Positive transformation angle (Figure 6.1); [±angle] for an angle–ply laminate; Relative humidity; or Angle between the inclined side and the vertical plane of a hat section
ψ	Slant or orientation angle between the major axis of an elliptic opening to the 2–axis of a laminated plate (Figure 20.1)
κ_y	Change in curvature
$\xi–\eta$	Reference coordinates of a laminated beam (Figure 22.1)
θ	Ply angle; or Negative transformation angle (Figure 6.1)
θ_0	Phase angle in Mohr's circle; i.e., orientation of the principal axes
$\{\sigma\}$	Stress components
$|\sigma|$	Effective or invariant (von Mises) stress
σ_b	Bearing stress in a bolted joint
σ_z	Clamping pressure in a bolted joint

$\sigma_q, \sigma_r, \sigma_s$	Shear stress components, subscript q for (2–3) plane, r for (3–1) plane, and s for (1–2) plane
σ_I, σ_{II}	Principal stress components
σ^*	Ratio of two normal stress components; σ_2/σ_1
$\{\sigma^*\}$	Stress in a laminte due to the presence of an opening
$\{\sigma^0\}$	Stress in a laminte due to an applied load at infinity
$\{\sigma\}^{(i)}$	Ply stress of the i–th ply group, or the i–th ply angle
$\{\sigma\}^z$	Ply stress at distance z from the mid–plane
$\{\sigma^0\}$	In–plane stress components
$\{\sigma^f\}$	Flexural stress components
$\{\sigma^m\}$	Mechanical stress components
$\{\sigma^n\}$	Nonmechanical stress components
$\{\sigma^r\}$	Residual stress components
$\sigma_i^{(0)n}$	Nonmechanical in–plane stress components; same as $\{\sigma^0\}^n$
$\sigma_i^{(0)r}$	Residual in–plane stress components; same as $\{\sigma^0\}^r$
$\sigma_{min}/\sigma_{max}$	Applied stress ratio in a constant amplitude fatigue test
$[\ ]^{cor}$	Property of the plate equivalent to the corrugation
$[\ ]^{Grid}$	Property of the plate equivalent to the grid
$[\ ]^{hat}$	Property of the plate equivalent to the hat type corrugation
$[\ ]^{lam}$	Property of a laminate
$[\ ]^{top}$	Stiffness of the top facing sheet of a sandwich panel
$[\ ]^{bot}$	Stiffness of the bottom facing sheet of a sandwich panel

Appendix B

UNIT CONVERSIONS AND PLY DATA

ITEMS	SI TO ENGLISH	ENGLISH TO SI
$\{\sigma\}$, [Q]	1 MPa = 145 psi = 0.145 ksi	1 ksi = 6.89 MPa
	1 GPa = 145 ksi = 0.145 msi	1 msi = 6.89 GPa
$\{N\}$, [A]	1 N/m = 0.00571 #/in	1 #/in = 175 N/m
	1 MN/m = 5710 #/in	1 kip/in = 0.175 MN/m
	= 5.71 kip/in	
$\{M\}$, [B]	1 N = 0.225 #	1# = 4.45 N
Length	1 m = 39.4 in	1 in = 0.0254 m
		= 2.54 cm = 25.4 mm
Work	1 J = 1 Nm = 8.85 #in	1 #in = 0.112 Nm

SUMMARY OF PLY AND FABRIC DATA IN SI UNITS

Type	CFRP	BFRP	CFRP	GFRP	KFRP	CFRTP	CFRP	CFRP	CCRP	CCRP
Fiber/cloth	T300	B(4)	AS	E-glass	Kev 49	AS 4	IM6	T300	T300	T300
Matrix	N5208	N5505	H3501	epoxy	epoxy	PEEK	epoxy	Fiberite 934		
						APC2		4-mil	13-mil	7-mil
Ply eng'g constants								tape	cloth	cloth
Ex, GPa	181.0	204.0	138.0	38.6	76.0	134.0	203.0	148.0	74.0	66.0
Ey, GPa	10.30	18.50	8.96	8.27	5.50	8.90	11.20	9.65	74.00	66.00
nu/x	0.28	0.23	0.30	0.26	0.34	0.28	0.32	0.30	0.05	0.04
Es, GPa	7.17	5.59	7.10	4.14	2.30	5.10	8.40	4.55	4.55	4.10
Other ply or fabric data										
v/f	0.70	0.50	0.66	0.45	0.60	0.66	0.66	0.60	0.60	0.60
rho	1.60	2.00	1.60	1.80	1.46	1.60	1.60	1.50	1.50	1.50
ho, mm	0.125	0.125	0.125	0.125	0.125	0.125	0.125	0.100	0.325	0.175
Quasi-isotropic constants										
E, GPa	69.68	78.53	54.84	18.96	29.02	51.81	78.35	56.24	52.67	47.07
nu	0.30	0.32	0.28	0.27	0.32	0.30	0.30	0.32	0.32	0.32
G, GPa	26.88	29.67	21.35	7.47	10.95	19.88	30.23	21.37	19.89	17.85
Max stress or strength, MPa										
X	1500	1260	1447	1062	1400	2130	3500	1314	499	375
X'	1500	2500	1447	610	235	1100	1540	1220	352	279
Y	40	61	51.7	31	12	80	56	43	458	368
Y'	246	202	206	118	53	200	150	168	352	278
S	68	67	93	72	34	160	98	48	46	46
Max strain, eps*, E-03										
x	8.29	6.18	10.49	27.51	18.42	15.90	17.24	8.88	6.74	5.68
x'	8.29	12.25	10.49	15.80	3.09	8.21	7.59	8.24	4.76	4.23
y	3.88	3.30	5.77	3.75	2.18	8.99	5.00	4.46	6.19	5.58
y'	23.88	10.92	22.99	14.27	9.64	22.47	13.39	17.41	4.76	4.21
s	9.48	11.99	13.10	17.39	14.78	31.37	11.67	10.55	10.11	11.22
Hygrothermal expansion coefficients, E-06/C and dimensionless										
alpha/x	0.02	6.10	-0.30	8.60	-4.00					
alpha/y	22.50	30.30	28.10	22.10	79.00					
beta/x	0.00	0.00	0.00	0.00	0.00					
beta/y	0.60	0.60	0.40	0.60	0.60					
Other empirical constants										
eta/y	0.516	0.215	0.516	0.516	0.516	0.516	0.516	0.516		
eta/s	0.316	0.282	0.316	0.316	0.316	0.316	0.316	0.316		
Fxy*	-0.50	-0.50	-0.50	-0.50	-0.50	-0.50	-0.50	-0.50		
Em* or DF	0.20	0.30	0.20	0.07	0.02	0.10	0.10	0.20		

SUMMARY OF PLY AND FABRIC DATA IN ENGLISH UNITS

Type	CFRP	BFRP	CFRP	GFRP	KFRP	CFRTP	CFRP	CFRP	CCRP	CCRP
Fiber/cloth	T300	B(4)	AS	E-glass	Kev 49	AS 4	IM6	T300	T300	T300
Matrix	N5208	N5505	H3501	epoxy	epoxy	PEEK	epoxy	Fiberite 934		
						APC2		4-mil	13-mil	7-mil
Ply eng'g constants								tape	cloth	cloth
Ex, msi	26.25	29.58	20.01	5.597	11.02	19.43	29.44	21.46	10.73	9.57
Ey, msi	1.49	2.68	1.30	1.20	0.80	1.29	1.62	1.40	10.73	9.57
nu/x	0.28	0.23	0.30	0.26	0.34	0.28	0.32	0.30	0.05	0.04
Es, msi	1.04	0.81	1.03	0.60	0.33	0.74	1.22	0.66	0.66	0.59
Other ply or fabric data										
v/f	0.70	0.50	0.66	0.45	0.60	0.66	0.66	0.60	0.60	0.60
rho	1.60	2.00	1.60	1.80	1.46	1.60	1.60	1.50	1.50	1.50
ho, mil	4.93	4.93	4.93	4.93	4.93	4.93	4.93	3.94	12.81	6.90
Quasi-isotropic constants										
E, msi	10.10	11.39	7.95	2.75	4.21	7.51	11.36	8.15	7.64	6.83
nu	0.30	0.32	0.28	0.27	0.32	0.30	0.30	0.32	0.32	0.32
G, msi	3.90	4.30	3.10	1.08	1.59	2.88	4.38	3.10	2.88	2.59
Max stress or strength, ksi										
X	217.5	182.7	209.8	154.0	203.0	308.9	507.5	190.5	72.4	54.4
X'	217.5	362.5	209.8	88.5	34.1	159.5	223.3	176.9	51.0	40.5
Y	5.8	8.8	7.5	4.5	1.7	11.6	8.1	6.2	66.4	53.4
Y'	35.7	29.3	29.9	17.1	7.7	29.0	21.8	24.4	51.0	40.3
S	9.9	9.7	13.5	10.4	4.9	23.2	14.2	7.0	6.7	6.7
Max strain, eps*, E-03										
x	8.29	6.18	10.49	27.51	18.42	15.90	17.24	8.88	6.74	5.68
x'	8.29	12.25	10.49	15.80	3.09	8.21	7.59	8.24	4.76	4.23
y	3.88	3.30	5.77	3.75	2.18	8.99	5.00	4.46	6.19	5.58
y'	23.88	10.92	22.99	14.27	9.64	22.47	13.39	17.41	4.76	4.21
s	9.48	11.99	13.10	17.39	14.78	31.37	11.67	10.55	10.11	11.22
Hygrothermal expansion coefficients, E-06/F and dimensionless										
alpha/x	0.01	3.38	-0.17	4.78	-2.22					
alpha/y	12.50	16.83	15.61	12.28	43.89					
beta/x	0.00	0.00	0.00	0.00	0.00					
beta/y	0.60	0.60	0.40	0.60	0.60					
Other empirical constants										
eta/y	0.516	0.215	0.516	0.516	0.516	0.516	0.516	0.516		
eta/s	0.316	0.282	0.316	0.316	0.316	0.316	0.316	0.316		
Fxy*	-0.50	-0.50	-0.50	-0.50	-0.50	-0.50	-0.50	-0.50		
Em* or DF	0.20	0.30	0.20	0.07	0.02	0.10	0.10	0.20		

SUBJECT INDEX

SUBJECT	SECTION